# Birnbaum's Europe for Business Travelers

**A BIRNBAUM TRAVEL GUIDE**

Alexandra Mayes Birnbaum
**EDITORIAL CONSULTANT**

Lois Spritzer
**Editorial Director**

Laura L. Brengelman
**Managing Editor**

Mary Callahan
**Senior Editor**

David Appell
Patricia Canole
Gene Gold
Jill Kadetsky
Susan McClung
**Associate Editors**

HarperPerennial
*A Division of HarperCollinsPublishers*

**To Stephen, who merely made all this possible.**

FIRST EDITION

ISSN 0749-2561 (Birnbaum Travel Guides)
ISSN 0749-4815 (Europe for Business Travelers)
ISBN 0-06-278189-8 (pbk.)

95 96 97 98 ❖/RRD 5 4 3 2 1

Cover design © Drenttel Doyle Partners

# Contents

## Glossary

Reykjavik
ICELAND
Norwegian Sea
ATLANTIC OCEAN
SWEDEN
NORWAY
Oslo
Stockholm
NORTHERN IRELAND
Edinburgh
North Sea
SCOTLAND
REPUBLIC OF IRELAND
Dublin
DENMARK
Copenhagen
THE NETHERLANDS
GREAT BRITAIN
WALES
ENGLAND
London
Amsterdam
Berlin
POLAND
English Channel
Brussels
BELGIUM
Bonn
GERMANY
Prague
CZECH REPUBLIC
Paris
LUXEMBOURG
SWITZERLAND
Vienna
Bay of Biscay
FRANCE
Bern
AUSTRIA
LIECHTENSTEIN
SLOV.
CROATIA
ANDORRA
SAN MARINO
PORTUGAL
MONACO
ITALY
Lisbon
Madrid
SPAIN
CORSICA
Rome
Adriatic Sea
SARDINIA
BALEARIC ISLANDS
GILBRALTAR
Mediterranean Sea
CANARY ISLANDS
SICILY
AFRICA
MALTESE ISLANDS

# Foreword

If there's one curse common to all business travelers, it's got to be that oft-heard line from non-traveling associates that goes, "Oh, you've got such a great job; you get to see so many countries/continents/the world." Envy seeps through every syllable; the only problem is that this perception is almost always totally wrong.

Anyone who has ever been on the road for business—whether the destination was foreign or domestic—knows that jet planes long ago eliminated what little romance ever existed in connection with on-the-job travel. Schedules are hectic and compressed, so it's hardly unusual to hear about a busy executive leaving New York in the evening for a morning meeting in Paris, working all day into early evening, then catching the *Concorde* back to New York to be at a mid-Manhattan desk shortly after 9 AM the next day. It may sound romantic in the telling, but it's more often the case that business travelers arrive feeling stiff and exhausted—as though they've been shipped home in a plain white envelope.

For a business traveler who actually gets to spend the night in an unfamiliar city, the thought of really looking around is seldom even considered. To begin with, easily accessible, reliable local information is usually notable by its absence, and while a busy business traveler carries a briefcase full of important papers, these documents rarely include any practical information about local life and environment. There's nothing about a particularly evocative restaurant or a nearby theater whose regional troupe presents truly notable performances. More often, the business traveler moves from airport to taxicab to meeting to hotel, feet seldom touching the ground.

Contemporary business travel schedules are understandably tight, but there's often a bit of spare time for working out, taking a peek at a local landmark, or savoring a bite of a foreign delicacy. It makes all the difference between actually having *been* to a world capital or merely having passed through.

Even in the case of business activities—including such simple-sounding matters as finding a bilingual secretary—not knowing the city can make awesome endeavors out of otherwise pedestrian chores. Sending a package across an ocean can suddenly seem the equivalent of scaling Everest, while getting a page translated into (or out of) a foreign language borders on the impossible. And the further complications of foreign travel—changing currency; catching a train, bus, or taxi to the airport; and figuring out the local protocol on whom to tip and how much—can exhaust even the hardiest business traveler.

The purpose of this special guide for the business traveler in Europe is, therefore, to answer such needs, as well as to give an often harried stranger a satisfying glimpse of what some of the world's most remarkable cities have to offer—beyond boardrooms and factory visits. We have organized our material into the most manageable size and format, eliminating superfluous data in favor of succinct descriptions of what we think is best and really worth seeing and doing. Scanning the pages that follow should provide insights into each European city that are sufficiently specific to make any business traveler's stay more productive—and more enjoyable.

Let me point out that every good travel guide is a living enterprise; that is, no part of this text is in any way cast in bronze. In each annual revision, we refine, expand, and further hone all our material to serve your needs even better. To this end, no contribution is of greater value to us than your reaction to what we have written, as well as information reflecting your experiences while trying our suggestions.

Please write to us at 10 E. 53rd St., New York, NY 10022. We sincerely hope to hear from you.

*Alexandra Mayes Birnbaum*

**ALEXANDRA MAYES BIRNBAUM, editorial consultant to the *Birnbaum Travel Guides*, worked with her late husband, Stephen Birnbaum, as co-editor of the series. She has been a world traveler since childhood and is known for her travel reports on radio on what's hot and what's not.**

# BIRNBAUM TRAVEL GUIDES

| | |
|---|---|
| Bahamas, and Turks & Caicos | London |
| Berlin | Los Angeles |
| Bermuda | Mexico |
| Boston | Miami & Ft. Lauderdale |
| Canada | Montreal & Quebec City |
| Cancun, Cozumel & Isla Mujeres | New Orleans |
| Caribbean | New York |
| Chicago | Paris |
| Country Inns and Back Roads | Portugal |
| Disneyland | Rome |
| Eastern Europe | San Francisco |
| Europe | Santa Fe & Taos |
| Europe for Business Travelers | South America |
| France | Spain |
| Germany | United States |
| Great Britain | USA for Business Travelers |
| Hawaii | Walt Disney World |
| Ireland | Walt Disney World for Kids, By Kids |
| Italy | Washington, DC |

## Contributing Editors

Judith Harris Ajello
Duncan Anderson
Carmen Anthony
Kathy Arnold
Melvin Benarde
Gunnar Berj
Patricia Bjaaland
Virginia Blackert
Barbara Bowers
Paolo Braghieri
Mark Brayne
John Buskin
Ron Butler
Count Jacob
 Coudenhove-
 Kalergi
Ann Campbell-Lord
Linda Carreaga
Rik Cate
David Cemlyn-
 Jones
Vinod Chhabra
Peter Collis
Roger Collis
Charles Cupic
Karen Cure
Stephanie Curtis
Roman Czajkowski
Martha de la Cal
Tom Fitzmaurice
 de la Cal
Claire Devener
Daniela Drazanova
Brad Durham
Thomas S. Dyman
William Echikson
Bjorn Edlund

Bonnie Edwards
Emily Emerson
Donna Evleth
Jackie Fierman
Brenda Fine
Ted Folke
Brenda Fowler
Joan Gannij
Fradley Garner
Lois Gelatt
Norman Gelb
Jerry Gerber
Andrew Gillman
Mireille Giuliano
Agnes Gottlieb
Don Graff
Patricia Graves
Petar Hadj-Ristic
Jessica Harris
Elizabeth Healy
Margaret Henderson
Jack Herbert
Marilyn Bruno
 Herrera
Ritva Hildebrandt
Brian Hill
Connie Hill
Elva Horvath
David Howley
Debra Immergut
Julian Isherwood
Bruce Johnston
Jill Jolliffe
Mark Kalish
Anne Kalosh
Leslie F. Kauffmann
Virginia Kelley

Lucy Koserski
Alexander Kushnir
Carole Landry
Robert Latona
Ann Rebecca
 Laschever
André Leduc
Richard Lee
Robert Levine
Howell Llewellyn
Sirrka Makelainen
Thomas C. Marinelli
Virginia McCune
Jan McGirk
Erica Meltzer
Diane Melville
Anne Millman
Tamara K. Mitchell
Jack Monet
Michael Moynihan
Martina Norelli
Ottar Odland
Carol Offen
Pat Patricof
A. E. Pedersen
Clare Pedrick
Samuel Perkins
Fred Poe
Alemka Porobic
Mark Potok
Everett Potter
Bogdan Preda
Jim Pressley
John Preston
Patricia Tunison
 Preston
Colin Pringle

Carol Reed
Susan Rock
Allen Rokach
Margery Safir
Jerrold L. Schecter
Patricia Schultz
Patrick Schultz
Richard Schweid
George Semmler
Hella Sessoms
Mike Shea
Frank Shiell
Jon Sigurdsson
Janet Steinberg
Janet Stobbart
Phyllis Stoller
Donald Stroetzel
Gillian Thomas
Nancy Patton
 Van Zant
Betty Vaughn
Florence Vidal
Toula Vlahou
Paul Wade
Richard Walbleigh
Ellen Wallace
Claudia Weber
Dennis Weber
Fred Weir
David Wickers
Mark Williams
Jennifer Wright
Derrick Young
Eleni Ziogas
Sonya Zalubowski
Emilia Zino

## Maps

Folio Graphics Co. Inc.
General Cartography Inc.

B. Andrew Mudryk
Mark Stein Studios

# Birnbaum's Europe for Business Travelers 95

# Amsterdam

## At-a-Glance

### SEEING THE CITY

The towers of two of Amsterdam's most historic churches offer the best views of the old city center areas. The early-14th-century *Oude Kerk* (Old Church; phone: 625-8284) is in the heart of the Walletjes district at Oudekerksplein. It's open daily in summer, Friday and Saturday afternoons only in winter; admission charge. The *Westerkerk* (Western Church; phone: 624-7766), Rembrandt's burial place, was completed in 1631 and sits amid Amsterdam's canals in the most beautiful part of the city at the Westermarkt. It boasts the city's tallest church tower (at more than 250 feet), with its distinctive gold crown. It can be toured Monday through Saturday from June 2 through September 12; open Sundays for services only.

For a spectacular, near-panoramic view of both the harbor and the historic city center, visit *Osaka,* a restaurant on the 12th floor of the *HavenGebouw* (Harbor Building; 7 De Ruyterkade; phone: 638-9833). To see the city's rooftops and canal configurations, try the coffee shop on the sixth floor of the *Metz* department store (455 Keizersgracht; phone: 624-8810).

### SPECIAL PLACES

The city's major sights are grouped conveniently around a few principal areas, all within walking distance of one another. Visitors armed with a good map and a guidebook should have no problem making their way around.

**DAM (DAM SQUARE)** The natural focal point of the city is this square. At the end of the Damrak—a street leading from the harbor and *Centraal Station*—the busy square is dominated by a distinctive war memorial constructed in 1956. In good weather, the steps ringing the monument are a sea of young people resting, singing, and socializing. The open plaza of the square opposite the monument attracts both spontaneous and organized activities: Festivals, jazz concerts, and free puppet shows are staged here one or two afternoons a week during the summer. But beware: Pickpockets and drug dealers often loiter around the square, too. Blue-uniformed "city watchmen," equipped with walkie-talkies, patrol the city's hot spots (Rembrandtsplein, Leidseplein, and Waterlooplein) and assist visitors who need directions or information.

**KONINKLIJK PALEIS (ROYAL PALACE)** The 13,659 wooden piles holding it up earned this palace the unofficial title of "Eighth Wonder of the World" after its completion in 1662. Its regal interior, decorated by the leading artists of the time, can be viewed daily from 12:30 to 4 PM in the summer and on Wednesdays at 1:45 PM in winter by

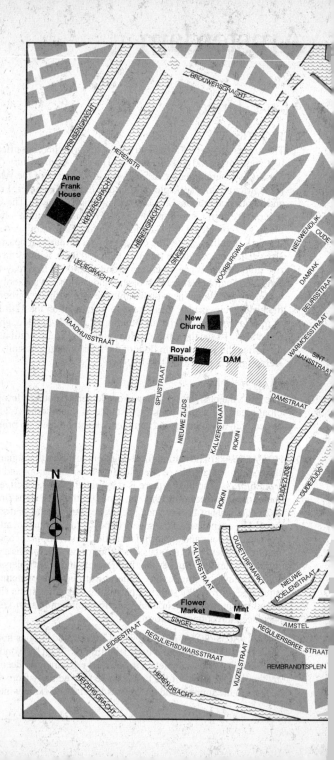

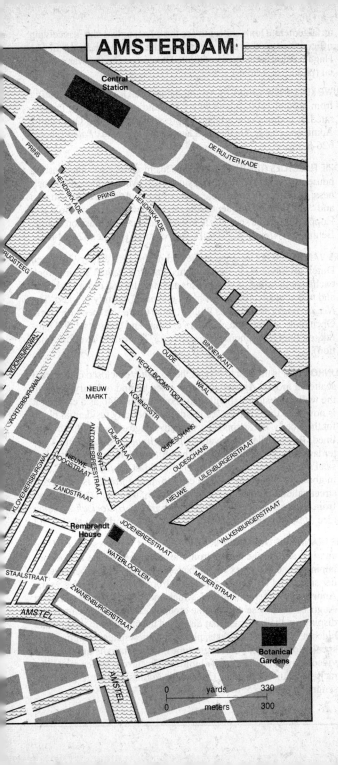

# AMSTERDAM

Central Station

PRINS

HENDRIKKADE

DE RUIJTER KADE

PRINS

HENDRIKKADE

BRUGSTEEG

VOORBURGWAL

ACHTERBURGWAL

BINNENKANT

OUDE

WAAL

RECHTBOOMSTOOT

NIEUW
MARKT

KONINGSSTR

KLOVENIERSBURGWAL

ANTONIESBREESTRAAT

DIJKSTRAAT

SINT J

OUDESCHANS

OUDESCHANS

NIEUWE UILENBURGERSTRAAT

NIEUWE
HOOGSTRAAT

ZANDSTRAAT

NIEUWE

VALKENBURGERSTRAAT

Rembrandt
House

JODENBREESTRAAT

WATERLOOPLEIN

MUIDER STRAAT

STAALSTRAAT

ZWANENBURGERSTRAAT

AMSTEL

AMSTEL

Botanical
Gardens

| 0 | yards | 330 |
| 0 | meters | 300 |

arrangement. Don't expect to see the queen unless she is receiving official visitors that day; she lives in the *Koninklijk Paleis* in The Hague. Admission charge. On the Dam, opposite the war memorial (phone: 624-8698).

**NIEUWE KERK (NEW CHURCH)** An imposing late Gothic church dating from around 1500, this is where Holland's monarchs are inaugurated. It features concerts and impressive exhibitions. Open daily. Admission charge. On the Dam, next to the *Koninklijk Paleis* (phone: 626-8168).

**DE DRIE FLESCHJES (THE THREE BOTTLES)** This historic, cask-lined tasting house has remained unchanged since 1650, when it opened for business. Make sure you sample some of the traditional Dutch snacks and "old Holland" liqueurs (the best-known brands are Bols and Hoppe) that are its specialty. Closed Sundays. No admission charge. Behind the *Nieuwe Kerk,* at 18 Gravenstraat (phone: 624-8443).

**BEURS VAN BERLAGE** Designed at the end of the 19th century by noted Dutch architect H. P. Berlage, this was Amsterdam's third stock exchange building. It now houses architecture and design exhibits, and two acoustically perfect halls, one made entirely of glass. The *Neederlands* (Netherlands Philharmonic Orchestra) performs here. Open daily. Admission charge to exhibits and concerts. 279 Damrak, on the Dam (phone: 626-5257; 627-0466 for ticket information).

**BEGIJNHOF** This is the best known of the 75 *hofjes* (enclosed courtyards) scattered around Amsterdam, concealed behind ordinary doors in the walls of residential buildings. Founded in 1346 as a cloister, it is now, like the other *hofjes,* an idyllic inner-city residential block for the elderly, but anyone may take advantage of its tranquil, bench-lined, flower-filled courtyard. The *Begijnhof* also contains Amsterdam's *Engels Kerk* (English Church), which regularly hosts classical music performances, as well as its oldest surviving house, built in about 1470, at No. 34. The easy-to-miss entrance is on a short street called Spui, leading from the Rokin, near the Dam. Or enter from the back courtyard of the *Amsterdams Historisch Museum* (see *Museums,* below) at 357 Nieuwe Zijds Voorburgwal.

**ANNE FRANK HUIS (ANNE FRANK HOUSE)** A short way west of the Dam and just around the corner from the *Westerkerk* is the house containing the secret annex where the teenage Anne Frank, her parents, her sister, and four other people hid from the Nazis for two years. Anne's diary traces the ordeal, which ended with a Gestapo raid in August 1944 that sent the whole group to extermination camps. On display are the bookcase that disguised the entrance to the upstairs hideout, and simple artifacts, photos, and newspaper clippings that speak eloquently of the tragic times. Downstairs is an excellent video show and changing exhibitions on current issues related to racism and discrimination. Open daily. Admission charge. 263 Prinsengracht (phone: 556-7100).

**WALLETJES** Immediately to the east of the Dam, this attractive old city center area is best known as Amsterdam's main red-light area. Along Oude Zijds (often abbreviated OZ) Voorburgwal, the Oude Zijds Achterburgwal, and the small neighboring streets, almost 1,000 prostitutes pose in windows, illuminated by real red lights, and there are live sex shows and sex shops all along Oude Zijds Voorburgwal. As would be wise in any city's "Times Square" area, watch out for pickpockets, drug dealers, and other criminals.

**WAAG (WEIGH-HOUSE)** Part of a gate and a fragment of the old city walls dating from 1488, the *Waag* later was converted into a weighing house. An anatomy lesson given here in the 17th century was the subject of Rembrandt's famous painting *The Anatomy Lesson of Dr. Tulp.* Currently the public is not admitted, but there are plans to open a children's book museum on the site (see the tourist office for details); in the meantime, the house can be viewed from the Nieuwmarkt.

**SCHREIERSTOREN (WEEPERS' TOWER)** Dating from 1569, this is another fragment of the original city walls. Henry Hudson departed from here on his voyage to North America in 1609. Tradition has it that the tower got its name from the sailors' wives who saw their husbands off from here. Between Walletjes and *Centraal Station,* at the corners of Prins Hendrikkade and Gelderskade.

**MUSEUM AMSTELKRING ONS'LIEVE HEER OP SOLDER ("OUR DEAR LORD IN THE ATTIC" AMSTELKRING MUSEUM)** During the repression of Catholics in the 17th century, at least 26 clandestine churches were built in city attics. This one extends through the joined attics of three houses and is equipped with everything from an organ to a Baroque altar. The entry house, set up in 1663, has one of the few perfectly preserved 17th-century living rooms in Amsterdam. Closed Sunday mornings. Guided tours by appointment; English guides available by request. Admission charge. In the heart of the Walletjes district, at 40 Oude Zijds Voorburgwal (phone: 624-6604).

**ZEEDIJK** Amsterdam's old sailors' quarter has been restored to its 17th-century grandeur, with the *Golden Tulip Barbizon Palace* hotel (see *Checking In*) and smart shops as its focal points. Amsterdam's Chinese community celebrates both *New Year's Eve* and the *Chinese New Year* with huge displays of fireworks on the bridge by the Zeedijk near the Gelderskade. Be cautious when walking down small side streets here; this neighborhood is in transition.

**JORDAAN** This is Amsterdam's colorful working class district. Devote a day to exploring the maze of narrow streets and alleys, with their innumerable small boutiques and arts and crafts shops sprinkled among more traditional businesses, and several nights to mingling with the Jordaaners in their characteristic neighborhood cafés (see *Nightclubs and Nightlife*). The major part of the Jordaan is bordered by the Rozengracht, Lijnbaansgracht, Brouwersgracht, and Prinsengracht, with the most interesting shops concentrated at 2e Anjeliersdwarsstraat, 2e Tuindwarsstraat, and 2e Egelantiersdwarsstraat.

For a taste of 17th-century Amsterdam visit the lively Monday market, with its array of knicknacks and second-hand clothes, on the Noordermarkt, at the corner of Prinsengracht and Noordermarkt. Or visit on Saturdays when the weekly "farmer's market" is held, its stalls filled with organic fruits, vegetables, cheeses, and snacks.

**HOLLANDSCHE SCHOUWBURG (DUTCH THEATER)** This former theater, built in 1892, was renamed the *Joodsche Schouwburg* (Jewish Theater) during the Nazi occupation of 1941 and was restricted to Jewish artists and audiences. A year later, the Nazis turned the building into an assembly point for Dutch Jews being shipped to concentration camps. After the war, it reopened briefly as a theater, but public revulsion at the idea of using the scene of such tragedy for entertainment shut it down. In 1993 the renovated structure was turned into a historical monument and memorial. A permanent exhibition examines the persecution of Dutch Jews. Open daily. No admission charge. 24 Plantage Middenlaan (phone: 626-9945).

**PORTUGESE SYNAGOGE** When it was constructed in 1675, this stately Sephardic house of worship was the largest synagogue in the world. The 17th-century interior is still intact, and weekly services are still conducted by candlelight. There is a slide show presentation in English, and the gift shop sells a unique collection of Judaica. Closed *Yom Kippur,* Sundays in winter, and Saturdays except for 8:45 AM services. Admission charge. 3 Mr Visserplein (phone: 624-5351).

**VLOOIENMARKT (FLEA MARKET)** This is Amsterdam's famous open-air secondhand market. A major part of the fun used to be haggling over the price of treasures unearthed from the random mounds, but these days there are few treasures to be found (though it's still possible to stumble across the unexpected among the curios). Closed Sundays. The market is located at the Waterlooplein (for which it was originally named), next to the *Stadhuis* (City Hall) and the *Muziektheater* (see below).

**REMBRANDTHUIS (REMBRANDT HOUSE)** The house where the artist Rembrandt Harmensz van Rijn (1606–69) lived and worked from about 1639 to 1658 is fully restored and furnished much as it was when he was in residence. Virtually all of his 250 etchings are on display here. Closed Sunday mornings. Admission charge. Near the *Vlooienmarkt,* at 4-6 Jodenbreestraat (phone: 624-9486).

**JOODS HISTORISCH MUSEUM (JEWISH HISTORICAL MUSEUM)** At a complex of four former German synagogues, the extensive collection focuses on the Holocaust and the customs and festivals of Jewish people in the Netherlands. Closed *Yom Kippur.* Admission charge. Near Waterlooplein, at 2-4 Jonas Daniël Meijerplein (phone: 626-9945).

**MUZIEKTHEATER** Overlooking the Amstel River (which the Dutch call simply "de Amstel"), this contemporary 1,600-seat complex is home to the *Nederlands Opera* (Netherlands Opera Company) and the *Nederlands Dans Theater* (Dutch National Ballet). Adjoining the *Stadhuis* (City Hall), at 22 Waterlooplein (phone: 625-5455).

**REMBRANDTPLEIN** Once the city's butter market, the Rembrandtplein now is a pedestrian-only precinct and a leading center of nightlife, known particularly for the piano bars, cafés, and striptease clubs that line the adjoining Thorbeckeplein. An open-air art market is held on Sundays. If you enter the Rembrandtplein from Amstelstraat you'll pass Engelse Pelgrimsteeg, a street to the right where English Pilgrims lived before leaving for America. Try to catch a film in the main hall of the *Tuschinski* (26 Reguliersbreestraat; phone: 575-1751), just before the square. This ornate Art Deco theater, now a multiplex, remains one of Europe's most beautiful. Tours are available on weekdays at 11 AM for a nominal charge.

**LEIDSEPLEIN** One of the city's major nightlife centers, this square also offers daytime diversions: In the summer its open terrace is a favorite gathering place for people watchers and beer drinkers. Street performers abound (including the Andean music groups ubiquitous throughout Europe). Next door is the *Stadsschouwburg* (see *Theater*), Amsterdam's oldest and most elegant municipal theater, where English-language performances are often given.

**ONTVANGSTCENTRUM HEINEKEN BROUWERIJ (HEINEKEN BREWERY)** Although the brewery is no longer in operation, visitors can tour the premises, see a video presentation and exhibits on this brewing dynasty, and sample the brew. Tours are offered for a nominal charge at 9:30 and 11 AM and at 1 and 2:30 PM weekdays from June 14 to October 16; the rest of the year, only the two morning tours are offered. Call first to make sure it is not a holiday, and get there early, as tours and tastings are on a first-come, first-served basis. No one under 18 is admitted. Tram Nos. 16, 24, and 25 stop near the entrance. 78 Stadhouderskade (phone: 523-9239).

**ALBERT CUYPMARKT (ALBERT CUYP MARKET)** A short walk from the brewery is Amsterdam's largest and most colorful street market, where practically everything imaginable is sold. It extends for blocks along the street for which it is named, starting at the Ferdinand Bolstraat, not far from the Museumplein. Beware of pickpockets. Closed Sundays. Tram Nos. 16, 24, or 25 stop near the market.

**VONDELPARK** Amsterdam's beautiful main park, named after the prolific poet and dramatist Jacob Vondel, has 120 acres of woodland, waterways, grassy fields, the *Nederlands Filmmuseum* (see *Museums*), and one of the best jogging tracks in town. In summer, it is transformed into just the kind of colorful human zoo Amsterdam would be expected to produce, with a number of open-air events presented on an almost daily basis (see *Special Events*). It is best to go before dark. In the Museumplein area, bordered by Constantijn Huygensstraat, Overtoom, Amstelveenseweg, and Koninginneweg/Willemsparkweg.

**RIJKSMUSEUM (NATIONAL MUSEUM)** This museum is probably best known for its Rembrandts, including *The Night Watch* and *The Anatomy Lesson of Dr. Tulp,* but it also has the world's greatest collection of

Dutch paintings from the 15th to the 19th century. There's more, but first-time visitors should stick with the Dutch masters—don't miss the superb Vermeer miniatures. Unfortunately, no 18th- and 19th-century paintings or Asiatic artworks will be on display until renovations on the south wing are completed (the target date is 1996). Closed Sunday mornings. Admission charge. In the Museumplein, at 42 Stadhouderskade (phone: 673-2121).

**STEDELIJK MUSEUM (CITY MUSEUM)** Amsterdam's museum of modern art, it features paintings and sculptures dating from the mid-19th century and changing exhibitions by contemporary international artists. Some exhibits may be closed this year, as a new wing is in the works. Open daily. Admission charge. In the Museumplein, at 13 Paulus Potterstraat (phone: 573-2911).

**VINCENT VAN GOGH MUSEUM** This newest of the city's "big three" museums (the others are the *Rijksmuseum* and the *Stedelijk*) occupies a building designed by the prominent Dutch architect Gerrit Rietveld. Its ultramodern facilities feature an unrivaled collection of 200 paintings and 400 drawings by the famous Dutch artist, as well as changing exhibitions of paintings related to his work. Also on display are some of the 19 canvases discovered by the museum in 1994 which had been recycled and painted over by van Gogh (a practice that was used by some painters to save having to buy new canvas). Closed Sunday mornings. Admission charge. In the Museumplein, at 7 Paulus Potterstraat (phone: 570-5200).

**SCHEEPVAART MUSEUM (MARITIME MUSEUM)** Ship models, nautical paintings, and charts pay tribute to the country's three centuries of globe-girdling exploits. A beautiful replica of an 18th-century trading ship is moored here, as is the elegant *Koninghssloop* (Royal Ship) that once carried the queen to ships she was boarding. Closed Sunday and holiday mornings, and Mondays from mid-September through mid-June. Admission charge. In the harbor area, at 1 Kattenburgerplein (phone: 523-2222).

**ARTIS** This 150-year-old park has a beautifully landscaped garden, as well as a zoo with some fascinating inhabitants. There also are a planetarium, an aquarium, a conservatory, a geological museum operated by the university, and a coffee shop/buffet. Open daily. Admission charge. In the Plantage district, at 38-40 Plantage Kerklaan (phone: 523-3400).

**HORTUS BOTANICUS (HORTUS BOTANICAL GARDEN)** Just minutes from the zoo and city center, this botanical garden provides a welcome break from the city's bustle. A spectacular glass house resembling a circus tent houses a collection of subtropical plants. Open daily. Admission charge. 2 Plantage Middenlaan (phone: 625-8411).

## EXTRA SPECIAL

Attending the morning flower auctions held in Aalsmeer, just outside Amsterdam, means rising before dawn, but the experience is well worth the effort. The auctions are held in a building said to be the largest under a single roof on this planet—it occupies an area greater than 50 football fields. More than 4,000 flower growers are part of the immense cooperative that supplies flowers as far as the eye can see: Acres and acres of freshly cut, fragrant roses sit beside equal acreages of tulips, carnations, freesia, and other blossoms. The flower auction is held weekdays from 7:30 to 11:30 AM. Hundreds of bidders occupy the steep grandstands above the constant parade of flower-filled carts. Any hotel in Amsterdam can help arrange transportation.

# Sources and Resources

## TOURIST INFORMATION

For brochures, general information, inexpensive maps showing all the major sights, lists of hotels and restaurants, and similar materials, go to one of the three offices of the *VVV (Vereniging voor Vreemdelingen Verkeer;* Organization for Tourist Traffic). There's one opposite *Centraal Station,* in the building called the *Koffie Huis* (Coffee House; 10 Stationsplein); another at 1 Leidseplein; and the third south of the city center, on Stadionplein across from the *Olympic Stadium.* The phone number for all three offices is 340-34066 and the fax number is 625-2869; there's a charge of about 50 Dutch cents per minute. All offices are open daily. The *US Consulate* is at 19 Museumplein (phone: 664-5661).

For information in the US, contact the *Netherlands Board of Tourism* (225 N. Michigan Ave., Suite 326, Chicago, IL 60601; phone: 312-819-0300; fax: 312-819-1740). The tourist board can provide information on the *Holland Leisure Card,* which provides discounts on car, train, and plane travel as well as breaks on shopping and attractions in the Netherlands.

The *Netherlands Embassy* is at 4200 Linnean Ave. NW, Washington, DC 20008-3896 (phone: 202-244-5300; fax: 202-537-5124).

**ENTRY REQUIREMENTS** A US citizen needs a current passport for a stay of up to 90 days.

**TIME** The time in Holland is six hours later than in US East Coast cities. Holland follows daylight saving time.

**LANGUAGE** The national language is Dutch, but English is spoken by many people.

**ELECTRIC CURRENT** 220 volts, 50 cycles, AC.

**MONEY** The guilder (abbreviated as f, Hfl, or Dfl; internationally as NLG) equals 100 Dutch cents. One-cent coins are no longer minted, so all prices are rounded to the nearest 5-cent denomination. At press time one American dollar bought 1.76 guilders.

**TIPPING** A 15% service charge is included in hotel and restaurant bills; if the service is good, leave an extra 5%. The porters at train stations get 1 NLG; bellhops expect less. Taxi drivers don't expect tips, but an extra 1 NLG is appropriate for long rides. The usual tip for other small services is 1 NLG.

**BANKING/BUSINESS HOURS** Most banks are open weekdays from 9 AM to 4 PM, but larger branches of Amro and ABN banks stay open until 5 PM. Foreign exchange offices in Amsterdam are open daily and have slightly longer hours. Most businesses are open weekdays from 9 AM to 5 PM.

**NATIONAL HOLIDAYS** *New Year's Day* (January 1), *Good Friday* (April 14), *Easter Sunday* (April 16), *Easter Monday* (April 17), *Queen's Birthday* (April 30), *Ascension Thursday* (May 25), *Whitsunday* and *Whitmonday* (June 4 and 5), *Christmas Day* (December 25), and *Boxing Day* (December 26).

**LOCAL COVERAGE** The best guides to what's happening are the biweekly *What's On in Amsterdam* in English, available from hotels and the *VVV,* and *Time Out,* a commercial publication available at many hotels and newsstands. The English-language monthly magazine *Holland Herald* covers activities of interest to visitors throughout the country and runs features on restaurants, shopping, special attractions, and Dutch life in general; it's available only on *KLM* flights. Most of Amsterdam's bookshops have books in English on various aspects of the city and the rest of the Netherlands. For the best selection, try *Scheltema Holkema Vermeulen* (20 Koningsplein; phone: 523-1411); *Athenaeum* (14 Spui; phone: 622-6248), which has an adjacent newsstand with long hours, including Sundays; *W. H. Smith* (152 Kalverstraat; phone: 638-3821), the English book and magazine store; or any *AKO* establishment around town. The *American Book Center* (185 Kalverstraat; phone: 625-5537) offers books, newspapers, and magazines seven days a week.

The most detailed commercial map (which includes the entire public transport system) is the *Falkplan,* available at any newsstand or at the tourist office.

**TELEPHONE** The city code for Amsterdam and surrounding areas is 20. When calling from one area to another within the Netherlands dial 0 + city code + local number. The country code for the Netherlands is 31. In an emergency, dial 0611 for an ambulance or the police.

## GETTING AROUND

**AIRPORT** *Luchthaven Schiphol* is about a 25-minute drive from the center of Amsterdam (double that time during rush hours). *Schiphol Line* trains (for train information call 06-9292; a call costs 50 Dutch cents per minute) leave every 15 minutes for the *Station Zuid* (Amsterdam South) railway terminals at the *WTC* (World Trade Center) and the *RAI Congres Centrum* (RAI Convention Hall)—both close to the city center—the terminal by the *Confectie Centrum* (Fashion Trade Center), and *Centraal Station. KLM* (phone: 649-1393) provides bus service from the airport to several central hotels. Call for times, as the schedule is subject to change. For airport information call 06-350-34050; the charge is about 50 Dutch cents per minute.

**BICYCLE** If you have nerves of steel, do as the Dutch do and rent a bike. Be aware that cars and taxis have the right-of-way, even though daring cyclists often ignore red lights. And leave your bike securely locked. One good source is *Take-a-Bike* at *Centraal Station* (33 Stationsplein; phone: 624-8391), but its bikes are almost always rented out by noon. Also try *Holland Rent-a-Bike* (247 Damrak; phone: 622-3207). If you prefer to seek safety in numbers, arrange to join a tour of the city or surrounding countryside by calling the *VVV* (see *Tourist Information*) or *Yellow Bike Guided Tours* (66 Nieuwe Zijds Voorburgwal; phone: 620-6940).

**BOAT** In addition to the glass-topped sightseeing boats (see *Tours,* below), water taxis accommodating up to eight people can be hired or flagged down year-round for transportation or sightseeing (phone: 622-2181). They charge either a flat hourly group rate or by the meter.

**BUS, TRAIN, AND TRAM** The *Centraal Station* (1 Stationsplein, at the end of Damrak) is the main train station as well as the hub for the city's local trams and buses. For train, bus, and tram information call 06-9292 (50 Dutch cents per minute). For information on international trains call 620-2266. Most hotels have free copies of the *City Transport Welcome Folder,* which lists all pertinent information in English.

The workhorse of Amsterdam's exemplary public transportation system is its network of frequently running trams, supplemented by bus routes and a subway line. The city is divided into tariff zones, and the same tickets and passes are good for all public transportation. Buy a 12-guilder (roughly $6) *dagkaart* (day card) from the driver or an 11-guilder ($5.50) *strippenkaart* (multiple card), which can be used for short trips during the week, at any tobacco shop or the bus office at *Centraal Station.* Tell the driver your destination, and he will stamp the appropriate strip for that zone. (Passengers over 65 and under 10 travel at half fare.) Cards can be purchased at reduced prices from the *GVB* (city transport) office in front of *Centraal Station,* where simplified maps of the system are available as well. All cards are good for unlimited transfers within the same zone for one hour after being stamped. After the normal system shuts down around midnight, the *nachtbus* (night bus network), covering the main routes through the city, is in service. The *Metro* (subway) runs from *Centraal Station* to the city suburbs and generally is used by commuters only.

**CAR RENTAL** *Avis, Budget, Hertz,* and many smaller firms are well represented at *Luchthaven Schiphol* and in the city, but driving in Amsterdam is no way to have a happy holiday, especially now. A city plan aimed at ultimately banning virtually all automobiles except taxis, police cars, and ambulances from the heart of the city is now in its first phase, which includes eliminating many of downtown's already scarce parking spaces, charging even higher prices for those that remain, lowering the speed limit to 18 miles per hour, widening sidewalks, and adding bike lanes, speed bumps, poles, and posts to already narrow streets. If you choose to drive regardless of such obstacles, here are some basic survival tips: (1) Trams have absolute right-of-way and enjoy exercising it; (2) all other traffic coming from the right usually has priority, and the Dutch regard yielding as a matter of dent before dishonor; and (3) stay out of marked cycle lanes and watch out for kamikaze cyclists who ignore red lights and ride without headlights. Rules of the road are contained in the *Welcome to Holland* brochure, published by the *Netherlands Board of Tourism* and available from most local tourist offices. For street parking, make sure to buy a parking ticket, issued by machines under a large yellow sign marked "P."

**TAXI** Taxis normally don't cruise for passengers, although you sometimes can flag one down. The best place to get a cab is at one of the many taxi stands around the center of town. Or call *Taxi Central* (phone: 677-7777). Fares are fairly reasonable.

**TOURS** Taking a boat tour of Amsterdam's canals may be a tourist cliché, but it's still the best way to get acquainted with the city. Several operators along the Rokin, the Damrak, Prins Hendrikkade, and the Nassaukade run tours that depart every half hour and last about an hour. Try *Lovers* (opposite *Centraal Station;* phone: 622-2181) or *Kooij* (near the Dam on the Rokin at the intersection with Spui; phone: 623-3810). Or take a cultural excursion on the *Museum Boat* (phone: 622-2181), which shuttles between such prominent museums as the *Rijksmuseum* and the *Scheepvaart* (Maritime) *Museum.*

Visitors can tour Amsterdam by bus through *Holland International* (phone: 625-3035), which also runs excursions out of the city to tulip fields, fishing villages, and windmill-dotted countryside. *Mee in Mokum* (phone: 625-1390) offers 2½-hour walking tours of historical and cultural sites led by friendly, well-versed locals, for a nominal charge.

## LOCAL SERVICES

**DENTIST (ENGLISH-SPEAKING)** Most dentists in Amsterdam speak English fairly well; call the *Central Dental Service* at 679-1821.

**DRY CLEANER/TAILOR** *Cleaning Shop Express* (22 Huidenstraat; phone: 623-1219); *Palthé* (59 Vijzelstraat and other locations; phone: 623-0337).

**LIMOUSINE SERVICE** *Doelen* (471 Kruisweg; phone: 653-0931), 24-hour service; *Van Delden & Son* (21-23 Visseringstraat; phone: 684-8408) also is available around the clock.

**MEDICAL EMERGENCY** *Central Doctors' Service* (phone: 06-350-32042); *Vrije University Hospital First Aid* (1117 de Boelelaan; phone: 548-9111).

**MESSENGER SERVICE** *City Courier* (phone: 684-8800), 24-hour service.

**NATIONAL/INTERNATIONAL COURIER** *DHL Worldwide Express,* near *Schiphol Airport* (563 Kruisweg, Hoofddorp; phone: 06-0552); *Federal Express* (phone: 06-022-2333).

**OFFICE EQUIPMENT RENTAL** *Ruad* carries audiovisual equipment (33 Kuiperbergweg; phone: 697-8191). *Wilson Office Machines* (70 Utrechtsestraat; phone: 623-8395).

**PHARMACY** For prescriptions: *Apollo* (19 Beethovenstraat; phone: 662-8108); *Dam* (2 Damstraat; phone: 624-4331). Pharmacies are open weekdays from 8:30 AM to 5:30 PM; they operate on a rotation basis for night and weekend service. Non-prescription items are found at the *drogist;* ask your concierge for the nearest one.

**PHOTOCOPIES** *Copy Net* (102 Singel; phone: 620-9503), open on Saturdays and Sundays, has computer, telex, and fax services; *Printerette* (91 Spuisstraat; phone: 625-1744; also other locations).

**POST OFFICE** The main branch (250 Singel; phone: 556-3311) is open weekdays from 9 AM to 6 PM and to 3 PM on Saturdays.

**SECRETARY/STENOGRAPHER (ENGLISH-SPEAKING)** *Eurobusiness Center* (two locations: 62-64 Keizersgracht; phone: 520-7500, and 95 Martinolaan, Maastricht; phone: 43-821500) has a multilingual staff and also provides temporary office space; *Manpower* (World Trade Center, 901 Strawinskylaan; phone: 662-5626) is an international company providing temporary services; *Regus Business Center* (Byzantium Bldg., 14 Stadhouderskade; phone: 607-7100).

**TELECONFERENCE FACILITIES** For conference calls, dial the *PTT Telehouse* at 30-555555 to make arrangements for up to 21 connections.

**TELEX** Telecommunications of all types are processed through *PTT Telehouse* (48-50 Raadhuisstraat; phone: 674-3654), open 24 hours.

**TRANSLATOR** *Mitaka BV* (213 Herengracht; phone: 620-0676).

**OTHER** Florist (it's considered a social blunder to visit a Dutch home without bringing blooms): *Ivy's* (35 Leidseplein; phone: 623-6561 or 626-5844); *Pompon* (8 Prinsengracht; phone: 622-5137). Men's formal attire rental: *John Huijer* (153 Weteringschans; phone: 623-5439); *Maison van den Hoogen* (88 Sarphatipark; phone: 679-8828). Professional photographer: *Capital Press and Photo* (35 Schipholdijk, Bldg. 106, *Schiphol Airport;* phone: 604-1046); *Ronald Roozen* (100 Nieuwlooiersstraat; phone: 620-9818). Relocation services: *Formula Two* (70 Jacob Obrechtstraat; phone: 672-2590) for short-term housing, orientation, itinerary preparation, and other services necessary for doing business in the Netherlands. Hair salon for men and women: *Hans Douglas* (*Grand Hotel Krasnapolsky;* phone: 627-3037).

## SPECIAL EVENTS

From March through September this year the city is holding a special tribute to its environment called *Amsterdam: City on the Water,* with various exhibitions and events held at different sites. *Sail '95,* a festival of tall ships held every five years, will run from August 10 through 14. One of the largest events in Europe, it attracts restored ships from all over the world, as well as more than five million visitors. The parade held on the first day of the festival is unforgettable. For details on these events, contact the *VVV* (see *Tourist Information*).

*New Year's Eve* in Amsterdam is a wild extravaganza, with fireworks exploding throughout the city, especially in the "red-light district" when the Chinese merchants around the Gelderskade have their own colorful displays. The *Queen's Birthday* (April 30) is another time of uninhibited celebration; festivities include street fairs with live music and ethnic food stands on the Dam (which becomes a sea of people), as well as a citywide "yard sale" of secondhand goods. Joining in the celebration can be a lot of fun, but don't try to leave or arrive in the city that day; public transportation comes to a virtual standstill. *Liberation Day* (May 4) marks Dutch liberation from the Nazis; that evening Queen Beatrix traditionally lays a wreath of flowers at the war memorial on the Dam as part of a moving tribute to the war dead.

During June the annual *Holland Festival* is a day-and-night marathon crammed with dance, music, and theater performances by top Dutch and foreign companies, and the same month, during *European Gay Pride Week,* the city puts on a well-attended party that draws participants from all over the continent. July's *Summer Festival* showcases young talent. Throughout the summer, music, mime, dance, theater, and special children's programs for all tastes are presented free in *Vondelpark.* The *Uitmarkt* is a free performing arts festival held at various locations the last weekend of August; simultaneously, all concert and theater organizations offer low prices to introduce the new season.

At the beginning of September the world's largest floral procession departs from Aalsmeer, site of the world's biggest flower auction (see *Extra Special*), winding its way to the Dam by late afternoon. In mid-September the two-week *Jordaan Festival* features markets, fairs, cabarets, and other festivities. In mid-November thousands line the streets as Sint Nicolaas, the original *Sinterklaas* (Santa Claus), makes his way through the city.

## MUSEUMS

Amsterdam has more than 50 museums, covering everything from classical art to torture and hash. A museum card offers entry to almost all museums in the Netherlands, excluding special exhibitions; cards can be purchased at any museum or *VVV* office. Among the interesting museums not mentioned under *Special Places* are the following:

**ALLARD PIERSON MUSEUM** An archaeological collection spanning several thousand years of classical culture. Closed Mondays and weekend mornings. Admission charge. 127 Oude Turfmarkt (phone: 525-2556).

**AMSTERDAMS HISTORISCH MUSEUM (AMSTERDAM HISTORICAL MUSEUM)**
In this former orphanage, dating from 1414, are changing exhibitions as well as permanent displays about the history of Amsterdam. Open daily; weekend hours 11 AM to 5 PM. Admission charge. 92 Kalverstraat (phone: 523-1822).

**BIJBELS MUSEUM (BIBLE MUSEUM)** Devoted to the history of the "book of books," it also includes archaeology exhibits in two elegantly restored 17th-century canal houses. Don't miss the models of the ancient tabernacle. Closed Mondays; Sunday hours 11 AM to 5 PM. Admission charge. 366 Herengracht (phone: 624-2436).

**KATTENKABINET (CAT'S GALLERY)** Housed in an elegant 17th-century canal house, this charming museum has a huge collection of paintings, prints, and sculptures depicting—you guessed it. There also are changing exhibitions throughout the year. Closed Sunday mornings and Mondays. Admission charge. 497 Herengracht (phone: 626-5378).

**KONINKLIJK INSTITUT VOOR DE TROPEN (ROYAL TROPICAL INSTITUTE)** A showcase for Third World culture, with permanent and changing exhibitions, dance and music performances, and an exotic café-restaurant, *De Soeterijn.* Closed weekend mornings. Admission charge. 2 Linnaeusstraat (phone: 568-8200).

**MADAME TUSSAUD WASSENBEELDENMUSEUM (MADAME TUSSAUD'S WAX-WORKS MUSEUM)** This affiliate of the London branch displays wax models of famous people. The "Golden Age of the 17th Century" exhibit, in which visitors come face-to-face with Rembrandt and walk through Vermeer's studio, is the most impressive. The huge round window on the top floor offers a spectacular view of the *Koninklijk Paleis*. Open daily. Admission charge. On the Dam (phone: 622-9949).

**NEDERLANDS FILMMUSEUM (NETHERLANDS FILM MUSEUM)** Features continuing exhibits on the history of film, as well as two daily showings of classic international films. The museum's *Café Vertigo* is a great spot to have a snack on the run, especially on the terrace in warm weather. Open daily. Separate admission charges for screenings and museum exhibits. 3 *Vondelpark* (phone: 589-1400).

**NINT TECHNOLOGY MUSEUM** Modern technology, from physics to computers, is the focus here. Closed weekend mornings. Admission charge. 129 Tolstraat (phone: 570-8111).

**THEATER MUSEUM** Housed in a magnificent canal house, it has a permanent exibition on Dutch theater history, including costumes, sets, drawings, and equipment. Closed Mondays. Admission charge. 168 Herengracht (phone: 623-5104).

**VAN LOON MUSEUM** Built in 1672, this opulent house was occupied during the 19th century by merchant-prince Hendrik van Loon. It now offers a vivid example of how wealthy Dutch families lived during the golden age. Open Sunday afternoons and Mondays only. Admission charge. 672 Keizersgracht (phone: 624-5255).

**VERZETS MUSEUM** A former synagogue houses permanent and rotating exhibitions on the 1940–45 Nazi occupation of Amsterdam and the Dutch resistance movement. Closed Mondays. Admission charge. 63 Lekstraat, near the Amstel and Victoriaplein (phone: 644-9797).

**WERF'T KROMHOUT** The shipyard, one of the oldest in Amsterdam, is still in operation. It offers exhibitions, plus a demonstration of 19th-century shipbuilding. Open weekdays. Admission charge. 147 Hoogte Kadijk (phone: 627-6777).

**WILLET-HOLTHUYSEN MUSEUM** Displays describe what the elegant homes lining the canals originally looked like. Open daily. Admission charge. 605 Herengracht (phone: 523-1822).

## SHOPPING

Amsterdam's finest stores are along the P. C. Hooftstraat, adjacent Van Baerlestraat, and on the Rokin. The Leidsestraat, between the Spui and Leidseplein, and the pedestrian-only Kalverstraat, from the Dam to the *Munt* (Mint), are other busy shopping districts. Some of the best shops also can be found on the small side streets connecting the canals—Herenstraat, Prinsenstraat, Runstraat, Huidenstraat—and along the Utrechtsestraat, Wolvenstraat, and Berenstraat. In addition, the *Magna Plaza Shopping Center* (182 Nieuwe Zijds Voorburgwal), in the beautifully restored former post office headquarters behind the *Koninklijk Paleis* and the Dam, houses unique shops and cafés. The world's largest duty-free shopping center is at Amsterdam's airport, *Schiphol.*

The city has had a long history as a center of the diamond industry, and a number of old firms are happy to show visitors how the precious gems are polished to perfection. Contact the *Amsterdam Diamond Center* (1-5 Rokin; phone: 624-5787); *Gassan Diamond House* (173-75 Nieuwe Uilenburgerstraat; phone: 622-5333); *Coster Diamonds* (2 Paulus Potterstraat; phone: 676-2222); *Herman Schipper* (3 Heiligeweg; phone: 623-6572); *Holshuysen-Stoeltie* (13-17 Wagenstraat; phone: 623-7601); or *Van Moppes Diamonds* (2 Albert Cuypstraat; phone: 676-1242). The city tourist office distributes an introductory brochure about the gems.

Other good buys are delftware (from the lovely old canal city of Delft), handicrafts, tulip bulbs, and antiques—but stick to the merchants recommended above and below or you might get stuck with fake diamonds or fake antiques. The greatest concentration of antiques shops is along the Nieuwe Spiegelstraat, Spiegelgracht, and adjacent streets near the *Rijksmuseum.* An indoor antiques market at 38 Looiersgracht, between the Leidseplein and Jordaan (phone: 624-9038), is open Mondays through Thursdays and Saturdays from 11 AM to 5 PM. Stamps and coins are featured every Wednesday and Saturday afternoon on the Nieuwe Zijds Voorburgwal between the Dam and the Spui, and old books are on sale Mondays through Saturdays at the historic Oudemanhuispoort, between Oude Zijds Achterburgwal and Kloveniersburgwal. On Fridays, a weekly antiquarian book market is held along the Spui. Those interested in Sunday browsing can try the book stalls on the Dam and the Waterlooplein. At the *Noordermarkt,* a bird market and *boerenmarkt* (farmers' market) take place Saturdays until 3 PM, and a popular flea market and textiles sale takes place Mondays until 1 PM. For information about other Amsterdam markets and for more about shopping in the Jordaan, see *Special Places.*

City shops (*winkel* is Dutch for "shop") are closed Sundays and Monday mornings; some are closed all day on Mondays. Usual shop hours are from 9 AM to 5:30 or 6 PM, with a slightly earlier closing time on Saturdays. Large stores and many smaller shops, especially in the center, remain open until 9 PM on Thursdays. *Avondverkoops* (night shops) generally are open evenings from 4 PM to 1 AM. Found throughout the city, they sell fresh fruits and vegetables, prepared foods, wines, and staples. Two of the best are *Sterk* (241 Waterlooplein; phone: 626-8810), across from the *Muziektheater,* and *Mignon* (127 Vijzelstraat; phone: 420-2687).

The following shops are especially recommended:

**Authentic Ship Models** A fascinating array of wooden model ships and maritime antiques, complemented by "do-it-yourself" model kits featuring windmills and Leonardo da Vinci machinery as well as ships. 1 Kattenburgerplein (phone: 624-6601).

**De Bijenkorf (The Beehive)** Amsterdam's renowned department store stocks the finest in contemporary fashions and furnishings, and the café and buffet restaurant offer good food at fair prices. At the Dam (phone: 621-8080).

**Bobb** A superlative collection of antique timepieces and distinctive leather watchbands. 27 Utrechtsestraat (phone: 625-8137).

**Bonebakker** The oldest and most respected gem merchant in the Netherlands, founded in 1792, this is a reliable place to buy diamonds. Although the premises are elegant, prices aren't a bit higher than anywhere else. 88-90 Rokin (phone: 623-2294).

**Capisicum** Delicate Indian and Thai silk fabrics in a brilliant assortment of hues. 1 Oude Hoogstraat (phone: 623-1016) and 5 Hartenstraat (phone: 624-6460).

**Christmas World** This cheerful shop sells unique *Christmas* items year-round. Behind the *Nieuwe Kerk,* at 137 Nieuwe Zijds Voorburgwal (phone: 622-7047).

**Christopher Clarke** An English designer who creates distinctive earrings and accessories in an exquisite shop that looks like a jewelry box. 4 Molsteeg (phone: 620-0017).

**Coppenhagen 1001 Kralen** More than 7,000 beads, plus semiprecious stones and tools for the hobbyist and jewelry maker. 54 Rozengracht (phone: 624-3681).

**Donald E. Jongejans** A spectacle of spectacles—from old-fashioned granny frames to chic sunglasses. 18 Noorderkerkstraat (phone: 624-6888).

**Focke & Meltzer** Headquarters since 1823 for famous European china, porcelain, and crystal. 65-67 P. C. Hooftstraat (phone: 664-2311).

**Fred de la Bretonière** This upscale shop stocks stylish Dutch-designed shoes for men and women, as well as beautifully crafted handbags. 20 St. Luciensteeg (phone: 623-4152) and 77 Utrechtsestraat (phone: 626-9627).

**French Moon** Original handmade leather bags and accessories. 236 Prinsengracht (phone: 627-3879).

**Hoeden Atelier Cachet** Monica van Dam sells her lovely hats here, along with antique hat pins. 256 Prinsengracht (phone: 627-4742).

**Intertaal** A comprehensive foreign-language bookshop; audio and video-tapes and computer software also are sold. 76 Van Baerlestraat (phone: 671-5353).

**De Klompenboer** You can watch wooden shoes being made here, or visit a museum on the premises devoted to the history of the practical footwear. 20 Nieuwe Zijds Voorburgwal (phone: 623-0632).

**De Knopenwinkel** Its name means "Button Shop," and this tiny spot has buttons of every kind—from glass to silk. On a charming shopping street behind the *Koninklijk Paleis,* at 14 Wolvenstraat (phone: 624-0479).

**De Kookboekhandel** An infinite variety of cookbooks from around the world, many in English. 26 Runstraat (phone: 622-4768).

**Kramer Kaarsen** A tantalizing assortment of hand-dipped, beeswax, and molded candles in both dazzling and subtle hues. Candle snuffers, wall sconces, incense, and scented oils also are available. 20 Reestraat, behind the *Koninklijk Paleis* (phone: 626-5274).

**Maison de Bonneterie** This elegant chandelier-hung Amsterdam institution, dating from the 19th century, specializes in high-quality fashions. 140-142 Kalverstraat (phone: 626-2162).

**P. G. C. Hajenius** "Everything for the smoker" since 1826, including custom-rolled Havana cigars. 92 Rokin (phone: 623-7494).

**De Porceleyne Fles** A fine selection of rare delftware produced at the royal factory, as well as new pieces. 170 Prinsengracht, across from the *Anne Frank Huis* (phone: 622-7509).

**P. W. Akkerman** An unusually tasteful collection of fountain pens, with prices ranging from the affordable to the astronomical. 149 Kalverstraat (phone: 623-1649).

**Silverplate** Just about everything in Kyra ten Cate's shop is silver-plated, from candlesticks to condiment holders. But there are also Victorian picnic hampers and fine patchwork quilts. 89 Nes (phone: 624-8339).

**Tesselschade** Handmade dolls and typical Dutch crafts. 33 Leidseplein (phone: 623-6665).

# SPORTS AND FITNESS

Sports facilities in the city are much in demand and largely restricted to members. Those listed here are open to the general public, but call first to make sure there's a place for you.

**BOATING** *Ottenhome* (phone: 2158-23331), in Oude Loosdrecht, outside Amsterdam, rents sailing equipment from March 15 to October 15. *Yacht Haven Robinson* (3 Dorpstraat, Landsmeer; phone: 2908-21346) has rowing equipment.

**CYCLING** There are special paths for exploring the *Amsterdamse Bos* woodland park south of the city; bikes can be rented at the park (phone: 644-5473).

**FISHING** There's angling at the Bosbaan artificial pond in the *Amsterdamse Bos* forest area. Obtain a license from the office there (10 Nikolaswetsanstr.; phone: 626-4988; open weekdays) or at any fishing supply store in the area.

**FITNESS CENTERS** The *Splash Club* (1 Kattengat; phone: 627-1044) and the *Marriott Health Club* (21 Stadhouderskade; phone: 683-5151) offer saunas, whirlpool baths, Turkish baths, and massages; the fitness centers in the *Golden Tulip Barbizon Palace* (see *Checking In*) and the *Victoria* (1-6 Damrak; phone: 623-4255) are open to the public as well. For aerobics classes conducted in English, try *H '88* (88 Herengracht; phone: 638-0650).

**GOLF** The *Amsterdam Golf Club* (4 Zwarte Laantje; phone: 694-3650) has a driving range and a nine-hole course. Non-members must present an official handicap from their home course to play the course. One of Amsterdam's newest golf complexes is *Golf Center Amstelborgh* (phone: 697-5000), 20 minutes from the city center off Highway A-2 (Amsterdam-Utrecht; "Oude Kerk aan de Amstel" exit). It has a nine-hole course, a restaurant, meeting facilities, locker rooms, and Europe's largest driving range (lit at night).

**HORSEBACK RIDING** *Amsterdamse Manege* (25 Nieuwe Kalfjeslaan, Amsterdam; phone: 643-1342) offers indoor and ring riding only. Horses rented at *De Ruif Manege* (675 Sloterweg; phone: 615-6667) can be ridden in the Amsterdam woods.

**JOGGING** Try *Vondelpark* in the city center (entrance at Stadhouderskade and Vossiusstraat) or run along the Amstel or in the *Bos* (wood) on the southern edge of town (take tram No. 12 or bus Nos. 171 or 172 to the river).

**SKATING** There's skating at the public Leidseplein rink, and the *Jaap Eden Rink* (64 Radioweg; phone: 694-9894) is open from November through February. There's also skating on the canals in winter when they freeze over, which happens rarely.

**SOCCER** Amsterdam is the home of the world-famous *Ajax* soccer team. It's easier to get tickets to heaven than to home games, but you always can try at *Olympic Stadium* (20 Stadionplein; phone: 671-1115).

**SWIMMING** The *Marnixbad* (9 Marnixplein; phone: 625-4843) is a glass-enclosed public pool; there's also a pool at the *Zuiderpad* (26 Hobbe-makade; phone: 671-0287).

**TENNIS AND SQUASH** *Frans Otten Stadium* (10 Stadionstraat; phone: 662-8767) has indoor tennis courts; there are also indoor and outdoor tennis courts at *Gold Star* (20 Karel Lotsylaan; phone: 644-5483). Squash courts can be found at *Squash City* (near *Centraal Station* at 6 Ketelmakerstraat; phone: 622-3575).

## THEATER

Several English-language companies perform contemporary plays in Amsterdam. One of the best is *Stalhouderij* (4 1e Bloemdwars-straat; phone: 626-2282), a small theater that presents international productions. Wednesday is comedy improvisation night. The *English Speaking Theater Amsterdam* plays the *Bellevue* (90 Leidsekade; phone: 624-7248) in winter months and the *Stadsschouwburg* (26 Leidseplein; phone: 624-2311) in summer. Amsterdam's oldest and most elegant theater, the *Stadsschouwburg* also presents many international shows in English throughout the year. The recently enlarged and renovated 106-year-old *Carré* (115-125 Amstel; phone: 622-5225) frequently has top international productions, performers, and groups. Current schedules are listed for all of these in the *What's On in Amsterdam* guide, and the *VVV* will make bookings (in person only). The *VVV* theater booking office, just in front of *Centraal Station,* is closed Sundays.

## MUSIC

The driest month for first-rate cultural events is July, although some excellent summer concerts are offered at *Vondelpark* and at various theaters, churches, and cafés. At other times of the year, the best in classical music usually is performed at the *Concertgebouw* (2-6 Concertgebouwplein; phone: 671-8345), the *Muziektheater,* or the *Beurs van Berlage* (see *Special Places* for details on the last two). Every Wednesday, a free noontime concert takes place in the small hall of the *Concertgebouw.* There are special music programs throughout the year at *Cristofori* (579 Prinsengracht; phone: 626-8485), a piano salon. A concert series is offered on Saturday afternoons at the *Engels Kerk* (English Church; in the Begijnhof; phone: 624-9665), and there are frequent concerts of all kinds at two churches, the *Waalse Kerk* (157 Oude Zijds Achterburgwal; phone: 623-2074) and the *Mozes en Aron Kerk* (205 Waterlooplein; phone: 622-1305). The *IJsbreker* café (23 Weesperzijde; phone: 668-1805), a popular place to look out on the Amstel in warm weather, features new classic and contemporary music in an adjacent concert hall. On the first Sunday of each month, the *Anthony Theater* (28 Oude Zijds Voorburgwal; phone: 627-0898) in the red-light district features Yiddish music in its small, cozy space.

Rock, salsa, and world music concerts by well-known groups are held at the *Paradiso* (6 Weteringschans; phone: 623-7348) and at the *Melkweg* (234 Lijnbahnsgracht; phone: 624-1777), a holdover from the 1960s, with more than incense in the air. Both clubs charge a nominal "membership fee" plus admission. Popular jazz clubs are *Bimhuis* (73 Oudeschans; phone: 623-1361), where international artists and aspirants hold sessions; *Café Alto* (115 Korte Leidsedwarsstraat; phone: 626-3249); and *Bourbon St. Jazz & Blues Club* (6 Leidsekruisstraat; phone: 623-3440), where good local players are showcased daily. Both have drink minimums. The courtyard at *Kapitein Zeppos* (5 Gebed Zonder End; phone: 624-2057) is great in summer for live jazz music on Sundays, and *Parker's* (5a Voetboogstraat; phone: 420-1711) is the newest small jazz venue, often featuring big-name artists. For folk and blues music in a time-warp setting, try *The String* (98 Nes; phone: 625-9015). Current performances are listed in *What's On.* For bookings and further information, contact the *VVV* or the *Uitburo* ticket office (26 Leidseplein; phone: 621-1211).

## NIGHTCLUBS AND NIGHTLIFE

The greatest concentration of cafés, nightclubs, and discotheques is around the Leidseplein, Rembrandtplein, and adjoining Thorbeckeplein, and many clubs keep going until 3 AM or later. Popular discos are *Mazzo* (114 Rozengracht; phone: 626-7500); *Escape* (11-15 Rembrandtsplein; phone: 622-1111); and the *Roxy* (465 Singel; phone: 620-0354), for the hip crowd. *Boston Club,* in the *Renaissance* hotel (1 Kattengat; phone: 624-5561), and *Juliana's,* at the *Hilton International* (138 Apollolaan; phone: 673-7313), attract an older, more mainstream crowd. There is generally a cover charge, and *Juliana's* has a dress code. Among the most popular gay discos are *Exit* (42 Reguliersdwarsstraat; phone: 625-8788) and *iT* (24 Amstelstraat; phone: 625-0111), the top spot of the moment, with an outrageous mixed crowd. For a more subdued evening out, the cozy *Piano Bar Le Maxim* (35 Leidsekruisstraat; phone: 624-1920) features a variety of music.

Visitors can try their luck at the *Holland Casino Amsterdam* (in the *Lido* complex at 62 Max Euweplein; phone: 620-1006), one of the largest gambling facilities in Europe. The *Lido Theater-Restaurant* (102 Leidsekade; phone: 626-2106) features a sophisticated international variety show and a lavish dinner, as well as an adjacent casino. And for those who want one last spin of the wheel, at press time *Holland Casino* was scheduled to have opened another casino at *Luchthaven Schiphol* for departing passengers only.

What really distinguishes Amsterdam's nightlife are its cafés. A full listing of the best would fill this chapter, but the sample that follows will get you started. For other recommended places, see the jazz cafés listed under *Music* and those serving food under *Eating Out.* *Hoppe* (18-20 Spui; phone: 623-7849), dating from 1670, is the most famous and most "in" of the traditional "brown cafés" (small, dark, Old World, intimate, and convivial); *De Beiaard* (90 Herengracht; phone: 625-0422) is a popular spot best known for its wide variety of Belgian Trappist beers; and *Maximiliaan Brouwhuis* (6-8 Kloveniersburgwasl; phone: 624-2778) is a café-brewery that serves fine house suds. *Papeneiland* (2 Prinsengracht; phone: 624-1989), which claims to be the oldest café in Amsterdam, is distinguished by a tunnel entrance in its cellar that was used by 17th-century Catholics secretly gathering to worship. *Nol* (109 Westerstraat; phone: 624-5380) is a typical Jordaan café that comes alive nightly in a special "Old Amsterdam" way, complete with an uninhibited sing-along that's not to be missed. Don't ring the bell, or you'll have purchased 10 rounds of beer for the house. At the small and cozy *De Twee Zwaantjes* (114 Prinsengracht; phone: 625-2729), the local brew for several generations has been served accompanied by a song.

Most Amsterdam cafés close at 1 AM on weekdays and an hour later on weekends. Many serve as congenial daytime gathering places as well, pleasant spots to start the day, though not until 10 or 11 AM. There also are some "night cafés" that are open from 10 PM to 3 or 4 AM. Stop in at *Koophandel* (49 Bloemgracht, in the Jordaan area; phone: 623-9843), which comes alive after 1 AM and features the best in Belgian beer, bottled or on tap.

# Best in Town

CHECKING IN

Visitors arriving without a hotel reservation (not recommended) should go to the *VVV,* which, for a nominal fee, can nearly always locate a room in one of Amsterdam's more than 200 hotels. Reservations can be made through the *Netherlands Reservation Center* (*NRC;* PO Box 404, Leidschendam 2260 AK, the Netherlands; phone/fax: 70-320-2500).

Expect to pay $180 or more per night for a double room at those places listed as expensive, $100 to $180 at those rated moderate, and from $45 to $100 at inexpensive lodging spots. Rates in most hotels vary according to the time of year. The big international hostelries add a charge for breakfast—which may be either continental (coffee and rolls) or Dutch (heartier, with bread, cheese, and a soft-boiled egg)—but more traditional Dutch hotels still include it as part of the basic room rate. Note that while the larger hotels and restaurants accept major international credit cards, plastic payment is not widely accepted in Holland. It is becoming more prevalent, however; note that businesses displaying the Eurocard logo also accept MasterCard and Visa. Guest rooms in the hotels listed below have private baths, telephones, TV sets, and air conditioning unless otherwise noted, and all telephone numbers are in the 20 city code.

### EXPENSIVE

**Americain** The spirit of Amsterdam is evoked nowhere more than in this 1882 landmark. Dutch and visiting celebrities find their way to one of its 188 rooms (Madonna slept here) and nearly everyone in town eventually visits its extensively renovated Art Deco café. A glass of beer costs about the same here as anywhere else in town, and the clientele ranges from jeans-clad students to the jet set. There's a fitness center with a sauna. Business facilities include 24-hour room service, meeting rooms for up to 400, an English-speaking concierge, foreign currency exchange, secretarial services in English, audiovisual equipment, photocopiers, computers, cable TV news, and translation services. 28 Leidseplein (phone: 623-4813; fax: 625-3236).

**Amstel Inter-Continental** This has been the grande dame of Amsterdam hotels ever since it opened in 1866 on the beautiful river of the same name. Celebrities and royalty stay here, and so should anyone who wants to find out what Old World opulence and service are really all about. The butlers even iron guests' newspapers on weekdays (sorry, never on Sunday) to prevent that pesky newsprint from soiling their hands. The hotel offers 79 sumptuous rooms and 19 suites, the *La Rive* restaurant, and a complete fitness club with swimming pool. Business facilities include 24-hour room service, meeting rooms for up to 400, an English-speaking concierge, foreign currency exchange, secretarial services, photocopiers, cable TV news, and express checkout. 1 Professor Tulpplein (phone: 622-6060; 800-327-0200; fax: 622-5808).

**Forte Crest Apollo** The English country-house atmosphere of this 228-room hostelry (whose rooms were completely renovated last year) is enhanced by its lobby, which faces the water. The waterside bar and outdoor terrace offer panoramic views of five canals. There's a nonsmoking floor, laundry and dry cleaning services, a restaurant, and a valet. Business facilities include 24-hour room service, meeting rooms for up to 200, an English-speaking concierge, foreign currency exchange, secretarial services in English, audiovisual equipment, photocopiers, computers, cable TV news, and translation services. 2 Apollolaan (phone: 673-5922; 800-225-5843; fax: 570-5744).

**Garden** Not far from the museum and concert hall neighborhoods, on a quiet street, this fine small hotel is known for its 98 well-appointed rooms, two suites, and personal service. There's a bistro-style restaurant. Business services include an English-speaking concierge, 24-hour room service, foreign currency exchange, cable TV news, and photocopiers. 7 Dijsselhofplantsoen (phone: 664-2121; fax: 679-9356).

**Golden Tulip Barbizon Palace** Nineteen landmark 17th-century homes close to the *Centraal Station* and the picturesque inner harbor were connected, fitted with an ultramodern interior behind their historic façades, and transformed into this 263-room luxury hotel. The *Vermeer* restaurant, with one Michelin star, is especially good (see *Eating Out*), and the café-restaurant, *Brasserie,* serves a fine Sunday brunch. There's also a shopping arcade, a fitness center, and a large new convention center in a restored 15th-century church. Business facilities include 24-hour room service, meeting rooms for up to 530, an English-speaking concierge, foreign currency exchange, secretarial services in English, audiovisual equipment, photocopiers, computers, cable TV news, translation services, and express checkout. 59-72 Prins Hendrikkade, at Zeedijk (phone: 556-4564; 800-344-1212; fax: 624-3353).

**Grand** This building has functioned at different times as a 15th-century nunnery, the town hall, and the home of Medici royalty. It is now a deluxe hotel featuring 166 rooms, all elegantly furnished and with mini-bars. Sixteen luxury apartments with living rooms and fully equipped kitchens were designed for long-staying guests. The excellent *Café Roux* serves innovative French specialties (see *Eating Out*). There's also a spa. Business facilities include 24-hour room service, meeting rooms for up to 400, an English-speaking concierge, foreign currency exchange, secretarial services, audiovisual equipment, and cable TV news. 197 Oude Zijds Voorburgwal (phone: 555-3111; fax: 555-3222).

**Grand Hotel Krasnapolsky** Built at the turn of the century, the "Kras" has grown over the years from a coffee shop run by a Polish immigrant to an Amsterdam institution. There are 330 rooms and a lobby with a café in the original building; a new extension adds another 95 rooms, a fitness center, and a shopping arcade. Many of the spacious guestrooms offer picture-postcard views; try to book Nos. 1026, 2026, 3026, or 4026, which overlook the Dam and the *Koninklijk Paleis* (Royal Palace). The *Brasserie Reflet* is a French-style bistro with Provençal specialties. The buffet breakfast served in the *Winter Garden* is gratis to hotel guests, and the lunch buffet is delicious. Business facilities include 24-hour room service, a modern convention center with meeting rooms for up to 2,000, an English-speaking concierge, foreign currency exchange, secretarial services in English, audiovisual equipment, photocopiers, computers, cable TV news, translation services, and express checkout. On the edge of Amsterdam's red-light district, this is the only hotel in Amsterdam actually on the Dam, at No. 9 (phone: 554-9111; 800-223-5652; fax: 622-8607).

**Holiday Inn Crowne Plaza** The first deluxe European property opened by the ubiquitous American chain began operations in 1987 with 270 rooms right in the city center. Amenities include the *Dorrius* restaurant featuring Dutch specialties and 17th-century furnishings, a pool, a sauna, a whirlpool, a fitness room, and valet parking. Business facilities include 24-hour room service, meeting rooms for up to 250, an English-speaking concierge, foreign currency exchange, secretarial services in English, audiovisual equipment, photocopiers, computers, cable TV news, translation services, and express checkout. 5 Nieuwe Zijds Voorburgwal (phone: 620-0500; 800-HOLI-DAY; fax: 620-1173).

**Pulitzer** Between 1968 and 1971, Peter Pulitzer, the grandson of US newspaper mogul Joseph Pulitzer, converted a group of 24 historic canal houses into an attractive hostelry, which now is owned by the Aga Khan's CIGA group. The 232 rooms and eight apartments are modern but by no means uniform, and the original roof beams have been retained. During the summer, guests can enjoy an afternoon champagne cruise on the hotel's canal boat, which is docked right out front. The restaurant serves dinner only. Business facilities include 24-hour room service, meeting rooms for up to 160, an English-speaking concierge, foreign currency exchange, secretarial services in English, audiovisual equipment, photocopiers, computers, cable TV news, and translation services. Parking is available. 315-331 Prinsengracht (phone: 523-5235; 800-344-1212; fax: 627-6753).

## MODERATE

**Ambassade** A pleasant, modern hotel whose 52 rooms, all with baths, telephones, and TV sets, are in eight historic canal houses, each furnished with antiques. About three-quarters of the rooms are accessible by elevator. There's no restaurant, but breakfast is included in the room rate. Business facilities include 24-hour room service, foreign currency exchange, and photocopiers. 341 Herengracht (phone: 626-2333; fax: 624-5321).

**Canal House** Operated by an American couple, this snug establishment in a 17th-century house has 26 cozy rooms, most of which overlook the canal. (Guestrooms on the third floor have the best views.) If you don't want to climb stairs, request accommodations on the mezzanine level, as the charming but antiquated elevator cannot reach every floor. Breakfast is included, but there's no restaurant. 48 Keizersgracht (phone: 622-5182; fax: 624-1317).

**Classic** This property housed in a former distillery in the city center between the Damrak and the *Koninklijk Paleis* offers 33 recently renovated rooms. Breakfast is included, but there's no restaurant. 14-16 Gravenstraat (phone: 623-3716; fax: 638-1156).

**Concert Inn** Just opposite the century-old *Concertgebouw* (Concert Hall), this family-run hotel has 25 rooms. No restaurant, but breakfast is included. 11 De Lairessestraat (phone: 675-0051; fax: 675-3934).

**Esthérea** Overlooking a canal, this charming family-run hotel has 73 modern, comfortable rooms. There's no restaurant, but breakfast (in a charming setting) is included. 303 Singel (phone: 624-5146; fax: 623-9001).

**Ibis** This recently opened hotel is conveniently located next to the train station. All of the 177 rooms are modern and efficient, some with good views of the canal. There's no restaurant, but there is a café-bar, and an extensive buffet breakfast is served at a reasonable price. Business services include an English-speaking concierge, fax machines, photocopiers, cable TV news, and foreign currency exchange. 49 Stationsplein (phone: 638-9999; fax: 620-0156).

**Jan Luyken** In the heart of the concert and museum quarter, this first class family-operated 63-room hotel was recently renovated and combines modern amenities with traditional Dutch hospitality. There's no restaurant, but there is room service, and breakfast is included. 54-58 Jan Luykenstraat (phone: 573-0730 or 573-0717; fax: 676-3841).

**Roemer Visscher** Just minutes from the Leidseplein shops and restaurants, this 55-room hotel offers singles and studios; some of the singles lack private bath, TV sets, and telephones. The dining room serves Dutch and Indonesian fare. 10 Roemer Visscherstraat (phone: 612-5511; fax: 612-6724).

**Toren** Centrally located near the historic Jordaan quarter and minutes from the *Anne Frank Huis,* this establishment features 43 comfortable, clean rooms and a bar overlooking a garden. Room 131 has a splendid canal view. Rates include breakfast; there's no restaurant. 164 Keizersgracht (phone: 622-6033; fax: 626-7905).

**Tulip Inn** Opened in 1994, this hostelry is in the heart of the city, surrounded by restaurants, galleries, bookshops, and cafés. The 208 rooms are set in five historic buildings from the 1920s and are comfortably furnished. There are a restaurant, a coffee shop, and a bar, and breakfast is included. Business facilities include foreign currency exchange, an English-speaking concierge, and cable TV news. 288-292 Suisstraat (phone: 420-4545; 800-344-1212; fax: 420-4300).

### INEXPENSIVE

**Filosoof** The decor in this establishment pays homage to such great philosophers as Aristophanes (a cloud-filled sky is painted on the ceiling) and Goethe (phrases from Faust adorn the walls). Of the 27 rooms, 21 have private baths. There's no restaurant, but breakfast is included. 6 Anna van den Vondelstraat, near the *Vondelpark* (phone: 683-3013; fax: 685-3750).

**Hoksbergen** This 14-room hotel is situated on the beautiful Singel canal in the heart of the city. No restaurant, but rates include breakfast. 301 Singel (phone: 626-6043; fax: 638-3479).

**Keizershof** A true Dutch atmosphere is offered at this cozy and friendly hostelry operated by the De Vries family. The 17th-century house, located on the picturesque Keizersgracht (Emperor's Canal), has a spiral staircase connecting four floors (alas, no elevator), and there is a grand piano in the parlor. The four rooms have private showers. A tasty Dutch breakfast is included. 618 Keizersgracht (phone: 622-2855; fax: 624-8412).

**The Seven Bridges** Each of the 11 guestrooms is pleasantly decorated, and some overlook the canal. Six rooms have private baths. Breakfast is included, but there is no restaurant. Near the Rembrandtplein, at 31 Reguliersgracht (phone: 623-1329).

**Van Onna** Two canal houses—one dating from 1644—provide 17 rooms in a very simple setting, with no private bathrooms, elevator, or restaurant. A recently constructed annex offers 21 modern rooms. Breakfast is included. Proprietor Loek van Onna can recount interesting anecdotes on the building's colorful history. In the Jordaan, at 102 Bloemgracht (phone: 626-5801).

**Wijnnobel** This family-operated hotel offers 12 unpretentious rooms in an elegant building minutes from shopping, restaurants, and the museum quarter. There's one full bathroom on each of the four floors; no elevator and no restaurant. Breakfast is included. Adjacent to the *Vondelpark,* at 9 Vossiusstraat (phone: 662-2298).

---

EATING OUT

Amsterdam is justly famed for its restaurants and for its ubiquitous rijsttafel ("rice table"), the delicious ceremonial Indonesian feast adopted by Dutch colonials and now Holland's de facto national dish. In a traditional rijsttafel, bowls of rice are surrounded by up to 20 small dishes of meat and chicken with a variety of sauces (such as peanut and coconut milk), prawns, fried bananas, cucumber in sour sauce, and other dishes, some spicy and some bland. For lighter fare try *bami goreng,* stir-fried noodles with strips of vegetables and meat, or *nasi goreng,* a plate of rice with vegetables and meat. All are served in Amsterdam's many Indonesian restaurants, and some can be modified for vegetarians. The city also offers some of the best Chinese restaurants in Europe (not that there's much competition).

Traditional Dutch foods and drinks also should be sampled. You probably already are familiar with gouda and edam, the popular Dutch cheeses. Vendors in the many open-air stalls around the city also hawk salted raw herring, a Dutch favorite. *Poffertjes* (tiny pancakes usually served with ice cream or a fruit topping) and *pannekoeken* (larger crêpe-like concoctions with toppings of rum or liqueur), either of which are wonderful with just a bit of butter and sugar, are sold at stands all around Amsterdam.

Meals in Holland are hearty, designed to warm you in winter. Especially good in cold weather is *erwtensoep,* classic Dutch split-pea soup. Also tasty are *capucijners,* an indigenous Dutch bean; *hutspot* (a stew made with leeks, carrots, potatoes, and beef); and *boerenkool met rookworst* (kale with potatoes and sausage).

Dutch beer is almost uniformly excellent, though many beer lovers prefer the stronger Belgian brews. The native liquor is *jenever* (a relative of gin); *oude* (old) *jenever* is aged gin, milder and mellower; *jonge* (young) *jenever* is stronger and plainer in taste.

For the best in inexpensive eating try one of the cafés listed below or a traditional *broodjeswinkel* (sandwich shop, not to be confused with modern junk-food snack bars). There also are window snack bars that sell Dutch fast-food, such as croquettes and *pommes frites* (french fries) with mayonnaise, as well as egg rolls and *satays* (Indonesian meat kebabs with peanut sauce).

At the restaurants rated as expensive be prepared to part with $150 or more for a complete dinner for two, including wine and coffee. Dinner for two at places in the moderate category will cost between $75 and $125; at eateries described as inexpensive expect to pay $35 to $60.

Note that any restaurant displaying the blue Tourist Menu sign must provide a three-course meal for the fixed price of about $9 to $13 (not including drinks). In Amsterdam, service charges and local taxes are usually included in the bill, although an extra 5% to 10% tip is always appreciated. Unless noted otherwise, the establishments below accept major credit cards and are open for lunch and dinner, and all telephone numbers are in the 20 city code.

**Beddington's** Jean Beddington's innovative cuisine includes combinations of French and Japanese specialties as well as variations on dishes from her native England. The clean, modern lines of this "power" dining spot do not upstage the food. Try the tandoori-style monkfish. Closed Sundays and Saturday and Monday lunch. Reservations necessary. 6-8 Roelof Hartstraat (phone: 676-5201).

**Il Buongustaio** Owner Enzo Rutigliano, a former interior designer, donned a chef's cap and found his true métier. His regional Italian dishes are subtle, simple, and superb. Begin with the *insalata caprese* (mozzarella and tomatoes with fresh basil and olive oil), then ask Enzo to surprise you. A new dining area features a low-priced menu of pasta and simple appetizers. Open daily. Reservations advised. 1A-B Koggestraat (phone: 622-4587).

**Christophe** This intimate, decidedly chic restaurant has earned one Michelin star. The fare is inspired by the south of France (proprietor Christophe Royer is from Toulouse), as is the wine list. Produce and crusty bread are brought directly from Paris. Try the eggplant terrine with cumin and the lobster with sweet garlic paste. Closed Sundays. Reservations necessary. 46 Leliegracht (phone: 625-0807).

**Gauguin** Located on the waterfront level of the *Lido* complex (see *Nightclubs and Nightlife*), this chic but reasonably priced spot offers Pacific Rim fare (including fresh fish flown in from Australia) prepared with a mélange of spices. The versatile menu changes according to the season, and there is an unusually good wine list. Closed Sundays and Mondays. Reservations advised. 10 Leidsekade (phone: 622-1526).

**De Gouden Reael** A small, modern-design restaurant housed in a former seafarer's pub, this place is known only to Amsterdam's cognoscenti. Hidden away on a small island not far from *Centraal Station* (walk over the Korte Prinsengracht bridge), it is a fine place to dine out on a warm summer evening. Seasonal French regional cooking is featured, as are fine wines from the Loire Valley and beyond. Open daily. Reservations advised. 14 Zandhoek (phone: 623-3883).

**Halvemaan** This one-Michelin-star waterside spot in the suburbs is owned and operated by John Halvemaan, long considered one of Amsterdam's best chefs. It has the tranquillity of a Japanese tearoom and a kitchen inspired by France, Italy, and the Orient. Closed Sundays and Saturday lunch. Reservations necessary. In the suburb of Buitenveldert, at 20 Van Leyenberghlaan (phone: 644-0348).

**Silveren Spiegel** Picturesque and charming are the only words to describe this intimate, antiques-furnished dining place set in two very crooked houses dating from 1614. The food is French-inspired with Dutch ingredients; the service, excellent. Begin with the delicious mustard soup, and try the Dutch lamb or fresh fish of the day. Ask the owner-host Ben van de Nieuwboer, a respected wine expert, to make a selection from the impressive wine list. Closed Sundays. Reservations advised. 4 Kattengat (phone: 624-6589).

**Vermeer** The pride of the *Golden Tulip Barbizon Palace,* this elegant dining room's decor was inspired by the master painter, and much of its original 17th-century atmosphere has been retained. Seasonal fish and game dishes are the specialty, and there is an extensive wine list, which includes a variety of half-bottles and champagnes. Open daily for dinner only. Reservations necessary. 59-72 Prins Hendrikkade (phone: 556-4564).

**D'Vijff Vlieghen (The Five Flies)** It's a bit of an adventure just finding this place. The main door doesn't open, so you must enter by way of a side street, also called D'Vijff Vlieghen. Once inside, you are transported back in time by a series of delightful dining rooms built in the 17th century, complete with Rembrandt drawings on the walls. The menu features "new Dutch cuisine," which uses only fresh local ingredients. Up a steep set of stairs is an intimate *jenever* bar for an aperitif or *digestif.* Open daily for dinner only. Reservations advised. 294 Spuistraat (phone: 624-8369).

### MODERATE

**Café Descartes** This authentic French eatery hidden in the 17th-century *Maison Descartes* cultural center seats 25 to 30 patrons in the building's original kitchen. Soup, salads, and house specialties such as coq au vin, rabbit stew, and cassoulet are offered at café prices. Save room for the *tarte du jour.* The lunch and dinner menu changes daily. Closed weekends. Reservations advised. Next to the *French Consulate* at 2 Vijzelgracht (phone: 622-1913).

**Café Roux** Renowned master chef Albert Roux is managing director of the *Grand Hotel* and consultant chef to its restaurants. His influence is seen here in the details and diversity of the menu. Fresh fish is a specialty, and the à la carte menu features excellent choices like fish soup, *tarte tatin,* and *salade Niçoise.* Open daily. Reservations necessary. In the *Grand Hotel,* 197 Oude Zijds Voorburgwal (phone: 555-3111).

**Shizen** A little bit Japanese, a little bit macrobiotic, this tranquil, cozy place is not far from the Leidsenplein. Fresh fish and vegetarian variations are the specialties. Closed Mondays. Reservations advised. 148 Kerkstraat (phone: 622-8627).

**Sluizer** The dependable fish dishes served in this Old World spot make it popular with Amsterdammers and visitors alike. The restaurant next door shares the same name and offers a menu with meat dishes. In warm weather, patrons can dine on the terrace in a secluded garden. Open daily. No reservations. 45 Utrechtsestraat (phone: 626-3557).

**Speciaal** This unpretentious Indonesian restaurant in the Jordaan attracts a loyal crowd of locals and their out-of-town guests. Besides rijsttafels, vegetarian dishes are served. Open daily. Reservations necessary. 142 Nieuwe Leliestraat (phone: 624-9706).

**Witteveen** A haunt for locals, this truly elegant Old World restaurant with attentive service is a trip back in time. Try the fresh fish or the *vispotje* (fish stew). Open daily for dinner only. Reservations advised. 256 Ceintuurbaan (phone: 662-4368).

### INEXPENSIVE

**De Blauwe Hollander** This restaurant features the kind of authentic dishes any Dutch grandmother makes, from *hutspot* to mashed potatoes and endive. Open daily for dinner only. Reservations advised. In the Leidseplein district, 28 Leidsekruisstraat (phone: 623-3014).

**Broodje van Kootje** The most famous of Amsterdam's traditional sandwich shops. The food is varied, wholesome, and inexpensive. Recommended for a quick lunch or snack. For breakfast, try an *uitsmijter* (basically a ham or beef sandwich topped with a fried egg). Open daily from 9:30 AM to 1:30 AM. No reservations. No credit cards accepted. 20 Leidseplein (phone: 232046); 12 Rembrandtsplein (phone: 623-6513); and 28 Spui (phone: 623-7451).

**Caffe Panini** A popular spot for simple and delicious Italian fare: focaccia sandwiches and salads during the day, pasta by night. Service is often slow, but the food's worth it. The mozzarella salad is a good choice; for dessert, try the tiramisù. Open daily. No credit cards accepted. 3 Vijzelgracht (phone: 626-4939).

**Ceren** This charming, unpretentious little Kurdish restaurant is a haven for vegetarians and fans of Middle Eastern cooking. Make a meal of the *mezes* (appetizers), an assortment of such dishes as hummus, chopped carrots with garlic, and white bean salad. Reservations advised, as there are only a few tables. No credit cards accepted. 40 Albert Cuypstraat (phone: 673-3524).

**De Jaren** This lively two-level café has a popular terrace for warm-weather socializing. The restaurant offers a tempting salad bar, and the à la carte menu lists pasta, vegetarian dishes, fresh fish, and steaks. Open daily. Reservations unnecessary. No credit cards accepted. 120 Nieuwe Doelenstraat (phone: 625-5771).

**Manchuria** This tastefully appointed establishment in a corner of the lively Leidseplein serves several delicious versions of rijstaffel, along with Thai and Chinese fare (the Hong Kong crispy duck is a favorite). Closed December 31. Reservations unnecessary. 10A Leidseplein (phone: 626-2105).

**Pompadour** A plush tearoom, it's the place to sample handmade chocolates by the piece and creamy pastries made daily. Closed Sundays. No reservations. No credit cards accepted. 12 Huidenstraat (phone: 623-9554).

# Athens

## At-a-Glance

### SEEING THE CITY

Likavitos (Lycabettus), the city's highest hill, opens up a panorama of Syntagma (Constitution Square) and the *Ethnikos Kipos* (National Gardens), the *Acropolis* and its surrounding hills, and, in the distance, the Saronic Gulf. The summit is crowned by the tiny 19th-century *Agios Georgios* (Chapel of St. George), visible from other parts of the city and worth a closer look. A café halfway up and a restaurant at the top provide unsurpassed views. Approaches to the summit include roads; a funicular (entrance at Ploutarchou and Aristipou in Kolonaki) that runs from 8 AM to midnight; bus No. 023, which departs from Kaningos and Kolonaki Squares; and footpaths.

### SPECIAL PLACES

Most of the interesting sights of Athens are within easy walking distance of one another. Archaeological sites are concentrated around the *Acropolis*. The narrow, winding streets of the adjacent Plaka district and Monastiraki square lend themselves to exploration on foot. The Greek words for "street," "avenue," and "square" are, respectively, *odós, leofóros,* and *plateía,* but in most cases Greeks drop these and use just the names (a style adopted in this chapter); in any case, Athens street signs are increasingly bilingual, in Greek and English.

Be aware that many of the ancient sites are open from 8:30 AM to only 3 PM.

**AKROPOLIS (ACROPOLIS)** Dominating the Athenian landscape, this monument of Western civilization is unsurpassed in its beauty, architectural splendor, and historical importance. In about 1500 BC, a Mycenaean ruler crowned the site with a citadel. During the same period, the first in a series of temples honoring Athena, goddess of the city, was built. In 480 BC, the Persians sacked the city and destroyed the *Acropolis*. Some 35 years later, Pericles, the renowned Athenian statesman, conceived a plan to rebuild the temple on a grand scale as the true capital of Greek civilization. Under the direction of the architects Iktinos and Kallikrates, structures were erected that endure today. The *Propylaea* (pronounced "pro-*pee*-lay-ah"), the monumental entrance on the west, was constructed between 449 and 444 BC. Though the roof was destroyed by a Venetian cannon volley in 1687, the rows of columns—Doric (without bases) on the outside and Ionic (with bases and more elaborate capitals) on the inside—still line the way. On the south side of the *Propylaea* stands *O Naos Tis Apterou Nikis* (Temple of the Wingless Victory), or simply *Athina Niki* (Athena of Victory), built between 425 and 422 BC

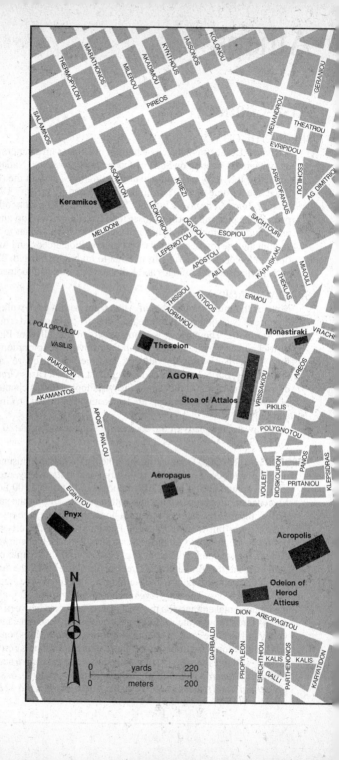

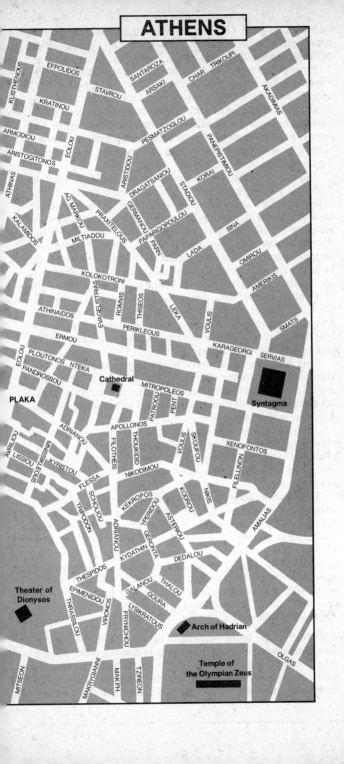

# ATHENS

KLISTHENOUS
EFPOLIDOS
KRATINOU
STAVROU
SANTAROZA
ARSAKI
CHAR TRIKOUPI
AKADIMAS

ARMODIOU
ARISTOGITONOS
EOLOU
PESMATZOGLOU
PANEPISTIMIOU

ATHINAS
AG MARKOU
PRAXITELOUS
ARISTIDOU
DRAGATSANIOU
GERMANOU
PAPARIGOPOULOU
STADIOU
KORAI
SINA

KALAMIDOS
MILTIADOU
PARN
LADA
OMIROU

KOLOKOTRONI
AMERIKIS

ATHINAIDOS
EVAGELISTRIAS
ROMVIS
THISSEOS
LEKA
VOULIS
SMATS

ERMOU
PERIKLEOUS
KARAGEORGI
SERVIAS

EOLOU
PLOUTONOS
NTEKA
PANDROSSOU
Cathedral
MITROPOLEOS
Syntagma

**PLAKA**
PATROOU
PENT

ADRIANOU
APOLLONOS
FILOTHEIS
THOUKIDID
VOULIS
SKOUFOU
XENOFONTOS

AVRILIOU
LISSIOU
MNISIKLEOUS
KYRISTOU
NIKODIMOU
FLELLINON

FLESSA
KEKROPOS
KODROU
NIKIS

SCHOLIOU
TRIPODON
ADRIANOU
YPERIDOU
ASTEROU
AMALIAS

KYDATHIN
GERONTA
DEDALOU

THESPIDOS
GALANOU
THALOU

Theater of
Dionysos
EPIMENIDOU
SONOS
GOURA
LYSIKRATOUS

THRASSLOU
VIRIONOS
FRYNICHOU
Arch of Hadrian

MITSEON
MAKRYGIANNI
MAKPH
TZIREON
Temple of
the Olympian Zeus
OLGAS

with Ionic columns. On the north side of the entrance is a Roman tower built in the 1st century as a votive offering by Agrippa, nephew of Emperor Augustus.

Beyond the *Propylaea,* on the highest part of the hill, stands the *Parthenon,* the main temple of the *Acropolis,* built between 447 and 432 BC. This is Athena's most sacred temple, and everything about it is a celebration of perfect order, from its Doric columns to the metopes (friezes with reliefs of mythological battles) that decorate it. From a distance the columns appear perfectly parallel and straight, an illusion sustained by a minor engineering trick: the turning of each column slightly inward.

To the north is the *Erechtheion,* a temple honoring Athena and Poseidon, god of the sea, who in ancient times lost out to Athena in the battle for the worship of the Athenians. The Ionic structure contains several architectural novelties, including the caryatids, sculptures of maidens that support a porch, and little friezes of palm flowers between the capitals and columns. Because of environmental damage, five of the six original caryatids have been replaced by copies; four of the originals can be seen at the *Mousion Akropoleos* (Acropolis Museum; see below). Athena gave humankind the gift of the olive, and her olive tree stands at the west side of the temple. Close inspection of the supporting wall directly north of the *Erechtheion* reveals several drums surviving from the first *Acropolis*; their purpose is to keep alive the memory of the catastrophic sack of Athens by the Persians.

Over the years, the *Acropolis* has undergone many alterations at the hands of conquerors. During the Byzantine era, the *Parthenon* and the *Erechtheion* were converted into churches; during the Turkish occupation, the *Parthenon* was used as a mosque and the *Erechtheion* as a harem.

Today air pollution and the high sulfur content of rainwater are turning the marble to soft gypsum. The *Erechtheion* has been rehabilitated; the limestone *Acropolis* rock base is being stabilized; and renovation of the *Parthenon,* which started in 1983, is progressing slowly.

The *Mousion Akropoleos* houses most of the works of art discovered in the *Acropolis* since excavation began in 1835. Highlights of the collection include fragments of the *Parthenon* frieze and numerous sculptures, including the *Kritian Boy,* the *Calf Bearer,* the *Rider and the Running Hound,* and the *Kourai* maidens. The *Acropolis* is open daily; weekend hours 8:30 AM to 2:45 PM. The museum hours are the same, except on Mondays it's open from 11 AM to 6:30 PM. One admission charge for both. Entrance on Areopagitou (phone: 321-0219). From Syntagma take bus No. 230 from Amalias and Othonos.

**PNIKA (PNYX)** This hill on the west side of the *Acropolis* is the true cradle of Athenian democracy. It was here, in classical times, that the men of Athens assembled to decide issues. All free male citizens were summoned to the hill. Officers carrying ropes covered with fresh paint rounded up those who didn't come, marking them for identification and punitive fines. Today the hill serves as the theater for a sound and light show—a dramatized history of the *Acropolis* delivered in ridiculously overblown language. But the view of the *Acropolis* is spectacular. Shows in English are held nightly at 9 PM from April through October. Admission charge. Entrance on Areopagitou, opposite the *Acropolis*.

**ARIOS PAGOS (AREOPAGUS)** The highest court of ancient Athens convened on this hill below the *Acropolis*. According to Aeschylus, Orestes was tried here for the murder of his mother, Clytemnestra. The jury split, and Athena broke the tie by throwing her support behind Orestes. In AD 51, St. Paul delivered his "Sermon of the Unknown God" from this site while proselytizing in Greece. Open daily. No admission charge. Just below the west slope of the *Acropolis*.

**AGORA AND THE STOA OF ATTALOS** The commercial and public center of ancient Athens spreads out below the *Acropolis*. During the classical age of Greece, leaders, philosophers, and common people gathered here to discuss current events and metaphysics. Sophocles taught here in the 5th century BC, and the plays of Aeschylus were performed in the theater. Much of what remains is in ruins, but you can re-create the scene in your mind's eye. No imagination is needed to evoke the ancient *Stoa of Attalos*, however. Originally built in the 2nd century BC by Attalos II, King of Pergamon, it has been reconstructed. Once an arcade of shops, the marble-colonnaded structure now serves as a museum housing Mycenaean artifacts excavated from the site, including early plans for the building of the *Acropolis* and a collection of marble statues and sculptures, coins, and vases. The *Naos Ifestou* (see below) sits atop the highest point of the *Agora*. Most of the ruins are scattered between the *Stoa* and the *Naos Ifestou*. The site is open daily; museum closed Mondays. Admission charge. Entrance at 24 Adrianou, Thission (phone: 321-0185).

**NAOS IFESTOU (TEMPLE OF HEPHAESTUS)** Also called the *Hephaesteion* or the *Theseion*, this structure was built in honor of the lame Greek god of blacksmiths and craftsmen. The first building in Pericles's ambitious program to be completed, it was designed by Kallikrates—who also built the *Athina Niki*—and was constructed between 444 and 442 BC. The *Naos Ifestou* is one of the best-preserved Doric temples in existence, despite the missing roof and worn Parian marble sculptures. The Doric hexagonal structure with slender columns offers good views of other great surrounding works; to the south along Ailou is the *Romaiki* (Roman Forum), an eastward extension of the *Agora* commissioned by Julius Caesar. The unique octagonal structure seen from the *Naos Ifestou* is the *Aerides* (Tower of the Winds), built during the 1st century BC as a combined weather vane and clock (see "Plaka District," below). During the 7th century, the *Naos Ifestou* was adapted to Christian use; it became *Aghios Georgios* (St. George's Church) around 1300. Closed Mondays. Admission charge. Entrance from the *Agora* (phone: 321-0185).

**KERAMIKOS** The cemetery of ancient Athens has some original graves in place, including the *Mnimio to Thexilo* (Memorial of Dexilos), honoring a knight killed in action at Corinth in the 4th century BC. Other graves, plus sculptures and vases found on the site, are in the *Mouseio Oberlaender* (Oberlaender Museum) beside the cemetery entrance. Closed Mondays. Admission charge. 148 Ermou, below Monastiraki (phone: 346-3552).

**THEATRO DIONISOU (THEATER OF DIONYSUS)** Built in the 4th century BC, this marble structure is the oldest of the Greek theaters. The plays of Sophocles, Euripides, Aristophanes, and Aeschylus were first performed here. Closed Mondays. Admission charge. Dionisiou Areopagitou, on the southern slope of the *Acropolis* (phone: 322-4625).

**ODION IRODOU ATTIKOU (ODEION OF HEROD ATTICUS)** Athens's other ancient (and smaller) theater was built in AD 160 by a rich Athenian philosopher. The structure illustrates the Roman influence on later Greek architecture. Open daily. No admission charge. On the southern slope of the *Acropolis* (phone: 922-6330).

**STILES OLIMPIOU DIOS (TEMPLE OF THE OLYMPIAN ZEUS)** Honoring Zeus, this massive temple, also known as the *Olympeion,* was built over a 700-year period beginning in the 6th century BC and ending under the Roman emperor Hadrian. The temple was the largest constructed in the elaborate Corinthian style. Only 14 columns remain intact, but they all are beautifully carved. Although it's surrounded by noisy streets, the historic location still provides a quiet haven for reflection. Closed Mondays. Admission charge. Vasilissis Olgas and Amalias (phone: 922-6330).

**PILI ADRIANOU (ARCH OF HADRIAN)** Hadrian had this arch built in AD 132 to demarcate the city he built from the earlier city, which was said to have been erected by the mythological King Theseus. Open daily. No admission charge. Vasilissis Olgas and Amalias (no phone).

**STADIO (OLYMPIC STADIUM)** On the site of the ancient Panathenean Stadium, this white marble structure was the site of the first modern *Olympic* games in 1896. Open daily. No admission charge. Opposite the eastern side of the *Zappeio* (Zappeion Gardens) at Vasileos Konstantinou and Agras.

**PLAKA DISTRICT** Hugging the north and northeast slopes of the *Acropolis,* this section of 19th-century Athens retains much of its original atmosphere. The narrow, winding streets are lined with restored houses, lively tavernas, and shops selling popular Greek art, pottery, jewelry, textiles, and ouzo. On the west side of the district are the *Romaiki* (Roman Forum) and the unusual *Aerides* (Tower of the Winds). Dating from the 1st century BC, this marble octagonal structure has eight reliefs, each personifying a wind blowing from a different direction. Open daily. No admission charge. Between Ermou and the north slope of the *Acropolis.*

**MONASTIRAKI SQUARE** This is the site of the *Monastiraki,* the Athens flea market, which carries on the traditions of leatherworking and metalsmithing first practiced within the city walls of the adjacent *Agora.* Numerous shops sell a variety of items, including antiques, jewelry, leather goods, copper, and bronze. Coppersmiths can be seen at work in the back of their shops. Bargaining for goods is an acceptable practice at some of the stores, but shop carefully, because many of the goods (and prices) are targeted specifically toward tourists eager to buy. The shops are open daily. On and around Ifestou.

**MITROPOLIS (GREEK ORTHODOX CATHEDRAL)** This has been the headquarters of the Greek Orthodox Church since 1864. The structure is composed of stones from 72 demolished churches, and the interior is impressively ornate. Open daily. Mitropoleos, between Syntagma and Monastiraki.

**SYNTAGMA (CONSTITUTION SQUARE)** The center of modern Athens, this is prime territory for watching the world go by. Sitting at one of the cafés, you can watch foreign businesspeople rushing in and out of luxurious hotels, office workers heading home, and persistent Greek men called *kamaki* (harpooners) trying to pick up female tourists. The *Vouli* (House of Parliament) and *Mnimio Agnosto Stratioto* (Memorial to the Unknown Soldier) flank the east side of the square. Twenty minutes before every hour, *evzones* (soldiers in traditional dress) perform the changing of the guard ceremony; Sundays at 11 AM, the entire regiment comes out in full regalia. Between Karageorgi Servias and Othonos.

**ETHNIKOS KIPOS (NATIONAL GARDENS)** Designed some 140 years ago at the urging of Queen Amalia, wife of King Otto, the gardens are home to peacocks and waterfowl, numerous nightingales, and hundreds of homeless cats. Adjacent is the *Zappeio,* Athens's version of the Paris's *Tuileries,* with broad promenades and formal gardens. Open daily. No admission charge. Entrances on Amalias, Vasilissis Sofias, and Irodou Attikou.

**ARCHEOLOGIKON MOUSION (NATIONAL ARCHAEOLOGICAL MUSEUM)** One of the world's greatest museums, this institution houses art treasures spanning 2,500 years of Greek civilization. Without a certain amount of scholarly preparation, you are not likely to be able to distinguish the Neolithic from the Cycladic from the Mycenaean—so just allow yourself to be overwhelmed by this matchless legacy of the most gifted civilization on record. You'll see sculptured bronze shields right from the pages of *The Iliad;* the *Death Mask of Agamemnon;* the *Anavissos Kouros,* the finest of the tradition of *kouroi,* sculptures of beautiful male youths; the bronze *Poseidon* discovered at Cape Artemisium in 1928; the statue of the *Youth from Marathon;* Minoan findings from excavations on the island of Santorini; and the *Jockey and Horse of Artemisium,* a bronze sculpture. Open daily. Admission charge. 44 Patission (phone: 821-7717).

# Sources and Resources

## TOURIST INFORMATION

The *Ellinikos Organismos Touristikos* (*EOT;* better known as the *National Tourist Organization of Greece* or *NTOG*) distributes free maps, brochures, and pamphlets. It has offices at 2 Amerikis, near Syntagma (phone: 322-3111), and inside the *Ethniki Trapeza* (National Bank) on Syntagma (phone: 322-2545). The *NTOG* also runs an information desk at *Hellinikon,* Athens's international airport (phone: 969-9500), and at the *Yeniki Trapeza* (General Bank; 1 Ermou; phone: 323-4130). The offices are open daily; hours are 7:30 AM to 3 PM in winter and 7 AM to 2:30 PM in summer.

Another source of tourist information and aid is the *Touristiki Astinomia* (Tourist Police), a branch of the metropolitan police that helps travelers find accommodations. They provide information in English 24 hours a day (phone: 171). The headquarters of the *Touristiki Astinomia* is at 77 Dimitrakopoulou (phone: 902-5992); other offices are at *Hellinikon* airport (phone: 970-2395), the airport's West Terminal (phone: 981-4093), and in the adjoining port of Piraeus (Pirreefs in Greek; phone: 418-4815). The *US Embassy* is at 91 Vasilissis Sofias (phone: 721-2951).

In the US the *National Tourist Organization of Greece* has several offices (168 N. Michigan Ave., Suite 600, Chicago, IL 60601; phone: 312-782-1084; fax: 312-782-1091; 611 W. Sixth St., Suite 2198, Los Angeles, CA 90017; phone: 213-626-6696; fax: 213-489-9744; and 645 Fifth Ave., Fifth Floor, New York, NY 10022; phone: 212-421-5777; fax: 212-826-6940). The *Greek Embassy* is at 2221 Massachusetts Ave. NW, Washington, DC 20008 (phone: 202-667-3168).

**ENTRY REQUIREMENTS** A US citizen needs a current passport for a stay of up to 90 days.

**TIME** The time in Greece is seven hours later than in US East Coast cities. Greece observes daylight saving time.

**LANGUAGE** Greek, though English is spoken on the tourist circuit.

**ELECTRIC CURRENT** 220 volts, 50 cycles, AC.

**MONEY** The drachma (Dr) is divided into 100 lepta. At press time there were 242 drachmas to the dollar.

**TIPPING** The minimum tip for a small service is 20 Dr. Service charges are included in most bills, but it is customary to add 5% to 10% more.

**BANKING/BUSINESS HOURS** Most banks are open weekdays from 8 AM to 2 PM. Government offices generally operate from 7:30 or 8 AM to 2:30 or 3 PM; private businesses usually are open from 8 or 9 AM to 4 or 5 PM.

**NATIONAL HOLIDAYS** *New Year's Day* (January 1), *Epiphany* (January 6), *National Independence Day* and *Feast of the Annunciation* (March 25), Greek Orthodox *Good Friday* (April 21), Greek Orthodox *Easter* (April 23), Greek Orthodox *Easter Monday* (April 24), *Labor Day* (May 1), *Whitmonday* (June 12), *Feast of the Assumption* (August 15), *National Day* (October 28), *Christmas Day* (December 25), and *Boxing Day* (December 26). Museums and archaeological sites are closed on *New Year's Day, National Independence Day, Good Friday* (afternoon), *Easter Monday,* and *Christmas Day.*

**LOCAL COVERAGE** The *Athens News* is the daily local English-language paper; the weekly *Greek News* and the bimonthly *Odyssey* also provide local news in English. Most leading foreign newspapers and magazines, including the *International Herald Tribune,* are available at hotels and at news kiosks surrounding Syntagma and Kolonaki squares. The *Athenian* is a monthly magazine in English with articles on contemporary Greece and thorough listings of entertainment events, points of interest, and restaurants. *This Week in Athens,* distributed by the *NTOG,* is a pamphlet with information on current activities and general information. *Greece's Weekly,* an English-language newsmagazine, focuses on politics.

**TELEPHONE** The city code for Athens and surrounding areas is 1. To use most public phones you will need to buy a telephone card at any newsstand (available for any amount of money desired). Since many telephone numbers in Greece have recently been changed (sometimes only by adding one digit), if you've gotten a wrong number wait until the resulting recording in Greek is finished, and an English-speaking operator should come on and give you the correct number.

When calling from one area to another within Greece dial 0 + city code + local number. The country code for Greece is 30. In an emergency dial 161 for an ambulance; 100 for the police.

## GETTING AROUND

**AIRPORT** *Aerolimenas Athina* (Athens Airport) at Hellinikon (the airport usually is referred to simply as *Hellinikon*) is 6½ miles (10 km) from Syntagma, about a half-hour drive. Inexpensive airport buses run from the West Terminal (for *Olympic Airways*) and East Terminal (foreign airlines) to Syntagma. From Athens, express buses leave from Syntagma and Omonia squares every 20 minutes from 6 AM to midnight for both terminals. News kiosks usually have information on bus stops. Note that a subway station is currently under construction at Syntagma.

**BUS** Some 40 bus and trolley routes serve central Athens and the outlying areas. Buses and electric trolleys run from 5 AM to midnight or 12:30 AM. They afford a convenient, inexpensive (75 drachmas, roughly 30¢), and fairly comfortable way to get around, provided you avoid them during rush hours: 7 to 9 AM, 2 to 3 PM, 5 to 6 PM, and 8 to 10 PM. Bus routes are outlined on the *NTOG* map of Athens; you also can check with the *NTOG* or the *Touristiki Astinomia* for information. Bus stops are marked *stasis.* Be aware that strikes frequently disrupt bus service in the city.

**CAR RENTAL** A valid international driver's license is required for Americans. Among the major firms represented in Athens are *Avis* (48 Amalias; phone: 322-4951); *Budget* (8 Syngrou; phone: 921-4771); *Avanti* (50 Syngrou; phone: 923-3919); *Hertz* (576A Vouliagmenis; phone: 994-2850); and *Pappas* (44 Amalias; phone: 322-0087). The *Elliniki Leschi Peririseos ke Autokiniton* (Automobile and Touring Club of Greece, usually referred to simply by its acronym, *ELPA*; phone: 174) can provide foreign motorists with information on road conditions and road service, insurance, legal aid, hotel reservations, and camping. For emergency service and a list of gas stations open after 7 PM, dial 104.

**SUBWAY** The system is called *ilektrikos* or *Metro* in Greek. Until the two subway lines now under construction are completed (scheduled for 1997), the city's only line passes through central Athens, linking Piraeus (Pirreefs), the major port, with the northern suburb of Kifissia. The line goes underground only downtown and emerges outside town. The fare is 75 drachmas (about 30¢). Trains run frequently between 5:30 AM and midnight.

**TAXI** Cab fares in Athens are inexpensive when compared with those in other major European cities. Most cabs are individually owned, but rates are standardized, so ask your hotel desk or the tourist office how much your intended trip usually costs. You can hail a cab in the street or pick one up at specially marked cab stands near the main squares, major hotels, or railway stations. Sharing a cab is a common practice, but you pay your full fare even if you share. Extra fare is charged for luggage. To call for a taxi 24 hours a day, dial *Proodos Radio-Taxi* (phone: 643-3400) or *Kosmos Radio-Taxi* (phone: 493-3811 or 492-0505).

**TOURS** Various companies offer sightseeing tours of Athens by air conditioned bus; two of the best are *C.H.A.T.* (4 Stadiou; phone: 322-2886) and *American Express* (2 Ermou; phone: 324-4975). Contact American historian David Hartman (phone: 659-0432) for walking tours of Attica's ancient sites. If you would like to hire a government-trained guide, contact the *NTOG,* a travel agent, or the hotel concierge.

**TRAIN** *Stathmos Larissis* (phone: 524-0646), the main train station, is a short cab ride from downtown. Trains to the Peloponnesus leave from the station on Pelopos (behind the main station). For schedules of trains departing from Athens for all domestic destinations, dial 145; for other parts of Europe, 147.

## LOCAL SERVICES

**DENTIST (ENGLISH-SPEAKING)** Dr. Dmitri Boutsias (phone: 894-7183) and Dr. John Lagos (phone: 894-9148).

**DRY CLEANER/TAILOR** *Star Dry Cleaning* (67 Panepistimiou, phone: 321-4721).

**LIMOUSINE SERVICE** *Limotours* (phone: 323-3957 or 323-7942).

**MEDICAL EMERGENCY** *Hygeia Hospital* (Kifissias and 4 Erythros Stavros, Marousi; phone: 682-7940); for 24-hour emergency medical assistance dial 166 or 161.

**MESSENGER SERVICE** *DHL Worldwide Express* is used for local deliveries (see below).

**NATIONAL/INTERNATIONAL COURIER** *DHL Worldwide Express* (44 Alinos; phone: 982-9691; or 28 Philellinon, Syntagma; phone: 323-9430); *Federal Express* (40 Vouleagmenis; phone: 995-0803).

**OFFICE EQUIPMENT RENTAL** *Executive Services Ltd.* (Athens Tower B, Suite 506, 2 Messogion; phone: 770-1062 or 778-3698).

**PHARMACY** *Pharmacy Panos Zamaloykas* (6 Stadiou; phone: 324-9589); *Pharmacy Safliani E. Efkleidou* (20 Akadimias at Voukourestiou; phone: 361-1010).

**PHOTOCOPIES** *Papachristou* (downstairs at 4A Valaoritou, phone: 363-8827).

**POST OFFICE** The main office (100 Aeolou; phone: 321-6023) and a branch (Syntagma, at Mitropoleos; phone: 324-3311 or 324-1014) are open from 7:30 AM to 8 PM.

**SECRETARY/STENOGRAPHER (ENGLISH-SPEAKING)** *Executive Services Ltd.* (see *Office Equipment Rental*); *International Business Services* (*IBS;* 29 Michalakopoulou; phone: 724-5541 or 729-1573).

**TELEX** *Executive Services Ltd.* (see *Office Equipment Rental*); *Greek Telecommunications Organization* (phone: 155 to send a telex within Greece; 165 to send it abroad).

**TRANSLATOR** *Executive Services Ltd.* (see *Office Equipment Rental*); *International Business Services* (see *Secretary/Stenographer*).

**OTHER** *American-Hellenic Chamber of Commerce and Business Library* (16 Kanari; phone: 363-6407); *American Library, American-Hellenica Union* (22 Massalias; phone: 362-9886), closed August.

## SPECIAL EVENTS

On *Megali Paraskevi* (Good Friday), one of the most solemn religious holidays (April 21 this year), an impressive candlelight *Epitaph Procession* leads from the *Mitropolis* (Greek Orthodox Cathedral) to Syntagma and back; the midnight mass on Saturday (actually early *Easter Sunday*) is just as impressive. Summer brings the *Festival Athinon* (Athens Festival)—a full complement of theater, music, opera, and ballet performed by renowned artists from Greece, Europe, and the US. Most of the events are held in the *Odion Irodou Attikou* (Odeion of Herod Atticus; see *Special Places*). Tickets for the festival are available at 4 Stadiou, in the arcade (phone: 322-1459 or 323-4467), or at the theater just before the performance. Held in a lovely pine-wooded park at Daphni, 7 miles (11 km) from Athens, the *Giorti Krasiou* (Wine Festival) runs from mid-July to early September. Admission entitles you to unlimited amounts of wine produced in all different regions of Greece. A few concessions and tavernas provide snacks and meals, and groups perform traditional and popular music and dances that get pretty merry as the night wears on. The *Diethnis Marathonas Athinon* (Athens Open International Marathon), usually on the fourth Sunday in October, follows the route of Pheidippides from near the *Tumvos Tou Marathona* (Tomb of Marathon) to the *Oliembiako Stadio* (Olympic Stadium).

## MUSEUMS

Note that at press time the *Mouseio Benaki* (Benaki Museum) was closed for renovation; check with the tourist office for updates. Besides those described in *Special Places,* the following museums may be of interest. All charge admission unless otherwise indicated. Note that many museums are open from 8:30 AM to only 3 PM.

**VIZANTINO MOUSEIO (BYZANTINE MUSEUM)** Religious art and icons from the period of Byzantine occupation, from the 3rd to 15th centuries. Closed Mondays. 22 Vasilissis Sofias (phone: 723-1570 or 721-1027).

**PINAKOTHIKI PIERIDI (PIERIDIS GALLERY)** Paintings, sculpture, and engravings by Greek and Cypriot artists. Closed Sundays. No admission charge. 29 Vasilissis Georgiou, Glyfada (phone: 894-8287 or 893-1496).

**MOUSEIO FISIKIS ISTORIAS GOULANDRIS (GOULANDRIS NATURAL HISTORY MUSEUM)** Greece's plant and animal life, geology, and paleontology. Closed Fridays. 13 Levidou in Kifissia (phone: 808-6405 or 801-5870).

**MOUSEIO LAIKIS ENDYMASIAS KAI PARADOSEOS (HISTORICAL GREEK COSTUME MUSEUM)** Traditional dress from all over the country. Open Mondays, Wednesdays, and Fridays from 9:30 AM to 1 PM. No admission charge. 7 Dimokritou, Kolonaki (phone: 362-9513).

**HISTORICAL AND ETHNOLOGICAL MUSEUM** Portraits, arms, and mementos of the heroes of the 1821 War of Independence, plus Lord Byron's sword and helmet. Closed Mondays. No admission charge on Thursdays. 13 Stadiou on Kolokotronis square, in the stately former parliament house (phone: 323-7617).

**EVREIKO MOUSEIO (JEWISH MUSEUM OF GREECE)** Judeo-Greek and Sephardic religious and folk art are represented. Closed Saturdays. No admission charge. 36 Amalias (phone: 323-1577).

**MOUSEIO KANELLOPOULOU (KANELLOPOULOS MUSEUM)** A private collection of pre- and post-Christian art and artifacts. Closed Mondays. Theorias and Panos, in the Plaka district (phone: 321-2313).

**MOUSEIO KYKLADIKIS TECHNIS (MUSEUM OF CYCLADIC AND ANCIENT GREEK ART)** Two thousand years of the Bronze Age Cycladic civilization, whose simple geometric lines and austere marble shapes have strongly influenced 20th-century sculpture. Closed Tuesdays and Sundays. 4 Neofytou Douka in Kolonaki (phone: 722-8321).

**LAIKIS ELLENIKIS TECHNIS (MUSEUM OF GREEK FOLK ART)** Traditional arts and crafts mainly from the 18th and 19th centuries, including embroidery, carved wooden objects, and paintings. Closed Mondays. 17 Kidathineion in the Plaka district (phone: 321-3018).

**SIDIRODROMIKO MOUSEIO ATHINON (ATHENS RAILWAY MUSEUM)** Old trains and related objects, including steam locomotives from the 1800s. Open Wednesdays from 5 to 8 PM and Fridays from 9 AM to 1:30 PM. No admission charge. 301 Liossion (phone: 524-6580).

**POLEMIKO MOUSEIO (WAR MUSEUM)** Weapons, uniforms, regimental flags, medals, and historical heirlooms of the battles of Greece. Closed Mondays. No admission charge. Vasilissis Sofias and Rizari (phone: 729-0544).

SHOPPING

Before you buy handicrafts, visit *EOMEH* (the National Organization of Hellenic Handicrafts; 9 Mitropoleos; phone: 325-1240), where items are exhibited in the summer (only the carpets are for sale). Goods from all over Greece—gold and silver jewelry, embroidered clothing, fabrics, *flokati* rugs of sheep's wool, wool blankets in rich colors, pottery, onyx, marble, alabaster, and leather goods, especially reasonably priced shoes—are for sale in the main shopping area downtown around Syntagma, Omonia, and Kolonaki squares, as well as in Monastiraki (see *Special Places*).

Two good shopping streets for something other than typical souvenirs are Voukourestiou and Tsakalof, which have pedestrian-only malls. The best pottery is available in Maroussi at shops along Kifissias Boulevard. For flowers, stop in *Flerianos* (3 Stadiou; phone: 322-1514); there also are several flower stalls behind the *Vouli* (House of Parliament) off Syntagma on Vasilissis Sofias. Also try *Alstromeria* (4 Dragatsaniou; phone: 322-7835). *Minion* (13 Patission; phone: 523-8901) is Greece's largest department store, with everything from bathing suits to carpets. Hours at downtown stores can be erratic, but most are closed Sundays and are open afternoons only on Mondays.

*Bibliopoleio Eleftheroudaki (Eleftheroudakis Bookshop)* Athens's oldest bookstore carries a wide selection of English-language books. 4 Nikis, between Ermou and Karageorgi Servias Sts. (phone: 322-9388).

*Brettos* An almost unlimited selection of ouzo, wines, and distilled specialties; take your camera to capture the ambience. In the Plaka district, on Kydathineon (phone: 323-2110).

*IKA (National Welfare Organization)* This nonprofit organization offers a wide variety of lovely crafts, from moderately priced copper and woven products to embroideries, jewelry, and rugs. Three locations: 6 Ypatias (phone: 325-0524, ext. 166); 135 Vasilissis Sofias (phone: 646-0603); and 352 Syngrou (phone: 942-7504).

*Karamichos-Mazarakis* Specializes in *flokati* rugs and other rugs from around the world, sometimes at low prices. Worldwide shipping is available. Near Syntagma, at 31 Voulis (phone: 322-4932).

**Lallaounis Elias** This internationally known jeweler fashions original and traditional Greek designs in gold and silver. Two locations: 6 Panepistimiou (phone: 361-1371) and 12 Voukourestiou (phone: 362-4354).

**Lyceum of Greek Women** The place for woven fabrics, embroidery, bedspreads, rugs, curtains, pillowcases, ceramics, and jewelry. 14 Dimokritou (phone: 361-1042).

**Maramenos and Pateras** A variety of exclusive jewelry designs. 2 Stadiou (phone: 324-6885).

**Mouseio Benaki (Benaki Museum)** While the museum itself was closed for renovations at press time, even if it hasn't yet reopened you can still browse in its shop. Prints and jewelry—reproductions of pieces in the museum's collection—are featured. A wide variety of other items—from matchbooks, scarves, and tablecloths to needlepoint kits—also is available. Closed Sundays. 1 Koumbari at the corner of 22 Vasilissis Sofias (phone: 361-1617).

**Music Box** Offers a diverse selection of Greek music, from classical to contemporary pop. 2 Nikis (no phone).

**Papapetrou** High-quality handbags at reasonable prices. 128 Patission (phone: 823-6918).

**Parissis** Luxury leather goods. 76 Alexandras (phone: 644-0418).

**Parthenis** A star among Greek designers, he was the first to export Greek women's fashions successfully on a large scale to the US and Europe. His designs are avant-garde and medium-priced. Dimokritou and Tsakalof in Kolonaki (phone: 363-0020) and Nikis (phone: 363-3158), near the Plaka district.

**Studio Mocassino** Stylish shoes for men and women. 7 Ermou (phone: 323-4744).

**XEN (YWCA)** The *YWCA* store has a small but attractive collection of handmade embroideries. 11 Amerikis (phone: 362-4291).

**Zolotas** An internationally renowned jeweler who creates original and traditional designs in silver and gold. 10 Panepistimiou (phone: 361-3782).

## SPORTS AND FITNESS

**FITNESS CENTERS** *Nautilus Gym* (30 Ioannis Metaxa, Glyfada; phone: 894-2111) is a small unisex health studio; *Bodyline* (Syntagma; phone: 324-4913) has beauty and fitness centers for women only throughout the country. In addition, many large hotels have fitness centers.

**GOLF** The *Golf Glyfadas* (Glyfada Golf Club, 8 miles/13 km from the center of Athens; phone: 894-6820) has a gradually sloping 18-hole course in the foothills of Mt. Hymettus, overlooking the Saronic Gulf. The 6,808-yard, par 72 layout has well-maintained fairways lined with pine trees. Clubs and carts are available for rent, and a city bus links the course with downtown.

**HIKING** *Ipethrios Zoi* (9 Vasilissis Sofias; phone: 361-5779), a mountaineering club, organizes outings every weekend at a minimal cost. All you'll need are good hiking shoes and a backpack. Another outfit is the *Ellinikos Orivatikos Synthesmio* (Greek Mountaineering Club; phone: 321-2429).

**HORSEBACK RIDING** The *Ippikos Omilos Tatoiou* (Tatoi Riding Club; Varimbombi; phone: 808-3008) has four open-air tracks. Slightly less expensive, and also open to visitors, is the *Ippikos Omilos Athinon* (Athens Riding Club; Gerakas, Aghia Paraskevi; phone: 661-1088).

**JOGGING** The *Ethnikos Kipos* (National Gardens) are honeycombed with dirt tracks, and the *Oliembiako Stadio* (Olympic Stadium) is a unique place to do some laps and stair climbing (see *Special Places* for details on both). For a real workout, try the hills around the *Acropolis.*

**SAILING AND WINDSURFING** Sailing is popular, particularly in Piraeus (Pireefs), where many residents maintain private boats in Mikrolimano, the small harbor, or in the larger *Zea Marina.* Many sailing regattas are held throughout the year. For information, contact the *Istioploikos Omilos Athinon* (Athens Sailing Federation; 15A Xenofontos; phone: 323-6813 or 323-5560). The *Ellinikos Omilos Istiosanidas* (Greek Windsurfing Association) can be contacted at 323-3696.

**SWIMMING** Within an hour's bus or cab ride from downtown Athens are clean, attractive beaches boasting lovely natural settings and complete facilities—changing rooms, refreshment stands, playgrounds, canoe and paddleboat rentals, and tennis, basketball, and volleyball courts. The *NTOG* operates a large, clean beach 25 miles (40 km) to the north at Porto Rafti (phone: 299-72572). There are two good *NTOG* beaches to the south, both 10 miles (16 km) from downtown at Voulas Alipedou (phone: 895-3248 and 895-9590). In addition, there's Vouliagmeni, 16 miles (26 km) from the center, a long and popular beach jutting out between sea and bay (phone: 896-0906); and Varkiza, 24 miles (38 km) from town, where bungalows are available (phone: 897-2102). Glyfada, 10 miles (16 km) from Athens, is a fashionable resort area with good beaches. Beaches are open year-round, though most people swim between May and October. There's a small admission charge to the *NTOG* beaches. Because of Greece's lack of treatment plants for sewage and industrial waste, the general rule is the farther from the city, the cleaner the water.

**TENNIS** Play and instruction in Athens are pleasantly inexpensive by US standards. The *NTOG* beaches listed above have outdoor tennis courts; only the court at Varkiza is open daily year-round. No equipment is provided, and a modest fee is charged. The courts at the *Athlitikis Egatastaseis Aghiou Kosma* (Aghios Kosmas Athletic Center) in Attica (phone: 981-2112) are open to non-members. Also try *AOK* in Kifissia (phone: 801-3100). More detailed information is available from the *Elliniki Omospondeia Tennis* (Greek Tennis

Federation; 89 Patission; phone: 821-0478) or the *Athens Tennis Club* (phone: 923-2872).

**WATER SKIING** Several training centers in Vouliagmeni provide instruction for beginners and equipment for those with experience. Try the *Nautikos Omilos* (Naval Club; phone: 896-2416); the *Scholi Lipiterakou* (Lipiterakou School; phone: 896-0743); or the *Scholi Kasidokosta* (Kasidokosta School; phone: 896-0820), at a hotel with a private beach.

## THEATER

Athens has a fairly active theater scene, but plays are presented almost exclusively in Greek. The state theatrical company, the *Ethniko Theatro* (National Theater; 20 Aghiou Konstantinou; phone: 522-0585 or 523-3322), performs modern and classical plays, as well as works by foreign playwrights (translated into Greek). During the summer, the company performs in the ancient Epidaurus amphitheater as part of the *Festival Athinon.*

Language is no barrier to appreciating or learning the folk dances performed by the renowned *Horoi Doras Stratou* (Dora Stratou Dance Company). Performances are held nightly year-round at the theater on Philopappou Hill (phone: 324-4395 from 8 AM to 2 PM; 921-4650 after 5:30 PM). For information about English-language performances and lectures, call the *Hellenic American Union* (22 Massalias; phone: 362-9886). The *British Council* (12 Kolonaki; phone: 363-3211) also sponsors a variety of cultural events.

## MUSIC

The *Orchistra Athinon* (Athens State Orchestra) gives classical concerts during the winter and spring. *Lyriki Skini,* the national opera company, performs operas with foreign stars during the winter and spring at the *Theatro Olympia* (Olympia Theater; 59 Akadimias; phone: 361-2461). The *Theatro Kollegiou Athinon* (Athens College Theater, Paleio Psychiko campus; phone: 671-7523) often hosts concerts by Greek and international artists. *Syllogos Parnasou* (Parnassos Hall; 8 Karitsi; phone: 323-8745) has regular recitals throughout the year. In the *Diethnis Politistiko Kentro Atheneum* (Athenaeum International Cultural Center) is the *Aithousa "Maria Kallas"* (Maria Callas Concert Hall; 8 Amerikis; phone: 363-3701), which hosts international music competitions and other cultural events. Spectacular acoustics characterize the *Megaro Mousikis Athinion* (Athens Concert Hall, on Vasilissis Sofias next to the *US Embassy;* phone: 723-1564 or 729-0391), which features a variety of concerts. The *Theatro Likavitou* (Lycabettus Amphitheater), at the foot of Likavitos (Lycabettus Hill) in the center of Athens, is the site of an annual music festival every June or July, as well as a series of summer concerts. For venues featuring traditional Greek bouzouki music, see *Nightclubs and Nightlife.*

## NIGHTCLUBS AND NIGHTLIFE

Athens has an active nightlife. Athenians tend to dine late, so very often things don't get rolling until after 10 PM. Whether you're interested in a simple evening sitting around a café or more elaborate dining and entertainment (which can get costly), you'll find numerous places to go and plenty of company. Bars and other nightspots close at 2 AM weekdays, 3 AM or later on weekends. But when the lights go off, candles are lit, and the crowd often stays until dawn.

The most celebrated of Greek social institutions are the tavernas, or restaurant-cafés. In summer, the dining is alfresco, beneath the stars and wandering vines. The emphasis is on eating, but there's often entertainment, usually folk songs and popular music. Among the more popular places are *Xynos* (4 Angelou Gerondos, in the Plaka district; phone: 322-1065), which features guitarists performing Greek songs; *Anixi* (272 Vouliagmenis; phone: 973-5012); and *Epistrefe* (in Nea Kifissias, west of the National Rd.; phone: 246-8166), for bouzouki and balalaika music. Another popular taverna is *To Terani* (at the intersection of Ragkava Tripodon and Epixarmov, in the Plaka district; no phone). The best boîtes also are concentrated in the Plaka district: *Apanemia* (4 Tholou; phone: 324-8580); *Esperides* (6 Tholou; phone: 322-5482); and *Zoom* (37 Kydathineon; phone: 322-5920).

If you're interested in a frenetic nightlife scene try *bouzoukia* (establishments where the emphasis is on traditional bouzouki music) or nightclubs. Most open at 10 PM and close around 2 or 3 AM. As the volume of the music increases, so does the pace: People burst balloons, toss flowers, and break into impromptu dances as the level of energy becomes almost as high as the tab for drinks, dinner, and entertainment. But beware of the overpriced tourist traps that streethawkers entreat you to enter, especially in the Plaka district. For classic bouzouki by renowned composers and singers, and *rembetika*—the Greek version of blues—try *Harama* (Endos Skopeftiriou in Kesariani; phone: 766-4869) or *Leoforos* (251 Syngrou; phone: 942-8237). Reservations are necessary.

Saturday night fever remains an integral part of Athens nightlife, in spite of government attempts to crimp its style. Among the classiest discos are *Barbarella* (253 Syngrou; phone: 942-5602); *Café 14* (14 Kolonaki; phone: 724-5938); *Bitchoulas* (2 Diadochou Pavlou, Glyfada; phone: 894-5560); *Rigel* (behind the *Hilton,* at 39 Michalakopoulou; phone: 724-1418); and *Make Up* (25 Ioannis; phone: 253-2806 or 251-8237). Make reservations.

For a change of pace try the *Jazz Bar Tsakalof* (Kolonaki, at 10 Tsakalof; phone: 360-5889), a supper club with jam sessions. Another popular spot, offering outdoor entertainment in summer, is *Giulietta e Romeo* (near Syntagma; phone: 322-2591), a sophisticated restaurant/piano bar. Or catch a variety show at *Diogeni's Palace* (258 Syngrou; phone: 942-4267), a music hall/restaurant.

For a more subdued evening, you can spend hours over coffee, drinks, and pastry at *Zonar's* (off Syntagma, on Panepistimiou; phone: 722-6374), a well-known café. Try the *galaktibouriko*—custard in phyllo dough. *Kafe Plaka* (Tripodon at Flessa and Lysion; no phone) is a popular place in the heart of the Plaka district. Or sip drinks at *Ratka* (24 Haritos, in Kolonaki; phone: 729-0746).

One of Athens's choicest wine bars is *Strofilia* (7 Karitsi; phone: 323-4803).

If you're interested in trying your luck, the *Mont Parnes Casino* (in the *Mont Parnes* hotel, 22 miles/35 km from Athens; phone: 322-9412) features baccarat, chemin de fer, blackjack, and roulette.

# Best in Town

## CHECKING IN

In all categories Greek hotels generally offer good value; many moderately priced and inexpensive hotels have such amenities as pools and rooftop sun decks, gardens, or bars with panoramic views of the city. In peak season expect to pay $140 to $300 per night for a double room in an expensive (deluxe) hotel; from $60 to $130 in a moderate place; and $50 or less in an inexpensive one. A number of hotels lower their rates by as much as 20% in the off-season (November through March), and group rates are available. Bear in mind, however, that as of April 1995 new rates will go into effect that—depending on the hotel—may be as much as 10% higher than the previous rates. Continental breakfast is often included in the price of a room. Unless otherwise indicated all rooms have private baths, TV sets, and telephones; in addition, all in the moderate and expensive categories have air conditioning. Note that although credit cards are more widely used here than in the past, some establishments still do not accept them. All telephone numbers are in the 1 city code.

### EXPENSIVE

**Andromeda Athens** Here are 17 deluxe rooms, four deluxe studios, five suites, and four penthouses in modern, beautifully maintained surroundings near the American Embassy. Each room has all the latest conveniences. There are also a fitness center, the *White Elephant* Polynesian restaurant, a bar, and on-site parking. Business facilities include 24-hour room service, meeting rooms for up to 250, an English-speaking concierge, foreign currency exchange, secretarial services in English, translation services, audiovisual equipment, photocopiers, computers, in-room fax machines, cable TV news, and express checkout. 22 Timoleontos Vassou, off Mavili (phone: 643-7302; fax: 646-6361).

**Athenaeum Inter-Continental** A massive glass atrium fills the huge lobby with light, and picture windows with views of the *Acropolis* illuminate separate living and sleeping areas in all 511 rooms and 48 suites. There are a French/continental restaurant; the *Café Pergola,* which offers the best Sunday brunch in town; and *Premier,* an eatery which serves cuisine of 21 different countries. Other amenities include shops, a pub, a coffee and tea lounge, a bar with live entertainment, and shuttle service to the airport and city center. Business facilities include 24-hour room service, meeting rooms for up to 1,500, an English-speaking concierge, foreign currency exchange, secretarial services in English, audiovisual equipment, photocopiers, computers, cable TV news, translation services, and express checkout. 89-93 Syngrou (phone: 902-3666; 800-327-0200; fax: 924-3000).

**Athens Chandris** Convenient to the airport and Pireefs (Piraeus), this modern hotel is 15 minutes from the city center. It has 372 rooms, and on the premises there are a rooftop pool, two restaurants, and two bars. A buffet breakfast is included. Hourly shuttle buses to the city center are available. Business facilities include 24-hour room service, meeting rooms for up to 500, an English-speaking concierge, foreign currency exchange, secretarial services in English, translation services, audiovisual equipment, photocopiers, and express checkout. 385 Syngrou (phone: 941-4824; fax: 942-5082).

**Athens Hilton International** A large, busy hotel located on one of Athens's noisiest thoroughfares, it has a big outdoor pool and a health club. The 453 rooms are a bit worn but comfortably appointed, some with views of the *Acropolis* or the mountains to the north. On the premises are the Greek restaurant *Ta Nissia* and the *Byzantine,* which offers a salad bar and a hot buffet. The bar features live piano music in a clubby atmosphere. Business facilities include 24-hour room service, meeting rooms for up to 1,200, an English-speaking concierge, foreign currency exchange, secretarial services in English, audiovisual equipment, photocopiers, computers, and express checkout. There's bus service to the airport and to the city center. 46 Vasilissis Sofias (phone: 725-0201; 800-HILTONS; fax: 725-3110).

**Grande Bretagne** This grand 132-year-old hotel is gradually regaining its old-fashioned elegance (through restoration) and once superior service. With 332 rooms and 23 palatial suites (some with *Acropolis* views), the hotel often is the scene of state receptions, and its guest list has included the most prominent personalities of the last 130 years. On the premises are an elegant dining room, the *G. B. Corner* coffee shop, a bar that attracts local movers and shakers, and a bank. The executive floor offers three suites, a lounge, and a staff that caters to the business traveler. Other business facilities include 24-hour room service, meeting rooms for up to 450, an English-speaking concierge, foreign currency exchange, secretarial services in English, audiovisual equipment, photocopiers, cable TV news, and express checkout. On Syntagma, at 1 Vasileos Georgiou (phone: 323-0251; 800-221-2340; fax: 322-8034).

**Ledra Marriott** This attractive establishment features attentive service. The 261 rooms are large, and each has a marble bath, three telephones, a mini-bar, and movies on the color TV sets; some have views of the *Acropolis.* One of Athens's only Polynesian restaurants, the *Kona Kai,* is here, as are a grill and a family-style eatery. The rooftop pool, whirlpool, and bar afford a splendid view of the *Acropolis* and the city. The hotel offers a shuttle bus to the center of town. Business facilities include 24-hour room service, meeting rooms for up to 500, an English-speaking concierge, foreign currency exchange, secretarial services in English, audiovisual equipment, photocopiers, computers, translation services, and express checkout. 115 Syngrou (phone: 934-7711; 800-228-9290; fax: 935-8603).

**Le N.J.V. Meridien** A marvel of French sophistication and modern efficiency, it features 177 superior rooms with balconies overlooking Syntagma. There are two restaurants, a bar, and shops. Business facilities include 24-hour room service, meeting rooms for up to 80, an English-speaking concierge, foreign currency exchange, secretarial services in English, translation services, audiovisual equipment, photocopiers, computers, and express checkout. Syntagma (phone: 325-5301; 800-543-4300; fax: 323-5856).

**Park** In a quiet section of town, this luxurious hotel is convenient to the *Archeologikon Mousion* (National Archaeological Museum). The building is crowned with a pool and a rooftop garden bar, both offering good views of Likavitos (Lycabettus Hill) and the *Acropolis*. The 146 rooms are equipped with mini-bars. The *Latina* restaurant serves Italian specialties; snacks are available around the clock at the coffee shop. There is a parking garage on the premises. Business facilities include 24-hour room service, meeting rooms for up to 700, and foreign currency exchange. 10 Alexandras (phone: 883-2712; fax: 823-8420).

### MODERATE

**Amalia** Across from the *Ethnikos Kipos* (National Gardens), this popular hotel is known for its friendly service. Some of the 98 modern rooms have balconies. There are a restaurant, a bar, a tearoom, and airport bus service. 10 Amalias (phone: 323-7301; fax: 323-8792).

**Athenian Inn** Very little traffic passes by this clean, attractive pension on a side street in the chic Kolonaki quarter. The friendly staff makes you feel at home. The 28 rooms, bar, and dining room are outfitted with the dark rustic furniture and fabrics of the Greek countryside. There is an English-speaking receptionist. 22 Haritos (phone: 723-9552; fax: 724-2268).

**Athens Gate** Overlooking the *Pili Adrianou* (Arch of Hadrian) and the *Stiles Olimpiou Dios* (Temple of Zeus), this brightly furnished Best Western affiliate offers 104 rooms with balconies and good views. The rooftop sun deck commands a panoramic vista of Athens. The restaurant serves traditional Greek dishes and international specialties. There's also a bar decorated in marble, leather, and chrome. 10 Syngrou (phone: 923-8302; 800-528-1234; fax: 923-7493).

**Electra** In the center of the city are 110 rooms, all simply and comfortably furnished. The rooftop pool commands good views of the *Acropolis*. There's a good bar and a restaurant serving both Greek and international cuisine. The service is first rate. 5 Ermou, just off Syntagma (phone: 322-3223; fax: 322-0310).

**Lycabette** Family-owned, this hotel with 39 rooms is minutes from Syntagma. The street is traffic-free, and the rooms are comfortably furnished. There is a restaurant. 6 Valaoritou (phone: 363-3514; fax: 363-3518).

**Novotel Mirayia Athenes** This establishment deserves praise for its 195 rooms, each cheerful, airy, spacious, and soundproof (a boon in noisy Athens). There are a good restaurant and a bar, a roof garden with an outdoor pool, and underground parking. Business facilities include 24-hour room service, meeting rooms for up to 600, an English-speaking concierge, foreign currency exchange, secretarial services in English, translation services, audiovisual equipment, and photocopiers. 4-6 Michail Voda (phone: 825-0422; 800-NOVOTEL; fax: 883-7816).

**Titania** Centrally located, this hotel is always bustling. The 398 rooms have contemporary decor and the top-floor piano bar and terrace afford stunning views. Other pluses are a 24-hour coffee shop and a restaurant. Business facilities include 24-hour room service, meeting rooms for up to 700, an English-speaking concierge, foreign currency exchange, secretarial services in English, translation services, audiovisual equipment, and photocopiers. Between Syntagma and Omonia, at 52 Panepistimiou (phone: 330-0111; fax: 330-0700).

**Zafolia** Near the *Archeologikon Mousion* (National Archaeological Museum), this place has a renovated neo-Byzantine decor, a much-frequented pool, and a garden. More than half of the 192 rooms have private baths, balconies, and air conditioning. There is a large bar, and the restaurant serves international fare. On-site parking is available, and there are meeting rooms for up to 180. 87-89 Alexandras (phone: 644-9012; fax: 644-2042).

### INEXPENSIVE

**Ava** Verging on the spartan, this small family-operated hostelry with 25 rooms is clean and quiet. Its main advantage is an ideal location, just below the *Acropolis* in the Plaka district. Some family suites with kitchens are available. There's no restaurant. 9-11 Lissi Kratous (phone: 323-6618; fax: 323-1061).

**Byron** A small, unpretentious 17-room hotel (only six of which have air conditioning) in the heart of the Plaka, yet on a quiet street. There's no restaurant, but breakfast is served. Ask for a room on the top floor, where the views of the *Acropolis* are spellbinding. 19 Vironos (phone: 323-0327; fax: 322-0276).

**Ermeion** In the center of town, this clean 29-room hostelry is five minutes from Syntagma and the *Monastiraki* flea market. The proprietors are friendly. The rooms, though, lack private baths and are not air conditioned. There's no restaurant, but breakfast is served. 66 Ermou (phone: 321-2753).

**Museum** Near the *Archeologikon Mousion* (National Archaeological Museum), it has 58 clean and comfortable rooms, a bar, and a recreation room, but no restaurant. 16 Bouboulinas and Tossitsa (phone: 360-5612; fax: 360-0507).

**Myrto** Here are 12 clean and basic rooms, but no restaurant. Near Syntagma, at 40 Nikis (phone: 322-7237).

**Nefeli** In the shadow of the *Acropolis,* this attractive property has 18 simply furnished (and non-air conditioned) rooms. Other facilities include a coffee shop and roof garden facing the *Acropolis.* Hyperidou in the Plaka district (phone: 322-8044).

**Niki** Small, it has 24 clean, standard rooms, but no restaurant. Near Syntagma, at 27 Nikis (phone: 322-0913).

---

## EATING OUT

In Greece, restaurants are more than places to have a bite before an evening's entertainment; very often they *are* the entertainment. Dinner usually doesn't start until at least 9 PM, when the tavernas begin to open. Then the parade of food begins: *mezethakia* (appetizers)—*horiatikosalata* (tomato, cucumber, olive, and feta cheese salad), *taramosalata* (a caviar spread), *fava* (a bean dish), *melitzanosalata* (eggplant salad), *spanakopita* (small spinach pies), *tzatziki* (a yogurt dip made with garlic and cucumbers), *tiropita* (cheese pies), and *dolmathakia* (grape leaves stuffed with meat, rice, and onions, served with a lemon sauce). For the entrée, there's a choice of grilled meat—lamb or beef, veal, or chicken—and a wide assortment of seafood—octopus, squid, red snapper, lobster, or *youvetsi* (a casserole), as well as moussaka, a dish of ground meat and eggplant baked with cheese. *Retsina* (a resinated wine) traditionally accompanies taverna meals, though locally brewed beers have become popular. In the winter the Greeks always eat *rathikia,* dandelion greens served with lemon and olive oil.

Adventurous carnivores should visit the meat market arcade (on Aristoghitonos, between Othiou and Omonia squares), where two 24-hour eateries serve traditional dishes in a genuine Greek atmosphere. *Stifatho* (stew), tripe, and various soups are the favorites of the regulars who make this last stop after a night at the bouzouki clubs. It's best to visit the meat market with a group, since it's located in a rough section of town. The market is closed Sundays.

For dinner for two expect to pay $75 or more in an expensive restaurant; $30 to $65 in a moderate place; and $20 or less in an inexpensive one. Prices include drinks and tips. Many restaurants are open only for dinner, so call ahead. Unless otherwise noted the restaurants listed accept major credit cards and all telephone numbers are in the 1 city code.

### EXPENSIVE

**Le Abreuvoir** The oldest French dining place in Athens serves lighter-than-air soufflés, snails, steak tartare, and tender swordfish steaks. In summer, dine in the garden under mulberry trees. The perfect spot for a secluded lunch. Open daily. Reservations necessary for dinner. 51 Xenokratous, Kolonaki (phone: 722-9061).

**Athenaeum** On the ground floor of the *Diethnis Politistiko Kentro Atheneum* (Athenaeum International Cultural Center), this soignée spot is frequented by a sophisticated crowd for snacks, lunch, and candlelit dinners. The menu offers everything from smoked salmon and caviar to steak tartare and pasta. Closed July, August, and Sundays. Reservations necessary. 8 Amerikis (phone: 363-1125).

**Bayazzo** Owned by a German chef who once cooked for the wife of the Shah of Iran, this is Athens's most elegant choice for nouvelle cuisine. Specialties include grape leaves stuffed with sea bass mousse and eggplant with ouzo-flavored mincemeat and yogurt. The truly sinful desserts deserve a visit just for themselves. Open for lunch and dinner; closed Sundays and *Christmas.* Reservations advised. 35 Ploutarchou at Dimokritou, Kolonaki (phone: 729-1420).

**Dionysos** Two restaurants with the same name but with different—though equally splendid—views: One offers a panorama from the top of Likavitos (Lycabettus Hill); the other, the *Acropolis.* The views make up for the usually mediocre menu. Stick to the *mezethakia* and the *tzatziki.* The waiters at both are multilingual. Open daily. Reservations unnecessary. Dionisiou Areopagitou, opposite the *Acropolis* (phone: 923-1936), and Lycabettus, accessible by the funicular that starts at the top of Ploutarchou, above Kolonaki (phone: 722-6374).

**Gerofinikas** One of the city's grand dames, it offers classic dishes from Greece and Turkey. We recommend the eggplant salad, *imam bayildi* (eggplant purée, onions, and tomatoes), and the best *ekmek* (a cake soaked in burnt-sugar syrup and chantilly cream) in Athens. Open daily for lunch and dinner. Reservations advised. 10 Pindarou (phone: 362-2719).

**Precieux Gastronomie** The cloying name belies the sumptuous fare served up in this fine dining establishment. French and German dishes are prepared with a deft hand; the pork filet in wine and mustard sauce and the foie gras with green apples are equally delightful to the palate and the eye. Closed Sundays. Reservations advised. In the city center, 14 Akadimias (phone: 360-8616).

### MODERATE

**Eden** One of the Plaka's best-kept secrets, this vegetarian restaurant features Greek specialties, including *melitzanosalata* (eggplant salad), hummus, and *tsatziki.* The moussaka and spinach tart are memorable. The owner uses only the freshest ingredients. Closed Tuesdays. No reservations. American Express accepted. 3 Lysiou and Minisikleous (phone: 324-8858).

**Ellinikon** Among the many trendy café-restaurants on Kolonaki this little place is where the elite meet. Of the continental and local dishes served our favorite is the lamb blanketed with a rich egg and lemon sauce spiked with wine. The pastries also are good. Open daily. Reservations unnecessary. No credit cards accepted. 19-20 Kolonaki (phone: 361-5866).

---

**Hermion** South of the *Mitropolis* (Greek Orthodox Cathedral), this stylish tavern is tucked away in an appealing cul-de-sac. The food is fresh, imaginative, and light on the oil. Try the eggplant croquettes. Open daily. Reservations unnecessary. Some credit cards accepted. 15 Pandrossou, off Kapnikareas near the Adrianou square (phone: 324-6725 or 324-7148).

**Palia Taverna** Established in 1896, this traditional taverna features delicous Greek specialties and live music. Open daily. Reservations advised. 35 Markou Mousourou, on the hill behind the *Stadio* (Olympic Stadium; phone: 902-9493).

**Ta Kalamia** One of the most famous tavernas in Greece, it relocated from central Athens to a breezy northern suburb. The first course—an array of wonderful *mezethakia*—is followed by a variety of imaginative meat dishes. In summer, dine alfresco in a bamboo-lined garden. Open daily. Reservations unnecessary. No credit cards accepted. Aghiou Georgiou and 26 Aiskilou, in Halandri (phone: 681-0529).

**To Kafenion** Athens's current equivalent to the Paris café *Les Deux Magots,* this is a perfect place to people watch and while away an afternoon. Dishes are simple, and the appetizers—start with the *keftethakia* (meatballs) and *kolokokeftethes* (zucchini with potato croquettes)—are filling. Closed Sundays. Reservations unnecessary. No credit cards accepted. 26 Loukianou, Kolonaki (phone: 722-9056).

**Vouli** The owner of this unpretentious restaurant-café bases his menu on what's fresh at the market, often putting an Asian or Italian spin on things. Open daily for lunch and dinner. Reservations advised. No credit cards accepted. 42 Haritos, Kolonaki (phone: 724-4713).

INEXPENSIVE

**Apotsos** This cozy indoor *ouzerie* is popular with locals, who come for the simple but tasty Greek dishes. The atmosphere is casual and cluttered. Closed Sundays. Reservations unnecessary. No credit cards accepted. Near Syntagma, in an arcade at 10 Panepistimiou, just west of Voukourestiou (phone: 363-7046).

**Brazilian** In the middle of town, this café specializes in tasty small sandwiches. The menu also features pastries and a variety of fresh coffees and teas—all served by an amiable staff. Closed Sundays. No reservations. No credit cards accepted. 1 Voukourestiou (phone: 323-5463).

**Delphi** A no-frills eatery, it serves fresh, light Greek food; try the moussaka and the stewed meat dishes. Open daily. Reservations advised. No credit cards accepted. In the Plaka district, on 13 Nikis (phone: 323-4869).

**O Platanos** A half-century-old taverna in the Plaka district, this place is off a small street away from the hectic crowd. Simply decorated, it offers a large selection of Greek foods; try the lamb and pasta or the veal with potatoes. Closed Sundays. No reservations. No credit cards accepted. 4 Diogenous (phone: 322-0666).

**Socrates' Prison** The owners of this unpretentious taverna—a former prison—claim it was the site of Socrates' internment. Good food, house wine, and boisterous conversation make it a jolly spot. Closed Sundays. Reservations unnecessary. No credit cards accepted. Across from the *Odion Irodou Attikou* (Odeion of Herod Atticus), 20 Mitseon (phone: 922-3434).

**Themistoklis** Delicious Greek fare is served in a brightly lit family atmosphere popular with locals. Sample the *mezethakia,* including *tzatziki,* and the *horta,* a dish of green vegetables. Open daily. No reservations. No credit cards accepted. 31 Vasilissis Georgiou, in the Pangrati neighborhood near the *Athens Hilton International* hotel (phone: 721-9553).

# Barcelona

## At-a-Glance

### SEEING THE CITY

Panoramic views of Barcelona, its harbor, the foothills of the Pyrenees, and the Mediterranean (on a clear day you can see the island of Majorca, some 125 miles away) can be enjoyed from the top of Tibidabo, a 1,745-foot hill on the northwest side of the city. To get there, take the *FFCC* train to Av. del Tibidabo, change to the *tramvia blau* (blue tram; operating from 7:05 AM to 9:35 PM daily), and take it one stop to Peu del Funicular, where you can take the funicular to the amusement park that's located on the hill. Check the park's opening hours with the tourist office beforehand, however, because it's not open daily and it closes fairly early. At other times, do as the locals do and after the tram ride walk across the square at the foot of Tibidabo to *La Venta* (Plaça Dr. Andreu; phone: 212-6455), a large restaurant with an attractive terrace whose contemporary Catalan and Basque dishes are decent but pricey. Or stop for drinks at one of the bars across the square: The *Mirablau* (phone: 418-5879) and *Merbeyé* (phone: 417-9279) both offer panoramic views of the city, especially dramatic at night, and a lively clientele. The top floor of the *Monument a Colom* (see *Special Places*) also affords an extraordinary view of the city.

### SPECIAL PLACES

Barcelona's oldest buildings of historic and artistic interest are located in the Barri Gòtic (Gothic Quarter), the medieval heart of the city. Southwest of the Barri Gòtic is the city's most colorful and animated promenade, La Rambla (also known, in the plural, as Les Rambles in Catalan, Las Ramblas in Spanish), alternately sordid and sophisticated as it stretches from the Plaça de Catalunya down to Barcelona harbor. In 1858, after the walls of the old city were razed, Barcelona expanded north and west into the Eixample (Ensanche in Castilian—literally, "enlargement"), a grid pattern of wide streets and boulevards designed by visionary city planner Ildefons Cerdà. The Av. Diagonal and the Gran Via de les Corts Catalanes, two of modern Barcelona's major streets, cut across this chessboard, which is the city's special pride because of the unparalleled late 19th- and early 20th-century *modernista* architecture found here, including a number of Gaudí's most interesting works. To the south of the Barri Gòtic and the Eixample, beginning to rise almost at the foot of La Rambla, is Montjuïc, a cultural and recreational area covering the slope of a large hill of the same name.

Keep in mind when planning visits that in Barcelona, as in other Spanish cities, churches, museums, historic sites, and other places of historic interest usually open from 9:30 or 10 AM to 1 or 2 PM, and then again from around 4 or 5 to 7 or 8 PM; some hours may change with the seasons. Some museums are open mornings only, and weekend hours are also often more abbreviated. Closing days tend to be Sundays or Mondays. Furthermore, many places close during July and/or August. If possible, it's best to call for exact hours or have a hotel or tourism office staffer do it for you (see *Tourist Information*).

## BARRI GÒTIC

**CATEDRAL DE BARCELONA** Barcelona's cathedral, dedicated to Saint Eulàlia, the 4th-century Barcelona-born martyr who is one of the city's patron saints, is an excellent example of Catalan Gothic architecture. It was begun in 1298 on the site of two earlier cathedrals. Though most of the present-day cathedral was completed by the mid-15th century, the façade and spired cupola that rises over it were added between 1887 and 1913, although they follow the original plans. The interior is laid out in classic Catalan Gothic form, with three aisles neatly engineered to produce an overall effect of grandeur. The church is comparatively bright inside, thanks to the flickering of thousands of votive candles and the shafts of light pouring through the stained glass windows.

In the enclosed choir are 14th- and 15th-century wooden stalls bearing the coats of arms of the Knights of the Golden Fleece. Also worthy of note is the 16th-century choir screen depicting scenes from the life of St. Eulàlia, who is allegedly interred in a crypt in front of the High Altar. The *Capella de Sant Benedicte* (St. Benedict's Chapel)—the third one beyond the caskets—is among the most notable of the many in the cathedral; it contains the nine-panel *Altarpiece of the Transfiguration* by the 15th-century Catalan artist Bernat Martorell. Another of the cathedral's treasures is the 15th-century polychrome tomb of St. Ramòn of Penyafort.

The adjoining cloister is a homey surprise. Accessible from within the cathedral through the *Cappella de Santa Llúcia* (St. Lucy's Chapel) or through doors from the street, it is an oasis of greenery, full of palm trees and inhabited by pigeons and a gaggle of white geese who reside beside a fountain and a pool. The cathedral is open daily; the museum is open daily from 11 AM to 1 PM. Separate admission charges to the enclosed choir and to the museum. Plaça de la Seu (phone: 315-3555).

**PALAU DE LA GENERALITAT (PALACE OF THE GOVERNMENT)** The former seat of the ancient Catalan parliament, this 15th-century Gothic structure now houses the executive branch of Catalonia's autonomous government. Among the notable rooms are a 15th-century Flamboyant Gothic chapel; the *Capella de Sant Jordi* (St. George Chapel, named for Catalonia's patron saint), with splendid 17th-century vaulting; and the 16th-century *Saló de Sant Jordi* (St. George Hall), in which the most important decisions of state have been handed down over the centuries. Unfortunately, this is a working building and is not open to the public, but arrangements can be made to see

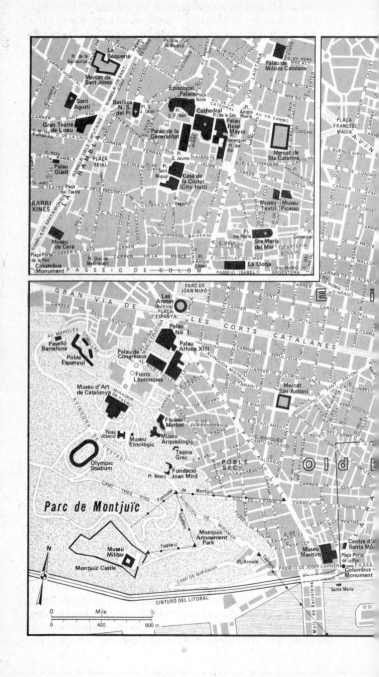

# BARCELONA

Casa-Museu Gaudí

Parc Güell

Gràcia

Eixample

Barcelona

- Museu de Música
- Casa Milà (La Pedrera)
- Centro Cultural de la Caixa
- Casa Batlló
- Casa Amatller
- Casa Lleó-Morera
- University
- Museu Taurí
- Plaça Monumental (Bellring)
- La Sagrada Família
- Cathedral
- BARRI GÒTIC FOR DETAILS SEE INSET MAP ABOVE
- Arc del Triomf
- Palau de Justicia
- Museu de Zoologia
- Museu de Geologia
- Parc de la Ciutadella
- Museu d'Art Modern
- Estació de França
- Pl. de las Armes
- Parlament de Catalunya
- Parc Zoològic

PLAÇA DE CATALUNYA

PLAÇA DE TETUAN

GRAN VIA DE LES CORTS CATALANES

Plaça de Glòries Catalanes

POBLE NOU

BARCELONETA

Olympic Village

it, on weekends only, by appointment. Contact the Protocolo (public relations) office. Plaça de Sant Jaume (phone: 402-4600).

**CASA DE LA CIUTAT (CITY HALL)** Like the *Palau de la Generalitat* across the square, this structure, also known as the *Ajuntament,* is a fine example of Gothic civil architecture. The façade on the square is 19th-century neoclassical; walk along the Carrer de la Ciutat side to see the building's original 14th-century Flamboyant Gothic façade. Closed to the public. Plaça de Sant Jaume.

**PALAU REIAL MAJOR (GREAT ROYAL PALACE)** This is the former palace of the Counts of Barcelona, who ruled the Catalan-Aragonese Confederation—and through it much of the Mediterranean world—from the 12th through the 15th centuries. A complex of buildings, dating mostly from the 14th century but built on 12th-century foundations, it is most notable for its *Saló de Tinell* (Dining Hall), which is over 50 feet high and 110 feet long and is defined by immense arches spanned by wooden beams. The Catalan Parliament met here for several years in the 1370s, and it is popularly believed that Columbus was presented to King Ferdinand and Queen Isabella here to report on his exploration of the Western Hemisphere. The room is closed to the public unless there is a concert or exhibition; then it is worth the price of admission just to see it and the stylized painting of the "Catholic Monarchs" sitting on the palace's great steps, surrounded by the heroic Columbus and the Native Americans he brought home on his return voyage. The palace is entered from the Plaça del Rei, a small and beautiful square almost completely surrounded by buildings, with a flight of shallow rounded stairs in one corner. The acoustics are excellent here, and the landing atop the stairs is sometimes used as a stage for jazz or chamber concerts. Plaça del Rei (phone: 315-1111 or 318-8599).

**MUSEU D'HISTÒRIA DE LA CIUTAT (MUSEUM OF CITY HISTORY)** Ensconced in the *Casa Clariana-Padellàs,* a 16th-century Gothic merchant's house, is a repository of Barcelona's history. Begin a tour in the basement, where pathways thread through an excavated section of Roman Barcelona, past remains of houses, storerooms, columns, walls, and bits of mosaic pavement. Upstairs rooms contain paintings, furniture, and municipal memorabilia, including the 16th-century Gran Rellotge, one of the six clocks that have occupied the cathedral bell tower. The museum also incorporates part of the Palau Reial Major. Closed Mondays. Admission charge. Plaça del Rei; enter on Carrer del Veguer (phone: 315-1111).

**MUSEU FREDERIC MARÈS** In another part of the *Palau Reial Major* (see above), this is an important collection of medieval art, particularly sculpture, which was donated to the city by Frederic Marès, a prominent local sculptor. The painted wooden religious statues, peculiar to this part of Iberia, are outstanding. On the upper floors, a display of artifacts ranging from costumes and combs to pipes and purses invites visitors to discover what everyday life was like in old Catalonia. Closed Mondays. Admission charge. 5-6 Plaça de Sant Iu (phone: 310-5800).

**MUSEU PICASSO** Although Picasso was born in Málaga and lived in France for 69 years, Barcelona was where he spent his student days, and it occupied a warm place in his heart and provided artistic inspiration throughout his life. This museum was founded in 1963 when Jaime Sabartés, a native of Barcelona and friend of Picasso's, presented his collection of the master's work to the city (Picasso himself donated 58 paintings). Housed in the beautiful 15th-century *Palau Aguilar,* which is nearly as interesting as the artist's works, the museum is not strictly within the Barri Gòtic, although it's quite near. A lovely Gothic-Renaissance courtyard opens to the roof, surrounded by tiers of arcaded galleries with pointed arches and slender columns. Lithographs and early works from the artist's years in Málaga and Barcelona constitute most of the collection; there's also a large exhibition of 44 variations on *Las Meninas,* the famous Velázquez painting in Madrid's Prado. Also notice examples of Picasso's warm and unpretentious ceramic work. Closed Mondays. Admission charge. 15 Carrer de Montcada (phone: 319-6310).

**MUSEU TÈXTIL I DE LA INDUMENTÀRIA (TEXTILE AND COSTUME MUSEUM)** The beautiful 14th-century palace of the Marquis of Lió holds a fascinating collection of fabrics and men's and women's everyday and ceremonial dresses from the 18th to the 20th century. Closed Mondays. Admission charge. 12 Carrer de Montcada (phone: 310-4516).

**ESGLÉSIA DE SANTA MARIA DEL MAR (CHURCH OF ST. MARY OF THE SEA)** At the foot of the Carrer de Montcada, where it meets Passeig del Born, is the back of what many consider to be the most beautiful Gothic church in Barcelona, if not in all Spain. Once the preserve of the city's wealthy shipbuilders and merchants, the church dates mostly from the 14th century. Walk around to the front entrance on the Plaça Santa Maria and note the perfectly proportioned and simply (but attractively) detailed façade. The interior of the church draws its great beauty from its simplicity and its high, slender proportions. Plaça Santa Maria (phone: 310-2390).

**PALAU DE LA MÚSICA CATALANA (PALACE OF CATALAN MUSIC)** Not far from the Barri Gòtic, this is quintessential *modernisme.* Designed by Lluís Domènech i Montaner and built from 1905 to 1908, this concert hall is as colorful as anything designed by the more famous Gaudí. But it's also less bizarre and, in the opinion of many, more beautiful. The interior, renovated and expanded by noted Barcelona architects Oscar Tusquets and Carlos Díaz, is partially illuminated by an elaborate stained glass dome; it's full of mosaics and rife with ceramic rosettes, garlands, and winged beasts. Tours are given in several languages and schedules vary, but attendance at part of a rehearsal by the *Orquesta Municipal de Barcelona* often is included; call for details. Or just amble in with the crowd on evenings when there is a performance and admire the foyer, a lovely space full of brick pillars that rise to ceramic capitals. In summer, when there are no concerts or tours, make sure to walk by the equally colorful exterior. Carrer d'Amadeu Vives (phone: 317-9982).

**PASSEIG DE GRÀCIA** Running from Plaça de Catalunya to Plaça de Joan Carles I, where it is cut off by Av. Diagonal, this is the widest boulevard in the grid-patterned Eixample. Lined with boutiques, banks, hotels, cinemas, and art galleries, it links the Barri Gòtic to what once was the old village of Gràcia, and it provides a pleasant backdrop for a stroll. Note the *fanals-banc,* combined lampposts and mosaic benches. Of much greater interest, however, are the *modernista* buildings located here, three of them on one block alone (see below).

**CASA LLEÓ-MORERA** This is one of three noteworthy buildings occupying the block between Carrer del Consell de Cent and Carrer d'Aragó, dubbed the *manzana de la discordia* ("apple of discord," also a pun meaning "block of discord") by locals who were shocked by the clashing avant-garde styles of the architecture. Designed by Domènech i Montaner and built in 1905, at the peak of the *modernista* movement, this structure has stone balconies carved in flower designs and winged lions. The façade is monochromatic, but step across the street to see the ventilator on top, which looks like an elaborate bonnet with a green, pink, and yellow flowered hat band. The interior is not open to the public. 35 Passeig de Gràcia, on the corner of Carrer del Consell de Cent.

**CASA AMATLLER AND CASA BATLLÓ** These two buildings, both designed as apartment complexes, make up the remainder of the "block of discord." The *Casa Amatller* (41 Passeig de Gràcia), completed in 1900, was designed by Josep Puig i Cadafalch, perhaps the best-known and most prolific of *modernista* architects and designers after Gaudí and Domènech i Montaner. The building contrasts dramatically with its neighbor, the *Casa Batlló* (43 Passeig de Gràcia), designed by Antoni Gaudí, leader of the *modernista* movement. Built circa 1907, it's a fairy-tale abode with mask-shaped balconies, sensuous curves in stone and iron, and bits of broken tile in its upper levels. Both buildings are closed to the public, though it may be possible to take a peek in the lobby.

**CASA MILÀ** Only a few blocks from the "block of discord," on the other side of the Passeig de Gràcia, is this apartment house, regarded as the classic example of Gaudí's *modernista* architecture. Popularly known as La Pedrera (the "Stone Quarry"), this sinuous yet geometric building seems to be making an almost sculptural attempt to distance itself from the harsh, square lines of its turn-of-the-century neighbors. Barcelona novelist Joan Perucho once wrote that the *Casa Milà* "gives the impression of a mountain eroded by the wind and the rain, excavated right into its entrails by the piercing blast of atmospheric accident." Be sure to visit the rooftop terrace, with its strange chimney caps. There is no elevator, but the six flights of stairs are worth the effort to see details of doorknobs and banisters en route. Conducted tours take place Mondays through Saturdays at 10 and 11 AM, noon, and 1 PM. No admission charge. 91 Passeig de Gràcia (phone: 487-3613).

**FUNDACIÓ ANTONI TÀPIES (ANTONI TÀPIES FOUNDATION)** Designed by Lluís Domènech i Montaner in an early *modernista* style with Mudejar (medieval Hispanicized Moorish) overtones, this museum houses a major collection of the internationally acclaimed, still-living Catalan artist's works—paintings, drawings, sculpture, assemblages, and ceramics. There also is a research library, as well as a basement gallery devoted to shows by other artists and photographers. But perhaps the main attraction is the huge Tàpies sculpture of metal wire and tubing on the roof of the building, taking up the entire width of the façade and adding 40-plus feet to its height. It's called *Cloud and Chair,* and if you're walking along the opposite side of the street, near Passeig de Gràcia, you can't help but notice it. Closed Mondays. Admission charge. 255 Carrer d'Aragó (phone: 487-0315).

**PARC GÜELL (GÜELL PARK)** Planned as a real estate development by Gaudí and his friend Count Eusebi Güell, a noted Barcelona industrialist and civic leader, Parc Güell is now a public park. At its core, resting on 86 pillars and edged with an undulating stone bench "upholstered" with a mosaic quilt of broken glass and tiles, is a plaza that was meant to be the development project's marketplace. Only two of the development's houses—the cottages flanking the park entrance—were ever built; a third, not designed by Gaudí but his home for the last two decades of his life, has been turned into the *Casa-Museu Gaudí,* containing drawings, models, furniture, and a number of his belongings. South of the park, the Passeig de Gràcia ambles past some impish turn-of-the-century houses. The park is open daily; the museum is closed Saturdays. Admission charge to the museum (phone: 284-6446). The park is located to the north and west of the Eixample. Bus No. 24 up Passeig de Gràcia leads to the Carretera del Carmel entrance, which is close to the museum, and also not far from the main park entrance (with pavilions), at Carrer de Llarrad and Carrer d'Olot. Metro line No. 3 runs from the intersection of Passeig de Gràcia and the Av. Diagonal to Plaça Lesseps (two stops); the main entrance is about a six-block (uphill) walk from there.

**TEMPLE EXPIATORI DE LA SAGRADA FAMÍLIA (EXPIATORY CHURCH OF THE HOLY FAMILY)** Antoni Gaudí was killed in a tram accident in 1926 before he could complete this religious edifice, his most famous and controversial work—and a structure that became an emblematic symbol of Barcelona. Begun in 1884 by Francesc de Pau Villar in a neo-Gothic style, in 1891 it was taken over by Gaudí, who changed the style dramatically. *La Sagrada Família* is in the great Gothic tradition of Flamboyant swirls, jutting gargoyles, allegorical façades—and lifetimes of construction. In fact, Gaudí's estimate that the completion of his final project would take 200 years may prove to be overly optimistic. Under construction for more than a century, the church still lacks four complete walls and a roof. Only the *Façana del Naixement* (Nativity Façade)—with its tall spires, stained glass windows, and sculpted figures—was completed before Gaudí died. Construction on the *Façana de la Passió* (Passion Façade), on the Carrer de Sardenya side, was begun in 1952. Still to come are a central dome, to rise more than 500 feet, along with several smaller domes.

Take the elevator (or the stairs) up the *Façana del Naiximent* side to the dizzying heights of the spires for views of the city and close-ups of the amazing architectural details. Steps go even higher, but beware if you suffer from vertigo or claustrophobia. The audio-visual show in the *Museu Monogràfic,* located in the crypt, traces the history of the church. There's also a scale model of the structure as it will be one day. Open daily. Admission charge, plus an additional charge for the elevator. Plaça de la Sagrada Família; entrance on Carrer de Sardenya (phone: 455-0247).

## MONTJUÏC

**POBLE ESPANYOL (SPANISH VILLAGE)** Built for the *1929 International Exposition* and revitalized for the *1992 Olympics,* this is a five-acre museum village (known in Castilian as the *Pueblo Español)* whose streets and squares are lined with examples of traditional buildings from every region of Spain, from Galician *casonas* (cottages) to whitewashed Andalusian villas with wrought-iron grilles. A walk through the "town" illustrates the diversity of Spanish architecture and offers a chance to see traditional artisans at work (see *Shopping,* below). There also is an interesting *Museu de les Arts Gràfiques* (Graphic Arts Museum), with displays of printing and engraving equipment both old and new, and samples of posters, playing cards, hand-printed books, and other items; and a *Museu de les Arts Populars, d'Industria i Tradició* (Museum of Popular Arts, Industry, and Tradition) with displays of historical and ethnological material from all over Catalonia and other parts of Spain, including a reconstructed antique pharmacy. Nightlife aficionados should check out the popular, high-tech *Torres de Avila* club here (see *Nightclubs and Nightlife,* below). The grounds open daily till the wee hours of the morning, but the shops, restaurants, museums, and other enterprises within the village keep their own, shorter hours. Admission charge. Av. del Marquès de Comillas (phone: 325-7866).

**MUSEU D'ART DE CATALUNYA (ART MUSEUM OF CATALONIA)** Occupying a section of the *Palau Nacional* (National Palace) and now being remodeled by Italian architect Gae Aulenti (also responsible for Paris's magnificent Musée d'Orsay), this museum is often referred to as "the Prado of Romanesque art." Its collection of Romanesque and Gothic altarpieces and sculpture is superb, but its chief treasure, a series of 12th- and 13th-century frescoes removed by Italian craftsmen from dank little churches in the Pyrenees and reinstalled magnificently here, is unparalleled in the world. The museum also contains works by Tintoretto, El Greco, Zurbarán, and the Catalan painter Antoni Viladomat. The museum was closed for renovations at press time with the exception of special exhibits, but was scheduled to reopen this year. Call to be sure. Mirador del Palau, *Parc de Montjuïc* (phone: 423-6199).

**FUNDACIÓ JOAN MIRÓ (JOAN MIRÓ FOUNDATION)** Set up in an ultra-modern building designed by the late Catalan architect José Luís Sert, this is a light, airy tribute to Catalonia's surrealist master, Joan Miró (who is buried in the nearby Montjuïc cemetery). Numerous painted bronze sculptures are displayed on terraces of the museum's upper level; in the galleries are works in various styles and mediums, including a haunting *Self Portrait,* which the artist began in 1937 and did not finish until 1960. The *Fundació* hosts frequent special exhibitions, and also has a library, a well-stocked art bookstore, and a good snack bar. Closed Mondays. Admission charge. Plaça Neptú, *Parc de Montjuïc* (phone: 329-1908).

**MUSEU ARQUEOLÒGIC (ARCHAEOLOGICAL MUSEUM)** Exhibits include relics found in the excavation of the Greco-Roman city of Empúries on the nearby coast; other remnants of Spain's prehistoric cultures; and a fine collection of Carthaginian, Greek, Iberian, Roman, and Visigothic artifacts, mosaics, and sculptures, most of them found in present-day Catalonia and the Balearic Islands. There also is an archaeological library. Closed Sunday afternoons and Mondays. No admission charge. Carrer de Lleida (phone: 423-2149).

**PAVELLÓ BARCELONA (BARCELONA PAVILION)** Designed by architect Mies van der Rohe as the German pavilion for the *1929 International Exposition,* this spare, very contemporary building is considered a landmark of modern architecture. Among the meager furnishings are a sensuous standing nude sculpture by Georg Kolbe and two prototype examples of the Barcelona chair—probably the most famous chair design of our century, done originally for this space and first sat in (according to tradition) by Alfonso XIII, the last king of Spain before the Franco era. Disassembled and put into storage in the 1930s, the pavilion was rediscovered after 50 years and reconstructed in 1986. Open around the clock. No admission charge. Av. del Marquès de Comillas (phone: 423-4016).

**ANELL OLÍMPIC (OLYMPIC RING)** Some 63 years after hosting the *1929 International Exposition* on its slopes, Montjuïc hosted the *1992 Summer Olympics.* The sports facilities in the *Anell Olímpic,* from which there is a panoramic view of the Mediterranean, include the 70,000-seat *Estadi Olímpic* (Olympic Stadium), built for the *International Exposition* but completely remodeled in the late 1980s. Also here are the 17,000-seat domed *Palau d'Esports Sant Jordi* (St. George Sports Palace), designed by noted Japanese architect Arata Isozaki, and the *Piscines Municipals B. Picornell* (B. Picornell Municipal Pools), open-air pools with seating for 5,000. The *Universitat d'Esport* (University of Sport) was built by controversial architect Ricardo Bofill and his associate Peter Hodgkinson in a neoclassical–post-*modernista* style. Alongside the stadium is the *Galeria Olímpica,* with videos, photos, and medals from the 1992 games. Admission charge. Call for hours. Av. de l'Estadi, *Parc de Montjuïc* (phone: 426-0660).

**MUSEU MILITAR (MILITARY MUSEUM)** Since time immemorial, there has been a fortress at the top of Montjuïc, and the 17th- and 18th-century castle currently occupying the spot now houses military uniforms, toy soldiers, models of castles and fortresses, and a collection of 17th- to 19th-century firearms. The castle can be reached by road as well as aboard the Montjuïc *telèferic,* a cable car (see *Getting Around*). The museum is closed Mondays. Admission charge. *Parc de Montjuïc* (phone: 412-0000).

ELSEWHERE

**LA RAMBLA** This is the city's favorite, and liveliest, promenade. Originally a drainage channel (a *rambla* is a watercourse), it is now a wide, tree-lined pedestrian esplanade, with a single lane of traffic and a sidewalk on each side, running at a gentle downhill angle from the Plaça de Catalunya to the harbor. Though popularly known simply as La Rambla or Les Rambles, the boulevard in fact changes its name en route (Rambla dels Caputxins, Rambla de Sant Josep, Rambla de Canaletes, and so on). A brisk 20-minute trot will cover it all, from the Plaça de Catalunya to the harbor, but the idea is to take it slowly, examining the flower stands, thumbing through books and magazines at the newsstands (which sell everything from Arabic-language newspapers to German brides' magazines), reading a favorite newspaper or magazine at a sidewalk café, or merely strolling and chatting with friends amidst the din. Notice the sidewalk mosaic by Miró at the Plaça de Boqueria, and be sure to visit *La Boqueria* (see below). You'll also pass the *Teatre del Liceu* (at the corner of Carrer de Sant Pau), one of Europe's great opera houses, which is closed indefinitely for reconstruction after burning down in 1994. On the right side of La Rambla (facing the sea), almost at the harbor, is the new *Centre d'Art Santa Mònica* (phone: 412-2279), a beautiful contemporary art exhibition space designed by Albert Viaplana and Helio Piñón on the site of a former convent. Hours vary according to the shows. Also see Gaudí's first major *modernista* work, the *Palau Güell* (3 Carrer Nou de la Rambla; phone: 317-3974), a few steps off La Rambla and now serving as the *Institut del Teatre* (Theater Institute). Unlike some of Gaudí's later works, the *Palau Güell* interior tends toward the massive and heavy. Of particular note is the remarkable roof, crowned by 20 cone-shaped mosaic chimneys (of which no two are alike). Guided tours are available, but call for hours. Admission charge.

## SEEING RED

**Just off the port, the triangle between La Rambla and the Av. del Paral·lel, with its little alleyways, is known as the Barri Xinès (Barrio Chino in Spanish), literally "Chinese district"—but it is actually the red-light district and should be avoided at night, when it can be dangerous.**

**LA BOQUERIA** Officially called the *Mercat de Sant Josep* (St. Joseph's Market), this is one of the most attractive and richly stocked public food markets in Europe. A huge, covered 19th-century ironwork structure that looks a bit like a turn-of-the-century French train station, it features displays of the finest food products of Catalonia and the rest of the world in an abundance and variety that are breathtaking. Mountains of bright vegetables, mounds of earthy mushrooms, oceans worth of fish displayed on ice, treasure chests of candied fruit and nuts, thick screens of sausages dangling from the butcher stalls—it's one glorious sight and smell after another. Merchants are happy to sell a single piece of fruit or a tiny bag of olives or almonds, so even the casual visitor can sample the wares. The market building is open 24 hours a day, but most of the individual shops and stands are open early mornings to mid-afternoons. Closed Sundays.

**WATERFRONT** The largest port in Spain, Barcelona has become a port of call for major international cruise ships. The Moll de la Fusta (Wooden Wharf), the quay where the Barri Gòtic meets the harbor, boasts a pedestrian promenade complete with palm trees, park benches, and unusual-looking contemporary bridges, as well as a row of indoor/outdoor restaurants and bars. Many locals consider most of these restaurants too expensive to patronize. Continue walking along the waterfront and beach of Barceloneta to the Port Olímpic (Olympic Port), site of Platja Barcelona, a beach built in 1992. There's also a yacht basin here, as well as a long raised pier featuring several good restaurants offering fine meals at moderate prices and lovely views of the sea. Below the pier along the edge of the yacht basin are more modest cafés with *tapas* and outdoor seating. Barcelonans flock to this new seaside spot to swim, sunbathe, and stroll.

**MONUMENT A COLOM (COLUMBUS MONUMENT)** Barcelonans are fond of Christopher Columbus (known as Cristòfol Colom in Catalan, Cristóbal Colón in Spanish), who allegedly first reported on his exploration of the Americas to King Ferdinand and Queen Isabella in this city (some even claim Columbus was actually Catalan). This 200-foot-high column and statue sits at the harbor end of La Rambla, anchoring one end of the Moll de la Fusta. It's the tallest tribute in the world to the noted explorer and, together with Gaudí's *Sagrada Família,* an emblematic symbol of Barcelona. Open daily. Admission charge. Plaça Porta de la Pau (phone: 302-5224).

**MUSEU MARÍTIM (MARITIME MUSEUM)** The old low, stone buildings behind the *Monument a Colom* are the *Drassanes Reials* (Royal Shipyards), fine examples of medieval Catalan industrial architecture. Built in the 13th and 14th centuries, they are believed to be the largest intact medieval shipyards in the world. Ships carrying the red-and-yellow Catalan flag to the far corners of the world were launched from these yards years before Columbus's bold discovery. Fittingly, the *Museu Marítim,* one of the city's finest museums, now occupies the yards. The immense and varied collections include old maps (including one drawn by Amerigo Vespucci) and navigational instruments, ships' figureheads, models of ancient fishing boats, freighters, and other vessels. Closed Mondays. Admission charge. 1 Plaça Porta de la Pau (phone: 318-3245).

**BARCELONETA** Created in the early 18th century on what had been an empty spit of land jutting into the harbor, lively "Little Barcelona" was originally a resettlement area for citizens who had been displaced by the huge citadel built by Philip V to keep rebellious Barcelonans in line. Today, it is virtually its own little town, bustling, colorful, and almost romantically tacky. The Passeig Nacional, lined with bars and every kind of eating establishment imaginable, forms the area's waterfront promenade on the city side. Behind it is a grid of streets strung with laundry drying from balconies and encompassing a few leafy plazas stretching to the Platja de la Barceloneta, the beach on the Mediterranean side. The beach is rather dirty and run-down, a fact that doesn't stop thousands of local citizens from frequenting it in hot weather. Somewhat to the north is Poble Nou (or New Village), an industrial, working class quarter, much of which was torn down to construct the *Villa Olímpica.* A new beach, the Platja de Sant Martí, with breakwaters creating two large coves, has been constructed at Poble Nou. Some people swim at these beaches; others claim the water is still too polluted. To reach Barceloneta, walk around the waterfront from the *Monument a Colom* past the Moll d'Espanya; take the metro (subway) line no. 4 to the Barceloneta stop and walk from there; take any of several buses; or take the Barceloneta *telèferic* from Miramar, at the foot of Montjuïc (see *Getting Around*).

**PARC DE LA CIUTADELLA** This open space was created for the *International Exhibition* of 1888, on the site of the hated citadel built by Philip V in 1716 and razed in 1868. The popular park features gardens, an artificial lake with an elaborate fountain and cascade (co-designed by Antoni Gaudí early in his career), and a zoo (phone: 221-2506) that's home to Copita de Nieve (Snowflake), said to be the only albino gorilla in captivity. There's also the *Palau de la Ciutadella,* which houses the Catalan Parliament and the *Museu d'Art Modern* (see below); the *Museu de Zoologia* (Zoology Museum), housed in a *modernista* building by Domènech i Montaner (closed Mondays; no admission charge for children under 18; phone: 319-6912); and the *Museu de Geologia* (Museum of Geology), Barcelona's oldest museum, with a large mineral collection and paleontology exhibits (closed Mondays; admission charge; phone: 319-6895).

**MUSEU D'ART MODERN (MUSEUM OF MODERN ART)** In the *Palau de la Ciutadella*, the collection includes a few works by such well-known Catalan artists as Dalí, Miró, and Tàpies, but consists mostly of 19th-century and early 20th-century paintings, graphic works, and sculptures by such less famous but talented local artists as Ramón Casas (a great portraitist), Santiago Rossinyol, Isidre Nonell, Miguel Utrillo, Pau Gargallo, and José Luís Sert. Closed Tuesdays. Admission charge. Plaça de las Armes (phone: 319-5728).

# Sources and Resources

## TOURIST INFORMATION

Brochures, maps, and general information are available at
Barcelona's *Oficina de Turisme* (658 Gran Via de les Corts Catalanes; phone: 301-7443; fax: 412-2570). It's closed Saturday afternoons and Sundays. Between late June and the end of September
there's also a tourist information office in the Barri Gòtic, at the
*Ajuntament* (City Hall), on Plaça de Sant Jaume; closed Saturdays
after 2 PM and Sundays. The tourist information offices at the *Estació
Barcelona Sants* and the *Estació de França* train stations, as well
as that at the *Aeroport del Prat* international arrivals hall (phone:
478-4704) are open daily year-round. "Casacas Rojas"—red-jack-
eted guides who patrol popular areas such as the Barri Gòtic, the
Passeig de Gràcia, and La Rambla—supply on-the-spot information from approximately mid-June to mid-September. The *US Consulate* is at 23-25 Passeig Reina Elisenda (phone: 280-2227).

In the US, there are four branches of the *National Tourist Office
of Spain* (San Vicente Plaza Bldg., 8383 Wilshire Blvd., Suite 960,
Beverly Hills, CA 90211; phone: 213-658-7188; fax: 213-658-1061;
Water Tower Place, 845 N. Michigan Ave., Suite 915E, Chicago,
IL 60611; phone: 312-642-1992; fax: 312-642-9817; 1221 Brickell Ave., Suite 1850, Miami, FL 33131; phone: 305-358-1992; fax:
305-358-8223; and 665 Fifth Ave., New York, NY 10022; phone:
212-759-8822; fax: 212-980-1053). The *Spanish Embassy* is at 2700
15th St. NW, Washington, DC 20009 (phone: 202-265-0190).

**ENTRY REQUIREMENTS** A US citizen needs a current passport for a stay of
up to 90 days.

**TIME** The time in Spain is six hours later than in US East Coast cities.
Spain observes daylight saving time.

**LANGUAGE** Catalan Spanish is the official tongue in Barcelona. Spain's
official language is Castilian Spanish. English is understood in principal hotels, restaurants, and shops.

**ELECTRIC CURRENT** 220 volts, 50 cycles, AC.

**MONEY** The peseta (pta) is the unit of currency. At press time the peseta
traded at 132 to $1 US.

**TIPPING** Though service charges of 15% are included in restaurant bills,
extra tips of between 5% and 10% are expected. Taxi drivers receive
5% of the meter and, in most cases, 50 to 100 pta is enough for
porters, bellhops, and (per night) for chambermaids.

**BANKING/BUSINESS HOURS** Most banks are open weekdays from 9 AM
to 2 PM and Saturdays to 1:30 PM; many are closed Saturdays during the summer. Most other businesses are open weekdays from 9
AM to 2 PM and from 4:30 to 7 PM, though some have changed to
an 8 AM to 3 PM schedule.

**NATIONAL HOLIDAYS** *New Year's Day* (January 1), *Epiphany* (January 6), *St. Joseph's Day* (March 19), *Good Friday* (April 14), *Easter Sunday* (April 16), *Easter Monday* (April 17), *Día del Trabajo* (Labor Day, May 1), *San Isidro Day* (May 15), *Feast of the Assumption* (August 15), *National Day* (October 12), *All Saints' Day* (November 1), *Constitution Day* (December 6), the *Feast of the Immaculate Conception* (December 8), and *Christmas Day* (December 25).

**LOCAL COVERAGE** The weekly *Guía del Ocio* and monthly Barcelona city magazine, *Vivir en Barcelona,* both available at newsstands, provide comprehensive listings of museums, nightspots, restaurants, and other attractions—in Spanish, though the latter does include some information in English in high-season editions. Watch the news in English on TV3 during the summer.

**TELEPHONE** The phone code for Barcelona and surrounding areas is 3. When calling from one area to another within Spain dial 9 + city code + local number. The country code for Spain is 34. Dial 091 or 092 for emergency assistance.

## GETTING AROUND

**AIRPORT** Barcelona's airport for domestic and international flights is *Aeroport Barcelona en Prat de Llobregat,* commonly known as *Aeroport del Prat* (phone: 478-5000), located 7½ miles (12 km) southwest of the city, or about 30 minutes from downtown by taxi. Shuttle flights to Madrid leave hourly on *Iberia* and other carriers such as *Air Europa* and *Spanair.* Trains run between the airport and *Estació Barcelona Sants,* the central railway station, connecting with the metro (subway) lines, every 20 minutes; the trip takes 15 minutes and the fare is 260 pesetas (roughly $1.95) weekdays and 300 pesetas ($2.25) weekends. There is bus service every 15 minutes from Plaça de Catalunya to the airport weekdays from 5:30 AM to 10 PM; weekends and holidays from 6 AM to 10 PM; the fare is 400 pesetas (about $2.90).

**BOAT** Ferries operated by *Transmediterránea* leave Barcelona for the Balearic Islands daily in summer, less frequently in winter. Ticket sales and departures are at the *Estació Marítima de Baleares* at the Moll de Barcelona near the *Monument a Colom* (phone: 317-4262). *Golondrinas* ("swallow boats") offering brief sightseeing jaunts in the harbor (out to the breakwater and back) depart from in front of the monument throughout the year. The trip takes about 15 minutes; buy tickets from the office at the water's edge (phone: 310-0342). Three or four times a day, *golondrinas* also leave from the Portal de la Pau to tour the Olympic harbor (phone: 412-5944).

**BUS** Although more than 50 routes crisscross the city, the system is easy to use since each stop is marked with a map of the routes that pass there. The fare is 120 pesetas (about 87¢). The best deal for the visitor is *Bus Cien,* the No. 100 bus that constantly circles around 12 well-known sites, including the cathedral and the *Sagrada Família.* A flat-rate full ticket (bought on the bus) lets you get on and off as often as you like, and also entitles the bearer to a discount at museums. The route operates only in high season, however, from approximately mid-June to mid-September. At other times buy a 10-ride ticket (called T-1, or Targeta Multiviatge 1) for 625 pesetas (about $4.50). It's valid on all buses, as well as on the metro (subway) and the interurban trains operated by the *Generalitat* that run to the suburbs. (The 10-ride T-2 ticket, which costs 600 pesetas, is good for the metro but not for the bus.) Buy tickets at the public transport kiosk in the *Estació Universitat (Metro L1)* ; at the *Estació Sants (Metro L5)*, where the *Guía del Transport Públic de Barcelona* (Guide to Barcelona's Public Transportation) also is available; or at any other metro station. After boarding the bus (enter through the front doors), insert the ticket in the date-stamping machine. Long-distance domestic and international buses depart from the *Estació de Autobuses Barcelona Nord* (80 Carrer Alimbe; phone: 265-7845). For information on city, interurban, or international buses, call 412-0000.

**CAR RENTAL** All the major international and local car rental firms have offices at the airport. Note that parking on the street can be a headache in downtown Barcelona.

**FUNICULARS AND CABLE CARS** In addition to the funicular to Tibidabo (see *Seeing the City*), a funicular makes the climb from the Parallel subway stop up to Montjuïc, where it connects with the Montjuïc *telèferic* (cable car; phone: 329-8613 or 441-4820) that swings out over the *Parc d'Atraccions de Montjuïc* and makes one interim stop before depositing passengers at the castle, belvedere, and restaurant at the top. The funicular, cable car, and amusement park operate daily in summer; weekends and holidays only in winter. Another *telèferic* (phone: 441-4820) connects Barceloneta's Muelle de los Astilleros with Miramar, at the foot of Montjuïc, making an interim stop at the *Torre de Jaume I* (a tower built on the Moll de Barcelona in 1930 as part of the *telèferic* system). The trip is a spectacular one across the harbor—passengers swing out over the cruise ships and hang over the water as though in a slow-moving airplane. Rides are available afternoons daily in summer.

**SUBWAY** A "Metro" sign indicates an entrance to Barcelona's modern, clean subway system. All four lines (*L1, L3, L4,* and *L5*) are easy to navigate. The fare is 125 pesetas (about 95¢); a 10-ride ticket (T-2, or Targeta Multiviatge 2) is a good idea if you plan to make multiple trips. It can be purchased at any metro station for 600 pesetas (roughly $4.55). The T-2 is not valid for buses.

**TAXI** Taxis can be hailed on the street or picked up at one of the numerous *paradas de taxi* (taxi ranks) throughout the city. For *Radio Taxi*, call 490-2222. During the day, *Lliure* or *Libre* in the window indicates that a cab is available; at night a green light shines on the roof. The city is divided into various fare zones, and fares generally are moderate.

**TRAIN** Barcelona is served by trains operated by *RENFE*, the Spanish national railways, and by trains operated by *Ferrocarrils de la Generalitat de Catalunya (FFCC)*. All four of the city's railway stations are undergoing long-term refurbishment. The stations are *Estació Barcelona Sants,* at the end of Av. de Roma, the main station for long-distance trains within Spain; *Estació de França,* on Av. Marquès de l'Argentera, for international trains; *Estació Passeig de Gràcia,* on Passeig de Gràcia at Carrer d'Aragó; and *Estació Plaça de Catalunya,* underneath the Plaça de Catalunya. For fare and schedule information, go to the *RENFE* office at *Barcelona Sants* or call the 24-hour-a-day information service (phone: 490-0202).

## LOCAL SERVICES

**DENTIST (ENGLISH-SPEAKING)** Ask the *US Consulate* or your hotel concierge for recommendations.

**DRY CLEANER** *Tintorería Aribau* (29 Carrer Aribau; phone: 453-8933).

**LIMOUSINE SERVICE** *International Limousine System* (24 Montmajor; phone: 429-1388; ask for Miguel Regol Font).

**MEDICAL EMERGENCY** *Hospital de la Santa Creu i de Sant Pau* (167 Sant Antoni María Claret; phone: 291-9000); ambulance (phone: 300-4000).

**MESSENGER SERVICE** *Mensajerías Barcelona Express* (4 Carrer de Berlín; phone: 322-2222).

**NATIONAL/INTERNATIONAL COURIER** *DHL Worldwide Express* (332-334 Carrer de Entença; phone: 336-4000 for pickup).

**OFFICE EQUIPMENT RENTAL** *Rigau* (Gran Via de les Corts Catalanes; phone: 318-7040) rents typewriters and office equipment.

**PHARMACY** *Farmàcia Maragall* (50 Passeig de Gràcia; phone: 216-0365). A variety of pharmacies operate on a rotating basis 24 hours a day; check newspapers for listings.

**PHOTOCOPIES** There are photocopy shops all over town.

**POST OFFICE** *Central de Correus* (Plaça Antoni López; phone: 318-3831), open weekdays from 8 AM to 10 PM; Saturdays from 9 AM to 2 PM; Sundays and holidays from 10 AM to noon.

**SECRETARY/STENOGRAPHER (ENGLISH-SPEAKING)** *OTAC* (45-47 Carrer de Sepúlveda; phone: 325-2546; contact José Luís Laborda).

**TAILOR** *Baseiria* (24 Carrer d'Aribau; phone: 454-6024).

**TELEX** At *Central de Correus* (see *Post Office,* above).

**TRANSLATOR** *OTAC* (see above); *Rosario Tauler de Canals* (50 Passeig de Sant Joan; phone: 301-7181).

**OTHER** Convention facilities: *Palau de Congresos* (Convention Center; Av. María Cristina; phone: 423-3101), at the *Barcelona Fair Grounds,* has full meeting and convention facilities, including an auditorium that holds 1,200. Convention information: *Barcelona Convention Bureau* (35 Passeig de Gràcia; phone: 215-4477) provides information for meetings and conventions at restaurants and historical sites around the city.

## SPECIAL EVENTS

The *Cavalcada de Reis* (Cavalcade of Kings) is held on January 5 with a parade of floats from the waterfront to Montjuïc commemorating the journey of the Wise Men (or Three Kings) to visit the baby Jesus. *Carnaval* commences every year on *Dijous Gras* (Fat Thursday), the week before *Dimecres de Cendre* (Ash Wednesday, in Spanish *Miércoles de Ceniza*) and runs for six days and nights with nonstop parades, concerts and theatrical performances, costume balls, and ceremonial gluttony. On March 19, the *Festa de Sant Josep* (Feast of St. Joseph), Valencian residents of Barcelona recreate the *fallas,* or ritual bonfires, for which their own city is famous, and everybody eats *crema catalana,* Catalan "burnt cream" (custard with a caramelized sugar topping), also known as *crema de Sant Josep.* On April 23, the *Festa de Sant Jordi* (Feast of St. George, the patron saint of Catalonia), Barcelonans give gifts to one another—books to friends, roses to lovers (real or hoped for). The Sunday after the *Festa de Sant Jordi* is the *Dia Universal de la Sardana* (Universal Day of the Sardana), celebrated all over Catalonia and dedicated to performances of the region's traditional dance and its accompanying music. Bonfires, fireworks, dancing, and revelry mark the nights before the *Festa de Sant Joan* (Feast of St. John) and *Festa de Sant Pere* (Feast of St. Peter), on June 24 and 28, respectively, and every bakery dispenses its version of the *coca de Sant Joan,* a large rectangular pastry covered with candied fruit, on the former occasion. On Thursdays from June through September, the Guardia Urbana (City Police force) dons scarlet tunics and white plumed helmets for a riding exhibition at 9 PM at the *Pista Hípica La Fuxarda* (Fuxarda Racetrack) in Montjuïc. The narrow streets of the Gràcia neighborhood are elaborately and colorfully decorated for the *Festa Major de Gràcia* (High Feast of Gràcia); for a week beginning on August 15 there are open-air concerts and theatrical performances. September 11 is *La Diada,* Catalonia's national day commemorating the defeat of the Catalans at the hands of Philip V and the fall of Barcelona in 1714. *La Festa de la Mercè* (The Feast of Our Lady of Mercy) is Barcelona's most extravagant annual festival. The feast day itself is September 24, but the week leading up to it is noisy, exhausting, and full of general gaiety. Included in the festivities are folk dancing, wine and gastronomic fairs, free concerts (often by major international stars) all over the city, fireworks displays, and *casteller* (human pyramid) competitions. Other observances include a *Ball de Gegants* (Giants' Ball), with parades of flamboyantly costumed papier-mâché figures 15 feet high and more, and the remarkable *Correfoc* (Fire Run), in which crowds ceremonially confront and try to turn aside fireworks-wielding teams of Barcelonans dressed as fantastical characters. *Nadal* (Christmas; *Navidad* in Spanish) is heralded by the two-week

*Fira de Santa Llúcia* (St. Lucy's Fair), when stalls selling greenery, decorations, gifts, and figurines for nativity scenes are set up
in front of the Gothic cathedral and the *Sagrada Família.*

## MUSEUMS

Besides those listed in *Special Places*, the following museums may
be of interest:

**CENTRE CULTURAL DE LA FUNDACIÓ CAIXA DE PENSIONS (CULTURAL CEN-
TER OF THE CAIXA DE PENSIONS BANK FOUNDATION)** Though not strictly
speaking a museum, this beautiful exhibition space is a must for art
lovers; there is always a well-mounted and sophisticated show here,
and there are chamber music concerts in an enclosed garden area,
plus a contemporary-style arts bookshop and café. The building itself
is one of *modernista* architect Josep Puig i Cadafalch's best, with
hints of Moorish and Catalan Gothic architecture incorporated seam-
lessly into the turn-of-the-century façade. Closed Mondays. Admission charge. 108 Passeig de Sant Joan (phone: 458-8905).

**MUSEU DELS AUTÓMATES (MUSEUM OF AUTOMATONS)** Mechanical dolls
and animals, amusement park figures, and model trains. Open weekends and holidays from 11 AM to 8 PM. Admission charge to the
*Parc d'Atraccions de Tibidabo* includes the museum. *Parc del Tibidabo* (phone: 211-7942).

**MUSEU DEL CALÇAT ANTIC (ANTIQUE SHOE MUSEUM)** A two-room collection in the Barri Gòtic of old shoes, including 1st-century slave
sandals and 3rd-century shepherd's footwear, plus famous people's
shoes. Open from 11 AM to 2 PM; closed Mondays. Admission charge.
Plaça Sant Felip Neri (phone: 302-2680).

**MUSEU DE LA CIÈNCIA (SCIENCE MUSEUM)** A popular, hands-on museum
with a small planetarium and an innovative children's section, which
features experimental exhibits about the body, matter, communication, and movement. Closed Mondays. Admission charge. 55 Carrer Teodor Roviralta, off Av. del Tibidabo (phone: 212-6050).

**MUSEU ETNOLÒGIC (ETHNOLOGICAL MUSEUM)** Good collections of ritual and religious art and everyday objects from Japan, New Guinea,
and Afghanistan. Closed Mondays. Admission charge. Passeig Santa
Madrona (phone: 424-6807).

**MUSEU DEL FÚTBOL CLUB BARCELONA (BARCELONA SOCCER CLUB
MUSEUM)** One of the most popular attractions in this sports-mad
town, this small collection of trophies and videos highlights the
local soccer team's illustrious history—located in the 120,000-seat
*Estadi Camp Nou,* the largest stadium in Europe. Closed Mondays
from November through March and Sundays from April through
October. Admission charge. *Estadi Camp Nou,* Carrer Arístides
Maillol (phone: 330-9411).

**MUSEU MONESTIR DE PEDRALBES (PEDRALBES MONASTERY AND MUSEUM)**
A 14th-century Gothic church known for its stained glass windows,
choir stalls, unusual three-story cloister surrounded by galleries,

and its overall elegant simplicity of design. This gem of medieval architecture also contains an impressive collection of Italian-influenced Catalan paintings and other art. The monastery is now the permanent home of 80 paintings and eight sculptures from the renowned Thyssen–Bornemisza collection (formerly in Lugano, Switzerland and the bulk of which is now in Madrid's new *Palacio de Villahermosa* museum). Closed Mondays. Admission charge. 9 Baixada del Monestir (phone: 203-9282).

**MUSEU DE LA MÚSICA (MUSEUM OF MUSIC)** An odd collection of antique instruments from many countries, dating from the 16th century to the present, in a *modernista* building by Puig i Cadafalch. Closed Mondays. Admission charge. 373 Av. Diagonal (phone: 416-1157).

**MUSEU TAURÍ (BULLFIGHTING MUSEUM)** Matadors' costumes, trophies, posters, bull-ranch branding irons, and other memorabilia. Open daily from April through September. Admission charge. 749 Gran Via de les Corts Catalanes (phone: 245-5803).

SHOPPING

A textile center for centuries, Barcelona also always has been a good place to buy leather goods. More recently, it's become a source of up-to-the-minute fashion as well.

Passeig de Gràcia and Rambla de Catalunya are lined with elegant shops selling leather goods, furs, accessories, and jewelry, as well as boutiques carrying Spain's *moda joven* (young fashion). More boutiques are housed in shopping centers or indoor arcades, of which the best known is the original *Bulevard Rosa* (55 Passeig de Gràcia)—an entire city block filled with shops selling everything from clothing and hats to unusual jewelry and paper goods. There's also a second *Rosa* complex—much smaller with just 40 stores (474 Av. Diagonal). Also at 55 Passeig de Gràcia is the government-sponsored *Centre Permanent d'Artesania* (phone: 215-7178 or 215-5814), where changing exhibitions of crafts by contemporary Catalan artists and artisans are held. What's on display is for sale, although it can't be taken away until the show closes. For more traditional crafts, visit the *Poble Espanyol* on Montjuïc, where some 35 stores feature pottery, carvings, glassware, leather goods, and other folk crafts made by artisans from all over Spain. Also visit the Ribera–El Born quarter around the *Museu Picasso* on Carrer de Montcada, known as the artists' and artisans' quarter.

Barcelona has two *El Corte Inglés* department stores (Plaça de Catalunya; phone: 302-1212; and 617 Av. Diagonal; phone: 419-5206); branches of the countrywide chain, they are known for reliable quality in everything from Lladró porcelain and leather gloves to other clothing, records, and books. Best of all, they are open during the long Spanish lunch hour, when smaller shops are closed. A 376,000-square-foot retail center called *L'Illa Diagonal* (565 Av. Diagonal) opened at the end of 1993, and offers 200 shops including well-known foreign names like *Marks & Spencer, Benetton,* and *Foot Locker.* The block-long edifice also incorporates offices and a hotel.

Somewhat smaller, but still carrying a wide range of merchandise, are the two *Galerías Preciados* stores (Porta de l'Angel; phone: 317-0000; and Plaça Francesc Macià; phone: 419-6262). Top avant-garde Spanish clothing designers are represented, as well as everyday goods from children's clothes and toys to food. In general, department stores are open from 10 AM to 8:30 PM; smaller shops close between 2 and 4:30 PM. All are closed—*tancat* in Catalan—on Sundays.

A visit to at least one of the city's markets is a colorful must, whether *La Boqueria* (see *Special Places*) or the *Mercat de Santa Caterina* (Carrer Francesc Cambó, near the Gothic cathedral), where the fresh, tempting produce puts big-city supermarkets to shame. *Els Encants* is Barcelona's principal flea market (held Mondays, Wednesdays, Fridays, and Saturdays from dawn to dusk on the Plaça de les Glòries Catalanes). An outdoor art market is held on the Plaça de Sant Josep Oriol on Saturdays from 10 AM to 10 PM and Sundays to 3 PM year-round. Spend Sunday mornings in Plaça Reial among the stamp and coin collectors (9 AM to 2:30 PM) or at the *Mercat de Sant Antoni,* leafing through old books and magazines (10 AM to 2 PM). There is an unusual organic food market, featuring bread, cheese, honey, tea, and such from the nearby mountains, on weekends and holidays from 10 AM to 2 PM on the Plaça de la Sagrada Família.

More than 150 antiques shops line the narrow streets of the Barri Gòtic. Major periods as far back as the 12th century are represented. One of the best shops is *Alberto Grasas* (14 Carrer Banys Nous and 10 *bis* Carrer Palla; phone: 317-8838), which sells antique paintings, furniture, and decorative objects, principally porcelain. For ceramics, one of the city's top showrooms is *Arturo Ramón* (25 Carrer Palla; phone: 302-5974). Its prized possessions include 18th-century furniture, as well as the highly valued ceramics from Manises. Look out for the monthly *subastas* (auctions) at *Sotheby's* (2 Passeig Domingo; phone: 487-5272). A Barri Gòtic antiques market, formerly held on the Plaça Nova, now takes place on the Plaça del Pi every Thursday (except during August) from 10 AM to 10 PM.

It is no coincidence that Catalonia has the highest literacy rate in Spain and can claim to be the only city in the country where the feast day of its patron saint, St. George (*Festa de Sant Jordi,* April 23) is celebrated with gifts of books to friends. In Barcelona, it sometimes seems as if there's a bookshop on every block. A good collection of English-language books can be found at *BCN Books* (277 Aragó; phone: 487-3123) and *The English Bookshop* (52 Calaf; phone: 200-4147). For secondhand books in English, try *K.O. and Simon's* (13 Carrer la Granja; phone: 238-3086).

Other shops worth exploring:

**Adolfo Domínguez** Menswear from one of Spain's internationally recognized designers. 89 Passeig de Gràcia (phone: 215- 1339).

**Artespanya** A high-quality selection of Spanish crafts, from handmade glass and leather goods to tables and chairs. 75 Rambla de Catalunya (phone: 215- 6146).

**BD Ediciones de Diseño** The showroom for one of Spain's top interior design firms, with furniture and accessories by major contemporary figures, as well as licensed reproductions of design classics by Gaudí, Josef Hoffman, and other 20th-century designers. 291-293 Carrer de Mallorca (phone: 458-6909).

**Camper** Women's shoes and handbags, the latest in styles and colors. Popular with the younger disco and nightclub set. 5 Av. Pau Casals (phone: 209-5846), 248 Carrer Muntaner (phone: 201-3188), and 249 Carrer de València (phone: 215-6390).

**Dos y Una** A glorified souvenir shop, full of Mariscal T-shirts, plus miniatures of Gaudí buildings and other local memorabilia. 275 Carrer del Rosselló (phone: 217-7032).

**E. Furest** Classy men's clothing, both neo-traditional and contemporary, from a wide selection of Spanish, other European, and American designers. 3 Av. Pau Casals (phone: 203-4204), 12 Passeig de Gràcia (phone: 301-2000), 468 Av. Diagonal (phone: 218-2665), and 609 Av. Diagonal (phone: 419-4006).

**Eleven** The largest selection of men's and women's shoes in Barcelona, featuring more than 2,000 styles, from traditional to way-out. 466 Av. Diagonal (phone: 218-4558).

**Enric Majoral** Unusual handmade jewelry in silver, gold, oxidized bronze, and even plastic. 19 Carrer de Laforja (phone: 238-0752).

**Gràfiques el Tinell** A sort of antique stationery store, with recently minted notepaper, letterheads, bookplates, prints, and the like, many hand-colored and/or made from original 18th- and 19th-century woodblocks and engraving plates. 1 Carrer Freneria (phone: 315-0758).

**Groc** Trendy designer Tony Miró's boutique, with men's clothing and chic, expensive women's evening and daywear, plus Miró shoes and Chelo Sastre jewelry. Will make to order in 15 days, but 20% is added to ready-to-wear prices. 100 Rambla de Catalunya (phone: 215-0180) and 385 Carrer de Muntaner (phone: 202-3077).

**Jean Pierre Bua** Fashion by young designers from Catalonia and elsewhere in Europe. Look for Roser Marcé's "modern classics" for men and women. 469 Av. Diagonal (phone: 439-7100).

**Joaquín Berao** Contemporary jewelry, often avant-garde, in an award-winning interior. 277 Carrer del Rosselló (phone: 218-6187).

**Jorge Juan** Well-priced women's shoes and handbags in distinctive designs. 125 Rambla de Catalunya (phone: 217-0840).

**Laie** An attractively designed bookshop/café specializing in books on the arts and humanities, with a particularly good section on the cinema. The upstairs café has a terrace, and books and newspapers for browsing. 85 Carrer de Pau Claris (phone: 318-1739).

**Loewe** Spain's best-known and most expensive purveyor of fine leather goods. 35 Passeig de Gràcia (phone: 216-0400). There are two other locations, one specializing in men's fashions, 570 Av. Diagonal (phone: 200-0920), and the other in women's apparel, 8 Carrer Johann Sebastian Bach (phone: 202-3150).

**La Manual Alpargatera** Handmade rope-soled espadrilles in contemporary colors and designs. 7 Carrer d'Avinyó (phone: 301-0172).

**Margarita Nuez** Sophisticated women's clothing in the finest fabrics. 3 Carrer de Josep Bertrand (phone: 200-8400).

**Matrícula** The latest in men's and women's clothing and accessories from Yamamoto, Rifat Ozbek, and noted Spanish designer Sybila, among other names. 24 Carrer de Pau Claris (phone: 201-2308) and *Bulevard Rosa de Pedralbes*, 609-615 Av. Diagonal (phone: 419-1100).

**Pilma** A large selection of contemporary home furnishings, Spanish and otherwise, including kitchen utensils, luggage, and fabrics. 403 Av. Diagonal (phone: 416-1399) and 1 Carrer de València (phone: 325-3572).

**Sara Navarro** Elegant, original, contemporary shoes and quality leather jackets and other accessories. 598 Av. Diagonal (phone: 209-3336).

**Tema** Fashions by Spanish designers Manuel Piña, Jesús del Pozo, and Jorge Gonsalves (a favorite of Spain's current queen, Sofía). 10 Carrer Ferran Agulló (phone: 209-5165).

**Teresa Ramallal** Stylish women's clothing, accessories, and shoes. 17 Carrer Mestre Nicolau (phone: 201-3998).

**Tocs** A large well-stocked bookshop, specializing in art, design, and architecture books. Also a wide selection of magazines, stationery and other paper goods, and CDs and cassettes. 341 Carrer del Consell de Cent (phone: 215-3121).

**Trau** Where society girls go for posh glad rags. 6 Carrer Ferran Agulló (phone: 210-4268).

**2 Bis** Amusing art pieces, including overweight terra cotta beauties and papier-mâché infants, as well as tabletop-size papier-mâché replicas of the fierce-looking *dracs* (dragons) featured in the *Correfoc* (fire walk) during Barcelona's September *Festa de la Mercé* (Feast of Our Lady of Mercy). Also some serious glassware and plates. Near the Gothic cathedral. 2 Carrer del Bisbe Irurita (phone: 315-0954).

**Vigares** A small but good selection of leather goods at tempting prices (including riding boots for about $90). 16 Carrer de Balmes (phone: 317-5898).

**Vinçon** Barcelona's number-one design and home furnishings store, it carries gifts and trinkets, kitchen gadgets, glassware and plates, fabrics, furniture and lighting, food and design books, and many other items. There is a delightful terrace upstairs, and an exhibition space with changing art shows. 96 Passeig de Gràcia (phone: 215-6050).

## SPORTS AND FITNESS

In addition to the *Annell Olímpic* facilities built for the *1992 Summer Olympics,* the city boasts many major facilities, including the 120,000-seat *Estadi Camp Nou,* Europe's largest sports stadium, and the *Piscines Municipals B. Picornell* (Picornell Municipal Pools) on Montjuïc. Other possibilities for the sports-minded include the following:

**BULLFIGHTING** Catalans claim to abhor bullfighting and, in fact, most of the spectators in the arena are immigrants from other parts of Spain—or tourists. The gigantic *Plaça Monumental* (743 Gran Via de les Corts Catalanes) has fights on Sundays at 6:30 PM from April to late September; additional fights are held on Thursdays at 6:30 PM in August. Advance tickets are available (at 24 Muntaner, at the corner of Carrer d'Aribau; phone: 453-3821).

**FITNESS CENTERS** *Squash Diagonal* (193 Carrer de Roger de Flor; phone: 458-3408) has a pool, sauna, and gym, besides squash courts.

**GOLF** The *Club de Golf El Prat* (phone: 379-0278), 10 miles (16 km) southwest of town near the airport, is the area's best course, used on the European pro tour. *Club de Golf Sant Cugat* (Sant Cugat del Vallès; phone: 674-3908; fax: 675-5152) is 12½ miles (20 km) away and hard to find in the hilly suburbs to the west. *Club de Golf Vall-romanes* (phone: 572-9064; fax: 568-4834) is 15½ miles (24 km) along the Masnou-Granollers road.

**JOGGING** *Parc de la Ciutadella,* near the center of town, has a good track. The paths surrounding Montjuïc also are popular jogging spots.

**SOCCER** The major passion of born and bred Barcelonans. The *Fútbol Club (F.C.) Barcelona* embodies the spirit of Catalonia, especially when the opponent is archrival *Real Madrid.* The world's greatest stars are signed up to play for the club, and infants are enrolled as club members at birth. More than 120,000 fans regularly attend home games, played at the *Estadi Camp Nou* (Carrer Arístides Maillol; phone: 330-9411). *Espanyol,* the other, less popular "major league" club in town, plays at *Estadi de Sarrià* (2 Ricardo Villa; phone: 203-4800).

**SWIMMING** Take a dip in the waters that hosted the *1992 Olympic* swimming events at *Piscines Municipals B. Picornell* (on Montjuïc, near the main stadium; phone: 325-9281). Open weekdays from 7 AM to 10 PM; Saturdays to 9 PM; Sundays from 7:30 AM to 2 PM; admission fee. Most people swim without hesitation at Platja Barcelona, the new beach near the *Villa Olímpica* (Olympic Village), though some are wary of pollution and will not swim near the city.

**TENNIS** Courts may be available at the *Centre Municipal de Tenis del Vall d'Hebron* (178 Passeig Vall d'Hebron; phone: 427-6500 or 427-8561). The nearby seaside town of Castelldefels, a few miles beyond the airport, is the site of many tennis clubs that rent courts to non-members. It's fun to play there and then go to the beach. Also just outside the city, in Sant Just d'Esvern, is *Club Canmalich* (Av. 11 de Setembre; phone: 372-8211).

## THEATER

The city has a strong theatrical tradition in Catalan, but it still embraces foreign playwrights such as Shakespeare and Chekhov.

At the *Teatre Lliure* (Free Theater; 47 Carrer Montceny; phone: 218-9251), Fabia Puigserver's cooperative troupe is so dynamic that language is no barrier when the works are familiar. Another Catalan troupe is the *Companyia Flotats,* led by Josep Maria Flotats, whose repertoire tends to be lighter (115 Poliorama Rambla; phone: 317-7599). Experimental theater can be seen in the impressive *Mercat de les Flors* (59 Carrer de Lleida; phone: 426-1875), the old Flower Hall built on Montjuïc for the *1929 International Exposition.* Higher up the hill, the open-air *Teatre Grec* (Passeig Santa Madrona; phone: 243-0062) hosts a festival every June and July, with classic Greek tragedies and other works. Many companies from around the world now make appearances. Unfortunately, the city's main opera house, *Gran Teatre del Liceu* (facing La Rambla) was destroyed by a fire in early 1994, and reconstruction is not expected to be completed until at least next year or possibly later.

## MUSIC

Barcelona is a music center year-round. From November through May, opera and ballet dominate, but there is a festival of some sort every month, from medieval music in May to the *Festa Internacional de Música* in October. The *Palau de la Música Catalana* (see *Special Places*), a gem of Art Nouveau style, is home to the *Orquesta Ciutat de Barcelona* (Barcelona City Orchestra), among other groups. There are two concert halls being built in the Plaça de les Arts complex, near Plaça de les Glòries Catalanes (no word yet on when they will be open; contact the tourist office for details).

## NIGHTCLUBS AND NIGHTLIFE

Barcelona has plenty of action, but be careful in the most popular after-dark centers, since the city has its share of muggers and purse snatchers. Also be wary of thieves on motorcycles and minibikes, who snatch purses from pedestrians and out of cars parked or stopped at traffic signals. The city's pubs, bars, and cafés begin to fill up between 10 and 11 PM, but these establishments merely serve as a warm-up for the clubs and discotheques, which open even later and don't kick into high gear until 1 or 2 AM. The Eixample has a greater concentration of bars than other neighborhoods. For flamenco, try *El Cordobés* (35 La Rambla; phone: 317-6653), *Andalucía* (27 Rambla; phone: 302-2009), and *El Patio Andaluz* (242 Carrer d'Aribau; phone: 209-3378). Shows are continuous from 10 PM to 3 AM, but really get going after midnight. Popular discotheques include the *Up and Down* (179 Carrer de Numancia; phone: 204-8809), with loud music downstairs and a restaurant and a more "sophisticated" club upstairs; and *Studio 54* (64 Av. del Paral-lel; phone: 329-5454), a weekends-only favorite, boasting lots of elbow room and the best light show in town.

Barcelona also boasts a number of "dance bars"—trendy places with contemporary interiors by some of the city's best designers and architects. Attracting young people and loud rock music—although dancing is usually downplayed (these aren't discos per se)—these nightspots are primarily venues for drinking and flirting. Two worth visiting are *Nick Havana* (208 Carrer del Rosselló; phone: 215-6591), the original of the genre and much copied; and *Velvet* (161 Carrer de Balmes; phone: 217-6714), small, loony, and fun. Other possibilities in the same style are *Otto Zutz* (15 Lincoln; phone: 238-0722), *292, KGB* (55 Carrer Alegre de Dalt; phone: 210-5904), *Network* (616 Av. Diagonal; phone: 201-7238), *Rosebud* (Carrer Adrià Margerit; phone: 418-8885), *Universal Bar* (Carrer Mariá Cubí; phone: 201-4658), and *Zeleste* (122 Carrer Almogàvers; phone: 309-1204).

For sheer spectacle and good music (no dancing), *Las Torres de Avila* (Av. de Marquès de Comillas, *Poble Espanyol,* Montjuïc; phone: 424-9309) features a rooftop terrace and an astral theme, with an electric moon circling the wall in sync with the music on one side, and an electric sun setting slowly on the other. For hot jazz, try the live jams at *Hot Club Otto Zutz* (see above). At the *Gran Casino de Barcelona* (Sant Pere de Ribes, 26 miles/42 km from the city near the seaside town of Sitges; phone: 893-3666), you have to be over 18, with a passport for identification, to enjoy the dining and gambling in a 19th-century setting.

# Best in Town

## CHECKING IN

Though Barcelona always was short on hotel space, the *1992 Olympics* spurred an expansion that resulted in the addition of 5,000 hotel rooms to the city's previous 14,000-room-plus hotel capacity. Expect to pay more than $300 a night for a double room at a hotel listed below as very expensive, between $190 and $300 for a double room at a hotel listed as expensive, between $75 and $100 at ones listed as moderate, and less than $75 at an inexpensive hotel. Unless otherwise noted, the hotels listed offer private baths, air conditioning, and in-room telephones and TV sets. All telephone numbers are in the 3 city code.

### VERY EXPENSIVE

**Arts** Ritz Carlton claims that this, its first European property, is the continent's tallest hotel. The new 455-room luxury hotel is located in one of the two twin towers 100 yards from Platja Barcelona, the new beach at the *Villa Olímpica* (Olympic Village). The hotel's public spaces are filled with Catalan modern art, and there's a formal restaurant, a café, a fitness center, and two outdoor swimming pools. Business services include 12 meeting rooms, an English-speaking concierge, secretarial services in English, foreign currency exchange, and 24-hour room service. 19 Passeig de Marina (phone: 221-1000; 800-241-3333; fax: 221-1070).

**Barcelona Hilton** Situated on a tree-lined avenue in one of the most stylish parts of the city, this hotel's architecture is modern, the decor classic, cozy, and restful. There are 300 rooms, including several executive floors, one of which is reserved exclusively for women.

Popular with business travelers, in addition to a health club and a restaurant it offers meeting rooms for up to 1,000, an English-speaking concierge, foreign currency exchange, secretarial services in English, audiovisual equipment, photocopiers, computers, translation services, 24-hour room service, and express checkout. 589 Av. Diagonal (phone: 419-2233; 800-HILTONS; fax: 405-2573).

**Rey Juan Carlos I** Named for the current king of Spain, this modern property near the university and the upscale Pedralbes neighborhood has 375 rooms and 17 suites, all surrounding a large open atrium. Facilities include a health club and an outdoor swimming pool, three restaurants (one of which is Japanese), two bars, 24-hour room service, secretarial services in English, six meeting rooms, and foreign currency exchange. 661-667 Av. Diagonal (phone: 448-0808; fax: 448-0607).

**Ritz** Built in 1919, this deluxe, recently refurbished aristocrat boasts a new face, and once again lives up to its reputation for superb service in an elegant, charming atmosphere. It's the hotel of choice for many international celebrities. All 161 rooms have high ceilings, and there also is a fine restaurant. Amenities include 24-hour room service, eight meeting rooms for 20 to 500 people, an English-speaking concierge, foreign currency exchange, secretarial services in English, audiovisual equipment, photocopiers, translation services, and express checkout. 668 Gran Via de les Corts Catalanes (phone: 318-5200; 800-223-6800; fax: 318-0148).

### EXPENSIVE

**Almirante** This small, modern hostelry is in the center of the city near the cathedral. There are 80 oversize rooms with luxury bathrooms, and amenities include a restaurant, 24-hour room service, six meeting rooms for up to 80, an English-speaking concierge, foreign currency exchange, secretarial services in English, a photocopier, and translation services. 42 Via Laietana (phone: 268-3020; fax: 268-3192).

**Avenida Palace** Polished brass and fancy carpets lend a tasteful, Old World atmosphere to this deluxe property. The 169 rooms are cheerful yet quiet, and have mini-bars. The public areas are adorned with sedate paintings, fine reproductions, and interesting antiques. There are a gym and a sauna, a restaurant, five meeting rooms for up to 300, an English-speaking concierge, foreign currency exchanges, secretarial services in English, audiovisual equipment, photocopiers, computers, translation services, 24-hour room service, and express checkout. The staff is well trained and attentive. 605 Gran Via de les Corts Catalanes (phone: 301-9600; fax: 318-1234).

**Calderón** In this longtime favorite with the business crowd, most of the 264 generously proportioned rooms have been equipped with the conveniences and services frequent business travelers expect. In addition there is a restaurant, 10 meeting rooms, an English-speaking concierge, foreign currency exchange, secretarial services in English, audiovisual equipment, photocopiers, translation services, and express checkout. The rooftop pool, sauna, and sun terrace command a splendid view of the city. 26 Rambla de Catalunya (phone: 301-0000; fax: 317-4453).

**Claris** The 19th-century Vedruna Palace, with its original regal façade intact, has been renovated with marble floors and teak paneling. Owner Jordi Clos owns the most important collection of Egyptian art in Spain, and he has installed 70 pieces of it in a second-floor gallery of the hotel. There are Egyptian or Indian pieces of art in the 124 rooms; the hotel also boasts two restaurants, a bar, an outdoor pool, a sauna, parking facilities, an English-speaking concierge, and foreign currency exchange. l50 Carrer Pau Claris (phone: 487-6262; 800-888-4747; fax: 487-8736).

**Colón** A renovated old favorite in the Barri Gòtic, right in front of the cathedral. Clean and pleasantly decorated, it has 146 rooms with high ceilings, including 10 on the sixth floor with terraces (three of them face the cathedral). A restaurant is on the premises, and other amenities include 24-hour room service, a meeting room for up to 100 people, and English-speaking concierge, foreign currency exchange, and translation services. 7 Av. de la Catedral (phone: 301-1404; fax: 317-2915).

**Condes de Barcelona** *Modernista* outside and modern inside, it's in a striking Art Nouveau building that was transformed into a luxury hotel in the mid-1980s, and proved so popular that it is already undergoing an expansion. The 183 rooms and suites contain all the expected amenities. Its location in the heart of the Eixample is ideal, and its *Brasserie Condal* is a good dining spot. There are five meeting rooms for 20 to 225 people, an English-speaking concierge, foreign currency exchange, secretarial services in English, audiovisual equipment, photocopiers, and translation services. 75 Passeig de Gràcia (phone: 484-8600; fax: 487-1442).

**Derby** This is an elegant establishment done in hushed colors, with diffused lighting and impressive wood trim and ornamentation. Affiliated with Best Western, it offers 117 rooms; those on the top floor have large terraces. The intimate piano bar adds an extra special touch; there's also a restaurant, three meeting rooms for up to 50 people, an English-speaking concierge, foreign currency exchange, secretarial services in English, a photocopier, and translation services. 21 Carrer de Loreto (phone: 322-3215; 800-528-1234; fax: 410-0862).

**Diplomatic** Dedicated to businesspeople with its excellent conference facilities, this modern 217-room establishment is conveniently located near the Pedrera and the Passeig de Gràcia shops. It offers an outdoor pool, a restaurant, 24-hour room service, five meeting rooms for up to 500, an English-speaking concierge, foreign currency exchange, secretarial services in English, audiovisual equipment, photocopiers, computers, translation services, and express checkout. 122 Carrer de Pau Claris (phone: 488-0200; fax: 488-1222).

**Ducs de Bergara** Stepping into the foyer, you'll find yourself 100 years back in time. Located next to the Plaça de Catalunya, this charming hotel boasts marble floors, pillars, cut-glass mirrors, molded ceilings, and 56 modern and stylish rooms, as well as a restaurant, 24-hour room service, two meeting rooms, an English-speaking concierge, foreign currency exchange, secretarial services in English, and photocopiers. 11 Bergara (phone: 301-5151; fax: 317-3442).

**Gran Hotel Havana** This luxury establishment has a neoclassical façade but a completely modern interior, featuring a dramatic six-story central atrium lined with shops, a piano bar, and a restaurant. Its 141 rooms are decorated with Italian marble and are equipped with satellite television. On the top floor are 10 deluxe suites and a private terrace garden. Other amenities include an English-speaking concierge, four large meeting rooms, audiovisual equipment, fax machines, and translation services. 647 Gran Via de les Corts Catalanes (phone: 412-1115; fax: 412-2611).

**Meliá Barcelona Sarrià** Near Plaça de Francesc Macià, this is a favorite with business travelers. All 312 rooms have king-size beds. The executive Piso Real floor features its own concierge. There is a restaurant, 24-hour room service, nine meeting rooms, an English-speaking concierge, foreign currency exchange, secretarial services in English, audiovisual equipment, photocopiers, and translation services. 50 Av. de Sarrià (phone: 410-6060; 800-336-3542; fax: 410-6173).

**Le Meridien Barcelona** A large (210-room), imposing link in the international chain, it provides expected standards of comfort and service. The Renaissance Club rooms on the top four floors are the finest, featuring computer terminals. Ideally located near the Barri Gòtic, it has two restaurants, 24-hour room service, an English-speaking concierge, foreign currency exchange, secretarial services in English, audiovisual equipment, photocopiers, computers, translation services, 10 meeting rooms, and express checkout. 111 La Rambla (phone: 318-6200; 800-543-4300; fax: 301-7776).

**Presidente** This 156-room modern luxury establishment is located away from the center of town but is, nevertheless, bustling with businesspeople, film stars, and other personalities. A restaurant serves Catalan and international fare, and other amenities include 24-hour room service, three meeting rooms for up to 150, an English-speaking concierge, foreign currency exchange, secretarial services in English, audiovisual equipment, photocopiers, and translation services. 570 Av. Diagonal (phone: 200-2111; fax: 209-5106).

**Princesa Sofía** Big, bustling, and modern, this convention-oriented hotel has an indoor pool, a gym, a sauna, and restaurants. It could be anywhere in the world, but is out near the university and the *Estadi Camp Nou*. The 511 rooms, decorated in contemporary style, have large tile bathrooms and mini-bars. Other amenities include 24-hour room service, 28 meeting rooms, and English-speaking concierge, foreign currency exchange, secretarial services in English, audiovisual equipment, photocopiers, computers, translation services, and express checkout. Plaça de Pius XII (phone: 330-7111; fax: 330-7621).

**Rivoli Rambla** Conveniently situated on La Rambla, this hotel is within easy walking distance of the Barri Gòtic, the Plaça de Catalunya, Passeig de Gràcia, and the waterfront. The 87 rooms are furnished in low-key contemporary style, with remote-control TV sets, room safes, mini-bars, and personal computers in the suites. There is a small fitness center, an attractive restaurant called *Le Brut,* showcasing specialties from all over Spain, a rooftop terrace, and the *Blue Moon* piano bar. 128 Rambla dels Estudis (phone: 302-6643; 412-5053 for reservations; fax: 317-5053).

### MODERATE

**Espanya** A well-priced hotel with a *modernista* dining room in a 19th-century building, it has antique plumbing, but it's clean, with 84 rooms and a restaurant. On the edge of the Barri Gòtic, at 9 Sant Pau (phone: 318-1758; fax: 317-1134).

**Gala Placidia** An apartment complex, it has 31 suites with small bedrooms, sitting rooms with fireplaces, dining areas, and refrigerators. 112 Via Augusta (phone: 217-8200; fax: 217-8251).

**Majestic** A Barcelona classic, it has 335 rooms with in-room English-language movies, hair dryers, and mini-bars. There is also a gym, a sauna, and a rooftop pool, in addition to 24-hour room service, nine meeting rooms, an English-speaking concierge, foreign currency exchange, secretarial services in English, audiovisual equipment, and photocopiers. The restaurant serves international cuisine. The location, in the heart of the Eixample (opposite the *Condes de Barcelona*) amid restaurants, shops, and *modernista* buildings, couldn't be better. 70 Passeig de Gràcia (phone: 488-1717; 800-332-4872; fax: 418-1880).

**Oriente** Right on La Rambla, so reserve a room in the back. Built in 1842 with fancy public rooms, its Old World charm has worn a bit thin, but its central location just about compensates. There are 142 rooms and a restaurant. 45 La Rambla (phone: 302-2558; fax: 412-3819).

**Rialto** In the heart of the Barri Gòtic, this simple but stylish place has 128 rooms and a restaurant. 42 Carrer de Ferrán (phone: 318-5212; fax: 315-3819).

### INEXPENSIVE

**Gaudí** Renovated and rather spartan, but handy for Montjuïc, the port, and the Barri Gòtic. There are 73 rooms; those on the top floor have great views of Montjuïc and the Gothic cathedral. A restaurant is on the premises. 12 Carrer Nou de la Rambla (phone: 317-9032; fax: 412-2636).

**Jardín** Overlooking two of the most picturesque squares in the Barri Gòtic, this 100-year-old establishment is simple, but scenic. Half of its 38 rooms have private baths. No restaurant. 1 Plaça de Sant Josep Oriol (phone: 301-5900; fax: 318-3664).

**Nouvel** Conveniently located on a pedestrians-only street near the top of La Rambla and the Plaça Catalunya, it has 54 rooms and a small restaurant. 18-20 Carrer Santa Anna (phone: 301-8274; fax: 301-8370).

------

## EATING OUT

Barcelonans are serious about eating, often taking coffee and a pastry for breakfast in a café, or *cafetería* (a sit-down coffee shop; our idea of a cafeteria is called a "self-service" in Spain); a Spanish-style potato omelette or a ham-and-cheese sandwich between 11 AM and noon; a late lunch (many restaurants don't even open until 2 PM); a round of *tapas* (see below) later in the day to take the edge off the appetite; and an even later dinner, beginning at 10 or 10:30 PM. (In the heat of the summer, and on weekends, this could be 11 PM.)

Barcelona boasts restaurants of every kind, including French, Italian, German, Chinese, Japanese, Argentine, Ecuadoran, Lebanese, and even American, as well as establishments serving specialties of the Basque country, Andalusia, Navarre, and virtually every other Spanish region (there are also more than a few American fast-food restaurants, as well as local knockoffs; if you're in this mode, try instead the chain of Catalan-style sandwich shops called *Pans & Company*). But as Catalan self-pride has blossomed, so has interest in the traditional cooking of Catalonia, as well as contemporary improvisations on the theme. Catalan food is unusual, and not much like other Spanish culinary idioms. Codified as early as the 14th century, influenced by the Romans, Visigoths, and Moors (and later by the French and Italians), it is exuberant, voluptuous, dense, baroque, and definitively Mediterranean. It freely and skillfully mixes fish and fowl, meat and fruit, garlic and chocolate; it adds nuts and aromatic spices to its savory sauces; combines salted fish (especially anchovies and salt cod) with fresh; and constructs elaborate culinary fantasies around pigs' trotters, snails, wild mushrooms, and squid—sometimes all in the same pot. It has remained closer to its medieval roots than any other Western European cooking today, but at the same time has admitted influences from Italy, France, even Asia, updating itself without losing its ancient soul. *Sarsuela,* an everything-but-the-kitchen-sink soup, or stew of fish and shellfish, is something of a tourist dish, often made with products past their prime. Instead, try the simpler *suquet,* a stew made with potatoes and just one or two varieties of fish. Paella, originally from Valencia, to the south, is popular in Barcelona; the version called *paella Parellada,* named for a local dandy, is a specialty, made without bones or shells. *Arròs negre* (black rice), made with inkfish (similar to squid but more flavorful), is a delicacy from the Costa Brava, well interpreted at several Barcelona restaurants. The most basic Catalan dish is *escudella i carn d'olla,* a hearty pot-au-feu of sausage, beans, meatballs, and assorted vegetables. The classic Catalan snack food is *pa amb tomàquet* (bread with tomato), good country bread moistened with olive oil and the juice of fresh tomatoes, usually accompanied by plump Costa Brava anchovies or mountain ham. *Crema catalana,* the ubiquitous caramel custard with the burnt-sugar top, often concludes a meal.

In restaurants classified as expensive, expect to pay $60 or more for a dinner for two; $30 to $60 in establishments in the moderate range, and less than $30 in inexpensive places. Prices include a bottle of house wine, as well as *servicio* (tip) and *IVA* (value-added tax), which are usually tallied directly into the bill. It's a good idea to check the daily fixed-price menu—the *menú del día*—which all restaurants are required to offer. Unless otherwise noted, the restaurants listed are open for both lunch and dinner, and all telephone numbers are in the 3 city code.

### EXPENSIVE

**Agut d'Avinyó** A favorite for both lunch and dinner, this beautiful multilevel restaurant in the Barri Gòtic has whitewashed walls, oak plank floors, and antique furnishings. Its traditional Catalan food—especially the duck with figs—is excellent. The award-winning owner-hostess, Mercedes Giralt, lends her considerable charm to it all. Closed Sundays, *Easter Week,* and the month of August. Reservations necessary. Major credit cards accepted. 3 Carrer de la Trinitat (phone: 302-6034).

**Azulete** Imaginative international dishes are served here, and the house, with its gardens and fountain, is a delight. The dining room of this former mansion is actually a glass-enclosed garden, with tables arranged around a decorative pool, surrounded by lush vegetation. Specialties include tiny medallions of pork crowned with mushroom purée, and broiled *lubina* (sea bass) with fresh dill. For dessert, try figs with strawberry-scented honey. Closed Saturday lunch, Sundays, holidays, the first two weeks in August, and from *Christmas* through *New Year's.* Reservations necessary. Major credit cards accepted. 281 Via Augusta (phone: 203-5943).

**Beltxenea** When he opened this place on the premises of the former *Ama Lur* restaurant, owner-chef Miguel Ezcurra began reviving the tradition of Basque cooking in Barcelona. His new approach to the typical dishes of Spain's North Atlantic coast offers a change from Catalan food. Fish in spicy sauce is a specialty. Closed Saturday lunch and Sundays. Reservations necessary. Major credit cards accepted. 275 Carrer de Mallorca (phone: 215-3024).

**Casa Isidre** Joan Miró's favorite restaurant in Barcelona while he was alive, this contemporary-and-traditional Catalan place offers impeccable seafood of many kinds. Choose from *espardenyes* (a kind of sea slug eaten only in this part of Catalonia), fava bean salad, very good foie gras from the Costa Brava, and superb calf's brains, among other delicacies. Awarded one Michelin star, it boasts good wines and the best selection of armagnacs in town. Closed Sundays, holidays, *Christmas Week, Easter Week,* and from mid-July to mid-

August. Reservations necessary at least two days in advance. Major credit cards accepted. 12 Carrer de les Flors (phone: 441-1139).

**Casa Leopoldo** A longtime favorite among Barcelonans, this family-run eatery features beautifully tiled walls and the freshest of seafood. Take a taxi: While the restaurant is top-shelf, the neighborhood is not. Closed Sunday dinner, Mondays, and August. Reservations advised. Major credit cards accepted. 24 Carrer de Sant Rafael (phone: 441-3014).

**Eldorado Petit** A recipient of the National Gastronomy Award, owner Lluís Cruanyas made a big hit with his first restaurant of the same name (in Sant Feliu de Guixols on the Costa Brava); menu specialties at his Barcelona dining place combine local and French dishes in such "new Catalan" concoctions as cold cod salad with cilantro and thyme, *bacallà* (salt cod) wrapped in bell peppers, salmon lasagna, and goose liver and duck liver pâtés. Dessert specialties include exquisite homemade ice creams and sherbets. Closed Sundays and the first two weeks in August. Reservations essential. Major credit cards accepted. 51 Carrer de Dolors Monserdá (phone: 204-5506).

**Florián** One of the city's most imaginative and consistent contemporary-style dining spots, this place offers fare that's modern-Mediterranean rather than strictly Catalan, but it has plenty of local flavors (and flavor). Wild mushrooms and beef from bullring bulls are specialties. Rosa Grau cooks while Xavier García-Ruano, her husband, minds the art-filled dining room. There are good wines, often reasonably priced. Closed Sundays, *Easter Week,* two weeks in August, and *Christmas.* Reservations necessary. Major credit cards accepted. 20 Carrer de Bertran i Serra (phone: 212-4627).

**Gorría** This first-rate old-line Barcelona establishment specializes in the food of Navarre. Though there are some good seafood dishes (including sautéed cod cheeks in garlic sauce), the best choices here are roasted meat, sausages, and anything involving white or red beans. Closed Sundays and August. Reservations necessary. Major credit cards accepted. 421 Carrer Diputació (phone: 245-1164).

**Hispania** A Catalan classic in a large roadside villa about a 20-minute drive up the coast, it offers light salt cod beignets, stuffed cabbage rolls with *botifarra* sausage, pig's trotters stewed with lentils, *suquet* of monkfish and clams, and wonderful *crema catalana,* among other dishes. It's definitely worth the trip. Closed Sunday dinner, Tuesdays, *Easter Week,* and during October. Reservations necessary. Major credit cards accepted. 54 Carretera Reial, Arenys de Mar (phone: 791-0457).

**Neichel** This dining spot boasts two Michelin stars and a dedicated local following. Among the French-tinged Catalan specialties are rare slices of duck breast with juniper berries and wild raspberries, lobster salad garnished with quail eggs and truffle strips, a wonderful seafood platter of *lluç* (hake), mollusks, and freshwater crab, filet of sea bass in cream of sea urchin, fish pot-au-feu with wine, and the best pastry cart in all of Spain. Closed Sundays, holidays, *Christmas Week,* and *Easter Week*, and during August. Reservations necessary. Major credit cards accepted. 16 *bis* Av. de Pedralbes (phone: 203-8408).

**Nostromo** Named (rather curiously) for Joseph Conrad's silver-grubbing South American dock foreman, this place boasts a bar and a nautical-theme bookshop upstairs and a good-looking dining room below. Ideas sometimes exceed execution in the young-minded kitchen here, but the warm tongue and lentil salad, the salt cod *de la catedral* (topped with puréed tomatoes and soufléed garlic mousseline), and the chicken and shrimp *canalons,* among other dishes, are excellent. Closed Saturday lunch and Sundays. Reservations advised. Major credit cards accepted. 16 Carrer de Ripoll (phone: 412-2455).

**La Odisea** This attractive, art-filled restaurant (whose owner-chef, Antonio Ferrer, is a well-known local poet) offers an imaginative assortment of Catalan and French-influenced dishes. Among the outstanding items are the marinated monkfish and vegetable salad, the classic *fideus* (noodles) in fish stock, and the remarkable stuffed rabbit loin with apple-honey *all-i-oli* (garlic sauce). The good wine selection includes numerous private labels. Closed Saturdays, *Easter Week,* and during August. Reservations advised. Major credit cards accepted. 7 Carrer de Copons (phone: 302-3692).

**Oliana** An upscale spinoff of *L'Olivé* (see below), with a light, airy, handsome upstairs dining room and an ample menu of Catalan specialties—including old standbys served at *L'Olivé* and such newer items as red peppers stuffed with hake and black-eyed peas sautéed with anchovies and onions. Closed Sundays. Reservations advised. Major credit cards accepted. 54 Carrer de Santaló (phone: 201-0647).

**Els Perols de l'Empordà** Excellent traditional cooking from the Empordà region of Catalonia—whence come many of the best and most unusual Catalan dishes. Duck (for which the Empordà is famous) is a specialty, the *escupinya* clams from Minorca are a revelation, and the rice dishes (including *arròs negre*) are glorious. Closed Sunday dinner, Mondays, and *Easter Week.* Reservations necessary. Major credit cards accepted. 88 Carrer de Villaroel (phone: 323-1033).

**Quo Vadis** Muted paneling, soft lights, and harmonious decor provide a pleasing ambience at this top establishment. The service is solicitous, and the highly original international cuisine is excellent. Closed Sundays. Reservations advised. Major credit cards accepted. 7 Carrer de Carmen (phone: 317-7447).

**Racó de Can Fabes** Hidden away in an old stone house is this creative restaurant, one of area's few two-Michelin-star restaurants. The Relais Gourmands establishment focuses on Mediterranean fare that features local ingredients—truffles, other fungi, and herbs—in such outstanding dishes as *raviolis de gambas al aceite de setas* (prawn ravioli with *porcini* mushrooms) and *lomo de cordero con* *hierbas del Montseny* (loin of lamb with local herbs). Closed Sunday nights, Mondays, two weeks at the end of January, and the first two weeks in July. Reservations necessary. Major credit cards accepted. North of the city, at 6 Carrer de Sant Joan, Sant Celoni (phone: 867-2851).

**Via Veneto** A grand, serious place with a rather silly interior—mock–Art Nouveau, padded in black leather—but excellent food, much of it genuinely Catalan. One traditional—and excellent—dish is a remarkable boneless pig's trotters stuffed with ground pork and herbs, wrapped in caul fat, and braised with wild mushrooms. The wine list is one of the best in town, especially strong in Rioja vintages. Closed Saturdays, Sunday lunch, and August 1 through 20. Reservations necessary. Major credit cards accepted. 10-12 Carrer de Ganduxer (phone: 200-7024).

### MODERATE

**Antigua Casa Solé** Also known as *Can Solé,* this is one of the relatively few non-tourist-trap seafood restaurants in portside Barceloneta, simple and always crowded. The choice of fish and shellfish changes daily. Closed Saturday dinner, Sundays, the first two weeks of February, and the first two weeks of September. Reservations advised. Major credit cards accepted. 4 Carrer de Sant Carles, Barceloneta (phone: 319-5012).

**Arcs de Sant Gervasi** One of Barcelona's favorite dining spots in the bustling neighborhood near Plaça de Francesc Macià. Try the gratin of eggplant, ham, and tiny shrimp, or the slices of rare duck with zucchini mousse and sliced pears. Open daily. Reservations advised. Major credit cards accepted. 103 Carrer de Santaló (phone: 201-9277).

**Asador de Aranda** North-central Spanish food, which means lots of rich sausages, grilled meat, suckling pig, and homemade bread, in one of the city's most notable *modernista* buildings—a veritable urban castle of a place, built between 1903 and 1913 by Joan Rubió i Bellvé. Closed Sunday dinner. Reservations advised. Major credit cards accepted. 31 Av. del Tibidabo (phone: 417-0115).

**La Bona Cuina** The decor looks a bit like a *modernista* parlor, with walls paneled in dark wood, lace curtains at the windows, and a huge Art Nouveau mirror, all gold swirls with a golden peacock on top, dominating the room. In the Barri Gòtic, behind the cathedral, it unabashedly caters to tourists, but delivers good Catalan food, especially fish and seafood, and good value. Open daily. Reservations advised. Visa accepted. 12 Carrer Pietat (phone: 315- 4156).

**Can Majó** Slightly fancier than other seafood spots in the neighborhood, it specializes in seafood-based rice dishes of several kinds. The *suquet* is excellent as well. Many Barcelonans say this is the best eatery in Barceloneta. Closed Sunday and holiday dinner, Mondays, and August. Reservations advised. Major credit cards accepted. 23 Carrer Almirall Aixada, Barceloneta (phone: 310-1455).

**Los Caracoles** At first glance this bustling, jovial place looks like a tourist trap, but the good solid Catalan cooking can be impressive. Try *caracoles* (snails) or the chicken that's always roasting on rotisseries outside; the langostinos are fresh and delicious. Open daily. Reservations necessary (but you'll still have to wait during rush hours). Major credit cards accepted. 14 Carrer dels Escudellers (phone: 302-3185).

**Chicoa** An attractive folkloric interior and a large menu of well-cooked traditional Catalan specialties are featured here. There are a number of excellent interpretations of *bacallà* (salt cod)—try the sampler plate. Closed Saturdays, Sundays, and August. Reservations necessary. Major credit cards accepted. 73 Carrer d'Aribau (phone: 453-1123).

**El Gran Café** A big, warm, turn-of-the-century bistro in the *modernista* style, featuring café-society piano music in the evenings, and decent food from a menu that is part traditional Catalan and part contemporary. Featured items include a tart filled with ratatouille-like *escalivada,* monkfish sautéed with scampi, and sweetbreads and kidneys in anchovy-cream sauce. Closed Sundays, holidays, and August. Reservations advised. Major credit cards accepted. 9 Carrer d'Avinyó (phone: 318-7986).

**El Mordisco** For a taste of post-modern Barcelona, this trendy eatery boasts contemporary interior design, paintings by Xavier Mariscal on the walls, and a simple Catalan-French menu full of imaginative salads and meat dishes. Closed Sundays. Reservations necessary. Major credit cards accepted. 265 Carrer del Rosselló (phone: 218-3314).

**Network Café** With a TV set at every table, loud rock music, and trendy decor, this place attracts a young, well-heeled crowd. Its menu is generally continental, offering dishes hard to find in Spain such as curried chicken salad and guacamole. Downstairs, there's a lively bar with billiard tables. Open daily for lunch and dinner. Reservations advised. Major credit cards accepted. 616 Av. Diagonal (phone: 201-7238).

**L'Olivé** Pure, straightforward Catalan cooking in a simple but attractive setting. Bread with tomato and anchovies, marinated salt cod, stewed calf's head with ratatouille-like *samfaina,* and veal with mushrooms are among the typical specialties. Closed Sundays. Reservations necessary. Major credit cards accepted. 171 Carrer de Muntaner (phone: 430-9027).

**Passadís del Pep** Tiny, hard to find (it's hidden down a long corridor off a busy square), and always jam-packed with local politicians and businessmen, this eatery features home-style cooking, with seafood the specialty. Menus exist, but regulars (and astute first-timers) just ask for little tastes of whatever's particularly good that day. Closed Sundays and holidays. Reservations necessary. Major credit cards accepted. 2 Plaça de Palau (phone: 310-1021).

**El Raïm** A tiny place, hard to locate, with a guest book filled with famous names and a kitchen offering plain, hearty, unadorned Catalan specialties—often including *escudella i carn d'olla,* this region's monumental version of pot-au-feu. Closed weekends. Reservations necessary. Major credit cards accepted. 6 Carrer de la Pescateria (phone: 319-2098).

**Senyor Parellada** A good-looking place near the *Museu Picasso,* it's built around the atrium of an early iron-frame *modernista* building. Owner Ramón Parellada comes from a restaurant family—his grandfather once ran *Set Portes,* and his father had the well-known *Fonda Europa* in the suburb of Granollers—and standards of food and service are high here. The menu is almost exclusively Catalan, with occasional contemporary improvisations. Closed Sundays and holidays. Reservations advised. Major credit cards accepted. 37 Carrer Argenteria (called Calle Platería on some maps; phone: 315-4010).

**Set Portes** Also known by its Spanish name, *Siete Puertas* ("Seven Doors"), this is more or less *La Coupole* of Barcelona—a big, bright bistro or brasserie kind of place, dating from the mid-19th century. The paellas and other rice dishes and simple roasted meat (goat chops, for instance) aren't bad, but people come here more for the piano and the lively atmosphere than for the cooking. It's a bit touristy, but does attract plenty of local clientele, too—and in any case the atmosphere is worth it. Open daily. Reservations advised. Major credit cards accepted. 14 Passeig de Isabel II (phone: 319-3046). Moderate.

**Ticktacktoe** A billiard parlor/restaurant, in a delicate post-modern mode. Some dishes are precious—salmon tartare with baby eels, or strawberries with black pepper—but the thin noodles with clams and the filet mignon with wild mushroom sauce are delicious, the dining room is luminous, and the scene is animated. Closed Sundays, holidays, and August 7 to 31. Reservations necessary. Major credit cards accepted. 40 Carrer de Roger de Llúria (phone: 318-9947). There is a new second location on the pier at Platja Barcelona. Closed Wednesdays and Sunday dinner. Reservations advised. Major credit cards accepted. Port Olímpic, 20-21 Moll del Grega (phone: 221-0066).

### INEXPENSIVE

**Bar Pinocho** Not a restaurant at all, but a little stand with nine or ten stools in *La Boqueria.* Somehow, though, the closet-size kitchen manages to produce market-fresh traditional Catalan food—black rice, stewed calf's head, salt cod in cream sauce, and the like—as good as that at most of the white-tablecloth eateries in town. Open for breakfast and lunch only (the stewed calf's head is a popular dish even at breakfast!). Closed Sundays. No reservations. No credit cards accepted (phone: 317-1731).

**Café de la Ribera** Near the Plà de Palau, this airy bi-level café is a real find. Noisy, bustling, and very popular with the under-30 crowd, it features a *menú del dia,* usually seafood-oriented. The walls are covered with framed watercolors, posters, and black-and-white photographs; there's often a line of people waiting to get in. Closed Sundays. No reservations. No credit cards accepted. 6 Plaça de les Olles (phone: 319-5072).

**Les Corts Catalanes** A wonderful vegetarian delicatessen, located one block from the Passeig de Gràcia, serving everything from vegetable lasagna to cheese and spinach empanadas. Open daily. No reservations. Visa accepted. 603 Gran Via de les Corts Catalanes (phone: 301-0376).

**Egipte** Very popular and definitely bohemian, the two branches of this eatery are favorites of students and artists. The Carrer de Jerusalem branch is located behind *La Boqueria* market, so order the dish of the day for some of the freshest food in town (this one is closed Sundays); both have long menus of Catalan specialties. No reservations. Visa accepted. 3 Carrer de Jerusalem (phone: 317-7480) and 79 La Rambla (phone: 317-9545).

**Quatre Gats** The third incarnation of the popular café (whose name means "Four Cats") near the Barri Gòtic. The original, which opened in 1897 in this landmark *modernista* building designed by Puig i Cadafalch, was a hangout for artists and writers of the *modernisme* movement. Picasso had his first show here and even made the place the subject of one of his paintings. There's café-society ambience still, especially in the pretty dining room, behind the café, which features Art Nouveau lamps, wrought-iron and marble tables, potted palms, and a candelabra on the baby grand. The limited menu features unpretentious (and occasionally less than inspiring) Catalan dishes; try the *Quatre Gats* salad for a new twist on diet food. Open daily. No reservations. Visa accepted. 3 Carrer de Montsió (phone: 302-4140).

**Tortilleria Flash-Pan** Owned by the proprietor of *Set Portes,* and specializing in Spanish *tortillas*—torte-like omelettes, 101 varieties in all. Open daily until 1:30 AM. No reservations. Major credit cards accepted. 25 Carrer de la Granada del Penedès (phone: 237-0990).

---

## TAPAS BARS

The Catalans did not invent *tapas,* the Spanish equivalent of dim sum; the Andalusians did. And many Catalans consider this kind of eating to be too frivolous to be worth their time; they like to sit down at a table with a knife and fork and plenty of real food. Nonetheless, Barcelona has numerous *tapas* bars, catering both to locals and to immigrants from other parts of Spain. You can eat *tapas* as a snack to stave off hunger waiting for Spain's late mealtimes, or you can indulge in a *tapeo,* which consists of making the rounds of *tapas* bars, downing a drink (beer, sherry, and wine are common choices) at each, and making an entire dinner of these delicious snacks.

Many of Barcelona's *tapas* bars are along or just off La Rambla and in the area surrounding the *Museu Picasso*. Some of the more popular choices—all beyond this zone—are *José Luis* (520 Av. Diagonal; phone 200-8312), which offers a wide selection of seafood and some of Spain's finest hams; *Casa Fernández* (46 Carrer Santaló; phone: 201-9308), a great place to sample a variety of beers, including their own brand; *Jamón Jamón* (off Plaça de Francesc Macià at 4 Carrer del Mestre Nicolau; phone: 209-4103), which serves what its name ("Ham Ham") implies, and it serves the best, from Jabugo; *Mundial* (1 Plaça Sant Agustín; phone: 331-2516), which specializes in seafood; *Belvedere* (in a quiet alleyway off Passeig de Gràcia, at 3 Passatge Mercader; phone: 215-9088), which offers a nice terrace and a wide selection; and *Bodega Sepúlveda* (173 Carrer de Sepúlveda; phone: 454-7094), where the proprietor's own wine accompanies cheese in oil and little salads. Don't avoid *tapas* bars because their floors look "dirty": throwing crumpled napkins on the floor is the tradition, and the messier a floor looks, the better a place usually is.

---

BARS AND XAMPANERIES

A hard-drinking town, Barcelona has a large number of old-style "American" bars specializing in 1930s-style cocktails, and a good many newer places called *xampaneries* (singular: *xampaneria*), devoted to *xampany* (champagne)—usually Catalonia's own champagne-method *cava* sparkling wine, often very good.

Among the best cocktail bars are *Antiquari* (13 Carrer Veguer; phone: 315-3109), a secret of the Barri Gòtic, near the Plaça del Rei, beautifully furnished with old-style chairs and tables, a sturdy wooden bar (dispensing fine mixed drinks), antique tiles, and even bits of Roman wall visible in the basement lounge; *Boadas* (1 Carrer Tallers; phone: 318-8826), on the corner of La Rambla, a tiny triangular-shape bar that has great cocktails, opened in 1933; *Dos Torres* (300 Via Augusta; phone: 203-9899), a handsome, easygoing drinking spot in a well-decorated *modernista* mansion with a terrace that is popular in summertime; and *Ideal Scotch* (89 Carrer d'Aribau; phone: 253-1028), a big, warm, popular Anglo-American–style bar with a formidable array of single-malt Scotch whiskies, opened in 1931 and presided over by well-known personality Josep Gotarda—known as "El Rey Gotarda," supposedly the local king of cocktail making. Top *xampaneries* include *La Cava del Palau* (10 Carrer Verdaguer i Callis; phone: 310-0938), just down the street from the *Palau de la Música Catalana* and featuring a wide choice of sparklers and excellent anchovies and duck-breast ham to nibble on, as well as piano music in the evenings; *El Xampanyet* (22 Carrer de Montcada; phone: 319-7003), near the *Museu Picasso*, beautifully tiled and serving sparkling cider in old-fashioned bottles in addition to *cava;* and *Xampu Xampany* (702 Gran Via de les Corts Catalanes; phone: 232-0716), which adds a number of complicated specialty drinks to the list of sparkling wines available.

# Berlin

## At-a-Glance

### SEEING THE CITY

The tallest structure in Berlin is the slender spire of the *Fernsehturm* (Television Tower; between Alexanderplatz and the Lustgarten; phone: 24040), which climbs to a height of 1,209 feet. Built in 1969, it is Europe's second-tallest tower. A revolving sphere at 655 feet is decked out with studio and transmission facilities, as well as with a good restaurant/café (see *Eating Out*), from which there is a magnificent view of the city. The tower is open daily; there's an admission charge.

The *Funkturm,* Berlin's radio tower (Messedamm; phone: 303-82996), is a steel-latticed spire 453 feet above the town that resembles the Eiffel Tower. An elevator ascends the structure to a viewing platform that, weather permitting, offers a good view of Germany's largest city; there is also a restaurant on a lower floor. The *Funkturm* is open daily; admission charge.

### SPECIAL PLACES

Berlin is easy to get around. Most of the downtown area was laid out in the late 19th century, and the streets form a sensible grid. You can see much of that part of the city by foot, if you familiarize yourself with the main thoroughfares. Running from east to west in the western part of the city are Kurfürstendamm (the closest thing to Main Street), Hardenbergstrasse, Kantstrasse, and Strasse des 17. Juni; the chief north-to-south connections are Potsdamer Strasse, Joachimstaler Strasse, and Wilmersdorfer Strasse. In Berlin's eastern section, the important downtown streets are Friedrichstrasse, which runs north to south, and Unter den Linden (which becomes Strasse des 17. Juni in "West" Berlin) and Karl-Marx-Allee, both running east to west. The city is divided into 23 districts, but most of the best-known tourist attractions are in Mitte, especially along Unter den Linden and around Potsdamer Platz. Berlin's historical center is on an island in the Spree (pronounced *Shpray*) River. To reach outlying areas of the city, use the *U-Bahn* (subway), buses, streetcars, or *S-Bahn* (aboveground trains). For more information, see *Getting Around.*

#### THE MITTE DISTRICT—AROUND UNTER DEN LINDEN

**UNTER DEN LINDEN** Some 1,500 yards long and almost 70 yards wide, this avenue is in the very heart of what was East Berlin. Originally laid out to connect the royal palace with the hunting preserve, the *Tiergarten,* it got its name from the rows of linden trees that were planted on both sides (and in the center) of the wide boulevard. In the 18th and 19th centuries, a number of magnificent structures

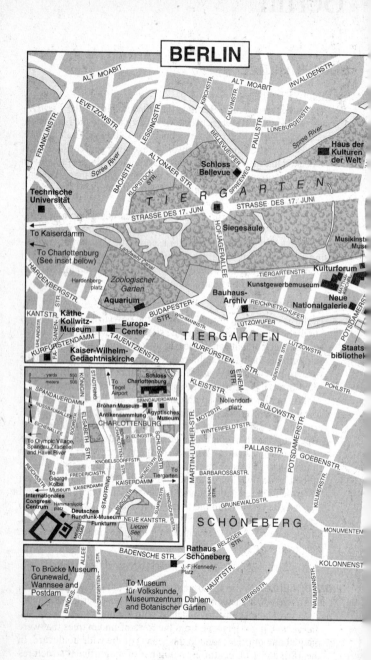

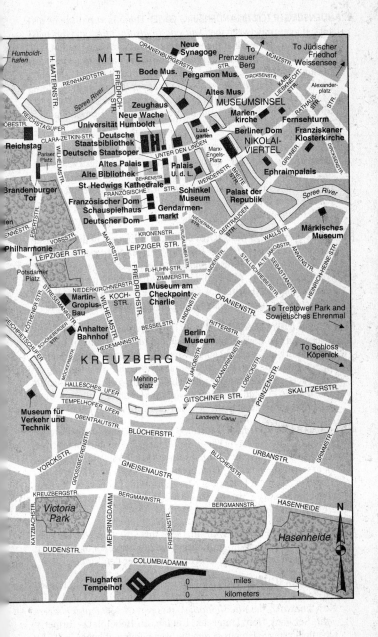

**MITTE**

Humboldt-hafen

H. MATERNSTR.
REINHARDTSTR.
ORANIENBURGERSTR.
FRIEDRICH STR.
Spree River

Neue
Synagoge

Prenzlauer
Berg

To
MÜNZSTR.

To Jüdischer
Friedhof
Weissensee

DIRCKSENSTR.

Alexander-platz

KARL-LIEBKNECHT-STR.

Bode Mus.
Pergamon Mus.

Altes Mus.

MUSEUMSINSEL

RATHAUS STR.

REICHSTAGUFER
ÖBESTR.
CLARA-ZETKIN-STR.

Reichstag

Zeughaus
Neue Wache
Universität Humboldt

Deutsche
Staatsbibliothek
Deutsche Staatsoper
Altes Palais
Alte Bibliothek
St. Hedwigs Kathedrale
Französischer Dom
Schauspielhaus
Deutscher Dom

Marien-kirche
Berliner Dom

Fernsehturm

Franziskaner
Klosterkirche

NIKOLAI-VIERTEL

Ephraimpalais

Lustgarten

Marx-Engels-Platz

UNTER DEN LINDEN

Palais
U. d. L.

WERDERSTR.

BEHRENSTR.

FRANZÖSISCHE

Schinkel
Museum

Palast der
Republik

Spree River

Gendarmen-markt

NIEDER-WALL-STR.

GERTRAUDEN-STR.

WALLSTR.

Märkisches
Museum

Brandenburger
Tor

Pariser
Platz

WILHELMSTR.

EBERTSTR.

NNESTR.

VOSSSTR.

Philharmonie

LEIPZIGER STR.

MAUERSTR.

KRONENSTR.

JERUSALEMER STR.

LINDENSTR.

ALTE JAKOBSTR.

STALLSCHREIBERSTR.

ANNENSTR.

HEINRICH-HEINE-STR.

Potsdamer
Platz

STRESEMANNSTR.

KÖTHENER STR.

LEIPZIGER STR.
FRIEDRICHSTR.
R.-HUHN-STR.
ZIMMERSTR.

NIEDERKIRCHNERSTR.
Martin-
Gropius-
Bau

KOCH-STR.

WILHELMSTR.

Museum am
Checkpoint
Charlie

ORANIENSTR.

To Treptower Park and
Sowjetisches Ehrenmal

REICHPIETSCHUFER
SCHÖNEBERGER STR.

MÖCKERNSTR.

Anhalter
Bahnhof

BESSELSTR.

HEDEMANNSTR.

LINDENSTR.

Berlin
Museum

RITTERSTR.

ALTE JAKOBSTR.

ALEXANDRINENSTR.

LOBECKSTR.

PRINZENSTR.

To Schloss
Köpenick

**KREUZBERG**

Mehring-platz

SKALITZERSTR.

HALLESCHES UFER
TEMPELHOFER UFER

OBENTRAUTSTR.

GITSCHINER STR.

Museum für
Verkehr und
Technik

BLÜCHERSTR.

Landwehr Canal

URBANSTR.

GRIMMSTR.

YORCKSTR.

GROSSBEERENSTR.

GNEISENAUSTR.

BLÜCHERSTR.

KREUZBERGSTR.

MEHRINGDAMM

BERGMANNSTR.

BERGMANNSTR.

HASENHEIDE

KATZBACHSTR.
Victoria
Park

FRIESENSTR.

*Hasenheide*

N

DUDENSTR.

COLUMBIADAMM

Flughafen
Tempelhof

| 0 | miles | .6 |
| 0 | kilometers | 1 |

were built along the boulevard. Although many were bombed during World War II, the former East German government faithfully restored those that survived.

**BRANDENBURGER TOR (BRANDENBURG GATE)** There is very little of historical interest between the *Deutsche Staatsbibliothek* and this massive Berlin landmark at the western end of Unter den Linden. The *Brandenburger Tor,* formerly inaccessible to cars and pedestrians because of the Wall, now is open to everyone; it turned 200 years old in 1991. The *Quadriga,* a beaten copper replica of the goddess of victory in a chariot drawn by four horses, was restored to the top of the gate for the bicentennial ceremonies. The triumphal arch is brilliantly lit at night. Pariser Pl.

**DEUTSCHE STAATSBIBLIOTHEK (GERMAN STATE LIBRARY)** Built in the early 20th century, the library occupies the site of the former *Preussische Staatsbibliothek* (Prussian State Library); the latter's stock of books that remained in Berlin during the war has been stored here. The rest are at the *Staatsbibliothek* (see below). Open daily. 8 Unter den Linden (phone: 203-8435).

**HUMBOLDT UNIVERSITÄT (HUMBOLDT UNIVERSITY)** Erected in the mid-18th century, it became *Friedrich-Wilhelm Universität* (Frederick William University) in 1810. Since 1949, this, the largest university in what was East Germany, has been known by its present name. Famous teachers included Hegel, Max Planck, and Einstein; Marx and Engels were students here. 6 Unter den Linden (phone: 20930).

**NEUE WACHE (NEW GUARDHOUSE)** Built in 1818, from 1960 until recently it served as an East German monument to the victims of fascism and militarism. The Kohl administration has transformed the monument into a memorial to *all* German war dead. An engraving on the neoclassical structure reads, "To the victims of war and the rule of violence." Inside there is a sculpture by Käthe Kollwitz. Open daily. No admission charge. 4 Unter den Linden (no phone).

**ZEUGHAUS (ARSENAL)** Built between 1695 and 1706, this lovely Baroque structure is the oldest on Unter den Linden. Set on the Spree River, it overlooks the historic *Museumsinsel* (Museum Island). Originally an arsenal, the building now houses the *Deutsches Historisches Museum* (German Historical Museum), with temporary displays about the country's history. Closed Wednesdays. Admission charge. 2 Unter den Linden (phone: 215020).

**ALTES PALAIS (OLD PALACE)** Built in 1836, this structure was the residence of Emperor William I during the last 50 years of his life. It is now used by *Humboldt Universität.* 9 Unter den Linden.

**ALTE BIBLIOTHEK (OLD LIBRARY)** This late-18th-century building housed the *Preussische Staatsbibliothek* (Prussian State Library) until 1914. Now known as the *Alte Bibliothek,* it is part of *Humboldt Universität.* Set back from Unter den Linden, on Bebelplatz (formerly Opernplatz, made famous during the Nazi burning of books in 1933).

**DEUTSCHE STAATSOPER (GERMAN STATE OPERA)** The opera house was built in 1743 and burned down 100 years later. Rebuilt, it was twice destroyed by bombs during World War II. It seats nearly 1,500 people (for ticket information, see *Music*). The interior is closed to the public except during performances. 7 Unter den Linden (phone: 203540).

**ST. HEDWIGS KATHEDRALE (ST. HEDWIG'S CATHEDRAL)** This Roman Catholic cathedral dates from the late 18th century and was built according to plans laid out by Frederick the Great (who was, by all appearances, impressed by the Pantheon in Rome). Gutted in the war, it has been just as carefully restored as most other Unter den Linden landmarks. Bebelpl.

**PALAIS UNTER DEN LINDEN (UNTER DEN LINDEN PALACE)** Converted from a house into a Baroque palace in the 17th century, it was known as the *Kronprinzenpalais* (Crown Prince Palace) until 1945. Emperor William II was born here in 1859, and during the Weimar Republic the handsome building was used as a museum of contemporary art. More recently—in August 1990—the Treaty of Unification between East and West Germany was signed here, and it is currently being considered as the official residence of Germany's federal president. The palace is reserved for state functions and is closed to the public; however, the adjacent and equally opulent *Opernpalais* (formerly the "Princesses' Palace," where the daughters of Queen Luise lived in the 19th century) houses two of the city's best restaurants, *Abend-Restaurant Königin Luise* and the *Operncafé* (see *Eating Out* for both). Unter den Linden (no phone).

**MUSEUMSINSEL (MUSEUM ISLAND)** On the north side of the Lustgarten, surrounded on three sides by the Spree River, is one of the world's largest and most magnificent museum complexes. The impressive buildings date to the 19th and early 20th centuries. The *Altes Museum* accommodates contemporary paintings and the *Kupferstichkabinett* (Cabinet of Engravings), which contains 135,000 prints by German and foreign masters (15th to 18th centuries), including Botticelli's illustrations of scenes from Dante's *Divine Comedy.* Also here is the *Pergamon Museum,* the site of three astounding architectural feats: the *Pergamon Altar,* named after the ancient Greek city in which it was discovered (south of the historic city of Troy in what is now Turkey) and including huge bas-reliefs of most of the major Greek gods; the *Market Gate,* from a Roman settlement at Miletus (also in what is now Turkey), which towers more than two stories high; and the Babylonian *Ishtar Gate* and processional way, the 2,600-year-old entrance to the legendary city of Babylon. These are among the most imposing sights on view at any museum anywhere. In this building, too, are the *Vorderasiatisches Museum* (Near Eastern Collection), the *Museum für Völkerkunde* (Museum of Ethnography), and the *Islamisches Museum* (Islamic Museum). At the northernmost tip of this island of museums is the *Bode Museum,* which now houses the *Ägyptisches Museum* (Egyptian Museum; there's another museum of the same name that houses the bust of Queen Nefertiti—see *Museums*), the *Gemäldegalerie*

(Picture Gallery), the *Museum für Bildhauerkunst* (Sculpture Collection), the *Münzekabinett* (Cabinet of Coins), and the *Museum für Vor- und Frühgeschichte* (Museum of Pre- and Proto-History). Among the treasures here are such masterpieces of German sculpture as the 12th-century *Naumburg Crucifix* and the *Winged Altarpiece* from *Minden Cathedral* (15th century). Closed Mondays and Tuesdays, except for the *Pergamon Museum,* which is open daily. Admission charge to each museum. 1-3 Bodestr. (phone: 203550).

**STAATSRATSGEBÄUDE (STATE COUNCIL BUILDING)** Not in use at press time (though it may reopen this year), this modern structure is still worth seeing from the outside; it's where the former East German government, the State Council, used to meet in the days of Communist boss Erich Honecker's rule. The centerpiece is one of the portals from the former royal palace. South side of the *Lustgarten.*

**BERLINER DOM (BERLIN CATHEDRAL)** This monumental (243 feet high and 116 feet in diameter), domed church was built around the turn of the century by the Hohenzollern family, whose palace stood across the street. After an 18-year, multimillion-dollar restoration, the lavish main sanctuary reopened in 1993; the crypt, containing the Hohenzollern mausoleum, also may be visited. *Lustgarten.*

**MARIENKIRCHE (ST. MARY'S CHURCH)** Just past the *Museumsinsel,* in the shadows of the *Fernsehturm* (Television Tower), is Berlin's second-oldest church. First erected in 1240, it is a pleasant combination of Gothic and neoclassical styles. Karl-Liebknecht-Str.

## OTHER MITTE LANDMARKS

**GENDARMENMARKT (GENDARMES' MARKET)** The square, which takes its name from the 18th-century gendarmes who quartered their horses here, was a lively marketplace until the onset of World War II. Now a lovely plaza with elegant cast-iron street lamps, geometric stone pavement, and a statue of playwright Friedrich Schiller, it is framed by two historic churches and a concert hall. The *Französischer Dom* (French Cathedral), on the northern side of the plaza, was built in the early 18th century by Berlin's Huguenot community, which left France following the revocation of the Edict of Nantes in 1685. You can climb to the tower's balustrade for a view of the Mitte district. The church also houses the *Hugenottenmuseum* (Huguenot Museum), with exhibits tracing the history of the exiled community. The museum is closed Mondays and Fridays; admission charge (phone: 229-1760). Facing the *Französischer Dom* and dating from the same period, the towers of the *Deutscher Dom* (German Cathedral) dominate the quarter. Severely damaged during World War II, its façade was restored in 1985, and its interior was still undergoing restoration when a fire destroyed its cupola in late 1994; no word yet on when it's due to reopen to the public. Between the two cathedrals stands the *Schauspielhaus.* Designed in 1818 by the renowned neoclassical architect Karl Friedrich Schinkel, this 1,650-seat concert hall, with its sparkling crystal and gold interior, offers classical music concerts (see *Music*).

**EPHRAIMPALAIS (EPHRAIM PALACE)** More a mansion than a palace, this elaborate home in the neighborhood known as the Nikolaiviertel (see below) was built in the 1760s as a gift from Frederick II to his court jeweler and banker, Heine Ephraim. Demolished in 1935, the rococo masterpiece was reconstructed in the 1980s and is used today for changing exhibits of local art and history. Museum hours vary, depending upon the exhibition, so call ahead for information. Admission charge. 16 Poststr. (phone: 238-0900).

**NIKOLAIVIERTEL (NIKOLAI QUARTER)** A charming 16th-century neighborhood, destroyed by bombs in World War II and later rebuilt, it's perfect for a leisurely stroll through narrow streets, replete with gas lanterns and several period taverns. Note the *Nikolaikirche* (St. Nicholas's Church; Nikolaikirchpl.); the oldest building in Berlin, it was founded around 1200 and renovated in 1812. Its twin steeples overlook the cobbles, nooks, and crannies of this charming quarter. Between the Spree and the *Rathaus* (City Hall).

**FRANZISKANER KLOSTERKIRCHE (FRANCISCAN CLOISTER CHURCH)** Founded in 1249, its walls are among only a few remnants of medieval Berlin. The structure was heavily bombed in 1945; the ruins remain a grim reminder of the war. Klosterstr.

**NEUE SYNAGOGE (NEW SYNAGOGUE)** Opened in 1866 as Berlin's main Jewish sanctuary (it once had 3,500 seats), this golden-domed, Moorish-style structure was plundered and set on fire during the anti-Jewish raids on *Kristallnacht* (November 9, 1938). It was further damaged by bombs during a 1943 air attack and torn down in 1958. The black marble plaques on its façade hauntingly recall the tragic events. Restoration work on the interior is scheduled for completion next year. The building will then reopen as the *Centrum Judaicum* (Jewish Cultural Center). 30 Oranienburger Str. (phone: 280-1253).

**DOROTHEENSTÄDTISCHER FRIEDHOF (DOROTHEENSTADT CEMETERY)** Not far from the *Friedrichstrasse* train station, this tranquil oasis is the final resting place of many notables of German culture, including Bertolt Brecht and his wife, the actress Helene Weigel. Other illustrious names on the tombstones include Georg Wilhelm Friedrich Hegel, Heinrich Mann, and Johannes Becher. 126 Chausseestr.

**BRECHT-WEIGEL-GEDENKSTÄTTE (BRECHT-WEIGEL MEMORIAL)** Bertolt Brecht and Helene Weigel's former apartment is located next to the *Dorotheenstädtischer Friedhof* (see above). Boasting its original furnishings, it's now a memorial and a study center devoted to Brecht's works. Closed Sundays and Mondays. Admission charge. 125 Chausseestr. (phone: 282-9916).

AROUND POTSDAMER PLATZ

**POTSDAMER PLATZ (POTSDAM SQUARE)** Ever since the demise of the Wall, Berlin has become a building contractor's dream, especially in this section of the city. Before World War II, it was the city's "Times Square," and Europe's busiest intersection. During the postwar years, Potsdamer Platz was a Cold War desert bisected by the Wall and chiefly frequented by East German border guards and a host of rabbits. During the next decade, this gigantic construction site will become Berlin's largest commercial and residential district. Offices, apartment buildings, hotels, a conference center, and a theater will be in place when it is completed.

**MARTIN-GROPIUS-BAU (MARTIN GROPIUS BUILDING)** This huge, red brick neoclassical building houses rotating history and contemporary art exhibits; the *Berlinische Gallerie* (Berlin Gallery), which features works by local artists; and a collection of religious items, photographs, and documents tracing the history of Berlin's Jewish community. Closed Mondays. Admission charge. 110 Stresemannstr. (phone: 254860).

**PRINZ-ALBRECHT-GELÄNDE (TOPOGRAPHY OF TERROR)** On this site stood the headquarters of Nazi terror mechanisms: the Gestapo and the SS. It now houses a moving and informative documentary exhibition devoted to the victims of the Third Reich. A 200-yard stretch of the Wall still stands here as a reminder of days past. Closed Mondays. No admission charge. 110 Stresemannstr. (phone: 254-86703).

**ANHALTER BAHNHOF (ANHALTER TRAIN STATION)** All that remains of what was once Berlin's busiest long-distance train station is a single broken portal, a haunting reminder of a lively neighborhood where hotels, cafés, restaurants, and bars were always packed. An unusual sight, and worth a look. Askanischer Pl.

**MUSEUM AM CHECKPOINT CHARLIE** The collection here chronicles the history of the Wall and of Berlin during the Cold War years, with a special emphasis on the creative ways East Germans tried to flee their country. The museum is next to the former site of Checkpoint Charlie, the most famous border crossing between eastern and western Berlin. A guard tower and a section of the Wall still stand here, but this may change when an American business center goes up at the site in a few years. Open daily. Admission charge. 43-44 Friedrichstr. (phone: 251-1031).

**PHILHARMONIE** The home of the world-renowned *Berliner Philharmonisches Orchester* (Berlin Philharmonic Orchestra) is just a few blocks south of the *Reichstag* (Parliament Building), at the southern fringe of the *Tiergarten*. The building's asymmetrical architecture has been controversial ever since it was completed in 1963. Smaller ensembles perform in the adjoining *Kammermusiksaal* (Chamber Music Hall; see *Music*). Free guided tours of the building (in German only) are given once every morning. Kemperpl. (phone: 254880).

**MUSIKINSTRUMENTEN MUSEUM (MUSEUM OF MUSICAL INSTRUMENTS)** This museum holds an intriguing collection of European instruments that date from the 16th century. Music lovers will particularly enjoy such rarities as Frederick the Great's flute and Edvard Grieg's piano. Closed Mondays. Admission charge. 1 Tiergartenstr. (phone: 254810).

**KUNSTGEWERBEMUSEUM (MUSEUM OF DECORATIVE ARTS)** Next door to the *Philharmonie,* in the city's developing cultural center, is this imposing museum that houses a unique collection of German crafts from the past 900 years. Closed Mondays. Admission charge. 6 Tiergartenstr. (phone: 266-2911).

**NEUE NATIONALGALERIE (NEW NATIONAL GALLERY)** Designed by Ludwig Mies van der Rohe in 1968, this striking glass-walled building houses the city's collections of late 19th- and 20th-century art. Spend some time in the quiet sculpture garden during the summer months. Closed Mondays. Admission charge for special exhibitions. 50 Potsdamer Str. (phone: 266-2662 or 266-2663).

**STAATSBIBLIOTHEK (STATE LIBRARY)** Directly opposite the *Neue Nationalgalerie* is the starkly modern *Staatsbibliothek,* Berlin's successor to the *Preussische Staatsbibliothek* (Prussian State Library). Its collection of more than three million volumes makes it one of the world's largest libraries. Exhibitions and lectures also are presented. Closed Sundays. No admission charge to exhibitions. 33 Potsdamer Str. (phone: 2661).

**GEDENKSTÄTTE DEUTSCHER WIDERSTAND (GERMAN RESISTANCE MEMORIAL)** Plaques and impressive statuary are grouped in the courtyard of this building—which housed the German Armed Forces Supreme Command during World War II—to honor the German officers who were shot here for the ill-fated uprising against Hitler on July 20, 1944. There also is a historical document center. Open daily. No admission charge. Near the *Neue Nationalgalerie,* at 14 Stauffenbergstr. (phone: 265-42202).

THE TIERGARTEN

**TIERGARTEN** This beautiful public park—far more extensive than the *Zoologischer Garten* (Zoological Garden; see below), which is at its western fringe—originally was the royal hunting preserve. It now is one of the world's largest and most beautifully landscaped urban parks and is dotted with charming lakes and ponds. The *Tiergarten* extends from the zoo to within several hundred yards of the *Brandenburger Tor,* a total length of about 2 miles (3 km).

**REICHSTAG** At the eastern edge of the *Tiergarten,* just north of the *Brandenburger Tor,* is Germany's once and future Parliament building, built in the late 19th century in Italian High Renaissance style. Gutted by fire by Hitler's supporters in 1933, it was rebuilt and currently is used for political conclaves. A permanent display is devoted to recent German history, and there is also the excellent *Im Reichstag* restaurant (see *Eating Out*). It will take several years to renovate the building to accommodate the Bundestag—the seat of Germany's government. By the end of this decade, the entire area around the *Reichstag* is scheduled to be occupied by new government buildings. Closed Mondays. No admission charge. Pl. der Republik (phone: 39770).

**SIEGESSÄULE (VICTORY COLUMN)** Completed in 1873 to commemorate the Prussian campaigns against Denmark, Austria, and France, this 223-foot-high monument stands at the center of the *Tiergarten.* At the top are an observation platform and a gold statue of Victory. The platform is closed November through March. Admission charge.

**HAUS DER KULTUREN DER WELT (HOUSE OF WORLD CULTURES)** A gift from the American people in 1957, the ultramodern structure stands in the *Tiergarten,* on the banks of the Spree. Always controversial because of its bold design, it offers exhibitions, concerts, and theater devoted to the world's ethnic groups. In addition, it has a charming riverside restaurant and café-bar. Nearby is a 140-foot-tall carillon, whose 68 bells resound daily at noon and 6 PM. Open daily; restaurant and café-bar closed Mondays. No admission charge. 10 John Foster Dulles Allee (phone: 397870).

**ZOOLOGISCHER GARTEN (ZOOLOGICAL GARDEN)** On the southeastern edge of the *Tiergarten,* one block north of the *Gedächtniskirche* (see below), is one of Berlin's two zoos (*Tierpark* is the other; see below). Germany's first, the zoological gardens were laid out in 1841 and still have more species than any other zoo in the world. Open daily. Admission charge. 8 Hardenbergpl. (phone: 254010).

**AQUARIUM** Next door to the *Zoologischer Garten,* it has the most comprehensive collection of marine animals in the world. In the *Tropical Hall* you can watch large numbers of alligators and crocodiles in their own environments; your vantage point is a bridge a mere 10 feet or so above the bloodthirsty creatures. Open daily. Admission charge. 32 Budapester Str. (phone: 254010).

THE CHARLOTTENBURG DISTRICT (WEST OF THE TIERGARTEN)

**KAISER-WILHELM-GEDÄCHTNISKIRCHE (KAISER WILHELM MEMORIAL CHURCH)** This huge neo-Romanesque church was built toward the end of the 19th century to honor Kaiser Wilhelm I. The structure was almost completely destroyed by Allied bombing during World War II, and it has only been partially rebuilt. Its hexagonal bell tower and the octagonal chapel were added in the 1960s. The old west tower, 207 feet tall, was preserved in its ruined state. Partially new, partially old, partially preserved, and partially destroyed, to Berliners the church has become a symbol of the city. Breitscheidpl.

**GEDENKSTÄTTE PLÖTZENSEE (PLÖTZENSEE MEMORIAL)** About 2 miles (3 km) northwest of the *Gedenkstätte Deutscher Widerstand,* tucked behind the *Gefängnis Plötzensee* (Plötzensee Prison), is a memorial to the people who died in the Holocaust. Here stand two small brick buildings where "undesirables," such as Jews, Gypsies, and homosexuals, as well as many members of the resistance movement against the Nazis, were executed. In front of the buildings are a small garden, a wall bearing a tribute to the victims, and a stone urn containing soil from all the Nazi concentration camps. Open daily. No admission charge. Hüttigpfad (phone: 344-3226).

**SCHLOSS CHARLOTTENBURG (CHARLOTTENBURG PALACE)** Begun in 1695 and completed 10 years later, this sprawling Baroque castle on the outskirts of Berlin was to Prussia what Versailles was to France: the sometime residence of the royal family. It was also a great stone monument to the aspirations of the Hohenzollern regime, and a bronze statue of the Great Elector Frederick William (1620–88), the iron-fisted tyrant who forged the Prussian juggernaut, sternly welcomes visitors to the *Ehrenhof* (Court of Honor). The cavernous bedrooms and endless hallways in this castle built for Queen Sophie-Charlotte are gracefully feminine, albeit not exactly cozy. Adjacent to the palace is the *Galerie der Romantik* (Gallery of Romantics) in the Knobelsdorff Wing, devoted to 19th-century art from the neo-classical, Romantic, and Biedermeier periods, including works by Caspar David Friedrich and Antoine Watteau. The *Galerie der Romantik* is closed Mondays. The palace also houses the *Museum für Vor- und Frühgeschichte* (Museum of Pre- and Early History; closed Fridays). The beautifully laid-out park behind the palace is one of the nicest areas in the city. The castle is open daily. Separate admission charges to the castle and museums. Luisenpl. (phone: 320911).

**INTERNATIONALES KONGRESSCENTRUM UND MESSEGELÄNDE (INTERNATIONAL CONGRESS CENTER AND FAIRGROUNDS)** The modern *ICC*, as it is called, is about 1½ miles (2 km) southwest of *Schloss Charlottenburg*. Across the street from this looming convention center and concert hall, and connected to it by a covered pedestrian walkway, are the rambling fairgrounds, the site of year-round fairs and exhibitions, which include *Internationale Grüne Woche* (International Green Week; see *Special Events*) and the German radio and TV exhibition. On the fairgrounds is the *Funkturm* (Radio Tower; see *Seeing the City*). Masurenallee and Messedamm (phone: 30380).

**OLYMPIASTADION (OLYMPIC STADIUM)** Another 2 miles (3 km) to the west of the *ICC*, this huge sports arena casts its shadow over the low-lying houses of a pleasant residential area. It was built for the *1936 Olympic Games,* and if you look hard, you can still make out the "royal" box from which Hitler and his cohorts took in the spectacle. Open daily unless a sports event is being held here. Admission charge. Olympischer Pl. (phone: 304-0676).

ELSEWHERE IN THE CITY

**TIERPARK** In the city's suburbs, this zoo was opened in 1955 on the grounds of *Schloss Friedrichsfelde* (Friedrichsfelde Palace; also see *Museums*). As much as possible, the animals are shown in herds or family groups in spacious enclosures that blend with the landscape. Open daily. Admission charge. 125 Am Tierpark (phone: 515310).

**SOWJETISCHES EHRENMAL (SOVIET WAR MEMORIAL)** In the suburbs of eastern Berlin, within the confines of verdant *Treptower Park* and not far from the left bank of the Spree, is this huge, impressive monument. Dedicated in 1949, it honors more than 5,000 Soviet soldiers who fell in the battle for Berlin in 1945. Much of the material used came from the ruins of Hitler's *Reich Chancellery*. Open daily. Entrance from Puschkinallee and Am Treptower Park.

**JÜDISCHER FRIEDHOF WEISSENSEE (JEWISH CEMETERY)** In the Weissensee district, this is said to be the largest Jewish cemetery in Europe. Restored by the former East German government, it contains thousands of graves, most marked by large, ornate tombstones in late 19th- and early 20th-century style. Male visitors must wear hats. Closed Saturdays. 45 Herbert-Baum-Str.

**EAST SIDE GALLERY** Shortly after the two Berlins were united, artists from over 20 nations were invited by city officials to paint sections of the longest extant piece of the Berlin Wall. Their creations are wildly different, but the central theme is the fall of the Wall. This "canvas" runs for more than a half mile along the Spree River in Friedrichshain. Mühlenstr., near the *Hauptbahnhof* (Main Train Station).

**MUSEUM FÜR VERKEHR UND TECHNIK (MUSEUM OF TRANSPORT AND TECHNOLOGY)** Across the Landwehrkanal (Landwehr Canal) and a bit east is this showplace, which houses a very interesting collection devoted to the historic development of the railroad, the automobile, the bicycle, and the airplane. Closed Mondays. Admission charge. 9 Trebbiner Str. (phone: 254840).

**RATHAUS SCHÖNEBERG (SCHÖNEBERG CITY HALL)** This building, Berlin's city hall, also functions as the seat of government for the borough of Schöneberg. In 1991, the mayor moved his offices here, and other government officials followed. The city council has since moved to larger quarters in eastern Berlin. There is a good panoramic view from the top of the spireless tower, which contains a replica of the American Liberty Bell, presented to the city by General Lucius Clay in 1950. On June 26, 1963, President John F. Kennedy made his *"Ich bin ein Berliner"* speech from the balcony here to a gathering of over 450,000 citizens. The tower is open Wednesdays and Sundays from April through September. No admission charge. John-F.-Kennedy-Pl. (phone: 7831).

**SPANDAU ZITADELLE (SPANDAU CITADEL)** Even farther west, on the Havel River, is this historic citadel. The oldest edifice on the grounds, the *Juliusturm* (Julius Tower) dates from the 14th century. The citadel, which has served as a fortification, a prison, and the royal treasury, now is a local history museum. Nazi war criminals were not housed here, but at the prison on Wilhelmstrasse, in the middle of the Spandau district; the prison was torn down in 1987, after the suicide of its sole remaining occupant, Rudolf Hess. Closed Mondays. Admission charge. Am Juliusturm (phone: 33911).

**MUSEUMSZENTRUM DAHLEM (DAHLEM MUSEUM CENTER)** To the south, in the fashionable and lovely section of Dahlem, is one of Berlin's largest museum complexes. Its extensive buildings accommodate several institutions, and you can spend at least a full day going through them: The *Gemäldegalerie* (Painting Gallery) houses masterpieces of European painting before 1800, with the Italian Renaissance and Dutch and Flemish collections the standouts. Also at *Museumszentrum Dahlem* is the *Museum für Völkerkunde* (Ethnology Museum), which displays cultural artifacts from around the world. The museum's accessible exhibits make it a great choice for families with young children. There is also a small sculpture department, with Byzantine and European sculpture from the 3rd to the 18th centuries, as well as the *Museum für Islamische Kunst* (Museum of Islamic Art), *Museum für Indische Kunst* (Museum of Indian Art), and *Museum für Ostasiatische Kunst* (Museum of Far Eastern Art), as well as a collection of prints and engravings. Closed Mondays. No admission charge on Sundays and holidays. 8 Lansstr. (phone: 83011).

**BOTANISCHER GARTEN (BOTANICAL GARDEN)** About half a mile east of *Museumszentrum Dahlem* is the largest botanical garden in Germany, and one of the world's most significant collections of flora. Of special interest are the geographical gardens, where plants from various parts of the world flourish in carefully maintained native environments. There is a fascinating botanic display at the museum, next to the entrance to the gardens. The gardens are open daily; the museum is closed Mondays. Separate admission charges to museum and gardens. 6 Königin-Luise-Str. (phone: 830060).

**GEDENKSTÄTTE HAUS DER WANNSEE-KONFERENZ (WANNSEE HOLOCAUST MEMORIAL CENTER)** In 1942, this peaceful lakeside mansion 5 miles (8 km) west of Berlin was the site of a grisly summit. Here members of the Nazi Party, including Adolf Eichmann, convened to discuss the "final solution to the Jewish question." More than 50 years later, the building serves as a Holocaust memorial and educational center, with a permanent exhibition that documents the history of Germany's acts of genocide. Closed Mondays. No admission charge. 56-58 Am Grossen Wannsee (phone: 805-0010).

## EXTRA SPECIAL

Largely unknown to most tourists, who rarely leave the downtown area, the outlying districts of Berlin are mostly forests, including the Grunewald and the Tegel and Spandau Wälder, and waterways, such as the Havel and Spree Rivers, the Tegeler See, and the Wannsee. To see the Havel and the forests, board one of the 70 ships that make daily trips on the river. Between *Easter* and the end of September, boats leave eight times a day from numerous points, including Wannsee Hafen (Wannsee Harbor) in the Zehlendorf district. The main cruise company in Berlin is *Stern und Kreisschiffahrt* (60 Sachtlebenstr.; phone: 810-0040).

Along the way, get off at any number of points and explore to your heart's content, then reboard a subsequent boat. Stopping-off points include the *Grunewaldturm* (Grunewald Tower), formerly known as *Kaiser-Wilhelm Turm* (Kaiser Wilhelm Tower), dating from the 19th century and affording a good view of Berlin from the top; Lindwerder Insel (Lindwerder Island), with restaurants offering snacks of beer, coffee, and cake; Pfaueninsel (Peacock Island), a beautiful example of an 18th-century formal garden with small pavilions, ponds, and a château dating from 1796 that is open to the public; and *Potsdam,* the former Prussian royal residence, just outside the city (for information, call the *Potsdam Tourist Office* at 331-21100). All stops on this trip are well provisioned with restaurants and beer gardens. (The only catch is that since these boats are mostly for Germans and rarely cater to foreign visitors, English usually is not spoken by the guides.)

A similar tour is offered on the Spree River, whose tributaries flow through the city for a total of 20 miles before joining the Havel. The white excursion ships run by *Stern und Kreisschiffahrt* (see above) ply the Spree and its tributaries every day from March through early October; you can get on and off as often as you wish. Along the way you might want to stop off at these sights: the *Müggelturm,* a 98-foot-high tower near Berlin's largest lake, Müggelsee; the *Mecklenburger Dorf,* in Köpenick, a replica of a 19th-century northern German village, offering typical snacks and beverages at very reasonable prices; and the *Rathaus,* a neo-Gothic brick structure built in 1904. Boats depart eight times a day from the piers on the Spree at the *Treptower Park S-Bahn* station. (Again, this trip is mostly for Germans, so English is rarely spoken on board.)

# Sources and Resources

## TOURIST INFORMATION

The *Verkehrsamt* (Tourist Office) is in the large complex of shops and restaurants at *Europa-Center* (entrance on Budapester Str.; phone: 21234; fax: 212-32520). It also maintains branches at *Flughafen Berlin-Tegel* (Tegel Airport; phone: 410-3145), as well as at the foot of the *Fernsehturm* (phone: 242-4675) and at the *Bahnhof Zoologischer Garten* train station (phone: 279-5209). The tourist offices will supply you with all sorts of free information in English about Berlin, including a general tourist map and numerous brochures. All branches are open daily. Another source of information is *Dial Berlin,* a private tourism reservation service that has a telephone hotline in the US (phone: 800-237-5469). The *US Consulate* is at 170 Clayallee (phone: 832-4087).

In the US, there are two branches of the *German National Tourist Office* (11766 Wilshire Blvd., Suite 750, Los Angeles, CA 90025; phone: 310-575-9799; fax: 310-575-1565; and 122 E. 42 St., 53rd Floor, New York, NY 10168; phone: 212-661-7200; fax: 212-661-7174). The *German Embassy* is at 4645 Reservoir Rd. NW, Washington, DC 20007-1998 (phone: 202-298-4000).

**ENTRY REQUIREMENTS** A US citizen needs a current passport for a stay of up to 90 days.

**TIME** The time in Germany is six hours later than in US East Coast cities. Germany observes daylight saving time.

**LANGUAGE** *Hochdeutsch* (High German) is the written language and the one that's commonly spoken throughout the country. English is the second language of the country.

**ELECTRIC CURRENT** 220 volts, 50 cycles, AC.

**MONEY** The deutsche mark (DM) equals 100 pfennigs. At press time the exchange rate was 1.5 DM to the dollar.

**TIPPING** A 10% to 12% service charge is included in restaurant checks; superior service may warrant an additional amount. Porters receive 1 DM per bag. Taxi drivers should get a 15% tip.

**BANKING/BUSINESS HOURS** Most banks are open weekdays from 9 AM to 1 PM, and also from 3:30 to 6 PM on Tuesdays and Thursdays. Some bank branches operate weekdays from 9 AM to 6 PM and on Saturday mornings. The *Berliner Bank* at *Tegel Airport* is open daily from 8 AM to 10 PM. Most other businesses operate weekdays from 9 AM to 5 PM.

**NATIONAL HOLIDAYS** *New Year's Day* (January 1), *Epiphany* (in Bavaria and Baden-Württemberg, January 6), *Good Friday* (April 14), *Easter Sunday* (April 16), *Easter Monday* (April 17), *Labor Day* (May 1), *Ascension Thursday* (May 25), *Whitmonday* (June 5), *Feast of Corpus Christi* (June 15), *Feast of the Assumption* (August 15), *German Unity Day* (October 3), *Day of Prayer and Repentance* (November 22), *Christmas Day* (December 25), and *Boxing Day* (December 26).

**LOCAL COVERAGE** There is no newspaper in English, but a monthly calendar of events called *Berlin Programm* is available at the tourist office and at newsstands; some of the information is in English. *Tip* and *Zitty,* two German-language biweekly city magazines, list local events along with information on places of interest in Berlin. Both are available at most newsstands. One of the best-detailed and most up-to-date local maps of Berlin is the *Berlin Stadtatlas,* available at many bookstores and larger newsstands for about 16 DM ($10).

We also immodestly suggest that before you leave home, you pick up a copy of *Birnbaum's Berlin 95* (HarperCollins; $12).

**TELEPHONE** The city code for Berlin is 30. When calling from one area to another within Germany dial 0 + city code + local number. The country code for Germany is 49. Dial 110 for emergency assistance.

## GETTING AROUND

**AIRPORT** *Flughafen Berlin-Tegel* (Tegel Airport), a 20- to 30-minute ride from downtown, handles most domestic and international flights. The No. 109 bus provides service from the airport to downtown and leaves from just outside Gate 8 every 15 minutes between 5:30 AM and midnight. *Flughafen Berlin-Schönefeld* (Schönefeld Airport), just outside the city and about a 45-minute drive to downtown, handles some international traffic. *S-Bahn* lines 9 and 10 run directly to *Schönefeld;* you can also take the No. 171 bus from Rudow (the last stop on *U-Bahn* line 7) to the *Schönefeld* air terminal. *Flughafen Tempelhof* (Tempelhof Airport), in the city center, caters to a limited number of domestic carriers; it's 15 minutes by taxi from downtown. The No. 119 bus also runs to *Tempelhof,* as does the *U-Bahn* line 6 to the *Platz der Luftbrücke Station.*

**CAR RENTAL** The major American firms are represented, as well as several European companies. Information can be obtained at any hotel.

**SUBWAY AND BUS** Berlin has one of the world's most efficient public transportation systems. The subway, or *U-Bahn,* with its snappy little yellow cars, has been a fact of life here since 1902, and its eight lines serve almost every part of the city. The *U-Bahn* is fast, clean, convenient, and one of the least expensive in Germany. Its eastern and western sections have been reunited, so trains now run from the *Olympiastadion* in the west to Pankow, northeast of the city. The "El," or *S-Bahn,* carried its first passengers in 1882, and is still in service today. Both lines travel to points in eastern Berlin. A ticket for about 3 DM (about $2) is valid for a trip from one end of the city to the other, and you can transfer as often as you wish within the *U-Bahn* system, the elevated *S-Bahn,* and to any of the many bus and streetcar lines that ply Berlin's streets. A *carnet,* valid for four rides, is available for 12 DM ($8). The *Berlin Transport Authority* also sells a ticket valid for 24 hours unlimited travel on all *U-Bahn, S-Bahn,* and bus lines throughout Berlin (11 DM/$7.30) and a six-day, unlimited-travel ticket (30 DM/about $20).

**TAXI** Berlin's cream-colored cabs are spacious and often luxurious (many are Mercedes-Benzes). Taxis can be hailed in the streets, and there are cabstands all over town and at the major hotels; fares are posted near the stands. To call a cab, which can be ordered around the clock and up to 24 hours in advance, call 69022, 210202, or 261026. Many dispatch operators understand English.

**TOURS** Several bus companies—among them *BVB* (phone: 885-9880), *BBS* (phone: 213-4077), and *Severin und Kühn* (phone: 883-1015)— offer two- and four-hour motorcoach tours of Berlin's major sights;

most coaches are equipped with headphones, allowing visitors to hear the commentary in their own language. Reservations are unnecessary; you'll see the ticket booths (most have a sign saying "Tours") all along the Ku'damm (Kurfürstendamm), at Breitscheidplatz, and on Unter den Linden. Tours leave approximately every half hour from 10 AM to 6 PM daily.

Though guided walking tours are plentiful, almost all of them are conducted in German. If you understand enough to get by, pick up a copy of *Tip* (see *Local Coverage*) for a daily schedule. *Stadtreisen Berlin* (4 Turmstr.; phone: 394-8354; fax: 394-7910) offers custom-designed, English-language tours for small groups.

**TRAIN** The city's main stations are *Bahnhof Zoologischer Garten* (also known as *Zoo Station;* Hardenbergpl.; phone: 19419) in western Berlin, and *Hauptbahnhof* (Holzmarkt; phone: 19419) in eastern Berlin. Though Germany still has two train companies—the Eastern German *Deutsche Reichsbahn (DR)* and the Western German *Deutsche Bundesbahn (DB)*—tickets to eastern destinations such as Dresden and Leipzig can be purchased at the *DB* offices. (The difference between the two systems is mostly in the age of the cars— the *DR*'s can be ancient.)

## LOCAL SERVICES

**DRY CLEANER/TAILOR** *Express* (28 Brandburgische Str.; phone: 881-4954); *Horst Marschall* (80 Uhlandstr.; phone: 861-4374).

**LIMOUSINE SERVICE** *Minex* (64A Detmolder Str.; phone: 853-3091).

**MEDICAL EMERGENCY** *Am Urban Krankenhausbetrieb von Berlin-Kreuzberg* (1 Dieffenbachstr.; phone: 6971); *Universitätsklinikum Steglitz* (30 Hindenburgdamm; phone: 7981); and *Westend DRK-Klinikum* (130 Spandauer Damm; phone: 30351). For emergency service dial 110.

**MESSENGER SERVICE** *Messenger Courier Service* (6 Pestalozzistr.; phone: 311-09311).

**OFFICE EQUIPMENT RENTAL** *Eischleb* (129 Uhlandstr.; phone: 860491); *Wegert Photographers* (30F Kolonnenstr.; phone: 250020) for audio-visual equipment.

**PHOTOCOPIES** *Copy-Center* (40 Bayreuther Str.; phone: 211-3411).

**POST OFFICE** Berlin's main branch is at the *Bahnhof Zoo* train station (phone: 313-9799).

**SECRETARY/STENOGRAPHER (ENGLISH-SPEAKING)** *Bürotel* (180 Kurfürstendamm; phone: 882-7031); *Regus Business Center* (11 Kurfürstendamm; phone: 884410).

**TELEX** The Winterfeldstrasse post office (21 Winterfeldtstr.; phone: 21710) is open daily from 9 AM to 2 PM.

**TRANSLATOR** *Bundesverband Dolmetscher und Übersetzer,* or *BDU,* the *Association of Interpreters and Translators* (phone: 882-7339).

**OTHER** Tuxedo and evening gown rental: *Runge* (99 Bismarckstr.; phone: 312-1187).

## SPECIAL EVENTS

Berlin's calendar is filled with a variety of annual celebrations, the most notable of which is its September music festival.

---

### FAVORITE FETE

**Berliner Festwochen (Berlin Festival Weeks)** Every September, the city prolongs the afterglow of summer with a month-long musical extravaganza (though theater and dance are featured as well). Orchestras, soloists, and chamber ensembles fill halls large and small throughout the city, as maestros Fischer-Dieskau, Brendel, and Giulini deliver the musical scripture of Beethoven and Brahms. And then there are the German music world's lesser-known performers, offering renditions of newly manuscripted works by not-yet-hallowed names. Most of the big-name performers appear at the *Philharmonie*. Kemperpl. (phone: 254880).

---

*Internationale Grüne Woche* (International Green Week), a 14-day agricultural and food festival, takes place at the convention hall in Charlottenburg in January. The annual two-week *Berlinale* (International Film Festival Berlin) is held in February. The *Theater-treffen Berlin,* a gathering of performers and directors from throughout the nation, takes place in May. The *Internationale Polo Turniers* (International Polo Tournaments) are held on the Maifeld at the *Olympiastadion* (see *Special Places*) in August. In September, runners thread their way through the streets of western Berlin in the 26-km *Berlin Marathon.* (Shorter races are also held on *New Year's Eve* and *New Year's Day.*) The *Berlin Oktoberfest* (in October, natch) brings food, drink, and a carnival atmosphere to the fairgrounds near the *Funkturm.* For two weeks in October, international soloists gather at bars and nightclubs across the city for *Jazz Fest Berlin.* November also marks Berlin's annual six-day *Sechstagerennen,* a cycling contest that attracts international competitors. And during the *Christmas* season, the city hosts several *Christkindlesmarkts* at various locations; the most famous one is held around the *Kaiser-Wilhelm-Gedächtniskirche* on Breitscheidplatz. For additional information and exact dates, check with the tourist office at *Europa-Center* (see *Tourist Information,* above).

## MUSEUMS

In addition to those described in *Special Places,* other museums worth seeing include the following:

**ÄGYPTISCHES MUSEUM (EGYPTIAN MUSEUM)** Directly opposite *Schloss Charlottenburg* is this unusual collection whose priceless treasures include the world-renowned bust of Queen Nefertiti and the magnificent *Kalabsha Gate,* which dates from 2000 BC and was found in a temple in Kalabsha, Egypt. Closed Mondays. Admission charge. 70 Schlossstr. (phone: 320911).

**ANTIKENSAMMLUNG (ANTIQUITIES MUSEUM)** Masterpieces of Greek, Roman, and Etruscan art, including sculpture, jewelry, and portraits, are displayed in a palatial building across from the *Schloss Charlottenburg* complex. Closed Fridays. Admission charge. 1 Schlossstr. (phone: 32011).

**BAUHAUS-ARCHIV** Housed in a striking white building, this collection of manuscripts, tools, and blueprints documents the work of the famed Bauhaus School of architecture and applied and graphic arts. Founded by Walter Gropius in 1919, the group counted Paul Klee, Marcel Breuer, Vassily Kandinsky, and Mies van der Rohe among its masters and students; the school was forced into exile by the National Socialist government in the 1930s. Closed Tuesdays. Admission charge. 14 Klingelhöferstr. (phone: 254-0020).

**BRÖHAN MUSEUM** Adjacent to the *Antikensammlung* (see above), this lovely, small facility features a collection of 20th-century art—especially *Jugendstil* paintings, sculptures, graphic arts, and furniture. Closed Mondays. Admission charge. 1A Schlossstr. (phone: 321-4029).

**BRÜCKE MUSEUM** This contemporary building in the Grunewald serves as a gallery and archive for the works of Die Brücke (The Bridge)—an influential group of early 20th-century German Expressionist artists. Displays include paintings, watercolors, drawings, and sculptures by Karl Schmidt-Rottluff and Ernst Ludwig Kirchner, among others. Closed Tuesdays. Admission charge. 9 Bussardsteig (phone: 831-2029).

**DEUTSCHES RUNDFUNK-MUSEUM (GERMAN RADIO MUSEUM)** Located at the base of Charlottenburg's radio tower, the exhibits offer a complete overview of German broadcasting history, from primitive radios to modern television sets. Closed Tuesdays. Admission charge. 1 Hammarskjöldpl. (phone: 302-8186).

**FRISEURMUSEUM (HAIRDRESSING MUSEUM)** A unique collection documenting over 500 years of the barber's art. Displays include a magnificent *Jugendstil* workstation from a hair salon that served members of the Prussian royal court, medieval surgical equipment, and elaborate powdered wigs. Closed Fridays. Admission charge. 8 Husemannstr. (phone: 449-5380).

**GEORG-KOLBE-MUSEUM** The former home and studio of one of Berlin's best-known sculptors houses a display of his works, along with those of his local contemporaries. Closed Sundays and Mondays. Admission charge. 25 Sensburger Allee, in Charlottenburg (phone: 304-2144).

**GRÜNDERZEITMUSEUM MAHLSDORF (MAHLSDORF FOUNDING ERA MUSEUM)** During the 1870s, when Germany was united by Iron Chancellor

Otto von Bismarck, the nation underwent a rapid period of industrialization, and the appearance of the German household changed enormously—factory-made furniture and such luxury items as gramophones came into widespread use. Furnishings, housewares, and other domestic treasures from this era are displayed in an old villa in the suburbs; there's also a pub in the basement that dates to the decadent 1920s. Open Sundays for guided tours (in English on request) beginning at 11 AM and noon, or by appointment. No admission charge. 333 Hultschiner Damm (phone: 527-8329).

**KÄTHE-KOLLWITZ-MUSEUM** The works of this eponymous local artist, including sculptures, drawings, prints, and posters, are housed in a charming villa just off the Ku'damm (Kurfürstendamm). Kollwitz's subjects included the city's downtrodden population; the collection is renowned for its emotional impact. Closed Tuesdays. Admission charge. 24 Fasanenstr. (phone: 882-5210).

**KUNSTGEWERBEMUSEUM IM SCHLOSS KÖPENICK (APPLIED ARTS MUSEUM AT THE KÖPENICK PALACE)** Built by Prince Friedrich in the late 17th century on the site of a medieval Slav castle, this historic palace on the Spree River houses a museum of European arts and crafts. The collection, which spans 900 years, include gold and silver work, glass, porcelain, and furniture. Closed Mondays and Tuesdays. No admission charge Sundays. About 12 miles (20 km) outside the city center at Schlossinsel Köpenick (Köpenick Palace Island; phone: 657-1504).

**MÄRKISCHES MUSEUM** One of the best of its kind in Europe, it surveys Berlin's history. Closed Mondays and Tuesdays. Admission charge. 5 Am Köllnischen Park (phone: 270-0514).

**MUSEUM BERLINER ARBEITERLEBEN (BERLIN LABOR MUSEUM)** Created by the former East German government, the exhibits chronicle the lifestyle of the city's proletariat at the turn of the century; there's also a replica of an apartment of the period. Closed Sundays and Mondays. Admission charge. 12 Husemannstr. (phone: 448-5675).

**MUSEUM FÜR VOLKSKUNDE (FOLKLORE MUSEUM)** A collection of tools, household goods, clothing, and furniture from the 16th century to the present. Closed Mondays. No admission charge Sundays. 6-8 Im Winkel (phone: 839-01287).

**OTTO-NAGEL-HAUS** This branch of the *Neue Nationalgalerie* (see *Special Places*) exhibits typical works of proletarian art from 1918 to 1945. Closed Fridays and Saturdays. No admission charge Sundays. 16-18 Märkisches Ufer. (phone: 279-1402).

**SCHINKEL-MUSEUM** The great local architect Karl Friedrich Schinkel changed the face of Berlin in the early 19th century. His life and works are depicted in this collection housed in one of Schinkel's churches—the neo-Gothic *Friedrichswerdersche Kirche.* Closed Mondays and Tuesdays. Werderstr., near Unter den Linden (phone: 208-1323).

**SCHLOSS BRITZ (BRITZ PALACE)** Originally part of an 18th-century country estate, this luxurious mansion displays the beautiful furniture and decorations of the Wilhelmine era (mid- to late 19th century). There also are rotating historical exhibits and exquisitely landscaped grounds. Closed Mondays and Tuesdays. Admission charge. 73 Alt-Britz (phone: 606-6051).

**SCHLOSS FRIEDRICHSFELDE (FRIEDRICHSFELDE PALACE)** This pink-and-white Baroque palace was built in 1695 by the Prussian royalty for members of their court. Sixteen of its rooms, which have been painstakingly restored, house displays on the art and culture of the 18th and 19th centuries. Open only for guided tours (in English on request) at 11 AM and 1 and 3 PM; closed Mondays. Admission charge. 125 Am Tierpark (phone: 510-0111).

**SCHWULES MUSEUM (GAY MUSEUM)** Located in the heart of Kreuzberg, this museum features rotating exhibits on gay history, art, and culture. Closed Mondays and Tuesdays. Admission charge. 61 Mehringdamm (phone: 693-1172).

---

### NOTE

The history of Berlin's Jewish community is not only a chronicle of persecution and tragedy, but of achievement and vitality as well. The graves of some of the city's most famous Jewish residents can be seen in the cemeteries in Prenzlauer Berg and Weissensee. Artifacts from the collection of the *Jüdisches Museum* (Jewish Museum) are temporarily being displayed in the *Martin-Gropius-Bau* (see *Special Places*) while a new home for the museum is being constructed next to the *Berlin Museum,* which is also currently closed; both facilities are scheduled to reopen in 1998.

In addition, two of Brandenburg's concentration camps are dedicated to the victims of the Nazis' attempt at genocide. The *Sachsenhausen* camp (Str. der Nationen, Oranienburg; phone: 3301-803715), where many Jews, political prisoners, homosexuals, Poles, and Russians were sentenced to forced labor, can be reached by taking the *S-Bahn* No. 1 line to the last stop in Oranienburg. From there, it's a short bus or cab ride to the camp. The camp is closed Mondays; no admission charge. The other camp, *Ravensbruck,* is located in Fürstenburg (phone: 33093-2025). To get there, take an *S-Bahn* train from *Lichtenberg Station* to *Fürstenburg-Havel Station*

---

(about an hour's ride) and take a taxi from there. *Ravensbruck* is also closed Mondays; no admission charge.

Today, Berlin's Jewish community is thriving, due in part to a large influx of Jews from the former Soviet republics. For a tour of the community, contact the *Stadtreisen Berlin* (4 Turmstr.; phone: 394-8354; fax: 394-7910).

## SHOPPING

Berlin has an abundance of interesting shops. There is hardly anything you cannot buy here, and some of the items offered for sale are truly unique. The best shopping is in the western part of the city. If you just want to browse before making up your mind, go through *Europa-Center,* at the foot of Kurfürstendamm in the middle of the downtown area. This city within a city has scores of small shops and boutiques offering a variety of typical German specialties. German cameras, including those by Leica, Rollei, and Zeiss, are available here, but it is necessary to do very careful comparison shopping; the same brands often are less expensive in the US. Optical goods such as binoculars, telescopes, and microscopes also are German specialties, and there are good buys in china and porcelain; great names in the latter are Meissen, Rosenthal, and KPM (Staatliche Porzellan Manufaktur Berlin, the state porcelain factory). Toys, cutlery, and clocks are good buys, too.

Berlin's antiques dealers have a reputation for expertise and honesty. The Keithstrasse is virtually one long row of antiques shops, with a variety of specialties. Some of the best stores include *Galerie St. Petersburg* (No. 15; phone: 211-9295), which features remnants of Czarist Russia; *Hedwig Lansch* (No. 8; phone: 218-6554), for bronze and silver pieces and jewelry; and *J. Schwandt* (No. 10; phone: 218-5017), with a stunning collection of *Jugendstil* and Art Deco silver serving pieces. Sumptuous 18th-century jewelry and silver abound at *Antiquitäten Kabinett* (73 Fasanenstr.; phone: 881-3550), and there are fine porcelain, glass, furniture, and oil paintings at *Galerie Westphal* (68 Fasanenstr.; phone: 882-1162). Art Deco jewelry is the specialty at *Bleibtreu Antik* (9 Ludwigskirchstr.; phone: 883-5212); furniture and glassware from the same period can be found at *Decorative Arts* (1 Niebuhrstr.; phone: 882-7373). For one-of-a-kind old travel equipment—steamer trunks, maps, compasses, and so on—visit *Ubu* (55 Bleibtreustr.; phone: 313-5115). There's a selective assortment of 18th- and 19th-century furniture, porcelain, and art at *W. Weick* (10 Eisenacher Str.; phone: 218-7500).

A sprawling secondhand market is held on weekends in the Strasse des 17. Juni, and an antiques and flea market is open daily except Tuesdays under the *S-Bahn* tracks of Friedrichstrasse (phone: 215-02129).

Most shops are open from 9 AM to 6:30 PM weekdays and 9 AM to 2 PM Saturdays; on the first Saturday of the month in summer, they stay open until 4 PM. Also, some stores operate until 8:30 PM on Thursdays and until 6 PM on Saturdays. Although you might want to do some exploring on your own, here is a small sample of recommended stores:

**Ararat** Over 32,000 different postcard designs. 99a Bergmannstr. and other locations (phone: 693-5080).

**Bannat** For the globetrotter, everything from Gore-Tex jackets to compasses and maps. 65 Lietzenburger Str. (phone: 882-7601).

**Berliner Zinnfiguren** Wonderful miniature toy soldiers and other collectible pewter figurines. 88 Knesebeckstr. (phone: 310802).

**Boris Schoenherr** Handmade musical instruments. 17 Sophienstr. (phone: 281-7064).

**Bücherbogen am Savignyplatz** Berlin's best source for art and architecture books. Savignypl., under the *S-Bahn* (phone: 312-1932).

**Design Pur** Sleek accessories for the home and office. 17 Dahlmannstr. (phone: 324-0756).

**Durchbruch** Designer Christina Ueckermann features quality casual womenswear. 54 Schlüterstr. (phone: 881-5568).

**FNAC** A household name in France, this unusual emporium carries books, records, cassettes, and CDs in both German and English. 20-24 Meinekestr. (phone: 884720).

**Freimuth** Traditional, well-made hats for men and women. 33 Kurfürstendamm (phone: 881-6865).

**Horn's** The latest in women's fashions. 213 Kurfürstendamm (phone: 881-4055).

**J. A. Henckels** Cutlery and top-of-the-line kitchen utensils. 33 Kurfürstendamm (phone: 881-3315).

**Jazzcock** LPs, cassettes, and CDs—a paradise for jazz fans. 17 Fürbringer Str. (phone: 693-6133).

**Jil Sander Boutique** Chic womenswear. 48 Kurfürstendamm (phone: 883-3730).

**KaDeWe** Germany's largest, grandest, and best-stocked department store (the name is short for *Kaufhaus des Westens*), it's simply got everything, including an enormous food shop with a score of lunch counters on the sixth floor. 21-24 Tauentzienstr. (phone: 21210).

**Kaufhaus Schrill** Fun fashions and outrageous ties and jewelry. 46 Bleibtreustr. (phone: 882-4048).

**Kiepert** Berlin's most comprehensive bookstore has an excellent selection of English books—everything from murder mysteries to romance novels. 4-5 Hardenbergstr. (phone: 311-0090).

**Kostumhaus** This eastern Berlin shop features clothes by young German designers. 22 Veteranenstr. (phone: 281-5224).

**Kramberg** Expensive designer clothing for men and women. 56 Kurfürstendamm (phone: 323-6058).

**Kunsthandwerk Stroh** Handmade *Christmas* tree ornaments, dolls, and other unique creations—all made from straw. 9 Sophienstr. (phone: 281-2888).

**Leysieffer** Fine cakes, preserves, and chocolates. Marzipan and flavored truffles are specialties. There's also a café serving these delicacies on the second floor. 218 Kurfürstendamm (phone: 882-7820).

**Marga Schoeller** English and American books. 33 Knesebeckstr. (phone: 881-1112).

**Musikalienhandlung Hans Riedel** The city's best sheet music selection, plus records. 38 Uhlandstr. (phone: 882-7395).

**Porzellan-Manufaktur Meissen** Porcelain from the famous Meissen factory. Two locations: 39b Unter den Linden (phone: 229-2691) and 30 Mohrenstr. (phone: 238-24150).

**Rogacki** Berlin's oldest smoked-fish shop. 145 Wilmersdorfer Str. (phone: 341-4091).

**Rosenthal Studio-Haus** Porcelain from modern to classic designs from one of Germany's top manufacturers. 226 Kurfürstendamm (phone: 881-7051).

**Rutz** Fine bedding and lingerie. 7b Tauentzienstr. (phone: 262-4055).

**Schuhtick** The city's best outlet for trendy shoes. Alexanderpl. (phone: 242-4012) and 11 Savignypl. (phone: 312-4955).

**Siedel und Sohn** Military and other fine antiques. 113 Eisenacher Str. (phone: 216-1850).

**Staatliche Porzellan Manufaktur Berlin (KPM)** Known until 1918 as *Königliche Porzellan Manufaktur* (Royal Porcelain Manufacturers), this company's beautiful china has been made in Berlin for centuries. 26a Kurfürstendamm (phone: 390090).

**Triebel** An outlet for traditional clothes from Bavaria and Austria, as well as hunting and riding outfits. 12 Schönwalder Str., Spandau (phone 335-5001).

**Virgin Megastore** True to its name, this shop carries an enormous selection of records, cassettes, and CDs. 14 Kurfürstendamm (phone: 880-0810).

**Vom Winde Verweht (Gone with the Wind)** An Anglo-American kite emporium featuring fascinating European kites at low prices. 43 and 81 Eisenacher Str. (phone: 784-7769 or 788-1992).

## SPORTS AND FITNESS

**BICYCLING** You can rent a bike by the hour for a jaunt through the expansive Grunewald Forest from *F. Damrau* (Schmetterlingspl.; phone: 811-5829; call before 9 AM). Also try *Fahrradbüro* (146 Hauptstr.;

phone: 783-5562) and *Räderwerk* (14 Körtestr.; phone: 691-8590); both companies require a 24-hour-minimum rental.

**FITNESS CENTER** *Fitness-Studio* (182-183 Kurfürstendamm; phone: 882-6301 or 881-3371) is open to visitors for a fee.

**GOLF** The *Golf und Landclub* (Stölpchenweg, Berlin-Wannsee; phone: 805-5075) has a nine-hole golf course.

**HORSE RACING** Berlin's renowned *Trabrennbahn Mariendorf* (222-298 Mariendorfer Damm; phone: 74010) has harness racing year-round on Wednesdays and Sundays. Harness racing at *Trabrennbahn Karlshorst* (129 Treskowallee; phone: 509-0891) is on Saturdays and Tuesdays year-round. Thoroughbreds race on weekends from April through October at the historic *Hoppegarten* (1 Goetheallee, Dahlwitz-Hoppegarten; phone: 559-6102).

**ICE HOCKEY** From November through April, you can see professional games at the *Eissporthalle* (Jafféstr.; phone: 30380). Berlin's resident teams are the *Preussen* (Prussians) and the *Eisbären* (Polar Bears).

**ICE SKATING** In the winter, there are various public indoor rinks in the city, including the *Sportforum Berlin* (Konrad-Wolf-Str.; phone: 97810) and the *Eisstadion Wilmersdorf* (9 Fritz-Wildung-Str.; phone: 823-4060).

**JOGGING** The best place is the *Tiergarten,* where there are trails. Farther out, runners prefer Grunewald Forest or the long, winding trails of the *Volkspark Wilmersdorf.*

**SOCCER** A very special sport here, as West Germany won the *1990 World Cup* in its final season before reunification. *Hertha* and *Blau-Weiss,* Berlin's professional soccer teams, play on autumn Saturdays at the *Olympiastadion* (Olympischer Pl.; phone: 304-0676).

**SWIMMING** Aquatic sports can be enjoyed at a number of indoor and outdoor pools; each of Berlin's 23 boroughs has at least one public facility. In addition, there is a sandy beach at Wannsee and another at Müggelsee.

**TENNIS** Courts can be reserved by the hour at *Tennis and Squash City* (53 Brandenburgische Str.; phone: 879097). In addition, the city has a number of indoor and outdoor public courts. For locations and hours of admission, consult the tourist office.

## THEATER

Theater in Berlin, still Germany's theatrical metropolis, is mostly an all-German affair. But some places are worth visiting despite a possible language barrier. For 30 years, *The Threepenny Opera* at the *Berliner Ensemble* (1 Bertolt-Brecht-Pl.; phone: 282-3160) was one of the best reasons to visit East Berlin. In the last few seasons, the *Ensemble* has been wooing talent from the German-speaking world's most lustrous institutions. Founded in 1883, the *Deutsches Theater* repertory company (13A Schumannstr.; phone: 284-41225) was long locked in the GDR and is now trying to claim its rightful throne in a unified Germany's theater world. Its longtime director was Gustav Gründgens, the actor who steered his career through the shoals of Nazi cultural policy and was the inspiration for the character played by Klaus-Maria Brandauer in Istvan Szabo's film *Mephisto.* The once subversive *Schaubühne am Lehninerplatz* (153 Kurfürstendamm; phone: 890020; 890023, box office) has shed its angry bent, but its bold productions are still the rage.

For an example of classical repertoire, go to the intimate *Kammerspiele* (same address as the *Deutsches Theater,* see above; phone: 287-1226), which was founded in 1906 by Max Reinhardt. Another small stage, the *Maxim Gorki Theater* (2 Am Festungsgraben; phone: 208-2783), offers both classical and contemporary dramas. Eastern Berlin's *Volksbühne* (Rosa-Luxemburg-Pl.; phone: 282-8978) features innovative productions of new and classic plays. Other prominent theaters are the *Renaissance* (6 Hardenbergstr.; phone: 312-4202); *Theater am Kurfürstendamm* (206 Kurfürstendamm; phone: 882-3789); *Komödie* (206 Kurfürstendamm; phone: 882-7893); and *Tribühne* (18-20 Otto-Suhr-Allee; phone: 341-2600). One of Europe's most successful children's theaters is *Grips* (22 Altonaer Str.; phone: 391-4004).

Berlin also boasts a variety of fringe theaters, whose productions range from the sublime to the ridiculous. An important venue for the avant-garde scene is the *Hebbel Theater* in Kreuzberg, a district on the outskirts of the city (29 Stresemannstr.; phone: 251-0144). Other well-respected alternative theaters are the *Vaganten-Bühne* (12a Kantstr.; phone: 312-4529); *Schmalen Handtuch* (91 Frankfurter Allee; phone: 588-4659); *Theater unterm Dach* (101 Dimitroffstr.; phone: 420-0610); *Fliegendes Theater* (54 Hasenheide; phone: 692-2100); and *Theater am Halleschen Ufer* (32 Hallesches Ufer; phone: 251-0941). The *Zan Pollo* in Schöneberg (45 Rheinstr.; phone: 852-2002) mounts rarely staged classics. Two of eastern Berlin's wildest experimental theaters are the *Tacheles* cultural center (53-56 Oranienburger Str.; phone: 282-6185), housed in a turn-of-the-century former shopping arcade, and the *Kesselhaus* in the *Kulturbrauerei* complex (36-39 Schönhauser Allee, entrance on Knaackstr.; phone: 440-9243). Several *Kneipen* (pubs) host theatrical performances, including *Rost Bühne* (29 Knesebeckstr.; phone: 881-1699). There's also the *Freunde der Italienischen Oper* (40 Fidicinstr.; phone: 691-1211), a tiny theater/cabaret in Kreuzberg that often has performances in English.

Tickets for all performances can be purchased at box offices (you can almost always call ahead for reservations); you also can buy tickets for the mainstream theaters at just about any ticket booth around town, including *Wildbad Kiosk* (1 Rankestr.; phone: 881-4507); *Theaterkasse Zanke* (16 Kurfürstendamm; phone: 882-6563); and the *Theaterkasse* in the *Radisson Plaza* hotel (see *Checking In*).

The best venues for ballet are the *Deutsche Oper* and the *Komische Oper* (see *Music,* below). Berlin's lively contemporary dance scene centers around the *Hebbel* (see above) and the *Tanzfabrik* (68 Möckernstr.; phone: 786-5861).

Should you feel a bit homesick, take in the latest Hollywood movie in English at the *Odeon* (116 Hauptstr.; phone: 781-5667). Other cinemas show movies in English on occasion; check the *Tip* or *Zitty* listings for showings labeled "OmU" (original version with German subtitles) or "OF" (original version). Beware: All other movie theaters show English-language films dubbed in German.

MUSIC

Berlin is one of the world's musical centers, with performances of everything from classical to pop and rock. The *Berliner Philharmonisches Orchester* (Kemperpl.; phone: 254880; no telephone ticket orders accepted) is quite simply the world's best orchestra. Whatever the program, the *Philharmonie* concert hall is filled with a sound that is no less than divine.

The 40-year rivalry between East and West has left Berlin with two of everything—except in opera, where there are three companies. The oldest, the *Deutsche Staatsoper* (7 Unter den Linden; phone: 200-4762)—which until a few years ago was East Germany's state opera—celebrated its 250th anniversary in 1992. Now restored to its imperial luster, the 18th-century scale of the opera house makes it far more intimate than larger, modern spaces that singers have to strain to fill. Unlike most of the rest of Germany, which was painstakingly reconstructed to look exactly like its prewar self, the gutted, turn-of-the-century opera house in the western suburb of Charlottenburg was rebuilt into the modern *Deutsche Oper* (35 Bismarckstr.; phone: 34381), which opened in 1961. In addition to performances by such luminaries as Lucia Aliberti, Alfredo Kraus, René Kollo, and Karan Armstrong, the *Deutsche Oper*'s productions are intermingled with evenings of ballet. The *Komische Oper* (55-57 Behrensstr.; phone: 229-2555) is the custodian of the repertoire's lyric froth, but it does not stick slavishly to jolly presentations. Recent productions have ranged from an acerbically updated version of Wagner's politically charged *Rienzi* to traditional versions of operas by Rimsky-Korsakov and Rossini.

Chamber music can be heard at the *Kammermusiksaal* (phone: 254880) in the *Philharmonie*. The *Schauspielhaus* (Gendarmenmarkt; phone: 209-02129), built in 1820, also hosts other world-famous orchestras. The *Rundfunk-Sinfonieorchester Berlin* (Berlin Radio Symphony Orchestra) gives most of its concerts at *Sender Freies Berlin,* the radio station (8-14 Masurenallee; phone: 302-7242). Concerts and recitals of classical music can be heard at the *Hochschule der Künste* (College of Arts; 1 Fasanenstr.; phone: 318-52374). Operettas and musicals are launched at *Theater des Westens* (12 Kantstr.; phone: 319-03193). Pop concerts, many by visiting international stars, are performed at the *ICC* (see *Special Places*), the *Metropol* (see *Nightclubs and Nightlife,* below), and the *Deutschlandhalle* (Messedamm; phone: 303-84387). For the latest in jazz and rock music, attend one of the concerts that are frequently given at *Tempodrom* (In den Zelten; phone: 394-4045) and at *Huxley's Neue Welt* (108-114 Hasenheide; phone: 786-6048). In the summer, the *Waldbühne* (Passenheimer Str.; phone: 305-5079), an open-air amphitheater, is a pleasant place to hear a concert, either rock or classical.

## NIGHTCLUBS AND NIGHTLIFE

Berlin's nightlife—immortalized in story, song, the cartoons of George Grosz, and films like *Cabaret*—is legendary. London's *Time Out* magazine once hailed Berlin as "Europe's most decadent city," and the description still fits. Even if decadence is not your style, Berlin's after-dark scene offers something for every taste, from the tame to the outlandish.

For some nostalgic cheek-to-cheek dancing, try *Clärchen's Ballhaus* (24-25 Auguststr.; phone: 282-9295) and *Ballhaus Berlin* (102 Chausseestr.; phone: 282-7575); the latter even has telephones on the tables so you can call that attractive person in the corner and ask for a dance. *Annabelle's* (64 Fasanenstr.; phone: 883-5220) in Charlottenburg is a chic club favored by the champagne set; you must ring the bell and get the doorman's approval before entering. *First* (26 Joachimstaler Str.; phone: 882-2686) is a popular club for those over 30; so are the *Bristol Bar* at the *Bristol Kempinski* hotel (27 Kurfürstendamm; phone: 884-34756) and *Salsa* (13 Wielandstr.; phone: 324-1642), which features Latin American music.

Those eager to sample Berlin's radical nightlife scene have a variety of choices. The demise of East Berlin resulted in the birth of discos in way-out settings: ruins, bunkers, abandoned underground restrooms, and so on. Many in what used to be West Berlin occupy factory space. *Neunzig Grad* (Ninety Degrees; 37 Dennewitzstr.; phone: 262-8984) offers a mixture of musical styles and decor. *Planet* (52 Köpenicker Str.; no phone) is housed in an old chalk factory on the Spree. *Tresor* (Leipziger Str. and Otto-Grotewohl-Str.; no phone) has an underground disco in the former treasury of an old bank.

Also popular with the young crowd, but housed in more conventional settings, are the huge *Metropol* (5 Nollendorfpl.; phone: 216-4122); *Orpheo* (2 Marburger Str.; phone: 211-6445); and *Abraxas* (134 Kantstr.; phone: 312-9493).

Local bands and those from abroad perform at *Knaack* (224 Greifswalder Str.; phone: 426-2351) and *Franz* in the *Kulturbrauerei* complex (36-39 Schönhauser Allee, entrance on Knaackstr.; phone: 448-5567), where the sounds range from Russian punk to an eclectic music mix called "African-Latin Jazz Rock." Try *Go In* (17 Bleibtreustr.; phone: 881-7218) or *Café Zapata* in the *Tacheles* cultural center (see *Theater,* above) for folk music.

Berliners love jazz, and the city boasts myriad first-rate jazz clubs. *Quasimodo* (12a Kantstr.; phone: 312-8086) attracts big names to its classic smoky cellar. *A-Trane* (1 Bleibtreustr., near Savignyplatz; phone: 313-2550) is the city's classiest hot spot. *Flöz* (37 Nassauische Str.; phone: 861-1000), *Lohmeyer's* (24 Eosanderstr.; phone: 342-9660), and *Badenscher Hof* (29 Badensche Str.; phone: 861-0080) offer intimate settings that attract laid-back jazz lovers. In Mitte, the *Podewil* cultural center (68-70 Klosterstr.; phone: 24030) and *Sophienclub* (6 Sophienstr.; phone: 282-4552) often have jazz on the musical menu. *Yorckschlösschen* (77 Yorckstr.; phone: 215-8070) offers live jazz on Sundays performed in its shady outdoor beer garden (weather permitting).

And don't forget Berlin's cabarets. Both *Stachelschweine* (*Europa-Center;* phone: 261-4795) and *Wühlmäuse* (Lietzenburger Str., corner of Nürnberger Str.; phone: 213-7047) put on interesting performances, devoted chiefly to literary and political satire. At *Kartoon* (24 Französischestr.; phone: 229-9305), the waiters, who perform as well as serve, specialize in skits that satirize German politics. As its name implies, *Chamäleon Varieté* (40-41 Rosenthaler Str.; phone: 282-7118) offers an ever-changing bill. Also good choices for an evening out are *BKA* (34 Mehringdamm; phone: 251-0112), housed in a Kreuzberg factory loft; *Bar Jeder Vernunft* (24 Schaperstr., phone: 883-1582), in an ornate circus tent in Charlottenburg; and *Die Distel* (101 Friedrichstr.; phone: 200-4704), once the state-sponsored cabaret of East Germany. The *Wintergarten* (96 Potsdamer Str.; phone: 262-7070) and *Friedrichstadtpalast* (107 Friedrichstr.; phone: 284-66474) feature flashy variety shows with scantily clad chorus girls.

Nightclubs featuring transvestite shows have long been a German specialty. If you like this sort of thing (if you think you don't, you may be pleasantly surprised) visit *La Vie en Rose* (in the *Europa-Center;* phone: 323-6006) or *Chez Nous* (14 Marburger Str.; phone: 213-1810). If gambling is one of your sins, visit the city's one and only licensed casino, on the ground floor at the Budapester Strasse side of *Europa-Center,* for roulette, baccarat, and blackjack. The casino is open daily from 3 PM to 3 AM (phone: 250-0890). Minimum age is 21; you must present your passport at the door. Jacket and tie are required.

Berlin is known for its multitude of *Kneipen* (pubs) and *Biergärten* (beer gardens), which dispense well-drawn glasses of beer, homemade schnapps, good eats, and lots of *Gemütlichkeit* (congeniality). Those worthy of mention include *Die Kleine Weltlaterne* (22 Nestorstr.; phone: 892-6585), which caters to an arty crowd; *Lutter und Wegener* (see *Eating Out*), a wine cellar of note; *Zwiebelfisch* (7-8 Savignypl.; phone: 317363), a haunt for journalists and students; and *Zur letzten Instanz* (14 Waisénstr.; phone: 212-5528).

# Best in Town

## CHECKING IN

In Berlin, visitors can choose from among one of the best assortments of hotels in all of Germany. Nearly all the hotels in the city's eastern section have been privatized (many are now run by US and other Western hotel chains), adding to the number of good-quality accommodations available. Since there always seems to be something happening in this scintillating city, it is always advisable to make advance reservations—either directly with the hotel of your choice or through the city's efficient tourist office; *Dial Berlin* can also help here (see *Tourist Information*).

Hotel accommodations in Germany are expensive, and Berlin is no exception. Should you prefer more modest, although somewhat less comfortable, rooms, check with the tourist office. The hotels listed below have a bath or a shower in every room, and in almost every case the rooms have telephones; breakfast is included in the rates, unless otherwise noted. For a double room in those hotels we have classed as expensive, expect to pay $200 or more; in places in the moderate category, from $100 to $200; and in inexpensive hotels, under $100. All telephone numbers are in the 30 city code unless otherwise indicated.

### EXPENSIVE

**Am Zoo** When Thomas Wolfe came to Berlin in the early 1930s, he stayed at this 145-room hotel, one of the traditional downtown establishments. It has a good restaurant. Business facilities include 24-hour room service, meeting rooms for up to 200, an English-speaking concierge, foreign currency exchange, secretarial services in English, audiovisual equipment, photocopiers, computers, cable TV news, translation services, and express checkout. 25 Kurfürstendamm (phone: 884370; fax: 884-37714).

**Berlin Hilton** Beautifully designed, this property in the eastern part of the city overlooks the *Deutscher Dom* and *Französischer Dom,* along with the 19th-century Gendarmenmarkt and the *Schauspielhaus* concert hall (see *Special Places*). The 505 rooms and suites are all luxuriously appointed. Several restaurants, taverns, and bars, as well as a pool, sauna, and fitness center are among the extensive amenities. Business facilities include 24-hour room service, meeting rooms for up to 350, an English-speaking concierge, foreign currency exchange, secretarial services in English, audiovisual equipment, photocopiers, computers, cable TV news, translation services, and express checkout. 30 Mohrenstr. (phone: 23820; 800-HILTONS; fax: 238-24269).

**Bristol Kempinski** Like so much in Berlin, the "Kempi" is a fine old name wrapped in a new package. At the corner of patrician Fasanenstrasse and the Ku'damm—Germany's best and brightest boulevard—this 358-room establishment is right in the middle of the city's golden mile. It also boasts a renowned restaurant, the *Kempinski Grill* (see *Eating Out*); and a table at the *Kempinski-Eck* café feels like sitting on the 50-yard line of all of Europe. Business facilities include 24-hour room service, meeting rooms for up to 600, an English-speaking concierge, foreign currency exchange, secretarial services in English, audiovisual equipment, photocopiers, computers, cable TV news, translation services, and express checkout. Breakfast is not included. 27 Kurfürstendamm (phone: 884340; 800-426-3135; fax: 883-6075).

**Curator** With an ideal location—between Savignyplatz and the Ku'-damm—this quiet, chic place is perfect for tourists or business travelers. Amenities such as king-size beds and telephones in the bathrooms make the 100 rooms especially comfortable; the

English-speaking concierge is very helpful. There's an elegant bar and a restaurant off the lobby. Business facilities include a conference room. 41-43 Grolmanstr. (phone: 884260; fax: 884-26500).

**Forum** In the eastern downtown area, its 994 rooms make it one of the largest in town. There is a fine restaurant (the *Panorama;* see *Eating Out*), plus a sauna and a garage. Although guestrooms are fairly small, the convenient location in front of Alexanderplatz is this establishment's main draw; closed to automobile traffic, the square is ringed by restaurants, stores, the *Fernsehturm,* and other public buildings. Business facilities include 24-hour room service, meeting rooms for up to 400, an English-speaking concierge, foreign currency exchange, secretarial services in English, audiovisual equipment, photocopiers, computers, cable TV news, translation services, and express checkout. Alexanderpl. (phone: 23890; fax: 212-6437).

**Grand Hotel Esplanade** With 400 rooms, plus 17 suites, this fine hostelry is idyllically set on the Landwehr Canal—but it's downtown Berlin, not Amsterdam, that's just around the corner. The rooms, service, and other amenities are well above standard, and the popular *Harlekin* restaurant (see *Eating Out*) is on the premises. Business facilities include 24-hour room service, meeting rooms for up to 450, an English-speaking concierge, foreign currency exchange, secretarial services in English, audiovisual equipment, photocopiers, computers, cable TV news, translation services, and express checkout. Breakfast is not included. 15 Lützowufer (phone: 261011; 800-223-5652; fax: 262-9121).

**Inter-Continental** In the heart of western Berlin—with wall-size windows to keep the weather out and the luxury in—this modern 600-room establishment is somewhat removed from the city's hustle and bustle. Request a room overlooking the green, expansive *Tiergarten;* you'll feel as if you're miles from the tumult of the Kurfürstendamm—but in fact you're only a short walk away. Acres of pale marble cover the lobby, and there's a fine selection of restaurants, including a rooftop dining room with live entertainment, as well as a popular ballroom. The hotel is located next to the *Zoologischer Garten.* Business facilities include 24-hour room service, meeting rooms for up to 1,600, an English-speaking concierge, foreign currency exchange, secretarial services in English, audiovisual equipment, photocopiers, computers, cable TV news, translation services, and express checkout. Breakfast is not included. 2 Budapester Str. (phone: 26020; 800-327-0200; fax: 260-80760).

**Maritim Grand Hotel Berlin** In the center of the historic downtown area in what was East Berlin, it offers the height of luxury and comfort. The 350 well-appointed rooms, spacious lobby, and six cafés and restaurants (especially good is *Silhouette;* see *Eating Out*) all seem so "Western" that it's hard to imagine that you're in the middle of what used to be a workers' state. Business facilities include 24-hour room service, meeting rooms for up to 100, an English-speaking concierge, foreign currency exchange, secretarial services in English, audiovisual equipment, photocopiers, computers, cable TV news, translation services, and express checkout. 158-164 Friedrichstr. (phone: 23270; 800-843-3311; fax: 232-7362).

**Metropol** This handsome 340-room high-rise was built in the mid-1970s by a Swedish firm. Extras are a fine dining room (see *Eating Out*), a sauna, and a garage. In former East Berlin, the hotel has always appealed to those used to Western European luxury. Business facilities include 24-hour room service, meeting rooms for up to 120, an English-speaking concierge, foreign currency exchange, secretarial services in English, audiovisual equipment, photocopiers, computers, cable TV news, translation services, and express checkout. 150-153 Friedrichstr. (phone: 23875; fax: 2387-4209).

**Mondial** In the heart of Ku'damm, it has 75 large, elegantly decorated rooms, plus a pool and a first-rate restaurant. Business facilities include foreign currency exchange, an English-speaking concierge, cable TV news, and a conference room. 47 Kurfürstendamm (phone: 884110; fax: 884-11150).

**Palace** Just behind the *Kaiser-Wilhelm-Gedächtniskirche* and within the orb of the *Europa-Center,* this imposing downtown hostelry has a large number of apartments and 160 well-appointed rooms, as well as a restaurant, a pool, and a sauna. Business facilities include 24-hour room service, meeting rooms for up to 600, an English-speaking concierge, foreign currency exchange, secretarial services in English, audiovisual equipment, photocopiers, computers, cable TV news, translation services, and express checkout. Breakfast is not included. 42 Budapester Str. (phone: 25020; fax: 262-6577).

**Penta** With 425 rooms, this is one of Berlin's largest and most modern properties. On the premises are a restaurant, a bar, a beer cellar, a pool, a sauna, a solarium, and an underground garage. Business facilities include 24-hour room service, meeting rooms for up to 780, an English-speaking concierge, foreign currency exchange, secretarial services in English, audiovisual equipment, photocopiers, computers, cable TV news, translation services, and express checkout. Breakfast is not included. Centrally located at 65 Nürnberger Str. (phone: 210070; 800-225-3456; fax: 213-2009).

**President** In a sleek, modern building, this 132-room hostelry boasts a prime location—across the street from the *Urania,* the city's famed lecture hall, and within easy walking distance of Wittenbergplatz and *KaDeWe,* the great department store. Its topnotch restaurant, *Die Saison* (see *Eating Out*), attracts business and theater people. Children under 14 stay free in their parents' room. Business facilities include conference rooms, services of an English-speaking concierge and secretaries, foreign currency exchange, photocopiers, cable TV news, and express checkout. 16-18 An der Urania (phone: 219030; fax: 214-1200).

**Radisson Plaza** Formerly the *Palast,* this 600-room hotel in the city's eastern section provides first class service, luxurious accommodations, and a good view of the city. Its restaurants serve a variety of ethnic fare, from Asian to French. Business facilities include 24-hour room service, meeting rooms for up to 780, an English-speaking concierge, foreign currency exchange, secretarial services in English, audiovisual equipment, photocopiers, computers, cable TV news, translation services, and express checkout. 5 Karl-Liebknecht-Str. (phone: 23828; 800-333-3333; fax: 2382-7590).

**Savoy** In a prewar building, this 128-room establishment radiates Old World charm with its plush lobby and elegant bar. The rooms on the sixth floor are especially posh, with TV sets that double as computers, and fresh flowers daily. Other amenities include a restaurant, 24-hour room service, conference rooms, an English-speaking concierge, foreign currency exchange, photocopiers, and cable TV news. 9-10 Fasanenstr. (phone: 311030; 800-63-SAVOY; fax: 311-03333).

**Schweizerhof** This 441-room establishment is opposite the *Inter-Continental* and is managed by that same chain. The motif is Swiss, as the name implies, and the service is excellent. There is a restaurant. Breakfast is not included. 21-31 Budapester Str. (phone: 26960; 800-327-0200; fax: 269-6900).

**Seehof** Only 2½ miles (4 km) down the road from the downtown area, on the lovely Lietzensee, this 80-room hotel overlooks a small park. There is a restaurant, and business facilities include 24-hour room service, meeting rooms for up to 600, an English-speaking concierge, foreign currency exchange, secretarial services in English, audiovisual equipment, photocopiers, computers, cable TV news, translation services, and express checkout. Breakfast is not included. 11 Lietzenseeufer (phone: 320020; fax: 320-02251).

**Steigenberger** This modern, comfortable establishment with 400 rooms—plus several restaurants and bars, a pool, a sauna, and a shopping arcade—is a link in one of Germany's largest hotel chains. The location is prime. Business facilities include 24-hour room service, meeting rooms for up to 600, an English-speaking concierge, foreign currency exchange, secretarial services in English, audiovisual equipment, photocopiers, computers, cable TV news, translation services, and express checkout. Breakfast is not included. Downtown, facing lovely Los Angeles Platz. 1 Los Angeles Pl. (phone: 21080; 800-223-5652; fax: 210-8117).

### MODERATE

**Am Studio** A modern place, it offers a magnificent view of the city from each of its 78 rooms. There's no restaurant, but breakfast is included. There's also an English-speaking concierge. 80 Kaiserdamm (phone: 302081; fax: 301-9578).

**Art Hotel Sorat** An unusual 75-room establishment that is a cross between a hotel and an art gallery. Modern paintings and sculpture by German artist Wolf Vostell enliven the building's façade and its unusually tasteful interior. Its equally attractive dining room, *Anteo,* serves fine continental fare (see *Eating Out*). Business facilities include

24-hour room service, meeting rooms for up to 100, an English-speaking concierge, foreign currency exchange, and photocopiers. 28-29 Joachimstaler Str. (phone: 884470; fax: 884-47700).

**Askanischer Hof** A favorite with journalists and actors, this 17-room property—a country inn in the heart of Berlin—has a charming, antiques-filled decor. The lobby and breakfast room, on the second floor of the prewar building, are cozy and welcoming. There's no restaurant. 53 Kurfürstendamm (phone: 881-8033; fax: 881-7206).

**Berlin** With 470 rooms (those in the older—circa 1960—section are especially spacious), this is one of the city's largest properties. An old-fashioned pub, the *Berlin Eck,* offers hearty snacks, while the *Globe* restaurant (see *Eating Out*) is considered one of the city's best hotel dining rooms. 17 Lützowpl. (phone: 26050; 800-843-6664; fax: 260-52716).

**Berlin Excelsior** Just off Kurfürstendamm in the center of town, this pleasant property offers 325 rooms with refrigerators; public rooms include a breakfast room, restaurant, bar, and banquet room. Business facilities include 24-hour room service, meeting rooms for up to 120, an English-speaking concierge, foreign currency exchange, secretarial services in English, audiovisual equipment, photocopiers, computers, cable TV news, translation services, and express check-out. 14 Hardenbergstr. (phone: 31550; fax: 315-1053).

**Börse** Right in the middle of downtown Berlin, this 44-room hotel offers little peace and quiet, as it's surrounded by shops, cafés, restaurants, theaters, and movie houses. But it's fine if you like a lively location. There's no restaurant, but breakfast is included. Business facilities include 24-hour room service, an English-speaking concierge, foreign currency exchange, and photocopiers. 34 Kurfürstendamm (phone: 881-3021; fax: 883-2034).

**Castor** Located on a quiet side street in the middle of Berlin's antiques district, just four blocks from the *KaDeWe* department store, is this unpretentious, no-frills hostelry. Each of the 78 small rooms is prettily decorated with French fabrics, and the corner rooms have porthole windows. A good restaurant serving fine regional fare is a plus. Other amenities include an English-speaking concierge and foreign currency exchange. 8 Fuggerstr. (phone: 213030; fax: 213-03160).

**Domus** Set on a charming side street in the city center, this pleasant establishment offers 70 comfortable rooms. There's no restaurant, but a generous buffet breakfast is included. 49 Uhlandstr. (phone: 882041; fax: 882-0410).

**Forsthaus Paulsborn** Housed in a former hunting lodge on the Grunewaldsee (Grunewald Lake), this 10-room gem offers a quiet and romantic atmosphere in a lovely setting. The vaulted-ceiling bar and restaurant feature lake views and fine German cooking. Am Grunewaldsee (phone: 813-8010; fax: 814-1156).

**Frühling am Zoo** Located on the busiest corner in town, this place can be noisy, but its prices are reasonable. The 66 guestrooms have high ceilings and comfortable beds. There's no elevator, however, and no restaurant. 17 Kurfürstendamm (phone: 881-8083; fax: 881-6483).

**Luisenhof** This comfortable, elegant hostelry is housed in a beautiful 19th-century building that was formerly used as a Communist Party training center. It has 28 rooms, a bar, and a restaurant. 92 Köpenicker Str. (phone: 279-1109).

**Novotel** With 187 rooms, and right next to *Flughafen Berlin-Tegel* (Tegel Airport), it provides efficiency without any sacrifice of comfort. There's a restaurant, sauna, solarium, and pool on the premises. Business facilities include meeting rooms for up to 25, an English-speaking concierge, and foreign currency exchange. 202 Kurt-Schumacher-Damm (phone: 41060; 800-221-4542; fax: 410-6700).

**Plaza** Just around the corner from the Kurfürstendamm is this 131-room alternative to more expensive accommodations. There is a restaurant, and business facilities include an English-speaking concierge and foreign currency exchange. 63 Knesebeckstr. (phone: 884130; fax: 884-13754).

**Residenz** A favorite of German TV stars who sometimes stay for months, this 90-room property boasts *Jugendstil* interiors, an excellent French restaurant, and a wonderful location—just off the Ku'damm. Ask about their special packages. 9 Meinekestr. (phone: 884430; fax: 882-4726).

**Riehmer's Hofgarten** This offbeat 25-room hostelry, which looks out onto the courtyard of a large turn-of-the-century apartment complex, is located in Kreuzberg, a neighborhood popular with artists. Guests enjoy comfort without frills. There is a restaurant on the ground floor (not connected to the hotel). 83 Yorckstr. (phone: 781011; fax: 786-6059).

**Viktoria Hotelschiff** For those who envision sailing over the bounding main but can't stand the sight of a wave, this floating hostelry on the River Spree is the perfect choice. Once a private yacht, this now-moored boat offers 38 cozy, comfortable rooms decorated with—what else?—a nautical theme. The on-board dining room serves good seafood dishes. Business facilities include 24-hour room service, an English-speaking concierge, and foreign currency exchange. Pier 3 at *Treptower Park* (phone: 272-7117 or 272-7873; fax: 272-7435).

### INEXPENSIVE

**Christliches Hospiz** Near *Friedrichstrasse Station* and the Scheunenviertel, this clean, well-run place has no frills, but its 70 rooms are comfortable and reasonably priced. The concierge speaks little English. The restaurant is open to the public on weekdays; to guests only on weekends. 82 Auguststr. (phone: 284970; fax: 284-97109).

**Econtel** Midway between *Flughafen Berlin-Tegel* (Tegel Airport) and downtown and near the *Deutsche Oper* and *Schloss Charlotten-*

*burg,* it puts its accent on simple comfort rather than luxury, but doesn't sacrifice modern facilities. Business facilities include meeting rooms for up to 25, an English-speaking concierge, and foreign currency exchange. There's no restaurant, but breakfast is included in the rate. 24-26 Sömmeringstr. (phone: 346810; fax: 344-7034).

---

## PENSIONS

The European tradition of the family-run pension is alive and well here. For travelers on a budget, a pension can be the perfect antidote to Berlin's sky-high hotel rates—a double room and breakfast costs from about $50 to $80 a night at a pension, depending on location and amenities. Even the least expensive establishments are usually spotlessly clean.

Here are some standouts (none has a restaurant, but breakfast is included at each):

**Alpina** Sixteen comfortable rooms (some with private baths) in a suburban setting near the Grunewald. 3 Trabener Str. (phone: 891-6090).

**An der Weide** Located in a quiet eastern Berlin neighborhood, this modern 14-room pension (a few with private baths) is run by a friendly family. 20 Alt-Mahlsdorf (phone: 527-7975).

**Charlottenburg** With 14 rooms (some with private baths), it's a wonderful bargain with a prime location near Savignyplatz. 32-33 Grolmanstr. (phone: 881-5254).

**Charlottenburger Hof** Clean, well-managed, and convenient, it offers 45 rooms, some with private baths. 14 Stuttgarter Pl. (phone: 324-4819).

**Kettler** This seven-room place is situated on one of the loveliest streets in the city; some of the units have private baths. 19 Bleibtreustr. (phone: 883-4949).

**Kleistspark** An exceptionally well maintained pension with 20 rooms (some with baths) in the pleasant Schöneberg district. 1 Belziger Str. (phone: 781-1189).

**Seeblick** Located near the lovely Lietzensee (Lietzen Lake), this 10-room place is within easy commuting distance of downtown Berlin. Some of the rooms have private baths. 14 Neue Kantstr. (phone: 321-3072).

---

## EATING OUT

At its best, German food is hearty and tasty; at its worst, it's as heavy as lead. Main courses usually consist of roasted or stewed meat with boiled potatoes or dumplings (called *Knödel,* which are very heavy) and sauerkraut, cabbage, or other vegetables, such as string beans. Wiener schnitzel and sauerbraten are well-known specialties.

Like other continentals, Germans like rolls for breakfast, occasionally the sweet, cruller-like pastries called *Krapfen* and *Berliner*

*Pfannkuchen.* At mid-morning, they often have a snack of sausages and bread for *Brotzeit* (literally, "breadtime").

Sausages are the specialty in Germany; they are made from pork, veal, and game. The frankfurter, which originated in Vienna, is longer, slimmer, and better than the American variety. *Weisswurst* is white sausage made mostly of veal; bratwurst is pork sausage; a *Regensburger* is a spicy pork sausage.

Interesting appetizers include herring, which is very popular and comes in many varieties, and *Lachs* (smoked salmon). Popular, substantial soups include *Leberknödelsuppe* (liver dumpling soup), *Erbsensuppe* (pea soup), and *Kohlsuppe* (cabbage soup). *Schwarzbrot,* or dark bread, is very tasty, especially Westphalian pumpernickel.

For a typical Berlin treat, stop in at a *Konditorei,* a little shop that offers excellent cakes and pastries with coffee or tea. Special desserts are *Schwarzwälder Kirschtorte,* a Black Forest cherry cake with whipped cream; *Kugelhupf,* a marvelous coffee cake; or *Käsekuchen,* a cheesecake. Another Berlin specialty is *Eisbein* (pigs' knuckles).

The past several years have seen a dramatic increase in the number of ethnic restaurants in the city, adding variety to Berlin's dining scene. Italian and Chinese establishments seem to be on every corner—but not all of them are good. More reliable bets are the Indian, Turkish, and Greek restaurants, with loads of bright vegetables and tasty grilled meat. Other treats include Afghan, Thai, and Japanese fare.

Germans are justifiably famous for their beer and wine. *Helles* (light) and *Dunkles* (dark) beers from southern Germany come in many sizes and varieties. Most beers come from Munich, but you might want to try *Berliner Weisse* in the summer, a whitish beer made from wheat and often served *mit Schuss* (with raspberry juice). *Bierkeller* (beer restaurants) serve food as well as beer.

Germany produces a lot of wine, some of it very good. You may be disappointed in *Liebfraumilch,* which is not a place-name (it means "Milk of Our Lady") and thus is not reliable. Best bets are the Moselles—light, pleasant, and often cheap—like *Wehlener Sonnenuhr, Piesporter,* or *Zeltinger.* Rhine wines, of course, are famous— some of the best are *Niersteiner, Oppenheimer,* and *Schloss Johannisberger.* Baden wines are equally renowned, especially *Weissherbst,* a rosé.

For a dinner for two expect to pay $100 or more at restaurants in the expensive category; between $40 and $100 at places in the moderate range; and less than $40 at places classed as inexpensive. Unless otherwise noted the restaurants listed below are open for lunch and dinner and accept major credit cards. Prices do not include drinks and wine. Taxes and tips are included in the bill, but leave a few extra deutsche marks (DM) for good service. All telephone numbers are in the 30 city code unless otherwise indicated.

Here is our culinary favorite, followed by our cost and quality choices, listed by price category.

**Bamberger Reiter** Although this rustic restaurant in the center of the city opened in 1984, the tasteful renovations and dark wood paneling give it a patina of antiquity. Austrian owners Franz and Doris Ranburger have created a sumptuous menu (honored with a Michelin star) which features perch in rosemary butter with spinach and pumpkin noodles, Breton lobsters, Italian truffles, and the more traditional pot roast and dumplings; the sommelier will have just the wine to go with all of it. Open for dinner only; closed Sundays and Mondays. Reservations necessary. No credit cards accepted. 7 Regensburger Str. (phone: 218-4282; fax: 214-2348).

## EXPENSIVE

**Alt-Luxemburg** The nouvelle cuisine at this cozy bistro near the city center (which has earned a Michelin star) has made this a favorite among locals and visitors alike. Try the seafood specialties—especially halibut topped with fresh greens and salmon with kumquat sauce. Closed Sundays, Mondays, and three weeks in July. Reservations advised. 31 Windscheidstr. (phone: 323-8730).

**Chalet Corniche** This beautiful former country mansion on the western fringe of the city in the Grunewald section, is a special place indeed. Not only does the impressive architecture give you the feeling of bonhomie (the house was built around a big old tree), but the view through the tall windows onto wide lawns and a beautiful lake is as soul-satisfying as the food. We recommend the veal steaks and the seafood specialties. Open daily. Reservations advised. 5B Königsallee (phone: 892-8597).

**Conti Fischstuben** As its name implies, this elegant, small dining room in the *Ambassador* hotel is for seafood lovers. Open for dinner only; closed Sundays and Mondays. Reservations advised. 42 Bayreuther Str. (phone: 219-02362).

**Daitokai** Close to the Kurfürstendamm, this Japanese dining place offers good food and friendly service. Guests can sit on the floor Japanese-style. Closed Mondays. No reservations. *Europa-Center,* Budapester Str. (phone: 261-8099).

**Ermeler Haus** Away from the hustle and bustle of downtown, this lovely rococo building in the eastern part of the city is one of only a few historic buildings still standing here (except for those on Unter den Linden). Housed on the building's second floor, the restaurant offers good continental dishes in intimate surroundings. The *Raabe-Diele* beer cellar and the first-floor café also are popular. Open daily for dinner only. Reservations advised. 10-12 Märkisches Ufer (phone: 279-4028).

**Frühsammers** Twenty minutes from downtown Berlin, this country cottage has none of the French ambitions of its tonier competition. Peter Frühsammer prides himself in dishing out the very best in local products—he works with farmers and fishers, urging them to grow the finest vegetables and herbs, raise free-range livestock, fish the region's lakes, and gather wild mushrooms and berries. These ingredients are then melded into subtle delights such as *Milchlammleber mit Ofenschalotten* (an appetizer of milk-fed lamb's liver with roasted shallots) and *Lendchen vom Neuland-Schwein in Sherryrahm mit Rösti* (roast pork loin in a sherried cream sauce, served with fried potatoes). Open for dinner only; closed Sundays. Reservations necessary. 101 Matterhornstr. (phone: 803-2720 or 803-8023).

**Globe** One of the best hotel dining rooms in town, with continental dishes served in elegant surroundings. You can dine either in the main dining room or in the smaller grillroom. Grillroom closed Sundays. Reservations advised. In the *Berlin Hotel,* 17 Lützowpl. (phone: 26050).

**Grand Slam** In a quiet suburb, about 7 miles (11 km) from downtown Berlin, it offers first-rate fare that has earned a Michelin star—we recommend the cream of spinach soup with a side dish of black truffle slices, or any one of several succulent lamb creations. This is one of the few restaurants in the Berlin area that requires men to wear jackets and ties. Closed Sundays and Mondays. Reservations necessary. 47-55 Gottfried-von-Cramm-Weg (phone: 825-3810).

**Harlekin** This stylish dining room in the *Grand Hotel Esplanade* features refined "New German" fare—try the lentils with saddle of rabbit or the lamb filet. The wine list boasts some unusual selections. Closed Sundays. Reservations advised. 15 Lützowufer (phone: 261011).

**Kardell** Specialties are leg of lamb, game, steaks, and fish. Owner Heinz Kardell runs the place with obsessive attention to detail—and it shows. Open daily; closed Saturday lunch. Reservations necessary. 24 Gervinusstr. (phone: 324-1066).

**Kempinski Grill** The candlelit glow, creamy decor, and piano music are all serenely old-fashioned in Berlin's number one hotel dining room. The menu features lobster (a Berlin obsession) in salads, soups, and sauces. Grilled fish and steaks also are recommended. Round off the evening with a stop at the hotel's soothing *Bristol Bar* (see *Nightclubs and Nightlife* above). Closed Sundays. Reservations necessary. 27 Kurfürstendamm (phone: 884-34792).

**Landhaus am Poloplatz** Overlooking a polo field in the exclusive northern suburb of Frohnau, this place serves classic German cooking. Closed Mondays and for three weeks during the summer (usually in July). Reservations necessary. 9 Am Polopl. (phone: 401-9035).

**Lutter und Wegener** One of the oldest dining spots in Berlin, this elegant place moved to its present location in Charlottenburg after its original 19th-century building in the Mitte district was bombed during

World War II. It offers well-prepared nouvelle cuisine, fine wine, and soft jazz in a relaxed setting. Try the stuffed roast lamb with rosemary served with zucchini and dumplings. Open daily for dinner only. Reservations advised. 55 Schlüterstr. (phone: 881-3440).

**Marjellchen** A cozy establishment specializing in East Prussian cuisine. The goose and the *Königsberger Klopse* (meatballs in a caper sauce) are especially good. Open daily for dinner only. Reservations advised. 9 Mommsenstr. (phone: 883-2676).

**Metropol** This elegant hotel dining room features rustic decor, *Gemütlichkeit* (a warm, welcoming atmosphere), and fine continental fare. Open daily. Reservations advised. Major credit cards accepted. 150-153 Friedrichstr. (phone: 22040 or 203070).

**Ming's Garden** If you crave Peking duck, this lushly decorated dining room is the place. But though it serves the city's finest Chinese cooking, don't expect the quality or variety available in most US cities. Open daily. Reservations advised. 16 Tauentzienstr., entrance on Marburger Str. (phone: 211-8728).

**Panorama** A fitting name for a restaurant on the 37th floor of the *Forum* hotel. The fare, which includes seafood dishes, pork, and steaks, almost equals the marvelous view. Try the daily specialties. Open daily. Reservations necessary. Alexanderpl. (phone: 238-94347).

**Paris-Bar** A traditional bistro that is a magnet for intellectuals and artists drawn by its equally traditional French cuisine. Closed Sundays. Reservations advised. 152 Kantstr. (phone: 313-8052).

**Paris-Moskau** Not far from the *Reichstag* in a somewhat undistinguished neighborhood, this nevertheless distinguished restaurant offers excellent continental dishes in three dining rooms in a charming two-story house. Open daily for dinner only. Reservations advised. 141 Alt-Moabit (phone: 394-2081).

**Restauration 1900** Located in Prenzlauer Berg, this renowned eastern Berlin eatery was named for the famous Bertolucci film. The city's cultural elite come here to dine and look. The food is continental-Mediterranean. Try the bouillabaisse. Open for dinner only; closed Sundays and Mondays. Reservations necessary. 1 Husemannstr. (phone: 449-4052).

**Rockendorf's** This turn-of-the-century villa in a northern suburb of Berlin is not a place to grab a bite between sights—a meal here is a production. There is something almost religious in the veneration with which each meal is borne out of the gleaming kitchen where Siegfried Rockendorf, one of Germany's high priests of gastronomy, watches over his potions. The fixed- (and high-) price menu changes daily, so call ahead if you're picky. Closed Sundays and Mondays. Reservations necessary. 1 Düsterhauptstr. (phone: 402-3099).

**Die Saison** In a plant-filled space lined with colorful paintings, an ever-changing menu of seasonal specialties makes this hotel dining room a favorite among locals and visitors alike. Our favorites are the asparagus soup and calf's liver with brandy. Open daily. Reservations advised. In the *President Hotel,* 16-18 An der Urania (phone: 219030).

**Silhouette** This dining room (with one Michelin star) is the pride of the *Maritim Grand* hotel. The food and decor are Thuringian, with such specialties as roast goose and grilled sausages with bacon-laden potato salad. Native red wines are featured. Open daily. Reservations necessary. 158-164 Friedrichstr. (phone: 209-2400).

### MODERATE

**Abend-Restaurant Königin Luise** Set in the handsome *Opernpalais* restaurant complex, formerly the "Princesses' Palace," where Queen Luise's three daughters lived in the early 19th century, this is one of Berlin's most elegant dining rooms. The exterior was recently restored to its former splendor; the decor is 19th-century imperial, with antique furnishings, china, and silver. The menu of nouvelle German fare is equally elaborate: Breast of guinea hen with walnut sauce and broccoli timbales, and filet of goat with rosemary sauce are just a few of the selections. Open daily for dinner only. Reservations necessary. 5 Unter den Linden (phone: 200-2269).

**Alter Fritz** One of Berlin's oldest restaurants, this former coach stop on the road north of the city serves up hearty German food and beer in a charming country atmosphere. Open daily. Reservations advised. 12 Karolinenstr. (phone: 433-5010).

**Anselmo** A must for devotees of Italian fare, this intimate spot has an imaginative and well-run kitchen, rustic decor, and a pleasant atmosphere. Closed Mondays. Reservations advised. 17 Damaschkestr. (phone: 323-3094).

**Anteo** Contemporary and avant-garde art adorn the walls of this hotel dining establishment. A continental menu offers simple, flavorful fare such as Greek hors d'oeuvres, tortellini with Gorgonzola sauce, and beef steaks with roasted potatoes. There's terrace dining in fine weather. Open daily. Reservations advised. In the *Art Hotel Sorat,* 29 Joachimstaler Str. (phone: 883-4407).

**Aphrodite** This dining place in the Prenzlauer Berg district offers continental dishes and wines at reasonable prices. Try the lamb filet with a glass of chardonnay. Open for dinner only; closed Sundays and Mondays. Reservations advised. 61 Schönhauser Allee (phone: 448-1707).

**Ax-Bax** The beautiful people often hang out in this nicely designed bar that has no identifying sign on the door. In addition to the drinks and glitter, it also has good pub-style food, including bratwurst and steaks. Open for dinner only; closed Mondays. Reservations advised. 34 Leibnitzstr. (phone: 313-8594).

**Blockhaus Nikolskoe** The perfect restaurant for fans of German history and good continental food, this place, high above the wide Havel River, was built in log cabin fashion in 1819 by Prussian King Friedrich Wilhelm III for his daughter Charlotte and her husband,

Grand Duke Nicholas (later Russian Czar Nicholas I). It looks like a Russian dacha. The location is remote, so ask directions when you make reservations. Closed Thursdays and in the winter after 7 PM. Reservations advised. On Nikolskoer Weg in Wannsee (phone: 805-2914).

**Bovril** This tony bistro is the best place in town for fine French-German food at a reasonable price. The menu changes daily; try the salad appetizers and the fresh fish dishes. Closed Sundays. Reservations advised. 184 Kurfürstendamm (phone: 881-8461).

**Chamisso** Situated on one of the city's few remaining perfectly preserved 19th-century squares, this charming Italian eatery specializes in fine pasta. Open daily for dinner only. Reservations advised. 25 Willibald-Alexis-Str. (phone: 691-5642).

**Don Quijote** Appropriately named, this eatery features first-rate Spanish fare in a friendly, festive atmosphere. Ask for the daily fish special—waiters present an assortment and let you choose. Other favorites include a *tapas* plate (a variety of Spanish appetizers) and garlic shrimp. Be sure to sample the sangria. Open daily for dinner only. Reservations advised. 41 Bleibtreustr. (phone: 881-3208).

**Exil** This out-of-the-way place is well worth the trip. On a canal in Kreuzberg, it features well-prepared Viennese dishes, including Wiener schnitzel and strudel. You can dine on the bower-like terrace, weather permitting. The service also is charmingly Viennese, and the ambience is sophisticated but relatively informal. Open for dinner only; closed Mondays. Reservations advised. No credit cards accepted. 44A Paul-Lincke-Ufer (phone: 612-7037).

**Fernsehturm** Europe's second-tallest tower (see *Seeing the City*) has a revolving café/restaurant that, in addition to offering decent international fare, affords diners a breathtaking panoramic view of Berlin. Good choices are the salads, pork cutlets, and sausages. Open daily. Reservations unnecessary. Alexanderpl. (phone: 212-3333 or 210-4232).

**Florian** A finely tuned crew maintains this admirable dining spot. The menu emphasizes French, Austrian, and Bohemian fare, and the wines and the service are as good as the food. The neighborhood is currently "in," so the place is frequented by artists, film people, and the so-called New Wave set. Open for dinner only; closed *Christmas Eve* through *New Year's Eve*. Reservations advised. No credit cards accepted. 52 Grolmanstr. (phone: 313-9184).

**Fofi's** A Greek-style bistro that has become a magnet for the "in" crowd; the attractions here are the Greek food and the clientele. Open for dinner only; closed *Christmas Eve.* Reservations advised. 70 Fasanenstr.—look for the *"estiatorio"* sign (phone: 881-8785).

**Foyer** Tucked in a rear courtyard just off the Ku'damm, this unpretentious dining spot is somewhat hard to find, but if you crave Turkish food, it's worth the effort. Open for dinner only; closed Sundays. Reservations advised. 28 Uhlandstr. (phone: 881-4268).

**Good Friends** This Chinese eatery boasts tasty barbecued pork and chicken, as well as efficient service and a convenient location. Open daily. Reservations advised. 210 Kurfürstendamm (phone: 881-5756).

**Hard Rock Café** Berlin's member of the ubiquitous Hard Rock dynasty, which extends from London to Singapore. Die-hard rock fans can eat to the beat, munching on hefty hamburgers and salty French fries while their favorite tunes fill the air. Rock 'n' roll memorabilia on the walls include the microphone first used by the *Beatles* in concert, Jimi Hendrix's vest, a poster of the *Who* signed by John Entwhistle and Keith Moon, and a tour jacket signed by Madonna. Open daily. Reservations unnecessary. 21 Meinekestr. (phone: 881-2995).

**Im Reichstag** One wing of this late 19th-century building, the former (and future) seat of the German Parliament (see *Special Places*), has been set aside as a restaurant. Solid German food is served in a historic setting. Closed Mondays. Reservations advised. No credit cards accepted. Pl. der Republik (phone: 397-73172).

**Istanbul** The food at Berlin's oldest Turkish restaurant is excellent, but the real attraction is the atmosphere. The rooms are ornate and colorful, and on weekends belly dancers work the crowd into a delighted frenzy. Open daily. Reservations advised. 77 Knesebeckstr. (phone: 883-2777).

**Katschkol** In the city's only Afghan eatery, diners can sit on the floor or at regular tables; dishes are wonderfully spiced and served with cool yogurt sauces. Service can be erratic, but the food is worth the wait. Open daily for dinner only. Reservations advised. 84 Pestalozzistr. (phone: 312-3472).

**Lanna** A friendly staff serves topnotch Thai food in this dimly lit, wood-paneled dining room. Try the octopus with basil and garlic, green curry chicken, or spicy Thai noodles. Open for dinner only; closed Sundays. Reservations advised (a few days in advance for Fridays and Saturdays). 4 Pfalzburger Str. (phone: 883-2373).

**Lucky Strike** Located just a few steps from the *Pergamon Museum,* this trendy eatery is Berlin's first foray into New Orleans–style cooking. Menu items include jambalaya, barbecued ribs, and seafood gumbo. An adjacent lounge features live jazz and blues by various artists. This spot is hopping well into the wee hours of the morning. Open daily; closed weekday lunch. Reservations advised. Georgestr., under the *S-Bahn* tracks (phone: 308-48822).

**Müggelsee-Perle** The fish, fowl, and game dishes are best; also try the Berlin pea soup. On the shore of the Grosser Müggelsee, the restaurant is accessible by excursion ship (see *Extra Special*) as well as by bus and car. Closed November through April. Reservations unnecessary. Am Grossen Müggelsee (phone: 65882).

**Mundart** In Kreuzberg, a former working class district that has gone arty, it features French cuisine, though Jacques, the imaginative chef, is no disciple of nouvelle. The decor, service, and excellent wines are also highly commendable. Open for dinner only; closed Mondays, Tuesdays, and July. Reservations advised. No credit cards accepted. 33-34 Muskauer Str. (phone: 612-2061).

**November** On the south bank of the Landwehrkanal, oppposite the *Neue Nationalgalerie,* this intimate, bistro-like place is a favorite of writers, artists, and others belonging to the cultural scene. The bohemian ambience is in charming contrast to the upmarket tone of the fare offered by an extremely obliging staff. Try the leg of lamb or game dishes. Open daily for dinner only. Reservations advised. 65 Schöneberger Ufer (phone: 261-3882).

**Offenbach Stuben** Intimate and cozy, this is one of the few eateries in the city's eastern section that always has been privately run. The German and continental fare are fine, as are the beverages. Closed Sundays and Mondays. Reservations necessary. 8 Stubbenkammerstr. (phone: 448-4106).

**Osteria No. 1** Always crowded, this Italian eatery offers fine pasta, seafood, and meat dishes in a bright and cheerful dining room. The ravioli is excellent. Open daily. Reservations advised. 71 Kreuzbergstr. (phone: 786-9162).

**Schipkapass** A rustically decorated Czech eatery, featuring those two mainstays of every good Bohemian kitchen: Prague ham and pilsener beer. You can feast on the large portions. Open daily for dinner only. Reservations advised. No credit cards accepted. 185 Hohenzollerndamm (phone: 871941).

**Shell Café** For elegantly presented fare served all hours of the day, this centrally located eatery is a real find. Set in a former gas station (and named for the oil company), it features brunch with American-style bacon and eggs. Open daily. No reservations, but the place gets very crowded after 4 PM, so expect a wait. 22 Knesebeckstr. (phone: 312-8310).

**Storch** Alsatian specialities offered here include *Flammenkuchen,* a crispy flat pastry topped with cheese, ham, and onions; as a dessert, it's covered with cheese and apples, then drizzled with Calvados and flambéed. The big wooden tables make this a good choice for large groups. Open daily for dinner only. Reservations advised. No credit cards accepted. 54 Wartburgstr. (phone: 784-2059).

**Terzo Mundo** A favorite of actors and journalists, its menu features hearty Greek fare; there's often an entertainer who sings Greek folk songs. Open daily for dinner only. Reservations advised. 28 Grolmanstr. (phone: 881-5261).

**Tres Kilos** Berlin's only good Tex-Mex restaurant, it's a great spot for hot summer evenings; the open-air terrace overlooks the lively Marheinekeplatz, and the margaritas are first-rate. The dining rooms are filled to overflowing almost every night. Open daily for dinner only. Reservations advised. 3 Marheinekepl. (phone: 693-6044).

**Tuk-Tuk** Indonesian food served in a tropical setting. Friendly service and a large selection of vegetarian dishes make this place a Schöneberg favorite. Open daily for dinner only. Reservations advised. 2 Grossgörschenstr. (phone: 781-1588).

**Weinstube am Savignyplatz** Grilled steaks and fresh fish, complemented by a carefully chosen list of French wines, are served in a warm, candlelit dining room. Near the *Theater des Westens,* it's a fine choice for a pre- or post-theater dinner. Open for dinner only; closed Mondays. Reservations advised. Corner of Savignypl. and Kantstr. (phone: 313-8697).

**Wirtshaus Schildhorn** Steaks cooked on the grill are a specialty at this upscale beer garden and outdoor restaurant. With its lovely location—on a tiny peninsula by the Havel River—it is very popular in summer. Open daily. Reservations advised on summer weekends. 4A Am Schildhorn (phone: 305-3111).

**Yukiguni** A delicate pale-wood interior provides the perfect setting for the chef's artful versions of Japanese specialties. There's also an excellent sushi bar. Closed Sunday lunch and Tuesdays. Reservations advised. 30 Kantstr. (phone: 312-1978).

### INEXPENSIVE

**El Bodegón** This lively Spanish *finca,* featuring a wide range of Iberian dishes, is much frequented by students, musicians, and artists. The atmosphere is genuinely Iberian, including guitar music, chiefly flamenco. Open daily for dinner only. Reservations unnecessary. 61 Schlüterstr. (phone: 312-4497).

**Brasserie** You will find a true French bistro here. The decor, food, and wine are typical of the Gallic provinces. There also is a small enclosed terrace. Open daily. Reservations unnecessary. 3 Wittenbergpl. (phone: 218-5786).

**Café Möhring** This traditional German *Konditorei* has two locations in the city. Here you can enjoy rich cakes, light Danish pastry, and other wonders from their own bakery to go along with your coffee or tea. Light hot meals also are available. Open daily. Reservations unnecessary. No credit cards accepted. 213 Kurfürstendamm (phone: 881-2075) and 55 Charlottenstr. (phone: 209-02240).

**Café Oren** Located near the *Neue Synagoge,* this popular vegetarian eatery features innovatively prepared Eastern European and Israeli dishes. The soups, especially the yogurt and the borscht, are outstanding. A great place to stop while touring the Scheunenviertel, but be prepared to wait in a long line. Open daily. Reservations necessary on weekends. 28 Oranienburger Str. (phone: 282-8228).

**Häagen-Dazs** A refreshing taste from home, its name notwithstanding. The same good ice cream (you won't have any trouble translating from the German *Eiscrem*); ask for one *Kugel* (scoop) or two *Kugeln.* Open daily. 224 Kurfürstendamm (phone: 882-1207).

**Hardtke** Two traditional restaurants with traditionally hearty German food such as fresh *Leberwurst* and *Blutwurst.* All meat dishes come from its own butcher shops. The atmosphere is rustic and friendly. A very good value. Open daily. Reservations advised. 27 and 27B Meinekestr. (phone: 881-9827).

**Hollandstüb'l** Dutch fare, with the accent on dishes from the East Indies (*nasi goreng, rijsttafel,* and so on). The decor is a holdover from the 1920s, when this was one of Berlin's more popular restaurants. Open daily. No reservations. 11 Martin-Luther-Str. (phone: 218-8593).

**India Haus** A bit out of the way, this place is worth the detour for its better-than-average Indian food. The butter chicken and curried lamb are scrumptious. Open daily; closed weekday lunch. Reservations unnecessary. 38 Feurigstr., at the corner of Dominicusstr. (phone: 781-2546).

**Jimmy's Diner** Right out of *American Graffiti,* this spot in the heart of town is a larger-than-life replica of the good old American diner, complete with canned music piped in everywhere, even in the WC. The menu is what you'd expect: luscious cheeseburgers, coleslaw (the only place in town that serves it), pasta, salads, sandwiches, and steaks. For dessert, have a slice of apple pie and a cup of coffee. Open daily. No reservations, and it's crowded in the evening. 41 Pariser Str. (phone: 882-3141).

**Kellerrestaurant im Brecht-Haus** The decor may be downscale, but this dining spot in the eastern part of town is a great place to grab a bite. Classic Austrian fare and a jovial atmosphere are in abundance here, not to mention a bit of history—German playwright Bertolt Brecht spent the last 10 years of his life in the upstairs rooms. Try the Wiener schnitzel with fried potatoes. Dinner only; closed Sundays. Reservations advised. 125 Chausseestr. (phone: 282-3843).

**Litfass** Not far from the Kurfürstendamm and the famous *Schaubühne* theater is this unpretentious Portuguese place. Among the specialties are shark steaks and potted chicken in garlic sauce. Open daily for dinner only. No reservations. No credit cards accepted. 49 Sybelstr. (phone: 323-2215).

**Luisen-bräu** Locals flock here for the hearty, traditional German fare, including homemade sausages, cabbage soup, and house-brewed beer (the waiters will keep refilling your small mug until you put a coaster on top of it—that's the signal for "enough already"). In the summer, guests may dine alfresco on big picnic tables. There's no extra charge for the fine view of *Schloss Charlottenburg,* directly across the street. Open daily. Reservations unnecessary. No credit cards accepted. 1 Luisenpl. (phone: 341-0232).

**Nordsee** Fish is the only dish served in this conveniently located place in the city center. Seafood also reigns supreme (but at slightly higher prices) at *Rendezvous für Feinschmecker,* a fancy grill located a floor below street level in the same building and under the same ownership. Open daily. Reservations unnecessary. Spandauer Str., at the corner of Karl-Liebknecht-Str. (phone: 212-3296).

---

## A BERLIN BREAKFAST

The first meal of the day is an event in Berlin, especially on weekends. The typical Berlin café breakfast consists of a large plate overflowing with slices of gouda and camembert cheese, slices of ham, chunks of fruit, jam and butter, and little bowls of yogurt or a fluffy cream called *Quark.* You may also be served a soft-boiled egg and a basket of fresh bread and rolls. Another specialty is the *Bauernfrühstück* (farmer's breakfast), a hearty omelette made with potatoes, onions, and ham or bacon.

It's a real delight to linger over Sunday breakfast as the Berliners do—eating a bit, reading a bit, then eating some more, as the morning stretches into afternoon. Many places serve until 2 PM, so the meal makes for an ideal brunch or lunch as well. If you do decide to forgo your hotel breakfast one morning, here are a few suggestions. All open at 10 AM unless otherwise noted. None accept credit cards.

**Café Einstein** This grand homage to the Viennese coffeehouse is set in a palatial villa with an outdoor terrace in back. A favorite of the established arts community, it's more expensive than most cafés, but it's worth every pfennig. Try the eggs Florentine for breakfast. 58 Kurfürstenstr. (phone: 261-5096).

**Café Tiago** Inexpensive and popular with students. 9 Knesebeckstr. (phone: 312-9042).

**Café Tomasa** One of the best breakfast spots in town; serves until 4 PM. 60 Motzstr. (phone: 213-2345).

**Operncafé** An extensive breakfast buffet is served from 8:30 AM to 2 PM in a beautiful Old World setting. 5 Unter den Linden (phone: 200-2269).

# Bratislava

## At-a-Glance

### SEEING THE CITY

Head for the Danube and begin with coffee and pastries in the futuristic *Bystrica* restaurant (1 Dunaj; phone: 850042), which towers above the modern Nový Most, formerly Most SNP (Bridge of the Slovak National Uprising). The vista unfolds and reveals the layout of Bratislava, which is built into a countryside dotted with small houses and family gardens. For a more regal perspective, the tower of *Bratislava Castle* on the opposite side of the Danube affords a spectacular view across the river and into Austria and Hungary.

### SPECIAL PLACES

Probably the best tool for traversing the city is a good, updated map, available at the airport and the city's main train station, bus terminal, and bookstores. In addition, *SATUR* (*Slovenská Agentura Pre Turistiku;* Slovak Tourist Agency), formerly part of the *Cedok* complex, offers a four-hour bus tour and a two-hour walking tour of the city (see *Sources and Resources*). A few Slovak words that may help with your navigations: *námestie* and *nábrežie* are the words for square or place; *ulica* means street.

#### STARÉ MÉSTO (OLD TOWN)

If you have the chance for only one close encounter with Bratislava, make it in the Old Town. Most of the sights of interest in the city can be found in this area on the banks of the Danube. Flanked by *Bratislava Castle* on the west, the Old Town stretches roughly to the south and east.

**BRATISLAVSKÝ HRAD (BRATISLAVA CASTLE)** Actually situated on a hill above the Old Town, this towering fortress on the southernmost spur of the Little Carpathian Range is the most visible and frequented tourist attraction in the city. Though the museum inside is of marginal interest (unless you're a Slovak nationalist), the view from the castle's tower is astounding. Remains of the Moravian civilization from the 9th century and of 10th- to 12th-century buildings are preserved near the eastern wall. The castle served as the seat of Hungarian royalty until it was gutted by fire in 1811. It has been reconstructed several times (most recently in 1968). The best way to enter is through the reconstructed Gothic *Sigmund's Gate.* Closed Mondays. Admission charge. Just west of the city center (phone: 311444 or 314508).

**MICHALSKÁ BRÁNA (MICHAEL'S GATE)** Enter the Old Town through this portal, built in the second half of the 13th century, the only remaining gate of the four that once protected the city. The view from its

18th-century Baroque tower is wonderful, and a collection of antique weaponry is housed inside. The tower and gate are the best-preserved portion of the city's former fortifications. On top of the tower's onion dome is a copper statue of *Michael the Dragonslayer.* Extending out from *Michael's Gate* is Michalská ulica (Michael's Street), where some of Bratislava's most beautiful buildings can be found. Closed Tuesdays. Admission charge.

**PRIMACIANSKÝ PALÁC (PALACE OF THE HUNGARIAN ROYAL CHAMBER)** Built in 1756, this palace was the meeting place of the Hungarian Parliament from 1802 to 1848. It currently serves as the university library. Serfdom in Hungary was abolished here officially in 1848. Closed Sundays. Admission charge. 1 Michalská ulica.

**MIRBACHOV PALÁC (MIRBACH PALACE)** This renovated palace houses a branch of the *Galéria Mesta Bratislavy* (Bratislava City Gallery). There are works of 17th- to 19th-century European art on the second floor and, occasionally, international exhibits on the first and third floors. Of special interest is the original stucco decoration of the palace ceilings, the richly decorated main staircases, and the original 18th-century decor in the first-floor exhibition rooms. The gallery is the site of concerts held every Sunday at 10:30 AM. Tickets are available a half-hour before the performance. Closed Mondays. 11 Františkánsko námestie (phone: 331556).

**KLARISKÁ KAPLE (CHAPEL OF THE SISTERS OF ST. CLAIR)** Built in the 14th century for the nuns of the Clarissine order, soon after their arrival in Bratislava, this church is one of the oldest Gothic buildings in the city. It features a single, elegant spire and a pentagonal tower supported by buttresses. Klariská ulica.

**VENTÚRSKA ULICA** Known as the "Street of Music," this avenue, lined with Renaissance buildings, is one of Bratislava's most picturesque. In the 18th century the palaces here were alive with the music of Liszt, Mozart, and many others.

**MESTSKÉ MÚZEUM (CITY MUSEUM)** Part of a complex of buildings comprising the *Old Town Hall,* this museum contains exhibits (none identified in English) dating from 5,000 years ago through the 20th century. The real gem on display is the midget-size piano of the child prodigy Mozart. Unfortunately, the keyboard is kept covered, so the instrument looks like a small table. Perhaps the most beautiful of the exhibits is the 18th-century furniture and glassware collection from the reign of the Austrian Hapsburg dynasty. Don't ignore the building itself, a striking bit of period architecture with arched arcades and courtyards teeming with flowers and statues. Closed Mondays. Admission charge. 1 Primaciálné námestie (phone: 331473). *Apony Palace,* home of the *Expozícia Vinohradnícko-Vinárska* (Slovakian Museum of Wine Production) is in the courtyard. Closed Tuesdays. Admission charge. 1 Radničná.

**PRIMACIONÁLNY PALÁC (PRIMATE'S PALACE)** Just outside the *Old Town Hall* courtyard (go out through the east gate) is Primaciálné námestie, site of this palace and its famous *Hall of Mirrors.* Napoleon and

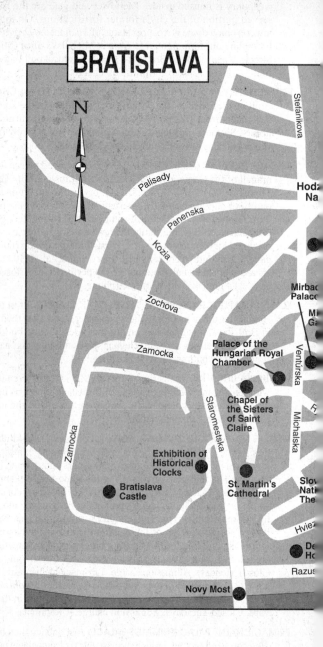

# BRATISLAVA

N

Štefánikova

Palisady

Panenska

Kozia

Hodž
Na

Zochova

Mirbac
Palace

Zamocka

Palace of the
Hungarian Royal
Chamber

Mi
Ga

Venturska

Staromestska

Chapel of
the Sisters
of Saint
Claire

Michalska

Zamocka

Exhibition of
Historical
Clocks

Bratislava
Castle

St. Martin's
Cathedral

Slo
Nat
The

Hvie

De
Ho

Razus

Novy Most

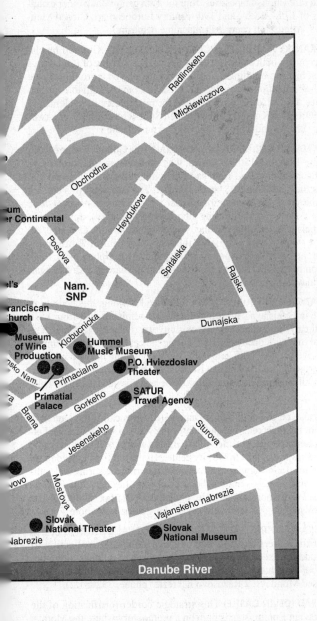

Radlinskeho

Mickiewiczova

Obchodna

Heydukova

...um
...r Continental

Postova

Spitalska

Rajska

...l's

**Nam. SNP**

...ranciscan
...hurch

Klobucnicka

Dunajska

**Museum of Wine Production**

Hummel Music Museum

...nsko Nam.

Primacialne

P.O. Hviezdoslav Theater

Primatial Palace

Gorkeho

SATUR Travel Agency

...a Brana

Jesenskeho

Sturova

...vovo

Mostova

Vajanskeho nabrezie

Slovak National Theater

Slovak National Museum

...Nabrezie

**Danube River**

the Austrian Emperor Franz I signed the Peace of Pressburg here after the Battle of Austerlitz in 1805. Currently the seat of President Michal Kovač, it has a gallery on the second floor adorned with rare English tapestries from the 17th century and other examples of 17th-, 18th-, and 19th-century European art. Closed Mondays. Admission charge. Primaciálné námestie.

**FRANTIŠKANSKY KOSTOL (FRANCISCAN CHURCH)** This Gothic Franciscan church, built at the end of the 13th century, is one of Bratislava's most historic buildings. The Franciscans played a prominent role in the coronation of royalty in Bratislava from the 16th to 19th centuries; they also were responsible for raising certain noblemen to the Order of Knights of the Golden Spur. The church has a two-story chapel and a crypt. Františkánskó námestie.

**DOM SV. MARTINA (ST. MARTIN'S CATHEDRAL)** This Gothic structure, built in the 14th and 15th centuries, was the coronation church of 11 Hungarian kings and eight spouses, symbolized by the crown that tops the 1,280-foot (384-meter) tower. The cathedral was erected on the site of the Romanesque *Savior's Church* and consists of three naves, a presbytery (housing members of the clergy), three Gothic chapels, a late Gothic entrance hall, and the Baroque *Chapel of St. John the Almoner.* Arguably the most beautiful of Bratislava's churches, it features a poignant, 18th-century sculpture of St. Martin on horseback, tearing his coat in half to share it with a beggar. Rudnayovo námestie.

**CORONATION ROUTE** At just over a mile (1.6 km) long, this pedestrian zone in Bratislava's historical district is a reminder that, from 1536 until early in the last century, this city was Hungary's capital. The regal road was opened in 1991 during the celebration of two important events: the 700th anniversary of the granting of town rights to Bratislava by King Andrew III of Hungary, and the second millennium of uninterrupted occupation of the land on which the city is built.

### THE DANUBE SHORE

A cruise on the not-so-blue Danube (Slovaks call it the Dunaj) is one of the most relaxing and interesting ways to see Bratislava. Ferries depart several times a day during warm weather from the *Danubus* travel port in the city center. Hydrofoil trips to Budapest, Komárno, and Vienna are also available during the spring and summer. Since space is limited, book in advance through *Blue Danube Travel* (2 Fajnorovo nábrežie; phone: 363501; fax: 333905). The following are the noteworthy sites along the river's shore:

**SLOVENSKÁ NARODNÁ GALÉRIA (SLOVAK NATIONAL GALLERY)** Located near the waterfront, this is Bratislava's major art collection. It includes an excellent Gothic section and is housed in an ultramodern building that incorporates an 18th-century palace into its design. Closed Mondays. 2 Rázusovo nábrežie (phone: 332081/2).

**DEVÍN HRAD (DEVIN CASTLE)** This strategic border fortification of the Moravian Empire stands high on a promontory where the Morava River meets the Danube, just across from the Austrian border. There has been a settlement here since Neolithic times. The Celts used the site as a military stronghold, and the Romans later established a military post here. In 1809 Napoleon's troops reduced the castle to ruins; some parts have been reconstructed and are now open to the public. About 6 miles (10 km) west of the city. Closed November through March, and Mondays year-round.

**SLOVENSKÉ NARODNÉ MÚZEUM (SLOVAK NATIONAL MUSEUM)** Built in 1928, the museum houses exhibits of anthropology, archaeology, natural history, and Slovakian geology. Located across from the hydrofoil and ferry terminal on the Danube at 2 Vajanského nábrežie (phone: 332985 or 330791).

### EXTRA SPECIAL

Year-round, the Sunday *Philharmonic* concerts held at the concert hall in *Bratislava Castle* are a melodious way to wind up the weekend. Since these musical events are very popular, book with *BIS* (*Bratislavská Informačná Služba;* Bratislava Information Service) or *SATUR* (see below for information on both) before you arrive, or with your hotel's information desk as soon as you check in.

# Sources and Resources

TOURIST INFORMATION
For general information, maps, brochures, and details about group tours and bookings, contact *SATUR* (5-9 Jesenského ulica; phone: 367624; fax: 367645); closed Sundays. The staff here also can be helpful in obtaining hotel reservations.

General information about Bratislava is the domain of *BIS* (Bratislava Information Service; 18 Pánská; phone: 333715 or 334370), which also will arrange accommodations in hotels, pensions, and private homes as well as provide guides and translation services. The service desk at your hotel also may be helpful in booking tours, obtaining theater tickets, and making restaurant reservations. The *US Embassy and Consulate* is at 4 Hviezdoslavovo námesti (phone: 330861).

For information in the US, contact *Cedok/SATUR* (10 E. 40th St., Suite 3604, New York, NY 10016; phone: 212-689-9720; 800-800-8891; fax: 212-481-0597). The *Slovak Embassy and Consulate* is at 2201 Wisconsin Ave. NW, Suite 380, Washington, DC 20007 (phone: 202-965-5161).

**ENTRY REQUIREMENTS** A US citizen needs only a current passport for a visit of up to 30 days.

**TIME** The time in Slovakia is six hours later than in US East Coast cities. The Slovak Republic follows daylight saving time.

**LANGUAGE** Slovak is the native language of Slovakia, and is extremely similar to Czech (as well as related to Polish). Those engaged in tourism speak English, and Russian is widely understood.

**ELECTRIC CURRENT** 220 volts, 50 cycles, AC.

**MONEY** Slovakia's currency is called the koruna (ks; plural *koruny*). Export of the currency is prohibited. At press time $1 US was worth about 30 korun.

**TIPPING** Restaurant bills don't include service charges, and at least 10% should be added; taxi drivers also expect 10% tips; 5 to 10 koruny should be given to porters and doormen.

**BANKING/BUSINESS HOURS** Banks generally are open weekdays from 8 AM to 4 PM; some are open until 6 PM twice a week and until noon once a week. Branches of Všeobecná Uverová Banka (one is at 15 SNP námestie) will exchange Czech for Slovak *koruny* (crowns). There is a 24-hour electronic exchange machine at the north end of Michalská ulica; in addition, hotels generally have currency exchange desks. Most other businesses are open weekdays from 8 AM to 4 PM.

**NATIONAL HOLIDAYS** *New Year's Day* (January 1), *Easter Sunday* (April 16), *Easter Monday* (April 17), *Labor Day* (May 1), *Anniversary of World War II Liberation* (May 8), *National Holiday* (July 5), *Day of National Uprising of World War II* (August 29), *Christmas Day* (December 25), and *Boxing Day* (December 26).

**TELEPHONE** The city code for Bratislava is 7. When calling from one area to another within the Slovak Republic dial 0 + city code + local number. The country code for Slovakia is 42. In an emergency, dial 155 for an ambulance and 158 for the police.

## GETTING AROUND

**AIRPORT** Most major Czech, Slovak, and Eastern European cities are served from Bratislava's *M. R. Stefáník Airport,* about 5 miles (8 km) northeast of the city (phone: 220036). The airport is small and quaint—after disembarking, passengers must negotiate a long staircase before reaching passport control. Bus No. 24 connects *M. R. Stefáník Airport* with the rail station.

**BUS/TROLLEY** Tickets are available throughout the city in vending machines, at stations, and at most newspaper kiosks. There is a 24-hour tourist pass available at the *DPB Transportation Office* (Grösslingová and Sturová ulica). For destinations outside of Bratislava, buses depart from the *Central Bus Station* (Stanica námestie).

**CAR RENTAL** American and Czech automobiles may be rented through *Hertz* at the *Forum* hotel (phone: 348155). *Hertz* also has an office at the airport (phone: 291482), as does *Europcar* (phone: 220285). Better rates are to be found at *Recar* (1 Stefániková; phone: 333420) and *Budget* (32 Vysoká; phone: 220328).

**TAXI** Cabs are not hard to find in Bratislava, and can be hailed in the street or booked by your hotel service desk. Officially, payment is in the Slovak koruna, but dollars are also welcome. The fares are reasonable.

**TRAIN** The main railroad station is *Hlavná Stanica* (1 Dimitrovo námestie; phone: 204-4484).

## LOCAL SERVICES

The desks at most large hotels are the best places to inquire about special services. The *Danube* and *Forum Inter-Continental* hotels provide dry-cleaning and some business services (see *Checking In*). Hotel concierges can prove useful as translators.

**MEDICAL EMERGENCY** The number to call for an ambulance is 155. English is not always spoken; it's best to ask the service desk at any major hotel to make the call for you. Emergency medical aid is provided at the clinics at 6 Pionierská ulica (phone: 44444), 5 Mýtná ulica (phone: 46580), 3 Bebravská ulica (phone: 242461), and 1 Robniaková ulica (phone: 825043).

**PHARMACY** There are 24-hour pharmacies at 3 Spitálská ulica (phone: 321447), 9 Mýtná ulica (phone: 496515), and 1 Bebravská (phone: 242101).

**POST OFFICE** Located at 35 SNP námestie (phone: 278111).

## SPECIAL EVENTS

Bratislava is a city steeped in music and enriched by a long history of visits from the greats—Mozart, Haydn, Beethoven, and Liszt, to name just a few. The city honors this tradition by staging several music festivals throughout the spring, summer, and fall. For rock 'n' roll fans the *Bratislava Rock and Pop Festival* (formerly the *Bratislava Lyre*) features a series of concerts in early June. *Bratislava Jazz Days* are held in October, as is the *International Music Festival,* during which the beautiful *Reduta Philharmony* (2 Paleckého; phone: 333351) hosts classical performances almost every night.

## MUSEUMS

In addition to those mentioned in *Special Places,* there are other interesting Bratislava museums you may wish to visit. All those listed below charge a nominal admission.

**HUDOBNA EXPOZÍCIA RODNÝ DOM J. M. HUMMELA (HUMMEL MUSIC MUSEUM)** The birthplace and onetime home of Johann Hummel, an early-19th-century composer. Concerts are held outside the house on summer weekends. Closed Mondays. 2 Klobučnícká ulica.

**MÚZEUM HODIN (EXHIBITION OF HISTORICAL CLOCKS)** A large collection for the timepiece buff. Closed Tuesdays. 1 Zidovská ulica.

**MÚZEUM ROMANSKEJ KULTURY (MUSEUM OF ROMAN CULTURE)** A relatively new exhibit that features treasures from the excavations of the Roman settlement of Gerulata. Located in Rusovce, across the Danube and several miles south of Bratislava. Ask *BIS* for directions. Also on the site is the neo-Gothic mansion of the Zichy family and a park with rare and exotic trees.

**PÁLFFYHO PALÁC (PALFFY PALACE)** This 19th-century palace houses a branch of the *Municipal Gallery of Bratislava*, featuring a collection of 19th-century European art as well as 19th- and 20th-century Slovak art. Originally the home of the powerful Palffy family, the palace has been restored entirely and maintains portions of its original Celtic, Moravian, and Gothic details. Closed Mondays. 19 Pánská ulica (phone: 333627).

## SHOPPING
Souvenirs from Slovakia include lovely crystal and lavish, gold-rimmed china, particularly tea sets. *Dom Odievania* (30 SNP námestie) and *Kmart* (1 Kamenné námestie) are the city's main department stores, carrying these and other souvenir items. Keep an eye out for the blue- and yellow-painted ceramics known as majolica, as well as hand-painted *Easter* eggs and gingerbread ornaments. Fine handicraft items can be found at *UL'UV* (The Center for Folkcrafts; 17 SNP námestie; phone: 323802; and 4 Michalská ulica; phone: 277-2332). Boutique items and exquisite examples of Slovak ceramics, glass, and paintings are offered at the *Dielo Centrum* (12 SNP námestie; phone: 368648). Try *Folkfolk* (2 Rybárská Brána; phone: 334874) for crystal and Swiss army knives. A good buy is classical music on cassette tape and compact disc, and don't overlook the high-quality vinyl pressings from the Opus label. A small selection of books in English is available at *Mestská Knižnica* (2 Obchodná ulica; no phone) and at *Slovenská Kniha* (1 Rybárská ulica; no phone).

## SPORTS AND FITNESS
The *Forum Inter-Continental* hotel, a visitor's premier recreation venue, features a swimming pool, a fitness center, and massage and sauna facilities. The new *Danube* hotel also has a pool, fitness center, and sauna. See *Checking In* for both. Several outdoor swimming pools open to the public include *Tehelné Pole* (Odbojárov ulica), *Matador* (Udernícká ulica), and *Delfin* (18 Ružová Dolina). The three major indoor pools open to the public are *Pasienky* (Vavnorská ulica), *Central* (2 Miletičová ulica), and *Grössling* (3 Kúpelná).

## THEATER
"Sold out" in Bratislavan theater parlance doesn't necessarily mean that seats to the performance in question are unavailable. Simply go to the theater and ask to speak with an usher or other employee; you will be told to return half an hour before the performance, whereupon seats magically will be found for you.

For non-Slovak speakers one of Bratislava's best theater experiences is the experimental *Divadelný Súbor Stoka* (Gutter Theater; 1 Pribinová ulica; phone: 201-3161). Other innovative, nontraditional theater can be seen at the *Nová Scéna* (New Stage; 20 Kollarovo námestie; phone: 321139), *Theatre Astorka* (17 Suche mýto; phone: 324062); and *Stúdio's* (51 Maja námestie; phone: 499552). The *Státné Bábkové Divadlo* (State Puppet Theater; 36 Dunajská; phone: 323668 or 323834) is charming and a wonderful venue regardless of the language barrier.

The *Slovenské Národné Divadlo* (Slovak National Theater; 1 Hviezdoslavovo námestie; phone: 321146 or 333890) presents operas and ballets. Tickets are available at the corner of Jesenského ulica and Komneského námestie. It has a second site for drama at the *P. O. Hviezdoslav Theater* (21 Laurinská ulica; phone: 333083), while the *Malá Scéna* (Small Stage; 7 Dostojevského ulica; phone: 323775) presents more innovative productions.

MUSIC

The chamber music concerts held every Sunday at 10:30 AM at *Mirbachov Palác* (Františkánsko námestie; phone: 331556) are local favorites. The *Slovak Philharmonic* is one of the finest orchestras in Eastern Europe. Its performances of the works of Smetana, Dvořák, and other composers are immensely popular, so book in advance. Concerts are given at two locations in the city: the *Koncertná Sieň Slovenskej Filharmónie Reduta* (Reduta Theater; 2 Paleckého; phone: 333351) and the *Moyzesová Sieň Slovenskej Filharmónie* (Slovak Philharmonic Concert Hall; 12 Vajanského nábrežie; phone: 3564130). Other venues are the concert hall at *Bratislava Castle* (phone: 313020); the *Rozhlasové Slovenského Kultúrne Centrum* (Slovak Radio Concert Hall; 1 Mýtna; phone: 44462); *Zichyho Plác* (9 Venturská; no phone); and *Vel'ký Evanjelickyý Kostol* (Evangelical Church; Panenská ulica). Tickets for all events may be purchased at *Slovak Concert* (10 Michalská; phone: 334757).

NIGHTCLUBS AND NIGHTLIFE

After-dark entertainment in Bratislava has much improved in the past several years, with more clubs featuring a variety of options. The *Forum Inter-Continental* and *Devín* hotels (see *Checking In*) offer floor shows nightly. Aficionados of blues, jazz, and country music should try *Mefisto* (24 Panenská; no phone). For hip rock music, concerts, and other cultural events try the smoky cavern of *Zbrojnoša* (Zamočnická ulica; no phone). By far the best place to quaff a Budvar (beer), sample Slovak pub food, and listen to the region's *dechovňka* (polka), country, and jazz music is *Stará Sladovňa;* known locally as *"Mamut,"* it's billed as Eastern Europe's largest beer hall (Laurinská; no phone).

# Best in Town

CHECKING IN

Hotel reservations may be made through *SATUR* or your travel agent. Happily, the image of the dreary Eastern-bloc hotel does not apply to many properties in Bratislava. Some are surprisingly modern and well-appointed and offer many Western amenities. For a double room expect to pay $130 or more per night at a very expensive hotel; between $70 and $125 at an expensive place; $40 to $70 at a moderately priced hotel; and about $30 at an inexpensive place. Be aware that the Slovak government has imposed a 25% tax on hotel rooms, so check in advance to see whether or not that has been included in the price you are quoted. In all of the following hotels, guestrooms have private baths. All telephone numbers are in the 7 city code unless otherwise indicated.

**Danube** This modern French-built luxury property is located directly on the banks of the Danube. There are 280 rooms, 36 suites, and four deluxe apartments, all decorated in pastels. Guests also enjoy the *Pressbourg* restaurant, a café, a bar overlooking *Bratislava Castle,* a nightclub, and a fitness center with pool and sauna. Business facilities include meeting rooms for up to 300, secretarial services in English, audiovisual equipment, photocopiers, computers, cable television news, translation service, and express checkout. 1 Rybničné námestie (phone: 340000 or 340833; fax: 314311).

**Forum Inter-Continental Bratislava** This hotel is one of the best-staffed properties in Eastern Europe—they'll arrange everything from restaurant reservations to theater tickets, and offer advice on interesting sights and places to shop. The entrance and lobby are large and attractively decorated in glass and chrome. The 210 rooms and 11 suites are comfortable, and all have mini-bars and color TV sets. There's also a fitness center with a pool, gym, and solarium; three bars; a nightclub; and three restaurants serving French, Slovak, and Hungarian cuisines, including the first-rate *Slovakia* (see *Eating Out*). Business facilities include meeting rooms for up to 200, foreign currency exchange, secretarial services in English, and translation services. 2 Hodžovo námestie (phone: 348115; 800-327-0200; fax: 314645).

**Perugia** This new hotel in the center of the Old Town, specifically catering to the business traveler, offers 11 luxury rooms with satellite TV and mini-bar, as well as a grand suite. A glass atrium brimming with lush foliage welcomes visitors in the reception area. The restaurant serves local and continental cuisine; there is is also a café and a nightclub. Business facilities include a meeting room for up to 25, photocopiers, computers, and translation services. 5 Zelená ulica (phone/fax: 330719).

**Devín** In the center of the Old Town right on the Danube, this modern hotel has 98 rooms, five suites, and three restaurants—Chinese, French, and Slovak—plus a café, wine bar, and terrace. Business facilities include a meeting room for up to 20 and secretarial services in English. 4 Riečná (phone: 330851/2/3/4; fax: 330682).

**Bratislava** This is the largest hotel in the Bratislava vicinity, but it is about 3 miles (5 km) outside of town. Its modern facilities include 344 rooms, a restaurant, two bars, and a nightclub. Business facilities include meeting rooms for up to 250 and secretarial services in English. 9 Seberiniho ulica (phone: 239000; fax: 236420).

**Gracia** Anchored in the river near the *Slovak National Gallery,* this 29-room, three-story "botel" boasts a modern blue- and-black decor and surprisingly large and comfortable cabins, all equipped with telephones, color TV sets, and mini-bars. There is a restaurant featuring continental dishes, and a summer terrace for dining and dancing. Rázsovo nábrežie (phone: 332132 or 332430; fax: 332131).

**Zochová Chata** Located 22 miles (35 km) from the city, this typical wood-and-stone *chata* (mountain cottage) has 15 small, comfortable rooms. It is best known for its wood-adorned *Koliba* restaurant, featuring an open-pit barbecue for spit-roasted meat and live folk and Gypsy music. There's access to a nearby swimming pool, tennis courts, and ski facilities. 900-01 Modrá-Piesok, Modra (phone: 704-923919; fax: 704-92291).

### INEXPENSIVE

**Gremium** If basics are all that you need, then you'll do well to stay in one of the five simply furnished rooms of this new pension across from the *National Theater.* Downstairs is a café-gallery for cappuccino, as well as contemporary art, jewelry, and ceramics by local artists. There's also a delightful restaurant (see *Eating Out*) and a pool room. 11 Gorkého námestie (phone: 321818; fax: 330653).

---

## EATING OUT

Heavy peasant food is standard fare throughout the Slovak Republic. Great stews, goulash (a thick, spicy soup here), filling *kapustnica* or *kapustová polievka* (cabbage soup), goose liver, breaded cutlets, cabbage, and sauerkraut are in abundance. Many meals are accompanied by a *knedliky,* a large dumpling. A particular Slovak specialty is *bryndzové halušky,* a small dumpling stuffed with cheese made from sheep's milk. Pastries are lavish, occasionally fruit- or cream-filled. Note that fried potato pancakes are sold at outdoor stands throughout the city, and though they may not appear appetizing at first blush—they're served in grease-soaked napkins—they are delicious; restaurants frequently serve them with apple sauce and sour cream. On the lighter side, Slovakia's streams contain some excellent trout. In addition, look for *morčacie prsia,* lightly sautéed turkey breast, which is very popular on most menus. Some restaurants, particularly those in the better hotels, offer something resembling continental cuisine, but they generally are not as colorful or authentic as the local spots.

Bratislava is ideally located in the middle of the country's best wine region. It is, therefore, no coincidence that the city's *vináreň* wine restaurants are the best places to eat and drink. Though many feature Slovak music and costumes and have become tourist haunts, Bratislavans continue to frequent them because of the good food, grog, and warm atmosphere.

Slovaks brew their own beer, the well-known Sopvar and Corgonň, but Czech brands—Budvar and Pilsner Urquell—are widely available as well. Your Slovak hosts may ask you to drink a toast of *slivovitz* (plum brandy) before dinner, or you may opt for

---

*borovička*. Made from juniper berries, it is as fragrant as a freshly cut *Christmas* tree. Cafés and coffeehouses are also plentiful, a legacy of the Turks, who introduced thick, sludgy coffee to Vienna and Bratislava during the heyday of the Ottoman Empire.

For dinner for two, including wine, expect to pay $40 or more at a very expensive restaurant (excluding other drinks and tip); $30 to $40 at an expensive restaurant; $15 to $30 at a moderately priced place; and less than $15 at an inexpensive one. Unless otherwise specified, all restaurants are open for lunch and dinner. All restaurants are in the 7 city code unless otherwise indicated.

### VERY EXPENSIVE

**Casablanca** If you crave good, fresh seafood, this is the best place in town. Choose from a wide variety—lobster, salmon, crayfish, swordfish, and oysters. Open daily. Reservations necessary. Major credit cards accepted. 53 Jeseniová ulica (phone: 371767).

**Slovakia** The *Forum Inter-Continental*'s finest restaurant features Slovak specialties. Polite and congenial waiters wear colorful folk costumes and recommend various dishes. At lunch there's a salad bar (rare in this country). Local music enhances the cheery atmosphere. Open daily. Reservations necessary. Major credit cards accepted. 2 Hodžovo námestie (phone: 348111).

### EXPENSIVE

**Arkádia** This first class dining spot and café perched on the side of a hill below *Bratislava Castle* offers fine Slavic fare in formal surroundings. Try the *masováme na ražni* (mixed meats on skewers). A terrace open in summer affords beautiful views of the city. Open daily. Reservations necessary. Major credit cards accepted. Zámocká ulica (phone: 335650).

**Cervený Rak (Red Crayfish)** Historic *Michael's Gate* is adjacent to this sleek and modern restaurant-bar. In the summer dine in view of the tower in the garden terrace. Seafood lovers should indulge in the crab with béchamel sauce. Vegetarians are invited to taste the delicately prepared spinach crêpes with garlic and cream sauce. Open daily. Reservations advised. Major credit cards accepted. 26 Michalská ulica (phone: 331375).

### MODERATE

**Auspic** This former rowing club was designed in 1930 by renowned Slovak architect Emil Bellusa. The lower level is paneled in floor-to-ceiling glass that slides open during summer months for outdoor dining overlooking the Danube River. Fish is the house specialty, including fresh carp, pike, and trout. Fill up at the salad bar and try a Slovak favorite: fried turkey Cordon Bleu. Open daily. Reservations advised. Major credit cards accepted. 24 Viedenská cesta (phone: 850916).

**Cínská Reštaurácia Cchang-Ccheng** Decorated with red-tasseled Chinese lamps and colorful dragons, this is one of the newest restaurants in the city. Savor the crisp egg rolls and fried dumplings, and the stir-fried vegetables with rice noodles spiced just right. The friendly staff makes dining here a pleasure. Open daily. Reservations advised. Major credit cards accepted. 59 Palisady (phone: 322157).

**Gremium** The pleasant, comfortable setting makes this a favorite with couples and businesspeople alike. Try the *basta* for two (a heaping platter of pork, beef, and lightly fried turkey breast on a bed of fresh vegetables and fruit). Or perhaps the *bryndzové halušky* might satisfy your appetite. Open daily. No reservations. No credit cards accepted. At the *Gremium Hotel,* 11 Gorkého námestie (phone: 321818).

**Korzo** At this combination café-restaurant located across from the *Danube* hotel, a pianist accompanies the first-rate fare and fine service in the spacious, candlelit dining room. Try the traditional *tatranská pochútka na zemiakovej placke* (pork loin with potato pancakes). Open daily. Reservations advised. No credit cards accepted. 11 Hviezdoslavovo námestie (phone: 334974).

**Slovenská Reštauracia pod Machnačom** From the exterior it's just another cement bunker; the charming interior, however, is designed as a Slovak peasant cottage. Costumed waitresses serve generous portions of traditional Slovak fare, including *česnaková* (garlic) soup. Folk music is performed nightly. A beer hall with oak tables is located downstairs. Open daily. Reservations advised. No credit cards accepted. 42 L. Svobody nábrežie (phone: 314580 or 314219).

### INEXPENSIVE

**Kavárna U Lizsta (Café Lizst)** The front room boasts a piano player, the back offers views of a garden courtyard of the building where Franz Liszt once had a salon. The menu is varied, with such specialties as fried turkey breast, pasta, and huge salads. The Algerian, Parisian, and Russian coffees are a real treat. Open daily. No reservations or credit cards accepted. 1 Klariská (phone: 334343).

**Klaštorna Vinárieň (Monastery Wine Cellar)** One of the very best cafés in the city is located in the picturesque, vaulted cellars of a former monastery in the Old Town, its walls adorned with ancient manuscripts and other "brotherly" paraphernalia. The regional specialties are excellent, as is the selection of Slovak and Moravian wines and world-renowned Czech beer. Closed Sundays. Reservations unnecessary. No credit cards accepted. 2 Františkánsko námestie (phone: 338282).

**Reštauracia pod Baštou (Restaurant under the Tower)** This cheerful wine cellar with brick, vaulted ceilings and oak benches joins others lining the small street to the left of *Michael's Gate.* Well-cooked meals, low prices, and a good selection of wines make this a favorite of Bratislava natives. Try the *misa bašta* for two (pork, beef, and chicken with bacon and mushrooms). Open daily. Reservations unnecessary. No credit cards accepted. Pod Bašton ulica (phone: 331765).

---

# Brussels

## At-a-Glance

### SEEING THE CITY

The *Palais de Justice,* at Place Poelaert, is on a hill that offers a lovely overview of Brussels, especially the older section of town. The *Palais* is one of the largest edifices built in Europe during the 19th century; it's open weekdays; no admission charge (phone: 508-6111).

### SPECIAL PLACES

Most of the interesting sights in town are situated within the inner circle of boulevards that enclose the central section; a great majority lie in the rather small area between the Grand' Place and *Parc de Bruxelles* and can easily be covered on foot.

#### IN TOWN

**GRAND' PLACE** Considered by some to be Europe's most beautiful square, Grand' Place is the historic heart of Brussels. It was a marketplace in the Middle Ages, when it was known by its Dutch name, Grote Markt (Great Market, a name still used by Flemish Belgians today). Most of the square—with the exception of the *Hôtel de Ville* (see below)—was destroyed by Louis XIV's armies in 1695 during a 35-hour bombardment, but it was rebuilt within three years.

Also around the square are the *Maison du Roi* (see below) and the guild halls, which were built between 1696 and 1698, after the originals were destroyed in 1695. Among the guilds represented are bakers, boatmen, haberdashers, butchers, and brewers.

Wander through the narrow, cobbled streets leading off the square. Their names—Rue du Pain/Broodstraat (Bread Street), Rue du Poivre or Peperstraat (Pepper Street), Rue au Beurre/Boterstraat (Butter Street)—date from when this area was one vast marketplace. And don't miss the bird market and the flower market, both held in the Grand' Place on Sunday mornings.

**HÔTEL DE VILLE (TOWN HALL)** Considered a symbol of the city's freedom, this Gothic structure (whose name in Dutch is *Stadhuis*) is one of the finest examples of 15th-century European architecture. Its spire (rebuilt after the 1695 bombardment) is topped by a statue of St. Michael, the city's patron saint. Inside is an excellent collection of tapestries. Open three days a week for guided tours only: Tuesdays from 10 to 11:30 AM, Wednesdays from 1:30 to 3:15 PM, and Sundays from 10 AM to 12:15 PM. Admission charge. Grand' Place (phone: 512-7554).

**MAISON DU ROI (KING'S HOUSE)** This historic building, which was rebuilt in the 1870s after being destroyed in the 1695 bombardment, stands on the site of a 13th-century bread market (its name in Dutch, *Brood-*

*huis,* means "Bread House"). It now houses the *Musée Communal* (Municipal Museum), which has exhibitions on the history and archaeology of the city. There also are examples of the applied arts of Brussels, such as tapestry, lace, and goldwork, and a display of the clothing for the *Manneken-Pis* (see below). Closed Fridays and weekend afternoons. Admission charge. Grand' Place (phone: 511-2742).

**MAISON DES BRASSEURS (BREWERY MUSEUM)** Set in the building of the ancient brewers' guild is a collection of old beer making equipment. Next door is a drinking house where you can taste the various beers. Open daily. Admission charge. 10 Grand' Place (phone: 511-4987).

**MANNEKEN-PIS** Jérôme Duquesnoy's small bronze statue of an impudent little boy urinating has stood southwest of the Grand' Place since 1619 and has become a symbol of the city's spirit. The statue has over 400 suits of clothing (which he sometimes wears), given to him by everybody from Louis XV of France to the Boy Scouts of America and the Allied Armies of World War II; they're displayed at the *Maison du Roi* (see above). Rue de l'Etuve, just off the Grand' Place.

**JEANNEKE-PIS** The female counterpart to *Manneken-Pis,* this fountain was created in 1985 by Denis Adrien Debouvrie to symbolize loyalty. In a little alley off the Rue des Bouchers, Impasse de la Fidélité.

**GALERIES ST-HUBERT** Built in 1847, this is the oldest shopping arcade in Europe. Located just north of the Grand' Place, it features elegant shops and restaurants. The nearby streets, such as the quaint, narrow Petite Rue des Bouchers, are known for their many dining establishments. Rue du Marché-aux-Herbes.

**PARC DE BRUXELLES (BRUSSELS PARK)** Near the *Musée d'Art Ancien* (see below), this historic park was the hunting ground of the Dukes of Brabant. It was laid out in the formal French manner during the 18th century. The *Palais du Roi,* the office of the sovereign, overlooks the park just east of the Place Royale, an elegant neoclassical square.

**MUSÉE D'ART ANCIEN (MUSEUM OF OLD MASTERS)** This is a large collection of paintings, mostly Flemish, from the 14th to the 17th centuries. Included are the works of Rubens, the Breughels, and Van Dyck, among others. Closed Mondays and public holidays. No admission charge. 3 Rue de la Régence (phone: 508-3211).

**MUSÉE D'ART MODERNE (MUSEUM OF MODERN ART)** Next to the *Musée d'Art Ancien,* this building showcases an extensive collection of art from 1880 to the present, including paintings by Picasso, Dalí, and De Chirico, along with works by Belgium's greatest modern artists— among them Paul Delvaux, James Ensor, and René Magritte. Together, the two museums form the *Musée des Beaux-Arts* (Royal Museums of Fine Arts), one of Europe's most impressive art complexes. Closed Mondays and public holidays. No admission charge. 1-2 Pl. Royale (phone: 508-3211).

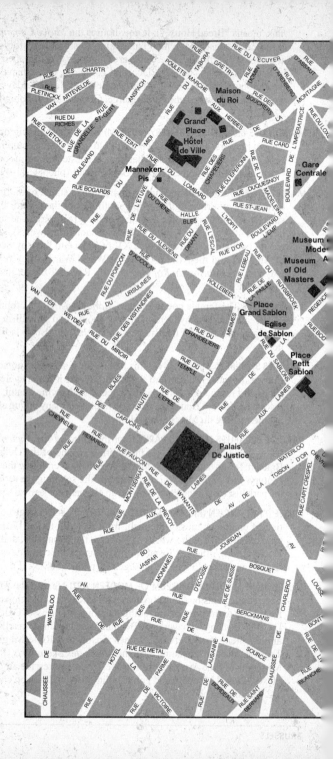

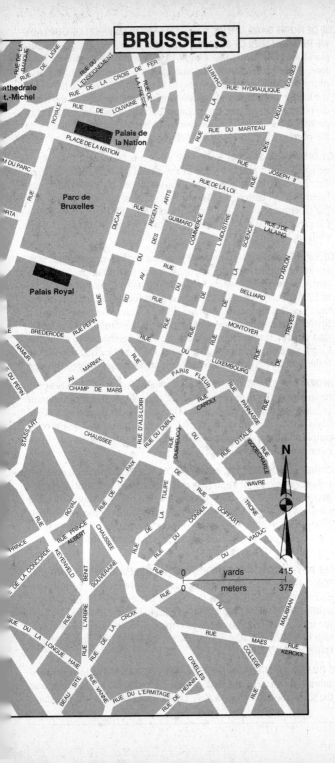

**EGLISE DE NOTRE DAME DES VICTOIRES DU SABLON (CHURCH OF OUR LADY OF THE VICTORIES OF SABLON)** This 15th-century church is an outstanding example of late Gothic architecture. According to local lore, a woman from Antwerp was told in a vision to bring a statue of the Virgin Mary from Antwerp to Brussels. The woman presented the statue to the guild of crossbowmen who practiced in the Place du Grand-Sablon, and their chapel became a popular pilgrimage destination. So many people came that in 1400 work was begun on the present church. Pl. du Petit-Sablon.

**PLACE DU GRAND-SABLON** Below the church is the heart of the city's antiques center, also the scene of a weekend book and antiques market. The bustling streets of this district (called Zavel in Dutch) are lined with art galleries, antiques shops, cafés, and restaurants. Just off the square is the Romanesque church of *Notre-Dame-de-la-Chapelle,* burial place of painter Pieter Breughel the Elder and the philosopher Spinoza.

**PLACE DU PETIT-SABLON** This square is dotted with 48 small bronze statues representing the medieval trade guilds. A formal garden slopes down from *Notre Dame du Sablon* and contains statues of the Counts of Egmont and Hoorn. In 1568 these great Flemish (Catholic) noblemen were beheaded in the Grand' Place for protesting to Philip II of Spain (who ruled the Low Countries at that time) about the persecution of Protestants. Egmont's courage was celebrated in a play by Goethe and an overture by Beethoven. Off the Place du Petit-Sablon is the Rue des Six-Jeunes-Hommes, which has some lovely old houses.

**CATHÉDRALE DE ST-MICHEL** Sitting majestically on top of a hill near the town center, the 13th-century Gothic national cathedral of Belgium is one of the oldest buildings in Brussels. Its 16th-century stained glass windows were donated by Emperor Charles V. The Baroque pulpit and the mausoleums also are worthy of note. Bd. de l'Impératrice at Pl. Ste-Gudule.

**COLONNE DU CONGRÈS (CONGRESS COLUMN)** Near the cathedral, the column was built in 1850 to honor the national constitutional congress held after the 1830 revolution. On top is a statue of King Leopold I. In front is the eternal flame that burns in memory of soldiers killed in both world wars. From the esplanade there is a good view of the entire city. Rue Royale, north of the *Cathédrale de St-Michel* at Pl. du Congrès.

**MUSÉES ROYAUX D'ART ET HISTOIRE (ROYAL MUSEUMS OF ART AND HISTORY)** In the *Parc du Cinquantenaire* (see below) at the northern end of town, this is one of the largest museums of its kind. It has exhibits on ancient civilizations, Belgian history and folklore, and the useful and decorative arts in Europe. Closed Mondays and certain holidays. No admission charge. 10 *Parc du Cinquantenaire* (phone: 741-7211).

**PARC DU CINQUANTENAIRE (FIFTIETH ANNIVERSARY PARK)** In a northern suburb of Brussels, this park (whose Dutch name is *Jubelpark*) was the site of the *1958 World's Fair.* The symbol of the fair was the *Atom-*

*ium,* a structure that represents an iron molecule magnified 165 billion times. There's an elevator to a restaurant at the top of the structure and escalators to various spheres with exhibits—most are dated now—on the peaceful uses of atomic energy. There also is a group of exhibit halls dating from the *1935* and *1958 World's Fairs.* Also on the site is the *Bruparck,* comprised of the *Oceadium,* an indoor aquatic amusement park; *Kinepolis,* with 23 movie theaters under one roof; the *Village,* whose cafés, restaurants, shops, and playground all evoke Brussels of the past; and *Mini-Europe,* with 400 models (scaled 1:25) of the Continent's most famous landmarks. Open daily. Admission charge. Heysel, Laeken (phone 477-0977).

## ART NOUVEAU

This city has many important examples of the sinuously graceful turn-of-the-century architectural style known as Art Nouveau. The *Musée Horta* (Horta Museum; 25 Rue Américaine; phone: 537-1692) was the museum/workshop of architect Victor Horta, one of Art Nouveau's foremost proponents. It's open from 2 to 5:30 PM; closed Mondays and holidays; admission charge. The *Hôtel Solvay* (224 Av. Louise), *Maison Stoclet* (281 Av. de Tervuren), and *Hôtel Tassel* (6 Rue Paul-Emile Janson, now the *Mexican Embassy*) are probably the most famous private buildings in the Art Nouveau style. Special group visits to the *Hôtel Solvay* and *Hôtel Tassel* occasionally are arranged by the *Musée Horta* (Horta Museum); the *Maison Stoclet* cannot be visited. Among the public Art Nouveau buildings worth seeing are two hotels, the *Astoria* (103 Rue Royale; phone: 217-6290) and the *Métropole* (31 Pl. de Brouckère; phone: 217-2300); a restaurant, *De Ultième Hallucinatie* (316 Rue Royale; phone: 217-0614); and the *Falstaff Café* (25-27 Rue Henri-Maus; phone: 511-8789). Excellent specialized tours can be arranged through *ARAU* (phone: 513-4761), which offers an assortment of architectural itineraries, or *Chatterbus* (phone: 673-1835), which offers three-hour guided tours on foot and public transportation from near the Grand' Place.

### ENVIRONS

**MAISON D'ERASME (ERASMUS'S HOUSE)** This was not, in fact, the house of the famous humanist, but the home of a friend, where Erasmus stayed in about 1521. Nevertheless, this residence evokes his spirit. Rooms are richly furnished in 16th-century style; there's a library and a walled garden as well as documents that illustrate Erasmus's life and work.

The house also includes a small but excellent collection of Renaissance paintings, including Hans Holbein's portrait of Erasmus. Closed Tuesdays and Fridays. Admission charge. 31 Rue du Chapitre, in the southwestern suburb of Anderlecht (phone: 521-1383).

**EGLISE DE SS PIERRE ET GUIDON (CHURCH OF ST. PETER AND ST. GUY)** Also in Anderlecht, not far from the *Maison d'Erasme,* is the this 15th-century Gothic church with an ancient crypt and Renaissance wall paintings. Place de la Vaillance, Anderlecht (phone: 521-8415). Just north of the church on Rue du Chapelain is a Flemish *begijnhof* (convent), founded in 1252 and restored in 1956 to its original appearance.

**WATERLOO** The site of the famous battle is only 12 miles (19 km) south of the city and is accessible by bus. If you climb the *Butte du Lion* (Lion Monument), you can see a somewhat obstructed view of the battlefield itself. Nearby there is a *Centre du Visiteur de la Bataille de Waterloo* (Battle of Waterloo Visitors' Center; Route du Lion; phone: 385-1912). It's open daily; admission charge.

A better sense of the battle can be gained from a visit to the town of Waterloo, which is about 2 miles (3 km) north of the battlefield. The *Wellington Museum* (147 Chaussée de Bruxelles; phone: 354-7806), once Wellington's headquarters, is very informative. It's open daily; admission charge.

To mark the 180th anniversary of the battle, this year during the weekend of June 17 and 18 the town of Waterloo will stage a sound-and-light show, a re-enactment, and a parade of period-clad thousands.

**VILLERS-LA-VILLE** The ruins of this 12th-century Cistercian abbey include the dining hall and brewery. Open weekends only from November through March; daily the rest of the year. Admission charge. About 15 miles (24 km) south of Waterloo (phone: 71-879555).

**CHÂTEAU DE BEERSEL (BEERSEL CASTLE)** This early-14th-century brick château-fort, set in the middle of a moat, has the obligatory drawbridge, lookout tower, and torture room. Closed January, Mondays from March to mid-November, and weekdays the rest of the year. Admission charge. Ten miles (16 km) south of Brussels (phone: 331-0024).

**GAASBEEK CASTLE** This historic 13th-century castle (many times restored) is 6 miles (10 km) southwest of Brussels. Though its exterior, with seven round towers, is medieval, its interior contains Renaissance tapestries, furniture, and objets d'art. The view from the garden terrace was painted by Breughel the Elder. It may be visited by guided tour only. Closed Mondays from April through October and Fridays year-round. Admission charge. 12 Groenstr., Lennik (phone: 532-4372).

# Sources and Resources

## TOURIST INFORMATION

For excellent maps and leaflets, calendars of tourist events, and assistance of any sort, visit the main office of the *Commisariat-*

*Générale au Tourisme/Commissariaat-Generaal voor Toerisme* (Belgian National Tourist Office; 63 Rue Marché aux Herbes; phone: 504-0390; fax: 504-0270) or the *Tourisme Information Bruxelles/Toerisme Informatie Brussel* (Brussels Tourist Office; in the *Hôtel de Ville,* Grand' Place; phone: 513-8940 or 513-8946; fax: 514-4091). Both are identifiable by green "i" signs jutting out of the façade. The *US Embassy and Consulate* is at 27 Bd. du Régent (phone: 513-3830).

For information in the US, contact the *Belgian Tourist Office* (780 Third Ave., New York, NY 10017; phone: 212-758-8130; fax: 212-355-7675). The *Belgian Embassy* is at 3330 Garfield St. NW, Washington, DC 20008 (phone: 202-333-6900).

**ENTRY REQUIREMENTS** A US citizen needs a current passport for a stay of up to 90 days.

**TIME** The time in Belgium is six hours later than in US East Coast cities. Belgium observes daylight saving time.

**LANGUAGE** Belgium has three official languages: Dutch (spoken by the Flemish), French (spoken by the Walloons), and German (spoken by a small minority). English is widely understood.

**ELECTRIC CURRENT** 220 volts, 50 cycles, AC.

**MONEY** The Belgian franc (BF) equals 100 centimes. At press time one US dollar was equal to 32.34 Belgian francs.

**TIPPING** A 16% service charge is added to restaurant bills and also is included on taxi meters; additional tipping is unnecessary. More and more hotels are including service charges on their bills. If they are not included, 50 BF per bag should suffice for bellhops; 100 BF per day for chambermaids. Railway station porters charge a fixed fee of 20 to 25 BF per bag. Restroom attendants expect at least 7 BF; coatroom attendants, 20 to 50 BF per article. Barber and beauty shop bills often include the tip.

**BANKING/BUSINESS HOURS** Most banks are open weekdays from 9 AM to 3 or 4 PM; some banks are open later on Fridays. Most other businesses are open weekdays from 9 AM to 5 PM; some banks and businesses close for an hour between noon and 2 PM.

**NATIONAL HOLIDAYS** *New Year's Day* (January 1), *Easter Sunday* (April 16), *Easter Monday* (April 17), *Labor Day* (May 1), *Ascension Thursday* (May 25), *Whitmonday* (June 5), *Independence Day* (July 21), *Feast of the Assumption* (August 15), *All Saints' Day* (November 1), *Armistice Day* (November 11), and *Christmas Day* (December 25).

**LOCAL COVERAGE** The best English-language publication is *The Bulletin,* a weekly in a newsmagazine format. It's available at local newsstands.

**TELEPHONE** The city code for Brussels and surrounding areas is 2. When calling from one area to another within Belgium dial 0 + city code

+ local number. The country code for Belgium is 32. In an emergency, dial 100 for an ambulance; 101 for the police.

## GETTING AROUND

**AIRPORT** *Aéroport Nationale de Bruxelles* (Brussels National Airport) at Zaventem (it's sometimes referred to simply as *Zaventem Airport*) is a 20-minute drive from downtown. At press time the airport was being expanded; the project should be completed by next year. Greater Brussels taxis (see *Taxi,* below) are more economical than those parked at the airport, but you must call for a pickup. An efficient train service links the airport directly with the city center; it operates every 20 to 30 minutes from 5:39 AM to 11:46 PM. City buses marked BZ or 3586 run from *Zaventem Airport* to the *Gare du Nord/Noord Station* (North Station).

**BUS, TRAM, AND MÉTRO** A detailed map is available at the tourist office. Fares are 50 Belgian francs (about $1.50 at press time) a ride; you can save money by purchasing a one-day unlimited ticket (120 Belgian francs, about $3.70), a five-ride card (230 francs/$7), or a ten-ride card (305 francs/$9.35). One of these cards is called simply a *carte* in French and a *metrokaart* in Dutch.

**CAR RENTAL** All major firms are represented.

**TAXI** Taxis are plentiful but expensive. The tip is included in the fare. You can pick one up at a taxi stand, or call *Autolux* (phone: 411-1221), *Taxis Oranges* (phone: 513-6200), or *Taxis Verts* (phone: 349-4949).

## LOCAL SERVICES

**DENTIST (ENGLISH-SPEAKING)** Dr. G. Trice (8 Bd. Brand-Whitlock; phone: 733-3314); or call the *Service de Garde Dentaire* (Dental Help Service; phone: 426-1026).

**DRY CLEANER/TAILOR** *DeGeest* (37-41 Rue de l'Hôpital; phone: 512-5978).

**LIMOUSINE SERVICE** *François Jacobs* (60 Rue F.-Séverin; phone: 215-9859) for chauffeured Mercedes-Benzes.

**MEDICAL EMERGENCY** *CUL, Cliniques Universitaires St-Luc* (10 Av. Hippocrates; phone: 764-1111). For emergency service dial 100.

**MESSENGER SERVICE** *Eurocolis* (130 Rue Picard; phone: 425-3801). Brussels taxi drivers also perform this service; call *Taxi Verts* (phone: 349-4949).

**NATIONAL/INTERNATIONAL COURIER** *DHL Worldwide Express* (210 Kosterstraat, Machelen-Diegem; phone: 720-9500); *Federal Express* (Building 119, 1820 Nelsbroek; phone: 752-7111).

**PHARMACY** *Grande Pharmacie de Brouckère* (10-12 Passage du Nord; phone: 218-0575). Pharmacies are open weekdays and Saturdays from 9 AM to 6:30 PM; they operate on a rotation basis for night and weekend service (at least one per neighborhood is on weekend duty).

**PHOTOCOPIES** *D-Copy* (17-25 Rue des Vierges; phone: 512-7010).

**POST OFFICE** *Monnaie Center* (Pl. de la Monnaie; phone: 226-2111), open Mondays through Saturdays from 8 AM to 8 PM; *Gare du Midi* (48A Av. Fonsny; phone: 538-4000) for 24-hour service.

**SECRETARY/STENOGRAPHER (ENGLISH-SPEAKING)** *Regus Business Center* (25A Bessenveldstraat; phone: 716-4711; 65 Ave. Louise; phone: 535-7800; and 45 Rue de Teves; phone: 238-7800); *Wings* (51 Rue Dejoncku; phone: 537-7240).

**TELECONFERENCE FACILITIES** *Hilton International Brussels* (see *Checking In*).

**TELEX** *Belgacom* (19 Bd. de l'Impératrice; phone: 511-6551), open from 8 AM to 10 PM.

**OTHER** Office space rental: *Burotel Belgium* (4 Rue de la Presse; phone: 217-8080); *European Business Facilities* (55 Blvd. Général Wahlis; phone: 511-7290). Tuxedo rental: *John Kennis* (12 Av. Marnix; phone: 513-2303).

## SPECIAL EVENTS
Brussels is the venue for a number of delightful activities.

---

### FAVORITE FÊTE

**Festival van Vlaanderen (Flanders Festival)** One of Europe's major music festivals, this event takes place from spring into October in several Belgian towns, with concerts often held in the towns' most beautiful buildings. During August, September, and early October, the festival comes to Brussels, bringing with it internationally known orchestras, soloists, operas, and dance companies. Tickets are reasonably priced. For information write to the *Festival of Flanders,* 18 Eugène Flageyplein, Brussels 1050 (phone: 640-1525).

---

In addition, each February the *Palais des Beaux-Arts* (23 Rue Ravenstein; phone: 512-5045) hosts the *Foire des Antiquaires de Belgique,* a two-week antiques fair featuring an array of pieces collected by antiques dealers around the country. Every spring, usually for two weeks straddling April and May, the *Serres Royales de Laeken* (Laeken Royal Palace Greenhouses) are open to the public. Located in Laeken, just a few miles north of downtown Brussels, the indoor gardens feature exotic flowering trees and plants. Call the tourist office for exact dates and hours. Starting officially in late June, but with a series of park concerts dubbed "kiosks à musique" beginning a month earlier, is the annual *Festival Musical d'Eté* (Summer Music Festival).

The *Ommegang* pageant takes place in the Grand' Place on the first Thursday in July at 9 PM. It is a centuries-old spectacle commemorating the miraculous arrival of a statue of the Virgin in the Sablon church. The word *ommegang* means "walk around." The oldest and noblest families take part in the procession, which is done much as it was in the 16th century. This splendid tradition is one of Belgium's most popular attractions. Tickets for bleacher seats go fast; see the tourist office for details.

The *Festival de Wallonie* (Festival of Wallonia), the Walloon counterpart to the *Flanders Festival,* takes place in June; contact the festival office for details (29 Rue du Jardin Botanique, Liège 4000; phone: 41-223248). There's also a month-long summer fair (mid-July to mid-August) on the Boulevard du Midi, featuring rides and local foods. In August, when the royal couple take their vacation, the ornate sitting rooms and splendid ballroom of the *Palais Royale* (Royal Palace, called the *Koninklijk Paleis* in Dutch), in front of the *Parc du Bruxelles,* are open to the public at no charge.

Every other year in September and October, Brussels has produced its own international arts festival, *Europalia.* The events focus on a single nation and attract the top names in their respective fields. The next festival, with Turkey as its subject, will take place in 1996.

## MUSEUMS

Besides those mentioned in *Special Places,* the following are some of the city's more interesting museums.

**AUTOWORLD** A spectacular collection of vintage cars. Closed *Christmas* and *New Year's Day.* Admission charge. Esplanade du Cinquantenaire, Etterbeek (phone: 736-4165).

**BIBLIOTHÈQUE ROYALE ALBERT I (ALBERT I ROYAL LIBRARY)** More than three million volumes as well as coins, maps, and splendid illuminated manuscripts are housed here. Closed Sundays, holidays, and the last week of August. No admission charge. Mont des Arts (phone: 519-5311).

**CENTRE BELGE DE LA BANDE DESSINÉE (BELGIAN CENTER OF THE COMIC STRIP)** Set in a cast-iron Art Nouveau building designed by Victor Horta, this museum features the work of many Belgian artists—including Hergé, who created the cartoon character Tintin. Closed Mondays, November 1, *Christmas Day*, and *New Year's Day.* Admission charge. 20 Rue des Sables (phone: 219-1980).

**MUSÉE COMMUNAL DES BEAUX ARTS D'IXELLES (MUSEUM OF FINE ARTS OF IXELLES)** Splendid Dürers, Toulouse-Lautrec posters, and works of French and Belgian Impressionists are featured. Closed Mondays, weekday mornings, and public holidays. No admission charge to the permanent collection. 71 Rue Jean-van-Volsem, Ixelles (phone: 511-9084).

**MUSÉE DU COSTUME ET DE LA DENTELLE (COSTUME AND LACE MUSEUM)** Exhibitions on the history of lace making in Brussels. The city's lace industry once employed 15,000 workers, producing some of the most intricate examples of the art. Open daily. Admission charge. 6 Rue de la Violette (phone: 512-7709).

**MUSÉE INSTRUMENTAL (MUSEUM OF MUSICAL INSTRUMENTS)** A collection of some 5,000 instruments from the Bronze Age to the present. Open Tuesday through Friday afternoons, plus Sunday mornings. No admission charge. 17 Pl. du Petit-Sablon (phone: 512-0848).

**MUSÉE ROYAL DE L'AFRIQUE CENTRALE (ROYAL MUSEUM OF CENTRAL AFRICA)** The brainchild of colonialist King Leopold II, it has an art gallery and a panorama of African life. Closed Mondays. No admission charge. 13 Leuvensesteenweg, Tervuren (phone: 769-5211).

**MUSÉE DES SCIENCES NATURELLES (MUSEUM OF NATURAL SCIENCE)** Noteworthy for its collection of well-preserved dinosaur skeletons, unearthed in western Belgium in 1878. Closed Mondays. Admission charge. 29 Rue Vautier, Ixelles (627-4211).

**PAVILLON CHINOIS (CHINESE PAVILION)** A first-rate collection of 17th- and 18th-century Chinese and Japanese porcelain. Closed Mondays and public holidays. Admission charge. 44 Av. Van Praet, Laeken (phone: 268-1608).

## SHOPPING

Brussels is not a city for bargain hunters, but you will get top quality for the price. Here and in other Belgian cities, look for Val St-Lambert, one of the world's finest crystals. Pewter and linen also are excellent values. Leather goods and women's clothing are *très* chic and equally *cher.* All the top couturiers are represented. Lace is abundant, especially in the souvenir shops around the Grand' Place. Some of the women who made Brussels lace world famous still are working, but alas, much of the lace now is machine-made in Hong Kong. This lace usually is used on cocktail napkins and placemats, which make inexpensive, easily portable gifts. Look carefully at tags to know what you are buying. Belgian carpets usually are made to a very high standard. In most cases, they are mechanically produced and offer a wide variety of styles and materials. To make sure that you're getting the best, look for the "T" mark on the carpet backing.

Most antiques are of excellent quality. The streets near the Place du Grand-Sablon (Rue Watteau, Rue Lebeau, Rue Ernest-Allard) are full of interesting shops, as is Chausée d'Ixelles, which runs roughly parallel to the Avenue Louise. Or try the Saturday and Sunday antiques and books market at the Place du Grand-Sablon. Usually there are some lovely things there, so it's fun even if you are "just looking."

Although there are fine shops all over the city, there are two main shopping districts. Shops with more modest prices are found in the area including the Boulevard Adolphe-Max, the Boulevard Anspach, Rue Neuve, Rue Marché-aux-Herbes, and Galeries St-Hubert. The other shopping district, where the chic boutiques are located, includes Avenue Louise, Avenue de la Toison d'Or, and the Boulevard de Waterloo. *Les Jardins du Sablon* (at 36 Pl. du Sablon and 6 Rue des Minimes) houses 36 shops and a tearoom under its skylit cupola. Anderlecht, a suburb of Brussels, has one of the largest suburban shopping centers in Europe.

Flea market shoppers enjoy the *Marché de la Brocante* at the Place du Jeu de Balle (Vossenplein) daily from 7 AM to 2 PM. The *Antiques Market* is held on Saturdays and Sundays from 9 AM to 2 PM at the Place du Grand-Sablon. Bimonthly auctions, featuring high-quality items, are held at the *Galerie Moderne* (3 Rue du Parnasse; phone: 513-9010). Another reputable auction house is *Nova* (35 Rue du Pépin; phone: 512-2494). A good place to get a sampling of everything is at *L'Innovation* (also known as *Inno*), Brussels's finest department store (111 Rue Neuve; phone: 211-2111). Standard shopping hours are 9 AM to 6 PM weekdays. Other shops to explore:

**Art et Sélection** Famous Val St-Lambert crystal. 83 Rue Marché-aux-Herbes (phone: 511-8448).

**Biot-Believre** Linen tablecloths and the like, hand embroidered on request. Rue Vilain XIV (phone: 646-9536).

**La Boutique de Tintin** Belgium's most famous comic strip character, the beloved early-20th-century boy reporter Tintin, appears on posters, jewelry, T-shirts, and other memorabilia (though these same Tintin knickknacks are available at lower prices elsewhere around the Grand' Place). 13 Rue de la Colline (phone: 514-4550).

**CBRS** The best of Belgian carpets from a variety of manufacturers. 431 Bd. Emile-Bockstael (phone: 479-9944).

**Corné Toison d'Or** Belgian chocolates for the connoisseur. 12 Av. de la Toison d'Or (phone: 512-8947), 24-26 Galerie du Roi (phone: 512-4984), and several other locations.

**Degand Tailleur-Chemisier** Fine men's suits, shirts, and accessories by Chester Barrie, Zimmerli, and Ballantyne, as well as tailor-made clothes. Degand's mother, Yvonne, runs the women's shop on the top floor. 415 Av. Louise (phone: 649-0073).

**Delvaux** *The* place for leather goods. 31 Galerie de la Reine (phone: 512-7198); 22-24 Bd. Adolphe-Max (phone: 217-4234); and 24A Av. de la Toison-d'Or (phone: 513-0502).

**Euroline** Watches, flags, umbrellas, and other souvenirs bearing the European Union flag emblem of 15 yellow stars on a blue field. 55 Blvd. A. Maxlaan (phone: 218-2993).

**F. Rubbrecht** Exquisite lace and linen. 23 Grand' Place (phone: 512-0218).

**Madymous** Official distributor of Huy pewter, considered Belgium's best. Look for the Huy hallmark (the town's castle mark) to be sure. 42B-C-D Rue du Noyer (phone: 733-5065 or 732-2358).

**Manufacture Belge de Dentelles** Lace and lace making demonstrations. 6-8 Galerie de la Reine (phone: 511-4477).

**Mary** The most exclusive chocolate-maker in Belgium, *chocolatier* to the royal court. 73 Rue Royale (phone: 217-4500).

**Rose's Lace** Blouses and lingerie made of Belgian lace and linen. 1 Rue des Brasseurs (phone: 512-1126).

**Textilux Center** Brussels tapestries in traditional and modern designs. 41 Rue du Lombard, near the *Manneken-Pis* (phone: 513-5015).

**Top Mouton** Chic home furnishings and accessories by top European and American designers. The English-speaking staff is knowledgeable and friendly. Galerie de la Reine (phone: 513-3599).

**Wittamer** Delectable chocolates and pastries. 12-16 Pl. du Grand-Sablon (phone: 512-3742).

**Wolfers** Fine jewelry and diamonds. 14 Blvd. Waterloo (phone: 511-6525 or 513-6150).

## SPORTS AND FITNESS

**FITNESS CENTERS** The facilities at the *Hilton International,* the *Radisson SAS Royal,* and the *Brussels Sheraton* can be used for a fee (see *Checking In*). The *Woluwé* sports center (near the *Forêt de Soignes* at 87 Av. Mounier; phone: 762-8522) has an Olympic-size swimming pool; there's an admission charge.

**GOLF** The *Royal Golf Club de Belgique* (Château de Ravenstein, Tervuren; phone: 767-5801) is the royal diplomats' club. The facilities are first-rate and only 7 miles (11 km) from downtown.

**HORSEBACK RIDING** Try *Royal Etrier Belge* (19 Chaussée du Vert-Chasseur; phone: 374-2860), or contact the *Fédération Royale Belge des Sports Equestres* (38 Av. Hamoir; phone: 374-4734).

**JOGGING** Best is *Parc de Bruxelles,* opposite the *Palais Royale* and bordered by Rue Royale (see *Special Places*). *Parc du Cinquantenaire* (take the *Métro* to the *Schuman* station and you'll spot the park just ahead) is larger. About a mile away on Avenue de Tervuren is the hilly *Parc Woluwé* (Woluwé Park; take tram No. 44 from the *Montgomery Métro* station). Farther afield is the *Forêt de Soignes* (Royal Forest; *Zoniënwoud* in Dutch), just outside the city (take tram No. 44 and signal the driver to stop as the woodland comes into sight). Due to the traffic, jogging is not recommended on the streets of Brussels. A 20-km race is held in June at the *Parc du Cinquantenaire (Jubelpark)* and the *Brussels Marathon* takes place each September.

**SOCCER** Known as football here, this is the city's most popular spectator sport. Major games are played at *Stadi Heysel* (Heysel Stadium; 135 Av. du Marathon; phone: 478-9300).

**SWIMMING** There are pools at *Bains de Bruxelles* (28 Rue du Chevreuil; phone: 511-2468); *Calypso* (60 Av. L.-Wiener, Boitsfort; phone: 673-3929); and *Poséidon* (2 Av. des Vaillants, Woluwé-St-Lambert; phone: 771-6655).

**TENNIS** Try the *Brussels Lawn Tennis Club* (890 Chaussée de Waterloo; phone: 374-9259).

## THEATER

The marionette theater, *de Toone* (21 Petite Rue des Bouchers; phone: 513-5486), is a must. Popular plays with puppet "actors" are performed in Brussels slang nightly except Sundays. Brussels has more than 20 theaters staging a variety of plays; most modern plays are in French or Dutch, though occasionally there is some amateur theater in English. Check the daily newspapers for schedules.

## MUSIC

One of the world's most prestigious music competitions is the *Concours Reine Elisabeth,* named for the grandmother of the present king. It takes place in May and usually is covered by TV and radio.

The *Théâtre Royal de la Monnaie* (Royal Mint Theater; Pl. de la Monnaie; phone: 218-1202) is the home of opera and ballet in Brussels, but it also is an important part of its history. The original building was built in the late 17th century on the site of the old mint (hence the name). The present building dates from 1817. In 1830, at a performance of the opera *La Muette de Portici* at the *Monnaie,* one of the patriotic songs ("Sacred love of the fatherland, give us courage and pride") so inflamed the audience that they left the opera house and commenced the rebellion that led to Belgium's independence. Recitals and concerts by world-famous musicians are given throughout the year in the *Palais des Beaux-Arts* (23 Rue Ravenstein; phone: 512-5045). Sunday morning concerts, generally by string quartets, are offered at the *Astoria* hotel's *Boîte à Musique* (103 Rue Royale; phone: 513-0965).

## NIGHTCLUBS AND NIGHTLIFE

Brussels is not exactly known for its swinging *vie nocturne,* and in what nightclubs that do exist prices often are high. *Le Mozart* (541 Chaussée d'Alsemberg; phone: 344-0809) is a pub that serves up jazz as well as food until 5 AM. You can have dinner until 6 AM at *Safir* (23 Petite Rue des Bouchers; phone: 511-8478), a classic all-night spot. Live jazz late into the night in the requisite smoky atmosphere is the Saturday-night staple at *Bierodrome* (21 Pl. Fernand-Cocq; phone: 512-0456). Popular dance clubs include *Le Crocodile Club,* at the *Royal Windsor* hotel (see *Checking In*); the trendy *Le Garage* (16-18 Rue Duquesnoy; phone: 512-6622); and Brussels's most outrageous disco, *Le Mirano Continental* (38 Chaussée de Louvain; phone: 218-5772), open Saturdays only.

Brussels also has some superb café-bistros, including *'T Spinnekopke* (1 Pl. du Jardin aux Fleurs; phone: 511-8695) and *De Ultième Hallucinatie* (316 Rue Royale; phone: 217-0614), an Art Nouveau marvel where fine food is served on weekends. For a pleasant nightcap, try *Au Roi d'Espagne* (in the Grand' Place; phone: 513-0807) or *Au Bon Vieux Temps* (12 Rue Marché-aux-Herbes; phone: 218-1546). The *Café Métropole* (31 Place de Brouckère; phone: 217-2300) has an Art Nouveau interior and an outdoor café heated for year-round dining. The *Falstaff Bistro* (near the Grand' Place at 17-23 Rue Maus; phone: 511-8789) has turn-of-the-century décor and a lively clientele. Scores of English beers are available for sampling at *La Houblonnière* (4 Pl. de Londres; phone: 502-1597), where Dixieland jazz is heard on Sunday nights.

# Best in Town

## CHECKING IN

As could be expected in Europe's diplomatic and commercial capital, accommodations in Brussels are high in quality—and price. A double room at a hotel in the very expensive category will cost from $300 to $485 per night; in the expensive category, from $165 to $275; in the moderate range, between $100 and $150; and in the inexpensive category (rare in this city), from $65 to $95. Rates include a 16% service charge and Value Added Tax. Significantly lower rates prevail on weekends and during July and August. Most Brussels hotels, particularly in the moderate category and up, offer rooms with private baths, air conditioning, telephones, and TV sets. All telephone numbers given are in the 2 city code.

### VERY EXPENSIVE

**Conrad Brussels** The choice for elegant surroundings and efficient service, this hotel has 268 rooms, including 15 suites. Also on the premises are a restaurant, a café, two lounges, and a well equipped health center. Facilities include nine fully equipped conference rooms, a ballroom accommodating up to 800 people, and state-of-the-art audiovisual equipment. Close to the Grand' Place, at 71 Ave. Louise (phone: 542-4242; fax: 542-4342).

**Royal Windsor** In the Grand' Place area, this 300-room member of the Leading Hotels of the World is Tudor in style, and its *Les Quatre Saisons* restaurant offers a splendid menu (see *Eating Out*). The atmosphere is very British and modern, and the rooms are soundproofed. Business facilities include 24-hour room service, meeting rooms for up to 250, an English-speaking concierge, foreign currency exchange, secretarial services in English, audiovisual equipment, photocopiers, computers, cable TV news, translation services, and express checkout. There's also an underground parking garage. 5-7 Rue Duquesnoy (phone: 511-4215; 800-223-6800; fax: 511-6004).

### EXPENSIVE

**Amigo** Gracious and comfortable, only one street away from the Grand' Place, it offers the charm (and sometimes the noise) of the square along with an aristocratic interior. There's a garage, a restaurant, a bar, and 183 spacious rooms and suites. Best are the sixth-floor apartments with terraces. Business facilities include 24-hour room service, meeting rooms for up to 200, an English-speaking concierge, foreign currency exchange, audiovisual equipment, photocopiers, and cable TV news. 1-3 Rue de l'Amigo (phone: 511-5910; fax: 513-5277).

**Astoria** Smaller than most in the city, with 128 comfortable rooms, this hostelry is a souvenir of the Belle Epoque. It has a restaurant, a bar done up like a Pullman car, and the *Boîte à Musique*, where classical music performances are held. Business facilities include 24-hour room service, meeting rooms for up to 320, an English-speaking concierge, foreign currency exchange, secretarial services in English, audiovisual equipment, photocopiers, computers, translation services, and express checkout. 103 Rue Royale (phone: 217-6290; 800-221-4542; fax: 217-1150).

**Brussels Sheraton** Brussels's largest property (530 rooms) has several dining rooms, including *Les Comtes de Flandres,* serving haute cuisine, and a coffee shop. It's a 31-story affair with a handsome lobby, good-size rooms, a discotheque, a fitness center, and a pool. On Fridays, Saturdays, and Sundays rates are quite moderate. Business facilities include 24-hour room service, meeting rooms for up to 1,000, an English-speaking concierge, foreign currency exchange, secretarial services in English, audiovisual equipment, photocopiers, cable TV news, and translation services. 3 Pl. Rogier (phone: 224-3111; 800-325-3535; fax: 224-3456).

**City Garden** Modern, spacious, and comfortable, this 96-room residential hotel offers kitchenettes and proximity to the *Métro* and European Community headquarters, but no restaurant. Business facilities include meeting rooms for up to 20, an English-speaking concierge, foreign currency exchange, secretarial services in English, photocopiers, and express checkout. Rates are moderate on weekends. 59 Rue Joseph-II (phone: 230-0945; fax: 230-6437).

**Le Dixseptième** Just off the Grand' Place, this is a welcome change from impersonal business hotels. It consists of three 17th-century houses around a small courtyard. There are just 17 rooms, some with beamed ceilings, and a restaurant. Rates are moderate on weekends. 25 Rue de la Madeleine (phone: 502-5744; fax: 502-6424).

**Hilton International Brussels** Another of the city's large (369 rooms) establishments, near the Avenue Louise shopping area. The duplex rooms here have balconies and full kitchens. The roof garden restaurant offers a superb view of the city, and there is an authentic French restaurant (*Máison du Boeuf;* see *Eating Out*), an English pub, and a bar-discotheque. Business facilities include 24-hour room service, meeting rooms for up to 450, an English-speaking concierge, foreign currency exchange, secretarial services in English, audiovisual equipment, computers, cable TV news, and express checkout. Rates are moderate on weekends and in July through August. 38 Bd. de Waterloo (phone: 504-1111; 800-HILTONS; fax: 504-2111).

**Holiday Inn Brussels Airport** Like any other member of the chain, this 310-room place is clean, convenient, and standardized. It has tennis courts, a pool, and a sauna, and courtesy buses run to the airport and into town. Business facilities include 24-hour room service, meeting rooms for up to 500, an English-speaking concierge, foreign currency exchange, secretarial services in English, audiovisual equipment, photocopiers, computers, cable TV news, translation services, and express checkout. Rates are inexpensive on weekends. 7 Holiday St., near the airport in Diegem (phone: 720-5865; 800-HOLIDAY; fax: 720-4145).

**Jolly Hotel Atlanta** Taking its name from the heyday of *Gone With the Wind,* this link in the Jolly hotel chain has a rooftop restaurant, *La Veranda*, with a good view of the city. The hotel is downtown and some of the 244 rooms can be noisy. Business facilities include meeting rooms for up to 50, an English-speaking concierge, foreign currency exchange, secretarial services in English, audiovisual equipment, and translation services. 7 Bd. Adolphe-Max (phone: 217-0120; fax: 217-3758).

**Jolly Hotel du Grand Sablon** Situated between the *Palais Royale* and the Place du Grand-Sablon, the heart of the antiques district, this 203-room hotel has every modern amenity. Rooms are soundproofed; there's a restaurant; and conference facilities can accommodate up to 100. 2-4 Rue Bodenbroek (phone: 512-8800; fax: 512-6766).

**Métropole** The city's last remaining 19th-century establishment, it has 410 rooms decorated in styles ranging from Art Deco to modern. The lobby, café, and *L'Alban Chambon* restaurant (see *Eating Out*) have been restored but retain last century's charm. Business facilities include 24-hour room service, meeting rooms for up to 500, an English-speaking concierge, foreign currency exchange, secretarial services in English, audiovisual equipment, photocopiers, cable TV news, translation services, and express checkout. Rates are moderate on weekends. 31 Pl. de Brouckère (phone: 217-2300; fax: 218-0220).

**Palace** Tastefully renovated, this 360-room hotel was built in 1910 and overlooks the *Jardin Botanique* (Botanical Gardens) adjacent to the *Gare du Nord*. The *Restaurant Le Bouquet* serves à la carte meals. Business facilities include meeting rooms for up to 500, an English-speaking concierge, foreign currency exchange, secretarial services in English, audiovisual equipment, photocopiers, cable TV news, and translation services. 3 Rue Gineste (phone: 217-6200; fax: 218-7651).

**Radisson SAS Royal** This 281-room property, a stone's throw from the Grand' Place and the Rue Neuve shopping area, has been designed around an atrium filled with light and plants. Guests can choose from different room styles. There is a piano bar, a 1950s American–style bar and grill (which on weekend nights fills up with young *Bruxellois* pretending to be American); a restaurant serving Belgian and Scandinavian specialties; and the *Sea Grill,* a highly regarded seafood restaurant (see *Eating Out*). Business facilities include 24-hour room service, meeting rooms for up to 250, an English-speaking concierge, foreign currency exchange, secretarial services in English, audiovisual equipment, photocopiers, computers, cable TV news, translation services, and express checkout. Rates are moderate on weekends. 47 Rue du Fossé-aux-Loups (phone: 219-2828; 800-333-3333; fax: 219-6262).

**Scandic Crown** It's one of the city's more gracious modern hotels, with 315 rooms, including four duplexes, seven junior suites, two presidential suites, and 15 executive suites. *Hugo's* restaurant serves French fare, and there is a breakfast room. The hotel also has complete health club facilities. Business facilities include 24-hour room service, meeting rooms for up to 350, an English-speaking concierge, foreign currency exchange, secretarial services in English, audiovisual equipment, photocopiers, computers, cable TV news, translation services, and express checkout. 250 Rue Royale (phone: 220-6611; fax: 217-8444).

**Stéphanie** Close to the *Palais de Justice* and to one of the best shopping districts in Brussels, this 142-room hostelry is convenient for shoppers, but its front rooms can be noisy. It has an indoor pool and a restaurant. Children under 12 stay free in an adult's room. Business facilities include 24-hour room service, meeting rooms for up to 180, an English-speaking concierge, foreign currency exchange, secretarial services in English, audiovisual equipment, photocopiers, translation services, and express checkout. Rates are moderate on weekends. 91-93 Av. Louise (phone: 539-0240; fax: 538-0307).

## MODERATE

**Novotel** Conveniently located just one block from the Grand' Place and within walking distance of many downtown sites, this 136-room property is a quiet place to stay, despite its busy location. Belgian and international dishes are served in the restaurant. Children under 16 stay free with their parents. Business facilities include meeting rooms for up to 30, an English-speaking concierge, foreign currency exchange, audiovisual equipment, photocopiers, computers, and cable TV news. 120 Rue Marché-aux-Herbes (phone: 514-3333; 800-221-4542; fax: 511-7723).

**Park** On the *Parc Cinquantenaire* in a quiet neighborhood, this 49-room, two-suite hotel offers a Jacuzzi and a sauna, as well as a bar and breakfast buffet service, but no restaurant. Business facilities include a meeting room for up to 35, an English-speaking concierge, foreign currency exchange, and cable TV news. Secretarial services can be arranged. 21-22 Ave. de l'Yser (phone: 735-7400; fax: 735-1967).

## INEXPENSIVE

**La Légende** Small (31 rooms) and lacking a restaurant, this property is centrally located, just a short walk from the *Manneken-Pis*. The concierge speaks some English. 35 Rue du Lombard (phone: 512-8290; fax: 512-3493).

---

# EATING OUT

The French like to make fun of the Belgians for being obsessed with *pommes frites* (French fries, with mayonnaise), but in fact Brussels rivals Paris as a culinary capital. Restaurateurs here pride themselves on good food, from elaborate haute cuisine to simply prepared fresh produce, and restaurants in Brussels go to exceptional lengths to please their patrons. Belgium's cooks are some of the best in the world, and Belgian food, once a stepchild of French cuisine, has developed its own specialties, both Gallic- and Flemish-inflected. These include the inevitable brussels sprouts (developed here in the 18th century), asparagus from Malines, *witloof* (usually—but inexactly—called endive in English) steamed *moules* (mussels), red cabbage prepared *à la flamande* (with apple), *carbonnades flamandes* (beef braised in beer), *boudin* (blood and white sausage), *waterzooï* (chicken or fish in a vegetable and cream soup), *anguilles au vert* (eels, served with herbs), and mussels served in a variety of ways. Belgian pastries are excellent, especially *pain à la grecque* (which resembles biscotti), *gaufres* (waffles, served with confectioner's sugar, jam, and a host of other goodies), and tarts made with custard, sugar, or rice. And don't miss the pralines, the famous Belgian chocolate with a variety of fillings. The *Bruxellois,* the people of Brussels, will tell you that their chocolate is the best in the world—and they may be right. Beer is special here too; among the fine Belgian brews are Faro, Gueuze-Lambic, Kriek-Lambic, and Trappiste (even some Germans and Dutch think Belgian beer is the best in Europe).

There are about 1,700 restaurants in this city, and while it's easy to spend a small fortune for a good meal, it's not necessary—rarely is a bad meal served anywhere in Brussels. A dinner for two, including wine (remember, most wine is imported), in a very expensive restaurant will cost $220 or more; in an expensive place, $160 to $220; in a moderate place, between $100 and $160; and in an inexpensive one, $70 to $100. Unless otherwise specified the restaurants listed take major credit cards and are open for lunch and dinner. All telephone numbers are in the 2 city code.

For an unforgettable culinary experience, we begin with our favorite Brussels dining spot, followed by our cost and quality choices of restaurants, listed by price category.

---

### DELIGHTFUL DINING

**Comme Chez Soi** This intimate urban restaurant, distinguished by a kitchen devoted to modern culinary delights, has been awarded three Michelin stars. The talented young chef considers the "new" in nouvelle cuisine an invitation to experiment, and almost any one of his adventures will provide not just superb value for your money but an evening's repast you will remember long and lovingly. Reservations necessary. Closed Sundays, Mondays, two weeks at *Christmas,* and July. 23 Pl. Rouppe (phone: 512-2921; fax: 511-8052).

---

## VERY EXPENSIVE

**Bellemolen** This rustic country mill house, built in 1149, is well worth the 15-mile (24-km) drive northwest of Brussels. The prix fixe menu offers seasonal specialties. During summer, seating is available in the garden. Closed *Christmas* through *New Year's Day* and July. Reservations advised. Exit 19A off the E40; turn left across the bridge and continue a quarter mile to 11 Stationstr., Essene-Affligem (phone: 53-666238).

**Bruneau** One of Brussels's finest restaurants, boasting three Michelin stars, it serves excellent French cuisine against a pleasant background. Try the *menu de dégustation,* a sampling of the house specialties with a selection of wines. Closed Tuesday dinner and Wednesdays. Reservations necessary. 73-75 Av. Broustin (phone: 427-6978).

**L'Ecailler du Palais Royal** Superbly prepared seafood dishes are served in a 16th-century guild house in the Grand Sablon. Closed Sundays, holidays, and August. Reservations necessary. 18-20 Rue Bodenbroek (phone: 511-9950).

**Le Trèfle à Quatre** Set on the picturesque shore of Genval Lake, this elegant establishment won a Brussels *Iris de la Gastronomie* award in 1990 for chef Michel Haquin's imaginative fare. Closed Mondays, Tuesdays, and January 10 to February 10. Reservations advised. Château du Lac, 87 Av. du Lac, Genval (phone: 654-0798; fax: 653-3131).

## EXPENSIVE

**De Bijgaarden** Imaginative fare is combined with superb management at this suburban dining spot. Closed Sundays, Saturday lunch, *Easter,* the last half of August, and the first two weeks of September. Reservations advised. 20 Isidoor Van Beveren Str., Groot Bijgaarden (phone: 466-4485).

**Eddie Van Maele** Set in a villa north of Brussels, this small establishment decorated in greens, whites, and grays serves imaginative creations prepared by one of Belgium's master chefs. Closed Saturday lunch, Sundays, Mondays, the last two weeks of June, and the first two weeks of July. Reservations advised. Near *Stadi Heysel,* 964-966 Chaussée Romaine, Wemmel (phone: 460-6145).

**La Maison du Cygne** Making its home in an exquisite 16th-century building, this elegant place is especially proud of its lobster cassoulet, pheasant with chicory, and milk-fed lamb. Closed Saturday lunch, Sundays, *Christmas Week, New Year's Day,* and three weeks in August. Reservations necessary. 2 Rue Charles-Buls, Grand' Place (phone: 511-8244; fax: 514-3148).

## MODERATE

**L'Alban Chambon** In the Art Nouveau setting of the *Métropole* hotel, chef Dominique Michou of the *Académie Culinaire de France* offers a wide selection of French specialties. Closed weekends and mid-

July to mid-August. Reservations necessary. 31 Pl. de Brouckère (phone: 217-2300).

**Auberge de Boendael** Make an excursion beyond the downtown area to enjoy this dining spot's delicious meat and fish specialties, grilled over a wood fire. Try to save room for homemade *café glacé* (coffee ice cream) or sorbet. Closed weekends and mid-July to mid-August. Reservations necessary. 12 Sq. du Vieux-Tilleul (phone: 672-7055; fax: 660-7582).

**Barbizon** This charming villa in the midst of the *Forêt de Soignes* serves such one-Michelin-star specialties as aspic-coated lobster, smoked salmon and asparagus, and duck and endive salad. Closed Tuesdays, Wednesdays, February, and mid-July to early August. Reservations necessary. 95 Welriekendedreef (phone: 657-0462; fax: 657-4066).

**Bernard** At first you may think you have wandered into a grocery store by mistake, but go up one flight to the small dining room where the tables are tucked nose to nose. The setting is unpretentious, but the clientele consists mostly of knowledgeable Belgian gastronomes. Closed Sundays, Monday dinner, holidays, and July. Reservations necessary. 93 Rue de Namur (phone: 512-8821).

**Délices de la Mer** Fresh seafood prepared in inventive ways is the specialty. Closed Sundays. Reservations necessary. 1020 Chausée de Waterloo (phone: 375-5467).

**Maison du Boeuf** In the *Hilton International Brussels,* overlooking the gardens of the Egmont Palace, this place, with one Michelin star, specializes in shellfish as well as game (in season) and beef. Open daily. Reservations advised. 38 Bd. de Waterloo (phone: 504-2874).

**L'Ogenblik** A small eatery with the feel of a Paris bistro. All the waiters wear floor-length aprons, and the menu changes daily. Closed Sundays. Reservations advised. 1 Galerie des Princes (phone: 511-6151).

**Les Quatre Saisons** The *Royal Windsor* hotel's award-winning French restaurant serves meals that are as elegant as its ambience. Try the duck liver, pigeon breasts, or sole (fish is the specialty here). Closed Saturday lunch, Sundays, and July 20 through August 20. Reservations advised. 5 Rue Duquesnoy (phone: 511-4215; fax: 511-5729).

**Sea Grill** The highly reputed French seafood chef Jacques Le Divellec comes to Brussels frequently to prepare food for the *Radisson SAS Royal* hotel's one-Michelin-star dining room. The menu offers a wonderful variety of fish and shellfish dishes. Closed Saturday lunch and Sundays. Reservations necessary. 47 Rue du Fossé-aux-Loups (phone: 219-2828).

**Villa Lorraine** Probably the country's most famous restaurant, it has two Michelin stars and is set in a lovely villa just outside the city center. The service is impeccable, the decor sumptuous, the food the sort of which dreams are made. Closed Sundays and most of July.

Reservations necessary. 75 Av. du Vivier-d'Oie (phone: 374-3163; fax: 372-0195).

## INEXPENSIVE

**Aux Armes de Bruxelles** This is one of the traditional Brussels restaurants. Located on a narrow street leading off the Grand' Place, its specialties are fish, *moules* (mussels), and shellfish. Closed mid-July to mid-August. Reservations advised. 13 Rue des Bouchers (phone: 511-5598; fax: 514-3381).

**Chez Léon** This 103-year-old spot is warm, unpretentious, and serves solid Belgian fare such as *waterzooï, carbonnades à la flamande,* and at least a dozen varieties of *moules* (mussels). Open daily. Reservations unnecessary. 18-24 Rue des Bouchers (phone: 511-1415).

**'T Kelderke** Congenial and rustic, this fun bistro serves hearty Belgian fare such as rabbit stewed in beer and *waterzooï,* a soup-like mixture of boiled chicken and vegetables. Open daily. No reservations. 15 Grand' Place (phone: 513-7344).

**La Quincaillerie** Located in a former turn-of-the-century hardware store, this lively spot has a steady clientele who come for the home-smoked salmon, the succulent baked oysters, and other seafood dishes. Closed Sundays. Reservations advised. 45 Rue du Page (phone: 538-2553).

**Au Vieux Saint-Martin** A favorite of artists, it is bright and cheerful, with newspapers and magazines to read if you are dining alone. The menu is simple, with Belgian specialties. Open daily. No reservations. Visa accepted. 38 Pl. du Grand-Sablon (phone: 512-6476).

**Le Vimar** Tucked into the corner of a busy square near EU headquarters, this small spot has long been a favorite of the *Bruxellois.* Try the turbot with leeks, mussels in white wine sauce, or seafood casserole. Closed Saturday lunch, Sundays and late July to mid-August. Reservations advised. 67 Pl. Jourdan (phone: 231-0949).

**Vincent** On one of the cobblestone streets near the Grand' Place, this is the place to go for Belgian specialties. Closed part of the month of August, *Christmas Eve,* and *Christmas.* Reservations advised. 8 Rue des Dominicains (phone: 511-2303).

# Bucharest

## At-a-Glance

### SEEING THE CITY

There is really no one spot from which to behold all of Bucharest, but the courtyard of the *Cathedral of the Patriarch*—perched on a quiet hillside overlooking the city just south of the *Palatul Voievodal* (Princely Court)—does offer a nice view of the Old City. Perhaps the best panoramic view of the city as a whole is from the *Balada* restaurant on the 22nd floor of the *Inter-Continental* hotel (see *Checking In*).

### SPECIAL PLACES

A visit to Bucharest affords an opportunity to witness a piece of history—though visitors must be willing to expend some energy and endure considerable discomfort. Getting a sense of the recent changes in the city is not all that difficult, however, as you will find many people eager to share their experiences with you. To hire an English-speaking guide and/or driver and a car, try the state-run travel agency, *Carpați* (see *Tourist Information*), and ask to be taken on a tour of the sites of the 1989 revolution. With a little luck, your guide/driver will have taken part in the December uprising. He or she can be your key to insights into the heart of Bucharest, which the official tours, heavy on ancient history, don't reveal. Note: *Strada* is the Romanian word for street, *aleea* means alley, *piața* means square, and *calea* and *bulevardul* mean avenue.

#### OLD BUCHAREST

The core of this district is the *Palatul Voievodal* (Princely Court), the central part of the original *Dîmbovița Citadel* and now a museum. Portions of the medieval ruins and its surrounding streets are being reconstructed; parts of the area are open for viewing. Other attractions of the Old City are the Lipscani trading area and several old houses of worship.

**PALATUL VOIEVODAL (PRINCELY COURT)** Once the home of the kings and princes of Walachia, it is now a historical museum, located almost entirely underground, showing the progressive building of the citadel from the 15th to the 18th century. The outlines of the original citadel are preserved in stone; later additions are brick. From the outside only chimneys and archways are visible, but inside are artifacts and portions of the original structures. Closed Mondays. Admission charge. 31 Strada Iuliu Maniu.

**CURTEA VECHE (OLD COURT CHURCH)** Orthodox masses are held daily in this 16th-century church located across from the *Princely Court*.

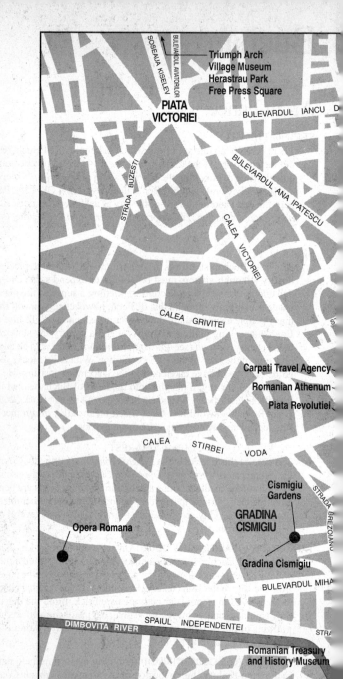

Triumph Arch
Village Museum
Herastrau Park
Free Press Square

**PIATA VICTORIEI**

SOSEAUA KISELEV

BULEVARDUL AVIATORILOR

BULEVARDUL IANCU D

BULEVARDUL ANA IPATESCU

STRADA BUZESTI

CALEA VICTORIEI

CALEA GRIVITEI

Carpati Travel Agency

Romanian Athenum

Piata Revolutiei

CALEA STIRBEI VODA

Cismigiu Gardens

**GRADINA CISMIGIU**

STRADA BREZOIANU

Opera Romana

Gradina Cismigiu

BULEVARDUL MIHA

DIMBOVITA RIVER

SPAIUL INDEPENDENTEI

STRA

Romanian Treasury
and History Museum

National Unity Square
"House of the People"
Unirea Department Store

NATI

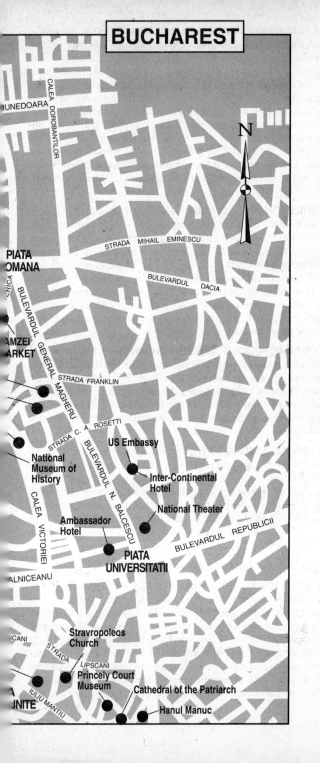

**BISERICA PATRIARHIEI (CATHEDRAL OF THE PATRIARCH)** This, the seat of the Patriarch of the Romanian Orthodox church, was built in 1658 and was later enlarged when the patriarchate was transferred from the province of Moldavia to Walachia. Inside, groups of old women dressed in black can be seen sitting on the floor sharing a lunch of bread, cheese, and melon; later they clean and decorate the cathedral with flowers. Though never closed by the Communist regime, like many houses of worship in the area it was slated for demolition and saved only by the 1989 revolution. The courtyard and cemetery, erected during the mid-19th century in memory of bishops and monks already dead for three centuries, are filled with headstones and crosses inscribed in ornate Old Slavonic. 21 Aleea Patriarhiei (phone: 615-6772).

**PARLAMENTUL ROMÂNIEI (ROMANIAN NATIONAL PARLIAMENT)** Situated across from the cathedral, this long, gray, neoclassical structure was built in 1907, and was formerly the seat of the rubber-stamp Grand National Assembly under the Communist regime. The building is open to the public when the Chamber of Deputies (Parliament's lower house) is in session (from September through July); parliamentary sessions themselves also are open to the public. The entrances are guarded by friendly Romanian soldiers dressed in sharp new khakis that replaced the old Soviet-style green uniforms. Aleea Parliamentului (phone: 638-5090).

**BISERICA STRAVROPOLEOS (STAVROPOLEOS CHURCH)** This 18th-century structure is a fine example of Brâncovenesc architecture, a uniquely Romanian style named after the illustrious 18th-century Walachian Prince Constantin Brâncoveanu. The curvy style, executed in both wood and stone, is a fusion of late Renaissance, Byzantine, and Romanian folk-art designs. Services are held here regularly. Strada Stavropoleos.

**STRADA LIPSCANI (LIPSCANI STREET)** Just two blocks from the *Princely Court* is the most historical part of Bucharest, the principal trading street of the Old City. It is a wonderful place to walk for its myriad small shops and outdoor stands, and also because the narrow lane so teems with people, pushcarts, bicycles, and street merchants that it is next to impassable for cars. Merchants and farmers from all over the Balkans used to bring their wares to trade in the district, which dates from the 18th century.

ELSEWHERE IN THE CITY

**VECHEA BURSĂ ROMÂNĂ (OLD ROMANIAN STOCK EXCHANGE)** One of the most ornate pieces of architecture in Bucharest, the *Bursă* was built in 1880 and restored by the Ceauşescu government a hundred years later. It's no longer used for its original purpose; a new stock exchange opened in 1991 at Free Press Square. The style reflects Byzantine and Romanesque features: Magnificent marble columns are topped with *dosserets* (sort of secondary capitals) of hammered copper. The floor is of patterned stone, the octagonal ceiling a mosaic of leaded glass stained in vibrant shades of blue. Iron gates, cherubs, and other finely carved statuary preside over the variety of shops now housed here. 18 Strada Lipscani, opposite the back entrance of the *National Bank.*

**PIAȚA UNIVERSITĂȚII (UNIVERSITY SQUARE)** North of Lipscani, at the intersection of Bulevarduls Nicolae Bălcescu and Republicii, this plaza, the seat of Bucharest's university, was the site of much of the fighting of the December 1989 revolution. Demonstrators, unhappy with the presence of former Communists in the new government, continued to gather here after the elections until they were forcibly and brutally removed by government-sponsored miners brought to the city for the purpose. A momumental flat tomb surrounded by ancient stone crosses was built in the middle of the square in memory of the victims of the revolution.

**GRĂDINA CIȘMIGIU (CIȘMIGIU GARDENS)** This grand 19th-century park is a picturesque place to escape the urban bustle. There's a lake with boats for hire and numerous gardens on the 34 acres. Off Bulevardul Republicii, west of Piața Universității.

**PIAȚA REVOLUȚIEI (REVOLUTION SQUARE)** Just northwest of University Square, this plaza, formerly called Piața Palatului (Palace Square), was first named for the former royal palace located here, which ultimately became a government building and a half of which now houses the *Museum of National Art.* Across from the palace is the Senate's headquarters (Parliment's upper chamber), formerly the headquarters of the Central Committee of the Communist Party, where Ceaușescu last spoke to his infuriated people, and from whose roof he and his wife, Elena, temporarily escaped by helicopter during the 1989 uprising. In front of the building lies a simple monument made of white marble. Bucharest residents, especially those who lost loved ones during the revolution, decorate it with fresh flowers each December. Before the monument was erected, the citizens themselves manufactured shrines in the memory of the victims. At that time one of these was a massive cross brought by an Orthodox priest and his followers from Timișoara, the city where the revolution began.

**ATENEUL ROMÂN (ROMANIAN ATHENAEUM)** Perhaps Bucharest's most beautiful building, home of the city's *Philharmonic Orchestra and Choir,* it was completed in 1888 under the supervision of French architect Albert Galleron; the funds to build it came from public donation. Here, more than anywhere else, you can get a taste of what Bucharest once was like—especially if you are lucky enough to attend one of the concerts that attract the capital's dignitaries. The alleys of the small park in front lead to the building's main entrances, guarded by Ionic columns. Once inside, note the 12 Doric columns of the main hall. Four circular staircases lead to the most fascinating part of this architectural jewel, the ornate, acoustically perfect, 1,000-seat concert hall ringed by circular frescoes which depict the country's illustrious history. 1 Strada Franklin (phone: 614-0899).

**CENTRUL CIVIC (CIVIC CENTER)** Ceaușescu razed thousands of old buildings just south of the Lipscani area to make way for this huge neo-classical complex, intended to house the Communist Party elite. Its main artery, connecting Piața Unirii (Union Square) to the gargantuan *House of the Republic,* now called the *Palace of the Parliament,* was to be named the Boulevard of the Victory of Socialism. Although widely condemned as an architectural atrocity, Bulevardul Libertății, as it is now called, has ironically become a center of the emerging capitalist class, with luxury car dealerships, bars, and galleries, all lit at night by the neon glare of signs advertising Japanese electronics. The former *House of the Republic* is worth a visit: Dubbed the *House of the People,* it cost more than $1 billion over a six-year period of construction. This monstrosity with thousands of rooms (some on a par with airplane hangars), intended as Ceaușescu's personal headquarters, is said to be the second-largest edifice in the world, second only to the *Pentagon.* The building is open only intermittently to the public; access to the inner rooms usually requires prearranging a tour through city officials (phone: 615-0100 or 615-3240; fax: 614-8091 or 312-0902).

**PIAȚA VICTORIEI (VICTORY SQUARE)** You can reach this square by either driving or walking north on Bucharest's oldest and nicest avenue, Calea Victoriei. The point from which most of Bucharest's main thoroughfares emanate, it is also where the government has its headquarters. Across the plaza is Soseaua Kiseleff, bordered on both sides by parkland and leading through the *Triumphal Arch* past Free Press Square into *Herăstrău Park,* Bucharest's largest nature preserve.

**ARCUL DE TRIUMF (TRIUMPHAL ARCH)** Modeled on Paris's *Arc de Triomphe,* this structure was erected in 1922 on the initiative of King Ferdinand and Queen Marie to celebrate the Allied victory in World War I and to honor Romania's war dead. (Unfortunately, you can't go up to the top.) Soseaua Kiseleff, north of Piața Victoriei.

**PIAȚA PRESEI LIBERE (FREE PRESS SQUARE)** This plaza used to be named Piața Scinteiei (Spark's Square) for the *Scinteiei,* the Communist Party journal published here for 40 years until the 1989 revolution (now it is the site of a non-Communist paper's offices). It took two cranes four days to remove the 7,000-pound bronze statue of Lenin that stood here. Soseaua Kiseleff.

**FOREST PARKS** Bucharest is blessed with extensive greenery and spacious parks, including several nature preserves and recreation areas. Perhaps the best known is *Herăstrău Park,* whose 1½-square-mile expanse is home to a large lake, more than a half-dozen pleasant restaurants, and the outdoor *Muzeul Satului* (Village Museum), a collection of houses, churches, and other structures from throughout Romania (see *Museums*). The pastoral settings provide a pleasant respite from urban Bucharest, and the museum displays a good cross section of the very different architectural styles found in the various regions of the country. Open daily.

*Băneasa Forest,* located within the city limits to the north of *Herăstrău,* has areas for picnicking and such outdoor games as volleyball and badminton, as well as the *Pădurea Băneasa* (Băneasa Forest) restaurant, which offers outdoor dining and Romanian folk shows. Nearby is the *Grădina Zoologica Băneasa* (Băneasa Zoo), Romania's largest, albeit poorly managed, zoo. Open daily.

## ENVIRONS

**LACUL SI MÂNĂSTIREA SNAGOV (SNAGOV LAKE AND MONASTERY)** A lovely recreation area located 20 miles (32 km) north of Bucharest, Snagov is very popular with the residents of the capital for family outings (as well as with the Romanian national sculling team for training). It's about a 30- to 40-minute drive from downtown, depending on traffic.

Snagov Island is in the middle of the lake and was formerly closed to the public because Ceauşescu had built a villa on its western shore; the island now is open to all and can be reached via an 85-person ferry (see below). Also on the small island is the 15th-century church and monastery founded by Vlad Tepeş (better known as Vlad the Impaler, or Dracula), who is buried in the crypt here. In the portrait of him that rests before the altar, the prince is long-lashed, wide-eyed, and somewhat demented looking. (Though certainly fierce and ruthless, even by the standards of five centuries past, Vlad is revered throughout Romania as one of the country's greatest rulers, and was not literally a bloodsucker; Count Dracula was a 19th-century fictional exaggeration dreamed up by Irish author Bram Stoker. Vlad did, however, earn the sobriquet "The Impaler," due to his fondness for skewering the bodies of thieves and of the invading Turks—nearly 20,000 of them—on long wooden spears.)

The church, with its monastery, originally dates from the 6th century. In 1383 it was christened the *Church of Princes* and was fortified, serving until 1418 as a fortress to defend Walachia. In 1456 Vlad Tepeş built the current *Snagov Monastery* and fortifications (including an underground escape tunnel to the shore, which is now in disrepair and unusable). The church's altar table is from the original 6th-century structure and has never been moved, as is customary in the Orthodox faith. On display in the church are a number of ancient ecclesiastical documents, including copies of the first Romanian Bible, printed at *Snagov* toward the end of the 17th century (the original is in Bucharest's *Romanian Academy*). The *Snagov Printing Press* was brought here in 1695. The monastery is still home to four monks, and Sunday and holiday services are held at 9 AM (Sunday mass is open to the public).

Also along the lakeshore are a number of small cafés, outdoor food stands selling barbecued meat and *mititei* (lamb sausage), and a restaurant at the Snagov Lake recreation area. Rowboats can be rented (don't try to row all the way out to the island, though, since there's no place to dock). A number of small villas on the island offer interesting tourist accommodations, which can be booked through *Carpaţi* (phone: 614-5160).

A note on the ferry: It operates during the summer on no particular schedule—just whenever the captain feels there are enough passengers for a run to the island, generally once every hour. *Carpați* will tell you it's impossible to visit the island during the winter, but you can arrange private passage with one of the weekly supply boats (again, on no particular schedule; you show up at the dock and ask around, or ask your guide to find out what day the boat leaves). Be sure to agree on a price before getting on the boat.

**MOGOȘOAIA PALACE** A visit to the elegant 18th-century estate of Prince Constantin Brâncoveanu, 9 miles (14 km) through the parks and forests to the northwest of the city, is one of Bucharest's finest day trips. Now a museum of medieval art and artifacts, the palace itself overshadows its contents. A formal structure, it was built on the scale of a Venetian palazzo, with ornately arched colonnades, a stately, close-cropped garden, and a quiet reflecting pond. Open daily. Admission charge. 1 Valea Parcului (no phone).

**WALACHIA** The most exotic and typical example of traditional Romanian life is found just outside the capital. Only a few miles from the center of Bucharest are villages where peasants still live off the land; where Gypsies roam the countryside in tarpaulin-covered wagons pulled by horses or oxen; and public wells are sheltered by brilliantly painted shrines.

Worthwhile excursions include the two-hour ride through rural Walachia to the lovely medieval monastery at Curtea de Argeș, once the seat of Walachia's rulers, and the trip to the red-roofed medieval Transylvanian town of Brașov, some 115 miles (184 km) north of Bucharest.

Accommodations in some of Moldavia's beautiful working monasteries and convents are available on a very limited basis. All prospective visitors must be screened well in advance for a stay of two to three days. Quarters are modest and clean, and the environment is one of complete peace and serenity. Apply through *Carpați* (see below).

# Sources and Resources

## TOURIST INFORMATION

In Bucharest the main branch of the *Oficiul National de Turism-ONT Carpați* (Carpați-București National Tourist Office) is located at 7 Bulevardul General Magheru (phone: 614-5160; fax: 312-2594). Hours and days of operation can be somewhat erratic, so be sure to call ahead. The tourist offices also will make hotel and other reservations for you, but your own travel agent may be more efficient and reliable. The *US Embassy* is at 7-9 Strada Tudor Arghezi (phone: 312-4042).

For information in the US, contact the *Romanian National Tourist Office* (342 Madison Ave., New York, NY 10173; phone: 212-867-5011; 800-223-6037). The *Romanian Embassy* is at 1607 23rd St. NW, Washington, DC, 20008 (phone: 202-232-4747).

**ENTRY REQUIREMENTS** A US citizen needs a valid passport and a visa to enter Romania. A tourist visa, good for a single-entry visit of up to six months, is available at any Romanian diplomatic office. It also can be obtained upon arrival at any border entry point or at *Otoponi Airport* in Bucharest.

**TIME** The time in Romania is seven hours later than in US East Coast cities. Romania follows daylight saving time.

**LANGUAGE** Romanian. English is becoming more common.

**ELECTRIC CURRENT** 220 volts, 50 cycles, AC.

**MONEY** The leu (plural lei) equals 100 bani. It still is illegal to enter or leave the country with Romanian currency. At press time the exchange rate was about 1,600 lei to $1 US.

**TIPPING** Though not expected, small tips (the equivalent of a dollar or two) are accepted for special services.

**BANKING/BUSINESS HOURS** Banks are open weekdays from 8:30 or 9 AM to 4:30 or 5 PM. Most other businesses are open weekdays from 8 AM to 4:30 PM.

**HOLIDAYS** *New Year's* (January 1 and 2), Greek Orthodox *Easter* (April 23), *National Day* (December 1), and *Christmas Day* (December 25).

**LOCAL COVERAGE** The most prominent daily is *Evenimentul Zilei* (The *Day's Event*), followed by *România Liberă* (Free Romania). An attempt to improve the standards of the Romanian press is now evident within the pages of another daily newspaper, *Ultimul Cuvănt* (The Last Word). If you need to follow both the development of domestic and international events, look for *Nine O'Clock,* an English-language daily. English-language publications such as the *International Herald Tribune* and *Time* magazine are available at most major hotels, where some French and German-language publications also are sold.

**TELEPHONE** The city code for Bucharest is 1. When calling from one area to another within Romania dial 0 + city code + local number. (Keep in mind that all city codes—except Bucharest's—were changed last year. For information regarding phone numbers, city codes, and so on, dial 930/1/2.)

The country code for Romania is 40. International calls can be made from most major hotels; to reach the international operator, dial 971. In an emergency dial 961 for an ambulance or 955 for the police.

## GETTING AROUND

Bucharest's roughly 43 square miles are easy to navigate, and are best covered on foot or in a rental or chauffeured car (parking spaces generally are available). Taxis are a good option, too, and drivers will often wait while you eat or sightsee. The most difficult area is Lipscani, where it's generally best to walk.

**AIRPORT** Buses leave *Otopeni International Airport* and *Băneasa Airport* (domestic flights only) for Bucharest about every hour. To get to the airport, take bus No. 783 from Piaţa Unirii (Union Square). For domestic flight information and reservations contact the Romanian airline, *TAROM* (59-61 Strada Buzeşti; phone: 659-4725 or 659-4185). *TAROM* also has international flights. For up-to-the-minute information on arrivals, departures, delays, weather conditions, and such at *Otopeni International Airport,* call 633-6602; for *Băneasa Airport,* 633-0030.

**BUS/TROLLEY/STREETCAR** They crisscross the city and are relatively inexpensive, but crowded and dirty. Buses are the least reliable form of transportation; often you will see crowds of people waiting for buses that never arrive.

**CAR RENTAL** Automobiles, with or without drivers, are available through *Carpaţi* (see above). Though costs are reasonable, you may be able to get an even better bargain by hiring a *Carpaţi* driver independently to take you around the city for a day. *Hertz* (2 Strada Cihoschi; phone: 611-0408) and *Europcar* (7 Bulevardul Magheru; phone: 613-1540) have outlets at major hotels. Many private travel agencies in Bucharest also rent cars; a complete list can be obtained from *Carpaţi.*

**SUBWAY** Three interconnected lines serve Bucharest: The first travels around the city in a circle, the second traverses it, and the third serves the outlying industrial areas. The system, called *metrou,* is clean, efficient, inexpensive, crowded, and runs daily. No maps are available, though there are some diagrams affixed to the walls in the stations.

**TAXI** State taxis can be ordered by phone from anywhere in Bucharest by dialing 953; the number is also marked on the cabs, making them distinguishable from private ones. Private, state-licensed taxis sometimes have signs on them reading "P Taxi" or "Taxi Particular," and are generally in much better condition. They charge more than the state taxis but are more readily available. Unlicensed cabs with no signs also will stop to pick up passengers—particularly handy at night, when there's a scarcity of regular taxis. Insist that drivers in state-run cabs run the newer digital meters. If the meters are "broken," agree on a price *before* getting in or be prepared to be taken for a ride you hadn't bargained for. Though the fare is generally in lei, drivers won't turn down dollars or other hard currency.

**TRAIN** The main station, through which 90% of rail traffic passes, is the *Gara de Nord,* which occupies an entire city block on Calea Griviţei. A handful of lesser stations provide service only to a few small towns around Bucharest. It's best to book train reservations and pay in advance with *Carpaţi* before leaving the US if you want to be assured of private, first class accommodations (if you really want to meet the Romanian people, consider traveling what is known as "regular class"). The local trains make a lot of stops, they don't take reservations, and are generally quite crowded, but eventually you'll find a seat. For *Gara de Nord* train schedule information dial 952 and ask for "informatii."

## LOCAL SERVICES

Most hotels will try to arrange for any special services a traveler might require.

**DENTIST (ENGLISH-SPEAKING)** Most hospitals have dental services, and many of their dentists speak some English. Inquire at your hotel for more information.

**DRY CLEANER** In addition to the hotels, there is a chain called *Nufarul,* with branches throughout the city; most dry cleaning takes two or three days.

**EMERGENCY** Dial 961 for an ambulance and 955 for the police.

**FAX** Most hotels and the main post office have fax facilities.

**LIMOUSINE SERVICE** Available through *Carpaţi* (see *Tourist Information,* above) and at any of the major hotels.

**MEDICAL EMERGENCY** The *Spidalul de Urgentă* (Emergency Hospital; 8 Calea Stefan cel Mare; phone: 212-0107) handles all emergencies in Bucharest.

**MESSENGER SERVICE** Available from any of the large hotels. The service is free if it is a matter of five or 10 minutes, but they charge for longer deliveries.

**NATIONAL/INTERNATIONAL COURIER** *DHL Worldwide Express* (63 Calea Victoriei; phone: 312-2787 or 312-2661) and *TNT Express Worldwide* (38 Grigore Mora; phone: 212-1210 or 312-6915) both offer reliable service.

**OFFICE EQUIPMENT RENTAL** Available from the larger hotels.

**PHARMACY** To find the all-night one closest to your hotel, call the 24-hour pharmacy hotline, 951. Most pharmacies have someone who speaks some English.

**PHOTOCOPIES** At the *Inter-Continental* hotel (4-6 Bulevardul Nicolae Bălcescu; phone: 613-7040 or 614-0400); some storefront services also are opening up—inquire at your hotel.

**POST OFFICE** The main post office is at 37 Calea Victoriei. All post offices throughout the city are open Mondays through Saturdays.

**SECRETARY/STENOGRAPHER (ENGLISH-SPEAKING)** Contact the *Chamber of Commerce* (22 Bulevardul Nicolae Bălcescu; phone: 615-4706/7).

**TAILOR** Inquire at your hotel.

**TRANSLATOR** Through *Carpaţi* or the *Chamber of Commerce* (address and phone above).

## SPECIAL EVENTS

The *Enescu Music Festival,* featuring the works of the world's famous composers and including those of Romanian Georges Enesco

(1881–1955), is held at the *Romanian Athenaeum* (see *Music,* below) in September every four years. The next festival is scheduled for next year. An international trade show primarily geared to businesses takes place twice a year, in May and October (1 Piaţa Presei Libere; phone: 617-6010; in the US call the *Romanian Trade Mission* at 212-682-9120). International folk and other festivals are held several times a year at the *Muzeul Satului* (Village Museum; see below). On the feast of St. Dumitru (October 26), the saint's relics are venerated at the *Church of the Patriarch* by thousands of faithful. But the most colorful and unusual events generally take place in the provincial villages, not in Bucharest. The *Feast of the Goat* (Capra) is a masked winter carnival held in many villages from *Christmas* through *New Year's Eve.* It is the peasants who also preserved Orthodox *Christmas* carols unaltered (especially in northern Moldavia and Maramureşş), and who offer the *Pluguşorul* (Plowing Feast) each *New Year's Eve.*

## MUSEUMS

Besides the museum of the *Palatul Voievodal* (Princely Court) listed in *Special Places,* other museums of interest include the following:

**MUZEUL NAŢIONAL DE ISTORIE (NATIONAL MUSEUM OF HISTORY)** In what once was the *Palatul Regal* (Royal Palace), the museum's superb collection of paintings and sculpture showcases the talent of such local artists as the 19th-century painter Grigorescu as well as Western European giants including Rubens and van Gogh. Works by the world-renowned, Romanian-born sculptor Constantin Brâncuşi (1876–1957) are also on display. Closed Mondays. Admission charge. Piaţa Revolutiei; entrance is at 4-3 Strada Stirbei Voda (phone: 614-9774).

**MUZEUL NATIONAL DE ISTORIE SI TREZORIE (ROMANIAN TREASURY AND HISTORY MUSEUM)** The worthwhile part of this museum is on the ground floor; to get in you will have to relinquish all cameras, notebooks, and anything else the soldiers standing guard think you might use to compromise Romania's national treasures. There is an exquisite collection of gold and jewelry, including the famous *Tezaurul de la Pietroasele* (Pietroasele Treasure), which dates as far back as the 4th century. Headdresses, icons, goblets, coins, and military and religious ornaments from the Dacian and Roman eras through the 19th century are here, too. Closed Mondays. Admission charge. 12 Calea Victoriei (phone: 613-7055).

**MUZEUL SATULUI (VILLAGE MUSEUM)** Just outside the city limits on the grounds of *Herăstrău Park* is this beautifully arranged "community" of several dozen peasant houses, a wooden church, wells, kiosks, and other structures brought here from every section of the nation's three provinces, starting in 1936. The spacious park is the perfect setting in which to learn about peasant life—particularly the different types of wooden houses from which the residents sell postcards and souvenirs to passersby throughout the country. Also quite charming are the Transylvanian houses, which feature peak-roofed side porches and outdoor kiosks that sell bread and water. In summer the "museum" hosts crafts demonstrations, including weaving, carving, wool spinning, and making *naiuri* (flutes). The park is also home to a large lake and several restaurants, making a trip here a pleasant respite from urban Bucharest. Open daily. Admission charge. 28-30 Soseaua Kiseleff, *Herăstrău Park* (phone: 617-5920).

## SHOPPING

Bucharest now boasts private shops selling all manner of Western-made goods, but your best bet for a wide selection is *Coleus,* a new citywide chain, whose main store is on 114 Bulevardul Dacia (phone: 210-3528). Open daily. No credit cards accepted.

A wide selection of Romanian products—such as gorgeous leaded crystal, handmade lace, woodcarvings, embroidery, pottery (including beautiful, shiny black Margina), wool sweaters, hats, and blankets—is available at *Comturist* shops located in major hotels throughout Bucharest and the rest of the country. They offer some decent bargains, especially on crystal. Payment is in hard currency *only*—cash or credit card. Most of what you'll probably want to take home from Romania will be bulky or breakable, so plan to leave some extra room in your luggage.

Stores where Romanians shop (and pay in lei) also can offer some interesting finds. Stores are generally open daily from 8 AM to 4 PM, though some are open from 8 AM to noon, close until 4 PM, then reopen from 4 to 8 PM. Food and department store hours are 8 AM to 8 PM.

**Cogsignația** The name refers to the several consignment stores among the wonderful little shops along Strada Lipscani. They sell everything from antiques to Western goods imported from Turkey and Greece. As you enter the street from the east, an alleyway on the left leads into a cobblestone courtyard with iron-shuttered windows, part of the original 15th-century marketplace. The shops are about eight doors down on the left-hand side of the courtyard. Strada Lipscani.

**Galerie de Artă Veche si Modernă (Old and Modern Art Gallery)** Romanian artifacts—from religious icons to dusty, centuries-old volumes on history and art—many of which were confiscated by the Communists from the Romanian bourgeoisie. 1 Bulevardul Unirii (phone: 615-0915).

**Librărie** The name simply means "bookstore." Both Romanian and foreign-language books are sold here, the latter mostly in French, English, and German (including some beautifully illustrated 20th-century texts). Locations at 15 Bulevardul Carol (phone: 615-8761) and 26 Bulevardul Magheru (phone: 611-2965).

**Muzică** Record albums, cassette tapes, and compact discs, some of them featuring great Romanian folk music and *Christmas* carols, are offered, as are wonderful woodcarvings at low prices. 41 Calea Victoriei (phone: 615-6088).

**Oficiu Poştal (Post Office Building)** Not only are stamps sold here, but also picture postcards and decorative envelopes. There are often long lines. Closed Sundays. 150 Calea Dorobanţilor (no phone); other branches located on Strada Nikos Beloinis, Strada Jean Louis Calderon, and Calea Dorobanţilor.

**Orizont** A gallery of fine paintings, sculpture, and Romania's famous glassware. Also on display are some examples of art done during the Soviet regime. Closed weekends. 23A Bulevardul Nicolas Bălcescu (phone: 615-8917).

**Piaţa Amzei (Amzei Market)** This huge indoor/outdoor market is open year-round, and in late summer and fall sells the fresh fruit and vegetables so noticeably absent at most restaurants. There also are booths for crafts, including hand-knit wool sweaters, blankets, and throws, as well as the bright, red-and-black embroidered table runners that decorate homes and restaurant walls. Strada Biserica Amzei (near the *Bucureşti* hotel).

**Unirea** The city's central department store has a good souvenir department. Sometimes you'll find handmade wool rugs, scarves, and national costumes and blouses. 1 Piaţa Unirii (phone: 311-1750 or 311-1756).

**Uniunea Artistilor Plastici (Union of Plastic Artists)** Look for this sign on the doors of a series of small art galleries located in the courtyard off Strada Lipscani. They sell cards and small prints, oil lamps, ceramics, jewelry, glassware, and paintings. Be sure to ask if you're allowed to take original art out of the country, since some valuable items are considered part of the "national patrimony." For more information, contact the *Union* (21 Nicolai Iorga; phone: 650-7180).

## SPORTS & FITNESS

Physical fitness and sports activities are considered fundamental for all Romanians—at school, in the factories, and in the villages. In the tennis world players Ion Tiriac and Ilie "Nasty" Năstase have had their share of aces. As elsewhere in Europe soccer is the national game here, and matches are played during spring, summer, and fall at several stadiums in Bucharest, including the *Dinamo* (7-9 Soseaua Stefan cel Mare; phone: 210-1288). Fitness centers and swimming pools can be found at the *Bucureşti, Flora, Inter-Continental* and *Parc* hotels (see *Checking In* for all four). About 3 miles (5 km) north of downtown is *Herăstrău Park,* where six clay tennis courts are available daily. Call for reservations (phone: 679-5948).

## THEATER

Tickets to shows and musical events are generally quite inexpensive and can be obtained at box offices, through most hotels and *Carpaţi,* and at ticket agencies around town. The *Caragiale National Theater* (2 Bulevardul Nicolae Bălcescu; phone: 615-1975) stages Romanian classics, Shakespeare, and other plays. Native son Eugène Ionescu's works are popular in Bucharest, and have been frequently presented at the *Theater of Comedy* (2 Strada Mândinesti; phone: 615-9137). Other famous venues in central Bucharest are the *Not-*

*tara Theater* (Bulevardul Magheru; phone: 659-5260) and the *Bulandra Theater* (76A Strada Jean Louis Calderon; phone: 611-9544). Opera and ballet fans should check the September-through-May schedule at the *Opera Română* (70 Bulevardul Mihail Kogălniceanu; phone: 613-1857). The only theaters open during the summer season (mid-June through mid-September) are puppet and comedy theaters; they present satire, very popular with Romanians.

## MUSIC

The *Ateneul Român* (Romanian Athenaeum; 1 Stradă Franklin; phone: 615-6875) is the home of the *Bucharest Philharmonic Orchestra and Choir,* which performs here during the winter. The *Rapsodia Română Artistic Ensemble Hall* (2 Strada Constantin Exarcu; phone: 615-0026) offers folkloric song and dance from Walachia, Moldavia, and Transylvania. Those with more contemporary tastes can take in pop and jazz concerts at the *Radiodifuziunea Română* (Hall of the Radio Building; 62-64 Strada General Berthelot; phone: 653055), where the *Bucharest Radio-Television Orchestra* also gives classical performances featuring many guest artists.

## NIGHTCLUBS AND NIGHTLIFE

The last four years have seen a surge in the nightlife scene, which was generally oriented toward cabarets and floor shows at the larger hotels. After-dark life usually begins around 9 PM and lasts until the wee hours. Popular among locals, especially the under-30 crowd, is the *Salion Spaniol* (120 Calea Victoriei; phone: 312-3999), with offerings ranging from amateur entertainment to special guest stars. For a blend of cabaret, vaudeville, and satire that can be entertaining even if you don't speak Romanian, try the *Casino Victoria* (174 Calea Victoriei; phone: 659-5865) and the *Savoy Theater* (Strada Academie). The *Bar Melody* (1 Strada Pictor Verona; phone: 611-8099) has floor shows. A new place in town, *Studio Martin* (Bulevardul Iancu de Hunedoara; phone: 321-4945) is a western-style disco that plays good music from 10 PM to 4 AM. Also try *Le Baron,* another new dance place (Parcul Patinoar Floreasca; phone: 633-1212), where the music is as hot as the beer is cold. *Vox Maris* (2 Bulevardul Kogŏlniceanu; phone: 615-5030) is a new, plush disco ensconced in quarters on the first floor of the army general staff building. The *Carioca Club* (97 Dacia; phone: 611-3126) is an elegant, minimally furnished bar that features live jazz Thursdays; reservations necessary. Although the *Insomnia Bar* (18 Bibescu Voda; phone: 614-8351) is in Ceaușescu's overwhelming *Civic Center,* it is basically an unpretentious, American-style place that attracts a mix of Romanians and foreigners—an ideal place for a late-night cheeseburger and beer; there's dancing to live music most nights. Although some might characterize the *Sarpele Rosu* (Red Snake; 133 Strada Galați; phone: 210-7825) as a dive, it is also one of the most fascinating places to spend an evening in Bucharest, featuring rousing jam sessions of live Gypsy music. The mostly local crowd often includes some unsavory types, but fear not: They are kept in check by the owner, who presides over his establishment from a corner table. The new American-style *Café Club 30* (14 Strada Batiştei; phone: 311-1038) boasts a pleasant piano bar and a large selection of drinks, including good German beer. Bridge, snooker, and pool may be played as well. Open daily until 4 AM, it is near the *US Embassy* and the *Inter-Continental* hotel.

# Best in Town

CHECKING IN

Without exception hotels in Bucharest and Romania's other major cities are the least expensive in Eastern Europe, and their quality is adequate to good, though hardly comparable to their counterparts in Western Europe. Hilton International will start to operate the veteran *Athénée Palace* early next year. The 1914 hotel's façades, pockmarked by bullets during the 1989 uprising, will be resurfaced, and the comfort of rooms improved under a $50 million restoration. Also scheduled to open next year is Radisson's *Grand* hotel, with 339 rooms, restaurants, a casino, nightclubs, and theaters.

Expect to pay $155 or more per night for a double room listed as very expensive; between $95 to $155 in a hotel listed as expensive; moderate accommodations run about $55 to $80. Reservations are particularly important during the summer months. In all of the following hotels guestrooms have private baths. All telephone numbers are in the 1 city code unless otherwise indicated.

### VERY EXPENSIVE

**Bucureşti** This modern, 447-room establishment is located on one of Bucharest's main thoroughfares and convenient to most sites in the city center. Its rooms and suites are small but comfortable. There's a good restaurant (see *Eating Out*) with a nightly Romanian music show, a brasserie, snack bar, and a good bar. Other amenities include indoor and outdoor swimming pools, saunas, a hairdresser, and a fitness center. Business facilities include meeting rooms for up to 250, foreign currency exchange, and photocopiers. 63-81 Calea Victoriei (phone: 615-5850; fax: 312-0927).

**Helveţa** The newest and one of the smallest hotels in Bucharest, it's what the French might call a chic place to stay. This retreat, near Bucharest's finest neighborhood and off the main entrance to *Herăstrău Park,* features 30 pleasant rooms with international direct-dial phones and color TV sets. Room service is very prompt. A good restaurant and bar are also here. Business facilities include an English-speaking concierge, foreign currency exchange, photocopiers, and computers. 4-6 Piaţa Aviatrilor (phone: 618-3790; fax: 312-0567).

**Inter-Continental** Bucharest's most modern property boasts 423 rooms at a great downtown location, but it has none of the Old World charm of the *Bucureşti* (see above). Many of the amenities are similar, though, including a pool and fitness center, three good restaurants serving Romanian and international food, two bars, a casino, and a nightclub complete with a floor show (admission is free to guests). Business facilities include meeting rooms for up 300, foreign currency exchange, and cable television news. 4-6 Bulevardul Nicolae Bălcescu (phone: 614-0400 or 613-7040; 800-327-0200; fax: 312-0486).

**Ambassador** Built in 1937, this 234-room hostelry is eminently serviceable, as well as conveniently located near Piaţa Universităţii and *Carpaţi*'s main office. There is a good restaurant and a wonderful pastry shop. Rooms are adequate, with bulky phones and TV sets. As for room service, it exists, but be patient. 8-10 Bulevardul Magheru (phone: 615-9087; fax: 312-1239).

**Capitol** The location more than makes up for the somewhat simple accommodations. All 80 rooms have telephones and TV sets, and there is a good restaurant serving Romanian fare along with a coffee shop on the premises. Just off Piaţa Universităţii, at 29 Calea Victoriei (phone: 613-9440; fax: 312-4169).

**Dorobanţi** This concrete structure located near Piaţa Romana may look unpretentious from the outside, but is in fact a perfect option for business travelers. All 298 rooms have TV sets and international direct-dial phones. In addition, there's a good restaurant serving continental and Romanian fare, as well as a bar. Business facilities include meeting rooms and foreign currency exchange. 1-7 Calea Dorobanţilor (phone: 211-5450; fax: 210-0150).

**Flora** A pleasant four-story hotel with 150 rooms and a lovely setting near *Herăstrău Park* on the outskirts of Bucharest. In addition to a restaurant, brasserie, cafeteria, and bar, facilities include a swimming pool and sauna. For jet-lagged travelers, skin-care and other therapeutic treatments are available for an additional fee. Business facilities include meeting rooms for up to 200 and foreign currency exchange. 1 Calea Poligrafiei (phone: 618-4640; fax: 312-8344).

**Lebăda (Swan)** A 127-room hotel on the site of a recently razed monastery on an island in Lake Pantelimon. There's a restaurant and bar, tennis courts, and a bowling alley. Business facilities include meeting rooms, foreign currency exchange, audiovisual equipment, and photocopiers. 3 Bulevardul Biruinţei, near the eastern edge of the city (phone: 624-3010; fax: 312-8041).

**Parc** Located near *Herăstrău Park,* next door to the *Flora,* this 257-room property is not quite as exclusive, but comfortable nonetheless, with modern amenities including a pool, sauna, indoor bowling center, outdoor tennis courts, a restaurant, cafeteria, brasserie, and bar with nightly entertainment. Business facilities include meeting rooms and foreign currency exchange. 3 Calea Poligrafiei (phone: 618-0950; fax: 617-7956).

**Sofitel** Located near Free Press Square, this is the capital's most modern facility. The hotel features 203 luxury rooms and suites; the *Darciee* restaurant, serving fine continental cuisine; a bar and coffee shop; and a nightclub. The hotel also offers a courtesy bus service to and from the airport. Business facilities include meeting rooms for up to 350, an English-speaking concierge, foreign currency exchange, secretarial services in English, audiovisual equipment, photocopiers, computers, and translation services. 2 Bulevardul Expozitiei (phone: 618-2828; 800-763-4835; fax: 212-0646).

### MODERATE

**Grivița** Thanks to reasonable prices and a convenient location near the *Gara de Nord* train station, all 62 rooms here are often full. Amenities are minimal, but there is a passable restaurant. 130 Calea Griviței (phone: 650-5380).

**Hanul lui Manuc (Manuc's Inn)** Built as an inn 300 years ago around a courtyard forming part of the city's old Princely Court, this historic, two-story wooden structure was first renovated in the 19th century. Located near the old market district, it has 32 guestrooms (try to get one that overlooks the courtyard) with TV sets and telephones. The on-site *Cramma* (wine cellar) serves Romanian and continental fare, as well as a wide variety of Romanian vintages. There's also a well-stocked bar and hair salon on the premises. Business facilities include meeting rooms and foreign currency exchange. 62 Strada Iuliu Maniu (phone: 613-1415; fax: 312-1811).

**Lido** This hotel affords 111 comfortable rooms that feature TV sets and international direct-dial phones. There's also an outdoor swimming pool famous for its artificial waves, the *Casa Lida* restaurant, and a bar. Business facilities include meeting rooms, foreign currency exchange, sercretarial services in English, photocopiers, computers, and translation services. 8-10 Bulevardul Magheru (phone: 614-4930; fax: 312-6544).

**Palas** A pleasant, 173-room hostelry within walking distance of Bucharest's theater district, it has a decent restaurant and cafeteria. 18 Strada C. Mille (phone: 613-6735).

**Triumf** Away from the downtown area in a quiet rose and statue garden surrounded by a wrought-iron fence is this three-story, red stone-and-brick hostelry. Originally built in 1938 to house the guests of King Carol II and later one of the Communist secret police's counterintelligence headquarters, its 93 rooms furnished in 19th-century style make it the best of the hotels in this category; suites boast Oriental carpets and antiques. Formerly called *Le President,* this is a favorite among members of the foreign diplomatic corps, particularly for its lovely restaurant (see *Eating Out*). Tennis courts near the summer terrace are available to guests. Business facilities include meeting rooms, foreign currency exchange, audiovisual equipment, photocopiers, computers, and translation service. 12 Soseaua Kiseleff (phone: 618-410; fax: 312-8411).

---

## EATING OUT

Though Bucharest was once a gastronomic capital of Europe, the city is struggling to regain even a soupçon of its former reputation.

Things are slowly improving, and a handful of restaurants are a cut above the rest.

Authentic Romanian food is usually simple but varied, due to multiple cultural influences—Slavic, Germanic, and French among them. Fish dishes abound. The favorite appetizer is *mititei,* a small, skinless lamb sausage spiced with garlic and herbs and grilled. *Ciorbă* is a hearty soup that comes in many varieties, including *ciorbă de perişoare* (a milky broth with meatballs and vegetables) and *ciorbă de burta* (a cream soup with veal tripe, rice, and vegetables, highly seasoned with vinegar and garlic). Perhaps the primary national staple is *mămăligă,* a creamy corn porridge that accompanies the entrée at lunch or is eaten by itself as a light supper, served with fresh unsalted cheese and sour cream. The best Romanian dishes are the desserts, like cream-filled chocolate pastries, mocha- or fruit-filled strudel, and rich Austrian-style tortes and honey-nut pies. Wash all this down with a selection of quite good red and white wines from Transylvania, Moldavia, and the Black Sea area. Murfatlar wines (mostly white) have won medals in worldwide competitions, and Cotnari, a northern Moldavian white, was a favorite of 15th-century Prince Stefan cel Mare (the Great). Another national drink is *tuică,* an aromatic (and very potent) plum eau-de-vie.

The major meal of the day is generally taken at noon, though many restaurants, including those listed here, serve a full menu at both lunch and dinner. To assure the widest selection have dinner as early as possible; even in good restaurants the best dishes are rarely available in abundance and are likely to run out later in the evening.

An expensive three-course dinner for two (including wine, drinks, and tip) will cost $30 to $50. At moderately priced establishments expect to pay between $20 and $30, and less than $20 for an inexpensive meal. Payment is in lei, but nobody will ever refuse hard currency or, in many cases, a major credit card. Unless otherwise specified all restaurants below are open for lunch and dinner. All telephone numbers are in the 1 city code unless otherwise indicated.

### EXPENSIVE

**Bucureşti** In the hotel of the same name, meals here are well prepared, with fresh, if not particularly imaginative, fare such as beef Stroganoff, roast pork, and lamb chops. A wonderful tradition left over from 19th-century Bucharest is the "show table," which allows diners to peruse the specials of the day before ordering (a boon for non-Romanian speakers). Desserts are creamy and irresistible. Entertainment includes a pop-rock band and folkloric song and dance. Open daily. Reservations advised. Major credit cards and hard currency accepted. 63-11 Calea Victoriei (phone: 615-5850).

**Capşa** Founded in 1852 by a Parisian restaurateur, this became the city's premier culinary institution, as well as an artistic and literary salon and magnet for Bucharest's aristocratic elite. Red velvet banquettes, gold-framed beveled mirrors, crystal chandeliers, and pink marble columns suggest some of the grandeur of a lost age. The food is continental, with a variety of Romanian specialties, and the kitchen makes as much use as possible of fresh local produce. There's also an elegant tearoom. Open daily. Reservations necessary. Major credit cards accepted by advance arrangement through *Carpaţi*. The side entrance at 16 Strada Edgar Quinet is used for the restaurant, while the front entrance at 36 Calea Victoriei mostly is for the tearoom (phone: 613-4482).

**Caru cu Bere (Beer Wagon)** It's a splendid German-style beer hall and good restaurant. Live folk shows tend to be too noisy sometimes, but it's definitely worth a visit for a glimpse at the spectacular interior and for the delicious *mititei*. Open daily. Reservations advised. No credit cards accepted. 3 Strada Stavropoleos (phone: 613-7560).

**Casă Lido** Originally built in 1890, this dining spot later received neoclassical touches; the focal point is a grand spiral staircase. The Romanian food is adequate rather than inspired, but the service is quite elegant, and there is a good selection of wines and cognacs. Open daily. Reservations necessary. Major credit cards accepted by advance arrangement through *Carpaţi*. 13 Strada C. A. Rosetti; entrance through a courtyard at 3 Bulevardul Magheru (phone: 615-5085).

**Casă Romana** Romanian specialties, some Italian dishes such as good spaghetti, as well as steaks are offered in this fine setting. Occasionally a shipment of Italian wine or German beer livens up the menu. Open daily. Reservations advised. Major credit cards accepted. 2 Calea Victoriei (phone: 614-6808).

**Doi Cocoşi (Two Roosters)** Three miles (5 km) from the city center, this lively eatery serves up delicious Romanian fare. Near *Băneasa Airport,* at 6 Soseaua Bucuresş-Târgovişte (phone: 667-1080).

**Elite** A former aircraft factory canteen located near *Băneasa Airport,* it now is a fine restaurant serving Romanian specialties, excellent pork filet, roast beef, and several French-inspired dishes. Open daily. Reservations advised. No credit cards accepted. Complexul Aviatiei Băneasa (phone: 312-9973).

**Nan Jing** Bucharest's best Chinese restaurant offers a fine menu that includes octopus with mushrooms, shrimp with bamboo, and the standard rice dishes. Open daily. Reservations advised. Major credit cards accepted. 2-4 Strada Locotenent Gheorghe Manu (phone: 650-6010).

**La Premiera** This gathering place for diplomats, foreigners, and assorted members of Romanian bohemia serves consistently high-quality continental and Romanian fare in a modern, pleasant atmosphere, in the back of the *National Theater Building.* During the summer, the terrace is the most "in" place in town for dinner or late-night drinks or snacks. Be sure to try the excellent quail and schnitzel, as well as a selection from the good wine list. Open daily. Reservations necessary. Major credit cards accepted. 16 Strada Tudor Arghezi (phone: 312-4397).

**Select** Good Romanian and international dishes are featured at this dining spot. Ask for the delicious foie gras. A first-class bar is located downstairs. Open daily. Reservations necessary. No credit cards accepted. 18 Aleea Alexandru (phone: 212-0492).

**Triumf** One of the establishments that is trying hard to restore some luster to the culinary arts in Bucharest—and it's succeeding. Romanian dishes mix with continental specialties, including superb chateaubriand, pâté, and cakes and pastries that taste as heavenly as they look. Open daily. Reservations necessary. Major credit cards accepted. At the *Triumf Hotel,* 12 Soseaua Kiseleff (phone: 618-4110).

**Velvet** This elegant dining room, decorated with plush, pink chairs and white, wooden tables, is an excellent place for dinner, offering French-inspired food that is probably the best in Bucharest. Try the chateaubriand or seafood salad. There is also an upstairs café. Open daily. Reservations necessary. No credit cards accepted. 2 Calea Stirbei Vodă (phone: 615-9241).

### MODERATE

**Casa Albă (The White House)** A popular indoor/outdoor place in a park setting, with a good menu. Recommended Romanian specialties include cold stuffed vegetable appetizers. Entertainment is provided by a five-piece band, and there's a folkloric show. A bit touristy, but you might spot a few Romanians here, too. Open daily. Reservations advised and should be made in person. No credit cards accepted. In *Băneasa Forest,* on Aleea Privighetorilor (phone: 679-5203).

**Dong Hai** One of the best of the dozen or so Chinese restaurants that have sprung up throughout the city. Try the spicy pork. Open daily. Reservations necessary. No credit cards accepted. 14 Strada Blanari (phone: 615-6494).

**Gogoşarul** No music and not much atmosphere, but the Romanian specialties are as close to homemade as you're likely to find anywhere. A favorite dinner spot for well-to-do locals. Open daily. Reservations advised. No credit cards accepted. 53 Strada Turda (phone: 617-3402).

**Pescăruş (Seagull)** This large, two-story dining spot on a lovely lake in *Herăstrău Park* is well suited for large groups, and evening folkloric shows can be arranged. The fare is a combination of international and Romanian dishes. Closed Mondays. Reservations necessary. Major credit cards accepted. Calea Aviatorilor (phone: 679-4640).

### INEXPENSIVE

**Panipat** Thick-crust pizza with all the fixings is available daily. No reservations or credit cards accepted. 204 Calea Victoriei (phone: 650-0641).

**Springtime** Similar to *McDonald's,* it serves the best hamburgers in town; cheeseburgers, fried chicken, egg muffins, ice cream, and soft drinks are other staples. Open daily. No reservations or credit cards accepted. Piaţa Victoriei (phone: 312-3514).

# Budapest

## At-a-Glance

### SEEING THE CITY

The best view of Budapest is from the top of Gellérthegy (Gellért Hill) on the Buda side, which can be climbed from Gellért tér (Gellért Square). From the balustrades of a stone fort built in 1850 you will enjoy a panorama of the Danube with its bridges—Margit híd (Margaret Bridge) to Margitsziget (Margaret Island) in the middle of the Danube, the recreational center of the city; the historic Széchenyi-lánchid (Chain Bridge) to Castle Hill on the Buda side, the oldest part of town; and the Erzsébet híd (Elizabeth Bridge) that connects Buda with the Inner City on the Pest side, the busy downtown commercial and shopping center. In front of the fort, or *Citadella,* is the gigantic *Liberation Monument,* a statue of a woman holding an olive branch, which is sometimes called Budapest's *Statue of Liberty;* it commemorates the Soviet liberation of Budapest from Nazi occupation in 1945.

Since Buda is built on seven hills, there are several other panoramas of the city. One of the best is from *Halászbástya* (Fishermen's Bastion) in the Castle Hill District, from which the Danube, Margaret Island, and the flat Pest side of the river, including the spectacular façade of *Parliament,* are all clearly visible.

Budapest is divided into numerous districts designated by a Roman numeral before the street address. Streets have been renamed, and on many corners visitors will find both the new and old signs; the older one, usually bearing the name of a Communist hero, has a red "X" drawn through it. *Utca, út,* and *útja* mean street in Hungarian; *tér* means square; *körút* refers to the concentric avenues radiating from the Danube in Pest; and *rakpart* is the name given to the quays that run parallel to the river.

### SPECIAL PLACES

Budapest, once actually three cities—Buda, Obuda, and Pest—sprawls along both banks of the Danube River and is difficult to explore on foot because of the distances involved. To make matters worse, Buda's streets are hilly and often cobbled. A detailed map, recently printed, is strongly advised (see *Sources and Resources*). Public transportation is good, and fares are low.

#### BUDA

**VÁRHEGY (CASTLE HILL)** Topped by monuments, this hill is the heart of medieval Budapest, with cobbled streets, narrow alleys, and lovely squares. Homes are painted in pastel colors that used to denote the trade of the owner. The Baroque and neoclassical public buildings, also painted in lovely pastels, now house famous restaurants, writers' studios, a student quarter, and many landmarks. Unfortunately, few Hungarians live in this area anymore; the charming district has become a visitor's paradise in which almost everyone speaks a foreign language. Much of the area was badly damaged during World War II, and restorations include a 19th-century funicular railway (Budavári Sikló) that climbs up the hill from the Danube. The funicular runs daily from just in front of the Széchenyi-lànchid at Clark Adám tér, taking about a minute each way.

**HALÁSZBÁSTYA (FISHERMEN'S BASTION)** Named for the fishermen of the city who protected this northern side of the *Royal Castle* from siege in medieval times, the bastion is a turn-of-the-century *Disneyland*-type version of Romanesque ramparts and turrets. Originally built as a showpiece for the 1896 *World's Fair,* today the structure affords good views of the Danube and the city. I, Hunyadi János út.

**MÁTYÁS TEMPLOM (MATTHIAS CHURCH)** This neo-Gothic edifice atop Castle Hill, where King Matthias was married twice, dates from the 13th century, although it has been rebuilt many times, most recently after World War II. Its proper name is the *Church of Our Lady.* With its 250-foot spire and colored tile roof, this coronation church of Hungarian kings has one of Europe's most memorable silhouettes. Inside, the splendor of the gilded Baroque nave is especially noteworthy, as are the original chalices and vestments in the treasury. During the Turkish occupation of Hungary in the 16th and 17th centuries, the church served as a mosque. There are frequent organ recitals. I, 2 Szentháromság tér.

**BUDAVÁRI PALOTA (ROYAL PALACE)** Reduced to rubble by bombs in 1944–45, the palace has been rebuilt carefully to incorporate all the styles of its historic past. Prior to the bombing it existed primarily as an 18th-century building with some Baroque touches; before that it had been destroyed and rebuilt several times and in several architectural styles since it was first constructed as a castle in the 13th century. It now houses the *Historical Museum of Budapest,* the *National Gallery,* the *National Library,* and the *Museum of Contemporary Times* (formerly the *Museum of the Worker's Movement*). On Várhegy, I, 2 Szent György tér (phone: 175-7533).

**BUDAPESTI TÖRTÉNETI MÚZEUM (HISTORICAL MUSEUM OF BUDAPEST)** In Wing E (the southern wing) of the *Royal Palace,* the museum contains archaeological remains of the ancient town and exhibits on the history of the palace's construction. Also on display are splendid furniture, sculpture, ceramics, glass, and china; the halls, dating from the 15th century, have Renaissance door frames carved of red marble. To appreciate the richness of this collection, one must remember that Hungary's King Matthias had a greater income at the end of the 15th century than either of the English or French kings. Closed Mondays. Admission charge. I, 2 Szent György tér (phone: 175-7533).

**NEMZETI GALÉRIA (NATIONAL GALLERY)** Also housed in the *Royal Palace,* this museum displays medieval stone carvings, early Gothic stat-

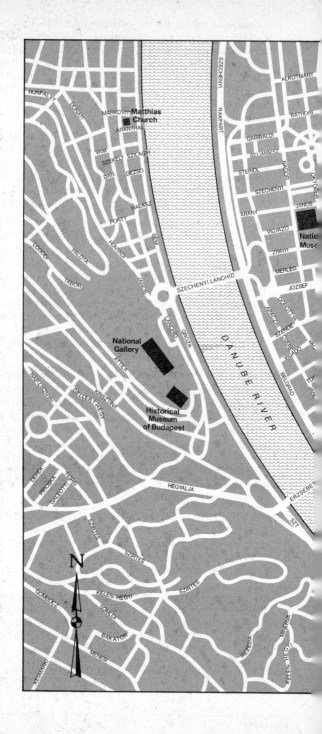

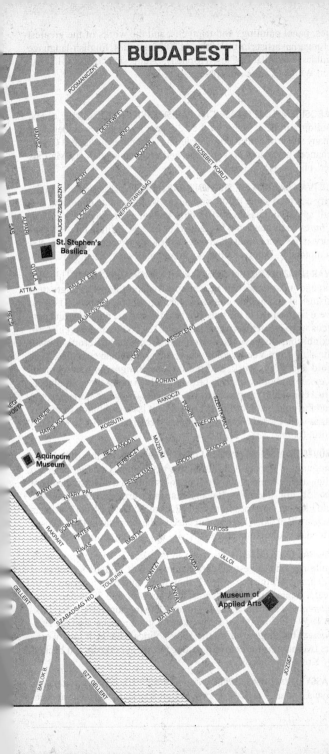

# BUDAPEST

ues, panel paintings and triptychs, and the works of the greatest Hungarian artists of the 19th and 20th centuries. English-language guides are available. Closed Mondays. Admission charge. I, 17 Dísz tér, Wings B, C, and D (phone: 175-7533).

## PEST

**BELVÁROSI TEMPLOM (INNER CITY PARISH CHURCH)** This is the oldest building in Pest, begun in the 12th century. It shows evidence of many styles of construction, including a Romanesque arch, a Gothic chancel, a Moslem prayer niche, and a Roman wall. V, 15 Március tér (phone: 118-3108).

**SZENT ISTVÁN BAZILIKA (ST. STEPHEN'S BASILICA)** The largest church in the city can hold some 8,500 worshipers. With its huge dome and two tall spires, the basilica (officially known as *St. Stephen's Parish Church*) dominates the flat landscape of Pest. Built in the 19th century, it has murals and altarpieces by leading Hungarian painters and sculptors. V, Bajcsy-Zsilinszky út (entrance on V, Szent István tér).

**MAGYAR NEMZETI MÚZEUM (HUNGARIAN NATIONAL MUSEUM)** This oldest and most important museum in Budapest houses the greatest historical and archaeological collections in the country. The first were bequeathed to the museum in 1802, and the buildings and gardens were erected between 1837 and 1847. One of the prehistoric exhibitions displays the most ancient remnant of European man, the skull from Vértesszölös. There are also Roman ceramics, Avar gold and silver work, and the famous *Hungarian Crown of St. Stephen* and other historic crown jewels. Among the gold objects are a chiseled Byzantine crown (called the *Crown of Monomachos*) and the gold baton of Franz Liszt. There is an exhibition of minerals as well. Closed Mondays. Admission charge. VIII, 14-16 Múzeum körút (phone: 138-2122).

**IPARMÜVÉSZETI MÚZEUM (MUSEUM OF APPLIED ARTS)** Another of the great museums of Budapest, its most important holdings are European and Hungarian ceramics, the work of goldsmiths and silversmiths from the 15th to 17th century, Italian Renaissance textiles, Turkish carpets, and Flemish tapestries from the 17th century. The museum's artifacts were a gift of Ödön Lechner (architect of the museum) in 1896. Closed Mondays. Admission charge. IX, 33-37 Ullöi út (phone: 117-5222).

**ORSZÁGHÁZ (PARLIAMENT)** Mirrored in the Danube, these impressive buildings on the Pest side are reminiscent of London's *Houses of Parliament.* Finished in 1902, they were built over a period of 17 years. A maze of 10 courtyards, 29 staircases, and 88 statues, *Parliament* is a favorite haunt for lovers (and the homeless) after dark. In 1950 the Communist Party placed a giant red star atop the *Parliament* buildings. During the 1989 political change it took workers two months to remove it. Along Széchenyi rakpart and backed by Kossuth Lajos tér.

**ANDRÁSSY ÚT (ANDRÁS STREET)** Named after 19th-century statesman Gyula Andrássy and also known as Embassy Row, this noble avenue, which runs from the inner city of Pest and crosses two concentric rings toward *Városliget* (City Park), has had many other names throughout Budapest's stormy past—among them Sugár (Radial) in the 19th century, Andrássy in the early 20th century, Stalin Avenue and Avenue of Hungarian Youth in 1956, Népköztársaság (People's Republic) in 1957, and Andrássy again in 1990. The avenue—built between 1871 and 1885—is lined with over 200 houses and palaces on both sides, many of which were designed by architect Miklós Ybl in the 1870s and 1880s; among these buildings are the neo-Renaissance *Hungarian State Opera House* at No. 22 and the building that once housed the Gestapo and the Communist secret police at No. 60.

**HÖSÖK TÉR (HEROES' SQUARE)** At the end of Andrássy is a large square marked by the *Millennial Monument,* begun in 1896 and finished in 1929 to celebrate Hungary's thousand-year anniversary. A semicircular colonnade displays a pantheon of Hungarian historical figures; on top of the 119-foot pillar in the middle of the square is a statue of the Archangel Gabriel, who, according to legend, offered a crown to King Stephen I, founder of the kingdom. On this square are the *Museum of Fine Arts* (see below) and the *Art Gallery* (phone: 122-7405).

**SZÉPMÜVÉSZETI MÚZEUM (MUSEUM OF FINE ARTS)** Here is the greatest collection of its kind in the country. The 1906 building is at the entrance of *Városliget* (City Park), on the left as you face the *Millennial Monument.* More than 100,000 works of art are housed in this neoclassical structure. Among the masterpieces are seven paintings by El Greco, five by Goya, the *Madonna Esterházy* by Raphael, and the *Sermon of St. John the Baptist* by Pieter Breughel the Elder. The museum also has permanent exhibitions of Egyptian and Greco-Roman antiquities and modern European painting and sculpture. Closed Mondays. Admission charge. XIV, Hösök tér (phone: 142-9759).

**VÁROSLIGET (CITY PARK)** This large park just behind Heroes' Square contains an artificial lake; the *Széchenyi Baths* (a public spa); a zoo; a botanical garden; an amusement park; and *Vajdahunyad Castle* (built for the 1896 *World's Fair*), which encompasses a conglomeration of architectural styles. In winter there's an ice skating rink.

**GALLERY 56** Opened in 1992 by Yoko Ono and Samuel Havadtoy, it showcases works of acclaimed contemporary artists from around the world. The gallery's minimalist interior and provocative exhibits make it a unique cultural spot in Budapest. V, 7 Falk Miksa utca (phone: 269-2529).

**MERLIN CULTURAL CENTER** What was once a private club of the Budapest City Council is now a trendy cultural center that houses a restaurant, a late-night jazz club, and, during the summer, a theater presenting plays in English and German. 4 Gerlóczy utca (phone: 267-3625).

**NYUGATI PÁLYAUDVAR (WESTERN STATION)** This glass-and-iron railroad station, designed by August de Serres between 1874 and 1877 and constructed by the Alexandre-Gustave Eiffel Company (of *Eiffel Tower* fame), is well worth a visit, even if you're not taking a train. VI, 57 Teréz Körút.

## OBUDA

**FŐ TÉR (MAIN SQUARE)** Located along the northwestern bank of the Danube River is Obuda, the city's most recently developed residential area, with its charming old houses and taverns intermingled with towering apartment complexes. Obuda's cobblestoned main square boasts a life-size sculpture called *Strollers in the Rain,* by contemporary artist Varga. Around the square are numerous art galleries, cafés, and the early-18th-century *Zichy Mansion* (No. 1 Fő tér), but restaurants, such as *Sipos Halászkert* (see *Eating Out*), are an even bigger attraction. Some have outdoor seating in the warm weather.

**AQUINCUM** Not far from Fő Tér is one of the most significant excavations of a Roman urban area outside Italy. *Aquincum* (meaning "Ample Water") in its heyday had almost 100,000 inhabitants. Its streets, houses, temple, and amphitheater have been unearthed 4 miles (6 km) upstream of the city center on the western bank of the Danube. The museum on the site has mosaics depicting public baths, jewelry, glass, and inscribed stones. Open from mid-April through mid-October. 139 M. Szentendrei út.

## ELSEWHERE IN THE CITY

**MARGITSZIGET (MARGARET ISLAND)** This resort and recreation island lies right in the middle of the Danube, accessible from both banks by the pedestrians-only Margit híd (Margaret Bridge). Cars and trains enter from Arpád Bridge to the north; on summer weekends a bus runs between the southern end of the island and the hotels near Arpád Bridge. The whole island is a park replete with more than 10,000 trees, a sports stadium, a large municipal swimming pool, a rose garden, a fountain, and several hotels, restaurants, and spas. During the summer, when theaters close, the performances move to outdoor quarters here; you can attend plays, concerts, films, and sports events. For specific programs inquire at the tourist office, *IBUSZ* (see *Tourist Information*).

**KEREPESI TEMETŐ (KEREPESI CEMETERY)** Once you've tired of walking from monument to church to museum, visit the *Kerepesi Cemetery,* an oasis of quiet and rest in this busy city. Wealthy Hungarians spent fortunes building mausoleums adorned with sculptures and decorations, and the century-old trees here offer pleasant shade. At one side of the cemetery are monuments to people who died during the 1919 revolution and the 1956 uprising. Off Kerepesi út.

---

### EXTRA SPECIAL

A boat trip on the beautiful (if not blue) Danube is an experience you will not soon forget. From May to September, *IBUSZ* (see below) offers several day tours to the Danube Bend area, about 31 miles (50 km) north of Budapest, where the river makes a hairpin turn, changing its course from west-east to north-south. The area is rich in scenery, with limestone hills and volcanic mountains, and in history, with communities that date from Roman times. Tours depart Wednesdays and Saturdays at 8:30 AM from the Vigadó tér landing dock (phone: 118-1223 or 129-5844; or call *IBUSZ*). From the middle of April through October there are daily hydrofoil trips between Budapest and Vienna, but it's necessary to reserve two to three months in advance. Contact *European Cruises* (241 E. Commercial Blvd., Fort Lauderdale, FL 33334; phone: 800-5-DANUBE). For information in Budapest call *MAHART* (V, Belgrád rakpart; phone: 118-1953 or 118-1706).

# Sources and Resources

TOURIST INFORMATION
For general information, brochures, and maps contact *IBUSZ*—Hungary's largest travel agency (V, 10 Ferenciektére; phone: 118-6866; 3 Petőfi tér; phone: 118-4842, both open 24 hours; at the *Budapest Tourist Office,* V, 5 Roosevelt tér; phone: 117-3555; and at most major hotels). You may also contact *Tourinform* (V, 2 Sütö utca; phone: 117-9800; fax: 117-9578), open daily. The *US Embassy* is at V, 12 Szabadsag tér (phone: 112-6450).

For information in the US contact *IBUSZ Travel* (1 Parker Plaza, Mezzanine, Ft. Lee, NJ 07024; phone: 201-592-8585 in NJ; 800-367-7878 elsewhere in the US; fax: 201-592-8736). The *Hungarian Embassy* is at 3910 Shoemaker St. NW, Washington, DC 20008 (phone: 202-362-6730).

**ENTRY REQUIREMENTS** No visa is necessary for a US citizen holding a valid passport for a stay of up to 90 days. For an extension beyond 90 days it is necessary to apply to a local police station in Hungary.

**TIME** The time in Hungary is six hours later than in US East Coast cities. Hungary follows daylight saving time.

**LANGUAGE** Hungarian (Magyar), a Finno-Ugric language distantly related to Finnish. German is the second language and Russian is still understood by some, but English is becoming increasingly common.

**ELECTRIC CURRENT** 220 volts, 50 cycles, AC.

**MONEY** The forint (ft) equals 100 fillér. At press time $1 US bought about 100 forint.

**TIPPING** Be prepared to add 15% to restaurant bills, taxi fares, and hotel service; 200 forints is the usual tip for strolling musicians in restaurants if you ask them to play.

**BANKING/BUSINESS HOURS** Banks and many offices are open weekdays from 8 or 9 AM to 2 or 4 PM. Currency exchange facilities outside the banks are numerous.

**NATIONAL HOLIDAYS** *New Year's Day* (January 1), *Anniversary of the 1848 Revolution* (March 15), *Easter Sunday* (April 16), *Easter Monday* (April 17), *Labor Day* (May 1), *St. Stephen's Day* (August 20), *1956 Revolution Day* (October 23), *Christmas Day* (December 25), and *Boxing Day* (December 26).

**LOCAL COVERAGE** *Programme in Hungary* (in English and German) and *Budapest Panorama* (in English, German, and Italian) are comprehensive monthly bulletins that list concerts, theater events, literary evenings, museum exhibits, sporting events, restaurants, and casinos. *Budapest Panorama* also carries information regarding airlines, credit cards, and rental cars. Both are available free at hotel desks. For a complete listing of all restaurants in Budapest, look for *Foglaljon Helyet!* (Have a Seat!), available in bookstores.

Budapest now has two weekly English-language newspapers: *Budapest Week* amd the *Budapest Sun,* available at newsstands and major hotels. International papers, such as the European edition of the *Wall Street Journal* and the *International Herald Tribune,* are sold at most kiosks throughout the city.

**TELEPHONE** The city code for Budapest is 1. Phonecards, available at all post office branches, are now used throughout the city for pay phones. When calling from one area to another within Hungary dial 0 + city code + local number. The country code for Hungary is 36. In an emergency, dial 04 for an ambulance and 07 for the police.

## GETTING AROUND

**AIRPORT** *Ferihegy Airport* handles all international flights. One terminal is for *MALÉV* (the Hungarian national carrier; phone: 118-4333). The drive from the airport to downtown Budapest takes about a half hour. Waiting taxi drivers are likely to overcharge you, as will gypsy cabs, which often have "less than accurate" meters. Hail an incoming cab or go upstairs to the domestic cab pickup area. The recently revamped *Airport Minibus* (phone: 157-8555 or 157-6283) is a much less expensive alternative. Reservations can be made in advance either by phone or at hotel desks.

**BUS/TRAM/SUBWAY** Public transportation is efficient and cheap. Tickets are sold at tobacco shops, kiosks, and ticket offices only (not on the vehicles). Each ticket, valid for one trip, must be punched in the machines inside the vehicles. Yellow tickets are good on the metro (subway), trams, and trolleybuses; blue tickets are for bus transportation only.

**CAR RENTAL** Automobiles may be rented with or without drivers from *IBUSZ-Avis* (V, Szeruta tér; phone: 118-6222); *Hertz* (VII, 24-28 Kertész utca; phone: 111-6116; and V, 4-8 Aranykéz utca; phone: 117-7533); and *Europcar* (V, 62 Ullöi út; phone: 113-1492). All companies have branches at the airport.

**TAXI** Taxi stands can be found throughout the city; rates vary widely by company as there is no fare regulation. Budapest's best cab companies include *Főtaxi* (phone: 222-2222) and *Volántaxi* (phone: 166-6666); both have drivers for guided tours. Also serving Budapest are *Tele5* (phone: 155-5555), *City Taxi* (phone: 153-3633), and *Budataxi* (phone: 120-2006).

**TOURS** You might wish to get acquainted with Budapest by taking the three-hour city tour offered daily by *IBUSZ* (see above). A four-hour *IBUSZ* tour, conducted Thursdays at 10 AM from Erzsébet tér, provides a look at the city's cultural life, with art studio and museum visits and concerts. *CityRama Budapest* (V, 27 Báthori utca; phone: 132-5344; fax: 112-5424) arranges private sightseeing tours of the city and environs. Of the many local agencies conducting tours of the country, *IPV Tourisme* (22 Angol utca; phone: 163-3406) has particularly imaginative packages with an accent on culture and history.

**TRAIN** The main office of the *Magyar Allamvasutak* (*MAV; Hungarian State Railways;* VI, 35 Andrássy út; phone: 122-8049) handles tickets, reservations, and general train information. Major stations are the *Eastern* (Baross tér; phone: 155-8657), for eastbound and most international trains, and the *Western* (Nyugati tér; phone: 149-0115), for trains headed west. A fast, dependable, and air conditioned *EuroCity (EC)* train—the *Lehár*—connects Budapest and Vienna in under three hours (phone: 122-4052).

## LOCAL SERVICES

The larger hotels are the best bet for travelers who like lots of services under one roof. Most of these provide dry cleaning and tailoring, photocopying, and more, along with a concierge who will help find anything the hotel can't supply.

**DENTIST (ENGLISH-SPEAKING)** Once there were only a few, but now there are many dental clinics in Budapest where English is spoken. *Dental-Coop* (XII, 60 Zugligeti út; phone: 176-0243) and *Superdent KFT XIII* (65 Dózsa György utca; phone: 129-0200); both clinics are open weekdays only. For additional recommendations ask your hotel concierge.

**DRY CLEANER/TAILOR** Recommended are *Cooperative Dry Cleaning* (*Flórián Shopping Center;* 6-9 Flórián tér) and the *Patyolat* dry-cleaning chain (look for the swan logo), found all over the city.

**LIMOUSINE SERVICE** Budapest has no limousine companies per se, but you can hire a car with driver from *IBUSZ-Avis* (phone: 118-6222) and *Főtaxi* (phone: 222-2222).

**MEDICAL EMERGENCY** Emergency cases are handled by hospitals on a rotating basis. Dial 04 for an ambulance, and it will take you to the facility on duty. There is also a 24-hour emergency medical service with English-speaking technicians (phone: 118-8212).

**MESSENGER SERVICE** Ask your hotel concierge.

**NATIONAL/INTERNATIONAL COURIER** *DHL Worldwide Express* (VIII, 1-3 Rakoczi út; phone: 266-7777 or 266-5555).

**OFFICE EQUIPMENT RENTAL** Check with the main hotels that offer conference rooms and other business services.

**PHARMACY** There is 24-hour service at *gyógyszertár* (pharmacies) located at VI, 41 Teréz körút (phone: 111-4439), and II, 22 Frankel Leó utca (phone: 115-8290).

**PHOTOCOPIES** At all major hotels.

**POST OFFICE** Post offices No. 62 (VI, 51 Teréz körút, near the *Western Railway Station*) and No. 70 (VII, 1 Verseny utca, at the *Eastern Railway Station*) have 24-hour service.

**SECRETARY/STENOGRAPHER (ENGLISH-SPEAKING)** Ask your hotel concierge.

**TRANSLATOR** Call *IBUSZ* (phone: 118-6866) or inquire at your hotel.

## SPECIAL EVENTS

The *Budapest Spring Festival,* from mid-March through mid-April, is the highlight of the cultural season and features concerts, folk dancing, and other performances. For tickets and information, contact the booking office (1 Vörösmarty tér; phone: 118-9570). In 1986 Hungary became the host country for the annual *Formula 1 Grand Prix* on the *Hungaroring* at Mogyoród, about a half-hour's drive southwest of Budapest. This international auto race takes place every year in August. Tickets are available at the *Autoclub* (phone: 115-8469). *Budapest Music Weeks,* in early fall, include international competitions for various types of musicians and many concerts. Late November marks *Kierkegaard Week,* which honors the life of Danish philosopher Søren Kierkegaard. Events include lectures, seminars, and concerts held throughout the city. For more information, contact the *Budapest Chamber Theater* (phone: 202-7587).

In addition to official celebrations, peaceful marches and demonstrations organized by opposition groups are the order of the day (motorists take note). Budapest also has announced that it will host the 1996 *World's Fair.* For general information about all special events, contact *IBUSZ* (see above).

## MUSEUMS

Several museums provide an introduction to Hungary's rich religious heritage: *Collections of Ecclesiastical Treasures* at the *Matthias Church* (I, Szentháromság tér; phone: 116-1453) and at *St. Stephen's Basilica* (V, Szent István tér); the *National Evangelical Museum* (V, 4 Deák tér; phone: 117-4173); and the *Bible Museum* (IX, 28 Ráday utca). In addition to these museums and those listed in *Special Places,* the following are worth a visit. All are closed Mondays and have a nominal admission charge.

**BARTÓK EMLÉKHÁZ (BÉLA BARTÓK MEMORIAL HOUSE)** Concerts are presented here on occasion. II, 29 Csalán utca (phone: 176-2100).

**BÉLYEGMÚZEUM (MUSEUM OF POSTAGE STAMPS)** An extensive collection that includes some very rare stamps. VII, 47 Hársfa utca (phone: 142-0960).

**LISZT FERENC MÚZEUM (FRANZ LISZT MUSEUM)** A collection of the composer's personal possessions displayed in his apartment in the old *Academy of Music.* Piano recitals occasionally are held here. VI, 35 Vörösmarty utca (phone: 122-9804).

**MAGYAR KERESKEDELMI ÉS VENDÉGLÁTÓIPARI MÚZEUM (MUSEUM OF HUNGARIAN COMMERCE AND CATERING)** A delightful small museum on Castle Hill featuring a replica of a turn-of-the-century confectioner's shop and odd artifacts—advertising signs, appliances, and other consumer goods—from Budapest's capitalist past. I, 4 Fortuna utca (phone: 175-6242).

**NÉPRAJZI MÚZEUM (ETHNOGRAPHIC MUSEUM)** A glimpse into the country's past. Concerts are held here on Sundays. V, 12 Kossuth tér (phone: 132-6349).

**SEMMELWEIS ORVOSTÖRTÉNETI MÚZEUM (SEMMELWEIS MUSEUM OF THE HISTORY OF MEDICINE)** A fascinating look at the development of European and Hungarian medicine from Roman times to the present. Dr. Ignác Semmelweis, the man responsible for the cure for childbed fever, was born in the building that now houses the museum. I, 1-3 Aprád utca (phone: 175-3533).

**VARGA IMRE GYÜJTEMÉNY (IMRE VARGA COLLECTION)** Monuments by the internationally famous sculptor are scattered throughout his native Hungary. Samples of his work are on permanent exhibition here, and sometimes the artist himself is on hand. III, 7 Laktanya utca (phone: 180-3274).

**ZENETÖRTÉNETI MÚZEUM (MUSICAL HISTORY MUSEUM)** An exhibition called "Béla Bartók's Workshop" traces the composer's creative process. In addition, a collection of historical musical instruments is on display and a concert series is presented. I, 7 Táncsics Mihály utca (phone: 175-9011 or 175-9487).

**ZSIDÓ MÚZEUM (JEWISH MUSEUM)** The history of Hungarian Jewry is shown through liturgical objects and documents. On the outside wall is a plaque honoring Theodor Herzl, founder of Budapest's Zionist movement, whose house once stood on this site. VII, 8 Dohány utca (phone: 142-8949).

## SHOPPING

The change from state-owned to private business is most apparent in the city's shops. Once stocked with limited amounts of goods, they are now brimming with every imaginable consumer item. Along Váci utca, the Hungarian approximation of Fifth Avenue, clothing stores that once sold few styles in even fewer colors now have racks of the latest fashions—many with well-known designer labels, but the best buys are those that are uniquely Hungarian. The many boutiques that line the streets of the Castle Hill District are also where you'll find traditional, folk-inspired garments—from embroidered peasant shirts and shawls to assorted leather goods and embroidered sheepskin jackets. Other local crafts include dolls in regional costumes and woodcarvings made by herdsmen. Pottery and porcelain are likewise plentiful in Budapest's tourist shops. Especially prized are Herend (produced by the world-famous factory), Zsolnay, and Arföldi porcelain. The best selections can be found at *Folk Art Centers* located throughout the city (including V, 14 Váci utca; and XIII, 26 Szent István körút) and at *Herend Porcelain* (V, 11 József Nador tér).

At any grocery store you can buy an authentic, inexpensive, and very portable souvenir—a packet of real Hungarian paprika, not the red dust generally sprinkled on as a decorative touch in the US. The towns of Kalocsa and Szeged are famous for growing this fragrant red pepper, available in both spicy and sweet varieties. Best for gifts are the small cloth bags of paprika decorated with a folkloric motif. Hungarian wine such as Tokay is another good buy available at grocery stores. *Esceri* is an interesting flea market (Nagykorosi út; open Saturdays only). Various gift items are sold at the many *Intertourist* shops scattered around town. For information about locations, call 122-7217. Falk Miksa utca, near *Parliament,* is the antiques district of Budapest. The street is lined with small shops filled to overflowing with furniture, paintings, carpets, and objets d'art from all over Eastern Europe.

Most shops are open daily from 10 AM to 8 PM. Below are some of particular interest.

**Amfora Crystal** A wide selection of crystal, porcelain, and other decorative items. V, 24 Károly körút (no phone).

**Antikvárium** A secondhand bookstore in the center of the city, it offers 16th- and 17th-century tomes in Latin, as well as old maps, prints, and photographs. V, 281 Váci utca (phone: 118-5673).

**Antiquitat** Art Nouveau–inspired porcelain, glass, and furniture. V, 3 Vitkovics M. utca (no phone).

**Artz Modell** A popular boutique for unique and trendy clothing by a young Hungarian designer. V, 2 Semmelweis utca (no phone).

**BAV** Antique furniture, glass, silver, watches, and porcelain. V, 12 Ferencek tér (phone: 118-3381).

**Bianca** Fashionable Hungarian- and Italian-made clothing for men and women. V, 2 Sütö utca (no phone).

**Equus** High-quality riding clothes and accessories at affordable prices. I, 2 Országház utca (phone: 156-0517).

**Helia D Studio** A wide selection of natural Hungarian-made beauty products. V, 19-21 Váci utca (phone: 138-2015).

**Libri Könyvesbolt** Centrally located, this bookstore has a wide array of English- and other foreign-language books, maps, and magazines. V, 32 Váci utca (phone: 118-2718).

**Luca Folklor Shop** A tiny treasure trove of gift items. Open daily. V, 7-9 Régiposta utca (no phone).

**Luxus** The foremost department store in the city, carrying designer labels. V, 3 Vörösmarty tér (phone: 118-2277).

**Museum Souvenir Antiques and Museum Copies** Beautiful reproductions. I, 7 Szentháromság utca (phone: 155-8165).

**National Center of Museums Shop** More reproductions of museum objects. V, 7 József Nádor tér (no phone).

**Rózsavölgyi** Hungarian classical and folk music. V, 5 Martinelli tér (no phone).

## SPORTS AND FITNESS

**BOATING** By arrangement with *IBUSZ* (see *Tourist Information*), you can rent a sailboat, dinghy, motorboat, small hydrofoil, and even water skis by the hour or by the day to enjoy the Danube.

**FISHING** Licenses are issued by the *National Federation of Hungarian Anglers* (*MOHOSZ;* V, 6 Október utca; phone: 132-5315; and at the fishing information bureau; II, 1 Bem József utca; no phone).

**FITNESS CENTERS** The facilities at both the *Forum* and the *Atrium Hyatt* hotels (see *Checking In*) are open to non-guests for a fee.

**GOLF** The *Budapest Golf Park and Country Club*, operated by the *Hilton* hotel, has a nine-hole island course set amid oak and acacia trees on Szentendrei Island in the Danube, just north of the city limits (phone: 117-6025). It is advisable to make advance reservations.

**GREYHOUND RACING** On the Danube embankment, just outside Budapest, there are races from May to September. Inquire at *IBUSZ* for details (see *Tourist Information*).

**HORSE RACING** There are trotting races at the track at *Ugetópálya* (VIII, 9 Kerepesi utca; phone: 134-2958) and flat racing at the *Kincsem Park* track (X, 9 Albertirsai utca; phone: 252-0888).

**HORSEBACK RIDING** A very popular pastime in this land of horsemen. There are schools and stables in and around Budapest, including the *Petneházy Riding School* (II, 5 Feketefej utca; phone: 176-5992). Information on riding tours is provided by *IBUSZ* (see *Tourist Information*) and *Pegazus Tours* (V, 5 Károlyi Mihály utca; phone: 117-1644).

**ICE SKATING** In winter there is a large outdoor rink in *Városliget* (City Park), near *Vajdahunyad Castle* (XIV, Stefánia út). Skating competitions and other athletic events take place at the *Budapest Sports Hall* (XIV, 1-3 Istvánmezei utca; phone: 251-1222).

**JOGGING** Margitsziget (Margaret Island), in the center of the city in the Danube River, is the best place to run. The island is roughly 2 miles long and half a mile wide, and most of it is given over to sports facilities. Either take a cab to the island's *Thermál* hotel (see *Check-*

*ing In*) and choose a path from there, or jog over on the pedestrians-only Margit híd (Margaret Bridge). Running is also pleasant along the foothills near the *Budapest* hotel (II, 47-49 Szilágyi Erzsébet fasor). For information on jogging, contact the *Futapest Club* (62-64 Váci utca; phone: 118-1638).

**SKIING** The Buda Hills, accessible by bus and funicular, have several slopes, the most popular of which is the *Szabadsághegy.*

**SOCCER** As in many European countries, soccer (called football) is the most popular spectator sport. The largest city stadium is the *Népstadion* (People's Stadium) near *Városliget* (City Park) in Pest, seating 96,000 (XIV, 1-3 Istvánmezei utca; phone: 252-7280). Information on games and other sports events is available from the ticket bureau (VI, 6 Andrássy út; phone: 112-4234).

**SPAS** Visitors from all over the world come to Budapest hoping that the waters will help ailments ranging from asthma to arthritis. Treatments include drinking cures (mineral waters), baths in lukewarm or very hot mineral pools, mud packs, and massages, all directed by specialists under the supervision of doctors.

The waters at *Aquincum* (94 Árpád Fejedelem útja; phone: 250-3360) have been known for centuries, but the hotel and spa facilities are relatively new and very luxurious. An attentive staff offers a wide variety of spa treatments (also see *Checking In*). The springs beneath the *Gellért* (XI, 1 Szt. Gellért tér; phone: 166-6166), Budapest's oldest spa-hotel (it was built in 1918), have been known for almost 2,000 years. Today, in addition to the thermally heated mineral water baths, there are treatments, an outdoor pool that ripples with mechanically produced waves, and a sun terrace (also see *Checking In*). The *Király* (I, 84 Fő utca; phone: 115-3000) is arguably the most exotic bath house in Budapest. It was built during the 16th-century Turkish occupation. With its cupola, domes, and elaborate design, this is one of Budapest's most interesting architectural gems—well worth taking the time for a dip and a good look at its fabulous (if steamy) interior. Built in the 15th century, the *Rác* (8-10 Hadnagy utca; phone: 156-1322) was reconstructed in the late 19th century according to the classical designs of famed architect Miklós Ybl. Today, it houses thermal baths and treatment and fitness rooms. Construction of the spa at *Rudás* (9 Döbrentei tér; phone: 156-1322) began during Turkish rule in the 16th century. Located near the Gellért Hill and Elizabeth Bridge, it remains a tranquil spot in the center of a busy city. *Széchenyi* (XIV, 11 Allatkerti körút; phone: 121-0310) is housed in a large, impressive building dating from 1913. It has both indoor and outdoor spas and pools. The outdoor spa pools are filled with thermally heated waters in which men and women bathe and play chess on floating cork chessboards—even if there's snow covering the ground. *Thermál Margitsziget* (XIII, Margitsziget; phone: 111-1000) offers a variety of treatments, as well as state-of-the-art fitness rooms. Located on Margaret Island, the spa facility is shared by both the *Thermál* and *Ramada Grand* hotels.

**SWIMMING** Budapest has many indoor and outdoor pools. (People swim in the Danube, but it is not too clean and sometimes has strong currents.) The largest public facility—both indoor and outdoor—is the *National Swimming Pool* on Margaret Island. In addition, many hotels have pools, both ordinary and thermal. The stately *Gellért*, for example (see *Checking In*), has an outdoor pool with artificial waves in a park setting. In the *Városliget* the turn-of-the-century *Széchenyi Baths* (see above) include three large outdoor pools, also open in winter.

**TENNIS** There are tennis courts near *Dózsa Stadium* on Margaret Island; at *FTC Sporttelep* (Sports Grounds; 129 Ullöi utca); and on Szabadság Hill, near the *Olympia* hotel (40 Eötvös út). Both the *Flamenco* and *Novotel* hotels (see *Checking In*) provide indoor courts for guests.

## THEATER

In Budapest everyone goes to the numerous theaters, which are subsidized by the state and are very inexpensive. Most performances are in Hungarian, but you still might enjoy seeing a Shakespearean or other familiar play. If not, the *Municipal Operetta Theater* (VI, 17 Nagymező utca in Pest; phone: 132-0535) offers performances of Kálmán, Lehár, Romberg, and other great operetta composers whose works need no translation. The *Allámi Bábszínház* (Main Puppet Theater; VI, 69 Andrássy út; phone: 121-5200) presents everything from the *Three Little Pigs* for children to *The Miraculous Mandarin* and revues and satires for adults. The *Fővárosi Nagy Cirkusz* (Municipal Grand Circus), open weekdays, is in *Városliget* (City Park; XIV, 7 Allatkerti körút; phone: 117-5935). Hungarian plays are performed in English from May through October at the *Merlin Cultural Center* (4 Gerlóczy utca; phone: 117-5935); the complex also houses a jazz club, a restaurant, and an art gallery.

For more details and tickets consult the current *Programme in Hungary* and contact *IBUSZ* (see *Tourist Information*) or the *Central Booking Agency for Theaters* (VI, 18 Andrássy út; phone: 112-0000).

## MUSIC

Budapest has a rich musical life; this city of Bartók and Kodály has two opera houses, several symphony orchestras, and a great many chamber groups. Built from 1844 to 1875, the *Hungarian State Opera House* (VI, 22 Andrássy út; phone: 153-0170) is part of the legacy of Franz Liszt and of Ferenc Erkel, composer of the Hungarian opera *Bank Ban.* The theater retains its original splendor and looks rather like the *Bolshoi* in Moscow, with domed ceilings, chandeliers, and ornate frescoes. Operas are performed in Hungarian. The *Erkel Theater* (VIII, 30 Köztársaság tér; phone: 133-0540) offers operas and ballets. Concerts are given at the *Academy of Music* (VI, 8 Liszt Ferenc tér; phone: 141-4788) and at the *Pest Concert Hall* (V, 1 Vigadó tér; phone: 117-6222), facing the Danube. The *Matthias Church* also has concerts; tickets may be purchased at the *Concert Ticket Office* (V, 1 Vörösmarty tér; phone: 117-6222).

On Sundays at 11 AM concerts are held at the *Néprajzi Múzeum* (Ethnographic Museum; V, 12 Kossuth tér; no phone), sometimes featuring children's folk dancing.

In the summer, the music moves outdoors to Margaret Island. For tickets and information about performances at the above-mentioned musical venues, contact *IBUSZ* or the *Central Booking Agency* (see *Theater*).

## NIGHTCLUBS AND NIGHTLIFE

Once virtually nonexistent, Budapest's nightlife is now flourishing. On any given night there is a host of venues—from traditional cabarets in hotels such as the *Duna Marriott* and *Buda-Penta* (see *Checking In* for these and all other hotels mentioned in this section) to after-dark activity at the *Maxim Varieté* (VII, 3 Alkácfa utca; phone: 122-7858). Other popular nightspots include *Biliárd Fél 10* (VII, 48 Maria utca; no phone), where you can hear great jazz and hang out with the "in" crowd; *Café Pierrot* (14 Fortuna utca; phone: 175-6971), a charming and romantic piano bar in the Castle Hill District; and the *Fondue Bar* (II, 25 Keleti Karoly utca; no phone), a small tavern with a lot of energy and a good place to hang out with some real local characters. *Fekete Lyuk* (VIII, 3 Golgota utca; phone: 113-0607), which literally means "Black Hole," is a punk-rock music club. For rock, there's *Hold* (XIII, 7 Hegedüs Gyula utca; no phone), which in Hungarian means "moon," and does indeed have an otherworldly atmosphere. A newcomer on the late-night scene, the *Jazz Café* (V, 25 Balassi Bálassi Bálint utca; phone: 111-3437) is a popular hangout for the under-25 set who come here to shoot pool and listen to rock 'n' roll. The *Made Inn* (V, 112 Andrássy út; phone: 132-2959) is another favorite watering hole for the young. Arguably the oldest nightclub in Budapest, the *Miniatur* (II, 1 Rózsahegy utca; no phone) is the most enduringly cool. This piano bar, where Hungarian interpretations of Cole Porter hits are de rigueur, is best after midnight. The piano bar and nightclub *Piaf* (VI, 20 Nagymező utca; phone: 112-3823) is one of the most exciting in the city. Located in *City Park,* the *Petőfi Csarnok* (XIV, 14 Zichy Mihaly utca; phone: 142-4327) attracts a younger crowd and is more a concert hall than a club, featuring rock bands from all over the world. The *Merlin Jazz Club* (4 Gerlóczy utca; phone: 117-5935) is part of the *Merlin Cultural Center* and a good place to visit into the wee hours. Though *Tilos Az A* (VIII, 2 Mik-száth tér; phone: 118-0684) literally means "Winnie the Pooh," this is no place for kids. The alternative rock club attracts interesting bands from all over Central Europe.

Folk dancing sessions known as "dance houses," which feature traditional songs and steps, are held in Budapest a few times a week from mid-September to mid-June. They're an interesting way to experience a bit of local culture, and some of the chain and round dances are simple enough even for rank beginners. Dance houses take place in community centers across the city, including the *Almássy Téri Szabadidő Központ* (Almassy Square Free Time Center; VII, 6 Almássy tér; phone: 142-0387); *Belvárosi Ifjusági Ház*

(Downtown Youth House; V, 9 Molnár út; no phone); *XII Kerület Polgármesteri Hivatal* (12th District Municipal Building; XII, 23-25 Böszörményi út; phone 153-6567); and *Szakszervezetek Fővárosi Müuvelödési Ház* (Union Culture House; XI, 47 Fehérvári út; no phone). A comprehensive schedule of dance house sessions appears in the English-language monthly *Programme in Hungary.*

Gamblers are in luck, as every new year sees at least one or two more casinos open their doors. In addition to the *Hilton*'s elegant *Casino Budapest,* the *Atrium Hyatt* has opened the *Las Vegas Casino*, and the *Béke Radisson* is now home to the *Orfeum Casino.* Other casinos include the *Casino Budapest Gresham* (V, 5 Roosevelt tér; phone: 117-2407), *Casino Budapest Schönbrunn* (1-3 Hess András tér; phone: 138-2016), *Casino Citadella* (XI, 4 Citadella Sétány; phone: 166-7686), and *Casino Vigadó* (V, 2 Vigadó utca; phone: 117-0869).

# Best in Town

## CHECKING IN

September is the peak season in Budapest, so it is advisable to make reservations well in advance, either directly, through your travel agent, or through *IBUSZ* (see *Tourist Information*).

Hotel prices in Budapest are reasonable compared with those in other European capitals. Hotels described below as expensive charge from $100 to $200 or more per night for a double room; places in the moderate category charge $50 to $100; and an inexpensive place charges under $50. Note that *IBUSZ* rents rooms in private homes (usually with shared baths) from $18 per day. Also, *American-International Homestays* (1515 W. Penn St., Iowa City, IA 52240; phone: 319-626-2125) arranges for stays with Hungarian families in Budapest and several other Eastern European cities. In all of the following hotels guestrooms have private baths unless otherwise specified, and all telephone numbers are in the 1 city code unless otherwise indicated.

### EXPENSIVE

**Aquincum** Built over one of the city's ancient sources of medicinal thermal waters, this spa-hotel on the Buda side of the Danube near the Árpád Bridge is elegant, luxurious, and absolutely modern. All of the 312 rooms have balconies and views of Margaret Island and the river. The restaurants, *Ambrosia* and *Apiciud,* both serve consistently good Hungarian fare, and there are drinks and snacks available at *Café Iris* and the *Calix Bar*. The spa includes diagnostic and therapeutic facilities. Business facilites include meeting rooms for up to 250 and audiovisual equipment. 94 Árpád Fejedelem útja (phone: 250-3360; fax: 168-8872).

**Atrium Hyatt** A central courtyard lined with hanging greenery is the focus of this 357-room luxury establishment. It has a top-floor VIP Regency Club, a swimming pool, a health club, and 24-hour room service.

Its *Old Timer* restaurant serves international cuisine, the *Tokaj* has Hungarian fare and Gypsy music, the *Atrium Terrace* is a coffee shop, and the rustic *Clark Brasserie* is very popular for snacks accompanied by draft beer. Business facilities include meeting rooms for up to 300, audiovisual equipment, photocopiers, and cable television news. V, 2 Roosevelt tér (phone: 266-1234; 800-233-1234; fax: 266-8658).

**Béke Radisson** A reconstructed old hotel with 246 rooms and a turn-of-the-century ambience, particularly evident in its beautiful *Zsolnay Café*. There's also a swimming pool and 24-hour room service. Business facilities include meeting rooms for up to 200 and cable television news. VI, 43 Teréz körút (phone: 132-3300; 800-333-3333; fax: 153-3380).

**Budapest Hilton International** This elegant establishment occupies one of the most historic sites in Buda, high on Castle Hill, overlooking the Danube. The 323 rooms are modern and comfortable, though not particularly lavish; the views from the picture windows are priceless. The construction of the building took 10 years, primarily because, as excavation proceeded, archaeologists kept uncovering ruins and artifacts dating from the 13th century, which the hotel incorporated into the new structure. As a result, the modern stone-and-glass building includes the walls and tower of a 13th-century Dominican church and a Jesuit monastery. Reflected in a rosy glass wall of the six-story hotel is the famous *Fishermen's Bastion,* a neo-Romanesque series of arches and towers overlooking the Danube. Its *Miklós Tower* (on the street side), once part of a church, has been converted into an elegant casino (hard currency only). Inside another tower is *Halászbástya* (see *Eating Out*), a restaurant that features Hungarian food, Gypsy music, and a fabulous view of *Parliament.* There's also the *Troubador,* with cabaret performances; a wine cellar dubbed *Dr. Faust;* a coffee shop with rustic decor; a two-level espresso bar with an outdoor terrace; the colorful *Kalocsa* restaurant; and the *Codex Bar,* which occupies the site of the country's first printing workshop, opened in the 15th century. Business facilities include meeting rooms for up to 1,000, audiovisual equipment, photocopiers, cable television news, and translation services. I, 1-3 Hess András tér (phone: 175-1000; 800-HILTONS; fax: 156-0285).

**Duna Marriott** This 362-room, former Inter-Continental property has been newly refurbished. It is on Pest's riverside Corso, a traditional promenade between the Chain and Elizabeth Bridges. Amenities include a pool with a view of the Danube, a fitness center, a squash court, a solarium, and a sauna, and 24-hour room service. Guests also enjoy the peasant inn–style *Csárda* restaurant, *Intermezzo* terrace café, a wine cellar, and a nightclub. Business facilities include meeting rooms for up to 1,000, secretarial services in English, audiovisual equipment, photocopiers, cable television news, and translation services. V, 4 Apáczai Csere János utca (phone: 266-7000; 800-228-9290; fax: 266-5000).

**Dunapart** Budapest's only floating hotel, this onetime merchant ship, permanently anchored on the Buda side of the Danube, offers spectacular views of *Parliament,* 32 rooms, a restaurant, and a bar. I, Szilágyi Dezsö tér (phone: 155-9001; fax: 155-3770).

**Flamenco** Popular with the business set, this Spanish-style hotel features 336 comfortable rooms. There's a small lake on the pleasant grounds as well as indoor tennis, a pool, a fitness center, two restaurants, and 24-hour room service. Business facilities include meeting rooms for up to 100, an English-speaking concierge, foreign currency exchange, secretarial services in English, audiovisual equipment, photocopiers, computers, cable TV news, translation services, and express checkout. Tas Vezer utca (phone: 161-2250; fax: 165-8007).

**Forum** This 408-room property has river views and an efficient staff. It's the hotel of choice for businesspeople; at night the lobby fills with wheeler-dealers. It also boasts a swimming pool and a health club with a bar. For dining choose between the elegant *Silhouette* restaurant and the informal *Forum Grill.* For pastries and coffee stop by the *Wiener Kaffehaus,* or take advantage of 24-hour room service. Business facilities include meeting rooms for up to 240, audiovisual equipment, photocopiers, cable TV news, and translation services. V, 12-14 Apáczai Csere János utca (phone: 117-8088; fax: 117-9808).

**Gellért** On the Buda side of the Danube near *Liberation Memorial Park,* this 235-room, Old World hotel at the foot of Gellért Hill makes up in history what it lacks in decor. Built in 1918 in ornate Art Nouveau style, the hotel was recently renovated, although the modern interior is not up to the original fairy-tale standards. What makes the *Gellért* special, however, is its old-fashioned spa (see *Sports and Fitness*). The restaurant is famous for Hungarian food served to the sounds of soulful Gypsy music. There also is an espresso bar, a beer hall, and a nightclub. Business facilities include meeting rooms for up to 400, audiovisual equipment, photocopiers, and cable TV news. XI, 1 Szt. Gellért tér (phone: 166-6166; fax: 166-6631).

**Grand Hotel Corvinus Kempinski** Within walking distance of Budapest's shopping, business, and cultural districts, this gray granite, 369-room hotel offers an array of amenities. All rooms are furnished with cable TV and telephones, and personal computer outlets are available upon request. The health club with a swimming pool, sauna, solarium, and exercise equipment is a particularly welcome feature for those who have overindulged at the hotel's dining room (there are also a pub, a coffee shop, and two bars). Business facilities include meeting rooms for up to 600, an English-speaking concierge, foreign currency exchange, secretarial services in English, audiovisual equipment, photocopiers, computers, cable TV news, translation services, and express checkout. V, 7-8 Erzsébet tér (phone: 226-1000; fax: 226-2000).

**Helia** This eight-story, 263-room property is set on the Pest side of the Danube embankment, just opposite Margaret Island (a bridge leads there from the hotel). It has two restaurants—*Jupiter,* a buffet-style eatery, and *Saturnus,* with an à la carte menu. Recreational pluses include a pool, tennis courts, a sauna, and a solarium. Business facilities include meeting rooms for up to 200, audiovisual equipment, and cable TV news. 62-64 Kárpát utca (phone: 270-3277; fax: 270-2262).

**Korona** Best Western runs this modern luxury property, which is in the main shopping and business area opposite the *Hungarian National Museum.* The two wings of the hotel are connected by a bridge, and the eight-story building has 443 rooms, a swimming pool, solarium, and sauna, as well as several restaurants. Business facilities include meeting rooms for up to 400 and photcopiers. 12-14 Kecskeméti utca (phone: 117-4111; 800-528-1234; fax: 118-3867).

**Nemzeti** Another Old World (1880s) establishment, it was restored a few years ago but could use additional touching up. This 76-room place has an elegant restaurant with Gypsy music and a beer hall. Take heed: The location is noisy. Cable television news is available. V, 4 József körút (phone: 133-9160; fax: 114-0019).

**Petneházy Country Club** Located in the Buda Hills in a country-like setting 8 miles (13 km) from the center of the city, this sports-oriented resort offers 45 individual Scandinavian-style luxury cabins equipped with private kitchens, terraces, and saunas. Tennis, bicycling, horseback riding, hunting, and swimming in an indoor pool are some of the options available here. The *Petneházy* restaurant serves international cuisine. A private minibus transports guests to and from the city. II, 2-4 Feketefej utca (phone: 176-5992; fax: 176-5738).

**Ramada Grand Hotel Margitsziget** On Margaret Island, this renovated spa dating from the 19th century is now a 162-room resort hotel; it's connected to its sister hotel, the *Thermál* (see below), by an underground passage. In former days the hotel reportedly housed famous spies-in-hiding. There are 3 restaurants. Business facilities include meeting rooms for up to 180. XIII, Margitsziget (phone: 131-7769; 800-2-RAMADA; fax: 153-3029).

**Thermál Hotel Margitsziget** This 340-room, luxury spa-hotel has health facilities with diagnostic and treatment centers and equipment for hydro- and physiotherapy. Business facilities include meeting rooms for up to 180. XIII, Margitsziget (phone: 111-1000; fax: 153-2753).

### MODERATE

**Astoria** This small, 130-room, renovated hostelry (it was built in 1912) is the best of the moderately priced hotels. There's a marvelous Art Deco café and restaurant. Business facilities include a meeting room for up to 15. V, 19 Kossuth Lajos utca (phone: 117-3411; fax: 118-6798).

**Buda-Penta** Near the *Southern Railway Station* and *Underground Terminal* in Buda, it has 395 rooms plus seven suites, a swimming pool and health club, a restaurant, coffee shop, beer hall, and nightclub. Business facilities include a meeting room for six people, audiovisual equipment, and photocopiers. I, 41-43 Krisztina körút (phone: 156-6333; 800-225-3456; fax: 155-6964).

**Erzsébet** An attractive, modern property with 123 rooms on the site of a much older one. The hotel's *János Beer Cellar* has, in fact, kept the furnishings of its popular predecessor. Business facilities include meeting rooms for up to 100, audiovisual equipment, and photocopiers. V, 11-15 Károlyi Mihály utca (phone: 138-2111; fax: 118-9237).

**Grand Hotel Hungária** This bustling, 1960s establishment opposite the *Eastern Railway Station* is the biggest hotel in the country, with 529 rooms (beware, the walls are paper thin), a restaurant, beer hall, wine cellar, the *Jugendstil* (Art Nouveau) café, and a nightclub. Business facilities include meeting rooms for up to 300, audiovisual equipment, and photocopiers. VII, 90 Rákóczi utca (phone: 122-9050; fax: 122-8029).

**Liget** A simple establishment opposite the zoo side of *Városliget* (City Park). The 140 rooms are clean and pleasant, though some are noisy. There's also a good restaurant, a gym, and a sauna. VI, 106 Dózsa György út (phone: 111-7050).

**Normafa** Set in an oak forest on the highest point in the Buda Hills, 15 minutes from downtown, this hotel has 71 rooms, all with balconies. The *C'est la Vie* restaurant serves international cuisine, while the *Mormafa Grill and Garden* prepares traditional Hungarian fare. The hotel has a fitness center, garden swimming pool, and tennis courts. Business facilities include meeting rooms and a banquet hall for up to 100. XII, 52-54 Eötvös út (phone: 156-8011; fax: 175-9583).

**Novotel Budapest** A quick drive from the city center, it has 324 rooms, a small pool, tennis courts, and several restaurants and bars. The *Budapest Convention Center* is next door. Business facilities include a meeting room for up to 15 and cable TV news. XII, 63-67 Alkotás utca (phone: 186-9588; 800-221-4542; fax: 166-5636).

**Olympia** On the outskirts of town in the residential Buda Hills, this pleasant property has 172 rooms (most with private baths), a swimming pool, health club, tennis court, restaurants, and a nightclub. Business facilities include meeting rooms for up to 120 and photocopiers. XII, 40 Eötvös út (phone/fax: 156-8720).

**Taverna** The main pedestrian shopping street in Pest boasts a well-designed, post-modern hotel with 324 rooms, a restaurant, beer hall, pastry shop, fast-food eatery, and a champagne bar. Business facilities include a meeting room for up to 130. V, 20 Váci utca (phone: 138-4999; fax: 118-7188).

**Victoria** Centrally located with striking views of the Danube, *Parliament,* and the Chain Bridge, this 24-room hotel offers comfortable accommodations, a restaurant, and 24-hour room service. Business facilities include audiovisual equipment and photocopiers. I, 11 Bem rakpart (phone: 201-8644; fax: 201-5816).

**Kulturinnov** Housed in a once-grand university building, this simply furnished, reasonably priced 15-room hostelry (only four have private baths) is ideally located in the center of the Castle Hill District. Attracting scholarly types, it offers two lecture rooms, each accommodating 140 people, and two smaller lecture halls, each seating 50. There are also nine rooms that can be used for seminars, a library, a reading room, and a cafeteria. I, 6 Szentháromság tér (phone: 155-0122; fax: 175-1886).

---

## EATING OUT

The justly celebrated cuisine of Hungary dates from ancient times. The most famous ingredient is paprika, the red pepper that comes in different strengths and is used copiously, most notably in *paprikás csirke* (chicken paprika) and in sauces. (Don't worry about paprika dishes being too hot; any restaurant will be glad to spice to your taste.) Another culinary distinction is the use of pork drippings, which—in concert with the ubiquitous sour cream—make meals here conspicuously caloric, as well as sometimes heartburn-inducing. Various Hungarian dishes have become world famous, particularly *gulyás* (goulash), which will not be what you expect if you have eaten it elsewhere. Here it is a very thick soup with meat (usually beef or pork), onions, carrots, sour cream, and a lot of paprika. If you like fish, try *halászlé,* Hungary's famous fish soup, made with *fogas* (a unique pike-perch caught only in Lake Balaton), carp, or bream, and seasoned with onions and many spices including paprika. Another traditional dish, *kolozsvári rakott káposzta* (layered cabbage), includes eggs and sausage, heaps of sour cream, and crisp pork chops.

Hungarian rye bread is superb, and *pogácsa,* a flaky biscuit strewn with bits of crackling pork, is delicious. Pastries are absolutely fabulous, whether filled with *barack lekvár* (apricot preserves), *aszalt szilva lekvár* (prune preserves), walnuts, hazelnuts, crushed poppy seeds, or chocolate. You might start with *rétes* (strudel) or *dobos torta* (a multilayered cake)—but the sky is the limit. Budapest is a place to let that diet go.

Hungarian wines are wonderful, especially Tokay, which is often sweet; *tokaji szamorodni* and *tokaji aszú* are famous dessert wines made from hand-picked, shriveled, "noble rot" grapes. A popular choice with meals is *egri bikavér* (bull's blood), a dry red wine. *Leányka* is a delicious white wine. There are also a number of fruit juices, including the delicious sour cherry.

Hungarians love to linger over small cups of strong coffee, called *eszpresszó,* or over *dupla kavé,* which is a strong, double-mocha brew. These are available everywhere—in pastry shops, cafés, and the *Mackó* shops, whose symbol is a bear cub.

Budapest has over 2,000 restaurants, cafés, pastry shops, wine cellars, beer halls, and taverns. A few of the highlights are listed below. There is an important distinction to be made among eating establishments in Budapest: whether the restaurant is privately owned or still state-run. The food at private establishments is generally of a higher quality, the service is better, and the price is sure to reflect it. The native word for "restaurant" is *étterem;* a *vendéglö* is a more informal establishment. For a dinner for two (including wine, drinks, and tip) expect to pay $80 to $100 in restaurants listed as expensive; $35 to $80 in those categorized as moderate; and $20 to $35 in places described as inexpensive. Reservations are highly recommended in Budapest; many restaurants won't seat you without them, even if the place is empty. Unless otherwise specified all restaurants are open for lunch and dinner and all telephone numbers are in the 1 city code.

For an unforgettable dining experience we begin with our culinary favorite, followed by our cost and quality choices, listed by price category.

## DELIGHTFUL DINING

**Gundel** Not only is this the cradle of Hungarian cooking, it's the place where this country's rich culinary traditions are kept alive. The restaurant, founded by Károly Gundel, perhaps the most highly esteemed chef in Budapest's history, is now owned by a Hungarian-born American, restaurateur/entrepreneur George Lang (owner of New York City's Café des Artistes), and Ronald Lauder, the former US Ambassador to Austria (and Estée's son). Recently reopened, it still possesses all the beauty and culinary excellence that have made it a legend since 1904. The turn-of-the-century building (including a main dining room, a Rococo ballroom, and six private dining rooms) has been fully refurbished and the park-like garden (with seating for 450) restored. The decor celebrates Hungarian culture with native paintings and antiques. Among chef Kálmán Kalla's featured dishes are *fogas,* Hungarian goose and goose liver from the restaurant's own farm, and game and game birds in season. There are also fresh fruits and vegetables, traditional breads, pastries, and desserts— including Károly Gundel's legendary *palacsinta* (crêpes filled with hazelnuts and cream and smothered with a bittersweet chocolate sauce)—and Tokay from the restaurant's own vineyards. Live entertainment, from a Gypsy orchestra to Hungarian operettas, completes the illusion that you've somehow stepped back into Budapest's golden age. Jackets and ties required. Open daily. Reservations necessary. Major credit cards accepted. XIV, 2 Allatkerti körút, in *Városliget* (phone: 122-1002; fax: 142-2917).

EXPENSIVE

**Alabárdos** In one of the most beautiful Gothic buildings in the Castle Hill District, and probably the best restaurant in the area, try the house specialty, flambéed meat served with great ceremony on a sword. Closed Sundays. Reservations necessary. American Express and Visa accepted. I, 2 Országház utca (phone: 156-0851).

**Les Amis** The perfect little bistro, it serves consistently good Hungarian staples such as goulash plus a selection of French-inspired dishes. Closed Sundays. No reservations. Major credit cards accepted. II, 12 Rómer Flóris utca (phone: 135-2792).

**Apostolok** This old brasserie decorated with carved wood and paintings by local artists is centrally located and very popular, especially for lunch. It's also a good place to have a few beers. Open daily. Reservations advised on weekends. No credit cards accepted. V, 4-6 Kígyó utca (phone: 118-3704).

**Barokk** This delightful dining spot, where the waitresses wear Baroque garb against a backdrop of taped Mozart music, authentic 18th-century furniture, oil paintings, and gilded plaster wainscoting, serves what may be the best food in Budapest. Dishes are based on 17th- and 18th-century recipes. Try the sublime fish crêpes in remoulade sauce or the filet of beef with goose liver. The vegetables, desserts, and other extras are all unusually good and innovative as well. Open daily. Reservations necessary. Major credit cards accepted. 12 Mozsar utca (phone: 131-8942).

**Halászbástya** This dining spot is located next to the *Hilton,* inside one of the towers of the *Fishermen's Bastion* (see *Special Places*). The fare is unexceptional, but the view of *Parliament* building and the town is fabulous. Hungarian food and Gypsy music are featured. Open daily. Reservations necessary. Major credit cards accepted. I, *Fishermen's Bastion* (phone: 156-1446).

**Kacsa (Duck)** This charming establishment features a large menu with excellent game including wild duck (hence the name) with pears and apples, a superb goulash, and grilled carp. There's also a good wine list. Open daily. Reservations necessary. Major credit cards accepted. I, 75 Fő utca (phone: 201-9992).

**Krónikás Etteremben** Budapest natives love this small, club-like restaurant which serves traditional fare as well as some non-Hungarian dishes (like shrimp and lobster). Open daily. Reservations necessary. No credit cards accepted. XIII, 2 Szent István körút (phone: 131-6278).

**Légrádi Testvérek (Légrádi Brothers)** Make reservations at least a week in advance for this fine, privately owned dining place favored by businesspeople. A good selection of hors d'oeuvres and traditional Hungarian specialties is prepared at the table. Open daily for dinner only. Reservations necessary. American Express accepted. V, 23 Magyar utca (phone: 118-6804).

**Lugas** Located in a former mansion in Buda, this new venture by pioneer restaurateur Béla Hegedus is the most Western establishment in town. Service is exceptional, and the food—Italian specialties and seafood—is not only good, but healthful. Try the lobster and zucchini ravioli or the salmon. There is also an excellent salad bar. Live music nightly. In summer dine in the garden. Open daily. Reservations necessary. Major credit cards accepted. II, 77 Szilágyi Erzsébet Fasor (phone: 156-4765).

**Ménes Csárda** This small, cozy establishment with an equestrian decor became an instant hit after it opened in 1982. It serves unusual Hungarian specialties—often prepared at your table—in attractive ceramic dishes made for the restaurant by a local artist. Try the stuffed filet of pork and the cherry or cottage cheese *túrós* (a strudel-like dessert). Good, light wines are available. While you dine a Gypsy *cimbalom* player performs. Open daily. Reservations necessary. Major credit cards accepted. V, 15 Apáczai Csere János utca (phone: 117-0803).

**New York/Hungária** A landmark since 1894, when it opened as the *Café New York*, this most famous of the city's restaurants is worth seeing, even if the food does not live up to the decor. Hidden on the outside by scaffolding, the interior is grand; with its gilt columns, frosted-glass globes, chandeliers, and glittering mirrors, you'll almost feel as if you're dining in an opera house, or even a palace. Among the specialties are *kengurufarokleves* (kangaroo tail soup), *crêpes à la Hortobagy* (stuffed with meat and served with a paprika sauce), and a dessert called "omelette surprise" (a parfait in sponge cake baked in a froth of meringue). As an alternative to an expensive but undistinguished meal, consider a snack or coffee in the café, where you still get the full benefit of the elaborate decor. There's also a nightclub. Be prepared, however, to see only a roomful of tourists. Open daily. Reservations necessary. Major credit cards accepted. VII, 9-11 Erzsébet körút (phone: 122-3849).

**Robinson** Located in *Városliget* (City Park) adjacent to a swan-populated, artificial lake, this privately owned dining spot is currently all the rage. Lace curtains and airy colors provide the background for classic Hungarian specialties. Open daily. Reservations necessary. Major credit cards accepted. *Városliget* (phone: 142-3776).

**Vadrózsa** In a private villa with a shady garden, it features charcoal-broiled specialties such as goose liver and pike-perch, plus other tempting dishes. This place is frequented by diplomats and, perhaps diplomatically, no longer lists prices on the menu. Very friendly service. Closed Mondays. Reservations necessary. Major credit cards accepted. II, 12 Pentelei Molnár utca (phone: 115-0044).

**Vasmacska** Popular with out-of-towners, the interior of this restaurant evokes the atmosphere of an officers' wardroom on a ship. The house specialty is a hearty bean dish with different kinds of smoked meat. Downstairs is a less expensive beer hall. Open daily. Reservations advised. No credit cards accepted. III, 3-5 Laktanya utca (phone: 188-7123).

**Vén Buda (Old Buda)** Serving traditional Hungarian dishes, this elegant, privately owned dining place is a favorite among locals and visitors alike. Closed weekends. Reservations necessary. Major credit cards accepted. II, 22 Eröd utca (phone: 201-2928).

## MODERATE

**Aranybárány Borozó (Golden Lamb Wine Bar)** Lamb dishes, naturally, are the specialty at this cellar eatery with a shepherd motif. Open daily. Reservations advised on weekends. No credit cards accepted. V, 4 Harmincad utca (phone: 117-2703).

**Aranymókus Kertvendéglö (Golden Squirrel Garden)** Traditional game dishes (but no squirrel) are served at this spot, a short taxi ride from the city center. Pleasant garden dining in the summer. Closed Mondays. Reservations advised on weekends. No credit cards accepted. XII, 25 Istenhegy utca (phone: 155-9594).

**Chicago** Popular with American expatriates, this restaurant is famous for its spectacular chicken wings, hamburgers, and beer. Open daily. No reservations. American Express accepted. VII, 2 Blaha Lujza-tér (phone: 269-6753).

**Dunakorzó** Situated near the riverside, this place offers an undistinguished decor but a great location and heaping portions of solid Hungarian fare. Open daily. Reservations advised on weekends. No credit cards accepted. V, 3 Vigadó tér (phone: 118-0913).

**Gresham Wine Bar** Near *Parliament,* here you can taste fine Hungarian wines such as Tokay, which is often sweet; *egri bikavér* (bull's blood), the famous dry red wine believed to have medicinal value; and *leányka,* a good white. Closed Sundays. Reservations advised on weekends. No credit cards accepted. V, Mérleg utca (phone: 117-4445).

**Kis Pipa** A brasserie atmosphere—bright lights, red tablecloths, and friendly chatter by diners who all seem to know each other—prevails at this privately owned eatery. It features an extensive menu of Hungarian specialties and almost anything else you might wish to eat. It's a five-minute taxi ride from the major hotels in Pest. Closed Sundays. Reservations necessary. Major credit cards accepted. 38 Akácfa utca (phone: 142-2587).

**Kisbuda Gyöngne** Don't look for anything formal or fancy here—this is an authentic Hungarian bistro. For starters try the crêpes filled with caviar and cheese. Among the excellent entrées is wild pheasant with cherries; the savory strudel is the dessert of choice. Open daily. Reservations advised on weekends. American Express accepted. III, 34 Kenyeres utca (phone: 168-6402).

**Kiskakukk** An extensive year-round menu of game dishes is the draw here. The decor, however, is plain, and the restaurant can get noisy. Closed Sundays during the summer. Reservations advised. Major credit cards accepted. XIII, 12 Pozsonyi utca (phone: 132-1732).

**Mátyás Pince** Tourists fill this ornately romantic beer cellar in central Pest, where the real attractions are copious quantities of wine and even richer servings of Gypsy music and old Budapest spirit. If you get hungry, the fish dishes are well known around the city. Open daily. Reservations advised on weekends. No credit cards accepted. V, 7 Március 15 tér (phone: 118-1650).

**Náncsi Néni** A must on any list of Budapest's eateries, this homey little restaurant has a devoted following. Dishes have unusual names—such as "Kammermeyer's (Budapest's first mayor) Happiness"—and all are unquestionably delicious. The restaurant is about 20 minutes from the city center but well worth the trip. Open daily. Reservations necessary. Major credit cards accepted. II, 80 Ordögárok út (phone: 176-5809).

**Pest-Buda** A good, informal dining option, this cozy eatery has occupied the same vaulted quarters in the Castle Hill District since 1880. Try the Wiener schnitzel. Open daily. Reservations advised on weekends. No credit cards accepted. I, 3 Fortuna utca (phone: 156-9849).

**Pilvax** An old café-restaurant in the heart of Pest, it is noted for its chicken broth, pastries, and cakes. Gypsy music accompanies the meal. Open daily. Reservations advised on weekends. No credit cards accepted. V, 1-3 Pilvax köz (phone: 117-5902).

**Régi Országház** This old inn on the north side of the castle in Buda offers many dining rooms with different decors, traditional fare, a wine cellar, Gypsy music, and jazz. Open daily. Reservations advised on weekends. No credit cards accepted. I, 17 Országház utca (phone: 175-0650).

**Seoul House** The food at this authentic Korean dining spot is exceptionally good, if not typically spicy. Delectable meat is flambéed at the table. The decor is simple and attractive. Open daily. Reservations advised. Major credit cards accepted. I, 8 Fő utca (phone: 201-7452 or 201-9607).

**Sipos Halászkert** Known as the *New Sipos*—to distinguish it from the original *Régi Sipos Halászkert* (Old Sipos; 46 Lajos utca; phone: 686480)—this branch serves first-rate fish dishes. There is music and a garden. Open daily. Reservations advised on weekends. Major credit cards accepted. Fő tér in the Obuda District (phone: 188-7745).

**Vegetárium Étterem** Until recently vegetarians have had a tough time in Budapest, but things are looking up. The selection of vegetables here is generally good, the decor clean and functional, and the preparation is at times quite interesting. Open daily. Reservations advised. Major credit cards accepted. IV, Cukor utca (phone: 138-3710).

INEXPENSIVE

**Alföldi** This is where Hungarians come for Sunday lunch; it's noisy and serves simple traditional fare. Open daily. No reservations or credit cards accepted. V, 4 Kecskeméti utca (phone: 117-4404).

**Fészek** Popular with the art crowd, this eatery offers tempting cold fruit soup, chicken paprika, veal stew, and *palascinta* (Hungarian crêpes). During the summer there is outdoor dining in the pretty, trellis-lined garden. Open daily. Reservations advised. No credit cards accepted. VII, 36 Kertész utca (phone: 122-6043).

**Kádár** At this very special lunch-only restaurant, you'll find an eclectic mix of students, workers, and artists, who come here for the large portions of good Kosher dairy food. There is no English menu, the place is small, and you might have to share a table with locals. Open Tuesdays through Saturdays from 11:30 AM to 3:30 PM. No reservations or credit cards accepted. VII, 9 Klauzál tér (no phone).

**Marxim** For the eat-and-run set, here's Budapest's best pizza—thick crust and all. Open daily. No reservations or credits cards accepted. III, 23 Kisrokus utca (no phone).

---

## CAFÉ SOCIETY

Just as they were at the turn of the century, Budapest's coffeehouses are places where people meet to discuss the day's events. They are also wonderful venues for visitors to experience a slice of life while sampling a wedge of delicious cake and sipping an espresso. Below are some worth visiting. All cafés listed are open daily, do not require reservations, accept local currency only, and are in the inexpensive category.

In the heart of Pest since 1858, facing a beautifully restored square bustling with tourists and street entertainers, *Café Gerbeaud* (V, 7 Vörösmarty tér; phone: 118-6823) is no mere pastry shop; it is an institution. Its decadent desserts and leisurely atmosphere are reminiscent of days gone by. Another special spot is the *Café Ruszwurm* (I, 7 Szentháromság tér; phone: 175-5284). Just down the block from *Matthias Church,* this fabulous 1827 pastry shop still serves the best baked goods in Central Europe. With displays of old utensils once used by pastry chefs, 19th-century signs, and Biedermeier cherrywood furniture, it has been designated a historic monument. Try *rétes* (strudel) vanilla slices; or Ruszwurm cake, a chocolate cake filled with chocolate cream and spiked with orange peel and rum. Also worth a visit is *Korona* (I, 16 Dísz tér; phone: 175-6139), a gathering place for literary types and tourists that features poetry readings and other bookish events, often in foreign languages. The *Angelika* (I, 7 Batthyány tér; phone: 201-4847), on the Buda side of the Danube, boasts an authentic Old World atmosphere; the popular bookstore café *Littea* (I, 4 Hess András tér; no phone) offers books and classical music disks along with a pot of tea; *Café l'Orient-Express* (I, 17 Fő utca; phone: 202-1133), a new place located on the second floor of the sleek French Institute, is a favorite of the city's young set; and the *Wiener Kaffehaus* (V, Apáczai Csere János utca; phone: 117-8088), in the *Forum* hotel, is popular with locals and visitors alike, who come for the delicious pastries and confections.

# Copenhagen

## At-a-Glance

### SEEING THE CITY

The *Rundetårn* (Round Tower; Købmagergade; phone: 33-936660), built in 1642 by King Christian IV as an observatory, offers a panorama of the spires and steeples of Copenhagen's central old quarter. In the 18th century, Peter the Great of Russia reportedly led a carriage containing the Czarina Catherine to the top of the *Rundetårn,* but today's visitors have to climb the 687-foot spiral walkway on foot. The tower is open daily, but the observatory on the roof is open for limited hours depending on the season, so call ahead. There's an admission charge.

There's also a spectacular view of Copenhagen from the *Top of Town* restaurant on the 25th floor of the *Radisson SAS Scandinavia* hotel (see *Checking In*).

### SPECIAL PLACES

Copenhagen is a pedestrian's paradise, and it is relatively easy to get oriented after finding Strøget (Strolling Street), which links Kongens Nytorv, the largest square in the harbor, with Rådhuspladsen (Town Hall Square), the largest square in the downtown area. Strøget is made up of five connecting pedestrian streets, none of which is actually named Strøget (from Rådhuspladsen, they are Frederiksberggade, Nygade, Vimmelskaftet, Amagertorv, and Østergade). But the medieval street plan of the old quarter is irregular, and once you leave the downtown area and familiar landmarks, it's easy to get lost. Danes generally are helpful, however, and nearly everyone speaks English. In addition to the tourist office, banks, hotels, and many stores give away city maps with street guides, both in English.

#### DOWNTOWN

**SLOTSHOLMEN** The island where Bishop Absalon built his fortress in 1167 is in the central part of Copenhagen. The best way to get there is to walk from Rådhuspladsen down Vester Voldgade, left on Stormgade, and across the bridge leading into Porthusgade, where *Thorvaldsens Museum* is on the left and, *Christiansborg Slot* (Christiansborg Palace) is on the right with the seat of the Danish parliament, the *Folketing,* on one side and *Royal Reception Rooms* on the other. Bertil Thorvaldsen was a famous Danish sculptor; in 1838 he donated his work to the city of his birth, and the city built the museum to house it. The collection also includes some of Thorvaldsen's personal effects. The museum is closed Mondays. No admission charge. English-language guided tours are available at 2 PM on Sundays from June through August (phone: 33-321532).

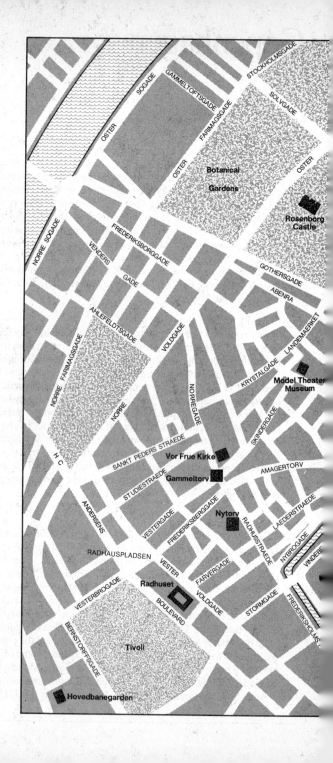

# COPENHAGEN

VOLDGADE

DELFINGADE
ELSDYRSGADE
SUENSONSGADE
HAREGADE
GRØNNINGEN

RIGENSGADE
FREDERICIAGADE
ADELGADE
BORGERGADE

ESPLANADEN

Museum of
Decorative Art

STORE KONGENSGADE

BREDGADE

Amalienborg
Castle

KRONPRINSESSEGADE
DRONNINGENS TVAERGADE
ADELGADE
BORGERGADE

AMALIENGADE

NY
ØSTERGADE
BREMERHOLM
PILESTRÆDE

KONGENS
NYTORV

NYHAVN

NYHAVN

KØBMAGERGADE
ØSTERGADE
ADMIRALGADE
NIKOLAJGADE

HEIBERGSGADE
TORDENSKJOLDGADE
PEDER SKRAMS
HERLUF TROLLES GADE
HOLBERGSGADE

KAN
NIELS JUELS GADE

HAVNEGADE

HOLMENS
VED STRANDEN

Thorvaldsen
Museum

Christiansborg
Castle

KNIPPELS BRO

N

CHRISTIANS
BRYGGE

INDERHAVNEN

| 0 | yards | 415 |
| 0 | meters | 375 |

*Christiansborg* was completed in 1740, burned in 1794, rebuilt in 1828, and burned down once more. The present palace, in a mixed Baroque/rococo design by Thorvald Jorgenson, was built from 1906 to 1928 (although the buildings around the riding ground date from the 1740s). Guided English-language tours of the royal reception rooms are available. Call ahead for times (phone: 33-926492). There's an admission charge. Underneath the palace are ruins of Absalon's fortress and its successor, *København Slot* (Copenhagen Castle). The ruins are open daily in summer, closed Mondays and Saturdays in winter. Admission charge.

**VOR FRUE KIRKE (OUR LADY'S CHURCH)** From Rådhuspladsen the old section of Copenhagen is reached by taking a left down Vester Voldgade and then a right on Studiestræde. Up ahead is *Vor Frue Kirke,* Copenhagen's neoclassical Catholic cathedral, which was completed in 1829. Statues of the 12 Apostles by Danish sculptor Bertel Thorvaldsen guard the porticoes inside, and a kneeling angel holds a seashell baptismal font. Services in English are held Sundays at 11 AM. Nørregade (phone: 33-144128).

**GAMMELTORV** Take a right on Nørregade in front of the *Vor Frue Kirke* to enter the oldest part of the city—the marketplace of Gammeltorv. The first marketplace in Copenhagen, Gammeltorv has been the site of jousting tournaments and public executions and still is a center for social activity. *Caritas* (Charity), the city's oldest fountain, donated by King Christian IV in 1609, is here. Nytorv, another market square, was added in 1606 as an extension of Gammeltorv, and originally was the site of public whippings.

**DUKKETEATERMUSEET (MODEL THEATER MUSEUM)** At the end of Skindergade, the street that runs through the Latinske Kvatir (Latin Quarter), Copenhagen's university area, this museum has a historical collection of toy theaters from different countries. Open afternoons only; closed Tuesdays, weekends and the month of April. Admission charge. 52 Købmagergade (phone: 33-151579).

**EKSPERIMENTARIUM (SCIENCE CENTER)** This exciting attraction offers visitors the chance to use computer technology to understand science. Some 225 lively and interesting demonstrations on topics ranging from the earth's ozone layer to food's calorie content have made this imaginative center a hit, especially with children. There are changing exhibits. Many displays are in English. Open daily. Admission charge. In the old bottling plant of the *Tuborg Brewery,* at 7 Tuborg Havnevej (phone: 39-273333).

**BOTANISK HAVE (BOTANICAL GARDENS)** Tropical and subtropical plants thrive in the park and greenhouses; in the summer, the "nature" on view includes topless sunbathers. Open daily. No admission charge. Entrance at Gothersgade and Sølvgade. 128 Gothersgade (phone: 35-322240).

**ROSENBORG SLOT (ROSENBORG CASTLE)** This Renaissance castle was built by Christian IV from 1606 to 1617. It houses the crown jewels and treasures of the Danish royal family from the 15th to the 19th centuries. The new *Grønne Kabinet* (Green Chamber) features 700 dazzling heirlooms including 16th-century Oriental ivory carvings. Be sure to see the sumptuous porcelain and crystal closets and the tiled bathroom with running water that King Christian installed in 1616. Open daily. Admission charge. 4A Øster Voldgade (phone: 33-153286).

**AMALIENBORG SLOT (AMALIENBORG PALACE) /GLÜCKSBORG MUSEET** The residence of the Danish royal family since 1794, *Amalienborg* is a spectacular example of Danish rococo, with four identical palaces set against the harbor background. When the royal family is in residence there is plenty of pomp during the daily changing of the guard. The royal guard leaves the *Rosenborg Slot* at 11:30 AM and marches through the streets to arrive at the *Amalienborg Slot* at noon. Several official and private rooms in the palace were opened to the public for the first time last summer. The rooms are known collectively as the *Glücksborg Museet* (Glückborg Museum) in honor of the reigning family, who ascended the throne in 1863. Some highlights are King Christian IX's study, a costume gallery, and a jewelry room. Open daily mid-April through mid-October; closed Mondays the rest of the year. Admission charge. Amaliegade and Frederiksgade (phone: 33-122186).

**NYHAVN (THE HARBOR)** Hans Christian Andersen found inspiration in his morning walks around Nyhavn, Copenhagen's old waterfront district, where he lived for some 20 years. The stately old merchant townhouses, the shabby sailor bars, the tattoo parlors, all the assorted arcana of dockside life—much of which remains—provided fertile soil for his imagination. Nyhavn is still a fascinating district, the haunt of all manner of characters, from sleek fashion models to the proverbial drunken sailor. The south side of Nyhavn, also known as the Charlottenborg side, has been an elegant residential area for many years. It was on the north side, at No. 67, that Andersen lived between 1845 and 1864 and wrote many of his famous fairy tales. In recent years, a number of good, small restaurants have emerged on both sides of Nyhavn.

**KUNSTINDUSTRIMUSEET (MUSEUM OF DECORATIVE AND APPLIED ART)** Founded in 1890, the museum contains European and Oriental applied art—wonderful furniture, porcelain, and crystal—from the Middle Ages to the present. The modern wing offers an overview of today's best Danish designers. Closed Mondays and mornings. Admission charge. 68 Bredgade (phone: 33-149452).

**FRIHEDSMUSEET (RESISTANCE MUSEUM)** In *Churchill Parken* (Churchill Park) just outside the entrance to *Kastellet* (the Citadel, Copenhagen's old harbor fortifications), the *Frihedsmuseet* contains relics from the resistance movement during the German occupation of 1940–45. Open daily May through mid-September, closed Mondays the rest of the year. No admission charge. *Churchill Parken* at Langelinie (phone: 33-137714).

**NY CARLSBERG GLYPTOTEK (NEW CARLSBERG SCULPTURE MUSEUM)** Gorgeous marble and mosaics adorn this building, which has a glass-roofed courtyard. In addition to halls with Egyptian mummies and rows of Greek, Etruscan, and Roman statues, there's a collection of 19th- and 20th-century European art, including Gauguin's *Vahine No Te Tiare* and works by van Gogh. Closed Mondays. No admission charge on Wednesdays and Sundays. 7 Dantes Plads (phone: 33-911065).

**LANGELINIE PROMENADE** One of the loveliest spots in Copenhagen is just opposite the *Kastellet,* overlooking the harbor. *Langelinie Pavillionen* (phone: 33-121214) is an elegant (and pricey) restaurant where you can gaze at the moonlit waters and dine and dance until the wee hours on Fridays and Saturdays. A walk along the promenade leads to *Den Lille Havfrue* (The Little Mermaid), the city's famous statue, erected in 1913 with a grant from *Carlsberg* beer magnate Carl Jacobsen.

**MEDICINSK-HISTORISK MUSEUM (MEDICAL HISTORY MUSEUM)** Reputed to be the world's largest medical history repository, this fascinating collection is housed in Copenhagen's former medical college. Dental, psychiatric, obstetrical, pharmacological, and surgical tools are on exhibit, and a guide explains past medical treatments, many of which seem outlandish today. Open Wednesdays, Thursdays, Fridays, and Sundays for guided tours only, in Danish and English, at 11 AM and 12:30 PM. No admission charge. 62 Bredgade (phone: 35-323800).

**CARLSBERG BRYGGERIERNE (CARLSBERG BREWERY)** Visitors are welcome at the brewery, a 20-minute walk from Rådhuspladsen (or take the No. 6 bus). Danes take their beer seriously—Elephant Beer, the world-famous Danish brew by Carlsberg, is about twice as strong as regular American beer (or even the Elephant Beer marketed in the US). Tours, featuring free tastings, are conducted at 11 AM and 2 PM; closed weekends. No admission charge. 140 Ny Carlsbergvej (phone: 33-271314).

**TUBORG BRYGGERIERNE (TUBORG BREWERY)** This brewery also welcomes visitors on weekdays, and can be reached by bus No. 6. Tours in English at 10 AM and 12:30 and 2:30 PM consist of an hour of walking and a half hour of quaffing; closed weekends. No admission charge. 54 Strandvejen, Hellerup (phone: 33-272212).

**TIVOLI** Copenhagen's most famous recreational area is on the south side of Rådhuspladsen. Built in 1843 on top of the old city ramparts, it's a tantalizing hybrid of an amusement park, gardens (400,000 flowers), lakes, theaters, dance halls, and restaurants, illuminated at night by over 100,000 colored lights. Whether you are looking for a first class restaurant such as *Belle Terasse,* a sandwich at *Grøften* (see *Eating Out* for both), or the tawdry company of a one-armed bandit, *Tivoli* has it all.

The season runs from late April to mid-September, from 10 AM to midnight daily (though rides may not be in operation during the winter season from mid-November through December). Internationally known artists perform on an outdoor stage every night. The concert hall features nightly concerts with orchestras and soloists, often free of charge. Other entertainment includes performances by the *Tivoligarden* (Tivoli Boy Guard) marching band, *Pantomimeteater,* children's theater, promenade concerts every night around the gardens, and amusement park rides. There's a fireworks show shortly before midnight three times a week. The *Tivoli Museet* (Tivoli Museum) tells the century-old park's history with pictures and displays. The museum is open daily during the *Tivoli* season; closed Mondays the rest of the year; admission charge. 3 Vesterbrogade, near Rådhuspladsen (phone: 33-151001).

**SØPAVILLION (LAKE PAVILION)** A 10-minute walk from Rådhuspladsen, the old pavilion on Lake Peblinge offers live music, cabaret, art shows, and international food and drink year-round. *Søpavillion* has much the same magic as *Tivoli*'s 19th-century *Pantomimeteater* (Pantomime Theater)—the same architect designed both. Three picture-perfect lakes draw sailors in summer, skaters in winter, and joggers in all seasons. Open daily for lunch and dinner; reservations advised. Admission charge for shows. 24 Gyldenløvesgade (phone: 33-151224).

**TYCHO BRAHE PLANETARIUM** Named for the famous 16th-century Danish astronomer, this planetarium features an impressive computer-controlled Zeiss star projector. The planetarium's 275-seat theater also features Omnimax films on a 360-degree screen. Both are extremely popular, so plan to purchase tickets in advance for these attractions. There are exhibitions on astronomy and space exploration, a restaurant, a bar, and a gift shop. Closed Mondays October to mid-June. Admission charge, plus an additional charge for films. 10 Gl. Kongevej, across the street from the *Sheraton* hotel (phone: 33-121224).

**NATIONAL MUSEET (NATIONAL MUSEUM)** This impressive museum contains a spectacular collection of Stone Age and Viking artifacts—including jewelry, tools, weapons, and clothing. Other collections focus on the Middle Ages, with church interiors and precious relics; ethnography of peoples from all over the world; and classical antiquities. There's a special mini-museum for children, a gift shop, a theater for films and cultural events, a café, and a restaurant. Closed Mondays. Admission charge. 10 Ny Vestergade, beside Frederiksholms canal (phone: 33-134411).

OUTSIDE THE CITY

**DRAGØR** This enchanting fishing village south of Copenhagen dates from the 16th century and is still in vintage condition. Its streets are paved with cobblestones, and 65 of its quaint, old, red-roofed houses are protected historical sites, making an address here both fashionable and expensive. The oldest house in the village is the home of the *Dragør Museum* (4 Strandlinien; phone: 32-534106), which is closed every afternoon, Mondays, and October through April. There is an admission charge. One old inn, the *Dragør Kro* (23 Kongev; phone: 32-530187), has a bar and a restaurant serving

Danish and French specialties. On the tip of the island of Amager, Dragør is about a 30-minute ride from Rådhuspladsen on either bus No. 30 or No. 33.

**FRILANDSMUSEET (OPEN-AIR MUSEUM)** An elaborate tribute to the joys of being down on the farm, this museum is a half-hour ride from the city via the No. 184 bus or the *S-train* to *Sorgenfri* station. Old houses from around Denmark have been dismantled and moved here, and efforts have been made to re-create the ecology of each kind of farm. In summer the visitor can watch sheep being sheared, wool being spun, and other examples of agrarian toil. There is a restaurant, as well as picnic tables and benches. Closed Mondays and October through March. Admission charge. 100 Kongevejen, Lyngby (phone: 42-850292).

**HELSINGØR (ELSINORE)** This town, which is about a 45-minute train ride north of Copenhagen, is home to *Kronborg Slot* (Kronborg Castle), which is presumed to have been the site of Hamlet's endless brooding. Dating from around 1426, the castle was completely rebuilt in 1585. Some rooms, including the king's and queen's apartments, are open to the public. The castle is closed Mondays and October through April. Admission charge (phone: 49-213078). Also on the castle grounds is the *Handels- og Sjøfartsmuseet* (Mercantile and Maritime Museum; phone: 49-210685).

**FREDENSBORG** About 5 miles (8 km) southwest of *Helsingør* is *Fredensborg Slot* (Fredensborg Palace), the spring and autumn home of the Danish royal family. The palace is open for tours on July afternoons only, but the magnificent grounds and gardens are open daily year-round.

**LOUISIANA MUSEUM OF MODERN ART** In the town of Humlebæk, 22 miles (35 km) north of Copenhagen, is the most important collection of modern Danish art in Europe. There are also works by other internationally renowned artists, as well as a new, interactive wing called *Children's House*. Open daily. No admission charge for those under 18. All-inclusive tickets for transportation and museum admission are sold at Copenhagen's central train station, *Hovedbanegården*. Take the train to Humlebæk or the No. 388 bus from *Klampenborg* station. 13 Gammel Strandvej, Humlebæk (phone: 42-190719).

**KAREN BLIXEN MUSEET, RUNGSTEDLUND** A museum devoted to the baroness and celebrated author (1885–1962) who under the pen name Isak Dinesen wrote the autobiographical *Out of Africa,* among other books. Located in the seaside town of Rungsted, about 15 miles (24 km) north of Copenhagen, *Rungstedlund* was Blixen's country manor birthplace. Closed Mondays and Tuesdays from October through April. No admission charge for those under 16. Take the *S-train* to Rungsted Kust, then catch the No. 388 bus to *Rungstedlund.* 111 Rungsted Strandvej, Rungsted (phone: 42-571057).

**BORNHOLM** A beautiful island in the Baltic between Denmark and Sweden, Bornholm is the secret summer retreat of nature-loving Danes and Swedes. An overnight ferry trip from Copenhagen, it offers several spectacular beaches, as well as more than 200 Viking burial mounds, 40 rune stones, and four round churches from the early Middle Ages. For more information, write to the *Bornholm Welcome Center*, 3 Ndr. Kystvej, 3700 Rønne, Denmark (phone: 56-959500; fax: 56-959568).

---

**EXTRA SPECIAL**

About 23 miles (36 km) north of Copenhagen, at Hillerød, lies the remarkable *Frederiksborg Slot* (Frederiksborg Palace, not to be confused with *Fredensborg Slot*, still a royal residence), widely considered to be Europe's most beautiful Renaissance castle. It's now the *Nationalhistoriske Museum* (National Historical Museum; phone: 42-260439). It's open daily. Admission charge. From Copenhagen, take the *S-train* to Hillerød.

---

# Sources and Resources

## TOURIST INFORMATION

The *København Touristinformation* (Copenhagen Tourist Information Bureau) is at 1 Bernstorffsgade, across the street from the *Hovedbanegården* (Central Station; phone: 33-111325; fax: 33-934969). It offers general information, brochures, and maps, as well as assistance in finding accommodations. Students may wish to consult the *Youth Information Center* (13 Rådhusstræde; phone: 33-156518). The *US Embassy and Consulate* is at 24 Dag Hammarskjöld Allé (phone: 31-423144).

In the US, contact the *Danish Tourist Board* (655 Third Ave., New York, NY 10017; phone: 212-949-2333; fax: 212-983-5260). The *Danish Embassy* is at 3200 Whitehaven St. NW, Washington, DC 20008-3683 (phone: 202-234-4300).

**ENTRY REQUIREMENTS** A US citizen needs a current passport for a stay of up to 90 days. The 90-day period begins on the date of entry into any one of the Nordic countries, which besides Denmark include Finland, Iceland, Norway, and Sweden.

**TIME** The time in Denmark is six hours later than in US East Coast cities. Denmark observes daylight saving time.

**LANGUAGE** Danish. English is spoken and understood throughout the country.

**ELECTRIC CURRENT** 220 volts, 50 cycles, AC.

**MONEY** The Danish krone (DKr) equals 100 øre. At press time there were 6 Danish kronen to $1 US.

**TIPPING** Service charges always are included in restaurant and hotel bills and in taxi fares. Railway porters and washroom attendants receive

---

small tips, but otherwise they are not expected unless a special service has been provided.

**BANKING/BUSINESS HOURS** Most banks are open weekdays from 9:30 AM to 4 PM; some banks are open to 6 PM on Thursdays. Most other businesses are open weekdays from 8 AM to 4 PM; government offices usually close on Fridays at 2 PM.

**NATIONAL HOLIDAYS** *New Year's Day* (January 1), *Maundy Thursday* (April 13), *Good Friday* (April 14), *Easter Sunday* (April 16), *Easter Monday* (April 17), *Labor Day* (May 1), *Common Prayers Day* (May 7), *Ascension Thursday* (May 25), *Whitmonday* (June 5), *Constitution Day* (June 5), *Christmas Day* (December 25), and *Boxing Day* (December 26).

**LOCAL COVERAGE** *Copenhagen This Week,* available at hotels and the tourist offices, lists events of interest. There are no English-language newspapers in Copenhagen, but the *International Herald Tribune* and *The European,* a London-based weekly, are available. News in English is broadcast on weekdays at 8:30 AM on Radio Denmark, Program III.

**TELEPHONE** The city codes for Copenhagen and surrounding areas are 31 through 49. Telephone numbers listed in this chapter include city codes. You must dial all 8 digits when making calls within the country. The country code for Denmark is 45. Dial 112 for emergency assistance.

## GETTING AROUND

**AIRPORT** *Københavns Lufthavn* (Copenhagen Airport) at Kastrup, with its restaurants, terrific (but pricey) duty-free boutiques, and other attractions, has been christened "Europe's most beautiful airport." It handles both international and domestic flights and is a 20-minute taxi ride from the center of town. Bus service operates every 15 minutes, starting on the hour, between the airport and Copenhagen's main railway station, *Hovedbanegården,* with a stop at the *Radisson SAS Scandinavia* hotel.

**BUS AND TRAIN** *HT/Copenhagen Transport,* the city bus system, is inexpensive and efficient, and is supplemented by a seven-line network of electric *S-trains* running throughout the city and on to the suburbs. Local buses and *S-trains* start running at 5 AM (6 on Sundays), and the last regular departures from downtown are at about 12:30 AM. All buses and railways in Copenhagen and environs operate under a collective fare system. This means that within defined zones tickets are good for a full hour's travel by bus or train with unlimited transfers. Buy your tickets from bus drivers or at train stations. A basic ticket is 10 kronen (about $1.60). Discount tickets, good for 10 trips, can be bought for 75 and 95 kronen (about $12 and $15, respectively, depending on what zones they cover) at stations, *HT* ticket offices, or from bus drivers. You stamp your ticket yourself by running it through the automatic machine at the front of the bus, where you board; when taking the train, you will see the machine on the platform. This is important, as tickets are checked now and again and those with invalid or unstamped tickets are fined. For more bus and *S-train* information, call 36-454545, then dial 3 for individual assistance.

The *Københavnerkortet* (Copenhagen Card) provides unlimited travel by bus or train in the metropolitan area, substantial reductions on fares for crossings to Sweden, and free admission to more than 50 museums. The card can be purchased at major railway stations, travel agencies, and the tourist information office. It's available for one day (140 kronen/$22.50), two days (230 kronen/$37), or three days (295 kronen/$47).

For interurban train travel the city's main railway station is *Hovedbanegården,* on Vesterbrogade (phone: 33-141701 for fares and schedules).

**CANAL TOURS** From late April through mid-September *Canal Tours Copenhagen* offers four different types of trips along the city's waterways, with or without guides, in open-air boats. The ticket office is at 26 Gammel Strand (phone: 33-133105).

**CAR RENTAL** To rent a car you must be at least 20 years old, although some firms set 25 as the minimum age. All major firms are represented.

**TAXI** Cabs are expensive but fast, and can be ordered by telephone (phone: 31-353535) or hailed on the streets. They are available when the green light on top is on; the tip is included in the fare.

## LOCAL SERVICES

**DENTIST (ENGLISH-SPEAKING)** Kirsten and Franklin Læssø (1 Herlev Torv, Herlev; phone: 44-940920); *Tandlægevagten* (14 Oslo Plads; phone: 31-380251) is a clinic for dental emergencies; no appointments taken.

**DOCTOR (ENGLISH-SPEAKING)** *Lægevagt* (Doctor's Watch; phone: 32-840041), a taxi radio service, dispatches quick medical assistance in Greater Copenhagen daily from 4 PM to 8 AM.

**DRY CLEANER/TAILOR** *Schleisner* (12 Vester Voldgade; phone: 33-110037); *Brødrene Andersen* (9 Østergade; phone: 33-151577), tailor.

**LIMOUSINE SERVICE** *Copenhagen Limousine Service* (2-4 Korlblomstvej; phone: 31-311234).

**MEDICAL EMERGENCY** Treatment at any hospital emergency room *(skadestue)* is free. *Kommunehospitalet* (5 Østerfarimagsgade; phone: 33-383338); *Rigshospitalet* (9 Blegdamsvej; phone: 35-453545).

**MESSENGER SERVICE** *Radio Codan Bilen* (phone: 31-317777) for deliveries by taxi.

**NATIONAL/INTERNATIONAL COURIER** *World Courier Service* (20 Flyver Vej; phone: 31-515031).

**PHARMACY** *Steno Apotek* (6C Vesterbrogade; phone: 33-148266).

**PHOTOCOPIES** There's a copy center in the *Hovedbanegården* (Central Station; entrance at 11 Reventlowsgade).

**POST OFFICE** The main post office (35-39 Tietgensgade) is open weekdays from 10 AM to 6 PM and Saturdays from 9 AM to 1 PM. There's also a branch in the *Hovedbanegården,* which is open even later and on Sundays. For information about any post office branch call 33-338900.

**SECRETARY/STENOGRAPHER (ENGLISH-SPEAKING)** *Copenhagen Business Center* (1 Graabrodre Torv; phone: 33-338833); *Regüs Business Center* (3 Larsbjørnsstræde; phone: 33-322525; fax: 33-324370).

**TRANSLATOR** *Translatør-Centret* (7 Danasvej; phone: 33-250144).

**OTHER** Tuxedo rental: *Amorin* (45 Vesterbrogade; phone: 31-212021 or 31-212158).

## SPECIAL EVENTS

The advent of spring in Copenhagen is heralded by the opening in late March of *Bakken,* Scandinavia's oldest (500 years old) festive amusement park in the *Dyrehaven* (Deer Park) north of Copenhagen, and of *Tivoli* in late April (see *Special Places*). On the *Dronningens Fødelsdag* (Queen's Birthday, April 16), the troops are decked out in full ceremonial dress for the changing of the guards at *Amalienborg Slot* (see *Special Places*) and the royal family appears on the balcony. Each June, Copenhagen celebrates *Carnival* with costumes, music, and parades. The swinging *Copenhagen Jazz Festival* is held in early July. In 1996, Copenhagen will host a full calendar of special events when it becomes the European Union's "Cultural Capital of Europe" for the year.

## MUSEUMS

In addition to those mentioned in *Special Places,* Copenhagen boasts a number of other well-organized museums, the most notable of which are the following:

**DET DANSKE FILMMUSEUM (DANISH FILM MUSEUM)** A comprehensive archive of films and related books. Open weekdays except Wednesdays from June through August; open Tuesdays only the rest of the year. No admission charge. 4 Store Søndervoldstræde (phone: 31-576500).

**GEOLOGISK MUSEUM (GEOLOGICAL MUSEUM)** Meteorites, fossils, and minerals. Closed Mondays. No admission charge. 5-7 Øster Voldgade (phone: 35-322345).

**KØBENHAVNS BYMUSEUM OG SØREN KIERKEGAARD-SAMLINGEN (COPENHAGEN'S CITY MUSEUM AND THE SØREN KIERKEGAARD COLLECTION)** The city's 800 years in pictures and mementos; also material related to native son Søren Kierkegaard (1813–55), theologian and father of existentialism. Closed Mondays. No admission charge. 59 Vesterbrogade (phone: 31-210772).

**LEGETØJSMUSEET (TOY MUSEUM)** Danish toys from generations ago. Closed Fridays. Admission charge. 13 Valkendorfsgade (phone: 33-141009).

**STATENS MUSEUM FOR KUNST (ROYAL MUSEUM OF FINE ARTS)** Danish and European works of art, including a Matisse collection. Out front, a group of odd-looking statues is known locally as the "Muppet Show" (its formal name is the *Human Wall*). Closed Mondays. No admission charge. Sølvgade at Øster Voldgade (phone: 33-912126).

**ZOOLOGISK MUSEUM (ZOOLOGICAL MUSEUM)** Animal life explained through exhibitions, models, and dioramas. Closed Mondays. No admission charge. 15 Universitetsparken (phone: 35-321000).

SHOPPING

With so many areas set aside for strolling (and shopping), Copenhagen is ideal for the consumer. Keep in mind that the 25% sales tax in Denmark is included in the price. To obtain a partial refund of this tax, have the goods sent to your US address, or present the sales slips and article(s) at the customs counter at the airport.

Denmark is world famous for beautifully designed wares for the home—furniture, sterling silver by Georg Jensen and others, and porcelain by Bing & Grøndahl and Royal Copenhagen. Copenhagen is also northern Europe's main fur trading center. It's wise to check the prices of these items before you leave home, as savings may not be substantial in Denmark.

Another Danish claim to fame is pastry, though the doughy, sticky pastry that Americans know as danish bears little resemblance to the original, crisp, buttery concoctions Danes call *wienerbrod* (Vienna bread). Follow your taste buds into the nearest bake shop for a whiff of *kanelstænger, snegle, tebirkes, borgmesterstænger,* and their caloric ilk. In the core of the old quarter is Copenhagen's oldest active bakery, now called *Skt. Peders Bageri* (29 Skt. Pedersstr.; phone: 33-111129), which traces its history back to 1652. For irresistible *kransekage* (Danish marzipan cake), prepared in every conceivable form, stop by *Kransekagehuset* (9 Ny Østergade; phone: 33-131902). At *J. Chr. Andersen's Eftf.* (32 Købmagergade; phone: 33-121345) you'll find from 450 to 500 different kinds of cheese, many of them homemade—or at least home-aged. Purchases can be vacuum-packed for the trip home.

Strøget is the most famous of the city's shopping streets; take a look at its side streets as well. Other pedestrian streets are Fiolstræde and Købmagergade in the old Latinske Kvatir (Latin Quarter), once the student district, now the place to go for antiques and rare books as well as boutiques and specialty shops. Bredgade, extending from Kongens Nytorv, is another antiques area. Be sure to investigate the extension of Pistolstræde, just off the Østergade section of Strøget. It has a charming little arcade with a pastry shop and other food stores, and designer boutiques. For folks who like their shopping a lot less formal, Copenhagen boasts a very appealing, low-pressure flea market that functions most Saturdays (in good weather) from May through October at the Israel Plads (at Romersgade). The following shops are also recommended. Stores generally are open weekdays 10 AM to 6 PM, Saturdays 9 AM to 2 PM, closed Sundays.

**A. Michelsen** High-quality silver. 10 Amagertorv (phone: 33-114080).

**Anthon Berg** Irresistible Danish chocolates. 1 Østergade (phone: 33-111564).

**Bing & Grøndahl** World-famous porcelain. 4 Amagertorv (phone: 33-122686).

**Birger Christensen** Perhaps the best furrier in Scandinavia. 38 Østergade (phone: 33-115555).

**Boghallen** For English-language paperbacks and the latest hardcovers. Also Denmark's largest selection of travel books. 37 Rådhuspladsen (phone: 33-118511).

**Georg Jensen Silver** Needs no introduction. 4 Amagertorv (phone: 33-114080).

**Hans Hansen Sølv** Silverware of similar quality and lower prices than *Georg Jensen,* plus more contemporary designs. 16 Amagertorv (phone: 33-156067).

**Holmegaards Glasværker** Denmark's distinctive designer of dramatic glassware. 15 Østergade (phone: 33-124477).

**Illum's** A popular department store with a selection of typical Danish wares; also a fine café. Don't miss the basement food hall. 52 Østergade (phone: 33-144002).

**Illums Bolighus** World-renowned furnishings center of modern design. Also the latest in china and stemware. 10 Amagertorv (phone: 33-141941).

**In Circus** A consortium of Danish designers provides the trendiest of ready-to-wear and costume jewelry. 17 Studiestr. (phone: 33-913392).

**Magasin du Nord** The city's largest, oldest, and best-known department store, with a great gourmet grocery. 13 Kongens Nytorv (phone: 33-114433).

**Paustian House** Modern furniture and decorative objects by renowned Scandinavian designers and architects. The prize-winning building was designed by Danish architect Joern Utzon (who did the *Sydney Opera House*). On Copenhagen's northernmost harborfront, 2 Kalkbrænderiløbskaj; take the *S-train* east to Nordhavn and walk (phone: 31-184511).

**Rosenthal Studio Haus A/S** Elegant crystal and porcelain, including a fine selection of Danish artist Bjørn Wiinblad's works. 21 Frederiksberggade (phone: 33-142101; fax: 33-142342).

**Royal Copenhagen** The maker of exquisite (and expensive) porcelain. 6 Amagertorv (phone: 33-137181).

## SPORTS AND FITNESS

Copenhagen does not have the variety of sports facilities found in many American cities, but the few sports popular in Denmark are *very* popular. Call the *Idrættens Hus* (Sports House; phone: 42-455555) for information on sports organizations.

**BICYCLING** A favorite mode of transportation here. Nearly all streets have separate lanes for bicycle traffic, and except for the worst winter months, it is often easier to ride a bicycle than to drive a car on Copenhagen's narrow streets. Bicycles can be rented at *Københavns Cyklebørs,* also called *DSB Cyclecenter* (at the *Hovedbanegården,* 11 Reventlowsgade entrance; phone: 33-140717) or from *Dan Wheel* (3 Colbjørnsensgade; phone: 31-212227).

**BICYCLE RACING** One of Denmark's most popular sports. *Ordrup Cykelbane* has races on Tuesdays; contact *Idrættens Hus* (see above) for more information. The exciting *Copenhagen Six-Day International Cycle Race* is held every year in late January or early February.

**FITNESS CENTERS** *Form & Figur* (70 Amager Bd.; phone: 31-542888) accepts non-members (for a fee), as do *Københavns Boldklub* (147 Peter Bangsvej; phone: 31-714180), where you can play tennis or cricket or use the pool and fitness room, and *Fitness Club Scala* (2E Vesterbrogade; phone: 33-321002), which has weights, step and aerobics classes, a pool, and saunas.

**HORSE RACING** *Klampenborg Galopbane* (40 Klampenborgvej, Klampenborg; phone: 31-637898) has races on Saturdays from mid-April through June and from August through mid-December; in July races are on Tuesdays.

**JOGGING** The parks, *Kongens Have* and *Fælledparken,* as well as the four Søerne (Central Lakes) are all good spots, 10 minutes from Rådhuspladsen.

**SOCCER** It's known in Denmark as *fodbold,* and professional matches take place every weekend from April through early May and August through early November. The Danish national team also plays *World Cup* qualifying matches in Copenhagen at *Idrætsparken* (Østerbro; phone: 31-421430). A local Copenhagen team plays matches here also.

**SWIMMING** The coast north of Copenhagen has many beaches, and the water is relatively warm in the latter part of the summer. South of Copenhagen, *Køge Bay Strandpark* is an area of beaches, marinas, and dunes. Topless, if not nude, bathing is the norm in Denmark, especially for the young. There are also a number of excellent Olympic-size public pools, both indoor and outdoor. From late May through August 31, try *Bavnehøj Friluftsbad* (90 Enghavevej; phone: 31-214900). For year-round indoor swimming, try *Kildeskovshallen* (25 Adolfsvej, Hellerup; phone: 31-682822).

**TENNIS** Ever since the success of Björn Borg, tennis has boomed in Scandinavia. Copenhagen's spring and summer climate is delightful for court capers, and a number of clubs offer temporary memberships, including *Boldklubben af 1893,* known locally as *B 93* (10 Per Henrik Lings Allé; phone: 31-381890); *Hellerup Idrætsklub* (37 Hartmannsvej, Hellerup; phone: 31-621428); and *Københavns Bold-*

*klub* (147 Peter Bangsvej; phone: 31-714180). Advance reservations are required. Additional information about facilities and tournaments is available from the courteous *Dansk Tennis Vorbund* (20 *Brøndby Stadion, Idrættens Hus;* phone: 42-455555).

## THEATER

Because the arts in Denmark are government subsidized, tickets are normally inexpensive. The famous *Det Kongelige Teater* (Royal Theater) at Kongens Nytorv is worth a visit. The national theater and opera companies perform here, in Danish, as does the *Kongelige Ballet* (Royal Danish Ballet), one of the world's foremost dance companies. There are three stages: the *Gamle Scene* (Old Stage), the *Nye Scene* (New Stage), and the even newer *Boltens*. For schedule information and for all bookings, contact the tourist office or box office (phone: 33-141002; 33-324444 for *Boltens*). In the summer there are lighter diversions, like cabarets at *Tivoli* (see *Special Places*) and beer hall entertainment at *Bakken* (see *Special Events*). The *Mermaid Theater* (27 Skt. Pedersstr.; phone: 33-114303) is Scandinavia's only permanent English-language stage, presenting Scandinavian plays in summer and British and American works in winter. A cabaret in the style of an old English musical is presented at *Christmastime.*

## MUSIC

Opera is performed at *Det Kongelige Teater* (see above). Classical music concerts performed by the *Radio Symfoniorkester* (Radio Symphony Orchestra) are presented in *Tivoli* at the *Radiohusets Konsertsal* (Radio House Concert Hall; phone: 35-203040) and the *Zealand Symphony Hall* (phone: 33-151012). Students of the *Kongelige Musikkonservatorium* (Royal Danish Academy of Music; phone: 33-124274) give regular concerts, usually free, at 1 Niels Brocksgade. During the winter, there also are modern music concerts at *Ny Carlsberg Glyptotek* and *Louisiana Museum of Modern Art* (see *Special Places*). The world's best rock bands often perform at *Falkonér Teatret* (9 Falkonér Allé; phone: 31-868501).

## NIGHTCLUBS AND NIGHTLIFE

*Nautilus* at the *Copenhagen Admiral* hotel is a traditional nightspot with food, live music, and dancing; *Restaurant Wiinblad* at the *d'Angleterre* hotel has a busy bar and serves good—but a tad pricey—food (see *Checking In* for details on both). The *Copenhagen Jazz House* (10 Niels Hemmingsensgade; phone: 33-152600) offers music from international jazz artists.

More informal are *Den Røde Pimpernel* (7 Hans Christian Andersen Blvd.; phone: 33-122032), with music for dancing, and the lively *HongKong* (7 Nyhavn; phone: 33-120765). If you like discotheques, there are several alternatives, but nothing that measures up to New York's finest. The best of the lot are *Annabel's* (16 Lille Kongensgade; phone: 33-112020), where there's a dress code—no jeans allowed—and *New Fellini Club* in the *Radisson SAS Royal* hotel (1 Hammerichsgade; phone: 33-933239). Another popular disco is *Privé* (14 Ny Østergade; phone: 33-137520), with a huge dance floor and two bars.

The music cafés are much friendlier than discos and a much better deal. Excellent jazz and big-name guest stars are featured at *Montmartre* (41 Nørregade; phone: 33-136966), the northern European jazz capital. Other good spots are *Daddy's* (5 Axeltorv; phone: 33-114679) for hip hop and pop music, and *La Fontaine* (11 Kompagnistræde; phone: 33-116098) for live music, usually jazz or swing. *Brønnum* (1 Tordenskjoldsgade at Kongens Nytorv; phone: 33-930365), just behind the *Royal Theater,* is another late-night bar-restaurant-café. *Sommersko* (6 Kronprinsensgade; phone: 33-148189) and *Dan Turell* (3 St. Regnegade; phone: 33-141047) are popular hangouts for intellectuals. *Café Victor* (8 Ny Østergade; phone: 33-133613) offers French food and is always packed, particularly at lunchtime and during happy hour. Down the street, *ZeZe Bar and Café* (20 Ny Østergade; phone: 33-142390) is fashionable with the younger crowd and draws many students. Gamblers can try their luck at the *Casino Copenhagen* in the *Radisson SAS Scandinavia* hotel (see *Checking In*), which opens daily at 2 PM. There's an entrance fee; jackets and ties required for men.

# Best in Town

## CHECKING IN

The few large luxury hotels in Copenhagen are expensive and often the rooms are on the small side. For a double room expect to pay $250 or more per night in a hotel in the very expensive category; $180 to $245 in a place described as expensive; $120 to $175 in a moderate hotel; and $120 or less in an inexpensive place. All rates include tax and, unless otherwise indicated, breakfast (usually a generous buffet), and all hotel rooms have private baths, TV sets, and telephones unless otherwise indicated. Book ahead during the peak summer season. If you arrive without reservations your best bet is to use the accommodations service at the tourist board office (see *Tourist Information*). There's a small fee, but there are often special room rates. Be aware that many of the less-expensive establishments are closed during the *Christmas–New Year's* holidays.

### VERY EXPENSIVE

**D'Angleterre** Built in 1775, this 126-room hostelry is the oldest and still the most venerable in town, and its new owner has renovated the façade, remodeled the lobby bar, and enlarged the reception area. An indoor pool and fitness center are planned. The old-fashioned paneled rooms and the location near Nyhavn give the place the ambience of an old ocean liner. There's a good, reasonably priced French restaurant; a café, the *Restaurant Wiinblad;* and a bar. Breakfast is not included. Business facilities include 24-hour room service, meeting rooms for up to 400, an English-speaking concierge, foreign currency exchange, and secretarial services in English. 34 Kongens Nytorv (phone: 33-120095; fax: 33-121118).

**Kong Frederik** In the heart of town, just a stone's throw from *Tivoli* and the *Rådhus* (Town Hall), are 110 rooms in a charmingly renovated building. The new owners (who also run the *d'Angleterre)* have spiffed up the lobby and added a new à la carte restaurant, while the *Queen's Pub* remains, as before, a popular watering hole. Breakfast is not included. Business facilities include meeting rooms, photocopiers, an English-speaking concierge, and cable TV news. 25 Vester Voldgade (phone: 33-125902; 800-223-6800; fax: 33-935901).

**Phoenix** Set in a graceful 17th-century building, this luxurious property offers 212 well-appointed rooms, including three suites with Jacuzzis and 52 executive rooms with their own fax machines, marble baths, and gold-plated fixtures. The hotel also has a fitness center with a sauna and indoor pool (a rarity in Copenhagen). Along with a first class international restaurant, there is a traditional Danish eatery, a British pub, and a bar. Breakfast is not included. Business facilities include 24-hour room service, meeting rooms for up to 100, an English-speaking concierge, and secretarial services in English. 37 Bredgade (phone: 33-959500; 800-888-4747; fax: 33-339833).

**Plaza** If fine antique furnishings, mahogany paneling, and luxurious comfort appeal to you, consider one of the 93 rooms at this Art Nouveau establishment. The high quality of decor and service make it a favorite of well-known visiting artists. You will need to reserve well ahead of time. The wood-paneled *Library Bar* is a cozy spot for a drink; there's also a restaurant. Business facilities include room service, meeting rooms for up to 60, and an English-speaking concierge. 4 Bernstorffsgade (phone: 33-149262; 800-223-6800 or 800-223-5652; fax: 33-939362).

**Sheraton Copenhagen** Another business-traveler-oriented establishment, with 471 rooms (including 36 suites), a charming view of the city, and the *King's Court Bar.* There is also an elegant restaurant, an English pub, and a café where cappuccino and fresh pastries are always available. Business facilities include 24-hour room service, meeting rooms for up to 1,500, an English-speaking concierge, and secretarial services in English. 6 Vester Søgade (phone: 33-143535; 800-325-3535; fax: 33-321223).

### EXPENSIVE

**Grand** This classic, 146-room hotel is conveniently located a few blocks from *Tivoli* and Rådhuspladsen, near the *Hovedbanegården.* Well-appointed rooms, a French-inspired sidewalk café, and an elegant Danish restaurant are among its features. Business facilities include meeting rooms for up to 100, an English-speaking concierge, and cable TV news. 9 Vesterbrogade (phone: 31-313600; 800-THE-OMNI; fax: 31-313350).

**Neptun** Formerly a sailor's hostel, this 136-room inn has been restored to offer first class amenities while retaining its 1860s charm. Fifteen apartments are available for long-term stays. There's a restaurant and an atrium where snacks are served in warm weather. In a lovely section of Nyhavn, near Kongens Nytorv. 14-20 Sankt Annæ Plads (phone: 33-138900; fax: 33-141250).

**Palace** A turn-of-the-century hotel with a renovated façade, it's right where the action is—overlooking Copenhagen's central Rådhuspladsen and only a two-minute walk to *Tivoli*. The 159 rooms are comfortably furnished, and there is a popular Danish buffet lunch and dinner. Business facilities include meeting rooms, an English-speaking concierge, photocopiers, and cable TV news. 57 Rådhuspladsen (phone: 33-144050; fax: 33-145279).

**Radisson SAS Scandinavia** This 542-room modern skyscraper is the largest in town. On the 25th floor is the *Top of Town* restaurant, which affords spectacular views of the city. Gamblers enjoy the *Casino Copenhagen*. The hotel caters primarily to the needs and tastes of businesspeople on the move and has airport bus service. Business facilities include 24-hour room service, meeting rooms for up to 1,200, an English-speaking concierge, and secretarial services in English. 70 Amager Blvd. (phone: 33-112324; 800-333-3333; fax: 31-570193).

### MODERATE

**Copenhagen Admiral** In an old corn warehouse on the waterfront near the *d'Angleterre* (and much less expensive), it has 366 modern rooms, a sauna, a bar, a restaurant, and the congenial *Nautilus* night-club downstairs. Breakfast is not included. Business facilities include room service for breakfast, meeting rooms for up to 80, and an English-speaking concierge. 24 Toldbodgade (phone: 33-118282; 800-223-9868; fax: 33-325542).

**Copenhagen Star** Near the *Hovedbanegården*, this hotel has 134 bright, modern rooms with convenient extras such as trouser presses and hair dryers. There's also a breakfast room, café, and bar. Business facilities include meeting rooms for up to 70. 13 Colbjørnsensgade (phone: 31-221100; 800-44UTELL; fax: 31-222199).

**Friendly Hotel Østerport** This long, low, 170-room hotel alongside the railroad tracks looks rather odd, but it provides comfortable accommodations and a good *smørrebrød* lunch. Business facilities include meeting rooms for up to 60 and an English-speaking concierge. 5 Oslo Plads (phone: 33-112266; fax: 33-122555).

**Opera** Located just behind *Det Kongelige Teater,* this Old Europe hostelry was formerly an apartment building. The 87 rooms have been redecorated, but many are small, so request a suite if spacious accommodations are a priority. The *Opera Bar* off the lobby has a comfortable, clubby atmosphere, and there is a good Danish-French restaurant. Business facilities include meeting rooms for up to 18. 15 Tordenskjoldsgade (phone: 33-121519; fax: 33-321282).

### INEXPENSIVE

**Absalon** Named for the city's founder, this is a clean, 260-room hotel near the *Hovedbanegården* for those on a limited budget. For even greater savings, some rooms are available with a shared bath. There's no restaurant, but breakfast is offered in the breakfast room. 19 Helgolandsgade (phone: 31-242211; fax: 31-243411).

**Cosmopole** Just a block south of *Tivoli* and convenient to the *Hovedbanegården*, this spot offers 208 rooms and a restaurant. 11 Colbjørnsensgade (phone: 31-213333; fax: 31-313399).

**Viking** An honorable old salt's hotel near Nyhavn, this 91-room property offers an address in the heart of the city's harbor section. There's no restaurant and the rate does not include breakfast. 65 Bredgade (phone: 33-124550; fax: 33-124618).

---

## EATING OUT

The Danes enjoy good food as well as good beer and *snaps* (aquavit). A number of established restaurants serve capital continental—especially French—fare. In addition there are many small taverns/inns, or *kro,* offering Danish specialties like open-face sandwiches or *smørrebrød.* The most distinctive Danish meal is *frokost* (lunch), usually a selection of sandwiches, scrambled eggs, or steak tartare with onion. Most restaurants have three-course *frokost* menus.

A Dane will never refuse a *snaps* with herring—and visitors may want to indulge as well. *Snaps* is imbibed icy cold, and is often chased by one of the many wonderful Danish beers. The best snaps are Aalborg's Jubileum and Harald Jensen.

The proper way to toast is to raise your glass to eye level, say *"skål,"* (pronounced "skoal"), and look your companions in the eye. Toss back the shot and, before returning the glass to the table, hold it at eye level again. Aquavit can also be added to coffee.

For a meal for two expect to pay $140 or more at a very expensive place; at least $110 at an expensive one; $70 to $100 at a restaurant in the moderate category; and $70 or less at an inexpensive eatery. Prices don't include wine and drinks, which are expensive and easily can double the tab. Your dinner bills in general may seem a bit high, but remember that the 25% sales tax and a 15% service charge are included in the total. Danes seldom leave an additional tip unless service is truly superb. Unless otherwise indicated, all restaurants listed below accept major credit cards and serve both lunch and dinner.

### VERY EXPENSIVE

**Kong Hans** Under the vaulted, whitewashed ceiling of a 14th-century wine cellar is this elegant one-Michelin-star restaurant. Young chef Daniel Letz proudly presides over salmon, silky pickled or smoked right on the premises; stuffed langoustines; *côte de boeuf;* and a selection of splendid desserts. The atmosphere is sophisticated, but Letz makes sure that everyone feels relaxed and comfortable, and the service is superb. Open for dinner only; closed Sundays and holidays, and July 15 to August 15. Reservations necessary. 6 Vingårdsstræde (phone: 33-116868).

**Belle Terasse** The most elegant restaurant in *Tivoli,* with lush gardens, live music, a romantic ambience, and French/Danish food. Dinner here is an experience, though an expensive one. Closed September through April. Reservations advised. *Tivoli* (phone: 33-121136; fax: 33-150031).

**Egoisten** A traditional restaurant with an enduring reputation for its haute cuisine. Closed Sundays. Reservations advised. 2 Hovedvagtsgd. (phone: 33-127971).

**Els** The murals date from the mid-19th century, when the restaurant was a coffeehouse. Lunch is primarily *smørrebrød;* the dinner menu, which changes daily, is nouvelle-inspired Danish and French with an emphasis on fish and game. Closed *Christmas* and *New Year's Day.* Reservations necessary. 3 Store Strandstræde (phone: 33-141341).

**Les Etoiles et une Rose** The lovingly prepared fish and game helped earn this fine restaurant a Michelin star. Five- and seven-course tasting menus change daily, while the à la carte list varies with the seasons. Closed Saturday lunch and Sundays. Reservations advised. 43 Dronningens Tværgade (phone: 33-150554).

**Kommandanten** A 17th-century house with enchanting doll-size rooms painted in copen blue is the setting for classic dining. Awarded one Michelin star, the chef's offerings might include a frothy, hot lobster soup with sorrel, a perfectly grilled piece of salmon (part of a three-course "fish menu"), or a six-course menu that will give diners a taste of the best of old and new Danish cooking. Closed Saturday lunch and Sundays. Reservations necessary. 7 Ny Adelgade (phone: 33-120990).

**Lumskebugten** Warm service and wonderful food are the hallmarks of this cozy nautical-theme dining establishment located near the waterfront. Seafood and shellfish are the big draws; for a real (and reasonably priced) treat, order the Russian caviar with sour cream and garlic toast. Closed Sundays. Reservations advised. 21 Esplanaden (phone: 33-156029).

**Restaurationen** Very noisy and very "in," especially with the young, chic, and moneyed, this is one of the most innovative of the city's newer restaurants. A fixed five-course menu changes weekly; it could feature such unusual dishes as salmon with red cabbage and apple beurre blanc. Meals may also be ordered à la carte. Diners may order certain wines by the glass (a rarity in Denmark), expertly chosen from the ample cellar. The desserts are fanciful and the service is excellent. Open for dinner only; closed Sundays and Mondays. Reservations necessary. 19 Møntergade (phone: 33-149495).

**Saison** Just a few miles north of the city in the village of Skovshoved, this critically acclaimed eatery is set in the historic and charming *Skovshoved* hotel. The bill of fare features freshly caught fish and seafood treats such as oysters in parsley bouillon, and turbot and forest mushrooms served with potatoes. Closed Sundays. Reservations advised. 203 Strandvejen (phone: 31-624842).

**Café Grønnegade** A variety of nooks and crannies in the basement and ground floor of a 17th-century townhouse is the setting for this informal and friendly café. The piping hot soups and the freshest of local fish and vegetables are fine choices. Open daily for buffet or à la carte lunch and for dinner. Reservations unnecessary. 39 Grønnegade (phone: 33-933133).

**Copenhagen Corner** Ask for a window table for a good view of pedestrian traffic past Rådhuspladsen. This pleasant spot, always packed, serves traditional Danish dishes. Closed *Christmas* and *New Year's Day.* Reservations advised for dinner. Rådhuspladsen (phone: 33-914545; fax: 33-910404).

**Grøften** Nothing fancy—just simple Danish cooking, reasonably priced. Besides the abundant *smørrebrød,* the heartiest (and best) dish on the menu is *skipperlabskovs,* a veal stew with potatoes and leeks. Closed September through April. Reservations unnecessary. *Tivoli* (phone: 33-121125; fax: 33-155125).

**Den Gyldne Fortun** This spot is famous for seafood; it also serves *smørrebrød* for lunch only and is popular with big groups (a minimum of 20 people is required for a group reservation). Closed at lunch on weekends. Reservations necessary. 18 Ved Stranden (phone: 33-122011).

**Krogs** Across the canal from *Christiansborg,* it serves some of the best seafood in Copenhagen. The bouillabaisse is an excellent choice, but is rather pricey. Closed Sundays and from December 20 to January 7. Reservations advised. 38 Gammel Strand (phone: 33-158915).

**Peder Oxe** This popular meeting place has a little something for everybody, but the specialties are meat dishes. A bottle of house wine is at every table, and guests are charged according to the amount they drink. Closed *Christmas Eve.* Reservations necessary. 11 Gråbrødre Torv (phone: 33-110077).

**Slotskælderen** Known locally as *Gitte Kik* (the name of the owner and granddaughter of the founder) and favored by politicians and businessmen, this basement spot is the ideal place to sample true *smørrebrød.* An ample selection of cold, open-face sandwiches (try the roast beef topped with soft fried onions), a variety of herring, and several hot dishes are among the choices, along with good Danish beer. Open for lunch only; closed Sundays. Reservations unnecessary. 4 Fortunstræde (phone: 33-111537).

**Parnas** A dark, smoky place with a piano bar, it's a friendly artists' haven and an ideal place to meet the natives. Hash with béarnaise sauce is a specialty. Open from noon until 3 AM; closed Sundays, *Christ-*

*mas Eve,* and *New Year's Eve.* No reservations. 16 Lille Kongensgade (phone: 33-114910).

**Wessels Kro** This quaint old tavern is the place to partake of the famous
Danish *store kolde bord* ("great cold table"). There's a wide assort-
ment of Danish hams and other cold cuts. Closed *New Year's Eve.*
Reservations unnecessary. 7 Sværtegade (phone: 33-126793).

# Dublin

## At-a-Glance

### SEEING THE CITY

Views of this essentially flat city are best from a number of restaurants in the surrounding hills; particularly nice is *Killakee House* in Rathfarnham (Killakee Rd.; phone: 493-2645 or 493-2917). Or see Dublin from the neighboring Wicklow Mountains.

### SPECIAL PLACES

Central Dublin is compact. Since traffic often moves slowly, the best way to see the city is on foot, on the splendid, signposted *Tourist Trail*. Walk the wide Georgian squares and avenues, meander down the cobblestone lanes near the Liffey Quays, stroll through the sylvan paths of St. Stephen's Green or along bustling Grafton Street, and stop at *Bewley's Café* (see *Eating Out*) for a cup of coffee or at the *Shelbourne* hotel (see *Checking In*) for a proper afternoon tea.

#### SOUTH DOWNTOWN

**MERRION SQUARE** The loveliest of Dublin's Georgian squares, it is a study in balance and elegance. Note particularly the variety of fanlights on doorways. At No. 1, the young Oscar Wilde lived with his celebrated parents, the surgeon Sir William Wills Wilde and the poetess Speranza; No. 58 was the home of Daniel O'Connell, the "Liberator" who won Catholic emancipation in 1829; at No. 70 lived Sheridan Le Fanu, author of sinister tales such as *Uncle Silas* and *Through a Glass Darkly* (after his wife's death in 1858, he shut himself up there, appearing only after nightfall to walk in the shadows of Merrion Square); No. 82 was the home of William Butler Yeats. Today the only house in the square used as a private dwelling is No. 71, where well-known couturière Sybil Connolly has her home and studio.

**NUMBER TWENTY-NINE** On one of Dublin's most fashionable 18th-century streets, this four-story brick building, restored and maintained by a joint effort of the *National Museum of Ireland* and the Irish Electrical Supply Board, gives visitors the opportunity to see the interior of a typical Georgian house. The furnishings reflect the home life of a middle class Dublin family during the late-18th and early-19th centuries. Open Tuesdays through Sundays year-round. No admission charge. 29 Lower Fitzwilliam St. (phone: 676-5831).

**LEINSTER HOUSE** When the young Duke of Leinster chose to build a mansion "on the other side of the River Liffey" in 1745, the location was questioned by many, for at that time the north side of the city was considered more fashionable. Undaunted, he went ahead with his plan, asserting prophetically, "Where I go, fashion will follow."

The house built by the Duke of Leinster is said to resemble (and may have inspired) the American White House, whose architect, James Hoban of Carlow, studied in Dublin after the completion of *Leinster House.* The building was purchased in the 19th century by the *Royal Dublin Society,* and in 1921 the Parliament of the new Irish Free State chose the building as its meeting place. *Leinster House* continues to be the meeting place of the Dáil (House of Representatives) and Seanad (Senate). When the former is in session, visitors may watch from the visitors' gallery. Sessions are held Tuesdays through Thursdays, except in July, August, and September. Apply for tickets at the main gate or by writing in advance. No admission charge. Kildare St., Merrion Sq. (phone: 678-9911).

**MUSEUM OF NATURAL HISTORY** The first sight to greet visitors is a huge preserved shark hanging from the ceiling. Also popular is the display of birds, as well as the three magnificent skeletons of giant Irish deer, believed to be about 10,000 years old. On the ground floor, the *Irish Room* displays Irish fauna and a new exhibition of Irish insects. An impressive collection of big-game heads and antlers from India and Africa in the galleries on the second floor transports museumgoers to late Victorian times. On the third floor are exotic shells, butterflies, and birds—plus skeletons of the extinct dodo, solitaire, and giant bird of Madagascar, with its 11.7-inch egg. A priceless assemblage of glass models of the invertebrates is also well worth seeing, as is an impressive geological collection consisting of Irish rocks and minerals. Admission charge. Closed Mondays. Merrion Sq. (phone: 661-8811).

**NATIONAL GALLERY** It has been called "the best small gallery in Europe," and considering its chronic shortage of funds, it certainly has a remarkable collection, with some outstanding examples of works from all the major schools, particularly the Italian and Dutch. In 1993, a priceless addition was made to the collection: a large painting, *The Taking of Christ,* formerly attributed to Honthorst and later discovered to be by Caravaggio; it is on indefinite loan to the gallery. A collection of more than 30 Turner watercolors is shown every January. The Irish School is brilliantly represented by the works of Jack Yeats and earlier painters such as Nathaniel Hone, Walter Osborne, William Orpen, and James Arthur O'Connor. Though staff shortages often cause a number of its rooms to be closed, the gallery is lively and interesting. There's a good research library, a bookshop, and an inexpensive restaurant that has become a popular Dublin meeting place. Open daily. Admission charge. Merrion Sq. (phone: 661-5133).

**NATIONAL MUSEUM** This massive Thomas Deane building on Kildare Street houses a remarkable collection of Irish antiquities, among them priceless collections of prehistoric gold artifacts, such as solid gold dress fasteners, torques, and *lunulae* made by the skilled craftsmen of the Bronze and Iron Ages. An exhibition area called *The Treasury* features the museum's important collection of early Christian metalwork, including the *Ardagh Chalice* and the *Cross of*

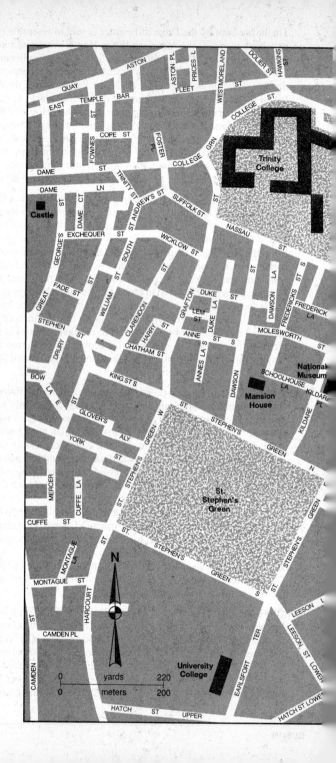

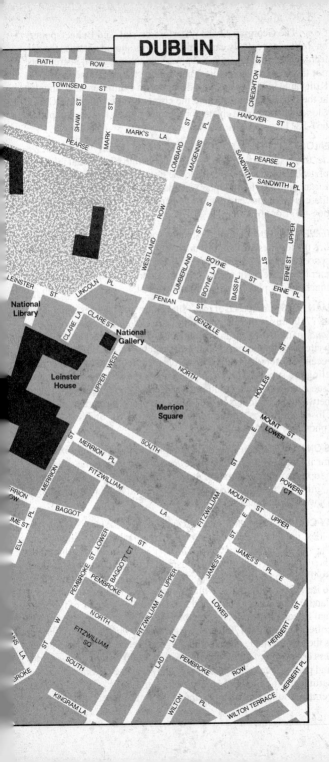

# DUBLIN

RATH ROW

TOWNSEND ST

CREIGHTON ST

HANOVER ST

SHAW ST

MARK ST

MARK'S LA

MAGENNIS PL

LOMBARD ST

SANDWITH

PEARSE ST

PEARSE HO

SANDWITH PL

WESTLAND ROW

S ST

CUMBERLAND ST

BOYNE

BOYNE LA

BASS PL

ST

ST

ERNE ST UPPER

ERNE PL

LEINSTER ST

LINCOLN PL

FENIAN ST

ERNE ST

**National Library**

CLARE LA

CLARE ST

DENZILLE

LA

ST

**National Gallery**

HOLLES

**Leinster House**

UPPER WEST

NORTH

**Merrion Square**

MOUNT ST LOWER

ST

E

MERRION ST

MERRION PL

SOUTH

ST

POWERS CT

RRION OW

FITZWILLIAM

MOUNT ST UPPER

JME ST

MERRION

BAGGOT

LA

FITZWILLIAM

E

ELY

PL

PEMBROKE ST LOWER

BAGGOTT CT

ST

JAMES'S

JAMES'S PL E

PEMBROKE LA

FITZWILLIAM ST UPPER

LOWER

HERBERT ST

NS LA

ST W

NORTH

**FITZWILLIAM SQ**

LAD LN

PEMBROKE

ROW

HERBERT PL

BROKE

SOUTH

WILTON PL

KINGRAM LA

WILTON TERRACE

*Cong.* The Georgian silver, Waterford crystal, and Belleek pottery on display are equally captivating. Visitors should not miss the collection of Irish harps, *uilleann* pipes, and other musical instruments, nor the Derrynaflan chalice, paten, and strainer, found in 1980 at Killenaule in Tipperary. Varied short-term exhibitions are mounted at the museum annex around the corner on Merrion Row. Closed Mondays. Admission charge for special exhibits. Kildare St. (phone: 661-8811).

**GENEALOGICAL OFFICE AND HERALDIC MUSEUM** Formerly in *Dublin Castle,* this is the domain of Ireland's chief herald (the official in charge of genealogy, heraldic arms, and the like) and the ideal starting point for an ancestry hunt. Open weekdays. No admission charge, but there is a fee for genealogical consultations. 2 Kildare St. (phone: 661-4877 or 661-1626).

**ST. STEPHEN'S GREEN** A couple of blocks southwest of Merrion Square lies the loveliest of Dublin's many public parks. The 22-acre green space contains gardens, a waterfall, and an ornamental lake. In summer it's an excellent place to sit and watch working Dublin take its lunch; bands play here in July and August.

**NEWMAN HOUSE** Composed of two 18th-century townhouses dating back to 1740, this is the historic seat of the *Catholic University of Ireland,* named for Cardinal John Henry Newman, the 19th-century writer and theologian and the first rector of the university. The recently restored plasterwork, marble tiled floors, and wainscot paneling are superb. The site also contains the *Commons* restaurant (see *Eating Out*), an outdoor terrace, and a "secret garden" tucked between the buildings in the back. Open June through September; closed Mondays. Admission charge. 85-86 St. Stephen's Green (phone: 475-7255 or 475-1752).

**MANSION HOUSE** Dublin preceded London in building a *Mansion House* for its lord mayor in 1715. The *Round Room,* was the site of the adoption of the Declaration of Irish Independence in 1919 and the signing of the Anglo-Irish Treaty of 1921. No admission charge. Dawson St. (phone: 676-2852).

**TRINITY COLLEGE** Dawson Street descends to meet *Trinity College,* the oldest university in Ireland, founded by Elizabeth I of England on the site of the 12th-century *Monastery of All Hallows.* Alumni of the college include Oliver Goldsmith, Edmund Burke, Jonathan Swift, Bishop Berkeley (pronounced *Bark-*lee)—who lent his name to Berkeley, California—William Congreve, Thomas Moore, Sheridan Le Fanu, Oscar Wilde, and J. P. Donleavy. No trace of the original Elizabethan structure remains; the oldest surviving part of the college dates from 1700. The *Long Room, Trinity*'s famous library, is the longest single-chamber library in existence. It contains a priceless collection of 800,000 volumes and 3,000 ancient manuscripts and papyri. The area of the library known as the *Colonnades* is the setting for the library's chief treasure, the *Book of Kells,* an 8th-century illuminated manuscript of the four gospels that has been described as the "most beautiful book in the world." The *Colonnades* is open daily, year-round. Admission charge. College Green (phone: 677-2941).

*Trinity College* also is the home of *The Dublin Experience,* a 45-minute multimedia program that traces the history of the city from earliest times to the present. In May through October it is shown daily in the *Davis Theatre.* Admission charge. Entrance on Nassau St. (phone: 677-2941, ext. 1688).

**PARLIAMENT HOUSE** Facing *Trinity College* is the monumental *Parliament House,* now the Bank of Ireland. Built in 1729 and regarded as one of the finest examples of the architecture of its period, this was the first of the great series of 18th-century public buildings in Dublin. It was erected to house the Irish Parliament in the century that saw the birth of Home Rule. Closed Sundays. No admission charge. College Green (phone: 677-6801).

**TEMPLE BAR** Just south of the River Liffey, stretching from Westmoreland to Fishamble Streets between *Trinity College* and *Christ Church Cathedral,* this eight-block area is ensconced in one of Dublin's oldest sections. The district, which has a distinctive blend of Georgian and Victorian ambience, owes its name to Sir William Temple, Provost of *Trinity College,* who maintained a house and gardens here in the early 17th century. Temple Bar is fast becoming Dublin's "Left Bank," with an assortment of avant-garde art galleries, shops, bars, cafés, and restaurants. The area is also the home of the *Irish Film Centre* (see below).

**IRISH FILM CENTRE** This complex is dedicated to the art of cinema culture—an exciting development for the Irish film industry, as well as for researchers, historians, students, and the general public. It houses two movie theaters, a *National Film Archive,* a film and television museum, a film information office, and film and video libraries, in addition to a restaurant and coffee shop. Film and video courses are conducted on site. Call for hours. Admission charge for films. 6 Eustace St. (phone: 677-8788).

**DUBLIN CASTLE** Dame Street leads west from *College Green* toward the older part of the city, where the early Viking and Norman settlers established themselves. Fortresses have stood on the site of *Dublin Castle* since the time of the Celts. The current structure was the center of English rule in Ireland for 400 years; for much of this time it had as grim a reputation as the Tower of London. Although the present building dates primarily from the 18th century, one of the four towers that flanked the original moated castle survives as the *Record Tower.* The 15th-century *Bedford Tower,* later reconstructed in 1777, was used as a state prison from 1918 to 1920. The *Georgian State Apartments,* formerly the residence of the English viceroys, have been beautifully restored; they now are used for state functions. *St. Patrick's Hall* in the *State Apartments* was the scene of the inauguration of Ireland's first president, Douglas Hyde. Open daily. Admission charge for the *Bedford Tower* and the *State Apartments.* Dame St. (phone: 677-7129).

**CHRIST CHURCH CATHEDRAL** Not far from *Dublin Castle,* this massive structure crowns the hill on which the ancient city stood. Founded in 1038 by Viking King Sitric Silkenbeard of Dublin, *Christ Church* was demolished in the 12th century and rebuilt by the Norman Richard Gilbert de Clare (Strongbow), who is buried within its walls. *Christ Church* today is the Church of Ireland (Protestant) cathedral for the diocese of Dublin. The vaulted crypt remains one of the largest in Ireland. Dubliners traditionally gather in front of the cathedral to ring in the *New Year.* Christ Church Pl. (phone: 677-8099).

**ST. AUDOEN'S ARCH AND THE CITY WALLS** The 13th-century *Church of St. Audoen* is Dublin's oldest parish church, founded by early Norman settlers who gave it the name St. Ouen, or Audoen, after the patron saint of their native Rouen. Close to the church is a flight of steps leading down to *St. Audoen's Arch,* the sole surviving gateway of the medieval city walls. High St. (phone: 679-1855).

**SYNOD HALL** Next door to *Christ Church Cathedral,* this building houses *Dublinia,* a multimedia re-creation of Dublin's formative medieval Anglo-Norman period from 1170 to 1540. Developed by the *Medieval Trust,* the exhibits are spread over several floors and include life-size replicas of buildings and objects unearthed during a recent archaeological dig. Open daily, May through October. Admission charge. At the corner of High and Wine Tavern Sts. (phone: 679-4611).

**ST. PATRICK'S CATHEDRAL** Although *Christ Church* stood within the old walled city, John Comyn, one of Dublin's 12th-century archbishops, felt that while he remained under municipal jurisdiction he could not achieve the temporal power for which he thirsted. Accordingly, he left the city walls and built a fine structure within a stone's throw of *Christ Church.* By the 19th century both cathedrals were in a state of considerable disrepair. Henry Roe, a distiller, restored *Christ Church* at his own expense; Sir Benjamin Lee Guinness of the famous brewing family came to the assistance of *St. Patrick's*— hence the saying in Dublin that "*Christ Church* was restored with glasses, *St. Patrick's* with pints!"

The most interesting aspect of this beautiful cathedral is its association with Jonathan Swift, author of *Gulliver's Travels* and dean of the cathedral for 32 years. Within these walls he is buried, beside his loving Stella. On a slab near the entrance is carved the epitaph Swift composed for himself: "He lies where furious indignation can no longer rend his heart." St. Patrick's now is used interdenominationally. Patrick St. (phone: 475-4817).

**MARSH'S LIBRARY** Adjoining St. Patrick's, this library dates from 1702. Its collection of 25,000 rare, magnificently bound old volumes and maps includes a copy of Clarendon's *History of the Great Rebellion,* once owned and annotated by Jonathan Swift. Closed Tuesdays and Sundays. No admisson charge (phone: 543511).

**GUINNESS BREWERY** Founded in 1759 by Arthur Guinness, this is the largest exporting stout brewery in the world. The *Guinness Hop-*

*store* (adjacent to the main brewery), once the storage building for the ingredients of the world-famous dark stout, is now a public hall that mounts temporary exhibits and art shows. In the same building is the *Guinness Museum,* which features old posters and other Guinness memorabilia, and the *Cooper's Museum,* which focuses on the casks and vats used in the brewing process. Next to the *Hopstore,* the visitors' center has an audiovisual presentation about the making of the famous brew, and offers free samples. Open weekdays. Admission charge. Crane St. (phone: 536700).

**IRISH MUSEUM OF ART (IMMA)** Housed in one of Ireland's finest 17th-century structures is a collection of contemporary and avant-garde works by such modern masters as Picasso, Miró, and Léger, as well as works by native artists including Jack Yeats and Louis le Brocquy. Originally a home for retired soldiers, the museum building was restored in the 1980s. The galleries are set around a large courtyard in the style of Les Invalides in Paris. The museum often hosts visiting visual, theatrical, performance, and musical exhibitions; check the Dublin newspapers for details. Closed Mondays. No admission charge (phone: 671-8666).

## NORTH DOWNTOWN

**FOUR COURTS** Almost directly across the river from the *Guinness Brewery* lies the stately *Four Courts of Justice,* dating from the apogee of the 18th century. The design of the building was begun by Thomas Cooley and completed by James Gandon, the greatest of all the Georgian architects. Supreme and High Court sittings are open to the public on weekdays. No admission charge. Inns Quay (phone: 872-5555).

**ST. MICHAN'S CHURCH** Not far from the *Four Courts* is this 17th-century church, built on the site of a 10th-century Viking church. The 18th-century organ is said to have been played by Handel when he was in Dublin for the first public performance of *Messiah.*

Of perhaps greater interest is the extraordinary crypt, with its remarkable preservative atmosphere: Bodies have lain here for centuries without decomposing, and visitors can, if they feel so inclined, shake the leathery hand of an eight-foot-tall Crusader. Open weekdays and Saturday mornings. Admission charge. Church St. (phone: 872-4154).

**IRISH WHISKEY CORNER** The story of the legendary liquid, known in Gaelic as *uisce beathadh* (water of life), is told at this former distillery warehouse. One-hour tours include an audiovisual presentation, a visit to an area with archival photographs and distillery memorabilia, a whiskey-making demonstration, and a tasting during which visitors can sample the various brands being brewed today. Tours are available weekdays at 3:30 PM. Admission charge. Bow St. (phone: 872-5566).

**MUNICIPAL GALLERY OF MODERN ART** Lord Charlemont, for whom this house was designed by Sir William Chambers in 1764, was a great patron of the arts; it is fitting, therefore, that his home has become a museum. It has an outstanding collection of Impressionist paintings, as well as works by Picasso, Utrillo, Bonnard, and such prominent Irish painters as Sir William Orpen, John B. Yeats (the poet's father), and Jack Yeats (the poet's brother). Closed Mondays. No admission charge. Beyond the Garden of Remembrance (a memorial to those who died for Irish freedom), on the north side of Parnell Sq. (phone: 874-1903).

**CUSTOM HOUSE** This masterpiece of Georgian architecture—restored and newly illuminated in 1991—adorns the north bank of the Liffey, east of O'Connell Street. The chef d'oeuvre of James Gandon, it is one of the finest buildings of its kind in Europe. Now occupied by government offices and closed to the public, it should nonetheless be seen at close range: The carved river heads that form the keystones of the arches and entrances are splendid. Custom House Quay (phone: 874-2961).

## ENVIRONS

**PHOENIX PARK** Northwest of the city center, this 1,760-acre park is beautifully planted with a great variety of trees. Within its walls are the residences of the President of the Republic and the US Ambassador. Among the attractions are the lovely *People's Gardens,* a herd of fallow deer, and the *Dublin Zoological Gardens.* The charming zoo, which has an impressive collection of animals, holds several records for lion breeding. Open daily. Admission charge for the zoo. Entrance on Park Gate St. (phone: 677-1425).

**JAMES JOYCE MUSEUM** Resembling other Martello towers that line the Irish coast, the one that houses this museum was built in 1804 to withstand a threatened Napoleonic invasion, and it would have remained an impressive but fairly anonymous pile of granite had it not been for James Joyce's *Ulysses.* The author lived in the tower briefly with Oliver St. John Gogarty, and in the opening scene of *Ulysses,* Stephen Dedalus lives here with Buck Mulligan. For many a Joyce fan, June 16, the day when the events described in *Ulysses* take place, is marked with a *Bloomsday* tour, with the first stop at the tower. In the tower museum is an eclectic collection of memorabilia: the writer's piano and guitar; his waistcoat, tie, and cane; and letters, manuscripts, photographs, and rare editions. But the chief exhibit is the tower itself, a squat structure looking across Dublin Bay to Howth. Open year-round, but by appointment only from October through April. Sandycove (phone: 280-9265 or 280-8571).

**CHESTER BEATTY LIBRARY** Founded by an American-born, naturalized British resident in Ireland, this library houses what is considered to be the world's most valuable and representative private collection of Oriental manuscripts and miniatures. Among the Islamic art and manuscripts are some 250 Korans, plus Persian, Turkish, and Indian paintings. There's also a collection of Chinese jade books, some 900 Chinese snuffboxes, and more than 220 rhinoceros horn cups. The collection of *nara-e* (Japanese illuminated manuscripts) ranks with the foremost in Europe, as does the collection of *surimono* (Japanese woodblock prints). The superb group of Western manuscripts includes illuminated books of hours and a volume of gospels from *Stavelot Abbey,* executed in Flanders around the year 1000. Eleven manuscript volumes of the Bible dating from the early 2nd to the 4th century are also on view. Closed Sundays and Mondays. No admission charge. 20 Shrewsbury Rd., Ballsbridge (phone: 269-2386).

**NATIONAL BOTANIC GARDENS** Nearly 50 acres of flowers, shrubs, and trees of some 20,000 species make this one of the most pleasant places to pass a few hours in Dublin. Among the most notable features are a rose bush grown from a cutting of national poet Thomas Moore's original "Last Rose of Summer"; the curvilinear mid-19th-century glass conservatories designed by Dublin architect Richard Turner, who also built the *Great Palm House* at London's Kew Gardens; a specimen of the Killarney fern *Trichomanes speciosum,* virtually exterminated in its native habitat by rapacious Victorian fern hunters; and a charming small rose garden reached by a bridge across a millstream. Lovers of English literature will be interested to note that the property previously belonged to *Spectator* founder Joseph Addison, who was secretary to the Earl of Sutherland in Dublin for a short while. Lovers of Victorian cemeteries should wind up their visit with a stop at *Glasenevin Cemetery* next door, where the headstones are like a roll call of key figures in Irish history, with O'Connell and Parnell at the top of the list. Open daily, year-round. No admission charge. Glasnevin (phone: 377596 or 374388).

**CASINO MARINO** This miniature masterpiece, an 18th-century architectural gem, was designed in 1761 for Lord Charlemont by Sir William Chambers as a summer retreat. Resembling a garden temple, the three-story structure features several reception rooms, bedrooms, and spacious kitchens depicting 18th-century life. Open daily, June through mid-September. Admission charge. Gardiner St. (phone: 33168).

**MALAHIDE CASTLE, PARK, AND GARDENS** No other property in Ireland was occupied by a single family as long as this one, which overlooks the Broadmeadow estuary and the Irish Sea. The Talbot family lived here continuously from 1185 until 1973 (when the last Lord Talbot died), with a break of only a few years in Cromwellian times. Despite the pedigree, this is a smallish, easily managed castle, although many additions have been made to the oldest surviving section, a 15th-century tower. The paneled 16th-century *Oak Room,* one of the finest in the country, is still well preserved. Throughout the castle, a number of portraits from the valuable *National Portrait Collection* are on display, along with a fine collection of Irish period furniture.

The 270-acre gardens and park are superb. The last occupant, Lord Milo Talbot de Malahide, was a horticultural enthusiast who specialized in plants of the Southern Hemisphere; he also owned an estate in Tasmania. Between 1948 and his death, he amassed a collection of some 5,000 species and varieties that flourished in the alkaline soil, Gulf Stream–warmed climate, fine breezes, and low rainfall, including the world's largest collection of olearias, good specimens of euphorbia, eryngium, and ceanothus, and a significant assortment of ozothamnus. He also persuaded many extremely tender plants from South America and Africa to prosper in the open here. Open year-round during seasonally varying hours. Admission charge. Malahide, about 12 miles (19 km) from Dublin on the Malahide road (phone: 845-2377 or 845-2337).

**NEWBRIDGE HOUSE AND PARK** Life upstairs and downstairs is the theme of this Georgian house designed by Edward Lovett Pearce's colleague Richard Castle and built from local stone in about 1740 for Charles Cobbe, Archbishop of Dublin. Although the house is now managed by the Irish government, Cobbe's descendants still live on a part of the estate, among curiosities from the lives of their forebears (furniture, portraits, dolls, and travel memorabilia upstairs; 18th-century kitchen and laundry implements downstairs). There are also some possessions of Jonathan Swift, who was dean of *St. Patrick's* in Dublin and a friend of the archbishop. The grounds include *Newbridge Farm,* a 20-acre re-creation of a Victorian farm with indigenous Irish produce and livestock (Kerry cows, Jacob sheep, Shannon goats, and Connemara ponies). The park surrounding the mansion is pleasant but not noteworthy, except for the remains of ancient and picturesque *Landestown Castle.* Open daily. Admission charge. About 12 miles (19 km) from the city center off the Dublin-Belfast road, N1, at Donabate (phone: 843-6534 or 843-6535).

# Sources and Resources

## TOURIST INFORMATION

For on-the-spot information and assistance, call the *Dublin Tourism Office* (at *Dublin Airport;* phone: 844-5387; or 14 O'Connell St.; phone: 284-4768 for general information; 284-1765 for hotel accommodations; and 800-600-800 for credit card bookings). The tourism office personnel offer advice on all aspects of a stay in Ireland and can make theater bookings and hotel reservations anywhere in the country.

The *Irish Tourist Board* publishes several useful guides, which are available at tourist board offices and most bookstores. They include *Dining in Ireland, The Dublin Guide,* and *Dublin Tourist Trail,* an excellent city walking guide (also see "Walking Tours," below). The best city map is the *Ordnance Survey Dublin Map.* The *US Embassy* is at 42 Elgin Rd., Ballsbridge (phone: 668-8777).

In the US, contact the *Irish Tourist Board* (345 Park Ave., New York, NY 10154; phone: 212-418-0800; fax: 212-371-9052). The *Irish Embassy* is at 2234 Massachusetts Ave. NW, Washington, DC 20008 (phone: 202-462-3939).

**ENTRY REQUIREMENTS** A US citizen needs a current passport for a stay of up to 90 days.

**TIME** The time in Ireland is five hours later than in US East Coast cities. Ireland observes daylight saving time.

**LANGUAGE** Irish is the national language, but English is spoken everywhere.

**ELECTRIC CURRENT** 220 volts, 50 cycles, AC.

**MONEY** The Irish pound (punt; IR£) equals 100 pence. Note that the Irish pound and the British pound are no longer tied to one another and are not interchangeable. Each has its own value in relation to world currencies, although as we went to press the Irish pound was trading at a level close to that of its British counterpart; one American dollar was equal to about 65 Irish pence.

**TIPPING** When the customary 10% to 15% service charge has been added to restaurant and hotel bills, no additional tip is necessary. Taxi drivers get 10% to 15%; porters, about 50 pence per bag.

**BANKING/BUSINESS HOURS** Most banks are open weekdays from 10 AM to 3 PM (to 5 PM on Thursdays). Most other businesses are open weekdays from 9 AM to 5 PM, some until 6 PM.

**NATIONAL HOLIDAYS** *New Year's Day* (January 1), *St. Patrick's Day* (March 17), *Good Friday* (April 14), *Easter Sunday* (April 16), *Easter Monday* (April 17), *May Day* (May 1), *Bank Holidays* (June 5, August 7, and October 30), *Christmas Day* (December 25), and *St. Stephen's Day* (December 26).

**LOCAL COVERAGE** The *Dublin Event Guide,* published biweekly and distributed free of charge at hotels, shops, tourist offices, and other public places, includes the latest information on theater performances, exhibitions, clubs, live music venues, and films. The journal *In Dublin,* sold in shops and at newspaper kiosks, is an excellent guide to what's going on in the city. The city's large daily newspapers are the *Irish Times,* the *Irish Independent,* and the *Irish Press,* which come out in the morning, and the *Evening Herald* and the *Evening Press.*

**TELEPHONE** The city code for Dublin and the immediate vicinity is 1. Be aware that Dublin phone numbers continue to be changed from six digits to seven. If you dial a number that has been changed since press time, a recording should inform you of the new number; otherwise, check with the local operator or the tourist office.

When calling from one area to another within Ireland dial 0 + city code + local number. The country code for the Republic of Ireland is 353. Dial 999 for emergency assistance.

## GETTING AROUND

**AIRPORT** *Dublin Airport* is north of the city at Collinstown. In normal traffic, a trip from the airport to downtown takes 35 to 40 minutes. The *CIE (Córas Iompair Eireann, National Transport Company)* operates bus service (see below) between the airport and the central bus station.

**BUS** *Bus Eireann,* a division of the *CIE,* operates service not only in Dublin but nationwide as well. *Dublin Bus,* the local division of *Bus Eireann,* offers extensive cross-city service. Passengers pay as they board; the fare is about IR55p (80¢). For more information regarding bus travel throughout the Republic call 635-5111. Official *Bus Eireann* and *Dublin Bus* timetables are available at newsstands.

**BUS TOURS** A good way to get one's bearings in Dublin is to take a guided tour. *Dublin Bus* operates half-day motorcoach tours through the city and the nearby countryside as well as full-day tours to more distant points, with very reasonable prices for a half-day or full-day trip. All tours leave from the *Central Bus Station* (*Busáras;* Store St.; phone: 677-1871). *Gray Line* (3 Clanwilliam Ter.; phone: 661-9666) also offers a limited number of tours.

The bus tour with the greatest flexibility is *Dublin Bus*'s *Heritage Trail,* which provides continuous guided bus service connecting 10 major points of interest, and is available for a flat per-day rate; it operates from mid-April through September. Passengers can get off the bus at whatever site they choose, take as much time as they like at each stop, and reboard another bus (they come by every 20 to 30 minutes) to continue the circuit at their own pace.

**CAR RENTAL** *Avis, Budget, Hertz,* and *National,* as well as a variety of local firms, offer excellent self-drive opportunities. *Dan Dooley* (42 Westland Row; phone: 677-2723; at the airport, 844-5156) and *Murray's/Europcar* (Baggot St. Bridge; phone: 668-1177; at the airport, 844-4179) are both dependable. Information and brochures are available from the tourism office.

**CARRIAGE TOURS** Horse-drawn carriage tours are among Dublin's newest and most popular form of sightseeing. The carriages vary in size and style (some are open and others closed) and can accommodate from two to five passengers plus a driver/guide. Tours depart from the Grafton Street corner of *St. Stephen's Green.* Visitors have their choice of a quick trip around the *Green;* a half-hour Georgian tour past the *National Museum, Mansion House,* the government buildings, Merrion Square, Grand Canal, and Leeson Street; or an hour-long historic route that takes in *St. Patrick's Cathedral, Christ Church Cathedral,* the *Four Courts,* and *Dublin Castle.* Carriages operate daily and some evenings, depending on the weather. No reservations necessary; tours are on a first-come, first-served basis. For more information, contact Bernard Fagan (phone: 872-6968) or Liam Stewart (phone: 661-3111); or ask at your hotel.

**TAXI** There are stands throughout the city, especially near main hotels, and cabs also can be hailed in the streets. Among the companies that have 24-hour radio service are *Blue Cabs* (phone: 676-1111), *Co-op Taxis* (phone: 676-6666), and *City Cabs* (phone: 286-8888).

**TRAIN** Although Dublin has no subway, a commuter rail system, *Dublin Area Rapid Transit (DART),* runs from central Dublin along the bay as far north as Howth and as far south as Bray. It is swift, dependable, and safe at all hours. Traveling from one end of the line to the other makes a delightful sightseeing trip of the bay area for a modest fare. Fares are determined by destination and are collected at entry points. For extended stays, purchase an Explorer Pass, which provides unlimited use of the *DART* system and of all buses and trains within a 20-mile (32-km) radius. *Irish Rail* provides nationwide service to all major points outside of Dublin. For more information regarding train travel throughout the Republic call 636-6222. Official *Irish Rail* timetables are available at newsstands.

**WALKING TOURS** Small and easily navigated on foot, Dublin lends itself to walking tours. Stop at the *Dublin Tourism Office* (see above) for a copy of the *Dublin Tourist Trail.* This booklet outlines a signposted pedestrian route that offers a basic orientation to the city. The tourism office also has designed four special-interest walking tours, each outlined in a separate booklet. The *Georgian Trail* explores the city's most attractive 18th-century streets, squares, terraces, and public buildings; the *Old City Trail* traverses the most historic enclaves, dating back to Viking times; the *Cultural Trail* rambles around the leading museums, galleries, theaters, parks, quays, churches, markets, historic houses, and literary sites; and the *Rock 'n' Stroll Trail* traces Dublin's contemporary music scene, including places associated with performers such as *U2,* the *Chieftains,* and the *Dubliners.*

Walking tours are conducted by several individuals and small firms as well. *Old Dublin Walking Tours* offers two-hour tours around the Liberties area, departing from *Christ Church Cathedral* daily during summer and on weekends the rest of the year. For reservations and information, call 532407. Babette Walsh, a guide registered with the *Irish Tourist Board,* knows every nook and cranny of the city and offers customized tours, including escorted shopping sprees. She is an irrepressible storyteller, and her often salty dialogue more than makes up for her occasionally creative view of Irish history. Walsh leads from two to 20 people on private half-day or full-day jaunts. Contact her in advance (at the *Cottage,* Balscaddon Rd., Howth, Co. Dublin; phone: 391869). The *Dublin Literary Pub Crawl* leads guests to haunts of the city's illustrious literary figures—Samuel Beckett, James Joyce, Brendan Behan, and Patrick Kavanaugh, a poet who wrote about the area. The tour begins at the *Bailey Pub* (Duke St.) Mondays through Thursdays, June through August (phone: 540228).

## LOCAL SERVICES

**DENTIST** Frank Allen (45 Fitzwilliam Sq.; phone: 676-2160); *McDonagh Bros.* (106 Marlboro St.; phone: 872-9721).

**DRY CLEANER/TAILOR** *Alteration Centre* (28 S. Anne St.; phone: 677-6258); *Baggot Dry Cleaners* (33 Upper Baggot St.; phone: 668-

1286); *Express Alteration* (53 Middle Abbey St.; phone: 873-0449); *Grafton Cleaners* (32 S. William St.; phone: 679-4309).

**LIMOUSINE SERVICE** *Murray's/Europcar* (Baggot St. Bridge; phone: 668-1777); *Vincent Russell* (42 Dromartin Park; phone: 298-2922).

**MEDICAL EMERGENCY** *St. Vincent's Hospital* (Elm Park; phone: 269-4533).

**MESSENGER SERVICE** *A-1 Courier Service* (*Palmerstown Shopping Centre,* Unit 16, Kennelsfort Rd.; phone: 626-7633); *Shamrock Couriers* (41 Lower Baggot St.; phone: 661-2800).

**NATIONAL/INTERNATIONAL COURIER** *AerFast* (Ashley House, Santry; phone: 842-6424); *City Skyway Express* (Unit 93, Newtown Industrial Estate, Coolock; phone: 848-4111); *DHL Worldwide Express* (*Dublin Airport;* phone: 844-4111); *Federal Express* (Unit 1, Willsborough Industrial Estate, Clonshaugh; phone: 848-2299); *TNT Express Worldwide* (Coolock Industrial Estate; phone: 847-3799); *UPS* (Walsh-Western Ltd., Santry Hall, Santry Industrial Estate; phone: 842-7766).

**OFFICE EQUIPMENT RENTAL** *Dublin Office Service* (58 Haddington Rd.; phone: 668-1355); *Executive Rentals* (Woodchester House, Golden La.; phone: 475-6691).

**PHARMACY** *Hamilton Long* (5 Lower O'Connell St.; phone: 874-3352), open until 6 PM; *O'Connell Pharmacy* (310 Harold's Cross Rd.; phone: 497-3977), open until 10 PM; *Roches* (165 Upper Rathmines Rd.; phone: 497-2693), open Mondays through Saturdays until 7:30 PM and Sundays 11 AM to 1:30 PM.

**PHOTOCOPIES** *Kwikprint Shop* (91 Morehampton Rd.; phone: 660-1366); and *Prontaprint,* two locations (38 Upper Baggot St., phone: 660-9500; and 3 Lower Leeson St., phone: 660-5480).

**POST OFFICE** Main branch (Lower O'Connell St.; phone: 872-8888) is open Mondays through Saturdays 8 AM to 8 PM and Sundays 10:30 AM to 6:30 PM.

**SECRETARY/STENOGRAPHER** *Active Business Partner Ltd.* (Haddington Hall, 80 Haddington Rd.; phone: 668-1748); *CO-SEC Secretarial Services* (IDA Enterprise Centre, Pearse St.; phone: 677-5655); *Regus Business Centre* (Europa House, Harcourt St.; phone: 475-4244).

**TELECONFERENCE FACILITIES** *Convention Bureau of Ireland* (Baggot St. Bridge; phone: 676-5871).

**TELEX** For telex or fax services, ask the concierge at your hotel.

**OTHER** Men's formal attire rental: *Dawson's Formal Wear* (20 Dawson St.; phone: 661-6707); *McGrath's Dress Hire* (13 Aston's Quay; phone: 677-5307); *Wicklow St. Dress Hire* (33 Wicklow St.; phone: 671-6533). Cellular car phone rental: *Cellrent* (*Dublin Airport;* phone: 842-4700).

## SPECIAL EVENTS

*St. Patrick's Day* (March 17) brings a parade and many other festivities, and May is the time for the *Spring Show,* a social and agricultural gathering. In early June, the *Festival of Music in Great Irish Houses* includes such events as operatic performances, plus chamber music concerts in splendid Castletown House; for details, contact Judith Woodworth, Festival Director, 4 Highfield Grove, Rathgar, Dublin 6 (phone: 962021). On *Bloomsday* (June 16), James Joyce aficionados from the world over follow the circuitous path through Dublin that Leopold Bloom took from morning until late at night in *Ulysses.* The *Horse Show,* the principal sporting and social event of the year, is held at the Royal Dublin Society grounds in Ballsbridge in July or August, when the *Irish Antique Dealers' Fair* also comes to town.

The last week in September and the first in October bring the *Dublin Theatre Festival,* when plays open daily. Increasingly, the festival has been a showcase for new works by Irish writers such as Tom Murphy, Hugh Leonard, Stewart Parker, Brian Friel, Frank McGuinness, and Billy Roche. For details, contact the *Dublin Theatre Festival,* 47 Nassau St., Dublin 2 (phone: 677-8439 or 679-2458). Finally, the *Dublin Marathon* takes place the last Monday in October. For details about these and other events, inquire at any tourist office.

## MUSEUMS

In addition to those described in *Special Places,* Dublin is the home of several smaller museums:

**DUBLIN CIVIC MUSEUM** Adjacent to the *Powerscourt Town House Centre,* it contains artifacts and memorabilia—from old maps and prints to street signs and wooden water mains—reflecting 1,000 years of Dublin history. Closed Mondays. No admission charge. 58 S. William St. (phone: 679-4260).

**DUBLIN WRITERS' MUSEUM** Dedicated to Dublin's literary heritage, this museum commemorates the work of some of its most famous native scribes, including Wilde, Swift, Shaw, Beckett, and Joyce. Besides housing a collection of rare editions and original manuscripts, the museum provides a haven for living writers to work and meet with their peers. Open daily. Admission charge. 18-19 Parnell Sq. (phone: 874-7733).

**IRISH JEWISH MUSEUM** Housed in a former synagogue, this museum traces the history of Jews in Ireland over the last 500 years. Documents, photographs, and memorabilia are on display. Open Sundays, Tuesdays, and Thursdays; Sundays only in winter. No admission charge, but donations are welcome. 3-4 Walworth Rd., off Victoria St. (phone: 676-0737).

**JAMES JOYCE CULTURAL CENTRE** In Joyce's *Ulysses,* Professor Dennis J. Maginni held dancing classes at 35 North Great George's Street. The Georgian townhouse at that address became derelict in the 1970s, but has been restored and refurbished by a group of Joyce enthusiasts. Although the library, lecture room, reading room, and bookshop are not yet fully operational, they are tended to each weekday by Ken Monaghan, the writer's nephew. Guided tours are available by appointment. 35 North Great George's St. (phone: 873-1984).

**MUSEUM OF CHILDHOOD** Exhibits include dolls, dollhouses, and doll carriages from all over the world, dating from 1730 to 1940. There also are other antique toys and rocking horses. Schedule varies, so call in advance. Admission charge. The Palms, 20 Palmerstown Park, Rathmines (phone: 497-3223).

**ROYAL IRISH ACADEMY LIBRARY** This small building houses a remarkable collection of ancient Irish manuscripts, including the *Annals of the Four Masters,* a comprehensive history of Ireland from 2242 BC to AD 1616. Open daily. No admission charge. 19 Dawson St. (phone: 676-2570).

**SHAW HOUSE** Born in this house in 1856, George Bernard Shaw lived here for the first decade of his life. The museum includes original furnishings and memorabilia. Open daily, May through September. Admission charge. 33 Synge St. (phone: 872-2077).

## SHOPPING

Neatly balanced on both banks of the Liffey, Dublin has two downtown shopping areas: one around O'Connell and Henry Streets, the other centered on Grafton Street and its environs (stores on the south side were traditionally regarded as more elegant, but such distinctions are less noticeable nowadays). *Arnott's* (phone: 872-1111), *Roche's* (phone: 873-0044 or 872-6500), and *Clery's* (phone: 878-6000) are reasonably priced department stores in the O'Connell and Henry Streets area; *Brown Thomas* (phone: 679-5666), *Marks & Spencer* (phone: 679-7855), and *Switzer's* (phone: 677-6821) are the main department stores on Grafton Street. The *Powerscourt Town House Centre,* just off Grafton Street, has a number of clothing stores and crafts shops in a courtyard built around a pretty townhouse. The top floor houses the showrooms of the *Craft Council of Ireland.* Good buys in Dublin include Aran sweaters, Donegal tweeds, Waterford and Galway crystal, and Belleek china.

Over the years, the antiques trade in Dublin has developed great sophistication, particularly in the fields of furniture, glass and china, table silver, and certain kinds of jewelry. The shops are clustered in several areas: Clare, Duke, Kildare, Molesworth, and South Anne Streets are lined with long-established antiques dealers; the *Powerscourt Town House Centre* has a number of antiques emporiums; and the Liffey Quays area, once a great source of underpriced treasures, still has quite a bit to see, mainly larger items. The antiques scene also has taken a firm hold on Francis and Patrick Streets, in the district known as the Liberties, among the city's oldest areas. Our favorite antiques shops include *Anthony Antiques* (7-9 Molesworth St.; phone: 677-7222), for fine French and English furniture; *H. & E. Danker Antiques* (18 S. Anne St.; phone: 677-4009), featuring high-quality jewelry; *Kenyon Fine Art & Antiques* (10

Lower Ormond Quay; phone: 873-0488), a 200-year-old establishment that offers treasures, but not necessarily bargains; *Oriel Gallery* (17 Clare St.; phone: 676-3410), which specializes in early-20th-century art; *Jenny Vander* (20 Market Arcade; phone: 677-0406), for clothing from the turn of the century; *Bits and Pieces* (78 Francis St.; phone: 541178), specialists in Art Deco and Art Nouveau lighting fixtures; *Lantern Antiques* (57 Francis St.; phone: 453-4593), which carries old framed theatrical and advertising prints and posters; and *Timepiece Antiques* (58 Patrick St.; phone: 540774), for vintage clocks and watches.

The following are other recommended shops (unless otherwise indicated, the stores are closed on Sundays):

**Anncraft** At the back entrance of the *Powerscourt Town House Centre,* this shop offers a wonderful assortment of products from the west of Ireland, including Claddagh rings, Foxford rugs, Kerry glass, and Connemara marble, as well as hand-knits, tweeds, crystal, china, oak carvings, and handmade toys. S. William St. (phone: 677-2609).

**Best of Irish** A wide range of Irish goods—crystal, china, hand-knit goods, jewelry, linen, and tweeds. Open daily May through September; closed Sundays the rest of the year. Two locations: next to the *Westbury* hotel, on Harry St., off Grafton St. (phone: 679-1233); and 5 Nassau St. (phone: 679-9117).

**Blarney Woollen Mills** A branch of the Cork-based family enterprise, this huge shop is known for its competitive prices. It stocks all the favorites, from tweeds and hand-knits to crystal, china, pottery, and souvenirs. Open daily. 21-23 Nassau St. (phone: 671-0068).

**Cathach Books** Sheer joy for collectors, this shop has a most comprehensive selection of old tomes and early editions of Irish literature. The oldest book here was printed in the 17th century, while hand-drawn maps are from the 16th century. The shop also has first editions of W. B. Yeats and James Joyce. 10 Duke St. (phone: 671-8676).

**Celtic Bookstore** This shop focuses on books about Irish history, language, and culture. It's housed on the ground floor of the *Conrad na Gaeilge Building,* a center of learning about all things Gaelic. 6 Harcourt St. (phone: 478-3814).

**Cleo Ltd.** For more than 50 years, this has been one of Dublin's most fashionable sources for hand-knit and handwoven cloaks, caps, suits, coats, and shawls. 18 Kildare St. (phone: 676-1421).

**Dublin Woollen Mills** Beside the Ha'Penny Bridge, this place overflows with quality woolens. 41 Ormond Quay (phone: 677-5014).

**Fergus O'Farrell Workshops** A showcase for top-quality Irish crafts—from woodcarvings and brass door knockers to beaten-copper art. 62 Dawson St. (phone: 677-0862).

**Fred Hanna** Bookseller to *Trinity College* and one of the finest in the country, it stocks new and used volumes, maps, and excellent books on Ireland. 28-29 Nassau St. (phone: 677-1255).

**Heraldic Artists** A good source for family crests, flags, scrolls, and genealogical books. 3 Nassau St. (phone: 676-2391).

**H. Johnston Ltd.** The place to purchase traditional blackthorn walking sticks. 11 Wicklow St. (phone: 677-1249).

**Hodges Figgis** A terrific bookstore, it has four stories stacked floor to ceiling with tomes on every subject. 57-58 Dawson St. (phone: 677-4764).

**House of Ireland** Top-quality Irish and European goods—from Aynsley, Lladró, Spode, Wedgwood, Hummel, and Waterford crystal and china to hand-knits, kilts, linen, and shillelaghs. Open daily in summer; closed Sundays the rest of the year. 64-65 Nassau St. and 6465 Dawson St. (phone: 671-4543).

**House of Names** For high-quality genealogical items; sweaters can be custom-ordered with a family crest and name. 26 Nassau St. (phone: 679-7287).

**Kevin & Howlin Ltd.** Men's ready-to-wear and made-to-measure clothing; some women's tweeds as well. 31 Nassau St. (phone: 677-0257).

**The Lace Lady** Here are yards of lace, antique and modern, as well as Irish linen tablecloths, bedcovers, pillowcases, handkerchiefs, and vintage clothes and accessories. 129 Upper Leeson St. (phone: 660-4537).

**Louis Copeland** Possibly Dublin's—if not Ireland's—best bespoke tailor. 18 Wicklow St. (phone: 677-7038).

**Malton Gallery & Bookshop** Focusing on the Ireland of old, this shop specializes in prints by 18th-century artist James Malton as well as placemats, coasters, greeting cards, and postcards. Also for sale here are hand-marked silver, pewterware, crystal, and books. 23 St. Stephen's Green (phone: 676-6333).

**Margaret Joyce** Women's sweaters, hand-knit in wool or cotton. *Powerscourt Town House Centre* (phone: 679-8037).

**Mullins of Dublin** Coats of arms emblazoned on parchment, plaques, and door knockers. 36 Upper O'Connell St. (phone: 874-1133).

**Patrick Flood** Silver and gold jewelry in traditional Irish designs. *Powerscourt Town House Centre* (phone: 679-4256).

**La Potiniere** Features a wide selection of Irish cheeses, mustards, and teas. *Powerscourt Town House Centre* (phone: 671-3000).

**Sheepskin Shop** High-quality sheepskin and lambskin coats are sold, along with leather trousers, suits, and jackets. 20 Wicklow St. (phone: 671-9585).

**Sleater's** A charming jewelry shop tucked in an alley between Grafton Street and the *Powerscourt Town House Centre.* 9 Johnson's Ct. (phone: 677-7532).

**Sweater Shop** A good source for high-quality Irish knitwear of all kinds, colors, styles, fibers, and patterns. 9 Wicklow St., off Grafton St. (phone: 671-3270).

**Sybil Connolly** Ireland's reigning couturière; her romantic ball gowns of finely pleated Irish linen are truly special. Open weekdays and by appointment. 71 Merrion Sq. (phone: 676-7281).

**Tower Design Craft Centre** Once a sugar refinery, this renovated 1862 tower houses the workshops of more than 30 craftspeople, with items ranging from heraldic jewelry, Irish oak carvings, and hand-cut crystal to Irish chocolates, stained glass, toys, and fishing tackle. There's also a self-service restaurant. An ideal stop for a rainy day. Pearse St. (phone: 677-5655).

**Trinity College Library Shop** Specializing in scholarly works and books on Irish subjects, this shop also carries reproductions, posters, and prints from the *Book of Kells.* Open daily. Nassau St. (phone: 677-2941).

**Waltons Musical Instrument Galleries** A great emporium, stocked full of sheet music, recordings, and musical instruments—pianos, Scottish bagpipes, *uilleann* pipes, harps, tin whistles, old violins, and *bodhráns.* 2-5 N. Frederick St. (phone: 747805).

**Waterstone & Co.** Another great bookshop, a branch of the British firm of the same name, with an array of volumes on international topics, as well as ceiling-high shelves on Irish history, literature, language, politics, cookery, and crafts. Open daily. 7 Dawson St. (phone: 679-1415).

**Weir & Sons** A tradition in Dublin, this classy shop offers the best in jewelry, gold, silver, antiques, glass, china, and leather goods. 96-97 Grafton St. (phone: 677-9678).

## SPORTS AND FITNESS

**BICYCLING** Irish Raleigh Industries operates *Rent-a-Bike* at a number of city locations (phone: 626-1333). Two downtown shops offering bicycle rentals are *USIT Rent-A-Bike* (58 Lower Gardiner's Row; phone: 872-5349) and *McDonald's* (38 Wexford St.; phone: 475-2586). Charges are per day or per week with a deposit required.

**GAELIC GAMES** Football and hurling are two fast, enthralling field sports; important matches are played at *Croke Park* (Jones Rd; phone: 363222). For details, consult local newspapers or the tourism office.

**GOLF** More than 30 golf courses are within easy reach of Dublin; visitors are welcome at all clubs on weekdays, but gaining admission can be more difficult on weekends.

---

**TOP TEE-OFF SPOTS**

**Portmarnock** This fabled layout, just outside Dublin, is perhaps the best single course in the Republic. The short flag sticks, set on springs to let them swing freely in the breeze, indicate something about the wind hazards here, and the last five holes are diabolically difficult. However, the quality of the course, especially the greens, is superb. Be prepared for the strong prevailing northeasterly wind, soaring scores—and a bracing outing. Portmarnock (phone: 846-2968).

**Royal Dublin** The "other" Dublin-area golfing magnet deserves a place among Europe's best. The winds blow here as well, and the rough grows to a size not normally known in the New World. Founded in 1885, the course is famous for its four short holes—the fourth, sixth, ninth, and 12th—all of which call for a keen eye and precision play; the demanding fifth hole, with its narrow valley of a fairway, once prompted the late comedian Danny Kaye to ask his caddie for a rifle. Dollymount (phone: 336346).

---

**GREYHOUND RACING** You can go to the dogs regularly at two tracks, *Shelbourne Park Stadium* and *Harold's Cross Stadium,* each an eight-minute ride from the city center. Details are available in local newspapers or at the tourism office.

**HORSE RACING** Six miles (10 km) south of the city in Foxrock is the *Leopardstown* racecourse (phone: 289-3607), a modern track with glass-enclosed viewing areas. The best-known course in the Dublin vicinity is the *Curragh* (phone: 454-1025), about a mile (1.6 km) or so outside the town of Kildare in County Kildare, about an hour's drive from Dublin. This modern complex hosts the *Irish Derby* in June and other high-stakes races throughout the year. The *Irish Racing Board* at *Leopardstown* (phone: 289-7277) can provide information about all local racing events.

**HORSEBACK RIDING** A list of riding establishments close to Dublin is available at the tourism office.

**TENNIS** The area's top tennis spot is the *Kilternan Country Club* (Kilternan; phone: 295-3742), in the sylvan Dublin Mountains, about 15 minutes south of the city. The multimillion-dollar national tennis center boasts eight courts (four indoor, four outdoor), which stay open from early in the morning until midnight. There are a few public courts, generally outdoors, where visitors can play for a small fee. The most central is *Herbert Park* (Ballsbridge; phone: 668-4364). During the second week of July, Dublin hosts the *Irish Open;* for information, contact *Tennis Ireland* (54 Wellington Rd.; phone: 668-1841).

## THEATER

There are at least 10 main theaters in the city center; smaller troupes perform at universities, suburban theaters, and occasionally pubs and hotels. For complete program listings, see the publications listed in *Tourist Information,* above.

CENTER STAGE

**Abbey Theatre** Alas, the original *Abbey Theatre,* founded by Yeats and Lady Gregory on the site of the old city morgue, is no more. In 1951, at the close of a performance of O'Casey's *Plough and the Stars*—a play that ends with Dublin blazing in the aftermath of rebellion—the theater itself caught fire and burned to the ground. The new *Abbey,* designed by Michael Scott, one of the country's foremost architects, opened in 1966 on the site of the original building. The lobby, which can be seen daily except Sundays, contains portraits of those connected with the theater's early successes. The *Abbey* still presents the best of contemporary Irish playwriting, including productions of works by Brian Friel, Hugh Leonard, and Thomas Murphy, as well as revivals of the classics that made the 85-year-old *Abbey Players* famous. Work of a more experimental nature is presented downstairs, in the *Peacock;* the opportunity to visit this wonderfully intimate auditorium should not be missed. Lower Abbey St. (phone: 878-7222).

A relative newcomer, the *Andrews Lane Theatre* (9-17 Andrews La.; phone: 679-5720) presents contemporary plays and avant-garde productions. An evening at the small *Focus Theatre* (6 Pembroke Pl.; phone: 676-3071) is never disappointing, whether the play is a classic by Chekhov or the latest offering of a young Irish writer. The opulent *Gaiety Theatre* (S. King St.; phone: 677-1717) counts among those who have lit up its stage Lily Langtry, Burgess Meredith, Siobhán McKenna, the *Bolshoi Ballet,* and Peter O'Toole. Today, the theater also serves as the spring and summer venue for the *Dublin Grand Opera Society.* You're as likely to see a play by Tennessee Williams as one by native Brian Friel in the beautifully decorated *Gate Theatre* (1 Cavendish Row; phone: 874-4045). The *Olympia Theatre* (72 Dame St.; phone: 677-7744) occupies a special place in the hearts of Dubliners, perhaps because of its connection with the music hall, the most popular form of theater here. Nowadays, the *Olympia* presents concerts (including rock concerts) and pantomimes, as well as plays, both Irish and foreign.

Other noteworthy theaters include the avant-garde *Project Arts Centre* (39 E. Essex St.; phone: 671-2321); the *Tivoli* (135-138 Francis St.; phone: 544472), which features controversial Irish plays and imports from London; and the *New Eblana* (Store St.; phone: 679-8404), a revived "pocket" theater in the basement of Busáras (the Central Bus Station), that's a venue for contemporary plays. The *Lambert Mews Puppet Theatre* in the suburb of Monkstown (Clifden La.; phone: 280-0974) proves irresistible to children.

It is always advisable to make reservations for theater performances in Dublin. You can make bookings at theaters, major department stores, and some record shops, such as *HMV Golden Discs*

(65 Grafton St.; phone: 677-1025). Most theaters accept telephone reservations and credit cards.

## MUSIC

Settling on an evening's entertainment (or an afternoon's, for that matter) can pose some problems in Dublin, as there are so many choices. The elegant *National Concert Hall* (Earlsfort Ter.; phone: 671-1888) is the center of Dublin's musical life and the home stage of the *Radio Telefis Eireann (RTE) Symphony Orchestra* and the *New Ireland Chamber Orchestra*. The *Royal Dublin Society (RDS)* stages recitals from November to March in the *Royal Dublin Society Concert Hall* (Ballsbridge; phone: 668-0645), which has also hosted such distinguished musicians as the *Smetana String Quartet* and Isaac Stern.

Traditional Irish music is a must in Dublin. *Seisiún* (sessions) are held at many places around the city by an organization called the *Comhaltas Ceoltóirí Eireann* (phone: 280-0295); informal sessions are held on Friday and Saturday nights at its headquarters (32 Belgrave Sq., in Monkstown; take *DART* to the Seapoint station; admission charge); ballad sessions are held nightly except Sundays in the *Barn* on the ground floor of the *Abbey Tavern* (Howth, 10 miles/16 km north of the city on the coast; phone: 322006 or 390307). Many pubs offer music informally; see *Sharing a Pint* for a list of the best. A new theater-cum-concert hall, *The Point* (E. Link Bridge; phone: 363633), presents everything from *U2* concerts to Broadway hits. Ticket prices are hefty here, and most events are booked well in advance.

## NIGHTCLUBS AND NIGHTLIFE

There is little in the way of large-scale cabaret-cum-dancing; swinging Dublin tends to congregate in the discotheques starting at 9 PM. Premises range from big, bustling places where an escort is not necessarily required to small, intimate clubs; most have only wine licenses. Among the more established discotheques on a rapidly changing scene are the large and lively *Annabel's* in the *Burlington* hotel (Leeson St.; phone: 660-5222), *Raffles in Sachs* (Northampton Rd.; phone: 668-0995), *Blinkers* at *Leopardstown* racecourse (phone: 896307), the *Night Train* (7 Lower Mount St.; phone: 676-1717), and the *Waterfront* (14-15 Sir John Roger's Quay; phone: 679-9258). Smaller, cozier clubs are mainly to be found in the Leeson Street area: *Styx* (phone: 676-1560) and *Cats* (phone: 661-6151) are two. Most exclusive is *Lillie's Bordello* (Grafton St.; phone: 679-9204)—not at all what the name implies. There's music at the *Place of Dame* (Old Harcourt St. Station; phone: 679-9114), and in the Temple Bar area there is *Rock Garden* (1 Crown Alley; phone: 679-9114). The most famous traditional cabaret in Dublin is the established *Jurys Cabaret*, performed nightly except Mondays from April through October at *Jurys* hotel (see *Checking In*). *Doyle's Irish Cabaret* is presented from April through October at the *Burlington* hotel (see above), and the *Clontarf Castle* hosts a dinner show (Castle Ave.; phone: 332271).

# Best in Town

## CHECKING IN

With the opening of several hotels in recent years, along with the refurbishment of still others, Dublin's accommodations have risen significantly in quality and can be compared with the finest almost anywhere. Expect to pay $250 or more per night for a double room at hotels classified as very expensive; $165 to $245 at an expensive place; $75 to $165 at places listed as moderate; and less than $75 at inexpensive ones. A room with Irish breakfast for two in a private home in a residential neighborhood will cost $60 or less. In all of the following listings, private baths are included unless otherwise specified. All telephone numbers are in the 1 city code unless otherwise indicated.

### VERY EXPENSIVE

**Berkeley Court** The flagship of the Doyle group and the first Irish member of the Leading Hotels of the World is close to the city in the leafy suburb of Ballsbridge. It combines graciousness with modern efficiency: Contemporary and antique furnishings harmonize, and the service is warm and friendly. There are 210 rooms and six suites (all with Jacuzzis); the excellent *Berkeley Room* (see *Eating Out*); a conservatory-style coffee shop; a health center with indoor pool and saunas; and a shopping arcade. Business facilities include 24-hour room service, meeting rooms for up to 400, a concierge, foreign currency exchange, secretarial services, audiovisual equipment, photocopiers, translation services, and express checkout. In the suburb of Ballsbridge, on Lansdowne Rd. (phone: 660-1711; 800-223-6800 or 800-44-UTELL; fax: 661-7238).

**Conrad** Opposite the *National Concert Hall* and across from St. Stephen's Green, the hotel has 192 bright and airy guestrooms (including 10 suites), all with bay windows. Each room has an executive desk, two or three telephones, a mini-bar, color TV set, and large marble bathroom. One floor is reserved for nonsmokers. Other facilities include a hair salon and a garage. The *Alexandra* (see *Eating Out*) is elegant; there also is an informal brasserie and a lively pub. Business facilities include 24-hour room service, eight meeting rooms for up to 370, a concierge, foreign currency exchange, secretarial services, audiovisual equipment, photocopiers, translation services, and express checkout. In the heart of the city, on Earlsfort Ter. (phone: 676-5555; 800-HILTONS; fax: 676-5076).

**Shelbourne** This venerable establishment, a nice mixture of the dignified and the lively, is more polished than ever after a $5-million face-lift. Some of the 164 rooms are truly splendid, particularly those in front on the second floor. The *Horseshoe Bar* is one of the livelier fixtures of Dublin pub life, while the main restaurant, with its 1826 plasterwork and Waterford crystal chandeliers, is a showcase for modern Irish cuisine. Business facilities include 24-hour room service, eight meeting rooms for up to 400, a concierge, foreign currency exchange, secretarial services, audiovisual equipment, photocopiers, translation services, and express checkout. 27 St. Stephen's Green (phone: 676-6471; 800-223-5672 in the continental US and Canada; fax: 661-6006).

**Westbury** The fashionable centerpiece of a chic mall of shops and restaurants, this hotel is also a member of the Doyle group. The management emphasizes elegance, and the 206 rooms and suites have canopied beds and mahogany and brass furnishings. Executive suites with Jacuzzis and balconies also are available. Public facilities include a restaurant, a coffee shop, a seafood pub, and a lobby lounge with pianist. There also is an arcade of shops and underground parking. Business facilities include 24-hour room service, five meeting rooms for up to 300, a concierge, foreign currency exchange, secretarial services, audiovisual equipment, photocopiers, translation services, and express checkout. Grafton St. (phone: 679-1122; 800-223-6800 or 800-44-UTELL; fax: 679-7078).

### EXPENSIVE

**Gresham** This 200-room hostelry once attracted Dublin's most distinguished visitors. Situated on one of the city's main streets, near shops, theaters, cinemas, and museums, it is still a popular place to stay. The restaurant features a good selection of seafood dishes; there's also 24-hour room service. Business facilities include 24-hour room service, six meeting rooms for up to 200, a concierge, foreign currency exchange, secretarial services, audiovisual equipment, and photocopiers. Upper O'Connell St. (phone: 874-6881; 800-223-0888 or 800-44-UTELL; fax: 878-7175).

**Jurys** This modern complex offers 290 rooms, plus 100 extra-large units in a newer wing known as the *Towers*. Each of the computer-key-accessible rooms has a bay window, mini-bar, three telephone lines, work area, satellite TV, marble bathroom, and either king- or queen-size bed. Two floors are nonsmoking. There are two restaurants, including the *Kish* (see *Eating Out*); a 24-hour coffee shop; two bars; an indoor/outdoor pool; and a health center. For entertainment, there is *Jurys Cabaret*, Ireland's longest running variety show. Business facilities include 24-hour room service, 12 meeting rooms for up to 850, a concierge, foreign currency exchange, secretarial services, audiovisual equipment, photocopiers, translation services, and express checkout. In Ballsbridge opposite the American Embassy, on Pembroke Rd. (phone: 660-5000; 800-44-UTELL or 800-THE-OMNI; fax: 660-5540).

**Longfields** Located on one of the city's most fashionable streets, this small hostelry is composed of two 18th-century Georgian townhouses originally owned by Richard Longfield, also known as Viscount Longueville, a member of the Irish Parliament more than 200 years ago. Completely restored and refurbished over the last five years, it now has 26 rooms decorated to reflect both the Georgian period and more modern influences; each has a phone, color TV set, mini-bar, and hair dryer. The *Number Ten* restaurant offers a fine menu of French cuisine. Business facilities include a meeting room accommodating up to 20, foreign currency exchange, secretarial services, and photocopiers. 10 Lower Fitzwilliam St. (phone: 676-1367; fax: 676-1542).

**Mont Clare** One of the city's oldest hotels, this Georgian-style property sits in the heart of the business district, close to Trinity College, the Irish government buildings, and museums. There are 80 rooms, each with a phone, TV set, radio, hair dryer, mini-bar/refrigerator, tea/coffee-maker, and trouser press. A restaurant, lounge, and enclosed parking lot are on the premises. Business facilities include 24-hour room service, five meeting rooms for up to 250, a concierge, foreign currency exchange, secretarial services, audiovisual equipment, and photocopiers. Merrion Sq. (phone: 661-6799; 800-44-UTELL; fax: 661-5663).

### MODERATE

**Anglesea Townhouse** In this Edwardian residence, guests are pampered with hearty breakfasts of fresh fish, homemade breads and scones, fresh-squeezed juices, baked fruits, and warm cereals. Heirlooms and family antiques add to the ambience of this jewel of a bed and breakfast guesthouse. All seven rooms have TV sets and direct-dial telephones. Near the American Embassy, at 63 Anglesea Rd., Ballsbridge (phone: 668-3877; fax: 668-3461).

**Ariel House** A country home in the city, this historic Victorian guesthouse is one block from the *DART* station, providing easy access to downtown. It has 27 rooms decorated with period furniture and original oil paintings and watercolors; each has a TV set, phone, and hair dryer. There's also a restaurant and wine bar on the premises. 52 Lansdowne Rd., opposite the *Berkeley Court* hotel, in Ballsbridge (phone: 668-5512; fax: 668-5845).

**Fitzwilliam** In the heart of Georgian Dublin and within walking distance of St. Stephen's Green, this spacious townhouse dates back to the mid-1700s. Originally a private residence, it has been restored and converted into a 12-room guesthouse. Each room is comfortably furnished and equipped with a phone and TV set. Facilities include a restaurant and a cozy parlor with a marble fireplace. 41 Upper Fitzwilliam St. (phone: 660-0199; fax: 676-7488).

**Georgian House** Recently renovated, this guesthouse is less than two blocks south of St. Stephen's Green. It offers 18 bedrooms with phone and TV set, but no elevator. There also is a basement-level seafood restaurant featuring Irish music at night, and an enclosed parking area. 20 Lower Baggot St. (phone: 661-8832; fax: 661-8834).

**Russell Court** Two Georgian houses have been transformed into this convenient place, steps from St. Stephen's Green. The decor in the public areas is Art Deco, and the 22 modern bedrooms are decorated in light woods and pastel tones. Facilities include a restaurant, a lounge, and a nightclub. 21-23 Harcourt St. (phone: 478-4066; 800-521-0643; fax: 478-1576).

**St. Aidan's** Managed by the O'Dwyer family, this Victorian house offers nine warm, comfortable rooms. A traditional Irish breakfast is served each morning. Situated in quiet Rathgar, close to the center of Dublin. 32 Brighton Rd. (phone: 490-2011 or 490-6178; fax: 492-0234).

**Stephen's Hall** These apartment-style accommodations, available on a short-term basis, are ideal for travelers who want to entertain in Dublin or just cook for themselves. The exterior is a replica of a Georgian building that formerly stood on the site, and the interior is modern and functional. Each of the 37 suites consists of a sitting room, a dining area, a well-equipped kitchen and one or two bedrooms with phone. Services include daily housekeeping and underground parking. 14-17 Lower Leeson St., Earlsford Ter. (phone: 661-0585; 800-223-6510; fax: 661-0606).

### INEXPENSIVE

**Egan's House** This comfortable guesthouse offers 23 rooms with TV sets, phones, and hair dryers. There is also a small restaurant. 7 Iona Park (phone: 830-3611; fax: 830-3312).

**Iona House** A guesthouse with 11 rooms, all with TV sets and direct-dial telephones. A traditional breakfast is included in the rate. 5 Iona Park (phone: 306217; fax: 306732).

**Jurys Christchurch Inn** Located in the heart of the city near *Christ Church Cathedral,* this modern, well-appointed facility offers 183 rooms. In addition, guests enjoy the *Arches* restaurant, which features fine Irish fare, and a lively bar. Christchurch Pl. (phone: 475-0111; fax: 475-0488).

**Mount Herbert** Close to the city center in a quaint neighborhood, this well-run, pleasant, family-owned Georgian mansion has 110 rooms (100 with private baths), a health facility, and a good restaurant. No bar (wine license only) but a pleasant atmosphere. Business facilities include 24-hour room service, five meeting rooms for up to 150, and audiovisual equipment. 7 Herbert Rd. (phone: 668-4321; fax: 660-7077).

**Northumberland Lodge** This gracious Georgian family home features six comfortable rooms with private baths. Near the US Embassy, in Ballsbridge (phone: 660-5270; fax: 668-8679).

## EATING OUT

Although traditional dishes such as Irish stew, Dublin coddle, and bacon and cabbage are rarely served in better restaurants, when it comes to meals prepared with the finest produce, Ireland's top restaurants can compare with the best anywhere. Dinner for two (excluding wine, drinks, and tip) will cost $100 or more in expensive restaurants; $45 to $90 in moderate places; and under $45 in inexpensive spots. Unless otherwise specified, all restaurants are open for lunch and dinner. All telephone numbers are in the 1 city code unless otherwise indicated.

**Alexandra** Small and intimate, this dining spot is like a private club, with open fireplaces, crystal chandeliers, brass fittings, and oil paintings. The imaginative menu includes salmon *paupiettes* in cabbage and spinach leaves, loin of lamb with truffle and caper juice, and medallions of veal in ginger. Open for dinner only; closed Sundays. Reservations advised. Major credit cards accepted. In the *Conrad Hotel,* on Earlsfort Ter. (phone: 676-5555).

**Berkeley Room** At this elegant, lavishly appointed dining room, the prize-winning chef produces highly satisfactory fare, including rack of lamb, roast duckling, and prime ribs carved tableside. Open daily. Reservations advised. Major credit cards accepted. *Berkeley Court Hotel,* Lansdowne Rd. (phone: 660-1711).

**The Commons** In the basement of 18th-century Newman House, the historic seat of the University of Ireland, this eatery has been totally restored in recent years. Its spacious interior has high ceilings and contemporary artwork, much of it featuring James Joyce. In the summer, guests can sit outdoors in a charming terraced garden. The menu, international with some Asian influences, includes minted prawns, grilled black sole with a mussel and chive ragout, steamed *paupiettes* of brill in champagne sauce, and medallions of veal with lime and ginger sauce. Closed Sundays. Reservations advised. Major credit cards accepted. 85-86 St. Stephen's Green (phone: 872-5597).

**Le Coq Hardi** This gracious Georgian establishment is run by John Howard, a gold-medal winner in the prestigious *Hotelympia/Salon Culinaire* contest. The highlight of the extensive à la carte menu is Howard's renowned duckling *à l'orange.* Open daily. Reservations necessary. Major credit cards accepted. 35 Pembroke Rd., Ballsbridge (phone: 668-9070).

**Dobbins** A wine-cellar atmosphere—sawdust-strewn floor, wooden benches, checkered linen—prevails at this relaxed bistro. On warm days there is seating on a tropical patio. The varied international menu includes salmon and sole with prawn tails and spinach soufflé, beef teriyaki, and breast of chicken with garlic and vodka butter. There often is live Irish harp music on weekends. Closed Sundays. Reservations advised. Major credit cards accepted. Stephen's La. (phone: 676-4670, 676-4679, or 661-3321).

**Ernie's** This place earned its reputation under the direction of the late seafood chef Ernie Evans, whose family carries on the restaurant's fine tradition. The menu still features *fruits de mer,* including Valentia scallops, garlic prawns, and fresh salmon. Closed Sundays and Mondays. Reservations necessary. Major credit cards accepted. Mulberry Gardens, Donnybrook (phone: 269-3300 or 269-3260).

**Les Frères Jacques** Situated downtown beside the *Olympia Theatre* and close to *Trinity College,* this busy eatery melds creative French fare with a relaxed Dublin atmosphere and live piano music. The menu includes filet of turbot with salmon ravioli, roast suckling pig with caramelized apple and cider sauce, and roast breast of free-range duck marinated with spices, soy sauce, and ginger root. Closed Sundays. Reservations necessary. Major credit cards accepted. 74 Dame St. (phone: 679-4555).

**Grey Door** This restaurant has achieved an enviable reputation for fine Russian and Finnish cuisine. The wine list is good, and the more adventurous imbiber can sample such rarities as Russian champagne. The setting, in the heart of Georgian Dublin, is intimate, like dining in a private home. There's also a small guesthouse on the premises. Closed Sundays. Reservations advised. Major credit cards accepted. 23 Upper Pembroke St. (phone: 676-3286).

**Kish** Seafood is the unmistakable star of the menu here. Specialties include baked sole stuffed with oysters, prawns, and lobster in anise sauce; Dublin Bay prawns wrapped in smoked salmon on cider butter; and filet of salmon in phyllo pastry on a yellow pepper and scallop sauce. Open for dinner only; closed Sundays. Reservations necessary. Major credit cards accepted. At *Jurys Hotel,* Pembroke Rd., Ballsbridge (phone: 660-5000).

**Locks** A French provincial eatery on the banks of the Grand Canal near Portobello Bridge. Only the freshest ingredients are used for such dishes as wild salmon and breast of pigeon. Closed Sundays. Reservations necessary. Major credit cards accepted. 1 Windsor Ter., Portobello (phone: 538352 or 543391).

**La Stampa** Popular with the young trendy set, this elegant dining room offers fine French cuisine. Try the *dodine de canard* (boned duck, rolled and served cold in aspic) or *gratin de fruits de mer* (seafood in a rich cheese sauce). Leave room for the exceptional *profiterole au chocolat* (puff pastry filled with custard and hot chocolate sauce). Open daily. Reservations advised. Major credit cards accepted. 35 Dawson St. (phone: 677-8611).

**Old Dublin** Scandinavian-style fish—Venalainen smokies (filets of hake, halibut, sea trout, or other fish smoked on the premises and served as an appetizer in a white wine, cream, and dill sauce) and salmon coulibiac—is the hallmark of this cozy eatery. Meat eaters will savor the filet à la Novgorod—chateaubriand with sauerkraut, fried kasha, spicy mushrooms, caviar, and sour cream. The atmosphere is clubby, with most patrons on a first-name basis. There also is a good wine list. Open weekdays for lunch and dinner; Saturdays for dinner only. Reservations advised. Major credit cards accepted. 91 Francis St. (phone: 542028 or 542346; fax: 541406).

**Patrick Guilbaud** A trendy place for classic and nouvelle French cuisine, served in bird-size portions. The chef's specialty is sea bass, pan-fried in saffron butter and served with herbs and an onion *confit.* Other delightful options include filets of hare sautéed in walnut oil and doused with a red wine and juniper sauce, and freshwater pike. Closed Sundays and Mondays. Reservations essential. Major credit cards accepted. 46 James Pl., off Baggot St. (phone: 676-4192).

**Chapter One** Given its location in the *Dublin Writers' Museum,* it is not surprising that this place exudes a literary ambience. The menu, enlivened with epicurean quotes by Irish writers, features a mix of traditional Irish dishes and creative new recipes, with choices such as Irish stew, and cockles and mussels, as well as breast of duckling with peppered pineapple, filet of beef wrapped in bacon with brandy-butter sauce, and oysters and prawns in pastry. Open daily. Reservations advised, especially for dinner. Major credit cards accepted. 18-19 Parnell Sq. (phone: 217766).

**Coffers** This small, comfortable eatery specializes in wild Atlantic salmon in season and steaks—varying from a plain filet to a pork steak cooked in fresh apples and Pernod. There's a pre-theater dinner daily except Sundays. Open for dinner daily, weekdays for lunch. Reservations advised. Major credit cards accepted. 6 Cope St. (phone: 671-5740).

**FXB's** This new eatery specializes in steaks, excellently prepared to order. The same meticulous attention also is paid to seafood: The shrimp are plump and glistening; the lobsters are unbelievably juicy. Closed Sundays. Reservations advised. Major credit cards accepted. Lower Pembroke St. (phone: 676-4606).

**Gallagher's Boxty House** Casual and unpretentious, this spot is a haven for traditional Irish cooking, from lamb stew to boiled cabbage and bacon. It also is a good place to try *boxty,* a traditional potato pancake rolled around a variety of non-traditional fillings such as chicken, ham, or vegetables. Open daily. No reservations. Major credit cards accepted. 20-21 Temple Bar (phone: 677-2762; fax: 676-8567).

**La Grenouille** Each dish on the limited menu at this French-style bistro is cooked to order. Choices include rack of lamb, chicken in blue cheese sauce, steaks, and duck. Open daily for dinner and for lunch on weekdays. Reservations advised. Major credit cards accepted. Next to the *Powerscourt Town House Centre,* at 64 S. William St. (phone: 677-9157).

**McGrattans' in the Lane** An elegant Georgian door is the entrance to this restaurant, tucked in an alley between Lower Baggot Street and Merrion Square. The interior is equally inviting, with a cozy living room–like cocktail area and a skylit, plant-filled dining room. The menu melds French recipes and Irish ingredients: poached salmon Florentine, crispy duck with walnuts and honey sauce, breast of chicken in pastry with citrus sauce, and noisettes of lamb diable (roast lamb with mustard and tarragon sauce). Open daily. Reservations advised. Major credit cards accepted. 76 Fitzwilliam La. (phone: 661-8808).

**Mitchell's** Set in the cellar of *Mitchell's Wine Merchants,* this is where swinging Dubliners come for lunch. The menu is somewhat limited, but the helpings are large, the cooking good, and the desserts mouth-watering. Get here before 12:30 PM, or you'll find yourself in for a long wait (which you can while away by sampling some of their splendid wines). Open for lunch only; closed Sundays year-round and Saturdays from June through August. No reservations. Major credit cards accepted. 21 Kildare St. (phone: 668-0362).

**Polo One** Steps from St. Stephen's Green and tucked between Kildare and Dawson Streets, this modern dining place features a white-and-blue decor, enhanced by a fine collection of paintings by local artists. The menu, a hybrid of Italian, Spanish, and American influences, incorporates fresh Irish cheeses, seafood, and fruit. Closed Sundays. Reservations advised. Major credit cards accepted. 5-6 Molesworth Pl. (phone: 676-6442).

**Roly's Bistro** Located in the Ballsbridge section of town, this new eatery offers a fine menu from chef Colin Daly. Most popular are the pigeon breast with marmalade onions and pan-fried turbot with mushrooms and cream sauce. Open daily. Reservations necessary. Major credit cards accepted. 7 Ballsbridge Ter. (phone: 668-2611).

### INEXPENSIVE

**Bad Ass Café** One of the brightest, liveliest eating spots to hit town in some time, it's famed as much for its (loud) rock music and videos as for its great pizza. Steaks are another specialty. Open daily. Reservations unnecessary. Major credit cards accepted. 9-11 Crown Alley, behind the Central Bank on Dame St. (phone: 671-2596).

**Beshoff** Owned by a family long known as purveyors of fresh fish, this is a classy version of the traditional Dublin fish-and-chips shop. The menu features chips (French fries) with salmon, shark, squid, turbot, or prawns, as well as the humble cod. Open daily. Reservations unnecessary. No credit cards accepted. 14 Westmoreland St. (phone: 677-8781).

**Bewley's Café Ltd.** This Dublin landmark is a purveyor of coffees and teas of all nations. It has a tempting candy selection, too, and sampling is encouraged. The sweet pastries are also addictive. There are five Bewley's cafés in the Dublin area, but only the one on Grafton Street has waitress service. Open daily for breakfast, lunch, and dinner. Major credit cards accepted. 78-79 Grafton St. (phone: 677-6761).

---

### SHARING A PINT

You have not truly experienced Dublin until you have been in a pub, the preferred venue for Dubliners intent on pursuing drinking and conversation. Plenty of traditional pubs remain—noisy, companionable places for the pursuit of friendly ghosts of bygone Dublin in an unhurried atmosphere. *Davy Byrne's* (21 Duke St.; phone: 711298)—the "moral pub" in which Leopold Bloom had gorgonzola cheese and a glass of burgundy on June 16, 1904—today bears little resemblance to the place Joyce was evoking when he wrote of Bloom's visit in *Ulysses*. At the hub of the main shopping and business district, it attracts a predictably varied clientele. The *Brazen Head* (20 Lower Bridge St.; phone: 679-5186) is a dark and intimate place, with hallways leading off in all directions, one of them into a little room where poetry and music sessions are held. At times claustrophobic, *Doheny & Nesbitt* (5 Lower Baggot St.; phone: 676-2945) fills up with trainee architects, students, and political pundits taking time off from reporting the proceedings in the Dáil around the corner. There's usually breathing space around noon, a good time to munch on a hot roast beef sandwich. *Mulligans* (8 Poolbeg St.; phone: 677-5582), in existence since the 1750s, serves nothing but plain drink, and the Guinness draft here is among the best in the country. The patrons run the gamut from journalists and students to dock workers. The back door of *Neary's* (1 Chatham St.; phone: 677-8596) opens directly opposite the stage door of the *Gaiety*, which makes for a clientele of actors, musicians, and visiting celebrities from both professions. The *Bailey* (2 Duke St.; phone: 677-0600), the watering place for generations of Dublin's writers and artists, is still as popular as ever. The best way to experience the pub is to come for drinks at noon and then, at about 1 PM (having reserved a table), to climb the stairs to the restaurant overhead. On the way up, don't miss the original door of Leopold Bloom's house at 7 Eccles Street, lovingly preserved by the *Bailey*'s former owner. *Stag's Head* (1 Dame Ct.; phone: 679-3701) generally draws a clientele from all strata of society; unfortunately, it's awkward to get to, even though it's in the heart of the city.

Among the Dublin pubs known for their traditional music, *O'Donoghue's* (15 Merrion Row; phone: 661-4303) is one of the most famous (and least comfortable). Others to try: *An Béal Bocht* (Charlemont St.; phone: 475-5614); *Slattery's* (Capel St.; phone: 872-7971); the *Baggot Inn* (Lower Baggot St.; phone: 676-1430); *Kitty O'Shea's* (23-25 Upper Grand Canal St.; phone: 660-9965). Other favorites—where drinking and talking are the primary amusements—include *Toner's* (139 Lower Baggot St.; phone: 676-3090); *Foley's* (1 Merrion Row; phone: 661-0115); the *Horseshoe Bar* in the *Shelbourne* hotel (see *Checking In*), favored by the uppity, horsey set; the *Palace Bar* (21 Fleet St.; phone: 677-9290), a traditional haunt of journalists and literati; the award-winning *Dubliner* in *Jurys* hotel (see *Checking In*), which offers an airy atmosphere with a fireplace and a section called the "Press Room," serving (lethal) seasonal drinks; and last, but certainly not least, the delightful *Ryans* (28 Parkgate St.; phone: 677-6097), with its shining mirrors, courteous barmen, and snugs where guests can drink quietly and enjoy first-rate pub grub.

# Edinburgh

## At-a-Glance

### SEEING THE CITY

On a clear day there are striking panoramas from the top of any of its extinct volcanoes. Another option is to climb the 143 steps to the top of the *Nelson Monument* (phone: 556-2716), built in 1815, on Calton Hill at the east end of Princes Street. It is closed Sundays; admission charge. To the north lies the sparkling Firth of Forth and, beyond it, the ancient kingdom of Fife. To the south are the lovely Pentland Hills and surrounding plowed farmlands. Look eastward to the giant Bass Rock, off the coast of Berwickshire. Look westward to see Ben Lomond, nearly on the west coast of Scotland. Or drive up Arthur's Seat (the road begins just by the *Palace of Holyroodhouse*), park at Dunsapie Loch, and walk to the uppermost height (a steep and furzy climb—wear flat shoes and watch out for falling sheep). If you have no car, view the city from *Edinburgh Castle,* or take an open-top tour bus from *Waverley Station* (see *Sightseeing Tours,* below).

### SPECIAL PLACES

The Royal Mile, the oldest part of the city, is the road that runs downhill from *Edinburgh Castle* to the *Palace of Holyroodhouse.* It comprises four contiguous streets: Castle Hill, the Lawnmarket, High Street, and the Canongate. Since the entire citizenry of Edinburgh lived and worked for centuries either on or just off these four streets, the Royal Mile is practically groaning with objects and sites of historic fascination.

#### THE ROYAL MILE

**EDINBURGH CASTLE** The oldest building in Edinburgh is part of the castle structure, a tiny chapel built in the 12th century by Queen Margaret, wife of the Malcolm who is featured in *Macbeth.* The Scottish Regalia, including Sceptre and Crown, are on display. The regalia disappeared after the union of Scotland with England and were found, more than a century later, by Sir Walter Scott in an old locked box. Also here are the *United Services Museum,* documenting Scottish participation in the British armed forces; two regimental museums, focusing on the Royal Scots Regiment and the Royal Scots Dragoon Guards; the *Great Hall,* built by King James IV in the 16th century and featuring a lofty wood-beamed ceiling and huge stained glass windows; and the *Scottish National War Memorial,* honoring Scots who died in the two world wars. At 1 PM Mondays through Saturdays, a gun is fired from the ramparts. Open daily. Admission charge (phone: 244-3101).

**OUTLOOK TOWER AND CAMERA OBSCURA** A short distance east of the castle, climb up 98 steps and find yourself face to face with church spires. Opened in 1853, the camera obscura, actually a periscope, throws a revolving image of nearby streets and buildings onto a circular table, while one of the tower's denizens gives an excellent historical talk. There also are exhibitions of holography and pinphotography—tiny photos taken through matchboxes. Downstairs is a very good bookshop. Open daily. Admission charge. 354 Castle Hill (phone: 226-3709).

**SCOTCH WHISKY HERITAGE CENTRE** Just next door to the entrance to *Edinburgh Castle,* this attraction features an hour-long tour, in an electric barrel-car, that shows the role of whisky in Scotland's turbulent past. You will emerge knowing exactly how whisky is made. The heritage shop stocks over 60 brands of malt and blended whiskies. Open daily. Admission charge. 354 Castle Hill (phone: 220-0441).

**PARLIAMENT HOUSE** Built from 1632 to 1640, this historic sanctum once housed Scotland's Parliament and is today the country's supreme court. Its showpiece is the *Great Hall,* with a fine hammer-beam roof and walls laden with portraits by Raeburn and other famous Scottish artists. Closed weekends. Admission charge for library. Upper High St. (phone: 225-2595).

**ST. GILES' CATHEDRAL** A church of some sort has stood here for over 1,000 years. The 12th-century building here was named for the Athenian saint Egidius (Giles). From 1559 to 1560, during the Reformation, soldiers were stationed at the church and many of its treasures hidden in private homes; Protestant nobles nonetheless ravaged the altars. Later, English troops joined them and stripped *St. Giles'* from top to bottom. It was at this stage that John Knox was made minister of *St. Giles'.* His unmarked grave is believed to be under Parliament Square, just outside the cathedral. Admission charge. Upper High St. (phone: 225-9442).

**MERCAT CROSS, OR MARKET CROSS** Near the east door of *St. Giles'* stands a monument restored in 1885 by Prime Minister W. E. Gladstone. Proclamations were read out and hangings took place at this site until well into the 19th century (and announcements are still made here on special occasions, such as the accession of a new monarch). It was also the commercial focal point of old Edinburgh, the place being so thick with butchers, bakers, merchants, lawyers, and other shopkeepers and businesspeople that the town council issued ordinances requiring each trade to occupy its own separate neighboring street or close (hence the names on the entrances to the closes: Fleshmarket Close, Advocates' Close, and so on). High St.

**ADVOCATES' CLOSE AND ANCHOR CLOSE** These are typical of the narrow alleys that gave access to the inns and taverns that were so much a part of Edinburgh's 18th-century cultural life. Doors to these places (taverns no longer) were topped by stone architraves dating from the 16th century and bearing inscriptions like "Blissit Be God

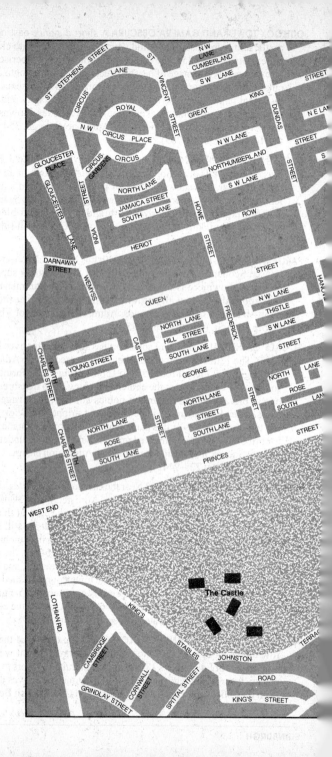

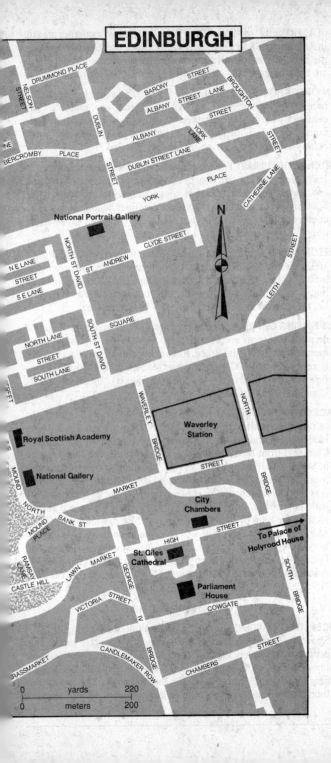

# EDINBURGH

DRUMMOND PLACE

NELSON STREET

BARONY STREET

ALBANY STREET LANE

BROUGHTON STREET

DUBLIN STREET

ALBANY STREET

YORK LANE

BERCROMBY PLACE

DUBLIN STREET LANE

PLACE

CATHERINE LANE

YORK

**National Portrait Gallery**

CLYDE STREET

N

LEITH STREET

N E LANE

NORTH ST DAVID ST

ST ANDREW

STREET

S E LANE

SQUARE

NORTH LANE

SOUTH ST DAVID

STREET

SOUTH LANE

WAVERLEY BRIDGE

**Waverley Station**

NORTH

■ **Royal Scottish Academy**

STREET

■ **National Gallery**

MARKET

MOUND

BRIDGE

**City Chambers**

NORTH MOUND PLACE

BANK ST

HIGH STREET

To Palace of Holyrood House

RAMSAY LANE

LAWN MARKET

**St. Giles Cathedral**

GEORGE IV

CASTLE HILL

SOUTH BRIDGE

■ **Parliament House**

VICTORIA STREET

COWGATE

BRIDGE

GRASSMARKET

CANDLEMAKER ROW

CHAMBERS STREET

| 0 | yards | 220 |
| 0 | meters | 200 |

of Al His Gifts" or "Spes Altera Vitae" (these two examples are still in Advocates' Close today). In Anchor Close was *Douglas's*, where the poet Robert Burns habitually drank. Entrances to both closes are from High Street.

**JOHN KNOX'S HOUSE** Legend says that Scotland's fieriest preacher lived here; history disagrees. However, legend has won, and this 15th-century dwelling was preserved when most of its neighbors were razed during the widening of High Street in 1849. Closed Sundays. Admission charge. 45 High St. (phone: 556-2647).

**SCOTTISH POETRY LIBRARY** For anyone who visits Britain to explore America's literary ancestry, an hour or two browsing here is richly rewarding. An extensive collection of books, magazines, and tapes with Scottish works in English, Scots, and Gaelic is housed in this 18th-century building in a courtyard off the Royal Mile. Closed Sundays. No admission charge. 14 High St. (phone: 557-2876).

**ACHESON HOUSE** When King Charles I was crowned at Edinburgh in 1633, Sir Archibald Acheson was his secretary of state. Acheson built this small courtyard mansion, the only one of its kind in Edinburgh, in the same year. Although the house is closed to the public, the exterior is well worth seeing. 140 Canongate.

**BRASS RUBBING CENTRE** Visitors may rub any of the brasses or stones on display. Materials are provided for a small fee. The brass commemorating Robert the Bruce, King of Scotland from 1306 to 1329, is very impressive. Closed Sundays (except during the *Edinburgh International Festival*—see *Special Events*). In Trinity Apse, Chalmers Close, off High St. (phone: 556-4364).

**PALACE OF HOLYROODHOUSE** A royal retreat since the 16th century, the stone palace is where Queen Elizabeth II stays when she is in residence in Edinburgh. Most of what you see of it now was built by Charles II from 1671, but it is chiefly associated with Mary, Queen of Scots, who lived in it for six years. The old part contains her bedroom and the supper room in which David Riccio, her secretary, was brutally murdered before her eyes by a gang that included her jealous husband, Lord Darnley. By the side of the palace are the picturesque ruins of *Holyrood Abbey* and the lodge known as *Queen Mary's Bath House*. A guide will take you through it all, sparing no gory details. Closed Sundays in February, March, November, and December; also closed January and when the queen is in residence. Admission charge. At the bottom of the Canongate (phone: 556-1096).

## BEYOND THE ROYAL MILE

**PRINCES STREET GARDENS** Princes Street is modern Edinburgh's Main Street, its Broadway, and its Fifth Avenue. The street can be surprisingly cold, in any season—deserving of its nickname, "The Valley of Winds." The gardens, lined with wooden benches, stretch nearly the street's whole length on the south side. The city spends thousands of pounds every year to keep the gardens opulent with flowers. In summer months there are concerts, children's shows, variety acts, and do-it-yourself Scottish country dancing (to professional bands). Gates close at dusk. Princes St.

**NATIONAL GALLERY OF SCOTLAND** One of a trio of *National Galleries of Scotland* within walking distance of each other, this museum stands on a manmade embankment known as the Mound at the center of *Princes Street Gardens*. Opened in 1859, it has a small but vital collection of European paintings, prints, and drawings that includes works by Poussin (*Mystic Marriage of St. Catherine*), Gauguin (*Vision After the Sermon*), Andrea del Sarto (*Portrait of Becuccio Bicchieraio*), Velázquez (*Old Woman Cooking Eggs*), Rembrandt (*Woman in Bed*), Vermeer (*Christ in the House of Martha and Mary*), Watteau (*Fêtes Vénitiennes*), and Degas (*Diego Martelli*), among others. The collection of works by Scottish artists is particularly good; visitors should not miss Henry Raeburn's *Rev. Robert Walker.* Open daily. No admission charge except for special exhibits (phone: 556-8921).

**SCOTTISH NATIONAL GALLERY OF MODERN ART** Scotland's choice collection of painting, sculpture, and graphic art of the 20th century features works of established masters such as Picasso, Matisse, Ernst, Kirchner, Dix, Moore; major Scottish artists; and leading figures of the national contemporary scene. Open daily. No admission charge. Belford Rd. (phone: 556-8921).

**SCOTTISH NATIONAL PORTRAIT GALLERY** On display are portraits—in all media—of people who have played a significant role in Scottish history from the 16th century to the present, rendered by the most famous artists of the day, as well as the *National Collection of Photography.* The gallery shares a splendid neo-Gothic building with the *Royal Museum of Scotland* (one of the *National Museums of Scotland*), whose collection includes a 14th-century longbow recently found in the Tweedsmuir Hills in southeast Scotland and several exhibits about science, technology, and natural history. Open daily. No admission charge. 1 Queen St. (phone: 556-8921).

**SCOTT MONUMENT** Sir Walter Scott is certainly one of Edinburgh's favorite sons—his face even decorates all Bank of Scotland notes, even though he was the most famous bankrupt in Scottish history. The elaborate 200-foot Gothic monument helps make Edinburgh's skyline an ornamental marvel. Its 287 steps take you to the top. Plans to clean the monument's grimy stonework have been postponed amid controversy about whether the process will cause damage. Closed Sundays. Admission charge. Princes St. (phone: 225-2424, ext. 6596).

**ST. JOHN'S CHURCH** At the west end of *Princes Street Gardens* is this stolid Episcopal church, built in 1818, with richly colored stained glass windows that are among the finest in Scotland. From time to time, large murals with a peace theme are painted on the outside walls (the artwork is sponsored by the church), causing a stir among staid passersby. The stone arched terrace on the far side of the church houses several shops, a café, and in August, a lively crafts market. Princes St. (phone: 229-7565).

**NEW TOWN** To the north of Princes Street lies the largest neoclassical townscape in Europe, built between the 1760s and 1830s. Assiduous conservation means that little has changed externally. Three of the more interesting places are Charlotte Square (designed by Robert Adam), Moray Place, and Ann Street. The *New Town Conservation Centre* (13A Dundas St.; phone: 557-5222) offers exhibitions, a reference library, and various publications; it is closed weekends.

**GEORGIAN HOUSE** On the most gracious square in the elegant New Town, the *National Trust for Scotland* has furnished a house in period style and opened it to the public. Fascinating audiovisual sessions on the New Town are included. Closed Sundays November through March. Admission charge. 7 Charlotte Sq. (phone: 225-2160).

**EDINBURGH ZOO** Opposite the Pentland Hills, away from the city center, is a zoo with a view and the world's most famous penguins, the largest colony in captivity. Every afternoon at 2:30, April through September, they perform their delightful Penguin Parade through the park grounds. Open daily. Admission charge. Corstorphine Rd., Murrayfield (phone: 334-9171).

**GRASSMARKET** This ancient street is flanked by many eateries, elegant shops, and flophouses. The West Bow, off the street's east end, has some intriguing boutiques and antiques shops. Leading from the Grassmarket is Cowgate, with the 16th-century *Magdalen Chapel;* to see it, contact the *Scottish Reformation Society* (phone: 220-1450).

**GREYFRIARS KIRK** This historic Presbyterian church, dedicated on *Christmas Day* in 1620, was the site of a pre-Reformation Franciscan friary. It is also where Presbyterians declared their opposition to the prescribed Episcopalianism of Charles I by signing the National Covenant in blood in 1638. Sunday services are given in English and in Gaelic. The church is closed (except on Thursdays and for services) October through February; the *Kirkyard* (graveyard) is open daily. George IV Bridge (phone: 225-1900).

**EDINBURGH CRYSTAL VISITORS CENTRE** Cut-glass items sell like hotcakes in Edinburgh, and here's a chance to see how they are made. Operating in a town about 12 miles south of Edinburgh, the center offers guided tours on weekdays. There is also a factory shop and a restaurant. Children under 10 are not allowed. Open daily. Admission charge. At Eastfield near Penicuik; take Straiton Rd. south out of town (phone: 1968-675128).

**ST. MARY'S CATHEDRAL** Consecrated in 1879, this Episcopal church has a lofty 270-foot main spire and two smaller ones at the west end which were added between 1913 and 1917 (named Barbara and Mary, after the women who paid for their construction). The rows of modern, light wood chairs brighten up the dark stone interior and the lectern's base is a pelican instead of the usual eagle. Palmerston Pl. (phone: 225-6293).

# Sources and Resources

## TOURIST INFORMATION

Located next to *Waverley Station,* the *Edinburgh and Scotland Information Centre* (3 Princes St., Edinburgh EH2 2QP; phone: 557-1700) has an accommodations desk, details of guided walking tours, and a ticket center for Edinburgh events. It also offers maps, leaflets, and all City of Edinburgh publications, some at a nominal charge. On sale here is the *Essential Guide to Edinburgh,* updated annually. The center is closed Sundays October through April. There is also a tourist information desk at *Edinburgh Airport* (phone: 333-1000); open daily. For information concerning travel in other parts of Scotland, drop by the *Scottish Tourist Board* (23 Ravelston Ter.; phone: 332-2433).

For information in the US, contact the *British Tourist Authority* (625 N. Michigan Ave., Suite 1510, Chicago, IL 60611; phone: 312-787-0490; fax: 312-787-7746; and 551 Fifth Ave., Suite 701, New York, NY 10176; phone: 212-986-2200; fax: 212-986-1188). The *British Embassy* is at 3100 Massachusetts Ave. NW, Washington, DC 20008 (phone: 202-462-1340).

**ENTRY REQUIREMENTS** A US citizen needs a current passport for a stay of up to six months.

**TIME** The time in Scotland is five hours later than in US East Coast cities. Scotland observes daylight saving time.

**LANGUAGE** English is the official language. Gaelic is widely spoken in the Outer Islands of Scotland.

**ELECTRIC CURRENT** 240 volts, 50 cycles, AC.

**MONEY** The pound sterling (£) equals 100 pence. Scotland prints its own banknotes, which are of equal value to the pound sterling and are interchangeable with comparable English bills. At press time the exchange rate was 63 pence to the American dollar.

**TIPPING** Service charges of between 10% and 15% usually are included in hotel bills, but it's wise to make sure. The tipping standard is between 10% and 15% in restaurants and taxis and 50 pence per bag for bellhops and porters.

**BANKING/BUSINESS HOURS** The Bank of Scotland is open weekdays from 9:30 AM to 4:45 PM and on Thursdays until 5:30 PM. The Royal Bank of Scotland is open weekdays from 9:30 AM to 3:30 PM (and from 4:30 to 5:30 PM on Thursdays). Most other businesses operate weekdays from 9 AM to 5 PM.

**NATIONAL HOLIDAYS** *New Year's Day* (January 1; public holiday, January 2), *Winter Bank Holiday* (January 3), *Good Friday* (April 14), *Easter Sunday* (April 16), *Easter Monday* (April 17), *May Day* (May 1, but to be observed this year on May 8), *Spring Bank Holiday* (May 29), *Summer Bank Holiday* (August 7), *Christmas Day* (December 25), and *Boxing Day* (December 26).

**LOCAL COVERAGE** The following publications are available: the *Scotsman,* morning daily; the *Edinburgh Evening News,* evening daily; the information center's free *Day by Day,* published monthly (except during the *Edinburgh International Festival,* when it's published every two weeks), listing forthcoming happenings; and *The List* (phone: 558-1191), a comprehensive biweekly Glasgow and Edinburgh events guide.

**TELEPHONE** The area code for Edinburgh is 131. When calling from one area to another within Scotland, dial 0 + city code + local number. The country code for Scotland (and for all of Great Britain) is 44. Dial 999 for emergency assistance.

## GETTING AROUND

**AIRPORT** *Edinburgh Airport* is about a half hour from the center of town. An *Airlink* bus (No. 100) travels from the airport to Waverley Bridge, making stops en route at Haymarket and Murrayfield (phone: 226-5087). The *Edinburgh Airbus* (phone: 556-2244), which also connects the airport and the city center, stops at most of the major hotels.

**BUS** *Lothian Region Transport* bus route maps and information are available from the information desk at the *Ticket Centre* on Waverley Bridge (phone: 220-4111), except for buses that run from St. Andrew Square (phone: 556-8464). Passengers can reach most places from Princes Street. Fares range from 40p (about 60¢) to £1.10 (about $1.65); exact change is required. The information center (see above) can provide information on bus tours of the city and countryside. Longer-distance buses leave from *St. Andrew Square Bus Station* (St. Andrew Sq.). The Edinburgh Touristcard provides unlimited bus travel for two or more days; it may be purchased at either the *Lothian Region Transport* office (14 Queen St.; phone: 554-4494) or the *Ticket Centre* (see above). A two-day pass costs £4.80 (about $7.20); a seven-day pass costs £8 (about $12).

**CAR RENTAL** Major firms represented include *Avis* (100 Dairy Rd.; phone: 337-6363); *Europcar* (24 E. London St.; phone: 661-1252); and *Hertz* (10 Picardy Pl.; phone: 556-8311).

**SIGHTSEEING TOURS** *Guide Friday* (Platform 1, *Waverley Station;* phone: 556-2244) and *Lothian Regional Transport* (see above) run hour-long tours of the city that leave every hour (every 15 minutes during peak time). Open-top, double-decker buses depart from various points; tickets are valid all day so you can get on and off as often as you like.

University-trained historians from *Mercat Tours* (14 Redford Ter.; phone: 661-4541) lead guided walks from the *Mercat Cross* next to *St. Giles'* on the Royal Mile. Guided walks around the Royal Mile also are offered, and ghosts are the subject of an evening walk that ends with a drink in a historic tavern; both tours are given once or twice daily, depending on the season. Another night walk along the "Ghost Hunter Trail" leaves once a day June through September to visit sites of reputed macabre and supernatural events.

*Robin's Tours* (60 Willowbrae Rd.; phone: 661-0125) leads several excursions, including Grand City, Royal Mile, 18th-century Edinburgh (April through October), and Ghosts and Witches tours. All leave from outside the information center. A Murder & Mystery tour led by a guide dressed as Adam Lyal, a highwayman executed in the city's Grassmarket in 1811, leaves from outside the *Witchery* restaurant in Castle Hill every evening (times vary); book in advance (phone: 225-6745).

**TAXI** There are cabstands at *St. Andrew Square Bus Station* (see above), *Waverley Station* (see below), opposite the *Caledonian* hotel (west end of Princes St.), and in front of the *Cameron Toll Shopping Centre* (Lady Rd.). To call a taxi, contact *Capital Castle* (phone: 228-2555), *Central Radio Taxis* (phone: 229-2468), or *City Cabs* (phone: 228-1211).

**TRAIN** The main railway terminal is *Waverley Station* (off Princes St.; phone: 556-2451). There is a 24-hour *British Rail* information service (phone: 556-2451).

## LOCAL SERVICES

**DENTIST** Dental emergencies are treated for a nominal charge at *Western General Hospital* (Crewe Rd. S.; phone: 332-2525).

**DRY CLEANER/TAILOR** *Pullar's* (23 Frederick St.; phone: 225-8095), four-hour dry cleaning; *Quick Stitch* (79 Rose St.; phone: 225-5840), for quick repairs, is just around the corner from *Pullar's*.

**LIMOUSINE SERVICE** *W. L. Sleigh* (6 Devon Pl.; phone: 337-3171).

**MEDICAL EMERGENCY** *Royal Infirmary,* Emergency Ward (Lauriston Pl.; phone: 229-2477).

**MESSENGER SERVICE** *QED* (*Dundonald House;* 5-7 Dundonald St.; phone: 557-3877; fax: 556-0215) operates 24 hours daily.

**NATIONAL/INTERNATIONAL COURIER** *Pony Express* (31A Albany St.; phone: 557-4300); *QED* (see *Messenger Service* above).

**OFFICE SERVICES** *Reception Business Centre* (21 Lansdowne Cresc.; phone: 226-2830); also rents office space on a short-term basis.

**PHARMACY** *Boots* (48 Shandwick Pl.; phone: 225-6757) is open Mondays through Saturdays from 8:30 AM to 9 PM and Sundays from 10 AM to 5 PM.

**PHOTOCOPIES** *Rank Xerox* (27 George St.; phone: 225-4388) is open weekdays from 9 AM to 5:30 PM.

**POST OFFICE** The main post office (2 Waterloo Pl., east of Princes St.; phone: 550-8229) is open weekdays from 9 AM to 5:30 PM, Saturdays until 12:30 PM. A second office (7 Hope St.; phone: 226-6823) has similar hours.

**SECRETARY/STENOGRAPHER** *Reception Business Centre* (see above).

**TELECONFERENCE FACILITIES** Edinburgh can handle multi-party calls. To make an appointment, call *British Telecom* (phone: 800-282429) weekdays from 8:30 AM to 5 PM.

**OTHER** Tuxedo rental: *Moss Brothers* (43 George St.; phone: 225-2625); should the occasion arise, they also have full Highland dress available for rent.

## SPECIAL EVENTS

There's plenty going on in Edinburgh all year, but several festivals are worth arranging your itinerary around.

---

### FAVORITE FETES

**Edinburgh International Festival** During its three-week run from mid-August to early September, this world-renowned festival offers a cornucopia of activities. The city's theaters, concert halls, museums, churches, community centers, and some schools are taken over for theater, dance, and opera performances; for lectures, master classes, conferences, exhibits, and other cultural affairs of global significance; and for nearly 1,000 presentations of the *Festival Fringe,* which the *Guinness Book of World Records* lists as the largest arts festival in the world. The *Fringe* nowadays embraces the traditional as well as the experimental and gives particular encouragement to comedians; past performers have included Eric Idle, Michael Palin, and Terry Jones (all later of *Monty Python*) as well as Dudley Moore. The colorful *Edinburgh Military Tattoo,* a spectacular pageant featuring a performance of the massed pipe bands of Her Majesty's Scottish regiments in full Highland dress, is equally popular; it takes place at the castle every night (except Sundays) for the last three weeks in August.

Coinciding with the first two weeks of the *International Festival* is the *Edinburgh International Film Festival.* Entries are screened at *Filmhouse* (88 Lothian Rd.; phone: 228-4051). The *Edinburgh International Jazz Festival* is held at various sites throughout the city during the first week of the *Tattoo;* for information, contact the festival office (116 Canongate; phone: 557-1642).

It's a good idea to reserve tickets—and hotel space—as far in advance as possible, especially for the most popular attractions; the film and jazz festivals are easier to get into on short notice. For details on events, contact the *Festival Society* (21 Market St., Edinburgh EH1 1BW, Scotland; phone: 226-4001), the *Edinburgh Military Tattoo* (22 Market St., Edinburgh EH1 1QB, Scotland; phone: 225-1188), and the *Festival Fringe Society* (180 High St., Edinburgh EH1 1QS, Scotland; phone: 226-5257).

---

Other events include *New Year's Eve,* or "hogmanay," which is celebrated with a three-day festival that includes torchlit processions through the streets, fairs, markets, and a huge party held in one of the major theaters. Folk music, dance, drama, a crafts fair, children's events, lectures, courses on traditional instruments, *ceilidhs,* workshops, and an Oral History Conference are the heart of the *Edinburgh International Folk Festival* (PO Box 528, Edinburgh EH10 4DU, Scotland; phone: 556-3181), which takes place over the 10 days that lead up to *Easter* weekend. The *Edinburgh Harp Festival* and the *Festival of European Piping* are an integral part of the event.

The world's only international science fair, the *Edinburgh Science Festival,* is held in early April; it includes films, talks, and conferences on such topics as superconductivity, high-tech wine making, and genetic engineering. For more details contact the *Science Festival Box Office* (1 Broughton Market; phone: 556-6446).

## MUSEUMS

In addition to those described in *Special Places,* the city runs two museums of local history: *Huntly House* (142 Canongate; phone: 225-2424, ext. 4143) and the *Lady Stair's House* (Lawnmarket; phone: 225-2424, ext. 6901), a Burns, Scott, and Stevenson museum. Both are closed Sundays (except during the *Festival*). Admission charge. Other museums include the following:

**LAURISTON CASTLE** A fine enlarged 16th-century tower, the castle overlooks the estuary of the Firth of Forth. The interior is filled with period furniture and collections of Derbyshire Blue Hogn, Crossley wool mosaics, and objets d'art. The castle may be visited on guided tours only. Open daily. Admission charge. Off Cramond Rd. S. (phone: 336-2060).

**MUSEUM OF CHILDHOOD** A treasure house of historic toys, dolls, and children's clothing, it also features a time tunnel with reconstructions of a schoolroom, a street scene, a fancy dress party, and a late 19th-century nursery. Closed Sundays (except during the *Festival*). No admission charge. 38 High St. (phone: 225-2424, ext. 6645).

**THE PEOPLE'S STORY** Tells the tale of the working class of Edinburgh through the centuries, including sections on the development of trade unions, health, welfare, and leisure. Operating days are the same as for the *Museum of Childhood* (above). No admission charge. At the *Canongate Tolbooth,* 163 Canongate (phone: 225-2424, ext. 4057).

## SHOPPING

Princes Street is Edinburgh's main venue, with some of Scotland's best shops as well as branches of several British department stores, though there are also some interesting shops on George Street, two blocks north, and on the Royal Mile. In addition, at the east end of Princes Street is *Waverley Market,* a large, modern shopping mall with *Waverley Station* at its base. The best buys are Scottish tartans and woolens.

Also worth a look are antiques on Dundas Street, West Bow (off Grassmarket), Randolph Place, Thistle Street, or in the area around St. Stephen's Street in Stockbridge—and three-day antiques fairs are held in January, April, August, and November in the *Roxburghe* hotel (see *Checking In*). *Phillips Scotland* (65 George St.; phone: 225-2266) has frequent antiques auctions. *Lyon and Turnbull* (51 George St.; phone: 225-4627) is another good auction house.

Bone china and Scottish crystal are attractive, and don't miss the shortbread, which is on sale everywhere. St. Mary's Street, leading off the Royal Mile, is rapidly becoming famous for shops selling secondhand clothes, jewelry, and objets d'art.

Most shops are open weekdays and Saturdays from 9 or 9:30 AM to 6:30 PM, and some also are open on Sundays (usually from 9 or 9:30 AM to 5:30 or 6 PM). Department stores and malls often stay open until 8 or 9 PM at least one day a week (usually Thursdays), and also may be open until 6:30 PM on Sundays.

Be sure to take your passport when you shop, and always inquire about the Value Added Tax (VAT) refund application forms when your total purchases in a store are over £50 (about $75). The VAT is a surcharge payable at the sales counter, but foreign customers usually will be reimbursed for it at home.

We especially recommend the following stores:

**Andrew Pringle** Old books, maps, and prints. 7 Dundas St. (phone: 556-9698).

**Belinda Robertson** High-quality cashmere tunics, sweaters, skirts, and other clothing in classic designs. 22 Palmerston Pl. (phone: 225-1057).

**Blackfriars Music** Folk music records, sheet music, and books, as well as all types of instruments from fiddles to bagpipes. 49 Blackfriars St. (phone: 557-3090).

**Bruntsfield Clocks** A tiny shop filled with old clocks of all shapes, sizes, and decorations. They also repair and restore. 7 Bruntsfield Pl. (phone: 229-4720).

**Burberrys Scotch House** Men's and women's clothing and accessories including women's kilts and splendid tartan umbrellas. 39-41 Princes St. (phone: 556-1252).

**Cashmere Store** The best place in town for cashmere sweaters and scarves. 2 St. Giles' St. (phone: 225-5178).

**Chit Chat** Antique cutlery and china, old prints, and rare books are featured at this small shop. 134 St. Stephen St. (phone: 225-9660).

**Cornerstone Bookshop** Books on religion, ecology, and women's issues are the main draw here; plus Celtic books and imaginative postcards. Behind *St. John's Church.* Princes St. (phone: 229-3776).

**Crabtree & Evelyn** Classical music plays quietly in this shop selling toiletries, chocolates, biscuits, and preserves. 4 Hanover St. (phone: 226-2478).

**Edinburgh Gallery** The best place in the city for contemporary paintings. 18A Dundas St. (phone: 557-5227).

**Edinburgh Woollen Mill** Good, inexpensive woolens such as kilts, sweaters, tweeds, scarves, shawls, and mohairs. Three locations: 62 Princes St. (phone: 225-4966); 453 Lawnmarket (phone: 225-1525); and 139 Princes St. (phone: 226-3840).

**Eric Davidson** Antique furniture, ceramics, paintings, and clocks. 183 Causewayside (phone: 662-4221).

**Festival Fringe Society** The *Fringe*'s headquarters and ticket office includes a small shop that sells colorful T-shirts and postcards. 180 High St. (phone: 226-5257).

**Gieves & Hawkes** The only branch in Scotland of the famous Savile Row tailors whose customers include the Prince of Wales. 48 George St. (phone: 225-7456).

**Hamilton & Inches** A grand, but friendly, jewelry shop that was established in 1866; the queen's silversmith and clock specialist. 87 George St. (phone: 225-4898).

**Hector Russell Kiltmaker** Everything in tartan including deerstalkers and caps and Scottish music in the background. 95 Princes St. (phone: 225-3315).

**Hugh Macpherson Ltd.** A family business that sells, in addition to bagpipes, Highland costumes handmade by local women on the premises. To go with the bagpipes, shoppers might buy a pipe band uniform or a custom-made tartan skirt or kilt. 17 W. Maitland St. (phone: 225-4008).

**James Pringle Weavers** Beautiful knitwear in cashmere, lamb's wool, and classic Shetland, as well as tartans and tweeds. Offering low prices for top-quality goods is the policy of this factory outlet, which also provides free taxi service from hotels in the city. 70-74 Bangor Rd. (phone: 553-5161).

**James Thin** Books, newspapers, magazines, and stationery since 1848. There is a quiet tearoom upstairs. 57 George St. (phone: 225-4495). There are also branches at *Waverley Market,* Princes St. (phone: 557-1378); and 53-59 S. Bridge (phone: 556-6743); the latter sells mostly textbooks.

**Jenner's** Sells everything, especially bone china and Scottish crystal. A particularly good selection of fine food items. Don't miss the china and glass shops in the lofty rear hall. The restaurant on the second floor has a good view of Princes Street. Princes and South St. David's Sts. (phone: 225-2442).

**John Dickson** This gunmaker and fishing tackle shop has been supplying sporting gear to Scotland's gentry since 1820. It also offers a fine selection of outdoor country wear. 21 Frederick St. (phone: 225-4218).

**Joseph H. Bonnar** A wide assortment of antique and modern jewelry. 72 Thistle St. (phone: 226-2811).

**Justerini & Brooks** Established in 1749, these wine merchants are suppliers to the queen. 39 George St. (phone: 226-4202).

**Kinloch Anderson** Serving the royal family, it's the place where Prince Charles, among others, obtains his kilts. Kilts for men and women can be made to order in some 400 of the tartans in existence; some ready-made kilts and accessories are available as well. 4 Dock St. (phone: 555-1371).

**Laurence Black Ltd.** A wide variety of Victorian Scottish antiques, including napkin rings, furniture, and knickknacks. 45 Cumberland St. (phone: 557-4545).

**Margaret Duncan Books** Antiquarian and other secondhand books sold by experts. 5 Tanfield (phone: 556-4591).

**One World Shop** Excellent selection of Third World crafts and small gift items from rugs to soaps. Behind *St. John's Church.* Princes St. (phone: 229-4541).

**Pine and Old Lace** A tiny shop specializing in antique lace garments, linen, and pine furniture. 46 Victoria St. (phone: 225-3287).

**Pitlochry Knitwear** Bargains in Scottish products, especially sweaters, kilts, and ladies' suits. 26 N. Bridge (phone: 225-3893).

**Ragamuffin** Designer knitwear for men and women, including women's jackets commissioned on the Isle of Skye. 276 Canongate (phone: 557-6007).

**Robert Cresser** This is the brush center of Edinburgh; everything from shaving brushes to brooms is made on the premises and sold here. 40 Victoria St. (phone: 225-2181).

**Royal Mile Whiskies** Paradise for whisky lovers—a huge selection from the Highlands, Lowlands, and the islands, ranging from miniatures to elaborate presentation bottles. Scottish foodstuffs, such as smoked salmon and haggis, also can be found here. 379 High St. (phone: 225-3383).

**Scottish Gems** Most of the traditional and modern jewelry in this shop is made in Scotland and depicts Celtic and Nordic influences; also Scottish pottery and glassware. 24 High St. (phone: 557-5731).

**Scottish Gifts, Curios, and Crafts** This tiny shop is the place to find genuine handmade Scottish goods (most are crafted in nearby workshops). It's stuffed to the rafters with antique jewelry, weapons, badges, kilts, bagpipes, and other items characteristic of Scotland. 499 Lawnmarket (phone: 225-6113).

**Second Edition Bookshop** Fine arts and literature books. 9 Howard St. (phone: 556-9403).

**Top Brass** Top-quality antique brass furnishings from candelabras to bedframes. 77 Dundas St. (phone: 557-4293).

**Waterstone's** The Edinburgh branches of this huge chain of bookstores, whose instant success is due mainly to an enterprising, well-informed staff and late hours (it's open weekdays until 9 PM). Three locations: 83 George St. (phone: 225-3436), 13 Princes St. (phone: 556-3034), and 128 Princes St. (phone: 226-2666).

## SPORTS AND FITNESS

**BICYCLING** Rentals are available from *Central Cycle Hire* (13 Lochrin Pl., Tolcross; phone: 228-6363).

**FITNESS CENTER** *Meadowbank Sports Centre* (139 London Rd.; phone: 661-5351) has a large gym with weights and exercise equipment, a 400-meter track, and classes in archery, boxing, fencing, and judo.

**GOLF** With more than 20 courses, Edinburgh is a good place to practice Scotland's national mania. One course in the area, however, is merely the greatest.

---

### TOP TEE-OFF SPOT

**The Honourable Company of Edinburgh Golfers** The single best course in Scotland is in nearby Gullane (pronounced *Gill*-in), and it boasts the golf club with the longest continuous history in the world, one that has grown in status with each decade since its formal beginnings in 1744. Tucked along the south shore of the Firth of Forth, the course—most commonly called *Muirfield*—is totally challenging as well as beautifully simple. (For an idea of just how challenging it can be, know that the House Committee has imposed a maximum handicap of 18 for men and 24 for women because so many visitors took longer than four and a half hours to get around the course.) Note that access is granted to non-members only by advance arrangement, and then only on Tuesday, Thursday, and Friday mornings (Tuesdays and Thursdays only in July and August); when writing, include alternate dates. For information or reservations, contact *The Honourable Company of Edinburgh Golfers* (Muirfield, Gullane; phone: 1620-842255).

---

A letter from your home club president or pro should get you into any of the city's courses; other fine venues are *Royal Burgess* and *Bruntsfield,* both in suburban Barnton, *Carrick Knowe* (in Glendevon Park; phone: 337-1096), and *Silverknowes* (Silverknowes Pkwy.; phone: 336-3843). Reserve tee-off times at these clubs ahead of arrival. Golf clubs can be rented. And if you can't get into any of these, the *Braids Hill Golf Centre* (91 Liberton Dr.; phone: 658-1755) has a driving range.

**JOGGING** A good bet is *Holyrood Park,* near the huge stone palace at the foot of Canongate. An especially popular run is around Arthur's Seat, the extinct volcano in the center of the park.

**SWIMMING** Have a dip in the luxurious *Royal Commonwealth Pool* (Dalkeith Rd.; phone: 667-7211), which features a water slide, re-created river rapids, a twister, and a stingray. Open daily.

## THEATER

Edinburgh's main venues are the *King's* (2 Leven St.; phone: 220-4349), which presents touring productions, including the finest from London's *National Theatre;* the *Playhouse* (20 Greenside Pl.; phone: 557-2590), which features a variety of plays, concerts, and musicals; and the *Royal Lyceum* (Grindlay St.; phone: 229-9697), which has a fine reputation for interesting productions of both classic and contemporary plays. Pop stars and extravaganzas are frequently presented at the *Edinburgh Exhibition Centre* (Ingliston; phone: 333-3036). The *Traverse* (Cambridge St.; phone: 228-1404) is a small theater which is internationally well known for its avant-garde pieces and for presenting the works of new playwrights from all over the world. The *Netherbow* (43 High St.; phone: 556-9579) and *Theatre Workshop* (34 Hamilton Pl.; phone: 226-5425) mount small-scale, artistic productions. In summer, open-air productions are performed at the *Ross Theatre* (phone: 220-4348) in *Princes Street Gardens.* Schedules are in the dailies, *Day by Day,* and *The List* (see *Local Coverage*), and tickets for most productions can be purchased at *Ticket Centre* (31-33 Waverley Bridge; phone: 225-8616), as well as at individual box offices.

## MUSIC

Classical music is the city's overriding passion. Highbrow musical events are held at *Usher Hall* (Lothian Rd.; phone: 228-1155), where the *Royal Scottish Orchestra* holds performances most Friday nights at 7:30. Internationally famous musicians and ensembles (both classical and nonclassical) perform at the *King's* and the *Playhouse* theaters (see above for both). The old *Empire Theatre* (famous for its Art Deco decor) recently reopened as the *Festival Theatre* (13 Nicholson St.; phone: 662-1112); boasting the largest stage in Great Britain (about 9,300 square feet), it hosts performances by the *Scottish Opera,* as well as classical music concerts and a variety of musicals and other plays. Concerts also are held at *Saint Cecilia's Hall* (Canongate; no phone). For chamber music and occasional jazz, try *Queen's Hall* (Clerk St.; phone: 668-2019). *St. Giles' Cathedral* regularly hosts organ recitals, and at *St. Mary's Cathedral,* evensong is sung on weekday afternoons at 5:15 by a trained choir with boy sopranos (see *Special Places* for both). Details on other musical events are available in the dailies, *Day by Day,* and *The List* (see *Local Coverage*).

## NIGHTCLUBS AND NIGHTLIFE

A number of nightspots have opened here in recent years. Discos usually are filled with a very young crowd, but you could risk the following if you're under 30: *Century 2000* (1 Lothian Rd.; phone: 229-7670); *Buster Brown's Disco* (25 Market St.; phone: 226-4224); and the *Red Hot Pepper Club* (3 Semple St.; phone: 229-7733). *Minus One,* the nightclub in the *Carlton Highland* hotel (see *Checking In*), attracts a somewhat older crowd (it's open only on Thursday, Friday, and Saturday nights). Jazz and folk music can be heard around the city; check the *Evening News*'s "Nightlife" page, *Day by Day* magazine, or *The List* (see *Local Coverage*).

Edinburgh also has several private casinos: *Berkeley* (2 Rutland Pl.; phone: 228-4446); *Stanley's* (5 York Pl.; phone: 556-1055); and *Stakis Regency* (14 Picardy Pl.; phone: 557-3585). Anyone who's 18 or older can join, but you must apply for membership (free) at least 48 hours before your visit.

# Best in Town

## CHECKING IN

In Scotland, it is practically impossible to get a room without an accompanying kippers-to-nuts Scottish breakfast (you usually pay for it whether you eat it or not). Expect to pay more than $190 per night for a double room (including private bath, phone, and TV set, unless otherwise indicated) in the hotels listed below as expensive; $115 to $190 for those in the moderate category; and less than $115 for inexpensive places. Lower rates are available on weekends at the larger hotels (except in August). You can make reservations in more than 70 hotels and guesthouses in the city by calling *Dial-a-Bed* (phone: 557-4365; 800-616947 toll-free within Britain). Should you find it impossible to get into any of our selected hotels, the tourist information center (see *Tourist Information,* above) has an accommodations service. All telephone numbers are in the 131 area code unless otherwise indicated.

### EXPENSIVE

**Balmoral Forte Grand** At the turn of the century, two rival railway companies raced to be the first to erect its own hotel; the *North British Railway Company* won, and its huge, Scottish baronial-style establishment began receiving guests in 1902. Locals still refer to the property (now part of the Forte chain), with 189 rooms and suites, as the "North British." Its Victorian features have been retained, although it has been revamped for the 21st century. There is a restaurant. Business facilities include 24-hour room service, meeting rooms for up to 400, a concierge, foreign currency exchange, secretarial services, audiovisual equipment, photocopiers, computers, cable television news, translation services, and express checkout. Princes St. (phone: 556-2414; 800-225-5843; fax: 557-3747).

**Caledonian** The city's other railroad hotel opened next to the *Caledonian Station* in 1903 (the station has since closed). The decor is very engaging, and some of the 238 rooms and suites have great views of *Edinburgh Castle.* Celebrities love it. The hotel's first class *Pompadour* dining room (see *Eating Out*) is nearly matched by the *Carriages* restaurant, with the old station clock proudly mounted on the wall. There also are three bars. In addition, the property is conveniently close to Edinburgh's new *International Conference Cen-*

*tre,* which is set to open this fall. Business facilities include 24-hour room service, meeting rooms for up to 300, a concierge, foreign currency exchange, secretarial services, audiovisual equipment, photocopiers, computers, translation services, and express checkout. Princes St. (phone: 225-2433; 800-641-0300; fax: 225-6632).

**Carlton Highland** Remarkably transformed from an old department store into a grand and sophisticated Victorian hotel with 207 rooms, two dining rooms, and a bar. Health facilities include a pool, squash courts, a gym, saunas, and a Jacuzzi, and there is dancing at the *Minus One* nightclub (see *Nightlife*). Business facilities include 24-hour room service, meeting rooms for up to 300, a concierge, foreign currency exchange, secretarial services, audiovisual equipment, photocopiers, cable television news, and translation services. North Bridge, off Princes St. (phone: 556-7277; fax: 556-2691).

**Howard** This luxurious, 16-room hotel, which deliberately has no reception desk, looks and feels like a splendid, elegantly decorated Georgian townhouse. The fabrics and furnishings are in soft Highland heather tones. Its restaurant serves a mix of continental and Scottish fare. Business facilities include 24-hour room service, meeting rooms for up to 24, secretarial services, audiovisual equipment, photocopiers, translation services, and express checkout. 36 Great King St. (phone: 557-3500; fax: 557-6515).

**Prestonfield House** One of Scotland's finest historic houses, this lovely 1687 mansion with its original furnishings is a very special place to stay. There are only five guestrooms (two with private baths), but the 13-acre gardens, where peacocks, pheasants, and partridges are familiar sights, make a stop here truly idyllic. The restaurant serves excellent fare (see *Eating Out*). An 18-hole golf course is also on the grounds. Business facilities include meeting rooms for up to 800 in an adjoining conference center. Located 2 miles southeast of the city center. Priestfield Rd. (phone: 668-3346; fax: 668-3976).

**Royal Terrace** A portrait of the Duke of Edinburgh over the open fire near the reception desk sets the tone for this luxurious 97-room hostelry. Occupying a row of beautiful Georgian houses, fully restored to their original grandeur, the establishment offers a lush decor, with marble fireplaces and crystal chandeliers. The *Conservatory* restaurant serves Scottish fare. There is a large landscaped garden, and a health club with a heated pool, gym, sauna, and massage room. Business facilities include 24-hour room service, meeting rooms for up to 100, a concierge, foreign currency exchange, secretarial services, audiovisual equipment, photocopiers, and translation services. 18 Royal Ter. (phone: 557-3222; fax: 557-5334).

**Scandic Crown** Located halfway between *Edinburgh Castle* and the Royal Mile in Edinburgh's Old Town, this establishment, though modern, has an antiquated air, which goes well with the neighboring architecture. Rooms have heated floors, security safes, satellite TV, free in-house movies, and mini-bars. The two restaurants serve a combination of Scandinavian and Scottish fare. There's also a health club with Finnish saunas. Business facilities include 24-hour room service, meeting rooms for up to 200, a concierge, foreign currency exchange, secretarial services, audiovisual equipment, photocopiers, computers, cable television news, translation services, and express checkout. 80 High St. (phone: 557-9797; 800-44-UTELL; fax: 557-9789).

**Sheraton Grand** Following a complete overhaul that gives it a thoroughly Scottish feel, this comfortable 263-room hotel is decorated with tartan and tweed fabrics, and the *Grill Room* restaurant serves authentic regional dishes. The airy *Terrace* brasserie overlooks the fountains of Festival Square, and diners might well enjoy their meals to the accompaniment of the pipes and drums of the Scots Guards. There are also lovely views of *Edinburgh Castle,* and many of the city's other attractions are a short walk away. Business facilities include 24-hour room service, meeting rooms for up to 485, a concierge, foreign currency exchange, secretarial services, audiovisual equipment, photocopiers, computers, cable television news, translation services, and express checkout. 1 Festival Sq. (phone: 229-9131; 800-334-8484; fax: 228-4510).

### MODERATE

**Braid Hills** Muriel Spark fans will remember that this is where Miss Jean Brodie, by then past her prime, took tea. An old, established, family-run, 68-room hotel with restaurant in the southern suburbs toward the Pentland Hills. Business facilities include 24-hour room service, meeting rooms for up to 100, a concierge, secretarial services, audiovisual equipment, photocopiers, cable television news, and translation services. 134 Braid Rd. (phone: 447-8888; fax: 452-8477).

**Bruntsfield** Set in a Victorian townhouse about a mile south of the city's center is this friendly 54-room hotel. Its *Potting Shed* restaurant specializes in tasty, light dishes, including crêpes, and the large bar attracts a lively crowd in the evenings. Business facilities include meeting rooms for up to 60, foreign currency exchange, secretarial services, audiovisual equipment, photocopiers, cable television news, and translation services. 69 Bruntsfield Pl. (phone: 229-1393; fax: 229-5634).

**Channings** Five fine Georgian townhouses have been joined to create this elegant hostelry on a quiet cobbled lane within walking distance of Princes Street. There are 48 beautifully appointed rooms with modern amenities, and the bar and brasserie offer Scottish and international dishes. Business facilities include 24-hour room service, meeting rooms for up to 20, foreign currency exchange, secretarial services, audiovisual equipment, photocopiers, computers, cable television news, and express checkout. S. Learmonth Gardens (phone: 315-2226; fax: 332-9631).

**George Inter-Continental** Located in the New Town between Charlotte and St. Andrew Squares, this gracious 19th-century establishment—

originally apartments for the aristocracy when the New Town of Edinburgh was created by architect Robert Adam and his pupils—retains a luxurious ambience. Now affiliated with the Inter-Continental hotel group, it has 195 bedrooms, two dining rooms, and the *Gathering of the Clans* bar. Business facilities include 24-hour room service, meeting rooms for up to 200, a concierge, foreign currency exchange, secretarial services, audiovisual equipment, photocopiers, computers, cable television news, translation services, and express checkout. 19-21 George St. (phone: 225-1251; 800-327-0200; fax: 226-5644).

**Holiday Inn** Located a mile northwest of the city center, this modern property has 120 comfortable rooms, a restaurant, and a small gym. Its friendly service, reasonable prices, and fine views of the city and the Firth of Forth from some rooms make up for its lack of historical ambience. Business facilities include meeting rooms for up to 60, foreign currency exchange, secretarial services, audiovisual equipment, photocopiers, cable television news, translation services, and express checkout. Queensberry Rd. (phone: 332-2442; 800-HOLIDAY; fax: 332-3408).

**Mount Royal** Located next to *Jenner's* department store, this 160-room hotel with a restaurant and café has splendid views of the *Scott Monument* right across the street and of *Edinburgh Castle* towering high above it. Be sure to ask for a room in the front. Business facilities include 24-hour room service, meeting rooms for up to 50, a concierge, foreign currency exchange, secretarial services, audiovisual equipment, photocopiers, translation services, and express checkout. 53 Princes St. (phone: 225-7161; fax: 220-4671).

**Norton House** Set in a secluded parkland on the edge of Edinburgh, this ornate Victorian mansion with 46 rooms was once the home of the Ushers (they founded the brewing firm). Dine in the lovely conservatory restaurant or the more informal *Norton Tavern,* located in what once was the walled garden. Business facilities include 24-hour room service, meeting rooms for up to 400, a concierge, foreign currency exchange, secretarial services, audiovisual equipment, photocopiers, translation services, and express checkout. In Ingilston, near *Edinburgh Airport* (phone: 333-1275; fax: 333-5305).

**Old Waverley** This pleasant 1870s hostelry has 66 rooms (ask for one at the front); *Cranston's,* its charming restaurant decorated in soft pink tones, has wonderful views of the *Scott Monument* and *Edinburgh Castle.* Business facilities include 24-hour room service, meeting rooms for up to 40, a concierge, foreign currency exchange, secretarial services, audiovisual equipment, photocopiers, cable television news, and translation services. 43 Princes St. (phone: 556-4648; fax: 557-6316).

**Roxburghe** One of the best examples of Robert Adam's townhouse architecture, this distinguished, tranquil oasis at the west end of Princes Street is where Scottish gentry with no townhouse of their own stay. Scottish seafood and game are the specialties in the *Consort* restaurant. There are 75 well-appointed rooms. Business facilities include 24-hour room service, meeting rooms for up to 300, a concierge, foreign currency exchange, secretarial services, audiovisual equipment, photocopiers, translation services, and express checkout. 38 Charlotte Sq. (phone: 225-3921; 800-528-1234; fax: 220-2518).

INEXPENSIVE

**Albany** Three elegant Georgian townhouses make up this comfortable hotel with 22 rooms of varying sizes and shapes. The staff is friendly and there is a restaurant and bar. 39 Albany St. (phone: 556-0397; fax: 557-6633).

**Bank** As its name implies, this hostelry, conveniently situated on the Royal Mile, used to be a bank. Still corporate-looking on the outside, it has been charmingly redecorated within, and today offers eight simply furnished guestrooms, plus a large, bistro-style café. 1 South Bridge (phone: 556-9043; fax: 558-1362).

**Donmaree** This establishment has nine rooms in the original 1830s house and eight more in a modern annex with a conservatory overlooking the gardens. The restaurant offers good, traditional dishes. 21 Mayfield Gardens (phone: 667-3641; fax: 667-9130).

**Galloway Guest House** Just off the panoramic Dean Bridge, this place has 10 rooms (six with private baths), but no restaurant (there's a breakfast lounge). There's also on-street parking. No credit cards accepted. 22 Dean Park Crescent (phone: 332-3672).

---

EATING OUT

While Scottish food cannot lay claim to culinary laurels, visitors might want to try cock-a-leekie soup (chicken and leek), salmon, haddock, trout, and Aberdeen Angus beef. Skip haggis (spicy intestines), except on a purely experimental basis. Scones originated in Scotland, and shortbread shouldn't be missed. There are a number of quality dining spots away from the center in the waterfront district of Leith. Restaurants usually keep the city's formal hours (lunch until 2:30, dinner anywhere from 6 on). The city's restaurants can get crowded during August, so call ahead. Expect to pay more than $60 for a dinner for two, excluding wine and tips, in establishments listed as expensive; $40 to $60 in moderate establishments; and less than $40 in inexpensive places. All restaurants listed below serve lunch and dinner, unless otherwise noted. All telephone numbers are in the 131 area code unless otherwise indicated.

EXPENSIVE

**L'Auberge** A discreet dining spot that serves French fare, most notably fish and game. Open daily. Reservations advised. Major credit cards accepted. 58 St. Mary's St. between Cowgate and Canongate (phone: 556-5888).

**Pompadour** The fascinating lunch menu provides a history of Scottish cooking, while dinner features French dishes (some of the recipes were used in the *Palace of Holyroodhouse* when Mary, Queen of Scots, was married to the heir to the French throne). Closed weekend lunch. Reservations advised. Major credit cards accepted. In the *Caledonian Hotel,* Princes St. (phone: 225-2433).

**Prestonfield House** A 300-year-old country estate within its own peacock-laden park grounds offers French fare in a candlelit dining room with tapestries, paintings, and an open fireplace. Open daily. Reservations necessary. Major credit cards accepted. Priestfield Rd. (phone: 668-3346).

**Stac Polly** This restaurant (formerly *Grindlay's*) is named after a Scottish mountain. The menu features well-prepared Scottish fare using fresh local ingredients such as salmon, mussels, and lamb. If you're in the mood to try haggis, this place offers an interesting version of it (wrapped in phyllo pastry). Conveniently located near the *Royal Lyceum Theatre* and *Usher Hall,* it's ideal for either pre- or post-performance dining. Closed Saturday lunch and Sunday evenings. Reservations necessary. Major credit cards accepted. 8-10 Grindlay St. (phone: 229-5405).

### MODERATE

**Atrium** Andrew Radford, formerly the chef on the luxurious *Royal Scotsman* touring train, oversees the kitchen at this elegant dining room in the foyer of the *Traverse Theatre.* The menu presents innovative versions of English and continental dishes, such as game casserole, shellfish bisque, and sticky toffee pudding. Closed Saturday lunch and Sundays. Reservations advised. Major credit cards accepted. Cambridge St. (phone: 228-8882).

**Bay of Bengal** Excellent tandoori dishes are cooked with delicate spices; there may be a bit of a wait, but it's well worth it. Closed Sunday evenings. Reservations advised. Major credit cards accepted. 164 High St. (phone: 225-2361).

**Merchant's** Trendy and French, with white tablecloths, silver, and crystal, this eatery is decorated in a minimalist style, with bare floorboards and white walls. Closed Sundays. Reservations advised. Major credit cards accepted. Off Candlemaker Row, 17 Merchant St. (phone: 225-4009).

**Patio** A trendy, attractive Italian place just off Princes Street, it serves steaks and seafood specialties along with good pizzas and pasta dishes. Closed Sundays. Reservations advised. Major credit cards accepted. 87 Hanover St. (phone: 226-3653).

**Skipper's Bistro** A jolly waterfront seafood spot in Leith, known for its imaginative preparations and fresh ingredients. Closed Sundays and Mondays. Reservations necessary. Major credit cards accepted. 1A Dock Pl., Leith (phone: 554-1018).

**Cornerstone Café** This tiny vegetarian restaurant also has tables on its outdoor terrace. Excellent salads, stuffed potatoes, rolls, and homemade cakes. Closed Sundays. No reservations. No credit cards accepted. Behind *St. John's Church,* Princes St. (phone: 229-0212).

**Harry Ramsden's** A branch of the nationwide chain of fish-and-chips eateries, this place has done a booming business ever since it opened a couple of years ago. Diners are also treated to a great view of Newhaven Harbour. Open daily. Reservations advised for large groups. Major credit cards accepted. *Newhaven Fishmarket* (phone: 551-5566).

**Pierre Victoire** Excellent fare such as salmon with raspberries and champagne and lobster in a light curry sauce, low prices, and informality have made this French-style bistro quite popular. Closed Sundays. Reservations advised. Major credit cards accepted. Three locations: 38-40 Grassmarket (phone: 226-2442), 8 Union St. (phone: 557-8451), and 10 Victoria St. (phone: 225-1721).

**Waterfront Wine Bar** A former ticketing office for ships houses this lively wine bar, which features interesting fish dishes such as smoked trout mousse. There are meats and vegetarian fare as well, and a good selection of wine and beer. Open daily. Reservations advised. Major credit cards. 1C Dock Pl., Leith (phone: 554-7426).

---

## SHARING A PINT

Edinburgh has more than 750 pubs to choose from. The largest concentration of pubs is in the waterfront district of Leith, but the most famous area is the narrow Rose Street, just a block north of Princes Street. The *Rose Brewery* (55 Rose St.; phone: 220-1227) serves Auld Reekie (named after the smell of coal smoke that used to cling to the city's buildings) that is brewed on the premises. Nearby is the *Café Royal Oyster Bar* (17 W. Register St.; phone: 556-1884), the longest bar in Britain; its stained glass windows and dark paneling were featured in the film *Chariots of Fire.* Also nearby is the *Guildford Arms* (1 W. Register St.; phone: 556-4312), a Victorian-style tavern with mahogany walls, a lovely plasterwork ceiling, and a gallery alcove where you can look down on the action in the main bar. If you enjoy folk music, try the *Fiddler's Arms* (9-11 Grassmarket; phone: 229-2665) or the *Auld Hundred* (100 Rose St.; phone: 225-1809). Another good pub with a turn-of-the-century atmosphere is the *Barony Bar* (81-85 Broughton St.; phone: 557-0546).

The large *Preservation Hall* (9 Victoria St.; phone: 226-3816) is ornamented with fine epigraphs against drink and offers rock and jazz music in the evenings. *Mather's* (25 Broughton St.; phone: 556-6754) is the ecumenical watering hole for left-wing, nationalist, and sexual politicos. Opulent barges sometimes carry licenses in tourist season on the Leith waterfront. Find out at the *Waterfront Wine Bar* (see *Eating Out*). Also try *Leith Oyster Bar* (57 The Shore, Leith; phone: 554-6294). Both offer bar lunches.

# Frankfurt

## At-a-Glance

### SEEING THE CITY

Unfortunately, the 1,086-foot *Europaturm* television tower (Western Europe's tallest)—the best place to get an overall view of the city and surrounding area—is temporarily closed for renovation; its reopening date was uncertain at press time. However, a good aerial view of Frankfurt can be seen from the tower of the *Dom* (Cathedral; see *Special Places*). You also can get a sense of the region by riding along the Main River on the historic *Eisenbahn* steam train, which runs one weekend per month. For information call 436093.

### SPECIAL PLACES

Central Frankfurt is on the right bank of a bend in the Main. Most of the commercial and historic areas are in a small area ringed by a series of green parks that follow the Altstadt (Old City) walls. Across the Main is a district called Sachsenhausen. Both these areas are ideal for exploring on foot.

#### DOWNTOWN

**AN DER HAUPTWACHE** This little square on the right side of the Main is considered the hub of Frankfurt. The centerpiece is the *Hauptwache,* a beautifully reconstructed Baroque building dating from 1730 that once served as a sentry house. You can get your bearings at the adjacent *Hauptwache Café* (phone: 281026), a lovely little eatery that serves coffee and cake and attracts locals and tourists alike; in spring and summer, tables are set up on the sidewalk outside. Just in front of the café is an escalator leading from the street to a huge underground shopping mall. Before leaving the square, you may want to visit the *Katharinenkirche* (St. Katharine's Church). Originally a convent and hospital when it was built in 1343, it has been destroyed and rebuilt several times; its main claim to fame, however, is that the poet Goethe was christened and confirmed here.

**GOETHE HAUS UND MUSEUM (GOETHE'S HOUSE AND MUSEUM)** A few blocks southwest of the Hauptwache is the home of Frankfurt's favorite son. Faithfully reconstructed after the war and furnished with many original possessions of the Goethe family, the house offers a fascinating peek at the place where the prolific poet and playwright did much of his work; it also gives visitors a sense of what 18th-century life was like in this wealthy, commercial city. In an adjoining museum are documents on Goethe's life and work as well as pictures and sculpture by well-known artists of his era. Closed weekends October through March. Admission charge. 23 Grosser Hirschgraben (phone: 282824).

**RÖMERBERG** South of the Hauptwache, on a broad square with a statue of Justice, are three adjoining burghers' houses that have served as Frankfurt's city hall since 1405. You can go in and look around on weekdays, but there are no tours. The three gabled façades and the row of seven medieval houses across the street are the symbol of the Römerberg; also here are statues of four German kaisers (Friedrich Barbarossa, Ludwig II, Charles IV, and Maximilian), as well as a sculpture of an eagle, the emblem of Frankfurt. History comes alive in the *Kaisersaal* (Imperial Hall), which is part of the complex of buildings that forms the city hall. During the imperial era, banquets were held here to celebrate the coronations of the Holy Roman Emperors; today, the *Kaisersaal* still hosts important functions. The hall is closed to visitors Mondays and when receptions are going on; admission charge. Nearby is the modern *Schirn Kunsthalle* (Schirn Hall of Fine Arts; see *Museums*). During the *Christmas* season, the city holds a special market here daily, selling locally made handicrafts, pretzels, and mulled wine.

**DOM (CATHEDRAL)** East of Römerberg Platz is this beautiful Gothic cathedral, once called the *Bartholomödom* (Cathedral of St. Bartholomew). Originally built between the 13th and 15th centuries on a Carolingian foundation dating from 852, it was destroyed by Allied bombing in 1944 and rebuilt in 1953. Now it has been completely renovated. The cathedral's outstanding features are its 15th-century dome and a tower that affords a fine view of the city. There is also a museum displaying religious vestments and exhibits about the history and architecture of the building. The museum is closed Mondays. Admission charge. Am Kaiserdom (phone: 289229).

**DER HISTORISCHE GARTEN (HISTORICAL GARDEN)** In 1953, the remains of a Roman settlement and a Carolingian imperial palace were found at this site in front of the main entrance to the *Dom.* It's the oldest site in Frankfurt. Open daily. No admission charge (no phone).

**ALT-SACHSENHAUSEN** A few steps from Römerberg, near where the ancient Franks forded the river, the Eiserner Steg footbridge leads across the river into another old section of the city. (*Sachsenhausen* means "Saxons' houses.") Here you can enjoy the jumble of half-timbered houses and rough cobbled streets with their inviting pubs and restaurants, as well as charming little squares and pretty fountains that are particularly lively meeting places at night and on weekends. There are also several museums along Schaumainkai near the river, including the *Deutsches Architekturmuseum* (Museum of German Architecture); *Deutsches Filmmuseum* (German Film Museum); and the *Museum für Völkerkunde* (Museum of Ethnology; see *Museums* for details on all three). A colorful flea market is held beside the river every Saturday, and there is a short but pleasant stretch of greenery where you can sit and gaze at the city skyline. Visit the local pubs for the special apple cider called *Stöffche* and the Frankfurt dishes *Rippchen* (pork ribs) or *Haxen* (pork foot and sauerkraut). For listings of pubs to visit in Alt-Sachsenhausen, see *Nightclubs and Nightlife.*

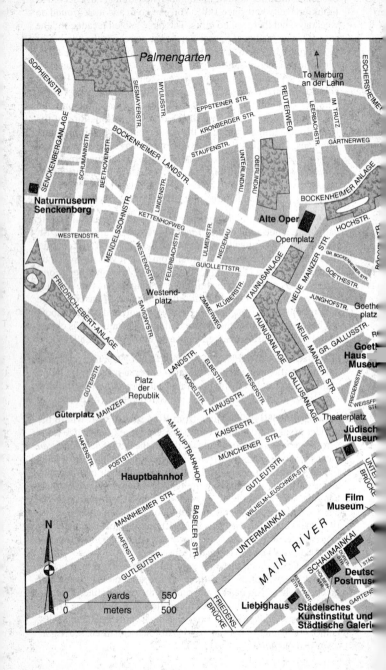

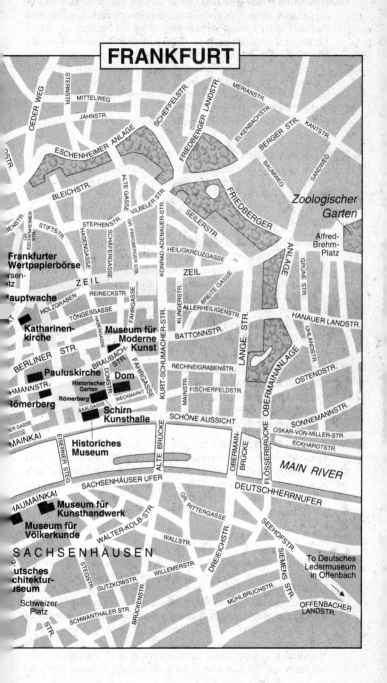

# FRANKFURT

OEDER WEG
STERNSTR.
MITTELWEG
JAHNSTR.
SCHEFFELSTR.
MERIANSTR.
FRIEDBERGER LANDSTR.
ELKENBACHSTR.
BERGER STR.
KANTSTR.
ESCHENHEIMER ANLAGE
BLEICHSTR.
BAUMWEG
SANDWEG
ALTE GASSE
VILBELER STR.
GR. FRIEDBERGER STR.
FRIEDBERGER
ANLAGE
Zoologischer
Garten
SEILERSTR.
GR. ESCHENHEIMER
STR.
STIFTSTR.
STEPHENSTR.
SCHÄFERGASSE
HASENGASSE
Alfred-
Brehm-
Platz
HEILIGKREUZGASSE
GRÜNE STR.

**Frankfurter
Wertpapierbörse**
rsen-
tz
ZEIL
ZEIL
KONRAD-ADENAUER-STR.

**auptwache**
HOLZGRABEN
REINECKSTR.
TÖNGESGASSE
BREITE GASSE
ALLERHEILIGENSTR.
KLINGERSTR.
HANAUER LANDSTR.

**Katharinen-
kirche**
FAHRGASSE
HASENGASSE
**Museum für
Moderne
Kunst**
BATTONNSTR.
LANGE STR.
UHLANDSTR.
OSTENDSTR.

BERLINER STR.
BRAUBACH STR.
DOMSTR.
FAHRGASSE
RECHNEIGRABENSTR.
OBERMAINANLAGE

**Pauluskirche**
**Historischer
Garten**
**Dom**
MAINSTR.
FISCHERFELDSTR.
SONNEMANNSTR.

HMANNSTR.
**Römerberg**
Römerberg
SAALGASSE
WECKMARKT
**Schirn
Kunsthalle**
OSKAR-VON-MILLER-STR.

er GASSE
SCHÖNE AUSSICHT
ECKHARDTSTR.

MAINKAI
EISERNER STEG
**Historiches
Museum**
ALTE BRÜCKE
OBERMAIN-
BRÜCKE
FLÖSSERBRÜCKE
MAIN RIVER

SACHSENHÄUSER UFER
DEUTSCHHERRNUFER

HAUMAINKAI
**Museum für
Kunsthandwerk**
GR. RITTERGASSE
SEEHOFSTR.

**Museum für
Völkerkunde**
WALTER-KOLB-STR.
WALLSTR.

**SACHSENHAUSEN**
DREIEICHSTR.
SIEMENS STR.
To Deutsches
Ledermuseum
in Offenbach

utsches
chitektur-
useum
STEGSTR.
GUTZKOWSTR.
WILLEMERSTR.
OFFENBACHER
LANDSTR.

Schweizer
Platz
STR.
SCHWANTHALER STR.
BRUCKENSTR.
MÜHLBRUCHSTR.

**PALMENGARTEN (PALM GARDEN)** One of Europe's most famous botanical gardens, these 55 acres of trees, meadows, ponds, gardens, and footpaths offer a welcome sanctuary from the bustling city. Over 12,000 varieties of plants grow in the park and thousands of orchids and cacti are displayed in its conservatories. A traditional Sunday afternoon entertainment in Frankfurt is a stroll through the flower gardens, perhaps pausing to listen to one of the concerts, followed by an elaborate ice-cream sundae on the flower-bedecked terrace of the *Palmengarten* restaurant (phone: 975-7510). The gardens are open daily. Admission charge. Entrance at Palmengartenstrasse (phone: 212-33939).

**ZOOLOGISCHER GARTEN (ZOOLOGICAL GARDEN)** This is one of Europe's oldest zoos, but nonetheless one of its most up-to-date. Founded in 1858, the zoo is noted for its beautifully landscaped open-air enclosures, its aviary, its collection of nocturnal animals, and its success in breeding rare species. Open daily. Admission charge. 16 Alfred-Brehm-Pl. (phone: 212-33735).

**FRANKFURTER WERTPAPIERBÖRSE (FRANKFURT STOCK EXCHANGE)** Frankfurt is one of the most important financial centers in the world. More than 400 German and overseas banks have headquarters or subsidiaries in the city. Although public access is extremely limited, no tour of the financial district would be complete without a visit to the spectators' gallery to watch the activity on the floor. Tours (available in English) are given weekdays at 10 and 11 AM and at noon, but reservations must be made at least a month in advance. No admission charge. Börsenpl. (phone: 299770).

**STÄDELSCHES KUNSTINSTITUT UND STÄDTISCHE GALERIE (STÄDEL ART INSTITUTE AND MUNICIPAL GALLERY)** Famous works of Flemish primitives and German masters of the 16th century are on display in the second-floor picture gallery. Closed Mondays. Admission charge. 63 Schaumainkai (phone: 605-0980).

**ALTE OPER (OLD OPERA HOUSE)** A victim of wartime bombing, this 100-year-old landmark was finally rebuilt in 1981. No opera is performed here, however; the ultramodern complex of rooms and halls now is used for concerts and conferences. The façade and the vestibule have been fully restored. The building is closed to the public except during performances. Opernpl. (phone: 13400).

## ENVIRONS

**WIESBADEN** The famous hot springs of this lovely spa city 19 miles (30 km) west of Frankfurt have been attracting visitors since Roman times. The mineral-laced waters are used for both bathing and drinking. A casino has been an added attraction in more recent times (see *Nightclubs and Nightlife*). The leafy Kurhausplatz in the center of town and elegant villas dating from the 19th century, both of which were largely untouched during World War II, also contribute to Wiesbaden's charm. As a special treat, dine at the superb, one-Michelin-star *Die Ente vom Lehel* in the elegant *Nassauer Hof* hotel

(3-4 Kaiser-Friedrich-Pl.; phone: 611-1330). The restaurant, which serves dinner only, is closed Sundays, Mondays, holidays, and July. Reservations necessary. Major credit cards accepted.

**DEUTSCHES LEDERMUSEUM (GERMAN LEATHER MUSEUM)** Exhibitions of the history of shoes and handbags are displayed in a wonderfully fragrant museum in Offenbach just 5 miles (8 km) southeast of Frankfurt. Open daily. Admission charge. 86 Frankfurterstr., Offenbach (phone: 813021).

**FREILICHTMUSEUM HESSENPARK (HESSENPARK OPEN-AIR MUSEUM)** Located in a northern suburb about 16 miles (25 km) from Frankfurt, this collection of typical dwellings and rustic buildings representing various regions of the state of Hesse includes houses, barns, stables, and even a church. The look is of a re-created 19th-century village. Tours are given in English, each focusing on a different craft, such as pottery or weaving. Open daily. Admission charge. Hessenpark, Neu Anspach, Taunus (phone: 6081-5880).

# Sources and Resources

TOURIST INFORMATION

For information, maps, brochures, hotel and restaurant listings, plus special sightseeing tours and tickets to local events, visit the *Frankfurter Verkehrsamt* (Frankfurt Tourist Board). It has information bureaus on the north side of the *Hauptbahnhof* (Main Train Station), opposite track 23 (phone: 212-38849 or 212-38851), and at 27 Römerberg (phone: 212-38708 or 212-38709). Both tourist information bureaus are open daily. The *US Consulate* is at 21 Siesmayerstr. (phone: 75350).

In the US there are two branches of the *German National Tourist Office* (11766 Wilshire Blvd., Suite 750, Los Angeles, CA 90025; phone: 310-575-9799; fax: 310-575-1565; and 122 E. 42nd St., 53rd Floor, New York, NY 10168; phone: 212-661-7200; fax: 212-661-7174). The *German Embassy* is at 4645 Reservoir Rd. NW, Washington, DC 20007-1998 (phone: 202-298-4000; fax: 202-298-4368).

**ENTRY REQUIREMENTS** A US citizen needs a current passport for a stay of up to 90 days.

**TIME** The time in Germany is six hours later than in US East Coast cities. Germany observes daylight saving time.

**LANGUAGE** *Hochdeutsch* (High German) is the written language and the one that's commonly spoken throughout the country. English is the second language of the country.

**ELECTRIC CURRENT** 220 volts, 50 cycles, AC.

**MONEY** The deutsche mark (DM) equals 100 pfennigs. At press time the exchange rate was 1.5 DM to the dollar.

**TIPPING** A 10% to 12% service charge is included in restaurant checks; superior service may warrant an additional amount. Porters receive 1 DM per bag. Taxi drivers should get a 15% tip.

**BANKING/BUSINESS HOURS** Most banks are open weekdays from 8:30 AM to 12:30 PM and from 1:30 to 3:30 PM; on Thursdays they close at 5:30 PM. Most other businesses throughout the country operate weekdays from 9 AM to 5 PM.

**NATIONAL HOLIDAYS** *New Year's Day* (January 1), *Epiphany* (in Bavaria and Baden-Württemberg, January 6), *Good Friday* (April 14), *Easter Sunday* (April 16), *Easter Monday* (April 17), *Labor Day* (May 1), *Ascension Thursday* (May 25), *Feast of Corpus Christi* (June 15), *Whitmonday* (June 5), *Feast of the Assumption* (August 15), *German Unity Day* (October 3), *Day of Prayer and Repentance* (November 22), *Christmas Day* (December 25), and *Boxing Day* (December 26).

**LOCAL COVERAGE** The tourist office issues *Journal,* a bimonthly publication in English that lists all special events, plus museum and restaurant information.

**TELEPHONE** The city code for Frankfurt is 69. When calling from one area to another within Germany dial 0 + city code + local number. The country code for Germany is 49. Dial 110 for emergency assistance.

## GETTING AROUND

Frankfurt has a clean, efficient, and quiet rapid-transit system of buses, streetcars, subways, and trains. The trip from the *Flughafen Frankfurt Main* (Frankfurt-Main Airport) to the city's main railway station takes only 12 minutes by train. The same kind of ticket is used for the entire system. Be advised that individual ride tickets are more expensive during morning and late afternoon–evening rush hours than they are during nonpeak hours (3 DM/$2 as opposed to 2.50 DM/$1.70). Buy tickets from automatic dispensers before boarding. There also are passes that allow unlimited travel for one day (6 DM/$4) or three days (17 DM/$11.30); they can be purchased at the tourist information bureaus (see *Tourist Information*). Maps and timetables are conveniently posted throughout the system. For information on service, contact the public transportation system (*FVV;* 15-19 Mannheimer Str.; phone: 269402).

**AIRPORT** Frankfurt's *Flughafen Frankfurt Main* (Frankfurt-Main Airport) handles both domestic and international flights. It's about a 20-minute drive from the airport to downtown. Various lines of the *S-Bahn* inter-urban train system speed their way to downtown Frankfurt in just 12 minutes (look for signs to the *S-Bahn,* and take the S-14 or S-15 train).

**BUSES AND STREETCARS** *Stadtbus* (city buses) and *Strassenbahn* (streetcars) transport passengers inexpensively to all parts of the city and to many suburbs.

**CAR RENTAL** Among major international firms represented are *Avis* (170 Mainzer Landstr.; phone: 230101); *Europcar* (at the airport; phone: 690-5464); and *Hertz,* with two locations (106-108 Hanauer Landstr.; phone: 449090; and at the airport; phone: 690-5011). If one reason for your visiting Germany is to drive a special German vehicle—Porsche, BMW, Mercedes—on the autobahn at top speed, get in touch with *Budget-Sixt* (52 Allerheiligenstr.; phone: 290066; or at the airport; phone: 697-0070), which offers luxury cars (despite its name).

**SUBWAYS AND TRAINS** The subway system, called the *U-Bahn,* and the fast trains to outlying areas, *S-Bahn,* get you where you want to go quickly and comfortably. The main stops are at Hauptwache and the *Hauptbahnhof* (Main Train Station).

**TAXI** There are stands near major hotels, stations, and at some intersections, and taxis (they are expensive) can easily be hailed on the streets. Most public telephone booths have a taxi call-number posted. For 24-hour service call 230001, 230033, or 545011.

**TOURS** The Frankfurt tourist board offers two-and-a-half-hour guided bus tours of the city which depart daily from in front of the office on Römerberg (see *Tourist Information*). *Gray Line Limousine and Coach Travel Service* (39 Wiesenhüttenpl.; phone: 230492) offers daily guided tours in English of Frankfurt and its neighboring cities. *Fahrgastschiff Wikinger II* (phone: 293960) offers Main River sightseeing cruises on steamers; the excursions leave from the dock at Eiserner Steg weekdays at 2, 3, and 4 PM (weather permitting); Sundays and holidays every half hour between 1 and 6 PM.

On weekends, you also can circle the city on the gaily painted streetcars of the *Ebbelwei Express* (phone: 213-22425). The tours are given every 30 minutes between 1:30 and 5:30 PM; commentary is available in English as well as German. You'll get music with your ride, and you can buy some of Frankfurt's famous *Apfelwein* (apple wine) to sip along the way. Hop aboard at any of the 18 *Ebbelwei Express* stops, including those in Willy-Brandt-Platz, at the *Hauptbahnhof* (Main Train Station), or at the intersection of Gartenstrasse and Schweizerstrasse in Sachsenhausen.

## LOCAL SERVICES

**DENTIST (ENGLISH-SPEAKING)** Many German dentists speak English; the *US Consulate* (see *Tourist Information*) has a list of English-speaking dentists. For emergency service, dial 660-7271.

**DRY CLEANER** *RNV Center* (41 Sandweg; phone: 233520).

**LIMOUSINE SERVICE** *Classic Limousines* (3 Am Siebenstein, Dreieich-Buchschlag; phone: 490-9220).

**MEDICAL EMERGENCY** All hospitals in Frankfurt have emergency rooms. For emergency service dial 110; to reach a doctor at any time of day or night call 19292. In addition, the *US Consulate* (phone: 75350) has a list of English-speaking physicians.

**NATIONAL/INTERNATIONAL COURIER** *DHL Worldwide Express* (20 Lyonerstr; 669040); *Federal Express* (Kelsterbach, 34 Langer Kornweg; phone: 6107-77050).

**OFFICE EQUIPMENT RENTAL** *Böhler* (Sulzbach, 12A Wiesenstr.; phone: 6196); *Max Neithold* (10 Schillerstr.; phone: 284626), for audiovisual equipment.

**PHARMACY** *Hirsch-Apotheke* (111 Zeil; phone: 281565). To find out which pharmacies are open at night, on weekends, or on holidays, dial 11500.

**PHOTOCOPIES** *E Reitz Color Copy* (27 Königsteinerstr.; phone: 303023).

**POST OFFICE** The post office at the *Hauptbahnhof* (Main Train Station; phone: 261-5113) is open 24 hours.

**SECRETARY/STENOGRAPHER (ENGLISH-SPEAKING)** *Büro-Service International* (37 Hermannstr.; phone: 555813); *Regus Business Center* (Business Zentrum, 23 Messezentrum; phone: 975447).

**TAILOR** *Flesch* (7 Martin-Luther-Str.; phone: 444777).

**TELEX** The post office at 14 Grosse Eschenheimerstr. (phone: 530-03425).

**TRANSLATOR** *Berlitz International* (66 Kaiserstr.; phone: 271040; fax: 297-7261).

**OTHER** Tuxedo and fur rental: *Amor* (43 Zeil; phone: 284271).

## SPECIAL EVENTS

Frankfurt is at its busiest during the more than a dozen trade fairs that draw some 1.2 million visitors to the city each year. The biggest of these are the *Internationale Frankfurter Messe Premiere* (International Frankfurt Trade Fair) held in winter, and the *Frankfurter Buchmesse* (Frankfurt Book Fair) in October. Most of these events are held at the *Messegelände* (Fairgrounds), a huge exhibition center near the main railway station. The tradition of trade fairs in Frankfurt dates back 800 years. There also are numerous public fairs, such as the *Main Messe* (Main Fair), held in August in the streets between the river and the *Paulskirche;* and *Dippemess,* a big country fair that takes place in front of the *Eissporthalle* (see *Sports*) in April and September, with colorful stalls of crockery being the main attraction. One other very special local holiday deserves mention: *Wäldchestag.* On the Tuesday afternoon following *Pfingstmontag* (Whitmonday—the seventh Monday after *Easter*), most Frankfurters leave the city to walk in the neighboring woods, eat sausages and drink beer, and dance in the *Oberforsthaus* (Forest House).

## MUSEUMS

In addition to those described in detail in *Special Places,* Frankfurt has a large number of interesting museums, the best of which are listed below. Unless otherwise noted, the museums listed are closed Mondays.

### DEUTSCHES ARCHITEKTURMUSEUM (MUSEUM OF GERMAN ARCHITECTURE)

The country's only museum specifically focusing on German architecture has exhibits on the country's building styles throughout history, as well as presentations on theoretical issues pertaining to architecture (ecology, responsibility to people, and more). The "house within a house," featuring several rooms of a house built within a self-contained exhibit, is especially interesting. No admission charge on Wednesdays. 43 Schaumainkai (phone: 212-38844).

**DEUTSCHES FILMMUSEUM (GERMAN CINEMA MUSEUM)** Offers permanent and changing displays about the history of films and filmmaking, both in Germany and all over the world. It also has a cinema that regularly shows movies (in German only), a bookstore, and a café. No admission charge on Wednesdays. 41 Schaumainkai (phone: 212-38830).

**DEUTSCHES POSTMUSEUM (GERMAN POSTAL MUSEUM)** Housed in two adjacent buildings are exhibits relating to the history of the communications industry in Germany, including the postal service and the development of telecommunications technology. There's also a large collection of postage stamps. No admission charge on Wednesdays. 53 Schaumainkai (phone: 60600).

**HISTORISCHES MUSEUM (HISTORICAL MUSEUM)** The life of Frankfurt and its people throughout the years is explored via models of the Altstadt, graphics, and coin collections, among other exhibits. There's also a children's museum, a library, and a café. No admission charge on Wednesdays. 19 Saalgasse, at the Römerberg (phone: 212-35599).

**JÜDISCHES MUSEUM (JEWISH MUSEUM)** Set in the magnificent palace of the Rothschilds, this museum details the social and cultural lives of Jews in Germany through permanent and temporary exhibitions, seminars, readings, and films. Admission charge. 14-15 Untermainkai (phone: 212-35000).

**LIEBIEGHAUS (LIEBIEG HOUSE)** Displays many types of sculpture, including those from ancient Greece, Egypt, and Rome. Periods covered include the Middle Ages and the Renaissance. No admission charge on Wednesdays. 71 Schaumainkai (phone: 212-38617).

**MUSEUM JUDENGASSE (JEWS' LANE MUSEUM)** Like the *Jüdisches Museum* (see above), this place has exhibits about Jewish life, but here they focus specifically on the history and culture of Frankfurt's Jewish quarter. Admission charge. 10 Kurt Schumacher Str. (phone: 297-7419).

**MUSEUM FÜR KUNSTHANDWERK (MUSEUM OF APPLIED ARTS AND CRAFTS)** Over 30,000 European books, prints, and handicrafts are housed in an elegant villa designed by American architect Richard Meier. The café here is a popular local meeting place. No admission charge on Wednesdays. 17 Schaumainkai (phone: 212-34037).

**MUSEUM FÜR MODERNE KUNST (MUSEUM OF MODERN ART)** One of Frankfurt's newer museums, it displays controversial works by international artists and examples of avant-garde architecture from the 1960s to the present. No admission charge on Wednesdays and Saturdays. 10 Domstr. (phone: 212-38819).

**MUSEUM FÜR VÖLKERKUNDE (MUSEUM OF ETHNOLOGY)** Changing exhibitions, with emphasis on the cultures of Third World countries. No admission charge on Wednesdays. 29 Schaumainkai (phone: 212-35391).

**NATURMUSEUM SENCKENBERG (SENCKENBERG MUSEUM OF NATURAL HISTORY)** Animals, plants, fossils, and geological items, including an impressive collection of dinosaurs and prehistoric whales, are displayed. Open daily. No admission charge on Wednesdays. 25 Senckenberganlage (phone: 75421).

**SCHIRN KUNSTHALLE (SCHIRN HALL OF FINE ARTS)** A museum that offers changing exhibits of modern painting and sculpture by internationally renowned artists. No admission charge on Wednesdays. Am Römerberg (phone: 299-8820).

## SHOPPING

As befits Europe's major transportation hub, Frankfurt is filled with goods from all over the world. It is said that more money passes through the cash registers of the well-stocked department stores on the Zeil than on any other street in Europe. The best-known department stores are *Kaufhof* (116 Zeil; phone: 21910) and *Hertie* (90 Zeil; phone: 29861). There are several pedestrian shopping streets besides the Zeil, including Grosse Bockenheimerstrasse, with its chic boutiques and elegant apparel stores. Incidentally, this street is known locally as Fressgass (a rough English equivalent is "Gluttony Alley") because it is lined with so many restaurants, wine bars, and delicatessens, including one of the best delis in town, *Plöger* (No. 30; phone: 20941). Two other streets, Goethestrasse and Schillerstrasse, offer a tempting variety of designer clothing stores and fine boutiques. The best buys are the well-known German cutlery, expensive but superbly made leather clothing, and Frankfurt's distinctive blue and gray pottery.

Most shops are open weekdays from 9 AM to 6:30 PM, Saturdays from 9 AM to 2 PM; on the first Saturday of the month in summer, they stay open until 4 PM. Also, some stores operate until 8:30 PM on Thursdays and until 6 PM on Saturdays.

*Cris Bittong* Distinctive women's clothing from this local designer, including silk blouses and shirts with asymmetrical patterns. 19 Oppenheimer Landstr. (phone: 628464).

*Fink Exklusiv Schühe* A local favorite, this shoe store is packed with high-quality footwear in conservative styles. 9 Goethestr. (phone: 289904).

*Francofurtensien* The perfect place to pick up a visual reminder of Frankfurt, this store is stocked with prints and paintings of local scenes, woodcuts, etchings, and even a map of the city in 1549. 11 Bethmannstr. (phone: 292324).

*Freiraum* Tin figures, glass jewelry, and decorative housewares, all locally designed and crafted. 15 Braubachstr. (phone: 296566).

*Friedrich* Brothers Christoph and Stephan Friedrich are among Germany's most famous jewelry designers; their pieces in gold, silver, and precious gems are beautiful, classic—and pricey. 17 Kaiserstr. (phone: 284353).

*Hut Lange* Hats, hats, and more hats, in a staggering variety of shapes and styles. 99 Fahrgasse (phone: 284687).

***Der Laden*** Vivi Leonhardt creates and sells wonderful leather items in her workshop, from handbags to backpacks, including custom-made pieces. 16 Danneckerstr. (phone: 617180).

***Lorey*** A veritable paradise of gift items, including Hummel, Meissen, and Rosenthal figurines. 16 Schillerstr. (phone: 299950).

***Pfuller Kinderhaus*** Children's clothing in classic, yet modern, styles. 12 Goethestr. (phone: 284547).

***Rosenthal am Kaiserplatz*** World-renowned porcelain. 38 Kaiserstr. (phone: 239822).

## SPORTS AND FITNESS

One out of every six Frankfurt residents belongs to some type of sports club, and walking and jogging along the river or the marked paths in the city forest and in the nearby Taunus Mountains are almost universal activities. Physical fitness is even sponsored by the state government, which maintains a *Trimm Dich* ("keep yourself trim") trail, a 1½-mile (2.5-km) illustrated course of exercises and jogging in the Stadtwald (City Forest; see *Jogging*).

**BICYCLING** Numerous cycling events are scheduled during the summer (check with the tourist office for details), and there are paths in the city parks and the forest. Bicycles can be rented at *Fahrrad Burger* (73 Bergerstr.; phone: 432453) and *Theo Intra* (273 Westerbachstr.; phone: 342780), which also rents touring and mountain bikes and tandems.

**FITNESS CENTER** Many major hotels have fitness facilities on their premises (see *Checking In*). In addition, two well-equipped fitness centers are *Sport- und Fitnesszentrum Judokan* (109 Zeil; phone: 280565) and *Sportschule Petrescu* (55-57 Bleichstr.; phone: 295906).

**FOOTBALL** Frankfurt's team, *Galaxy,* faces fellow members of the World League of American Football at the *Waldstadion* (362 Mörfelder Landstr.; phone: 530-9935) between April and June.

**GOLF** The 18-hole course at *Frankfurter Golfclub* is just west of *Waldstadion* (41 Golfstr.; phone: 666-2318); to play here, you must be a member of a golf club at home.

**HORSE RACING AND HORSEBACK RIDING** Flat races and steeplechase races are held at *Frankfurt-South Racecourse* in suburban Niederrad (Schwarzwaldstr.; phone: 678-7018). Horses can be rented by the hour from *Frankfurter Reit- und Fahrclub* (85 Hahnstr.; phone: 666-7585) and *Reiterbund Frankfurt* (87 Hahnstr.; phone: 666-7485).

**ICE SKATING** You can skate or just watch other people at various rinks, including one at the *Waldstadion* (362 Mörfelder Landstr.; phone: 678040) and another at the spacious *Eissporthalle Frankfurt* (Am Bornheimer Hang; phone: 212-30825).

**JOGGING** There are paths through the Stadtwald, south of the Main River and 4 miles (6 km) from downtown; take streetcar No. 14; exit Oberschweinstiege.

**SOCCER** Frankfurt is a major soccer city. Its professional club, *Eintracht,* plays to large, enthusiastic crowds at the *Waldstadion* (see *Football*) almost every other weekend from September through January.

**SWIMMING** Several hotels have swimming pools, and there are numerous indoor and outdoor pools throughout the city. For indoor swimming, visit *Rebstockbad* (7 August-Euler-Str.; phone: 708078 or 708079) or *Brentanobad* (Rödelheimer Parkweg; phone: 212-39020).

**TENNIS** Exhibition matches are played at *Waldstadion* (see *Football*) and the *Festhalle* at the *Messegelände* (Fairgrounds); contact the tourist office (see *Tourist Information*) for details. It is difficult for visitors to get court time at parks and clubs because of local demand, but three places usually have open times: *Tennisanlage Füssenich* (Sigmund-Freud-Str.; phone: 542318); *Tennisplätze Eissporthalle* (Am Bornheimer Hang; phone: 419141); and *Tennis & Squash Park Europa* (49 Ginnheimer Landstr.; phone: 532040).

## THEATER

Frankfurt has more than 20 theaters. Most performances are in German, but there are some English-language theaters, including the *Theater in Bornheim* (*TIB;* 35 Bornheimer Landwehr; phone: 493-0503) and the *English Theater* (52 Kaiserstr.; phone: 242-31620). *The Städtisches Theater* (City Theater) is in the *Städtische Bühnen* complex on Theaterplatz (phone: 236061). The *Fritz Rémond-Theater* is at the *Zoologischer Garten* (16 Alfred-Brehm-Pl.; phone: 435166), and often produces current British and American hits in German. The *Theater am Turm (TAT)* offers drama (2 Eschersheimer Landstr.; phone: 154-5110); light comedy is the specialty at *Die Kömodie* (18 Neue Mainzer Str.; phone: 284580). *Ballet Frankfurt,* a local company under the direction of American choreographer William Forsythe, presents avant-garde, often provocative productions at the *Oper* (11 Untermainanlage; phone: 236061)—not to be confused with the *Alte Oper* on Opernplatz.

## MUSIC

Whatever your taste in music, from opera or jazz to punk or pop, you'll hear it in Frankfurt. The *Städtische Opera* (City Opera) performs on the stage of the theater in the *Städtische Bühnen* arts complex (see *Theater*). There are frequent choral, symphony, and chamber music concerts at *Hessischer-Rundfunk* (8 Bertramstr.; phone: 1551), at the huge *Jahrhunderthalle* in suburban Hoechst (phone: 360-1240), and at the *Alte Oper* (see *Special Places*). Upcoming music events are posted on billboards around the city and in the daily newspaper.

## NIGHTCLUBS AND NIGHTLIFE

All of Frankfurt's big hotels offer music and dancing, and discotheques are cropping up all over the city. One of the most popular discos is *Dorian Gray* (at the airport; phone: 690-2212), modeled after New York's late *Studio 54. Tiger-Palast* (16-20 Heiligkreuzgasse; phone: 289691) features an international circus-style show with magic acts, acrobats, and juggling; there's also a bar and a restaurant where locals gather. Other good clubs include *Chamäleon* (13 Kaiserhofstr.; phone: 289977); *Cooky's* (4 Am Salzhaus; phone: 287662); *Omen* (14 Junghofstr.; phone: 282233); and *Plastic* (14 Seilerstr.; phone: 285055).

Jazz lovers will love Frankfurt, which is purported to have more than 100 daily performances, ranging from traditional New Orleans to modern jazz. *Der Jazzkeller* (18A Kleine Bockenheimerstr.; phone: 288537) is the best-known club, but you should also stop in at *Jazzkneipe* (70 Berlinerstr.; phone: 287173); *Sinkkasten Arts Club* (9 Brönnerstr.; phone: 280385); *Jazzhaus* (12 Kleine Bockenheimerstr.; phone: 287194); *Jazz-Life Podium* (22 Kleine Rittergasse; phone: 626346); and *Lorbascher Tal* (49 Grosse Rittergasse; phone: 616459).

Pub-hopping in Sachsenhausen gets merrier and merrier as the night wears on. Look for the traditional green wreath hanging over the door to identify taverns that serve Frankfurt's special *Apfelwein* (apple wine). Among the most authentic are *Mutter Ernst* (12 Alte Rothofstr.; phone: 283822), which serves beer, *Apfelwein,* and such local fare as veal cutlets, wurst, and potato salad; *Zum Gemalten Hause* (67 Schweizerstr.; phone: 614559), which has a garden; *Apfelweinwirtschaft Wagner* (71 Schweizerstr.; phone: 612565); *Zur Germani* and *Zum Kanonesteppel* (16 Textorstr.; phone: 613336), together known as *Die Insel* (The Island); *Lorsbacher Tal* (in the center of Sachsenhausen, 49 Grosse Rittergasse; phone: 616459), which has its own apple winery; and, in the nearby suburb of Seckbach, *Zum Rad* (2 Leonhardsgasse; phone: 479128), a local favorite for its friendly ambience and attractive garden terrace.

Located 10 miles (16 km) north of the city, the *Spielbank Bad Homburg* casino (phone: 61-721-70170) in Bad Homburg's *Kurpark,* occupies a special place in European gaming history. The world's first gambling casino—established in 1841 under the aegis of the celebrated brothers Blanc, who went on to create the casino at Monte Carlo 20 years later—the glittering casino served as the setting of that famous novelette of compulsive gambling, *The Gambler,* whose author, the great Russian master Fyodor Dostoyevsky, managed to run through a nonfictional fortune of his own. There's gambling—plus dining and dancing—nightly. Another casino in the area is the *Spielbank Wiesbaden* (1 Kurhauspl.; phone: 611-536100) in Wiesbaden, 19 miles (30 km) west of Frankfurt.

# Best in Town

## CHECKING IN

Although Frankfurt has a total of 200 hotels and pensions, with over 20,000 beds, only the most confident traveler comes here without a reservation. Space always is tight, and empty hotel rooms are nearly nonexistent during the big trade fairs, when, incidentally, the highest prices normally prevail. At other times, however, hotels have plenty of empty rooms on weekends, and most offer cut-rate special packages for at least Friday and Saturday nights. At an expensive hotel, expect to pay from $250 to $350 a night for a double room. Moderate hotels charge from $150 to $250; places in the inexpensive category charge less than $150 a night. Hotel rooms have private baths and TV sets, unless otherwise indicated. Virtually all hotels in Frankfurt, regardless of price, share the German virtue of cleanliness. Be aware that most of the large luxury hotels no longer include breakfast in their rates; expect to pay about $20 per person for breakfast from the buffet. Smaller hotels generally still include breakfast in the price of the room. All telephone numbers are in the 69 city code unless otherwise indicated.

## EXPENSIVE

**Arabella Grand** With 378 spacious, modern rooms, this luxury property is conveniently located in the city center. Close to the Zeil, the main shopping street, the hotel has several restaurants, a pool, and massage facilities. Business facilities include 24-hour room service, meeting rooms for up to 1,000, an English-speaking concierge, foreign currency exchange, secretarial services in English, audiovisual equipment, photocopiers, computers, cable television news, and translation services. 7 Konrad-Adenauer-Str. (phone: 29810; fax: 298-1810).

**Frankfurt Inter-Continental** One of the largest hotels in Germany, with American-style service and 849 luxuriously appointed rooms (ask for one on the river side). There are several restaurants, including the elegant *Rôtisserie*. Fitness facilities include a pool, a sauna, and a solarium. Business facilities include 24-hour room service, meeting rooms for up to 800, an English-speaking concierge, foreign currency exchange, secretarial services in English, audiovisual equipment, photocopiers, cable television news, and express checkout. 43 Wilhelm-Leuschner-Str. (phone: 26050; 800-327-0200; fax: 252467).

**Frankfurt Marriott** The tallest hotel in Germany is near the fairgrounds, but its decor is more sophisticated than you might expect from a place that caters to conventioneers. There are 585 guestrooms, several restaurants, a small disco, and a seductive piano bar, *Die Bibliotheke*. There's even a bakery on the premises. Business facilities include 24-hour room service, meeting rooms for up to 1,450, an English-speaking concierge, foreign currency exchange, secretarial services in English, audiovisual equipment, photocopiers, cable television news, and express checkout. 2-10 Hamburger Allee (phone: 79550; 800-228-9290; fax: 795-52432).

**Gravenbruch Kempinski** Advise the management of your flight arrival and they will send a limousine to whisk you to the pastoral sophistication of this elegant, 288-room hotel in a small town about 7 miles (12 km) outside Frankfurt. A perimeter of private parkland, graced by a willow-ringed pond, and a battalion of service staff will welcome you, and if there's a chill in the air, there's sure to be a well-stoked fire crackling in the lobby's hearth. Once settled in, you can decide between a wurst washed down by *Weizbier* (wheat beer) in the homey, stone-and-wood *Tor Schänke,* or the finer fare of the *Forsthaus* served under wrought-iron chandeliers. There's also an outstanding, multi-course Sunday brunch. Business facilities include meeting rooms for up to 500, an English-speaking concierge, foreign currency exchange, audiovisual equipment, photocopiers, and express checkout. Neu Isenberg (phone: 6102-5050; 800-426-3135; fax: 6102-505445).

**Sheraton Frankfurt** Walk right in from the airport's central terminal. An extension has made this one of Germany's largest hotels, with 1,050 rooms. There are three restaurants, including *Papillon,* which has an extensive continental menu and a good wine list. There's also an indoor pool and sauna. Business facilities include 24-hour room service, meeting rooms for up to 1,200, an English-speaking concierge, foreign currency exchange, audiovisual equipment, photocopiers, and express checkout. Central terminal, *Flughafen Rhein-Main* (phone: 69770; 800-334-8484; fax: 697-72230).

**Steigenberger Frankfurter Hof** Built in the tradition of grand European hotels, it was refurbished and restored to its prewar charm after serving as headquarters for the Allied occupation forces. Its 347 guestrooms are attractively furnished and feature plenty of luxury amenities. It's easy to find an attractive spot here where a waiter will bring a drink, a newspaper, or a message. International movers and shakers from the political and financial worlds dine in the elegant *Français* restaurant, while the less expensive *Frankfurter Stubb* has an extensive menu and offers excellent service (see *Eating Out* for both). Bicycle rentals are available. Business facilities include 24-hour room service, meeting rooms for up to 500, an English-speaking concierge, foreign currency exchange, secretarial services in English, audiovisual equipment, photocopiers, translation services, and express checkout. 17 Kaiserpl. (phone: 21502; 800-223-5652; fax: 215900).

### MODERATE

**Admiral** In a nice location near the zoo, this 60-room hostelry offers good service, reasonable rates, and a restaurant. Business facilities include an English-speaking concierge and photocopiers. 25 Hölderlinstr. (phone: 448021; fax: 439402).

**Am Berg** Once a private villa and now a designated historical monument, this property offers 20 large rooms, rebuilt after World War II to their original 1900 style. There's no restaurant. 23 Grethenweg (phone: 612021; fax: 615109).

**Am Dom** Although in the historic downtown area, this smallish hostelry (25 rooms) is an oasis of quiet. There is no restaurant. 3 Kannengiessergasse (phone: 282141; fax: 283237).

**Diana** Near the city center, this small (24 rooms) place offers the standard comforts, but no extras. There's no restaurant. 83 Westendstr. (phone: 747007; fax: 747079).

**Florentina** Small (28 rooms), and in a pleasant neighborhood not far from the main train station. There's no restaurant. 23 Westendstr. (phone: 746044).

**Frankfurt** A motel in the city center is a rarity in Germany. This one, with 66 rooms, is convenient and offers good service and reasonable rates. There's also a restaurant. 204 Eschersheimer Landstr. (phone: 568010).

**Maingau** In Sachsenhausen, on the south bank of the Main River, this is a particularly reasonably priced 100-room hotel with a restaurant. Business amenities include meeting rooms that seat up to 40, an English-speaking concierge, and photocopiers. 38-40 Schifferstr. (phone: 617001; fax: 620790).

**Mozart** This charming 35-room hostelry is next to the US military headquarters (the quieter rooms are in the back). There's a restaurant, and business facilities include an English-speaking concierge, foreign currency exchange, and photocopiers. 17 Parkstr. (phone: 550831).

### INEXPENSIVE

**Kautz** Located on the Sachsenhausen side of the river, this small hotel has 15 comfortably furnished rooms and a restaurant. 17 Gartenstr. (phone: 618061; fax: 613236).

**Weisses Haus** This small, pleasant 32-room hotel is conveniently located just outside the city center. No frills here, but there is a restaurant on the premises, and the rooms certainly live up to German standards for comfort and cleanliness. 18 Jahnstr. (phone: 554605; fax: 596-3912).

## EATING OUT

Though Frankfurt is not noted for its culinary artistry, local specialties are prepared just as well in restaurants as in private homes. The large population of foreign-born residents inspires a wide spectrum of European and Asian offerings. Lunch, often the main meal of the day, is served in most places between 11 AM and 3 PM. Restaurants then close until about 5:30 PM. Except in big hotel restaurants, it is difficult to just drop in anywhere for a late lunch. However, there is a late afternoon *Kaffee* ritual, at which Frankfurters fortify themselves with coffee and pastry or a snack at a *Konditorei*. A local specialty that is a perfect nosh with beer or *Apfelwein* (apple wine) is *Handkäs mit Musik:* soft limburger cheese mixed with vinegar, oil, a bit of onion, and a few caraway seeds. And whether the frankfurter originated here or not, you still can buy the best franks in Frankfurt, on the freshest rolls, from a cart right outside the *Kaufhof* department store. For a three-course lunch or dinner for two, you'll pay between $160 and $225 at restaurants in the expensive category; $95 to $155 at places in the moderate range; and less than $70 at inexpensive places. Prices do not include drinks, wine, or beer. Taxes and the tip always are included in the bill; however, it is customary to add a small extra amount for good service. All restaurants listed below are open for lunch and dinner unless otherwise noted. All telephone numbers are in the 69 city code unless otherwise indicated.

### EXPENSIVE

**Bistro Rosa** Owner Dinah Oehler has run this charming eatery for the last 10 years, and the decor reflects her fondness for pigs—there are lots of porcine paintings, prints, and sculptures, all in shades of *rosa* (pink). The menu changes seasonally, but no matter when you go, you can feast on such well-prepared delicacies as breast of duck in rhubarb sauce and marinated asparagus. Though the list of French wines is rather short, the vintages are a splendid complement to the food. Closed Sundays and holidays. Reservations necessary. Major credit cards accepted. 25 Grünebergweg (phone: 721380).

**Bistrot 77** One of the city's top restaurants, it has been run by brothers Guy and Dominique Mosbach since 1977 and features excellent presentations of French fare in a simple, tasteful setting. The menu changes frequently, but possible entrées could include perch with lentils and duck prepared in several ways. The wine list features a number of Alsatian vintages from the Mosbach vineyard. Closed Sundays (except during trade fairs) and Saturday lunch. Reservations necessary. Major credit cards accepted. 1-3 Ziegelhüttenweg (phone: 614040).

**Daitokai** Formerly *Kikkoman,* this is an elegant Japanese restaurant. Open daily; dinner only on Saturdays and holidays. Reservations advised. Major credit cards accepted. Zoo Passage, 1 Friedberger Anlage (phone: 499-0021).

**Erno's Bistro** This place has been a Frankfurt favorite for 20 years. French, with checkered tablecloths and superior cooking, it offers such outstanding entrées as filet of beef in red wine sauce and salmon with a sesame crust. Be sure to leave room for the exquisite desserts (like the tarte tatin with ice cream) and fine cheeses that await at the end of the meal. There also is an excellent and extensive wine list. Even with a reservation in hand, you may have to wait for your table (the place can get crowded), but it's worth it. Closed weekends. Reservations advised. Major credit cards accepted. 15 Liebigstr. (phone: 721997).

**Français** Well-prepared game, French cuisine, and excellent service have made this one-Michelin-star dining room at the *Steigenberger Frankfurter Hof* a particular favorite of those used to eating the best. Closed Sundays, Mondays, holidays, and for four weeks during the summer. Reservations advised. Major credit cards accepted. 17 Kaiserpl. (phone: 21502).

**Weinhaus Brückenkeller** This restaurant, especially popular with international visitors, has been awarded two Michelin stars for its first-rate continental fare. The elegant dining room is tastefully decorated with antique furniture. Among chef Alfred Friedrich's most successful dishes are salmon and turbot roulade served with caviar sauce and baby goat with green and white *Spargel* (asparagus). There's also an impressive wine list, and the service is impeccable. Open for dinner only; closed Sundays (except during trade fairs). Reservations necessary. Major credit cards accepted. 6 Schützenstr. (phone: 284238).

## MODERATE

**Alte Brückenmühle** On the Sachsenhausen side of the river, this cozy eatery's decor is in the traditional, Old German style. The menu features the choicest cuts of veal, beef, pork, poultry, game, and fish—all prepared according to old Frankfurt recipes. Lunch specials are especially reasonable. Closed Saturday lunch. Reservations advised. Major credit cards accepted. 10 Wallstr. (phone: 612543).

**Altes Zollhaus** Travelers who could not make it through the Frankfurt city gates in time once found refuge for the night in this former customs house, dating from the 18th century. It's now a restaurant specializing in local dishes. Closed Mondays. Reservations advised. Major credit cards accepted. 531 Friedberger Landstr. (phone: 472707).

**Frankfurter Stubb** German specialties are beautifully prepared in this well-appointed cellar restaurant at the *Steigenberger Frankfurter Hof.* The decor is inspired by Goethe, including a window from his childhood house and framed anecdotes and prints depicting the great poet's life. During May, when white *Spargel* (asparagus) from the Schwetzinger area south of Frankfurt is in season, it is presented here in an imaginative array of dishes, served with wine chosen to complement its delicate flavor. Diners also can enjoy Franconian specialties such as boiled beef with green sauce and *Handkäs mit Musik* (cheese served with raw onions in vinaigrette). Closed Sundays. Reservations advised. Major credit cards accepted. 33 Bethmannstr. (phone: 215679).

**Gargantua** Despite its name, this charming bistro is an intimate place that attracts diners who come for—and receive—first class continental fare at reasonable prices. The prix fixe menu, featuring four to six courses with fine wines, is an especially good deal, but dishes are available à la carte as well. Closed Sundays (except during trade fairs) and Saturday lunch. Reservations advised. Major credit cards accepted. 3 Friesengasse (phone: 776442).

## INEXPENSIVE

**Altes Café Schneider** In business since 1906, this eatery/bakery has an Old World charm that sets it apart from other, more modern cafés in the city. Though especially popular for its sumptuous pastries (best enjoyed over a hot cup of coffee in the afternoon), the breakfast and lunch menus offer good local specialties at excellent prices. Open for breakfast and lunch only; closed Sundays and holidays.

No reservations. No credit cards accepted. 12 Kaiserstr. (phone: 281447).

**Da Pang** This little Chinese restaurant is an ideal place to grab a quick, inexpensive lunch or snack. Menu items include various kinds of soup, spring rolls, and Szechuan-style meat and seafood dishes. *Note:* Since the neighborhood can get very rough after dark, it's best to come here for lunch. Open daily. Reservations advised. Major credit cards accepted. 17 Weserstr. (phone: 235483).

**Harvey's** A relatively recent addition to Frankfurt's restaurant scene, this café on the north side of the city offers good food and a quirky ambience that have quickly endeared it to locals. The highlight of the dramatic decor is the gilded bar and the striking modern murals on the walls; the menu offers a wide selection of seafood, meat, and vegetarian dishes. A good breakfast is served here, too. Open daily. No reservations. No credit cards accepted. 64 Bornheimer Landstr. (phone: 497303).

**Klein Markthalle** Located above the international food market hall, this restaurant is one of the best kept secrets in town. Locals flock here to partake of genuine home cooking in a friendly, home-style setting. The fare, including veal cutlets, fried potatoes, and omelettes, is hearty and very tasty. Open for breakfast and lunch only; closed Sundays. No reservations. No credit cards accepted. 5 Hasengasse (phone: 293498).

**Künstlerkeller** Set in the cellar of a former Carmelite monastery dating from the 13th century, this place serves a menu of well-prepared local dishes. The convivial patrons will make you feel both comfortable and welcome. Closed Mondays. No reservations. Major credit cards accepted. 1 Münzgasse (phone: 292242).

**Saladin** Here is an informal eatery with a buffet of salads, soups, vegetarian entrées, and meat and seafood dishes, all freshly prepared and served cafeteria-style. Closed Sundays. No reservations. No credit cards accepted. 6 Adalbertstr. (phone: 779005).

**Steinernes Haus** This traditional beer hall, set in a rustic stone house built in the 15th century, serves up a menu of hearty specialties, including steak grilled tableside and liver dumplings with sauerkraut and mashed potatoes, along with a wide variety of beers and ales. Open daily. No reservations. No credit cards accepted. 35 Braubachstr. (phone: 283491).

# Geneva

## At-a-Glance

### SEEING THE CITY

The best view of the town and its surroundings is from the north tower of *Cathédrale St-Pierre;* on a clear day it is worth the 153 steps and the price of admission; the panorama of city, lake, Alps, and Jura Mountains is spectacular. Another superb view—and the one most often photographed—is from the Quai du Mont-Blanc near the bridge; on the sailboat-dotted lake you can see the famous *Jet d'Eau,* pride of Geneva, with the Alps as a backdrop.

### SPECIAL PLACES

Geneva can easily be explored on foot.

#### VIEILLE VILLE (OLD TOWN)

Built on a hill around its famous Reformation-era *Cathédrale St-Pierre* (St. Peter's Cathedral), the Vieille Ville was important in medieval times as the site of international fairs. Stroll down the narrow, cobblestone streets, discovering delightful corners like Place du Bourg-de-Four, the former market square. Have coffee or a snack in one of the cafés and browse in the antiques stores. In summer regular walks in the Vieille Ville with English-speaking guides are offered; ask at the tourist office for details.

#### CAROUGE

Just across the River Arve, less than half a mile from the downtown area, is a little old town with low houses, shady squares, fountains, and pubs. Although this enchanting place is within the city limits, the residents here live quiet lives independent of busy Geneva. Carouge is becoming more and more popular after dark, however, when folks fill its cafés and small theaters.

#### DOWNTOWN

**CATHÉDRALE ST-PIERRE (ST. PETER'S CATHEDRAL)** Built in the 12th and 13th centuries on the site of earlier churches, the *Cathédrale St-Pierre* later was reconstructed; John Calvin preached here, and his chair is displayed. The archaeological excavations of a 4th-century church under the present structure are open to the public. Closed Mondays and at lunchtime. Admission charge to view the excavations. Cour St-Pierre.

**AUDITOIRE CALVIN (CALVIN AUDITORIUM)** Next door to *Cathédrale St-Pierre* is a Gothic church where the Scottish Protestant John Knox once preached; it was restored in 1959 for the 450th anniversary of John Calvin's birth. Rue de la Taconnerie.

**MAISON TAVEL** A few steps from the *Auditoire Calvin* is the oldest house in Geneva. Inside, the *Musée de la Vieille Genève* (Museum of Old Geneva) features a collection of historic engravings as well as changing exhibitions on the Vieille Ville. Closed Mondays. No admission charge. 6 Rue du Puits-St-Pierre (phone: 282900).

**HÔTEL DE VILLE (TOWN HALL)** This is where the Geneva Convention was signed in 1864. (Ask the guard to show you the room where the signing took place.) Its oldest part is *Tour Baudet* (Baudet Tower), erected in 1455. Rue de l'Hôtel-de-Ville.

**EGLISE ST-GERMAIN (ST. GERMAIN CHURCH)** On the site of an early Christian basilica, it is a fine example of 15th-century Gothic architecture. The beautiful stained glass windows are modern. Rue des Granges.

**MUR DES RÉFORMATEURS (REFORMATION MONUMENT)** Under the ramparts that used to surround the town, in a pleasant park belonging to the university, is a long, plain wall, erected in 1917, with statues of the main Protestant Reformation leaders and other important personages. Bas-reliefs and tablets tell the story of John Calvin. Promenade des Bastions.

**THE QUAYS** Quai du Mont-Blanc (see *Seeing the City*) is a good place to start a tour of the quays. It's the site of several hotels, a landing pier, and a monument to the Duke of Brunswick, who left his fortune to the town about 100 years ago (with the condition that he get a monument). Don't miss the panoramic table on the quay, a map of nearby and distant peaks that are especially beautiful when the sun sets on the Alps. To the north, the quay ends at the *Jardins Botaniques* (Botanical Gardens), a series of manicured parks. Along the riverfront west of the Pont (Bridge) du Mont-Blanc runs the Quai des Bergues, with the charming Ile Rousseau (Rousseau Island) just off it. On the other side of the Pont du Mont-Blanc is the *Jardin Anglais* (English Garden), with a huge clock whose face is composed of living flowers; it keeps the exact time. From the *Jardin Anglais,* the Quai Gustave-Ador eventually runs into the delightful *Parc de la Grange,* with one of the finest rose gardens in Europe.

**PALAIS DES NATIONS** The former *League of Nations* palace, as big as *Versailles,* now houses the European section of the *UN* as well as a small museum of diplomatic history and a philatelic museum. There are daily guided tours. Closed for the two weeks following *Christmas.* Admission charge. Av. de la Paix (phone: 734-6011). Nearby are the headquarters of the *World Health Organization* (20 Ave. Appia; phone: 791-2111); the *International Red Cross* (19 Ave. de la Paix; phone: 734-6001); and the *International Labor Office* (4 Rue des Morillons; phone: 799-6111). The latter building has an especially striking interior. Visits to the three organizations' offices can be arranged for groups by special request.

**MUSÉE D'ART ET D'HISTOIRE (MUSEUM OF ART AND HISTORY)** The archaeological section of this museum features medieval furniture, sculpture, an armory; and the fine arts collection also is excellent. A highlight is Conrad Witz's *Miraculous Fishing*—painted in 1444 for an

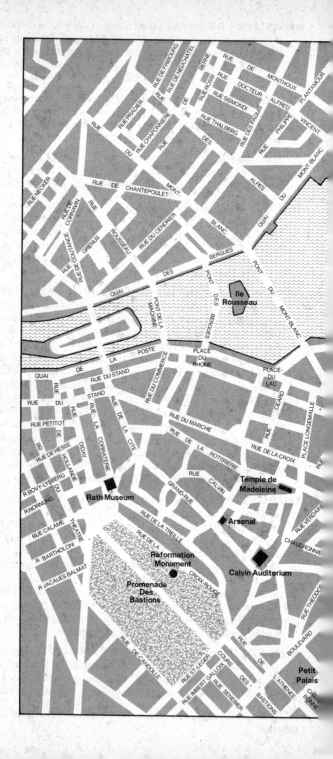

# GENEVA

LAKE GENEVA

PROMENADE DU LAC

**Jardin Anglais**

QUAI GENERAL GUISAN

RUE DU RHONE

D'ITALIE

RUE DE RIVE

RUE

ROND-POINT DE RIVE

RUE PIERRE FATIO

RUE VERSONNEX

R. DE LA SCIE

RUE MUZY

QUAI

RUE DU LAC

QUAI GUSTAVE ADOR

GUSTAVE ADOR

RUE DU ROVERAY

RUE DU TRENTE - ET-UN-DECEMBRE

RUE DES EAUX-VIVES

RUE BLANVALET

RUE DE LA MAIRIE

RUE DE MONCHOISY

RUE DU NANT

**To Parc de la Grange**

BD HELVETIQUE

RUE DES GLACIS DE RIVE

DU PARC

AV DE FRONTENEX

RUE DE LA TERRASSIERE

RUE ST-LAURENT

RUE ADRIEN LACHENAL

RUE DE VILLEREUSE

RUE DELAVALLEE

RUE DALCROZE

RUE FERDINAND

AMI LULLIN

HODLER

LEFORT

BOULEVARD

RUE

RUE CHARLES

GALLAND

RUE MONT- DE-SION

BOULEVARD DES TRANCHEES

RTE DE MALAGNOU

RUE DE MONNETIERRE

RUE VICTOR

**Museum of Art and History**

**Museum of Old Musical Instruments**

N

| 0 | | yards | 330 |
| 0 | | meters | 300 |

altar of the cathedral—which depicts medieval Geneva in the background. Closed Monday mornings. No admission charge. 2 Rue Charles-Galland (phone: 290011).

**MUSÉE DE L'HORLOGERIE (WATCH MUSEUM)** This is an exquisite collection of watches, clocks, and enamel works from the 16th century on, with emphasis on artisans from Geneva. The setting is a charming townhouse and park. Closed Tuesdays. No admission charge. 15 Rte. de Malagnou (phone: 736-7412).

**COLLECTIONS BAUR (BAUR COLLECTIONS)** In the home of the original owner, this is a private collection of superb Chinese and Japanese ceramics. Closed mornings and Mondays. Admission charge. 8 Rue Munier-Romilly (phone: 461729).

**MUSÉE BARBIER-MUELLER (BARBIER-MUELLER MUSEUM)** An outstanding private collection of primitive art, it has exhibits of African, Indonesian, Pacific, and pre-Columbian items. Closed mornings, Sundays, and Mondays. Admission charge. Rue Jean-Calvin (phone: 786-4646).

**MUSÉE D'INSTRUMENTS ANCIENS DE MUSIQUE (MUSEUM OF OLD MUSICAL INSTRUMENTS)** This private collection was bought by the city, but its former owner is still the curator. All the instruments, however old, can be played, and on occasion visiting musicians do just that. Open Tuesdays, Thursdays, and Fridays; call ahead to check hours. Admission charge. Next to the Russian church at 23 Rue Lefort (phone: 469565).

**MUSÉE DE L'HISTOIRE DES SCIENCES (MUSEUM OF THE HISTORY OF SCIENCE)** A collection of mathematical, medical, astronomical, and other scientific instruments and souvenirs displayed in a lovely setting. Closed mornings and from November through March. No admission charge. Villa Bartholoni, 128 Rue de Lausanne (phone: 731-6985).

**INSTITUT ET MUSÉE VOLTAIRE** Voltaire's former residence is filled with his furniture, art objects, manuscripts, correspondence, and works. Closed mornings and weekends. No admission charge. 25 Rue des Délices (phone: 447133).

**MUSÉE INTERNATIONALE DE LA CROIX-ROUGE (INTERNATIONAL RED CROSS MUSEUM)** A collection of Red Cross documents from 1863 to the present. Closed Tuesdays. Admission charge. 17 Av. de la Paix (phone: 734-5248).

**MUSÉE JEAN-JACQUES-ROUSSEAU (JEAN-JACQUES ROUSSEAU MUSEUM)** The manuscripts, letters, pictures, and death mask of Rousseau (1712–78) can be seen here. Closed Saturday afternoons and Sundays. No admission charge. *Bibliothèque Universitaire* (University Library), Salle Lullin, Promenade des Bastions (phone: 208266).

ENVIRONS

**BIBLIOTHÈQUE BODMER (BODMERIAN LIBRARY)** In the luxurious villa of Zurich millionaire Martin Bodmer, in the suburb of Cologny (about 2 miles/3 km east of Geneva), this is a unique private collection of rare manuscripts, first editions, and incunabula (books printed before 1501). The exhibitions change occasionally. The villa also houses a research institute and offers a panoramic view of the lake and the town. Open Thursday afternoons and the first Tuesday of the month. Admission charge. Rte. du Guignard, Cology (phone: 736-2370).

**CHÂTEAU DE PENTHES** In a lovely park, this 18th-century private château features views of the Alps and lake. It houses the *Musée des Suisses à l'Etranger* (Museum of Swiss Expatriates), with documents from the Middle Ages to the 1980s. The *Musée Militaire Genevois* (Geneva Military Museum) is in an adjoining pavilion. Closed Mondays. Admission charge. 18 Chemin de l'Impératrice, Pregny-Chambésy, about a mile (1.6 km) outside the city (phone: 734-9021).

**LAC LEMAN (LAKE GENEVA) AND THE RHÔNE** Beautiful Lake Geneva, 45 miles long, with Geneva on its western end, Lausanne in the middle, and Vevey and Montreux to the east, has been popular with nature lovers since the days of Rousseau. Its southern shore is in France; the northern shore in Switzerland is the more famous part. The Romantics loved Lake Geneva, particularly the area around Vevey and Montreux, and the list of greats who've lived here includes Byron, Goethe, Hugo, and Balzac. The *Château de Chillon*—celebrated by Byron in "The Prisoner of Chillon"—can be visited by boat. This 9th-century castle held François Bonivard prisoner; he was chained to a pillar for four years (1532–36) for delivering Protestant sermons.

A trip on the lake is a must. Cruises of varying lengths are offered several times a day (except in winter); lunch cruises also are recommended. In addition, there are daily trips down the shores of the Rhône River. For details inquire at the tourist office (see *Tourist Information,* below); at *Navigation Mouettes Genevoises* (8 Quai du Mont-Blanc; phone: 732-2944); or at *Compagnie Générale de Navigation* (*Jardin Anglais;* phone: 311-2521).

**CHÂTEAU DE COPPET** On Lake Geneva, in the charming town of Coppet, is the residence of the Paris-born Baroness Germaine de Staël (1766–1817), the meeting place of some of the greatest minds of the 18th and early 19th centuries. Madame de Staël led a complicated and unconventional life, which she described in her autobiography. She wrote several successful novels and a study of German Romanticism that so enraged Napoleon that he destroyed an entire edition as "un-French"; in 1803 she was forced to flee France to Geneva. Closed November through January and Mondays. Admission charge. Coppet, about 7 miles (11 km) north along the lake from Geneva (phone: 776-1028).

---

### EXTRA SPECIAL

Nearby Mt. Salève looms 4,000 feet over the lake and seems close enough to touch, but it's actually in France, about 4 miles (6 km) away. Drive or take the No. 8 bus (catch it at the *Gare Cornavin,* the main

---

train station) to Veyrier, where a cable car ride affords a view of the Vallée d'Arve (Arve Valley), Geneva, and Mont-Blanc. In warm weather, Mt. Salève is a center for hang gliding.

# Sources and Resources

## TOURIST INFORMATION

For general information, brochures, and maps contact the *Office du Tourisme de Genève* at the main train station, *Gare Cornavin* (Pl. Cornavin; phone: 738-5200; fax: 731-9056), or at 1 Tour-de-L'Ile (phone: 310-5031; fax: 311-8965). A branch office of the *US Embassy* is at 1-3 Ave. de la Paix, Chambesy/Geneva (phone: 799-0211).

In the US, the *Swiss National Tourist Office* has three branches (150 N. Michigan Ave., Suite 2930, Chicago, IL 60601; phone: 312-630-5840; fax: 312-630-5848; 222 N. Sepulveda Blvd., Suite 1570, El Segundo, CA 90245; phone: 310-335-5980; fax: 310-335-5982; and 608 Fifth Ave., New York, NY 10020; phone: 212-757-5944; fax: 212-757-6116). The *Swiss Embassy* is at 2900 Cathedral Ave. NW, Washington, DC 20008 (phone: 202-745-7900).

**ENTRY REQUIREMENTS** A US citizen needs a current passport for a stay of up to 90 days.

**TIME** The time in Switzerland is six hours later than in US East Coast cities. Switzerland observes daylight saving time.

**LANGUAGE** French, German, Italian, and Romansh, a Romance language derived from Latin, are all spoken in Switzerland. The more than two dozen Swiss-German dialects, called collectively Schweizerdeutsch, vary from region to region. English is widely understood.

**ELECTRIC CURRENT** 220 volts, 50 cycles, AC.

**MONEY** The Swiss franc (SFr) equals 100 centimes or rappen. The exchange rate at press time was 1.28 Swiss francs to the dollar.

**TIPPING** A 15% service charge is included in hotel, restaurant, and bar bills, as well as taxi fares, so that only porters and bellhops require tips (about 1 SFr per bag).

**BANKING/BUSINESS HOURS** Most banks are open weekdays from 8:30 AM to 4:30 PM. Most other businesses are open weekdays from 9 AM to 5 PM, but many offices close between noon and 2 PM.

**NATIONAL HOLIDAYS** *New Year's Day* and the day after (January 1 and 2), *Good Friday* (April 14), *Easter Sunday* (April 16), *Easter Monday* (April 17), *Ascension Thursday* (May 25), *Whitmonday* (June 5), *Independence Day* (August 1), *Jeûne Fédéral* (Fasting Day, the first Thursday in September; September 7 this year), and *Christmas* (celebrated December 25 and 26).

**LOCAL COVERAGE** *This Week in Geneva,* a bilingual publication, is good for practical and cultural information and advertisements; it also contains a concise "guided tour" of the city. There are no local newspapers in English, but the daily *International Herald Tribune* is available for world news.

**TELEPHONE** The city code for Geneva and surrounding areas is 22. When calling from one area to another within Switzerland dial 0 + city code + local number. The country code for Switzerland is 41. In an emergency, dial 144 for an ambulance; 117 for the police.

## GETTING AROUND

**AIRPORT** *Aéroport Cointrin* (Cointrin Airport; phone: 799-3111) handles both domestic and international traffic. It's about a 15-minute drive from downtown. There is train service between the airport and the main train station, *Gare Cornavin.*

**BUS** Buses are numerous and frequent. Buy tickets from the vending machines found at all stops (you cannot buy a ticket on the bus, and you are fined if found without one). Tickets cost between 1.60 and 3 Swiss francs (roughly $1.25 to $2.25), depending on the number of zones traveled. One-, two-, or three-day passes for unlimited transport on buses and trolleys are available, and Swiss Pass holders may use their passes for city transport. Booklets with bus routes are sold at *Gare Cornavin* (Pl. Cornavin). Bus No. 1, which leaves from *Gare Cornavin,* offers a sightseeing tour in English.

**CAR RENTAL** All major firms are represented at the airport and in the city. Note that while the rates are among the highest in Europe, unlike elsewhere on the continent no Value Added Tax is levied.

**TAXI** Taxis are much more expensive than in the US, but the tip is included in the fare. They can be hailed all over the city; the light on top indicates availability.

**TRAIN** The main train station is *Gare Cornavin* (Pl. Cornavin; phone: 731-6450).

## LOCAL SERVICES

**DENTIST (ENGLISH-SPEAKING)** *Alliance des Cliniques Dentaires* (5 Rue Mallombré; phone: 466444) provides names and addresses around the clock.

**DRY CLEANER/TAILOR** *Baechler* (3 Pl. Molard; phone: 311-6039) and other locations.

**LIMOUSINE SERVICE** *Globe SA* (36 Rue de Zurich; phone: 731-0750).

**MEDICAL EMERGENCY** *Hôpital Cantonal Universitaire* (24 Rue Michel-du-Crest; phone: 372-3311 or 382-3311). *Permanence Médicale* (21 Rue de Chantepoulet; phone: 731-2120), dispensary and surgery open 24 hours; major credit cards accepted.

**MESSENGER SERVICE** *DHL Worldwide Express* is used for local deliveries (see below).

**NATIONAL/INTERNATIONAL COURIER** *DHL Worldwide Express* (40 Av. Aïre; phone: 344-4400).

**OFFICE EQUIPMENT RENTAL** *Thiéry* (8 Rue des Corps-Saints; phone: 732-4911); also, ask your hotel concierge.

**PHARMACY** *Pharmacie Centrale* (9 Rue du Mont-Blanc; phone: 731-9740 or 731-3856).

**PHOTOCOPIES** *TEX SA* (1 Pl. St-Gervais; phone: 732-6704 or 731-6681).

**POST OFFICE** The main post office (18 Rue du Mont-Blanc; phone: 739-2111) is open from 7:30 AM to 10:45 PM.

**SECRETARY/STENOGRAPHER (ENGLISH-SPEAKING)** *Manpower* (4 Rue Winkelried; phone: 731-6800); *Recipa* (14 Rue de la Corraterie; phone: 310-9188); *Regus Business Center* (14 Rue du Rhône; phone: 311-2768).

**TELEX** Go to the telegraph window at the main post office (see above), and other post offices (at Rue du Stande, Pl. de la Poste).

**TRANSLATOR** *Intercongress* (54 bis, Rte. des Acacias; phone: 343-5179); *Traducta* (2 Rue Môle; phone: 732-6393).

**OTHER** Tuxedo rental: *Balestra* (20 Av. Mail; phone: 328-4140), by appointment.

## SPECIAL EVENTS

The *International Motor Show,* held for 10 days in early March, is one of the most important in Europe. With a display of the latest products, the *Salon International de la Haute Horlogerie* (International Watch and Jewelry Show) will be held from April 20 to 26 this year. The *Fête d'Indépendance* (Independence Day Celebration, August 1) commemorates the founding of the Swiss Confederation and is celebrated with bonfires on the hills. The *Fête de Genève* takes place on a long weekend in mid-August; there are fairs and processions, culminating in fireworks on the lake. The *Escalade* (on or around December 13) is the most typically Genevois celebration; it marks the city's 1602 victory over the Savoyard enemy with a colorful evening torchlight pageant, medieval costumes, and all-night partying.

## MUSEUMS

Besides those described in *Special Places,* the following museums may be of interest. All are closed Mondays unless otherwise indicated.

**MUSÉE D'ETHNOGRAPHIE (ETHNOGRAPHIC MUSEUM)** A rich worldwide collection. No admission charge. 65-67 Bd. Carl-Vogt (phone: 281218).

**MUSÉE D'HISTOIRE NATURELLE (NATURAL HISTORY MUSEUM)** The most modern natural history display in Europe. No admission charge. 1 Rte. de Malagnou (phone: 735-9130).

**MUSÉE HISTORIQUE DE LA RÉFORMATION (MUSEUM OF THE REFORMATION)** A monument to the most important figures of the Protestant Reformation, located in the *Salle Lulin* of the *Bibliothéque Universitaire* (University Library). No admission charge. Promenade des Bastions (phone: 208266).

**PETIT PALAIS** Art from 1890 to the present, with an emphasis on works by Renoir and Picasso. Closed Monday mornings. Admission charge. 2 Terr. St-Victor (phone: 461433).

## SHOPPING

The main shopping area, with the best and most expensive stores, is around Rue du Rhône and its parallel and side streets. Other shopping streets are *les rues basses,* literally "lower streets," near the lake: A few of these are Rue du Marché, Rue de la Confédération, and Rue de Rive. In addition, many new (and expensive) boutiques and gift shops have opened on the small streets around Place du Bourg-de-Four in the Vieille Ville. Antiques shops are concentrated on Rue de la Cité, Rue de l'Hôtel-de-Ville, and Grande Rue.

Geneva's version of New York City's Trump Tower, the *Centre Commercial de la Confédération* (Rue de la Confédération), features several levels of shops and cafés in an attractive Art Nouveau decor. The city's best-known department stores are *Placette* (9 Rue Grenus; phone: 731-7400) and *Grand Passage* (50 Rue du Rhône; phone: 206611).

Geneva's best buys are watches—the most famous in the world— jewelry, toys, clothes, and the ubiquitous Swiss Army knives. There is a flea market on Wednesdays and Saturdays on the Plain de Plainpalais and a flower and vegetable market on Saturday mornings on the streets of *les rues basses.*

General shopping hours are weekdays from 9 AM to 6:30 PM (to 9 PM on Thursdays), and Saturdays from 9 AM to 4 PM. Other recommended shops:

*Les Ambassadeurs* This shop specializes in Audemars-Piguet watches. 39 Rue du Rhône (phone: 285566).

*B&B* For timepieces by Ebel. Quai du Mont-Blanc (phone: 732-3118).

*Bally Scheurer* A good selection of famous footwear. 62 Rue du Rhône (phone: 328-1066).

*A la Bonbonnière* The place to find Geneva's best chocolates. 11 Rue de Rive (phone: 216196).

*Bon Génie* Fashion for men and women. At several locations, including the *Inter-Continental Hotel,* 7-9 Chemin du Petit-Saconnex (phone: 733-4545).

*Bucherer* Watches and jewelry. 45 Rue du Rhône (phone: 311-6266).

*Centre Genevois de l'Artisanat* Swiss crafts. 2 Ave. du Mail (phone: 329-1144).

*Au Chalet Suisse* Lace blouses and tablecloths, and hand-embroidered accessories. 18 Quai du Général-Guisan (phone: 218210).

**Chocolat Arn** Another of the city's luscious chocolate shops. 12 Pl. du Bourg-de-Four (phone: 204094).

**Chocolaterie du Rhône** World class sweets, including the quintessential chocolate truffle. 3 Rue de la Confédération (phone: 311-5614).

**Collet** Still more fine jewelry. 8 Pl. du Molard (phone: 210877).

**Confiserie Hautlé** Yet another windfall for the chocoholic. At 21 Pl. du Bourg-de-Four (phone: 203773).

**Davidoff** The original home of these famous cigars. 2 Rue de Rive (phone: 289041).

**Elm Books** A well-stocked English bookstore. 5 Rue Versonnex (phone: 736-0945).

**Galerie Catherine van Notten** Swiss paintings. 17 Grande Rue (phone: 280-3932).

**Gérard Père & Fils** A paradise for cigar smokers. At the *Noga-Hilton,* 19 Quai du Mont-Blanc (phone: 732-6511).

**Gübelin** More fine watches and jewelry. 1 Pl. du Molard (phone: 288655).

**Jouets Weber** Miniature replicas of trains and cars for grownups. 12 Rue Croix-d'Or (phone: 284255).

**Librairie des Amateurs** English, German, and French classic books. 15 Grande Rue (phone: 213313).

**Ludwig Muller** Original jewelry designs. Rue de Chaudronniers (phone: 202930).

**Aux Mille Cadeaux** Lovely gifts, music boxes, and cuckoo clocks. 11 Rue Céard (phone: 213010).

**Naville** The biggest international bookstore in Geneva has four branches. 5 Rue de la Confédération (phone: 292133) and 5-7 Rue Lévrier (phone: 732-2400) are the most central. The other two are at 11 Rue Prince (phone: 280111) and 61 Rte. Flourissant (phone: 310-0111).

**Patek Philippe** The famous timepieces and jewelry. 22 Quai du Général-Guisan (phone: 781-2448).

**Piaget** More timepieces and jewelry. 40 Rue du Rhône (phone: 310-7388).

**Salomé** Art Deco and contemporary furnishings and accessories. 5 Rue de Chaudronniers (phone: 311-0370).

**Schmitt** An antiques shop in the Vieille Ville specializing in English furniture, silverware, plates, and lamps. 3 Rue de l'Hôtel-de-Ville (phone: 310-3540).

**Sturzenegger** Fine Swiss embroidery and linen. 3 Rue du Rhône (phone: 289534).

**Tabbah** Pricey jewelry and other trifles. 25-27 Rue du Rhône (phone: 281860).

*Teuscher* Fabulous chocolates in the *Confederation Center*. 8 Rue de la Confédération (phone: 310-4410).

## SPORTS AND FITNESS

**FITNESS CENTER** The *John Valentine Fitness Club* (12 Rue Gautier; phone: 732-8050) offers a day pass for visitors.

**GOLF** Geneva has no public courses. The 18-hole *Golf Club of Geneva* (phone: 735-7540), in a magnificent setting in Cologny, is private but accepts guests who call in advance. It's closed December through February.

**ICE SKATING** Indoor and outdoor skating is offered only in winter, at *Les Vernets* skating rink at Quai des Vernets (phone: 438850).

**JOGGING** Best for running are *Parc Mon Repos, Parc Bertrand, Parc des Eaux-Vives,* and the quays on both sides of the lake.

**SAILING** The obvious sport in Geneva; rentals are available all along the quays, especially Quais Mont-Blanc, Wilson, and Gustave-Ador.

**SKIING** There are excellent runs, very crowded on weekends, within an hour's drive of Geneva at the marvelous resorts of Haute Savoie in France. The best known are Chamonix (phone: 50-530024) and Megève (phone: 50-212728), about an hour away; the newest resort, Flaine (phone: 50-908001), is even closer. The closest good skiing in Switzerland is in Champéry (phone: 25-791141) or on the glacier of Les Diablerets (phone: 25-532348), about 1½ hours away.

**SOCCER** Football, as it's called in Europe, is very popular here. Matches are held at *Stade des Charmilles,* on Chemin des Sports in the district of Les Charmilles, and at other stadiums (see the tourist office for schedule information).

**SWIMMING** Beaches on the lake are open in summer; they include Plage de Genève (Geneva Beach) on Quai Gustave-Ador, Pâquis Plage (Pâquis Beach) on the Quai du Mont-Blanc, and two beaches on the Route de Lausanne. An indoor pool, *Les Vernets,* is in the suburb of Acacias (4-6 Rue Hans-Wilsdorf; phone: 438850).

**TENNIS** There are several clubs; courts must be reserved in advance. Try the *Geneva Tennis Club* at *Parc des Eaux-Vives* (phone: 735-5350).

## THEATER

The major theaters are the *Théâtre de Carouge* (Rue Joseph-Girard; phone: 434343) and *Le Caveau* (Av. Ste-Clotilde; phone: 281133). Performances usually are in French; some visiting companies perform in other languages. International theatrical shows occasionally are presented at the *Grand Casino* at the *Noga-Hilton* hotel (see *Checking In*).

## MUSIC

Operas are performed in the *Grand Théâtre* (Pl. Neuve; phone: 212311) from October through May (not daily); there's one production per month and the quality is greatly varied. There are also excellent ballets here. The *Orchestre de la Suisse Romande* (Orchestra of French Switzerland) performs regularly, often with renowned guest artists. Most of the performances are at *Victoria Hall* (Rue Hornung; phone: 289193); tickets are somewhat difficult to get. There also are frequent concerts and recitals in churches, and open-air concerts in season. During the summer free concerts are held on Thursdays at 12:30 PM at the *Musée Internationale de la Croix-Rouge* (International Red Cross Museum; 17 Av. de la Paix; phone: 734-5248). For further details about concert activity contact the tourist office's concert line (phone: 786-3611).

During the *Montreux Jazz Festival* in July, a number of the performers appear in concert or in clubs in Geneva (Montreux is about 50 miles/80 km away). Call the concert line for details.

## NIGHTCLUBS AND NIGHTLIFE

Geneva has the most active nightlife in Switzerland (which isn't saying much), and it's enjoyed mainly by visiting and resident foreigners. The best spots are the private clubs, which non-members can also get into with a bit of waiting. *Griffins* (36 Bd. Helvétique; phone: 735-1218) is a favorite, with good food. Several of the better hotel restaurants, such as the *Richemond,* have dance floors (see *Checking In*). *Régine's,* a member of the chic, international discotheque chain, is attached to the *Noga-Hilton's Grand Casino* (see *Checking In*). At the *Hilton* and other Swiss casinos, you can wager only about five Swiss francs, so most gamblers go to Divonne-les-Bains in France, 12½ miles (20 km) away, where the top bet is higher. The minimum age for admittance is 18, and a passport is required.

# Best in Town

## CHECKING IN

There are many hotels, but charming, inexpensive ones with atmosphere are rare; the rule is either old-time luxury or functional modern. Unless otherwise indicated, the hotels listed have private baths and accept major credit cards. Most offer telephones, radios, and TV sets in guestrooms. Expect to pay $275 or more for a double room at a place in the expensive category; $130 to $250 at hotels described as moderate; and $85 to $130 at inexpensive places. Lower rates can be found on the outskirts of town. Reservations are strongly advised. All telephone numbers are in the 22 city code unless otherwise indicated.

### EXPENSIVE

**Les Armures** In a 17th-century building in the Vieille Ville, this is considered by many the most charming hotel in Geneva. There are 24 rooms and four suites. Decor is rustic-elegant, with beamed ceilings and vaulted doors. The popular restaurant is the oldest in town (see *Eating Out*). 1 Rue du Puits-St-Pierre (phone: 310-9172; fax: 310-9846).

**Beau-Rivage** This place has retained its Old World charm in spite of a recent renovation. There are 120 rooms, some with lakefront views, and a justifiably famous restaurant, *Le Chat Botté* (see *Eating Out*). Business facilities include 24-hour room service, meeting rooms for up to 200, an English-speaking concierge, foreign currency exchange, secretarial services in English, audiovisual equipment, photocopiers, computers, cable TV news, and translation services. 13 Quai du Mont-Blanc (phone: 731-0221; fax: 738-9847).

**Des Bergues** A grand, splendidly renovated property in a choice location near the lake, it has 109 rooms, eight suites, the elegant *Amphitryon* restaurant (see *Eating Out*), and room service from 6 AM to midnight. Business facilities include meeting rooms for up to 500, an English-speaking concierge, foreign currency exchange, secretarial services in English, audiovisual equipment, photocopiers, computers, cable TV news, and translation services. 33 Quai des Bergues (phone: 731-5050; fax: 732-1989).

**La Cigogne** One of the most unusual hotels in the city center; 100 yards from the lake, it was built in 1903 as a bordello. The decor of each of its 50 rooms is different, and some are furnished with collectors' items, such as the beds of onetime visitors Cary Grant and Barbara Hutton. There's a restaurant, and room service is available around the clock. 17 Pl. Longemalle (phone: 311-4242; fax: 311-4065).

**Geneva Penta** Equidistant from the airport and downtown, this property has 320 rooms, a restaurant, and a fitness center with a sauna. Business facilities include meeting rooms for up to 650, secretarial services in English, and audiovisual equipment. 75-77 Av. Louis-Casaï (phone: 798-4700; fax: 798-7758).

**Inter-Continental** Close to the European headquarters of the *UN* and *Palexpo,* the exhibition center, this hostelry overlooks Geneva's lakeshore and the city center. All 353 rooms, 60 of which are suites, are air conditioned, with color TV sets offering cable programming in five languages. The restaurant, *Les Continents,* boasts a Michelin star and serves fine French food. There also is a coffee shop, a piano bar, a bar next to the swimming pool, a shopping arcade, a fitness center, a *Swissair* desk, and a beauty salon. Business facilities include 24-hour room service, meeting rooms for up to 450, an English-speaking concierge, audiovisual equipment, photocopiers, computers, and translation services. 7-9 Chemin Petit-Saconnex (phone: 734-6091; 800-327-0200; fax: 734-2864).

**Noga Hilton** Sleek and modern, with 377 rooms right on Lake Geneva, this is currently the most expensive hotel in the city. Guests can enjoy a sauna, a heated pool, boutiques, a nightclub, a discotheque, and numerous restaurants (among them *Le Cygne,* one of the best in town; see *Eating Out*). Business facilities include 24-hour room service, meeting rooms for up to 1,400, an English-speaking concierge, foreign currency exchange, secretarial services in English, audiovisual equipment, photocopiers, computers, cable TV news, translation services, and express checkout. Parking is available. 19 Quai du Mont-Blanc (phone: 731-9811; 800-HILTONS; fax: 738-6432).

**Du Rhône** A favorite of vacationers and businesspeople alike, this modern establishment has 234 cheerful rooms (most with views), two restaurants, a terrace, and superb service. The hotel is headquarters for the *International Wine Academy* and frequently hosts the *Trophée des Barmen,* an international wine-tasting competition held in *Le Neptune* restaurant (see *Eating Out*). The famous wine cellar houses 200,000 bottles of mostly French and Swiss wines. Business facilities include 24-hour room service, meeting rooms for up to 200, an English-speaking concierge, foreign currency exchange, secretarial services in English, audiovisual equipment, photocopiers, computers, cable TV news, and translation services. Quai Turretini (phone: 731-9831; 800-223-6800; fax: 732-4558).

**Le Richemond** It's still the most prestigious hotel in town, abounding in understated elegance. There are 67 rooms, and the restaurant, *Le Gentilhomme,* is first-rate, with dance music at night (see *Eating Out*). Business facilities include 24-hour room service, meeting rooms for up to 500, an English-speaking concierge, foreign currency exchange, secretarial services in English, audiovisual equipment, photocopiers, computers, cable TV news, and translation services. *Jardin Brunswick* (phone: 731-1400; 800-223-6800; fax: 731-6709).

### MODERATE

**Amat-Carlton** A very comfortable property, it offers 123 spacious rooms with balconies. There's also a restaurant, and apartments with kitchens are available for longer stays (10-day minimum). 22 Rue Amat (phone: 731-6850; fax: 732-8247).

**Du Midi** In an excellent location, this modern hotel has 85 comfortable rooms, some with river views; a brasserie; a tavern; and a café. Pl. Chevelu (phone: 731-7800; fax: 731-0020).

**La Tourelle** About 10 minutes from the center of town (direct bus service) in luxurious, residential Vésenaz, this villa features 24 attractive, comfortable rooms, a garden, and a view of the lake. Closed December and January. 26 Rte. d'Hermance, Genève-Vésenaz (phone: 752-1628; fax: 752-5493).

### INEXPENSIVE

**Le Grenil** Connected with the *YMCA,* this modern hotel not far from the city center is an excellent value. Most of its 50 rooms have private baths. Facilities include a snack bar and meeting rooms for up to 200. 7 Av. Ste-Clotilde (phone: 328-3055; fax: 321-6010).

**Lido** A "best buy," this is an excellently run no-frills (no restaurant) hotel with 32 rooms in a central location. 8 Rue de Chantepoulet (phone: 731-5530; fax: 731-6501).

**Des Tourelles** Not related to *La Tourelle* (above), this is a modest, family-type hotel with 24 rooms but no private baths and no restaurant. Sunny and pleasant, the place offers a view of the river. No credit cards accepted. Centrally located, at 2 Bd. James-Fazy (phone: 732-4423; fax: 732-7620).

---

## EATING OUT

Geneva has more than 1,100 eating establishments in all price categories. French cooking dominates, with Italian second. Definitely try the French-Swiss cheese dishes, such as fondue and raclette (a puddle of delicious cheese melted on an open fire in individual portions and eaten with tiny potatoes), which are served in inexpensive pubs. Also sample the excellent lake fish, including *perche* (perch) and, if available, the rare *omble chevalier* (grayling), found only in Lake Geneva. Tips are included in bills, but it is customary to add a bit more. For a three-course dinner for two, without drinks, wine, or coffee, expect to pay $150 to $300 at places described as expensive, $100 to $150 at restaurants in the moderate category, and $50 to $90 at inexpensive spots. Set lunch menus are often considerably less expensive. Unless otherwise indicated restaurants are open for lunch and dinner and all telephone numbers are in the 22 city code.

### EXPENSIVE

**Amphitryon** Fine French food is served in this elegant dining place at *Des Bergues* hotel. Closed Saturdays and Sundays. Reservations advised. Major credit cards accepted. 33 Quai des Bergues (phone: 731-5050).

**Le Béarn** With two Michelin stars, this small and elegant restaurant serves fresh, imaginative dishes and delicious warm desserts. Closed Saturday lunch, Sundays, and mid-July through mid-August. Reservations necessary. Major credit cards accepted. 4 Quai de la Poste (phone: 321-0028).

**Le Chat Botté** "Puss in Boots," set in the *Beau-Rivage* hotel, is a notable eatery that's earned a Michelin star. Specialties include mousseline of lobster and artichokes. Closed Saturdays, Sundays, holidays, two weeks at the end of March and beginning of April, and during the *Christmas–New Year's* holidays. Reservations necessary. Major credit cards accepted. 13 Quai du Mont-Blanc (phone: 731-6532).

**Chez Valentino** This lively Italian place features a flower-filled terrace for alfresco dining in spring and summer. Closed Mondays, Tuesday lunch, and August. Reservations advised. Major credit cards accepted. Three miles (5 km) from the city center, at 63 Rte. de Thonon, Vésenaz (phone: 752-1440).

**Le Cygne** Another one-Michelin-star spot, this French restaurant in the *Noga Hilton* is one of the best in town. Open daily. Reservations advised. Major credit cards accepted. 19 Quai du Mont-Blanc (phone: 731-9811).

**La Favola** The best of French and Italian fare is found in this relaxed restaurant in the Vieille Ville. Owner-chef Gabriel Martinoli makes

---

his own pasta and risotto, taking full advantage of seasonal produce. Closed Saturdays, Sundays, and July. Reservations advised. Major credit cards accepted. 15 Rue Jean-Calvin (phone: 311-7437).

**Le Gentilhomme** "The Gentleman" is one of the most celebrated eating places in a city of fine restaurants. The menu offers an unbeatable selection of caviar, and there is a wide variety of meat and fish dishes. Closed weekends. Reservations advised. Major credit cards accepted. In *Le Richemond Hotel, Jardin Brunswick* (phone: 731-1400).

**Hostellerie de la Vendée** The interior is functional and sober, but the service and food are outstanding and have earned a Michelin star. Open for dinner only; closed Sundays. Reservations advised. Major credit cards accepted. On the outskirts of town, 28 Chemin de la Vendée, Petit Lancy (phone: 792-0411).

**Le Lion D'Or** The place for elegant dining overlooking the lake. Seafood is the specialty at this two-Michelin star restaurant. Closed weekends. Reservations necessary (preferably far in advance). Most credit cards accepted. 5 Pl. Gauthier (phone: 736-4432).

**Le Neptune** In the *Hôtel du Rhône,* this elegant dining spot is a member of the Chaîne des Rôtisseurs and a favorite of Geneva businesspeople. It features creative variations on classic French food. There is an open-air terrace, and private dining rooms may be reserved. Closed weekends. Reservations advised. Major credit cards accepted. Quai Turrettini (phone: 731-9831).

**L'Olivier de Provence** An intimate, elegant French dining spot in Carouge. In summer there's dining in the big tree-shaded garden. Closed Sundays. Reservations advised. Major credit cards accepted. 13 Rue Jacques-Dalphin (phone: 342-0450).

**La Perle du Lac** On the lake, in *Parc Mon Repos;* in summer you can dine outside and enjoy the ravishing view; in winter meals are served in the intimate, elegant, and candlelit dining room. A less expensive café adjoins the restaurant. Closed Mondays. Reservations necessary. Most credit cards accepted. 128 Rue de Lausanne (phone: 731-7935).

### MODERATE

**Les Armures** The oldest restaurant in Geneva, rich in atmosphere (with plenty of old wood beams and medieval suits of armor), this is a good place for raclette or fondue. Closed Monday lunch. Reservations advised. Major credit cards accepted. In the heart of the Vieille Ville at *Les Armures Hotel,* 1 Rue du Puits-St-Pierre (phone: 310-9172).

**Auberge de la Mère Royaume** A cozy, paneled, Old Geneva–style place serving French specialties. Closed Saturday lunch and Sundays. Reservations advised. Major credit cards accepted. 9 Rue des Corps-Saints (phone: 732-7008).

**Cave Valaisanne et Chalet Suisse** Cozy and friendly, it offers excellent fondue, as well as other good cheese dishes. Open daily. Reservations unnecessary. Major credit cards accepted. 23 Bd. Georges-Favon (phone: 328-1236).

**Edelweiss** A Swiss chalet featuring folk music and regional specialties. Open daily. Reservations unnecessary. Major credit cards accepted. 2 Pl. de la Navigation (phone: 731-4940).

**La Fenice** Tasty Venetian specialties are served in a homey atmosphere. Closed Sundays, Mondays, and the first two weeks in August. Reservations necessary. Major credit cards accepted. 78 Avenue de Châtelaine (phone: 797-0370).

**Mortimer** Antique advertising signs hang on the walls of this popular Parisian-style bistro. The fare is plain but satisfying, with hearty soups, salads, and steaks with *pommes frites.* Open daily. Reservations unnecessary. Major credit cards accepted. 2 Pl. du Bourg-de-Four (phone: 310-1398).

**Au Pied de Cochon** Named after the well-known restaurant in the old Les Halles neighborhood in Paris, this lively, crowded dining spot offers hearty Lyonnais cooking. Open daily. Reservations advised. Major credit cards accepted. 4 Pl. du Bourg-de-Four (phone: 310-4797).

### INEXPENSIVE

**Café des Beaux-Arts** Modest but lively, this bistro is very popular with locals. Potato au gratin is a specialty. Closed Mondays and the second Sunday of the month. Reservations unnecessary. No credit cards accepted. 32 Rue de Carouge (phone: 329-1501).

**Café du Centre** This pleasant brasserie is on historic Place du Molard and serves a huge variety of dishes till well after midnight. (There is a more expensive section upstairs.) Open daily. Reservations unnecessary. No credit cards accepted. 5 Pl. du Molard (phone: 311-8586).

**Palais de Justice** An unassuming little place specializing in fondue. On the romantic square of the Vieille Ville, it has lots of local color. Closed Sundays. Reservations advised. No credit cards accepted. 8 Pl. du Bourg-de-Four (phone: 310-4254).

# Helsinki

## At-a-Glance

### SEEING THE CITY
From the steps of Helsinki's majestic cathedral, the *Tuomiokirkko* (see *Special Places*), you can scan the entire old section of the city. In front of the church is the spacious Senaatintori (Senate Square), designed during the early 19th century in neoclassical style. Its *Sederholmin talo* (Sederholm House), built in 1755–57, is the oldest stone building in the city. On the west side of the square is *Helsingin Yliopisto* (Helsinki University); on the east side is the *Valtioneuvosto* (Government Palace). Nearby is *Esplanadi puisto* (Esplanade Park), center of Helsinki's business activities. The wide tree-lined promenade, with avenues on either side, begins at Kauppatori (Market Square) and ends several blocks north at Mannerheimintie (Mannerheim Street).

### SPECIAL PLACES
Downtown Helsinki is compact, making it easy to explore the city on foot.

#### DOWNTOWN

**FINLANDIA-TALO (FINLANDIA HALL)** Don't miss this $9-million marble edifice built in the early 1970s, the last triumph of the great Finnish architect Alvar Aalto. Guided tours of the concert and convention halls are available by appointment. Admission charge. In *Hesperian puisto* (Hesperia Park) facing Mannerheimintie, almost directly across from the *Kansallismuseo* (National Museum), at 4 Karamzininkatu (phone: 40241).

**SIBELIUKSEN-MONUMENTII (SIBELIUS MONUMENT)** Dedicated to Finland's revered composer Jean Sibelius (1865–1957), this giant sculpture of tubular steel pipes built in the mid-1960s is in a park, also named after the composer, northwest of downtown. To the side is a head of the composer molded by sculptress Eila Hiltunen. Lighted at night, it's a dramatic sight. *Sibelius puisto* (Sibelius Park).

**TUOMIOKIRKKO (LUTHERAN CATHEDRAL)** The cornerstone of Carl Ludwig Engel's cathedral was laid in 1830 and the building was consecrated in 1852. A parish church to this day, it is also the scene of festive national services. Closed Sunday mornings. Senaatintori (phone: 656365).

**USPENSKIN KATEDRAALI (GREEK ORTHODOX CATHEDRAL)** This classic example of Byzantine-Slavic brick architecture was completed in 1868 and restored for its 100th anniversary. Closed Mondays, as well as Saturdays from October through April. 1 Kanavakatu at Katajanokka Hill (phone: 634267).

**TEMPPELIAUKION KIRKKO (ROCK CHURCH)** This Lutheran house of worship is breathtakingly beautiful in its simplicity. Designed in 1969 by two brothers, Timo and Tuomo Suomalainen, it was carved out of solid rock and occupies most of a city block. The interior is pink and gray granite with vertical glass strips cut into the ceiling, through which light enters in dramatic shafts. The copper dome spans 70 feet. Closed Sunday mornings, during concerts, and to non-worshippers during services. 3 Lutherinkatu (phone: 494698).

**EDUSKUNTATALO (PARLIAMENT HOUSE)** Guided tours of this stately neoclassical building, constructed in the late 1920s, are offered in English (call for specific times). Closed weekdays September through June. No admission charge. 30 Mannerheimintie (phone: 4321).

**KANSALLISMUSEO (NATIONAL MUSEUM)** This monument to Finland's National Romantic style was designed in 1910 by the noted Finnish architects Eliel Saarinen, Herman Gesellius, and Armas Lindgren, and its foyer is decorated with frescoes by the National Romantic artist Akseli Gallen-Kallela. It houses an extensive library; thousands of archaeological items from the Stone, Bronze, and Iron Ages in Scandinavia and Russia; thousands more historical items, including Finnish costumes, textiles, weapons, metals, and coins; and extensive ethnic collections tracing life in Finland from prehistoric times to the present. Closed Mondays. Admission charge. 34 Mannerheimintie (phone: 40501).

**ATENEUMINTAIDEMUSEO (ATHENEUM ART GALLERY)** Among the paintings, sculptures, drawings, and etchings housed in this stately century-old neo-Renaissance building are a comprehensive collection of paintings by prominent modern Finnish artists, including Gallen-Kallela, Albert Edellelt, and Hugo Simberg. The collection also includes older works from the Finnish archives. Closed Mondays. Admission charge. On Rautatientori (Railway Square; phone: 173361).

**SUOMALAISEN MUOTOILUN EDISTÄMISKESKUS (DESIGN FORUM)** A gallery featuring changing exhibitions of Finnish designers' textiles and other applied arts. Open daily. No admission charge. 10 Fabianinkatu (phone: 629290).

**YLIOPISTON KASVITIETEELLINEN PUUTARHA (UNIVERSITY BOTANICAL GARDENS)** Established in 1833, this lush park holds Finland's largest botanical collection. There are a variety of trees, shrubs, and grasses common to Finland; the greenhouses showcase exotic tropical plants. Park open daily. Greenhouses open afternoons except Fridays from May through August, weekend afternoons only the rest of the year. Admission charge. 44 Unioninkatu (phone: 1911).

**SUOMEN KANSALLIS OOPERA (FINNISH NATIONAL OPERA)** This magnificent opera house, inaugurated in 1993, features two halls (the larger seating 1,365) for ballet, concerts, and recitals, in addition to opera.

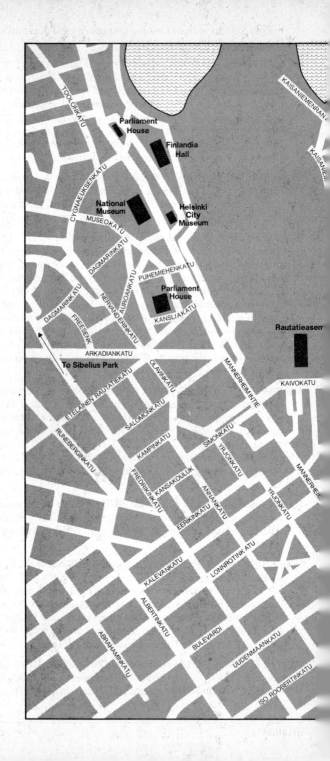

TOOLONKATU

Parliament House

Finlandia Hall

CYGNAEUKSENKATU

National Museum

Helsinki City Museum

MUSEOKATU

DAGMARINKATU

PUHEMIEHENKATU

DAGMARINKATU

NERVAND ERINKATU

AUROANKATU

Parliament House

FREESENK

KANSLIAKATU

Rautatieasem

ARKADIANKATU

To Sibelius Park

KAIVOKATU

ETELAINEN RAUTATIEKATU

OLAVINKATU

SALOMONKATU

MANNERHEIMINTIE

RUNEBERGINKATU

KAMPINKATU

FREDRIKINKATU

KANSAKOULUK

SIMONKATU

YRJONKATU

EERIKINKATU

ANNANKATU

YRJONKATU

MANNERHEIM

LONNROTINK ATU

KALEVANKATU

ALBERTINKATU

BULEVARDI

UUDENMAANKATU

ABRAHAMINKATU

ISO ROOBERTINKATU

KAISANIEMENRAN

KAISANIE

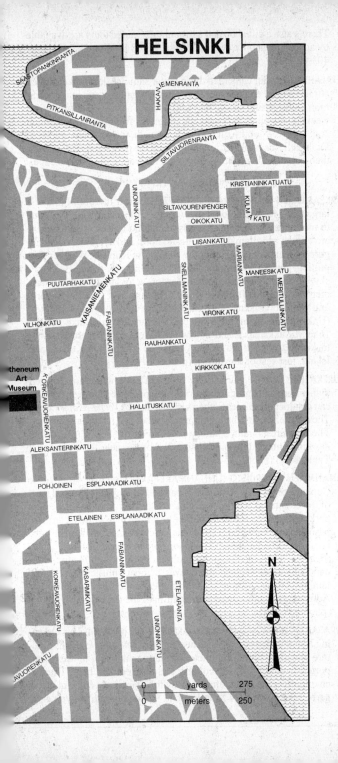

There's also a gift shop and a restaurant. Guided tours are available by appointment only. Admission charge. 58 Helsinginkatu (phone: 403-02350).

**HIETALAHTI** Take your camera to this popular summer flea market, which attracts a loyal and colorful following. Bargains are no longer common, but a careful search may still unearth a treasure or two. Open weekday evenings and weekend mornings from mid-May through August. Head southwest on Eteläesplanadi, the southern branch of Esplanadi (the boulevard running along the park *Esplanadi puisto*), then continue down Bulevardi to the market on the water's edge.

## ELSEWHERE IN THE CITY

**KORKEASAAREN ELÄINTARHA (HELSINKI ZOO)** Built in 1888, Finland's largest zoo (and said to be the world's northernmost) is the home to more than a thousand animals, including those native to northern climes, plus llamas, bison, bears, lions, and a number of endangered species, among them the rare snow leopard. Weather permitting, guests can have lunch in an open-air café facing Helsinki's skyline and Eteläsatama (South Harbor) across the sea. In the summer ferry service from the shore of Kauppatori (Market Square) and motorboat service from the shore of Hakaniemiementori (Hakaniemi Square) are available. Visitors may also take bus No. 16 to Mustikkamaa Island and then walk across the pedestrian bridge to *Korkeasaari*. Open daily. Admission charge. On Korkeasaari Island, just east of downtown (phone: 19981).

**HEUREKA** This science and activity center offers a wide range of permanent and changing exhibitions on modern technology. Visitors can conduct experiments, then visit the domed *Verne-teatter* (Verne Theater), where fascinating films on science and nature are screened. There is a restaurant, a café, a bar, and a gift shop. Closed Mondays in winter. Admission charge. In Vantaa, near the airport, at 1 Tiedepuisto (phone: 857999).

**LINNANMÄEN HUVIPUISTO (LINNANMÄKI PARK)** Helsinki's answer to Copenhagen's *Tivoli Gardens* is patronized by Finns from all parts of the country as well as foreign tourists. This popular amusement park includes 25 rides, including a turn-of-the-century carousel. Also on the premises are restaurants, cafés, a dance pavilion, assorted kiosks, and two stages. The indoor *Linnanmäen Peacock Teatteri* (Peacock Theater) and an open-air auditorium both feature internationally known comedians, clowns, acrobats, musicians, and marionettes. Closed Mondays and from September through mid-May. Admission charge; there's an additional fee for rides. Tivolikuja (phone: 750391).

**SEURASAARI ULKOMUSEO (SEURASSAARI OPEN-AIR MUSEUM)** This charming island park and open-air museum provides a representative picture of early Finland, complete with farm and manor houses transported from all over the country and reassembled here. There is entertainment in the summer, mostly folk dancers in colorful native garb. Take bus No. 24 from Erottaja Square downtown; you enter by a footbridge. The park is open daily, but the houses are open and guided tours available only from May through mid-September. Admission charge. Seurasaari Island (phone: 484712).

**OLYMPIASTADION (OLYMPIC STADIUM)** Distinguished by a 236-foot-high tower, this stadium was designed by Yrjö Lindegren and Toivo Jäntti for the 1940 *Olympics* (which never took place due to World War II) but was eventually used for the *Summer Olympics* in 1952. It's still used for track and field and other sports events. In front is Wäinö Aaltonen's statue of runner Paavo Nurmi, a world-famous medalist of the 1920s. The stadium tower is open to the public. Open daily from March from December. Admission charge. 3 Eteläinen Stadionintie (phone: 440363).

**SUOMENLINNA** This intriguing fortification on a group of five rocky islands in the Gulf of Finland just southeast of Helsinki was built in 1748, when Finland was part of Sweden. Known as the "Gibraltar of the North," it is reputed to be the largest sea fortress in the world. The fortress, which the Swedes named *Sveaborg,* capitulated to the Russians in 1808 but defended itself successfully against an Anglo-French fleet in 1855 during the Crimean War. The *Walhalla* restaurant here (phone: 668552), open in the summer only, is a pleasant place to dine. A ferry from Kauppatori in Eteläsatama (South Harbor) to Suomenlinna leaves hourly, usually on the half-hour, and the 1½-mile crossing takes about 15 minutes. In summer tours start at the information kiosk near where the boat docks (phone: 668341, summer; 668154, winter).

From Suomenlinna visitors can cross by footbridge to explore the forts, casements, parks, and walks of nearby Susisaari (Wolf Island) and Kustaanmiekka (Gustav's Sword). On Susisaari the *Ehrensvärd Museo* (Ehrensvärd Museum; phone: 668131) has exhibits on Suomenlinna's history. It's closed weekdays in October and November, as well as from December through April. The *Armfelt Museo* (Armfelt Museum; phone: 668154) on Kustaanmiekka depicts the life of the 19th-century Finnish gentry; it's closed September to mid-May. Also on Kustaanmiekka is the *Rannikkotykistömuseo* (Coastal Defense Museum; phone: 161295), which is closed October to mid-May. Within walking distance of the museum, in a harbor near the bay of Kustaanmiekka Island, sits the World War II submarine *Vesikko*. All sites charge for admission.

## EXTRA SPECIAL

Since Finland is a country of 188,000 lakes and 180,000 islands, it would be a shame not to spend some part of your visit here on water. Leisurely paced sightseeing cruises and archipelago tours past innumerable little islands and around peninsulas depart daily from Kauppatori from June through August. Choices range from brief 1¼-hour trips to five-hour excursions, including lunch. For more information contact the *Helsinki City Tourist Office* (see *Tourist Information*, below).

# Sources and Resources

## TOURIST INFORMATION

For general information, brochures, and maps contact the *Matkailun Edistämiskeskus* (Finnish Tourist Board; 4 Eteläesplanadi; phone: 403-01300; fax: 403-01333) or the *Helsingin Kaupungin Matkailutoimisto* (Helsinki City Tourist Office; 19 Pohjoisesplanadi; phone: 169-3757; fax: 169-3839). The "Helsinki Today" telephone information line (phone: 700-8058) lists events in the city, recorded in English. The *US Embassy and Consulate* is at 14A Itainen Puistotie (phone: 171931).

In the US, contact the *Finnish Tourist Board* (655 Third Ave., New York, NY 10017; phone: 212-949-2333; fax: 212-983-5260). The *Finnish Embassy* is at 3216 New Mexico Ave. NW, Washington, DC 20016 (phone: 202-363-2430).

**ENTRY REQUIREMENTS** A US citizen needs a current passport for a stay of up to 90 days. The 90-day period begins on the date of entry into any one of the Nordic countries, which besides Finland include Denmark, Iceland, Norway, and Sweden.

**TIME** The time in Finland is seven hours later than in US East Coast cities. Finland observes daylight saving time.

**LANGUAGE** Finland has two official languages: Finnish and Swedish. English is the country's most widely spoken foreign language.

**ELECTRIC CURRENT** 220 volts, 50 cycles, AC.

**MONEY** The Finnish markka (FIM) equals 100 pennis. At press time there were about 5 markkaa to the American dollar.

**TIPPING** Restaurants add a 14% service charge (15% on Sundays and holidays), but you can leave a bit extra for the waiter, and make sure to tip the restaurant doorman about 3 FIM. Hotel bills also include a service charge. Porters receive 3 FIM; others, including cab drivers, don't expect tips.

**BANKING/BUSINESS HOURS** Banks are open weekdays from 9:15 AM to 4:15 PM. Most other businesses are open weekdays from 8:30 AM to 4 or 4:30 PM, but government office hours are 8 AM to 4:15 PM (3:15 in summer).

**NATIONAL HOLIDAYS** *New Year's Day* (January 1), *Epiphany* (January 6), *Good Friday* (April 14), *Easter Sunday* (April 16), *Easter Monday* (April 17), *Walpurgis Night* (April 30), *May Day* (May 1), *Ascension Thursday* (May 25), *Midsummer's Eve* (June 25), *Midsummer's Day* (June 26), *All Saints' Day* (November 1), *Independence Day* (December 6), *Christmas Eve* (December 24), *Christmas Day* (December 25), and *Boxing Day* (December 26).

**LOCAL COVERAGE** The *International Herald Tribune* and *The European* (a London-based pan-European weekly) are available at better hotels, newsstands, and the airport. The *Akateeminen Kirjakauppa* (Academic Book Store; see *Shopping*) carries a large selection of newspapers and magazines in many languages. A summary of world news in English is broadcast on radio stations YLE 3 and YLE 4 daily at 10:55 PM.

**TELEPHONE** The city code for Helsinki and surrounding areas is 0. When calling from one area to another within Finland dial 9 + city code + local number. The country code for Finland is 358. Dial 112 for emergency assistance.

## GETTING AROUND

**AIRPORT** *Helsinki-Vantaa Lentoasema* (Helsinki-Vantaa Airport), 12 miles (19 km) north of the city, handles domestic and international traffic. *Finnair* buses travel between the airport and the air terminal adjoining the *Inter-Continental* hotel (21 Töölönkatu; phone: 818-7670) or the city bus terminal between the *Rautatieasema* central train station and the post office (3 Asema Aukio; phone: 818-7757). The buses run two to four times an hour from 5 AM to midnight, and the fare is 22 markkaa (roughly $4.25). *Yellow Line* (phone: 220-02500) is a minibus service providing door-to-door service between the airport and the Helsinki area.

**CAR RENTAL** *Avis, Budget, Hertz, InterRent/Europcar,* and others operate rental desks at the airport and in many hotel lobbies.

**TAXI** Cab stands, clearly marked "Taksi," are found at every few corners, and there are usually plenty of empty cabs at each (except from around midnight to 3 AM, when the bars close). You may hail a cab if its sign is illuminated. Fares are relatively low; no tip is expected but give the driver 2 to 10 markkaa if you wish. There is an extra charge from 6 PM (2 PM on Saturdays) to 6 AM.

**TRAIN** The city's main train station is *Rautatieasema* (13 Vilhonkatu; phone: 100121), built in 1914. With its splendid Art Deco architecture and good restaurants, the station is a destination in itself.

**TRAM AND BUS** Trams 3T and 3B, which can be boarded anywhere along their routes, offer a tour of the business and residential areas of the capital. A brochure available at the *Helsinki City Tourist Office* describes sights along the way. A basic ticket for all public transport is 9 markkaa (about $1.75). A 24-hour tourist ticket, which can be purchased at the tourist office, entitles the holder to unlimited travel on trams and buses. The *Helsinki-kortti* (Helsinki Card) buys unlimited travel for 24, 48, or 72 hours on trams, buses, subways (linking the city center and the eastern suburbs), and ferries, as well as free admission to 48 museums, discount theater and concert tickets, and weekend discounts at hotels, shops, and restaurants. Depending on the time of year, it costs about 85 markkaa ($16.40 at press time) to 165 markkaa ($32)—half-price for children—and can be purchased at the airport, the *Helsinki City Tourist Office,* and hotels.

For additional details on trams and buses call the *Helsingin Linja-autoasema* bus station (3 Simonkatu; phone: 600-4000).

## LOCAL SERVICES

**DENTIST (ENGLISH-SPEAKING)** *Forum Dentists' Centre* (20B Mannerheimintie; phone: 129-6611); for emergency service from 9 AM to 9 PM call 736166.

**DRY CLEANER/TAILOR** *Lindström Forum* (20 Mannerheimintie; phone: 694-3085); *Lindström Oy* (City Passage, 2nd Floor; phone: 657251); or ask your hotel concierge.

**LIMOUSINE SERVICE** *Limousine Service* (7 Tuulimyllyntie; phone: 288650).

**MEDICAL EMERGENCY** *Helsinki University Hospital* (4 Haartmaninkatu; phone: 4711) or *Töölö Hospital* (5 Topliuksenkatu; phone: 4711). To contact a doctor (they all speak English) in an emergency, dial 112; for 24-hour information about medical services call 735001.

**MESSENGER SERVICE** *Transpoint* (phone: 148-79300).

**NATIONAL/INTERNATIONAL COURIER** *DHL Worldwide Express* (16 Niitylänpolku; phone: 777991).

**OFFICE EQUIPMENT RENTAL** *International Business Center,* in the *Inter-Continental* hotel (46 Mannerheimintie; phone: 405-5268), arranges international teleconferencing, rents fully equipped offices, and provides secretarial services. Also try *Office Center Forum* (20A Mannerheimintie; phone: 693501). Both advise reserving several weeks in advance.

**PHARMACY** *Yliopiston Apteekki* (96 Mannerheimintie; phone: 415778) is open 24 hours daily.

**PHOTOCOPIES** *Office Center Forum* (see *Office Equipment Rental,* above) and *Stockmann* (52 Aleksanterinkatu; phone: 1211); most hotels also have photocopiers.

**POST OFFICE** The main post office (11 Mannerheimintie; phone: 195-5117) is open weekdays from 9 AM to 5 PM; *Poste Restante* (general delivery) hours are weekdays from 8 AM to 9 PM, Saturdays from 9 AM to 6 PM, and Sundays from 11 AM to 9 PM (phone: 195-5123).

**SECRETARY (ENGLISH-SPEAKING)** *Office Center Forum* (see *Office Equipment Rental,* above).

**TELEX** *Teleservice,* at the main post office (11B Mannerheimintie; phone: 195-5022, 195-5353, or 195-5387), is open weekdays from 9 AM to 10 PM and Saturdays from 10 AM to 4 PM; a telex also can be sent at any time by dialing 92021.

**TRANSLATOR** Diana Tullberg at *The English Centre* (14A Tenppelikatu; phone: 449200).

**OTHER** Formal wear rental: *Juhla-Asu* (13 Fabianinkatu; phone: 666024). Professional photographer: *Lehtikuva Press Photo Agency & Studio* (9B Erottajankatu; phone: 605588).

## SPECIAL EVENTS

More than a decade ago Finland introduced some 800 summer festivals in cities and towns across the country. The events range from symphony and opera performances in a 15th-century castle courtyard to folk, jazz, and pop music concerts to seminars on world affairs. The *Helsingin Juhlaviikot* (Helsinki Festival) comprises as many as 100 events between late August and early September. Perhaps its most popular event is the *Taiteiden Yö* (Night of the Arts), when art galleries are open to the public and there's free music and entertainment throughout the city center. The date varies yearly, but it's held in August or September. For program information contact *Helsingin Juhlaviikot* (28 Unioninkatu; phone: 659688). For information on festivals in Helsinki and other cities contact *Finland Festivals* (40 B49 Mannerheimintie; phone: 445686 or 445763). Other traditional holidays include *Vappu* (May Day, April 30 through May 1), with a carnival-style celebration, folkloric dancing, sports and musical events, and horse races; and the *Lucia Festivaali* (St. Lucia's Day) on December 13, with concerts and a children's procession.

## MUSEUMS

Besides those described in *Special Places,* the following museums may be of interest.

**AINOLA** The former home of composer Jean Sibelius. Closed Mondays, Tuesdays, and October through April. Admission charge. Järvenpää (phone: 287322).

**AMOS ANDERSONIN TAIDEMUSEO (AMOS ANDERSON ART MUSEUM)** Contemporary Finnish art plus European works from earlier centuries. Open daily. Admission charge. 27 Yrjönkatu (phone: 640221).

**CYGNAEUS GALLERIA (CYGNAEUS GALLERY)** Finnish art from the 19th century, housed in its former collector's villa. Closed Mondays and Tuesdays. Admission charge. In *Kaivo puisto* (Spa Park), 8 Kalliolinnantie (phone: 656928).

**DIDRICHSENIN TAIDEMUSEO (DIDRICHSEN ART MUSEUM)** Pre-Columbian and Oriental paintings, sculptures, and graphics are featured in a modern setting. Open Wednesdays from 1 to 4 PM and Sundays from 4 to 6 PM. Admission charge. 3 Kuusilahdenkuja, on Kuusisaari Island (phone: 489055).

**GALLEN-KALLELA** The castle-like former studio and home of Akseli Gallen-Kallela (1865–1931), the first painter to use Finnish epics as his subject matter (including the great mythical *Kalevala* cycle from pre-Christian times), is a must-see. Closed Mondays from mid-January through mid-May. Admission charge. Take tram No. 4 to Munkkiniemi, a scenic, tranquil spot by the sea, then walk west along the seaside path for about a mile or take bus No. 33 (weekdays only). Espoo (phone: 513388).

**HELSINGIN KAUPUNGIN MUSEO (HELSINKI CITY MUSEUM)** Pictures and objects portray the city's history from its founding to the present. Closed Mondays and Tuesdays. Admission charge. The main collection is housed in a private villa at 6 Tomisto Dagmarinkatu; the rest can be seen at 2 Karamzininkatu (phone: 169-3444 for both).

**HVITTRÄSK** Set in a forest beside a beautiful lake, the former studio and residence of architects and designers Eliel Saarinen, Armas Lindgren, and Herman Gesellius now serves as a cultural center. Closed Mondays from mid-January through March. Admission charge. Bus No. 166 from platform 62 at the central bus station, the *Helsingin Linja-autoasema,* gets you there in 40 minutes. Luoma, Kirkkonummi (phone: 297-5779).

**KIRPILÄIN TAIDEKOKOELMA (KIRPILÄ ART COLLECTION)** Housed in Juhani Kirpilä's former residence in a stately neighborhood, this museum showcases the late physician's collection of portraits and sculptures by Finnish artists. Open Wednesday and Sunday afternoons; closed July. Admission charge. 7 Pohjoinen Hesperiankatu (phone: 494436).

**MANNERHEIM MUSEO (MANNERHEIM MUSEUM)** Originally the home of Finland's great early-20th-century war hero and post–World War II president, Marshal Carl Gustav Emil Mannerheim (1867–1951), this intriguing museum features his military medals and memorabilia he collected from around the world. Open Friday through Sunday afternoons and by appointment. Admission charge includes a guided tour (available in English). In *Kaivo puisto,* 14 Kalliolinnantie (phone: 635443).

**RAKENNUSTAITEEN MUSEO (MUSEUM OF FINNISH ARCHITECTURE)** Archives and exhibitions of Finnish architecture past and present. Closed Mondays. Admission charge. 24 Kasarmikatu (phone: 661918).

**SUOMEN VALOKUVATAITEENMUSEO (PHOTOGRAPHIC MUSEUM OF FINLAND)** Works by both Finnish and international photographers. Closed Mondays. Admission charge. 1 Tallberginkatu (phone: 694-1343).

**TAIDETEOLLISUUSMUSEO (MUSEUM OF APPLIED ARTS)** Finnish industrial design and native handicrafts. Closed Mondays. Admission charge. 23 Korkeavuorenkatu (phone: 174455).

**URHO KEKKONEN MUSEO (URHO KEKKONEN MUSEUM)** The home of the late Urho Kekkonen, Finland's president from 1956 to 1981, showcases the gifts he received from various world leaders and includes a visit to the sauna house where he entertained some of them. Closed Mondays from September through June. Admission charge. Adjacent to the *Seurasaari Ulkomuseo,* Seurasaari Island (phone: 480684).

**VILLA GYLLENBERG** A private collection of Finnish art exhibited in a splendid villa, once the home of prominent art collectors Signe and Ane Gyllenberg. Open from 4 to 8 PM Wednesdays and noon to 4 PM Sundays. Admission charge. 11 Kuusisaarenpolku (phone: 647390).

## SHOPPING

Finland offers some of the best buys in Europe on textiles, ceramics, glassware, jewelry, handicrafts, furs, and leather goods. Marimekko and Anniki Karvinen clothes and fabrics, Arabia glass and pottery, and Aarikka wooden toys are exceptional. Due to an economic downturn and the devalued Finnish markka, the dollar goes further here than it used to.

Helsinki's main shopping area is near the large hotels, particularly along Aleksanterinkatu and *Esplanadipuisto* (Esplanade Park) and their side streets. Kauppatori (Market Square), at Eteläsatama (South Harbor) across from the 19th-century *Presidentinlinna* (Presidential Palace), is the venue for a bustling open-air marketplace where everything from fresh flowers and produce to inexpensive furs and handicrafts is sold. Be sure to try the freshly brewed coffee and hearty Finnish pastries. The *Senaatin Tori* is a complex of bazaars, art galleries, shops, and cafés in the revived 18th-century Old Town buildings at Aleksanterinkatu, Unioninkatu, and Sofiankatu. For flea-market mavens, *Hietalahti* (see *Special Places*) offers colorful sights. Among Helsinki's better department stores are *Aleksi 13* (corner of Aleksanterinkatu and Mikonkatu; phone: 131441); *City Sokos* (2 Asema-Aukio; phone: 12561); and *Stockmann* (52 Aleksanterinkatu; phone: 1211), Scandinavia's oldest.

Most shops and boutiques are open weekdays from 9 AM to 5 PM, Saturdays to 2 or 3 PM; department stores are open weekdays from 9 AM to 8 PM, Saturdays to 5 or 6 PM. Hours and closing days are subject to change.

A Value Added Tax (VAT) of 12% is included in the price of many items. Department stores and finer shops provide a tax-refund receipt for purchases by foreign visitors. Refunds are made at the "Tax Free" counters at the airport and ferry terminals.

Some of our favorite Helsinki shops:

**Aarikka** Toys, jewelry, animals, and other articles in wood and silver designed by Kaija Aarikka. 27 Pohjoisesplanadi (phone: 652277) and 8 Eteläesplanadi (phone: 175462).

**Agora** A shopping patio surrounded by elegant boutiques filled with jewelry, crystal, sculpture, furs, fashions, and Finland's only genuine tearoom. 30 Unioninkatu (no phone).

**Akanvirta** Wonderful wool sweaters and vests in fall colors. At the *Senaatin Tori* (phone: 602963).

**Akateeminen Kirjakauppa (Academic Book Store)** One of the world's largest bookstores, it was designed by Alvar Aalto. Some English-language books are sold here. Books in Finland are very expensive, so buy only what you won't find back home. 39 Pohjoisesplanadi (phone: 12141).

**Annikki Karvinen** The best textiles in Helsinki, including clothing, hand-woven blankets, pillows, wall hangings, and placemats. 23 Pohjoisesplanadi (phone: 633837).

**Artek** Housed in the Rautatalo building, designed by Alvar Aalto, it offers Aalto home furnishings, including furniture, lamps, textiles, and assorted design products. 18 Eteläesplanadi (phone: 177533).

**Forum** A modern four-story shopping plaza packed with boutiques, cafés, and shops. 20 Mannerheimintie.

**Fuga** A well-stocked music store specializing in traditional Finnish and classical music. 28 Unioninkatu (phone: 631181).

**Galerie Björn Weckström** Renowned sculptor Björn Weckström is the principal designer of the avant-garde Lapponia jewelry that's often made with gold nuggets and spectrolite from Lapland. In the *Agora* gallery at 30 Unioninkatu (phone: 656529).

**Hackman Shop Arabia** Helsinki's best selection of Iittala glass, as well as ceramics, crystal, and exquisite china. 25 Pohjoisesplanadi (phone: 170055). Visit the *Arabia Museum Gallery and Factory Store* at the same location for discounted prices. 135 Hämeentie (phone: 39391).

**Kalevala-Koru** An extensive selection of traditional folk jewelry in gold, silver, and bronze, as well as handmade knitwear and textiles. 25 Unioninkatu (phone: 171520).

**Kankurin Tupa** Handmade clothing, rugs, jewelry, crystal, wall hangings, and kitchen accessories. 40 Mannerheimintie (phone: 492535).

**Kaunis Koru** Interesting jewelry, some made of Finnish spectrolite. 28 Aleksanterinkatu (phone: 626850).

**Kiseleff Bazaar Hall** A charming shopping gallery in the city center at Senaatintori, with a variety of clothes and handicrafts, a flea market, and an exhibition of toys from the 1930s through the 1960s. 28 Aleksanterinkatu (no phone).

**Marimekko** Brightly colored fabrics and clothing in the spirit of the internationally famous Finnish designer of the same name, who sold the chain a few years ago. 31 Pohjoisesplanadi and across the street at 14 Eteläesplanadi (phone: 177944 for both).

**Pentik** Exclusive clothing designs in leather. Two central locations: *Forum* mall, 20 Mannerheimintie (phone: 694-8817), and 27 Pohjoisesplanadi (phone: 625558).

**Rahikainen Boutique** A fine selection of Finnish furs, including many one-of-a-kinds by the acclaimed Finnish designer. 48 Kasarmikatu (phone: 631353).

**Sauna-Soppi-Shop (Sauna Shop)** Wonderful bath accessories, including robes, soaps, and towels. At the *Senaatin Tori* shopping complex (phone: 634733).

**Schröder, Hellbom and Degerlund** A wide variety of reasonably priced Rapala fishing lures for the serious angler. 23 Unioninkatu (phone: 656656).

**Sirkka Könönen** Handmade sweaters. 17 Liisankatu (phone: 135-5302).

**Suomen Käsityön Ystävät Ry (Friends of Finnish Handicrafts)** Rya rugs and embroidery items. 11E Yrjönkatu, inner yard (phone: 607622).

**Tarja Niskanen** Reputed to be the best furrier in the city, Ms. Niskanen designs sporty, luxury, and reversible models. In the *Agora* gallery at 30 Unionkatu (phone: 624022).

**Wahlman** A variety of hats, including fur, in Russian styles. 35 Pohjois-esplanadi (phone: 639939).

**Wanha Satama (Old Harbor Market)** These two warehouses, built in 1897 and now beautifully restored, house boutiques, restaurants, and crafts exhibitions. At the harbor east of the *Presidentinlinna*.

## SPORTS AND FITNESS

The single most popular venue for outdoor activities in Helsinki is the forested *Keskuspuisto* (Central Park), a 2,470-acre network of greenery of which *Hesperian puisto* forms the southernmost section, starting near *Finlandia-talo* (Finlandia Hall) at the south tip of Töölönlahti (Töölö Bay) and stretching northward. It's filled with trails ideal for strolling, jogging, cycling, horseback riding, and cross-country skiing in winter.

**BICYCLING** Aside from the *Keskupuisto* (see above), the city has special bicycle lanes and a number of prescribed biking routes. There also are some old country roads in good cycling condition. Check with the *Helsinki City Tourist Office* for information, including where to rent a bike, or call *Cat Sport Oy* (phone: 692-3676).

**BOATING** A boat or canoe can be rented at one of the many yachting clubs on the islands right outside Helsinki, but the reefy waters are tricky. Check with the *Yachting Association* or the *Motor Boat Association* (both at 20 Radiokatu; phone: 1581). You can rent a boat with or without a crew from the *Nautic Center* (9 Itälahdenkatu; phone: 670271). The *Finnish Canoe Association* (20 Radiokatu; phone: 158-2363) has canoes for rent.

**FISHING** Both deep-sea and inland fishing are possible year-round. General fishing licenses can be obtained on weekdays at the *Pääposti* (Main Post Office; 11 Mannerheimintie). For further information, check with the *Helsinki City Tourist Office*.

**FITNESS CENTER** Try *Alexium* (15 Aleksanterinkatu, second floor; phone: 175757), offering free weights, the latest machines, aerobics, and step classes.

**GOLF** There are some 22 courses in the Helsinki area. In summer, when there are almost 24 hours of light, you can tee off as late as 10 PM and still finish all 18 holes in daylight. For course information contact the *Suomen Golfliitto ry* (Finnish Golf Union; 20 Radiokatu; phone: 158-2244). Visitors should bring club membership cards from home.

**HORSEBACK RIDING** You won't have trouble finding a horse to ride. Check with the *Suomen ratsastajain liitto ry* (Finnish Equestrian Federation; 20 Radiokatu; phone: 158-2318).

**ICE SKATING** Practice your triple Salkows at the *Helsingin jäähalli* (Helsinki Ice Hall) on Nordenskiöldinkatu near the *Olympiastadion* (phone: 418122) or at one of three outdoor arenas: Oulunkylä, Lassila, or Kallio. Contact the *Suomen Valtakunnan Urheiluliitto* (Finnish Sports Federation; phone: 1581) for information on outdoor rinks.

**JOGGING** There are paths close to *Olympiastadion,* at *Kaivo puisto* (Spa Park) in the southern part of the city, around *Hesperia Park* near the city center, and throughout *Keskuspuisto* (Central Park), which stretches north from *Hesperia Park* for miles into the suburbs (see above).

**SAUNAS** Most hotels have their own saunas; the most popular are at the *Kalastajatorppa, Inter-Continental, Grand Marina,* and *Strand Inter-Continental* (see *Checking In*). Since the hotel saunas are open to the public, it is advisable to book in advance. Contact the *Helsinki City Tourist Office* for information on public saunas, which usually do not accept reservations.

**SKIING** In Finland, skiing mostly means Nordic (cross-country) skiing. Marked and often illuminated, ski trails of varying lengths and difficulty are found all over the country. In the dead of winter, when the Gulf of Finland is solidly frozen, you can put on your skis and follow tracks on the gulf to the nearby islands. There are also numerous downhill slopes with ski lifts. Several winter sports centers, with both cross-country and downhill ski trails, are within 70 miles or so of Helsinki, including *Messilä* (65 miles/104 km away; phone: 18-86011), near the site of international skiing competitions in February; *Kulomäki* (in Hyvinkää, about 40 miles/64 km away; phone: 14-88283); and the *Peuramaa* ski center (phone: 298-1011), just a half-hour ride (18 miles/30 km) from Helsinki. Ski equipment can be rented at *Stadionin Retkeilymaja* (3B Pohjoinin Stadionintie; phone: 496071) and at all ski centers. For further information about skiing in and around Helsinki contact the local sports association, *Suomen Latu* (7 Fabianinkatu; phone: 170101); the *Helsinki City Tourist Office;* or any travel agent in Helsinki. The peak season for skiing in the Helsinki area is January through March.

**SLEDDING** *Kaivo puisto* (Spa Park) has plenty of hills for this popular winter activity; you can buy a sled or a round piece of plastic in any sporting goods store.

**SOCCER** In summer there are games between Finland and other countries at various locations around the city. Check *Helsinki This Week* for schedules and locations.

**SQUASH** For information on the 600 squash courts throughout Finland contact the *Suomen Squashliitto* (Finnish Squash Racquets Association; 20 Radiokatu; phone: 158-2400) or *Töölön Kisahalli* (Töölö Sports Hall; 41 Topeliuksenkatu; phone: 417761).

**SWIMMING** There are several outdoor and indoor locations; in summer try *Uimastadion* (Swimming Stadium; Hammarskjöldintie; phone: 402-9383) or *Töölö Kisahalli* (41 Topeliuksenkatu; phone: 412752 for pool).

**TENNIS** Helsinki boasts more than 30 tennis clubs. To book a court or for information call the *Suomen Tennisliitto* (Finnish Tennis Association; 20 Radiokatu; phone: 1581). Equipment rentals are available, but it's best to bring your own racket.

## THEATER

The top two theaters in town for performances in Finnish are the *Kansallisteatteri* (Finnish National Theater; Asema-aukio, Rautatientori; phone: 173-31331) and *Helsingin Kaupunginteatteri* (Helsinki City Theater; 5 Eläintarhantie; phone: 394022). The *Svenska Teatern* (Swedish Theater; 2 Pohjoisesplanadi; phone: 170438) stages performances in Swedish. In summer there are only open-air performances.

## MUSIC

There's always an excellent choice of concerts by symphony orchestras, chamber groups, and jazz artists, especially during the *Helsingin Juhlaviikot* (Helsinki Festival; see *Special Events*). Don't be surprised if you find a group of Japanese instrumentalists playing one concert and the *New York Philharmonic* at another. Major concert venues include *Finlandia-talo* (Finlandia Hall; see *Special Places*); the *Kulttuuritalo* (House of Culture; 4 Sturenkatu; phone: 77081); *Sibelius Akatemia* (Sibelius Academy; 9 P. Rautatiekatu; phone: 405441); and the *Ritarihuone* (House of Nobility; 1 Ritarikatu; phone: 625413). There's also the *Suomen Kansallis Oopera* (Finnish National Opera; see *Special Places*), where operas are sung in their original languages and concerts, recitals, and ballets are presented.

## NIGHTCLUBS AND NIGHTLIFE

Finns are nightlifers—especially those under 50, who are endowed with seemingly limitless endurance. Crowds flock to "nightclubs," as dance spots are called here, at various locales around the city. There often are lines to get in and a doorman usually decides who enters. Men may be required to wear jackets in some clubs. Expect to tip the people who check your coat and call a taxi for you. Three of the liveliest spots in the city are the *Storyville Jazz Club* (8 Museokatu; phone: 408007); *Old Baker's* (12 Mannerheimintie; phone: 641579); and the *Fizz* in the *Marski* hotel (next door to *Old Baker's;* see *Checking In*). Also popular are *Fanny and Alexander* (2 Siltasaarenkatu; phone: 753-2332) and *Vanha Maestro* (51 Fredrikinkatu; phone: 644303), which offers a real glimpse of traditional Helsinki, with tango and "ladies' nights." The discos at the *Grand Marina, Inter-Continental,* and *Strand Inter-Continental* hotels (see *Checking In*) draw a younger, wilder crowd. *Café Adlon* (14 Fabianinkatu; phone: 664611) is one of the city's most sophisticated nightclubs. For a noisy, devil-may-care atmosphere, visit *Wäinämöinen,* an old sailing ship anchored in Hietalahti harbor (phone: 685-1840). The *Ateljee* bar in the *Sokos Hotel Torni* tower (see *Checking In*) is the best place to enjoy a drink and an incredible view of the city rooftops. You'll find roulette wheels in many hotels and nightspots, but if you're looking for a full-tilt casino try the *Casino Ray* in the *Ramada Presidentti* (see *Checking In*).

# Best in Town

## CHECKING IN

Most of the city's accommodations are centrally located, modern, and equipped with a full range of amenities—and all the hotels listed below have at least one sauna. Reservations should be made in advance, especially during the summer. Seasonal discount accommodations coupons, called *Finncheques,* are available to summer travelers. These are good for considerably reduced rates and a full breakfast at 250 hotels across the country. *Finncheques* can be purchased in the US from *Cosmos Travel/Fenno Tours* (phone: 407-585-6870 or 800-535-6714); *Holiday Tours of America* (phone: 212-832-8989 or 800-677-6454); *Rahim Tours* (phone: 407-585-5305 or 800-556-5305); *ScanAm World Tours* (phone: 201-835-7070 or 800-545-2204); and *Scantours* (phone: 310-451-0911 or 800-223-SCAN).

For a double room expect to pay $160 to $235 per night (including tax) at a hotel in the expensive category; $90 to $160 at one in the moderate category; and less than $90 at one in the inexpensive category. Unless otherwise noted breakfast is included in the rate and rooms have private baths, air conditioning, TV sets, and telephones. Credit cards are accepted everywhere. All telephone numbers are in the 0 city code unless otherwise indicated.

### EXPENSIVE

**Inter-Continental** With 555 rooms and 30 luxury suites, this is a popular hotel for international business travelers. A terrace adjoining the sauna on the top floor overlooks the city. Guests may dine at the *Galateia* (see *Eating Out*), browse the shopping arcade in the lobby, or swim in the pool. Business facilities include 24-hour room service, meeting rooms for up to 650, secretarial services in English, audiovisual equipment, photocopiers, computers, cable TV news, translation services, and express checkout. Breakfast is not included. The *Finnair* bus terminal adjoins the rear entrance. 46-48 Mannerheimintie (phone: 40551; 800-327-0200; fax: 405-5255).

**Kalastajatorppa** In a park bordered by the blue waters of the Gulf of Finland, this 235-room property is spacious and ultramodern. The double rooms in the annex have views of the gulf, and several handsome suites connect to the older section via a whitewashed rock tunnel. A romantic formal garden invites a stroll between dancing sessions in the main dining room or the disco. Tennis courts, a private beach, and two indoor pools also are available. Business facilities include room service, meeting rooms for up to 550, secretarial services in English, audiovisual equipment, photocopiers, and translation services. Breakfast is not included. Outside the city center, at 1 Kalastajatorpantie (phone: 45811; fax: 458-1668).

**Marski** A business hotel, it offers many desirable extras, including three saunas. All 232 rooms have mini-bars, hair dryers, and pants presses; some have their own saunas. The upstairs dining room is very good, and the popular *Fizz* nightclub, *CinCin* bar, and cellar restaurant attract lively crowds. Business facilities include room service, meeting rooms for up to 400, secretarial services in English, audiovisual equipment, photocopiers, computers, cable TV news, and translation services. There's also a parking garage. In the center of town, at 10 Mannerheimintie (phone: 68061; fax: 642377).

**Palace** A Best Western affiliate, this older hostelry near the Eteläsatama (South Harbor) and the Kauppatori (Market Square) has 59 comfortable rooms and three saunas. Its *Palace Gourmet* dining room (see *Eating Out*) and Italian restaurant serve excellent fare, and the *American Bar* on the top floor is a delight. In summer you can have lunch or a drink on the terrace overlooking a wide expanse of sea. Business facilities include 24-hour room service, meeting rooms for up to 300, secretarial services in English, audiovisual equipment, photocopiers, cable TV news, translation services, and express checkout. Breakfast is not included. 10 Eteläranta (phone: 134561; 800-528-1234; fax: 654786).

**Radisson SAS Royal** Here you'll find 260 deluxe rooms with mini-bars, saunas, and two restaurants, one of which serves one of the best buffet breakfasts in town. Business facilities include meeting rooms for up to 300, secretarial services in English, audiovisual equipment, photocopiers, and computers. Breakfast is not included. 2 Runeberginkatu (phone: 69580; 800-333-3333; fax: 695-87100).

**Ramada Presidentti** Five hundred rooms, three saunas, a good steakhouse and several other restaurants, and the *Casino Ray,* Finland's first complete casino (offering roulette, blackjack, and slots) are the draws here; there's also an indoor pool. Business facilities include room service, meeting rooms for up to 400, secretarial services in English, audiovisual equipment, photocopiers, cable TV news, translation services, and express checkout. Breakfast is not included. Centrally located, at 4 Eteläinen Rautatiekatu (phone: 6911; 800-2-RAMADA; fax: 694-7886).

**Seurahuone-Socis** This establishment has traditional Old Europe charm, but feels a little dusty these days. There's a good restaurant (don't miss the excellent breakfast buffet), a classic Art Deco café and pub, and 118 rooms with modern conveniences. Business facilities include a meeting room for up to 70, secretarial services in English, audiovisual equipment, photocopiers, computers, cable TV news, translation services, and express checkout. Breakfast is not included. At an ideal location across from the railway station, at 12 Kaivokatu (phone: 170441; fax: 664170).

**Strand Inter-Continental** Elegant and intimate, this 200-room hotel is located on the waterfront near the old city center. The top floor has four saunas—each with its own terrace—and an indoor pool; there also is an elegant glass atrium and an excellent choice of restaurants (including *Pamir;* see *Eating Out*). Business facilities include 24-hour room service, meeting rooms for up to 250, secretarial services in English, audiovisual equipment, photocopiers, computers, cable TV news, translation services, and express checkout. *Finnair* passengers can check luggage and receive boarding passes in the lobby. Breakfast is not included. 4 John Stenberginranta (phone: 39351; 800-327-0200; fax: 393-5255).

## MODERATE

**Anna** This quiet, comfortable place has 60 rooms with all the usual amenities. There's no restaurant, but breakfast is included. In the center of town, at 1 Annankatu (phone: 648011; fax: 602664).

**Grand Marina** Designed in 1911 by noted Finnish architect Lars Sonck, this hostelry on the island of Katajanokka was once a warehouse. Each of the 462 modern rooms (including 28 suites) is decorated in exquisite taste and equipped with a mini-bar, pants press, and hair dryer. There are five good restaurants and a heated parking garage. Business facilities include meeting rooms for up to 50, audiovisual equipment, photocopiers, and cable TV news. Breakfast is not included. 7 Katajanokanlaituri (phone: 16661; fax: 664764).

**Helka** A Best Western property, it has 164 comfortable, modern rooms, a lobby bar, a restaurant, a sauna, a Jacuzzi, and a solarium. In the center of town, at 23 Pohjoinen Rautatienkatu (phone: 440581; 800-528-1234; fax: 441087).

**Holiday Inn Garden Court** This modern airport hotel geared to the business traveler offers 313 comfortable rooms with such conveniences as mini-bars and pants presses. There also is a cafeteria-style restaurant that serves breakfast and dinner, a no-frills bar, two saunas, a fitness room, parking, and a courtesy bus to and from the airport. Business facilities include meeting rooms for up to 50, cable TV news, and photocopiers. Near the airport in Vantaa, at 2 Ralssitie (phone: 870800; 800-HOLIDAY; fax: 870-90101).

**Lord** Designed in 1903, this granite castle is a fine example of Finnish Art Nouveau. With only 46 rooms, two suites, and two saunas in its connecting annex, it offers a quiet refuge. The small but well-furnished rooms include whirlpool baths and mini-bars. There are two restaurants and a bar. Business amenities include a meeting room featuring a private sauna in which 20 people can convene, and other meeting rooms that accommodate up to 150 people. There's also a parking garage. In the heart of the old city, at 29 Lönnrotinkatu (phone: 680-1680; fax: 680-1315).

**Rivoli Jardin** Charming and cozy, this well-run establishment with 54 rooms has no formal restaurant, but it does have a bar, a café, a winter garden, a solarium, and a sauna. In addition, snacks are available through room service (until midnight) and breakfast is included. Meeting rooms are available for up to 250. 40 Kasarmikatu (phone: 177880; fax: 656988).

**Seaside** Friendly service and excellent value are hallmarks of this 325-room Best Western property located right on the shore and the downtown tram line. Three categories of rooms, ranging from basic to spacious suites with terraces and kitchenettes, are very competitively priced. An informal lobby restaurant, a bar, and a 10th floor VIP sauna with a view are additional features. Business facilities include a 24-hour business center offering secretarial services in English, photocopiers, and computers; room service; meeting rooms for up to 60; and cable TV news. Rates include morning sauna. 3 Ruoholahdenranta (phone: 69360; 800-528-1234; fax: 693-2123).

**Sokos Hotel Torni** Those seeking serene surroundings and friendly service should stay at this venerable hostelry, built in 1903. The 155 rooms, all furnished with antiques, offer such modern amenities as mini-bars and hair dryers. *Ritarisali,* the restaurant (see *Eating Out*), has a loyal following. Be sure to visit the 13th-floor bar, the highest in Helsinki, for a fabulous view of the city's rooftops and harbor. Breakfast is not included. Business facilities include meeting rooms for up to 40. 26 Yrjönkatu (phone: 131131; fax: 131-1361).

**Sokos Klaus Kurki** Catering to businesspeople, this hotel has 134 comfortable rooms, a quiet bar, a pleasant restaurant, and an unpretentious wine cellar serving quick lunches. Its personal, friendly service makes it a favorite with frequent visitors to the city. Business facilities include room service, meeting rooms for up to 16, audiovisual equipment, photocopiers, and express checkout. Breakfast is not included. 2-4 Bulevardi (phone: 618911; fax: 608538).

### INEXPENSIVE

**Arthur** Formerly called *Hospiz,* this hotel near the center of town is a good choice for a family on a budget. There are 155 rooms and a restaurant (no liquor license). Meeting rooms are available for up to 250. 17 Vuorikatu (phone: 173441; fax: 626880).

**Aurora** In the heart of Helsinki, this small (70 rooms), dependable Best Western inn has a restaurant, a bar, a pool, and a sauna. 50 Helsinginkatu (phone: 717400; 800-528-1234; fax: 714240).

**Eurohostel** On Katajanokka Island by the ferry terminals, this no-frills hostel is convenient for those traveling by ship. There are 135 rooms (singles, twins, and triples); each floor has a shared toilet, shower, and kitchen. There also are two saunas, a laundry, and a café. Breakfast is not included. 9 Linnankatu (phone: 664452; fax: 655044).

**Marttahotelli** Near the business district, this quiet 45-room hotel run by the *Finnish Housewives' Association* has a restaurant and room service but no liquor license. 24 Uudenmaankatu (phone: 646211; fax: 680-1266).

---

## EATING OUT

Although Finnish cuisine shows marked Eastern (Russian) and Western (French and Swedish) influences, some dishes are uniquely Finnish. *Voileipäpöytä,* the Finnish version of Swedish smorgasbord, is popular, especially for lunch. Fish dishes also are common, especially *lohi* (salmon), whitefish, and Baltic herring. Not to be missed are fried Baltic herring and the delicious little native *rapu* crayfish, similar to American lobster but even tastier; the crayfish are in season from mid-July through August. *Poro* (reindeer meat) is served in many forms, but especially tasty is reindeer tongue, served smoked or in a madeira sauce. *Vorschmack* (a blend of herring, mutton, beef, and onions) is served with sour cream and a baked potato. Other typical dishes are *karjalanpiirakka* (a pastry dough of rye flour) filled with rice or potato, and *kalakukko* (a rich fish and pork pie). The national dessert is *ohukainen,* a Finnish version of crêpes. Also delicious are fresh berries—especially strawberries and *lakka* (cloudberries, a kind of yellowish raspberry)—and chewy Lapp cheese, which is served warm with a berry sauce. Finns drink their own high-quality beer and vodka, as well as brandy, Scotch, and Campari. Finnish after-dinner liqueurs made with berries include *mesimarja* (from brambleberries), *lakka* (from cloudberries), and *karpalo* (from cranberries). For a real jolt try the Finnish vodka Koskenkorva, and before tossing it back be sure to say *"Kippis!"* ("Cheers!").

Helsinki has a number of appealing restaurants near water or on small islands, open only in summer, that are great for dinner and dancing. The *Walhalla* on the island fortress of Suomenlinna is one of the most charming (see *Special Places*). Check at the concierge's desk at your hotel or at the *Helsinki City Tourist Office* for a complete list.

For dinner for two with drinks expect to pay $100 to $150 at an expensive restaurant; $50 to $100 at a moderate one; and less than $50 at an inexpensive one. A service charge is included in the bill, but leaving a small additional gratuity is a common practice. In Finland spirits are highly taxed and their sale is controlled by Alko, the state-run liquor monopoly (hence the popularity of package "drinking tours" across the border to Russia, where alcohol is inexpensive). Do as the Finns do and drink local beer or mineral water when eating out: A bottle of wine in a restaurant often costs more than a meal (though many establishments now serve wine by the glass, as well). Unless otherwise noted the restaurants below accept most major credit cards and are open for lunch and dinner. All telephone numbers are in the 0 city code unless otherwise indicated.

## EXPENSIVE

**Alexander Nevski** The decor is elegant and the service attentive at this Russian dining place near Eteläsatama (South Harbor). Closed Sunday dinner. Reservations advised. 17 Pohjoisesplanadi (phone: 639610).

**Bellevue** Not far from Kauppatori near the Greek Orthodox cathedral, this elegant establishment is one of the best Russian restaurants in Helsinki. Start your meal with a visit to the caviar bar. The chicken Kiev is memorable, as is the filet of beef for two. Closed January and February. Reservations advised. 3 Rahapajankatu (phone: 179560).

**Galateia** The *Inter-Continental* hotel's ninth-floor dining room features seafood, a panoramic city view, and a luminous interior. Closed weekends. Reservations advised. 46-48 Mannerheimintie (phone: 405-5900).

**Havis Amanda** This cellar restaurant has an elegant atmosphere, good service, and a reputation for excellence. Fresh seafood and luscious desserts are featured. Closed Saturday dinner and Sundays. Reservations advised. 23 Unioninkatu (phone: 666882).

**Kynsilaukka** Garlic is the specialty of this bistro-style restaurant where everything—soup, bouillabaisse, baked lamb, reindeer filets, and even ice cream—is prepared with a delicate touch of the clove. Go with someone you love—or at least like being near. Open daily. Reservations advised. 22 Fredrikinkatu (phone: 651939).

**Palace Gourmet** This restaurant in the *Palace* hotel is among the city's best, with both international and Finnish fare. Try the steamed salmon in lime and butter sauce or the smoked elk tartare, preceded by a bowl of rich forest mushroom bouillon. Ask for a window table with a harbor view. Closed weekends. Reservations necessary. 10 Eteläranta (phone: 134561).

**Pamir** Imaginative Finnish fish and game dishes are served in a tranquil setting, with muted colors and Saarinen furniture. In summer there's waterfront dining on the terrace. Closed weekends. Reservations advised. In the *Strand Inter-Continental Hotel,* 4 John Stenberginranta (phone: 39351).

**Piekka** The authentically Finnish food and atmosphere here attract hordes of businesspeople entertaining out-of-town guests. The menu features rich soups, fresh fish, seasonal game, and tasty desserts of local berries and cheeses. Open daily. Reservations advised. 2 Sibeliuksenkatu (phone: 493591).

**Ritarisali** White tablecloths and romantic violin music create a charming atmosphere in the "Hall of Knights." Fresh dishes such as eel filet pickled in juniper berries, and salmon and cod tournedos with crab ravioli are the mainstays of the menu. A prix-fixe, seven-course *menu du chevalier* is offered in the evenings. The Sunday buffet luncheon is also very popular. Closed Saturdays and July; open for buffet only Sundays. Reservations necessary. *Sokos Hotel Torni,* 5 Kalevankatu (phone: 131131).

**Säkkipilli** A busy downtown spot, it features two restaurants serving Finnish food (reindeer and the like), a pub, and a disco. Closed weekends. Reservations advised. Corner of Kalevankatu and Mannerheimintie (phone: 605607).

**Savoy** In the center of town at the top of an office building designed by Alvar Aalto, this is a popular spot for business luncheons. It serves both international and Finnish specialties—and a good *vorschmack.* Closed weekends. Reservations advised. 14 Eteläesplanadi (phone: 628715).

---

**Elite** Striking functionalist decor was restored with loving care to create this restaurant frequented by artists, writers, and Finnish celebrities. Order local specialties such as Baltic herring or *vorschmack,* or just try the soup and salad bar. The house wines are excellent. Open daily. Reservations necessary. 22 Eteläinen Hesperiankatu (phone: 495542).

**Galleria Hariton** Colorful chef Hariton Ivanovits, formerly of *Alexander Nevski,* returned from a stint at Moscow's *Savoy* hotel to open this cozy restaurant. It's usually noisy and packed with locals who come for the wild mushroom *pelmeny* (Russian ravioli). Ask for a grand portion of mixed *pelmeny* with sour cream on the side, or try the lamb Wellington for two. Open daily. Reservations advised. In the city center, at 44 Kasarmikatu (phone: 622-1717).

**Kasvisravintola** This is a basic vegetarian eatery, with a health food shop on the premises. Open daily. Reservations unnecessary. 3 Korkeavuorenkatu (phone: 179212).

**Kosmos** A slice of Finnish bohemian life—the patrons are painters, poets, and philosophers—this eatery has a versatile bistro menu. Try the escargots *vorschmack.* The beefy men at the door act as bouncers and check coats; local protocol dictates that you tip them about five markkaa. Closed weekends. Reservations necessary. 3 Kalevankatu (phone: 647255).

**Messenius** Helsinki's oldest restaurant, this is a meeting place for a colorful crowd of poets, painters, film people, and neighborhood folk. They come for the homestyle cooking—bowls of hearty soup or grilled *fogasch,* a kind of fish. Plays often are staged here on weekends. Open daily. Reservations necessary. 7 Messeniuksenkatu (phone: 414950).

**Namaskaar** This Indian restaurant is a good place to go for lamb *vindaloo* or chicken *tikka.* The crowd is lively. Open daily. Reservations advised. 100 Mannerheimintie (phone: 477-1960).

**Rivoli** A charming, cheerful spot devoted to traditional Finnish cooking. The sweetbreads in mustard sauce are a good choice, as is any seafood dish. Open daily. Reservations necessary. 38 Albertinkatu (phone: 643455).

**Wellamo** The literati and other locals come to this floating restaurant for hearty soups and daily specials, which change according to the whim of the flamboyant proprietress. The art on the walls is for sale. Closed Mondays. Reservations advised. 9 Vyokatu (phone: 663139).

**Aurora** A popular tearoom, it serves light fare in a cozy atmosphere. Open daily. Reservations unnecessary. In the *Aurora Hotel,* 50 Helsinginkatu (phone: 717400).

**Café Ursula** A sunny seaside café with good pastries and snacks. Open daily. No reservations. Alongside the Kaivopuisto shore (phone: 652817).

**Ekberg** A Helsinki institution, this is the spot for breakfast, lunch, or tea. Baked goods are made daily on the premises and sold at the bakery next door. Try the fresh berry tarts, salads, or a vegetable quiche. Closed Sundays. Reservations unnecessary. 9 Bulevardi (phone: 605269).

**Fazer** This tearoom/sweetshop, one of several run by the famed chocolate manufacturer, serves light meals, scrumptious pastries, and the best ice-cream sundaes in town. A great place for people watching. Closed Sundays. No reservations. 3 Kluuvikatu (phone: 665348).

**Rafaello** Always crowded, this cozy bar and brasserie offers a good value thanks to its generous portions. The menu features pasta and meat dishes and a few vegetarian entrées. With its central location, it's also a convenient place to stop for a beer or cappuccino. There's an outdoor terrace with live music during the summer. Open daily. Reservations unnecessary. 46 Aleksanterinkatu (phone: 653930).

# Lisbon

## At-a-Glance

### SEEING THE CITY

A city built on hills, Lisbon frequently surprises visitors with lovely views that emerge unexpectedly as you turn a corner. It has 17 natural balconies—called *miradouros*—from which to view the city. Foremost of these is the hilltop on which the ruins of *Castelo São Jorge* (see *Special Places,* below) stand. All of the squares are laid out beneath: Praça do Comércio, on the banks of the Tagus; Praça Rossio, with its fountains and flower stalls; Praça da Figueira, the bustling market square; Praça dos Restauradores, with its monument to Portugal's independence; the circular Praça Marquês de Pombal, at the end of the broad Avenida da Liberdade; and beyond that, the lovely *Parque Eduardo VII.* On a clear day, it is possible to see the castles of Sintra far to the west.

Another vantage point that's worth a pause is Largo de Santa Luzia, in the Alfama district, between the castle and the cathedral. Although the view from here—over the Alfama's red-roofed buildings down to the port—presents a less sweeping panorama than the one from the castle, the esplanade is charming, lined with *azulejos* (glazed tiles) and decked with flower beds and a trellis-topped colonnade. (Those who prefer not to walk may take the No. 28 *eléctrico,* or tram.) A third *miradouro* is the terrace on Rua de São Pedro de Alcântara, on the hill opposite Largo de Santa Luzia across the city in the Bairro Alto. From here, see a picture-postcard view of the castle, with the Alfama district spread down the slopes below its walls.

Ponte 25 de Abril (April 25 Bridge) across the Tagus provides another breathtaking view. Now named for the date of the military coup that began the 1974 revolution, it was originally called Ponte Salazar after Portugal's former dictator, who had it built in the 1960s. The third-longest suspension bridge in the world, it is particularly spectacular at night when its cables, the ships in the river, and the city are brightly lit. On the other side, there is a marvelous panorama of the Tagus estuary from the top of the 360-foot statue of *Cristo Rei* (Christ the King), built to commemorate Portugal's neutrality in World War II. An elevator takes visitors up. The statue is open daily. There is an admission charge. Those without a car can cross the river by ferry from Praça do Comércio and take a bus from Cacilhas to the statue.

### SPECIAL PLACES

In earliest times and later under the Moors, Lisbon was contained within walls that surrounded the hill where the *Castelo São Jorge* now stands. Today, that area is the Alfama, the oldest part of the city, where traces of the picturesque Judiaria (Jewish Quarter) and Mouraria (Moorish Quarter) still can be seen, along with remains of Roman structures. The Alfama has been destroyed several times by earthquakes and always was rebuilt along the original plan, its tortuous, narrow streets spiraling down from the top of the hill to the Baixa below. The Baixa, to the west of the Alfama, is the main shopping and commercial district of Lisbon. Built in a grid pattern after the 1755 earthquake, it stretches northward from Praça do Comércio by the river to the top of the Praça Rossio, one of the city's main squares. It includes Rua da Prata (Silver Street) and Rua Aurea (Gold Street), which is generally called and appears on most maps as Rua do Ouro (also translated as Gold Street); the streets are aptly named since each is lined with banks and fine jewelry stores. Up the hill and west of the Praça Rossio is the part of the Baixa known locally as the Chiado, which encompasses not much more than 10 square blocks. Here, landmark buildings gutted by a 1988 fire are in the last stages of restoration. The Chiado is a popular shopping district, dotted with coffeehouses and outdoor cafés.

Higher up is the Bairro Alto (Upper Quarter), above and to the west of Praça dos Restauradores and the Praça Rossio. The once wealthy and later seedy residential district in recent years has been taken over by the avant-garde. It's become the center of nightlife in downtown Lisbon, with fine restaurants, typical *tascas* (taverns or eateries), and *fado* houses, where the famous, sad Portuguese songs are heard. West of the Bairro Alto are the Madragoa and Lapa districts, largely residential areas where restaurants, government buildings, embassies, several museums, and art galleries can be found. Modern Lisbon, with contemporary residential areas, museums, and the zoo stretches to the north and east of the downtown area.

The Belém quarter is along the riverbank west of the above districts. Because it suffered little in the 1755 earthquake, many of its fine, old palaces and monuments still stand. Belém also is home to several museums and many restaurants.

Many of the city's churches, museums, historical sites, and shops close for an hour or two at midday.

## CASTELO DE SÃO JORGE AND THE ALFAMA

**CASTELO DE SÃO JORGE (ST. GEORGE'S CASTLE)** Built on one of Lisbon's highest hills, this castle with 10 towers is considered the cradle of the city. An Iron Age *castro* (fortified hilltop town) probably was located here, succeeded by Roman fortifications (Roman walls and other remains are under excavation), a fortress built by the Visigoths during the 5th century, and later, a fortified Moorish town. The present castle was built during the 12th century. On the grounds are lovely gardens where peacocks roam free, the remains of an Arabian palace where the kings of Portugal lived from the 14th to the 16th century, and the *Casa do Leão* restaurant (see *Eating Out*). Open daily. No admission charge. On Rua Costa do Castelo.

**ALFAMA** The old quarter slopes downhill from *São Jorge*. The cobbled labyrinth, where some streets are so narrow that pedestrians must

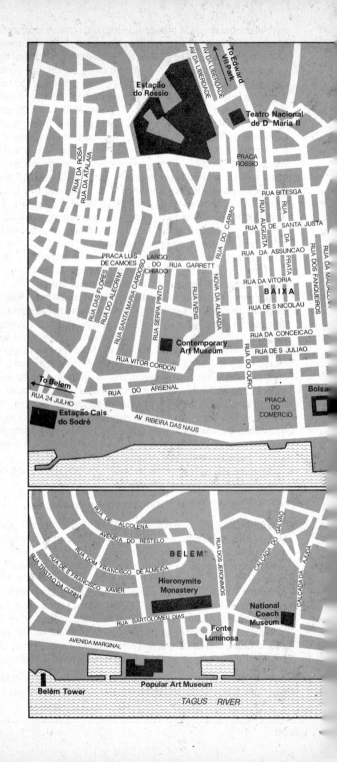

walk single file, is one of the most colorful spots in Europe. Its streets are overhung with balconies ablaze with scarlet geraniums from spring through fall and lined with little taverns decorated with strings of peppers, garlic, and cheese. By day, caged canaries on the balconies sing in the sun; at night, wrought-iron lamps light the scene; and on wash days, the buildings are strung with clotheslines and laundry. Most of the houses date from the late 18th century, after the earthquake of 1755. The best times to see the Alfama are in the morning, when the markets come alive; late in the afternoon, when the streets and squares fill with people; and on a moonlit evening. The quarter stretches north to south from the castle to the banks of the Tagus, and west to east from the cathedral to the vicinity of *Igreja de São Vicente de Fora.*

**SÉ (CATHEDRAL)** Lisbon's oldest church, built just after the Christian reconquest in the 12th century, suffered enormous earthquake damage in 1755, but it was rebuilt during the 18th century and restored during this one. It is a typical fortress church of solid, massive construction, with battlements and towers. The plain façade is Romanesque, the ambulatory chapels and the cloister are pure Gothic, and the choir is Baroque. In the enclosure of *azulejos* just inside the door is the *Pia Baptismal de Santo Antonio* (Baptismal Font of St. Anthony); Portugal's patron saint was born and baptized here, although he is known as St. Anthony of Padua because he spent much of his life in Italy. In the chapel to the left is a *presépio* (nativity scene) by Joaquim Machado de Castro. Relics of St. Vincent, the patron saint of Lisbon, also are housed in the cathedral, but they're brought out only on special occasions. In addition, there is a collection of religious vestments and ecclesiastical gold, which can be seen only by prior arrangement. Closed Mondays. Admission charge to the cloister. On Largo da Sé (phone: 886-6752).

**MUSEU-ESCOLA DE ARTES DECORATIVAS (MUSEUM-SCHOOL OF DECORATIVE ARTS)** Around the bend from the Largo de Santa Luzia *miradouro* and housed in a 17th-century palace that survived the great earthquake, this museum contains Portuguese porcelain, silver, crystal, paintings, tapestries, and furniture, most from the 17th and 18th centuries and all arranged as the furnishings of an aristocratic Lisboan home of the time. The foundation that created the museum also runs a school and crafts workshops (phone: 872429) for the reproduction and restoration of antiques. Visitors may tour the workshops, which are adjacent to the museum, but an appointment is required. The museum is closed Sundays and Mondays. Admission charge. On 2 Largo das Portas do Sol (phone: 886-2184).

**IGREJA DE SÃO VICENTE DE FORA (CHURCH OF ST. VINCENT OUTSIDE THE WALLS)** From Largo das Portas do Sol, follow the *eléctrico* tracks down Escadinhas de São Tomé and then up again to this church, which was built during the late 16th and early 17th centuries by Filippo Terzi. A remnant of an old monastery, it is notable for its Mannerist façade of distorted proportions and its cloisters, lavishly lined with 18th-century *azulejos.* Beyond, set up in the old monastery refectory, is the *Panteão Real* (Royal Pantheon), the mausoleum of the Bragança family, rulers of Portugal from 1640 to 1910. Most of the Bragança kings and queens, including Portugal's last monarchs, are buried here. Closed Mondays. Admission charge to the cloisters and pantheon also gains entrance to an ornate sacristy. Largo de São Vicente (phone: 886-2544).

**IGREJA DE SANTA ENGRÁCIA (CHURCH OF ST. ENGRÁCIA)** Begun during the 17th century but not completed until 1966, this church gave rise to the Portuguese expression *"obras de Santa Engrácia"* ("works of St. Engrácia"), to describe any seemingly endless task. The grandiose structure, with a Baroque façade and a richly decorated interior of marble, now serves as the *Panteão Nacional* (National Pantheon). It contains the tombs of three Portuguese presidents and three famed writers, and memorials to other esteemed men not buried here, including Prince Henry the Navigator, Luís de Camões, and Vasco da Gama. It's within easy walking distance of the *Igreja de São Vicente,* although on Tuesdays and Saturdays you may find yourself caught up by the flea market set up on the street between the two. Closed Mondays. Admission charge. Campo de Santa Clara (phone: 871529).

**MUSEU MILITAR (MILITARY MUSEUM)** Housed in an 18th-century arsenal (the huge, saffron-yellow building in front of the Santa Apolónia train station), it contains cannon, guns, swords, armor, and uniforms, as well as paintings, sculptures, coin collections, and other mementos of Portugal's wars. One room is dedicated to the discoveries of Vasco da Gama, the Portuguese explorer who made the first sea voyage from Western Europe around Africa to the East. Closed Mondays. Admission charge. Largo dos Caminhos de Ferro (phone: 886-7131).

**IGREJA DA MADRE DE DEUS (CHURCH OF THE MOTHER OF GOD)** Although the convent complex here was founded in 1501, most of what is seen today dates from the 18th century. The church is resplendent with ornate, gilded Baroque woodwork, oil paintings, and *azulejos.* But the attractions don't end there: The *Museu Nacional do Azulejo*—a must-see for tile lovers—is installed in the rooms around two cloisters, one of which is a small gem in itself. Exquisite examples of the art of the tile, both Portuguese and foreign, and dating from the 15th century to the present, are displayed. Among its treasures, the museum possesses a long tile frieze dating from about 1730 that shows a panoramic view of Lisbon before the great earthquake. There's even a pleasant cafeteria that's decorated with 19th-century kitchen tiles. Closed Mondays. Admission charge. Bus No. 104 from Praça do Comércio goes to the convent at Rua da Madre de Deus (phone: 814-7747).

**IGREJA DA CONCEIÇÃO VELHA (CHURCH OF THE CONCEPTION)** Built during the early 16th century on the site of Lisbon's ancient synagogue, this church was completely devastated in the 1755 earthquake, but its original Manueline portal survived. That beautiful doorway, richly carved with limestone figures, was retained for the new church, which otherwise has little of note. On Rua da Alfândega.

**PRAÇA DO COMÉRCIO** This impressive riverside square, planned by the Marquês de Pombal after the 1755 earthquake, is edged on three sides by arcaded neoclassical buildings. It's also known as Terreiro do Paço (Palace Square), after the royal palace that stood here before the great quake, and, to the English, as Black Horse Square, after the bronze equestrian statue of King José I by the 18th-century sculptor Joaquim Machado de Castro that stands in the middle. The triumphal arch on the north side of the square, leading to Rua Augusta and the rest of the Baixa, was finished during the late 19th century. The square was the scene of the assassination of Portugal's monarch, King Carlos I, and his eldest son in 1908.

**PRAÇA ROSSIO** Its official name is Praça de Dom Pedro IV, after the 19th-century king who is the subject of the statue at the center, but the name never stuck. The square is still invariably called only O Rossio (The Place) or Rossio (Place), and though it's located at the northern limit of the Baixa, it is the heart of the city. As early as the 13th century, it was the city's marketplace, but after it was destroyed by the earthquake of 1755 it was newly laid out. On the north side is the 19th-century *Teatro Nacional de Dona Maria II* (see *Theater,* below), standing on the site of a royal palace that during the 16th century was the seat of the Inquisition in Portugal. The square is cheery now, graced with flower stalls, fountains, and open-air cafés.

**ELEVADOR DE SANTA JUSTA (SANTA JUSTA ELEVATOR)** This lacy, gray iron structure—sometimes erroneously attributed to Alexandre-Gustave Eiffel—was designed by Raoul Mesnier, a Portuguese engineer of French descent, and erected in 1898. It not only spares visitors the climb from Rua do Ouro (occasionally called Rua Aurea, its official name) to Largo do Carmo in the Chiado district, but it also provides a panoramic view of the city from the top. As you exit, you pass under a flying buttress of the *Igreja do Carmo.* The elevator runs from 7 AM to 11 PM; Sundays from 9 AM. Rua do Ouro to Largo do Carmo.

**IGREJA DO CARMO (CARMO CHURCH)** Built during the 14th century, this had been an imposing, majestic structure overlooking the city until it was largely destroyed by the 1755 earthquake. The remaining shell of the church, with Gothic arches and a doorway, is floodlit at night. The ruins have been turned over to the *Museu Arqueológico do Carmo,* which operates in the church's remains, housing prehistoric, Roman, Visigothic, and medieval artifacts, as well as medieval sculpture, *azulejos,* and inscriptions. Closed Sundays. Admission charge. Largo do Carmo (phone: 346-0473).

**SOLAR DO VINHO DO PORTO (PORT WINE MANOR)** This comfortable bar run by the *Instituto do Vinho do Porto* (Port Wine Institute) is a good place to sample Portugal's famous sweet, fortified wine, *vinho do Porto*—called port in English—without making a trip to the northern city for which it was named. It's stocked with all types and vintages of port (more than 200 kinds, although the whole list is rarely available), many of which may be ordered by the glass. Open daily. Take the funicular streetcar from Praça dos Restauradores. 45 Rua de São Pedro de Alcântara (phone: 347-5707).

**IGREJA DE SÃO ROQUE (CHURCH OF ST. ROCH)** This 16th-century church is best known for the Baroque *Capela de São João Baptista* (St. John the Baptist Chapel), the fourth chapel on the left. The chapel was commissioned during the mid-18th century by King João V, and designed, assembled, and blessed by the pope in Rome. It was then dismantled, shipped to Portugal, and rebuilt here. Its lapis lazuli, marble, alabaster, ivory, and other precious and semiprecious materials were extravagant even for a king, and the workmanship is flawless. Note the *Baptism of Christ,* which appears to be an oil painting is, in fact, an exquisite mosaic. The *Museu de São Roque* adjoining the church contains paintings and richly embroidered vestments as well as other liturgical objects. The museum is closed Mondays. Admission charge. Largo Trindade Coelho (phone: 346-0361).

## NORTHERN AND WESTERN LISBON

**PARQUE EDUARDO VII (EDWARD VII PARK)** Downtown Lisbon's largest green space is this formally landscaped park at the northern end of Avenida da Liberdade, just beyond Praça Marquês de Pombal. From the esplanade at the top of the park, the view extends over the lower town to the Rio Tajo (Tagus River). In the northwest corner is the charming *Estufa Fria* (Cold Greenhouse), where plants and flowers from across the globe grow in luxuriant abundance alongside pathways, tunnels, streams, goldfish ponds, and waterfalls. A slatted roof protects them from the extremes of summer and winter and filters the sun's rays, suffusing the greenhouse with a magically soft light. Within the *Estufa Fria* is the *Estufa Quente*, a hothouse filled with tropical plants. Open daily; the *Estufa Quente* closes a half-hour earlier. Admission charge (phone: 682278).

**MUSEU CALOUSTE GULBENKIAN (CALOUSTE GULBENKIAN MUSEUM)** When the Armenian oil tycoon Calouste Sarkis Gulbenkian died in 1955, he left most of his estate and his enormous art collection to Portugal, the country to which he fled during World War II and where he spent the last years of his life. His legacy is *Fundação Calouste Gulbenkian* (Calouste Gulbenkian Foundation), located in a modern complex that houses not only the museum but auditoriums, a library, and exhibition space. Don't miss the museum, a repository of a half century of astute collecting—6,400 pieces, including works from the Hermitage that Gulbenkian purchased during the 1920s when the Soviet Union needed foreign currency. The treasures include fine European paintings, sculpture, 18th-century French furniture, Chinese vases, Greek coins, medieval ivories, illuminated manuscripts, Middle Eastern carpets and ceramics, and more. There also is a marvelous collection of small Egyptian pieces and a display of unique Art Nouveau jewelry by René Lalique. Closed Mondays year-round and Wednesday and Saturday mornings in winter. Admission charge. 45 Av. de Berna (phone: 797-4167).

**CENTRO DE ARTE MODERNA (MODERN ART CENTER)** Located in the gardens behind the *Museu Calouste Gulbenkian* is an impressive collection of 19th- and 20th-century Portuguese paintings and sculpture, including works by Portuguese Modernist José de Almada Negreiros, as well as 20th-century British art. There also are frequent temporary exhibits. A sinuous sculpture by Henry Moore and the oversize tapestries of Negreiros are among the permanent fixtures. A cafeteria overlooks the gardens. Closed Mondays year-round and Wednesday and Saturday mornings in winter. Admission charge. Rua Dr. Nicolau de Bettencourt (phone: 793-5131).

**JARDIM ZOOLÓGICO (ZOO)** Set in a 65-acre park, the zoo is home to some 2,000 animals, including an elephant who rings a bell for money. Other amusements include pony rides for children, rowboats, and a small train. Open daily. Admission charge. Parque das Laranjeiras (phone: 726-8041).

**PALÁCIO DOS MARQUESES DA FRONTEIRA (PALACE OF THE MARQUESSES OF FRONTEIRA)** West of the zoo, on the edge of the Parque Florestal de Monsanto, is a palace built during the second half of the 17th century and originally used by its aristocratic owners as a hunting lodge. It's notable for the great number of *azulejos* that cover its walls—inside as well as outside in the formal gardens—many of them depicting historical events. A public tour of the privately owned palace is offered daily, except Sundays and holidays. Admission charge. 1 Largo de São Domingos de Benfica (phone: 778-2023).

**AQUEDUTO DAS AGUAS LIVRES (AQUEDUCT OF FREE-RUNNING WATERS)** The aqueduct was built during the first half of the 18th century to transport water the distance of 11 miles (18 km) from Caneças in the northwest to a Lisbon reservoir. It not only survived the devastating 1755 earthquake but to this day supplies the city with drinking water, delivering it to a reservoir near the present-day *Centro Comercial das Amoreiras*. A quarter of the aqueduct runs underground, and there are 109 stone arches aboveground. The most impressive stretch, with one arch 214 feet high, is the section crossing the Alcântara Valley on the edge of the city. Look for it as you cross the viaduct out of town on the road (N7) that leads to Estoril and Sintra. The *Museu de Agua* (Water Museum; 12 Rua de Alviela; phone: 813-5522), located not far from the *Igreja da Madre de Deus,* organizes group visits within the aqueduct. It also chronicles the history of Lisbon's water supplies, going back to Roman times. The museum is closed Sundays and Mondays. There's an admission charge.

**BASÍLICA DA ESTRELA (STAR BASÍLICA)** Queen Maria I built this house of worship between 1779 and 1790 to fulfill the vow she had made to God while petitioning for the birth of a son. The dome is one of

Lisbon's landmarks; the tomb of the founder is inside. The sculptures in the church reflect the school founded at Mafra by the Italian sculptor Alessandro Giusti; Joaquim Machado de Castro, one of Giusti's Portuguese pupils, created the manger figures here. Open daily. Praça da Estrela.

## MUSEU NACIONAL DE ARTE ANTIGA (NATIONAL MUSEUM OF ANCIENT ART)
One of Lisbon's most important museums, it is housed partially in a 17th-century palace (once the home of Marquês de Pombal, an influential 18th-century prime minister) and partially in an adjacent 20th-century building. Although it contains numerous foreign works, such as a celebrated Bosch triptych titled *The Temptation of St. Anthony,* the museum is most notable for its paintings of the Portuguese school, especially of the 15th and 16th centuries. The prizes in this group—and perhaps the most famous paintings in all Portugal—are the pair of triptychs known as the *Panéis de São Vicente de Fora* (St. Vincent Panels), masterpieces by Nuno Gonçalves, the most important Portuguese painter of the 15th century. The only Gonçalves painting still extant, the triptychs are highly valued for their great artistic merit, and because they document Portuguese society of the time. Also housed in the museum are sculptures; Portuguese, European, and Oriental ceramics; objects of silver and gold; jewelry, furniture, and tapestries; plus the entire gilt-and-tile-laden *Capela de Santo Alberto* (St. Albert Chapel), an architectural leftover from a Carmelite convent that once occupied this spot. Worthy of special attention, too, are the Japanese painted screens portraying the first Portuguese visitors to Japan. Closed Mondays. Admission charge. 95 Rua das Janelas Verdes (phone: 397-2725).

BELÉM

## MOSTEIRO DOS JERÓNIMOS (HIERONYMITE MONASTERY) One of Lisbon's
great landmarks, this white marble monastery was founded in 1502 by King Manuel I to give thanks for the successful return of Vasco da Gama's fleet from the Indies and also to commemorate all the great voyages of Portugal's explorers during the Age of Discovery. Because Vasco da Gama had sailed from Belém, it was the site chosen for the original small mariners' chapel that was said to have been "built by pepper" because its funding came from the lucrative spice trade. The seashells, ropes, anchors, and other motifs of the sea carved throughout the monastery are the decorative elements that characterize Manueline architecture, a uniquely Portuguese style that served as a transition from the Gothic to the Renaissance styles and was named after the king, Dom Manuel. Built on the site of the mariners' chapel, the church complex includes adjoining cloisters and tiny monks' quarters and is considered the country's finest example of Manueline architecture: The two portals, extremely slender columns, and characteristic network vaulting of the church, plus the richly sculpted two-story cloister are exceptionally beautiful. King Manuel I and several other monarchs are buried in the church, as is Vasco da Gama, whose tomb just inside the entrance

is marked by a ship. Opposite it, marked by a lyre and quill pen, is a monument to Luís de Camões, Portugal's most famous poet, whose bones may or may not rest inside. (After the poet's death in Africa, the wrong bones may have been brought back.) The long galleries west of the monastery, neo-Manueline from the 19th century, contain the *Museu Nacional de Arqueologia e Etnologia* (National Museum of Archaeology and Ethnology; phone: 362-0000; open daily; admission charge) and, around the corner, the *Museu de Marinha* (see below). Modern annexes across the courtyard from the entrance to the *Museu de Marinha* contain a collection of boats and a planetarium, the *Planetario Calouste Gulbenkian* (phone: 362-0002), which has presentations several days a week (times are posted outside; admission charge). The monastery is closed Mondays. Admission charge to the cloister. Praça do Império (phone: 362-0034).

**MUSEU DE MARINHA (NAVAL MUSEUM)** In the 19th-century galleries attached to the *Mosteiro dos Jerónimos,* the museum displays small models of boats from all eras of Portuguese history—from the earliest caravels of the Age of Discovery to warships, trading ships, and submarines—along with naval uniforms and other marine paraphernalia. Actual-size boats are exhibited in the hangar-like extension, where the star attraction is the late–18th-century *galeota* (galley), built for the wedding day of Crown Prince João (who became João VI) to a Spanish princess and rowed by 71 red-coated figures. Examples of traditional boats from various regions include a *rabelo* boat from the Rio Douro (Douro River), a *moliceiro* from the Ria de Aveiro, and fishing boats from the Algarve. Closed Mondays. Admission charge. Praça do Império (phone: 362-0010).

**MUSEU NACIONAL DOS COCHES (NATIONAL COACH MUSEUM)** Probably the finest collection of coaches in the world is now housed in the building of the former riding school of the *Palácio de Belém.* The coaches date from the 16th through 19th centuries, and although a few are simple (such as the one that carried Philip III of Spain when he came to claim the throne as King Philip II of Portugal), most are intricately carved, gilded works of art especially designed to transport royal personages or their emissaries. (Note the three Italian-made 18th-century Baroque extravaganzas used by the Portuguese ambassador to the Holy See.) The museum also houses an important collection of livery, harnesses, and bullfighting costumes. Open daily. Admission charge. Praça Afonso de Albuquerque (phone: 363-8022).

**PADRÃO DOS DESCOBRIMENTOS (MONUMENT TO THE DISCOVERIES)** On the river in front of the *Mosteiro dos Jerónimos,* this modern monument was put up in 1960 to commemorate the 500th anniversary of the death of Prince Henry the Navigator. It's shaped like the prow of a Portuguese caravel, with the prince as a figurehead leading a sculptured frieze of personages of his time seaward. Inside there's exhibition space and an elevator to a belvedere on top, from which the view extends up and down the Tagus River and over formal green lawns to the monastery and the rest of Belém. Outside is a marble mosaic on the ground that represents a compass; in the center is a map of the world. Open daily. Admission charge to the belvedere. On Praça do Império.

**TORRE DE BELÉM (TOWER OF BELÉM)** This quadrangular five-story tower, which resembles a huge chess piece, stands on the banks of the Tagus, west of the *Padrão dos Descobrimentos.* It is the Portuguese symbol of their brave past, and its image often is used on official papers. Built during the 16th century to protect the river from pirates (it was at one time surrounded by water, but land has been reclaimed from the river since then), the tower later functioned as a prison. It is a good example of Manueline architecture, richly decorated with sea motifs, statues, stone tracery, and Moorish balconies. Temporary exhibitions are sometimes held inside. Visitors may climb to the top for a view of the Tagus from the outside terrace. Closed Mondays. Admission charge. Off Avenida Marginal (phone: 616892).

**PALÁCIO NACIONAL DA AJUDA (AJUDA NATIONAL PALACE)** In the hills behind Belém, this former royal palace, built in the early 19th century, is a treasure-trove of furniture, paintings, sculpture, and objets d'art, left as they might have been when royalty occupied the premises. The widow of King Luís, Maria Pia of Savoy, who died in 1911, was its last royal inhabitant, but the palace is still used occasionally by the Portuguese government for state dinners. Closed Mondays. Admission charge. Largo da Ajuda (phone: 363-7095).

ENVIRONS

**ESTORIL** This seaside suburb about 15½ miles (25 km) west of Lisbon became internationally famous during World War II, when both Allied and Axis spies were here, tripping over each other, most notably at the *Palácio* hotel. Portugal was neutral, and a gentlemen's agreement developed: Allied diplomats could play golf at the local clubs on certain days, Axis diplomats on others. Immediately after the war, Estoril became home to numerous members of Europe's exiled royalty, lending it a touch of glamour. The crowned heads are gone now, but Estoril, with its bars, cafés, and gambling casino (see *Nightclubs and Nightlife,* below), is still alluring. Its large turn-of-the-century mansions, hidden away behind spacious lawns and gardens flanked by winding, hilly streets and wide avenues, impart a decidedly Old World air. The *Parque do Estoril,* a lovely garden of stately palm trees and purple-red bougainvillea, faces the seaside esplanade and the beach. The modern, elegant *Casino Estoril* (phone: 268-4521) sits at the top of the park. The residential district of Monte Estoril, west of the park, tends to merge with the town of Cascais (see below). By train, Estoril can be reached easily from Lisbon's *Estação Cais do Sodré.* By car, take either the beach highway (Estrada Marginal—EN6) or the A5 toll highway that links Lisbon with Cascais and the towns in between. The *Posto do Turismo de Estoril* (Estoril Tourist Office) is located on Arcadas do Parque (phone: 468-0113).

**CASCAIS** Once a simple fishing village where picturesque brightly painted boats could be seen heading out to sea each morning, Cascais (pronounced Kash-ka-ish) evolved during this century into a beach resort and home to deposed royalty and dictators, as well as to thousands of British and other European expatriates. Although this fast-growing town just west of Estoril now flourishes on tourism, the fishermen remain, and it's interesting to watch the fish auction that takes place on weekday evenings at the market by the beach.

Cascais has a few monuments to detain sightseers. There is one important church, the Manueline *Igreja de Nossa Senhora da Assunção* (Church of Our Lady of the Assumption; on Largo da Assunçao), with 18th-century *azulejos* and paintings by Josefa d'Obidos. Also of note are the *Cidadela,* a 17th-century fortress on Estrada da Boca do Inferno overlooking the sea (closed to the public), and the *Museu-Biblioteca Condes de Castro Guimarães* (Museum-Library of the Counts of Castro-Guimrães; Av. Rei Humberto de Italia; phone: 483-0856), with paintings, sculpture, furniture, and objets d'art set up in an old mansion (closed Tuesdays; no admission charge).

The town has plenty of other distractions. The bullfights held on summer Sundays at the *Monumental de Cascais* (on Bairro do Rosario) attract many visitors; your hotel can arrange tickets. Water sports and sailing are available in the bay and the Atlantic; there are also riding stables, tennis courts, and golf courses in the vicinity. The town and surrounding coastal area are noted for seafood restaurants, many of which overlook the bay and the sea. There is no dearth of nightlife, either—Cascais is full of bars and discos.

A tourism kiosk is in the town's center (Av. Marginal; phone: 486-8204); it is open daily. Cascais can be reached by train from Lisbon's *Estação Cais do Sodré.*

**QUELUZ** This town 7½ miles (12 km) northwest of Lisbon on the road to Sintra is known for its lovely pink rococo *Palácio Nacional,* where guests of the Portuguese government often are housed. The palace was begun in 1747 under the auspices of the Infante Dom Pedro, who later became Pedro III and consort of Queen Maria I. The queen lived here after going mad following the deaths of both Pedro and her eldest son. Designed by Mateus Vicente de Oliveira, a pupil of the architect of the *Mafra Monastery*, the royal residence took decades to finish and was restored after being partially destroyed by fire in this century. Its rooms are filled with Portuguese furnishings and tapestries, Italian glassware and marble, Dutch tiles, Chinese screens, Austrian porcelain, and other exquisite antiques; its gardens are laid out to resemble those of Versailles (Queen Maria once had been engaged to Louis XV), with fountains, statuary, and *azulejos.* Among the more striking rooms are the *Sala do Trono* (Throne Room), *Sala dos Embaixadores* (Hall of the Ambassadors), *Sala da Música* (Music Salon), and *Toucador da Rainha* (Queen's Dressing Room). In summer, cultural events are staged here to re-create the ambience of Queen Maria's 18th-century court—with costumed dances, chamber music concerts, equestrian exhibitions, and even games in which visitors may take part. The palace is closed Tuesdays. Admission charge (phone: 435-0039). Queluz can be reached by train from Lisbon's *Estação de Rossio*.

The beauty of Sintra, a town on the north slope of the Serra de Sintra about 17½ miles (28 km) northwest of Lisbon, has been sung through the ages, most notably by poet Luís de Camões in *The Lusiads,* and by Lord Byron, who called it a "glorious Eden" in "Childe Harold's Pilgrimage." The town has an enchanting setting, swathed in towering trees, dense ferns, and plants and flowers brought by the Portuguese from every corner of their once far-flung empire—all kept green by springs gushing from the rocks and little waterfalls that tumble down the mountain. Mists from the nearby Atlantic Ocean often envelop its heights, lending the town an ethereal air and producing a pleasant climate in summer, although from time to time they obscure the majestic views. Among the oldest towns in Portugal, Sintra was occupied by the Moors, who built two castles, one in the center of the present town and the other winding from pinnacle to pinnacle around the side of the mountain. After Sintra was taken from the Moors in the 12th century, it became a favorite summer residence of the Portuguese monarchs. Over the centuries, they built the imposing *Palácio Nacional de Sintra* (Sintra National Palace) in town on the site of a former Moorish castle, and the whimsical, even Disneyland-like *Palácio Nacional da Pena* (Pena National Palace) on the very peak of the mountain, where it can be seen from as far away as Lisbon and the Arrábida Peninsula.

The *Palácio Nacional de Sintra* is also popularly referred to as both the *Palácio da Vila* (Town Palace) and the *Palácio Real* (Royal Palace). It stands in the main square where it was built by King João I in the late 14th century and added to by King Manuel I in the early 16th century. The palace received still further additions later on, creating in the enormous structure a survey of styles from Moorish through Mudejar, Gothic, Manueline, and Renaissance to Baroque. In addition to the twin conical chimneys that dominate the town, the most notable features of the palace's exterior are the characteristic Manueline windows. Facing the walls throughout the palace interior are the striking *azulejos,* some of the finest in the country. A particularly interesting room is the *Sala dos Brazões* (Hall of the Coats of Arms), built during Manuel's reign; its ceiling is an octagonal wooden cupola with painted panels showing the coats of arms of the king, his eight children, and the 72 noble families of Portugal of the time. In the *Sala das Pêgas* (Hall of the Magpies), the ceiling is decorated with 136 magpies, which were painted on the orders of João I, so the story goes, after his wife, Philippa of Lancaster, found him kissing a lady-in-waiting. (The work was designed to end the gossiping of the queen's 136 ladies-in-waiting.) The palace is closed Wednesdays. There's an admission charge (phone: 923-0085).

The *Palácio Nacional da Pena,* standing on the highest peak above Sintra, is reached via a spectacular road of hairpin curves through beautiful parks and woods. After religious orders were expelled from Portugal in 1832, Ferdinand of Saxe-Coburg-Gotha, consort of Queen Maria II, purchased a small 16th-century monastery that stood on this spot and commissioned a German architect, Baron Eschewege, to create a medieval palace around it. Inspired by the Bavarian castles of his own country, the architect combined their style with Moorish, Gothic, and Manueline elements to create a fantastic building complete with gold-topped domes, turrets, crenelated walls, parapets, and a drawbridge. The cloister and chapel of the monastery were preserved; the latter has a black alabaster and marble altarpiece executed in the 16th century by Nicolas Chanterène and 19th-century German stained glass windows. The rooms of the palace proper contain a delightful mixture of Indo-Portuguese and Sino-Portuguese furnishings, and they remain much as they were when the palace was last occupied by the royal family, who used it as their summer home before fleeing into exile in 1910. The views from the verandahs are spectacular, and the *Parque da Pena* surrounding the palace, first laid out in the 19th century with plants and trees from all over the world, is impressive.

The palace is closed Mondays. There is an admission charge (phone: 923-0227).

The *Castelo dos Mouros* (Moorish Castle) is located off the same road that leads to the *Palácio Nacional da Pena,* about halfway up the mountain. It was originally built by the Moors in the 8th or 9th century and was restored after the Christian reconquest in the 12th century and later by King Fernando I. It has five rather dilapidated towers, a keep, and long walls undulating over a great part of the mountain; it's always open. About 2 miles (3 km) from Sintra via N375 is the *Quinta de Monserrate,* a palace and park built by a 19th-century Englishman, Sir Francis Cook. The palace is an odd-looking three-domed structure, but the wonderful gardens, landscaped on a steep slope, are the prime attraction here. The palace and gardens are open daily. There's an admission charge. Another interesting sight is the 16th-century *Convento dos Capuchos* (Capuchin Monastery), 4 miles (6 km) from Sintra via N247-3. The monks' cells, which were carved out of rock, are lined with cork to keep out the dampness. The monastery is open daily (ring the bell for the caretaker). There's an admission charge. Still another of Sintra's palaces, the *Palácio dos Seteais,* has been turned into a luxury hotel (see *Checking In*).

Sintra is very crowded in summer and on weekends. It can be reached by car on N117 and N249 or by train from the *Estação do Rossio* station. Those who come by train can take a taxi to visit the palaces that are located at some distance from the center; the *Posto de Turismo da Câmara Municipal* (Town Hall Tourism Office; 3 Praça da República; phone: 923-1157) provides maps for those who choose to walk. There also are horse-drawn carriages that take visitors sightseeing around town. Good restaurants and hotels abound, as do excellent shops selling handicrafts, especially rugs, porcelain, and straw goods. The *Feira de São Pedro de Sintra* (St. Peter of Sintra Fair), a market that takes place on the second and fourth Sundays of every month, has everything imaginable for sale. The *Festival de Música* (Music Festival), held from mid-June to mid-July, draws crowds to the town each summer (see *Special Events*).

# Sources and Resources

## TOURIST INFORMATION

Maps, brochures, shopping guides, monthly listings of events, and other information can be obtained from the *Postos de Turismo* (Tourist Posts) run by the *Direcção-Geral do Turismo* (Directorate General for Tourism), headquartered at 86 Av. António Augusto de Aguiar. A tourist post is located at the same address (phone: 575086); it's open weekdays. The most convenient *Posto de Turismo* in downtown Lisbon is at *Palácio Foz* (Praça dos Restauradores; phone: 346-3624); open daily. There also is a *Posto de Turismo* at the *Aeroporto de Portela de Sacavém* (phone: 893689) for arriving passengers only. The posts have English-speaking staff members to answer questions and to help make hotel reservations. It is possible to hire English-speaking guides through the tourist posts or by calling the guides union, the *Sindicato Nacional da Actividade Turística, Tradutores e Intérpretes* (National Union of Tourism Activity, Translators and Interpreters; phone: 342-3298). The *US Embassy* is at Av. das Forças Armadas, Sete Rios (phone: 726-6600).

For information in the US, contact the *Portuguese National Tourist Office* (590 Fifth Ave., Fourth Floor, New York, NY 10036; phone: 212-354-4403; fax: 212-764-6137). The *Portuguese Embassy* is at 2125 Kalorama Rd. NW, Washington, DC 20008 (phone: 202-328-8610).

**ENTRY REQUIREMENTS** A US citizen needs a current passport for a stay of up to 60 days.

**TIME** The time in Portugal is five hours later than in US East Coast cities. Portugal follows daylight saving time.

**LANGUAGE** Portuguese is the official tongue; English is spoken in major tourist areas.

**ELECTRIC CURRENT** 220 volts, 50 cycles, AC.

**MONEY** The escudo, which equals 100 centavos. The symbol for the escudo is a dollar sign, which takes the place of the decimal point in our currency (for example, 1$00). There were 158 escudos to the dollar at press time.

**TIPPING** Tips in the 10% to 15% range are expected, even though a 10% service charge normally is added to hotel and restaurant bills. Porters and bellhops should receive from 100 to 120 escudos per bag.

**BANKING/BUSINESS HOURS** Banks are open weekdays from 8:30 AM to 2:45 PM. Most other businesses are open weekdays from 9 AM to 1 PM and from 3 to 7 PM.

**NATIONAL HOLIDAYS** *New Year's Day* (January 1), *Mardi Gras* (February 15), *Good Friday* (April 14), *Easter Sunday* (April 16), *Freedom Day* (April 25), *Labor Day* (May 1), *Camões Day* (June 10), *Feast of the Assumption* (August 15), *Day of the Republic* (October 5), *All Saints' Day* (November 1), *Independence Day* (December 1), *Feast of the Immaculate Conception* (December 8), and *Christmas Day* (December 25).

**LOCAL COVERAGE** The leading dailies are *Diário de Notícias* and *Público,* both morning papers. *Semanario* and *Expresso* are two of the most prestigious weekly papers. English-language newspapers and magazines are sold at most hotels and many central newsstands.

**TELEPHONE** The city code for Lisbon is 1. When calling from one area to another within Portugal dial 0 + city code + local number. The country code for Portugal is 351. Dial 115 for emergency assistance.

## GETTING AROUND

Although various sections of the city, such as the Alfama, are ideal for strolling, keep in mind that Lisbon is built on hills, so visitors probably will want to ride from one section to another. Parking is problematic, so public transportation and taxis are the better options.

**AIRPORT** Lisbon's airport for both domestic and international flights, *Aeroporto de Portela de Sacavém* (phone: 802060), is 5 miles (8 km) northeast of the center, a drive of 15 to 30 minutes. An express service of 18-seater minibuses called *AERO-BUS* runs between the airport and the central Praça de Restauradores, stopping at major points downtown along the way; the minibus departs from the airport every 20 minutes between 7 AM and 9 PM. The local office of the national airline, *TAP Air Portugal,* is at 3A Praça Marquês de Pombal (phone: 386-4080 for information; 386-1020 for reservations). The independent company *Portugalia* (170 Rodrigues Sampaio; phone: 352-5336) has flights to Porto and Faro as well as to foreign destinations. The private airline *Aerocondor* (phone: 444-2668), operating out of *Aeroporto de Tires* (Cascais), has flights on small planes (eight seats) daily to Porto and Bragança and can arrange charters to other cities.

**BOAT** Ferryboats, carrying both passengers and cars, cross the Tagus every few minutes from the Praça do Comércio and Cais do Sodré ferry terminals for Cacilhas, Barreiro, and other points. Short cruises on the Tagus take place from April through October; for information, contact the tourist office.

**BUS** City buses are run by *CARRIS (Companhia Carris de Ferro de Lisboa;* phone: 363-9343). Board buses via the front door, buy a ticket for 140 escudos (about 85¢ at press time) from the driver, and cancel it in the machine. Maps and other information can be obtained at the window at the side of the *Elevador de Santa Justa,* just off Rua do Carmo. Tourist passes for four or seven days of unlimited travel by bus, tram, subway, ferryboat, and the *Elevador de Santa Justa* can be bought at the *Praça dos Restauradores* and *Praça Marquês de Pombal* subway stations, at the *Elevador de Santa Justa,* and at *CARRIS* kiosks throughout the city. Long-distance bus service is provided by *Rodoviária Nacional,* whose terminal is at 18 Avenida Casal de Ribeiro (phone: 545439).

**CAR RENTAL** Many major firms have offices in Lisbon and at the airport: *Avis* (12C Av. Praia da Vitória; phone: 346-2676 or 500-1002, toll-free in Portugal; at the airport; phone: 849-4836; at the *Santa Apolónia* train station; phone: 876887; and at the *Ritz Inter-Continental* hotel; phone: 692020); *Hertz* (phone: 941-1090, central reservations; 10 Av. 5 de Outubro; phone: 579077; 10 Av. Visconde Seabra; phone: 797-2944; at the *Novotel* hotel, 1642 Av. José Malhoa; phone: 726-7221; and at the airport; phone: 849-2722); and *Budget* (phone: 89-803490, central reservations; 6 Av. Fontes Pereira de Melo; phone: 537717; and at the airport; phone: 801785 or 803981).

**ELEVATOR** The *Elevador de Santa Justa* takes passengers from Rua do Ouro (Rua Aurea) in the Baixa to Largo do Carmo in the Chiado. The Portuguese also refer to several funicular (cable) streetcars that travel a steep route as "elevators"; among them is the *Elevador da Glória,* running from Calçada da Glória, on the west side of Praça dos Restauradores, to the Bairro Alto. The unlimited-travel tourist pass is valid on elevators (see *Bus*); individual rides cost 140 escudos (85¢ at press time).

**SUBWAY** The Lisbon underground system is called the *Metropolitano.* A large "M" aboveground designates the stations—*Rossio* and *Restauradores* are the most central ones. The fare to any point is 65 escudos (38¢), slightly less if the ticket is bought in a machine. The unlimited-travel tourist pass is valid underground (see *Bus*). Beware of pickpockets.

**TAXI** Cabs, metered and inexpensive, charge a slightly higher rate from 10 PM to 6 AM. Look for an explanation of the fare system posted inside each cab. For trips outside Lisbon a set rate per kilometer is charged beyond the city limits. Taxis can be hailed on the street or picked up at cabstands conveniently scattered around town. (Note that by law passengers must enter and exit on the sidewalk side, never on the street side, and drivers may charge extra for luggage.) To call a cab dial 825060 or 825422.

**TRAIN** Frequent, fast electric trains connecting Lisbon with Belém, Estoril, and Cascais leave from the *Estação Cais do Sodré* (phone: 347-0181), by the river near Praça do Comércio. Trains to Queluz and Sintra operate from the *Estação do Rossio* (phone: 877092), just off the Praça Rossio. (The train station is the 19th-century building with the charming, elaborately carved neo-Manueline façade just across from the side of the *Teatro Nacional.* Confusingly, it's hardly ever referred to by its real name, *Estação Central,* which is carved in neo-Manueline letters around its circular doors.) Trains for most of the rest of Portugal and elsewhere in Europe leave from *Estação Santa Apolónia* (phone: 876025), which is located along the river east of the Alfama district; it's not within walking distance of the center, so take a bus or tram. The station for trains to the Algarve is *Estação Sul e Sueste* (phone: 877179), on the river at Praça do Comércio. The southbound trains actually leave from Barreiro, on the south bank of the Tagus, but tickets include the price of the ferry ride from the station. Trains between Lisbon, Porto, and Faro have air conditioned coaches with bars and restaurant service. For information on all trains except those leaving from the *Estação Cais do Sodré,* call 888-4025.

**TRAM** Like the city buses, Lisbon's trams are run by *CARRIS.* Many of the charming vintage vehicles travel through the more historic parts of the city, providing inexpensive tours. No. 28 is a particularly picturesque ride across the city to the Alfama district. *CARRIS* also offers two separate two-hour tram tours from Praça do Comércio: One circuit shows off the city and the other tour travels to Belém. Contact *CARRIS* (phone: 363-9343) for information.

**WALKING TOURS** One excellent way to see the city is to join the three-hour walking tour sponsored by the *Centro Nacional de Cultura* (National Culture Center; 68 Rua António Maria Cardoso; phone: 346-6722). Guided tours—in English and Portuguese—take in the Chiado, Alfama, and Belém districts.

## LOCAL SERVICES

**DENTIST (ENGLISH-SPEAKING)** The *US Embassy* (Av. das Forças Armadas; phone: 726-6600) has a list of English-speaking practitioners.

**DRY CLEANER/TAILOR** *Lavandarias AmoreiraSec* (*Amoreiras Shopping Center,* Av. Eng. Duarte Pacheco; phone: 692384).

**MEDICAL EMERGENCY** Lisbon has three state hospitals with general emergency facilities: *Hospital São Francisco Xavier* (phone: 301-7351); *Hospital São José* (phone: 886-0131); and *Hospital de Santa Maria* (phone: 797-5171). The emergency help line for poisoning is 795-0143, and the nationwide number to call for an ambulance is 115.

**MESSENGER SERVICE** *Pony Express* (18-1 Av. Marquês de Tomar; phone: 522336).

**NATIONAL/INTERNATIONAL COURIER** *DHL Worldwide Express* (37 Av. Marechal Gomes da Costa; phone: 859-9522; 859-9017 for pick-ups; and at the airport, Rua C, Edifício 124; phone: 890009).

**PHARMACY** *The Farmácia Azevedo* is on Lisbon's central square, the Rossio (31 Praça de Dom Pedro IV; phone: 342-7478). Pharmacies take turns for weekend and after-hours service; each one posts on its door the names of the shops on duty.

**PHOTOCOPIES** The following provide multi-format and color copying services: *Xecopex* (106 Av. António Augusto Aguiar; phone: 577904) and *Xerox Portugal* (16 Rua Pedro Nunes; phone: 577110; and 160 Rua dos Correiros; phone: 342-8420). Simple facilities also are widely available in stationery shops and the like.

**POST OFFICE** There are two main downtown post offices. The one on Praça dos Restauradores is open weekdays from 8 AM to 10 PM, and the one on Praça do Comércio is open weekdays from 8:30 AM to 6:30 PM.

**SECRETARY/STENOGRAPHER (ENGLISH-SPEAKING)** *American Typing Services* (38 Rua Castilho, 1st Floor; phone: 539650); *Intess* (62 Rua São Julião, 1st Floor; phone: 888-2506; fax: 871820). Both companies also can supply translators.

**TELEX** At two post office locations. The one on Praça dos Restauradores is open weekdays from 9 AM to 7 PM; the one in the *Forum Center* (48C Av. Fontes Pereira de Melo; phone: 524030) is open daily from 9 AM to 7 PM.

**TRANSLATOR** *American Typing Services* and *Intess* (see *Secretary/Stenographer,* above), as well as Lynn de Albuquerque (phone: 419-2383).

**OTHER** Tuxedo rental: *Guarda Roupa Anahory* (Rua Madalena; phone: 872046).

## SPECIAL EVENTS

The ancient celebrations of the summer solstice have been subsumed here by the *Festas dos Santos Populares* (Feasts of the Popular Saints), Christian rites in honor of São João (St. John), São Pedro (St. Peter), and Santo António (St. Anthony). On the eve of the *Festa de Santo António* (June 13), Lisbon's old quarter comes alive. In the Baixa, members of neighborhood associations bedecked in traditional costumes parade down Avenida da Liberdade, each attempting to outdo the display of the others. For the *Festa de São João* (June 23 and 24), celebrants build bonfires, sprinkle them with scented herbs and thistles, and jump over the flames to prove their daring in a modern version of an ancient fertility rite. The final celebration is the *Festa de São Pedro* (June 29).

The international *Feira de Artesanato* (Handicrafts Fair) is held for 10 days during July. One of the finest fairs of its kind in Europe, it features lace, wicker, pottery, jewelry, hand-knitted items, ceramic and copper dishes, embroidered tablecloths, crystal, the famous Arraiolos rugs, and much more. It takes place in the *Feira Internacional de Lisboa* building, Praça das Indústrias (phone: 362-0130).

In Sintra, the *Festival de Música* (Music Festival) is held from mid-June to mid-July each year. The music is classic though not strictly classical (from Baroque to modern with a chamber music bent), and a number of the concerts are performed in the town's historic palaces.

## MUSEUMS

In addition to the museums discussed above in *Special Places,* the following may be of interest. (Many that charge an admission fee are free on Sundays.)

**MUSEU DA CIDADE (CITY MUSEUM)** Maps, engravings, and other objects telling Lisbon's history are set up in an 18th-century palace. Closed Mondays. Admission charge. 245 Campo Grande (phone: 759-1617).

**MUSEU NACIONAL DO TEATRO (NATIONAL THEATER MUSEUM)** Costumes, scenery, drawings, programs, posters, and other theatrical memo-

rabilia are displayed. Closed Mondays. Admission charge. 10-12
Estrada do Lumiar (phone: 757-2547).

**MUSEU NACIONAL DO TRAJE (NATIONAL COSTUME MUSEUM)** Changing
exhibitions of Portuguese and foreign costumes, accessories, and
fabrics are on view in a lovely old suburban house about a mile
north of the *Museu da Cidade.* Closed Mondays. Admission charge.
5 Largo São João Baptista, Parque de Monteiro-Mor, Lumiar (phone:
759-0318).

**MUSEU RAFAEL BORDALO PINHEIRO** This museum is named for and devoted
to the works of the 19th-century caricaturist, ceramist, and painter.
Closed Mondays. Admission charge. 382 Campo Grande (phone:
795-0816).

## SHOPPING

The most important shopping area in Lisbon is the Baixa, the zone
between Praça Rossio and the river, with the mosaic-paved, pedestrians-only Rua Augusta as the main thoroughfare. Rua do Carmo,
which leads from this area to the part known as the Chiado, has many
fashionable shops. Numerous antiques shops also are located in this
area: Rua Dom Pedro V, in the Bairro Alto, is the city's antiques row,
but shops also are congregated along Rua do Alecrim, Rua da Misericórdia, Rua São Pedro de Alcântara, and Rua da Escola Politécnica. (Outside Lisbon, in São Pedro, near Sintra, antiques shops are
open all day at the market on Largo Primeiro de Dezembro.)

Downtown shops are open weekdays from 9 AM to 1 PM and 3
to 7 PM, Saturdays from 9 AM to 1 PM. Lisbon's most famous shopping center, with sophisticated stores and boutiques of all kinds—
more than 300 of them—is the *Centro Comercial das Amoreiras*
(Av. Engenheiro Duarte Pacheco; phone: 692558), a postmodernist
complex with huge towers in pinks and greens and glass, designed
by architect Tomás Taveira. *Centro Comercial Fonte Nova* (497
Estrada de Benfica; phone: 714-4654), just outside the city, has 80
stores, including excellent housewares, home decorating, and leather
goods shops. The 45 shops at *Centro Comercial Alvalade* (Praça
de Alvalade; phone: 848-0224) offer a classy assortment of giftware, clothing, shoes, and general merchandise. Savvy Lisbon shoppers often head for one of the hypermarkets, enormous emporiums
that stock everything from car parts to shoes. The two biggest, most
popular hypermarkets are *Pão Açúcar* (on EN 117 toward Sintra)
and *Continente* (on EN 240 in the direction of Amadora).

Also offering a wide variety of goods is the *Feira da Ladra*
(Thieves' Market), a flea market where anything from collectors'
items to ready-to-wear can be found. Portuguese Gypsies peddle
closeout items and leftover stock from top Portuguese clothing manufacturers and boutiques at the market (also look for them selling
from stands on street corners). The *Feira da Ladra* is held on Largo
de Santa Clara, at the edge of the Alfama, Tuesdays and Saturdays
from sunrise until noon. Show up early—the bargains go quickly.

Among the best buys in Lisbon are gold, silver, and jewelry.
Prices are relatively low, and the gold or silver content of each piece

is guaranteed. Rua da Prata and Rua Augusta are two of the better streets for jewelry. Accompanying a Lisbon renaissance in painting, tapestry making, and ceramics has been the opening of many new galleries to exhibit the works. Tile making has also seen a revival; many shops sell *azulejos* that are reproductions of 17th- and 18th-century designs. Hand-stitched rugs from Arraiolos, lace from Madeira, fine glass and crystal, copperware, fishermen's sweaters, and baskets are other good buys, along with fashionable clothing, shoes, and other leather goods. Shops often offer shipping service.

The following are our favorite buying and browsing spots in the Portuguese capital. (Note that many of the shops listed have branches in *Centro Comercial das Amoreiras.*)

**A. Chave de Prata** Well-stocked shelves of porcelain and glass giftware and some interesting bronze objects. 174 Rua da Prata (phone: 877915).

**Almorávida** A wide variety of regional crafts, pottery, and filigree jewelry plus an extensive collection of Portuguese-style, custom-made rugs. 10-14 Rua do Milagre de Sto. António (phone: 862261).

**Ana** Antique *azulejos* and small 18th-century plaques. *Ritz Inter-Continental Hotel,* 88 Rua Rodrigo da Fonesca (phone: 658767).

**Ana Salazar** Clothes by Portugal's most famous avant-garde designer for women, who draws artistic inspirations from the turn of the century and the 1940s. 87 Rua do Carmo (phone: 347-2289).

**António Campos Trindade** Antique Portuguese, English, and French furniture, as well as Chinese porcelain and paintings. 18 Rua do Alecrim (phone: 342-4660).

**Artesanato Arameiro** A wide variety of regional handicrafts—lace, rugs, ceramics, copperware, and filigree. 62 Praça dos Restauradores (phone: 342-0236).

**Atlantis** Fine crystal tableware from Alcobaça. *Centro Comercial das Amoreiras* (phone: 693670).

**Casa dos Bordados da Madeira** Embroidery and lace from Madeira, and an array of other Portuguese handicrafts. 135 Rua Primeiro de Dezembro (phone: 342-1447).

**Charles** A wide selection of shoes—it's the only store in Portugal that carries women's half sizes. It also specializes in Italian designer brands. 105 Rua do Carmo (phone: 347-7361) and 109 Rua Augusta (phone: 347-7360).

**Charlot** A very fashionable boutique, with designer labels from Portugal, Italy, and France. 28 Rua Barata Salgueiro (phone: 573665).

**Diadema** Lovely gold and silver jewelry. 166 Rua do Ouro (phone: 342-1362).

**Fábrica de Cerâmica Viúva Lamego** Makes and sells reproductions of *azulejos* from the 15th through the 18th centuries; its bird and animal motifs are famous. It also creates tiles with modern designs, as well as a variety of planters, dishes, lamp bases, and pottery. 25 Largo do Intendente Pina Manique (phone: 315-2401).

**Galeria Comicos** A good gallery showing avant-garde paintings. 1B Rua Tenente Raul Cascais (phone: 677794).

**Galeria 111** The longest established of Lisbon's art galleries, selling works of the best of today's Portuguese artists. 111 Campo Grande (phone: 797-7418).

**Galeria Sesimbra** Lisbon's second-oldest art gallery, known for hand-stitched Agulha tapestries, made from designs by leading contemporary Portuguese artists. 77 Rua Castilho (phone: 387-0291).

**Helio** Top-quality shoes for men and women. 93 Rua do Carmo (phone: 342-3171).

**Jalco** A good place for beautiful antique Arraiolos rugs. 44 Rua Ivens (phone: 342-8095).

**The King of Filigree** Silver filigree items, some dipped in gold, made in Porto. 58 Rua da Prata (phone: 877441).

**Livraria Buchholz** A large stock of foreign and Portuguese books. 4 Rua do Duque de Palmela (phone: 315-7354).

**Luvaria Ulisses** Quality leather gloves. 87 Rua do Carmo (phone: 315-7354).

**Madeira Gobelins** Embroidery, woven tapestries, and carpets from Madeira. 40 Rua Castilho (phone: 356-3708).

**Madeira House** Lisbon's oldest shop dealing in genuine Madeira embroidery and lace, it also sells less expensive embroidered linen. 137 Rua Augusta (phone: 342-6813).

**O Mundo Do Livro** Original maps and lithographs from the 16th through the 18th centuries are featured at Lisbon's oldest, and most famous, bookstore. 11 Largo da Trindade (phone: 346-9951).

**Ourivesaria Aliança** Antique silver trays and tea service sets. 50 Rua Garrett (phone: 342-3419).

**Ourivesaria Diadema** Gold, filigree, and souvenirs. 166 Rua do Ouro (phone: 342-1362).

**Ourivesaria Pimenta** Fine jewelry, watches, and silver. 257 Rua Augusta (phone: 342-4564).

**Príncipe Real Enxoval** Specializes in handmade embroidery from one of the finest factories in Madeira. 12 Rua da Escola Politécnica (phone: 346-5945).

**Quintão** Handmade Arraiolos rugs that are truly works of art. 30 Rua Ivens (phone: 346-5837).

**Sant'Anna** Founded in 1741, this store carries fabulous reproductions of 17th- and 18th-century *azulejos,* made in the shop's own factory.

95 Rua do Alecrim (phone: 342-2537). The factory, at 96 Calçada da Boa Hora, can be visited, but call first (phone: 363-8292).

**Solar** The largest selection of antique Portuguese *azulejos,* arranged by century, beginning with the 15th, as well as a fine collection of pewter and furniture. 68-70 Rua Dom Pedro V (phone: 346-5522).

**Vidraria da Marinha Grande** One of the largest selections of glass and crystal in the country. 38 Rua de São Nicolau (phone: 342-1840).

**Vista Alegre** The makers of Portugal's finest porcelain, from dinnerware to figurines. (Some of the samples and discontinued designs sold downstairs at the shop on the Chiado are great values.) 52-54 Rua Ivens (phone: 342-8581) and 18 Largo do Chiado (phone: 346-1401).

**W. A. Sarmento** Antique and modern gold jewelry. 251 Rua do Ouro (phone: 342-6774).

## SPORTS AND FITNESS

**BULLFIGHTING** Portuguese bullfighting, quite different from the Spanish version, is more a spectacle of horsemanship than a fight. Bulls are never killed in the ring, and the fighting is done mostly on horseback, with the *cavaleiros* wearing magnificent 18th-century costumes as they ride against the bulls. Although there is a bullfight at *Easter,* the season doesn't begin in earnest until June and then generally runs through September, with contests usually held on Thursdays, Sundays, and holidays. The most important fights take place at the *Praça de Touros do Campo Pequeno* (Campo Pequeno Bullring; Av. da República; phone: 793-2093), a mosque-like structure with minarets all around its walls, and at the *Monumental de Cascais* (Bairro do Rosario).

**FISHING** Boats for deep-sea fishing can be rented from the fishermen at Sesimbra, a fishing village 27 miles (43 km) south of Lisbon, or at Cascais.

**FITNESS CENTERS** Branches of *Health Club Soleil,* a chain, are open to non-members for a fee and can be found in the *Centro Comercial das Amoreiras* (Av. Engenheiro Duarte Pacheco; phone: 692907) and in several hotels: the *Lisboa Sheraton,* the *Palácio* in Estoril, and the *Estoril-Sol* in Cascais (see *Checking In,* below).

**GOLF** There are several prime golf courses within easy reach of Lisbon; visitors are generally welcome on weekdays, but weekend admission can be difficult. Just 11 miles (18 km) from Lisbon across the river on the Setúbal Peninsula is the Frank Pennick–designed 18-hole course at *Aroeira Clube de Campo de Portugal* (Quinta da Aroeira, Fonte da Telha; phone: 297-1314), with its challenging 11th and 14th greens, both seemingly surrounded by lakes and bunkers. The *Clube de Golfe do Estoril* (Av. da República, Estoril; phone: 468-0176) features 27 holes with wonderful views of the sea, the countryside, and the mountains. (On weekends, only nine holes are open to non-members). The 6,684-yard, 18-hole *Clube* *de Golfe da Marinha* (Quinta da Marinha, Cascais; phone: 486-9881), designed by Robert Trent Jones Sr., is the centerpiece of a deluxe residential resort complex. Lastly, at the foot of the Sintra Mountains is the *Estoril-Sol Golf Club* (Estrada da Lagoa Azul, Sintra; phone: 923-2461). Short (4,644 yards) yet challenging, it offers nine holes with 18 tees.

**HORSEBACK RIDING** Equestrians can be accommodated at the *Clube da Marinha* (Cascais; phone: 289282), at the *Clube de Campo de Lisboa* (south of Lisbon; phone: 226-1802 or 226-1060), at the *Pony Club Cascais* (Quinta da Bicuda; phone: 284-3233), and the *Clube de Campo Dom Carlos I* (Estrada Areia, Praia do Guincho; phone: 285-1403). *Nuno Veloso,* in Cascais (phone: 486-9084), organizes riding circuits and can provide details on horse-jumping competitions that are open to spectators.

**JOGGING** Attractive as it might seem, jogging in Lisbon's central *Parque Eduardo VII* is not recommended, especially alone or at night. Instead, run along the riverside between the Ponte 25 de Abril and Belém, or on the median strip of Avenida da Liberdade from the Praça Marquês de Pombal toward the Baixa. Another good place is the fitness circuit in the *Estádio Nacional* (National Stadium) area on the outskirts of the city on the way to Estoril, where the track winds through pleasant pine woods. (Don't jog alone or at night here, either.) The *Parque do Estoril* and the seafront in Cascais are other good jogging spots.

**SOCCER** Portugal's most popular sport is ruled by a triumvirate of top clubs: *Sporting* and *Benfica,* from Lisbon, and *Porto,* from the northern capital of the same name. Rivalries are intense, so any games involving one of the top three should be exciting. The season runs from August until the end of June, and matches are played on Sundays at various stadiums; ask at your hotel desk for help with tickets.

**SWIMMING** Sandy beaches are found south of Lisbon across the river, and along the entire coast west of the city (see the towns of "Estoril" and "Cascais" in *Special Places,* above). However, pollution is a problem on some beaches between Lisbon and Estoril, so check first for possible health hazards. (Don't go in the water unless the blue safety flag is flying.) In Estoril, the *Tamariz* restaurant, on the beach, provides changing rooms. In addition, many hotels have private swimming pools (see *Checking In,* below).

**TENNIS** The *Clube de Tenis de Estoril* (Av. Conde de Barcelona, Estoril; phone: 466-2770 or 468-1613) boasts two of the best facilities in the country, including four hard and 14 clay courts (11 are floodlit for night playing). At *Quinta da Marinha* in Cascais (Casa 36, Quinta da Marinha; phone: 486-9881) are six courts, three of them floodlit. There also are two public courts at the *Clube de Campo Dom Carlos I* (Estrada Areia, Praia do Guincho; phone: 285-2362) and at the *Estadio Nacional* (National Stadium; Estrada Marginal—EN6, Cruz Quebrada; phone: 419-7212).

## THEATER

Some of the most important classical and contemporary plays are staged (in Portuguese) at the *Teatro Nacional de Dona Maria II* (Dona Maria II National Theater; Praça Dom Pedro IV; phone: 347-1078). There are no performances in July. Check the publications listed in *Local Coverage,* above, for information about other theatrical presentations. Increasingly popular is the *revista* (revue), a Lisbon tradition that encompasses topical sketches, satire, music, and dance in something of an old-fashioned vaudeville format. *Revistas* can be entertaining even for those who don't understand the language.

## MUSIC

The focus of Portugal's musical life is *fado,* the country's unofficial national ballad, which pours out of the city's nightspots (see *Nightclubs and Nightlife,* below). Equally important are the many opera and ballet performances that take place in the city. Among the recommended venues are the *Grande Auditório de Fundação Calouste Gulbenkian* (Calouste Gulbenkian Foundation Grand Auditorium; 45 Av. de Berna; phone: 793-5131 or 793-4167), which presents orchestral, choral, and solo works, plus ballet performances; the *Teatro Municipal de São Luís* (Rua António Maria Cardoso; phone: 342-7172), site of *Companhia Nacional de Bailado* (National Ballet Company) and *Orquestra Metropolitana de Lisboa* (Lisbon Metropolitan Orchestra) performances; the Chiado's *Teatro Nacional de São Carlos* (9 Rua Serpa Pinto; phone: 346-5914), the city's premier concert hall/opera house and one of Europe's prettiest; and the huge new complex, the *Centro Cultural de Belém* (Belém Cultural Center; Praca do Imperio; phone: 301-9606; fax: 362-2689), whose main auditorium alone seats 1,500 for concerts, opera, and ballet.

## NIGHTCLUBS AND NIGHTLIFE

Begin your evening with a pre-dinner glass of dry, white port at *A Brasileira* (122 Rua Garrett; phone 346-9541), one of Lisbon's traditional old cafés. Take a seat at one of the tables outdoors and watch the world go by. The bronze gentleman seated at the bronze table is a statue of the poet Fernando Pessoa (1888–1935), placed here on the 100th anniversary of his birth. A second old café that's favored with the old guard is *Café Nicola,* on the Praça Rossio (phone: 346-0579).

Lisbon's popular *fado* houses—restaurants featuring *fado* music—are scattered throughout the Alfama and Bairro Alto districts. *Fado,* which translates as "fate," is the name for the anecdotal, satirical, sentimental, and occasionally happy songs, usually performed by a woman swathed in black (the *fadista*), to the accompaniment of one or more 12-stringed guitars. Although *fado* has become commercialized and many restaurants beef up their shows with folk dancing and popular music, a visitor may be lucky enough to hear the real thing. Do not make a sound during the singing—neither the singers nor the spectators permit it. Some particularly good spots are *Senhor Vinho* (18 Rua do Meio à Lapa; phone: 397-2681), where the *fado* is pure; *O Faia* (54 Rua da Barroca; phone: 342-1923), one of the best-known *fado* houses; *Adega Machado* (91 Rua do Norte; phone: 346-0095), entertaining because it offers spirited folk dancing in addition to moving renditions of *fado; Lisboa à Noite* (69 Rua das Gáveas; phone: 346-8557); and *A Severa* (51-61 Rua das Gáveas; phone: 346-4006). *Senhor Vinho* is in the Lapa district west of the Bairro Alto; the rest are in Bairro Alto. Those not dining should arrive after 10 PM. Reservations are essential.

*Fado* still draws loyal fans, but over the years discotheques have become the most popular spots for Lisbon's midnight-oil burners. The clientele is cosmopolitan, and the action continues into the wee hours of the morning. On busy nights, it may be difficult for non-regulars to get into the more conservative top discotheques, which are frequented by local socialites. Provided there's room, though, a traveler who is properly dressed (no shorts or jeans) won't have trouble gaining admission. Among the longest-established (and starchiest) of the haunts in downtown Lisbon are *Stones* (1 Rua do Olival; phone: 396-4545) and *Ad Lib* (18 Rua Barata Salgueiro; phone: 356-1717). For the trendy, the scene is a dockside area close to Alcântara just west of the center, clustered around Avenida 24 de Julho. The current favorites here include *Alcântara Mar* (11 Rua da Cozinha Económica; phone: 362-1226); *Kapital* (68 Av. 24 de Julho; phone: 395-5963); and *Kremlin* (5 Escadinhas da Praia; phone: 608768). In a category of its own is the very fashionable *Bar Bairro Alto* (50 Travessa dos Inglesinhos; phone: 342-2717), which features shows and other special events. For fans of African music, *Clave di Nos* (100 Rua do Norte; phone: 346-8420) is a bar-restaurant in the Bairro Alto that has live music—and cuisine—from the Cape Verde Islands.

Bars to try when you're in Estoril include the *Founder's Inn* (11D Rua Dom Afonso Henriques; phone: 468-2221) and the *English Bar* (Estrada Marginal, Monte Estoril; phone: 468-0413). And don't miss a night at the world-famous *Casino Estoril* (phone: 268-4521), in a shiny, modern building in the *Parque do Estoril.* The gaming rooms (open daily from 3 PM to 3 AM to those over 21 presenting a passport) offer slot machines and all the European and American games: roulette, baccarat, chemin de fer, blackjack, French bank, and bingo. The roulette stakes are higher than in Portugal's other casinos, and the slot machines sometimes spit out jackpots of more than $200,000. But gambling is only one of the casino's attractions. The glittering restaurant-nightclub resembles the *Lido* in Paris, with balconies and a main floor seating 800 for its international show.

Cascais, too, has a spirited nightlife, with many bars and cafés. Among our favorites are the *John Bull* (32 Praça Costa Pinto; phone: 483-3319), an English-style pub; *Tren Velho* (Av. Duquesa de Palmela; phone: 486-7355), a converted train coach beside the station; and *Bar 21* (1A Travessa da Misericórdia; phone: 486-7518), an attractive cocktail lounge. Popular discos include *Coconuts* (7 Boca do Inferno; phone: 284-4109), with an outdoor terrace by the sea; *Julianas* (10 Av. 25 de Abril; phone: 486-4052); and the very snooty *Van Gogo* (9 Travessa da Alfarrobeira; phone: 483-3378). For *fado* in Cascais, try *Forte Dom Rodrigo* (Estrada de Birre; phone: 285-1373) or *Picadeiro Maria d'Almeida* (Quinta da Guia, Torre; phone: 486-9982).

# Best in Town

## CHECKING IN

A visitor's primary decision will be whether to stay right in Lisbon, to commute (with thousands of *lisboetas*) from Estoril or Cascais via the clean, inexpensive trains that run into the city about every 20 minutes, or to stay in Sintra, about 17½ miles (28 km) northwest of Lisbon. Whichever your choice, a double room will cost from $150 to $260 a night at hotels in the expensive category, from $85 to $140 at places in the moderate range, and less than $75 at properties described as inexpensive. But bargaining—even for corporate rates—is not uncommon, and charges for rooms generally drop in the autumn and winter months, and sometimes even in the summer at some hotels. Unless otherwise noted the hotels listed have private baths, air conditioning, TV sets, and phones; breakfast is generally included in the room rate. All telephone numbers are in the 1 city code unless otherwise indicated.

### LISBON

#### EXPENSIVE

**Altis** This nine-story modern hotel has 303 rooms, a good view from its rooftop grill, a heated indoor pool, and a health club. Business services include 24-hour room service, meeting rooms for up to 400, an English-speaking concierge, foreign currency exchange, secretarial services in English, audiovisual equipment, photocopiers, and translation services. Halfway between the *Rossio* train station and *Parque Eduardo VII,* at 11 Rua Castilho (phone: 522496; fax: 548696).

**Lapa** A handsomely converted palace surrounded by gardens and with a harmoniously designed modern annex, it has 102 rooms (including eight suites), with views over the old Lapa embassy quarter and the Tagus River. All rooms have satellite TV and direct-dial telephones, and 24 of them have Jacuzzis. Among the pluses are two pools, a fitness center, and a good restaurant with a chef who specializes in French fare. Business services include 24-hour room service, meeting rooms for up to 230, an English-speaking concierge, foreign currency exchange, secretarial services in English, translation services, and fax machines in the rooms on request. 4 Rua Pau da Bandeira (phone: 395-0005; fax: 395-0665).

**Lisboa Sheraton** One of the best of the chain in Europe, this 400-room high-rise offers comfortable accommodations, marble bathrooms, and elegant public areas and lounges. There is a heated, open-air pool, plus several restaurants (including *Panorama* on the 29th floor), bars, shops, and a health club. Business services include 24-hour room service, meeting rooms for up to 550, an English-speaking concierge, foreign currency exchange, secretarial services in English, audiovisual equipment, photocopiers, computers, and translation services. It's located a bit away from the city center, a few blocks north of Praça Marquês de Pombal. 1 Rua Latino Coelho (phone: 575757; 800-334-8484; fax: 547164).

**Meridien** This sparkling modern luxury hotel with 350 rooms overlooks *Parque Eduardo VII.* The decor runs to chrome, marble, and splashing fountains, and the restaurants feature French cooking, hardly unusual in a hotel run by a subsidiary of *Air France.* Business services include 24-hour room service, a fitness center, an English-speaking concierge, foreign currency exchange, secretarial services in English, audiovisual equipment, photocopiers, computers, cable TV news, and translation services. 149 Rua Castilho (phone: 690900; 800-543-4300; fax: 693231).

**Ritz Inter-Continental** On a hill overlooking *Parque Eduardo VII,* next door to the *Meridien,* this luxury establishment is contemporary on the outside (built in the 1950s), but traditional within. The appointments are opulent—silks, satins, and suedes—in the 260 rooms and 40 suites, some furnished with antique reproductions. There's a lovely piano bar overlooking the park, fine shops, a tearoom, a grill, a coffee shop, and a beauty parlor. Soundproofed bedrooms are equipped with mini-bars and in-house movies. Rooms with balconies overlooking the park are pricier. Business services include 24-hour room service, meeting rooms for up to 700, an English-speaking concierge, foreign currency exchange, secretarial services in English, audiovisual equipment, photocopiers, computers, cable TV news, and translation services. 88 Rua Rodrigo da Fonseca (phone: 692020; 800-327-0200; fax: 691783).

**Sofitel Lisboa** The perfect base for touring the neighboring Alfama district, this modern hostelry has 170 rooms and four suites, all tastefully decorated in pastel colors. There's also a restaurant offering Portuguese and international fare and a piano bar. Business services include seven meeting rooms for up to 300, an English-speaking concierge, foreign currency exchange, photocopiers, computers, and cable television news. 123-125 Avenida da Liberdade (phone: 342-9202; 800-763-4835; fax: 342-9222).

### MODERATE

**Carlton** This small, charming hostelry is only a block from the *Museu Calouste Gulbenkian.* All 72 rooms have satellite TV, safes, mini-bars, hair dryers, and a decor that features lots of marble. While the hotel has no restaurant, guests may breakfast in the pleasant indoor patio, dominated by a spreading palm tree. There's an English-speaking concierge. 56 Av. Conde Valbom (phone: 795-1157; fax: 795-1166).

**Diplomático** Well situated near *Parque Eduardo VII,* it has 90 rooms equipped with mini-bars. There's also a restaurant, a bar, and private parking. Business services include 24-hour room service, meeting rooms for up to 80, an English-speaking concierge, foreign currency exchange, audiovisual equipment, and photocopiers. 74 Rua Castilho (phone: 386-2041; fax: 386-2155).

**Dom Rodrigo** A centrally located apartment-hotel, a few blocks south of the *Ritz,* it features nine penthouses, 39 suites, and nine studios with twin beds. The soundproofed rooms all have satellite TV and fully equipped kitchenettes. For those who prefer to stay out of the kitchen, there is a coffee shop—but no restaurant. There's also an outdoor pool. Business services include an English-speaking concierge, secretarial services in English, and translation services. 44-50 Rua Rodrigo da Fonseca (phone: 386-3800; fax: 386-3000).

**Holiday Inn Crowne Plaza** If flight logistics are a consideration, choose this modern, well-appointed hotel. It's five minutes from the airport—though a bit far from the city center. The 221 rooms are all soundproofed, with satellite TV and electronic safes. One floor is reserved for nonsmokers, and the executive floor offers special amenities. There's a handsome restaurant, and a bar with live music. Business services include a fitness center, 24-hour room service, meeting rooms for up to 200, an English-speaking concierge, foreign currency exchange, secretarial services in English, audiovisual equipment, photocopiers, computers, cable television news, translation services, and express checkout. At the end of *Campo Grande,* the park just off the main road to the airport. 390 Avenida Marechal Craveiro Lopes (phone: 759-9639; 800-HOLIDAY; fax: 758-6949).

**Lisboa Plaza** Centrally located off Avenida da Liberdade and redecorated by a leading Portuguese designer, this elegant, family-owned and -operated property has 94 rooms and 12 suites, all soundproofed and with mini-bars. In addition to the *Quinta d'Avenida* restaurant, there is a bar that's a popular meeting place. Business services include 24-hour room service, an English-speaking concierge, foreign currency exchange, secretarial services in English, photocopiers, and translation services. 7 Travessa do Salitre (phone: 346-3922; fax: 347-1630).

**Rex** This modern 70-room establishment is on the edge of *Parque Eduardo VII,* near the more prestigious *Ritz* and *Meridien* hotels. Half of the rooms have balconies overlooking the park. There are two restaurants (one with a panoramic view) and a bar. Business facilities include meeting rooms for up to 200, foreign currency exchange, audiovisual equipment, photocopiers, and translation services. 169 Rua Castilho (phone: 388-2161; fax: 388-7581).

**Senhora do Monte** A real find, this small place is in the Old Graça quarter northeast of *Castelo São Jorge.* It has fine views of Lisbon from many of its 27 rooms. Not every room is air conditioned, there's no restaurant, and it's not in the heart of things, but old hands swear by it for its offbeat location and amiable ambience. Business facilities include an English-speaking concierge and foreign currency exchange. 39 Calçada do Monte (phone: 886-6002; fax: 877783).

**Tivoli** Right on the main downtown avenue, this hotel has 350 rooms and suites. Because it's conveniently located, the lobby is a popular meeting place for businesspeople and travelers, and the bar just off the lobby is a favorite with local journalists. There is a restaurant plus a popular rooftop grillroom, a small pool set in a garden, and tennis courts on the grounds. Business services include 24-hour room service, meeting rooms for up to 200, an English-speaking concierge, secretarial services in English, audiovisual equipment, photocopiers, cable TV news, and translation services. 185 Av. da Liberdade (phone: 5356-1300; fax: 579461).

**Tivoli Jardim** On a quiet street behind its sister *Tivoli* (above), this hotel is much quieter and its prices somewhat lower. It has 120 rooms (many with balconies), a restaurant, a bar, and a parking lot. The service is first rate, and guests have access to the *Tivoli*'s pool and tennis courts. Business services include 24-hour room service, meeting rooms for up to 200 at the *Tivoli*, an English-speaking concierge, foreign currency exchange, secretarial services in English (also at the *Tivoli*), photocopiers, and translation services. 7-9 Rua Júlio César Machado (phone: 353-9971; fax: 355-6566).

**York House** Like *Senhora do Monte* (above), this is an insider's inn. One of the most attractive places to stay in Lisbon, it is some distance west of the heart of the city, close to the *Museu Nacional de Arte Antiga*. Housed in a 17th-century building that was once a convent, this lovely, antiques-filled *pensão* has a restaurant and a nice bar with tables in the garden. It's a particular favorite of British visitors, writers, and embassy personnel. Across and down the street a bit, in an 18th-century house (No. 47) that once belonged to the writer Eça de Queirós, there's an equally old-fashioned and aristocratic 17-room annex, making a total of 62 rooms (not all with private baths). Business services include an English-speaking concierge, foreign currency exchange, and photocopiers. 32 Rua das Janelas Verdes (phone: 396-2435; fax: 397-2793).

### INEXPENSIVE

**Dom Carlos** A good place to stay at Praça Marquês de Pombal. The 73 rooms are comfortable and come equipped with mini-bars. There's no restaurant on the premises, but there is a breakfast room and a bar. Business services include 24-hour room service, an English-speaking concierge, foreign currency exchange, and photocopiers. 121 Av. Duque de Loulé, at Praça Marquês de Pombal (phone: 353-9071; fax: 352-0728).

**Príncipe** Located northeast of *Parque Eduardo VII,* this hotel is simple yet comfortable, with many of its 70 rooms overlooking the park. It also offers the convenience of a restaurant and a bar. 201 Av. Duque de Avila (phone/fax: 353-6151).

**Torre** Modern and attractive, this little place is a 15-minute taxi ride from the center of Lisbon, but convenient for sightseeing in Belém, where it's right beside the *Mosteiro dos Jerónimos*. There are 50 rooms (not all air conditioned), and the hotel has a restaurant and a bar. Business services include an English-speaking concierge and foreign currency exchange. 8 Rua dos Jerónimos (phone: 363-7332; fax: 645995).

**Zurique** In an excellent location, near the *Campo Pequeno* bullring, this modern establishment has 252 rooms and a full range of facilities, including a pool, restaurant, and bar. Business services include meeting rooms for up to 280, an English-speaking concierge, secretarial services in English, and translation services. 18 Rua Ivone Silva (phone: 793-7111; fax: 793-7290).

ESTORIL

### EXPENSIVE

**Palácio** Imagine Allied and Axis spies peering around pillars during World War II and the jewels of exiled royalty glinting in the light of crystal chandeliers; that's the ambience of this gracious Old World hotel. The public rooms are majestic; the staff seems to remember everyone who has ever stayed here; and there are 200 rooms and suites featuring traditional furnishings mixed with the contemporary. In addition to a dining room, there is the superlative *Four Seasons Grill* (see *Eating Out,* below). A heated pool and cabañas are in lovely gardens behind the hotel; the beach on the Atlantic is a five-minute walk away. Temporary membership in the nearby *Clube de Golfe do Estoril* is available (hotel guests get a 60% discount on greens fees), and next door there are tennis courts at a private club (again, there are special rates for hotel guests). Business services include 24-hour room service, meeting rooms for up to 300, an English-speaking concierge, foreign currency exchange, secretarial services in English, audiovisual equipment, photocopiers, and translation services. Parque do Estoril (phone: 468-0400; 800-223-6800; fax: 468-4867).

### MODERATE

**Alvorada** A modern hostelry, near the casino, it has 51 rooms, each with a balcony. There's a solarium on top, and the hotel is only 200 yards from the beach. It has no restaurant, but there's a breakfast room and a bar. Business services include an English-speaking concierge, foreign currency exchange, and photocopiers. 3 Rua de Lisboa (phone: 468-0070; fax: 468-7250).

**Atlántico** Located in the pleasant residential district of Monte Estoril, this modern hotel is almost directly on the sea—only train tracks run between it and the beach. There are 175 rooms (some with balconies overlooking the Atlantic), a terrace with a large saltwater pool, an excellent restaurant, a bar, a nightclub, and a billiards room. Business services include meeting rooms for up to 80, an English-speaking concierge, foreign currency exchange, audiovisual equipment, and photocopiers. Estrada Marginal, Monte Estoril (phone: 468-5170; fax: 468-3619).

**Grande** On a hill overlooking the sea, this is a modern establishment of 73 rooms (some with balconies), a bar, a restaurant, and a covered pool. Business services include foreign currency exchange and photocopiers. Av. Sabóia, Monte Estoril (phone: 468-4838; fax: 468-4834).

**Inglaterra** A charming turn-of-the-century private-home-turned-hotel, it's set in gardens near the *Palácio*. Inside, the 45 rooms are decorated in a spare, contemporary style; there's a bar, a restaurant, and a pool. Business services include an English-speaking concierge, foreign currency exchange, and photocopiers. 1 Rua do Porto (phone: 468-4461; fax: 468-2108).

**Lennox Country Club** A hillside *estalagem* (inn) stands in a garden setting overlooking the coast. There are 34 rooms, either in the main building, which was once a private home, or in modern additions. It has a very good restaurant with excellent service, and a kidney-shaped heated outdoor pool. The inn caters to golfers—memorabilia of the sport decorate it—and will provide transportation to the area's courses for a small fee. 5 Rua Engenheiro Alvaro Pedro de Sousa (phone: 468-0424; fax: 467-0859).

### INEXPENSIVE

**Founder's Inn** British-owned and also known as the *Estalagem do Fundador,* it has 10 pleasant rooms, individually furnished and with satellite TV. The restaurant serves excellent international fare; there's also a bar. A freshwater pool is on the grounds, which are located on a hillside and set back from the beachfront. Other amenities include an English-speaking concierge and foreign currency exchange. 11 Rua Dom Afonso Henriques (phone: 468-2221; fax: 468-8779).

**Lido** Comfortable and modern, this hostelry is in a quiet spot on a hillside away from the beach, but not far from the casino and park. Each of the 62 rooms and suites has a balcony (but no TV set); and there is a restaurant, bar, large pool, solarium, and terrace with a view of the ocean. Business services include an English-speaking concierge, foreign currency exchange, and photocopiers. 12 Rua do Alentejo (phone: 468-4098; fax: 468-3665).

**Pica-Pau** Here's a nice inn in a pretty old, white-painted villa with a red tile roof, near the *Lido* and the *Founder's Inn.* There are 48 modern rooms (no TV sets), a bar, a restaurant, and a pool. Other amenities include an English-speaking concierge and foreign currency exchange. 48 Rua Dom Afonso Henriques (phone: 468-0803; fax: 467-0664).

**Smart** A *pensão* in a large old house, it has 16 rooms—most with private baths (the rest have washbasins). Not far from the beach, it also has a garden complete with palm trees. There's a breakfast room (but no restaurant). There's also an English-speaking concierge. 3 Rua José Viana (phone: 468-2164).

## CASCAIS

### EXPENSIVE

**Albatroz** Perched on the rocks at water's edge, this luxury property boasts a choice location, which is not surprising since the core of the hotel was built during the 19th century as a villa for the royal family. Between the original building and a newer balconied addition, there are 37 rooms plus three suites, all with satellite TV and mini-bars. An excellent restaurant (see *Eating Out,* below) and a bar, each overlooking the sea, plus an outdoor pool are further attractions. Business facilities include meeting rooms for up to 30, an English-speaking concierge, foreign currency exchange, secretarial services in English, audiovisual equipment, photocopiers, and translation services. 100 Rua Frederico Arouca (phone: 483-2821; fax: 484-4827).

**Estalagem Muchaxo** Set on the high cliffs above *Praia de Guincho* (Guincho Beach), this charming inn has views of Cabo de Roca—the westernmost point of land in Europe. In addition to 63 rooms with mini-bars, there is an excellent restaurant, *Muchaxo,* with a panoramic view and a seafood menu (see *Eating Out,* below). The property also offers a seawater pool, a sauna, squash courts, and a conference room. Praia do Guincho (phone: 487-0221; fax: 487-0444).

**Estoril-Sol** The biggest hotel on the coast, it has 317 rooms and suites, all with satellite TV and mini-bars. East of town, between the center of Cascais and Monte Estoril, the property is separated from the water only by the electric train tracks (an underground passage leads directly to the beach). There is a large rooftop restaurant with panoramic views, as well as five bars, a disco, and shops. Sports facilities include an Olympic-size pool set in gardens, a children's pool, a health club, a sauna, and squash courts; guests have privileges at a nearby nine-hole golf course. Business services include 24-hour room service, meeting rooms for up to 1,200, an English-speaking concierge, foreign currency exchange, secretarial services in English, audiovisual equipment, photocopiers, cable TV news, and translation services. *Parque Palmela* (phone: 483-2831; 800-843-6664; fax: 483-2280).

**Guincho** The waves crash against three sides of this restored 17th-century fortress that looks out to sea from a rocky promontory 5½ miles (9 km) northwest of Cascais, near the westernmost point of continental Europe. The location is spectacular, with beach on both sides, although walking along the sand is recommended over going in the water since the undertow is treacherous. The 36 rooms and suites in this elegant establishment all have old brick-vaulted ceilings and mini-bars, and some have balconies. There is a bar and a restaurant with a panoramic view (see *Eating Out,* below). Business services include an English-speaking concierge, foreign currency exchange, secretarial services in English, audiovisual equipment, photocopiers, and translation services. Praia do Guincho (phone: 487-0491; 800-843-6664; fax: 487-0431).

## MODERATE

**Baia** In the heart of town, this property is right on the beach at the spot where the fishermen tie up their painted boats. There are 113 renovated rooms, most with balconies, and all with satellite TV and mini-bars. A restaurant, terrace bar, and pool round out the amenities. Business services include an English-speaking concierge, foreign currency exchange, and photocopiers. Av. Marginal (phone: 483-1033; fax: 483-1095).

**Cidadela** Near the center of town and a short stroll from the waterfront, this hotel has 140 rooms and some apartments, each with its own sea-view balcony. Facilities include a good restaurant, a bar, and a pool set amid gardens. Business services include 24-hour room service, meeting rooms for up to 100, an English-speaking concierge, foreign currency exchange, audiovisual equipment, photocopiers, and translation services. Av. 25 de Abril (phone: 483-2921; fax: 486-7226).

**Farol** This charming *estalagem* (inn) in a building that was once the private house of an aristocratic family is located by the sea, just west of the center along the road to Boca do Inferno and Praia do Guincho. Each of the 15 rooms has a mini-bar; also on the premises are a pool, tennis court, bar, snack bar, and restaurant overlooking the water. Business amenities include an English-speaking concierge and foreign currency exchange. 7 Estrada da Boca do Inferno (phone: 483-0173; fax: 284-1447).

## INEXPENSIVE

**Dom Carlos** In the center of Cascais, this *pensão* occupies a restored house built in 1640, and decor of that period has been retained in the breakfast room and chapel. There are 18 rooms, with a salon for watching TV, and a tree-filled garden. 8 Rua Latino Coelho (phone: 486-8463; fax: 486-5155).

**Valbom** An *albergaria* (inn) located in the center of Cascais and near the train station, it's far more inviting inside than out. There are 40 rooms with a bar (but no restaurant). Business amenities include an English-speaking concierge and foreign currency exchange. 14 Av. Valbom (phone: 486-5801; fax: 486-5805).

## SINTRA

### EXPENSIVE

**Cesar Park** This luxury establishment overlooks the fairways of its own 18-hole golf course set in the Sintra foothills. It has 136 rooms and 41 suites that range from duplexes opening onto gardens to decidedly imperial quarters. Amenities include a swimming pool (enclosed and heated in winter), a health club, tennis courts, and a jogging course. There are two restaurants, one specializing in traditional

Japanese fare, the other offering international and traditional Portuguese dishes. Business services include 24-hour room service, meeting rooms for up to 300, an English-speaking concierge, foreign currency exchange, secretarial services in English, audiovisual equipment, photocopiers, computers, and translation services. Estrada da Lagoa Azul, Linho (phone: 924-9011; fax: 924-9007).

**Palácio dos Seteais** One of the loveliest and most romantic hotels in Europe, it was built at the end of the 18th century for the Dutch consul in Lisbon, sold to the fifth Marquês de Marialva, and visited often by royalty. Marble gleams underfoot, and murals line the walls of the public rooms. The 29 guestrooms and one suite are beautifully decorated with antiques, handwoven rugs, and tapestries, but there are no TV sets or mini-bars to destroy the neoclassical illusion. Located just outside of Sintra, the hotel has a TV lounge, a bar, a pool, tennis courts, a well-known restaurant that overlooks spacious gardens (see *Eating Out,* below), and a formal, windowed salon with views of the Sintra Valley. Business services include meeting rooms for up to 12, an English-speaking concierge, foreign currency exchange, audiovisual equipment, and photocopiers. 8 Rua Barbosa do Bocage (phone: 923-3200; fax: 923-4277).

### MODERATE

**Tivoli Sintra** The best in town, it is situated off the main square of Sintra, right by the *Palácio Nacional da Pena.* The modern building comes with all the latest conveniences, along with traditional Portuguese touches in the decor. There are 75 rooms with balconies. *Monserrate,* a highly regarded restaurant with a view (see *Eating Out,* below), is among the highlights here, and there are lounges, bars, and a garage. Business services include 24-hour room service, meeting rooms for up to 220, an English-speaking concierge, foreign currency exchange, secretarial services in English, audiovisual equipment, photocopiers, cable TV, and translation services. Praça da República (phone: 923-3505; fax: 923-1572).

### INEXPENSIVE

**Central** Located on the main square in front of the palace, this hotel is short on rooms (only 14, 11 with private baths, none with air conditioning or TV sets), but it's long on charm. There is a pleasant restaurant with a terrace that's used for lunch in the summer as well as a tearoom. 35 Praça da República (phone: 923-0063).

**Sintra** In São Pedro de Sintra, a 10-minute walk from downtown, this *pensão* has 10 rooms (some with private baths, but none with air conditioning). There's also a pool, a TV room, and a breakfast room (no restaurant). Business amenities include an English-speaking concierge and a foreign currency exchange. Travessa dos Avelares, São Pedro de Sintra (phone: 923-0738).

### STATELY HOMES AND MANOR HOUSES
Portugal's *Turismo no Espaço Rural* (Tourism in the Country) program provides visitors with a network of private homes that take

in small numbers of paying guests. There are three categories of properties: the *Turismo de Habitação* (Manor House Tourism) category, which includes elegant, old aristocratic estates and manor houses; the *Turismo Rural* (Rural Tourism) category, which consists of simpler but still fine country homes; and the *Agroturismo* (Farm Work Tourism) category, which features working farms. There are many properties in the latter two categories in the rural north, but travelers interested in the intimate and unusual lodgings in the *Turismo de Habitação* category, all of which are moderately priced, can find several in the Lisbon area. Among them, by the sea in Estoril, is the charming *Casal de São Roque* (Av. Marginal, Estoril 2765; phone: 268-0217), which was built at the beginning of the century. Furnished in period style, it has six guest rooms, four with private baths; the hosts serve meals on request. In the center of Cascais, there's the *Casa da Pérgola* (13 Av. Valbom, Cascais 2736; phone: 284-0040), set in lovely gardens and offering one luxurious suite and five bedrooms with private baths.

Among the Sintra estates, the *Quinta de São Tiago* (Estrada de Monserate, Sintra 2710; phone: 923-2923) is an imposing noble house several centuries old, surrounded by vast lawns with a pool, near the *Palácio dos Seteais*. Luxuriously furnished with antiques, it offers eight double bedrooms with private baths; the owner serves meals on request. The *Quinta da Capela* (Estrada de Monserrate, Sintra 2710; phone: 929-0170; fax: 929-3425), located beyond the *Palácio dos Seteais* and the *Quinta de Monserrate,* is another impressive old noble house surrounded by gardens. Six beautifully furnished bedrooms with private baths plus two cottage apartments are available; only breakfast is served. The *Vila das Rosas* (2-4 Rua António Cunha, Sintra 2710; phone: 923-4216) is a large, white 19th-century house with a red tile roof on the northern outskirts of Sintra; four double rooms with bath, a suite of three rooms with a private bath, and a cottage in the garden are available. In summer, breakfast is served in the cool wine cellar; other meals are served on request. Finally, the *Casa da Tapada* (Quinta das Sequoias, Sintra 2710; phone/fax: 923-0342) is a 19th-century country mansion situated on a mountaintop, with a view of the Pena and Mouros palaces from the front. There are five large rooms, all with private baths; dinner can be arranged upon request.

---

## EATING OUT

Portuguese food offers a surprising variety of tastes. Over the centuries, this seagoing nation's cuisine has come under the influence of far-flung countries, from Asia to Africa and the Americas, as well as from neighboring Spain and nearby France, and this heritage is reflected in Lisbon's restaurants—with many regional permutations. Fish and other seafood abound and usually are fresh and delicious, but they're luxury dishes that will often double your meal tab. Those who want to splurge may order steamed lobster or grilled prawns, or a dish such as *arroz de marisco* (rice with shellfish). Stuffed crab and boiled sea spider (served with a wooden mallet to crack open the shell) are flavorful, and codfish, salted and dried, is a great local favorite. It's said the Portuguese have as many ways to prepare codfish as there are days in the year, one of the best being *bacalhau à Gomes de Sá,* named for a Porto restaurant owner's baked medley of cod, potatoes, onions, eggs, and herbs. The best restaurants serve delicious smoked swordfish, sliced very thin, with lemon and capers, but for something uniquely Portuguese, sample the charcoal-grilled sardines, a tasty treat at summer festivities. Lisbon's meat is best grilled, but other typical dishes such as *cozido à portuguesa* (a stew of boiled vegetables, sausages, and other types of meats popular in the north) and *iscas à portuguesa* (thin slices of calf's liver marinated in wine, garlic, and bay leaves, and then cooked in an earthenware dish) are well worth trying. Desserts, most based on eggs, sugar, and almonds, may be too sweet for some palates; if so, there are good cheeses—queijo da Serra, from northeastern Portugal, and serpa, from the Alentejo, are two of the best. While vintages from all over the country appear on the city's wine lists, the regions to look for are Bairrada, which produces a number of forceful reds; Dao, known for mellow reds and fruity whites; Douro, the home of great table wines; and Alentejo, recognized for its fruity red wines and now emerging as a producer of fine whites. As a rule of thumb, Portuguese reds are at their best before five years, but whites, and particularly the northern *vinhos verdes,* should be drunk much before then.

If you steer clear of pricey seafood, dinner for two, with a local wine, averages from $110 to $150 at restaurants listed below as expensive, from $60 to $100 at moderate places, and from $40 to $60 at inexpensive restaurants. Customary dining time begins no earlier than 7:30 PM, and many restaurants close their kitchens at 11 PM. Lunch is served between noon and 2:30 PM. Unless otherwise noted, all restaurants are open for lunch and dinner, and all telephone numbers are in the 1 city code.

For an unforgettable dining experience, we begin with our culinary favorites (two in Lisbon, one in Queluz), followed by our cost and quality choices, listed by price category.

---

**DELIGHTFUL DINING**

**Aviz** When the elegant, turn-of-the-century *Aviz* hotel closed its doors during the early 1960s, its chef and maître d' joined forces and started a new restaurant—but with the same name and the same decor as the hotel—in a former tailor's shop. Legend has it that the Armenian oil millionaire Calouste Sarkis Gulbenkian, a frequenter of the hotel, contributed to the venture, but whatever the case, the restaurant's clients continue to be captains of industry, who like its subdued intimacy, refined Belle Epoque decor, and flawless service. Guests have a choice of dining rooms: the cozy silk-lined *Salão Verde* (Green Room) or the lighter *Salão Amarelo* (Yellow

Room), decorated with old musical instruments. Parties of 14 to 18 persons can retire to the intimacy of a private salon under the watchful eye of a 19th-century wooden statue of Pocahontas. Other attractions are the pub-like wooden bar and the tile-lined marble staircase. The chef's enticing culinary creations—such as smoked swordfish, gratinéed cod *Conde de Guarda*-style, rack of lamb with ground herbs, and chilled *bôlo de ananás* (pineapple cake)—make the restaurant one of Portugal's dining landmarks. Closed Saturday lunch, Sundays, and holidays. Reservations advised. Major credit cards accepted. 12B Rua Serpa Pinto (phone: 342-8391).

**Cozinha Velha** This is the former royal kitchen of the *Palácio Nacional* at Queluz (the name means "old kitchen"), now an air conditioned restaurant with considerable atmosphere. It has high stone arches, a 15-foot-long marble worktable, a walk-in fireplace, enormous spits, and walls lined with copper pots and utensils, many of them originals and bearing the royal seal. Wood-vaulted ceilings, red tile floors, iron lamps, refined service, and soft background music provide the elegant backdrop for such delectables as *terrina de casa* (veal pâté); *linguado suado* (steamed sole) served in a delicate onion, carrot, mushroom, and sour cream sauce; and souffléed, oven-baked *bacalhau espiritual* (codfish). The codfish dish takes 40 minutes to prepare and should be ordered in advance. Guests have a good choice of wines from all over the country, including neighboring Colares, which produces the light-bodied *tavares rodrigues*. The restaurant's pièces de résistance are its desserts, fashioned from ancient convent recipes. Try the *doce real* (royal sweet), which comes stamped with the Portuguese royal seal in confectionery sugar and is made of squash, eggs, and nuts. Closed *Labor Day* (May 1). Reservations necessary. Major credit cards accepted. *Palácio Nacional de Queluz* (phone: 435-0232).

**Tágide** This is a favorite with businesspeople and government officials, including the president. A beautiful staircase leads from the small dining room on the first floor to a second-floor dining area where picture windows afford a great view of the Tagus. The combination of stark white walls, leather chairs, and 18th-century tiles depicting mythological characters gives the dining room a classical elegance. Other attractions are a wine list of over 70 vintages, spanning Portugal's eight main wine regions, and the fish delicacies, including the house salmon pâté and *cherne no forno com coentros* (oven-baked stone bass with coriander). Meat lovers can savor the succulent *churrasco de cabrito* (grilled kid) or *carne* *de porco à alentejana* (Alentejo-style pork), an ingenious dish of pork and clams prepared with wine, garlic, red pepper, coriander, and oil. The fruit and almond crêpes, topped with vanilla sauce, provide a sweet finish. Closed weekends. Reservations necessary. Major credit cards accepted. 18 Largo da Biblioteca Pública (phone: 342-0720).

## LISBON

### EXPENSIVE

**Casa da Comida** This discreetly elegant restaurant is in a converted house, with tables set around a charming enclosed garden and an adjoining period bar. The food is delicious and beautifully presented; specialties include pheasant and shellfish dishes. Closed Saturday lunch and Sundays. Reservations advised. Major credit cards accepted. 1 Travessa das Amoreiras (phone: 388-5376).

**Casa do Leão** The dining room, once part of the living quarters of Portugal's first king, Dom Afonso Henriques, is decorated with 17th-century tiles. Try Chef João Santos's monkfish with lemon, or beef filet with shrimp and cheese sauce. The menu changes in the summer and winter. Open daily. Reservations advised. Major credit cards accepted. Its location, with spectacular views of the city and the Tagus River from the nearby castle ramparts, is a bonus. *Castelo de São Jorge* (phone: 875962).

**Club dos Empresarios–António Clara** Located in the 19th-century Art Nouveau mansion that is now a municipal monument, this dining spot specializes in Portuguese fare and fine fish dishes. It also boasts a good wine cellar and a piano bar that is open until 2 AM. Closed Sundays. Reservations necessary. Major credit cards accepted. 46 Av. da República (phone: 796-6380).

**Conventual** The menu is based on old Portuguese convent and monastery recipes, some of which date back to the 17th century, and ecclesiastical objects decorate the premises. Typical dishes include *bacalhau com coentros* (cod with coriander) and *ensopado de borrego* (lamb stew). Closed Saturday lunch and Sundays. Reservations advised. Major credit cards accepted. 45 Praça das Flores (phone: 609196).

**Michel** The owner, a well-known chef on Portuguese television, specializes in nouvelle cuisine, Portuguese-style, and traditional French dishes, too. Handsomely decorated, this place is in the Alfama, just below the *Castelo São Jorge.* Closed Saturday lunch and Sundays. Reservations necessary. Major credit cards accepted. 5 Largo de Santa Cruz do Castelo (phone: 886-4338).

**Restaurante 33** Behind its elegant clapboard façade, the hallmarks of this well-appointed eatery are good international food and a pleasant atmosphere. A pianist plays as you dine. Closed Sundays. Reservations advised. Major credit cards accepted. 33 Rua Alexandre Herculano (phone: 546079).

**Sua Excelência** Knock on the door to gain entry, and, on request, the attentive owner will read out the entire menu in English. He serves a very good *açorda* (a combination of seafood, bread, eggs, and coriander) and Mozambique prawns in a peppery sauce. Closed Wednesdays, weekends at lunch, and September. Reservations advised. Major credit cards accepted. In the Lapa district, near the embassy residences. 42 Rua do Conde (phone: 603614).

### MODERATE

**A Paz** This is the quintessential insider's restaurant, where the appointments are unpretentious but the fish served up by the skillful chefs is exceptional. Closed weekends. Reservations advised. No credit cards accepted. In the Ajuda quarter near the *Palácio Nacional da Ajuda*. 22B Largo da Paz (phone: 363-1915).

**Gondola** A long-established Italian eatery near the *Museu Calouste Gulbenkian,* it is a favorite with visitors. Portuguese dishes are also on the menu. There's a lovely vine-covered garden for summer dining. Closed Saturday dinner and Sundays. Reservations advised. Major credit cards accepted. 64 Av. de Berna (phone: 797-0426).

**Rosa dos Mares** Grilled fish is the specialty at this attractive restaurant just around the corner from *Mosteiro dos Jerónimos* in Belém. Ask for seating in the more spacious and elegant upstairs dining room. Closed Wednesdays. Reservations advised. Major credit cards accepted. 110 Rua de Belém (phone: 364-9275).

**Varina da Madragoa** Transformed from an old tavern, this blue-and-white tiled restaurant in the old Madragoa quarter near *Palácio de São Bento* (Parliament) serves delicious Portuguese food, including excellent *bacalhau* (codfish). Closed Saturday lunch and Mondays. Reservations advised at lunchtime. Major credit cards accepted. 36 Rua das Madres (phone: 396-5533).

### INEXPENSIVE

**Bomjardim** It's considered the best at preparing *frango na brasa,* chicken that's charcoal-broiled on a rotating spit, and dipped in *piri piri* (a fiery chili sauce) if desired. This is one of Lisbon's most popular— and least expensive—culinary delights. There are two *Bomjardim* restaurants facing each other just off Praça dos Restauradores, both noisy and crowded at lunchtime. Open daily. Reservations advised at lunch. Major credit cards accepted. 10-11 Travessa de Santo Antão (phone: 342-7424).

**Bota Alta** Traditional Portuguese cooking is served up here in a cheery bistro atmosphere. It's in the midst of all the Bairro Alto nightlife, and usually very busy. Closed Sundays. Reservations advised (or go early). Major credit cards accepted. 35-37 Travessa da Queimada (phone: 342-7959).

ESTORIL

EXPENSIVE

**Casino Estoril** The glittering, balcony-lined restaurant here is known for its international show at 11:30 PM every night, but it's also commendable for the excellent food and service. It has a long menu listing Portuguese and international dishes. Open daily. Reservations advised. Major credit cards accepted. *Parque do Estoril* (phone: 468-4521).

**Choupana** On a cliff overlooking the sea a bit over a mile (2 km) east of Estoril, this eatery specializes in seafood, but has a varied menu of other dishes as well. The air conditioned dining room is large, with a panoramic view. Later at night, there is a show and music until all hours. Closed Mondays. Reservations advised. Major credit cards accepted. Estrada Marginal, São João do Estoril (phone: 468-3099).

**English Bar** This brown-and-white building overlooks the water, with windows all around. It's cozily decorated in the English manner, serves very good Portuguese and international dishes, and has a popular bar. Closed Sundays. Reservations advised. Major credit cards accepted. Estrada Marginal, Monte Estoril (phone: 468-0413).

**Four Seasons Grill** Widely considered to offer the finest dining in Estoril, this place has a long menu of Portuguese and international dishes that changes seasonally, as do the china, the decor, and the waiters' uniforms. It is run by the *Palácio* hotel next door. Open daily. Reservations advised. Major credit cards accepted. Rua do Parque (phone: 468-0400).

**A Maré** Located by the sea and offering a lovely panoramic view, this dining spot features a varied menu. There is a large air conditioned dining room and, in summer, an outside barbecue. Open daily. Reservations unnecessary. Major credit cards accepted. Estrada Marginal, Monte Estoril (phone: 468-5570).

MODERATE

**Ferra Mulinhas** An unusual mix of good Portuguese and Hungarian cooking is featured here. Open for dinner only; closed Sundays. Reservations unnecessary. Major credit cards accepted. 5A Rua Viveiro (phone: 468-0005).

CASCAIS

EXPENSIVE

**Albatroz** The dining room of the hotel of the same name is set on rocks at the edge of the sea (the picture windows afford wonderful views). It's known for a varied menu, including paella and good seafood. There is piano music nightly and harp and flute music on weekends. Open daily. Reservations necessary. Major credit cards accepted. 100 Rua Frederico Arouca (phone: 483-2821).

**Baluarte** By the sea, two air conditioned dining rooms feature splendid views. Seafood is the specialty, but many other Portuguese and international dishes are on the menu. Open daily. Reservations advised. Major credit cards accepted. 1 Av. Marechal Carmona (phone: 486-5471).

**Guincho** In a cliff-top hotel that was once a fortress guarding continental Europe's westernmost extremity, this dining spot is surrounded by windows looking onto the crashing Atlantic. The location makes it a wonderful lunch or dinner spot for those on a day's outing along the coast, but the excellence of the food—particularly the seafood—and the fine service alone are worth the trip. Open daily. Reservations advised. Major credit cards accepted. Located 5½ miles (9 km) northwest of Cascais. Praia do Guincho (phone: 487-0491).

**Muchaxo** One of the most famous seafood spots on the Lisbon coast is set in an *estalagem* (inn) of the same name. Right by the sea, it offers a marvelous view over the water. Open daily. Reservations unnecessary. Major credit cards accepted. Praia do Guincho (phone: 487-0221).

**Pescador** A charming place near the fish market, it is decorated in a nautical motif. The fish and seafood are very good here. Open daily. Reservations advised. Major credit cards accepted. 10B Rua das Flores (phone: 483-2054).

### MODERATE

**O Batel** Nicely decorated in a rustic fashion, this is another good seafood restaurant, near the fish market. Closed Wednesdays. Reservations unnecessary. Major credit cards accepted. 4 Travessa das Flores (phone: 483-0215).

**Beira Mar** One of the oldest of the seafood eateries near the fish market, it is decorated with blue and white tiles and serves international fare in addition to good seafood. Open daily. Reservations unnecessary. Major credit cards accepted. 6 Rua das Flores (phone: 483-0152).

**John Bull** This well-known English pub has a good little restaurant attached; it serves international fare. Open daily. Reservations advised. Major credit cards accepted. 31 Praça Costa Pinto (phone: 483-3319).

**Morgados** By the bullring, this large, air conditioned place specializes in grilled meat. Closed Mondays. Reservations unnecessary. Major credit cards accepted. Praça de Touros (phone: 486-8751).

**O Pipas** A smart seafood spot in the center of town near the fish market, it has a small air conditioned dining room decorated with wine barrels and hanging garlic braids and sausages. Open daily. Reservations advised. Major credit cards accepted. 18 Rua das Flores (phone: 486-4501).

**Galegos** Near the center of town, this simple place specializes in Portuguese and seafood dishes. Closed Wednesdays. Reservations unnecessary. Major credit cards accepted. 3 Av. Valbom (phone: 483-2586).

SINTRA

### EXPENSIVE

**Monserrate** The floor-to-ceiling windows of this air conditioned hotel restaurant afford a panoramic view of the valley below Sintra. The menu features international dishes. Open daily. Reservations necessary. Major credit cards accepted. In the *Tivoli Sintra Hotel*, Praça da República (phone: 923-3505).

**Palácio dos Seteais** This 18th-century palace makes a lovely setting for lunch on a sunny day, particularly when the garden terrace is open. The very elegant restaurant, with tall windows that overlook the valley, serves well-prepared Portuguese and international dishes. Open daily. Reservations necessary. Major credit cards accepted. In the hotel of the same name, at 8 Rua Barbosa do Bocage (phone: 923-3200).

### MODERATE

**Adega do Saloio** Aptly named, this "countryman's wine cellar" has a rustic decor, with braids of onions and garlic hanging from the ceiling, two fireplaces, and an open kitchen. Meat, fish, and seafood grilled on a spit are the specialties. Located at the entrance to Sintra from Lisbon or Estoril. Closed Tuesdays. Reservations advised on weekends. No credit cards accepted. Chão de Meninos (phone: 923-1422).

**Café Paris** On the square facing the palace, this old-fashioned café-restaurant is one of the best dining places in the center of town; meat and fish dishes are featured. There is alfresco dining in the summer on the terrace. Open daily. Reservations unnecessary. Major credit cards accepted. Praça da Republica (phone: 923-2375).

**Cantinho de São Pedro** In São Pedro de Sintra, a 10-minute walk from downtown, this rustic restaurant has three large dining rooms and a wine cellar. Order seafood, game, or one of the many French dishes on the menu. Closed Mondays. Reservations advised. Major credit cards accepted. 18 Praça Dom Fernando II, São Pedro de Sintra (phone: 923-0267).

**Dos Arcos** Typical Portuguese dishes are served in an attractive setting that includes a waterfall. It's located in an old part of town just a 10-minute walk from the center. Closed Wednesday dinner and Thursdays. Reservations unnecessary. Major credit cards accepted. 4 Rua Serpa Pinto, São Pedro de Sintra (phone: 923-0264).

**Galeria Real** Above a gallery of antiques shops, this lovely dining room is filled with antiques. Portuguese and French food are served. Open daily. Reservations unnecessary. Major credit cards accepted. Rua Tude de Sousa, São Pedro de Sintra (phone: 923-1661).

**Solar de São Pedro** Two large dining rooms with fireplaces and a menu of French and Portuguese selections keep this place busy. Closed Tuesday dinner and Wednesdays. Reservations advised. Major credit cards accepted. 12 Praça Dom Fernando II, São Pedro de Sintra (phone: 923-1860).

**Tacho Real** Located in what once were the stables and coach house of a mansion in the historic center of town, this restaurant exudes atmosphere. Try the *caldeirada à Tacho Real* (the house rendition of the traditional fish stew) or the beefsteak with shrimp sauce. Closed Wednesdays, Thursday lunch, and from mid-October to mid-November. Reservations advised on weekends. Major credit cards accepted. 14 Rua Ferraia, Vila Velha de Sintra (phone: 923-5277).

---

## TEA SHOPS

The Lisbon tradition of the late afternoon tea break is almost as hidebound as London's, a reflection of the city's long-standing ties to England. Every weekday at around 5 PM, the city's handsome tea shops fill up with clerks taking a break from work; friends and housewives getting together to discuss the latest news; students doing homework while nibbling sticky cakes; and shoppers giving their feet a rest. Visitors to the city should be sure to join the convivial scene. Most tea shops offer a variety of snacks, from cakes and cream pastries to such savory tidbits as *pasteis de bacalhau* (codfish croquettes) and *folhados com salsicha* (sausage pastries). The grande dame of them all—going strong for more than 60 years—is the high-ceilinged, chandelier-and-mirror-filled *Versailles* (15A Av. da República; phone: 546340), whose formal, immaculately uniformed waiters serve customers from old silver-plated tea services. But even older is *Pastelaria Bénard,* in the Chiado shopping area (104 Rua Garrett; phone: 347-3133). *Pastelaria Ferrari* (2 Calçada Nova de São Francisco; phone: 346-2741) is another Chiado teatime tradition. Some of the best pastries in the country are made by *Pastéis de Belém* (84 Rua de Belém; phone: 363-7423), an Old Europe—style confectionery famous for its delicious cinnamon-sprinkled offerings and a good cup of tea. Most tea houses are closed on Sundays, except for the *Versailles,* which is open daily from 7:30 AM to 10 PM.

# London

## At-a-Glance

SEEING THE CITY

London has, for the most part, resisted the temptation to build high. Aside from a handful of modest gestures toward skyscraping, there are few towering structures to obscure panoramic views of the city from its vantage points, which include the following:

**LONDON HILTON INTERNATIONAL** There were discreet noises of disapproval from *Buckingham Palace* when it was realized that the view from the roof bar of the *Hilton* included not only the palace grounds but, with high-powered binoculars, the inside of some of the royal chambers as well. In fact, the view over Mayfair, *Hyde Park*, and Westminster is breathtaking. 22 Park La., W1 (phone: 171-493-8000). Underground: *Hyde Park Corner*.

**WESTMINSTER CATHEDRAL** Not to be confused with *Westminster Abbey*, this is London's Roman Catholic cathedral. The top of its bell tower overlooks a broad expanse of the inner city. An elevator takes visitors up for a token charge (April through September only). Off Victoria St. near the station, at Ashley Pl., SW1 (phone: 171-834-7452). Underground: *Victoria*.

**HAMPSTEAD HEATH** Climb to the top of Parliament Hill, on the southern rim of this "wilderness" in north London. On a clear day, the view south from the *Heath* makes the city look like a vast village. Underground: *Belsize Park* or *Hampstead*.

**SOUTH BANK CENTRE** On the south bank of Waterloo Bridge is this large, bunker-like complex of cultural buildings, including the *Royal Festival Hall*, the *Royal National Theatre*, the *National Film Theatre*, and the *Hayward Gallery*. For a view of London, look across the Thames—upriver to the *Houses of Parliament*, downriver to *St. Paul's Cathedral*. Underground: *Waterloo*.

**TOWER BRIDGE WALKWAY** The upper part of one of London's most famous landmarks is open to visitors. In addition to the viewing gallery, there is a museum with state-of-the-art animated figures and the bridge's original Victorian steam pumping engines—which still work. Open daily. Admission charge (phone: 171-403-3761 or 171-407-0922). Underground: *Tower Hill*.

**ST. PAUL'S CATHEDRAL** The reward for climbing the 538 steps to the dome—the largest in the world after St. Peter's in Rome—is a panoramic view of London. Galleries are closed Sundays and for special services. Admission charge to cathedral, except on Sundays; admission charge to galleries. *St. Paul's Churchyard*, EC4 (phone: 171-248-2705). Underground: *St. Paul's* or *Mansion House*.

**THE MONUMENT** This 202-foot-high obelisk (commemorating the Great Fire of 1666) affords a good view of nearby churches and across to *Canary Wharf* in the Docklands, as well as to *St. Paul's* and the *Telecom Tower.* Note that there is no elevator. Closed Sundays October through March. Admission charge. Monument St., EC3 (phone: 171-626-2717). Underground: *Monument.*

**GREENWICH PARK** The lone hill in this large expanse across the Thames in Greenwich provides a panorama over the Docklands and the rest of the city in the distance. The best view is from General Wolfe's statue near the *Old Royal Observatory;* on a clear day you can see the dome of *St. Paul's.* Greenwich can be reached by tube (*Greenwich Station*), *British Rail,* or boat from *Charing Cross, Westminster,* or *Tower Piers.*

## SPECIAL PLACES

Even the most jaded will appreciate London's wealth of sights, most of which are clustered reasonably close together in or near the inner districts of Westminster, the City, and Kensington. Another area worth exploring is the neighborhood of Chelsea, with quiet, pretty side streets and a long, often frenetic shopping thoroughfare called King's Road.

### WESTMINSTER

**CHANGING OF THE GUARD** This famous ceremony takes place daily April through mid-July (every other day the rest of the year) promptly at 11:30 AM in the *Buckingham Palace* forecourt and at 11:15 AM at *St. James's Palace.* (It is usually canceled in inclement weather.) Arrive early, as it can get crowded (for more information, phone: 839-123411; costs between 36p/about 55¢ and 48p/about 75¢ per minute).

**HORSE GUARDS** If you haven't had enough, you can see a new guard of 12 members of the Household Cavalry troop in with trumpet and standard, Mondays through Saturdays at 11 AM and Sundays at 10 AM, on the west side of Whitehall. Incidentally, they come from stables not far from *Hyde Park* and make a daily parade along the south roadway of *Hyde Park,* past *Buckingham Palace,* and then on to Trafalgar Square to turn into Whitehall. Their progress is as much fun to watch as the actual ceremony.

**BUCKINGHAM PALACE** The royal standard flies from the roof when the monarch is in residence at her London home. Although George III bought it in 1762, *Buckingham Palace* did not become the principal regal dwelling until 1837, when Queen Victoria moved in. The gate that originally was built for the entrance, too narrow for the coaches of George IV, now marks the *Hyde Park* end of Oxford Street and is known as *Marble Arch.*

Part of the palace is now open to the public—for a price. During August and September (when the royals are vacationing), visitors may view 18 of the state rooms; on display are many of the works in the nonpareil *Royal Collection* (also see the *Queen's Gallery,*

# LONDON

N

ISLINGTON N1

KING'S CROSS ROAD

PENTONVILLE ROAD

FINSBURY EC1

Myddelton Square Sadler's Wells

HOXTON N1

HACKNEY ROAD

SHOREDITCH N1

OLD STREET

CLERKENWELL EC1

BETHNAL GREEN

CLERKENWELL RD

OLD STREET

GOSWELL ROAD

CITY ROAD

EASTERN STREET

KINGSLAND ROAD

ckens House

Gray's Inn

ROSEBERY AVE

FARRINGDON ROAD

ST JOHN STREET

CENTRAL STREET

LEVER STREET

BATH STREET

BUNHILL ROW

WORSHIP STREET

HOXTON STREET

SHOREDITCH HIGH ST

WORSHIP STREET

HANBURY ST

SPITALFIELDS E1

CORALD'S

HOLBORN WC2

Sir John Soane's Museum

Lincoln's Inn

Law Courts

STRAND

Fleet Street

The Courtauld Temple Institute

EMBANKMENT

SMITHFIELD

Smithfield Market

St. Bart's Hospital

HOLBORN VIADUCT

Dr. Johnson's House

Old Bailey

St. Paul's Cathedral

LUDGATE HILL

Mermaid Theatre

Blackfriars Station

BEACH ST CHISWELL ST

Barbican Centre BARBICAN EC2

Museum of London LONDON EC2

CITY EC2

Guildhall

GRESHAM ST

CHEAPSIDE

POULTRY

QUEEN VICTORIA

UPPER THAMES STREET

Finsbury Circus

MOORGATE WALL

Bank of England

Stock Exchange

CORNHILL

THREADNEEDLE

Mansion House

Cannon St. Station

CANNON STREET

LOMBARD STREET

Lloyds

FENCHURCH

LEADENHALL ST

ALDGATE

Liverpool Street Station

Petticoat Lane Market

LIVERPOOL ST

BISHOPSGATE

MIDDLESEX ST

HOUNDSDITCH

LAMB ST

HANBURY ST

Whitechapel Art Gallery

WHITECHAPEL E1

ALDGATE

MANSELL ST

MINORIES

LEMAN ST

Fenchurch St. Station

River   Thames

National Theatre

Royal National Theatre

South Bank Centre

BANKSIDE ST

Globe Theatre

SOUTHWARK SE1

Southwark Cathedral

BLACKFRIARS

STAMFORD STREET

WATERLOO ROAD

Young Vic Theatre

Old Vic Theatre

THE CUT

Waterloo Station

WESTMINSTER BRIDGE

SOUTHWARK STREET

UNION STREET

SOUTHWARK HIGH ST

TOOLEY STREET

ST THOMAS STREET

London Bridge Station

The Monument

LOWER THAMES STREET

BYWARD ST

Tower of London

Tower Bridge

To Greenwich

Yacht Basin

BERMONDSEY SE1

rchbishop's Park

ambeth Palace

seum of den tory

LAMBETH SE11

Imperial War Museum

KENNINGTON LANE

KENNINGTON PARK RD

KENNINGTON SE11

Kennington Park

KENNINGTON ROAD

Oval Cricket Ground

---

Portobello Rd Market

NOTTING HILL W11

NOTTING HILL GATE

MOSCOW ROAD

BAYSWATER W2

BAYSWATER ROAD

LANCASTER GATE

BAYSWATER

QUEENSWAY

INVERNESS TERR

PEMBRIDGE

KENSINGTON PALACE GDNS

Kensington Palace

Kensington

Round Pond

Gardens

Serpentine

ROTTEN ROW

Continuation on the main map

Holland Park

HOLLAND PARK

AUBREY WALK

PEEL ST

KENSINGTON CHURCH STREET

HOLLAND ST

KENSINGTON W8

Albert Memorial

Royal Albert Hall

KENSINGTON PALACE GATE

PRINCE CONSORT RD

GLOUCESTER ROAD

Imperial College

Science Museum

Natural History Museum

Victoria and Albert Museum

Brompton Oratory

EXHIBITION ROAD

SOUTH KENSINGTON SW7

KENSINGTON HIGH STREET

EARL'S COURT ROAD

VICTORIA ROAD

STANFORD ROAD

Edwardes Sq.

CORNWALL GARDENS

EARL'S COURT SW5

CROMWELL ROAD

below)—including paintings by Rubens and Van Dyck and the greatest collection of porcelain in the world (acquired by George IV). Other highlights are the *Blue Drawing Room,* with its ice-blue color scheme and exquisite chandeliers; the *State Dining Room,* featuring several royal portraits; the *Throne Room;* the *Music Room;* and the majestic, sweeping staircase to the second floor. Open daily. The steep admission charge is going toward the restoration of *Windsor Castle;* time-specific tickets are sold each day (for that day only) at a kiosk in *St. James's Park,* opposite the palace (phone: 171-930-5526). Underground: *St. James's Park* or *Victoria.*

**Queen's Gallery** The *British Royal Collection*—one of the world's greatest—was inaccessible to most people until 1962, when this gallery was created at *Buckingham Palace,* and even now only a fraction is on view. The exhibitions here never fail to impress, whether they are devoted to a subject such as royal children, animal paintings, or British soldiers; to single artists—Leonardo da Vinci or Gainsborough or Canaletto or Holbein, to name a quartet of past shows; or to groups of painters—the Italians or the Dutch. Exhibitions change about once a year. Closed Mondays. Admission charge. Buckingham Palace Rd., SW1 (phone: 171-799-2331). Underground: *Victoria.*

**ROYAL ACADEMY** Britain's oldest fine arts institution is housed in the former home of Lord Burlington. Its permanent collection includes works by Turner, Gainsborough, and West. The Summer Exhibition of living painters has been a tradition for over 200 years. Special displays this year include exhibitions of works by French artists Nicolas Poussin (1594–1665) and Odilon Redon (1840–1916). Open daily. Admission charge. *Burlington House,* Piccadilly, W1 (phone: 171-439-7438). Underground: *Green Park* or *Piccadilly Circus.*

**ROYAL MEWS** The mews is a palace alley where the magnificent bridal coach, other state coaches, and the horses that draw them are stabled. The public is admitted from noon to 4 PM Wednesdays and Thursdays mid-April through mid-July; Wednesdays through Fridays mid-July through September; and Wednesdays only from early October to just before *Christmas.* Admission charge. Buckingham Palace Rd., SW1 (phone: 171-799-2331). Underground: *Victoria.*

**ST. JAMES'S PALACE** Built originally for Henry VIII, this forbidding brick palace has decorative chimneys and gates; still serving royalty (Prince Charles has an office here), it is the *Court of St. James,* where new monarchs are proclaimed. The entrance under the clock tower, dating from 1832 during William IV's reign, is guarded by two sentries from rotating regiments who wear scarlet uniforms with busbies (black bearskin hats) and chain chin straps. In 1649, Charles I walked from the palace to his execution at Whitehall. The palace is not open to the public. Pall Mall, SW1. Underground: *Green Park.*

**ST. JAMES'S PARK** Londoners love parks, and this is one of the nicest. At lunch hour on a sunny day you can see impeccably dressed London businesspeople lounging on the grass, their shoes off and their sleeves rolled up. With its sizable lake (designed by John Nash) inhabited by pelicans and other wild fowl, *St. James's* was originally a royal deer park laid out as a pleasure ground for Charles II. Underground: *St. James's Park.*

**THE MALL** This wide avenue (rhymes with "pal"), parallel to Pall Mall, is lined with lime trees and Regency buildings and leads from Trafalgar Square to *Buckingham Palace.* It is the principal ceremonial route used by Queen Elizabeth and the Household Cavalry for the State Opening of Parliament (October/November) and the *Trooping the Colour* (see *Special Events*). It is closed to traffic on Sundays. Underground: *Trafalgar Square.*

**PICCADILLY CIRCUS** Downtown London finds its center here in the heart of the theater district and on the edge of Soho. This is the London equivalent of Times Square, and at the edge of the busy "circus," or traffic circle, is a statue of Eros, which was designed in 1893 as *The Angel of Christian Charity,* a memorial to the charitable Earl of Shaftesbury—the archer and his bow are a pun on his name. The *Criterion* restaurant (see *Eating Out*) and the *Criterion Theatre* are on the south side; opposite is the *Trocadero,* a converted three-story shopping and entertainment complex whose latest addition is *Planet Hollywood* (see *Eating Out*), a link in the famous restaurant chain. At the *Rock Circus* (phone: 171-734-8025), on the top four floors of the *London Pavilion,* rock music's immortals—from the *Beatles* to the *Who*—are brought to life with lighting, narration, and music. The *Rock Circus* also houses Europe's largest revolving auditorium, where "performances" are offered by rather remarkable robotic figures that move in rhythm to the music. Another popular exhibition is the *Guinness World of Records* display. Both are open daily. Separate admission charges (phone: 171-439-7331). Underground: *Piccadilly Circus.*

**TRAFALGAR SQUARE** One of London's most heavily trafficked squares is built around *Nelson's Column*—a 145-foot-high monument bearing a 17-foot statue that honors Lord Horatio Nelson, who won the Battle of Trafalgar in 1805. At the base are four huge bronze lions and two fountains. Flanked by handsome buildings, including the *National Gallery* and the 18th-century *Church of St. Martin-in-the-Fields* (have lunch or tea in the *Café in the Crypt;* see *Eating Out*), the square is a favorite gathering place for political rallies, tourists, and pigeons. Underground: *Trafalgar Square.*

**NATIONAL GALLERY** Among the world's greatest art museums, the *National Gallery* was instituted in 1824, when connoisseur Sir George Beaumont persuaded the government to buy the three dozen–plus paintings offered for sale after the death of merchant-collector John Julius Angerstein—among them Rembrandt's *The Woman Taken in Adultery* and *The Adoration of the Shepherds,* Rubens's *The Rape of the Sabine Women,* and Titian's *Venus and Adonis.* Subsequent gifts and acquisitions have added jewels such as Leonardo da Vinci's great cartoon *The Virgin and Child with St. Anne and St. John the Baptist,* Botticelli's *Venus and Mars,* Raphael's *Crucifixion,* and

Jan van Eyck's *Arnolfini Marriage*. Most of the more than 2,000 works are organized according to nationality and hang in chronological order. Nearly every item is on view at all times; a computer system enables visitors to locate any painting. Guidebooks are available in the shop, including *Twenty Great Paintings,* featuring photographs and descriptions of the gallery's most famous masterpieces. There are free, hour-long guided tours weekdays at 11:30 AM and 2:30 PM and Saturdays at 2 and 3:30 PM. And to give the footsore art lover a break, the *Sainsbury Wing Brasserie* offers light lunches and wine (phone: 171-389-1769). The museum is open daily. Admission charge to special exhibitions. Trafalgar Sq., WC2 (phone: 171-839-3321). Underground: *Trafalgar Square.*

**NATIONAL PORTRAIT GALLERY** Established in 1856, this museum is devoted to the portraits of the most important figures in British arts, letters, history and politics, military life, science, and various other fields. In all, over 9,000 likenesses, arranged chronologically, stare down from the walls. Elizabeth I is here as a young woman and a dowager, not far from Shakespeare. Mary, Queen of Scots; Thomas More; Milton; Pope; Dickens; and the Brontë sisters are depicted as well. Also shown here are such contemporary faces as Peter O'Toole and the Prince and Princess of Wales. Special shows on historical themes or individual artists are mounted frequently as well; every summer, the gallery displays a special collection of portraits by up-and-coming international artists. Open daily. Admission charge to special exhibitions only. 2 St. Martin's Pl., WC2 (phone: 171-306-0055). Underground: *Trafalgar Square.*

**WHITEHALL** A broad boulevard stretching from Trafalgar Square to Parliament Square, lined most of the way by government ministries and such historic buildings as the *Banqueting House* (completed in 1622, with a ceiling painted by Rubens). This is also where the daily changing of the Horse Guards takes place (see above). Underground: *Trafalgar Square* or *Westminster.*

**DOWNING STREET** Behind an ornate gate off Whitehall lies a street of small, unpretentious Georgian houses that include the official residences of some of the most important figures in British government—in particular the prime minister at No. 10 and the chancellor of the exchequer at No. 11. Underground: *Westminster.*

**CABINET WAR ROOMS** This underground complex was Winston Churchill's auxiliary command post during World War II, which he used most often during the German Luftwaffe's blitz on London. Most of the rooms contain their original furnishings. Of special note are the *Map Room;* the *Cabinet Room,* where the prime minister met with his staff; and the cramped *Transatlantic Telephone Room* (No. 63) used only by Churchill himself. Open daily. Admission charge. Clive Steps, King Charles St., SW1 (phone: 171-930-6961). Underground: *Westminster.*

**WESTMINSTER ABBEY** It's easy to get lost among the endlessly fascinating tombs and plaques and not even notice the abbey's splendid architecture, so do look at the structure itself. The early English Gothic edifice, begun in the 13th century, took almost 300 years to build. Don't miss the cloisters, which display the abbey's Gothic design to best advantage. Note also the fine Tudor chapel of Henry VII, with its tall windows and lovely fan-tracery vaulting, and the 13th-century chapel of St. Edward the Confessor, containing England's *Coronation Chair* and Scotland's ancient coronation *Stone of Scone* (pronounced *Skoon*).

Ever since 1066, when William the Conqueror was crowned in the Norman church that previously stood here, the abbey has been the traditional place where English monarchs are crowned, married, and buried. Its tombs and memorials honor sovereigns, soldiers, statesmen, and many other prominent English personages. *Poets' Corner,* in the south transept, contains the tombs of Chaucer, Tennyson, Browning, and many others—plus memorials to nearly every English poet of note and to some Americans, such as Longfellow and T. S. Eliot.

Guided tours are offered six times every weekday and three times on Saturdays. The nave and cloisters are open daily; the *Royal Chapel* is closed Sundays. Admission charge to some parts of the abbey and for tours. Broad Sanctuary, off Parliament Sq., SW1 (phone: 171-222-5152). Underground: *Westminster.*

**HOUSES OF PARLIAMENT** The imposing neo-Gothic, mid-19th-century buildings of the *Palace of Westminster,* as it is sometimes called, look especially splendid from across the river. There are separate chambers for the *House of Commons* and the *House of Lords,* and visitors are admitted to the *Strangers' Galleries* of both houses by lining up at St. Stephen's Entrance, opposite *Westminster Abbey. Big Ben,* the world-famous 13½-ton bell in the clock tower of the palace, which is illuminated when Parliament is in session, still strikes the hours. Although the buildings are otherwise closed to the public, there are limited tours outside session hours on Friday afternoons. To make tour arrangements, write in advance to *The Public Information Office* (1 Derby Gate, London SW1A 1DG, England). Particularly impressive are *Westminster Hall,* with its magnificent hammer-beam roof, and the gold-and-scarlet *House of Lords.* No admission charge. Parliament Sq., SW1 (phone: 171-219-4272). Underground: *Westminster.*

**TATE GALLERY** Built in 1897 on the site of Millbank Prison, the gift of the sugar broker and art collector Sir Henry Tate, this national collection of British painting and 20th-century artwork was established when bequests had swelled the size of the *National Gallery*'s collection to an extent that there was no longer room for all the paintings. The works here are arranged in chronological order. The magnificent *Clore Gallery*—designed by James Stirling and set in a newer wing—houses the extensive collection of works by Turner. The group of sculptures offers excellent examples of the artistry of Rodin, Maillol, Mestrovic, Moore, and Epstein. The *British Collection* contains the world's most representative collection of works by Blake, as well as works by Hogarth, George Stubbs, John Constable, and the Pre-Raphaelites. The *Modern Collection* includes works of conceptual, minimal, optical, kinetic, British figurative, pop, and abstract art; it incorporates the most extensive survey of British art of its period in any public collection, including selected examples of very recent art. Rothko, Nevelson, Bacon, Ernst, and Picasso are represented. Rex Whistler, the noted trompe l'oeil painter, is responsible for the decor of the gallery's very good restaurant (see *Eating Out*). Mondays through Saturdays, there are free, hour-long guided tours of several of the collections: "The British Collection before 1900," "Early Modern Art," "Later Modern Art," and "Turner." A tour given once on Sundays highlights all the collections. Open daily. No admission charge, except for special exhibitions. Millbank, SW1 (phone: 171-887-8000; 171-887-8008 for recorded information). Underground: *Millbank*.

**SOHO** This area of London is lively, bustling, and noisy by day, and indiscreetly enticing by night. Its name comes from the ancient hunting cry used centuries ago when the area was parkland. Once infamous for striptease clubs and tawdry sex, Soho has again become one of London's liveliest bohemian areas. Shaftesbury Avenue is lined with theaters and movie houses. Gerrard Street abounds with Chinese restaurants (the *Dumpling Inn* remains one of our favorites— see *Eating Out*), and it is the place to go for *Chinese New Year* celebrations. Frith Street is a favorite Italian haunt, the best place for cappuccino and a view of Italian TV at the *Bar Italia*. Old Compton Street has several good delicatessens, as well as cafés and brasseries. Underground: *Leicester Square*.

**COVENT GARDEN** Tucked away behind The Strand, *Covent Garden* was the site of London's main fruit, vegetable, and flower market for over 300 years. The area was immortalized in Shaw's *Pygmalion* and the musical *My Fair Lady* by the scene in which young Eliza Doolittle sells flowers to the ladies and gents emerging from the *Royal Opera House*. The *Opera House* is still here, but the market moved south of the river in 1974, and the *Garden* has since undergone extensive redevelopment. The central market building has been converted into a Victorian-style shopping center with about 40 of the old *Covent Garden*'s original wrought-iron trading stands, from which the home-produced wares of English craftspeople are sold. In the former flower market is the *London Transport Museum,* whose exhibits include a replica of the first horse-drawn bus and a steam locomotive built in 1866 (phone: 171-379-6344; open daily; admission charge). Underground: *Covent Garden*.

**BLOOMSBURY** Known for its squares—Bloomsbury Square, Bedford Square, Russell Square, and others—this area has long been home to intellectuals. Within its confines are the *British Museum* and the *University of London*. The Bloomsbury group of writers and artists included Virginia Woolf and her husband, Leonard Woolf; her sister Vanessa Bell and her husband, Clive Bell; Lytton Strachey; E. M. Forster; Roger Fry; and John Maynard Keynes. Unfortunately, only a few of the original buildings have survived, although nearby

Bedford Square remains complete. Virginia Woolf lived at 46 Gordon Square before her marriage. Underground: *Russell Square.*

**BRITISH MUSEUM** Founded in 1753 around the lifetime accumulations of Sir Hans Sloane, a British physician and naturalist, this is Britain's largest and most celebrated institution, consecrated to the whole of human history. The crown jewels of the collection are the renowned *Elgin Marbles,* massive sculpture and reliefs from the Parthenon that Lord Elgin bought, in the early 19th century, from the Turkish sultan and carted off to civilized England, where they were purchased by the government for £35,000 and presented to the museum. Other treasures include the *Rosetta Stone,* the black basalt tablet that provided the key to Egyptian hieroglyphs; the deep blue and white cameo-cut *Portland Vase,* a marvel of the glassmaker's art dating from Roman times; the *Tomb of Mausolus* from Halicarnassus, which brought the word "mausoleum" into the English language; the *Temple of Diana* from Ephesus; and many mummies.

Seven sculpture galleries exhibit some 1,500 Greek and Roman treasures, including two of the seven wonders of the ancient world and representing the bulk of the museum's Greek and Roman collection. The *Departments of Western Asiatic Antiquities and Oriental Antiquities* are magnificent. The *British Library* displays the *Magna Carta* in its manuscript room and a Gutenberg Bible in its *King's Library.* (The library is in the process of moving to new quarters on Euston Road near *St. Pancras Station.*)

The *British Library Reading Room,* where Karl Marx did research for *Das Kapital,* is accessible only to those who come well recommended (preferably by a scholar of some note) and who apply in advance for a ticket. But visitors, accompanied by a warder, may view the *Reading Room* briefly on weekdays at 2:15 and 4:15 PM. Guidebooks to various parts of the collections, for sale in the main lobby, are good investments, as are the one-and-a-half-hour guided tours (offered several times daily). Open daily. Admission charge for tours. Great Russell St., WC1 (phone: 171-636-1555; 171-636-1544 for the *British Library;* 171-323-7766 for information about the library's move). Underground: *Holborn* or *Tottenham Court Road.*

**OXFORD, REGENT, BOND, AND KENSINGTON HIGH STREETS** London's main shopping streets include large department and specialty stores (*Selfridges, Debenhams, John Lewis, Liberty, D. H. Evans*), chain stores offering good value in clothes (*Marks & Spencer, C & A, British Home Stores*), and scores of popular clothing chains (*The Gap, Laura Ashley, Benetton, Principles*).

**BURLINGTON ARCADE** A charming covered shopping promenade dating from the Regency period (early 19th century), it contains elegant, expensive shops. (The gates are down and the arcade is closed off on Sundays.) One entrance is on Piccadilly St.; the other is near Old Bond St., W1. Underground: *Green Park.*

**HYDE PARK** London's most famous patch of greenery (361 acres) is particularly well known for its Speakers' Corner at *Marble Arch,* where crowds gather each Sunday morning to hear impromptu diatribes and debates. Among the other attractions are sculptures by Henry Moore; an extensive bridle path; a cycle path; Serpentine Lake, where boats can be rented and where there's swimming in the summer; a bird sanctuary; and vast expanses of lawn. Underground: *Hyde Park Corner* or *Marble Arch.*

**MADAME TUSSAUD'S** The popularity of this wax museum is undiminished by the persistent criticism that its effigies are a little bland; visitors are quite likely to find themselves innocently addressing a waxwork attendant—or murderer. The museum includes many modern and historical personalities and the gory *Chamber of Horrors,* with its murderers and hangmen. Another fun attraction takes visitors on a "cab ride" through the 400 years of London's history between the reigns of Elizabeth I and the current queen, with sights, sounds, and smells. Open daily. Admission charge. Marylebone Rd., NW1 (phone: 171-935-6861). Underground: *Baker Street.*

**LONDON PLANETARIUM** During 30-minute shows, visitors travel through space and time under a huge starlit dome. Interesting commentary accompanies the display. As you wait to get into the star shows, you can enjoy the Space Trail, which is a series of video screens showing how the earth is seen from satellites in space. Open daily; call ahead for show times. Admission charge, but guests can save money by purchasing a combination ticket to the planetarium and *Madame Tussaud's*—both at the same address. Note: As at *Madame Tussaud's,* the lines to get into the planetarium can be long. Marylebone Rd., NW1 (phone: 171-486-1121). Underground: *Baker Street.*

## THE CITY

London and the City of London are, in fact, two distinctly different entities, one within the other. The City of London, usually called only the City, covers the original Roman London. It is now the "square mile" financial and commercial center of the great metropolis. With a lord mayor (who serves only in a ceremonial capacity), a police force, and a rapidly growing number of developments, it is the core of Greater London.

**ST. PAUL'S CATHEDRAL** The cathedral church of the London Anglican diocese stands atop Ludgate Hill and is the largest church in London. This Renaissance masterpiece by Sir Christopher Wren took 35 years to build (1675–1710). Its majestic domed exterior is a landmark. The interior contains particularly splendid choir stalls, screens, and inside the dome, the *Whispering Gallery,* with its strange acoustics. Nelson and Wellington are buried in a crypt beneath the main floor, and there is a fine statue of John Donne, metaphysical poet and dean of *St. Paul's* from 1621 to 1631. Wren himself was buried here in 1723, with his epitaph inscribed beneath the dome in Latin: *"Si monumentum requiris, circumspice"* ("If you seek his monument, look around you").

Though damaged by bombs during World War II, the cathedral became a rallying point for the flagging spirits of wartime Londoners. More recently, *St. Paul's* was the site of the 1981 wedding of Prince Charles and Lady Diana Spencer. Guided tours are available. The cathedral, the galleries, and the crypt are closed Sundays. Separate admission charges. *St. Paul's Churchyard,* EC4 (phone: 171-248-2705). Underground: *St. Paul's* or *Mansion House.*

**OLD BAILEY** This is the colloquial name for London's *Central Criminal Court,* on the site of the notorious Newgate prison. Visitors are admitted to the court, on a space-available basis, to watch the proceedings and to see barristers and judges clad in wigs and robes. No children under 14 admitted. Closed weekends. No admission charge. Old Bailey, EC4 (phone: 171-248-3277). Underground: *St. Paul's.*

**MUSEUM OF LONDON** A fine introduction to London's history. Exhibits include Roman remains, Anglo-Saxon artifacts, Renaissance musical instruments, a cell from old Newgate prison, Victorian shops and offices, an audiovisual re-creation of the Great Fire of 1666, and the Lord Mayor's Golden Coach. Closed Mondays. Admission charge. 150 London Wall, EC2 (phone: 171-600-3699). Underground: *Barbican* or *St. Paul's.*

**BARBICAN CENTRE** The modern *Barbican Centre* complex includes 6,000 apartments, the *Guildhall School of Music and Drama,* and the restored *St. Giles' Church* (built in 1390). The center also features the 2,026-seat *Barbican Hall,* doubling as conference venue (with simultaneous translation system) and concert hall *(London Symphony Orchestra);* the 1,166-seat *Barbican Theatre* and a 200-seat studio theater (the *Royal Shakespeare Company*'s London performance venues); a sculpture courtyard; art exhibition galleries; three cinemas; two exhibition halls; restaurants; and bars. Silk St., EC2 (phone: 171-628-4141, ext. 7537 or 7538 for general information; 171-628-2295 for recorded information; 171-638-4141 for guided tours; 171-638-8891 for the box office). Underground: *Barbican, St. Paul's,* or *Moorgate.*

**BANK OF ENGLAND** Banker to the British government, holder of the country's gold reserves, controller of Britain's monetary affairs, the "Old Lady of Threadneedle Street" is the world's most famous bank. Its clerks and messengers wear traditional livery. The bank is not open to the public, but the *Bank of England Museum* here can be visited. It is closed Saturdays year-round and Sundays October through *Easter.* No admission charge. Threadneedle St., EC2; museum entrance on Bartholomew La. (phone: 171-601-5792). Underground: *Bank.*

**MANSION HOUSE** Built in the 18th century in Renaissance style, the official residence of the Lord Mayor of London contains his private apartments. It is difficult to gain admission, but you may request permission by writing, well in advance of your visit, to the *Principal Assistant Office* (*Mansion House,* London EC4N 8EH, England). Mansion House St., EC4 (phone: 171-626-2500). Underground: *Mansion House* or *Bank.*

**THE MONUMENT** This fluted Doric column, topped by a flaming urn, was designed by Sir Christopher Wren to commemorate the Great Fire of London (1666) and stands 202 feet tall. (Its height was determined because it was allegedly 202 feet from the bakery on Pudding Lane where the fire began.) The view from the top is worth the 311-step climb up a narrow staircase—there is *no* elevator. Closed Sundays October through March. Admission charge. Monument St., EC3 (phone: 171-626-2717). Underground: *Monument.*

**TOWER OF LONDON** Originally William the Conqueror's fortress to keep "fierce" Londoners at bay and to guard the river approaches, this complex of buildings has served as a palace, a prison, a mint, and an observatory. Today, the main points of interest are the *Crown Jewels,* which recently have been moved to the *Jewel House* (in the Waterloo Block), allowing as many as 20,000 visitors daily to view the dazzling gems, as well as displays about the British monarchy and the coronation ceremony; the *White Tower* (the oldest building), with its exhibition of ancient arms, armor, and torture implements; *St. John's Chapel,* the oldest church in London; the *Bloody Tower,* where the two little princes disappeared in 1483 and Sir Walter Raleigh languished from 1603 to 1616; an exhibit of old military weapons; *Tower Green,* where two of Henry VIII's queens, Anne Boleyn and Catherine Howard, as well as Lady Jane Grey, were beheaded; and *Traitors' Gate,* through which boats bearing prisoners entered the castle. During World War I, German spies were executed in the courtyards, and in 1941, Rudolf Hess, Hitler's deputy, was imprisoned here for a few days. The yeoman warders ("Beefeaters") still wear historic uniforms. They also give informative, often theatrical recitals of that segment of English history that was played out within the *Tower*'s walls. You can see the wonderful *Ceremony of the Keys* here every night at 9:30 PM; reserve tickets several months ahead. (Send a self-addressed envelope to Resident Governor, *Queen's House, HM Tower of London* EC3N 4AB, England, and enclose the appropriate international postage coupons.) Open daily. Admission charge (phone: 171-709-0765 for general inquiries; 171-488-5718 for recorded information). Underground: *Tower Hill.*

**FLEET STREET** Most native and foreign newspapers and press associations once had offices here, but none remain because of the exodus to more technologically advanced plants elsewhere. The street also boasts two 17th-century pubs, *Ye Olde Cheshire Cheese* (No. 145), where Dr. Samuel Johnson held court, and the *Cock Tavern* (No. 22).

**JOHNSON'S HOUSE** In Gough Square is the house where Dr. Johnson wrote his famous *Dictionary;* the house is now a museum of Johnsoniana. Closed Sundays. Admission charge. 17 Gough Sq., EC4 (phone: 171-353-3745). Underground: *Blackfriars.*

**INNS OF COURT** Quaint and quiet precincts house the ancient buildings, grounds, and gardens that mark the traditional center of Britain's legal profession. Only the four *Inns of Court—Gray's, Lincoln's,* and the *Inner* and *Middle Temples—*have the right to call would-be barristers to the bar to practice law. John Donne once preached in the *Lincoln's Inn* chapel, designed by Inigo Jones. The chapel can be seen on weekdays between 12:30 and 2:30 PM; ask at the *Gatehouse* (Chancery La., WC2; phone: 171-405-1393). Also lovely are the gardens of *Lincoln's Inn Fields,* laid out by Inigo Jones in 1618. The neo-Gothic *Royal Courts of Justice* in The Strand, better known as the *Law Courts,* house the *High Court* and the *Court of Appeal of England and Wales,* which pass judgment on Britain's most important civil cases. Sessions are from 10:30 AM to 1 PM and 2 to 4 PM. No admission charge. Underground: *Holborn, Chancery Lane,* or *Temple.*

## OTHER LONDON ATTRACTIONS

**REGENT'S PARK** The sprawling 472 acres just north of the city center include beautiful gardens, vast lawns, a pond with paddleboats, and one of the finest zoos in the world. Until last year, the zoo was in danger of closing because of a lack of funds, but it was rescued by a £21-million donation from a London doctor as a memorial to his daughter, who died as a young girl 25 years ago. Among several new additions is a children's zoo which depicts how people and animals have lived together throughout history. Open daily. Admission charge to the zoo (phone: 171-722-3333). Underground: *Camden Town.*

**KENWOOD, THE IVEAGH BEQUEST** The collection assembled here includes works by Cuyp, Gainsborough, Hals, Rembrandt, Reynolds, Romney, Turner, and Vermeer. What makes this institution particularly interesting is its setting, a late-17th-century house on *Hampstead Heath* remodeled beginning in 1764 by the Scottish architect Robert Adam. The stately neoclassical villa was rescued from demolition in 1925 by the first Earl of Iveagh, who then presented the house and the better part of his collection to the nation. It has the atmosphere of an 18th-century country house, and in summer frequently offers chamber recitals, poetry readings, and open-air concerts. Closed *Christmas Eve* and *Christmas.* No admission charge. Hampstead La., NW3 (phone: 181-348-1286). Underground: *Highgate, Golders Green,* or *Archway* (note, however, that the underground stops are a long walk away).

**KEW GARDENS** Here are the *Royal Botanic Gardens,* with tens of thousands of trees and other plants. Located by the Thames, the gardens are intended primarily to serve the botanical sciences by researching, cultivating, identifying, and experimenting with plants. There are shaded walks, floral displays, and magnificent Victorian greenhouses—especially the *Temperate House,* with some 3,000 different plants, including a 60-foot Chilean wine palm. Open daily. Admission charge (phone: 181-940-1171). Underground: *Kew Gardens.*

**VICTORIA AND ALBERT MUSEUM** An offspring of the *Great Exhibition* of 1851, this museum was originally a repository of the world's finest craftsmanship. The collection, dating from ancient times, was intended to lend inspiration to leatherworkers and ceramists, furniture makers and woodcarvers, architects and dressmakers, silversmiths and goldsmiths, and other artisans working in the applied arts in the 19th century. Though the original function has not been abandoned, the collections are a bit broader in scope: In addition to textiles and furniture there are also watercolors and paintings—including Constable's *Salisbury Cathedral from the Bishop's Grounds.* The collections of British art (including the *Constable Collection,* presented to the museum by the artist's daughter) stand out for their scope and comprehensiveness. Of particular interest are the Raphael cartoons (designs for tapestries for the Siştine Chapel); the period rooms; the world's oldest known teapot; and the intricately carved, abundantly graffiti-covered *Great Bed of Ware,* which Shakespeare's Sir Toby Belch mentioned in *Twelfth Night* and which (measuring about 11 feet square) was purportedly big enough to sleep a dozen couples. Other galleries include the *Medieval Treasury* (note the intricately embroidered bishop's cope); the *T. Tsui Gallery of Chinese Art* (you may touch the serpentine head); the *Nehru Gallery of Indian Art* (the finest collection outside the subcontinent); and the *Toshiba Gallery of Japanese Art.* Guided tours are given Mondays through Saturdays. This museum has something to interest everyone. Don't forget to admire the statues outside. There's also a restaurant and two fine museum shops. Open daily. Donation suggested. Cromwell Rd., SW7 (phone: 171-938-8441; 171-938-8349 for information on current exhibits). Underground: *South Kensington.*

**IMPERIAL WAR MUSEUM** Tanks, planes, cannons, submarines, rockets, artifacts, and war paintings are housed in this four-floor museum, which covers the history of war from Flanders to the Falklands to the Gulf War. Wartime events are brought to life via films, videos, and telephones that visitors can pick up to hear people describing their wartime experiences. The 20-minute-long "Blitz Experience" confines groups of 20 people in a damp, cramped re-creation of a bomb shelter during a World War II air raid, while "Operation Jericho" is a bumpy simulation of a World War II bombing raid; also see the World War I "Trench Experience." A souvenir shop and a café are also on the premises. Open daily. No admission charge on Fridays. Lambeth Rd., SE1 (phone: 171-416-5000; 171-820-1683 for recorded information). Underground: *Lambeth North, Elephant,* or *Castle.*

**DOCKLANDS** This area has been developed to such an extent that it even includes its own railroad; modern apartment, commercial, and office buildings stretch seemingly without end. The *Docklands Light Railway (DLR),* an overhead train, runs from the *Bank* tube station to *Island Garden,* Greenwich, speeding over the fast-developing and fascinating terrain. The Docklands also is home to the *Design Museum* (Butler's Wharf, 28 Shad Thames, SE1; phone: 171-403-6933; 171-407-6261 for recorded information). Open daily. Admission charge. Fascinating walking tours of the Rotherhithe district, where the *Mayflower* returned from its journey in 1621, are offered by local historian Jim Nash; for details, contact *Karisma Travel* (21

Hayes Wood Ave., Hayes, Bromley, Kent BR2 7BG, England; phone: 181-462-4953; call a week in advance). The new, 800-foot *Canada Tower* at *Canary Wharf,* containing the offices of the *Daily Mirror* and the *Daily Telegraph* as well as many other businesses, is the tallest building in England (it is closed to the public). The *London Docklands Visitor Centre* (3 Limeharbour, E14; phone: 171-512-1111), near the *Crossharbour* stop on the *DLR,* has a model of the area and other useful information; it is open daily. Further development plans for the Docklands, including the addition of several shopping plazas and other businesses, extend to 1998.

**GREENWICH** This Thameside borough is traditionally associated with British sea power, especially when Britain "ruled the waves." Here, along Romney Road, is the *Royal Naval College* (phone: 181-858-2154); its beautiful painted hall and chapel are closed Thursday afternoons, when the college is in session. No admission charge. Also here are the *National Maritime Museum,* the *Queen's House,* the *Old Royal Observatory,* and the *Cutty Sark* clipper ship (see the *National Maritime Museum* entry below for details on all four). In addition, there's the *Fan Museum* (10-12 Crooms Hill, SE10; phone: 181-858-7879), a collection of 12,000 unusual and beautiful antique fans from all over the world. Closed Mondays. Admission charge. *Greenwich Park* is 200 acres of greenery with splendid views from the hill across to the Docklands and the rest of London. Greenwich can be reached by tube (*Greenwich Station*), *British Rail,* or boat from *Charing Cross, Westminster,* or *Tower Piers.*

**NATIONAL MARITIME MUSEUM** This institution tells the story of Britain's long involvement with the sea. Galleries in the West Wing explore "Discovery and Seapower" and the "Development of the Warship," and the world's largest ship in a bottle is on display in *Neptune Hall.* There, too, are the steam paddle tug *Reliant;* the *Donola,* a 60-foot steam launch; and the smaller *Waterlily.* Next door in the *Barge House,* Prince Frederick's barge glitters in golden livery. Another must-see: the uniform that Lord Nelson wore when he was shot at the Battle of Trafalgar in 1805, complete with bullet hole and bloodstains. Nearby are the *Queen's House,* a beautifully proportioned white structure designed in 1618 by Inigo Jones for James I's consort, Anne of Denmark; and the newly refurbished *Old Royal Observatory*—the home of the Greenwich Meridian—which is centered around Sir Christopher Wren's 1675 *Flamsteed House* and has exhibits that illustrate the history of nautical astronomy, timekeeping, and Greenwich mean time, as well as the largest refracting telescope in the United Kingdom; the *Cutty Sark,* a 19th-century ship that was once the fastest clipper in existence (Cutty Sark Gardens, SE10; phone: 181-858-3445); and the *Gipsy Moth IV,* the 53-foot ketch that, between 1966 and 1967, bore Sir Francis Chichester—solo—around the world. Open daily. There's a separate admission charge to each attraction, but a single "Passport" can be bought which includes entry to the museum, *Queen's House,* the *Old Royal Observatory,* and the *Cutty Sark.* Romney Rd., SE10, Greenwich (phone: 181-858-4422). Greenwich can be reached by tube (*Green-*

*wich Station*), *British Rail,* or boat from *Charing Cross, Westminster,* or *Tower Piers.*

**RICHMOND PARK** The largest urban park in Britain is one of the few with herds of deer roaming free. (Hunting them is illegal, though this was once a royal hunting preserve established by Charles I.) From nearby Richmond Hill there is a magnificent view of the Thames Valley. The park can be reached by tube (*Richmond Station*) or *British Rail.*

**SPENCER HOUSE** This 1756 mansion owned by the Spencer family—the Princess of Wales is the former Lady Diana Spencer—has been restored and opened to the public. There are nine spectacular state rooms filled with artwork and furniture from the family's wide collection. The neoclassical state rooms were among the first to be so designed in Europe. No children under 10 admitted. Open only for guided tours, which are given on Sundays; closed January and August. Admission charge. St. James's Pl., SW1 (phone: 171-499-8620). Underground: *Green Park.*

**HAMPTON COURT PALACE** Along the Thames, this sumptuous palace and adjoining gardens are in Greater London's southwest corner. Begun by Cardinal Wolsey in 1514, the palace was appropriated by Henry VIII. Its architecture—including Wolsey's constructions, the modifications made by Henry VIII, and additions designed by Christopher Wren for William III in 1689—represents the very best of England's designers of the 16th and 17th centuries. The equally fine gardens, designed for William and Mary by Henry Wise and George London, comprise a maze and vinery (the Great Vine was planted in 1769). Still a royal palace, its attractions include a picture gallery, tapestries, Tudor kitchens—restored to the grandeur of Henry VIII's day, re-creating the *Feast of St. John the Baptist* on a midsummer day in 1542—the original tennis court, and a moat. Henry VIII's *State Apartments* reopened recently after being restored to their original Tudor splendor. Among the rooms that can be visited are the *Great Hall,* the royal chapel, and a gallery that is reportedly haunted by Catherine Howard, the monarch's fifth wife. Tours led by guides in authentic costume are given twice daily. There are even two apartments for overnight stays (see *Checking In*). Open daily. Admission charge. East Molesey, Surrey (phone: 181-977-8441). The quickest way to get here is by *British Rail* (32 minutes from *Waterloo Station*), but you can take a bus or even a boat from *Westminster Pier* during the summer.

**FREUD MUSEUM** This was the London home of the seminal psychiatrist after he left Vienna in 1938. His antiquities collection, library, desk, and famous couch are all on display. Closed Mondays and Tuesdays. Admission charge. 20 Maresfield Gardens, NW3 (phone: 171-435-2002). Underground: *Finchley Road.*

**HIGHGATE CEMETERY** The impressive grave of Karl Marx in the eastern cemetery attracts countless visitors, although the Victorian-style western cemetery is older and more historically interesting. Open daily. Entrance to the western cemetery, with its overgrown gravestones and catacombs of the not-so-famous, is by guided tour only. Admission charge to the western cemetery. Highgate Hill, NW3 (phone: 181-340-1834 for times). Underground: *Archway.*

**THAMES FLOOD BARRIER** This massive defense structure is located across the river at Woolwich Reach near Greenwich. Boats regularly leave *Barrier Gardens Pier* (or the riverside promenade nearby) for visits up close. Visitors are not allowed on the barrier itself, but audiovisual displays at the visitors' center, on the river's south bank, explain its background and illustrate the risk to London of exceptionally high tides. Open daily. Admission charge. 1 Unity Way, Woolwich (phone: 181-854-1373). Accessible from London by road, by river (from *Westminster Pier* to *Barrier Gardens Pier*), and by *British Rail* (to *Charlton Station*).

## EXTRA SPECIAL

*Windsor Castle* is the largest inhabited castle in the world. Reputed to be the queen's favorite among her five principal residences, it was founded by William the Conqueror in 1066 after his victory at the Battle of Hastings. Despite the ravages of a fire in 1992, *Windsor*'s exterior still looks like a picturebook fairytale castle. Thirteen of the 15 *State Apartments* were miraculously unharmed by the fire and can be toured daily (unless there is a state visit); they are splendidly decorated with paintings, tapestries, furniture, and rugs. Queen Mary's dollhouse is displayed in another room. In the *Waterloo Chamber,* visitors can look through glass doors into *St. George's Hall* and the *Grand Reception Room,* which were gutted by the fire. There's a small exhibit recounting the damage. Separate admission charges to the castle complex and to see the dollhouse. For information call 1753-831118.

The castle is bordered by 4,800 acres of parkland on one side and the town on the other. The *Savill Gardens*—35 acres of flowering shrubs, rare flowers, and woodland—make for a lovely summer walk. Open daily. Admission charge (phone: 1784-435544).

The train from *Paddington* stops right in the center of Windsor (travel time is 39 minutes); the *Green Line* coach from *Victoria* takes one and a half hours.

# Sources and Resources

## TOURIST INFORMATION

The *London Tourist Board and Convention Bureau,* with an office in the forecourt of *Victoria Station,* is a good source of information for attractions and events. Other branches are at the tube station at *Heathrow Airport*'s Terminals 1, 2, and 3 and at *Selfridges* department store (see *Shopping*). Many brochures about the city's landmarks and events are available. Staff is also on hand to answer questions; however, the offices do not handle telephone inquiries. All three centers are open daily. Accommodations and tours can be reserved by telephone using credit cards Mondays through Saturdays (phone: 171-824-8844 for reservations only).

The *British Travel Centre* (4 Lower Regent St., W1; phone: 171-730-3400) books travel tickets, reserves accommodations and theater tickets, and sells guidebooks. It has numerous free leaflets with information about walking tours, London's lesser-known museums and attractions, and canal tours. It also offers a free information service covering all of Britain. It's open daily. The *US Embassy* is at 24 Grosvenor Sq. (phone: 171-499-9000).

In the US, contact the *British Tourist Authority* (625 N. Michigan Ave., Suite 1510, Chicago, IL 60611; phone: 312-787-0490; fax: 312-787-7746; and 551 Fifth Ave., Suite 701, New York, NY 10176; phone: 212-986-2200; fax: 212-986-1188). The *British Embassy* is at 3100 Massachusetts Ave. NW, Washington, DC 20008 (phone: 202-462-1340).

**ENTRY REQUIREMENTS** A US citizen needs a current passport for a stay of up to six months.

**TIME** The time in Great Britain is five hours later than in US East Coast cities. Great Britain observes daylight saving time.

**LANGUAGE** English is the official language.

**ELECTRIC CURRENT** 240 volts, 50 cycles, AC.

**MONEY** The pound sterling (£) equals 100 pence. At press time the exchange rate was 63 pence to the American dollar.

**TIPPING** Service charges of between 10% and 15% usually are included in hotel bills, but it's wise to make sure. The tipping standard is between 10% and 15% in restaurants and taxis and 50 pence per bag for bellhops and porters.

**BANKING/BUSINESS HOURS** Banks are open weekdays from 9:30 AM to 3:30 PM; some major branches of Barclays, National Westminster, and Midland are open Saturday mornings from 9 AM to noon. Most other businesses throughout the country operate weekdays from 9 or 9:30 AM to 5 or 5:30 PM.

**NATIONAL HOLIDAYS** *New Year's Day* (January 1; public holiday, January 2), *Good Friday* (April 14), *Easter Sunday* (April 16), *Easter Monday* (April 17), *May Day* (May 1, but to be observed this year on May 8), *Spring Bank Holiday* (May 29), *Summer Bank Holiday* (August 28), *Christmas Day* (December 25), and *Boxing Day* (December 26).

**LOCAL COVERAGE** Of London's several newspapers, the *Times,* the *Guardian,* the *Independent,* and the *Daily Telegraph* (all dailies) and the *Sunday Times* and the *Observer* (Sundays only) are the most useful for visitors. Also helpful are the weekly magazines *What's On* and *Time Out.* The *Evening Standard,* published weekdays, is the only "local" newspaper for London. For business news, read the *Financial Times* (daily) and the *Economist* magazine (weekly).

London A-Z (Geographers' A-Z Map Co.) and *Nicholson's Street Finder* (Robert Nicholson), pocket-size books of street maps (the cost varies depending on map size), are useful for finding London addresses; they can be purchased in bookstores and from most newsagents. Also helpful are maps of the subway system and bus routes and the *London Regional Transport Visitors Guide*—all available free from the *London Transport* information centers at several stations, including *Victoria, Piccadilly, Charing Cross, Oxford Circus,* and *Heathrow Central,* and at the ticket booths of many other stations (phone: 171-222-1234 for information).

We also immodestly suggest that before you leave home, you pick up a copy of *Birnbaum's London 95* (HarperCollins; $12).

**TELEPHONE** London has two area codes: inner London, 171; outer London, 181. All telephone numbers listed in this chapter, therefore, include the appropriate city code.

When calling from one area to another within Great Britain (including Scotland and Northern Ireland) dial 0 + city code + local number. The country code for Great Britain is 44. Dial 999 for emergency assistance.

## GETTING AROUND

**AIRPORT** London has four airports. The two main airports are *Heathrow,* 15 miles and about 50 minutes from downtown, and *Gatwick,* 29 miles and about 1 hour from downtown. The others are *Stansted,* 30 miles northeast of the city, and *London "City" Airport,* 6 miles from downtown. Airport transportation options include taxis, the London underground (subway), trains, and car services.

**BOAT** For a leisurely view of London from the Thames, tour boats leave roughly every half hour from *Westminster Pier* (near the *Westminster* tube station) and from *Charing Cross Pier* (across from the *Embankment* tube station); they sail (*Easter* through September) upriver to *Kew Gardens* and *Hampton Court Palace* or downriver to the *Tower of London,* Greenwich, and the massive Thames flood barrier. You also can travel by boat to Marlow, Cookham, or Henley (where the first rowing regatta in the world was held in 1839). A journey along Regent's Canal through north London is offered (summers only) by *Jason's Trip* (opposite 60 Blomfield Rd., Little Venice, W9; phone: 171-286-3428). Also, *Bateaux London* (phone: 171-925-2215), a French-based company, runs lunch and dinner cruises on the Thames in wide riverboats similar to those used in Paris; food is included in the price. The evening trip features after-dinner dancing to live music, and the boat illuminates the buildings along the shoreline with floodlights. For further information about these and other boat trips, contact the *London Tourist Board*'s *River Boat Information Service* (phone: 839-123432; costs between 36p/about 55¢ and 48p/about 75¢ per minute).

**BUS AND UNDERGROUND** The subway, called the underground or tube, and bus lines cover the city pretty well—though buses suffer from traffic congestion, and the underground is lacking south of the Thames (however, aboveground trains partially compensate for this shortcoming). Avoid the hideous rush-hour traffic from 8:30 to 9:30 AM and from 5 to 6 PM. The tops of London's famous red double-decker buses offer delightful views of the city and its people. The underground is easy to understand and to use, with clear directions and poster maps in all stations. Pick up free bus and underground maps from tourist offices or underground ticket booths.

The fares on both trains and buses are set according to length of the journey. On some buses, conductors take payment after you tell them where you're going; others require that you pay as you enter. Underground tickets are bought on entering a station. Retain your ticket; you'll have to surrender it when you get off (or have to pay again), and bus inspectors make spot checks. *Red Arrow* express buses link the main-line *British Rail* stations, but you'll have to check stops before you get on. With a few exceptions, public transport comes to a halt around midnight; it varies according to underground line and bus route. If you're going to be traveling late, check available facilities. For 24-hour travel information, call 171-222-1234.

A London Visitor Travelcard is available for travelers to London; it must be purchased in the US from travel agents, at the *British Travel Bookshop* (551 Fifth Ave., Eighth Floor, New York, NY 10016; phone: 212-490-6688 or 800-448-3039), or at the *BritRail Travel International* offices in New York (1500 Broadway, New York, NY 10036; phone: 212-575-2667). The card provides unlimited travel on virtually all of London's bus and underground networks and costs $25 for three days, $32 for four days, and $49 for seven days (lower fares for children under 15). Also included is transportation to and from *Heathrow Airport* on the underground's *Piccadilly* line, a ride on the *Docklands Light Railway,* and a book of discount vouchers for many of the city's sights. In London, daily (costing £2.70/about $4) and weekly (£10.20/about $15.30) passes are available from newsagents, underground ticket offices, and *London Transport* offices for travel on buses and the underground in the central London area after 9:30 AM weekdays and all day on weekends; for the weekly card, a passport-size photo must be provided.

One of the least expensive and most comprehensive ways to tour the city is to take the *Original London Transport Sightseeing Tour* (phone: 171-918-3456), a one-and-a-half-hour unconducted bus tour, which leaves every hour from four sites: *Marble Arch,*

Piccadilly Circus, *Baker Street* tube station, and *Victoria Station.* Other guided bus tours are offered by *Frames Rickards* (phone: 171-637-4171), *Harrods* (phone: 171-581-3603), and *Evan Evans* (phone: 181-332-2222).

**CAR RENTAL** The major international rental agencies have desks at the city's airports as well as at numerous locations in town.

**SIGHTSEEING BY PLANE** Sightseeing tours by small airplane are available (by advance reservation only) from *Flights Over London, Biggin Hill Aerodrome,* Kent (phone: 959-540079).

**TAXI** Those fine old London cabs are gradually being supplemented with more "practical" models, many of which have dashboard computers that allow communication between driver and dispatcher. Whether you end up in a computerized or "regular" cab, taxi fares in London are increasingly expensive (and you can find yourself stuck in horrendous traffic jams, with the meter ticking away); there is a surcharge for luggage, and a 15% tip is customary. Be aware that taxi rates are higher after 8 PM (and sometimes even higher after midnight) and on weekends and holidays.

Tell the driver where you're going *before* entering the cab. When it rains or is late at night, an empty cab (identifiable by the glow of the roof light) is often difficult to find, so it is wise to carry the telephone number of one or more of the "minicab" companies that respond to calls by phone. These taxis (which look like regular cars) operate on a fixed-fare basis, which varies from company to company. Hotel porters or reception desks usually can arrange to have such a cab pick you up at a specified time and place.

Several firms and taxi drivers offer guided tours of London; details are available at information centers. You can arrange for the personal services of a member of London's specially trained "Blue Badge Guides" by contacting *GALS* (phone: 171-370-5063) or *Town Guides* (phone: 171-495-5504).

**TRAIN** London has 11 principal train stations, each the starting point for trains to a particular region, with occasional overlapping of routes. The stations you are most likely to encounter include *King's Cross* (phone: 171-278-2477), the departure point for eastern and northeast England and eastern Scotland, including Edinburgh; *Euston* (phone: 171-387-7070), serving the Midlands and north Wales, with connections to Northern Ireland and the Republic, northwest England, and western Scotland, including Glasgow; *Paddington* (phone: 171-262-6767), for the West Country and south Wales, including Fishguard and ferries to Rosslare, Ireland; *Victoria* (phone: 171-928-5100), for *Gatwick Airport* and, along with *Charing Cross Station* (phone: 171-928-5100), for departures to southeast England; and *Liverpool St. Station* (phone: 171-928-5100), for departures to East Anglia and to Harwich for ferries to the Continent, including Scandinavia. All of these stations are connected via London's underground.

**WALKING TOURS** A trained guide can show you Shakespeare's London or that of Dickens or Jack the Ripper, among other themes. These reasonably priced tours last up to two hours, generally in the afternoon or evening. *City Walks* offers several tours, including a Sherlock Holmes, Jack the Ripper, and Legal London (phone: 171-700-6931). *Citisights* (phone: 181-806-4325) tours start from many places, including the *Museum of London* (London Wall). *Streets of London* (phone: 181-346-9255) tours start from various underground stations. *Londoner Pub Walks* (phone: 181-883-2656) start from *Temple* underground station (*District* and *Circle* lines) on Fridays at 7:30 PM. *The Original London Walks* (phone: 171-624-3978) provides more than 50 tours a week on various subjects (including the *Beatles*). A tour of the Docklands' Rotherhithe district is offered by local historian Jim Nash (see *Special Places*).

## LOCAL SERVICES

**BABY-SITTING SERVICES** Nannies are readily available in London. Two baby-sitting agencies are *Childminders* (phone: 171-935-9763 or 171-935-2049) and *Universal Aunts Ltd.* (phone: 171-738-8937). Whether the sitter is hired directly or through an agency, ask for and check references.

**DRY CLEANER/TAILOR** *Anderson Sheppard* (30 Savile Row, W1; phone: 171-734-1420); *Jeeves* (8-10 Pont St., SW1; phone: 171-235-1101).

**LIMOUSINE SERVICE** *Guy Salmon* (Dolphin Sq., SW1; phone: 171-834-8415).

**MEDICAL EMERGENCY** *University College Hospital* (Grafton Way, W1; phone: 171-387-9300) and *St. Bartholomew's Hospital* (West Smithfield, EC1; phone: 171-601-8888) have "casualty" departments providing 24-hour emergency service. For emergency service dial 999.

**MESSENGER SERVICE** For pickup contact *Churchill Express* (phone: 181-993-2211).

**OFFICE EQUIPMENT RENTAL** *Programmes Unlimited* (*Imperial House,* 15-19 Kingsway, WC2; phone: 171-240-9006).

**PHOTOCOPIES** *Kall Kwik* (at several locations, including 21 Kingly St., W1; phone: 171-434-2471).

**POST OFFICE** London's main post office is at 24-28 William IV St., WC2 (phone: 171-930-9580); other offices include the Lombard Street branch (3 Lombard St., EC3; phone: 171-626-1820) and the Mount Pleasant branch (Roseberry Ave., EC1; phone: 171-239-2362).

**SECRETARY/STENOGRAPHER** *Drake International* (5 Regent St., W1; phone: 171-437-6900).

**TELECONFERENCE FACILITIES** The *Inter-Continental* hotel (see *Checking In*) has a teleconference link.

**TELEX** *Kensington Business Centre* (7-11 Kensington High St., W8; phone: 171-938-1721 or 171-938-2151) is open weekdays from 8:30 AM to 8 PM.

**OTHER** Business services: *Channel 5* (5 Roslin Sq., Roslin Rd., W3; phone: 181-752-1003), which provides direct mail services; and *Thomas Cook Heathrow Business Centre* (next to Terminal 2, *Heathrow Airport;* phone: 181-759-2434), which offers walk-in service at the airport. Camera rental and repair: *Keith, Johnson, and Pelling* (93-103 Drummond St., NW1; phone: 171-380-1144). Tuxedo rental: *Moss Bros.* (27 King St., WC2; phone: 171-379-1023).

## SPECIAL EVENTS

While London's festival calendar is full year-round, one annual event eclipses all others.

---

### TENNIS, ANYONE?

**Wimbledon** Britain practically closes down in late June and early July, the fortnight of the *All England Lawn Tennis Championships*—also known as *Wimbledon*. Ticket scalpers do a brisk trade outside the gate, and those who aren't lucky enough to secure tickets watch the competition on television. This year, *Wimbledon* will take place from June 26 to July 9 (excluding Sunday, July 2) at the *All England Lawn Tennis and Croquet Club* in Wimbledon. A magnet to players who compete for much bigger cash prizes elsewhere, this tourney is an experience even for those who have never held a racquet. Grass courts, strawberry teas, and the legendary *Centre Court* make for such a spectacle that visitors may find the world class matches no more than a diversion. Advance seat tickets for *Centre Court, Number One Court,* and *Court 14* are distributed by lottery. Ticket applications, available from September 1 of the previous year, can be obtained by sending a self-addressed, stamped envelope to the *All England Lawn Tennis and Croquet Club* (PO Box 98, Church Rd., Wimbledon SW19 5AE, England; phone: 181-944-1066). The club must receive completed forms by midnight, December 31. For the first nine days of the tournament, some tickets are available on the day of play for *Number One Court;* for *Number Two Court* and the remaining outside courts, tickets are always available on the day of play. For more details, contact the *All England Lawn Tennis and Croquet Club* (address and phone number above); include a self-addressed, stamped envelope or international postage coupons. The most certain and efficient means of seeing the match of your choice is to purchase one of the many packages from *NAA Events International* (1730 NE Expwy., Atlanta, GA 30329; phone: 404-329-9902 or 800-278-6738).

---

Late March/early April is the time for the *Oxford* and *Cambridge* rowing "eights" race from Putney to Mortlake, an important competition for the two universities. In April, London hosts the annual

*London Marathon,* the world's largest; last year, there were 36,500 participants. The world-famous *Chelsea Flower Show* takes place in late May. In early June, enjoy the annual *Trooping the Colour,* England's most elaborate display of pageantry—including a Horse Guards parade with military music and much pomp and circumstance—all in celebration of the queen's official birthday. You can see some of the parade without a ticket, but for the ceremony you must book before February 28 by writing to the Ticket Office (Headquarters, Household Division, Chelsea Barracks, London SW1 H8RF, England); you must include the appropriate international reply coupons—do not send money. The *Lufthansa Festival of Baroque Music* presents classical concerts at *St. James Church* in Piccadilly throughout June, and the *Greenwich Festival,* a two-week event in mid-June, features mime and dance performances, concerts, and poetry readings. Also in June is the *Spitalfields Festival,* a varied program of 15th- to 20th-century classical music held for three and a half weeks in the *Parish Church of Spitalfields* in the East End. The *City of London Festival* runs for two and a half weeks in July within the Old City; London's own festival takes advantage of the area's many fine halls and churches for concerts of serious music featuring performers of international repute. A program of jazz, dance, street theater, poetry, and exhibitions runs concurrent with the festival. The *Henley Royal Regatta,* in early July (at Henley-on-Thames, an hour's train ride from London), is an international rowing competition and one of the big social events of the year. Watch from the towpath (free) or from within the *Regatta* enclosure (admission charge). For nearly three weeks every July, Britain's armed forces stage the *Royal Tournament,* a spectacular military pageant in the huge indoor *Earl's Court* arena; the queen and the leading royals attend each year.

The *Henry Wood Promenade Concerts,* better known as "the *Proms,*" are so named because they offer a large number of "promenade" or standing places at reasonable prices. Held at the *Royal Albert Hall* from mid-July to mid-September, the *Proms* attract crowds from all over the world. At the *Punch and Judy Festival,* held the first Sunday in October, the 160 members of the *Punch and Judy Fellowship* gather at *St. Paul's Cathedral* to celebrate the traditional puppet show. For six weeks in the fall (the exact dates vary from year to year), the *Dance Umbrella* festival attracts participants from all over the world. October or November is the time for the *State Opening of Parliament; Guy Fawkes Day* is on November 5, when fireworks and bonfires mark the anniversary of the plot to blow up both the *Houses of Parliament* and King James I in 1605. On the first Sunday in November, the *London-to-Brighton Veteran Car Run* features shiny antique autos undertaking a 57-mile drive. The second Saturday in November sees the *Lord Mayor's Procession,* in which the new lord mayor rides in a golden carriage, followed by bands and wacky, colorful floats. On *Remembrance Sunday,* the Sunday nearest to November 11 (*Armistice Day*), a moving and solemn parade of veterans passes before the queen after she lays a red poppy wreath at the base of the *Cenotaph,* on Whitehall.

Also in November, the best of British and international movies from the latest international film festivals are presented at the *London Film Festival*, with lectures and discussions led by participating film directors after many of the screenings. The *National Film Theatre* on the South Bank is the principal location, but other London houses are used as well.

## MUSEUMS

In addition to those described in *Special Places,* other museums of note include the following:

**BETHNAL GREEN MUSEUM OF CHILDHOOD** It's an impressive collection of more than 4,000 items, including dolls and dollhouses, Victorian-era children's clothing, antique nursery toys, games, and puppets. Open daily. No admission charge. Cambridge Heath Rd., E2 (phone: 181-980-3204). Underground: *Bethnal Green.*

**COURTAULD INSTITUTE GALLERIES** A remarkable collection of French Impressionist and post-Impressionist paintings (artists include van Gogh, Gauguin, Cézanne, Manet, and Seurat), as well as 20th-century British art, is displayed in a lovely and comfortable setting for visitors. Open daily. Admission charge. *Somerset House,* The Strand, WC2 (phone: 171-873-2526). Underground: *Temple.*

**DESIGN MUSEUM** Examples of everyday items from today's consumer society are on display at this museum in the Docklands. There is also a library, auditorium, and riverside café. Open daily. Admission charge. *Butler's Wharf,* SE1 (phone: 171-403-6933). Underground: *London Bridge.*

**DICKENS HOUSE MUSEUM** The author's early works and personal memorabilia are displayed. Closed Sundays. Admission charge. 48 Doughty St., WC1 (phone: 171-405-2127). Underground: *Russell Square.*

**DULWICH COLLEGE PICTURE GALLERY** Works by European masters are exhibited in one of England's most beautiful art galleries. Among others, there are works by Rembrandt, Cuyp, Gainsborough, Rubens, Watteau, and Raphael. The college itself boasts such famous alumni as P. G. Wodehouse and Raymond Chandler. Guided tours are offered on weekends. Closed Mondays. Admission charge. College Rd., SE21 (phone: 181-693-5254; 181-693-8000 for recorded information). Accessible by *British Rail* (*West Dulwich Station*).

**FLORENCE NIGHTINGALE MUSEUM** Not for nurses only, this museum offers a fascinating look at the life of the "Lady with the Lamp." Closed Mondays. Admission charge. 2 Lambeth Palace Rd., SE1 (phone: 171-620-0374). Underground: *Westminster* or *Waterloo.*

**GUARDS MUSEUM** Close to *Buckingham Palace,* this small collection at Wellington Barracks houses exhibits of memorabilia relating to the Brigade of Guards, including uniforms and weapons—even a cat-o'-nine-tails. Closed Fridays. Admission charge. Birdcage Walk, SW1 (phone: 171-930-3271). Underground: *St. James's Park.*

**HAYWARD GALLERY** Temporary exhibitions of British and international art are shown in a modern building. Open daily. Admission charge. At the *South Bank Centre* on Belvedere Rd., SE1 (phone: 171-928-3144; 171-261-0127 for recorded information). Underground: *Waterloo.*

**HORNIMAN MUSEUM** In a striking Art Nouveau building, the exhibits illustrate the cultures, traditions, and changing living conditions of the peoples of the world, focusing on current environmental issues. There's also an excellent natural history collection and a 16-acre park. Open daily. No admission charge. London Rd., Forest Hill, SW2 (phone: 181-699-2339). Accessible by *British Rail* (*Forest Hill Station*).

**INSTITUTE OF CONTEMPORARY ARTS** Exhibitions of the latest art, film, and theater are shown. Open daily. Admission charge. *Nash House,* Duke of York Steps, The Mall, SW1 (phone: 171-930-3647). Underground: *Charing Cross.*

**JEWISH MUSEUM** Art and antiques illustrate Jewish history. Closed Fridays and Saturdays. No admission charge. *Raymond Burton House,* 129 Albert St., NW1 (phone: 171-388-4525). Underground: *Camden Town.*

**KENSINGTON PALACE** William and Mary were the first royals to live in the present-day home of Princess Margaret and other members of the royal family. The *Court Dress Collection* and the *State Apartments* are open to the public daily. Admission charge. *Kensington Gardens,* W8 (phone: 171-937-9561). Underground: *High Street Kensington.*

**LEIGHTON HOUSE** Surrounded by a private, peaceful garden, this house was built in the 1860s by Lord Leighton, a painter and President of the *Royal Academy.* In addition to his own paintings, the walls are hung with works by Sir John Millais, Sir Edward Burne-Jones, and other Victorian artists; but don't miss the *Arab Hall,* replete with patterned tiles. Closed Sundays. No admission charge. 12 Holland Park Rd., W14 (phone: 171-602-3316). Underground: *High Street Kensington.*

**LINLEY SAMBOURNE HOUSE** This terraced house behind Kensington High Street looks the same as when the *Punch* cartoonist Edward Linley Sambourne lived here early this century. It is filled with Victorian pictures and knickknacks. Open Wednesdays and Sundays March through September. Admission charge. 18 Stafford Ter., W8 (phone: 181-994-1019). Underground: *High Street Kensington.*

**MUSEUM OF GARDEN HISTORY** Set in tiny *St. Mary-at-Lambeth Church,* the museum houses a collection of antique gardening tools and horticultural exhibits. A 17th-century–style garden (out back) contains a tulip tree and trumpet honeysuckle. Captain Bligh—who lived down the road—is buried right in the garden's center! Closed Saturdays year-round and the second Sunday in December through the first Sunday in March. No admission charge. Lambeth Palace Rd., SE1 (phone: 171-261-1891). Underground: *Waterloo.*

**MUSEUM OF MANKIND** Ethnographic exhibitions from the *British Museum* are housed in this structure next to the *Burlington Arcade* in Piccadilly, including items such as bronzes from Nigeria, Maori jade ornaments, and a crystal skull probably made by the Aztec. There's also a popular café. Open daily. No admission charge. 6 Burlington Gardens, W1 (phone: 171-323-8043). Underground: *Green Park.*

**MUSEUM OF THE MOVING IMAGE** The museum has over 50 exhibits and over 1,000 clips from various old and recent films and TV shows. There's also plenty of movie memorabilia, including Charlie Chaplin's hat and cane—and hands-on exhibits. But arrive early, before it gets too crowded. Open daily. Admission charge. *South Bank Centre,* SE1 (phone: 171-928-3535). Underground: *Waterloo.*

**NATIONAL POSTAL MUSEUM** A philatelist's dream—the collection of stamps from all over the world runs into the millions and includes a complete sheet of Penny Blacks printed in 1840, examples of forgeries, and changing exhibits. Closed weekends. No admission charge. King Edward St., EC1 (phone: 171-239-5420). Underground: *St. Paul's.*

**NATURAL HISTORY MUSEUM** Featured here are high-tech, hands-on exhibits, as well as specimens in glass cases for natural historians of all ages. The huge dinosaur skeleton at the entrance is a favorite with children, who also love the *Creepy Crawlie Gallery* and the *Ecology Gallery.* The *Earth Galleries* feature a simulated earthquake, a collection of gemstones, and an explanation of the solar system. Open daily. Admission charge. Cromwell Rd., SW7 (phone: 171-589-6323). Underground: *South Kensington.*

**POLLOCK'S TOY MUSEUM** Upstairs there's a museum full of miniatures, dolls, dollhouses, and other toys; downstairs is a shop that offers similar items. Closed Sundays. No admission charge for children on Saturdays. 1 Scala St., W1 (phone: 171-636-3452). Underground: *Goodge Street.*

**ROYAL AIR FORCE MUSEUM** A full exhibition of military planes from the time of the Wright brothers to the present. There also is a special

"Battle of Britain" display. Open daily. Admission charge. Grahame Park Way, NW9 (phone: 181-205-2266). Underground: *Colindale.*

**SCIENCE MUSEUM** Worth more than a single visit to see the seven floors of exhibits here. Get a free map to locate your favorites from among such exhibits as "The Exploration of Space," "Land Transport," "Children's Gallery," and "Photography." Open daily. Admission charge. Exhibition Rd., SW7 (phone: 171-589-3456). Underground: *South Kensington.*

**SIR JOHN SOANE'S MUSEUM** Its eclectic collection of arts and antiques, occupying two houses designed by the famous architect, includes Hogarth's series *The Rake's Progress,* Flemish woodcarvings, and the world's greatest collection of 17th- and 18th-century architectural drawings—works by Sir Christopher Wren, Robert Adam, George Dance, and Soane himself, among others. Closed Sundays and Mondays. No admission charge. 13 *Lincoln's Inn Fields,* WC2 (phone: 171-405-2107; 171-430-0175 for recorded information). Underground: *Holborn.*

**THEATRE MUSEUM** Britain's most comprehensive collection of theatrical material comprises everything from circus to pop, straight theater to Punch and Judy and pantomime. Closed Mondays. Admission charge. 1E Tavistock St., WC2 (phone: 171-836-7891). Underground: *Covent Garden.*

**WALLACE COLLECTION** Sir Richard Wallace's fine collection of European paintings, sculpture, porcelain, and armor is displayed in his former home. Painters represented include Fragonard, Gainsborough, Rembrandt, Rubens, Titian, Van Dyck, Velázquez, and Watteau. Open daily. No admission charge. *Hertford House,* Manchester Sq., W1 (phone: 171-935-0687). Underground: *Bond Street.*

**WELLINGTON MUSEUM** Set in *Apsley House,* home of the first (and current) Duke of Wellington, this recently renovated museum contains many fine paintings, including portraits of the Iron Duke's fellow commanders from the victorious campaign against the French and a nude (!) statue of Napoleon Bonaparte. Closed Mondays. Admission charge. *Apsley House,* 149 Piccadilly, W1 (phone: 171-499-5676). Underground: *Hyde Park Corner.*

**WHITECHAPEL ART GALLERY** An East End haven for temporary exhibitions featuring the works of 20th-century artists. Closed Mondays. No admission charge. 80 Whitechapel High St., E7 (phone: 171-377-0107). Underground: *Aldgate East.*

## SHOPPING

Stores generally are open weekdays and Saturdays from 9 AM to 6:30 PM; some also are open on Sundays. Department stores often stay open until 8 or 9 PM at least one day a week (usually Thursdays), and also may be open from 9 AM to 6:30 PM on Sundays. Some shops in the Chelsea and Knightsbridge areas stay open until 9 PM on Wednesdays; in the West End, evening hours are on Thursdays. Although London is traditionally one of the most expensive cities in the world, savvy shoppers still can find good buys. The current lure, however, is more for fine British workmanship and style than low prices.

Devoted bargain hunters know that the best time to buy British is during the semiannual sales that usually occur from *Boxing Day* (December 26) through the early part of the new year and again in early July. Many stores remain open on *New Year's Day* to accommodate the bargain hunters, and the best-publicized single sale is that held by *Harrods* for about three weeks beginning the first Wednesday in January.

Though scattered about the city, London's most appealing shops tend to center in the West End area, particularly along Old and New Bond Streets, Oxford, South Molton, Regent, and Jermyn Streets, St. Christopher's Place, and Piccadilly. Other good shopping areas are the King's Road, Kensington High Street, and Kensington Church Street, along with Knightsbridge and *Covent Garden.* The *Princes* and *Piccadilly Arcades* on the other side of Piccadilly are shorter than the Regency-style *Burlington Arcade* (see *Special Places*), but they offer similar stores.

Beauchamp Place (pronounced *Beech*-um), a short walk from *Harrods* off Brompton Road, is a boutiques-filled block known for designer clothes and jewelry, trendy shops and shoppers; nearby Walton Street is similarly packed. Pedestrian streets are special fun. Lively Carnaby and Rupert Streets are gradually discarding a decades-old "tacky" image. Brick Lane is the London equivalent of New York City's Lower East Side—a strip of inexpensive ethnic stores, including great bagel shops, Indian restaurants, and a pets market on Sundays.

London is a city of markets. Camden Passage, a quaint pedestrian alleyway off Upper St. in Islington (N1), has an open-air market—pushcarts selling curios and antiques—on Wednesdays, Thursdays (books), and Saturdays. Portobello Road, one of the largest street markets in the world, is well known for its antiques shops, junk shops, and outdoor stalls, which are out on Saturdays only. Also notable is *Camden Lock Market* (Camden High St., NW1) on weekends for far-out clothes, leather items, antiques, and trinkets. The *Jubilee Market,* on the south side of *Covent Garden*'s square, is one of the largest indoor markets in the country. The stalls, barrows, and small shops sell mainly crafts, clothes, and gifts, while all around the perimeter are cafés, wine bars, and small restaurants. Or get up early on a Sunday morning and head for the East End to *Petticoat Lane* (Middlesex St., E1) for food, inexpensive clothes, crockery, and even the proverbial kitchen sink. *Columbia Road* (Shoreditch, E2) has been London's top flower market for over 50 years; open daily.

Be sure to take your passport when you shop, and always inquire about the Value Added Tax (VAT) refund application forms when your total purchases in a store are over £50 (about $75). The VAT is a surcharge payable at the sales counter, but foreign customers usually will be reimbursed for it at home.

**Fortnum & Mason** Boasts one of the most elegantly stocked grocery departments in the world. There's also a soda fountain-cum-restaurant (plus a second eatery), and rather dowdy designer originals. 181 Piccadilly, W1 (phone: 171-734-8040).

**General Trading Company** Good for one-stop shopping, it offers everything from a bridal registry (London's social set shops here) to a place to pick up a wooden crocodile or *Christmas* tree toothbrush. There is also a small café in the basement. 144 Sloane St., SW1 (phone: 171-730-0411).

**Hamleys** The world's largest toy store, with an extensive selection of games, dolls, model cars, teddy bears, and other playthings, it's a must-see even if you don't have kids. 188 Regent St., W1 (phone: 171-734-3161).

**Harrods** The ultimate department store, although it does tend to be quite expensive and you'll always be jammed elbow-to-elbow with fellow tourists. It has everything, even a bank, and what it doesn't stock it will get for you. The "Food Halls" particularly fascinate visitors. 87-135 Brompton Rd., Knightsbridge, SW1 (phone: 171-730-1234).

**Harvey Nichols** Princess Di's favorite luxury department store specializes in women's haute couture; its high-tech food halls are a marvel. Knightsbridge, SW1 (phone: 171-235-5000).

**Heal's** Trendy and modern, this store stocks high-quality furniture (including handmade beds), home decorations, and jewelry. Large purchases can be shipped abroad at an additional charge. 96 Tottenham Court Rd., W1 (phone: 171-636-1666).

**Joseph** A trend-setting spot that sells everything from luggage and housewares to men's and women's clothing, now with several branches around town. Try the largest, 77 Fulham Rd., SW3 (phone: 171-823-9500), or the one at 26 Sloane St., SW1 (phone: 171-235-5470).

**Marks & Spencer** Locally nicknamed "Marks & Sparks," this chain specializes in clothes for the whole family, made to high standards and sold at very reasonable prices. Its sweaters (especially cashmere and Shetland) are still among the best buys in Britain; plus linens and their own first-rate cosmetics line. Terrific fresh produce and grocery items, too. 458 Oxford St., W1, and many other branches (phone: 171-935-7954).

**Peter Jones** Another good, well-stocked department store, offering moderately priced, tasteful goods. Sloane Sq., SW1 (phone: 171-730-3434).

**Selfridges** This well-known emporium offers somewhat less variety than *Harrods,* but it has just about everything, too—only a bit less expensive. The extensive china and crystal department carries most patterns available. 400 Oxford St., W1 (phone: 171-629-1234).

**Whiteleys of Bayswater** Once a department store rivaling *Harrods,* the original building has undergone a total renovation and is now a beautiful, enclosed Edwardian mall housing branches of shops such as *Marks & Spencer,* as well as designer boutiques. The top tier has cafés, bars, and restaurants. Queensway, W2 (phone: 171-229-8844).

## ANTIQUES SHOPS

**Alexander Juran** While the showrooms are small and shabby, the textiles, rugs, and carpets here can be exceptional. 74 New Bond St., W1 (phone: 171-493-4484 or 171-629-2550).

**Alfie's Antique Market** Housed in what was once a Victorian department store, this warren of 370 stalls, showrooms, and workshops is London's biggest covered antiques market—and likely its least expensive, since it is where the dealers shop. 13-25 Church St., NW8 (phone: 171-723-6066).

**Antiquarius Antique Market** Over 60 vendors with specialties ranging from theatrical items and delft to faïence and finds from the 1950s. 135-141 King's Rd., SW3 (phone: 171-351-5353).

**Bond Street Antique Centre** Finely worked antique jewelry, watches, portrait miniatures, silver, porcelain, and other objets d'art. 124 New Bond St., W1 (phone: 171-351-5353).

**Chelsea Antique Market** The original indoor antiques market, and still one of the best. 253 King's Rd., SW3 (phone: 171-352-1424).

**Chenil Galleries** Though widely known as a center for Art Deco and Art Nouveau objects, this gallery also sells Gothic furniture, tapestries, textiles, 18th-century paintings, scientific instruments, and fine porcelain. 181-183 King's Rd., SW3 (phone: 171-351-5353).

**Grays Antique Market** Here are dozens of stands selling a fine selection of antique jewelry, as well as antiquarian books, maps, prints, arms and armor, lace, scientific instruments, and thimbles (58 Davies St., W1; phone: 171-629-7034). Around the corner, *Grays in the Mews* (1-7 Davies Mews; same phone) has Victorian and Edwardian toys, paintings and prints, and Orientalia.

**Grosvenor Prints** More than 100,000 prints, on all subjects. In April, the shop holds an annual portrait exhibition of famous social and historic figures, though prints on other topics are also available at that time. 28-32 Shelton St., *Covent Garden,* WC2 (phone: 171-836-1979).

**John Keil** Offers a large selection of lovely (but expensive) antiques. 154 Brompton Rd., SW3 (phone: 171-589-6454).

**London Silver Vaults** A maze of antique silver and jewelry shops below ground, housed in what once were real vaults. (A few shops sell new silver or silver plate, too.) Prices range from astronomical to affordable. 53-64 Chancery La., WC2 (phone: 171-242-5506).

**Lucy B. Campbell** Here are 17th- to 19th-century decorative prints, as well as contemporary watercolors. 123 Kensington Church St., W8 (phone: 171-727-2205).

**Mallett and Son** A veritable museum in miniature, it specializes in the finest English furniture, choosing every item with consummate taste (141 New Bond St., W1; phone: 171-499-7411). A branch, selling French and continental furniture and a large, eclectic stock of artwork and decorative items, is at *Bourdon House,* 2 Davies St., W1 (phone: 171-629-2444).

**Milne and Moller** Deals in British and continental watercolors by 19th- and 20th-century artists. By appointment only. 35 Colville Ter., W11 (phone: 171-727-1679).

**Partridge Ltd.** The absolute best in 18th-century French and English furniture, paintings, and objets d'art can be found here. 144-146 New Bond St., W1 (phone: 171-629-0834).

**Pickering and Chatto** Antiquarian books in English literature of the 17th through 19th centuries, economics, science, and medicine. 17 Pall Mall, SW1 (phone: 171-930-2515).

**S. J. Phillips** Silver, jewelry, and objets d'art from the 16th to the early 19th centuries. 139 New Bond St., W1 (phone: 171-629-6261).

**Temple Gallery** Byzantine, Greek, and early Russian icons. By appointment only. 6 Clarendon Cross, W11 (phone: 171-727-3809).

## BOOKS, MAPS, AND STATIONERY

**Dillon's** One of London's most academically oriented bookstores, though it also stocks general-interest books. 82 Gower St., WC1 (phone: 171-636-1577).

**Filofax Shop** The famous brand-name personal organizers. 21 Conduit St., W1 (phone: 171-499-0457).

**Foyle's** London's largest bookstore. 119 Charing Cross Rd., WC2 (phone: 171-437-5660).

**Hatchard's** Founded in 1797, this is London's oldest bookseller—and one of the most civilized. It currently stocks more than 150,000 titles on its four floors. It has several branches, but the main store is at 187 Piccadilly, W1 (phone: 171-439-9921).

**Henry Sotheran Ltd.** The large stock here includes volumes on voyages and travel, architectural books, finely bound literature, and children's books. 2 Sackville St., W1 (phone: 171-439-6151).

**Maggs Bros. Ltd.** The friendly staff at this quaint bookshop will help you find your way through three floors of antiquarian books on travel, military and naval history, and 17th-century English literature. 50 Berkeley Sq., W1 (phone: 171-493-7160).

**Map House** Antique maps (and reproductions), as well as atlases, engravings, prints, and travel books are sold here. 54 Beauchamp Pl., SW3 (phone: 171-589-4325).

**Smythson of Bond Street** The world's best place to buy leather diaries, notepads, stationery, and calendars also offers esoteric ledgers for recording odd data. 44 New Bond St., W1 (phone: 171-629-8558).

**Stanford's** The proprietors contend that it's the world's largest map shop, and they just may be right. If you want a topographical map of the mountains you've just walked, a yachting chart for an area you want to cruise, or a road map of the byways you plan to cycle, this is the place. 12 Long Acre, WC2 (phone: 171-836-1321).

**Traveller's Bookshop** A good source for guidebooks, secondhand books, and travel information. 25 Cecil Court, WC2 (phone: 171-836-9132).

**W. H. Smith's** Newspapers, magazines, and stationery supplies are sold at many branches throughout the city, including 118 Oxford St., W1 (phone: 171-436-6282).

**Waterstone's** Look for the signature maroon canopy of this huge chain of bookstores, whose instant success is due mainly to an enterprising, well-informed staff and late hours. There are many branches, including: 68-69 Hampstead High St., NW3 (phone: 171-794-1098); 99-101 Old Brompton Rd., SW7 (phone: 171-581-8522); 121-125 Charing Cross Rd., WC2 (phone: 171-434-4291); and 193 Kensington High St., W8 (phone: 171-937-8432).

## CHINA

**Reject China Shop** Here you'll find good buys in name-brand china, including some irregular pieces, as well as glassware, crystal, and flatware. For a fee, the shop will ship your purchases back home. There are several branches throughout the city, including: 134 Regent St., W1 (phone: 171-434-2502); 33-34 Beauchamp Pl., SW3 (phone: 171-581-0737); and 183 Brompton Rd., SW3 (phone: 171-581-0739).

**Thomas Goode and Company** London's best china and glass shop first opened in 1827. Even if you don't plan to buy anything, you may want to look at their beautiful 1876 showroom. 19 S. Audley St., W1 (phone: 171-499-2823).

**Waterford Wedgwood** A full selection of Waterford crystal and Wedgwood bone china (what else?). 158 Regent St., W1 (phone: 171-734-7262).

## CLOTHING, ACCESSORIES, AND FABRICS

**Anderson and Sheppard** Reputable "made-to-measure" tailor for men's clothes. 30 Savile Row, W1 (phone: 171-734-1420).

**Aquascutum** Famous for raincoats and jackets for men and women. 100 Regent St., W1 (phone: 171-734-6090).

**Austin Reed** Classic English menswear, plus an old-fashioned barber shop in the basement. Some womenswear, too. 103 Regent St., W1 (phone: 171-734-6789).

**Bellville Sassoon** This boutique's client list reads like a chapter from *Debrett's;* the Princess of Wales, who chose a saucy sailor dress for her first official picture with the queen, is a loyal customer. The specialty is glamorous evening wear specifically designed for the shop. 18 Culford Gardens, SW3 (phone: 171-581-3500).

**Browns** Designer clothes for men and women in eight shops along a tiny, pedestrians-only street. S. Molton St., W1 (phone: 171-491-7833).

**Burberrys** Superb, expensive raincoats and traditional clothes for men and women, and home of the now nearly ubiquitous plaid that began life as a raincoat lining. 18-22 Haymarket, SW1 (phone: 171-930-3343).

**Caroline Charles** Perfect women's styles for *Ascot* and other very social events. 56-57 Beauchamp Pl., SW3 (phone: 171-589-5850).

**Cordings** Sportswear for the quintessential country squire—plus a branch of *Hackett* (see below), a major source of elegant menswear. 19-20 Piccadilly, W1 (phone: 171-734-0830).

**Courtenay House** Particularly beautiful Swiss cotton and silky lingerie. 22 Brook St., W1 (phone: 171-629-0542).

**Douglas Hayward** A reputable made-to-order men's tailor. 95 Mount St., W1 (phone: 171-499-5574).

**Farlows** Perhaps the best spot in London to buy the completely waterproof and windproof Barbour jackets and hats and other casual wear for a day in the country. 5 Pall Mall, SW1 (phone: 171-839-2423).

**Feathers** French and Italian designer clothing for women. 40 Hans Crescent, SW1 (phone: 171-589-0356).

**Gieves and Hawkes** Over 200 years old, this establishment provides traditional English tailoring—from formal dress to the proper attire for hunting and fishing. The queen, Duke of Edinburgh, and Prince Charles are regular patrons. You can get a suit either custom-made or ready-to-wear. 1 Savile Row, W1 (phone: 171-434-2001), and 18 Lime St., EC3 (phone: 171-283-4914).

**Gucci** Outposts of the famous Italian fashion, leather goods, and shoe manufacturer are found at 32-33 Old Bond St., W1 (phone: 171-629-2716), and at 17-18 Sloane St., SW1 (phone: 171-235-6707).

**Hackett** Menswear in these elegant but welcoming shops is neither boring nor predictable. There are branches at several locations, including: 137 Sloane St., SW1 (phone: 171-730-3331); *Cordings,* 19-20 Piccadilly, W1 (phone: 171-734-0868); and 65b New King's Rd., SW6 (phone: 171-731-7964).

**Harvie and Hudson** Custom-made men's shirts, not to mention a selection of color-coordinated silk ties. Three branches: 77 Jermyn St., SW1 (phone: 171-930-3949); 97 Jermyn St., SW1 (phone: 171-839-3578); and 55 Knightsbridge, SW3 (phone: 171-235-2651).

**Jaeger** Tailored (and expensive) men's and women's clothes. 202-206 Regent St., W1 (phone: 171-734-8211), and 163 Sloane St., SW1 (phone: 171-235-2505).

**James Smith and Sons** Believed to be the oldest umbrella shop in Europe, it was opened in 1830 by James Smith, and in 1857 it moved to its current address. It also carries walking sticks and whips. A couple of blocks from the *British Museum.* 53 New Oxford St., WC1 (phone: 171-836-4731).

**Katharine Hamnett** Beautiful—but pricey—womenswear. 20 Sloane St., SW1 (phone: 171-823-1002).

**Kent & Curwen** The place to buy authentic cricket caps, Henley club ties, and all sorts of similarly preppy raiment. 39 St. James's St., SW1 (phone: 171-409-1955), and 6 *Royal Arcade* (for *Wimbledon* wear), W1 (phone: 171-493-6882).

**Laura Ashley** Romantically styled skirts, dresses, and blouses, plus a plethora of decorating essentials. 256 Regent St., W1 (phone: 171-437-9760), and other branches including 47-49 Brompton Rd., SW1 (phone: 171-823-9700).

**Liberty** Famous for print fabrics. Scarves and ties a specialty. 210 Regent St., W1 (phone: 171-734-1234).

**Moss Bros.** Men's formal attire (including dress tartans) and high-quality riding clothes for sale and hire. 88 Regent St., W1 (phone: 171-494-0666), and 27 King St., WC2 (phone: 171-240-4567).

**Paul Smith** Britain's number one men's designer has four adjacent shops (one sells womenswear) in *Covent Garden.* 41-44 Floral St., WC2 (phone: 171-379-7133).

**Scotch House** Famous for Scottish cashmeres, sweaters, tartans—a wide selection of well-known labels. 2 Brompton Rd., SW1 (phone: 171-581-2151), and several branches.

**Shirin** The best designer cashmeres in town. 51 Beauchamp Pl., SW3 (phone: 171-581-1936).

**Simpson (Piccadilly)** Classic and safe English looks for men and women, including their own famous "DAKS" label. 203 Piccadilly, W1 (phone: 171-734-2002).

**Turnbull and Asser** Famous for their made-to-order shirts, but they also sell ready-made luxury menswear, as well as womenswear next door. 71-72 Jermyn St., SW1 (phone: 171-930-0502).

**Vivienne Westwood** Innovative women's clothing from one of Britain's most influential designers. 41 Conduit St., W1 (phone: 171-439-1109).

**Westaway and Westaway** Cashmere and Shetland wool kilts, sweaters (their great doubleknit Shetlands are half the price of *Hackett*'s), scarves, and blankets. Mail order, too. 65 Great Russell St., WC1 (phone: 171-405-4479; 800-345-3219 for inquiries and mail orders).

**Zandra Rhodes** The designer's ultra-feminine creations are sold here. By appointment only. 87 Richford St., W6 (phone: 181-749-3216).

## COSMETICS

**Floris** Old-fashioned English scents, soaps, potpourri, and more in a charming Victorian shop. 89 Jermyn St., SW1 (phone: 171-930-2885).

**Penhaligon's** This chain of Victorian shops offers an extensive range of classical scents, toilet water, soaps, and bath oils for ladies and gentlemen—along with antique scent bottles and old English silver for the dressing table. 41 Wellington St., WC2, and four other locations (phone: 171-836-2150).

## FOOD AND DRINK

**Charbonnel et Walker** Sumptuous candies in beautiful packages. You can get Prince Philip's favorite chocolate here—a Mocha Baton. 28 Old Bond St., W1 (phone: 171-491-0939).

**Ferns** The carved mahogany shelves of this old-fashioned store are crammed with teas, tea caddies, and more, and the drawers are packed with beans of all types. 27 Rathbone Pl., W1 (phone: 171-636-2237).

**Justin De Blank** Excellent specialty foods, especially cheese and take-out dishes. 42 Elizabeth St., SW1 (phone: 171-730-0605).

**Paxton and Whitfield** This establishment shows cheeses the way some shops display jewelry. All of it is superb. 93 Jermyn St., SW1 (phone: 171-930-0250).

**Prestat** The best chocolates in all of London. Try the truffles. 14 *Princes Arcade,* SW1 (phone: 171-629-4838).

**Rococo Chocolates** London's most eccentric candy store: fresh cream truffles, pralines, and Swiss chocolates (made in London); plus chocolate engagement rings. Tea is served in summer by appointment only. 321 King's Rd., SW3 (phone: 171-352-5857).

**Twinings** London's oldest tea shop (est. 1706) sells tea in bags, balls, and bulk; there's also a large selection of coffee. 216 The Strand, WC2 (phone: 171-353-3511).

## FURNITURE, HOUSEWARES, AND BIBELOTS

**The Conran Shop** Sir Terence Conran has transformed the beautiful *Michelin Building* into a grander, more exclusive and expensive version of his well-known *Habitat* stores. However, the export of larger furniture and furnishings is probably better arranged through a US branch. 81 Fulham Rd., SW3 (phone: 171-589-7401).

**Halcyon Days** The best place to find authentic enameled Battersea boxes—both antique and new. 14 Brook St., W1 (phone: 171-629-8811).

***Irish Linen Co.*** Plain and fancy bed and table linen and handkerchiefs. 35 *Burlington Arcade,* W1 (phone: 171-493-8949).

***Naturally British*** Its stock includes tapestries from Wales, hand-knits from Scotland, and many wooden items such as rocking horses and traditional pub games. 13 New Row, *Covent Garden,* WC2 (phone: 171-240-0551).

## GOLD, SILVER, AND JEWELRY

***Asprey & Company*** Fine jewelry and silver (plus luggage and leather accessories). 165-169 New Bond St., W1 (phone: 171-493-6767).

***Mappin & Webb*** Elegant and traditional gold and silver jewelry. 170 Regent St., W1 (phone: 171-734-5842).

## GUNS AND SPORTING EQUIPMENT

***Gidden's of London*** Founded in 1806, it sells saddles and other riding equipment to the queen. On three floors, near New Bond St. at 15d Clifford St., W1 (phone: 171-734-2788).

***Holland and Holland*** Here, gunmaking is high art. It's worth a peek, if only to inspect the binoculars, folding earmuffs, and other appurtenances of hunting and shooting. 33 Bruton St., W1 (phone: 171-499-4411).

***James Purdey and Sons*** The place to go for custom-made shotguns and other shooting gear. 57 S. Audley St., W1 (phone: 171-499-1801).

***Lillywhites*** The whole gamut of sporting goods, from cricket bats to shuttlecocks. Piccadilly Circus, SW1 (phone: 171-930-3181).

***Swaine Adeney*** Riding gear and their famous pure silk umbrellas. 185 Piccadilly, W1 (phone: 171-734-4277).

## HATS

***Bates*** Our favorite gentlemen's hat shop. Check out the eight-part caps. 21A Jermyn St., SW1 (phone: 171-734-2722).

***Hat Shop*** Berets, cloches, deerstalkers, fedoras, flying caps, panamas, pillboxes, tam-o'-shanters, even baseball caps with earflaps, along with hats made by designers. Two locations: 58 Neal St., *Covent Garden,* WC2 (phone: 171-836-6718), and 18 St. Christopher's Pl., W1 (phone: 171-935-0820).

***Herbert Johnson*** Men's and women's hats. (It's worth a look just to see the shop's vividly expressive mannequins—they're the most clever in London.) 30 New Bond St., W1 (phone: 171-408-1174).

***James Lock and Company, Ltd.*** The royal hatters. They fitted a crown for the queen's coronation, and they'll happily fit you for your first top hat. Plus headgear for fishermen, hunters, groundskeepers, and—for the first time in 300 years—women. 6 St. James's St., SW1 (phone: 171-930-8874).

# MUSIC

**Chappell** London's largest supplier of sheet music, from Bach to rock. It also sells pianos, electronic keyboards, guitars, and metronomes. 50 New Bond St., W1 (phone: 171-491-2777).

**58 Dean Street Records** Offers a wide selection of show tunes and movie soundtracks, and the staff is very helpful. 58 Dean St., W1 (phone: 171-734-8777).

## SHOES

**Church's** Superior men's shoes (and some women's shoes) in various locations, including 58-59 *Burlington Arcade,* W1 (phone: 171-493-8307).

**John Lobb** World-famous for men's made-to-order shoes—at stratospheric prices—that will last 10 years or more, with proper care. 9 St. James's St., SW1 (phone: 171-930-3664).

**Shellys Shoes** A wide selection of trendy street footwear from thigh-high suede boots to platform shoes. 159 Oxford St., W1 (phone: 171-437-5842).

## TOBACCO

**Alfred Dunhill** Not only does this store offer the best in precision lighters, pipes, tobacco, and cigars, it claims to provide almost anything that a man can carry or wear—including luxury leather accessories, watches, writing instruments, and casual clothes. The Humidor Room features Havana and other cigars for connoisseurs. 30 Duke St. (near Piccadilly), SW1 (phone: 171-499-9566).

**James Fox and Robert Lewis** Specializes in cigars from around the world, including Havana. Cigars mature to peak condition in the on-premises humidifying rooms. 19 St. James St., W1 (phone: 171-493-9009).

# SPORTS AND FITNESS

Soccer (called football hereabouts) and cricket are the most popular spectator pastimes, but London offers a wide variety of other sports.

**CRICKET** The season runs from mid-April to early September. The best places to watch the matches are at *Lord's Cricket Ground* (St. John's Wood Rd., NW8; phone: 171-289-1615) and *The Oval* (Kennington, SE1; phone: 171-582-4911).

**FITNESS CENTERS** *Pineapple Dance Studios* (7 Langley St., WC2; phone: 171-836-4004); the *Albany Health and Fitness Club* (Little Albany St., NW1; phone: 171-383-7131); *Earls Court Gym* (254 Earls Court Rd., SW5; phone: 171-370-1402); and other locations around town. Several hotels have good fitness centers; see *Checking In.*

**GOLF** These courses, which are among the finest in England, are within 40 miles of London.

**Sunningdale** While the *Old Course* is considered the championship layout here, the *New* is probably the more challenging of the two. When you play them, you will discover that the decision on difficulty is an arbitrary one at best. Fairways and greens are meticulously maintained, and this is perhaps the finest single brace of courses in England. Private but approachable for play on weekdays; call well in advance and have a letter from your home club pro or president ready. Ridgemount Rd., Sunningdale (phone: 1344-21681).

**Wentworth** Generally considered the prettier of the layouts here, the *East* course can do wonders for a shaky backswing. But it's the *West* course, with its relatively narrow tree-lined fairways, that is sometimes not so affectionately called the "Burma Road." For a high-handicap player, the *West* is not unlike putting an innocent's head into a lion's mouth. The *World Match Play Championship* has been held here every year since 1964. Again, it's a private club; access is available to traveling players on weekdays with prior notice—upon presentation of your own club membership card with a handicap certificate and a letter from your club pro or president. Virginia Water, Surrey (phone: 1344-842201).

Aside from the private facilities described above, there are several municipal courses, some of which rent clubs. Try *Addington Court* (Featherbed La., Addington, Croydon; phone: 181-657-0281); *Beckenham Place Park* (Beckenham, Kent; phone: 181-650-2292); *Bush Hill Park* (Winchmore Hill, Middlesex; phone: 181-360-5738); and *Pickett's Lock Center* (Pickett's Lock La., N9; phone: 181-803-3611).

**HORSE RACING** Nine major racecourses are within easy reach of London, including *Epsom,* where the *Derby* (pronounced *Dar*-by) is run, and *Ascot,* where the *Royal Ascot* races take place—both in June. The flat racing season is from March to November; steeplechasing, August to June. Check the daily papers for details.

**HORSEBACK RIDING** Try *Richard Briggs Riding Stables* (63 Bathurst Mews, W2; phone: 171-723-2813) and *Ross Nye's Riding Establishment* (8 Bathurst Mews, W2; phone: 171-262-3791); *Hyde Park* is a fine place to ride.

**ICE SKATING** There is the *Queen's Ice Skating Club* (17 Queensway, W2; phone: 171-229-0172) and *Streatham Ice Rink* (386 Streatham High Rd., SW16; phone: 181-769-7771).

**JOGGING** Most pleasant for running are *Hyde Park,* bordered by Kensington Road, Park Lane, and Bayswater Road; *Hampstead Heath,* North London; and *Regent's Park,* bordered by Prince Albert Road, Albany Street, Marylebone Road, and Park Road. Do not jog after dark.

**RUGBY** An autumn-through-spring spectacle at local clubs throughout Greater London. Major international matches are staged at the Rugby Union world headquarters on Whitton Rd., Twickenham (phone: 181-892-8161).

**SOCCER** *The* big sport in Britain. The season is autumn to spring and the most popular local clubs are *Arsenal* (*Highbury Stadium,* Avenell Rd., N5; phone: 171-226-0304); *Chelsea* (Stamford Bridge, Fulham Rd., SW6; phone: 171-385-5545); and *Tottenham Hotspur* (White Hart La., N17; phone: 181-808-8080).

**SWIMMING** Excellent indoor public pools include *Swiss Cottage Center* (Adelaide Rd., NW3; phone: 171-413-6490) and *The Oasis* (167 High Holborn, WC1; phone: 171-836-9555). There is outdoor swimming in *Hyde Park*'s Serpentine Lake and at *Hampstead Heath* in the summer.

**TENNIS** Aside from private clubs, more than 50 London public parks have tennis courts available to all. Get information from the *Lawn Tennis Association* (phone: 171-385-4233) or the *London Tourist Board and Convention Bureau* (see *Tourist Information*). For information on *Wimbledon,* see *Special Events.*

## THEATER

London remains the theater capital of the world, with about 50 stages in and around its West End theater district and a collection of vigorous "fringe" theaters in various parts of town. Listed below are our favorite venues in this most dramatic of cities.

### CENTER STAGE

**Barbican Centre** An apparent tribute to modern architecture, this 1982 structure looks like a maze of concrete towers and corridors from the outside. Inside, the complex design and the breadth of artistic activity generated are overwhelming. This is the London home of the *Royal Shakespeare Company,* along with the *London Symphony Orchestra.* There are two theaters, cinemas, an art gallery, two shops, and a concert hall that hosts regular performances of classical music, opera, and more. The *Waterside Café,* which offers snacks by the fountains in summer, *Café on Six* (the *Barbican*'s wine bar), and the more formal *Searcey's* all make for delightful interludes. Silk St., EC2 (phone: 171-638-4141 for general information; 171-638-8891 for the box office).

**Royal Court Theatre** One of the most famous of London's small stages, this one has made theatrical history more than once—first around 1904, with Harley Granville Barker's stagings of Arthur Pinero farces and George Bernard Shaw plays, and again in the late 1950s, when George Devine's *English Stage Company* presented John

Osborne's *Look Back in Anger*. Even today, the theater is associated with very modern works, producing the plays of such contemporary writers as Caryl Churchill and Snoo Wilson. And despite the chronic shortage of money, standards are always high. The *Royal Court* is a great place for spotting talent, and the audience is lively. Stephen Daldry, the theater's new artistic director, has shown a marked preference for contemporary American playwrights; recent productions include David Mamet's *Oleanna* and John Guare's *Six Degrees of Separation*. Sloane Sq., SW1 (phone: 171-730-1745).

**Royal National Theatre** Anyone who visits this trio of houses in a handsome, large, Thameside drama complex is sure to have plenty to talk about. Such luminaries as Maggie Smith, Albert Finney, John Gielgud, Ian McKellen, and Paul Scofield have appeared here. The building itself is wonderful, too, with an interior that feels like a walk-through sculpture, a huge foyer with bars that seems to be London's answer to Paris's sidewalk cafés, and all manner of walks, terraces, and restaurants with fine views of *Somerset House* and the river curving off toward *St. Paul's*. Guided tours are given several times a day Mondays through Saturdays for a small charge. Before performances, ensembles and soloists play for free in the foyers, and you can browse through art exhibitions while listening. There are often so-called platform performances—brief plays, readings, poetry, music, and mime—in all three theaters: the 400-seat *Cottesloe*, which is otherwise mainly used for works requiring small-scale staging, the 890-seat proscenium-arch *Lyttelton*, and the 1,160-seat open-stage *Olivier*. South Bank, SE1 (phone: 171-928-2252 for the box office; 171-633-0880 for tour information).

---

A perfect way to spend a summer evening in London is to attend a performance of Shakespeare (or a musical) in the *Open Air Theatre* (*Regent's Park*, NW1; phone: 171-486-2431). Since 1962, the *New Shakespeare Company* has made its home here, offering three plays (two by Shakespeare) every season (May through September).

The *Sadler's Wells Theatre* (Rosebery Ave., EC1; phone: 171-278-6563 for general information; 171-278-8916 for the box office), built on the site of mineral springs discovered in 1683 by Richard Sadler, is one of the capital's oldest more or less continuously operating halls. It once hosted the world premiere of Benjamin Britten's *Peter Grimes* and, in its time, also has been home to the *Royal Ballet* and the *English National Opera*. Today, it hosts touring opera and dance companies from all over the world. The London seasons of the country's leading dance troupes—including the *Rambert Dance Company*, the *London Contemporary Dance Theatre*, and the *National Youth Music Theater*—also take place here.

Built to showcase Gilbert and Sullivan's operettas, the *Savoy Theatre* (The Strand, WC1; phone: 171-836-8117) saw the likes of such luminaries as Noël Coward, Ralph Richardson, and Paul Robeson on its stage. Gutted by fire in 1990, it has since risen like the proverbial phoenix. The theater underwent an Art Deco transformation in 1929, and it is to this era that the architects and designers, in renovating the structure, have returned; the decor is now a veritable show in itself.

Architects, bombs, and ill-advised alterations had left the *Old Vic* (Waterloo Rd., SE1; phone: 171-928-7616) a mishmash until 1982, when Canadian entrepreneur "Honest" Ed Mirvish bought the theater, transforming it into one of the most elegant and comfortable in central London. The façade was returned to its 1818 incarnation, and the interior was restored to a semblance of its 1880s self. The remarkable restoration alone makes a visit worthwhile.

The productions at the *Theatre Royal* (Drury Lane; Catherine St., WC2; phone: 171-494-5062 for the box office; 171-836-3352 for tours) may not be London's most innovative, but the theater—with its beautiful symmetrical staircase and domed entranceway—is definitely one of London's most historic. The *Theatre Royal* (Haymarket, SW1; phone: 171-930-8800), built in 1821, has been the setting for plays by everyone from Ibsen to Terence Rattigan. The *Young Vic Theatre* (66 The Cut, SE1; phone: 171-928-6363), founded in the late 1970s, is renowned for bringing fresh interpretations to Shakespeare and modern classics. Among its most recent successes have been the European premiere of *The Last Yankee* by Arthur Miller and *The Plough and the Stars* by Sean O'Casey.

The long-awaited, much-ballyhooed restoration of the *Globe Theatre,* the oval-shaped stage where many of Shakespeare's works were first performed, has been struggling with financial difficulties but is scheduled to be completed this spring. The open-air theater, on the south bank of the Thames, will be re-created in the Elizabethan style of the original (which was destroyed by fire in 1613) and will hold about 1,500 people; there will be some tiered seating, but most theatergoers will have to stand, as Shakespeare's audiences did in the 16th century. The project was spearheaded by the late American actor/director Sam Wanamaker, who felt Shakespeare deserved an important memorial in London, where so many of his plays were first produced. For more information, contact the *Shakespeare Globe Trust* (Bear Gardens, SE1; phone: 171-620-0202).

Visitors from the US often find attending theater in London easier—and a little less expensive (depending on the exchange rate)—than it is at home. Except for the small handful of runaway box-office successes, tickets usually are available for all performances. In most cases, you can reserve by telephone, but tickets must be picked up well before curtain time. The *Society of London Theatre* operates a half-price ticket kiosk in Leicester Square. It posts a list of shows for which remaining seats (usually in the orchestra) are available at half price on the day of the performance. Ticket agencies that offer tickets to all shows, charging a (sometimes hefty) commission, include *Edwards & Edwards* (*Palace Theatre,* Cambridge Circus, W1; phone: 171-379-1564; or 1 Times Sq. Plaza, New York, NY 10036; phone: 212-944-0290 or 800-223-6108), *Ticketmaster* (phone: 171-379-4444), *London Theatre Bookings* (96 Shaftesbury Ave.; phone: 171-439-3371 or 171-439-4061), and *First Call* (phone: 171-497-9977). Another service, *Theatre Tonight* (phone: 171-753-0333), offers tickets for same-night performances, which can be charged to MasterCard or Visa; there's no booking fee or ticket surcharge. A phone service, *Theatreline,* offers information on West End performances (phone: 836-430959 for plays; 836-430960 for musicals; 836-430961 for comedies; 836-430962 for thrillers; 836-430963 for children's shows; 836-430964 for opera, ballet, and dance); calls can be placed from anywhere in Great Britain, and there is a charge per call—36p (about 55¢) to 48p (about 75¢), depending on the time of day.

If you want to reserve specific tickets before you arrive in London, there are agencies in the US that keep a listing of what's on in London. For a service charge (again, it may be a bit steep—as much as 30% of the ticket price), they will sell you the best seats. Contact *Edwards & Edwards* (see address and phone number above) or *Keith Prowse & Co., Ltd.* (234 W. 44th St., Suite 1000, New York, NY 10036; phone: 212-398-1430 or 800-669-7469).

The quality of London's fringe theater varies from accomplished and imaginative to amateurish. Theaters in pubs are at the *King's Head* (115 Upper St., Islington, N1; phone: 171-226-1916) and the *Bush* (in the *Bush Hotel,* Shepherd's Bush Green, W6; phone: 181-743-3388). The *Riverside Studios* (Crisp Rd., Hammersmith, W6; phone: 181-748-3354), the *Tricycle Theatre* (269 Kilburn High Rd., NW6; phone: 171-328-1000), and the *New End Theatre* (27 New End, Hampstead, NW3; phone: 171-794-0022) have established excellent reputations; their productions often move on to the West End and sometimes even directly to Broadway. Also keep an eye on the *Donmar Warehouse* for major transfers from the *Edinburgh Festival Fringe* or for exciting avant-garde companies such as *Cheek by Jowl* (call 171-793-0153 for information). And try to catch a performance at *St. Martin's* (West St., Cambridge Circus, WC2; phone: 171-836-1443), the home of Agatha Christie's *The Mousetrap,* which has been running since 1952.

Musical nostalgia can be found at the *Players Theatre* (The Arches, off Villiers St., WC2; phone: 171-839-1134), just off The Strand at *Charing Cross Station,* which offers old-fashioned Victorian music hall entertainment.

Check *Time Out* to get comprehensive lists of current productions, plot summaries, and theater phone numbers. Daily papers list West End performances.

The best of London's ballet performances are presented at *The Place* (17 Duke's Rd., WC1; phone: 171-387-0031), home of the *London Contemporary Dance Theatre* and the *London School of Contemporary Dance;* the *Royal Opera House* (see *Music*), home of the *Royal Ballet;* the *London Coliseum* (St. Martin's La., WC2; phone: 171-836-3161), London's largest theater; and *Sadler's Wells* (see above), though the original company has moved to Birmingham. Details about concert, recital, opera, and ballet performances are listed in the arts sections of *Time Out.* Tickets to London ballet performances can be obtained in the US by contacting *Edwards & Edwards* (see above).

## MUSIC

Few cities offer a greater variety of musical performances. The *Royal Albert Hall* (Kensington Gore, SW7; phone: 171-589-8212 for the box office; 891-500252 for recorded information) was opened by Queen Victoria in 1871 as a memorial to her consort, Prince Albert. Today, it is the venue for the annual *Henry Wood Promenade Concerts* (see *Special Events*), for performances of the *BBC Symphony Orchestra* during most of its season, and for concerts by many other orchestras and ensembles. Most concerts at the *Hall* have remarkably low ticket prices. The *Royal Opera House* (Covent Garden, WC2; phone: 171-240-1066 for the box office), informally known as *Covent Garden,* has hosted the best divas in the world— among them Nellie Melba, Joan Sutherland, Maria Callas, and Kiri Te Kanawa. The hall ranks among the world's half-dozen true greats. The *Royal Opera* shares the house with the *Royal Ballet,* one of the world's most noted companies. In addition to operatic productions at *Covent Garden,* the *English National Opera Company* performs in English at the *London Coliseum* (see *Theater*) from October to June; to obtain opera tickets before departing from the US, contact *Edwards & Edwards* (see *Theater*).

Opened in 1951, the *Royal Festival Hall* (South Bank, SE1; phone: 171-928-8800), London's premier concert venue, seats an audience of 3,000. The permanent home of the renowned *London Philharmonic,* it is part of the *South Bank Centre,* which also comprises the *Royal National Theatre* (see *Theater*), the *Museum of the Moving Image* and the *Hayward Gallery* (see *Museums* for both), Jubilee Gardens, the *National Film Theatre,* and two smaller concert halls.

One of Europe's most elegant and intimate concert settings, *Wigmore Hall* (36 Wigmore St., W1; phone: 171-935-2141) is a fine example of the Art Nouveau style. Famous for its nearly perfect acoustics, the hall attracts artists such as Olaf Bär, Shura Cherkasky, and the *Beaux Arts Trio.* Another fine venue for classical fare is the *Barbican Centre* (see *Theater*), home of the *London Symphony Orchestra.* Concerts also are often held in the dignified, splendid setting of *St. John's Church* (Smith Sq., SW1; phone: 171-222-1061). During the summer, outdoor concerts are given at *Kenwood, Crystal Palace,* and *Holland Park,* and bands play in many of London's parks.

Good live popular music can be heard in London's music pubs. Among the best of them are the *Dublin Castle* (94 Parkway, NW1; phone: 171-485-1773); *King's Head* (4 Fulham High St., SW6; phone: 171-736-1413); *Hare and Hounds* (181 Upper St., N1; phone: 171-226-2992); and *Half Moon* (93 Lower Richmond Rd., SW15; phone: 181-788-2387). If you are interested in purchasing tickets in the US to see pop and rock concerts featuring superstar performers in London, contact *Keith Prowse & Co., Ltd.* (see *Theater*).

# NIGHTCLUBS AND NIGHTLIFE

London offers a lively and often wild nightlife, including nightclubs, jazz clubs, historical feasts, comedy clubs, and gambling casinos. Some wind up around midnight; most go on until well into the early morning hours. In *Covent Garden* and still-trendy Chelsea, particularly along King's and Fulham Roads, are fashionable pubs, wine bars, and restaurants. Two nightclubs with cabarets are *The Talk of London* (Drury La., WC2; phone: 171-408-1001) and *L'Hirondelle* (199 Swallow St., W1; phone: 171-734-1511). The best jazz clubs are *Ronnie Scott's* (47 Frith St., W1; phone: 171-439-0747) and *The 100 Club* (100 Oxford St., W1; phone: 171-636-0933). For jazz and a slice, try *Pizza Express* (10 Dean St., W1; phone: 171-437-9595) or *Pizza on the Park* (11 Knightsbridge, SW1; phone: 171-235-5550).

For a special (if touristy) treat, London offers the medieval banquet, with traditional meals served by costumed waiters and waitresses. Try *Beefeater* (St. Katherine's Dock, E1; phone: 181-405-1516) and *The Cockney Cabaret* (161 Tottenham Court Rd., W1; phone: 171-224-9000); the first is a traditional banquet, while the second is a medieval floor show with dinner.

The disco scene is ever-changing, and many places—such as the pricey *Annabel's* (44 Berkeley Sq., W1; phone: 171-629-1096)— are open only to members. Clubs of the moment include the *Hippodrome* (Charing Cross Rd., WC2; phone: 171-437-4311); *Stringfellows* (16-19 Upper St. Martin's La., WC2; phone: 171-240-5534); *Legend's* (29 Old Burlington St., W1; phone: 171-437-9933); *Crazy Larry's* (Lots Rd., SW10; phone: 171-376-5555); and *Limelight* (136 Shaftesbury Ave., W1; phone: 171-434-0572). A smart club in West London is the *Broadway Boulevard* club (in Ealing; phone: 181-840-0616), particularly convenient for guests at the nearby *Heathrow Airport* hotels.

London's comedy scene took root in the early 1980s with the *Comedy Store* (cofounded by Mike Myers, later seen on "Saturday Night Live" and in the movie *Wayne's World*), which featured both stand-up performers and improvisational humor. Over the years, other similar clubs sprang up throughout the city, and nowadays there are more than 50 to choose from. The *Comedy Store* (1 Oxenden St., WC1; phone: 426-914433 for information), which has moved from its original home in Leicester Square into a larger venue, is still one of the best; top stand-up comedians appear here regularly, and the *Comedy Store Players,* the club's resident troupe, perform clever improvised skits based on audience suggestions. Other good venues are the *Canal Café Theatre* (*The Bridge House,* Delamere Ter., W2; phone: 171-289-6054) and *Jongleurs Battersea* (*The Cornet,* 49 Lavender Gardens, SW11; phone: 171-924-2766). *Time Out* has a complete listing of clubs and current performers.

Female impersonators regularly perform at the *Black Cap* (171 Camden High St., NW1; phone: 171-485-1742). For the latest on what's where in the gay scene, consult *Time Out* or call the *Lesbian and Gay Switchboard* (phone: 171-837-7324).

# Best in Town

## CHECKING IN

Visitors arriving in London between early spring and mid-autumn without hotel reservations are in for an unpleasant experience. For many years now there has been a glaring shortage of hotel rooms in the British capital during the prime tourist season. (For a small fee the *London Tourist Board and Convention Bureau* offices at *Victoria Station* and at the underground station in *Heathrow* will try to help you locate a room; see *Tourist Information.*) This fact, plus years of inflation, is largely responsible for often excessive hotel charges, generally out of keeping with other costs in Britain. (Because of the current recession, however, room rates have stayed at the same level for the past several years. Also, some hoteliers may be willing to strike a deal with you; there's no harm in asking.) Very expensive and expensive hotels do not include breakfast; moderate, inexpensive, and very inexpensive hotels generally include continental or full English breakfast. In our selections prices are $375 or more per night for a double room (including private bath, phone, and TV set unless otherwise noted, and sometimes including VAT and a 10% service charge) in a very expensive hotel; $250 to $350, expensive; $150 to $250, moderate; $100 to $150, inexpensive; and less than $100, very inexpensive.

For an unforgettable experience in London we begin with our favorite lodging places (they're pricey, but worth it), followed by our cost and quality choices, listed by price category.

### GRAND AND BABY GRAND HOTELS

**Claridge's** Here is the final bastion of the British Empire. Despite its sober red brick façade, its supreme, traditional elegance is as much a part of the London experience as the Horse Guards and the *Crown Jewels.* The 136 rooms and 54 suites are beautifully decorated in Art Deco or traditional style; the bathrooms are worth fighting for. When visiting royalty is in residence here—which is often—the flags of their countries are flown outside, beside the Union Jack. The concierge, however, accords the same personalized attention to monarchs and commoners alike: Regulars will find their favorite soaps and shampoos—even their pillow preferences—waiting in their rooms. Female guests are welcome to use the fitness and pool facilities at the *Berkeley* hotel (see below), since only men are granted entry to the *Bath and Racquet Club* located behind *Claridge's.* There is also fine dining in two restaurants. Business facilities include 24-hour room service, meeting rooms for up to 800, foreign currency exchange, secretarial services, audiovisual equipment, photocopiers, computers, translation services, and express checkout. Brook St., W1 (phone: 171-629-8860; 212-838-3110 in New York City; 800-223-6800 elsewhere in the US; fax: 171-499-2210).

**Connaught** Another stronghold of 19th-century Britain, luxurious and intimate, that soon will have you feeling like a distinguished guest at Lord Hyphen's townhouse. Most impressive are the small details—like tea served in a private lounge reserved only for guests, and the white linen mats laid out every night at your bedside. Small (only 90 rooms and suites)—with a tenaciously faithful clientele—it sometimes seems to be booked several generations in advance. Some may be put off by the hauteur. The two dining rooms each have earned a Michelin star (see *Delightful Dining*). Business facilities include 24-hour room service, a concierge, secretarial services, photocopiers, and foreign currency exchange. Carlos Pl., W1 (phone: 171-499-7070; 212-838-3110 in New York City; 800-223-6800 elsewhere in the US; fax: 171-495-3262).

**Dorchester** The grande dame of London hostelries is more elegant than ever. All 252 rooms and 55 suites have beautiful bed linen and superbly designed bathrooms with Italian marble. (If you can, get the Oliver Messel Suite, whose bedroom, bath, and sitting room were decorated by the great theater designer.) Treat yourself to an elegant afternoon tea in the pink marble *Promenade*. Tuxedoed waiters serve a variety of sandwiches, as well as excellent teas, scones with clotted cream, the best strawberry jam in London, and pastries. And dinner at the *Grill* or *Terrace* restaurant is always a treat. The *Oriental* restaurant has earned a Michelin star (see *Eating Out*), and there is an exclusive basement nightspot—the *Dorchester Club*. The *Dorchester Spa,* featuring Elizabeth Arden products, is a luxurious health club. Business facilities include 24-hour room service, meeting rooms for up to 550, a concierge, foreign currency exchange, secretarial services, audiovisual equipment, photocopiers, computers, translation services, and express checkout. Park La., W1 (phone: 171-629-8888; 800-727-9820; fax: 171-409-0114).

**Ritz** One of the city's finest and most elegant hostelries, this property recently came under the management of Mandarin Oriental, a Hong Kong–based hotel group. The 129 luxurious guestrooms and suites are lavishly decorated. Tea here is as vital a British ritual as the coronation: In probably the most formal tearoom in the city, gracious white-tied waiters carrying silver trays serve guests in the lovely Louis XIV–style *Palm Court* (reservations necessary at least two weeks in advance for weekends and a week in advance for weekdays). The dining room is equally splendid, with its lovely interior columns, opulent ceiling frescoes, and a view of *Green Park.* Business facilities include 24-hour room service, meeting rooms for up to 80, a concierge, foreign currency exchange, secretarial services, audiovisual equipment, photocopiers, computers, translation services, and express checkout. Piccadilly, W1 (phone: 171-493-8181; 800-526-6566; fax: 171-493-2687).

**Savoy** This 200-room hostelry is to theater what the *Sacher* in Vienna is to music. On The Strand, and very near *Covent Garden* and Waterloo Bridge, this grande dame (she's now 106) remains one of *the* places to stay in London; its lobby is often a *Who's Who* of the international entertainment world. The atmosphere is gently Edwardian, but the management is contemporary—and adept at catering to the demands of plutocrats from every part of the planet. A health club is cleverly sited above the famous *Savoy Theatre,* restored to its former grandeur after the damage caused by a 1990 fire. In addition, there's the *River* restaurant, with a splendid view of the Thames and *Big Ben,* and the legendary *Savoy Grill* (see *Eating Out*); hotel guests can have tea in an open foyer off the lobby. Business facilities include 24-hour room service, meeting rooms for up to 600, a concierge, foreign currency exchange, secretarial services, audiovisual equipment, computers, translation services, and express checkout. The Strand, WC2 (phone: 171-836-4343; 800-63-SAVOY; fax: 171-240-6040).

---

### VERY EXPENSIVE

**Berkeley** Remarkably understated, this 160-room hotel in Knightsbridge manages to preserve its impeccably high standards while keeping a low profile. There is a restaurant featuring classic French fare, a health club and a rooftop gym with pool. Business facilities include 24-hour room service, meeting rooms for up to 200, a concierge, foreign currency exchange, secretarial services, translation services, audiovisual equipment, photocopiers, and express checkout. Wilton Pl., SW1 (phone: 171-235-6000; 212-838-3110 in New York City; 800-223-6800 elsewhere in the US; fax: 171-235-4330).

**Fortyseven Park Street** Once one of our most cherished secrets, this now very popular hotel (a Relais & Châteaux member) combines English character with French flair. The 52 large, beautifully decorated apartments, featuring full kitchens and marble baths, are ideal for long-term stays. The luxurious furnishings are in the best English taste; after a recent £3-million renovation, the decor now features muted, autumnal colors. Breakfast alone is worth crossing the Atlantic to experience, since "room service" here is provided by the elegant *Le Gavroche* restaurant downstairs (see *Delightful Dining*). The location, roughly between *Hyde Park* and Grosvenor Square, also is ideal. A drawback is that the lounge has no liquor license. Business facilities include 24-hour room service, meeting rooms for up to 20, a concierge, foreign currency exchange, secretarial services, audiovisual equipment, photocopiers, computers, and translation services. 47 Park St., W1 (phone: 171-491-7282; 800-451-5536; fax: 171-491-7281).

**Four Seasons** Don't be deceived by the modern exterior; everything is traditional (and wonderful) within. A fine example of the superb service routinely offered by members of the Canadian chain, this hotel offers 228 rooms (including 27 suites) that are comfortable, tastefully furnished, and spacious. The breakfast buffet is delightful, the restaurant is first-rate, and there is a fully equipped fitness center. Business facilities include 24-hour room service, meeting rooms for up to 400, a concierge, foreign currency exchange, secretarial services, audiovisual equipment, photocopiers, computers, translation services, and express checkout. Hamilton Pl., off Piccadilly, W1 (phone: 171-499-0888; 800-332-3442; fax: 171-493-1895).

**Grosvenor House** This elegant 454-room (including 77 suites and 144 apartments with kitchenettes) grande dame facing *Hyde Park* has a health club, a pool, some interesting shops; the much-lauded and Michelin-starred *Nico at 90* restaurant (see *Eating Out*); the *Park Lounge,* which serves traditional afternoon tea; and the exclusive *Crown Club* on the seventh floor for members only—usually businesspeople who require special services. Business facilities include 24-hour room service, meeting rooms for up to 1,500, a concierge, foreign currency exchange, secretarial services, audiovisual equipment, photocopiers, computers, translation services, and express checkout. Park La., W1 (phone: 171-499-6363; 800-225-5843; fax: 171-493-3341).

**Inter-Continental** Right on Hyde Park Corner, with a view of the Horse Guards as they trot off for the Changing of the Guard, this hotel has just completed a £3.4-million renovation; its 467 well-proportioned rooms (including 38 suites) are equipped with luxurious amenities, including refrigerated bars. Modern and comfortable, *Le Soufflé* restaurant is an added lure. Business facilities include 24-hour room service, meeting rooms for up to 1,000, a concierge, foreign currency exchange, secretarial services, audiovisual equipment, photocopiers, computers, translation services, and express checkout. 1 Hamilton Pl., Hyde Park Corner, W1 (phone: 171-409-3131; 800-327-0200; fax: 171-493-3476).

**Lanesborough** Just steps from the *Wellington Gate* in the tony Belgravia area, this luxury hotel at Hyde Park Corner is built within the landmark structure that was *St. George's Hospital* from 1734 to 1980. The interior design re-creates the feeling of an elegant 19th-century residence. There are 95 superbly appointed guestrooms, including 46 suites, some with steam showers and Jacuzzis. Dinner dances on Fridays and Saturdays and Sunday brunches with live jazz are held in the somewhat LA-ish *Conservatory,* which also offers light meals and afternoon tea. Both the club-like Library and the Withdrawing Room have bars. Business facilities include 24-hour room and butler service, meeting rooms for up to 50, a concierge, foreign currency exchange, secretarial services, in-room fax machines, two-line telephones, audiovisual equipment, photocopiers, computers, translation services, and express checkout. Knightsbridge and Grosvenor Crescent, SW1 (phone: 171-259-5599; 800-999-1828; fax: 171-259-5606).

**Langham Hilton** Originally opened in 1865 as "the first grand hotel of London," it was known for its "rising rooms" (elevators) and famous guests, including Mark Twain, Arturo Toscanini, and Oscar Wilde. The property offers 385 rooms (including 26 suites), and its several restaurants include the *Palm Court,* serving light meals and snacks around the clock, and *Tsar's,* specializing in vodka and caviar. Business facilities include 24-hour room service, meeting rooms for up to 320, a concierge, foreign currency exchange, secretarial services, audiovisual equipment, photocopiers, computers, translation services, and express checkout. 1c Portland Pl., W1 (phone: 171-636-1000; 800-HILTONS; fax: 171-323-2340).

**London Hilton International** Off Hyde Park Corner, near shopping and West End theaters, this contemporary high-rise offers comfortable accommodations (448 rooms, including 54 suites) and views of the park and the city. Special attention to executives includes a conference and business floor, multilingual switchboard, and private dining rooms. There's every conceivable service, plus three restaurants—the rooftop *Windows,* with a stunning view of the city; *Trader Vic's* (Polynesian); and the *Brasserie.* Business facilities include 24-hour room service, meeting rooms for up to 2,000, a concierge, foreign currency exchange, secretarial services, audiovisual equipment, photocopiers, computers, translation services, and express checkout. 22 Park La., W1 (phone: 171-493-8000; 800-HILTONS; fax: 171-493-4957).

**Le Meridien** Located between the *Royal Academy* and Piccadilly Circus, this hotel has a lofty, Edwardian marble entrance hall that leads to the 263 rooms, including 41 suites. Some of the accommodations here are on the smallish, dark side. The one-Michelin-star *Oak Room* restaurant offers fine French fare. The *Terrace* restaurant, on the second floor, has a glass roof, and the space beneath the hotel has been transformed into a very good health club. Business facilities include 24-hour room service, meeting rooms for up to 250, a concierge, foreign currency exchange, secretarial services, audiovisual equipment, photocopiers, computers, translation services, and express checkout. Piccadilly, W1 (phone: 171-734-8000; 800-543-4300; fax: 171-437-3574).

**St. James's Club** For $675 for the first year ($450 thereafter) and an introduction by a member, you can join this exclusive residential club in the heart of London (though you don't need to bother for your first stay). Guests have full use of club suites. Good food is served in the downstairs dining room. Business facilities include 24-hour room service, meeting rooms for up to 50, a concierge, foreign currency exchange, secretarial services, audiovisual equipment, photocopiers, computers, and translation services. 7 Park Pl., SW1 (phone: 171-629-7688; fax: 171-491-0987).

### EXPENSIVE

**Abbey Court** In the Notting Hill Gate area near *Portobello Market,* this elegant hotel has 22 guestrooms of various sizes, all with hair dryers and trouser presses. Breakfast is served in the room, and 24-hour room service is available. No restaurant. Business facilities include meeting rooms for up to 20, a concierge, secretarial services, and photocopiers. 20 Pembridge Gardens, W2 (phone: 171-221-7518; fax: 171-792-0858).

**Athenaeum Hotel and Apartments** Reopened last year after a $12-million renovation, this property is ideally located in the heart of the stylish Mayfair district, overlooking *Green Park* and *Buckingham Palace.* The 111 guestrooms and 12 suites are decorated in traditional English style with antique furnishings and floral fabrics; amenities include marble baths, mini-bars, in-room safes, satellite TV, compact disc players, and VCRs. The luxurious *Athenaeum Apartments,* located in a row of Edwardian townhouses next to the hotel, are also available. The 33 one-, two-, and three-bedroom apartments are equipped with a full kitchen (including a microwave oven), living and sitting rooms, and a washing machine and dryer; in addition, residents have access to all of the hotel's facilities. *Bullochs,* the hotel dining room, serves Mediterranean fare in an informal atmosphere; and the *Windsor Lounge* offers light snacks and teas around the clock. There's also the Scottish-style *Malt Whisky Bar,* which boasts a selection of 56 rare whiskies. Other facilities include 24-hour room service, complimentary transportation from the airport, baby-sitting services, and a health club. Business facilities include meeting rooms for up to 55, a concierge, secretarial services, audiovisual equipment, photocopiers, computers, and translation services. 116 Piccadilly, W1 (phone: 171-499-3464; 800-335-3300; fax: 171-493-1860; 800-335-3200).

**Basil Street** A relic with a reputation for graceful, old-fashioned service and antique furnishings to match. It draws a faithful international clientele who, if they can reserve one of its 94 smallish rooms, prefer staying here to patronizing any of the newer hotels. It sits just down the street from *Harrods.* Business facilities include 24-hour room service, meeting rooms for up to 300, a concierge, foreign currency exchange, secretarial services, audiovisual equipment, photocopiers, and computers. 8 Basil St., SW3 (phone: 171-581-3311; fax: 171-581-3693).

**Beaufort** Tranquil and elegant, it is composed of two Victorian houses in the heart of fashionable Knightsbridge. It offers 52 comfortable and attractive rooms, each with stereo/cassette player, hair dryer, magazines and books, a decanter of sherry, and even a teddy bear for the youngsters. Breakfast is brought on a tray each morning; there is no restaurant, but there are many in the area. All drinks and snacks are included. Convenient to shopping (*Harrods* is around the corner). Business facilities include a fax machine. 33 Beaufort Gardens, SW3 (phone: 171-584-5252; 800-888-1199; fax: 171-589-2834).

**Blake's** Popular with visiting Hollywood royalty, this 52-room complex of Victorian townhouses (including nine suites) offers charming accommodations in an Old World setting. The hotel also boasts a first-rate restaurant. Also offered is some of the most attentive service in town, as well as features such as laundry service, 24-hour room service, a concierge, foreign currency exchange, secretarial services, audiovisual equipment, photocopiers, computers, and translation services. 33 Roland Gardens, SW7 (phone: 171-370-6701; fax: 171-373-0442).

**Britannia** Mahogany furniture, velvet armchairs, rooms painted in colors you might choose at home—all tasteful and solid. This link in the Inter-Continental chain has 316 rooms and suites, as well as three restaurants. Business facilities include 24-hour room service, meeting rooms for up to 100, a concierge, foreign currency exchange, secretarial services, audiovisual equipment, computers, translation services, and express checkout. Grosvenor Sq., W1 (phone: 171-629-9400; 800-327-0200; fax: 171-629-7736).

**Brown's** As English as you can get, it's been renovated, yet still retains a pleasing, quaint, Victorian charm. With 109 rooms (including six suites), this hotel is strong on service. If it's an English tea you're after, this is the place (casual dress is acceptable, but not shorts). Business facilities include 24-hour room service, meeting rooms for up to 40, a concierge, foreign currency exchange, secretarial services, photocopiers, and translation services. Dover St., W1 (phone: 171-493-6020; fax: 171-493-9381).

**Cadogan** A comfortable 75-room place, redolent of Edwardian England. Oscar Wilde was arrested here, and Lillie Langtry, who was having an affair with the Prince of Wales (later Edward VII), lived next door. The furniture and decor are original, but modern conveniences are offered as well. There is a restaurant. Business facilities include 24-hour room service, meeting rooms for up to 40, a concierge, foreign currency exchange, secretarial services, photocopiers, and express checkout. 75 Sloane St., SW1 (phone: 171-235-7141; fax: 171-245-0994).

**Capital** This intimate hostelry, just steps from *Harrods*, has 48 cozy rooms and suites with Ralph Lauren–like decor, a wonderful wood-paneled bar, and one of the finest dining places in London (see *Eating Out*). And it's one of only two London hotels in the prestigious Relais & Châteaux group (*Fortyseven Park Street* is the other—see above). The eight suites are homey in the very best sense. Long-term visitors (which means a minimum of three *months*) also can choose to stay in one of the hotel's super-luxurious apartments, located just steps away from the main building. These comfortable suites include a choice of one, two, or three bedrooms, living rooms with ample dining tables, and fully equipped kitchens. Residents here may take advantage of all of the hotel's amenities, which include 24-hour room service, foreign currency exchange, meeting rooms for up to 24, a concierge, secretarial services, audiovisual equipment, photocopiers, computers, translation services, and express checkout. 22 Basil St., SW3 (phone: 171-589-5171; 800-926-3199; fax: 171-225-0011).

**Chesterfield** In the heart of Mayfair and near *Hyde Park,* this small Georgian mansion has an exclusive elegance. Its 110 bedrooms are modernized and well equipped. There's a restaurant, a wood-paneled library, and a small bar that opens onto a flower-filled patio. Business facilities include 24-hour room service, meeting rooms for up to 110, a concierge, foreign currency exchange, audiovisual equipment, photocopiers, and computers. 35 Charles St., W1 (phone: 171-491-2622; fax: 171-491-4793).

**Churchill** Still thought of as an "American"-style hotel, it remains a favorite among travelers headed to London from the US. This is a well-run 448-room place, with a pleasant restaurant and a snack room that serves the best bacon and eggs in London. Business facilities include 24-hour room service, meeting rooms for up to 300, a concierge, foreign currency exchange, secretarial services, audiovisual equipment, photocopiers, fax machines, translation services, and an executive floor. Portman Sq., W1 (phone: 171-486-5800; fax: 171-486-1255).

**Cranley** Sister hotel of *One Cranley Place* (see below), this is larger, with 36 rooms and suites and plusher furnishings. The unusual decor is bolder than that found in most townhouse hotels. With microwave ovens in the kitchenettes, plus showers and firm mattresses straight from the US, the aim is to provide the comforts of home. Secretarial services and photocopiers are available. 10-12 Bina Gardens, SW5 (phone: 171-373-0123; 313-995-4400 in Michigan; 800-553-2582 elsewhere in the US; fax: 171-373-9497; 313-995-1050).

**Delmere** This lovely, late Georgian hostelry was designed by architect Samuel Pepys Cockerell, a student of Benjamin H. Latrobe, who designed the south wing of the Capitol building in Washington, DC. Its 40 rooms have private showers or baths, hair dryers, and the makings for tea and coffee. There is also a bar and an Italian restaurant, *La Perla. Paddington Station,* where trains depart to Bath and south Wales, is a mere five-minute walk away, as is *Hyde Park.* Business facilities include room service, a small meeting room, a concierge, secretarial services, audiovisual equipment, photocopiers, and translation services. 130 Sussex Gardens, W2 (phone: 171-706-3344; fax: 171-262-1863).

**Draycott** The 26 rooms here are each distinctively decorated. While there's no restaurant, there is 24-hour room service, as well as a drawing room. Staying here is like living in a fashionable London townhouse, and guests must register 48 hours before arrival to become members upon their first visit. Business facilities include meeting rooms for up to 20, a concierge, foreign currency exchange, secretarial services, audiovisual equipment, photocopiers, computers, translation services, and express checkout. 24-26 Cadogan Gardens, SW3 (phone: 171-730-6466; fax: 171-730-0236).

**Dukes** Despite its modest size (only 38 rooms and 26 suites), this establishment exudes prestige. All the guestrooms and public areas are decorated with great taste and warmth, and the snug location, down a quiet cul-de-sac, makes guests feel protected and private. Some of the suites are actually former apartments, with their own small—but complete—kitchens. Piccadilly, *Buckingham Palace,* Trafalgar Square, Hyde Park Corner, and the shops of Bond Street and the *Burlington Arcade* are all within walking distance. Business facilities include 24-hour room service, meeting rooms for up to 70, a concierge, foreign currency exchange, secretarial services, audiovisual equipment, photocopiers, translation services, and express checkout. 35 St. James's Pl., SW1 (phone: 171-491-4840; 800-222-0939; fax: 171-493-1264).

**Egerton House** Overlooking two garden squares, this property in Knightsbridge is set in a fashionable townhouse. The 30 spacious guestrooms are individually decorated with antiques, traditional English floral fabrics, porcelain, and oil paintings; among the amenities are marble baths, mini-bars, and satellite TV. The atmosphere has an old-fashioned tranquillity, and the service is friendly and attentive. There is a restaurant. Business services include 24-hour room service, photocopiers, and secretarial services. 17-19 Egerton Ter., SW3 (phone: 171-589-2412; 800-473-9492; fax: 171-584-6540).

**Gatwick Hilton International** This 550-room hotel provides much-needed accommodations for the ever-increasing number of visitors using the *Gatwick* gateway. It is connected to the terminal by an enclosed walkway. There are two restaurants, two bars, a health club, and lounge service. Business facilities include 24-hour room service, meeting rooms for up to 400, a concierge, a bank, secretarial services, audiovisual equipment, photocopiers, computers, and express checkout. *Gatwick Airport* (phone: 1293-518080; 800-HILTONS; fax: 1293-528980).

**Halcyon** The two Belle Epoque mansions that are the foundations of this property have been restored to their original glamour. Some of the 44 guestrooms feature four-poster beds and Jacuzzis. Its restaurant is one of London's best hotel dining spots. Business facilities include 24-hour room service, meeting rooms for up to 40, a conference center, a concierge, foreign currency exchange, secretarial services, audiovisual equipment, translation services, and express checkout. 81 Holland Park, W11 (phone: 171-727-7288; fax: 171-229-8516).

**Halkin** This intimate property in the Belgravia area, right near *Buckingham Palace* and *Hyde Park,* boasts 41 individually designed rooms and suites, furnished with a mixture of contemporary and antique pieces. The hotel's restaurant serves fine Italian food. Business facilities include 24-hour room service, meeting rooms for up to 35, a concierge, foreign currency exchange, secretarial services, audiovisual equipment, photocopiers, computers, fax machines in each room, translation services, and express checkout. 5-6 Halkin St., SW1 (phone: 171-333-1000; 800-345-3457; fax: 171-333-1100).

**Heathrow Hilton** A first-rate hotel at *Heathrow Airport,* with its own covered walkway to Terminal 4. It has a five-story glass atrium enclosing a waterfall; there also are three restaurants. The 400 rooms are amazingly quiet (given the location); amenities include everything from trouser presses to an in-room review of accounts and express checkout—on your TV screen. The health club has a pool, gym, steamrooms, and saunas. Business facilities include 24-hour room service, meeting rooms for up to 240, a concierge, foreign currency exchange, secretarial services, audiovisual equipment, photocopiers, and express checkout. Terminal 4, *Heathrow Airport,* Hounslow, Middlesex (phone: 181-759-7755; 800-HILTONS; fax: 181-759-7579).

**Holiday Inn Mayfair** The Regency-style architecture is unusual for this hotel chain. In London's prestigious Mayfair neighborhood, the property has 185 rooms and the à la carte *Nightingale's* restaurant, with a pianist in the cocktail bar in the evenings. Business facilities include 24-hour room service, meeting rooms for up to 70, a concierge, foreign currency exchange, secretarial services, audiovisual equipment, photocopiers, computers, translation services, and express checkout. 3 Berkeley St., W1 (phone: 171-493-8282; 800-HOLIDAY; fax: 171-629-2827).

**Hyde Park** The only hotel in *Hyde Park,* this establishment hosted Rudolph Valentino in the 1920s and George VI and Queen Elizabeth in 1948. The 186 spacious bedrooms and suites feature antique furniture and modern baths. Some rooms also have spectacular views of the park. With huge windows providing panoramic views of *Hyde Park,* the *Park Room* restaurant offers delicious meals, including breakfast—but avoid afternoon tea here. A second dining room, *The Restaurant,* is run by renowned chef Marco Pierre White (see *Eating Out*). Business facilities include 24-hour room service, meeting rooms for up to 250, a concierge, foreign currency exchange, secretarial services, audiovisual equipment, photocopiers, and express checkout. 66 Knightsbridge, SW1 (phone: 171-235-2000; 800-225-5843; fax: 171-235-4552).

**London Marriott** Close to the US Embassy and West End shopping, it's bright and busy, with 223 comfortable rooms and a full range of facilities—a restaurant, café-lounge, shops, a fitness center, and attentive staff. Business facilities include 24-hour room service, meeting rooms for up to 1,000, a concierge, foreign currency exchange, secretarial services, audiovisual equipment, photocopiers, computers, translation services, and express checkout. Grosvenor Sq., W1 (phone: 171-493-1232; 800-228-9290; fax: 171-491-3201).

**Montcalm** A mid-size, elegant hostelry that has a lovely Georgian façade, an interior, and topnotch service. Its 98 rooms have all the usual comforts, and its 14 suites are especially luxurious. There's a bar and *Les Célébrités* restaurant. Business facilities include 24-hour room service, meeting rooms for up to 70, a concierge, foreign currency exchange, secretarial services, audiovisual equipment, and computers. Great Cumberland Pl., W1 (phone: 171-402-4288; fax: 171-724-9180).

**Number Sixteen** In four adjoining townhouses, this comfortable 36-room spot accents personal service. Rooms (some of which have terraces overlooking a conservatory and gardens) feature fresh flowers; most have private baths or showers (though a few singles do not). Continental breakfast is served in all rooms. There is a small bar, but no restaurant. Because of its quiet atmosphere, it is not suitable for small children. Photocopiers are available. 16 Sumner Pl., SW7 (phone: 171-589-5232; fax: 171-584-8615).

**Park Lane** If you don't mind street noise, the site of this hotel, in the heart of the West End, is appealing. Some of the 300 rooms (including 56 suites) have views of *Green Park* across the street, and there is a gym. *Bracewell's* restaurant is an elegant dining spot, and *Brasserie on the Park* is a less formal option. Business facilities include 24-hour room service, meeting rooms for up to 500, a concierge, foreign currency exchange, secretarial services, audiovisual equipment, photocopiers, computers, translation services, and express checkout. Piccadilly, W1 (phone: 171-499-6321; fax: 171-499-1965).

**Pelham** Actually two joined mid-Victorian townhouses in South Kensington that offer 34 stylish (though smallish) rooms and three suites, just steps away from the *Victoria and Albert, Natural History,* and *Science Museums.* There is also a restaurant and two lounges. Business facilities include 24-hour room service, a concierge, foreign currency exchange, secretarial services, photocopiers, audiovisual equipment, and express checkout. 15 Cromwell Pl., SW7 (phone: 171-589-8288; 800-553-6671; fax: 171-584-8444).

**Radisson Mountbatten** The life of Earl Mountbatten of Burma is the theme throughout this hotel's public rooms: Even the restaurant is called *L'Admiral,* since the earl was a navy man. All 127 rooms feature Italian marble bathrooms, satellite TV, and in-house movies; seven suites have Jacuzzis. A vegetarian tea (scones without animal fat) is served in the country-house–style drawing room. Business facilities include 24-hour room service, meeting rooms for up to 75, a concierge, foreign currency exchange, photocopiers, and express checkout. 20 Monmouth St. at Seven Dials, *Covent Garden,* WC2 (phone: 171-836-4300; 800-333-3333; fax: 171-240-3540).

**Regent** One of London's newest ultra-posh hotels is also one of its oldest. Originally opened in 1899 next to *Marylebone Station,* this hotel had its career cut short by World War II, but it is now restored to its former splendor. The 309 rooms are richly decorated with Victorian-era furnishings, but modern amenities abound (including two-line telephones and fax machines). The dining room serves French and northern Italian dishes; *Cellars* and the glassed-in *Winter Garden* (which incorporates the original courtyard) serve light fare. Business facilities include 24-hour room service, meeting space for up to 350, a concierge, 24-hour foreign currency exchange, a fully equipped business center, translation services, and express checkout. 222 Marylebone Rd., NW1 (phone: 171-631-8000; 212-838-3110 in New York City; 800-223-6800 elsewhere in the US; fax: 171-631-8080).

**Stafford** In a quiet side street close to the city center, this property (owned by Cunard) is where many American media organizations often lodge visiting correspondents. The main building has 62 rooms; in addition, the 18th-century stables down the alleyway have 12 "Carriage House" rooms which are decorated in smashing style (complete with compact disc and stereo systems and fax lines). Enjoy tea in the cozy drawing room, complete with fireplaces and comfortable furniture. Business facilities include 24-hour room service, meeting rooms for up to 80, a concierge, foreign currency exchange, secretarial services, audiovisual equipment, photocopiers, computers, translation services, and express checkout. 16 St. James's Pl., SW1 (phone: 171-493-0111; 800-525-4800; fax: 171-493-7121).

**22 Jermyn Street** Nestled in the heart of the West End, on one of the city's most fashionable streets, this privately owned, club-like hostelry offers intimacy, charm, and attentive service just a stone's throw from London's best shopping, theater, and other attractions. The 18 rooms and suites are decorated with modern and antique furniture; amenities include cable TV, two direct-dial phones, fax machines, and luxurious marble bathrooms. There's no restaurant (although a complimentary breakfast and 24-hour room service are provided). Other features include a concierge, valet service, access to a nearby health club, meeting space for up to 12, foreign currency exchange, and a full business center. 22 Jermyn St., SW1 (phone: 171-734-2353; 800-682-7808; fax: 171-734-0750).

**Whites** What used to be three 19th-century merchant bankers' private homes now make up one of London's most charming small hostelries, with 54 rooms. It has a cobbled forecourt, a glass-and-iron-covered entryway, even a wood-paneled writing room where afternoon tea is served. Choose a front room overlooking *Hyde Park,* and take breakfast on the balcony. Business facilities include 24-hour room service, meeting rooms for up to 30, a concierge, foreign currency exchange, secretarial services, audiovisual equipment, photocopiers, computers, translation services, and express checkout. 90-92 Lancaster Gate, W2 (phone: 171-262-2711; fax: 171-262-2147).

### MODERATE

**Academy** Not far from the *University of London* and the *British Museum,* this 33-room property in three Georgian townhouses scores for its handy location. Colorful modern art and pretty floral curtains and bedspreads make the rooms cheery whether they are on the ground floor or upstairs. Paperbacks can be borrowed from the library, which overlooks a small patio garden at the back. The stylish restaurant and bar are in the basement. Another attraction—there is an "American Friends" discount (about 10%) for travelers from the US. 17-21 Gower St., WC1 (phone: 171-631-4115; 800-678-3096; fax: 171-636-3442).

**Claverley** A favorite with Americans, this establishment in Knightsbridge has 32 rooms (including five suites), most of which have private baths; some rooms have four-poster beds. Guests are invited to help themselves to newspapers, coffee, tea, and cookies in the reading room. A fine British breakfast (including kippers and kedgeree) is served in the morning (however, there is no restaurant). Just a block from *Harrods.* Secretarial service and photocopiers are available. 13 Beaufort Gardens, SW3 (phone: 171-589-8541; fax: 171-584-3410).

**Copthorne Tara** Situated on a quiet corner of Kensington, this 825-room giant is just minutes from bustling High Street and within walking distance of the *Albert Hall,* the *Victoria and Albert Museum,* and the *Natural History Museum.* The rooms are on the small side, but all have hair dryers. There also are six fully equipped business suites, four restaurants, a nightclub, a baby-sitting service, and a garage, plus 24-hour room service, meeting rooms for up to 500, a concierge, foreign currency exchange, secretarial services, audiovisual equipment, photocopiers, computers, translation services, and express checkout. Wright's La., W8 (phone: 171-937-7211; 800-44-UTELL; fax: 171-937-7100).

**Diplomat** Small and charming, with an 1882 white façade, it has 27 rooms. It is comfortable, friendly, and affordable. There is a breakfast room, but no restaurant. In Belgravia at 2 Chesham St., SW1 (phone: 171-235-1544; fax: 171-259-6153).

**Dorset Square** Set on a lovely garden square (formerly Thomas Lord's own private cricket grounds) in the heart of London, this Georgian house is one of the city's more charming hotels. Guests can choose from 37 rooms and suites. There is a restaurant and 24-hour room service. Photocopiers and secretarial services are available. 39-40 Dorset Sq., NW1 (phone: 171-723-7874; fax: 171-724-3328).

**Durrants** This elegant Regency-style hotel has a splendid location behind the *Wallace Collection.* It has been family-run for over 70 years, and all 95 rooms have retained their character while being kept comfortably up-to-date. Business facilities include 24-hour room service, meeting rooms for up to 45, a concierge, foreign currency exchange, audiovisual equipment, secretarial services, fax machines, and photocopiers. George St., W1 (phone: 171-935-8131; fax: 171-487-3510).

**Ebury Court** A quaint hotel with smallish but cozy rooms and an intimate atmosphere (the owners dine with guests in the restaurant). Its faithful clientele testifies to its comfort, suitability, and "country-house" touches. Half of the 42 rooms have private baths or showers. There is meeting space for up to 40, a concierge, and photocopiers. 28 Ebury St., SW1 (phone: 171-730-8147; fax: 171-823-5966).

**Forte Crest St. James'** This modern 254-room property offers one of the best locations in central London, a block from Piccadilly. There is a restaurant and a pleasant bar. Business facilities include 24-hour room service, meeting rooms for up to 80, a concierge, foreign currency exchange, a full business center, translation services, and express checkout. 81 Jermyn St., SW1 (phone: 171-930-2111; 800-225-5843; fax: 171-839-2125).

**Gore** Ten-foot-tall potted palms and a collection of 5,000 prints on the walls set the tone in this 54-room hostelry, just five minutes from *Albert Hall* and the shopping on Kensington High Street. Wall safes are an unusual addition to conveniences such as hair dryers and mini-bars in the rooms. If you can't stay in the Judy Garland room, with its carved medieval-style bed, at least ask to see it. The *Bistro 190* is a popular dining spot, and room service delivers from 7:30 AM to 12:30 AM. Business facilities include meeting rooms for up to 14, a concierge, foreign currency exchange, secretarial services, audiovisual equipment, photocopiers, and express checkout. 189 Queen's Gate, SW7 (phone: 171-584-6601; fax: 171-589-8127).

**Harewood** This modern property is well maintained by a pleasant, efficient staff. Some of its 93 rooms have private terraces, and there's a clubhouse-style lounge that serves food. Business facilities include meeting rooms for up to 30, secretarial services, audiovisual equipment, and photocopiers. Harewood Row, NW1 (phone: 171-262-2707; fax: 171-262-2975).

**Hazlitt's** Formerly the nurses' quarters for the *Royal Women's Hospital* during Victorian times, this row of three adjacent Georgian terrace houses now serves as a cozy bed and breakfast establishment. The *National Trust* building has 23 rooms, each individually decorated in Victorian flavor. Hung on the walls are 2,000 prints depicting Victorian London. Photocopiers are available. 6 Frith St., W1 (phone: 171-434-1771; fax: 171-439-1524).

**L'Hotel** Owned by the same folks as the wonderful *Capital* just a step away, this comfortable 12-room bed and breakfast place has a New England colonial–style decor, with pine furniture and a huge patchwork quilt hung over the stairs. All rooms have mini-bars and kettles for making tea or coffee; four rooms have fireplaces. Complimentary continental breakfast is served in *Le Metro* bistro next door or in your room, and laundry and dry-cleaning services are available. Business facilities can be arranged through the *Capital*. 28 Basil St., SW3 (phone: 171-589-6286; 800-926-3199; fax: 171-225-0011).

**One Cranley Place** Set among a row of Regency houses in South Kensington, this charming and personal bed and breakfast establishment is like a private home. Unique antique pieces furnish the 10 rooms (from double rooms to luxury double suites), and fireplaces in some rooms and the common areas make for a cozy atmosphere. Breakfast is served in the dining room or guests' rooms; tea and light snacks also are available. Guests have access to the services of its sister property, the *Cranley* (see above). 1 Cranley Pl., SW7 (phone: 171-589-7944; 313-995-4400 in Michigan; 800-553-2582 elsewhere in the US; fax: 171-225-3931; 313-995-1050).

**Pastoria** In the heart of the West End, near all theaters, this pleasant, comfortable little hotel has 58 rooms, a bar, and a restaurant. Business facilities include 24-hour room service, meeting rooms for up to 60, a concierge, foreign currency exchange, secretarial services, photocopiers, and translation services. St. Martin's St., WC2 (phone: 171-930-8641; fax: 171-925-0551).

**Pembridge Court** Recommended by bed and breakfast aficionados, this cozy Victorian townhouse has a variety of room sizes, from large doubles to tiny singles. The bistro serves English breakfasts and French fare for dinner. Business facilities include meeting rooms for up to 20, a concierge, and photocopiers. 34 Pembridge Gardens, W2 (phone: 171-229-9977; fax: 171-727-4982).

**Portobello** Antiques are a main feature in this hostelry, converted from two Victorian row houses, located near the *Portobello Market*. The 25 rooms come in all shapes and sizes; the bathrooms tend to be quite small. There is an informal restaurant and bar. Business facilities include photocopiers and express checkout. 22 Stanley Gardens, W11 (phone: 171-727-2777; fax: 171-792-9641).

### INEXPENSIVE

**Bickenhall** This Georgian townhouse near the *Baker Street* tube station boasts 18 comfortable rooms and bathrooms with showers and hair dryers (three rooms on the top floor share a bath), as well as a quiet location. No restaurant. 119 Gloucester Pl., W1 (phone: 171-935-3401; fax: 171-224-0614).

**Blandford** Another pleasant bed and breakfast establishment, this one has 33 rooms, decorated in pastel greens and pinks. No restaurant. 80 Chiltern St., W1 (phone: 171-486-3103; fax: 171-487-2786).

**Camelot** In this quaint townhouse hotel, each of the 44 rooms is a different size and shape, and each features different amenities—for example, one of the guestrooms has a four-poster bed and another a little balcony. In the basement dining room (which serves breakfast only), the wood floor, fireplace, and pine tables lend a rustic look. 45-47 Norfolk Sq., W2 (phone: 171-723-9118; fax: 171-402-3412).

**Elizabeth** Overlooking a pretty garden square, this family-run hotel offers 40 neat rooms of varying sizes. Though short on fancy amenities (the rooms do not have phones or TV sets, and only 28 have private baths), this place provides good, basic accommodations for a reasonable price. No restaurant. 37 Eccleston Sq., SW1 (phone: 171-628-6812).

**Hallam** Incorporated into a modern office complex near Oxford Circus, this well-run establishment has 25 guestrooms that are small, but clean and nicely decorated. No restaurant. 12 Hallam St., W1 (phone: 171-580-1166; fax: 171-323-4527).

**Hotel la Place** This is a fine bed and breakfast place with 24 rooms, each featuring one king-size or two double beds; some rooms also have mini-bars. A full English breakfast is served in the morning; there is also a restaurant. Business facilities include 24-hour room service, meeting rooms for up to 30, a concierge, photocopiers, and translation services. 17 Nottingham Pl., W1 (phone: 171-486-2323; fax: 171-486-4335).

**Winchester** Near *Victoria Station,* this 18-room bed and breakfast place is in an old townhouse with a Victorian-style façade. Guests are treated to an English breakfast in the morning. No restaurant. 17 Belgrave Rd., SW1 (phone: 171-828-2972; fax: 171-828-5191).

**Windermere** Here is an attractive hotel with 23 nicely furnished and appointed guestrooms (19 have private baths). Several of the rooms are equipped with small refrigerators in addition to the usual amenities. There's also a good dining room decorated with some surprisingly elegant touches, such as fine china and fresh flowers. 142-144 Warwick Way, SW1 (phone: 171-834-5163; fax: 171-630-8831).

### VERY INEXPENSIVE

**Alfa** Antiques and interesting knickknacks give this small establishment an eclectic charm. The 33 rooms are simply but attractively furnished. No restaurant. 78-82 Warwick Way, SW1 (phone: 171-828-8603; fax: 171-976-6536).

**Jenkins** A cozy bed and breakfast place conveniently nestled in the heart of London. The 15 small bedrooms are pleasant, with mini-fridges (no TV sets), though only seven have private baths. There is a breakfast room (prettily decked out in blue and white lace tablecloths), but no restaurant. 45 Cartwright Gardens, WC1 (phone: 171-387-2067; fax: 171-383-3139).

**Mabledon Court** A former college dormitory, this property has 32 comfortable rooms, a breakfast room, and a lounge (but no restaurant). 10 Mabledon Pl., WC1 (phone: 171-388-3866; fax: 171-387-5686).

**Sandringham** Some of the 15 guestrooms in this Victorian house have a lovely view of the city and adjacent *Hampstead Heath.* The decor is charming and homey, as is the welcome of the American couple who run the place. No restaurant. 3 Holford Rd., NW3 (phone: 171-435-1569; fax: 171-431-5932).

## REGAL RENTAL

If you're curious about what it's like to live in a royal palace, here's an opportunity to find out. At *Hampton Court Palace,* two self-catered apartments are available for rent at a moderate price. Each flat sleeps six to eight people and features a full kitchen and living room; guests have complimentary access to the rest of the palace during its normal operating hours. (For details on the palace, see *Special Places*.) To book accommodations, contact the *Landmark Trust,* Shottesbrooke, Maidenhead, Berkshire SL6 3SW, England (phone: 1628-825925).

---

EATING OUT

Once upon a time a scarce few London restaurants were known for their excellent cooking—and some visitors of times past might call that a charitable overstatement. But there's been a notable transformation. While restaurants offering really good English cooking—and not simply "chips with everything"—are still rare (and tend to be upscale and pricey), there has been a veritable explosion of good ethnic dining places.

A dinner for two will cost $200 or more at a restaurant listed as very expensive; $150 to $190, expensive; $90 to $130, moderate; and $80 or less, inexpensive. Prices do not include drinks, wine, or tips. Most London restaurants have developed the continental habit of automatically adding a service charge to the bill, so make certain you're not tipping twice. All restaurants listed below serve lunch and dinner unless otherwise noted.

For an unforgettable culinary experience we begin with our favorites (they're expensive, but you'll get your money's worth), followed by our cost and quality choices of restaurants, listed by price category.

---

**DELIGHTFUL DINING**

**Connaught** With one Michelin star apiece, the two dining rooms at the eponymous hotel are as well mannered as you'd expect at a traditional British establishment. The best dishes are those on which the empire was founded: roast beef and Yorkshire pudding, Lancashire hot pot, and gooseberry pie. After dinner, you will feel as if the gentlemen should retire to the library with a glass of port and a cigar; many still do. Closed weekends and holidays. Reservations necessary. Major credit cards accepted. Carlos Pl., W1 (phone: 171-499-7070).

**Le Gavroche** After over 70 years of rating restaurants, the *Guide Michelin* gave its first three-star rating in Britain to this most French of restaurants; though it has now lost one star, the establishment is still very special. Proprietor Albert Roux, once the chef for the Rothschild family as well as the royal household, has passed the cooking duties to his son Michel. The wine card is exceptionally long and inviting (listing over 400 items, including a 1945 Château Lafite-Rothschild for about

$1,000, though many modest vintages are available for less than $25). Closed weekends, and late December to early January. Reservations necessary (well in advance). Major credit cards accepted. 43 Upper Brook St., W1 (phone: 171-408-0881).

**Quaglino's** Yet another triumph for style magnate/restaurateur Sir Terence Conran. Named after an eatery that was *the* meeting place for London's high society in the 1930s (Edward VIII had many tête-à-têtes with Wallis Simpson here), it also occupies the same location, off Piccadilly. The decor, however, is more reminiscent of a chic French brasserie: marble, mosaics, mirrors, and gleaming metal. The bistro-style menu includes a generous seafood platter, braised oxtail, and spiced lamb with roasted onions. There's dancing on Fridays and Saturdays until the wee hours. This place is one of the city's hot spots, so plan ahead. Open daily. Reservations necessary. Major credit cards accepted. 16 Bury St., SW1 (phone: 171-930-6767).

**La Tante Claire** Run by chef Pierre Koffman and his wife, Annie, this airy, attractively decorated establishment has been awarded three Michelin stars *and* is a member of Relais & Châteaux—which puts it among very select company indeed in Britain. While fish dishes are the specialty, everything—especially the duck, calf's liver, and *pied de cochon farci aux morilles* (pig's foot stuffed with foie gras and mushrooms)—is excellent. The prix fixe lunch is a remarkably good value at about $45. Closed weekends. Reservations necessary. Major credit cards accepted. 68 Royal Hospital Rd., SW3 (phone: 171-352-6045).

## VERY EXPENSIVE

**Bibendum** Located on the second floor of *Michelin House,* it is stylishly decorated by Sir Terence Conran of the *Habitat* chain of stores. Chef Simon Hopkinson's good taste evokes English dreams of France; he serves the best roast beef in town. Open daily. Reservations necessary. Major credit cards accepted. 81 Fulham Rd., SW3 (phone: 171-581-5817).

**Chez Nico at 90 Park Lane** Popularly known as *Nico at 90,* this *très elegante,* two-Michelin-star dining room at the *Grosvenor House* hotel features the gastronomic talents of temperamental but brilliant Nico Ladenis. The excellent menu includes such French specialties as smoked salmon with trout mousse, quail pie, and langoustines with garlic butter and ginger. The wine list here is among London's best (and most expensive), and the service is superior. Closed Saturday lunch and Sundays. Reservations necessary. Major credit cards accepted. 90 Park La., W1 (phone: 171-409-1290).

**The Restaurant** The revamped (but rather blandly decorated) dining room of the *Hyde Park* hotel is presided over by renowned chef Marco Pierre White (formerly of *Harvey's*). His previous efforts have been showered with two Michelin stars, and he's still up to his old tricks, presenting high-quality continental fare. Saddle of rabbit with asparagus and leeks, terrine of pork and foie gras, and mille-feuille are only a few of the menu's highlights. Closed Saturday lunch, Sundays, the last week in December, and the first week in January. Reservations advised. Major credit cards accepted. 66 Knightsbridge, SW1 (phone: 171-259-5380).

### EXPENSIVE

**Bice** Imaginatively prepared Italian specialties are served in an Art Deco setting at this fashionable restaurant. Outstanding choices from the menu include risotto with saffron and sausage in red wine sauce, linguine with baby clams, and baked bream served with white wine sauce and black olives. Closed Saturday lunch and Sundays. Reservations advised. Major credit cards accepted. 13 Albemarle St., W1 (phone: 171-409-1011).

**Capital** Serving some of the best French fare this side of the English Channel (it's earned a Michelin star), this small 35-seat hotel dining room specializes in gracious service and first-rate dishes, including grilled beef filet and root vegetables with foie gras and rosemary sauce, honey roasted French Barbary duckling with red wine sauce, and baked filet of sea bass with thyme and orange sauce. Open daily. Reservations necessary. Major credit cards accepted. 22-24 Basil St., SW3 (phone: 171-589-5171).

**Clarke's** It's London's answer to the San Francisco Bay area's *Chez Panisse*, with set menus of California-style cooking from owner/chef Sally Clarke presented in a lovely, light, basement eatery. Closed weekends. Reservations necessary. Major credit cards accepted. 124 Kensington Church St., W8 (phone: 171-221-9225).

**L'Escargot** A few years ago, this Soho landmark was in danger of closing; however, two award-winning chefs, David Cavalier and Garry Hollihead, have joined together to save it. The restaurant now features a formal dining room upstairs and a brasserie downstairs; both serve tempting menus of French-influenced dishes. Samples of Cavalier's and Hollihead's handiwork include pot-au-feu, *boudin blanc* (chicken and foie gras sausages), and *cassoulet toulousain* (a stew with pork, sausage, mutton, goose, and green beans). Closed Saturday lunch and Sundays; the formal dining room is also closed Mondays. Reservations advised. Major credit cards accepted. 48 Greek St., W1 (phone: 171-437-2679).

**Greenhouse** At this garden-style eatery tucked away in a Mayfair mews, chef Gary Rhodes (who had earned a Michelin star at Taunton's *Castle* hotel restaurant) delivers traditional flavors with style, from a simple poached egg with black pudding, bacon, and salad greens to *confit* of duck on butter beans. Leave room for the feather-light steamed jam sponge and custard. After the prix fixe Sunday lunch (which we heartily recommend), take a walk in nearby *Hyde Park.* Closed Saturday lunch. Reservations necessary. Major credit cards accepted. 27a Hay's Mews, W1 (phone: 171-499-3331).

**Green's** Pinstripes rule at this establishment, which serves some of the best oysters in London, and some would say the best English food. Open daily. Reservations necessary. Major credit cards accepted. 36 Duke St., SW1 (phone: 171-930-4566).

**Greig's Grill** Superlative steaks—and plenty of them—are the order of the day at this small restaurant, a favorite among Americans. Diners get to choose from a display of raw Scottish beef, lamb chops, or smoked salmon, plus fresh vegetables and what just may be the world's biggest and best baked potato. Open late, this is a good place for an after-theater feast. Save room for the Turkish delight. Closed Saturday lunch and Sundays. Reservations necessary. Major credit cards accepted. 26 Bruton Pl., W1 (phone: 171-629-3064).

**Hilaire** With light and flavorful dishes drawing on the Mediterranean, the Far East, and the chef's native Wales, this place offers a multicultural dining experience. Don't miss the lemon tart with toffee banana. Closed Sundays. Reservations necessary. Major credit cards accepted. 68 Old Brompton Rd., SW7 (phone: 171-584-8993).

**Ivy** Since 1911, this has been one of *the* restaurants of London's theater elite. Especially interesting are the commissioned works of contemporary art that contrast with the stained glass and oak paneling. International specialties are served along with British classics like grilled Dover sole, Cumberland sausages, and smoked salmon with scrambled eggs. Some dishes border on the just-too-trendy. Open daily. Reservations necessary. Major credit cards accepted. 1 West St., WC2 (phone: 171-836-4751).

**Ken Lo's Memories of China** The premier Chinese eatery in London, where Ken Lo, well-known Chinese author and tennis player, and his chefs prepare a wide range of fine dishes from all regions of China, from dim sum to Szechuan food. Closed Sundays (though brunch is served on Sundays at the Chelsea restaurant) and bank holidays. Reservations advised. Major credit cards accepted. Two locations: 67 Ebury St., SW1 (phone: 171-730-7734); and Harbour Yard, Chelsea Harbour, SW10 (phone: 171-352-4953).

**Langan's Brasserie** Still trendy after all these years, this spot is a haunt for celebrities. Ask for a downstairs table and take your time studying the lengthy menu. (For a lighter menu, try *Langan's Bistro;* see below.) Closed Saturday lunch and Sundays. Reservations necessary. Major credit cards accepted. 1 Stratton St., W1 (phone: 171-493-6437).

**Leith's** For over 20 years, this continental, one-Michelin-star restaurant in an out-of-the-way Victorian building northwest of *Kensington Gardens* has served superb entrées, hors d'oeuvres, and desserts as part of a fine prix fixe dinner. There's also an excellent vegetarian menu and a good wine list. Though its stuffy "dinner party" style is less than trendy, this is still a popular place. Open daily for dinner only. Reservations necessary. Major credit cards accepted. 92 Kensington Park Rd., W11 (phone: 171-229-4481).

**Lindsay House** For an unforgettable evening, few places can match this combination of plush, 17th-century decor and traditional English dishes with a twist. The Edwardian house has separate dining rooms furnished with huge gilt mirrors, fireplaces, and drapes, and flamboyant fare to match—cold carrot and orange soup, smoked salmon with creamed chives, and Westend lamb with basil sweetbread mousse in Madeira sauce. Open daily. Reservations advised. Major credit cards accepted. 21 Romilly St., W1 (phone: 171-439-0450).

**One Ninety Queensgate** Just a few years old, these two eateries at the *Gore* hotel are crowded with diners eager to try chef Antony Worrall-Thompson's refined fare—including sea bass with fish mousse and hot crab pancakes. His *Bistrot 190* upstairs serves modern French food at very reasonable prices (but to hotel guests only); *Downstairs at 190* specializes in seafood. Restaurant closed Saturday lunch and Sundays; bistro open daily. Reservations necessary in the restaurant; no reservations in the bistro. Major credit cards accepted. 190 Queen's Gate, SW7 (phone: 171-581-5666).

**Oriental** London's most glamorous Chinese restaurant is a sparkling jewel in the *Dorchester* hotel's crown; its excellent Cantonese cooking has earned it a Michelin star. The menu features sesame prawns with lemon sauce, medallions of beef, and shredded coconut tarts; the house specialty is Chinese mushrooms stuffed with prawn mousse. Closed Saturday lunch and Sundays. Reservations advised. Major credit cards accepted. Park La., W1 (phone: 171-629-8888).

**Pied-à-Terre** Richard Neat, the young chef of this hip French bistro, has earned a Michelin star for his innovative creations. The country-style fare includes masterfully prepared rabbit, pigeon, filet of turbot, scallops, and lamb chops; there are several prix fixe lunch and dinner selections, and the wine list is extensive, with both pricey and more affordable vintages. The decor is a bit spare except for some fine artwork on the walls (including a few Warhols), but the dining experience itself provides plenty of distraction. Closed Saturday lunch and Sundays. Reservations necessary. Major credit cards accepted. 34 Charlotte St., W1 (phone: 171-636-1178).

**Le Pont de la Tour** Sir Terence Conran (of *Habitat* store fame and *Quaglino's*—see above) has designed a "gastrodome" complex overlooking the Thames at Tower Bridge that houses a restaurant, bar/grill, oyster bar, food and wine shops, and a bakery. The innovative restaurant features traditional Arbroath smokies au gratin (smoked Scottish haddock) with fresh tomato, lobster pot-au-feu, baked apple, and citrus fruit salad. Open daily. Reservations necessary. Major credit cards accepted. 36 Shad Thames, Butler's Wharf, SE1 (phone: 171-403-8403).

**St. Quentin** The chef at this popular brasserie with mirrored walls and leather banquettes prepares traditional French fare, adapting the menu to make the best use of seasonal fish and produce. But the focus is not solely on fish; the homemade quenelles and *andouillettes* (spicy, smoked sausages) are also delicious. However, service can be erratic. Open daily. Reservations advised. Major credit cards accepted. 243 Brompton Rd., SW3 (phone: 171-589-8005 or 171-581-5131).

**Savoy Grill** It's renowned as a celebrity watching ground, but this eatery actually is patronized mostly by businesspeople. Although the menu features some classic French dishes, the English grills and roasts are the house specialties. Perfect for before and especially after theater. Closed Saturday lunch and Sundays. Reservations necessary. Major credit cards accepted. At the *Savoy Hotel,* The Strand, WC2 (phone: 171-836-4343).

**Wilton's** Good food is skillfully prepared and elegantly served in a plush, rather formal Victorian setting. Specialties include game, fish, oxtail, steak and kidney pie—what the best English cooking is about. Closed Saturday lunch, Sundays, and three weeks in August. Reservations necessary. Major credit cards accepted. 55 Jermyn St., SW1 (phone: 171-629-9955).

### MODERATE

**Alastair Little** The decor is minimalist but chic, and many find the chef here to be the most natural cook in the city. The eclectic menu changes twice daily and features French, Japanese, and Italian dishes. Closed Saturday lunch and Sundays. Reservations advised. Major credit cards accepted. 49 Frith St., W1 (phone: 171-734-5183).

**Bloom's** This kosher restaurant has a bright and bustling atmosphere, a bit like the dining room of a large hotel, with waiters who almost—but not quite—throw the food at you. The popular take-out counter serves the best hot salt beef (like corned beef) sandwiches in town. The house wine is Israeli. Closed Friday evenings and Saturdays. Reservations advised. Major credit cards accepted. 90 Whitechapel High St., E1 (phone: 171-247-6001), and 130 Golders Green Rd., NW11 (phone: 181-455-1338).

**Bombay Brasserie** At lunchtime there is an Indian buffet; at dinner, classic dishes from all over the land of the Moguls, including Goanese fish curry and Kashmiri lamb curry. And the setting is lovely, with lots of banana plants, wicker chairs, and ceiling fans. Popular with both the American and British show-biz colonies. Open daily. Reservations necessary. Major credit cards accepted. Courtfield Close, Courtfield Rd., SW7 (phone: 171-370-4040).

**Chiang Mai** Thai restaurants used to be a rarity in London. This one always has been easy to spot since it's the only eatery in Soho (and probably the whole of Britain) with a carved wooden elephant poised on the sidewalk. The menu offers such dishes as coconut chicken and *galanga* soup. Those unfamiliar with northern Thai cooking should inquire about the spiciness of individual dishes before ordering. Open daily. Reservations advised. Major credit cards accepted. 48 Frith St., W1 (phone: 171-437-7444).

**Chuen Cheng Ku** At this huge restaurant in the heart of Chinatown, the overwhelming majority of the clientele is Chinese. The specialty here is Cantonese-style dim sum; also try the pork with chili and salt, duck webs, and steamed lobster with ginger. Open daily. Reservations necessary. Major credit cards accepted. 17 Wardour St., W1 (phone: 171-437-1398).

**Chutney Mary** This Anglo-Indian eatery offers delicious echoes of the Raj. Just a few years old, its culinary crossovers include tandoori ginger lamb chops and Sindhi-style fried potatoes. Open daily. Reservations necessary. Major credit cards accepted. 535 King's Rd., SW10 (phone: 171-351-3113).

**Criterion** Considered *the* place to meet for many years (even Sherlock Holmes and Watson rendezvoused here), this eatery has now reopened after a lengthy renovation. Though the long bar still remains, most of the decor has been updated, with mirrors, hand-painted tables, and gilded mosaics. The Italian-American menu offers pizza with caramelized onions and olives, liver and onions with rosemary mashed potatoes, and fried spaghetti; traditional English tea also is served. Open daily. Reservations advised. Major credit cards accepted. Piccadilly Circus, W1 (phone: 171-925-0909).

**Dell'Ugo** Another culinary endeavor of Antony Worrall-Thompson, the man behind *One Ninety Queensgate* (see above), this trendy, three-level Italian eatery in Soho was an overnight success. And no wonder: The adventurous menu (served in the elegant dining rooms on the top two floors) includes roasted bell pepper and anchovy spaghetti, *tagliarini* (long, thin noodles) with grilled squid, and chicken with zucchini and garlic potatoes; a casual café on the ground floor offers fare that is lighter, but no less delicious. Closed Sundays. Reservations advised for the restaurant; no reservations for the café. Major credit cards accepted. 56 Frith St., W1 (phone: 171-734-8300).

**Gay Hussar** Among the best Hungarian restaurants this side of Budapest, it has a substantial menu with a varied selection: chicken ragout soup, goulash, roast pork, and lots more. The food here is extremely filling as well as delicious. The atmosphere is informal, with a regular clientele drawn from London's political and publishing worlds. Closed Sundays. Reservations necessary. American Express accepted. 2 Greek St., W1 (phone: 171-437-0973).

**Kensington Place** Here's a good example of the new breed of London restaurants, set behind a huge glass front, so you can see and be seen. A mix of "Californian new English" cookery from partridge and cabbage to foie gras, oysters, and delicious desserts. Frenzied atmosphere, sensible wine list. Open daily. Reservations necessary. Major credit cards accepted. 201 Kensington Church St., W8 (phone: 171-727-3184).

**Kettner's** As you check your coat, you have to decide—should you have a bottle of champagne at the bar (25 labels in stock), a humble but tasty salad in the brasserie-style café, or a pizza in the beautifully furnished dining room reminiscent of an Edwardian hotel? Whichever you choose, you can't go wrong. Open daily. Reservations unnecessary. Major credit cards accepted. In Soho, 29 Romilly St., W1 (phone: 171-437-6437).

**Langan's Bistro** Slightly simpler and less expensive dishes are prepared in the same style as *Langan's Brasserie* (above). Closed Saturday lunch and Sundays. Reservations advised. Major credit cards accepted. 26 Devonshire St., W1 (phone: 171-935-4531).

**Museum Street Café** It's near the *British Museum,* but there's nothing antiquarian about the fare served by American Gail Koerber and her English partner, Mark Nathan. They've cut out the frills (no liquor license; diners may bring their own alcoholic beverages), but left in the inspiration, with dishes such as salmon with lemon sauce, lamb on a skewer with pesto, and zabaglione. The bread is homemade. Closed weekends. Reservations necessary. No credit cards accepted. 47 Museum St., WC1 (phone: 171-405-3211).

**Porters** A very English eatery in *Covent Garden,* it's famous for home-cooked pies—steak, mushroom, and vegetable are the specialties. Leave room for such sticky British desserts as treacle and syrup sponge. Open daily. Reservations advised, especially for lunch. Major credit cards accepted. 17 Henrietta St., WC2 (phone: 171-836-6466).

**River Café** The first "new wave" Italian restaurant in London is hidden away (but overlooks the Thames) in Hammersmith, in a high-tech former architect's canteen serving stylish Tuscan peasant dishes. Closed Monday lunch and weekend evenings. Reservations necessary. Major credit cards accepted. *Thames Wharf,* Rainville Rd., W6 (phone: 171-381-8824).

**Rules** Approaching its bicentennial, this eatery has been at the same site since 1798. The Lillie Langtry Room, where the actress dined with the Prince of Wales (later King Edward VII), is reserved for private parties. The downstairs retains its Victorian atmosphere and decor. Walls are covered with signed photographs and cartoons of actors and authors. Another *must* for visitors to London, with better-than-average British fare. Start with smoked pheasant with spiced apricots, move on to whatever game and fish are in season, and finish with the treacle sponge pudding. Open daily. Reservations necessary. Major credit cards accepted. 35 Maiden La., WC2 (phone: 171-836-5314).

**Simply Nico** It's Nico Ladenis's not-so-snooty steak-and-chips joint. Closed Saturday lunch, Sundays, *Christmas* through *New Year's Day,* four days at *Easter,* and bank holidays. Reservations necessary. Major credit cards accepted. 48A Rochester Row, SW1 (phone: 171-630-8061).

**Smollensky's Balloon** A family place, this cocktail bar/restaurant with a 1930s piano-bar atmosphere is guaranteed to make Americans feel homesick. Steaks and fries figure importantly on the menu, offset by some interesting vegetarian dishes. Magicians and clowns entertain the younger set on weekends. You might even see Princess Di and her children here. Open daily. Reservations unnecessary. Major credit cards accepted. 1 Dover St., W1 (phone: 171-491-1199). There is a branch at 105 The Strand, WC2 (phone: 171-497-2101).

**Stephen Bull** Light in decor and fare, this clean-cut, modern eatery offers creatively prepared dishes, as well as service pared to essentials for true enjoyment and sensible tabs. Closed Saturday lunch and Sundays. Reservations necessary. Major credit cards accepted. 5-7 Blandford St., W1 (phone: 171-486-9696).

**Sweetings** A special London experience, this fish restaurant is one of the great attractions in the financial district. You may have to sit at a counter with your lobster, brill, or haddock, but it will be fresh and perfectly prepared. Open for lunch only; closed weekends. No reservations, so expect a wait. No credit cards accepted. 39 Queen Victoria St., EC4 (phone: 171-248-3062).

**Tate Gallery Restaurant** Who would expect one of London's better eateries to be in a fine art museum? But here it is—a genuine culinary outpost (leaning toward French fare), with a good wine list. Enjoy the famous Rex Whistler murals as you dine. Open for lunch only; closed Sundays. Reservations necessary. Visa accepted. *Tate Gallery,* Millbank, SW1 (phone: 171-834-6754).

**Upper Street Fish Shop** Try this dining spot for decent salmon, as well as traditional fish-and-chips. Expect to share a table. Closed Sundays. Reservations unnecessary. No credit cards accepted. 324 Upper St., N1 (phone: 171-359-1401).

**Wheeler's** A link in the national chain of seafood restaurants, this is the original—an old-fashioned, narrow (and very friendly and unpretentious) establishment on three floors. One of the best places in the city to enjoy finny fare, it specializes in a variety of ways of preparing real Dover sole and Scotch salmon. The oyster bar is our favorite perch. Closed Sundays. Reservations advised. Major credit cards accepted. Duke of York St. at Apple Tree Yard, SW1 (phone: 171-930-2460).

### INEXPENSIVE

**Bangkok** Known for its *satay*—small tender slices of beef marinated in a curry and soy sauce and served with a palate-destroying hot peanut sauce. From your butcher block table you can watch your meal being prepared in the windowed kitchen. Closed Sundays. Reservations advised. Major credit cards accepted. 9 Bute St., SW7 (phone: 171-584-8529).

**Café in the Crypt** Perhaps the best food value in central London is at this self-service eatery in the crypt of the *St. Martin-in-the-Fields Church* right on Trafalgar Square. A simple but good buffet offers many hot dishes and salads. Closed Sunday evenings. No reservations. MasterCard and Visa accepted. *St. Martin-in-the-Fields Church,* Trafalgar Sq., WC2 (phone: 171-839-4342).

**Calabash** West African fare gives this place a unique position on London's restaurant map, especially since it's in the bubbling *Covent Garden* district. The service is accommodating and helpful, and the food is both good and different. Closed Saturday lunch and Sundays. Reservations advised. Major credit cards accepted. Downstairs at London's *Africa Centre,* 38 King St., WC2 (phone: 171-836-1976).

**Chicago Pizza Pie Factory** In the early 1980s, an American advertising executive turned his back on the US ad world to bring London deep-dish pizza Windy City–style, along with Budweiser beer and chocolate cheesecake. Londoners beat a path to his door and haven't yet stopped clamoring to get in. Open daily. Reservations unnecessary. Major credit cards accepted. 17 Hanover Sq., W1 (phone: 171-629-2669).

**Chicago Rib Shack** Under the same ownership as *Chicago Pizza Pie Factory* (above), this is a great place for ribs. Open daily. Reservations unnecessary. Major credit cards accepted. Two locations: 1 Rafael St., SW7 (phone: 171-581-5595), and 13-17 Bear St., WC1 (phone: 171-839-4188).

**Cranks** There are several branches of this self-service vegetarian eatery. All are popular and serve good homemade desserts, as well as salads, quiches, and other hot food. Drop in for coffee or afternoon tea. Reservations advised. Major credit cards accepted. Some of the more central branches include 8 Marshall St., W1 (phone: 171-437-9431), closed Sundays; 11 The Market, *Covent Garden,* WC2 (phone: 171-379-6508), open daily; Tottenham St., W1 (phone: 171-631-3912), closed Sundays; Unit 11, Adelaide St., WC2 (phone: 171-836-0660), closed Sundays; 23 Barrett St., W1 (phone: 171-495-1340), closed Sundays; and 17-19 Great Newport St., Leicester Sq. (phone: 171-836-5226), open daily.

**Dumpling Inn** This Peking-style restaurant serves excellent Oriental dumplings, and most of the other dishes are equally good. Try the fried seaweed; it's got lots of vitamins and tastes terrific. The service, though efficient, is a bit brisk. Open daily. Reservations unnecessary. Major credit cards accepted. 15A Gerrard St., W1 (phone: 171-437-2567).

**Geales'** Truly fresh fish-and-chips are served in a setting that looks like a 1930s tearoom. Expect to wait in line, because this spot is no secret. Closed Sundays, Mondays, and the last three weeks in August. No reservations. Major credit cards accepted. 2 Farmer St., W8 (phone: 171-727-7969).

**Hard Rock Café** The original. With a loud jukebox and good burgers, this American-style eating emporium is still crowded after 23 years—the lines stretch well out into the street. As much a T-shirt vendor (at the shop around the corner) these days as a restaurant. Open daily. No reservations. Major credit cards accepted. 150 Old Park La., W1 (phone: 171-629-0382).

**Planet Hollywood** Another branch of the chain of eateries owned by Arnold Schwarzenegger, Sylvester Stallone, and Bruce Willis, it features displays of film memorabilia that are as popular as its down-to-earth menu of burgers, fries, and shakes. Several gadgets from the many James Bond movies can be seen here, including a model of the flying car from *The Man with the Golden Gun.* The atmosphere is boisterous and crowded. Open daily. No reservations. Major credit cards accepted. 13 Coventry St., W1 (phone: 171-287-1000).

**Standard** Possibly the best Indian restaurant value in London, so it tends to get crowded quickly. Open daily. Reservations advised. Major credit cards accepted. 23 Westbourne Grove, W2 (phone: 171-727-4818).

**Tuttons** A popular and lively brasserie in a former *Covent Garden* warehouse, this place is a handy snack spot for theatergoers. Open daily. Reservations advised. Major credit cards accepted. 11 Russell St., WC2 (phone: 171-836-4141).

---

### SHARING A PINT

There are several thousand pubs in London, the vast majority of which are owned by the six biggest brewers. Most pubs have two bars: the "public," which is for the working man who wants to get on with the business of drinking, and the "saloon" or "lounge," which makes an attempt at providing comfort and may serve food and wine as well as beer. Liquor at the latter may cost more. All pubs listed below are open daily unless stated otherwise.

Prince Albert stands holding a flower on the sign outside the *Albert* (52 Victoria St., SW1; phone: 171-222-5577), a smart but genuine Victorian pub with gas lamps and wrought-iron balconies. Office workers crowd in on weekdays at lunchtime, particularly for the interesting bar snacks. The small, excellent-value carvery upstairs is popular with politicians.

*Dirty Dick's* (202 Bishopsgate, EC2; phone: 171-283-5888) is galleried and spacious, with wood everywhere and sawdust on the floors. Plain rather than plush (much like the East End surrounding it), it's a supremely restful place to quench a thirst after a hectic Sunday morning's bargaining along nearby Petticoat Lane.

The *Grenadier* (18 Wilton Row, SW1; phone: 171-235-3074) used to be the Officers' Mess for the Duke of Wellington's soldiers; the exterior is chauvinistically red, white, and blue, and access from the north is via narrow Old Barracks Yard. Since it's an ideal place to stop for lunch after a trip to *Harrods* or a boutique browse up Brompton Road, the clientele is unceasingly posh.

Arthur Conan Doyle knew the *Sherlock Holmes* (10 Northumberland St., WC2; phone: 171-930-2644) when it was called the *Northumberland Arms* hotel (he set a scene in his *Hound of the Baskervilles* here). Drawings and photographs of actors playing Holmes and of scenes from Conan Doyle's works adorn the downstairs bar; upstairs is a replica of Holmes' Baker Street study.

Perfectly positioned between the east and west sides of *Hampstead Heath,* the *Spaniards Inn* (Spaniards La., NW3; phone: 181-455-3276) attracts Sunday walkers, visitors to nearby *Kenwood House,* wealthy local residents, and casual passersby. The pretty building has a large outdoor garden dotted with wooden tables and chairs.

*Ye Olde Cheshire Cheese* (145 Fleet St., EC4; phone: 171-353-6170) is the perfect place to rest during a tour of the nearby *Inns of Court.* Dr. Samuel Johnson lived around the corner, and his intimate circle—notably Boswell, Reynolds, and Gibbon—frequented "The Cheese." The pub's character has remained remarkably intact despite its place on many tourist itineraries and a recent renovation that included the addition of a snack bar.

Other fine spots include the *Audley* (41 Mount St., W1; phone: 171-499-1843), a favorite luncheon stop in the high-rent district, with fresh sandwiches and salad plates in an atypically hygienic environment; and the elegant *Antelope* (22 Eaton Ter., SW1; phone: 171-730-7781), where the Bellamys (or even Hudson, their butler) might have sipped a lager on the way home to nearby 165 Eaton Place. *Dickens Inn* by the *Tower* (St. Katherine's Way, E1; phone: 171-481-1786) is a converted warehouse overlooking a colorful yacht marina and serving shellfish snacks; *George Inn* (77 Borough High St., SE1; phone: 171-407-2056) dates from 1676 and retains the original gallery for viewing Shakespearean plays in the summer; *The Flask* (77 Highgate West Hill, N6; phone: 181-340-7260) serves drinks at three paneled bars and on its outside patio; *The Lamb* (94 Lambs Conduit St., WC1; phone: 171-405-0713) is also paneled and hung with photos of past music hall performers; *Museum Tavern* (49 Great Russell St., WC1; phone: 171-242-8987) is across from the *British Museum* and decorated with hanging flower baskets; and *Princess Louise* (208 High Holborn, WC1; phone: 171-405-8816) has live music, cabaret, and a good Thai restaurant. *Bull and Bush* (North End Way, NW3; phone: 181-455-3685) owes its fame to the Edwardian music hall song "Down at the Old Bull and Bush"; former customers include Thomas Gainsborough and Charles Dickens. *Prospect of Whitby* (57 Wapping Wall, E1; phone: 171-481-1095), London's oldest riverside pub, was once the haunt of thieves and smugglers (now it draws jazz lovers); *Anchor* (34 Park St., Bankside, SE1; phone: 171-407-3003) was possibly one of Shakespeare's haunts—the sites of the *Globe* and *Rose* theaters are close by; and *Black Friar* (174 Queen Victoria St., EC4; phone: 171-236-5650) is decorated in Art Nouveau style (closed weekends). On the south bank of the Thames, in the district of the Docklands called Rotherhithe, are two special pubs, the *Mayflower* (117 Rotherhithe St., SE16; phone: 171-237-4088) and the *Angel* (101 Bermondsey Wall E., SE16; phone: 171-237-3608). The former has been around since the 17th century when the *Mayflower* sailed for the New World and returned to Rotherhithe; today, the partially rebuilt Tudor inn is still a good spot to enjoy beer and ale. The *Angel* is set on stone pillars overlooking the Thames, and the cozy, dark interior hasn't changed much since the days when it was patronized by Samuel Pepys and Captain Cook.

---

## WINE BARS

Growing in popularity on the London scene, these bars serve wine by the glass or bottle, accompanied by such light fare as quiche and salad, and occasionally full meals. Prices tend to be lower in wine bars than in restaurants, and tables often can be reserved in advance. Here's a selection of the finest: *Café Suze* (1 Glenworth St., NW1; phone: 171-486-8216) combines rustic decor with good homemade food (closed weekends); *Cork and Bottle* (44-46 Cranbourn St., WC2; phone: 171-734-6592) is patronized by the London wine trade and serves good hot and cold dishes; *Draycott's* (114 Draycott Ave., SW3; phone: 171-584-5359) has tables grouped outside on the pavement and is frequented by the smart London set; *Ebury Wine Bar* (139 Ebury St., SW1; phone: 171-730-5447), in the heart of Belgravia, serves good food (try the English pudding) and offers live music nightly; *Shampers* (4 Kingly St., W1; phone: 171-437-1692), near the famous *Liberty* department store, is popular with the British media and public relations people; *Skinkers* (42 Tooley St., SE1; phone: 171-407-9189) is an atmospheric spot with sawdust on the floor, serving hearty food (closed weekends); *Café des Amis* (11-14 Hanover Pl., WC2; phone: 171-379-3444) is a crowded watering hole in fashionable *Covent Garden* (closed Sundays); *Brahms and Liszt* (19 Russell St., WC2; phone: 171-240-3661) always has good wines, food, and music; *Julie's* (137 Portland Rd., W11; phone: 171-727-4585) has become a landmark for aging hippies; *El Vino* (47 Fleet St., EC4; phone: 171-353-6786), once a journalists' haunt famous for refusing to serve women, is now full of legal eagles and PR folk in a nice Old World atmosphere; *Bubbles* (41 North Audley St., W1; phone: 171-491-3237) near the US Embassy serves champagne by the glass; *Dover Street Wine Bar* (8-9 Dover St., W1; phone: 171-629-9813) is a place to party with live music at night (closed Sundays); *Jimmy's Wine Bar* (18 Kensington Church St., W8; phone: 171-937-9988) serves claret and traditional English food and plays live music; *Le Metro* (28 Basil St., SW3; phone: 171-589-6286)—owned by the *Capital* hotel's David Levin—is across from *Harrods* and has a fine range of wines, good food, and reasonable prices; and near *St. Paul's*, *Balls Brothers* (6-8 Cheapside, EC2; phone: 171-248-2708), one of several around the city, serves over 60 kinds of wine and huge sandwiches stuffed with meat, fish, and cheese (closed weekends).

---

## TAKING TEA

The renaissance of afternoon tea in Britain has especially taken hold in its capital. A round of the best London teas would begin at the following hotels: *Brown's, Dorchester, Dukes, Grosvenor House,* the *Langham Hilton, Le Meridien,* the *Regent,* the *Ritz* (make reservations at least 10 days in advance), the *Savoy,* and the *Stafford* (see

*Checking In,* above, for addresses and phone numbers). Fine tea shops include *Daquise* (20 Thurloe St., SW7; phone: 171-589-6117); *Maison Bertaux* (28 Greek St., W1; phone: 171-437-6007); and *Pâtisserie Valerie* (44 Old Compton St., W1; phone: 171-437-3466). For those who prefer taking tea at home, *Heritage Touring (GB)* offers travelers the opportunity to enjoy the experience of an English cream tea with a London family. For more information, contact *Heritage Touring (GB),* 754 The Square, Cattistock, Dorchester, Dorset DT2 OJD, England (phone: 1300-320671; fax: 1300-321042).

# Madrid

## At-a-Glance

### SEEING THE CITY

For a romantic view of Madrid, watch the sun set from the roof garden and pool of the *Plaza* hotel on the Plaza de España (see *Checking In*). The vivid "Velázquez sky," portrayed in the artist's famous paintings, is usually tinted with a golden hue. Looking over the tile rooftops, visitors will see a fine view of the *Palacio Real* and, to the north, the distant Sierra de Guadarrama. The hotel's terrace and pool are open daily during the summer months; there's an admission charge.

### SPECIAL PLACES

The bustling Puerta del Sol and the Plaza de Cibeles traffic circle are two focal points at the heart of Madrid. The *Atocha* railroad station and traffic circle mark the southern extremity of this zone, the *Palacio Real* and the *Parque del Buen Retiro* form its western and eastern borders, respectively, and Plaza de Colón marks its northern limit. One major tree-lined avenue, with three names, bisects the entire city from top to bottom. Its southern section, between the *Atocha* train station and Plaza de Cibeles, is called Paseo del Prado. From Cibeles north to Plaza de Colón, its name is Paseo de Recoletos. At Plaza de Colón, it becomes the long Paseo de la Castellana, which runs through modern Madrid to the north end of the city beyond Plaza de Castilla and the *Chamartín* railroad station. The two major east–west arteries are Calle de Alcalá and the Gran Vía; the latter angles northwest to Plaza de España.

The best way to see Madrid is by walking. One good stroll is from Puerta del Sol to Plaza Mayor, then downhill to Plaza de Oriente. Keep in mind that opening hours for museums, churches, and many other places of touristic interest usually run from 9 or 10 AM to 1 or 2 PM, then resume from 4 or 5 to 7 or 8 PM; hours may vary with the season. Weekend schedules are often shorter than during weekdays. Most museums close on Mondays, some at midday, and smaller ones for the entire month of August. When possible it's a good idea to call for hours or have a hotel or tourism office staffer do it for you.

**PLAZA MAYOR** The grandiose main square of downtown Madrid is closed to vehicular traffic and easily missed on foot if you don't aim for it and go in through one of the nine arched entryways. Built in 1617–18 by order of King Felipe III and executed by Juan Gómez de Mora along the lines of Juan de Herrera's design for the imposing palace monastery of *El Escorial,* it is the quintessence of Hapsburg Madrid—cobblestones, tile roofs, and imposing austere buildings. The plaza was the stage for a wide variety of 17th-and 18th-century spectacles—audiences of more than 50,000 witnessed hangings, burnings, and the decapitation of "heretics," as well as canonizations of saints, jousting tournaments, plays, circuses, and even bullfights. The 477 balconies of the surrounding buildings served as spectator "boxes" for royalty and aristocrats. Beautifully refurbished, the Plaza Mayor is still lively, with *la tuna* (strolling student minstrels in period costume), other amateur musicians, artists, and portrait painters selling their works, as well as summer concerts and ballets, and outdoor cafés for watching it all. The plaza's most important edifice is the *Casa de la Panadería* (Bakers' House), occupying most of the north side and now housing a cultural center, and the *Casa de la Carnicería* (Butchers' House) on the south side. All the city's major trade guilds were represented under the arches around the perimeter. Continuing this tradition, myriad shops—many over a century old—still line the arcade, and on Sunday mornings philatelists and numismatists set up shop under the arches, to the delight of stamp and coin collectors. During the yuletide season, numerous stands sell lovely *Christmas* ornaments. Visitors can easily lose their sense of direction inside this vast enclosure, so it's helpful to know that the bronze equestrian statue of Felipe III in the center is facing east (toward the *Prado* museum). The landmark *Arco de Cuchilleros* entrance, with its huge arch, is at the southwest corner.

**PUERTA DEL SOL** This vast oblong plaza is the bustling nerve center of modern Madrid. Among the 10 arteries that converge here are Alcalá, San Jerónimo, Mayor, and Arenal. On the south side is the imposing heaquarters of the government of the Greater Madrid Autonomous Region. Near the curb in front of its main entrance a famous emblem in the sidewalk marks "kilometer zero," the central point from which all Spanish highways radiate and from which their distance is measured. Directly across the plaza stands the venerated bronze statue of *el oso y el madroño* (the bear and the madrona berry tree), the symbol and coat of arms of Madrid since the 13th century, when central Madrid was wooded and it wasn't unusual to see bears roaming around.

**MUSEO NACIONAL DEL PRADO (PRADO NATIONAL MUSEUM)** One of the world's supreme art museums, the *Prado* is a treasure house of over 4,000 universal masterpieces, most of which were acquired over the centuries by art-loving Spanish monarchs. The wealth of Spanish paintings includes famous works by El Greco (including the *Adoration of the Shepherds*), Zurbarán, Velázquez (including *The Spinners* and the famous *La Meninas,* "The Maids of Honor"), Murillo, Ribera (including the *Martyrdom of St. Bartholomew*), and Goya (including his renowned *Naked Maja* and *Maja Clothed*). On the ground floor, a special section is devoted to the tapestry cartoons designed by Goya for the palace-monastery outside the town of San Lorenzo de El Escorial and to his extraordinary *Disasters of War* etchings, which serve as his commentary on Spain's War of Independence. Visitors also will find Goya's stunning *Second of*

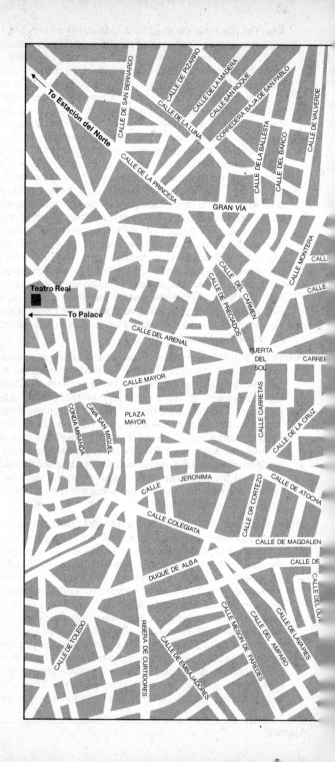

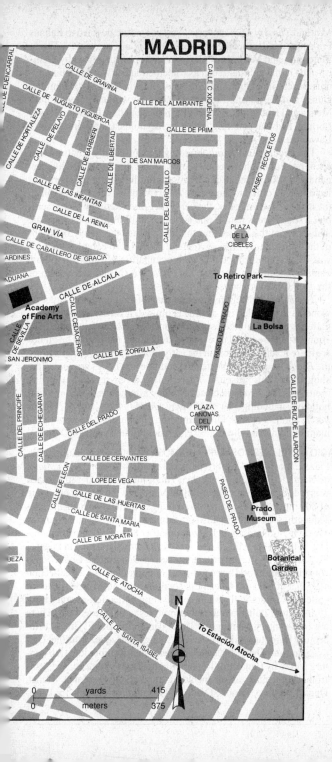

*May* and *Third of May* canvases. Vast rooms are devoted to Italians Fra Angelico, Botticelli, Raphael, Correggio, Caravaggio, Titian, Tintoretto, and Veronese. Other rooms display paintings by Flemish and German masters such as Rubens, van der Weyden, Hieronymus Bosch (including *The Garden of Earthly Delights*), Memling, Dürer, and Van Dyck. From the Dutch are works by Rembrandt, Metsu, and Hobbema. French art is represented by Poussin, Claude Lorrain, and Watteau; English art by Reynolds, Gainsborough, and Lawrence.

The neoclassical *Prado* building was originally a natural sciences museum, conceived by Carlos III in 1785. In 1819, King Fernando VII converted it into a museum to house the royal art collection. In addition to the main *Prado* (in the *Villanueva* building), the museum has an annex, the *Casón del Buen Retiro,* which resembles a small Greek temple and is just up a hill from the Goya statue that stands at the *Prado*'s north façade. Once the stately ballroom of the 17th-century *Palacio Real del Buen Retiro* complex—which was destroyed during the French occupation of Madrid—it now contains the *Museo Nacional del Siglo XIX* (National Museum of the 19th Century; phone: 468-0481).

The *Prado* collection is so vast that it is impossible to savor its wonders in a single visit. If time is limited, it is best to select a few galleries of special interest or hire one of the knowledgeable government-licensed freelance guides at the main entrance. The guides are more readily available in the early morning. Reproductions from the *Prado*'s collection, postcards, and fine arts books are sold at the shop inside the museum. There's also a bar-restaurant on the premises. The *Prado* is closed Sunday afternoons, Mondays, and holidays, including *New Year's Day, Good Friday, May 1, November 1,* and *Christmas.* One admission charge grants access to the main building and the annex. Paseo del Prado (phone: 420-2836).

**PALACIO DE VILLAHERMOSA (VILLAHERMOSA PALACE)** Diagonally across Plaza Cánovas del Castillo (the square with the *Fuente de Neptuno,* or Neptune Fountain) from the *Prado,* this splendid 1806 palace was redesigned by architect Rafael Moneo as the permanent home of 800 masterpieces (primarily paintings), initially on loan and subsequently sold to the Spanish government by Baron Hans Heinrich Thyssen-Bornemisza de Kaszon (another 80 are on permanent display in Barcelona's *Mostir de Pedralbes*). Formerly located in Lugano, Switzerland's Villa Favorita, the *Thyssen-Bornemisza Collection* is considered the world's second-most important private art collection after that of Britain's Queen Elizabeth II. In its airy, modern interior galleries visitors will find an astonishing collection ranging from 13th-century Italian and Dutch primitives to the present day. There are 16th-century paintings by Titian, Tintoretto, and El Greco; 17th-century Baroque works by masters such as Velázquez, Murillo, Caravaggio, Van Dyck, Brueghel, Rubens, and Rembrandt; 18th-century pieces by Canaletto, Tiepolo, Reynolds, and Watteau; and gems from 19th-century artists including Sargent, Goya, Manet, Monet, Degas, Pissarro, Renoir, Cézanne, Gauguin, van Gogh, Toulouse-

Lautrec, and Matisse. The 20th century is represented by Picasso, Chagall, Gris, Klee, Miró, Giacometti, de Kooning, O'Keeffe, Dalí, Hopper, Magritte, Bacon, Freud, Kandinsky, and Braque. On the premises there is a coffee shop, a book and souvenir shop, and a conference room. Closed Mondays. Admission charge. 9 Paseo del Prado (phone: 420-3944).

**REAL JARDÍN BOTÁNICO (ROYAL BOTANICAL GARDEN)** The garden was designed in 1774 by Juan de Villanueva, the same architect who designed the *Prado* (whose south façade it faces). Twenty manicured acres contain some 30,000 species of plants and flowers from Spain and throughout the world. Carlos III commissioned the project as part of his urban refurbishment program, and, by his order, therapeutic and medicinal plants and herbs were distributed free to those in need. Between the *Prado* and the entrance to the garden is the small Plaza de Murillo, which has a bronze statue of the 17th-century painter and the *Cuatro Fuentes,* four fountains of mythological triton cherubs playing with dolphins. Open daily. Admission charge. On Paseo del Prado at Plaza de Murillo (phone: 420-3568).

**PALACIO REAL (ROYAL PALACE)** The Moors chose a strategic site overlooking the Río Manzanares to build their *alcázar,* or castle-fortress. After the 11th-century Reconquest, Christian leaders renovated it and moved in, and Philip II made it the royal residence after proclaiming Madrid the capital of Spain in 1561. After the *alcázar* was destroyed by fire on *Christmas Eve* 1734, a new palace was built. It took 26 years to complete the colossus of granite and white limestone, with walls 13 feet thick, more than 2,800 rooms, 23 courtyards, and magnificently opulent interiors. At the north side are the formal *Jardines de Sabatini* (Sabatini Gardens); and down the slopes on the west side is the *Campo del Moro*—20 acres of forest, manicured gardens, and fountains, now a public park. The main entrance is on the south side, through the tall iron gates leading into an immense courtyard called the Plaza de la Armería (Armory Square), a setting for the pageantry of royal occasions. The imposing structure at the courtyard's south end is the *Catedral de la Almudena,* Madrid's cathedral honoring the patroness of the city (see *Museums*).

The palace is seen by guided tour, with different sections covered on different tours, led by Spanish- and English-speaking guides. The king and queen of Spain live in the *Palacio de la Zarzuela* on the outskirts of Madrid, but the *Palacio Real* still is used for official occasions and is closed to the public at those times (which are not always announced in advance). Normally the palace is open daily; Sundays and holiday hours from 9 AM to 2:15 PM. Admission charge. Plaza de Oriente (phone: 559-7404).

**MUSEO NACIONAL CENTRO DE ARTE REINA SOFÍA (QUEEN SOFÍA NATIONAL MUSEUM OF ART)** This gargantuan 18th-century building was the *Hospital General de San Carlos* until 1965. Following a tremendous reconstruction project, the building was inaugurated in 1986 as a museum devoted to contemporary art, named in honor of the present queen of Spain. Since then, it has taken its place among the world's leading contemporary art galleries and modern art museums. The collection encompasses that of the former *Museo Español de Arte Contemporáneo* (Spanish Contemporary Art Museum)—3,000 paintings, 9,000 drawings, and 400 sculptures, including works by Picasso, Miró, Dalí, Juan Gris, and Julio González. A recent addition to its permanent collection is Picasso's monumental *Guernica* (moved here from the *Prado*). The museum also contains the foremost contemporary art library in Spain, with state-of-the art braille facilities, videos, photography collections, research systems, and workshops. Throughout the year, prominent exhibitions are mounted at the museum's two landmark annexes in *Parque del Buen Retiro,* the *Palacio de Velázquez* and *Palacio de Cristal*. Closed Tuesdays; Sunday hours 10 AM to 2:30 PM. Admission charge. 52 Calle Santa Isabel (phone: 467-4761 or 467-5215).

**PLAZA DE LA CIBELES** Dominating Madrid's favorite traffic circle is the fountain and statue of the Greek fertility goddess Cybele, erected during the reign of Carlos III. It's a Madrid custom to "say hello to La Cibeles" upon arriving in town. The imposing turn-of-the-century wedding cake *Palacio de Comunicaciones* (the city's central post and telecommunications office) on the plaza almost eclipses Cibeles.

**PARQUE DEL BUEN RETIRO ("FINE RETREAT" PARK)** During the early 17th century, this was a royal retreat and the grounds of a royal palace complex and a porcelain factory, then on the outskirts of town. Now Madrid's foremost public park, the *Retiro* encompasses 300 peaceful acres of forest, manicured gardens, statuary, fountains, picnic grounds, and cafés. On a sunny Sunday afternoon, it seems all Madrid comes to jog, hug, gossip, or walk the dog around the lakeside colonnade. Art exhibitions are held at the *Palacio de Cristal,* a 19th-century jewel of glass and wrought iron, and at the *Palacio de Velázquez,* named for its architect, not for the painter. During July and August, as part of the city-sponsored cultural program "Verano en la Villa" (Summer in the City), classical and flamenco concerts are staged in the *Jardines Cecilio Rodríguez* (Cecilio Rodríguez Gardens) near the Menéndez Pelayo entrance at 10 PM and midnight, and the outdoor cinema (entrance on Alfonso XII) screens Spanish and foreign (including US) films (schedules change from year to year; check with the tourist office). We recommend savoring a *coupe royale*—a deluxe ice cream—among the statues of kings. The park's loveliest entrance is through the wrought-iron gates at Plaza de la Independencia, also referred to as the *Puerta de Alcalá.*

**PLAZA DE LA VILLA** This is one of Madrid's most charming squares, and its architectural diversity makes it especially interesting. Dominating the west side, the 17th-century neoclassical *Casa de la Villa,* also called the *Ayuntamiento* (City Hall), was designed by Juan Gómez de Mora, the architect who planned the Plaza Mayor. Its carillon chimes the hour with *zarzuela* melodies and plays 20-minute concerts every evening. The *Casa de la Villa*'s splendid museum collection is open to the public every Monday (except holidays) from 5 to 7 PM, with free tours provided by the tourist board (phone: 588-0002). Along the back of the square is the 16th-century Plateresque *Casa de Cisneros,* a palace built by the nephew and heir of the cardinal regent of the same name. On the east side are the old *Hemeroteca* (Periodicals Library), with a large Mudejar doorway, and the massive medieval *Casa de los Lujanes,* one of the oldest buildings in Madrid (King François I of France was once imprisoned in the tower by Holy Roman Emperor Charles V). It's now the *Academia de Ciencias Morales y Políticas* (Academy of Moral and Political Sciences). Separating these two structures, the tiny Calle del Codo (Elbow Street) angles down to the tranquil Plaza del Cordón, surrounded by historic noble mansions.

**MUSEO DE LA REAL ACADEMIA DE BELLAS ARTES DE SAN FERNANDO (MUSEUM OF THE ST. FERDINAND ROYAL ACADEMY OF FINE ARTS)** Housed in a splendid 18th-century palace just east of the Puerta del Sol, the academy's permanent collection comprises some 1,500 paintings and over 800 sculptures. There are works by El Greco, Velázquez, Zurbarán, Murillo, Goya, and Sorolla, as well as Italian and Flemish masters. Open Tuesdays through Fridays from 9 AM to 7 PM; weekends and Mondays to 3 PM; during the summer, open daily from 9 AM to 2 PM. Admission charge. 13 Calle de Alcalá (phone: 522-1491).

**MONASTERIO DE LAS DESCALZAS REALES (ROYAL MONASTERY OF THE BARE-FOOT CARMELITES)** Behind its stark stone façade is an opulent interior filled with an astonishing wealth of artistic treasures and ornamentation bestowed by kings and noblemen. Founded in 1559 by Princess Juana of Austria, sister of Philip II, the convent welcomed disconsolate empresses, queens, princesses, and *infantas,* including Juana's sister María, Empress of Germany. The grandiose stairway is a breathtaking example of *barroco madrileño,* every centimeter lavishly decorated with frescoes and carved wood. Art treasures include works by El Greco, Zurbarán, Titian, and Sánchez Coello, as well as Rubens tapestries. The windows of the upper floor afford a lovely view over the tranquil rooftop garden, where the cloistered nuns grow their vegetables as they have for centuries. Visitors are escorted by resident Spanish-speaking guides; tours in English should be arranged in advance through the municipal tourist office (see *Tourist Information*). Hours, which vary according to the season, are limited because the cloistered nuns often use the museum sections in their daily life; opening hours are usually Tuesdays through Saturdays from 10 AM to 1:30 PM. Admission charge includes the tour. Plaza de las Descalzas Reales (phone: 559-7404).

**MONASTERIO DE LA ENCARNACIÓN (MONASTERY OF THE INCARNATION)** Built by order of Queen Margarita of Austria, wife of King Felipe III, this Augustinian convent was founded in 1616. It was designed in the severe classical style by Juan Gómez de Mora, and its façade belies the bounteous religious and secular art treasures inside. The dazzling reliquary room displays some 1,500 religious relics contained in priceless gold and silver urns and jeweled cases. Among them is a vial of the powdered blood of the 3rd-century St. Pantaleón, which is said to liquefy every year on his feast day, July 27. This is another active cloistered convent, so individuals and groups must be escorted by resident guides; tours in English can be arranged in advance through the *Oficina de Museos* (Museums Office; phone: 248-7404). Open Tuesdays through Saturdays from 10 AM to 1:30 PM. Admission charge includes the tour. Plaza de la Encarnación (phone: 247-0510).

**MUSEO MUNICIPAL (MUNICIPAL MUSEUM)** Devoted to the history of Madrid, this fine museum will enhance any visitor's awareness of the city's evolution, culture, and personality. It is filled with art, furnishings, porcelains, photographs, engravings, and meticulously detailed maps and models of the city during the 17th, 18th, and 19th centuries. The museum building, declared a national monument in 1919, was originally an 18th-century hospital, and its elaborately ornate entrance is a memorable sight; its style is called "Churrigueresque," named after a distinctly Spanish Baroque dynasty of architects and artists. Closed Mondays; Sunday hours 10 AM to 2:30 PM. Admission charge. 78 Calle Fuencarral (phone: 521-6656).

**REAL FÁBRICA DE TAPICES (ROYAL TAPESTRY FACTORY)** Established early in the 18th century, this factory-museum continues to use traditional techniques in producing handmade Spanish tapestries and rugs. In addition to the permanent collection, visitors can see the workshops and watch master artisans at work weaving tapestries from cartoons by Goya and other artists, knotting luxuriant rugs, or doing intricate restoration work. Rugs and tapestries can be purchased by special order, and even can be custom-made from the customer's own design. Open weekday mornings; closed August. Admission charge. 2 Calle Fuenterrabía (phone: 551-3409).

**MUSEO DEL EJÉRCITO (ARMY MUSEUM)** An amazing array of more than 27,000 items related to war throughout Spain's history—uniforms, armor, cannon, swords (including one belonging to El Cid), stupendous collections of miniature soldiers, and portraits of heroines and heroes—are displayed here. Housed in the vast Baroque interior of one of the two surviving buildings of the 17th-century Royal Retiro Palace complex, this museum is well worth seeing. Open from 10 AM to 2 PM; closed Mondays. Admission charge. 1 Calle Méndez Núñez (phone: 522-0628).

**MUSEO ARQUEOLÓGICO NACIONAL (NATIONAL ARCHAEOLOGICAL MUSEUM)** The star among the Iberian and classical antiquities here is the enigmatic *Dama de Elche,* a dramatic Iberian bust of a priestess, or perhaps an aristocrat, estimated to have been sculpted during the 4th century BC. Also on display are basket weavings and funeral objects of early Iberians, as well as Neolithic, Celtic, ancient Greek, Roman, and Visigothic artifacts and handicrafts. In the garden at the entrance is an underground replica of Cantabria's famous

*Altamira Caves* and their prehistoric paintings. Closed Mondays; Sunday and holiday hours 9:30 AM to 2:30 PM. Admission charge includes entrance to the *Biblioteca Nacional* (see below), at the opposite side of the same building. 13 Calle Serrano (phone: 577-7912).

**BIBLIOTECA NACIONAL (NATIONAL LIBRARY)** With more than six million volumes, this is one of the world's richest libraries. Statues of Cervantes, Lope de Vega, and other illustrious Spaniards of letters stand at the classical columned entrance. Scheduled and seasonal exhibits of publications and graphics are held in the ground floor galleries. Closed Mondays; Sunday and holiday hours 10 AM to 2 PM. Admission charge includes entrance to the *Museo Arqueológico Nacional* (see above), at the opposite side of the same building. 20 Paseo de Recoletos (phone: 580-7800).

**CASA DE CAMPO** Once the private royal hunting grounds, this 4,300-acre forested public park on the right bank of the Río Manzanares is a playground for *madrileños* and visitors alike. It has a zoo (complete with a panda and more than 7,000 other animals), picnic and fair grounds (important trade fairs and conventions are held here), and a giant amusement park, the *Parque de Atracciones Casa de Campo,* with rides, open-air entertainment, and a spirited carnival atmosphere. Other highlights include a concert stadium, an all-encompassing sports complex, a small lake, and the bullpens of *La Venta de Batán* (for bullfight practice and previews of the bulls). The zoo is open daily April through September; weekends and holidays only October through March. The amusement park is closed in winter and Mondays the rest of the year. Admission charge to attractions. The park is easily reached by bus, metro, taxi, or the *teleférico* (cable car) that runs from Paseo del Pintor Rosales in *Parque del Oeste* (near Plaza de España). Casa de Campo (phone: 463-2900).

**REAL BASÍLICA DE SAN FRANCISCO EL GRANDE (ROYAL BASILICA OF ST. FRANCIS THE GREAT)** A few blocks south of the *Palacio Real,* this neoclassical church is one of the largest and most richly decorated in Madrid. Another project of King Carlos III, it was designed by the city's finest 18th-century architects. Six side chapels (the first on the left was painted by Goya) line its circular interior, which is topped by a cupola 108 feet in diameter. The museum inside the church contains a wealth of religious art. Museum closed Sundays, Mondays, and holidays. Admission charge to the museum. Plaza de San Francisco (phone: 265-3800).

# Sources and Resources

## TOURIST INFORMATION

Information, good city maps, and brochures can be obtained from the *Patronato Municipal de Turismo* (Municipal Tourism Board; 69 Calle Mayor, entrance on Calle Traviesa; closed weekends;

phone: 588-2900 or 559-1955; fax: 588-2930); information on the city, the rest of the province, and the entire country also is available from the *Oficina de Información Turística* of the Comunidad de Madrid (2 Duque de Medinaceli, near the *Palace* hotel; closed Saturday afternoons and Sundays; phone: 429-4951). Other provincial information offices (with similar hours) are at the downtown Torre de Madrid skyscraper on the Plaza de España (phone: 541-2325), at *Barajas* airport (phone: 305-8656), and at the *Chamartín* train station (phone: 315-9976). The *US Embassy* is at 75 Calle Serrano (phone: 577-4000).

In the US, there are four branches of the *National Tourist Office of Spain* (San Vicente Plaza Bldg., 8383 Wilshire Blvd., Suite 960, Beverly Hills, CA 90211; phone: 213-658-7188; fax: 213-658-1061; Water Tower Place, 845 N. Michigan Ave., Suite 915E, Chicago, IL 60611; phone: 312-642-1992; fax: 312-642-9817; 1221 Brickell Ave., Suite 1850, Miami, FL 33131; phone: 305-358-1992; fax: 305-358-8223; and 665 Fifth Ave., New York, NY 10022; phone: 212-759-8822; fax: 212-980-1053). The *Spanish Embassy* is at 2700 15th St. NW, Washington, DC 20009 (phone: 202-265-0190).

**ENTRY REQUIREMENTS** A US citizen needs a current passport for a stay of up to 90 days.

**TIME** The time in Spain is six hours later than in US East Coast cities. Spain observes daylight saving time.

**LANGUAGE** Castilian Spanish is the official tongue, but there are a number of regional languages such as Catalan, Basque, and Galician. English is understood in principal hotels, restaurants, and shops.

**ELECTRIC CURRENT** 220 volts, 50 cycles, AC.

**MONEY** The peseta (pta) is the unit of currency. At press time the peseta traded at 132 to $1 US.

**TIPPING** Though service charges of 15% are included in restaurant bills, extra tips of between 5% and 10%, depending on the attention you receive, are expected. Taxi drivers receive 5% of the meter and, in most cases, 50 to 100 pta is enough for porters, bellhops, and (per night) for chambermaids.

**BANKING/BUSINESS HOURS** Most banks are open weekdays from 9 AM to 2 PM and Saturdays to 1:30 PM; many are closed Saturdays during the summer. Most other businesses are open weekdays from 9 AM to 2 PM and from 4:30 to 7 PM, though some have changed to an 8 AM to 3 PM schedule.

**NATIONAL HOLIDAYS** *New Year's Day* (January 1), *Epiphany* (January 6), *St. Joseph's Day* (March 19), *Good Friday* (April 14), *Easter Sunday* (April 16), *Easter Monday* (April 17), *Día del Trabajo* (May 1), *San Isidro Day* (May 15), *Feast of the Assumption* (August 15), *National Day* (October 12), *All Saints' Day* (November 1), *Constitution Day* (December 6), the *Feast of the Immaculate Conception* (December 8), and *Christmas Day* (December 25).

**LOCAL COVERAGE** *El País* (liberal) and *ABC* (conservative), among Spain's principal Spanish-language dailies, offer local, national, and international news, along with arts and entertainment listings. The *Guía del Ocio* ("Leisure Guide"), also in Spanish, is the most complete weekly guide to restaurants, entertainment, culture, and sports. The city government publishes a quasi-bilingual monthly guide called *¿Qué Hacer en Madrid? (What's On in Madrid?)*. The *International Herald Tribune,* the international edition of *USA Today,* and some US and British newspapers are widely available downtown (especially in and around the Puerta del Sol).

**TELEPHONE** The city code for Madrid and surrounding areas is 1. When calling from one area to another within Spain dial 9 + city code + local number. The country code for Spain is 34. Dial 091 or 092 for emergency assistance.

## GETTING AROUND

**AIRPORT** The *Aeropuerto Internacional de Barajas,* 10 miles (16 km) from downtown Madrid, handles international and domestic flights. It is about a 20-minute taxi ride from the center of the city, depending on traffic. Public buses run every 15 minutes between the airport and the air terminal in the center of the city under Plaza de Colón; the buses are yellow and are marked "Aeropuerto." *Iberia* airlines has an office at the *Palace* hotel, and another at 130 Calle Velázquez (phone: 411-1011 for domestic reservations; 563-9966 for international reservations).

**BUS** Excellent bus service is available throughout Madrid. There is normal service from 6 AM to midnight; between midnight and 6 AM buses run every 30 minutes from Plaza de la Cibeles and Puerta del Sol. Signs clearly marking the routes are at each bus stop. Buy individual tickets from the driver (fare is 125 pesetas, roughly 95¢). Discounted *bonobus* passes good for ten rides can be bought for 600 pesetas (about $4.55) at *Empresa Municipal de Transportes (EMT)* kiosks all over the city, including one on the east side of Puerta del Sol and another at the south side of Plaza de la Cibeles; upon boarding the bus, insert the pass into the date-stamping machine behind the driver. For information on the city bus system, call *EMT* at 401-9900. Inter-city and international bus service is available from several stations; the *Estación Sur de Autobuses* (17 Calle Canarias; phone: 468-4200), serving Andalusia and other points south, is the largest.

**CAR RENTAL** Most international and Spanish firms have offices at Madrid's *Aeropuerto Internacional de Barajas,* and some are based at the *Chamartín* and *Atocha* train stations. In the city are *América* (23 Calle Cartagena; phone: 246-7919); *Atesa* (59 Gran Vía; phone: 247-0202; and 25 Calle Princesa; phone: 241-5004); *Avis* (60 Gran Vía; phone: 247-2048; and in the airport bus terminal under Plaza de Colón; phone: 576-2862); *Europcar* (29 Calle Orense; phone: 445-9930; and 12 Calle García de Paredes; phone: 448-8706); *Hertz* (88 Gran Vía; phone: 248-5803; and in the *Castellana Inter-Con-*

*tinental Hotel,* 49 Paseo de la Castellana; phone: 319-0378); and *Ital* (31 Calle Princesa; phone: 241-9403).

**SUBWAY** Madrid's clean, efficient metro runs from 6 AM to 1:30 AM. Stops along all 10 lines are clearly marked, and the color-coded maps are easy to read. Tickets are purchased from machines and inserted into electronic turnstiles, or they're bought at pass-through booths. (Do not discard the ticket until the end of the ride.) A single ride costs 125 pesetas (roughly 90¢) and ten-ride *bonobus* tickets also are available at metro stations for 600 pesetas (about $4.35). For subway information, call 435-2266.

**TAXI** Metered cabs are white with a diagonal red line. If a cab is available, it will have a windshield sign that says *libre* (free) and an illuminated green light on its roof. Fares are moderate; note that taxis charge an additional 55 pesetas (about 40¢) for picking up passengers at the airport, as well as another 30 pesetas (20¢) per bag. There is also a 55-peseta surcharge for all rides from about 11:30 PM to 6 AM, as well as all day on Sundays and holidays. Taxis can be hailed on the street, picked up at cab stands, or summoned by phone. Call *Radio-Teléfono Taxi* (phone: 247-8200); *Radio-Taxi* (phone: 404-9000); or *Tele-Taxi* (phone: 445-9008).

**TOURS** Companies offering half-day motorcoach tours of the city include *Juliá Tours* (68 Gran Vía; phone: 541-9125); *Pullmantur* (8 Plaza de Oriente; phone: 541-1805); and *Trapsatur* (23 Calle San Bernardo; phone: 542-6666). *Juliá Tours* also can be booked in the US through their US representative, *Bravo Tours* (182 Main St., Ridgefield Park, NJ 07760; phone: 800-272-8764). A new city-operated *Madrid Vision Bus* is a great way to see the major sights. Starting and finishing in front of the *Prado,* it makes 15 stops, at monuments, plazas, major museums, and shopping locations. Passengers may remain on board for the entire hour-and-a-half tour or get off at any stop and reboard a later bus. Multilingual on-board guides narrate and answer questions using a special audio system with individual headsets. There are four tours daily, two in the morning and two in the afternoon (morning only on Sundays and Mondays). Tickets are purchased on board. For more information inquire at tourism offices or hotel desks.

**TRAIN** The two major stations of *RENFE,* the Spanish national railway, are *Estación de Chamartín* at the north end of Madrid (north of Plaza de Castilla) and *Estación de Atocha* at the south end (near Plaza Emperador Carlos V). Both serve long-distance trains, as well as commuter trains to surrounding areas. West of Plaza de España, a third station, *Estación Príncipe Pío* (also called *Estación del Norte*), serves some lines to northern Spain. *RENFE*'s main city ticket office is located at 44 Calle de Alcalá (phone: 429-0518 for information; 429-8228 for reservations). Tickets also can be purchased at the train stations and at the city's two other *RENFE* stations: *Estación Nuevos Ministerios* (Paseo de la Castellana and Calle de Villa Verde Raimundo Fernández) and *Estación de Recoletos* (Paseo de Recoletos).

*RENFE*'s new bullet train, the *AVE* (*Alta Velocidad Española*), makes the trip to Seville in two and a half hours, departing *Estación de Atocha* every hour on the hour. Prices vary according to time of day, and there are three classes of service: *turista, preferencia* (business class), and *club* (first class). Reservations should be made at *RENFE* offices, through a Madrid travel agent, or in the US through *Marketing Ahead* (433 Fifth Ave., New York, NY; phone: 212-686-9213 in New York City; 800-223-1356 elsewhere in the US; fax: 212-686-0271).

## LOCAL SERVICES

**DENTIST (ENGLISH-SPEAKING)** Ask at the *US Embassy* (phone: 577-4000) or your hotel concierge.

**DRY CLEANER** *El Corte Inglés* department store (3 Calle Preciados; phone: 532-1800) also does laundry.

**FAX SERVICE** At the *Palacio de Comunicaciones* (Plaza de Cibeles; phone: 521-4004 or 521-8195) or the *Regis Business Center* (93 Paseo de la Castellana; phone: 555-8772).

**LIMOUSINE SERVICE** *American Express* (2 Plaza de las Cortes; phone: 322-5500) makes arrangements with English-speaking drivers.

**MEDICAL EMERGENCY** *British American Hospital* (1 Paseo de Juan XXIII; phone: 234-6700); *La Paz Hospital* (Paseo de la Castellana; phone: 734-2600); *Red Cross Central Hospital* (22 Av. Reina Victoria; phone: 233-3900; 233-7777 for emergencies).

**MESSENGER SERVICE** *Mensajeros Express* (5 Calle Berlín; phone: 255-3300).

**NATIONAL/INTERNATIONAL COURIER** Near *Barajas* airport: *DHL Worldwide Express* (17 Torres Quevedo, Polígono Fin de Semana; phone: 747-3400); *Federal Express* (3 Calle Campezo, nave 5, Polígono de las Mercedes; phone: 329-1444). *DHL* also has a downtown office at 1 María de Molina (phone: 561-7127).

**OFFICE EQUIPMENT RENTAL** *El 7* (39 Calle de Hortaleza; phone: 522-5943) for typewriters; *Telson* (64 Pradillo; phone: 413-4463) for audiovisual equipment.

**PHARMACY** To find the all-night pharmacy closest to your hotel, call the 24-hour pharmacy hotline, 098. Pharmacy hours also are listed in the newspapers; look under "Farmacias de Guardia."

**PHOTOCOPIES** There are shops throughout the city. Outstanding is *Prontaprint* (at two locations: 15 Jacometrezo, just off the Gran Vía, between Plaza Callao and Plaza Santo Domingo; phone: 248-9958; and 56 María de Molina; phone: 411-0823). It's open weekdays from 10 AM to 7 PM.

**POST OFFICE** The main post office is the *Palacio de Comunicaciones* at Plaza de Cibeles (phone: 521-4004 or 521-8195). Hours vary according to the service provided; stamps can be purchased from 9 AM to 10 PM.

**SECRETARY/STENOGRAPHER (ENGLISH-SPEAKING)** *CADRESSA* (33 General Margallo; phone: 270-3077); *Regus Business Center* (see *Fax Service,* above).

**TAILOR** *Galeote M. Córdova* (10 Calle Manuel de Falla; phone: 457-7539).

**TRANSLATOR** *CADRESSA (see Secretary/Stenographer,* above*); Intercom English SA* (19 Calle General Martínez Campos; phone: 445-4751); and *Siasa Congresos* (134 Paseo de la Habana; phone: 457-4891).

**OTHER** Convention facilities: The *Parque Ferial Juan Carlos I* is a vast, multifaceted convention and exhibition complex near *Barajas International Airport.* The center is already in use, although its completion is not scheduled until the year 2000, when it will rank as the most modern trade fair complex in Europe. For information call the *Madrid Convention Bureau* (phone: 588-2930; fax: 588-2914) or Madrid's trade fair association, *IFEMA (Instituto Federal de Madrid;* phone: 722-5180 or 722-5000). In addition, the *Palacio de Congresos* (99 Paseo de la Castellana; phone: 555-1600 or 555-4906) has two auditoriums that can be joined for a total capacity of 2,684 people, an amphitheater for up to 900, eight meeting rooms for up to 320, audiovisual equipment, closed-circuit TV, a cafeteria, banquet hall, and private dining rooms for 100; total capacity is 10,000 people. *Casa de Campo,* located on the outskirts of Madrid, has facilities on its fairgrounds and in its auditorium space for hundreds of stands, and the meeting hall has a capacity for 608. For information call *Auditorio del Recinto de la Casa de Campo* (Av. Portugal; phone: 463-6334). The *Madrid Convention Bureau* (69 Calle Mayor; phone: 588-2930) offers full assistance for every aspect of meeting and convention arrangements.

## SPECIAL EVENTS

Madrid has a distinctive, exuberant way of celebrating Spain's national holidays, as well as its own year-long calendar of local fairs and festivals. *Madrileños* go all out for *Carnaval,* a weeklong nonstop street fiesta of parades and dancing that climaxes on *Miércoles de Ceniza* (Ash Wednesday) with the *Entierro de la Sardina* (Burial of the Sardine), in which a cardboard image of a sardine is burned to symbolize the end of *Cuaresma* (Lent), with its restrictions on eating meat. The *Festival Internacional del Teatro* and the *Festival Internacional del Cine* (International Theater Festival and International Film Festival) are held in April. On the *Dos de Mayo* (Second of May) at Plaza 2 de Mayo in the Malasaña district, processions and events commemorate the city's uprising against the invading French, which Goya portrayed so dramatically. Even more *madrileño* are the *Fiestas de San Isidro* (Feast Days of St. Isidro)— 10 days of nonstop street fairs, festivals, concerts, special daily bullfights, and more, all in celebration of Madrid's male patron saint, whose feast day is on May 15. On June 13, the *Verbena de San Antonio* (St. Anthony's Fair) takes place at the shrine of *San Antonio de la Florida* (5 Paseo de la Florida; closed Mondays; phone: 542-0722) with outdoor singing, dancing, and traditional drinking from the fountain of the *Ermita de San Isidro* (Hermitage of St. Isidro).

Despite the mass exodus of summer vacationers Madrid is lively during the summer. During July, August, and early September, the city government presents *Veranos en la Villa* ("Summers in Town"), two-plus months of countless events and performances featuring international superstars and local talent—ballet, symphonic music, opera, jazz, rock, pop, salsa, *zarzuelas,* films, and many diverse exhibitions—in open-air and theater settings throughout the city. There are also colorful *verbenas* (street fairs) on the feast days of three of Madrid's most popular saints: San Cayetano (August 3), San Lorenzo (August 5), and La Virgen de la Paloma (August 15). In such *barrios castizos* as Lavapiés, Embajadores, and Puerta de Toledo, *madrileños* dress in the traditional attire of *chulos* and *chulapas* reminiscent of the period of 19th-century *zarzuelas.* They gather at lively street fairs to eat, drink, and dance the *chotis* and *pasodoble,* enjoying folk music performances, organ-grinders, processions, and *limonada* (not lemonade, but a kind of white-wine sangria). The world class *Festival Internacional de Jazz de Madrid* is held in late October and/or early November.

From October to the beginning of December, the *Festival de Otoño* (Autumn Festival) presents concerts and performances by top international and Spanish companies at Madrid theaters and concert halls. On November 9 the city celebrates St. Isidro's female counterpart, Madrid's patroness, La Virgen de la Almudena. During the season of *Navidades* (Christmas), the streets are bedecked with festive lights, and the Plaza Mayor fills with countless stands selling decorations, figurines for nativity scenes, candies, wreaths, and *Christmas* trees. On *Noche Vieja* (New Year's Eve), throngs gather at the Puerta del Sol to swallow one grape at each stroke of the clock at midnight, wishing for 12 months of good luck in the new year. The *Christmas* season lasts until January 6, the *Epifanía* (Feast of the Epiphany), also known as the *Día de los Reyes Magos* (Three Wise Men's Day), on the eve of which is the *Cabalgata de los Reyes,* the procession through the city streets by the gift-giving Reyes Magos, who are in Spain what Santa Claus is in the US (though even in Spain Kris Kringle is making inroads).

## MUSEUMS

The city's major museums are described in *Special Places.* Included in the following list of additional museums are certain churches that, because of their high artistic quality, should not be overlooked. Hours of many museums may vary during the summer, and smaller museums may be closed during July and August; contact the *Oficina de Museos* (Museums Office; phone: 248-7404) for up-to-date information.

**BASÍLICA DE SAN MIGUEL (BASILICA OF ST. MICHAEL)** An unusual 18th-century church with an air of Italian Baroque in its convex façade and graceful interior. Open daily. No admission charge. 4 Calle de San Justo (phone: 548-4011).

**CASA-MUSEO DE LOPE DE VEGA (LOPE DE VEGA HOUSE-MUSEUM)** The home and garden of Spain's great golden age dramatist. Hours are erratic; call in advance. Closed Sundays. Admission charge. 11 Calle Cervantes (phone: 429-9216).

**IGLESIA DE SAN ISIDRO (CHURCH OF ST. ISIDRO)** This imposing 17th-century church was temporarily designated Madrid's cathedral in 1885, pending the completion of the *Catedral de la Almudena*—which after more than a century of reconstruction was finally completed in 1993. The entombed remains of St. Isidro, Madrid's male patron saint, and those of his wife, Santa María de la Cabeza, are on the altar. Open daily. No admission charge. 37 Calle Toledo (phone: 369-2386).

**ESTUDIO Y MUSEO SOROLLA (SOROLLA STUDIO AND MUSEUM)** The house in which Joaquín Sorolla, the Valencian Impressionist "painter of light," lived, worked, and finally died in 1923. The studio and library remain intact. There's also a collection of his works. Closed Mondays. Admission charge. 37 Calle General Martínez Campos (phone: 410-1584).

**IGLESIA Y CONVENTO DE SAN JERÓNIMO EL REAL (ROYAL CHURCH AND CONVENT OF ST. JEROME)** This giant Gothic temple overlooking the *Prado* was built by order of King Ferdinand and Queen Isabella in 1503 (at the time, outside the city walls). With its Mudejar brickwork façade, *San Jerónimo* has become even more impressive after three renovations. Open daily. No admission charge. 19 Calle Ruiz de Alarcón (phone: 420-3578).

**MUSEO CERRALBO** The palatial 19th-century mansion of the Marquis of Cerralbo houses an important collection of art, antiques, ceramics, tapestries, and ancient artifacts. Outstanding among the paintings are works by El Greco, Ribera, Velázquez, Zurbarán, and Van Dyck. Closed Mondays and August. Admission charge. 17 Calle Ventura Rodríguez (phone: 547-3646).

**MUSEO DE LA CIUDAD (CITY MUSEUM)** This museum testifies to the evolution of Madrid. Open daily; weekend hours 10 AM to 2 PM. 140 Calle Príncipe de Vergara (phone: 588-6582).

**MUSEO LÁZARO GALDIANO** Named for its founder, whose palatial mansion houses his extraordinary collection of art, jewelry, ivory, and enamel. Open from 10 AM to 2 PM; closed Mondays and August. Admission charge. 122 Calle Serrano (phone: 561-6084).

**MUSEO NACIONAL DE ARTES DECORATIVAS (NATIONAL MUSEUM OF DEC-ORATIVE ARTS)** Four floors of furniture, porcelains, jewelry, Spanish tiles and fans, a full Valencian kitchen, and handicrafts from the 16th through 19th centuries. Closed Mondays and during summer. Admission charge. 12 Calle Montalbán (phone: 521-3440).

**MUSEO NACIONAL FERROVIARIO (NATIONAL RAILROAD MUSEUM)** Madrid's first train station, the *Estación de las Delicias,* now is a museum complete with intact antique trains, royal cars, and other predecessors of the modern railroad. Closed Mondays; Sunday and holiday hours 10 AM to 2 PM. Admission charge. 61 Paseo de las Delicias (phone: 227-3121).

**MUSEO PANTEÓN DE GOYA (PANTHEON MUSEUM OF GOYA)** Goya painted the magnificent religious frescoes on the dome and walls of this small 18th-century church, also called the *Ermita de San Antonio* (St. Anthony's Hermitage), which became his tomb. Closed Mondays and holidays; weekend hours 10 AM to 2 PM. No admission charge. Glorieta de San Antonio de la Florida (phone: 542-0722).

**MUSEO ROMÁNTICO (ROMANTIC MUSEUM)** Paintings, furniture, and decor of 19th-century Madrid, housed in an 18th-century mansion. Closed Mondays and August; Sunday hours 10 AM to 2 PM. Admission charge. 13 Calle San Mateo (phone: 448-1071).

**MUSEO TAURINO (BULLFIGHTING MUSEUM)** A major collection of bullfighting memorabilia. Open daily except Mondays from 9:30 AM to 1 PM during bullfighting season (May through October). Admission charge. Plaza de Toros Monumental de las Ventas, Patio de Caballos, 237 Calle de Alcalá (phone: 555-1857).

**TEMPLO DE DEBOD** A gift from the Egyptian government in the 1970s, this 2,500-year-old Egyptian temple was shipped to Madrid in 1,359 cases and reassembled, towering over a reflecting pool. Theater and music performances are held here in summer. Closed weekend afternoons, Mondays, and holidays. No admission charge. Calle Ferraz, Parque del Oeste (no phone; for information call the city tourist office).

## SHOPPING

Madrid's 54,000 stores and shops offer everything imaginable, from high fashion to flamenco guitars. Handicrafts, fine leather goods, embroidery, ceramics, Lladró porcelain, art, and antiques are among the enticing buys available throughout the city. Everything goes on sale twice a year—after the *Christmas* season (which in Spain means January 7, the day after *Epiphany*) and during the summer. The big summer sales (*rebajas*) begin in July, and prices are reduced even more during the first three weeks of August. Shops generally open at 9:30 AM, close from 1:30 to 4:30 PM for lunch and the siesta, and close for the night at 8 PM. The huge flagship stores of Spain's two major department store chains—*El Corte Inglés* (3 Calle Preciados; phone: 532-1800) and *Galerías Preciados* (1 Plaza de Callao; phone: 536-8000)—are next to each other in the pedestrian shopping area between the Gran Vía and Puerta del Sol. Unlike most retailers, they remain open during the lunch and siesta hours, and they provide such services for tourists as English-speaking escorts to accompany shoppers and coordination of shipping services to hotel or home. Branch stores of *El Corte Inglés* are at 42 Calle Princesa (phone: 542-4800), 76 Calle Goya (phone: 577-7171), and

79 Calle Raimundo Fernández Villaverde (the biggest of all, just off the Paseo de la Castellana; phone: 556-2300). Branches of *Galerías Preciados* are at 10-11 Calle Arapiles, 87 Calle Goya, 47 Calle Serrano, and at the *La Vaguada* shopping center in northern Madrid.

Madrid's antiques row is the Calle del Prado, near the *Prado*. Worth a look is *Luis Rodríguez-Morueco* (16 Calle del Prado; phone: 429-5757), which features treasures from the 16th, 17th, and 18th centuries, and *Durán* (12 Calle Serrano; phone: 431-9777), one of Madrid's oldest antiques shops and considered the finest. On the first Sunday of every month, the *Wellington* hotel (see *Checking In*) at 8 Calle Velázquez hosts an antiques fair featuring an array of jewelry, books, and furniture. For more concentrated antiques browsing and buying, try *Centro de Anticuarios Lagasca* (36 Calle Lagasca). It has 11 antiques shops under one roof, including *Luis Carabe* (phone: 431-5872), which has an interesting collection of crystal. *Alcocer* (5 Calle Santa Catalina, 68 Calle Pelayo, and 104 Calle Hortaleza) is a fourth-generation antiques dealer specializing in furniture, paintings, and other objects, including antique Spanish silver. The bibliophile can savor the experience of *Luis Bardón Mesa* (3 Plaza San Martín; phone: 521-5514), which counts among its 50,000 volumes masterpieces by authors such as Cervantes, Lope de Vega, and Calderón de la Barca. Also try *Librería del Callejón* (4 Callejón de Preciados; phone: 521-7167).

Other places to browse or buy include *La Galería del Prado* (phone: 429-7551), a sparkling addition to the *Palace* hotel (7 Plaza de las Cortes); it's a glamorous assembly of 38 top fashion boutiques, art galleries, jewelers, and gift shops, as well as a fancy food shop, a beauty salon, a bookstore, and a buffet-style restaurant. Another shopping mall is *Moda Shopping* (40 Av. General Perón), just off Paseo de la Castellana, with more than 60 establishments selling everything from high fashion to sporting goods, plus plenty of restaurants and bars. *La Vaguada* (Av. Ginzo de Lima and Monforte de Lemos) is an enormous 350-shop complex, complete with movie houses, restaurants, discos, amusement rides, and parking for 4,000 cars.

*El Rastro,* Madrid's legendary outdoor flea market (open Sundays and holiday mornings only), spreads for countless blocks in the old section of the city, beginning at Plaza de Cascorro and fanning south along Ribera de Curtidores to Ronda de Toledo. Hundreds of stands sell everything from canaries to museum-piece antiques; bargaining—preferably in Spanish—is customary. (Guard wallets and purses from pickpockets.) The *Cuesta de Moyano,* on a stretch of Calle de Claudio Moyano (along the south side of the *Real Jardín Botánico),* has a string of bookstalls selling new, used, and out-of-print books. It's open daily year-round. On Sunday mornings, the arcades of the Plaza Mayor overflow with stamp and coin dealers, buyers and sellers.

Other recommended shopping spots:

***Artespaña*** Government-run, with a wide range of handicrafts and home furnishings from all over Spain. 3 Plaza de las Cortes, 14 Calle Hermosilla, 33 Calle Don Ramón de la Cruz, and *La Vaguada*, Av. Ginzo de Lima and Monforte de Lemos (phone for all locations: 413-6262).

***El Aventurero*** A small bookstore specializing in guidebooks, maps, books on the art of bullfighting and other Spanish subjects, and an ample selection in English. Just off Plaza Mayor at 15 Calle Toledo (phone: 266-4457).

***Canalejas*** Top-quality men's shirtmakers, specializing in the classic European formfitting cut. 20 Carrera de San Jerónimo (phone: 521-8075).

***Casa Bonet*** A variety of handmade embroidery, including beautiful items from Palma de Mallorca. The prices are reasonable. 76 Calle Núñez de Balboa (phone: 575-0912).

***Casa de Diego*** Founded in 1858, this old-time store makes hand-painted fans, frames for displaying them, canes, and umbrellas. Two locations: 12 Puerta del Sol (phone: 522-6643) and 4 Calle Mesonero Romanos (phone: 531-0223).

***Casa Jiménez*** Another store specializing in fans, plus *mantones de manila*, fine lace shawls. 42 Calle Preciados (phone: 548-0526).

***Casa del Libro*** Madrid's biggest book store. 29 Gran Vía (phone: 521-1932). A newer branch, with four floors, is at 3 Calle Maestro Vitoria (phone: 521-4898).

***Cerámica el Alfar*** A large assortment of regional ceramics and earthenware; glazed-tile reproductions of famous Spanish paintings are a specialty. 112 Calle Claudio Coello (phone: 411-3587).

***Cortefiel*** A leading purveyor of men's and women's fashions and accessories. Branches at 180 Paseo de la Castellana (phone: 359-5713), 27 Gran Vía (phone: 522-0093), and 76 Gran Vía (phone: 547-1701) specialize in men's fashions only; the store at 146 Paseo de la Castellana (phone: 250-3638) caters exclusively to women; shops for both sexes are at 43-45 Raimundo Fernández Villaverde (phone: 554-2658) and 40 Calle Serrano (phone: 431-3342).

***Fernando Durán*** One of the city's most prestigious shops for antique furniture, sculpture, china, and a wide variety of silver items. 11 Calle Conde de Aranda (phone: 431-3806).

***Gil, Sucesor de Antolín Quevedo*** Spanish and international celebrities purchase work-of-art shawls, mantillas, and embroidery at this generations-old establishment. 2 Carrera de San Jerónimo (phone: 521-2549).

***Gritos de Madrid*** A fine ceramics shop, this is the place to buy works by the owner, master craftsman Eduardo Fernández, who's responsible for the restoration of Madrid's interesting hand-illustrated tile street signs and whose ceramic mural of 17th-century Madrid hangs in the museum of the *Casa de la Villa* (City Hall). 6 Plaza Mayor (phone: 265-9154).

**Horno del Pozo** Established in 1830, this small shop has the best *hojaldres* (puff pastries) in town. 8 Calle del Pozo (phone: 522-3894).

**Jesús del Pozo** One of Spain's top "jet-set" designers for men and women, and famed for his elegant evening gowns. 28 Almirante (phone: 531-6676).

**José Ramírez** They have supplied *madrileños* with fine classical and flamenco guitars for generations. 2-5 Calle Concepción Jerónima (phone: 227-9935).

**Loewe** Fine leather fashions, accessories, and luggage. At several locations, including 8 Gran Vía, 26 Calle Serrano, and at the *Palace* hotel; the shop at 34 Calle Serrano carries men's fashions exclusively (phone for all locations: 435-3023).

**Manuel Contreras** One of the city's largest collections of guitars and other musical instruments. 80 Calle Mayor (phone: 248-5926).

**Manuel Herrero** A popular leather outlet, offering a wide selection and good prices. 7 and 23 Calle Preciados (phone: 521-2990).

**María Vico** A small, enticing shop with an inimitable selection of small antiques, priceless collector's-item books, and engravings. Passageway at 3 Conde de Aranda (phone: 435-2882).

**Maty** For dance enthusiasts: authentic regional (including flamenco) costumes for men, women, and children. Dance shoes and boots are also sold. 2 Calle Maestro Vitoria (phone: 479-8802).

**México II** Over 200,000 books here from the 16th century to the 18th, as well as drawers full of historical prints and maps. 17 Calle Huertas (phone: 532-7664).

**Musgo** Five row houses filled with contemporary clothing and furnishings. 36 Calle Hermosilla (phone: 431-1156). Three additional locations: 15 Calle O'Donnell (phone: 575-3223); 34 Paseo de la Habana (phone: 562-8624); and 23 Santa Hortensia (phone: 519-5038).

**Plata Meneses** Spain's leading silver manufacturer, featuring a huge line of giftware and place settings. 3 Plaza de Canalejas (phone: 429-4236).

**Seseña** Founded in 1901, this store manufactures a fine line of capes for men and women. 23 Calle Cruz (phone: 531-6840).

**Sybilla** Famed in Spain and the rest of Europe as well as in the US, this young Spanish designer excels in bold and colorful pret-à-porter women's fashions. 12 Calle Jorge Juan (phone: 578-1322).

**Turner English Bookshop** An impressive collection of English, French, and Spanish titles. 3 Calle Génova, on Plaza de Santa Bárbara (phone: 319-2037).

## SPORTS AND FITNESS

**BASKETBALL** Madrid plays host to much of the finest basketball played in Europe. The city is represented by two professional teams, *Real Madrid* and *Estudiantes*, and also is the home of the Spanish national and Olympic squads. The most important games are played at the *Pabellón de Deportes del Real Madrid* (259 Paseo de la Castellana; phone: 315-0046); the *Palacio de Deportes de la Comunidad de Madrid* (19 Av. Felipe II; phone: 401-9100), and at the *Polideportivo Collado Villalva* (in Collado Villalva, a suburb of Madrid; phone: 850-5311).

**BULLFIGHTING** Madrid's bullring, *Plaza de Toros Monumental de las Ventas* (237 Calle de Alcalá; phone: 356-2200), seats 22,300 people. The season runs from mid-May through October. Tickets may be purchased the day of the event at a counter at 3 Calle Vitoria (near the Puerta del Sol), at the bullring, or through a hotel concierge.

**FISHING** There are fishing reserves along the Lozoya, Madarquillos, Jarama, and Cofio Rivers not far from Madrid. They are populated mostly by trout, carp, black bass, pike, and barbel. The Santillana reservoir is good for pike. For season and license information, contact the *Dirección General del Medio Rural* (39 Calle Jorge Juan; phone: 435-5121).

**FITNESS CENTERS** Madrid has 27 municipal gymnasiums; for information on the one nearest your hotel, call 464-9050. A number of major hotels also have gyms and fitness centers, though many of these are reserved for guests.

**GOLF** Among the city's top tee-off spots are the rambling 18-hole, par 72 course at the *Club de Golf de Las Lomas–El Bosque* (Villaviciosa de Odón; phone: 616-7427); the prestigious *Real Club de la Puerta de Hierro* (Av. Miraflores in metro Madrid; phone: 316-1745), which features two 18-hole courses; and the 18-hole *Club de Golf la Herrería* (near *El Escorial* monastery on Carretera Robledo–San Lorenzo de El Escorial; phone: 890-5111). There's also the *Club de Campo Villa de Madrid* (about 2½ miles/4 km outside Madrid on the Carretera de Castilla; phone: 207-0395), with 18-hole and nine-hole courses; the Jack Nicklaus–designed 18-hole course at the *Club de Golf La Moraleja* (7 miles/11 km north of town along the Burgos–Madrid highway; phone: 650-0700); and the 18 holes of the *Nuevo Club de Golf de Madrid* (at Las Matas, 16 miles/26 km west of town via the Carretera de La Coruña; phone: 630-0820). The *Federación Española de Golf* (9 Calle Capitán Haya; phone: 555-2682) has details on most of the area's facilities; hotels also can provide information regarding the use of the clubs by non-members.

**HORSE RACING** The *Hipódromo de la Zarzuela* (4 miles/7 km north of the center, along Carretera de La Coruña; phone: 207-0140) features Sunday afternoon races during spring and fall meets. Buses for the track leave from the corner of Calle Princesa and Calle Hilarión Eslava.

**JOGGING** *Parque del Buen Retiro* and *Casa de Campo* both have jogging tracks.

**SKIING** The mountain resort *Puerto de Navacerrada* (37 miles/60 km north of Madrid; phone: 852-1435) has 12 ski runs and six lifts.

**SOCCER** One of Spain's most popular teams, the capital's *Real Madrid,* plays its home games at the *Estadio Santiago Bernabeu* (1 Calle Concha Espina; phone: 250-0600); its rival, *Atlético de Madrid,* takes the field at the *Estadio Vicente Calderón* (6 Paseo Virgen del Puerto; phone: 266-2864).

**SWIMMING** Madrid has 150 public pools, including those indoors and outdoors at *Casa de Campo* (Av. del Angel; phone: 463-0050). Another nice outdoor pool is at *La Elipa* (Av. de la Paz; phone: 430-3358), which also has an indoor pool and an area set aside for male and female nude sunbathing. For information on other municipal pools call 463-5498.

**TENNIS** Among the hundreds of public and private tennis courts in town are the 35 courts at the *Club de Campo Villa de Madrid* (Carretera de Castilla; phone: 207-0395) and the 28 courts of the *Club de Tenis Chamartín* (2 Calle Federico Salmón; phone: 345-2500); and the *Club Internacional de Tenis* (Km 3, Carretera el Plantío–Majada-honda; phone: 639-2401). These are private clubs, but it's worth inquiring about short-term memberships.

## THEATER

Theater productions are in Spanish. Anyone fluent and interested in the Spanish classics should check the *Guía del Ocio* for what's playing at the *Teatro Español* (25 Calle del Príncipe; phone: 429-0318). Nearby, at *Teatro de la Comedia* (14 Calle del Príncipe; phone: 521-4931), the *Compañía Nacional de Teatro Clásico* (National Classical Theater Company) also puts on a fine repertoire of classic Spanish plays, as well as modern ones and foreign adaptations. The *Teatro Nacional María Guerrero* (4 Calle Tamayo y Baus; phone: 310-2949) is still another venue for both modern plays and classics of the Spanish and international repertoires. For the strictly modern and avant-garde, there's the *Centro Nacional de Nuevas Tendencias Escénicas* (National Center of New Theater Trends), housed at the *Sala Olimpia* (Plaza de Lavapiés; phone: 237-4622). Ballets, operas, and *zarzuelas* present fewer difficulties for nonspeakers of Spanish. Check listings for the restored *Teatro Nuevo Apolo Musical de Madrid* (1 Plaza Tirso de Molina; phone: 369-0637), home base for director José Tamayo's *Nueva Antología de la Zarzuela* company; *Teatro Lírico Nacional de la Zarzuela* (4 Calle Jovellanos; phone: 429-8225), which hosts opera, ballet, and concerts, as well as traditional *zarzuela;* and the *Centro Cultural de la Villa* (Plaza de Colón; phone: 575-6080), which presents both theater and *zarzuela.*

# MUSIC

Among the best of Madrid's numerous excellent flamenco *tablaos* (cabarets) are *Corral de la Morería* (17 Calle Morería; phone: 265-8146), a simply furnished cellar in the old quarter; *Café de Chinitas* (7 Calle Torija; phone: 547-1502), an intimate club frequented by Madrid's beautiful people; *Torres Bermejas* (11 Calle Mesonero Romanos; phone: 532-3322), a dinner-theater considered by many to put on the most authentic flamenco show in town; and *Venta del Gato* (about 5 miles/8 km outside Madrid on the road to Burgos, at Km 12.1 Carretera de Burgos; phone: 760-6060). *Café Central* (10 Plaza del Angel; phone: 468-0844) offers live jazz, classical, salsa, or folk music nightly, as well as late dinner. A classical music ambience (including concerts and recitals) can be enjoyed at the 19th-century *Palacio Gaviria* (see *Nightclubs and Nightlife,* below). Madrid's main hall for classical concerts is the *Auditorio Nacional de Música* (146 Calle Príncipe de Vergara; phone: 337-0100), the home of the *Orquesta Nacional de España* (Spanish National Orchestra) and the *Coro Nacional de España* (Spanish National Chorus). Symphonic, choral, chamber, and solo works are offered in either of its two theaters during the May-to-October season. Home base for the *Orquesta y Coro de Radio-Televisión Española* (Spanish Radio-Television Orchestra and Chorus) is the *Teatro Monumental* (65 Calle Atocha; phone: 429-1281). The opera season, which runs from January through May, brings a host of performances to the *Teatro Lírico Nacional de la Zarzuela* (see *Theater,* above). The *Teatro de la Opera* (Plaza de Oriente; phone: 547-1405), formerly the *Teatro Real,* will host international opera performances upon completion of its seemingly eternal renovation (at press time no end was in sight). Classical music can also be heard at several other locations, including the *Fundación Juan March* (77 Calle Castelló; phone: 435-4250). For a list of theaters presenting *zarzuela,* Spain's traditional form of operetta, see *Theater* above.

# NIGHTCLUBS AND NIGHTLIFE

Nightlife in Madrid can continue long into the early morning hours. Cover charges at cabarets and nightclubs include one drink, dancing, and floor shows that are becoming more risqué by the minute. Top choices include *Scala–Meliá Castilla* at the *Meliá Castilla* hotel (phone: 571-4411) and *Florida Park* (in the *Parque del Buen Retiro;* phone: 573-7804). For a night of gambling, dining, dancing, and entertainment, the *Casino Gran Madrid* has it all (Km 28.3, Carretera de la Coruña, Torrelodones; phone: 856-1100; free buses to the casino leave from 6 Plaza de España; the trip takes about 20 minutes). The latest dance rage in Madrid is the *sevillanas.* *Madrileños* have adopted the delightful dance music of their Andalusian cousins as their own, and *sevillanas* music plays at many discos. Among the best of dozens of *salas rocieras*—nightclubs dedicated to dancing and watching the *sevillanas*—are *El Portón* (25 Calle López de Hoyos; phone: 262-4956), *Al Andalus* (19 Calle Capitán Haya; phone: 556-1439), *La Caseta* (13 Calle General Castaños; phone: 419-0343), and *Almonte* (35 Calle de Juan Bravo; phone: 411-6880). *La Maestranza* (16 Calle Mauricio Legendre, near Plaza de Castilla; phone: 315-9059) features star *sevillanas* performers in its floor shows and also serves outstanding Andalusian dishes. Some discotheques and boîtes run two sessions a night, at 7 and 11 PM until the wee hours. Among the more popular are *Pachá* (11 Calle Barceló; phone: 446-0137) and *Joy Eslava* (11 Calle Arenal; phone: 266-5440), where ballroom dancing is now the fad. There's late dining and an energetic downstairs disco at *Archy* (11 Calle Marqués de Riscal; phone: 308-3162), while the latest gathering spot for the glitterati is *Teatriz* (15 Calle Hermosilla; phone: 577-5379). The *Cervecería Alemana* (6 Plaza Santa Ana; phone: 429-7033), a tavern that's an old Ernest Hemingway hangout, remains a favorite nightspot. For late-night jazz there's the popular *Clamores* (14 Calle Albuqyerque; phone: 445-7938); *Cock* (16 Calle Reina; no phone) draws an avant-garde set. Classical music lovers can drink it in to their hearts' content in the sumptuous salons of the *Palacio Gaviria* just off the Puerta del Sol (9 Calle Arenal; phone: 526-6069) in the converted palace of a 19th-century marquis (and alleged lover of Queen Isabel II); special concerts and recitals are also held here. *Madrileños* love to *pasear,* or stroll along the streets, and from April through October thousands of *terrazas*—outdoor cafés lining plazas, parks, and avenues—are jumping with nocturnal activity. Late revelers usually cap the evening with thick hot chocolate and *churros* (fried dough sticks) at *Chocolatería de San Ginés* (phone: 365-6546), which is open all night at 13 Calle Arenal just off Puerta del Sol in the alley behind an 18th-century church, the *Iglesia de San Ginés*.

# Best in Town

## CHECKING IN

Modern Madrid boasts at least 50,000 hotel beds in more than 800 establishments, with accommodations ranging from "grand luxe" to countless *hostales* and *pensiones.* Reservations are nonetheless recommended, especially between May and September and during such special events as national and local festivals, expositions, and conventions. Expect to pay $190 to $250 or more a night for a double room in a hotel listed as very expensive, from $130 to $180 in an establishment listed as expensive, from $55 to $120 in a moderately priced hotel, and $45 or less in an inexpensive one. Unless otherwise noted, the hotels listed offer private baths, air conditioning, telephones, and TV sets, and are in the 1 city code.

For an unforgettable experience in Madrid, we begin with our favorite, followed by our cost and quality choices of hotels, listed by price category.

**Ritz** The epitome of elegance, luxury, and Belle Epoque grace, this impeccably maintained classic was built at the behest of King Alfonso XIII. No two of the 156 rooms and 28 suites are alike, but all are adorned with paintings, antiques, and tailored handwoven carpeting from the Royal Tapestry Factory. Jacket and tie are appropriate for men in the bar and the exquisite *Ritz* restaurant, one of Madrid's finest (see *Eating Out*). The casual *Ritz Garden Terrace* also offers delightful dining, cocktails, and *tapas*. Business facilities include 24-hour room service, meeting rooms for up to 500, an English-speaking concierge, foreign currency exchange, secretarial services in English, audiovisual equipment, photocopiers, computers, cable TV news, translation services, and express checkout. 5 Plaza de la Lealtad (phone: 521-2857; 212-838-3110 in New York City; 800-223-6800 elsewhere in the US; fax: 232-8776).

## VERY EXPENSIVE

**Santo Mauro** This exquisite all-suite addition to Madrid's supreme echelon of *gran lujo* hotels is located in what was originally the turn-of-the-century palatial mansion of the Duques de Santo Mauro, and several embassies. It's centrally situated in Madrid's elegant Almagro–Castellana section in a faithfully restored French-style building. The interior decor, created by Madrid's hottest designers, is the last word in Art Deco. The 37 suites all feature a compact disc and cassette stereo system and satellite TV (VCRs are available on request). Other facilities include a sauna, an indoor pool, a summer terrace restaurant, and, in the mansion's original library, the *Belagua* restaurant (see *Eating Out*). Business facilities include 24-hour room service, an English-speaking concierge, foreign currency exchange, photocopiers, translation services, and express checkout. 36 Zurbano (phone: 319-6900; fax: 308-5417).

**Villa Magna** A Park Hyatt hotel, this property with 164 rooms and 18 suites is set amid landscaped gardens in the heart of aristocratic Madrid, right around the corner from the US Embassy. A multi-million-dollar remodeling project added unequaled luster—and technology—to the rooms. The *Champagne Bar* boasts one of Europe's finest selection of the bubbly, and the *Villa Magna* restaurant is celebrated for its imaginative specialties (see *Eating Out*). Richly decorated private salons accommodate meetings and banquets. Business facilities include 24-hour room service, meeting rooms for up to 250, an English-speaking concierge, foreign currency exchange, secretarial services in English, audiovisual equipment, photocopiers, computers, cable TV news, translation services, and express checkout.. 22 Paseo de la Castellana (phone: 576-7500;

800-233-1234; fax: 575-3158 for reservations; fax: 575-9504 to reach hotel guests).

**Villa Real** Among Madrid's newer establishments, its design and atmosphere embody Old Europe grace; marble, bronze, handcrafted wood, works of fine art, and antique furnishings create a seignorial interior decor. All 115 luxurious rooms and 19 suites feature satellite TV and three or more high-tech telephones. Elegantly furnished top-floor duplexes have two bathrooms—one with a sauna, the other with a Jacuzzi—and large private balconies overlooking the *Palacio de las Cortes Españolas* (Spanish Parliament Palace), the *Fuente de Neptuno* (Neptune Fountain), and the *Palacio de Villahermosa*. The hotel's choice setting—between Paseo del Prado and Puerta del Sol—couldn't be better. Business facilities include 24-hour room service, meeting rooms for up to 300, an English-speaking concierge, foreign currency exchange, secretarial services in English, audiovisual equipment, photocopiers, computers, cable TV news, translation services, and express checkout. 10-11 Plaza de las Cortes (phone: 420-3767).

EXPENSIVE

**Barajas** This hotel, close to Madrid's *Aeropuerto Internacional de Barajas*, offers 230 rooms and 18 suites, plus a garden swimming pool, a bar, a restaurant, and a health club. Free transportation is provided to and from the nearby airport terminals. Business facilities include 24-hour room service, meeting rooms for up to 675, an English-speaking concierge, foreign currency exchange, secretarial services in English, audiovisual equipment, photocopiers, computers, cable TV news, translation services, and express checkout. 305 Av. Logroño (phone: 747-7700).

**Castellana Inter-Continental** Its 310 rooms, all with modern accoutrements, are large and nicely decorated in pleasant pastels. Adjacent to the stately, marble-pillared lobby are car rental, airline, and tour desks, boutiques, a health club, and a business services department. *Los Continentes* restaurant and *La Ronda* piano bar are agreeable spots for meeting and eating. Business facilities include 24-hour room service, meeting rooms for up to 350, an English-speaking concierge, foreign currency exchange, secretarial services in English, audiovisual equipment, photocopiers, computers, cable TV news, translation services, and express checkout. 49 Paseo de la Castellana (phone: 410-0200; 800-327-5853; fax: 319-5853).

**Eurobuilding** A well-designed modern complex off the northern section of the Paseo de la Castellana near the *Palacio de Congresos* (Convention Center) and the *Estadio Santiago Bernabéu*. In addition to the 421-room hotel building, the *Eurobuilding 2* tower comprises 154 apartment-style units. There also are two outdoor pools, a health club, a hair salon, stores, and four restaurants. Business facilities include 24-hour room service, meeting rooms for up to 900, an English-speaking concierge, foreign currency exchange, secretarial services in English, audiovisual equipment, photocopiers, computers, cable TV news, translation services, and express checkout. 23 Calle Padre Damián (phone: 457-1700; 800-645-5687; fax: 457-9729).

**Holiday Inn Madrid** This modern and busy establishment with 313 rooms has an outdoor pool, health club, gymnasium, shopping arcade, and restaurants. It is near the *AZCA* shopping and commercial complex, the *Palacio de Congrsos* (Convention Center), *Estadio Santiago Bernabeu,* and the Paseo de la Castellana. Business facilities include meeting rooms for up to 450, an English-speaking concierge, foreign currency exchange, secretarial services in English, audiovisual equipment, photocopiers, computers, cable TV news, translation services, and express checkout. 4 Plaza Carlos Trías Bertrán (phone: 597-0102; 800-465-4329; fax: 597-0292).

**Meliá Castilla** With nearly 1,000 rooms and 17 suites, this modern highrise just off the Paseo de la Castellana in northern Madrid's business section is the largest hotel in Spain. Facilities and meeting rooms cater primarily to executive travelers. There is an outdoor pool, a gym, a sauna, a shopping arcade, several restaurants and bars, and a Las Vegas–style nightclub, the *Scala–Meliá Castilla.* Business facilities include 24-hour room service, meeting rooms for up to 800, an English-speaking concierge, foreign currency exchange, secretarial services in English, audiovisual equipment, photocopiers, computers, cable TV news, translation services, and express checkout. 43 Calle Capitán Haya (phone: 571-2811; 800-336-3542; fax: 571-2210).

**Meliá Madrid** Ideally located near the Plaza de España and very well run, this gleaming white, modern building has 266 tastefully decorated rooms and 23 suites. The dining room, grill, bar, and *Bong Bing* discotheque are popular meeting places. There's also a gym and a sauna. Business facilities include 24-hour room service, meeting rooms for up to 380, an English-speaking concierge, foreign currency exchange, secretarial services in English, audiovisual equipment, photocopiers, computers, cable TV news, translation services, and express checkout. 27 Calle Princesa (phone: 541-8200; 800-336-3542; fax: 541-1988).

**Miguel Angel** Conveniently located near Paseo de la Castellana, this 278-room, 26-suite property combines modern luxuries with 17th-, 18th-, and 19th-century paintings, tapestries, and furniture. Most rooms have balconies. Facilities include a health club with saunas, a Jacuzzi, a gym, and a heated indoor swimming pool. There are two restaurants and a bar. Business facilities include 24-hour room service, meeting rooms for up to 650, an English-speaking concierge, foreign currency exchange, secretarial services in English, audiovisual equipment, photocopiers, computers, cable TV news, translation services, and express checkout. 31 Calle Miguel Angel (phone: 442-8199; 800-423-6902; fax: 442-5320).

**Palace** This aristocratic Madrid landmark maintains its Belle Epoque elegance while offering the utmost of modern facilities in the spacious 518 rooms and 29 suites. Located in the heart of the city, the hotel overlooks the *Fuente de Neptuno* (Neptune Fountain) and Paseo del Prado. The lobby, embellished with trompe l'oeil painting, leads to a cozy lounge, which is topped by an immense painted-glass rotunda—an inviting setting for cocktails or informal dining at *El Ambigú,* with a musical backdrop of piano and violin until 2 AM. *El Bar del Palace* is *the* gathering place for politicians on break from their duties at the *Cortes* (Parliament) across the street. On the ground floor is the *Galería del Prado,* a collection of more than 40 fine boutiques, galleries, and shops, as well as *La Plaza,* a self-service restaurant. Business facilities include 24-hour room service, meeting rooms for up to 1,500, an English-speaking concierge, foreign currency exchange, secretarial services in English, audiovisual equipment, photocopiers, computers, cable TV news, translation services, and express checkout. 7 Plaza de las Cortes (phone: 429-7551; 212-838-3110 in New York City; 800-223-6800 elsewhere in the US; fax: 429-8655).

**Suecia** Expansion of this Swedish-managed hotel has added modern rooms and suites within the same building, but the original ones are still well maintained and very comfortable; today its rooms number 128. Ernest Hemingway lived here, enjoying the great advantage of the location—on a quiet street just west of Paseo del Prado, around the corner from Calle de Alcalá. Smoked salmon and smorgasbord are main attractions in the *Bellman* restaurant. Business facilities include meeting rooms for up to 150, an English-speaking concierge, foreign currency exchange, secretarial services in English, audiovisual equipment, computers, and translation services. 4 Calle Marqués de Casa Riera (phone: 531-6900; 800-528-1234; fax: 521-7141).

**Tryp Fénix** This aristocrat once again is counted among the city's finest. Ideally situated on the tree-lined Castellana at Plaza de Colón, it has 228 rooms and 12 suites with amenities including satellite TV and refrigerators—all enhanced by an air of sparkling elegance. There's a restaurant on the premises. Business facilities include 24-hour room service, meeting rooms for up to 200, an English-speaking concierge, foreign currency exchange, secretarial services in English, audiovisual equipment, photocopiers, computers, translation services, and express checkout. 2 Calle Hermosilla (phone: 431-6700; fax: 576-0661).

**Wellington** A classic, this hostelry with 295 spacious rooms and 29 suites is nicely located in the upscale Salamanca district, with fine boutiques, galleries, and the *Parque del Buen Retiro* practically at the doorstep. In summer, the outdoor swimming pool and the garden, with its restaurant, bar, and health club, are lively gathering spots. Business facilities include 24-hour room service, meeting rooms for up to 250, an English-speaking concierge, foreign currency exchange, secretarial services in English, audiovisual equipment, photocopiers, computers, translation services, and express checkout. 8 Calle Velázquez (phone: 575-4400; fax: 576-4164).

**Alcalá** On the north edge of *Parque del Buen Retiro* and Plaza de la Independencia, in the genteel Salamanca district, this 153-room property is within easy walking distance of fine shops and restaurants on Calle Serrano, as well as the *Prado* and other museums. The restaurant serves Basque specialties. Business facilities include meeting rooms for up to 60, an English-speaking concierge, foreign currency exchange, secretarial services in English, audiovisual equipment, photocopiers, computers, and translation services. 66 Calle de Alcalá (phone: 435-1060; 800-528-1234; fax: 435-1105).

**Arosa** Although it's on the bustling Gran Vía, this member of the Best Western chain has the charm, peaceful mood, and personalized service of a small luxury establishment. The 139 rooms—no two exactly alike—are tastefully decorated; luxurious bathrooms feature built-in hair dryers and fabulous showers in the bathtubs. The atmosphere is delightful in the bar, lounge, and restaurant. A parking garage is available. Business facilities include an English-speaking concierge, foreign currency exchange, and translation services. 21 Calle de la Salud (phone: 532-1600; 800-528-1234; fax: 531-3127).

**Carlos V** Conveniently located, this 67-room property, also a Best Western member, is in the lively pedestrian area between the Gran Vía and Puerta del Sol, near the *Convento de las Descalzas Reales* and *El Corte Inglés* department store. Rooms have satellite TV and mini-bars. Business facilities include an English-speaking concierge and foreign currency exchange. 5 Calle Maestro Vitoria (phone: 531-4100; 800-528-1234; fax: 531-3761).

**Carlton** This 112-room establishment is in a unique location in the southern part of central Madrid, near the *Atocha* train station complex, within easy walking distance of the *Museo Nacional Centro de Arte Reina Sofía*, the *Real Jardín Botánico,* and the *Prado.* A restaurant is on the premises. Business facilities include 24-hour room service, meeting rooms for up to 200, an English-speaking concierge, foreign currency exchange, secretarial services in English, audiovisual equipment, photocopiers, computers, and translation services. 26 Paseo de las Delicias (phone: 539-7100; fax: 539-8510).

**Don Diego** A well-kept *pensión* near the *Parque del Buen Retiro* in Madrid's lovely Salamanca district. The 58 rooms are nicely furnished, and several have ample balconies. There are no in-room TV sets and no restaurant, but there is a TV lounge and a bar that serves sandwiches and breakfast. 45 Calle Velázquez (phone: 435-0760).

**Emperador** Centrally located right on the Gran Vía, with 232 rooms. Unusual among the many hotels in the immediate area, it boasts a rooftop garden with a swimming pool and excellent views of the city. There is breakfast service but no restaurant. Business facilities include 24-hour room service, meeting rooms for up to 200, an English-speaking concierge, foreign currency exchange, secretarial services in English, audiovisual equipment, photocopiers, computers, and translation services. 53 Gran Vía (phone: 547-9600; fax: 547-2817).

**Escultor** Conveniently located near the Paseo de la Castellana in a quiet residential area, each of the 82 apartment-style units of this Best Western–affiliated property has a separate sitting room, complete kitchen, satellite TV, and a mini-bar. Business facilities include meeting rooms for up to 250, an English-speaking concierge, foreign currency exchange, secretarial services in English, audiovisual equipment, photocopiers, computers, and translation services. 3 Calle Miguel Angel (phone: 310-4203; 800-528-1234; fax: 319-2584).

**Galiano** A converted mansion, complete with marble floors, antique paintings, tapestries, and carved-wood furniture in the lobby and lounge. On a tranquil side street just off the Paseo de la Castellana and Plaza de Colón, it has 29 comfortable singles, doubles, and suites. Breakfast and TV sets are optional, and there's no restaurant. There is an English-speaking concierge. 6 Calle Alcalá Galiano (phone: 319-2000).

**Mayorazgo** Excellent service and 200 well-appointed, comfortable rooms are featured at this hostelry, just a step from the central Gran Vía. The dining room serves breakfast, lunch, and dinner. Business facilities include meeting rooms for up to 300, an English-speaking concierge, foreign currency exchange, secretarial services in English, audiovisual equipment, photocopiers, computers, and translation services. 3 Calle Flor Baja (phone: 247-2600; fax: 541-2485).

**Plaza** Located within the gigantic *Edificio España* landmark building of the early 1950s, this 306-room hotel is usually swarming with tour groups. The 26th-floor swimming pool and terrace restaurant offer marvelous panoramic views of the city. Business facilities include 24-hour room service, meeting rooms for up to 500, an English-speaking concierge, foreign currency exchange, secretarial services in English, audiovisual equipment, photocopiers, computers, and translation services. 2 Plaza de España (phone: 247-1200; 800-645-5687; fax: 248-2389).

**Reina Victoria** Run by the Tryp hotel chain, this 201-room remodeled Madrid classic was built in 1923 and later designated a "building of national historic interest." Its unaltered six-story façade, elaborate with pilasters, turrets, wrought-iron balconies, and bay windows, dominates the entire west side of the picturesque Plaza Santa Ana. The *Bar Taurino* revives the hotel's decades-old tradition as a rendezvous for bullfighters, breeders, and aficionados. A formal restaurant serving breakfast, lunch, and dinner is on the premises. Business facilities include meeting rooms for up to 500, an English-speaking concierge, foreign currency exchange, secretarial services in English, audiovisual equipment, photocopiers, computers, and translation services. 14 Plaza Santa Ana (phone: 531-4500).

**Serrano** Small and tasteful, refined and immaculate, this 34-room hotel stands on a quiet street between the Castellana and the boutique-lined Calle Serrano. Its marble-floored lobby is comfortably furnished and richly decorated with antiques (including a large 17th-century tapestry) and huge arrangements of fresh flowers. There's no restaurant, but snacks and sandwiches are available at the bar. Business facilities include an English-speaking concierge, foreign currency exchange, and translation services. 8 Calle Marqués de Villamejor (phone: 435-5200; fax: 435-4849).

**Tryp Ambassador** Formerly an aristocratic mansion, this fine hotel has 181 rooms, six suites, and all the latest conveniences. The six-story building is located near the *Teatro de la Opera,* Plaza de Oriente, and the *Palacio Real.* The restaurant serves Spanish and international fare. Business facilities include 24-hour room service, meeting rooms for up to 290, an English-speaking concierge, foreign currency exchange, secretarial services in English, audiovisual equipment, photocopiers, computers, translation services, and express checkout. 5 Cuesta Santo Domingo (phone: 541-6700).

### INEXPENSIVE

**Jamic** A small 19-room *pensión* centrally located across the street from the *Palace* hotel and near the *Prado.* The non-air conditioned rooms have telephones only, and some have full bath while others just offer sinks. Breakfast is served in a small dining room. 4 Plaza de las Cortes (phone: 429-0068).

**Lisboa** This well-run residential *hostal* has 23 non-air conditioned rooms, all with recently renovated private baths (they don't have TV sets, but there is a TV lounge for guests). The location—just off the Plaza Santa Ana in charming old Madrid, yet a short walk to the *Palace,* the *Ritz,* and the *Prado*—is terrific. There's no dining room, but fine restaurants of all price ranges line the street. English is spoken. 17 Calle Ventura de la Vega (phone: 429-9894).

---

## EATING OUT

*Madrileños* eat their main meal during the work break from 2 to 4 PM. A *merienda* (early-evening snack) such as wine and *tapas, chocolate con churros,* or coffee and sweets, takes the edge off appetites until a light supper is eaten after 10 PM. For those who can't adjust to the Spanish schedule, there are always *cafeterías* and snack bars, and many restaurants start serving dinner at about 8:30 PM to accommodate non-Spaniards. Dinner for two with wine will cost $135 or more at restaurants described below as very expensive; from $70 to $120 at places listed as expensive; between $30 and $60 at moderate eateries; and $30 or less at inexpensive ones. Most restaurants offer a set menu *(menú del día),* a complete meal for an economical price. Most restaurants include the *IVA* (value added tax) and *servicio* (tip) in their menu prices. Unless otherwise noted all restaurants listed are open for lunch and dinner, and all telephone numbers are in the 1 city code. Bear in mind that some restaurants close for vacation during the month of August.

For an unforgettable dining experience we begin with our culinary favorite, followed by our cost and quality choices, listed by price category.

---

### DELIGHTFUL DINING

**Zalacaín** Probably the finest restaurant in all of Spain, it was the first in the country to win three Michelin stars. Imaginative Basque and French haute cuisines are served here, with an emphasis on seafood. Try the fish and shellfish soup and the pig's feet stuffed with lamb. Owner Jesús Oyarbide often travels to the Rioja, Navarre, and Aragon regions in search of new ingredients and additions to his wine cellar. Luxuriously decorated, the restaurant shimmers with polished silver, gleaming glass, and fresh flowers. Impeccable service and an irresistible dessert cart also contribute to a memorable dining experience. Closed Saturday lunch, Sundays, August, *Easter Week,* and holidays. Reservations necessary at least two days in advance. Major credit cards accepted. 4 Calle Alvarez de Baena (phone: 561-4840).

---

### VERY EXPENSIVE

**Horcher** Operated for generations by the Horcher family, this remains one of Madrid's most elegant dining places, serving continental fare with an Austro-Hungarian flavor. Dining here is an indulgence that should include such delicacies as *chuletas de ternasco a la castellana* (baby lamb chops), endive salad with truffles, and crêpes Sir Holten for dessert. Diners might even try the classic goulash. Closed Sundays. Reservations necessary for lunch and dinner. Major credit cards accepted. 6 Calle Alfonso XII (phone: 532-3596).

**Jockey** A Madrid classic, intimate and elegant, and a recipient of the National Gastronomy Award. The continental cuisine is superb, as are traditional dishes such as *cocido madrileño,* a savory stew. Other specialties include *perdiz española* (partridge), *lomo de lubina* (filet of sea bass), and *mousse de anguila* (eel mousse). Closed Sundays and August. Reservations necessary. Major credit cards accepted. 6 Calle Amador de los Ríos (phone: 319-1003).

**Ritz** The sumptuous restaurant of the luxurious *Ritz* hotel serves French as well as traditional *madrileño* cuisine. The separate *Ritz Garden Terrace* offers more casual dining, or simply afternoon tea or *tapas.* Open daily for breakfast, lunch, and dinner. Reservations necessary. Major credit cards accepted. 5 Plaza de la Lealtad (phone: 521-2857).

**Villa Magna** The remodeling of Madrid's *Villa Magna* hotel placed its restaurant among the city's finest. Cristóbal Blanco, the prize-winning chef, designs such nouvelle delicacies as grilled scallops with caviar in basil sauce. The china was designed by Paloma Picasso. The *Champagne Bar* dispenses 252 French and Spanish vintages. Open for breakfast, lunch, and dinner. Reservations necessary. Major credit cards accepted. 22 Paseo de la Castellana (phone: 261-4900).

EXPENSIVE

**La Basílica** Once an old Baroque church, this elegant restaurant serves international, nouvelle, and Spanish cuisines in the see-and-be-seen main dining room or in secluded alcoves. It's located on a narrow street in old Madrid, near Plaza Mayor. Closed Saturday lunch and Sundays. Reservations necessary. Major credit cards accepted. 12 Calle de la Bolsa (phone: 521-8623).

**Belagua** When it reopened in the *Santo Mauro* hotel in 1992, this renowned eatery already had an elite *madrileño* following from its previous location in the *Sanvy* hotel. The same Basque-Navarrese fare that has long attracted locals is served in the sophisticated atmosphere of the restored library of a turn-of-the-century French palatial mansion, redecorated in glowing Art Deco. Traditional specialties include monkfish and spider crab stew; entrées with oxtail, pig's feet, lobster, or blood sausage; and exquisite desserts. Open daily; Sundays exclusively for hotel guests. Reservations advised. Major credit cards accepted. 36 Zurbano (phone: 308-4743).

**Cabo Mayor** The owner and chef both have won the National Gastronomy Award, and for good reason: Their fresh seafood from the northern region of Cantabria is imaginatively prepared, and the vegetable dishes are superlative. If it's on the menu, try the *cigalas y langostinos con verduras al jerez sibarita* (crayfish and prawns with green vegetables in sherry sauce). Closed Sundays and during August. Reservations advised. Major credit cards accepted. 37 Calle Juan Ramón Jiménez (phone: 350-8776).

**Café de Oriente** Anything from *tapas* to French haute cuisine can be enjoyed here in a delightful *madrileño* atmosphere. It is an ideal place for afternoon tea or cocktails in the café, which has sidewalk tables overlooking the square and the *Palacio Real* (reservations unnecessary); for fine Castilian dining downstairs in the vaulted 17th-century *Sala Capitular de San Gil* (Chapter House of St. Guy; reservations advised); or for superb French-Basque cuisine in the adjacent restaurant (reservations advised) or one of the private dining rooms frequented by royalty and diplomats (reservations necessary). Closed Monday lunch, Sundays, and August. Major credit cards accepted. 2 Plaza de Oriente (phone: 541-3974).

**Casa de América** Situated in the sumptuous 19th-century *Palacio de Linares,* which houses the cultural center for Latin American countries, this relatively new, modern-style restaurant is as exquisite as its scenic setting, overlooking Plaza de la Cibeles. Superb traditional Spanish as well as Latin American specialties are offered amidst intimate, friendly *madrileño* ambience and service. There's also a lovely private dining room seating 18. Closed Sunday dinner. Reservations advised on weekends. Major credit cards accepted. Plaza de la Cibeles (phone: 547-4540).

**El Cenador del Prado** Favored by aficionados of nouvelle cuisine, this place is artistically decorated in a style reminiscent of an elegant conservatory, allowing indoor dining under the stars. Try *patatas a la importancia con almejas* (potatoes with clams) or the *pato al vinagre de frambuesas* (duck with raspberry vinegar). Closed Saturday lunch, Sundays, and the first two weeks in August. Reservations necessary. Major credit cards accepted. 4 Calle del Prado (phone: 429-1561).

**La Dorada** Fresh seafood of every imaginable variety is flown in daily from the Mediterranean to this mammoth establishment, which serves Andalusian fare. Particularly noteworthy is the fish baked in a crust of salt, an Andalusian practice that results, surprisingly, in a dish that's not salty. Closed Sundays and August. Reservations necessary (this place is always crowded—and you'll enjoy the food even more if you reserve one of the private dining rooms). Major credit cards accepted. 64-66 Calle Orense (phone: 576-0575).

**La Gamella** Dedicated to new Spanish cuisine, American owner-chef-host Richard Stephens imaginatively combines choice ingredients in such dishes as slices of cured duck breast with Belgian endive and walnut oil, and *pastel de chorizo fresco y pimientos rojos* (sausage and red pepper quiche), followed by turbot in wild mushroom sauce with a tomato *coulis*. Irresistible desserts and a fine wine round out the dining adventure. Closed Sundays, holidays, and August. Reservations advised. Major credit cards accepted. 4 Calle Alfonso XII (phone: 532-4509).

**Gure-Etxea** One of the best for Basque dishes in Madrid, serving specialties such as *porrusalda* (leek and potato soup with cod) and a variety of fish dishes. Both the atmosphere and the service are pleasant. Closed Sundays and August. Reservations advised. American Express and Visa accepted. 12 Plaza de la Paja (phone: 265-6149).

**Lhardy** A Madrid institution since 1839, and the decor, atmosphere, and table settings haven't changed much since then. One specialty in the upstairs dining rooms and private salons is *cocido madrileño,* the typical stew. At *merienda* time in the late afternoon, the street-entrance restaurant and stand-up bar fill with regulars who serve themselves the *caldo* (broth) of the *cocido* from a silver tureen, and also enjoy finger sandwiches, canapés, cold cuts, pastries, cocktails, or coffee. Closed Sunday and holiday dinners; also closed Mondays in summer. Reservations necessary for the private dining rooms. Major credit cards accepted. 8 Carrera de San Jerónimo (phone: 522-2207).

**Paradís Madrid** This branch of a well-known Barcelona eatery is in a turn-of-the-century mansion alongside Plaza de las Cortes. The menu is primarily Catalan-Mediterranean: mushrooms served in several delicious ways (one stuffed with duck liver), five variations of *bacalao* (cod), and a "catch of the day." A separate menu features original dishes of illustrious Basque and Catalan chefs. The bar serves *tapas* and typical Catalan *pa amb tomàquet* (bread coated with tomato and olive oil) until 1:30 AM. Closed Sunday dinner. Reservations advised. Major credit cards accepted. 14 Marqués de Cubas (phone: 429-7303).

**Platerías** Its intimate low-key elegance in the heart of old Madrid creates a pleasant atmosphere for enjoying authentic Spanish dishes such as *callos a la madrileña* (succulent tripe, Madrid style), *chipirones* (cuttlefish in its own ink), and remarkable vegetable plates. Closed Sundays. Reservations advised. Major credit cards accepted. 11 Plaza Santa Ana (phone: 429-7048).

**La Trainera** Another favorite of seafood lovers. All the fish and shellfish is extremely fresh; try the grilled sole. Closed Sundays and August. Reservations advised. MasterCard and Visa accepted. 60 Calle Lagasca (phone: 576-0575).

### MODERATE

**El Callejón** A bust of Hemingway and walls chockablock with photos attest to the number of celebrities who have enjoyed the friendly atmosphere and home-cooked food here in the past. An informal old Madrid place, it serves a different regional specialty each day of the week, but *callos a la madrileña* (tripe Madrid style) is always on the menu, and *tapas* abound. Open daily. Reservations unnecessary. Major credit cards accepted. 6 Calle Ternera (phone: 531-9195).

**Casa Botín** One of Madrid's oldest restaurants—founded in 1725—is still an excellent value. It's famous for its Castilian-style *cochinillo asado* (roast suckling pig) and baby lamb, one of which is usually featured on the *menú del día*. Lunch and dinner seem to fall into two shifts, with the early-eating tourists first, followed by *madrileños*. Open daily. Reservations unnecessary. Major credit cards accepted. 17 Calle Cuchilleros (phone: 266-4217).

**Casa Lucio** This casual restaurant in old Madrid has become an institution among the elite who enjoy fine Spanish food—especially seafood. There are specialties from on land, too, such as *cordero asado* (roast lamb) and *callos a la madrileña*. Closed Saturday lunch and August. Reservations necessary. American Express and Visa accepted. 35 Calle Cava Baja (phone: 365-3252).

**Casa Paco** The steaks served in this old tavern are excellent. Other specialties include typical *madrileño* dishes. Closed Sundays and August. No reservations. Visa accepted. 11 Calle Puerta Cerrada (phone: 266-3166).

**La Chata** This typical *mesón* (inn) bears the nickname of Madrid's adored Infanta Isabel (the youngest child of Queen Isabel II), who is depicted on the hand-painted tile façade by Eduardo Fernández. Delicious morsels are served at the *tapas* bar, and the small restaurant specializes in roast suckling pig and lamb dishes. Closed Sunday dinner and Wednesdays. No reservations or credit cards accepted. 25 Calle Cava Baja (phone: 266-1458).

**Los Galayos** A typical tavern serving fine Castilian roast suckling pig and lamb, with a *tapas* bar and an outdoor café right alongside the Plaza Mayor. Open daily. Reservations unnecessary. Major credit cards accepted. 1 Plaza Mayor (phone: 265-6222).

**El Ingenio** This unpretentious, family-run restaurant, decorated with Don Quixote and Sancho Panza memorabilia, serves impeccably fresh seafood and locally grown pork, lamb, and beef. Closed Sundays and holidays. Reservations unnecessary. Major credit cards accepted. Just off the Plaza de España at 10 Calle Leganitos (phone: 541-9133).

**El Mentidero de la Villa** Inventive food and friendly service characterize this delightful restaurant, whose Japanese chef has created a distinctive French menu with both Spanish and Japanese influences. The salads are superb, as is *pato con manzana* (duck with apple) and *rollo de primavera con puerros y gambas* (spring rolls with leeks and shrimp). For dessert try the homemade chocolate mousse. Closed Sundays. Reservations advised. Major credit cards accepted. Just off the bustling Paseo de la Castellana. 6 Calle Santo Tomé (phone: 419-5506).

**La Mesa Redonda** A small eatery on one of old Madrid's most charming little streets. Its American owners serve the best *Thanksgiving* dinner in town. Other specialties include beef bourguignon and stews. Open for dinner only; closed Sundays. Reservations unnecessary (except for *Thanksgiving*). No credit cards accepted. 17 Calle Nuncio (phone: 265-0289).

**Posada de la Villa** Although the three-story building is relatively new, this authentic eatery dates back to 1642, when it was originally a *posada* (inn) for out-of-towners. It has retained its tradition of hospitality and still offers fine typical dishes such as *cocido madrileño* and roast pig and lamb. Closed Sunday dinner. Reservations unnecessary. Major credit cards accepted. 9 Calle Cava Baja (phone: 266-1860).

**La Quinta del Sordo** The façade of this award-winning restaurant is adorned with fine hand-painted tile mosaics. Its name means "house of the deaf man," referring to the place where Goya lived in Madrid. Reproductions of Goya art and memorabilia add to the decor. An array of fine Castilian dishes offers memorable dining in a pleasant atmosphere. Closed Sunday dinner. Reservations unnecessary. Major credit cards accepted. 10 Calle Sacramento (phone: 248-1852).

**Riazor** An unpretentious turn-of-the-century establishment with a cordial atmosphere, fine traditional fare, and a cornucopia of hot and cold *tapas* served at the bar. Open daily. Reservations unnecessary, except for groups. Visa accepted. Located one short block south of Plaza Mayor at 19 Calle Toledo (phone: 266-5466).

**Taberna del Alabardero** A Madrid classic, this once was the tavern of the guards of the *Palacio Real*. There is a wonderful *tapas* bar, and succulent Spanish and Basque dishes are served in cozy dining rooms reminiscent of 19th-century Madrid. Open daily. Reservations unnecessary. Major credit cards accepted. 6 Calle Felipe V (phone: 547-2577).

### INEXPENSIVE

**El Granero de Lavapiés** Good vegetarian food in one of old Madrid's most typical neighborhoods, Lavapiés, just south of Gran Vía. Closed Saturdays during the month of August. No reservations. No credit cards accepted. 10 Calle Argumosa (phone: 467-7611).

**Mesón Museo del Jamón** Any restaurant with 4,000 hams dangling from its ceiling and draping its walls deserves the name "Ham Museum," and there are four such pork paradises in central Madrid. Fine hams from the regions of Jabugo, Murcia, Salamanca, and Extremadura are served in various ways, including sandwiches, at the stand-up bars and at dining tables. Also featured are an array of cheeses, a great deli, and roast chicken. Any dish can also be prepared to take out. No reservations. No credit cards accepted. 6 Carrera San Jerónimo (phone: 521-0340); 72 Gran Vía (phone: 541-2023); 44 Paseo del Prado (phone: 230-4385); and 54 Calle Atocha (phone: 227-0716).

**Taberna de Antonio Sánchez** Genuinely typical of the *Madrid de los Austrias* (old Hapsburg Madrid), it has been a venerated favorite ever since it was founded by a legendary bullfighter more than 150 years ago. The small, unpretentious dining rooms are charming, the wonderful fare—seafood, Spanish cuisine, salads, and desserts—served with care. Closed Sunday dinner. No reservations. Visa accepted. 13 Calle Mesón de Paredes (phone: 239-7826).

---

### TAPAS BARS

*Tapas* probably originated in Seville, but today *el tapeo* (enjoying *tapas*) is a way of life throughout Spain, especially in Madrid, where there are literally thousands of places to do so. Practically every bar (not to be confused with pubs or *bares americanos,* which are for drinks only), *taberna, mesón, tasca, cervecería,* and even *cafetería* serves *tapas*—everything from little plates of green olives to an array of cheeses, sausages, hams, seafood, eggs, and vegetables that have been sliced, diced, wrapped, filled, marinated, sauced, or sautéed for hot or cold consumption. Most establishments specializing in *tapas* also have a few tables or even dining rooms in addition to their stand-up bar. Toothpicks and fingers are the most common utensils; shrimp, langoustine, mussel, and clam shells, olive pits, napkins, and almost everything else are dropped on the floor, which is swept and scoured after each surge (usually from 1 to 3 PM and 7 to 9 PM).

A *chato* (glass of wine) or *caña* (draft beer) customarily is served with a free *tapita.* If you're hungry for more and the vast array of *tapas* on display is overwhelming, just point to what you want. If you prefer a larger portion, ask for a *ración,* which can be a small meal in itself. Don't pay until you've completely finished; the bartender probably will remember everything you consumed, even if you don't. He'll deliver your change on a saucer; leave a few *duros* (five-peseta coins) as a tip, and always say *gracias* and *adiós* when you depart.

*Tapas* bar hopping is at its best in the central and old sections of Madrid. One of the city's best is *La Trucha* (with two locations, both just off Plaza Santa Ana: 3 Calle Manuel Fernández y González; phone: 429-5833; and 6 Calle Núñez de Arce; phone: 532-0809). They're jammed at *tapas* time, and with good reason: Everything from bull tails to succulent red pimentos, as well as *trucha* (trout), is served with gusto. Nearby, the *Cervecería Alemana* (6 Plaza Santa Ana; phone: 429-7033) is, despite its name ("German Beer Parlor"), thoroughly *madrileño,* which is why the ubiquitous Hemingway frequented it, and artists, intellectuals, and students continue to flock here. Among the *tapas* are good hams, sausages, and cheeses. Around Puerta del Sol are *Casa Labra* (12 Calle Tetuán; phone: 532-1405), which was founded in 1860 and has been jam-packed ever since—among the specialties is fluff-fried *bacalao* (cod) that melts in the mouth—and *Mejillonería El Pasaje* (3 Pasaje de Matheu; phone: 521-5155), which deals in mussels exclusively, fresh from Galicia. *La Torre del Oro* (26 Plaza Mayor; phone: 266-5016) is a lively Andalusian bar appropriately decorated with stunning bullfight photos and memorabilia, with recorded *sevillanas* music adding to the ambience; the *tapas* include such delicacies as baby eels and fresh anchovies, fried or marinated. In the same vicinity are *Valle del Tiétar* (5 Calle Ciudad Rodrigo; phone: 248-0511), in the northwest arcade entrance to the plaza, which offers *tapas,* Avila-style, with suckling pig and kid goat specialties; *El Oso y el Madroño* (4 Calle de la Bolsa; phone: 522-7796), with an authentic atmosphere and jovial clientele; and the unpretentious *El Chotis* (11 Calle Cava Baja; phone: 265-3230), south of Plaza Mayor. Elsewhere, there's *Cervecería Monje* (21 Calle del Arenal; phone: 248-3598), a showcase of fresh seafood as well as lamb sweetbreads, and *La Mi Venta* (7 Plaza Marina Española; phone: 248-5091), where a friendly neighborhood atmosphere prevails and fine hot and cold *tapas* and *raciones* are served, with select hams the specialty. At *Bocaíto* (4 Calle Libertad; phone: 532-1219), north of the Gran Vía and Calle de Alcalá, animated *tapas* makers behind the bar prepare a limitless selection of outstanding treats, and giant Talavera ceramic plates on the walls are painted with fine reproductions of Goya's *Wine Harvest.*

# Milan

## At-a-Glance

### SEEING THE CITY

For a grand view of Milan, the surrounding Lombard plain, the Alps, and the Apennines, climb the 166 steps, or take an elevator, to the roof of the *Duomo* (see *Special Places,* below). From here, more stairs take you to the topmost gallery at the base of the cathedral's central spire, 354 feet from the ground. Enter the stairway to the roof from the south transept near the Medici tomb, or enter the elevator from outside the church, on the north side (toward the *Rinascente* department store); an elevator on the south side is sometimes also in operation. Both elevators are open daily and charge admission. A seventh-floor addition to *Rinascente* boasts a *caffè* whose vast windows bring the *Duomo*'s gargoyles within, it would seem, sipping distance of your *aperitivo*. Here your admission charge for a unique view is the price of a cup of coffee. There also is a 350-foot viewing tower in *Parco Sempione* (Sempione Park), just beyond the *Castello Sforzesco* (see *Special Places*).

### SPECIAL PLACES

The huge Piazza del Duomo (Cathedral Square), with its perennial pigeons (note that it is forbidden to feed them) and ever-present pensioners, is one of the city's few pedestrian oases and the heart of this bustling metropolis. North of the piazza toward Piazza della Scala is the elegant glass-domed *Galleria Vittorio Emanuele II.* Built between 1865 and 1877 under the direction of architect Giuseppe Mengoni, the arcade has for decades been considered the *salotto* (salon) for Milan's exclusive shops, bookstores, *caffès,* and fashionable restaurants.

Some of the city's tourist attractions are too far from the center to reach comfortably on foot, but *ATM,* the local bus and tram system, connects these sites efficiently, as does the clean subway system (see *Getting Around,* below).

Note that many sites of interest in Milan close for a midday break, usually from noon or 12:30 PM to 2:30 or 3 PM; we suggest calling ahead to check exact hours.

#### DOWNTOWN

**DUOMO (CATHEDRAL)** The most magnificent Milanese monument is its rose-tinged marble cathedral, with 135 spires and more than 2,200 sculptures decorating the exterior. From the roof, reached by an elevator or a 166-step climb, you can study the details of its pinnacles and flying buttresses. The interior, divided into five main aisles by an imposing stand of 58 columns, contains another 2,000 sculptures. Seen from the inside, the stained glass windows depicting

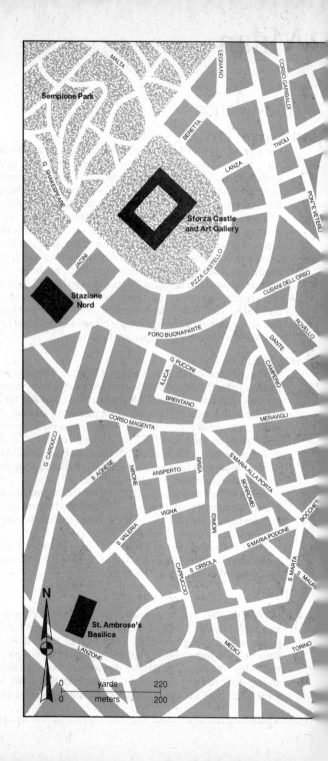

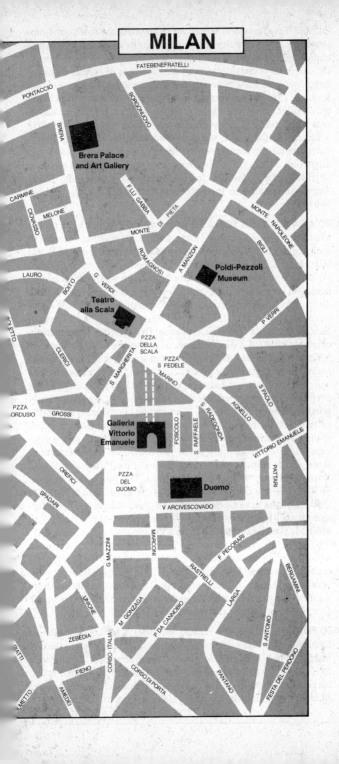

Old and New Testament scenes are so huge that the roof seems supported by shafts of colored light. On the site of an early Christian church located in the center of the then Roman city of Mediolanum, the cathedral is considered the finest example of Gothic architecture in northern Italy, although its architectural peculiarities—it was begun in 1386 but not completed until 1813—prevent it from being pure Gothic. Only *San Pietro* in Rome is larger. Next to the cathedral is the modern *Museo del Duomo,* which beautifully displays Milanese artifacts from the early Middle Ages, including illuminated manuscripts, parchments, statuary, architectural plans, and tapestries. A plus is the air conditioned *ambiente.* The *Duomo* is open daily; the museum is closed Mondays and for a midday break. Admission charge to the museum. Piazza del Duomo (phone: 860358).

**TEATRO ALLA SCALA (LA SCALA)** Built between 1776 and 1778 on the site of the *Chiesa di Santa Maria della Scala* and then restored to rococo glory in 1948 after Allied bombing damaged it during World War II, *La Scala* has always been a queen among opera houses. Works by Donizetti, Rossini, Bellini, and Verdi were first acclaimed here, and it was here that Arturo Toscanini, conductor and artistic director for years, reintroduced the works of Verdi. The house has never lost its aristocratic aura, and its opening night on *Festa di Sant'Ambrogio* (Feast of St. Ambrose; December 7) is a glittering, celebrity-studded gala, with special dinners offered by the tony Milanese restaurants that publish opera soirée menus in the newspapers. With legendarily perfect acoustics, a performance here is truly exhilarating—and also expensive. Tickets for each season's performances, presented December through May, are passionately pursued and hard to come by. They can be purchased—with difficulty—from the box office in advance; at the last minute, concierges at the city's deluxe hotels often can get positive results for a consideration. There also are ballet performances from September through November and concerts featuring the *Filarmonica della Scala,* perhaps Italy's finest orchestra. The box office (phone: 807041/2/3/4) is open from 10 AM to 1 PM and 3:30 to 5:30 PM (to 9:30 PM on the day of a performance); closed Mondays. For information, call 809120 or 720-03744; for credit card purchases, call 809126. The theater can be visited by appointment (phone: 887-9377). The adjacent *Museo della Scala* (La Scala Museum) houses a rich collection of manuscripts, costumes, and other *La Scala* memorabilia. It's closed for a midday break, and Sundays from November through March. Admission charge. The theater and museum are north of Piazza del Duomo, through the *Galleria Vittorio Emanuele II,* at 2 Piazza della Scala (phone: 805-3418).

**MUSEO POLDI-PEZZOLI (POLDI-PEZZOLI MUSEUM)** A Milanese nobleman bequeathed his home and exquisite private art collection to the city in 1879. The works include some prime examples of Renaissance to 17th-century paintings and sculpture, Oriental porcelain, Persian carpets, and tapestries. There also are a Botticelli portrait of the Madonna, paintings by Giovanni Battista Tiepolo, Pollaiuolo, and

Fra Bartolomeo, as well as Giovanni Bellini's *Pietà.* Closed Mondays and for a midday break. Admission charge. A short walk from *La Scala,* at 12 Via Manzoni (phone: 794889).

## PALAZZO E PINACOTECA DI BRERA (BRERA PALACE AND ART GALLERY)

One of the most important state-owned galleries in Italy, and Milan's finest, is housed in this 17th-century palace. Its 38 rooms contain a broad representation of Italian painting, with particularly good examples from the Venetian and Lombard Schools, including such masterpieces as Andrea Mantegna's *Dead Christ,* Raphael's *Wedding Feast of the Virgin,* and Caravaggio's *Dinner at Emmaus.* The palace also has an important library (founded in 1770) of incunabula and manuscripts, plus a collection of all books printed in the Milanese province since 1788. In the courtyard is a monumental statue of Napoleon I, depicted as a conquering Caesar. The art gallery is closed Mondays and Sunday afternoons. Admission charge. The library is closed Sundays. A few blocks north of *La Scala,* at 28 Via Brera (phone: 722631).

## CASTELLO SFORZESCO E CIVICI MUSEI (SFORZA CASTLE AND CIVIC MUSEUMS)

In the mid-15th century, Duke Francesco Sforza built this large, square brick castle on the site of a castle of the Visconti that had been destroyed. It became a fortress after the fall of the Sforzas and was damaged repeatedly in sieges before restoration began in the 19th century. Further damaged during World War II, it has been repaired and today houses a museum complex that includes the *Museo d'Arte Antica.* One of its treasures is the unfinished *Rondanini Pietà,* Michelangelo's last work. Enter the museum from the courtyard of the residential part of the castle, the *Corte Ducale.* The castle also houses important collections of art, musical instruments, and manuscripts and, occasionally, well-publicized temporary exhibitions. Beyond the castle is the beautiful 116-acre *Parco Sempione,* with an aquarium, sports arena, and neoclassical *Arco della Pace* (Arch of Peace), a triumphal arch with statues and bas-relief. Inspired by Rome's *Septimius Severus,* the arch marks the beginning of the historic Corso Sempione through the Alps to France, which was built by order of Napoleon. Closed Mondays. No admission charge. West of the *Palazzo e Pinacoteca di Brera,* on Piazza Castello (phone: 6236, ext. 3940).

## BASILICA E MUSEO DI SANT'AMBROGIO (ST. AMBROSE'S BASILICA AND MUSEUM)

The basilica was founded in the 4th century by Bishop Ambrose (later St. Ambrose), who baptized St. Augustine here. The bas-relief on the doorway dates from the time of Sant'Ambrogio, and the two bronze doors are from the 9th century. The basilica was enlarged in the 11th century, and its superb atrium was added in the 12th century. Two other early Christian saints—Gervase and Protasius—are buried with Sant'Ambrogio in the crypt. The ceiling of the apse is decorated with 10th-century mosaics. Above the portico is the *Museo di Sant'Ambrogio,* where you can see a 12th-century cross, a missal of Gian Galeazzo Visconti, and other religious treasures. The museum is open Mondays and Wednesdays through Fridays, with a long midday break; weekends from 3 to 5 PM; closed Tuesdays. Admission charge. South of the *Castello Sforzesco,* at 15 Piazza Sant'Ambrogio (phone: 872059).

**SANTA MARIA DELLE GRAZIE (CHURCH OF ST. MARY OF GRACE)** The interior of this restored brick and terra cotta church, representing a period of transition from Gothic to Renaissance, is decorated with some fine 15th-century frescoes. But the church, though beautiful in itself, usually is visited because Leonardo's *The Last Supper* (known as the *Cenacolo Vinciano*) is on a wall of the refectory of the former Dominican convent next to it. Commissioned in 1495 by Ludovico il Moro, Duke of Milan, *The Last Supper* took two years to paint. Leonardo chose the relatively slow-drying (and less durable) tempera instead of fresco technique (paint onto wet plaster) to gain time. The result was a meditative but fragile work of art. Although restoration was begun not long after its completion and has continued through the years, the painting has suffered considerable deterioration. The current restoration is well past the midway point, and, despite the problems, the pale colors seem to glow (visitors can see quite a bit of the masterpiece, notwithstanding the presence of some scaffolding). Open Tuesdays through Sundays from 9 AM to 1:45 PM. Admission charge. A few blocks northwest of the *Basilica e Museo di Sant'Ambrogio,* on Piazza Santa Maria delle Grazie (phone: 498-7588).

## ENVIRONS

**CERTOSA DI PAVIA (CHARTERHOUSE OF PAVIA)** Gian Galeazzo Visconti founded this Carthusian monastery in 1396 as a family mausoleum. With its façade of multicolored marble sculpture and its interior heavily decorated with frescoes, Baroque grillwork, and other ornamentation, the monastery is one of the most remarkable buildings in Italy. Closed Sundays, Mondays, and late afternoons. No admission charge, but donations are welcome. Sixteen miles (26 km) from Milan, just off the Milan-Pavia Road (phone: 925613, guided tours).

**PAVIA** On the banks of the Ticino, this gracious city (5 miles/8 km south of the *Certosa di Pavia*) was the capital of the Lombard kingdom and later a free commune, until it fell to the Visconti in 1359. The famous *Università di Pavia* (University of Pavia) was officially founded in the same century, although its origins go back to the 9th century. The 15th-century *Duomo* (Piazza del Duomo), with a 19th-century façade, is flanked by an 11th-century tower and backed by the 16th-century *Broletto* (Town Hall). Don't miss the house of Renaissance master painter Andrea Mantegna. Pavia's main street, the Strada Nuova, is lined with elegant shops and ends at the river, which is crossed by a postwar reconstruction of a 14th-century covered bridge. The *APT* tourist bureau is at 1 Corso Garibaldi (phone: 382-27238).

**MONZA** The world-famous Monza *Autodromo* is the scene of the Italian *Grand Prix Formula One* race early in September each year. Except during race-preparation times, visitors can drive around the course, with its well-known "seven corners" (admission charge). The *Autodromo* is in a splendid, 2,500-acre park that was once part of the *Villa Reale* (Royal Villa, open to the public only during special events), and now has golf courses, a racecourse, and a pool, besides the auto track. The historic cathedral here (Piazza del Duomo), built during the 13th and 14th centuries, has a notable façade. The *Museo Serpero* (Piazza del Duomo; phone: 393-23404) houses an interesting collection of precious medieval works in gold from the cathedral, including the famed *corona ferea* (iron crown) of Theodolinda, which Napoleon used to crown himself emperor. It is open Tuesdays through Saturdays, with a long midday break; Sundays from 10:30 AM to noon; closed Mondays. Admission charge. Monza is easily reached by bus or *Metropolitana;* by road, it is 7 miles (11 km) northeast of Milan on S36.

---

**EXTRA SPECIAL**

Until the early part of this century, Milan was criss-crossed by *navigli* (canals). Today, only two—the Grande Naviglio and the Pavese Naviglio—remain, and their environs are perhaps the most picturesque in Milan. A stroll through this romantic quarter of art galleries, colorful shops, charming restaurants, *caffès,* and jazz spots is not to be missed. It provides a marked contrast to the rest of this modern, bustling city. On the last Sunday of every month a fascinating antiques market, the *Mercatone del Naviglio,* takes place along the *navigli.* It's a fair walk: From the Piazza del Duomo, follow Via Torino and Corso di Porta Ticinese, or take a taxi.

# Sources and Resources

## TOURIST INFORMATION

General tourist information is available at the extremely helpful *Azienda Provinciale per il Turismo (APT)*, conveniently located at the corner of Piazza del Duomo (1 Via Marconi; phone: 861287; fax: 720-22432) and at the *Stazione Central* (Piazzale Duca d'Aosta; phone: 669-0432 or 669-0532). Both offices are closed from 1 to 3 PM. The *APT* will provide information on hotels, current exhibits, and events. A good introduction to the city is the free video presentation offered at the *APT* office by the *Duomo.* The *US Consulate* is at 2-10 Via Principe Amedeo (phone: 290351)

In the US, the *Ente Nazionale Italiano di Turismo* (Italian Government Travel Office) has several branches (500 N. Michigan Ave., Suite 1046, Chicago, IL 60611; phone: 312-644-0990; 12400 Wilshire Blvd., Suite 550, Los Angeles, CA 90025; phone: 310-820-0098; fax: 310-820-6357; and 630 Fifth Ave., Suite 1565, New

York, NY 10111; phone: 212-843-6880; fax: 212-586-9249). The *Italian Embassy* is at 1601 Fuller St. NW, Washington, DC 20009 (phone: 202-328-5500).

**ENTRY REQUIREMENTS** A US citizen needs a current passport for a stay of up to 90 days.

**TIME** The time in Italy is six hours later than in US East Coast cities. Italy observes daylight saving time.

**LANGUAGE** Italian is the official tongue, though the Milanese dialect and others still are spoken.

**ELECTRIC CURRENT** 220 volts, 50 cycles, AC, but there are some 110-volt outlets. Sometimes both voltages are found in hotel guestrooms.

**MONEY** The Italian currency unit is the lira (abbreviated either L. or Lit.); the plural of lira is lire. At press time the lira traded at 1,626 to the American dollar.

**TIPPING** Keep a handful of lire notes ready. Despite the 15% to 18% service charges at hotels and the 15% usually added to restaurant bills, you'll be expected to give 1,000 to 1,500 L. or more to chambermaids for each night you stay, and at least 1,500 L. to bellhops for each bag they carry. Waiters and wine stewards get an extra 10% of the bill. When eating or drinking at a *caffè* counter the procedure is to pay at the cash register first, then take the small receipt over to the counter, where you leave it with 100 to 200 L. (depending on what you're having). Then place your order. Taxi drivers receive 15% of the meter, hairdressers 15% of the bill. Even service station attendants expect about 1,000 L. for cleaning windshields and giving directions. Theater ushers are tipped 1,000 L.

**BANKING/BUSINESS HOURS** Most banks are open weekdays from 8:30 AM to 1:30 PM and 3:30 to 4:15 PM (some are open from 2:30 to 3:30 PM). On days preceding holidays, banking hours are from 8:30 to 11:30 AM.

A welcome convenience to travelers low on lire are automatic foreign exchange machines where you can change US dollar bills (as well as many other currencies) into local tender. The exchange rate is usually about what banks offer, and there is a fixed commission fee comparable to what financial institutions charge. A few of the many locations for these ATMs are at the airports; the tourist office (2 Via Marconi); the Banca Cesare Ponti (19 Piazza del Duomo); and the 24-hour ATM for credit card advances at the Banca Commerciale (Piazza della Scala). Another place to get a good exchange rate for US bills is at the main post office (4 Piazza Cordusio).

Government offices generally operate from 8 AM to 2 PM. Most other businesses are open from 9 AM to 1 PM and again from 3:30 or 4 to 7:30 or 8 PM. (Places that remain open all day generally close at 6:30 PM.)

**NATIONAL HOLIDAYS** *New Year's Day* (January 1), *Epiphany* (January 6), *Good Friday* (April 14), *Easter Sunday* (April 16), *Easter Monday* (April 17), *Liberation Day* (April 25), *Labor Day* (May 1), *Fer-*

*ragosto/Feast of the Assumption* (August 15), *All Saints' Day* (November 1), *Feast of the Immaculate Conception* (December 8), *Christmas Day* (December 25), and *St. Stephen's Day* (December 26).

**LOCAL COVERAGE** The tourist board can provide copies of *Milan Is,* a useful guide in English, which includes activities, facts, phone numbers, and listings of restaurants and discos. The monthly English-language *A Guest in Milan,* distributed by many hotels, has bulletins on special events, and *Viva Milano,* a weekly entertainment newspaper in Italian, provides up-to-date information on shops, fairs, restaurants, and discos.

Several books in Italian provide listings of restaurants and food and wine shops throughout Italy. Some of the better annually published guides are *La Guida d'Italia* (published annually by *L'Espresso*); *I Ristoranti di Bell'Italia* (published annually by Mondadori); *Gambero Rosso* (published by *Il Manifesto*); and *Osterie d'Italia* (published by Arcigola/Slow Food). They all are sold on newsstands and are available only in Italian.

**TELEPHONE** The city code for Milan is 2. When calling from one area to another within Italy dial 0 + city code + local number. The country code for Italy is 39. Dial 112 for an ambulance; 113 for the police.

## GETTING AROUND

Much of the center of Milan is closed to traffic, so it is most convenient for visitors to use public transportation. Inexpensive day tickets that allow unlimited travel on the bus and tram system can be purchased at the *ATM Ufficio Abbonamenti* at the *Piazza del Duomo* and *Cadorna* subway stations; the *Stazione Centrale;* and the *APT* on Via Marconi.

**AIRPORTS** *Malpensa Airport* (phone: 268-00606, national flights; 268-00627, international flights; 748-54215, lost luggage) is about 28 miles (45 km) and less than an hour's drive from the center of Milan; a taxi ride into town can be prohibitively expensive. Far less expensive buses to *Malpensa* leave from *Stazione Centrale,* on the east side of the *Galleria delle Carrozze,* every half hour (phone: 868008 or 331-797480). They also stop at the east entrance of *Porta Garibaldi* station en route.

*Linate Airport* (phone: 281-06300, national flights; 281-06324, international flights; 701-24551; lost luggage) handles domestic traffic, as well as some international—but not intercontinental—flights. *Linate* is 5 miles (8 km) and 15 minutes (longer if traffic is heavy) from downtown; taxi fare into the center of the city is reasonable. The less expensive *ATM* bus No. 73 leaves for the airport from Corso Europa (near Piazza San Babila) and *Porta Garibaldi* station every 15 minutes between 5:40 AM and midnight (phone: 875495). *Doria Agenzia* (phone: 664-0836) has inexpensive buses that leave from *Stazione Centrale* every 20 minutes from 5:40 AM to 8:30 PM.

Although there is no regular transportation between *Malpensa* and *Linate Airports, Alitalia* occasionally provides group transfers when two connecting *Alitalia* flights are involved. For information on all flights, call 26853; for fog information, call 701-25959.

**BUS AND TRAM** The local bus and tram service, *ATM* (phone: 875495), efficiently connects various points of this sprawling city. Tickets, which must be purchased in advance, are sold at tobacconists and newsstands throughout the city. They are valid for 75 minutes, thus permitting transfer to other lines, and can be used for the subway (see below) as well.

**CAR RENTAL** Most international firms are represented.

**SUBWAY** The efficient, clean *Metropolitana Milanese (MM)* has three lines. The most useful for tourists is line *M3,* which directly links the main railway station, through Piazza del Duomo, and the Porta Romana. Tickets are sold at coin-operated machines in each station and at many tobacconists.

**TAXI** Cabs can be hailed while cruising, picked up at a taxi stand, or called (phone: 8388, 8585, 6767, or 5251). Expect a surcharge after 10 PM, on Sundays and holidays, and for baggage.

**TOURS** *Agenzia Autostradale* (phone: 801161) conducts a three-hour bus tour in English of the city that leaves daily from the Piazzetta Reale. Tickets are available from most hotels and travel agencies, or directly on board. From April through October, the company also offers an all-day tour of the Lombardy lakes. Pick-up points are at Piazza Castello and the *Stazione Centrale.* The *Gestione Governative Navigazione Laghi* (21 Via Ariosto; phone: 481-6230 or 481-2086) arranges boat trips on the lakes.

**TRAIN** Milan's main train station is *Stazione Centrale* (Piazzale Duca d'Aosta; phone: 675001 or 67711). Several smaller stations serve local commuter lines. The largest of these is *Porta Garibaldi,* the departure point for trains to Turin, Pavia, Monza, Bergamo, and other points (phone: 655-2078). The northern line is *Ferrovie Nord Milano* (phone: 851-1608).

## LOCAL SERVICES

**BABY-SITTING SERVICES** *Centro Baby-sitter* (3 Via Vittadini; phone: 826-3845) weekdays or *ABC Baby Sitter* (29/A Via Tadino; phone: 295-16499) Mondays through Saturday mornings.

**DENTIST (ENGLISH-SPEAKING)** Dr. Lucia Calinescu (7 Piazza Giovanni delle Bande Nere; phone: 406241).

**DRY CLEANER** *Guritz* (7-9 Via Sant'Andrea; phone: 760-02129).

**LIMOUSINE SERVICE** *Pini* (28 Piazza Aspromonte; phone: 294-00555) or *VIP Limousine* (5/A Via A. di Tocqueville; phone: 659-2158).

**MEDICAL EMERGENCY** *Ospedale Fatebenefratelli* (23 Corso di Porta Nuova; phone: 657-2898 or 636-3469) or *Ospedale Maggiore Policlinico* (38 Via Francesco Sforza; phone: 55031; 551-1655, emergency first aid). In cases of extreme emergency, call 3883 for a house call or 33 or 113 for an ambulance or medical assistance. Two English-speaking physicians are Dr. Larry Burdick (4 Corso XXII Marzo; phone: 204-9167) and Dr. Bettina Sturlese (19 Via S. Eufemia; phone: 805-7831).

**MESSENGER SERVICE** *Agenzia Scatto* (19 Via Val Bregaglia; phone: 400-92702); *Carry Express* (phone: 6331); *City* (phone: 5430); and *Motopost* (9 Via Parini; phone: 6224).

**NATIONAL/INTERNATIONAL COURIER** *DHL Worldwide Express* (15 Via Agnello and 21 Via Fantoli; phone: 57571); *Emery Worldwide* (in Segrate; phone: 213-4613; fax: 213-6451); and *Federal Express* (10 Via Albricci; phone: 863222; 1-678-33040 toll-free in Italy; fax: 502341).

**OFFICE EQUIPMENT RENTAL** Most large hotels will arrange for short-term rentals (a day or two) of typewriters and computers. For long-term rentals contact *Executive Services Business Center* (8 Via Monti; phone: 481-94271 or 480-13060) or *Tiempo Instant Office Center* (6 Via Cherubini; phone: 498-8321; fax: 480-08459).

**PHARMACY** The main floor of the *Stazione Centrale, Galleria delle Partenze,* has a 24-hour pharmacy (phone: 669-0735). *Duomo* (Piazza Duomo; phone: 870795) and *Farmacia Boccaccio* (26 Via Boccaccio; phone: 469-5281) also are open 24 hours.

**PHOTOCOPIES** Try *Copisteria Tecnocopy* (17 Via Grossich; phone: 236-0475), which stays open in August, or *Rank Xerox* (3 Via Restelli; phone: 688-8941; and 21 Via Pisanello; phone: 406084 or 400-73709). Many photocopy centers send and receive faxes.

**POST OFFICE** The main post office (4 Piazza Cordusio; phone: 160) is open weekdays from 8 AM to 8 PM; Saturdays from 8 AM to noon. The railway post office (8-10 Via Aporti; phone: 670-2846) is open for registered letters weekdays from 8 AM to 10 PM; Saturdays from 8 AM to noon.

**SECRETARY/STENOGRAPHER (ENGLISH-SPEAKING)** *Congress Service 2000* (1 Via G. Marazzani; phone: 261-11435 or 261-11451; fax: 261-11440) and *Copisteria Manara* (28 Porta Vittoria; phone: 540-1047).

**TAILOR** *A. Caraceni* (16 Via Fatebenefratelli; phone: 655-1972) and *Luisa Corvino* (6 Corso Concordia; phone: 266-4253).

**TRANSLATOR** *Agenzia ATD* (24 Via Settembrini; phone: 294-02888); *ASAP* (8 Via Gallina; phone: 761-10150; fax: 701-02986) for technical translations and desktop publishing; *International Translation Center* (19 Via Monte Cervino, Monza; phone: 39-744611); and *Pronto-Mondo* (phone: 669-84862) for telephone interpreters.

**OTHER** Milan has numerous "congress centers" that are equipped with audiovisual devices, simultaneous translation systems, and other services, including *Athena* (36 Via Spartaco; phone: 599-00918); *Castello di Macconago Meeting Center* (38 Via Macconago; phone: 539-1053), a 14th-century castle 15 minutes from downtown; *Centro Congressi Milanofiori* (207 Viale Milano Fiori, Assago; phone:

824791); and *Villa Castelbarco* (Vaprio d'Adda 20069; phone: 909-65282; fax: 909-65212), located in a 12th-century monastery. Fully equipped offices can be rented through *Centro Italiano Congressi* (121/A Corso di Porta Romana; phone: 551-87057); *Executive Service* (8 Via V. Monti; phone: 480-12700); and *International Business Centre* (12 Corso Europa; phone: 760-13731). For jet rental, contact *Executive Jet Italiana* (65 Viale dell'Aviazone; phone: 702-09990); for formal-wear and costume rental, try *Lo Bosco Casa d'Arte* (7 Corso Venezia; phone: 760-00585).

## SPECIAL EVENTS

On *Epiphany* (January 6), a parade of the Three Kings proceeds from the *Duomo* to the *Chiesa di Sant'Eustorgio.* The annual *Fiera di Milano*, held in late April since the 1920s, has put Milan squarely on the international business map. Although this is the city's biggest, there are various other trade fairs and exhibitions (including the showings of designer collections, the twice yearly fashion fair, and the September furniture fair) almost every month except July and August. Obtain information, a copy of the useful bilingual periodical *In Fiera,* and a year-round calendar of events from the main *Trade Fair* office (1 Largo Domodossola; phone: 49971). On the first Sunday in June, the *Festa dei Navigli* (Canal Festival) takes place on Milan's two *navigli* and in Darsena—Milan's port—with music, food, and folklore. In July and August, the city sponsors a variety of outdoor cultural events; sometimes restaurants join in by serving regional specialties in the parks. Via Ripamonti is the site of a truffle festival the last Sunday in October. The city's most important antiques fair, the annual *Fiera di Sant'Ambrogio,* takes place in Piazza Sant'Ambrogio and adjoining streets for 15 days beginning on December 7.

## MUSEUMS

In addition to those listed in *Special Places,* several other museums and churches in Milan are worth a visit. All except the *Basilica di San Lorenzo Maggiore* charge admission.

**BASILICA DI SAN LORENZO MAGGIORE** Built in the 4th century, this church is the oldest in the West. Open daily, with a long midday closing. 39 Corso di Porta Ticinese (no phone).

**GALLERIA D'ARTE MODERNA (MODERN ART GALLERY)** Italian and international contemporary art. At press time, the gallery was closed for restoration after it was severely damaged by a bomb in 1993; call for information on reopening. 16 Via Palestro (phone: 760-02819).

**MUSEO E CASA DI MANZONI (MANZONI MUSEUM AND HOUSE)** The former home of Alessandro Manzoni, author of the 19th-century classic *I Promessi Sposi* (The Betrothed). Closed Saturdays through Mondays, and for a midday break. 1 Via Morone (phone: 864-60403).

**MUSEO DI MILANO (MUSEUM OF MILAN)** This collection of artworks and artifacts traces the city's development, from the Roman era through the Renaissance. Closed Mondays. 6 Via Sant'Andrea (phone: 760-6245).

**MUSEO DEL RISORGIMENTO NAZIONALE (NATIONAL MUSEUM OF THE RISORGIMENTO)** Here are archives and memorabilia dating from Napoleon's first Italian campaign in 1756 through Italy's unification. Closed weekends. 23 Via Borgonuovo (phone: 869-3549).

**MUSEO DELLA SCIENZA E DELLA TECNICA LEONARDO DA VINCI (LEONARDO DA VINCI MUSEUM OF SCIENCE AND TECHNOLOGY)** Some of these exhibits on inventions and ideas for scientific machines date back centuries. Closed Mondays. 21 Via San Vittore (phone: 480-10040).

**PALAZZO REALE (ROYAL PALACE)** A beautiful 18th-century building, it houses the *Civico Museo dell'Arte Contemporaneo* (Civic Museum of Contemporary Art) and prestigious temporary exhibitions. Closed Mondays. 12 Piazza del Duomo (phone: 620-83943).

## GALLERIES

Milan's scores of art galleries feature interesting shows. They generally are open from 10:30 AM to 1 PM and 4 to 8 PM; closed Mondays. The following offer an excellent selection of contemporary and early-20th-century Italian art:

**ANGOLARE** 4 Via Urbana III (phone: 837-6239).

**ANNUNCIATA GALLERIA** 44 Via Manzoni (phone: 796026).

**ARTE CENTRO** 11 Via Brera (phone: 864-62213).

**CAFISO** 1 Piazza San Marco (phone: 654864).

**CHRISTIE'S** 3 Via Manin (phone: 290-01374).

**GIAN FERRARI** 19 Via Gesù (phone: 760-05250).

**HARRY SALAMON** 2 Via Damiano (phone: 760-13142).

**SOTHEBY'S** 19 Via Broggi (phone: 295001).

**STUDIO MARCONI** 15-17 Via Tadino (no phone).

## SHOPPING

With the explosion of Italian design and fashion, Milan is an international style center full of enticing, if expensive, shops, including showrooms and boutiques of many of Italy's major contemporary clothing designers. It also is a center for antiques and home furnishings. The main shopping area comprises the streets near Piazza del Duomo and *La Scala,* particularly the elegant Vias Montenapoleone, della Spiga, and Sant'Andrea. The *Galleria Vittorio Emanuele II* (between the Piazza del Duomo and the Piazza della Scala) is a good place to window shop, dine, or people watch at a *caffè.* Boutiques offering modern fashions and antique clothes also are scattered throughout the old Brera quarter—Milan's Left Bank— and around the *Basilica di Sant'Ambrogio. Caffè Moda Durini* (14 Via Durini), the only mini-shopping mall in the city, is filled with fashions by designers such as Valentino (for men). Most shops are open from 9 or 9:30 AM to 12:30 PM and 3:30 to 7:30 PM; closed Sundays and Monday mornings.

Milan also has several outdoor markets. Tuesday mornings and Saturdays, there are clothing stalls on Viale Papiniano and Via V. Marcello in the Naviglio area—go early for the bargains. On the third Saturday of every month, the *Mercato di Brera* sells antiques, real and otherwise, from 10 AM to 11 PM in and around Piazza Formentini. A pre-*Christmas* flea market and fair near the *Basilica e Museo di Sant'Ambrogio* is a beloved tradition.

**Algani** Newspapers from all over the world. 11 *Galleria Vittorio Emanuele II* (phone: 864-60652).

**Beltrami** Shoes, handbags, and beautifully styled women's ready-to-wear. 4 Piazza San Babila (phone: 760-00546) and 16 Via Montenapoleone (phone: 760-02975).

**Blumarine** Women's sportswear with a difference. 42 Via Spiga (phone: 795081).

**Borsalino** Hats for her and him, with a dash. 92 *Galleria Vittorio Emanuele II* (phone: 874244).

**Brigatti** Milan's finest men's sportswear shop also has a ski boutique for the entire family. 15 Corso Venezia (phone: 760-00273) and 67 *Galleria Vittorio Emanuele II* (phone: 878346).

**Bulgari** High-style jewelry made from gold, silver, platinum, and precious stones. 6 Via della Spiga (phone: 760-05406).

**Byblos** The fashionable women who shop here don't mind paying high prices. 35 Via Senato (phone: 760-02109).

**Calderoni** Exquisite jewelry and silver. 8 Via Montenapoleone (phone: 760-01293).

**Centenari** Fine old prints and paintings. 92 *Galleria Vittorio Emanuele II* (no phone).

**Cignarelli** Wonderful homemade herbal liqueurs. 65 Corso Buenos Aires (phone: 204-3564).

**Dolce e Gabbana** Women's clothing and funky shoes. 10/A Via Sant'Andrea (phone: 799988).

**Drogheria Solferino** A converted 1930s spice-and-perfume shop that now sells moderate-priced contemporary clothes for men and women. 1 Via Solferino (phone: 878740).

**Emporio Armani** The designer's less expensive boutique line. For men and women: 9 Via Sant'Andrea (phone: 760-22757); for kids: 24 Via Durini (phone: 794248).

**Enrico Coveri** Sophisticated clothing for the whole family by one of Italy's top designers. Boutique at 12 Corso Matteotti (phone: 760-01624).

**Ermenegildo Zegna** Designer menswear. 3 Via Verri (phone: 760-06437).

**Fendi** High-fashion silk shirts, purses, and furs designed by Karl Lagerfeld. 9 Via della Spiga (phone: 760-21617).

**Franco Maria Ricci** Beautifully printed and illustrated art books. 19 Via Durini (phone: 798444).

**Frette** Luxurious linen for bed and bath, as well as silk negligees. 21 Via Montenapoleone (phone: 760-03791) and 11 Via Manzoni (phone: 864339).

**Galtrucco** Shimmering silks from Como, by the meter or ready-to-wear. 27 Via Montenapoleone (phone: 760-02978).

**Gianfranco Ferré** The Italian who designs haute couture for Dior sells his own luxurious clothing here. 11 Via della Spiga (phone: 760-09999).

**Gianni Versace** Vibrant, sometimes outrageous high fashion clothing. For men: 11 Via Montenapoleone (phone: 760-08528); for women: 4 Via della Spiga (phone: 760-05451).

**Gioelleria Buccellati** Jewelry famed for its finely chased, engraved gold. Inside the courtyard at 12 Via Montenapoleone (phone: 760-02153).

**La Gravure** An impressive selection of engravings from the 16th through the 20th centuries. 7 Via Laghetto (phone: 760-23500).

**Gucci** Leatherwear, clothing, and shoes for men and women from the famous maker. 5 Via Montenapoleone (phone: 760-13050).

**Immaginazione** Surrealist Fornasetti's famed designs are crafted into all manner of articles—from silk scarves to furniture and housewares. 16 Via Brera (phone: 864-62271).

**Krizia** High-fashion ready-to-wear. Women's boutique at 23 Via della Spiga (phone: 760-08429); menswear at 17 Via Manin (phone: 655-9629).

**Legatoria Artistica** Cleverly crafted gifts, including hand-bound books and notebooks. 5 Via Palermo (phone: 720-03632).

**Mastro Geppetto** Dolls, toys, models, and a life-size Pinocchio. 14 Corso Matteotti (no phone).

**Max Mara** Women's sportswear—look for the terrific jackets. Several locations include Corso Vittorio Emanuele and *Galleria de Cristoforis* (phone: 760-08849) and 6 Via Simpliciano (phone: 875426).

**Mila Schön** Women's fashions from Milan's own contemporary clothing designer; her store for men is a few steps away. 2 Via Montenapoleone (phone: 760-01803).

**Missoni** Sumptuous knitwear for men and women. 2 Via Sant'Andrea (phone: 760-03555) and 14 Via Durini (phone: 760-20941).

**Moschino** High-fashion ready-to-wear for women. 12 Via Sant'Andrea (phone: 760-00832).

**Officina Alessi** The ultimate in wooden and stainless steel household objects, in a tiny shop designed by Sottsass, Italy's most famous architect. 9 Corso Matteotti (phone: 390-39145).

**Prada** The place for shoes with the shape of things to come. 1 Via della Spiga (phone: 760-08636) and 21 Via Sant'Andrea (phone: 760-01426).

**Pratesi** Luxurious linen. 21 Via Montenapoleone (phone: 760-12755).

**Provera** Fine northern Italian wines are sold by the bottle or the glass in a 1920s shop that also has a few tables for tasting. 7 Corso Magenta (phone: 864-53518).

**Roxy** Pure silk ties for gents and scarves for women at realistic prices, with a great selection. 10 Via Tommasi Grossi (phone: 874322).

**Salvatore Ferragamo** Shoes for women, and accessories, including silk ties for men. 3 Via Montenapoleone (phone: 760-00054); for men: 20 Via Montenapoleone (phone: 760-06660).

**Salviati** Exquisite hand-blown Venetian glass in decorator bottles, designer desk lamps, and vases. 29 Via Montenapoleone (phone: 783926).

**Lo Scarabattolo** Fine antiques. 14 Via Solferino (phone: 659-0253).

**Shara Pagano** The bijoux are not the real thing, but are gems nonetheless. 7 Via della Spiga (no phone).

**T & J Vestor** For Missoni's carpets and wall hangings, and tablecloth and napkin sets. 38 Via Manzoni (phone: 760-03530).

**Tanino Crisci** The best in finely crafted men's and women's footwear. 3 Via Montenapoleone (phone: 760-21264).

**Trussardi** High-fashion leatherwear for men and women. 5 Via Sant'Andrea (phone: 760-20380).

**Valentino Donna** Women's clothing by the famous designer (3 Via Santo Spirito; phone: 760-06478). Men's fashions sold at *Valentino Uomo* (3 Via Montenapoleone; phone: 760-20285).

**Venini** Hand-blown glass from perfume bottles to chandeliers, made by one of Venice's foremost artisans. 9 Via Montenapoleone (phone: 760-00539).

**Vittorio Siniscalchi** One of Milan's best custom shirtmakers for men. 1 Via C. Porta (phone: 290-03365).

## DISCOUNT SHOPS

The following are select outlets where fine Italian goods and fashions are often found at far less than the prices in fancier shops. And for indefatigable bargain hunters, a good guide is *Bargain Hunting in Milan, Le Occasioni di Milano,* available at bookstores and some newsstands.

**Diecidecimi** Men's and women's fashions, all discounted 50%, including a large selection of leather jackets and sheepskin coats. 34 Via Plino (phone: 204-6782).

**Emporio** Discounted classic, spirited clothing from previous and current seasons; *not* part of *Emporio Armani.* 11 Via Prina, near Corso Sempione (phone: 349-1040).

**Mimosa** Samples from the salons of name designers. 1 Via Pi da Cannobio (phone: 860581).

**Il Salvagente** Armani, Valentino, and other famous designer clothes in two warehouse-like stores. Men's and women's labels at 16 Via Fratelli Bronzetti (phone: 761-10328); children's attire at 28 Via Balzaretti (phone: 266-80764).

## SPORTS AND FITNESS

Downtown Milan is small and has little green space, few gyms, and a scarcity of public parks. But it has an efficient municipal sports organization. For information on what sports are offered and where, contact the *Ufficio Sport e Ricreazione* (1/A Piazza Diaz; phone: 801466). The staff (some English-speaking) will explain how you can arrange to participate in many sports, including tennis (or ask your hotel concierge to do it for you). The closest and largest green space for jogging, paddling a boat, swimming in a large public pool, picnicking, sunbathing, and *caffè* sitting with Milanese families is the *Idroscalo Parco Azzurro* (Azzurro Park and Boat Landing) near Linate. Its waters are filtered and reportedly not polluted. The city bus No. ID leaves daily from Piazza Fontana for the park at frequent intervals.

**BICYCLING** Rentals by the hour, day, or month are available at *Cooperativa Il Picchio* (49 Corso San Gottardo; phone: 837-7926 or 837-2757).

**FITNESS CENTERS** *American Health Fitness Center* (various locations include 10 Via Montenapoleone; phone: 760-05290; and 1/A Piazza Reppublica; phone: 655-2728) and *Skorpion Center* (24 Corso Vittorio Emanuele; phone: 799449).

**GOLF** The largest and most accessible course in the Milan area is the *Golf Club Milano* (phone: 39-303112). These 27 holes are in the heart of the *Parco di Monza,* 7 miles (11 km) northeast of Milan, on the former estate of Umberto I (who was assassinated here in 1900). The site of several major tournaments, it boasts pros who rank among Italy's best, and the physical facilities are first-rate. Closed Mondays. Call the *Federazione Italiana Golf* (44/B Via Piranesi; phone: 701-07410) for information on other courses. Most are closed Mondays, and some do not allow guests on weekends.

**HORSE RACING** Thoroughbred (March through October) and trotting (year-round) races are run at the internationally famous *Ippodromo San Siro* (phone: 482161), on the eastern outskirts of Milan.

**HORSEBACK RIDING** There are two riding stables in Milan: the *Centro Ippico Amrosiano* (106 Via Verro; phone: 569-5394) and the *Centro Ippico Milanese* (20 Via Macconago; phone: 539-2013).

**JOGGING** Try *Parco Sempione* (behind the *Castello Sforzesco);* the *Giardini Pubblici* (Public Gardens; Bastioni di Porta Venezia); or the *Idroscalo Parco Azzurro* (see above).

**SOCCER** From September through May, both *Inter* and *Milan* play at *Stadio Comunale Giuseppe Meazza* (5 Via Piccolomini; phone: 487-07123).

**SWIMMING** Indoor public pools include *Cozzi* (35 Viale Tunisia); *Mincio* (13 Via Mincio); and *Solari* (11 Via Montevideo). Open-air pools include *Lido* (15 Piazzale Lotto, near the *Stadio San Siro;* phone: 7398). *Argelati* (6 Via Segantini; phone: 581-00012) is a beach establishment with showers.

**TENNIS** Book public courts well ahead of time. There are courts at *Bonacossa* (74 Via Mecenate; phone: 506-1277); *Centro Polisportivo* (48 Via Valvassori Peroni; phone: 236-1066); the private *Country Sporting Club* (about 5 miles/8 km from town, at 68 Via G. Pepe Paderno Dugnano; phone: 918-0789); *Lido di Milano* (15 Piazzale Lotto; phone: 392-66100); and *Ripamonti* (4 Via Iseo; phone: 645-9253).

## THEATER

Although you can take in classical Italian theater productions in various venues throughout the city, we give the following rave reviews, beginning with our favorite.

---

### CENTER STAGE

**Piccolo Teatro** Since its creation just after World War II, the so-called *Little Theater* has been the most vital force of the Italian stage. The mission of its ever-active founder and godfather, and arguably Europe's finest stage director, Giorgio Strehler, was to make the theater a medium of popular culture; to that end, the repertory is eclectic and international, the staging vigorous and imaginative, and its public the same patrician group glimpsed the evening before at *La Scala*. After more than a decade of debate, a larger and brand-new theater is being built at a different location; the new quarters are expected to be finished in 1996. 2 Via Rovello, *Palazzo del Broletto* (phone: 877663).

---

Other places to enjoy classic Italian theater include the *Manzoni* (40 Via Manzoni; phone: 760-00231) and the *Teatro Lirico* (14 Via Larga; phone: 866418). Purchase tickets at the box offices or at the following agencies (for a 10% fee): *La Biglietteria* (61 Corso Garibaldi; phone: 659-8472; and 58 Corso Lodi; phone: 573-01358) or *Virgin Megastore* (Piazza del Duomo; phone: 720-03354).

## MUSIC

The renowned *La Scala* is an obvious must for an opera fan lucky enough to have tickets in hand (or to have made the acquaintance of a sharp concierge who knows the ropes), but ballet and concerts also are held here from September through November (for more details, see *Special Places*). Concerts also are held at the *Auditorium Angelicum* (2 Piazza Sant'Angelo; phone: 632748) and the *Conservatorio di Musica* (12 Via Conservatorio; phone: 760-01755). Tickets to the *Angelicum* are sold at 4 Via Gustavo Favo or at *Ricordi Music Shop* (2 Via Berchet).

## NIGHTCLUBS AND NIGHTLIFE

Milan has a variety of nightclubs offering both dinner and dancing. For impromptu jazz spots, music with a sandwich, or just people watching, stroll through the Naviglio or Brera quarters. Popular nightclubs include *Charley Max* (2 Via Marconi; phone: 871416); *L'Angelo Azzuro* (11 Ripa di Porta Ticinese; phone: 581-00992), a favorite with jazz and R&B fans; *Budineria* (53 Via Chiesa Rossa; phone: 846-7268), a piano bar; and the funky *Nepentha* (1 Piazza Diaz; phone: 804837), open to 3 AM. Top discos include *American Disaster* (48 Via Boscovich; phone: 225728); *Amnesia* (2 Via Callini; phone: 540-0958), where the "look-makers" hang out; the trendy and crowded *Holliwood* (2 Corso Como; phone: 659-8996); *Lizard* (Largo la Fappa; phone: 659-00890), where fashion models cavort; *Al Vascello* (Piazza Greco; phone: 670-4353); and *Calipso Club* (120 Viale Umbria; phone: 256-0553). Live music, including jazz, can be heard regularly at numerous clubs, among them *Capolinea* (119 Via Ludovico il Moro; phone: 891-22024), the city's oldest jazz spot, where internationally acclaimed musicians perform, and *Ca'Bianca* (117 Via Ludovico il Moro; phone: 891-25777), an excellent music and cabaret spot near the Naviglio Grande. Milanese folk tunes and ballads are performed at *Osteria Amici Miei* (14 Via Nicola d'Apulia; phone: 261-45001). *Zelig* (140 Via Monza; phone: 255-1774) is very popular with the fashion-model set (closed Mondays; reservations necessary). *El Brellin* (14 Alzaia Naviglio Grande; phone: 581-01351) features a social scene in the evenings with snacks and a piano bar.

Milan has many cozy piano bars that are ideal for a late drink and snack. Try *Golden Memory* (22 Via Lazzaro Papi; phone: 548-4209); *Gershwin's* (10 Via Corrado il Salico; phone: 849-7722); or the elegant *Momus* (8 Via Fiori Chiari; phone: 805-6227).

# Best in Town

## CHECKING IN

An international business center, Milan offers a wide range of accommodations, from traditional old-fashioned hotels to efficient, modern, and commercial ones. Because of the many fairs and fashion showings some hotels are fully booked in peak periods a year ahead; summer reservations are sometimes easier to obtain. Milan's hotel prices are very high. In high season (summer and *Easter*) very expensive hotels here will cost $575 or more a night for a double room; expensive hotels will cost from $350 to $550; moderate places charge $200 to $350; and inexpensive ones charge between $100 and $200. Off-season rates are about 10% lower. All hotels feature air conditioning, private baths, TV sets, and telephones unless otherwise indicated. All telephone numbers are in the 2 city code unless otherwise noted.

**Pierre Milano** Slightly off the beaten track, this luxurious 47-room hotel is nevertheless a favorite of the VIP business crowd. On the premises is an American bar and a restaurant. Business facilities include 24-hour room service, meeting rooms for up to 20, an English-speaking concierge, foreign currency exchange, secretarial services in English, audiovisual equipment, photocopiers, cable TV news, translation services, and express checkout. 32 Via de Amicis (phone: 805-6221; fax: 805-2157).

### EXPENSIVE

**Diana Majestic** A lovely Art Nouveau building is the site of this charming, intimate hostelry near the *Giardini Pubblici.* Some of the 94 rooms and the bar overlook a private beautiful garden. No restaurant. A member of the CIGA hotel chain, it usually makes a limited number of tickets to *La Scala* available to guests booking from the US. Business facilities include meeting rooms for up to 50, an English-speaking concierge, foreign currency exchange, secretarial services in English, audiovisual equipment, photocopiers, computers, cable TV news, translation services, and express checkout. 42 Viale Piave (phone: 295-13404; 800-221-2340; fax: 201072).

**Doria Baglioni** Near the *Stazione Centrale,* this luxurious establishment has 116 soundproof rooms and two suites, all elegantly furnished. No restaurant, but there is a nice bar and covered parking. Business facilities include 24-hour room service, meeting rooms for up to 175, an English-speaking concierge, foreign currency exchange, secretarial services in English, audiovisual equipment, photocopiers, computers, cable TV news, translation services, and express checkout. 22 Viale Andrea Doria (phone: 290-06363 or 669-6694; fax: 669-6669).

**Excelsior Gallia** Built by the Gallia family in the early 1930s, this luxury hotel with 242 spacious rooms and 10 suites has an Art Nouveau façade and is decorated in the grand style. Its service is efficient and friendly; its restaurant, quite good. Another plus is the health club with a sauna, a gym, and massage. Business facilities include meeting rooms for up to 800, an English-speaking concierge, foreign currency exchange, secretarial services in English, audiovisual equipment, photocopiers, computers, translation services, and express checkout. Near the central train station at 9 Piazza Duca d'Aosta (phone: 6785; 800-225-5843 or 800-44-UTELL; fax: 656306).

**Four Seasons Milan** Opened in 1992, this member of the Canada-based chain has zoomed to Milan's top spot, so reserve early. It was constructed on the site of a 15th-century monastery, *Santa Maria del Gesù,* and some of the building's original architecture has been preserved—there are four columns in the hall, and a large, beautiful cloister sheds light into the main floor drawing rooms. (Some rooms overlook the cloister.) Although the 98 rooms and a vast presidential suite are decorated in contemporary Italian design, some 15th-century accents have been incorporated into the decor. Northern Italian fare is served in the fine *Il Teatro* restaurant and in a second eatery, *La Veranda*. Business facilities include 24-hour room service, meeting rooms for up to 200, an English-speaking concierge, foreign currency exchange, secretarial services in English, audiovisual equipment, photocopiers, computers, cable TV news, translation services, and express checkout. 8 Via Gesù (phone: 77708; 800-332-3442; fax: 770-85000).

**Grand Hotel Duomo** If modern industrial Italy has a heart, you can watch it beating in this hotel right next to the cathedral. It's here that the country's *pezzi grossi* (big businesspeople) meet to make the country's most important deals. The 156 guestrooms are arranged on two levels—a lower living room section furnished with contemporary pieces and elegant touches of marble, Oriental carpeting, and burnished wood, and a bedroom above. It's in the center of town, just off Piazza del Duomo, but on a pedestrian street that ensures quiet. The restaurant's food is quite good, and there's 24-hour room service. Business facilities include meeting rooms for up to 20, an English-speaking concierge, foreign currency exchange, secretarial services in English, audiovisual equipment, photocopiers, computers, and translation services. 1 Via San Raffaele (phone: 8833; fax: 864-62027).

**Hilton International** This attractive 321-room hotel in the commercial center facing the *Stazione Centrale* is tastefully decorated in a mixture of Italian provincial and modern styles. There is also a colorful, moderately priced Italian restaurant, 24-hour room service, and a discotheque. The service is first-rate. Business facilities include meeting rooms for up to 240, an English-speaking concierge, foreign currency exchange, secretarial services in English, audiovisual equipment, photocopiers, computers, cable TV news, translation services, and express checkout. 12 Via Galvani (phone: 69831; 800-HILTONS; fax: 667-10810).

**Jolly President** A superb location downtown, a handsome lobby, topflight services, 235 comfortable rooms, and a good restaurant make this a reliable favorite of Milan's executive set. Business facilities include 24-hour room service, meeting rooms for up to 110, an English-speaking concierge, foreign currency exchange, audiovisual equipment, photocopiers, and translation services. 10 Largo Augusto (phone: 7746; fax: 783449).

**Palace** Part of the reliably luxurious and efficient CIGA chain, each floor of this hostelry has a different color scheme; the 193 rooms and 13 suites are decorated in ultramodern style, while some suites come with a Laura Ashley–decorated children's room. The smaller new wing is more conventional than the renovated older section. Dining is on the roof garden or in the attractive *Casanova Grill,* and there's 24-hour room service. A limited number of tickets to *La Scala* can be booked (well ahead) through CIGA's US office. Underground parking is available. Business facilities include meeting rooms for up to 200, an English-speaking concierge, and foreign currency exchange. 20 Piazza della Repubblica (phone: 6336; 800-221-2340; fax: 654485).

**Principe di Savoia** Just north of the *Duomo* and within walking distance of the train station and boutique-lined Via Montenapoleone, this classic deluxe hotel, a member of the CIGA chain, has a lovely renovated façade, lobby, and reception area. The 294 guestrooms and four suites boast antiques, thick rugs, and marble baths. There are also 40 apartments with kitchenettes and balconies. Two floors house a fitness club with a pool, gym, and sauna. The well-recommended *Galleria* restaurant serves regional fare. A limited number of *La Scala* tickets are offered to guests who reserve in advance through their US office. Business facilities include meeting rooms for up to 500, an English-speaking concierge, foreign currency exchange, and secretarial services in English. 17 Piazza della Repubblica (phone: 6230; 800-221-2340; fax: 659-5838).

### MODERATE

**Blaise & Francis** Fifteen minutes from the center of Milan, it has 110 well-maintained and efficient rooms and a garage, but no restaurant. Business facilities include 24-hour room service, meeting rooms for up to 45, an English-speaking concierge, foreign currency exchange, and photocopiers. 9 Via Butti (phone: 668-02366; fax: 668-02909).

**Bonaparte** Formerly a residential hotel (now fully refurbished), this 56-room hostelry with a restaurant is luxuriously appointed. Business facilities include meeting rooms for up to 25, an English-speaking concierge, foreign currency exchange, audiovisual equipment, photocopiers, computers, cable TV news, and translation services. 13 Via Cusani (phone: 8560; fax: 869-3601).

**Century Tower** Near the train station, this very comfortable, 148-room hotel has a garden, a restaurant, a bar, and 24-hour room service. Business facilities include meeting rooms for up to 80, an English-speaking concierge, secretarial services in English, audiovisual equipment, photocopiers, computers, cable TV news, and translation services. 25/B Via Fabio Filzi (phone: 67504; fax: 669-80602).

**Fieramilano** Across the street from the fairgrounds, it has 238 rooms, a dining room, and private parking. Business facilities include meeting rooms for up to 50, an English-speaking concierge, foreign currency exchange, secretarial services in English, audiovisual equipment, photocopiers, cable TV news, translation services, and express checkout. 20 Viale Boezio (phone: 336221; fax: 314119).

**Manin** The newer rooms in this 119-room hostelry have a modern decor; the older guestrooms are not impressive but are spacious and comfortable. A few seventh-floor rooms overlook gardens. There's also a very good restaurant and bar. Business facilities include meeting rooms for up to 100, an English-speaking concierge, foreign currency exchange, audiovisual equipment, photocopiers, cable TV news, and express checkout. About a half mile from *La Scala* at 7 Via Manin (phone: 659-6511; fax: 655-2160).

**Spadari al Duomo** Chic, sleek, and small (38 rooms), this recently renovated hostelry has a tiny *caffè* for guests only. Its contemporary art collection adds to the tony ambience. 11 Via Spadari (phone: 20123; fax: 861184).

**Starhotel Ritz** Efficient and comfortable, this 205-room hotel aims to please the business traveler. There are a restaurant, a bar, and parking. Business facilities include meeting rooms for up to 320, an English-speaking concierge, foreign currency exchange, secretarial services in English, audiovisual equipment, photocopiers, computers, cable TV news, and translation services. 40 Via Spallanzani (phone: 2055; fax: 295-18679).

### INEXPENSIVE

**Antica Locanda Solferino** This delightful hostelry with only 11 rooms (no TV sets) is in the old Brera quarter a few blocks north of *La Scala*. Once a tavern, the place retains much Old World fin de siècle charm in its furniture and decor. No restaurant. 2 Via Castelfidardo (phone: 290-05205; fax: 657-1361).

**Manzoni** Small, pleasant, and quiet, it's right in the city's center and boasts a garage. The 52 rooms have no TV sets, and there's no restaurant, but room service provides snacks. There's an English-speaking concierge, and a shopping mall nearby. 20 Via Santo Spirito (phone: 760-05700; fax: 754212).

**Napoleon** This small hotel in a nearby suburb offers good value. On the metro line just southeast of the train station, it has 41 soundproof rooms, friendly service, and a pleasant decor, but no restaurant. 12 Via Ozanam (phone: 295-20366; fax: 295-20388).

---

## EATING OUT

Milan's restaurants are among the world's finest. Like much northern fare, *la cucina milanese* differs from other Italian food in that butter is used more often than olive oil. Look for special dishes made with the fabulous *tartufi bianchi* (white truffles) from the neighboring Piedmont region, in season between September and *Christmas.* Rice from the region's plantations is used as a food base, with saffron-perfumed *risotto alla milanese* the favorite provender—best eaten with a steaming osso buco (veal shank). The Milanese also love fresh fish. In September, try delicious white peaches; in December, panettone, a classic sweet brioche filled with candied fruits, is a must. Expect to pay $300 or more for dinner for two at very expensive restaurants—among the priciest in Italy; from $190 to $300 at an expensive place; from $100 to $180 at a moderately priced restaurant; and from $50 to $100 at an inexpensive one. Prices don't include drinks, wine, or tips. It is a good idea to check whether the restaurant you select accepts credit cards. All telephone numbers are in the 2 city code unless otherwise indicated.

All restaurants are open for lunch and dinner unless otherwise noted. For an unforgettable dining experience we begin with our culinary favorites, followed by our cost and quality choices, listed by price category.

## DELIGHTFUL DINING

**Aimo and Nadia** Gastronomes in search of light, full-flavored food with a Tuscan accent travel from far and wide to this refined and much-praised spot on the outskirts of the city. The menu, which varies with the season, features specialties such as risotto with zucchini blossoms and truffles, ricotta-stuffed zucchini flowers, super-fresh raw tomato soup, spaghetti with a sauce of baby onions and tomatoes, stuffed swordfish, and pheasant with wild mushrooms. Exceptional cheeses and luscious desserts provide the grand finale. Closed Saturday lunch, Sundays, and August. Reservations necessary. Major credit cards accepted. 6 Via Montecuccoli (phone: 416886).

**Antica Osteria del Ponte** In an old-fashioned inn by a bridge along a picturesque *naviglio* (canal) is one of Italy's few restaurants to be awarded three Michelin stars, plus kudos from all major Italian culinary guides; indeed, it may be Italy's best. Look for creative presentations of classic risotto, as with zucchini blossoms laced with saffron or drenched under precious truffles (in season); ravioli (try the ravioli stuffed with lobster and covered with a lobster sauce); and new and interesting preparations of fresh fish. The wine list and desserts are outstanding. The intimate, antiques-furnished dining room is warmed by a fireplace. Closed Sundays, Mondays, *Christmas* to January 12, and August. Reservations necessary. Major credit cards accepted. Near Abbiategrasso, 15 miles (24 km) from Milan, at 9 Piazza Castello, Cassinetta di Lugagnano (phone: 942-0034).

## VERY EXPENSIVE

**Biffi Scala** Since 1931, this restaurant has been a favorite for late-night suppers, particularly after the opera. The decor is sumptuous, the fare Lombard and international. Closed Sundays, two weeks in August, and *Christmas* week. Reservations necessary. Major credit cards accepted. Piazza della Scala (phone: 866651).

**Savini** La Callas used to dine here with Arturo Toscanini, and this place still hits the high notes. Today's diners can enjoy some of the style at easier prices by ordering the *menu degustazione*. Otherwise, go for Milanese specialties like an impeccable risotto with saffron or

the *cotoletta milanese,* a breaded veal cutlet that is to that traditional dish what La Callas was to *Tosca:* perfection. Vegetables,
salads, and desserts off a cart also merit applause. Closed Sundays,
10 days in mid-August, and 10 days at *Christmas.* Reservations
advised. Major credit cards accepted. *Galleria Vittorio Emanuele
II* (phone: 720-03433; fax: 864-61060).

### EXPENSIVE

**Bice** Years ago, Tuscan-bred Bice Mungai opened a tiny shop in which
she served staples from home, such as *ribollita* (vegetable soup
made with purple cabbage). From such beginnings evolved one of
Milan's most chic restaurants, now run by her children, with branches
in Paris, New York, and Washington, DC. Today's wide menu features both meat and fish specialties, including *risotto al pesce* (with
fish). In season, wild mushrooms, stuffed pheasant, and truffle toppings are served. Closed Mondays, Tuesday lunch, and part of
August. Reservations advised. Major credit cards accepted. 12 Via
Borgospesso (phone: 760-02572).

**Boeucc** Artists dine next to financiers in this traditional and very elegant downtown restaurant. In the local dialect, *boeucc* means "hole-
in-the-wall," but the clientele, service, traditional menu (here's the
place for the real Milanese, saffron-perfumed risotto), and vast wine
list belie the name. Closed Saturdays and Sunday lunch. Reservations advised. Major credit cards accepted. 2 Piazza Belgioioso
(phone: 760-20224).

**Don Lisander** On summer evenings, downtown diners can enjoy the courtyard garden at this reliable old favorite. It offers a sampler menu
of impeccably prepared traditional Italian dishes. Closed Sundays
and two weeks at *Christmas.* Reservations advised. Major credit
cards accepted. 12/A Via Manzoni (phone: 760-20130).

**Al Garibaldi** This relatively unpretentious eatery caters to Milan's chic
young businessfolk. The kitchen dispenses topnotch inventive food
with great professionalism. Open until 1 AM. Closed Fridays, Saturday lunch, August, and *Christmas*. Reservations advised. Major
credit cards accepted. 7 Viale Montegrappa (phone: 659-8006).

**Giannino** So famous that some people reserve six months in advance,
this bastion of traditional Italian fare includes fish, homemade pasta,
and pastries, though it's not as good as it used to be. Elegant private dining rooms are available. Closed Sundays and August. Reservations necessary. Major credit cards accepted. 8 Via Amatore Sci-
esa (phone: 551-95582).

**Gli Orti di Leonardo** In this smart, brick-vaulted eatery, specialties include
fish hors d'oeuvres and "little risotti," made with surprising ingredients. A rich choice of wines is available. Closed Sundays and most
of August. Reservations advised. Major credit cards accepted. 6-8
Via Aristide de Togni (phone: 498-3476).

**Peck** Around the corner from the *Duomo,* this is an offshoot of the eponymous, elegant food emporium. With its masterful blend of the clas-

sics and the creative, it is taking over the block, with an adjacent delicatessen, a pricey takeout, and separate (and reasonably priced) counter service also worth trying. Closed Sundays, holidays, early January, and the first three weeks of July. Reservations advised. Major credit cards accepted. 4 Via Victor Hugo (phone: 876774).

**Sadler-Osteria di Porta Cicca** In one of the oldest parts of the city, this eatery with only 11 tables serves truly innovative fare. Favorites in season are *tagliolini* with zucchini blossoms and chunks of salmon, and ravioli with mixed wild mushrooms. Closed Sundays, alternate Mondays (when the restaurant offers cooking classes), the first half of January, and August. Reservations advised. Major credit cards accepted. 51 Ripa di Porta Ticinese (phone: 581-04451).

**La Scaletta** The *nuova cucina* at this outstanding, elegantly appointed two-room restaurant with seating for only 30 diners is so popular among the Milanese that reservations are necessary. Closed Sundays, Mondays, August, *Christmas,* and *New Year's.* No credit cards accepted. 3 Piazza Stazione Porta Genova (phone: 581-00290).

**Solferino** Milanese tradition holds sway in this pleasant eatery in La Brera, the artists' quarter. The menu, which varies with the season and the inspiration of the kitchen, includes intriguing potato soup with wild mushrooms; the house specialty, *risotto alla milanese*; and the real thing when it comes to the Milanese cutlet. Closed Saturday lunch, Sundays, and in mid-August. Reservations advised. Major credit cards accepted. 2 Via Castelfidardo (phone: 659-9886).

**L'Ulmet** Milanese adore this place for its successful combination of traditional and creative Italian fare. It was built on ancient Roman foundations, and its roof incorporates a 1,600-year-old plinth. Wild game is served in season. For dessert, try the crêpes with honey and pine nuts. Closed Sundays, Monday lunch, and August. Reservations advised. Major credit cards accepted. 21 Via Olmetto (phone: 864-52712).

### MODERATE

**Antica Trattoria della Pesa** Founded in 1881, this old favorite retains a gaslit atmosphere. Offered are Lombard favorites such as saffron-hued risotto and garlic-flavored lamb shanks. Closed Sundays. Reservations advised. Major credit cards accepted. 10 Viale Pasubio (phone: 655-5741).

**Bagutta** A big and cheery Tuscan *osteria,* it serves good food, although the waiters can be brusque at times. Under the massive chestnut beams the walls are crammed with paintings from the artists who made this their hangout. Today it's always chockablock with businesspeople dining on polenta with *porcini* mushrooms, the classic *risotto alla parmigiana* with a dusting of truffles in season, or brains with artichokes. The dessert tray is laden with the restaurant's homemade *dolci.* Good chianti wines wash it all down. A patch of garden courtyard is open in the summer. Closed Sundays. Reservations unnecessary. Major credit cards accepted. 14 Via Bagutta (phone: 760-02767).

**Bistrot di Gualtiero Marchesi** The lacy marble fretwork of the *Duomo* roof seems close enough to touch from this eatery on the seventh floor of *La Rinascente* department store. Italy's most famous chef presides over a place that is simple, chic, and a good value. The prix fixe menu offers traditional Milanese dishes that vary according to season. Valuable modern art adorns the walls. Adjacent is a pleasant but sometimes noisy coffee shop with the same magnificent view. Closed Sundays, Monday lunch, and August. Reservations advised. Major credit cards accepted. During store hours take the escalator; in the evening, enter from 2 Via San Raffaele (phone: 877120).

**La Briciola** High-fashion models, journalists, and young Milanese-about-town enjoy the light touch of host Giorgio Valveri's homemade pasta, salads, and fresh fish. Good value for the money. Closed Sundays and Monday lunch. Reservations necessary. Most credit cards accepted. 25 Via Solferino (phone: 655-1012).

**Alla Clausura** Swiss-Italian fare is served in this extremely popular establishment. Specialties of the intimate dining room include *penne alle melanzane* (pasta with eggplant) and *filetto al midollo e rosti* (steak with marrow and Swiss potatoes). The desserts, such as *pinolata* (cream cake topped with pine nuts), are excellent. Closed Sundays and one week in August. Reservations advised. Major credit cards accepted. 13 Via Navarra (phone: 837-8366).

**Le Colline Pisane** A spot for Tuscan fare, this lively trattoria serves fine food in pleasant surroundings. Closed Sundays and August. Reservations advised. Major credit cards accepted. 5 Largo la Foppa (phone: 659-9136).

**Giardino** Near the banks of the Naviglio River, this restaurant serves simple but delicious food in an atmosphere reminiscent of a 19th-century Milanese tavern or *osteria.* There is alfresco dining in summer. Closed Tuesdays. Reservations unnecessary. No credit cards accepted. 36 Alzaia Naviglio Grande (phone: 894-09321).

**Alle Langhe** This popular family-style trattoria serves Piedmontese fare that makes visitors feel welcome. Closed Sundays and most of August. Reservations advised. Major credit cards accepted. 6 Corso Como (phone: 655-4279).

**Osteria del Binari** Elegant, with an impressive choice of traditional dishes from several Italian regions. The hot soup is topped with an incredibly light puff pastry. Closed for lunch, Sundays, and three weeks in August. Reservations advised. Major credit cards accepted. 1 Via Tortona (phone: 894-06753).

### INEXPENSIVE

**Al Materel** It's rustic Lombardy at its best, with old family recipes, homemade pasta, polenta, and wild game and wild mushrooms in season. Closed Tuesdays, Wednesday lunch, and July. Reservations advised. No credit cards accepted. Corner of Via Laura Solera Montegazza and Corso Garibaldi (phone: 654204).

**Montenero** This former trattoria is now gussied up and trendy, but it still offers bargains. There are two tasting menus, one expensive and the other less so. The desserts are worth the calories. Closed Sundays and August. Reservations advised. Most credit cards accepted. 34 Via Montenero (phone: 550-19104).

**Il Mozzo** Pizza is made the right way here, in a wood-burning oven. Brave the evening crowds to try the *pizza alla romana* (tomato, mozzarella, ricotta, and fresh basil in season) or *alla fiamma* (onions, rosemary, and hot red pepper). Closed Wednesdays. Reservations advised. No credit cards accepted. 22 Via Marghera (phone: 498-4676).

**Al Pont de Ferr** This wine shop/food emporium is hard by an iron bridge crossing the Naviglio Grande (hence its name), a colorful grand canal. House specialties include pasta, gnocchi, and a few meat dishes. Let the sommelier guide you through the excellent wine list. Closed lunch, Sundays, August, and *Christmas*. Reservations advised. Most credit cards accepted. 55 Ripa di Porta Ticinese (phone: 890-46277).

**Rigolo** Large and friendly, it's a favorite of local journalists and businesspeople. Tuscan specialties (such as thick, grilled steaks) and a superb selection of homemade desserts are the chief draws. Closed Mondays and August. Reservations advised. Major credit cards accepted. 11 Via Solferino (phone: 804589).

**La Risotteria** Here's the spot—small, friendly, and always crowded—to test Milan's all-time favorite dish, risotto, in its myriad forms, from the classic Milanese version bright with saffron to trendy fruit-laced concoctions. The variety of salads is interesting, and the desserts are homemade. Closed Saturday dinner, Sundays, and August. Reservations advised. Some credit cards accepted. 2 Via Dandolo (phone: 551-81694).

**La Topaia** This restaurant features specialties from Liguria, the former Yugoslavia, and the French countryside. With a new verandah for alfresco dining, it is a summertime favorite. Closed Sundays and for lunch. Reservations advised. Major credit cards accepted. In the Naviglio canals quarter, at 46 Via Argelati (phone: 837-3469).

**Trattoria Milanese** Founded in 1919, it's still a repository of genuine gastronomic tradition, including *risotto alla milanese* and mixed boiled meats. Closed Tuesdays, August, and *Christmas*. Reservations advised. Most credit cards accepted. 11 Via Santa Marta (phone: 864-51991).

**Trattoria Toscana Pagni** Traditional Tuscan cuisine is served in this family eatery. Try a platter of salami as a starter and then the homemade *pappardelle ai carciofi* (flat noodles with artichoke sauce), or make a single dish of the wild boar with polenta (winter only).

Closed Saturday dinner, Sundays, and August. Reservations advised. Some credit cards accepted. 7 Via Orti (phone: 550-11267).

---

## BARS AND CAFFÈS

After a full day of gallery-hopping or nonstop shopping, Milan's many *caffès* and pastry shops are good places to stop for lighter meals and to satisfy those with a sweet tooth. Our favorite is *Cucchi* (1 Corso Genova; phone: 839-9793; closed Mondays), where you can sip a Bellini (fresh peach juice and champagne) outdoors in the summer and eye Armani-clad executives, or nurse a Negroni (red vermouth and gin) indoors in the winter, amid 1930s-era pink velvet and chandeliers. You might want to time your visit for 7:45 AM to sample brioche fresh from the oven. Milan also boasts some of Italy's best *paninerie* (sandwich shops), which offer a variety of hot and cold sandwiches. Try *Montanelli American Bar* (inside the courtyard by *Buccellati* at 12 Via Montenapoleone; no phone); *Bar Magenta* (13 Via Carducci; phone: 805-3808); or *Paninomania* (12 Corso Porta Romana; phone: 576827). Most frequented by local office and fashion industry workers are the tiny coffee bars inside some of downtown Milan's charming courtyards. Some also offer inexpensive, pleasant lunches—a plate of pasta, a cooked vegetable, and a glass of wine.

For Milan's best coffee visit *Marches* (Via Meravigli); customers must stand at the bar, but they linger over hand-dipped chocolates and the Milanese *Christmas* specialty, the panettone. For tea and chocolates, the *Sant'Ambroeus* (7 Corso Matteotti) is the place to go—big, old-fashioned, and charming, with immense Venetian chandeliers and matrons in furs. The 166-year-old *Cova* (near *La Scala* at 8 Via Montenapoleone; phone: 760-00578) has pink damask tablecloths and waiters in black tie; try the hand-dipped *kikingerli*-filled (sour cherry) chocolates, and take home some candied violets. Conveniently located in the shopping district off a courtyard is *Babington's* (8 Via Sant'Andrea), a sister in spirit to the English tearoom in Rome, with Victorian decor. At the *Café Radetzky* (105 Corso Garibaldi), a 15-minute walk from downtown, the atmosphere of Milan 150 years ago, when the Austrians ruled, has been lovingly re-created in a stylish coffee shop. And sundowners say "cheers" at *Caffè Milano* (1 Piazza Mirabello; phone: 290-03300).

Wheat germ, honey, and pine nuts are only a few of the tempting ice-cream flavors offered at *Gelateria Ecologica Artigiana* (40 Porto Ticinese; phone: 581018), whose name roughly translates as "Craftsman's Environmental Ice Creamery." It stays open until well after midnight.

# Moscow

## At-a-Glance

### SEEING THE CITY

The lookout point in front of *Moscow State University* in Lenin Hills affords the best panorama of the city. Below are the Moskva River and the *Luzhniki* sports complex, while in the distance are the gold and silver domes of *Novodevichiy Monastyr* (New Maiden Convent) and the *Kremlin* complex (see *Special Places*), and the seven look-alike skyscrapers built by Stalin as monuments to himself. The university is near the *Leninskiy Gory* metro stop. There's a fine view of Red Square and the *Kremlin* from the *Rossiya* restaurant on the top floor of the 21-story tower wing of the *Rossiya* hotel (phone: 298-1562 or 298-5400).

Russian is an almost completely phonetic language, so when you sound out the letters on signs, you will recognize many English and French cognates. Here are a few Russian words to help you in your travels: *Ulitsa* is the Russian word for street; *prospekt* means avenue; *bulvar* means boulevard; *naberezhnaya* is embankment; *proyezd* is passage; *shosse* means highway; *ploshchad* is the word for square; and *pereulok* means lane.

It has become almost commonplace for Russian streets and squares to be renamed, and hotels and restaurants to have changed hands. Many of those newly deposed statues are now resting in an impromptu park behind the newly opened *Tretyakov Gallery*, across from *Gorky Park*. Also, after years of neglect under a Communist regime, Russia's cultural institutions and cathedrals are now undergoing much-needed repair. Many already have been closed for several years, with no scheduled dates for reopening. Check with hotel service bureaus for up-to-date schedules of museums and cathedrals.

### BE PREPARED!

At press time, prompted by the increase in reported cases of diphtheria in Russia, travelers are advised to update their immunizations before entering the country. For further information call the US State Department's *Citizen's Emergency Center* at 202-647-5225.

### SPECIAL PLACES

Moscow grew up in concentric rings around the *Kremlin,* and much of what is of interest to the visitor is within the area bounded by the Bulvar Koltso (Boulevard Ring). However, there is also much to explore in the area between the Boulevard Ring and the outlying Sadovoye Koltso (Garden Ring), which roughly follows the line of an old earthen wall that was demolished early in the last century. Moscow's main thoroughfare, Gorkovo Ulitsa, now renamed Tverskaya Ulitsa, runs from the *Byelorusskiy* railway terminal to Manezh Square, adjacent to Red Square.

## INSIDE THE KREMLIN

**KREMLIN COMPLEX** Kremlins, or fortresses, can be found in a number of old Russian towns. None, however, is as well known as the Moscow *Kremlin,* which occupies 69 acres overlooking the Moskva River. For most of the 20th century the seat of the central Soviet government, it is once again the stronghold of the Russian state. The entire complex is surrounded by a red wall studded with towers. Atop five of these towers are gigantic ruby-red stars that are lighted at night. Buried in the *Kremlin* walls are the ashes of various Russian heroes and two Americans—John Reed, whose book *Ten Days That Shook the World* is an eyewitness account of the Russian Revolution of 1917, and William ("Big Bill") Haywood, founder of the International Workers of the World (IWW), forerunner of the American Communist Party. There are guided tours of the *Kremlin* complex, or you can walk through the grounds on your own. Closed Thursdays. Admission charge.

**KAFEDRAINAYA PLOSHCHAD (CATHEDRAL SQUARE)** The central square in the *Kremlin* takes its name from the three principal cathedrals situated here. The largest, *Uspenskiy Sobor* (Assumption Cathedral), with its white limestone walls and five gilded domes, was built around 1475. This was the private cathedral of the czars, many of whom were crowned here, but when Napoleon occupied Moscow, his men used it for a stable and burned some of its icons for firewood. *Blagoveshchenskiy Sobor* (Annunciation Cathedral) had three cupolas when it was built in early-Moscow style between 1484 and 1489. When six new domes were added during reconstruction after a fire in the 16th century, it became known as the "golden-domed" cathedral. The five domes of *Arkhangelskiy Sobor* (Archangel Michael Cathedral), built between 1505 and 1509, are painted silver. All the pre-Romanov czars, with the exception of Boris Godunov, are buried here (the Romanovs are buried in St. Petersburg). Also on the square are the *Granovitaya Palata* (Granovitaya Palace), the oldest public building, dating from 1473 to 1491; the bell tower of Ivan the Great; and several other early cathedrals. Tickets for admission to all cathedrals may be purchased at a kiosk in the square.

**BOLSHOI KREMLEVSKIY DVORETS (GRAND KREMLIN PALACE)** Once the residence of the imperial family in Moscow, the palace is now a government building. The Supreme Soviet of the USSR and of the Russian Federation met here until the abortive coup of August 1991. From the outside the yellow-and-white-walled palace (built from 1838 to 1849) appears to have three floors; actually there are only two—the second floor has two tiers of windows. Not open to the general public except by special arrangement (phone: 929-7990).

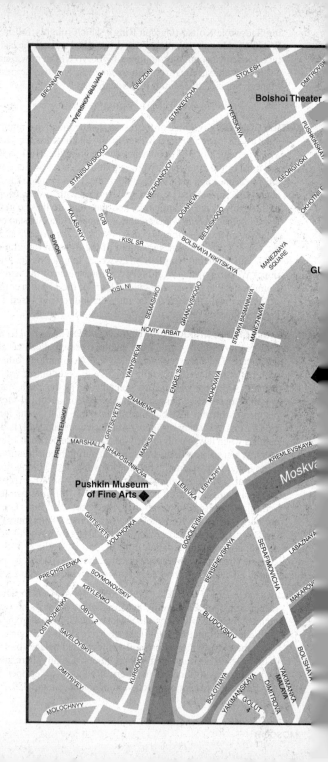

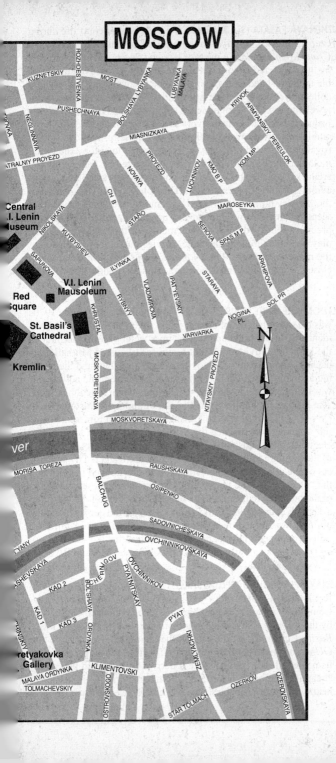

# MOSCOW

**Central I.I. Lenin Museum**

**Red Square**

**St. Basil's Cathedral**

**Kremlin**

**V.I. Lenin Mausoleum**

**Tretyakovka Gallery**

N

**ORUZHENAYA PALATA (STATE ARMORY)** The luxury of court life during czarist times comes alive in the halls of this museum next to the *Grand Kremlin Palace.* Lovers of *War and Peace,* and those intrigued by the checkered history of Russian royalty—from Ivan the Terrible to the ill-fated Romanovs—will be fascinated by the splendid collection of royal regalia: arms and armor; clocks and carriages; jewel-encrusted robes of priceless silk, velvet, and brocade; thrones, including Ivan the Terrible's ivory seat and the throne of Czar Alexei, emblazoned with over 2,000 precious and semi-precious stones; royal crowns; and the many gifts presented to and by the czars, including the beautiful bejeweled eggs created by Fabergé. If you are lucky, you may be able to join one of the very small tour groups admitted to the *Almazniy Fond* (Diamond Fund). This section of the *Armory* holds Catherine II's diamond-encrusted crown, her scepter with its Orlov diamond, and her golden orb, as well as other precious gems. Advance arrangements for this tour (in English) may be made through your hotel service bureau or by contacting the museum directly. The *Diamond Fund* and *Armory* are both closed Thursdays. Admission charge to both (phone: 921-4720).

OUTSIDE THE KREMLIN

**BYELI DOM (THE WHITE HOUSE)** This 21-story building built in the 1970s was the site of two major clashes in the 1990s. In August 1991 President Yeltsin and his supporters set up a center of resistance here to the hard-line Soviet coup that temporarily ousted Mikhail Gorbachev. About 20,000 Muscovites staged a vigil around the building and vowed to defend Yeltsin and his ministers and advisors. It was their defiance, in the end, that brought down the coup plotters. The Parliament building was the site of another confrontation in October 1993, this between Yeltsin's government forces and hard-line deputies who rejected the Russian leader's order to hold new elections to the legislature. Yeltsin sent tanks to destroy the façade of the building following a night of violence triggered by supporters of the dissolved Parliament. Muscovites dubbed the building the "black-and-white house" after smoke darkened several floors of the building. In the aftermath of the October revolt, Yeltsin hired a Turkish construction firm to quickly repair the damage, and the building was turned over to the government to house its offices. Yeltsin opponents have demanded, however, that the *White House* be given back to Parliament. Overlooking the Moskva River on Novy Arbat Ulitsa.

**KRASNAYA PLOSHCHAD (RED SQUARE)** This enormous square—2,280 feet long by 426 feet wide—is the heart of Moscow and of Russia. Completely repaired, the cobblestone area is bounded on the west by the *Kremlin* wall and the *Lenin Mausoleum;* on the south by *St. Basil's Cathedral;* on the east by the mammoth department store *GUM;* and on the north by the *State History Museum.* Red Square—its name will not change, since it derives from a word that meant "beautiful" before it meant "red," as in communism—is steeped in history. Centuries ago the square was chiefly used as a marketplace.

Only later did it become the venue for official proclamations and public events. On the southeast quadrant, between *St. Basil's* and *GUM,* is a circular platform known as the *Lobnoye Mesto* (Place of the Execution). Official decrees were read here, but it was better known as the spot where high-profile executions were carried out. For over seven decades the chief festivals—*May Day* on May 1 and *Revolution Memorial Day* on November 7—rumbled through here amid much flag waving and under the smug approval of the nation's rulers standing atop the *Lenin Mausoleum.* (Both have since been redesignated nonpolitical holidays.) In recent years *Red Square* also has been the site of demonstrations both in favor of and against the government's program of economic reforms.

**MAUZOLEY V. I. LENIN (V. I. LENIN MAUSOLEUM)** The body of V. I. Ulyanov, or Lenin, the Russian revolutionary and founder of Bolshevism, is still displayed in its glass sarcophagus; the impressive changing of the guard ceremony still takes place in front of it every hour; and incredible numbers of people still pass through the mausoleum each week to view the body. But Lenin's days in this huge, red-and-black, stepped memorial in Red Square seem numbered. With the death of the Soviet Union and the Communist Party, authorities have contemplated moving Lenin's remains and burying them elsewhere. (In all probability, it won't be in Moscow, since Lenin specifically requested to be interred with other members of his family in St. Petersburg.) Until then it's symbolic of the changing times in Moscow that the traditionally long line to get into the tomb has been eclipsed in length by the queue to the counter at *McDonald's,* a 10-minute walk away. No cameras are allowed, and no talking is permitted once inside. Closed Mondays. Krasnaya Ploshchad (phone: 224-5115).

**POKROVSKIY SOBOR (ST. BASIL'S CATHEDRAL)** Although this Moscow landmark houses numerous frescoes, icons, and other artifacts, the building itself is much more interesting than any of its collections. With its distinctive multicolored onion-shaped domes, *St. Basil's* has become *the* symbol of Moscow, gracing numerous books and providing the backdrop for countless television news reports. Located on the south side of Red Square, it was built at the bidding of Ivan the Terrible in the mid-16th century to celebrate the liberation of the Russian state from the Tatar yoke. According to legend Ivan had the architects blinded when it was finished, so they could never build a finer church.

The cathedral actually encompasses nine churches—a central building that stands more than 100 feet high surrounded by eight domed chapels. First walk around the exterior of the building, noting both its complex structure and its intricately painted decorations in blue, yellow, red, green, and gold (these were added in the late 17th century—the church was originally white with gilded domes). Take time to go inside and wander through the narrow passages to the tiny but extensively frescoed chapels. Though it was used as a museum (an annex of the *State History Museum* directly across Red Square; see *Museums*) after the Bolshevik Revolution,

*St. Basil's* and the *Kremlin* cathedrals were returned to the Russian Orthodox church in 1992. *Christmas* and *Easter* services once again are celebrated here. Closed Tuesdays. Admission charge. Krasnaya Ploshchad (phone: 298-3304).

**GORKY PARK** To most Muscovites, this massive park along the banks of the Moskva River is the centerpiece of their city. Year-round it's the place parents take their children for a special outing. In summer there is horseback riding available, as well as carnival rides for kids of all ages. In winter Muscovites test their skills at cross-country skiing and ice skating here. Open daily until sunset. The main gate is just off Krymskiy Val.

**GUM** One of the largest, best-known department stores in the world, *GUM* (pronounced *Goom*) was built in the late 19th century as an arcade for nearly a thousand small shops. It is said that some 350,000 shoppers wander through the three levels of this emporium each day. The store, which celebrated its 100th anniversary in 1992, is attempting to remodel itself into Moscow's premier shopping mall: The building, with its vaulted glass ceiling, etched-glass storefronts, and wrought-iron railings has been undergoing a face-lift since privatization. Shops now include *Botany 500, Samsonite, Benetton, Yves Rocher, L'Oréal, Estée Lauder, Arrow Shirts*, and *Galeries Lafayette*. The coming of capitalism to this venerable venue presages more interesting changes to come. Closed Sundays. 3 Krasnaya Ploshchad (phone: 926-3471).

**METRO** In addition to being a generally clean and efficient means of transportation, Moscow's subway system is actually one of the city's most interesting museums. Each of its more than 100 stations has its own aesthetic qualities: Stained glass windows, mosaics set with gold, crystal chandeliers, marble and stainless steel columns, and bronze statues are some of the decorative elements. Most interesting and beautiful are the *Mayakovskaya, Kievskaya,* and *Komsomolskaya* stations. The first *Metro* line opened in 1935; the newer the station, the less ornate it is likely to be. Some of the platforms, reached by fast escalators, are as much as 300 feet underground. For a single, very small fare, you can ride the entire system, getting off at every station for a look. Since trains arrive every two to four minutes, you can cover much of the system in a short time. The most central stop is a junction of three stations—*Manezh Ploshchad, Teatralnaya Ploshchad,* and *Okhotniy Ryad*—joined by underground passages. Open daily from 6 AM to 1 AM.

**NOVODEVICHIY MONASTYR (NEW MAIDEN CONVENT)** Recently renovated and rededicated by the Russian Orthodox church, this richly endowed convent was part of a ring of fortress-monasteries and convents that formed a protective circle around the *Kremlin*. Founded in 1524 to commemorate the liberation of Smolensk, it has a long and varied history. Boris Godunov was proclaimed czar from this convent; Peter I's sister, Sophia, was imprisoned here when she encouraged rebellion against her brother; and noble families sent their unmarried daughters and widowed (or unwanted) wives to live here. (When he grew tired of her, Peter the Great sent his first wife to the *Lopukhin Palace,* a brick building on the right near the convent entrance.) There is a functioning Russian Orthodox church here, but the convent's *Smolensky Cathedral* now serves as a museum of Russian applied arts from the 16th and 17th centuries. Chekhov, Gogol, Prokofiev, Stanislavsky, Khrushchev, and other famous Russians are buried in the cemetery. Closed Tuesdays and the first Monday of the month. Admission charge. Near the *Sportivnaya* metro station. Also reached by trolley No. 11 or 15, and by bus No. 64, 132, or 808. 1 Novodevichiy Proyezd (phone: 246-8526).

**MOSKOVSKIY UNIVERSITET (MOSCOW STATE UNIVERSITY)** South of the convent, across the Moskva River, this monumental university towers above the city from its 415-acre site in Lenin Hills. Statistics offer the best summary of its status as the world's largest bastion of learning. The buildings put up during the late Stalinist period (between 1949 and 1953) contain 45,000 rooms connected by some 90 miles of corridors. The main building is 787 feet tall and its façade is 1,470 feet long. The university was founded in 1755 by Russian scientist Mikhail Lomonosov and officially bears his name. Near the *Universitet* and *Leninskiy Gory* metro stops. Also reached by bus and trolley. Universitetskiy Prospekt (phone: 939-1000).

**GOSUDARSTVENNIY MUZEY IZOBRAZITELNIKH ISKUSSTV IMENI A. S. PUSHKINA (PUSHKIN MUSEUM OF FINE ARTS)** Near the *Kremlin,* this museum houses an eclectic collection of 550,000 pieces of ancient Eastern, Greco-Roman, Byzantine, European, and American art (including several works by 20th-century American painter, illustrator, and Communist sympathizer Rockwell Kent) as well as a library of 200,000 volumes. Its most important collections are its ancient Oriental and Renaissance art and 19th- and early-20th-century French paintings, including works by Cézanne, Monet, and Utrillo. Closed Mondays. Admission charge. 12 Volkhonka Ulitsa (phone: 203-6974).

ENVIRONS

**KOLOMENSKOYE ESTATE-MUSEUM** Established as a country estate for the ruling family in the 14th century, Kolomenskoye is on a hill beside the Moskva River, about 10 miles (16 km) southeast of the *Kremlin.* The first stone church in the Russian "tent roof" style was erected here by Czar Ivan Kalita in 1532, and several churches and buildings from the 16th and 17th centuries also can be seen here. The museum has interesting exhibitions of door locks and keys, ceramic tiles and stones, and carved-wood architectural details. Closed Mondays and Tuesdays. Admission charge. The buildings can be seen from the main road, but the entrance is from a dirt road off the Kashirskoye Shosse. 39 Andropova Prospekt (phone: 115-2713).

**KUSKOVO ESTATE** One of the best collections of 18th-century Russian art can be found in the palace of this estate that once belonged to the Sheremetiev family, among the oldest Russian noble families. The palace, built by serf craftsmen, has pine-log walls faced with painted boards. Since 1932 this also has been the site of the *State Museum of Ceramics,* with collections of Russian porcelain, glass, china, and majolica. There is also a 70-acre formal French garden. The estate is about 6 miles (10 km) from central Moscow, along the Ryazanskoye Shosse. Closed Mondays and Tuesdays. Admission charge. 2 Yunosti Ulitsa (phone: 370-0160).

# Sources and Resources

## TOURIST INFORMATION

*Intourservice* (4 Belinskovo Ulitsa; phone: 202-9975 or 203-8943; fax: 200-1243) provides general information, brochures, and maps, as well as English-speaking guides for general and specific sightseeing in Moscow and its environs, including tours of the *Kremlin* grounds and cathedrals.

Most visitors agree, however, that the city is not tourist-friendly. There are very few signs in English, even in the *Metro,* and ticket sellers at key tourist attractions do not speak English. In response to this shortcoming, privately owned tour companies have sprung up. One, *Patriarchy Dom* (phone: 255-4515), has knowledgeable, English-speaking guides to take you to the historic Arbat District, the cultural hub of Moscow; to modern galleries; as well as to places outside of the city. The *US Embassy* is at 19-23 Novinskiy Bulvar (phone: 252-1898).

In the US, Contact *Intourist USA* (610 Fifth Ave., Suite 603, New York, NY 10020; phone: 212-757-3884; 800-982-8416; fax: 212-459-0031). The *Russian Embassy* is at 1825 S. Phelps Pl. NW, Washington, DC, 20008 (phone: 202-939-8907).

**ENTRY REQUIREMENTS** A US citizen needs a valid passport and a visa to enter Russia. At present there are three kinds of visas: tourist, ordinary (for business or family visits), and transit. A visa application can be filed through a travel agent or directly with a consular office in the US; allow a minimum of 14 days before your departure. An itinerary that describes the time and duration of all stops within the country, travel arrangements, and hotel reservations must be submitted along with a fee (there is an additional fee for processing within a week or for a 24-hour turnaround); processing fees vary between consular offices.

**TIME** The time in most of western Russia, including Moscow, is eight hours later than in US East Coast cities. Russia follows daylight saving time.

**LANGUAGE** Russian, the official language, uses the Cyrillic alphabet. Tourism industry personnel and workers in the hotel and restaurant industries speak English.

**ELECTRIC CURRENT** 220 volts, 50 cycles, AC.

**MONEY** One ruble is made up of 100 kopecks. At press time $1 US was worth about 3,385 rubles. Although the ruble is convertible, the exchange rate is very unstable, so check rates before departing. Many prices are quoted in US dollars or German marks.

Economic turmoil, including frequent and steep price increases on many goods and services, makes it impossible to provide accurate information on prices, including the costs of basic services such as public transportation and the telephone. New currency regulations came into force on January 1, 1994, requiring all businesses to accept cash payments in rubles only. Payment by credit card can be made in dollars. The measure was aimed at putting an end to economic segregation between shops and restaurants that accepted foreign currency and those that accepted rubles. However, businesses can request payment in rubles at a fixed exchange rate that is considerably higher than the bank rate. Travelers are advised to pay by credit card to avoid the extra cost incurred due to unfavorable exchange policies.

**TIPPING** Tipping is not officially sanctioned, though tips are not refused.

**BANKING/BUSINESS HOURS** There are banking branches for currency exchange at major hotels, open weekdays from 9 AM to 5 PM. There's a foreign exchange bank on Tverskaya Ulitsa; it is open from 8:45 AM to noon and from 12:50 to 7:50 PM. Most other businesses are open weekdays from 9 AM to 5 or 6 PM.

**NATIONAL HOLIDAYS** *New Year's Day* (January 1), Russian Orthodox *Christmas* (January 8), *Soviet Army Day* (February 23), *International Women's Day* (March 8), *Day of Spring and Labor* (May 1), *Victory Day* (May 9), *Independence Day* (June 12), and *Anniversary of the 1917 Bolshevik Revolution* (November 7).

**LOCAL COVERAGE** Moscow's English-language newspapers, *The Moscow Times* and *The Moscow Tribune,* feature local and international news and survival tips for foreigners. The *International Herald Tribune, Time, Newsweek,* and other European and North American dailies and weeklies often can be purchased at kiosks and hotels, although not necessarily on the day of publication. For local coverage of the economy and Western business ventures, Russia's premier publication is the English-language edition of *Commersant,* available at hotels and kiosks throughout the city. In addition, several US newspapers, including *The New York Times,* now publish editions in Russian.

*The Moscow Times* publishes a quarterly magazine that offers suggestions on restaurants, cultural events, nightlife, and sightseeing. It's available at all hotels and at the *Times* office (24 Pravdy Ulitsa; phone: 257-2513 or 257-2550).

The *Falkplan City Map of Moscow* (Falk-Verlag; $7.95) is a good backup to local maps and is available in bookstores throughout the US. An invaluable tool for negotiating the streets of Moscow, it includes public transportation routes; lists of hotels, museums, and theaters; as well as a street index.

**TELEPHONE** The city code for Moscow is 095. When calling from one area to another within Russia dial 8 + city code + local number. The country code for Russia is 7. In an emergency, dial 03 for an ambulance and 02 for the police.

A word about telephones: The Russian telephone system is notoriously bad. There are no residential telephone directories, although a number of English-language business directories such as *Information Moscow* and the *All Moscow Directory* are available. Your hotel service bureau can contact Moscow information for residential numbers. If you speak Russian dial 09 for local information.

If your hotel does not have direct-dialing service, the desk can book an overseas call for you. If there is direct dialing, just dial 8, wait for the tone, then dial 10, the country code (the country code for the US and Canada is 1), the area code, and local number. Another certain, although more expensive, way of getting a direct international line is at any of 25 *Comstar* telephone booths around town (call 979-1692 or 210-0962 for their locations), which take American Express, Visa, or a prepaid phone credit card issued by *Comstar.* Finally, if you're determined to use rubles (quite a bargain if you have the patience), go early in the day to the *Central Telephone and Telegraph Office* (7 Tverskaya Ulitsa), which has international lines.

If you are going to be doing business in Moscow, you can rent a cellular phone at the *Americom Business Center,* located on the second floor of the *Radisson Slavyanskaya* hotel (phone: 941-8427).

## GETTING AROUND

Moscow has an efficient and exceptionally inexpensive public transportation system that includes a *Metro* (subway), buses, trams, trolleys, and even boats in summer.

**AIRPORTS** *Sheremetevo I* (phone: 155-0922 for domestic flights) and *Sheremetevo II* (phone: 578-7518 or 578-7816 for international flights) are about 30 minutes from downtown by taxi. Three other airports, *Domodedovo, Bykovo,* and *Vnukovo,* serve domestic flights and are from 40 minutes to an hour from downtown Moscow.

**BOAT** From late spring through early fall, low-priced boats cruise along the Moskva River, stopping to drop off and pick up passengers in different parts of the city. The view of the *Kremlin* and *St. Basil's* from the water around sundown, with the day's last flickers of light glinting off the gilded domes, is one to remember. The main dock is to the rear of the *Rossiya* hotel (6 Varvarka Ulitsa; no phone).

**BUS/TRAM/TROLLEY** These transport lines operate daily and are inexpensive to ride. Bus tickets can be obtained from the driver in units of 10 or from a hotel newsstand. Riders punch their own tickets and retain them until the end of the ride. (There are random inspections to enforce the honor system of paying the fare.) Maps showing the routes for all lines are available at hotels and many street kiosks.

**CAR RENTAL** Automobiles, with or without drivers, may be rented through major hotels. A word of caution: Roads—especially in the center of Moscow—are often in need of repair. To complicate matters further, there are myriad obscure traffic rules designed to bedevil you.

For instance, there are no left turns except at a handful of designated intersections, and driving with headlights on at night is prohibited (only parking lights are permitted).

Agencies for foreign-made cars include Russo-Japanese *InNis* (32 Bolshaya Ordynka Ulitsa; phone: 155-5021); *Business Car* (18-1 Ovchinnikovskaya Naberezhnaya; phone: 233-1796), which is open 24 hours; *Hertz,* under the licensee *MTD Service* (152 Gorbunovo Ulitsa; phone: 448-8035); *Avis* (7 Vernadskovo Prospekt; phone: 578-5676); *Rozec-Car* (phone: 241-5393 or 241-7715); and *Mosrent* (79 Krasnobogatirtskaya Ulitsa; phone: 248-0251).

**METRO** The subway has seven interconnected lines. One runs in a circle; the others radiate out to different parts of the city. Though much else may be unraveling in this city, the *Metro* is still generally clean, efficient, and inexpensive. Trains arrive and depart at the various stations frequently and operate from 6 AM to 1 AM.

**TAXI** Visitors will find that all taxi fares are expensive, but are subject to negotiation. Taxis are generally yellow, black, or white Volga sedans with a checkered pattern on the door. However, expect several rejections before you find one willing to take you where you want to go. Cabs also can be ordered in advance through your hotel service bureau or, if you speak Russian, by calling 927-0000 or 927-2108. It is best to order a taxi at least an hour in advance.

> **BE ALERT!**
>
> There has been an increasing number of reports of tourists being robbed by bands of young adults commonly known as Russian "mafia," who lurk outside major hotels and restaurants posing as taxi drivers. The best advice is never get into a taxi with other passengers, and quickly walk away if anything looks or sounds suspicious. Recent car bombings also pose a threat to travelers.

**TRAIN** Moscow supports over a dozen railroad stations. The *Intourservice* telephone number for train information and reservations in English is 921-4513, or ask your hotel service bureau for information about locations, fares, and schedules. The stations tourists are most likely to frequent are *Sankt Peterburgskiy* (1 Kalanchovskaya Ploshchad; phone: 262-4281), where trains depart for and arrive from St. Petersburg, Finland, and Estonia; *Byelorusskiy* (Byelorusskaya Ploshchad; phone: 253-4908), with trains to and from Berlin, London, Warsaw, Paris, and Lithuania; *Kievskiy* (Kievskaya Ploshchad; phone: 240-7622), with arrivals from and departures for Ukraine and Central Europe; and *Yaroslavskiy* (Kalanchovskaya Ploshchad; phone: 266-0595), with trains to and from the Far East, including the *Trans-Siberian* line.

For those who want to explore beyond Moscow, *Cox & Kings* organizes 11-, 13-, and 14-day tours on their *Bolshoi Express* steam locomotive to the Golden Ring cities of historic monasteries and churches, St. Petersburg, and the Baltic States. Accommodations and meals are provided. For more information contact *Cox & Kings* (511 Lexington Ave., New York, NY 10017; phone: 212-935-3854).

## LOCAL SERVICES

**BUSINESS SERVICES** International phone lines, fax machines, conference rooms, comprehensive bilingual secretarial services, and other business services are available at the major Western-style hotels (see *Checking In*); the British-Russian *Comstar Business Center* (10 Petrovka Ulitsa, Suite 301; phone: 924-0892 or 924-1385); the *Retour Business Center* (6 Savelyevskiy Pereulok; phone: 202-7610 or 202-2662); and the *Americom Business Center* in the *Radisson Slavyanskaya* hotel (2 Berezhkovskiy Naberezhnaya; phone: 941-8427 or 941-8815). The new *Red Square Business Center* on the second floor of the *GUM* department store (phone: 921-0911; fax: 921-4609) offers international phone service, faxing, and photocopying.

   Computer supplies can be purchased at *Future Technology* (6A-22 Festivalnaya Ulitsa; phone: 453-4204); *Computerland* (8 Kutuzovskiy Prospekt; phone: 243-3553); and *Computer Supply Services* (35 Prechistenka Ulitsa; phone: 202-0480). The only official Apple dealership in Russia is *InterMicro* (39 Nizhnaya Krasenoselskaya; phone: 267-4352 or 267-3210). Repairs on IBM-compatible computers can be made through the *Hewlett Packard Repair Center,* opposite the *Cosmos* hotel (150 Mira Prospekt; phone: 184-8002).

**CURRENCY EXCHANGE** The best places to exchange dollars for rubles are hotel service bureaus and larger souvenir shops. Cash traveler's checks for rubles or dollars (but not to convert rubles into dollars) at the Dialog Bank in the *Radisson Slavyanskaya* hotel (phone: 941-8349 or 941-8434). Bring your passport, customs declaration form, and a lot of patience. You will not be able to use traveler's checks in most restaurants and shops, so it is best to bring cash instead. It is also very unwise to deal with just anyone who approaches you on the street or inside a store; they may shortchange you or, worse, give you counterfeit money. Visa installed the first ATM (automatic teller machine) in the lobby of the *Metropol* hotel (see *Checking In*). In addition, there are banks in several hotels, including the *Mir* (phone: 252-9519) and the *Ukraina* (phone: 243-3030). At press time, however, these locations did not cash traveler's checks.

**DENTIST (ENGLISH-SPEAKING)** Dental problems should be taken to *Medical Interline* (5 Tverskaya Ulitsa, Room 2030; phone: 203-8631), a Swiss-Italian-Belgian-Hungarian-Russian joint venture with a multilingual staff, Western equipment, and reasonable prices. A new clinic, the *Adventist Health Center of Moscow* (21-60 Letiya Oktybrya Prospekt; phone: 126-3391), has an English-speaking dentist and English-speaking dental lab technicians.

**DRY CLEANING** Dry cleaning outlets can be found at the *Aerostar, Mezhdunarodnaya, Olympic Penta, Pullman Iris,* and *Savoy* hotels (see *Checking In*).

**MEDICAL EMERGENCY** Most hotels have a doctor on call (some speak English). For serious problems go directly to the *American Medical Center* (3 Shmitovskiy Proyezd; phone: 256-8212 or 256-8378). It offers Western-trained doctors and nurses, an emergency room with life-saving equipment, a laboratory, X-ray facilities, and a pharmacy; closed Sundays. The *European Medical Clinic's Polyclinic No. 6* (3 Gruzinskiy Pereulok; phone: 253-0703 or 240-9999) has both Russian and Western staff members, all of whom speak English. The *Sana Medical Center* (65 Nizhnaya Pervomaiskaya Ulitsa; phone: 464-1254 or 464-2563) is open daily and caters to foreigners, although there are few on staff who speak English—bring your own translator. As a last resort try the *Botkin Hospital* (2 Botkinskiy Proyezd; phone: 255-0015), formerly reserved for Western diplomats. For information on medical evacuations contact *Delta Consulting* (12 Berezhkovskaya Naberezhnaya; phone: 434-4389).

**NATIONAL/INTERNATIONAL COURIER** Moscow has become crowded with couriers, including *DHL Worldwide Express* (two locations: the *Olympic Penta* hotel; phone: 971-6101; and the *Mezhdunarodnaya* hotel; phone: 253-1194); *Federal Express* (12 Krasnopresnenskaya Naberezhnaya; phone: 253-1641); *TNT* (3 Baltiyskiy Pereulok; phone: 156-5771); and *UPS* (15A Bolshaya Ochakovskaya Ulitsa; phone: 430-7069 or 430-6373).

**PHARMACY** There are several reputable drugstores in Moscow. Among the best are the pharmacy of the *American Medical Center* (3 Shmitovskiy Proyezd; phone: 256-8212 or 256-8378); *Eczacibasi* (2-15 Moroseika Ulitsa; phone: 928-9189); the Swiss-operated *International Pharmacy of Moscow* (4 Tchernyakhovskava Ulitsa; phone: 155-7080 or 155-8780); the German *Seidel Medizin GmBH* (59A Beskudnikovsiy Bulvar; phone: 905-4227); and *Unipharm* (13 Skaterniy Pereulok; phone: 202-5071).

**PHOTOCOPIES** An American/Canadian outpost of quality printing services is *Alphagraphics* (50 Tverskaya Ulitsa; phone: 251-1208 or 251-1215), which makes photocopies, business cards, and passport pictures in a flash. Their fax services are competent but expensive. Several hotels also offer photocopying services.

**TRANSLATOR** The city's translation services are largely provided by *Intourservice* and most Western hotels. Also check the classified ads in *The Moscow Times. Inlingua* (2-1 Semyonovskaya Naberezhnaya; phone: 360-0847) and *IP Interpret* (1 Kaidashevskiy Pereulok; phone: 231-1020) are private agencies offering translators and interpreters.

## SPECIAL EVENTS

Although April 22 commemorates Lenin's birthday, not surprisingly, this day—and other old Soviet holidays such as May 1, *International Labor Day*—no longer are observed officially in post-Communist Russia. The *Moscow Film Festival* is held annually in June and July. The *Russian Winter Festival,* a major arts event, runs from December 25 to January 5.

# MUSEUMS

Besides those mentioned in *Special Places,* Moscow has numerous museums devoted to Russian art and folk crafts, the work of famous writers and composers who lived here, and various aspects of Russian history. Unless otherwise noted, those below do not have an admission charge.

**FILIAL MUZEY L. N. TOLSTOVO (LEO TOLSTOY HOME)** The restored home of the writer, who lived here from 1882 to 1909. The museum has three rooms filled with antiques, porcelains, and paintings that the author collected during his extensive travels throughout Europe. Closed Mondays and the last Friday of the month. 21 Lva Tolstovo Ulitsa (phone: 246-9444).

**GOSUDARSTVENNIY MUZEY ISKUSSTV NARODOV VOSTOKA (STATE MUSEUM OF ORIENTAL ART)** Crafts of the Russian Far East, plus Chinese, Indian, and Japanese art. Closed Mondays. 12A Suvorovskiy Bulvar (phone: 202-4953 or 202-4555).

**GOSUDARSTVENNIY MUZEY ISTORIL (STATE HISTORY MUSEUM)** Reopened last year, Moscow's oldest museum documents the history of the country and contains such relics as clothes worn by Ivan the Terrible, Peter the Great's carriage, Napoleon's saber, and decrees written by Lenin after the revolution. It also houses the country's largest archaeological collection as well as coins, medals, and precious ornaments. For further information check with your hotel service bureau. 1-2 Krasnaya Ploshchad (phone: 928-8452). For further information check with your hotel service bureau.

**GOSUDARSTVENNIY TSENTRALNIY MUZEY MUSIKALNOY KULTURI IMENI M. I. GLINKI (GLINKA STATE CENTRAL MUSEUM OF MUSICAL CULTURE)** Dedicated to Mikhail Ivanovich Glinka and other Russian composers of the 19th century, the collection includes 1,500 musical instruments. Closed Mondays and the last day of the month. 4 Fadeyeva Ulitsa (phone: 972-3237).

**KVARTIRA MUZEY DOSTOEVSKOVO (DOSTOYEVSKY APARTMENT-MUSEUM)** Memorabilia of the great author. Closed Mondays, Tuesdays, and the last day of the month. 2 Dostoyevskaya Ulitsa (phone: 281-1085).

**MUZEY ANDREYA RUBLOVA (ANDREI RUBLEV MUSEUM OF OLD RUSSIAN ART)** A good collection of restored icons, housed in Moscow's oldest cathedral. Included are works by students and contemporaries of Rublev, but none by the 14th-century master himself. The museum was undergoing renovation at press time; inquire at your hotel service bureau or call ahead before going. Closed Wednesdays and the last Friday of the month. 10 Andronyevskaya Ploshchad (phone: 278-1489).

**MUZEY CHEKHOVA (CHEKHOV MUSEUM)** Exhibitions relating to Russia's greatest playwright, Anton Pavlovich Chekhov. Closed Mondays and Tuesdays. 6 Sadovaya-Kudrinskaya Ulitsa (phone: 291-6154).

**MUZEY GORKOVO (MAXIM GORKY MUSEUM)** The writer's life in letters, manuscripts, and pictures. Closed Mondays and Tuesdays. 25A Povarskaya Ulitsa (phone: 290-5130).

**MUZEY L. N. TOLSTOVO (LEO TOLSTOY MUSEUM)** In the former Lopukhin mansion, it contains manuscripts and other memorabilia. Closed Mondays and the last Friday of the month. 11 Prechistenka Ulitsa (phone: 202-2190).

**MUZEY MAYAKOVSKOVO (MAYAKOVSKY MUSEUM)** The former home of Russian poet/playwright/painter Vladimir Vladimirovich Mayakovsky is now Moscow's most innovative museum. Mayakovsky's personal effects are arranged in such a way that the building resembles an avant-garde gallery of modern art. The author of such poems as *A Cloud with Trousers* and such plays as *The Bedbug* would have approved of the disorienting effect this gallery has on the senses. Closed Wednesdays and the last Friday of the month. Admission charge. 3-6 Serova Proyezd, near Lubyanka (formerly Dzerzhinsky) Ploshchad (phone: 921-6607).

**MUZEY NARODNOVO ISKUSSTVA (MUSEUM OF FOLK ART)** Embroidery, enamelwork, and woodcarvings are displayed here. Closed Fridays. 7 Stanislavskovo Ulitsa (phone: 291-8718).

**NOVAYA TRETYAKOVSKAYA GALEREYA (NEW TRETYAKOV GALLERY)** Modern (post-Soviet) Russian art is the focus of this new branch of the *Tretyakov Gallery* (below). Paintings, sculpture, and documents are featured. Closed Mondays. 10 Krymskiy Val (phone: 231-1352).

**PAVILION-MUZEY LENINSKIY PAKHORONIY POEZD (LENIN FUNERAL TRAIN PAVILION-MUSEUM)** The railway car that transported Lenin's coffin to his funeral, with an exhibit of Lenin memorabilia. Closed weekends. Located at the *Paveletskiy Station,* 1 Lenina Ploshchad (phone: 235-2898).

**TRETYAKOVKA GALEREYA (TRETYAKOV GALLERY)** One of the most extensive collections of native art in the world—a veritable *Who's Who* of Russian art from the 10th through the 20th century. However, even though this world-renowned gallery was slated to reopen last year after major renovations, funds have not been available to finish the work. At press time, only one wing of the gallery was open to the public displaying select works from various collections. Closed Mondays. 10 Lavrushinskiy Pereulok (phone: 231-1362).

**TSENTRALNIY MUZEY REVOLYTSIY (CENTRAL MUSEUM OF THE REVOLUTION)** Formerly the *English Club* for Russian noblemen, since 1923 this building has featured exhibits on the 1905 and 1917 revolutions. Though still open at press time, its future is uncertain. Closed Mondays. 21 Tverskaya Ulitsa (phone: 299-6724).

## SHOPPING

Despite all you may have heard or read, there are many interesting and desirable items to buy in Russia: amber, furs, samovars, lacquer boxes, balalaikas, caviar, and that ultimate Russian souvenir, *matryoshka* dolls, families of festively decorated wooden dolls hidden one inside the other (*matryoshkas* featuring Russian and Soviet leaders—from Yeltsin all the way back to Lenin—nesting inside one another are quite popular these days). And don't forget to take home some Russian vodka, which comes in several flavors, including lemon, pepper (very hot!), and a pleasantly aromatic variety called "hunter's vodka." Russian porcelain is very attractive, both the colorful hand-painted cups, saucers, and teapots, and the distinctive blue-and-white pottery from the nearby Gzhel region (be sure it has the Gzhel marking on the bottom). In addition to diamonds, pearls, sapphires, and semi-precious stones, scout out antiques shops and commission stores for unexpected good buys. If you're in the market for good souvenirs, don't miss the small arts and crafts shops set up inside the churches behind the *Rossiya* hotel (6 Varvarka Ulitsa).

The city has a weekend flea market at *Izmailovskiy Park* on the northeast edge of the city (see below). Payment is in rubles.

Moscow's art galleries sell works both old and new (some are listed below). Good deals can be found, considering Russian works are now in vogue in the world's art circles. Exporting art from Russia is a little tricky, however. If you buy from an established gallery, the paperwork will be done for you. Otherwise, before you attempt to take your purchase out of the country, it should first be appraised by the city export commission (29 Chekhova Ulitsa, open only on Tuesdays from 10 AM to 2 PM). Bring two small photos of the item with you (those planning to buy art in Moscow might consider bringing along a Polaroid camera for this purpose), and expect to pay a small fee. No items made before 1945 or books printed prior to 1977 may be taken out of the country. Visitors are advised to keep the receipts for *all* purchases. Unless otherwise noted, shops listed below are open weekdays from 8 AM to 7 PM, with a one-hour break for lunch. Many accept credit cards in addition to rubles.

Visitors from the West no longer have to travel to Moscow like packhorses, loaded down with cheese, fruit, Pepto-Bismol, and cartons of cigarettes. For groceries and other food items the city's joint-venture supermarkets—the lifeline for Moscow's burgeoning foreign community—are recommended. *Stockmann's* (4-8 Zatsepskiy Val Ulitsa; phone: 233-2602 or 231-1924), a Finnish-Russian outpost of the Helsinki department store, is always well stocked with fresh fruit and vegetables, frozen meat, milk and other dairy supplies, household appliances, a heady selection of liquor, foreign publications, and other items ordinarily found in Western supermarkets. Open daily; only major credits cards accepted (you will have to bring your passport). A second, more modern supermarket with ample parking is the *Sadko Arcade* (at the *ExpoCenter* on Krasnaya Presnya Naberezhnaya; phone: 256-2213). Even more centrally located is the *Irish Store* (19 Novy Arbat Ulitsa, Second Floor), which has the distinct advantage of carrying goods with labels in English; it's usually crowded—especially on Saturdays. The same management runs a second store, the *Garden Ring Supermarket* (1 Bolshaya Sadovaya; phone: 209-1572), stocked with fresh fruit and vegetables; open daily. Down the street is *Colognia*, a German-Russian venture located in the *Peking* hotel (phone: 209-6561), stocked with cheeses from almost every region of Europe. In the same neighborhood is the *Lavash* bread co-op (3-6 Bolshaya Sadovaya; no phone), offering a great selection of freshly baked flat bread from the Caucasus.

Some other shops—both Western and Russian—of interest in Moscow include the following:

**Detskiy Mir (Children's World)** Once the Russian version of *Toys 'R' Us,* this onetime kids' emporium has diversified and offers games for children of all ages. 5 Teatralniy Proyezd, near the *Bolshoi Theater* and the *Metropol* hotel (phone: 927-2007).

**Dom Knigi (House of Books)** Beautiful souvenir books about Moscow and Russia and colorful political posters and postcards can be purchased here. Souvenir stamps and some English-language books are available on the second floor. Closed Sundays. 26 Novy Arbat Ultisa (phone: 290-4507).

**Galerie du Vin** Moscow's first specialty wine shop, located on an embankment along the Moskva River, within walking distance of the *Radisson Slavyanskaya* hotel. Closed Sundays. 1-7 Kutuzovskiy Prospekt (entrance is off Tarasa Shevchenko Naberezhnaya; phone: 243-0365 or 243-7256).

**GUM** Moscow's huge, government-run department store (see *Special Places*). Closed Sundays. 3 Krasnaya Ploshchad (phone: 926-3471).

**Izmailovskiy Park** An outdoor weekend art market, it offers a wide range of contemporary paintings by both amateurs and accomplished artists. Crafts, jewelry, antiques, and such timeless favorites as *matryoshka* dolls, lacquered chess sets, boxes, and military garb also are for sale. Be prepared to bargain, beware of forgeries (there seems to be very little control), and bring loads of rubles. Barbecued kebobs and street jazz add to the lively atmosphere here. Open weekends. 17 Narodniy Prospekt, a five-minute walk from the *Izmailovskiy Park* metro station (phone: 166-7909).

**Magasin Gzhel** Hard to find (there's no sign outside) but worth it, this is *the* best place in Moscow to buy traditional blue-and-white Gzhel pottery, including dishes, vases, and ornaments. Closed Sundays and Mondays. In a mustard-colored building on the corner of Tverskaya Ulitsa (phone: 200-6478).

**Melodiya** As its name suggests, this is where to buy recordings of some of those catchy Russian folk songs you've been hearing since you arrived. Closed Sundays. 40 Novy Arbat Ulitsa (phone: 291-1421). *Melodiya*'s other branch carries compact discs. 11 Leninskiy Prospekt (phone: 237-4801).

**Petrovskiy Passage** Renovated to its prerevolutionary glory with lots of marble and wrought-iron staircases, this mall near the *Bolshoi Theater* offers everything from Russian souvenirs and fur coats to Japanese cars. One shop, a salon on the ground floor named *Valentin*

*Yudashkin* after its proprietor, has a particularly good selection of creative hats, coats, shoes, and dresses. Shops on the second floor carry a wide assortment of things Western. Closed Sundays. 10 Petrovka Ulitsa (phone: 921-5777, 921-3117, or 923-2398).

**Philatelist Shop** A good stop for collectors, if you can get into the front door without being inundated by stamp merchants trying to sell you their grandfathers' collections. Open daily. 1 Tara Shevchenko Ulitsa (phone: 243-0162).

**Ptichy Rynok (Pet Market)** Russians love animals—the bigger the better—and there is no finer place than this colorful market near Taganka Ploshchad. Locals flock here to admire the many animals—dogs, cats, rabbits, reptiles, and birds are just a few of the species for sale. Open daily. 42A Bolshaya Kalitnikovskaya Ulitsa (no phone).

**Russkiy Souvenir (Russian Souvenir)** The best collection of Russian souvenirs under one roof in the entire city. Offered are *matryoshkas,* jewelry, painted metal trays, chess sets, wooden toys, pottery, and huge blue Uzbek platters. Closed Sundays. No credit cards accepted. 9 Kutuzovskiy Prospekt (phone: 243-6985).

**Russkiy Uzory (Russian Patterns)** Jewelry and handicrafts made in traditional Russian styles. Also an excellent selection of souvenirs. Closed Sundays. No credit cards accepted. 16 Petrovka Ulitsa, near *Petrovskiy Passage* (phone: 923-3964).

**Sovmehkastoria** Furs and leather goods, including hats, jackets, and coats, from sheepskin to sable. Closed Sundays. Major credit cards accepted. 14 Bolshaya Dorogomilovskaya Ulitsa (no phone).

**Tsentralniy Rynok (Central Market)** Flowers and produce are available year-round at this market (including remarkable bargains on saffron and caviar). Farmers from the now-independent southern republics converge here to sell their goods. Open daily. 15 Tsvetnoy Bulvar (phone: 923-8687).

**TSUM** Another big department store, near Red Square and about a mile from *GUM.* Amid the kitsch is an occasional gem, perhaps a piece of amber, a fur hat, or a rug from Central Asia. Closed Sundays. 2 Petrovka Ulitsa (phone: 292-7600).

**Yantar (Amber)** A wide assortment of jewelry. Closed Sundays. 14 Gruzinskiy Val (phone: 252-4430).

**Zwemmer Books** Moscow's first English-language bookstore, selling Russian art and travel books, as well as novels and thrillers for those long train and plane rides. Closed Sundays. Kuznetskiy Most (phone: 928-2021).

## SPORTS AND FITNESS

Muscovites are avid sports fans, particularly of ice hockey, soccer, and horse racing. Attending such events is a good way to see Russian citizens at leisure. Schedules and tickets are available through your hotel service bureau. The *Olimpiyskiy Sportivniy* (Olympic Sports Complex; 16 Olimpiyskiy Prospekt; phone: 288-5663) includes the *Olimpiyskiy Stadion* (Olympic Stadium), the largest indoor stadium in Europe and the site of numerous soccer matches.

There is also a major sports facility in *Luzhniki Park,* across the Moskva River from *Moscow State University.* The *Tsentralniy Stadion Luzhniki* (Luzhniki Central Stadium; 24 Luzhnikovskaya Naberezhnaya; phone: 201-0155 or 201-0995) seats 103,000 people and is used for soccer matches, track and field meets, international competitions, and occasionally for rock concerts. Several Western hotels now have fitness clubs; the one in the *Radisson Slavyanskaya* hotel (phone: 941-8031) sells memberships to non-guests.

After exercising, or even if you don't, there is nothing more Russian than relaxing in a *banya,* or sauna. Moscow boasts several, the best known being the *Tsentralnaya Banya* (3 Teatralnaya Proyezd; no phone); closed Mondays. Bring your own towel and toiletries.

**FOOTBALL** Gridiron rivalry has hit the Moscow sports scene. The American-style lineup includes the *Russian Czars,* the *Siberian Devils,* and the *Moscow Mustangs.* The season runs through the dead of winter, but, fortunately, games are played in an indoor sports complex. Though some of the coaches are American, all the players are Russian. This year the second annual *Kremlin Bowl* will be played in December at *Olympic Stadium.* For further information contact the *US Embassy* (phone: 252-2451) or your hotel service bureau.

**GOLF** The Swedish-built *Tumba Golf Club* (1 Dovzhenko Ulitsa; phone: 147-6254) is located in the Lenin Hills near *Tsentralniy Stadion Luzhniki* and *Moscow State University.* The nine-hole course is open to the public. The club also has a restaurant featuring continental fare. Another choice is the *Park* hotel's 18-hole, Robert Trent Jones Jr. course at Nahabino, 19½ miles (31 km) west of the *Kremlin* (see *Checking In*).

**HORSE RACING** Harness and thoroughbred racing with low-stake pari-mutuel betting takes place on Sundays, Wednesdays, and Fridays at the *Hippodrome* racecourse (22 Begovaya Ulitsa; phone: 945-4516). At the *Ramenskiy Hippodrome* (phone: 8-246-36489 or 8-246-30331; about 31 miles/50 km from Moscow on Kazanskoe Shosse), there are races on Saturdays. In winter, exciting troika races are held on the snow and ice.

**ICE HOCKEY** The most popular ice hockey teams in Moscow are *Spartak, Dynamo,* and *CSKA.* Ticket and schedule information is available from your hotel service bureau.

**SOCCER** This sport is a passion with many Muscovites. The *Dynamo Stadium* (36 Leningradskiy Prospekt; phone: 212-7092 or 212-2252) holds 60,000 people and was built for one of Moscow's powerhouse teams, but the main events are held at the *Tsentralniy Stadion Luzhniki* (see above).

**SWIMMING** The water in the *Otkryty Baseyn Moskva* (Moscow Open-Air Swimming Pool; 37 Prechistenka Naberezhnaya; phone: 202-4725) is heated so the pool can be used all year. In winter, when steam gathers over the pool, it may look like something from Dante's

*Inferno,* but this protects swimmers from the cold. Open daily. Swimming competitions take place at the *Dvoretz Vodnikh Sportov* (Palace of Water Sports; 27 Mironovskaya; phone: 369-2925). Several hotels also have swimming pools, such as the *Cosmos* (150 Mira Prospekt; phone: 217-0785/6).

**TENNIS** Court space is available at *Druzhba Hall* (phone: 246-5515), located next to the *Luzhniki Central Stadium* (see above), and the *Chaika Tennis Club* (1-2 Korobeynikov Pereulok; phone: 202-0474).

## THEATER

Your hotel service bureau can provide schedules and tickets, but don't expect to get seats for popular events, such as the ballet, unless you book well ahead of time. Also check *The Moscow Times* for theater listings, or try the *IPS Theater Box Office* in the *Metropol* hotel (phone: 927-6728/9); open daily. Here are some Moscow venues that rate our applause.

---

### CENTER STAGE

**Bolshoi** The *Bolshoi* dance tradition goes back to the mid-19th century. Highpoints of its history include the early 20th century, when it was revitalized by Alexander Gorsky; the 1930s, when Igor Moiseyev experimented with folk-dance ballets; and after World War II, when the troupe danced to such works as Sergei Prokofiev's *Cinderella* and *The Stone Flower.* The company is based at the magnificent *Bolshoi Theater,* one of several imperial-style buildings built after Alexander I established a special commission to reconstruct Moscow in 1825. All crystal chandeliers, red plush, and ornate gold, just being here is a big part of the pleasure of a night at the ballet. Though the *Bolshoi* has lapsed into a financial crisis since the demise of the USSR, this great Russian cultural institution is now under the personal jurisdiction of President Yeltsin while it considers finding private sponsors. The *Bolshoi* also performs at the 6,000-seat *Palace of Congresses Theater,* inside the *Kremlin* complex. Book as far ahead as possible. Note: A three-year refurbishment of the *Bolshoi Theater* is set to begin in 1997 and will shut down productions. *Bolshoi Theater,* 8-2 Teatralnaya Ploshchad (phone: 292-9986); *Palace of Congresses Theater* (The *Kremlin;* phone: 227-8263).

---

Long renowned for its breathtaking aerial feats, nimble acrobats, special animal acts (bears on bicycles and roller skates, and the like), and spectacular finales, in recent years the *Moskovskiy Tsirk* (Moscow Circus; 7 Vernadskovo Prospekt; phone: 930-2815) has added more contemporary elements, including modern dance numbers and dazzling light shows. But this circus is perhaps best loved for its clowns. Performances start at 7 PM.

*Moskovskiy Teatr Dramy i Komedy* (Moscow Drama and Comedy Theater; 76 Zemlyanoy Ulitsa; phone: 272-6300), also known as *Taganka,* is Russia's most famous experimental theater. Tickets for musical and dramatic performances are difficult to come by, so try to order in advance through your travel agent. Upstairs, the *Taganka Café* serves light suppers, champagne, and beer.

On Teatralnaya Ploshchad are the *Maly Teatr* (Small Theater; 1-6 Teatralnaya Ploshchad; phone: 923-2621), which stages Russian classics, and the *Tsentralniy Detskiy Teatr* (Central Children's Theater; 2-7 Teatralnaya Ploshchad; phone: 292-0069), which often presents such children's classics as *Pushkin Tales.*

One of the oldest and most famous theaters in Russia is the *MKAT* (pronounced *Mkhut*), an acronym for *Moscovskiy Khudozhestvenniy Academicheskiy Teatr* (Moscow Art and Academic Theater; 3 Kamergerskiy Pereulok; phone: 229-8760), which features classical and modern dramas. The *Muzykalniy Academicheskiy Teatr imeni Stanislavskovo i Nemirovitcha-Danchenko* (Stanislavsky and Nemirovich-Danchenko Academic Musical Theater; 17 Pushkinskaya Ploshchad; phone: 229-0649) is reviving the prerevolutionary Russian appetite for satirical theater while also hosting regular musical performances and ballet. The *Tsyganskiy Teatr "Romen"* (Gypsy Roman Theater; 32-2 Leningradskiy Prospekt; phone: 250-7334) is the only one of its kind in Russia. It stages plays about the lives of Gypsies and their folk music; Shakespeare also is performed here. Marionettes are featured at the *Teatr Studio Marionette* (Theater-Studio Marionette; 37 Starokonushennaya Pereulok; phone: 202-2483) and puppets at the *Gosudarstvenniy Tsentralniy Kulolniy Teatr* (State Central Puppet Theater; 3 Sadovaya-Samotechnaya Ulitsa; phone: 299-3310). Finally, Moscow's famed prerevolutionary cabaret theater, *Lietutchaya Mysh* (The Bat; 10 Bolshoi Gnezdikovskiy Pereulok; phone: 229-7087)—which reopened in 1990 after a 69-year hiatus—once again is delighting cabaret lovers with its irreverent, bawdy performances.

## MUSIC

Ticket and schedule information is available from your hotel service bureau. The three most important concert halls in Moscow are the *Moskovskiy Gosudarstvennaya Konservatoriya* (Moscow State Conservatory; 13 Gertzenaya Ulitsa; phone: 229-7412 for information; 229-8183 for reservations); the *Konsertniy Zal imeni Tchaikovskovo* (Tchaikovsky Concert Hall; Mayakovskiy Ploshchad; phone: 299-3681); and the *Kolonniy Zal* (Hall of Columns) in the *Trade Union House* (1 Pushkinskaya Ulitsa; phone: 292-0178 for information; 292-0956 for reservations). Opera is performed at the *Bolshoi Theater* and the *Stanislavsky and Nemirovich-Danchenko Academic Musical Theater* (see *Theater*).

## NIGHTCLUBS AND NIGHTLIFE

A number of new nightclubs, pubs, and bars have opened their doors recently, bringing a much needed boost to Moscow's nightlife scene, which usually begins around 9 PM. On the northwest corner of the

*Rossiya* hotel, a group of New Yorkers have opened *Manhattan Express* (6 Varvarka Ulitsa; phone: 298-5354/5), a supper club that features excellent food and a great dance floor. For sheer fun drop by *Rosie O'Grady's* (9 Znamenka Ulitsa; phone: 203-9087), an Irish pub with the best draft beer this side of Dublin. Also popular is the *Shamrock Pub* (19 Novy Arbat Ulitsa; phone: 291-7641). For live music and some good Mexican fare there's *Armadillo* (1 Khrustainy Pereulok; phone: 298-5091). For a quiet drink after a night at the *Bolshoi*, try *Artists* at the *Metropol* hotel (1-4 Teatralniy Proyezd; phone: 927-6159).

If you want to see Moscow's well-to-do at play, drop by *Night Flight* (17 Tverskaya Ulitsa; phone: 229-4165), a Swedish-owned club with two floors, three bars with the latest hits on the sound system, and plenty of dancing. The club, which would be right at home in New York or Paris, is open from 9 PM to 5 AM.

Casinos are very popular, but you're best off playing at your hotel. The *Savoy* hotel opened the first casino in the Soviet Union—back when it was the Soviet Union (see *Checking In*). Its three tables—two for blackjack and one for roulette—are open from 8 PM to 4 AM. Gamblers at the *Casino Royale* (at the *Hippodrome* racecourse, 22 Begovaya Ulitsa; phone: 945-1410) have their choice of blackjack, roulette, poker, slot machines, and *punto banco* (Spanish baccarat). The casino offers free transportation from major hotels.

# Best in Town

## CHECKING IN

Hotel accommodations in Moscow, which can be booked directly or through numerous travel agencies, come in two varieties—Western and Soviet. Western hotels, while still partly owned by Russian or Moscow government agencies, are operated by major hotel chains, such as Penta, Radisson, and Inter-Continental.

Also on the Moscow accommodations scene are several bed and breakfast establishments, which offer foreigners rooms with private baths and opportunities to experience life with Russian families. Contact *IBV Bed & Breakfast Systems* (13113 Ideal Dr., Silver Spring, MD 20906; phone: 301-942-3770; fax: 301-933-1124), *American-Russian Homestays* (15115 W. Penn St., Iowa City, IA 52240; phone: 319-626-2125), or *ITS Tours & Travel* (1055 Texas Ave., Suite 104, College Station, TX 77840; phone: 409-764-9400; 800-533-8688; fax: 409-693-9673). At *ITS* properties at least one member of the host family speaks English. The company also rents furnished apartments, for those visitors on extended stays. *Room with the Russians* arranges home stays, an airport greeting, a car ride to your host's home, and a guarantee that at least one member of the family speaks English. Some families provide evening meals as well as breakfast. The company has a London office (phone: 181-472-2694; fax: 181-964-0272).

Accommodations in Moscow hotels usually are available in two classes: first class double rooms and deluxe two- and three-room suites. A few hotels also have spacious, super-deluxe suites—usually with duplexes. The dramatically fluctuating Russian economy makes it difficult to provide accurate rates for hotels. Foreigners must pay by credit card or in rubles at the set exchange rate. (Be sure to check the exchange rate immediately prior to your departure.) Be aware, too, that the Russian government has imposed a 23% tax on rooms, so check in advance to see whether or not that has been included in the price you are quoted. Many hotels include breakfast in the room rate. Most take major credit cards, but you should confirm that in advance as well. In all of the following hotels, guestrooms have private baths unless otherwise indicated. All telephone numbers are in the 095 city code unless otherwise indicated.

### DELUXE

**Aerostar** Recently opened and one of Moscow's choice locations, it has 417 well-appointed rooms, in addition to a fully equipped fitness center. The *Borodino* restaurant features live lobster from Nova Scotia, as does the more casual *Café Taiga* (see *Eating Out*). Business facilities include five meeting rooms, an English-speaking concierge, photocopiers, computers, and translation services. On the road to the international airport. 37 Leningradskiy Prospekt (phone: 155-5030; fax: 200-3286).

**Baltschug** It has taken three years and $80 million to renovate this yellow-and-cream building, once the old *Bucharest* hotel. Located across the river from the *Kremlin* and *St. Basil's,* the view is great—especially from the hotel's eighth-floor *Mansard Bar*. The best of the 234 rooms and suites are in the "round tower" overlooking the river and facing the *Kremlin.* Amenities include international direct dialing from each room; shops; a hairdresser; laundry and cleaning services; plus a pool, sauna, solarium, whirlpool, and fitness studio. There's even a library on the top floor with 2,500 books in English, German, and Russian. On site are two restaurants, a bistro, and a nightclub in the basement that stays open until 3 AM. Business facilities include meeting rooms for up to 150, secretarial services in English, audiovisual equipment, photocopiers, computers, and translation services. 1 Baltschug Ulitsa (phone: 230-6500; 800-426-3135; fax: 230-6502).

**Metropol** Completely restored and renovated by *Intourist* and now managed by Inter-Continental Hotels, this Moscow grande dame is close to the *Bolshoi* and *Maly Theaters.* The façade of the turn-of-the-century building is decorated with a marvelous majolica relief that reproduces artist Mikhail Vrubel's *Dream Princess.* There are 403 rooms and suites, many of which are decorated with antique and period furniture. All have TV sets, mini-bars, radios, and computer hook-up capabilities. There are three restaurants, including the *Lobster Grill,* the *Metropol Room* (where Lenin made spirited speeches and where portions of *Doctor Zhivago* were filmed), and the *Boyarskiy Zal* (see *Eating Out* for all three); four bars; a coffee shop; and, during the warm-weather months, a friendly outdoor café. The health club has a pool, fitness room, and saunas. Business facilities include 11 meeting rooms for up to 350, an English-speaking concierge, audiovisual equipment, photocopiers, cable television news, and translation services. 1-4 Teatralniy Proyezd (phone: 927-6000/1/2; 800-327-0200; fax: 975-2355).

**Olympic Penta** Recently opened, this joint venture of *Intourservice* and the Penta group has 500 rooms and suites; all have international direct-dial phones, satellite TV, and mini-bars. The 12-story establishment also offers a sauna, pool, solarium, gym, and car rental office. There are two restaurants, a brasserie, and an authentic German beer hall, *Die Bierstube*, which serves draft beer and pub food. *The Bakery* offers freshly baked cakes, pastries, and croissants daily. Business facilities include 12 meeting rooms for up to 300, an English-speaking concierge, secretarial services in English, photocopiers, computers, cable television news, and translation services. 18 Olympiyskiy Prospekt (phone: 971-6101 or 971-6301; 800-225-3456; fax: 230-2597).

**Palace** Opened last year, this is a joint venture between the Austrian Marco Polo group and the *Russian Academy of Sciences,* which once owned the building. There are 221 guestrooms and suites (including a two-story presidential suite decorated in Art Nouveau style), three restaurants (including the *Anchor* seafood restaurant; see *Eating Out*), and a health club. Business facilities include five meetings room for up to 100, an English-speaking concierge, audiovisual equipment, photocopiers, computers, and translation services. 19 Tverskaya Ulitsa (phone: 956-3152; fax: 931-3151).

**Park** To escape from the city bustle, locals and foreign travelers alike stay at this hotel set in forested grounds at Nahabino, about 19 miles (30 km) west of the *Kremlin.* Along with a boat pond, the four-story property offers 85 rooms, a restaurant serving Russian fare, a bar, a billiard room, a sauna, massage facilities, and a hair salon. The hotel's 18-hole Robert Trent Jones Jr. golf course is nearby. Business facilities include meeting rooms for up to 240, an English-speaking concierge, foreign currency exchange, audiovisual equipment, photocopiers, computers, cable television news, and translation services. 1 Nahabino (phone: 563-0598 or 561-2975; fax: 563-3456).

**Pullman Iris** Overlooking a beautiful atrium, this very comfortable property offers 195 rooms and suites (including a presidential suite). There is a French restaurant (the *Champs-Elysées*), a coffee shop, and a bar. Other amenities include a fitness club, a pool, a sauna, laundry and dry cleaning services, safe-deposit boxes, a beauty salon, and shops. Business facilities include meeting rooms for up to 300, secretarial services in English, audiovisual equipment, photocopiers, and translation services. 10 Korovinskoe Shosse (phone: 488-8000; 800-221-4542; fax: 906-0105).

**Radisson Slavyanskaya** On the banks of the Moskva River, this is Russia's first American-managed hotel, a joint venture of Radisson Hotels International, the Americom International Corporation, and

*Intourservice.* There are 430 rooms, four restaurants (including the *Exchange* steakhouse; see *Eating Out*), a health club, a swimming pool, a car rental office, and shops. The furniture is spare but functional; the rooms are a good size. Business facilities include meetings rooms for up to 600 with simultaneous interpretation in five languages, an English speaking concierge (many of the hotel employees speak English), foreign currency exchange, audiovisual equipment, photocopiers, computers, and express checkout. 2 Berezhkovskaya Naberezhnaya (phone: 941-8020; 800-333-3333; fax: 240-6915).

**Savoy** Moscow's first real nod toward Western-style luxury is this renovation of the former *Berlin* hotel, just a five-minute walk from the *Kremlin.* There are 86 guestrooms with tiled baths, mini-bars, and TV sets. Also here are the first gambling casino to open in the former USSR, several designer shops, an art salon, and car rental facilities. The luxurious dining room is one of the best places in town to enjoy elegantly presented Russian, Scandinavian, or international fare (see *Eating Out*). The surest way of obtaining a hard-to-get room reservation is to fly into Moscow via *Finnair,* which runs the hotel. The hotel has a weekend vacation center outside Moscow at Voskresenskoye, where you can go sleighing, skiing, and skating in the winter, and top off the day with a Russian sauna. It also arranges yacht cruises from May to September. Business facilities include meeting rooms for up to 600, an English-speaking concierge, audiovisual equipment, photocopiers, computers, cable television news, and translation services. 3 Rozhdestvenka Ulitsa (phone: 929-8500 or 929-8555; fax: 230-2186).

### FIRST CLASS

**Marco Polo Presnaya** A former Communist Party hotel, this Austrian-run establishment is in one of the prettiest locations in Moscow—just off Patriarch's Pond. All 68 rooms are rather plain, but the service is excellent. The dining room is one of Moscow's best. Business facilities are available through the *Palace* hotel (see above). 9 Spiridonyvesky Pereulok (phone: 202-0381 or 202-2848).

**Mezhdunarodnaya I and II** Known locally as the *Mezh*, this hotel attracts business travelers. Offered here are 540 rooms, five restaurants (serving Russian, continental, and Japanese food), three bars, an English pub, saunas, a pool, a bowling alley, a variety of shops, and a car rental counter. Business facilities include three meeting rooms for up to 1,200, an English-speaking concierge, foreign currency exchange, secretarial service in English, audiovisual equipment, translation services, and express checkout. 12 Krasnopresnenskaya Naberezhnaya (phone: 253-1316 or 253-6303; fax: 253-1071/2).

**Novotel Sheremetyevo** This 488-room property (including five rooms for disabled guests) is one of the newest members of Europe's largest hotel chain. The *Efimoff* restaurant features fine local and international fare. Business facilities include eight meeting rooms for up to 250, an English-speaking concierge, audiovisual equipment, photocopiers, cable television news, and translation services. At *Sheremetyevo Airport,* 35 miles (56 km) from downtown Moscow; free airport shuttle service (phone: 578-9401; 800-221-4542; fax: 578-2794).

**Tsaritsino** Located in the southern Moscow, this Swiss-run establishment—with its one- to five-room self-catering apartments—is a worthwhile option for those planning a longer stay. The rooms are furnished to Western standards with separate, fully equipped kitchens. A restaurant is now under construction. 47-1 Shipilovskiy Prospekt (phone: 343-4343 or 343-4373).

---

## EATING OUT

Moscow is experiencing a restaurant boom. Japanese, French, Italian, Greek, and American eateries are overtaking the purveyors of old-fashioned Russian fare served Soviet-style by indifferent waiters. The newer Russian restaurants have taken their cue from Western-run establishments, offering excellent national cuisine in comfortable surroundings. One drawback though: Restaurant entrepreneurs are passing on the price of imported produce and high operating costs to the customers.

With the opening of new dining places and the quality of their cuisine as unstable as the ruble, it is advisable to check with your hotel service bureau or with friends and/or contacts before you go. A new currency regulation came into effect on January 1, 1994, which calls for all cash payments to be made in rubles only. Payment in dollars can be made by credit cards, but be sure to bring along rubles for those places where credit cards are not accepted.

Though Russian cuisine is simple it boasts the finest of all delicacies: *ikra* (caviar), usually served on black bread with lots of butter or with thin, light pancakes, called *blini,* smothered with sour cream. Most Russian meals feature a large selection of appetizers, or *zakuski,* plus a main course. Aside from caviar, which can be black (sturgeon or beluga) or red (salmon), *zakuski* include a rich potato salad *(stolichny)* and various cold meats such as beef tongue and salami. Russians are fond of their salads, most of which are prepared with lots of mayonnaise, fresh eggs, and can incorporate crab or chicken. Don't pass up the "julienne," a dish of mushrooms baked in cheese and sour cream. Menus feature basic main dishes, mainly fried chicken and fish and the ever-popular "cutlet," which is in fact a fried ground beef patty. The *zakuski* are far more interesting. Dining is an evening-long affair, and most establishments expect customers to linger several hours. If you're pressed for time at lunch, choose a Western-run café.

The dramatically fluctuating Russian economy makes it difficult to provide accurate prices for restaurants; we suggest that you check costs—and the operative exchange rate—immediately prior to your departure. Although reservations are almost always advised, it may be difficult to make them on your own, unless you speak some Russian. However, your hotel service bureau can make the arrangements for you. Unless otherwise specified, all restaurants are open for lunch and dinner and all telephone numbers are in the 095 city code.

**Alexander Blok** A British-managed restaurant aboard a boat moored by the *Mezhdunarodnaya* hotel, it offers Greek and continental fare. On the menu are Greek favorites—moussaka, *tiropita* (small triangles of filo pastry stuffed with feta cheese), baklava, and Greek coffee. There's a casino next door. Open daily. Reservations advised. American Express and Visa accepted. 12 Krasnopresnenskaya Naberezhnaya (phone: 255-9284).

**Anchor** A beautiful, dark-wood restaurant that is a seafood lover's paradise. Everything on the menu is fresh, flown in from Scandinavia and Western Europe. Aside from the seafood platter of lobster, shrimp, and oysters, there is poached eel, Dover sole, salmon steak, and an excellent Spanish paella loaded with everything found in the sea. This is also the place for frog legs and snails, both expertly prepared. The wine list is extensive. For dessert try the white chocolate mousse, considered the best in Moscow. Open daily. Reservations advised. Major credit cards accepted. In the the *Palace Hotel,* 19 Tverskaya Ulitsa (phone: 956-3152).

**Arlecchino** A Russian-Italian venture, this upscale eatery decorated in pink and black offers a menu of good Italian dishes, including *medalyoniy telyachiy po-milanski* (fried veal medallions served with spaghetti, grated cheese, and tomato sauce), *spaghetti nizza* (with tomato sauce), and *salat Arleccino* (greens with olive oil). The risottos are also respectable. A variety show is featured on weekend evenings. Open daily. Reservations advised. American Express and Visa accepted. 15 Druzhinnikovskaya Ulitsa (phone: 205-7088).

**Armadillo** Great atmosphere and good food just off Red Square. The menu features both vegetarian and meat chili, guacamole, and Mexican beer. Open daily. Reservations necessary. No credit cards accepted. 1 Khrustalny Pereulok (phone: 298-5091).

**Azteca** Another intimate Mexican eatery (only five tables), serving enchiladas, chili, burritos, and tacos; the bar features lethal margaritas and Mexican beer. This is a good stop for a bite while touring nearby Red Square and the *Kremlin.* Open daily. Reservations necessary. Major credit cards accepted. At the *Intourist Hotel,* 3-5 Tverskaya Ulitsa (phone: 956-8489).

**Boyarskiy Zal** If money is no object, this elegant dining room in the *Metropol* hotel is the place to go. An enormous stuffed bear greets guests at the entrance and a five-piece folk instrumental group serenades from the balcony, all setting an appropriately Russian tone for the traditional fare served here—*pelymeni* (meat-stuffed dumplings), *piroshki* (small meat-filled turnovers) with vintage brandy sauce, or beef Stroganoff. The bad news is that the food is a bit bland and disappointing considering the steep prices. Open Mondays through Saturdays for dinner only. Reservations necessary. Major credit cards accepted. *Metropol Hotel,* 4 Teatralniy Proyezd (phone: 927-6452 or 927-6000).

**Café Margarita** Smack in the middle of the Margarita section of Moscow, the setting for Mikhail Bulgakov's monumental novel, *The Master and Margarita,* this little café on the corner has long been the haunt of Moscow's arty, trendy types. Patriarch's Pond, where the memorable opening scenes of the book take place, is across the street. A perfect place for coffee and homemade pastry or, if something more substantial is required, mushroom *plov* (pilaf). Open daily. No reservations or credit cards accepted. 28 Malaya Bronnaya Ulitsa (phone: 299-6534).

**Café Taiga** Lobster flown in live from Nova Scotia is the specialty of this restaurant in the *Aerostar* hotel. There are vodka and caviar happy hours daily, as well as champagne brunches on Sundays. Open daily. Reservations advised. Major credit cards accepted. 37 Leningradskiy Prospekt, the road to the airport (phone: 155-5030, ext. 2428).

**Le Chalet** Moscow's only Swiss restaurant, located at the *Chaika Tennis Club* on the Moskva River (although there are no river views). The menu features beef and cheese fondues, raclette, Caesar salad, carpaccio, and steak tartare. There is an extensive, and expensive, wine list. The management provides free transportation to and from your hotel. Live entertainment nightly. Open daily. Reservations necessary. Major credit cards accepted. 1-2 Korobeynikov Pereulok, on the corner of Prechistenka Ulitsa, near the Krimsky Bridge (phone: 202-0106).

**Danilovsky** Tucked away in the middle of the *Danilovsky Monastery,* this restaurant serves traditional Russian fare such as *pelymeni* and pickled mushrooms. The place is a nonsmoking establishment. Open daily. Reservations necessary. No credit cards accepted. 5 Bolshoi Staryanilov Pereulok (phone: 954-0566).

**Delhi** The Indian dishes are appropriately spicy, and even if the restaurant runs out of staples like yogurt, it doesn't seem to matter much. The waiters are elegantly dressed in Nehru jackets, and the bar stocks a wide range of liquors and liqueurs. Open daily. Reservations necessary. Major credit cards accepted. 23B Krasnopresnenskaya Naberezhnaya (phone: 255-0492).

**Exchange** The *Radisson Slavyanskaya* hotel's steakhouse has a menu that will capture the hearts and appetites of those who can't live without beef. This is the place for prime ribs, filet mignon, sirloin for two, or a whopping porterhouse. Other touches of Americana such as iceberg lettuce and baked potatoes are served in an elegant atmosphere. Open daily. Reservations advised. Major credit cards accepted. 2 Berezhkovskaya Naberezhnaya (phone: 941-8333 or 941-8020, ext. 3269).

**Flamingo Chicken House** A good alternative to pricier eateries, this place features good salads and chicken prepared six ways. Try the specialty: flamingo chicken stuffed with apricots. Homemade cakes are a must for dessert. Open daily. No reservations or credit cards accepted. 48 Mira Prospekt (phone: 280-4711).

**Glazur** An intimate dining spot with live jazz, this Russo-Danish venture specializes in seafood, including shrimp, salmon, and herring. The food is well prepared and delicious. The list of international wines is also impressive. Open daily. Reservations advised. Major credit cards accepted. 12-19 Smolenskiy Bulvar (phone: 248-4438).

**Iberia** Delicious Georgian food served in a cozy, candlelit restaurant near the *Savoy* hotel. Artwork (which is for sale) decorates the walls, and a piano player and wandering violinist provide the entertainment. Menu choices include *lobio* (marinated bean salad) and *khachapuri* (cheese-filled bread); don't try the chicken intestines unless you're adventurous. Open daily. Reservations necessary. No credit cards accepted. 5-7 Rozhdestvenka Ulitsa (phone: 928-2672).

**Imperial** Regal touches, such as the double-headed eagle of czarist Russia, accent this newly renovated dining spot. Diners sit at tables surrounding a fountain and partake of good Russian fare—veal Romanoff (cooked with cheese and tomatoes), beef Stroganoff, mutton Zhivago (with mushrooms), and chicken filet Potemkin. The house specialty is the Czar's Plate—pork, chicken, and veal with vegetables and potatoes—which serves four. A pianist or violinist provides background music. Open daily. Reservations necessary. Major credit cards accepted. 9-5 Ryleyeva Ulitsa (phone: 231-6063).

**Kombi's** Made-to-order sandwiches on thick French bread or croissants make this place popular with locals and visitors alike. Open daily. No reservations or credit cards accepted. 32-1 Tverskaya-Yamskaya Ulitsa (phone: 280-6402).

**Kropotkinskaya 36** The food is strictly Russian and quite good—try the caviar, *blini,* salads, and sturgeon. The upstairs dining room is elegant and formal; downstairs is cozier, with strolling violinists. Open daily. Reservations necessary. Major credit cards accepted. 36 Prechistenka Ulitsa (phone: 201-7500).

**Lazaniya** For respectable Italian food, this comfortable restaurant just across the river from the *Kremlin* is the place to go. The cooperative's menu features over 50 items, including its namesake, lasagna. During the warm months there is outdoor seating amid the beauty of this ancient neighborhood. Open daily. Reservations advised. Major credit cards accepted. 40 Pyatnitskaya Ulitsa (phone: 231-1085).

**Livan** Exquisite Lebanese food served in a dining room within a state-run restaurant called *Baku*. You can make an entire meal of the appetizers—several kinds of hummus; tabbouleh; pastries stuffed with meat, cheese, or spinach. It's a good idea, however, to save room for delicious cakes or baklava. Reservations advised. Major credit cards accepted. 24 Tverskaya Ulitsa (phone: 299-8506).

**Lobster Grill** Everything on the menu of this upscale restaurant located in the *Metropol* hotel is flown in fresh: lobsters from Canada, oysters from France. The classic seafood dishes include grilled salmon steak, lobster Thermidor, and Dover sole. To top the meal, Campari sorbet is truly delightful. Open daily for dinner only. Reservations advised. Major credit cards accepted. 1-4 Teatralniy Proyezd (phone: 927-6739).

**Lomonssov** Moscow's best buffet-style restaurant captures the imagination with such dishes as mussels in white wine sauce, as well as many caviar dishes. The dessert tables are brimming with custards, pies, and cakes. Open daily. Reservations advised. Major credit cards accepted. 19 Tverskaya Ulitsa (phone: 956-3152).

**Manhattan Express** This American-style eatery serves enormous portions of such classic meals as grilled steak with mushrooms and veal Madeira. Save room for scrumptious desserts, including apple pie with cheese or ice cream. Dancing nightly. Open daily. Reservations advised. Major credit cards accepted. 9 Varvarka Ulitsa, near Red Square (phone: 298-5355).

**Manila** Continental and Filipino fare are served in this cozy, peach-colored dining room. The menu offers a wide variety of à la carte items, including sizzling shrimp and good sweet and sour pork. Begin with a daiquiri at the bar. Open daily. Reservations necessary. Major credit cards accepted. 81 Vavilova Ulitsa (phone: 132-0055).

**McDonald's** Russians and foreign travelers alike have gotten their fill of *Big Mekys, kartofel* (French fries), and *kokteyli* (milk shakes) since the first of several planned franchises opened its doors in Moscow in early 1990. The grill and 29 computerized cash registers are manned by Russian employees who wait on customers at what was briefly the world's largest branch (it's been eclipsed by the one in Beijing), with seating for 700. Go early to avoid the lines (during the warm-weather months the wait can be as long as an hour). Open daily. No reservations or credit cards accepted. In Pushkinskya Ploshchad (phone: 200-0590 or 200-1655). Two more locations as well: One seats only 35 and is on the ground floor of the new 12-story *McDonald's Building* on the corner of Tverskaya Ulitsa and Ogareva Ulitsa, across from the *Central Post Office.* The newest outlet is a 500-seater located near the *Kremlin.*

**Metropol Room** Lenin once made postrevolutionary speeches to party members in this lavish dining room, with its stunning stained glass ceiling. (It was re-created for some scenes in the film *Doctor Zhivago.*) Today it is the site of what is probably the best brunch in Moscow. The buffet includes eggs Florentine and Benedict, smoked salmon, caviar, sausages, stuffed tomatoes, brie, fruit, champagne, and more. The feasting is accompanied by a seven-piece jazz band. Open daily for breakfast and lunch; brunch on Sundays only. Reservations advised. Major credit cards accepted. *Metropol Hotel,* 4 Teatralniy Proyezd (phone: 927-6452 or 927-6000).

**Moscow Bombay** Not far from Red Square, this Indian eatery serves reasonably priced curry, *daal,* tandoori chicken, and *biryani* rice. The garlic *naan* bread is excellent. Service is friendly and attentive. Open daily. Reservations advised. No credit cards accepted. 3 Nemirovich-Danchenko Ulitsa (phone: 292-9731).

**Peking** If you suddenly get the urge for Chinese food, this is where Chinese diplomats and journalists in Moscow eat. About 70 different dishes are prepared by Chinese cooks at this 600-seat, Sino-Russian venture. German beer also is available, and there is music and dancing at night. The barbecued bean curd is very hot and covered with spices; the chicken strips with lemon and five-spice marinade is also very good. Open daily. Reservations advised. No credit cards accepted. 1 Sadovaya Bolshaya (phone: 209-1865).

**Pescatore** Favorites of the expatriate community, these Italian restaurants feature a wide selection of pasta dishes (including penne with vodka), veal, and rabbit, but, as the name suggests, the emphasis is on seafood. Skip the lobster fettuccine and concentrate on the fish and prawns. White wines are moderately priced (by Moscow standards), but others are quite expensive. Though there is an English-language menu, the staff speaks only Russian and a smattering of Italian—don't worry, just point. Open daily. Reservations necessary. Major credit cards accepted. Two locations: across the street from the *Savoy Hotel,* 7-5 Pushechnaya Ulitsa (phone: 924-2058), and 26 Mira Prospekt (phone: 280-2400).

**Pizza Hut** Another US fast-food eatery becomes part of the Russian lifestyle. You know the menu. Open daily. No reservations or credit cards accepted. Two branches: 17 Kutuzovskiy Prospekt (phone: 243-1727, 243-7978, or 243-7960), and 12 Tverskaya Ulitsa (phone: 229-2013 or 299-7840).

**Praga** Located in the center of Moscow, this huge, state-run restaurant, which predates the 1917 revolution, serves uninspired Russian, Czech, and other Eastern European dishes to as many as 970 guests at a time. The turn-of-the-century decor is impressive: You've hit pay dirt if you find yourself at a balcony table overlooking the city. A dance band plays in the evening. Open daily from noon to midnight. Reservations advised. No credit cards accepted. 2 Novy Arbat Ulitsa (phone: 290-6171).

**Razgulya** Living up to its name, which means "cheer up," this dining place has a variety of creatively decorated rooms. One has Khokloma-style folk art, including red-and-gold paintings on Russian lacquerware. Another room, with a blue-and-white color scheme and wood-beam ceiling painted with blue flowers, is reminiscent of the Gzhel region, known for its blue-and-white pottery. A third room, the Beresta, has red tablecloths, colorful paintings, and hanging baskets. The menu features a variety of traditional Russian dishes, such as Razgulya salad (crab, rice, and nuts predominate). Live Russian and Gypsy music. Open daily. Reservations advised.

Major credit cards accepted. In the northeast part of the city at 11 Spartakovskaya Ulitsa (phone: 267-7613).

**El Rincón Español** As its name suggests, Spanish food is the thing in this ground floor restaurant at the *Moskva* hotel. (There is a little-known annex on the second floor, but the menu is limited.) The only place in town where you can get sangria and San Miguel beer, this trendy eatery has become a favorite with the expatriate community. Open daily. Reservations necessary. Major credit cards accepted. 7 Okhotniy Ryad (phone: 292-2893).

**Sadko Arcade** This mall next to the *Sadko* grocery store includes a spate of good restaurants. Best bets are the *German Beer House,* which offers excellent pea soup (phone: 940-4062), and the *Trattoria Italian Restaurant* (phone: 940-4066). Located along Krasnaya Presnya Naberezhnaya, near the *Mezhdunarodnaya* hotel. Open daily. No reservations or credit cards accepted. 1 Krasnogvardeisky Proyezd.

**Sapporo** This fine Japanese restaurant serves all the standard fare, including tempura, sukiyaki, and sushi. Open daily. Reservations advised. Major credit cards accepted. 12 Mira Prospekt (phone: 207-8253).

**Savoy** The luxurious dining room in the hotel of the same name is one of the best places in town to enjoy a quiet, elegant meal of Russian, Scandinavian, or international fare (the menu changes every six months). A prix fixe lunch includes appetizer, main course, and tea. Open daily. Reservations advised. Major credit cards accepted. *Savoy Hotel,* 3 Rozhdestvenka Ulitsa (phone: 929-8500).

**Sedmoe Nebo (Seventh Sky)** Moscow's only revolving restaurant, located atop the *Ostankino TV Tower.* There are three dining rooms, all at separate levels: the *Bronzovi Zal* (Bronze Hall), the *Zolotoi Zal* (Golden Hall), and the *Serebryani Zal* (Silver Hall). Each completes a revolution every 45 minutes. The prix fixe meal is part of a package that includes admission to the observation deck and an English-speaking guide who points out important buildings (you get a chance to see all of Stalin's "wedding cake" constructions). The security is so tight, however, that foreigners must bring their passports with them, and no bags or briefcases are allowed. The food is filling, if not fancy—start with pastry snacks and sausages, continue with mushrooms in sauerkraut and chicken cutlets, and end with ice cream. Vodka, champagne, and caviar can be ordered for an additional charge. Open daily. Reservations advised. No credit cards accepted. 15 Akademika Korolyeva Ulitsa (phone: 282-2293 or 282-2038).

**Skazka** The name means "fairy tale," and if good eating plus extravagant entertainment is what you're after, this is the spot. The atmosphere is warm, candlelit, and very Russian, and the acts range from performing cossacks and Gypsies to jazz musicians to an accordionist accompanied by a man playing spoons. *Zakuski* and single menu items are available. The *pelymeni* (Siberian meat dumplings in sour cream) are excellent here. Also recommended is boar cooked in wine, *veal perestroika* (marinated, then cooked on a spit), and *pozharskiy cutlet* (slices of veal and chicken stuffed with butter). Be sure to save room for some homemade pastries. There's also an art gallery with works for sale. Open daily. Reservations advised. No credit cards accepted. 1 Tovarishchevskiy Pereulok (phone: 271-0998).

**Stanislavsaya 2** This petite, lace-festooned spot is a real charmer. The veal, mushroom soup, and *blini* also are endearing. A violinist and pianist play softly in the background, and for a while the bustle of Moscow disappears. Open daily for dinner only. Reservations advised. No credit cards accepted. 2 Stanislavsaya Ulitsa (phone: 291-8689).

**Strastnoy-7** Chic and expensive, the most elegant of Moscow cooperatives boasts a stark neoclassical decor, warmed by lavish table accessories, quiet music, and professional, friendly service. There is no menu; diners are served daily specials, which make the most of limited ingredients. One such dish consists of tomatoes piled high with fresh herbed cream cheese, served with a tangy potato and cucumber salad; another is Old Moscow–style *roulette*—well-garnished platters of lightly fried, meat-and-ham-filled crêpes. Open daily. Reservations advised. Major credit cards accepted. 7 Strastnoy Bulvar (phone: 299-0498).

**Tanganka Bar** The entertainment—cossack and Russian singers who roam this dark, dungeon-like place in their elaborate garb, belting out folk melodies—overshadows the food. Belly dancers slither from one businessman to the next. Nevertheless, the ordinary Russian *zakuski* are tolerable and reasonably priced. Open daily for dinner only. Reservations advised. No credit cards accepted. 15 Radishchevskaya Ulitsa (phone: 272-4351).

**Tren-Mos** The name is a shortened version of Trenton-Moscow. Operated by a father-son team of Ukrainian descent from Trenton, New Jersey, this is a place where homesick Americans can relax over a good, home-style meal. US state flags, along with other related memorabilia, cover the walls, and the menu offers familiar dishes, such as chili, T-bone steaks, and apple pie. The French chef has quite a range of specialties, from cannelloni *al forno* to Texas-style boar. There's live piano music, too. Open daily. Reservations advised. Major credit cards accepted. 21 Komsomolskiy Prospekt (phone: 245-1216).

**Tren-Mos Bistro** The ambience is decidedly American, but the food and wine are European bistro fare—individual pizzas, lots of pasta dishes, and Italian-style meat, served by efficient and courteous waiters. Open daily. No reservations. Major credit cards accepted. 1-9 Ostozhenka Ulitsa (phone: 202-5722 and 202-3540).

**U Babushki** Literally meaning "Grandma's" and run by two Russian women, this is one of Moscow's most charming restaurants. The cozy dining area is filled with pictures of family and friends, books, and other memorabilia. The menu is strictly Russian and includes *pelymeni* and steaming borscht, homemade pastries and cakes top off the meal. Open daily. Reservations necessary. No credit cards accepted. 42 Bolshaya Ordynka Ulitsa (phone: 239-1484).

**U Pirosmani** This Georgian restaurant is a Moscow favorite. Named after the Georgian primitive painter Nikolai Pirosmanashvili, this cozy spot is decorated with copies of the painter's works, as well as wood beams and tables, stucco walls, an old piano and gramophone, and a fireplace. Ask for a table in the more attractive outer room. The menu offers spicy Georgian dishes including *khachapuri* (cheese-stuffed bread), *lobio* (marinated bean salad), marinated mushrooms, and pickled vegetables. There are usually only two main courses—if you still have room—shashlik and huge, meat-stuffed dumplings. Open daily. Reservations advised. Major credit cards accepted. Near *Novodevichiy Monastyr.* 4 Novodevichiy Proyezd (phone: 246-1638 or 247-1926).

**Vstrecha** A popular cooperative serving Georgian and Italian fare, it also features live music and a bar. Specialties include shashlik and *chakhohbili iz kuritsi* (stewed chicken with potatoes and tomatoes, cayenne, coriander, and saffron). Open daily. Reservations advised. Major credit cards accepted. 3 Gilyarovskogo Ulitsa (phone: 208-4597).

# Munich

## At-a-Glance

### SEEING THE CITY

An exceptional view of Munich and the Bavarian Alps is available from the *Olympiaturm* (Olympic Tower), located just northwest of the city at *Olympiapark*. The 951-foot television tower was erected to facilitate televising the *1972 Summer Olympics*. An elevator will take you to the tower terrace at 623 feet, with its impressive panorama of the city. There's also the *Tower* restaurant (phone: 308-1039), which revolves for a 360° view. The tower and restaurant are open daily; admission charge.

### SPECIAL PLACES

Marienplatz, with its tall white column of the Virgin Mary, the city's patron, is the heart of Munich. Many of the streets leading from it have been closed to traffic and turned into a *Fussgängerzone* (pedestrian zone). About eight blocks west of Marienplatz is the central square, Karlsplatz, known locally as Stachus, where buses, trams, and subways to all parts of the city arrive and depart. Visitors often are confused because street names change abruptly in central Munich for no apparent reason. You always can get back to the center again, though, because there are numerous signs pointing the way and the spires and towers of landmark churches stand out above the lower red-roofed buildings that constitute the heart of Munich. The Isar River cuts through the city's eastern section, and a walk north along its banks will lead to a huge, lovely park, the *Englischer Garten* (English Garden). On the west side of the park lies the Schwabing district.

### DOWNTOWN

**SCHWABING** At the turn of the century, it had a reputation as an artistic and intellectual center. Today this district to the north of the *Universität München* (University of Munich) is known to most visitors as the place "where the action is" in Munich. By day Schwabing resembles any other German residential district, but around 6 PM people swarm into its streets looking for a good time. The sidewalks along Leopoldstrasse, Schwabing's main street; Amalienstrasse; and Türkenstrasse take on a festive air. You'll see a confusion of sights: painters displaying their art, street musicians, poets offering their latest verses, barbers giving haircuts on the sidewalk, palm readers, quick-sketch artists. You can buy sandals, copper jewelry, ceramics, beads, belts—just about anything, in fact, including genuine and bogus antiques. Schwabing has more than 200 restaurants, with Greek, Yugoslavian, Italian, and Bavarian the most popular. There are countless discotheques, jazz *Kellers,* cafés, and bou-

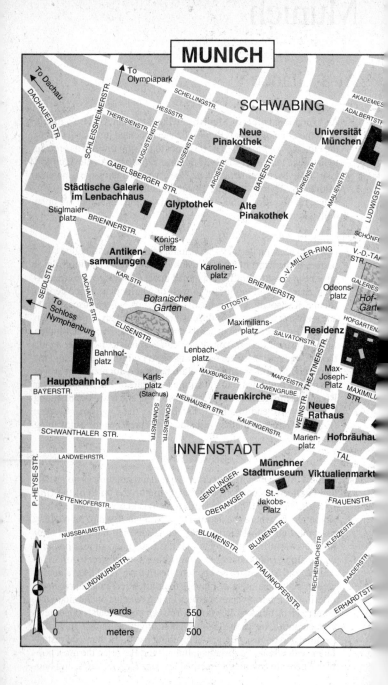

# MUNICH

To Dachau

To Olympiapark

DACHAUER STR.

SCHLEISSHEIMERSTR.

THERESIENSTR.

AUGUSTENSTR.

LUISENSTR.

SCHELLINGSTR.

HESSSTR.

**SCHWABING**

ARCISSTR.

BAYERSTR.

TÜRKENSTR.

AMALIENSTR.

AKADEMIES

ADALBERTSTR.

**Universität München**

Neue **Pinakothek**

GABELSBERGER STR.

**Städtische Galerie im Lenbachhaus**

Stiglmaier-platz

BRIENNERSTR.

**Glyptothek**

**Alte Pinakothek**

LUDWIGSTR.

SCHÖNFE

**Antiken-sammlungen**

Königs-platz

KARLSTR.

SEIDLSTR.

DACHAUER STR.

*Botanischer Garten*

Karolinen-platz

BRIENNERSTR.

O.-V.-MILLER-RING

V.-D.-TA STR.

GALERIES

Odeons-platz

*Hof-Gart*

To Schloss Nymphenburg

ELISENSTR.

OTTOSTR.

Maximilians-platz

SALVATORSTR.

THEATINERSTR.

HOFGARTEN.

**Residenz**

Bahnhof-platz

Lenbach-platz

MAXBURGSTR.

**Hauptbahnhof**

Karls-platz (Stachus)

NEUHAUSER STR.

MAFFEISTR.

LÖWENGRUBE

WEINSTR.

Max-Joseph-Platz

MAXIMILI STR.

BAYERSTR.

KAUFINGERSTR.

**Frauenkirche**

**Neues Rathaus**

SCHWANTHALER STR.

SONNENSTR.

Marien-platz

**Hofbräuhau**

P.-HEYSE-STR.

LANDWEHRSTR.

**INNENSTADT**

TAL

PETTENKOFERSTR.

SENDLINGER STR.

**Münchner Stadtmuseum**

**Viktualienmarkt**

OBERANGER

St.-Jakobs-Platz

FRAUENSTR.

NUSSBAUMSTR.

BLUMENSTR.

BLUMENSTR.

REICHENBACHSTR.

KLENZESTR.

BAADERSTR.

LINDWURMSTR.

FRAUNHOFERSTR.

ERHARDTSTR

N

| 0 | yards | 550 |
| 0 | meters | 500 |

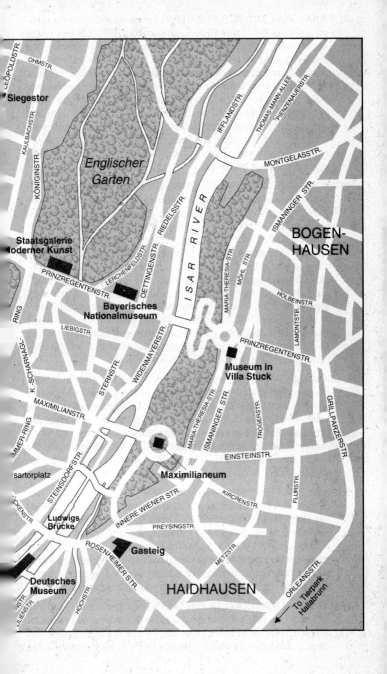

ular. There are countless discotheques, jazz *Kellers,* cafés, and boutiques.

**ALTE PINAKOTHEK (OLD PICTURE GALLERY)** Temporarily closed for renovation until 1997, this huge Renaissance building is one of the world's great art galleries; until it reopens, most of its paintings are displayed at the *Neue Pinakothek* (see *Museums*). The gallery's artworks include large and important collections of Dutch and Flemish painting from the 14th to the 18th century. The museum was built from 1826 to 1836 to house paintings gathered by the Dukes of Wittelsbach. Ludwig I made numerous other acquisitions that enhanced the museum's reputation. Among its treasures are major works by Albrecht Dürer and Peter Paul Rubens, as well as *Battle of Issus* by Albrecht Altdorfer and *Saint Erasmus and Saint Maurice* by Mathias Grünewald.

**DEUTSCHES MUSEUM (GERMAN MUSEUM)** Considered the largest technical museum in the world, it sits on Isarinsel (Isar Island) in the Isar River southeast of the city center. Included among its massive displays are the original 139-foot U-boat built in 1906, locomotives from the *Bavarian State Railway,* a collection of antique pianos and organs, a Messerschmitt 267 jet fighter from 1944, a planetarium, salt and coal mining exhibits in actual caverns, and an aeronautical and space center (including a full-size model of a lunar module). There are plenty of hands-on exhibits that can be activated by the spectator. Unfortunately, detailed descriptions are available only in German, but it's still very much worth a visit. Closed *New Year's Eve* and *New Year's Day.* Admission charge. Reached by subway (*Isartor* station) or by walking across one of several bridges connecting the island with the city. Isarinsel (phone: 21791).

**GASTEIG** High on the right bank of the Isar River, just 400 yards from the *Deutsches Museum,* this cultural center is one of Munich's newest attractions. It unites under one roof a philharmonic hall, two smaller concert halls, the *Richard Strauss Musikschule* (Richard Strauss Music Conservatory), and the municipal library. The $130-million building has an ultramodern design, a sharp contrast to the surrounding neighborhood. Open daily. 5 Rosenheimer Str. (phone: 480-98614).

**ENGLISCHER GARTEN (ENGLISH GARDEN)** This 18th-century garden, one of the oldest landscaped parks on the Continent, is a favorite meeting place. It has lakes, pavilions, riding trails, a site frequented by nude sunbathers, a Japanese teahouse, and a *Chinesischer Turm* (Chinese Tower). At the base of the tower is the city's largest beer garden, where the favorite pastime is quenching one's thirst with a liter of beer while enjoying the passing scene. The park is northeast of the city's center, between Schwabing and the Isar River.

**FRAUENKIRCHE (CATHEDRAL OF OUR LADY)** The onion domes atop two 325-feet symmetrical towers have made this late-Gothic cathedral Munich's most distinctive landmark. Its dull red brick façade was damaged extensively during air raids in 1944, but the exterior has been completely restored to its original appearance. The cathedral contains a rich depository of religious works of art, relics, sacred tombs, and the mausoleum of Emperor Ludwig IV. An elevator takes passengers to the top of the south tower, from which there is a good view of the city. 1 Frauenpl.

**RESIDENZ (PALACE)** Although damaged during World War II, the royal palace has regained much of its glory. Built for the Dukes of Wittelsbach, the palace has been extended over the centuries to form a complex of buildings with seven inner courts. There are state rooms and royal suites decorated in Renaissance, rococo, and neoclassical styles, and displays of royal treasures. Closed Mondays. Admission charge. Entrance at 3 Max-Joseph-Pl. (phone: 290671).

**BAYERISCHES NATIONALMUSEUM (BAVARIAN NATIONAL MUSEUM)** The vast array of art and historical memorabilia from the Middle Ages to the 19th century on display here should give you an excellent introduction to Bavarian culture. The museum has what may be the most extensive collection of arts and crafts in the world. Along with its tapestries and woodcarvings, the museum is best known for its unique *Krippenschau Collection* of *Christmas* crèches (nativity scenes). Closed Mondays. Admission charge. 3 Prinzregentenstr. (phone: 211241).

**HOFBRÄUHAUS (BEER HALL)** This immense structure is a dance palace, a restaurant, and a national monument to the good life. In the beer garden, you'll be part of a scene people around the world associate with Munich: cheerful waitresses and waiters in peasant costumes—often carrying as many as 10 steins of beer at once—moving through a noisy crowd selling pretzels stacked on long sticks, or white *Radis* (radishes) cut into fancy spirals—both suitably salty to help you work up a thirst. It's not expensive, and is a must on any visitor's sightseeing agenda. Open daily. 9 Am Platzl (phone: 221676).

**NEUES RATHAUS (NEW CITY HALL)** Built in the 19th century, Munich's *Neues Rathaus* dominates Marienplatz. Each day throngs of people peer up at its famous *Glockenspiel,* waiting to see the mechanical knights and their squires joust while the carillon signals to the city that it is 11 AM. It is a delightful diversion, not to be missed. This is also the site of the city's annual *Christkindlesmarkt* (Christmas Market)—another must-see, even if you don't buy any of the trinkets, ornaments, or tasty food items for sale. Marienpl.

**VIKTUALIENMARKT (VICTUALS MARKET)** In this open-air market, farmers, butchers, bakers, and other purveyors of food specialties set out their wares Mondays through Saturdays. It's the perfect place to browse, take pictures, and buy a snack or picnic fixings. Located a few blocks south of Marienpl.

SUBURBS

**OLYMPIAPARK (OLYMPIC PARK)** Built for the *1972 Olympic Games,* it also was the scene of the terrorist kidnapping of Israeli athletes.

The modern sports complex includes swimming pools, tracks, and gymnasiums. The park also has an 80,000-seat stadium—under an extraordinary skin-like roof—and an artificial lake. The Olympic Village, which housed the *Olympic* athletes and officials, is now a major residential suburb. Guided tours are available in German (and in English for groups by prior arrangement), and you even can swim in one of the pools that Mark Spitz made famous in 1972. The park can be reached easily by bus or subway. Admission charge. Oberwiesenfeld (phone: 3067-2424).

**SCHLOSS NYMPHENBURG (NYMPHENBURG PALACE)** Just west of the city limits stands a splendid 495-acre park with lakes, hunting lodges, and *Schloss Nymphenburg,* once the residence of the Bavarian kings. The great hall of the palace is decorated with frescoes by Johann Baptist Zimmermann, and the *Marstallmuseum* in the south wing of the palace houses state carriages and sleighs. The *Porzellanarbeitsschutzgesetz Nymphenburg* (Nymphenburg China Factory), with showrooms open to the public, is on the north crescent of the grounds. Outdoor concerts are presented here during summer months, and it is a particularly lovely spot to visit when the rhododendron are in bloom from May through June. Closed Mondays. Admission charge. Entrance from Menzingerstrasse (phone: 179080).

**TIERPARK HELLABRUNN (HELLABRUNN ZOO)** The nearby city of Hellabrunn keeps its extensive collection of animals in Europe's largest zoo, a 173-acre natural setting of forestland and rivers. It's famous for breeding rare animals and for its anthropoid ape section. There is regular bus and subway service from Marienplatz. Guided tours (in German) are given on Wednesdays; tours in English are available to groups by reservation. Open daily. Admission charge. Four miles (6 km) south of Munich at 30 Tierparkstr. (phone: 625080).

**DACHAU** Though the town itself is an attractive place near a misty heath, its name has evoked nothing but horror since this first Nazi concentration camp was built in 1933. During World War II, some 200,000 prisoners and deportees were held here, and an estimated 32,000 of them died or disappeared. The old administration building is now used as a museum where photos, memorabilia, and exhibitions document the camp's cruel history. Closed Mondays, *Christmas Eve,* and the afternoons of *New Year's Eve* and *Shrove Tuesday.* No admission charge. Dachau, 14 miles (22 km) northwest of Munich, can be reached by the Petershausen commuter train *(S-2)* from the *Hauptbahnhof* (main railway station). There is a direct bus (No. 722) from the station to the camp; get off at the Robert Bosch stop (phone: 8131-1741).

## EXTRA SPECIAL

It's said that over 650 kinds of beer are brewed in Bavaria, including those made privately. Munich is the home of six of Germany's major producers; one of them, Spaten (which alone makes nine different labels), will arrange tours (by advance appointment only). During a half-hour walk through the plant, accompanied by an English-speaking guide, guests learn the various steps of beer making—from germination of the barley to bottling the brew. The tour is an essential preliminary to enlightened imbibing. Admission charge. 48 Marsstr. (phone: 51220 for reservations).

# Sources and Resources

TOURIST INFORMATION

The *Munich Tourist Office* has information counters at the *Hauptbahnhof* (Bayerstr.; entrance 2; phone: 239-1256) and at the *Flughafen Franz Josef Strauss* (Franz Josef Strauss Airport; phone: 975-92815; also see *Getting Around*, below). Both offices are open daily until late evening. For information in English on museums and other sights call the tourist office at 239162 or 239172. The *US Consulate* is at 5 Königinstr. (phone: 2-8880).

In the US, there are two branches of the *German National Tourist Office* (11766 Wilshire Blvd., Suite 750, Los Angeles, CA 90025; phone: 310-575-9799; fax: 310-575-1565; and 122 E. 42nd St., 53rd Floor, New York, NY 10168; phone: 212-661-7200; fax: 212-661-7174). The *German Embassy* is at 4645 Reservoir Rd. NW, Washington, DC 20007-1998 (phone: 202-298-4000).

ENTRY REQUIREMENTS A US citizen needs a current passport for a stay of up to 90 days.

TIME The time in Germany is six hours later than in US East Coast cities. Germany observes daylight saving time.

LANGUAGE *Hochdeutsch* (High German) is the written language and the one that's commonly spoken throughout the country. English is the second language of the country.

ELECTRIC CURRENT 220 volts, 50 cycles, AC.

MONEY The deutsche mark (DM) equals 100 pfennigs. At press time the exchange rate was 1.5 DM to the dollar.

TIPPING A 10% to 12% service charge is included in restaurant checks; superior service may warrant an additional amount. Porters receive 1 DM per bag. Taxi drivers should get a 15% tip.

BANKING/BUSINESS HOURS Most banks are open weekdays from 8:30 AM to 12:30 PM and from 1:30 to 3:30 PM; on Thursdays they close at 5:30 PM. The bank at Munich's main train station is open daily from 6 AM to 11:30 PM. Most other businesses operate weekdays from 9 AM to 5 PM.

NATIONAL HOLIDAYS *New Year's Day* (January 1), *Epiphany* (in Bavaria and Baden-Württemberg, January 6), *Good Friday* (April 14), *Easter*

*Sunday* (April 16), *Easter Monday* (April 17), *Labor Day* (May 1), *Ascension Thursday* (May 25), *Whitmonday* (June 5), *Feast of Corpus Christi* (June 15), *Feast of the Assumption* (August 15), *German Unity Day* (October 3), *Day of Prayer and Repentance* (November 22), *Christmas Day* (December 25), and *Boxing Day* (December 26).

**LOCAL COVERAGE** The twice-weekly *Munich Times* and the monthly *Munich Found* are English-language newspapers. The tourist office publishes an official monthly program, *München,* that lists theater, museum, and concert schedules, special exhibitions, hotels, restaurants, camping facilities, and other useful information, but it is published only in German. However, many hotels provide literature in English focusing on Munich's activities and entertainment programs.

**TELEPHONE** The city code for Munich is 89. When calling from one area to another within Germany dial 0 + city code + local number. The country code for Germany is 49. Dial 110 or 558661 for emergency assistance.

## GETTING AROUND

Munich has an integrated rapid-transit system; the tickets that you buy from the blue dispensers at stations, streetcar stops, and on those vehicles bearing a white-and-green "K" sign can be used on buses, streetcars, subways, and local trains. You can cancel the tickets yourself in automatic canceling machines at the barriers of stations and in streetcars and buses bearing a yellow-and-black "E." A single ride costs 2.50 DM (about $1.70) or more, depending on how many zones you're traveling through; however, there is a reduced-rate ticket for about 10 DM ($6.66) that permits unlimited transport in a 24-hour period. These special tickets are sold at the tourist offices and all ticket offices.

**AIRPORT** The *Flughafen Franz Josef Strauss,* 18 miles (28 km) northeast of downtown Munich, is the terminus for all domestic and international flights into Munich. A rapid-transit train line *(S-8)* connects the city center with the airport, and leaves approximately every 20 minutes from the *Hauptbahnhof.* Buses also leave from the *Kieferngarten* subway station every 40 minutes for the airport; the trip takes approximately 25 minutes. For airport flight information call 975-21313.

**BUS AND STREETCAR** The Karlsplatz is the main junction for Munich's streetcars, and the *Ostbahnhof* (East Railway Station) across the Isar from central Munich is the terminal for many of the city's blue-and-white buses.

**CAR RENTAL** There are international and local rental firms in downtown Munich and at the airport. If you do drive, you should know that in some areas of Munich traffic-light poles contain two sets of lights: one on top for cars and a bottom set for bicycles. Munich also employs "motorbike" women, easily recognized by their light blue jumpsuits, who patrol the highways to aid lost or stranded motorists.

Fluent in several languages, these women carry maps, tourist information, and other helpful material.

**SUBWAY AND TRAIN** The subway, called the *U-Bahn,* crosses the city in a north-south direction and has its central stops at Marienplatz and the *Hauptbahnhof.* Like most European underground rail systems, the *U-Bahn* is clean, modern, and efficient. The *S-Bahn,* which connects with the *U-Bahn* at Marienplatz and *Hauptbahnhof,* is the interurban express line. It runs underground across the city in an east-west direction. Outside the city, it branches out over the whole national railway network. For information on *S-Bahn* trains call 557575. For information on trains to other parts of the country call 19419 (schedules) or 55414 (fares).

**TAXI** Munich's taxis are expensive. It will cost you about 5 DM ($3) just to have the driver flip down the arm of the meter. Taxis can be hailed on the street, or you can get one radio-dispatched by dialing 21610 or 19410.

## LOCAL SERVICES

**DENTIST (ENGLISH-SPEAKING)** Most German dentists speak English; the *US Consulate* (see *Tourist Information*) has a list of English-speaking dentists.

**DRY CLEANER/TAILOR** *Paradies-Sofortreinigung* (12 Lerchenfeldstr.; phone: 223465); *Tommaselli* (102 Landsbergerstr.; phone: 505564).

**LIMOUSINE SERVICE** *Sixt* (9-11 Seitzstr.; phone: 222829).

**MEDICAL EMERGENCY** Munich's hospitals all have emergency rooms. For emergency service, dial 110 or 558661. In addition, the *US Consulate* (see *Tourist Information*) has a list of English-speaking physicians.

**MESSENGER SERVICE** *Alpha Kurier* (16 Schraudolphstr.; phone: 273-0303).

**NATIONAL/INTERNATIONAL COURIER** *DHL Worldwide Express* (5 Carl-Zeiss-Str., Garching; phone: 320-8111); *Federal Express* (20 Diesel-str., Garching; phone: 130-7573).

**OFFICE EQUIPMENT RENTAL** *Bürozentrum Schulz* (192 Dachauer Str.; phone: 14820); *Pini* (1 Schützenstr.; phone: 594361), for audiovisual equipment.

**PHARMACY** *Bahnhof-Apotheke* (2 Bahnhofpl.; phone: 594119 or 598119). To find out which pharmacy is open at night, on weekends, or on holidays, call 594475.

**PHOTOCOPIES** *Copy Shop* (75 Amalien Str.; phone: 284734); *Uni-Kopie* (18 Adalbertstr.; phone: 333363).

**POST OFFICE** The main branch (1 Bahnhofpl.; phone: 5454-2732) is open 24 hours a day.

**SECRETARY/STENOGRAPHER (ENGLISH-SPEAKING)** *Conference Hostesses* (15 Connollystr., *Olympic Village;* phone: 351-4374); *Günther*

*Büroservice* (28 Leopoldstr.; phone: 391155 or 333200); and *Manpower* (17 Sonnenstr.; phone: 551030).

**TELEX** Services are available from 7 AM to 11 PM at the main branch of the post office (see above).

**TRANSLATOR** *Bundesverband der Dolmetscher und Ubersetzer* (*BDU,* the Association of Interpreters and Translators; 45 Amalienstr.; phone: 283330).

**OTHER** Tuxedo rental: *Cinyburg* (16 Lindwurmstr.; phone: 534412).

## SPECIAL EVENTS

In addition to *Oktoberfest* (see below), Munich is famous the world over for its annual bow to operatic excellence.

---

### FAVORITE FETES

**Munich Opera Festival** In July, while most of Europe's opera houses have their summer siesta, Munich sets out a month-long musical feast. The rich diet of Wagner is washed down with sparkling Donizetti, and bubbling *bel canto*—as *Figaro* weds, *Carmen* beds, *La Traviata* dies, and *Rigoletto* has the last sob. Most performances by the *Bayerische Staatsoper* (Bavarian State Opera) take place in the monumental *Nationaltheater* (Max-Joseph-Pl.; phone: 221316), but a few are held in the *Cuvilliés Theater,* an ornate 18th-century venue inside the *Residenz* (1 Residenzstr.; phone: 290671).

**Oktoberfest** No self-respecting lager lover should miss *Oktoberfest;* celebrated from late September through the first Sunday in October, it is 16 riotous days of beer drinking, sausage eating, and merrymaking at *Théresienwiese* (Theresa's Meadow), a fairgrounds where local breweries set up gaily decorated beer-garden buildings, brass bands oom-pah-pah continuously, and oxen are roasted on open spits. Unbelievable quantities of beer are drunk: Some 750,000 kegs are tapped.

---

*Fasching*—another longtime tradition which has been celebrated in Munich since the 14th century—hints more of indulgence in forbidden pleasures of the flesh (there is a traditional agreement that husbands and wives overlook one another's indiscretions during *Fasching*), but it, too, is characterized by lots of drinking and endless fun-seeking. The nonstop street reveling is all the more colorful for the outlandish costumes the celebrants don for fancy balls and an enormous parade through the city.

## MUSEUMS

Besides those mentioned in *Special Places,* notable museums in Munich include the following:

**ANTIKENSAMMLUNGEN (ANTIQUES COLLECTION)** Classical art, including Joseph Loeb's collection of Etruscan gold and silver. Closed Mondays. Admission charge. 1 Königspl. (phone: 598359).

**BMW-MUSEUM** Cars, motorcycles, and airplane engines of the Bavaria Motor Works. Open daily. Admission charge. 130 Petuelring (phone: 389-53307).

**GLYPTOTHEK** Greek and Roman sculpture. Closed Mondays. Admission charge. 3 Königspl. (phone: 286100).

**JÜDISCHES MUSEUM (JEWISH MUSEUM)** Exhibits devoted to Jewish history, culture, and traditions. Closed Fridays through Mondays and on Jewish holidays. No admission charge. 36 Maximilianstr. (phone: 297453).

**KUNSTHALLE (ART GALLERY)** Its space is used to show temporary, visiting exhibitions of paintings and sculpture. Open daily. No admission charge. 15 Theatinerstr. (phone: 224412).

**MÜNCHNER STADTMUSEUM (CITY MUSEUM)** Exhibits here cover Munich's history since the Middle Ages. Closed Mondays. Admission charge. 1 St.-Jakobs-Pl. (phone: 233-22370).

**MUSEUM IN VILLA STUCK** Turn-of-the-century and contemporary art are displayed. Closed Mondays. Admission charge. 60 Prinzregentenstr. (phone: 455-5510).

**NEUE PINAKOTHEK** A collection of 19th- and early 20th-century art; in addition, this gallery displays most of the paintings from the *Alte Pinakothek* (which is closed until 1997; see *Special Places*). Closed Mondays. Admission charge. 29 Barerstr. (phone: 238-05195).

**STAATSGALERIE MODERNER KUNST (STATE MUSEUM OF MODERN ART)** This recently renovated museum houses a collection of 20th-century sculpture and painting. Closed Mondays. Admission charge. 1 Prinzregentenstr. (phone: 292710).

**STÄDTISCHE GALERIE IM LENBACHHAUS (MUNICIPAL GALLERY IN LENBACH-HAUS)** Kandinsky and the Blue Rider School are featured. Closed Mondays. Admission charge. 33 Luisenstr. (phone: 233-0320).

**VALENTIN MUSEUM** Dedicated to one of Munich's legendary entertainers, Karl Valentin. Open daily. Admission charge. Gate Tower, Isartorpl. (phone: 223266).

## SHOPPING

Munich is such an elegant shopping city that some visitors confess to losing all sense of proportion once turned loose in the pedestrian zone. Shops tempt you with Bavarian beer steins, wonderful antiques, marvelous German porcelain, and items of German steel, as well as Parisian fashions. Munich's most elegant shops can be found along Maximilianstrasse and Briennerstrasse and the small streets between Marienplatz and Odeonsplatz. Most of the antiques shops are concentrated in Neuturmstrasse, near Marienplatz. The city's leading department stores are *Oberpollinger* (off Karlspl.; phone:

290230), which is affiliated with the national *Karstadt* chain of stores, and *Kaufhof* (Marienpl.; phone: 269072). Most shops are open from 9 AM to 6:30 PM weekdays and 9 AM to 2 PM Saturdays; on the first Saturday of the month in summer, they stay open until 4 PM. Also, some stores operate until 8:30 PM on Thursdays and until 6 PM on Saturdays. *Auer Dult* is a wonderful flea market for secondhand goods, antiques, and curiosities, set up three times a year—usually in May, July, and October at 2 Mariahilfplatz, across the Isar in the southeastern district of Au.

**Alois Dallmayr** A world-famous fancy food store. 14-15 Dienerstr. (phone: 21350).

**Anglia English Bookstore** The biggest selection of English-language paperbacks in southern Germany. 3 Schellingstr. (phone: 283642).

**Beck** Famous for textiles, womenswear, and Bavarian handicrafts. 11 Marienpl. (phone: 236910).

**Biebl** Solingen carving sets and other items made of this renowned German steel. 25 Karlspl. (phone: 597936).

**Dieter Stange-Erlenbach Pelze** Famed for its timeless and fashionable furs—for him and for her. 21 Maximilianstr. (phone: 535974).

**Dirndlkönigin** An interesting display of Bavarian handicrafts, including the best selection of Bavarian folk costumes in Munich. 18 Residenzstr. (phone: 293804).

**Kunstring** Contemporary and antique dinnerware. 4 Briennerstr. (phone: 281532).

**Loden-Frey** Men's and women's loden coats. 7-9 Maffeistr. (phone: 236930).

**Ludwig Mory** A huge and varied stock of interesting beer steins, as well as a collection of pewter objets d'art. 8 Marienpl. (phone: 224542).

**Maendler** High fashion for women. 7 Theatinerstr. (phone: 291-3322).

**Moderne Creation München (MCM)** The latest in chic fashion accessories. 11 Nicolaistr. (phone: 331096).

**Moshammer's** Clothing for men. 14 Maximilianstr. (phone: 226924).

**Obletter** Germany's largest toy store. 11-12 Karlspl. (phone: 231-8601).

**Pini** The city's largest store for cameras and allied equipment. Am Stachus (phone: 594361).

**Rosenthal** Home of the marvelous china, crystal, and cutlery. 8 Theatinerstr. (phone: 220422 or 227547).

**Staatliche Porzellan Manufaktur (State Porcelain Factory)** The main distributor of Nymphenburg porcelain. 1-2 Odeonspl. (phone: 172439 or 282428).

**Wallach Haus** Bavarian furniture, dirndls, and peasant dresses. 3 Residenzstr. (phone: 220871).

**Walter** Leather clothing for men and women. 9 Amalienstr. (phone: 282294).

**Wesely** Ornately decorated wax candles typical of this region. 1 Rindermarkt (phone: 264519).

## SPORTS AND FITNESS

The excellent facilities built for the *1972 Summer Olympics* are used by a variety of professional teams in Munich, providing visitors with an opportunity to see everything from European soccer and basketball to ice hockey and track and field events. Sports schedules are listed in the monthly tourist office program, *München* (see *Local Coverage*).

**BICYCLING** Bikes can be rented at the entrance to the *Englischer Garten* (at the corner of Königinstrasse and Veterinärstrasse; phone: 529943); the garden is a very pleasant place to cycle through. *Park & Bike* (18 Häberlstr.; phone: 539697), *Radius Touristik* (9 Arnulfstr.; phone: 596113), and *City Hopper Tours* (95 Hohenzollern Str.; phone: 272-1131) also rent bicycles.

**FITNESS CENTERS** The *Sportstudio* (16 Hansastr.; phone: 573479) is a gym that is open to non-members.

**JOGGING** Try the *Englischer Garten,* which stretches north from Prinzregentenstrasse and is easily accessible from downtown.

**SOCCER** *Bayern München,* one of Europe's top soccer teams, plays its home games year round (except January, June, and July) at the *Olympiastadion* (Olympic Stadium). For information and tickets contact *Olympiapark* (see *Special Places*) or the tourist office.

**SWIMMING** The *Olympia Schwimmhalle* (Olympic Swimming Hall) in *Olympiapark* (see *Special Places*) is open to the public daily.

## THEATER

Munich has been known for centuries as a theater city. You can see everything from Greek tragedy to classical ballet to modern experimental drama in the numerous theaters here. The chief theaters are the *Residenz Theater* (1 Max-Joseph-Pl.; phone: 225754) and the *Münchner Kammerspiele* (Munich Chamber Theater) in *Schauspielhaus* (26 Maximilianstr.; phone: 237-21328). Other venues include the *Cuvilliés Theater* in the *Residenz* (1 Residenzstr.; phone: 290671); *Theater in Marstall* (Marstallpl.; phone: 225754); *Prinzregententheater* (Prince Regent's Theater; 12 Prinzregentenpl.; phone: 221316); the *Münchner Marionettentheater* (Munich Puppet Theater; 29A Blumenstr. at Sendlinger-Tor-Pl.; phone: 265712); and the *Münchner Theater für Kinder* (Munich Theater for Children; 46 Dachauer Str.; phone: 595454 and 593858).

## MUSIC

The first opera was performed in Munich in 1650, and the names of Wagner, Mozart, and Richard Strauss (Strauss was born in Munich) are linked closely with the *Bayerische Staatsoper* (Bavarian State Opera), which performs in the *Nationaltheater* (Max-Joseph-Pl.; phone: 221316).

The *Munich Opera Festival,* with performances held at the *Nationaltheater* and the *Cuvilliés Theater* (see *Special Events*), is the highlight of the city's summer opera offering; opera also can be heard at the *Staatstheater am Gärtnerplatz* (3 Gärtnerpl.; phone: 201-6767). Hardly a day passes without a classical concert at one of the halls at the *Gasteig* (see *Special Places*).

## NIGHTCLUBS AND NIGHTLIFE

Nightlife and Schwabing are almost interchangeable terms. You can dance over an aquarium filled with sharks at *Hamlet Light* in the *Holiday Inn Crowne Plaza* (see *Checking In*); disco at *Cadillac* (1 Theklastr.; phone: 266974) and at *Charly M.* (5 Maximilianspl.; phone: 595272); or rock the night away at *Nightclub* in the *Bayerischer Hof–Palais Montgelas* (2-6 Promenadepl.; phone: 212-0994). Music and other entertainment is offered at *Clip* (25 Leopoldstr.; phone: 394578), and *Domicile* (19 Leopoldstr.; phone: 399451) offers jazz and rock. There's usually an interesting program of live music or cabaret-style satire on tap at *Nachtcafé* (5 Maximilianspl.; phone: 595900), as well as at the *Riem Airport* (400 Töginger Str., Riem; phone: 906322), housed (as its name implies) in the city's former airport terminal. A disco that appeals to trendy *Müncheners* is *Bubbles* (25 Oskar-von-Miller-Ring; phone: 281182); *Sunset* (69 Leopoldstr.; phone: 390303) is another popular dance spot. At *Harry's New York Bar* (9 Falkenturmstr.; phone: 222700) you can gawk at celebrities while imbibing one of 500 different drinks.

Biting humor and satire are the offerings at the literary cabaret *Lach-und Schiessgesellschaft* (Ursulastr.; phone: 391997); and don't miss the vocal renditions of Gisela (who only goes by one name, à la Cher or Madonna) at her bistro, *Schwabinger Gisela* (38 Herzog-Heinrich-Str.; phone: 534901). Jazz can be heard at clubs such as *Saint Thomas* (302 Tegernseer Landstr.; phone: 690-5456) and *Unterfahrt* (96 Kirchenstr.; phone: 448-2794). For rock and pop, try *Music Hall Epikero* (2 Detmoldstr.; phone: 351-0869) and *Schwabinger Podium* (1 Wagnerstr.; phone: 399482). *Waldwirtschaft Grosshesselohe* (3 Georg-Kalb-Str.; phone: 795088) offers great Bavarian beer as well as live jazz. On Monday evenings you can hear some of the best Irish and British folk music at the *Irish Folk Pub* (9 Fraunhofer Str.; phone: 679-2481).

If you'd like to test your luck, take the *Garmisch Casino's Blitz Bus* or one of the other buses the casinos run to bring players from Munich to the Garmisch area at the foot of the Alps, 54 miles (87 km) away. The buses leave from the north side of the *Hauptbahnhof* at 5 PM on weekdays and at 2 PM Sundays. They leave Garmisch at 11 PM for the return to Munich. The trip takes about an hour and 35 minutes each way. For information contact the tourist office at the *Hauptbahnhof* (see *Tourist Information*).

# Best in Town

## CHECKING IN

Except during *Oktoberfest* and *Fasching,* there is plenty of hotel space in Munich. Top hotels will cost a minimum of $150 a night for a double, and most of their rooms go for much higher prices; moderate-priced hotels charge between $90 and $140 a night; and anything below $90 must be considered inexpensive. The hotels listed below have a bath or a shower in every room, and in almost every case the rooms have telephones; room rates do *not* include breakfast unless specified. Be sure to make reservations well ahead if you're coming for *Oktoberfest* or *Fasching.* Munich also has many delightful, inexpensive pensions. They don't have all the conveniences of a modern hotel, such as private baths, but they do have *Gemütlichkeit*—the typical warmth and geniality that is one of the best reasons to visit Munich. All telephone numbers are in the 89 city code unless otherwise indicated.

### EXPENSIVE

**Bayerischer Hof–Palais Montgelas** Overlooking the verdant, flower-filled Promenadeplatz, this stately 442-room property has maintained its reputation for excellent service and high standards ever since once of its early guests, King Ludwig I, came here to bathe (the royal palace didn't have bathtubs). The bustle in the lobby is reminiscent of a movie set. There's a pool on the roof, and in the basement, *Trader Vic's* offers spareribs and Polynesian cocktails. The *Garden* restaurant is an idyllic oasis in summer (see *Eating Out*), while the baronial lounge—with its fireplace—is a warm refuge in winter. The guestrooms are equipped with plenty of amenities, including mini-bars. Business facilities include 24-hour room service, meeting rooms for up to 1,200, an English-speaking concierge, foreign currency exchange, secretarial services in English, audiovisual equipment, photocopiers, computers, cable TV news, translation services, and express checkout. 2-6 Promenadepl. (phone: 21200; 212900, reservations; 800-223-6800; fax: 212-0906).

**Grand Hotel Continental** Formerly the *Continental Royal Classic,* this 145-room property is a favorite of those who know the city well. Close to the center of town, it's still known affectionately as the *"Conti."* Filled with flowers and priceless antiques, the hotel is part of a group of buildings known as the *Kunstblock,* the center of the Munich art and antiques market. There are two restaurants, and business facilities include 24-hour room service, meeting rooms for up to 600, an English-speaking concierge, foreign currency exchange, secretarial services in English, audiovisual equipment, photocopiers, computers, cable TV news, translation services, and express checkout. 5 Max-Joseph-Str. (phone: 551570; fax: 551-57500).

**Hilton Park** Close to the picturesque *Englischer Garten,* this 500-room hostelry is designed to meet the particular needs of the international business traveler. There are several restaurants, a pool, a sauna, a shopping arcade, and a massive underground garage. Business facilities include 24-hour room service, meeting rooms for up to 1,000, an English-speaking concierge, foreign currency exchange, secretarial services in English, audiovisual equipment, photocopiers, computers, cable TV news, translation services, and express checkout. 7 Am Tucherpark (phone: 38450; 800-HILTONS; fax: 384-51845).

**Holiday Inn Crowne Plaza** A 360-room hotel on Schwabing's main thoroughfare, it's the home of the *Hamlet Light* disco (see *Nightclubs and Nightlife*), as well as a restaurant. Business facilities include 24-hour room service, meeting rooms for up to 600, an English-speaking concierge, foreign currency exchange, secretarial services in English, audiovisual equipment, photocopiers, computers, cable TV news, translation services, and express checkout. 194 Leopoldstr. (phone: 381790; 800-HOLIDAY; fax: 381-79888).

**Königshof** Despite its central location, this traditional and comfortable 132-room establishment is quiet. It also boasts one of Munich's best hotel restaurants, which has a great view of busy Karlsplatz. Business facilities include 24-hour room service, meeting rooms for up to 100, an English-speaking concierge, foreign currency exchange, secretarial services in English, audiovisual equipment, photocopiers, computers, cable TV news, translation services, and express checkout. 25 Karlspl. (phone: 551360; fax: 551-36113).

**Penta** Part of a European chain and designed to cut down on rapidly soaring hotel prices, this huge 740-room property caters to a predominantly business clientele. Guests carry their own baggage to their rooms. A unit in each room dispenses drinks, snacks, and even continental breakfast. There is an extensive shopping arcade and restaurant complex under the hotel, which is near the *Deutsches Museum*. Business facilities include meeting rooms for up to 600, an English-speaking concierge, foreign currency exchange, secretarial services in English, audiovisual equipment, photocopiers, computers, cable TV news, translation services, and express checkout. 3 Hochstr. (phone: 48030; fax: 4488-8277).

**Platzl** On the site of an old historic mill, this 170-room hotel has been modernized, with conveniences such as phones and mini-bars in all the guestrooms and a large parking garage. There's no restaurant, however. It's located in the center of the Altstadt, across the street from the *Hofbräuhaus* (see *Special Places*). Business facilities include 24-hour room service, meeting rooms for up to 120, an English-speaking concierge, foreign currency exchange, secretarial services in English, audiovisual equipment, photocopiers, computers, cable TV news, translation services, and express checkout. 1 Platzl (phone: 237030; fax: 237-03800).

**Queen's** Idyllically set on the right bank of the Isar River, near some of Munich's lushest greenery, this property offers 150 tastefully furnished rooms and a restaurant. Business facilities include 24-hour room service, meeting rooms for up to 320, an English-speaking concierge, foreign currency exchange, secretarial services in English, audiovisual equipment, photocopiers, computers, cable TV news, translation services, and express checkout. 99 Effnerstr. (phone: 927980; fax: 983813).

**Rafael** Centrally located, this elegant establishment occupies a remarkable 19th-century building that formerly housed ballrooms and then the *Antik Haus* art galleries. The 74 rooms and suites, as well as the public rooms, are decorated in a luxurious, late 19th-century style. *Mark's* is the intimate hotel dining room. There is a rooftop swimming pool with a sweeping view of the Bavarian capital. Business facilities include 24-hour room service, meeting rooms for up to 100, an English-speaking concierge, foreign currency exchange, secretarial services in English, audiovisual equipment, photocopiers, computers, cable TV news, translation services, and express checkout. 1 Neuturmstr. (phone: 290980; fax: 222539).

**Sheraton** East of the center of town, this 650-room link in the international chain is clearly geared to the convention trade. There's a restaurant, and business facilities include 24-hour room service, meeting rooms for up to 1,200, an English-speaking concierge, foreign currency exchange, secretarial services in English, audiovisual equipment, photocopiers, computers, cable TV news, translation services, and express checkout. 6 Arabellastr. (phone: 92640; 800-334-8484; fax: 916877).

**Vier Jahreszeiten Kempinski** In the mid-19th century, king and urban-planner Maximilian II mapped out the broad boulevard that now bears his name and commissioned this jewel of a hostelry for the wayside. Today, this grand, 325-room hotel (now part of the Kempinski chain) would still satisfy the whims of any sovereign. The *Vier Jahreszeiten,* whose name is German for "Four Seasons," is so close to Munich's theaters and opera that you can be wiping off the shaving cream as the house lights dim and still make it to your seat before the curtain goes up. After the show, join the cast for a drink in the basement bar, where the spectacle of people watching makes the *Jahresezeitenkeller* Munich's true center for the performing arts. Its restaurant is among the best in the city (see *Eating Out*). Business facilities include 24-hour room service, meeting rooms for up to 450, an English-speaking concierge, foreign currency exchange, secretarial services in English, audiovisual equipment, photocopiers, computers, cable TV news, translation services, and express checkout. 17 Maximilianstr. (phone: 230390; 800-426-3135; fax: 230-39693).

### MODERATE

**Biederstein** Probably Munich's quietest hostelry, this charming 32-room place is on the fringe of Schwabing, next to the *Englischer Garten.* There's no restaurant, but there is 24-hour room service. Business facilities include foreign currency exchange, an English-speaking concierge, secretarial services in English, and photocopiers. 18 Keferstr. (phone: 395072; fax: 348511).

**Daniel** A good value: Here are 85 plain but clean and comfortable guestrooms, plus a great location near the train and subway stations and within walking distance of most shopping. There's no restaurant. Business facilities include an English-speaking concierge, foreign currency exchange, and secretarial services in English. 5 Sonnenstr. (phone: 554945; fax: 553420).

**Englischer Garten** A homey guesthouse with 27 cheerfully decorated rooms, its location—overlooking a canal on one side and the beautiful *Englischer Garten* on the other—and its very reasonable rates make it popular with tourists. There's no restaurant. Business facilities include an English-speaking concierge and foreign currency exchange. 8 Liebergesellstr. (phone: 392034; fax: 391233).

**Intercity** This comfortable 260-room hotel is in the *Hauptbahnhof,* but it's surprisingly quiet. There's no restaurant. Business facilities include 24-hour room service, meeting rooms for up to 160, foreign currency exchange, an English-speaking concierge, secretarial services in English, audiovisual equipment, photocopiers, computers, cable TV news, translation services, and express checkout. 10 Bayerstr. (phone: 545560; fax: 596229).

**Leopold** This 80-room hotel, on the fringe of Schwabing, is in an old 19th-century house. The back wing is quieter and faces a garden. There's no restaurant. Business facilities include 24-hour room service, an English-speaking concierge, foreign currency exchange, secretarial services in English, and photocopiers. 119 Leopoldstr. (phone: 367061; fax: 893-67061).

**Letti** Centrally located, this hostelry has 35 rooms (ask for one in the newer wing). Breakfast is included in the room rate (there's a breakfast room, but no restaurant). Business facilities include 24-hour room service, an English-speaking concierge, foreign currency exchange, secretarial services in English, and photocopiers. 53 Amalienstr. (phone: 283026; fax: 280-5318).

**Mariahilf** A particular favorite with English tourists, this 25-room pension is in a quiet sector of the city across the Isar from central Munich. There's no restaurant. Business facilities include meeting rooms for up to 50, an English-speaking concierge, foreign currency exchange, and secretarial services in English. 83 Lilienstr. (phone: 484834; fax: 489-1381).

**Splendid** Alongside the calm Isar River, this pleasing little hotel is also close to the theater, museum, and shopping district. All 40 rooms are well equipped and unusually quiet. There's no restaurant, but 24-hour room service is available. Business facilities include an English-speaking concierge, foreign currency exchange, secretarial services in English, and photocopiers. 54 Maximilianstr. (phone: 296606; fax: 291-3176).

**Uhland** A charming little 37-room hotel in a lovely old building on a street near *Theresienwiese* (Theresa's Meadow). There's no restaurant. Business facilities include 24-hour room service, meeting rooms for up to 60, an English-speaking concierge, foreign currency exchange, and photocopiers. 1 Uhlandstr. (phone: 539277; fax: 531114).

**Mariandl** This charming pension near *Theresienwiese* has 25 quiet rooms and a restaurant famed for its classical music in the evenings. Business facilities include an English-speaking concierge and foreign currency exchange. 51 Goethestr. (phone: 534108 or 535158).

**Theresia** Very close to the museums, this well-run establishment has 24 rooms. There's no restaurant. Business facilities include an English-speaking concierge and foreign currency exchange. In Schwabing, 51 Luisenstr. (phone: 523-3081 or 521250; fax: 532323).

---

## EATING OUT

Bavarian cuisine is hearty and heavy, and most of it seems created to make you consume inordinate amounts of beer. *Leberknödel* (liver dumplings) are the most famous of more than four score Bavarian dumplings. *Leberkäse* translates as liver cheese but is neither; it's a baked pâté of beef and bacon. *Schweinswürstl mit Kraut* (pork sausages and sauerkraut) is another unforgettable local dish. Munich is the wurst (sausage) capital of the world. *Weisswurst,* a veal-based white sausage, is sold throughout the city by street vendors as well as in beer gardens. You'll also want to taste some of the local pretzels and salt rolls and sticks sold under such names as *Brez'n, Römische,* and *Salzstangerl.* Another specialty here is a large, tasty white *Radi* (radish), cut in spirals and sold with plenty of salt. If all of this makes you very thirsty, order *ein Mass Bier;* that's a liter. Otherwise, *eine Halbe* (a half liter) should suffice. If you need a break from Bavarian fare, you can choose from a wide variety of other ethnic foods, especially in the conglomeration of foreign restaurants in Schwabing, some of them the best in Germany.

Dining out can be expensive in Munich; even beer-hall fare, once the staple of budget-minded students, can add up quickly to $15, $18, or more. At expensive restaurants expect to pay a minimum of $85 for a meal for two, not including drinks or wine; $40 to $85 at places in the moderate price range; and less than $40 at the eateries we describe as inexpensive. Prices include taxes and tip, though you should leave an extra mark or two for good service. Unless noted otherwise, the restaurants listed are open for lunch and dinner and accept major credit cards. All telephone numbers are in the 89 city code unless otherwise indicated.

For an unforgettable dining experience we begin with our culinary favorite, followed by our cost and quality choices, listed by price category.

---

### DELIGHTFUL DINING

**Vier Jahreszeiten Kempinski** Everything about this restaurant is tastefully discreet, from its half-lit glow to its creamy decor and hushed carpeting. The dining room in the *Vier Jahreszeiten Kempinski* hotel offers Bavaria's most elegant and sophisticated fare, and when you've had the *Lachsforelle mit Kerbelsahne glaciert* (salmon trout glazed with chervil cream) or the *Kalbsfilet und Morcheln in Blätterteig* (filet of veal and morels in puff pastry in broccoli cream), you'll forget all about the last time you saw Paris. Closed Saturdays, Monday lunch, and August. Reservations necessary. 17 Maximilianstr. (phone: 230390).

### EXPENSIVE

**Boettner** A tiny wine restaurant in a high-ceilinged, paneled room behind a caviar-lobster shop, it has only about 10 tables and always is crowded. The specialty here is lobster. Closed Saturday evenings, Sundays, and holidays. Reservations necessary. 8 Theatinerstr. (phone: 221210).

**Garden** This elegant hotel dining room offers continental fare with Alsatian accents—onion quiche, baked scallops, smoked salmon lasagne in vermouth sauce, wurst and sauerkraut, and roasted venison·in red pepper sauce. Open daily. Reservations necessary. *Hotel Bayerischer Hof–Palais Montgelas,* 2-6 Promenadepl. (phone: 212-0993).

**Kaferschänke** What started out as a corner grocery store has worked itself up to one of Europe's largest delicatessens and Germany's biggest catering service, and now includes a popular restaurant upstairs over the sprawling store. You can get anything from *Presskopf* (homemade head cheese) to bass from the Mediterranean. Closed Sundays. Reservations advised. 73 Prinzregentenstr. (phone: 41680).

**Sabitzer** A favorite of Munich's beautiful people, decorated all in white with turn-of-the-century art hung on the walls, this fine, small spot serves nouvelle cuisine. Closed Sundays. Reservations advised. 21 Reitmorstr. (phone: 298584).

**Tantris** A thick aroma of truffles—scattered in paper-thin slices over a salad of scallops and leeks—hovers in this shrine of high-art cookery. The sleek decor is the perfect setting for the newest of nouvelle cuisine, streamlined dishes artfully composed from the day's market harvest by chef Hans Haas. Keeper of the wine cellar Paula Bosch, who presides over the annual gathering of Munich's nobly robed Knights of the Brotherhood of Bordeaux Wines, will also help you select the perfect accompaniment to your dinner. Closed Sundays and Mondays. Reservations advised. 7 Johann-Fichte-Str. (phone: 362061 or 362062; fax: 361-8469).

**Austernkeller** If you're marooned in landlocked Bavaria with a longing for seafood, descend into the vaulted Oyster Cellar. Here you'll find oysters of every type and temperature, smoked salmon, bouillabaisse, spits of grilled king prawns, lobster casseroles—probably even mackerel sherbet. The setting is Nautical Deco, the atmosphere is animated, almost raucous, and the place is great fun. If you have a play or a plane to catch, there's an oyster bar near the entrance where you can always grab six quick *fines de claire* and a glass of Muscadet. Closed Mondays. Reservations advised. 11 Stollbergstr. (phone: 298787).

**Bistro Terrine** The latest culinary vogue in Munich is the bistro, and this one is in the middle of swinging Schwabing. Its continental fare is complemented by the heady Mediterranean atmosphere. Closed Sundays and holidays. Reservations advised. 89 Amalienstr.; entrance is on Türkenstr. (phone: 281780).

**Goldene Stadt** Bohemian dishes are served in the four adjoining dining rooms here. A photomural of the Charles Bridge in Prague dominates the main dining room. Closed Sundays. Reservations advised. 44 Oberanger (phone: 264382).

**Halali** Not far from Schwabing, this eatery serves high-quality nouvelle cuisine with a hearty Bavarian touch at remarkably reasonable prices. Well-prepared game dishes are the house specialty. Closed Sundays. Reservations advised. 22 Schönfeldstr. (phone: 285909).

**Mifune** Ever since actor Toshiro Mifune opened this place, it's been a must for lovers of Japanese food. Closed Saturday evenings and Sundays. Reservations advised. 136 Ismaninger Str. (phone: 987572).

**Spatenhaus** A fine example of a typical Bavarian *Gaststätte* (inn), with its whitewashed walls, pine tables and chairs, and many cozy niches. A delicious dinner here might include roast duck, suckling pig, or hare with mushrooms in cream sauce; dessert could be the flaky apple strudel or crisp apple fritters. Open daily. No reservations. No credit cards accepted. 12 Residenzstr. (phone: 290-7060).

**Spöckmeier** This popular *Gasthaus*—which some say serves the best veal sausages in town—has two dining rooms: The vast, whitewashed and raftered hall downstairs bustles with shoppers and sightseers, and the smaller, paneled room upstairs hums with the quiet conversation of elegant drinkers. Closed Sundays from June through August. No reservations. No credit cards accepted. 9 Rosenstr., just off Marienpl. (phone: 268088).

**Weisses Bräuhaus** Perhaps the most traditional of Munich's restaurants, this inn has been serving hearty food and wheat beer at the same site for over 400 years. A best bet is the roast pork with dumplings. Open daily. No reservations. No credit cards accepted. 10 Tal (phone: 299875).

**Zum Alten Markt** Just a stone's throw from the colorful *Viktualienmarkt,* this downtown eatery is a must for lovers of good, but reasonably priced, continental fare. The emphasis is on fish and veal dishes. Closed Sundays and *Christmas* through mid-January. Reservations advised. No credit cards accepted. 3 Dreifaltigkeitspl. (phone: 299995).

## INEXPENSIVE

**Alte Börse** Nestled in a quiet passageway between two busy streets is this rare German hybrid—a café/restaurant that serves pastries and coffee or full-course dinners. True, it closes early and the menu is solidly German, but the pastries are heavenly continental concoctions. Try their famous Russian punch cake. Closed after 6 PM and Sundays. Reservations unnecessary. No credit cards accepted. Entrances on 3 Maffeistr. and 17-18 Schäfflerstr. (phone: 226795).

**Bratwurstherzl** Around the corner from the *Viktualienmarkt* (see *Special Places*), this is one of the last truly Bavarian establishments in swinging Munich. It serves only lunch—and be sure to be seated by 11 AM, since its traditional local specialties are very popular with *Müncheners.* Closed Sundays. No reservations. No credit cards accepted. 3 Heiliggeiststr. (phone: 226219).

**Donisl** A visit here is a Munich must: This centuries-old beer hall is where many *Müncheners* come for their daily brew and sausage ration, usually in the late morning. Open daily. No reservations. Next to the *Neues Rathaus.* 1 Weinstr., at Marienpl. (phone: 220184).

**Mariannenhof** At the edge of downtown Munich, this unpretentious place offers good food at reasonable prices in a comfortable atmosphere. Both continental and traditional Bavarian fare is served. Attached to the restaurant are a bar and a tavern. Closed Saturday and Sunday lunch. No reservations. No credit cards accepted. 1 Mariannenstr. (phone: 220864).

**Pfälzer Weinprobierstube** This tradition-laden wine cellar, located in the *Residenz* (see *Special Places*), features vintages from the Pfalz (Palatinate) region. The hearty food is also from that former part of Bavaria. Open daily. No reservations. No credit cards accepted. 1 Residenzstr. (phone: 225628).

**Sofia Grill** Somewhat off the beaten path—south of downtown and near the wholesale meat market—this friendly, casual eatery is well worth the trip. Though many of the dishes have a Bulgarian flavor—*shopska* salad with sheep's cheese, for example—the extensive menu also includes Balkan and Viennese entrées—Wiener schnitzel, goulash, and *rasniçi* (meat kebabs). Closed Mondays. Reservations unnecessary. No credit cards accepted. 157 Lindwurmstr. (phone: 775717).

## BIERGÄRTEN

One of the pleasures of summertime Munich is the garland of beer gardens strung out across the city—cool and companionable oases in the middle of the urban oven. Tree-shaded, open-air dining spaces with long wooden tables and benches, these reasonably priced establishments offer everything from just plain beer and pretzels to grilled chicken and barbecued spareribs. The air is redolent with eucalyptus and bratwurst, and *Müncheners* will loll for hours in these places, nursing a single stein of beer. Among the most characteristic: *Königliche Hirschgarten* (1 Hirschgarten; phone: 172591); *Taxisgarten* (12 Taxis; phone: 156827); *Augustiner* (on Neuhauser Str., near the *Hauptbahnhof;* no phone); and the sprawling *Menterschwaige Garten* (4 Menterschwaigstr.; phone: 640732), located outside of town on the banks of the Isar River.

# Oslo

## At-a-Glance

### SEEING THE CITY

There are spectacular views of the city and the Oslo Fjord from vantage points in Oslomarka, the hilly, wooded area on the east, north, and west of the city. Perhaps the best panorama is from *Tryvannstårnet*, a 390-foot observation tower on the 1,600-foot-high Tryvann Hill (see "Frognerseteren" in *Special Places*). The *Summit 21 Lounge & Bar* atop the *Radisson SAS Scandinavia* hotel (see *Checking In*) offers a fine view of the city from downtown. An even more stunning view can be found at *Plaza Sky Bar* (see *Nightclubs and Nightlife*), on the 33rd floor of the 37-story *Oslo Plaza* hotel, the tallest in Scandinavia.

### SPECIAL PLACES

In addition to the specific sights listed below, the city has a number of distinct areas of interest to travelers. Oslo Harbor's bustling Rådhus Gate (City Hall St.) is the site of many of the city's finest 17th- and 18th-century private and public residences. The streets directly behind the *Slottet* (Royal Palace), such as Inkognitogata and Oscars Gate, evoke images of Victorian Oslo. Called Homansbyen, this area is a protected historical enclave. In the late 19th century the district's well-heeled residents tried to outdo each other by building ever grander and more unusual houses. Drammensveien, the street just south of the *Slottet,* boasts many such buildings; some are still residences, but most are embassies or offices.

The Bygdøy peninsula offers a glimpse of modern Oslo's good life, with expensive homes and swimming beaches side-by-side with several maritime museums. The peninsula, which juts into the fjord southwest of the harbor, can be reached by bus No. 30 or, in summer, by one of the ferries that leave from near the *Rådhuset* (City Hall). To experience the Oslo of the outdoor enthusiast, take the tram up to Holmenkollen, where there are miles and miles of untouched forest and the world's widest network of ski trails.

### DOWNTOWN

**OSLO HAVN (OSLO HARBOR)** Stroll along the modern waterfront to see the graceful white cruise ships that ply the fjords along with ferries and private boats. In summer don't miss the chance to snack on tasty, tiny shrimp sold by fishermen who cook them aboard their boats.

**RÅDHUSET (CITY HALL)** A spacious square with fountains and sculpture separates this landmark from the harbor. Oslo's *City Hall* is lavishly embellished with contemporary Norwegian sculpture, woodcarvings, paintings, and tapestries. Free guided tours in English are available. Open daily May through September; closed Sundays the rest of the year. No admission charge. Rådhusplassen (phone: 22-861600).

**AKER BRYGGE** Oslo's "Fisherman's Wharf" is a favorite gathering point for residents and visitors. It features many little shops, fast-food stands and ethnic-food eateries, a theater, a multi-cinema complex with adjacent cafés, several major department stores, and pricey penthouse apartments. Underneath it all is a huge parking garage. There are outdoor jazz concerts in summer. On the waterfront near Rådhusplassen.

**AKERSHUS FESTNING OG SLOTT (AKERSHUS CASTLE AND FORTRESS)** Built by King Haakon V about 1300, this is one of the most important relics of medieval Norway. Rebuilt in Renaissance style under King Christian IV in the 17th century, it has been restored and now is used for state occasions and festivities; there also are Sunday afternoon concerts in the chapel. The ramparts offer a bird's-eye view of the harbor. Also in the complex is the stirring *Norges Hjemmefront Museet* (Norwegian Resistance Museum), with materials and memorabilia from the German occupation of Norway (1940–45) during World War II (phone: 22-403280; open daily; admission charge). The other fortress buildings are open daily from May 2 to September 15; Sunday afternoons only the rest of the year. Admission charge. Guided tours in English are available. The grounds are open daily; no admission charge. Entrance from Rådhus Gate, a short stroll from the *Rådhuset* (phone: 22-403917).

**DOMKIRKEN (OSLO CATHEDRAL)** Although both its exterior and interior have been restored since the cathedral was built in the late 17th century, the altarpiece and pulpit are original, dating from 1699. Also of interest are the bronze doors, the stained glass windows by Emanuel Vigeland, and the modernist ceiling decorations. Open daily. The former stables around the cathedral have been converted to small antiques shops and studios where artists and artisans create and sell their work. Stortorvet (phone: 22-412793).

**MINNEPARKEN (RUIN PARK)** The foundation stones of *Sankt Hallvard Kirke* (St. Hallvard Cathedral), along with archaeological excavations from medieval Oslo, can be seen in this park. At the park's edge is *Ladegård,* a private residence built in 1725 on the ruins of a bishop's palace dating from 1200. Call ahead for tour times. Open daily, the park is best reached by taxi or by tram No. 8 to St. Hallvards plass. Oslo Gate at Bispegata (phone: 22-194468).

**OSLO'S MARKETS** Three large, colorful outdoor markets are favorite spots for picture taking in the summer. Garden and greenhouse plants are sold in Stortorvet, a square near the cathedral; vegetables, fruits, and flowers are on sale in the other two squares, Grønland Torg and Youngstorget. All three markets are closed Sundays.

**GAMLE AKER KIRKE (OLD AKER CHURCH)** Built in 1100, this is by far the oldest building in Oslo and the oldest stone church in Scandinavia

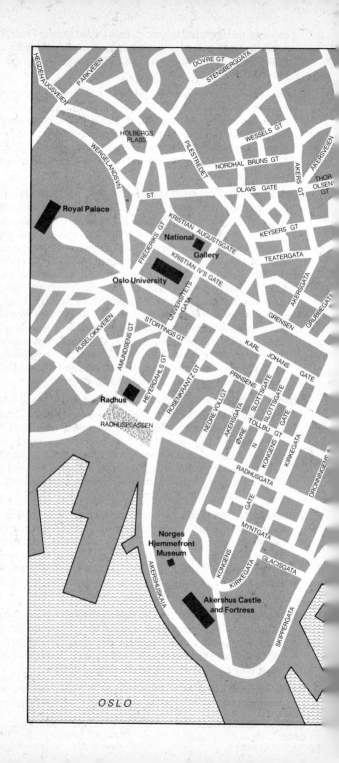

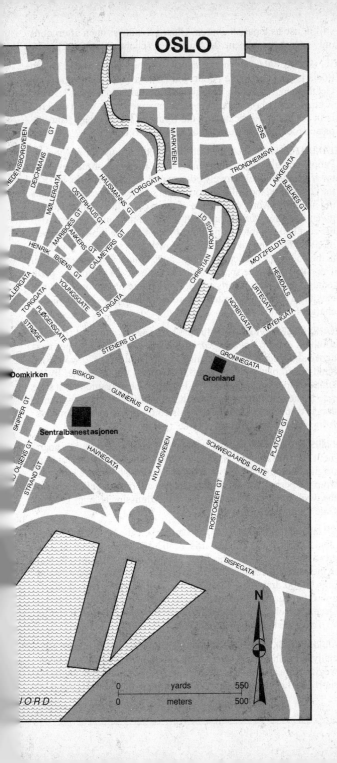

still in use as a parish church. Closed Sundays; open afternoons only or by appointment. 25 Akersveien (phone: 22-693582).

**SLOTTET (ROYAL PALACE)** The residence of King Harald V and Queen Sonja is not open to the public, but visitors can walk the grounds. Get there in time for the changing of the guard each day at 1:30 PM. A brass band plays during the ceremony weekdays when the king is in residence (indicated by the flying of his standard from the palace roof). At the west end of Karl Johans Gate.

**VIGELANDSLEGGET (VIGELAND SCULPTURE PARK)** A must for any visitor. People and animals sculpted in granite, iron, and bronze by Gustav Vigeland inhabit a lovely 80-acre park in western Oslo. In 1921 the city offered the brilliant Norwegian sculptor a free hand in carving his masterwork, a depiction of the cycle of human life. He was given a studio, workers, assistants, and all the funds he needed— the cost had run into the millions by the time the job was finished in 1943. Vigeland takes on birth, growth, joy, suffering, and death in the 650-piece collection of huge, nude figures in metal and stone. The park, a favorite spot of Oslo residents, has a swimming pool, tennis courts, and a sports arena. Two restaurants are open in summer and a cafeteria operates year-round. Open daily. No admission charge. Frogner.

**VIGELAND MUSEET (VIGELAND MUSEUM)** Just across the road from the southern end of *Vigeland Park* is Gustav Vigeland's former residence and studio, which contains 1,650 sculptures, 420 woodcuts, hundreds of plates for woodcuts, and some 11,000 sketches by the eminent Norwegian artist (1869–1943), whose romantic-realist style was in the tradition of the French sculptor Rodin. In the summer, concerts are held in the museum's courtyard. Closed Mondays. Admission charge. 32 Nobels Gate (phone: 22-441136).

**IBSEN MUSEET (IBSEN MUSEUM)** This was the famous playwright's apartment from 1895 until his death in 1906. Only his study contains original belongings, but the rest of the furnishings are authentic from the period. Closed Mondays; open afternoons only the rest of the week for guided tours on the hour. Admission charge. 1 Arbins Gate (phone: 22-552009).

**MUNCH MUSEET (MUNCH MUSEUM)** Edvard Munch, the Norwegian expressionist painter and graphic artist (1863–1944), bequeathed all his art to the city of Oslo. This light, airy, spacious museum was built in the eastern section of the city to house the almost 1,100 oil paintings, 4,500 drawings, 15,000 prints, and notes, letters, sketches, and other materials in the collection. Open daily June through December; closed Mondays the rest of the year. Admission charge. 53 Tøyen Gate (phone: 22-673774).

**DE NATURHISTORISKE MUSEER (NATURAL HISTORY MUSEUMS)** Children especially enjoy this group of excellent museums, with displays of Norwegian flora and fauna. Closed Mondays. No admission charge. A short stroll from the *Munch Museet* through the *Botanisk Hage og*

*Museum* (Botanical Gardens), 1 Sars Gate, Tøyen (phone: 22-851600).

**NASJONALGALLERIET (NATIONAL GALLERY)** Norway's principal art collection focuses on Norwegian artists, but there is a representative sample of international artists, particularly the French Impressionists. A star attraction is Edvard Munch's most famous opus, *Skriket* (The Scream; 1893), which was brazenly stolen in early 1994 and recovered three months later. Closed Tuesdays. No admission charge. 13 Universitets Gate (phone: 22-200404).

**ASTRUP FEARNLEY MUSEET FOR MODERNE KUNST (ASTRUP FEARNLEY MUSEUM OF MODERN ART)** Oslo's newest museum features changing exhibits of postwar works by Norwegian and international artists. Guided tours in English are available. Closed Mondays. Admission charge. 9 Grev Wedels Plass; enter at Dronningens Gate (phone: 22-936060).

**MUSEET FOR SAMTIDSKUNST (MUSEUM OF CONTEMPORARY ART)** This branch of the *Nasjonalgalleriet* (National Gallery) is devoted to modern paintings, sculpture, and photography. The innovative collection is updated annually so that it only includes works from the last 40 years; older acquisitions go to the *Nasjonalgalleriet*. The stately building was formerly a bank. Closed Mondays. No admission charge. 4 Bankplassen (phone: 22-335820).

**UNIVERSITAS OSLOENSIS (OSLO UNIVERSITY)** The main attraction at the university—also known in Norwegian as the *Universitetet i Oslo*—is the old festival hall, called the *Aula,* with its Munch paintings. Located at the downtown campus, this is where the award ceremony for the Nobel Peace Prize usually takes place in December (all the other Nobels are presented in Stockholm). For visiting times contact the *Norway Information Center* (see *Tourist Information* below). No admission charge. 47 Karl Johans Gate.

THE PENINSULA

**VIKINGSKIPSHUSET (VIKING SHIPS HOUSE)** Three longships, the *Gokstad,* the *Tune,* and the *Oseberg,* from AD 800–900, will take you back to the days when Vikings roamed the seas. The upswept prow of the *Oseberg,* with a striking pattern of carved animals, represents the finest workmanship of the period. The museum also has collections of utensils, gold and silver jewelry, and other objects from the Viking period. Open daily. Admission charge. 35 Huk Aveny (phone: 22-438379).

**NORSK FOLKEMUSEUM (NORWEGIAN FOLK MUSEUM)** Some 150 wooden buildings from all over Norway have been placed in a charming park near the *Vikinskipshuset.* One of the museum's treasures is a hand-hewn wooden stave church from 1200. Also on view are household furniture and utensils from various periods and a collection of antique toys. Park open daily; buildings open daily from March through October. Admission charge. 10 Museumsveien (phone: 22-437020).

**KON-TIKI MUSEET (KON-TIKI MUSEUM)** The balsa raft *Kon-Tiki,* used by Thor Heyerdahl and his crew on their 1947 voyage east across the Pacific Ocean, is preserved here along with Easter Island statues and an underwater shark exhibit. Also on display is the papyrus boat *Ra II,* on which Heyerdahl crossed the Atlantic Ocean in 1970. Open daily. Admission charge. 36 Bygdøynesveien, Bygdøy; take the No. 30 bus from downtown or the ferry from the *Rådhuset* (phone: 22-438050).

**NORSK SJØFARTSMUSEUM (NORWEGIAN MARITIME MUSEUM)** Norway's long maritime tradition is recalled by the collections here. Among the most fascinating exhibits are the authentic ships' interiors. Outside the building is Roald Amundsen's Polar ship, *Gjøa,* the first vessel to navigate a northwest passage, a feat accomplished in 1903–06. Guided tours (in English) are available. Open daily. Admission charge. A short walk from the *Kon-Tiki Museet,* 37 Bygdøynesveien, Bygdøy (phone: 22-438240).

**POLARSKIPET FRAM (POLAR SHIP FRAM MUSEUM)** The third ship museum in the area houses the *Fram,* built for Fridtjof Nansen's polar expedition of 1893–96 and also used by Roald Amundsen on his voyage to the South Pole in 1910–12. Closed January and February. Admission charge. Bygdøy (phone: 22-438370).

SUBURBS

**SKIMUSEET (SKI MUSEUM)** The world's oldest ski museum is inside the takeoff structure on the giant Holmenkollen ski-jumping hill. The collection traces the history of skiing from the ski tip found in a bog and believed to be some 2,500 years old to modern equipment. Open daily. Admission charge. A 20-minute ride by the *Holmenkollen Railway* from central Oslo and a 10-minute walk from the *Holmenkollen Station.* 5 Kongeveien, Holmenkollen (phone: 22-923200).

**FROGNERSETEREN** A 20- to 30-minute walk up the hill from the *Skimuseet* will take you 1,460 feet above sea level to a lookout point with a panoramic view of Oslo and the fjord. There's a cozy lodge-restaurant here, the *Frognerseteren Kafé* (see *Eating Out*). Another 20 minutes of uphill walking brings you to the 390-foot-high *Tryvannstårnet,* the highest lookout tower in Scandinavia (or take the *Holmenkollen Railway* to *Voksenkollen* station). Tower open daily. Admission charge. Holmenkollen. (phone: 22-146711).

**EMANUEL VIGELAND MUSEET (EMANUEL VIGELAND MUSEUM)** This small, two-room, church-like museum was built and decorated by Emanuel Vigeland, artist Gustav's younger brother. The most notable work is the main chamber's principal fresco, entitled *Vita.* Open Sunday afternoons only. No admission charge. 8 Grimelundsveien, a seven-minute walk from the *Slemdal* stop on the *Holmenkollen Railway* (phone: 22-149342).

**INTERNASJONALE BARNEKUNST MUSEET (CHILDREN'S ART MUSEUM)** A collection of 70,000 children's drawings, paintings, ceramics, and sculpture from around the world. There are workshop and musical activities for children; adults will enjoy the museum, too. Closed Mondays, Fridays, Saturdays, and mid-August to September 9. Admission charge. 4 Lille Frøens vei (*Frøen* stop—on request—on the *Holmenkollen Railway*; phone: 22-468573).

**NIELS ONSTADS–SONJA HENIE KUNSTSENTER (NIELS ONSTAD–SONJA HENIE ART CENTER)** Located 7 miles (11 km) west of Oslo near *Fornebu Airport,* the recently expanded center houses a permanent collection of 20th-century art donated by the international skating star and her husband. Included are works by Picasso, Miró, Villon, and Munch. Exhibitions and lectures on current trends in film, music, architecture, literature, and applied arts are scheduled regularly. One room features Sonja Henie's trophies and prizes. Open daily. Admission charge. Reached by bus from central Oslo. 31 Sonja Henies vei (phone: 67-543050).

**EKEBERG PARK** There's a fine view of Oslo and the fjord from this park's 685-foot hill, the site where the oldest works of art in the city—Stone Age carvings some 3,000 years old—were found in 1915. The rock carvings can be seen between the *Merchant Navy Academy* here and Kongsveien. Just southeast of the city, the park is easily reached by the *Ljabru* tram (lines 1 and 8).

**TUSENFRYD** The name of Oslo's amusement park means "A Thousand Delights." It has a roller coaster, clowns, music, miniature golf, movie theaters, restaurants, and more. Open from May through September; call for hours. Admission charge. *Dyreparken* in east Oslo—take E6 south to E18, or catch the free buses leaving hourly from the *Rådhuset* (phone: 64-946363).

# Sources and Resources

## TOURIST INFORMATION

The *Norges Informasjonssenter* (Norway Information Center; 1 Vestbaneplassen; phone: 22-830050; fax: 22-838150) is located at *Vestbanen,* the large yellow building between the Aker Brygge wharf and the *Rådhuset.* The office provides free information and maps. It's open daily in summer, weekdays only in winter. Another smaller tourist information office at *Oslo S* (Central Station; 2 Jernbanetorget) is open daily and can help you with hotel reservations (see *Checking In*). Guide service can be arranged by calling 22-427020. The *Oslo Kortet* (Oslo Card) is a pass that combines admission to museums and tourist sites, unlimited travel on all public transportation, free or discounted car parking, reduced fees on sightseeing tours, lower fares for train travel to or from Oslo, and other discounts. Cards—available for one day (110 krone, or about $16), two days (190 krone/$28), or three days (240 krone/$35)—are sold at the *Norway Information Center*, as well as at hotels, campsites, and other locations. Children's cards are half-price. The *US Embassy and Consulate* is at 18 Drammensveien (phone: 22-448550).

In the US, contact the *Norwegian Tourist Board* (655 Third Ave., New York, NY 10017; phone: 212-949-2333; fax: 212-983-5260). The *Norwegian Embassy* is at 2720 34th St. NW, Washington, DC 20008 (phone: 202-333-6000).

**ENTRY REQUIREMENTS** A US citizen needs a current passport for a stay of up to 90 days. The 90-day period begins on the date of entry into any one of the Nordic countries, which besides Norway include Denmark, Finland, Iceland, and Sweden.

**TIME** The time in Norway is six hours later than in US East Coast cities. Norway follows daylight saving time.

**LANGUAGE** Norwegian is the national language. English is common-place among the younger generation and those in the tourist industry.

**ELECTRIC CURRENT** 220 volts, 50 cycles, AC.

**MONEY** The Norwegian krone (NOK) equals 100 øre. The exchange rate at press time was 6.72 krone to the US dollar.

**TIPPING** Between 2 and 3 NOK is the usual tip for bellhops, porters, chambermaids (per night), and cloakroom personnel. A 15% service charge usually is added to restaurant bills.

**BANKING/BUSINESS HOURS** Most banks are open weekdays from 8:15 AM to 3:30 PM, Thursdays to 5 PM. During the summer, banks close weekdays at 3 PM. Most other businesses are open weekdays from 8 or 9 AM to 3 or 4 PM.

**NATIONAL HOLIDAYS** *New Year's Day* (January 1), *Maundy Thursday* (April 13), *Good Friday* (April 14), *Easter Sunday* (April 16), *Easter Monday* (April 17), *Labor Day* (May 1), *Constitution Day* (May 17), *Ascension Thursday* (May 25), *Whitmonday* (June 5), *Christmas Day* (December 25), and *Boxing Day* (December 26).

**LOCAL COVERAGE** The monthly English-language guide *What's On in Oslo* lists special attractions such as concerts and sporting events. There's also the more comprehensive but less timely *Oslo Guide,* published annually. Both are available at most hotels, travel agencies, and at the tourist office. Oslo has an English-language monthly newspaper, *The Norway Tribune,* and American and British periodicals as well as the *International Herald Tribune* are widely available; look for them at *Narvesen* kiosks. *Aftenposten,* one of Norway's foremost newspapers, carries a summary of the day's news in English in the summer. "Norway Today," an English-language radio broadcast with international news and features, is aired daily at 7 AM, 9 AM, 7 PM, and 9 PM; tune to 93 FM.

**TELEPHONE** The main city code for Oslo and surrounding area is 22, but the codes for some areas are 82 or 67. City codes are incorporated into all eight-digit numbers and always must be included, regardless of where the call is made. Telephone numbers in this chapter include city codes. The country code for Norway is 47. In an emergency, dial 003 for an ambulance; 002 for the police.

# GETTING AROUND

**AIRPORT** *Fornebu Lufthavn* (Fornebu Airport), which handles domestic and international flights, is a 20-minute trip from downtown. Buses (phone: 67-596220) operate between the airport and the *Oslo M* bus station on the ground floor of the *Galleri Oslo* on Biskop Gunnerusgate; the central railway station, *Oslo S;* the *Radisson SAS Park Royal* hotel; the *Radisson SAS Scandinavia* hotel; and the *Nasjonaltheateret* (National Theater) on Stortings Gate.

 *Gardermoen Lufthavn* (Gardermoen Airport), 33 miles (51 km) north of the city, handles charters as well as all nonstop transatlantic flights and is scheduled for expansion. The trip downtown takes almost an hour and can be very expensive by taxi. Bus service at a fraction of the price operates between the airport and downtown.

**CAR RENTAL** All major American and European firms are represented.

**FERRY AND BOATS** Boats and ferries leave from various piers along the harbor. For information on timetables, call the *Norway Information Center* (see *Tourist Information* above).

**SUBWAY (T-BANE), TRAM, AND BUS** The main bus terminal is *Oslo M* at the *Galleri Oslo* shopping complex on Biskop Gunnerusgate. Most of the buses running through the city center stop at Wessels Plass and by Universitetsplassen (University Square), or at the *Nasjonaltheateret.* The city *T-Bane* (subway) has eight lines and there are five tram lines. The *Nasjonaltheateret* and the *Stortinget* stations are the central stops for most electrified trams and the suburban railway to the forested park areas on the outskirts of Oslo. Standard fare for the *T-Bane*, trams, and buses is 15 krone (about $2.20) and half that for children. A "flexicard" of eight tickets costs 100 krone ($14.90), and a pass for a day of unlimited public transportation costs 30 krone ($4.40). For more information about public transportation timetables and fares contact the *Norway Information Center* or *Trafikanten,* the transportation information center at the main entrance to the *Oslo S* train station at Jernbanetorget (phone: 22-177030).

 *Note:* Public transportation in Oslo operates on an honor system, with occasional spot checks. Travel without a valid ticket results in a hefty fine. If you are using a discount card, be sure to validate it in the special machines on the waiting platforms or in the buses and trams themselves.

**TAXI** You can call a taxi by dialing 22-388090, or find one at any taxi stand. You can hail a cab on the street, but drivers are not allowed to pick up passengers near a taxi stand. When ordering a cab by phone, be sure to call at least an hour ahead (phone: 22-388080). For transportation for the disabled call 22-388070.

**TRAIN** Oslo has one major railway station, the *Sentralbanestasjonen,* or *Oslo S,* in the Jernbanetorget railway square at the end of Karl Johans Gate. It has a bank, a post office, a tourism and accommodations center, a restaurant, cafés, and kiosks. The *Nasjonaltheateret* station and the main *Stortinget* subway station handle local trains to Skien, Moss, Eidsvoll, and other destinations. For all train information call 22-171400.

## LOCAL SERVICES

**DENTIST (ENGLISH-SPEAKING)** *Oslo Kommunale Tannlegevakt* (near *Tøyen Center,* 18 Kolstadgate; phone: 22-673000) offers emergency dental care from 8 to 11 PM and also from 11 AM to 2 PM on weekends and holidays.

**DRY CLEANER** Most Oslo dry cleaners take a week and are generally very expensive ($10 for a pair of pants). *Oslo American Rens* (1 Griniveien; phone: 22-505741) offers 24-hour service.

**LIMOUSINE SERVICE** *Bislet Limousine* (10 Hoffsveien; phone: 22-570057; fax: 22-732833).

**MEDICAL EMERGENCY** *Legevakt* (40 Storgata; phone: 22-117070), open 24 hours. For ambulance service dial 003.

**MESSENGER SERVICE** *Securitas Express A/S* (51 Ostensjøveien; phone: 22-681120).

**NATIONAL/INTERNATIONAL COURIER** *DHL Worldwide Express* (10 Oksenøyveien, Lysaker; phone: 67-525500). Some Oslo hotels also offer courier service.

**PHARMACY** *Jernbanetorget Apotek* (4B Jernbanetorget; phone: 22-412482), open 24 hours; ring the doorbell at night.

**PHOTOCOPIES** *Rank Xerox* (11 Gjerdrumsveien; phone: 22-953000; fax: 22-953001).

**POST OFFICE** The main post office (15 Dronningensgt.; phone: 22-407802) is open weekdays from 8 AM to 8 PM and Saturdays from 9 AM to 3 PM; there also is a branch at 1 Jernbanetorget (phone: 22-407399).

**SECRETARY/STENOGRAPHER (ENGLISH-SPEAKING)** *Manpower A/S* (10 Dronning Mauds Gate; phone: 22-835100).

**TRANSLATOR** *Forenede Translatorer* (15 Kongens Gate; phone: 22-425640).

**OTHER** Convention information and facilities: *Chamber of Commerce* (30 Drammensveien; phone: 22-557400); *Oslo Convention Bureau* (4 Grev Wedels Plass; phone: 22-334386; fax: 22-334389). Formal wear rental: *Diva Utleiesalong* (3 Professor Dahls Gate; phone: 22-600002).

## SPECIAL EVENTS

In January the *Monolitten* (Monolith Meet), a major cross-country ski race, takes place in the *Vigelandsanlegget* (Vigeland Sculpture Park). The annual *Holmenkollen Skifestival,* which attracts the cream of the world's cross-country skiers and ski jumpers, occurs in March. *Holmenkollendagen* (Holmenkollen Day) is the last Sunday of the festival, when as many as 100,000 spectators make their way to the

*Holmenkollbakken* (Holmenkollen Ski Jump) to watch a special competition. *Påske* (Easter) is a special time of year for Norwegians, and most towns and cities are deserted over the long holiday weekend as the entire population takes off for a last fling on the slopes—something a traveler should keep in mind. A few major hotels and restaurants may remain open, but the majority are closed. *Grunnslovsdagen* (Constitution Day, May 17) is Norway's biggest holiday and one of the few days each year when national dress is worn. The children's parade up Karl Johans Gate to the *Slottet* (Royal Palace) is the highlight of the celebration. Hotel reservations must be made very far in advance. One of Norway's favorite events is *Sankthansaften* (Midsummer Night's Eve, June 21). Bonfires are lit everywhere on this festive evening. The *Bislet Games,* world class track and field events held each July at *Bislet Stadion* (Bislet Stadium), attract top international athletes. July is the main summer vacation month in Norway, and Oslo is pitiably devoid of Norwegians during these weeks. Each year in December, the Nobel Peace Prize is presented at *Oslo University* (see *Special Places*).

## MUSEUMS

In addition to those listed in *Special Places,* other notable Oslo museums include the following:

**HISTORISK MUSEET (HISTORICAL MUSEUM)** The university's collection of antiquities. Closed Mondays. No admission charge. 2 Frederiks Gate (phone: 22-859300).

**KUNSTINDUSTRIMUSEET (MUSEUM OF APPLIED ART)** Applied art—including crafts, design, and costumes—from the Middle Ages to the present. Closed Mondays. Admission charge. 1 St. Olavs Gate (phone: 22-203578).

**NORSK TEKNISK MUSEET (NORWEGIAN SCIENCE AND INDUSTRY MUSEUM)** Science and technology exhibits, including many working models. Open daily in July; closed Mondays the rest of the year. Admission charge. 143 Kjelsåsveien, Etterstad (phone: 22-222550).

**NORSK TOLLMUSEET (NORWEGIAN CUSTOMS MUSEUM)** The *Customs House,* depicted in exhibitions and models. Open Tuesday and Thursday afternoons. No admission charge. 1A Tollbugate (phone: 22-860999).

**POSTMUSEET (POSTAL MUSEUM)** Covering three centuries of communications. Open weekdays. No admission charge. 20 Kirkegate (phone: 22-408059).

**TEATERMUSEET I OSLO (OSLO THEATER MUSEUM)** Historic costumes, set designs, and props from Oslo's theater productions. Open Sunday afternoons and Wednesdays from 11 AM to 3 PM. Admission charge. 1 Nedre Slottsgate (phone: 22-418147).

## SHOPPING

Oslo is not a haven for bargain hunters. Prices are high, but you can get good value for your dollar if you concentrate on typically Norwegian items: arts and crafts, pewter, enameled silver, ski sweaters, and Norwegian blue fox and black Saga mink fur coats. Major department stores carry many of the same items as specialty shops do, often at lower prices. Shops generally are open 9 AM to 5 PM (department stores from 10 AM to 6 PM) on weekdays; to 6 or 7 PM on Thursdays. Most stores close at 1 or 2 PM on Saturdays. The *Oslo City* shopping complex (1 Stenergate) is open weekdays from 9 AM to 8 PM and Saturdays from 9 AM to 6 PM; its restaurants are open daily.

There are three main traditional shopping areas. The first is downtown Oslo, along Karl Johans Gate from Jernbanetorget to the *Slottet* (Royal Palace) and adjacent streets. One chic little shopping center in the area is *Paléet,* tucked into the northwest side of Karl Johan (enter at Nos. 37-41).

Another popular shopping district is Victoria Terrasse (called Vika by locals), a few minutes' walk from downtown Oslo, south of the *Slottet.* Built just before the turn of the century, this rather elite plaza was named after England's Queen Victoria. Its exclusive shops and colorful boutiques make it a favorite strolling area.

The third shopping district is along Bogstadveien Gate, linking the northernmost corner of the grounds of the *Slottet* with Majorstua, a major transportation crossroads north of downtown. Its attractive shops and boutiques make the street a favorite with Oslo's well-to-do, and its site off the beaten track means few tourist items.

Among the fine assortment of shops and boutiques in Oslo, we suggest the following:

**Brødrene Thorkildsen** For fine furs. 8 Øvre Slottsgate (phone: 22-332105).

**Brukskunstsentret i Basarhallene** A string of small crafts stores and workshops behind the *Domkorken* (Oslo Cathedral). Dronningensgate and Karl Johans Gate.

**David Andersen** Synonymous with Norwegian silver, and particularly noted for enameled silver. 20 Karl Johans Gate (phone: 22-416955) and in *Oslo City* (phone: 22-170934).

**Erik W. Abelson** An elegant little boutique for Scandinavian crystal, bronze, and silver jewelry, as well as tableware, wooden items, fabrics, and more. 27 Skovveien (phone: 22-555594).

**Format** Unusual designs in textiles, ceramics, glass, jewelry, and furniture by contemporary Norwegian artists. Closed Mondays, but open Sundays. In the *Norway Information Center,* 1 Vestbaneplassen (phone: 22-837312; fax: 22-837313).

**Freia** Norway's favorite chocolatier. 31 Karl Johans Gate (phone: 22-427466).

**GlasMagasinet** One of Oslo's most tempting department stores, renowned for having the city's best selection of crystal and tableware. 9 Stortorvet (phone: 22-425305).

**Husfliden** Norway's "official" arts and crafts shop offers homespun fabrics, hand-sewn clothing, wooden utensils, and pewterware. 4 Møllergaten (phone: 22-421075).

**J. Tostrup** The capital's oldest silverworks shop, with an adjacent boutique. 20 Karl Johans Gate, second floor, above *David Andersen* (phone: 22-428534).

**Maurtua** A less expensive alternative to *William Schmidt* (see below), featuring hand-knit sweaters and a variety of Norwegian souvenirs. 9 Fr. Nansens Plass (phone: 22-413164).

**N. M. Thune** Pewter in every conceivable form. 12 Ø. Slottsgate (phone: 22-414115).

**Norway Crafts** A fine selection of traditional pewterware, wooden items, ceramics, jewelry, and more. Closed Mondays, but open Sundays. Beside the *Norway Information Center*, 2 Vestbaneplassen (phone: 22-832480).

**Norway Designs** Ceramics, glassware, jewelry, clothing, and decorative art—all by Scandinavian designers. 28 Stortingsgate—downstairs (phone: 22-831100).

**Oslo Sweater Shop** For the largest selection of sweaters in town. At the *Radisson SAS Scandinavia* hotel, 5 Tullinsgate (phone: 22-112922), and the *Royal Christiania* hotel, 3 B. Gunnerus Gate (phone: 22-424225).

**Steen & Strøm** The department store for everything from eiderdowns, clothing, and cosmetics to ski gear and Scandinavian deli items. 23 Kongensgate (phone: 22-004000).

**Tanum** Oslo's best bookstore, with a huge English-language section. The place to buy travel guides, Scandinavian cookbooks, maps, translations of Norse sagas, and Norwegian classics. 37 Karl Johans Gate (phone: 22-411100).

**William Schmidt & Co.** Norwegians think it's overpriced, but visitors love the wide selection of high-quality items—sweaters, gift items, and more. 41 Karl Johans Gate (phone: 22-420288).

## SPORTS AND FITNESS

**BOATING** Sailing or boating on the Oslo Fjord can be a delightful experience. *Norway Yacht Charter* (1 H. Heyerdahlsgate; phone: 22-426498; fax: 22-426232) offers large sailboats with crews. Smaller boats, sailboats, and canoes can be rented by the hour, day, or week. Inquire at the *Norway Information Center* for current listings.

**CAMPING** Two campsites are close to the city. *Ekeberg Camping* (phone: 22-198568) is at Ekebergsletta, less than 2½ miles (4 km) from the center of town, and offers a great view of Oslo and the fjord. It has a riding school, a children's pool, a recreation and sports ground, a kiosk, and a shop, and is open from June through August. *Bogstad Camping* (phone: 22-507680; fax: 22-500162), near Bogstad Lake about 6 miles (10 km) from the city, is open all year and has winter-insulated cabins for rent. It also has shops, a cafeteria, a post office (open only in summer), a gas station, and other conveniences.

**CURLING** There are several curling clubs in Oslo, and members of foreign clubs are welcome to use their rinks. For information contact the *Norges Curlingforbund* (Norwegian Curling Association; phone: 67-154700).

**CYCLING** Cycling is enjoyable in the wooded Oslomarka area. Suggested cycle tours of the area can be obtained from the *Norges Cykleforbund* (Norwegian Cycling Association; 60 Maridalsvn.; phone: 22-719293). Many local tourist offices and hotels rent bicycles, as does *Den Rustne Eike* (near the *Norway Information Center* at Vestbanen; phone: 22-837231; fax: 22-836359). Be prepared to leave a credit card imprint or pay a hefty refundable deposit.

**FISHING** There is good trout fishing in the hills north of Oslo. A fishing license is available for a fee at local sports stores, but first a national permit must be purchased at a post office. *Pimpling* (ice fishing) is popular in the Oslomarka area and on the Oslo Fjord when the ice is safe. Bring your own equipment, as it can't be rented.

**FITNESS CENTERS** *Friskoteket A/S* (9A Bogstadveien; phone: 22-460090) has weights and exercise equipment, squash courts, a sauna, and a staff physical therapist. *High Energy* (10 Osterhausgate; phone: 22-360600) is an American-style gym, and *Friskis & Svetlis* (16 Munkedamsveien; phone: 22-609165) is *the* place for aerobics. For a low-impact workout try *Fitness Network* (2 Olaf Helsets Vei; phone: 22-297016). Larger hotels, like the *Radisson SAS Scandinavia* (see *Checking In*), have facilities on the premises. Guests at the *Oslo Plaza* hotel (see *Checking In*) can enjoy fabulous views while working out on the 35th floor, which has a sauna, a solarium, a pool, and a fitness room.

**GOLF** The best-known links are the *Oslo Golfklubb*'s *Bogstad* golf course, near Bogstad Lake and the Bogstad camping grounds (phone: 22-504402). To play visitors must show membership in an established golf club and pay greens fees; equipment may be rented. Also try *Groruddalen* golf club at Tokeruddalen (phone: 22-216718).

**HIKING** There is a network of about 1,860 miles of paths for hikers in the Oslo area. July and August are the best months for mountain walking. *Midtstuen* and *Frognerseteren* stations on the *Holmenkollen Railway* are good starting points. *Den Norske Turistforening* (*DNT;* Norwegian Tourism Association; 28 Stortings Gate; phone: 22-832550 or 82-052020) publishes excellent maps with suggested routes; *DNT* also will organize group tours with guides and reasonably priced lodging in mountain huts.

**ICE SKATING** The skating season lasts from December to mid-March. There are some 150 city-maintained outdoor rinks. There is also a rink open to the public from mid-October to mid-March at *Valle Hovin*, a sports ground in an eastern section of Oslo known as Bryn (phone: 22-657937). Admission to the rinks is free, but there is a small fee for the use of changing rooms. Ice hockey, speed skating, and figure skating competitions are held frequently at the *Bislet, Frogner,* and *Jordal Amfi* stadiums and the *Oslo Spektrum,* a 9,000-

seat arena near the *Oslo City* shopping center. Details of such events are listed in *What's On in Oslo* (see *Local Coverage*).

**JOGGING** A good choice is *Frognerparken,* five to 10 minutes from downtown. For a more rural setting, try any of the paths at *Holmenkollen* (*Holmenkollen Railway* to *Frognerseteren* stop). Many paths are clearly marked with destination and distance. *Nordmarka,* about 20 minutes north of Oslo, is a wilderness area ideally suited for joggers who wish to escape the crowds.

**SKIING** Skiing is the national pastime in Norway, and Oslo maintains more than 1,300 miles of ski trails through the woods and hills of Oslomarka. These are primarily for cross-country skiing, but hills for ski jumping and alpine skiing are available, too. Most alpine hills, including the popular *Tryvannskleiva,* are lighted for night skiing. Many of the choice spots are only a short ride by bus or suburban railway from downtown Oslo. The *Sognsvann Railway* line goes to Lake Sognsvann, a starting point for ski tourers. Buses leave the capital about every hour for Skansebakken in the Sørkedalen district and Skar in the Maridalen district, two other convenient starting points for cross-country skiers. There also are buses to such slalom centers as *Kirkerudbakken* in neighboring Baerum and Ingierkollen at Kolbotn. *Tomm Murstad's* ski school (at Øvreseter, near the *Voksenkollen* terminal of the *Holmenkollen Railway;* phone: 22-144124) is one of several that rents equipment and provides instruction in cross-country and slalom skiing. Information on skiing and related activities in the Oslo area is available from the *Skiforeningen* (Ski Association; 5 Kongev.; phone: 22-923200).

**SWIMMING** Besides several beaches on the Bygdøy peninsula, there are a number of public swimming pools, including an outdoor pool, *Frognerbadet,* at *Vigelandparken* with a spacious lawn surrounding it and a slide complex for kids (28 Middelthunsgate; phone: 22-447429). There are nudist bathing beaches on the northeast side of Svartkulp, a small lake north of Oslo; outside the city on the south side of Langøyene in Oslo Harbor, reached by ferry from the Oslo docks; and on the south side of Bygdøy, near Huk. Three public swimming pools near the center of the city are *Tøyenbadet* (90 Helgesens Gate; phone: 22-671889), *Bislet Bad* (60 Pilestredet; phone: 22-464176), and *Engergibadet* (1 Sommerogate; phone: 22-440726); all have saunas.

**WINDSURFING** The most popular area is around Bygdøy peninsula. Rent equipment from *Seasport Sportscenter* (1 Dronning Mauds Gate; phone: 22-837928). You can also windsurf and rent equipment at the *Bogstad* campground near Bogstad Lake, about 6 miles (10 km) from Oslo (phone: 22-507680). Instruction is available.

## THE GREAT OUTDOORS

Land Rover excursions through the Oslo forests, including rambling, canoeing, and fishing in the summer and skiing and tobogganing in the winter, are

offered to adventureous visitors. Half- and full-day
programs are available; make arrangements through
the *Norway Information Center* (see *Tourist Information,* above).

## THEATER

Programs are published in the daily press and in *What's On in Oslo.*
Most performances start at 7:30 PM and are in Norwegian. You can
see an Ibsen play at the *Nasjonaltheateret* (National Theater; 15
Stortings Gate in *Studenterlunden Park;* phone: 22-412710), Norway's principal theater. The *Dukketeatret* (Puppet Theater; 67 Frogn-
erveien; phone: 22-421188), in the same building as the *Oslo Bymuseum* (Oslo City Museum), is a delight not only for children. *Det
Norske Teatret* (8 Kristian IVs Gate; phone: 22-424344) produces
foreign plays and musicals in the language known as *ny norsk,* or
new Norwegian; *Oslo Nye Teater* (10 Rosenkrantz Gate; phone:
22-421188) features classic and modern comedy. *Chat Noir* (5
Klingenberggate; phone: 22-832202) presents cabaret acts; *ABC-
teatret* (3 St. Olavsplass; phone: 22-112166) is the place for light
comedy and cabaret, including classics in summer; and the
*Bryggeteatret* at Aker Brygge (phone: 22-838820) offers musicals
and comedies. Fine dining and revues are tastefully combined at
*Mølla* (21 Sagveien; phone: 22-375450). Internationally famous
shows such as *La Cage aux Folles* usually are performed at *Château
Neuf* (7 Slemdalsvn.; phone: 22-569500). Those in search of English-language productions must watch for special guest appearances by visiting groups. To reserve tickets for most theatrical productions, call *Billetservice* (phone: 81-033133). Foreign films
shown in Norway are screened in their original language and sub-
titled in Norwegian.

## MUSIC

The band of the *Kongens Garde* (King's Guard) plays outside the
*Slottet* (Royal Palace) at the changing of the guard at 1:30 PM whenever King Harald V is in residence, usually between October 1 and
June 24. Museums and libraries also schedule public concerts regularly. The *Oslo Filharmoniske Orkester* (Oslo Philharmonic Orchestra) performs in the autumn and winter seasons. Many of the concerts are held in the university's festival hall (see *Special Places*)
or at the *Oslo Konserthus* (Oslo Concert Hall; 14 Munkedamsveien;
phone: 22-833200); in July and August, the concert hall's *Lille Sal*
(Small Hall) is the site of Norwegian folk dancing on Mondays and
Thursdays at 9 PM. *Den Norske Opera* (21 Storgate, on Youngstorget; phone: 22-427724, advance sales) hosts ballets as well as operas.
A particularly charming venue for recitals and small concerts is the
historic *Gamle Logen* (Old Lodge; 2 Grev Wedels Plass; phone:
22-335470). Oslo's largest concert hall, *Spektrum*, near the *Oslo
City* shopping complex, hosts both rock concerts and classical events;
the ticket office (phone: 22-178050) is open weekdays. Tickets for
most concert and theater performances also can be obtained through
*Billetservice* (see *Theater*).

## NIGHTCLUBS AND NIGHTLIFE

Oslo nightlife has blossomed, and the capital is losing its sleepy reputation. Wine bars, discos, and supper clubs—offering fine dining at one level and live dance bands or cabaret shows at another—abound. *Humla* (26 Universitetsgate; phone: 22-424420), is a popular supper/dance club where visitors over 40 won't feel out of place. At the same address (and phone) is *Barock* for dining and disco dancing, and the new cabaret club *Dizzie.* The disco *Bonanza* at the *Grand* hotel; the dance-restaurant *El Toro* in the *Bristol* (see *Checking In*); and *Frascati* (20 Stortingsgate; phone: 22-336565), a restaurant/bar with dance music, all cater to more mature crowds, while *Galaxy* in the *Radisson SAS Scandinavia* hotel (see *Checking In*) is popular with the younger set. *Smuget* (24 Rosenkranzgate; phone: 22-425262) is a three-level establishment with an eatery serving until 3:15 AM, a disco, and a live jazz/blues/rock section. A slightly more sedate crowd gathers for wine, beer, or dinner at *Josefine Vertshus* (16 Josefines Gate; phone: 22-603126), a pub housed in an old villa in historic Homansbyen.

There are a number of good jazz clubs. Try *Oslo Jazzhus* (69 Toftesgate; phone: 22-383765) or ask at your hotel for current favorites. Two pleasant café–wine bars are *Café Sjakk Matt* (5 Haakon VIIs Gate; phone: 22-834156) and *Fru Blom's* (41B Karl Johans Gate; phone: 22-427300), both of which serve vintage wines by the glass, pâtés, cheeses, and other tasty snacks. After an evening on the floodlit *Trysvannskleiva* ski run, skiers gather around the blazing log fire at the lakeside *Trysvannstua Lodge* (phone: 22-144134). On summer evenings, young people cruise the outdoor cafés at Studenterlunden, bordering Karl Johans Gate. The *Plaza Sky Bar,* 33 floors up at the *Oslo Plaza* hotel (see *Checking In*), is a late-night must for the view alone. Closed Sundays, it's open from 5 PM to 3:30 AM the rest of the week; after 8 PM there's a cover charge, and jackets are required for men.

# Best in Town

## CHECKING IN

Oslo is rife with good, modern hotels, but rates, unfortunately, remain high and reservations must be made early if you plan to visit in the busiest ski periods (February, March, or *Easter*), *Constitution Day* (May 17), or at the height of the summer tourist season. For advance hotel bookings, call or write to *Tourist Information,* Oslo Central Station, Jernbanetorget, Oslo 0154 (phone: 22-171124; fax: 22-176613). If you do arrive without a place to stay, the tourist information office at *Oslo S* (Central Station; 2 Jernbanetorget), open daily, makes room reservations at hotels, pensions, and private homes for a small fee and a refundable deposit. Show up at the center in person on the day you require the room.

For a double room expect to pay $225 or more per night (including tax) at hotels decribed below as very expensive; from $150 to $225 at places in the expensive category; from $95 to $145 at moderate hotels; and less than $95 at inexpensive places. Breakfast—usually a generous buffet—is included, and hotel rooms have private baths, TV sets, and telephones unless otherwise indicated. Many of Oslo's best hotels offer special weekend rates (sometimes as much as 50% less). The *Oslo Package* is a program offering discounts at 29 hotels in the Norwegian capital plus the free transportation and sightseeing benefits of the *Oslo Card*. Contact your travel agent or, in Oslo, the *Norway Information Center* (see *Tourist Information*). For budget travelers there are some simple *pensiones* and two youth hostels. All telephone numbers include city codes, which you must dial when making a local call.

### VERY EXPENSIVE

**Continental** Centrally located, this first-rate property is a city landmark with 169 rooms and 12 suites, as well as *Annen Etage,* one of Oslo's best restaurants, and *Theatercaféen,* one of the city's most popular old-fashioned cafés (see *Eating Out* for both). Business facilities include 24-hour room service, meeting rooms for up to 300, an English-speaking concierge, foreign currency exchange, audiovisual equipment, photocopiers, and cable TV news. 24-26 Stortings Gate (phone: 22-419060; 800-223-6800; fax: 22-429689).

**Grand** Oslo's most prestigious hotel: dignified, traditional, and offering excellent service. It has 300 spacious rooms, three bars, five elegant restaurants—including *Etoile* and the *Grand Café* (see *Eating Out*)—a pool and exercise facilities, and a perfect location. If money is no object, book the *Nobel Suite,* which houses each year's Nobel Peace Prize winner, or the *Tower Suite.* There are also 25 junior suites. Business facilities include 24-hour room service, meeting rooms for up to 300, an English-speaking concierge, foreign currency exchange, secretarial services in English, audiovisual equipment, photocopiers, and cable TV news. 31 Karl Johans Gate (phone: 22-429390; 800-223-5652; fax: 22-421225).

**Oslo Plaza** With 712 luxurious rooms and suites, it's by far the country's largest hotel. The 37-story glass structure, the tallest hotel in Scandinavia, towers over Oslo, with the *Plaza Sky Bar* on the 33rd floor. There is a restaurant on the premises, and business facilities include 24-hour room service, meeting rooms for up to 900, an English-speaking concierge, foreign currency exchange, secretarial services in English, photocopiers, cable TV news, and translation services. 3 Sonja Henies Plass (phone: 22-171000; fax: 22-177300).

**Radisson SAS Scandinavia** A large, high-rise hotel near the *Slottet* (Royal Palace), it has 500 rooms, many with lovely views. Facilities include a health club and a swimming pool, a gallery of shops, five restaurants—including *Holbergs Årstidene* (see *Eating Out*)—and several bars, the most notable of which is the *Summit Bar* on the 21st floor. Business facilities include 24-hour room service, meeting rooms for up to 1,200, an English-speaking concierge, secretarial services in English, audiovisual equipment, photocopiers, translation services, cable TV news, express check-in/checkout, and express laundry. 30 Holbergs Gate (phone: 22-113000; fax: 22-113017).

**Royal Christiania** Its mood and decor inspired by the 300-year history of Christiania (Oslo's former name), this 456-room property features 100 suites, including the sumptuous two-story *Royal Suite.* There are shops, a trattoria, a wine bar, a piano bar, and a café, which is housed in the spacious marble-and-brass atrium. Business facilities include 24-hour room service, meeting rooms for up to 700, an English-speaking concierge, foreign currency exchange, secretarial services in English, audiovisual equipment, photocopiers, computers, translation services, and cable TV news. 3 B. Gunnerus Gate (phone: 22-429410; fax: 22-424622).

### EXPENSIVE

**Ambassadeur** This charming 42-room Best Western hostelry in the west end of the city is popular with diplomats and has suites and demi-suites, each distinctively decorated. There are also a restaurant and a small indoor pool. Business facilities include room service, meeting rooms for up to 25 (plus use of a nearby historic villa for up to 205), an English-speaking concierge, and cable TV news. 15 Camilla Collettsvei (phone: 22-441835; 800-528-1234; fax: 22-444791).

**Bristol** A very traditional European stopping place, set right in the center of town, it offers 141 large, pleasant rooms, an inviting lobby bar with comfy leather chairs, and a grillroom with Spanish decor and a dance floor. Business facilities include meeting rooms for up to 200, an English-speaking concierge, foreign currency exchange, audiovisual equipment, photocopiers, and cable TV news. 7 Kristian IVs Gate (phone: 22-415840; 800-4UTELL; fax: 22-428651).

**Holmenkollen Park Hotel Rica** Storybook-style and timber-beamed, this property has 191 comfortable (but small) rooms, and an excellent view of Oslo from its lovely setting on Holmenkollen Hill. A huge fireplace dominates its public salon, some rooms have terraces, and its attractive restaurant (*De Fem Stuer;* see *Eating Out*) features Norwegian specialties. Business facilities include 24-hour room service, a conference center in a separate building for up to 400, an English-speaking concierge, foreign currency exchange, audiovisual equipment, photocopiers, computers, cable TV news, and simultaneous interpretation facilities. Reached by car or the *Holmenkollen Railway* line. 26 Kongeveien, Holmenkollåsen (phone: 22-922000; 800-223-5652; fax: 22-146192).

**Nobel** Convenience is the keynote at this centrally located 85-room Best Western property. Room service is available, and there is a bar but no restaurant. Business facilities include meeting rooms for up to 25, a photocopier, and cable TV news. 33 Karl Johans Gate (phone: 22-427480; 800-528-1234; fax: 22-4205195).

**Rica Hotel Oslofjord** This 245-room hotel, about 20 minutes from the city center, overlooks the Oslo Fjord. Don't let the spartan exterior put you off. The garden café is airy and pleasant, while the *L'Orchidée* restaurant (open for dinner only) is Art Deco in style. There also is a sauna and a fitness center. Business facilities include room service, meeting rooms for up to 350, an English-speaking concierge, audiovisual equipment, photocopiers, and cable TV news. 184 Sandviksveien (phone: 67-545700; fax: 67-542733).

**Rica Victoria** Conveniently located near the *Stortingbygningen* (National Assembly Building), this elegant hotel offers 155 well-appointed rooms and six suites, plus a large restaurant and a bar. Breakfast is not included. Business facilities include 24-hour room service, meeting rooms for up to 70, an English-speaking concierge, and photocopiers. 13 Rosenkrantzgate (phone: 22-429940; fax: 22-429943).

**Scandic Crown** Not far from the *Slottet* (Royal Palace) and the *US Embassy,* it has 185 rooms that are quite small, a good restaurant, and a bar. Business facilities include meeting rooms for up to 200, audiovisual equipment, photocopiers, computers, and cable TV news. 68 Parkveien (phone: 22-446970; 800-4UTELL; fax: 22-442601).

### MODERATE

**Cecil** Convenient to the *Stortingbygningen* and Karl Johans Gate, this no-frills property is geared toward the business traveler. One hundred of the 112 spotless, modern rooms are singles—all with extra-large desks, mini-bars, trouser presses, and hair dryers. There's a breakfast room, and lunch is served in the atrium. Business facilities include two meeting rooms for up to six and cable TV news. 8 Stortingsgate (phone: 22-427000; fax: 22-422670).

**Gabelshus** A quiet, established hotel with 50 rooms, the aura of a stately home, an impeccable restaurant, and a loyal clientele. Business facilities include meeting rooms for up to 100 and a photocopier. A 15-minute walk from the city center. 16 Gabels Gate (phone: 22-552260; fax: 22-442730).

**Stefan** Centrally located, this clean, modest, 130-room hostelry has a restaurant that offers a good noontime buffet. Business facilities include room service, meeting rooms for up to 70, audiovisual equipment, photocopiers, and cable TV news. 1 Rosenkrantz Gate (phone: 22-429290; fax: 22-337022).

### INEXPENSIVE

**Anker** A no-frills establishment favored by students, it offers 120 rooms plus a breakfast room, but no restaurant. Business facilities include meeting rooms for up to 35 and photocopiers. It's right on the tram line and within walking distance of downtown. 55 Storgate (phone: 22-114005; fax: 22-110136).

**Munch** Almost all the conveniences of a hotel in a far higher price range are available here. There are 180 rooms and a breakfast room, but no restaurant. 5 Munchs Gate (phone: 22-424275; fax: 22-206469).

# EATING OUT

Norwegian cuisine features fish and seafood in addition to game. Norwegian trout and salmon are musts, but you also will find delicious meals of cod, haddock, and coalfish. *Gravlax* (marinated raw salmon) is a classic, but if it strains the budget, try another Norwegian delicacy: warm smoked mackerel. Sample the beer: *brigg* and *lettøl* are the weakest, lager is called *pils,* and *export* or *gold* is the strongest. *Akevitt* (the Norwegian spelling of aquavit), made from potatoes, herbs, and spices, accompanies special meals (with a beer chaser). Both reindeer and moose steaks are superb, especially in the fall hunting season. Breakfast ranges from the simple continental to the traditional Norwegian *koldtbord*—a buffet that includes assorted herring dishes, salmon, paper-thin slices of roast beef, and much more. For a particularly good *koldtbord* try the *Stefan* or the *Scandic Crown* hotels (see *Checking In*).

Best bet for a quick and inexpensive lunch is a *konditori,* or bakery/tearoom, where the Norwegians themselves go. Enticing sandwiches, cakes, coffee, and tea can be enjoyed at small tables or counters, or taken out for a picnic in a park.

Aker Brygge at the harbor and the *Oslo City* shopping center, located near the *Oslo S* central rail station, both have a large selection of cafés and informal restaurants offering a choice of different cuisines at varying prices.

Dining out in Oslo is expensive. For dinner for two, expect to pay $120 or more at a place in the expensive category; about $70 to $120 at a moderate restaurant; and less than $70 at the inexpensive place. The high price of beer and wine can quickly shoot a tab up into the $200 range. All the restaurants below accept major credit cards and are open for lunch and dinner unless otherwise noted. Many close during the *Christmas* and *Easter* holidays. All telephone numbers include city codes, which you must dial when making a local call.

### EXPENSIVE

**Annen Etage** This elegant and traditional Norwegian-European dining room has been awarded two stars by Michelin for its superb French and Norwegian cuisine. Closed Saturdays and Sunday lunch. Reservations advised. At the *Continental Hotel*, 24-26 Stortings Gate (phone: 22-419060).

**D'Artagnan** Honored with two Michelin stars for its exquisite French menu, this exclusive establishment reigns as one of Oslo's most fashionable. Dishes range from crab salad with avocado garnish to wild duck with cherries, oranges, and pineapple. Closed Sundays. Reservations necessary. 16 Øvre Slottsgade (phone: 22-415062).

**Bagatelle** The only Oslo restaurant to have earned three stars in the Michelin guide, it serves fine French food and has a distinguished wine cellar. Open for dinner only; closed Sundays. Reservations necessary. 3-5 Bygdøy Allé (phone: 22-446397).

**Blom** Decorated with the shields of members of the *Norwegian Society of Artists* (look for Charlie Chaplin's and Liv Ullmann's), this place is worth a visit for the art and antiques alone. It specializes in fish and game and has a popular lunchtime buffet. There's also a light post-theater menu. Closed Sundays. Reservations advised. 41B Karl Johans Gate (phone: 22-427300). .

**Bygdøystuene** Located near the *Norske Folkemuseum* (Norwegian Folk Museum), it has a classic interior and traditional Norwegian menu. In summer it becomes a charming open-air restaurant. Open daily. Reservations advised. 2 Strømborgveien, Bygdøy peninsula (phone: 22-440080).

**Det Blå Kjokken** The traditional Norwegian menu at this intimate, elegant eatery features first-rate fish and game dishes. Open for dinner only; closed Sundays. Reservations necessary. 30 Drammensveien (phone: 22-442650).

**Engebret Café** Founded in 1857, this cozy restaurant treats its guests with old-fashioned care, from the silver candelabra on each table to the lovingly prepared seafood, game, and meat. There's a noontime sandwich buffet, popular with well-heeled businesspeople. Closed Sundays. Reservations advised. 1 Bankplassen, near the *Museum for Samtidskunst* (Museum of Contemporary Art; phone: 22-336694).

**Etoile** On the sixth floor of the *Grand* hotel, with a glass roof and a terrific city view, this first class dining spot serves French and Norwegian food, and has a fine wine list. There's a lunch buffet featuring fish and seafood. Open daily. Reservations advised. 31 Karl Johans Gate (phone: 22-429390).

**Feinschmecker** A popular contemporary eatery, it features Michelin starrated Norwegian and continental fare in a cozy setting of candlelight and antiques. The service is impeccable. Open daily. Reservations necessary. 5 Balchensgate (phone: 22-441777).

**De Fem Stuer** Another of Oslo's top places—the lunch buffet is one of the city's best. Traditional Norwegian fare is served, with salmon and game featured. The decor, also traditional Norwegian, is attractive; the view over the city and its environs outstanding. Open daily. Reservations advised. In the romantic *Holmenkollen Park Hotel Rica*, 26 Kongeveien, Holmenkollåsen (phone: 22-146090).

**Holbergs Årstidene** An excellent grill restaurant with an international à la carte menu. Open for dinner only; closed Sundays. Reservations advised. In the *Radisson SAS Scandinavia Hotel*, 30 Holbergs Gate (phone: 22-113000).

**Kastanjen** An informal brasserie, with a more elegant dining room downstairs, it features modern versions of Norwegian classics, especially fish dishes. Open for dinner only; closed Sundays. Reservations advised for downstairs. 18 Bygdøy Allé (phone: 22-434467).

**La Mer** Perhaps the best fish and seafood spot in Oslo. Call two days ahead and order the house special, bouillabaisse. Open for dinner only; closed Sundays. Reservations advised. 31 Pilestredet (phone: 22-203445).

**Mølla** In an old textile mill on the banks of the River Akerselva, this fine fish and game place was the setting for Oskar Braaten's novels about factory workers' lives in the beginning of the century. After dinner, there's dancing, and musical revues are presented in the bar area. Open for dinner only; closed Sundays. Reservations advised. 21 Sagveien (phone: 22-375450).

**Theatercaféen** A place to see and be seen, this Oslo favorite, frequented by artists, is in the *Continental* hotel. Window tables are the most fashionable. The lunch buffet, consisting mostly of open-face sandwiches, is very popular; ask to see the menu if you want a more filling dish. The desserts are simply tantalizing. Reservations advised for dinner. 24-26 Stortings Gate (phone: 22-333200).

### MODERATE

**Café Sjakk Matt** One of Oslo's most enduring cafés. Open daily for lunch; snacks are served after 3 PM. Reservations unnecessary. 5 Haakon VIIs Gate (phone: 22-834156).

**Costa** This trendy brasserie-cum-Italian eatery is always crowded. The pasta is not the best you'll ever taste, but this is still one of *the* places to be seen in Oslo—and the homemade sorbets are delectable. Open daily for dinner only; closed Sundays in the summer. Reservations necessary. 4 Klingenberggaten (phone: 22-424130).

**Frognerseteren Kafé** Both à la carte restaurant and cafeteria, this establishment at Holmenkollen Hill has the feel of a ski lodge. Try the fresh salmon. In the summer, crowds gather on the terrace above Oslo Fjord to soak up the sun; in winter, skiers flock to tables by the fireplace for hot chocolate and the famous *eplekake,* pastry layered with apples and topped with a mound of whipped cream. Open daily. Reservations unnecessary, but expect crowds on the weekends. 200 Holmenkollen (phone: 22-143736). Restaurant, moderate; cafeteria, inexpensive.

**Grand Café** A busy dining place in the *Grand* hotel, it has large murals of life in Old Christiania at the turn of the century, when it was Ibsen's destination twice daily. The menu features continental fare and Norwegian specialties. Buffet breakfast begins at 6:30 AM, and there's piano music after 7 PM. Open daily. Dinner reservations necessary. 31 Karl Johans Gate (phone: 22-429390).

**Håndverkeren Bar and Grill** A meeting place for artists and journalists who flock here for the daily lunchtime sandwich buffet. The cooking is traditional Norwegian. Closed Sundays. Reservations advised. 7 Rosenkrantz Gate (phone: 22-420750).

**Tostrupkjelleren** A cellar meeting place for politicians, journalists, and businesspeople, it serves traditional Norwegian fare. On some evenings there's live jazz. Closed Sundays. Reservations unnecessary. 25 Karl Johans Gate (phone: 22-421470).

INEXPENSIVE

**Holmenkollen** The kitchen features Norwegian dishes, the dining room a spectacular view of the city and fjord. Try the large lunch buffet. Open daily. Reservations unnecessary. Reached by the *Holmenkollen Railway* line. 119 Holmenkollveien, Holmenkollåsen (phone: 22-146226).

# Paris

## At-a-Glance

### SEEING THE CITY

The most popular view of Paris is from the top of the *Eiffel Tower* on the Rive Gauche; on a clear day, you can see for more than 50 miles. The tops of *Notre-Dame*'s towers offer close-ups of the cathedral's Gothic spires and flying buttresses, along with a magnificent view of the Ile de la Cité and the rest of Paris. The observatory of the *Tour Montparnasse* also presents a striking panorama.

The most satisfying vantage point, if not the highest, is the top of the *Arc de Triomphe*, which commands a view of the majestic sweep of Baron Haussmann's 12 stately avenues radiating from the Place Charles-de-Gaulle, including the splendid vista down the Champs-Elysées to the Place de la Concorde, with the *Louvre* beyond. Visitors can take the elevator or climb the 284 steps up. Other Rive Droite sites offering stunning views are the terrace of *Sacré-Coeur,* the landing at the top of the escalator at the *Centre Georges-Pompidou,* and the observation deck of *La Samaritaine,* the six-floor department store at the foot of the Pont-Neuf (see *Shopping*). For details on the other sites described above see *Special Places.*

Another spectacular cityscape can be seen from the *Grande Arche de la Défense,* to the west of the city (1 Cour de la Défense, Puteaux; phone: 49-07-27-57). The Grande Arche completes the axis that starts at the *Louvre* and runs through the Champs-Elysées and the *Arc de Triomphe.* It is open daily. There's an admission charge.

### SPECIAL PLACES

Getting around this sprawling metropolis isn't difficult once you understand the layout of the 20 *arrondissements* (districts). Most bookshops and newsstands stock *Paris Indispensable* and *Plan de Paris par Arrondissement.* These little lifesavers list streets alphabetically and indicate the nearest *Métro* station on individual maps and an overall plan. Street addresses of the places mentioned throughout this chapter are followed by their *arrondissement* number (1er means 1st *arrondissement,* 2e means 2nd *arrondissement,* 3e means 3rd *arrondissement,* and so on).

---

**JUST THE TICKET**

The *Carte Musées et Monuments* (Museum and Monuments Pass) allows sightseers and art lovers to bypass ticket lines at 65 museums in and near Paris (though it's not valid for certain special exhibits).

---

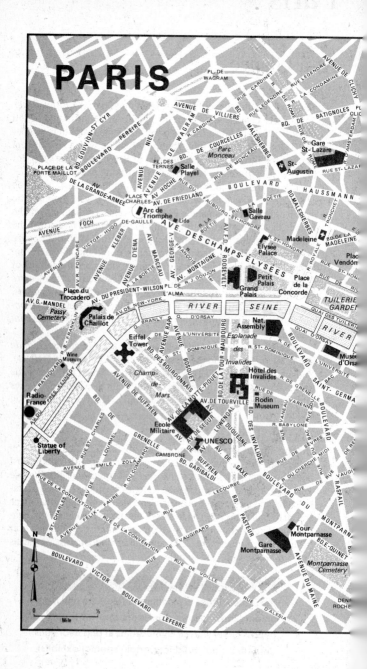

# PARIS

PL. DE WAGRAM

AVENUE DE VILLIERS

AVENUE DE CLICHY

PLACE DE LA PORTE MAILLOT

BD. DE GOUVION-ST CYR
BOULEVARD PEREIRE
NIEL
AV. DE WAGRAM
RUE CARDINET
PL. DE TERNES
BD. DE COURCELLES
DE MALESHERBES
Parc Monceau
RUE DE MONCEAU
RUE LEGENDRE
RUE LEGENDRE
RUE DE ROME
RUE LA CONDAMINE
BD. DE BATIGNOLES
RUE D'AMSTERDAM

Gare St-Lazare

Salle Pleyel
St-Augustin
RUE ST-LAZARE

AV. DE LA GRANDE-ARMEE
AVENUE
PLACE CHARLES-AV. DE FRIEDLAND
AV. HOCHE
RUE DU FAUBOURG-ST-HONORE
BOULEVARD HAUSSMANN
BD. MALESHERBES
R. TRONCHET

Arc de Triomphe
DE-GAULLE
Lido
R. LA BOETIE
Salle Gaveau
Madeleine
BD. DE LA MADELEINE

AVENUE FOCH
AVENUE VICTOR-HUGO
AVENUE KLEBER
AV. D'IENA
AV. MARCEAU
AV. GEORGE-V
AVE DESCHAMPS-ÉLYSÉES
AV. F.D. ROOSEVELT
R. ST-HONORE
R. ROYALE
Élysée Palace
Place Vendôme
RUE ST-HON.
RUE DE RI

AVENUE DU PRESIDENT-WILSON
AV. DE LA BOETIE
AV. MONTAIGNE
PL. DE L'ALMA
R. J. GOUJON
Petit Palais
Grand Palais
Place de la Concorde
RUE DE RI
TUILERIE GARDEI

Place du Trocadéro
AV. DU PRESIDENT-WILSON
AV. DE NEW-YORK
R. BRANLY
RIVER D'ORSAY
SEINE
QUAI DES TUILERI
RIVER

AV. G.-MANDEL
Passy Cemetery
AV. R. POINCARE
B. FRANKLIN
Palais de Chaillot
AVENUE RAPP
AVENUE BOSQUET
L'UNIVERSITE
R. ST-DOMINIQUE
Nat. Assembly
R. ST-DOMINIQUE
QUAI D'ORSAY
BOULEVARD
Musée d'Orsa

Eiffel Tower
Wine Museum
BD. DE LA TOUR MAUBOURG
Esplanade des Invalides
L'UNIVERSITE
SAINT-GERMA

Champ de Mars
AVENUE DE SUFFREN
BD. DE LA TOUR
AV. DE LA MOTTE-PIQUET
Hôtel des Invalides
RUE DE GRENELLE
R. DE VARENNE
BOULEVARD

Radio-France
AVENUE KENNEDY
BD. DE GRENELLE
AV. DE TOURVILLE
Rodin Museum
RUE DE GRENELLE
R. BABYLONE

Statue of Liberty
RUE ST-CHARLES
RUE LOURMEL
Ecole Militaire
AV. DE SEGUR
AV. DE SAXE
AV. DE TOURVILLE
AV. DE SUFFREN
BD. GARIBALDI
AV. DUQUESNE
DE TOMENDAL
DES INVALIDES
RUE DE SEVRES
RUE DU CHERCHE-MIDI

AVENUE EMILE-ZOLA
CAMBRONE
UNESCO
RUE DE VAUGI

RUE DE LA CONVENTION
RUE ST-CHARLES
AVENUE FELIX-FAURE
RUE DU COMMERCE
BD. GARIBALDI
LECOURBE
BD. DE VAUGIRARD
BOULEVARD DU
RASPAIL

AVENUE DE LA CONVENTION
RUE
RUE DE VAUGIRARD
RUE DE VOILLE
PASTEUR
Tour Montparnasse
Gare Montparnasse
BD. DU MONTPARN.
BD.E.-QUINET

N

BOULEVARD VICTOR
BOULEVARD
RUE D'ALESIA
AVENUE DU MAINE
Montparnasse Cemetery
DENF ROCHE

LEFEBRE

0 ½
Mile

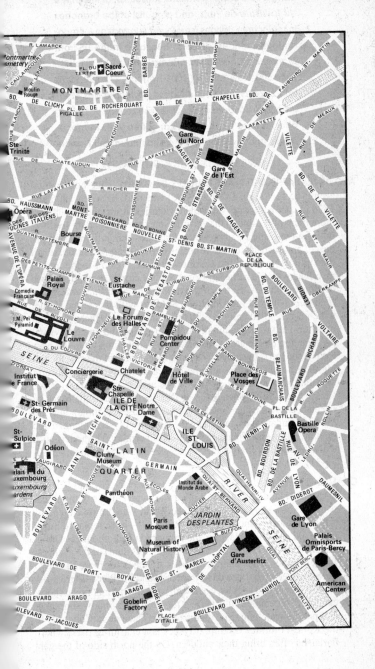

Available in one-, three-, or five-day passes, the *carte* is sold in *Métro* stations, museums, at the *Office du Tourisme de Paris,* and at tourist office branches in major train stations (see *Tourist Information* for more on tourist offices). It's also available in the US from *Marketing Challenges International* (10 E. 21st St., Suite 600, New York, NY 10010; phone: 212-529-9069; fax: 212-529-4838). The *Caisse Nationale des Monuments Historiques et des Sites* (see *Le Marais,* below) offers a card good for a year of free visits to monuments and sites both in Paris and throughout France.

## LA RIVE DROITE (THE RIGHT BANK)

**ARC DE TRIOMPHE AND PLACE CHARLES-DE-GAULLE** This monumental arch (165 feet high, 148 feet wide) was built between 1806 and 1836 to commemorate Napoleon's victories (it was then the largest monument of its kind in the world). Note the frieze and its six-foot-high figures—the 10 impressive sculptures symbolizing triumph, peace, and resistance, and especially Rude's *La Marseillaise,* on the right as you face the Champs-Elysées. Also note the arches inscribed with the names of Bonaparte's victories, as well as those of Empire heroes. Beneath the arch is the *Sépulture du Soldat Inconnu* (Tomb of the Unknown Soldier) with its eternal flame, which is rekindled daily at 6:30 PM. Inside the arch there's a small museum featuring documents and engravings and an audiovisual presentation on the arch's history. A 284-step climb up to the platform at the top is rewarded by a magnificent view of the city, including the Champs-Elysées and the *Bois de Boulogne.* (The platform also can be reached by elevator.) The arch is the center of Place Charles-de-Gaulle, once Place de l'Etoile (Square of the Star), so called because it is the center of a "star," whose radiating points are the 12 broad avenues, including the Champs-Elysées, planned and built by Baron Haussmann in the mid-19th century. The arch is open daily. Admission charge. Pl. Charles-de-Gaulle, 8e (phone: 43-80-31-31).

**CHAMPS-ELYSÉES** Paris's legendary promenade, the "Elysian Fields," was swampland until 1616. It once was synonymous with all that was glamorous in the city, but since World War II movie theaters, schlocky shops—and the "Golden Arches"—have replaced much of the old *élégance.* Happily, the restoration and greening of what Parisians call the "Champs" have brought back some of the avenue's former cachet. The Champs-Elysées stretches for more than two miles between the Place de la Concorde and the Place Charles-de-Gaulle. The broad avenue, lined with rows of chestnut trees, shops, cafés, and cinemas, still is perfect for strolling, window shopping, and people watching. The area from the Place de la Concorde to the Rond-Point des Champs-Elysées is a charming park, where Parisians often bring their children. On the north side of the gardens is the *Palais de l'Elysée* (Elysée Palace), the official home of the president of the French Republic. Ceremonial events such as the *Bastille Day Parade* (July 14) frequently take place along the Champs-Elysées.

**GRAND PALAIS (GREAT PALACE)** Off the Champs-Elysées, on opposite sides of Avenue Winston-Churchill, are the elaborate turn-of-the-century *Grand Palais* and *Petit Palais* (see below), built of glass and stone for the *1900 World Exposition*. With its stone columns, mosaic frieze, and flat glass dome, the *Grand Palais* contains the *Galeries Nationales* (a large area devoted to temporary exhibits), the *Palais de la Découverte,* as well as a science museum and planetarium. Parts of the *Grand Palais* will be closed for structural repairs throughout this year. The *Galeries Nationales* are closed Tuesdays; the *Palais de la Découverte* is closed Mondays. Admission charge for both. Av. Winston-Churchill, 8e (phone: 44-13-17-17).

**PETIT PALAIS (LITTLE PALACE)** Built at the same time as the *Grand Palais,* it has exhibits on the city's history and a variety of fine and applied arts, plus special shows. Closed Mondays and holidays. Admission charge. Av. Winston-Churchill, 8e (phone: 42-65-12-73).

**PLACE DE LA CONCORDE** Surely one of the most magnificent in the world, this square is grandly situated in the midst of equally grand landmarks: the *Louvre* and the *Tuileries* on one side, the Champs-Elysées and the *Arc de Triomphe* on another, the Seine and the Napoleonic *Palais Bourbon* on a third, and the pillared façade of the *Madeleine* on the fourth. Designed by Gabriel for Louis XV, the elegant square was where his unfortunate successor, Louis XVI, lost his head to the guillotine, as did Marie-Antoinette, Danton, Robespierre, Charlotte Corday, and others. It was first named for Louis XV, then called Place de la Révolution by the triumphant revolutionaries. Its present name, "Concorde," or "peace," signifies France's hope of overcoming the violent history that the square symbolized. Ornamenting the square are eight colossal statues that represent important French provincial capitals and the 3,300-year-old, 75-foot-high *l'Obélisque de Lougsor* (Obelisk of Luxor), which was a gift from Egypt in 1831.

**JARDIN DES TUILERIES (TUILERIES GARDENS)** Carefully laid out in patterned geometric shapes, with clipped shrubbery and formal flower beds, statues, and fountains, this is one of the finest examples of French garden design (in contrast to informal English gardens, exemplified by the *Bois de Boulogne*). It is currently undergoing extensive renovations, due to be completed in 1997. Along the Seine, between the Place de la Concorde and the *Louvre.*

**ORANGERIE** A museum on the southwestern edge of the *Jardin des Tuileries,* it displays Monet's celebrated paintings of water lilies, plus the art collection of Jean Walter and Paul Guillaume, with works by Cézanne, Renoir, Matisse, Picasso, and others. Closed Tuesdays. Admission charge. Pl. de la Concorde and Quai des Tuileries, 1er (phone: 42-97-48-16).

**JEU DE PAUME** This building was refurbished and reopened as a gallery for contemporary art in 1991 as part of the *Louvre* renovation project that began with the opening of the I. M. Pei pyramids. Facing the Place de la Concorde on the northeastern corner of the *Jardin des Tuileries* opposite the *Orangerie*—and originally an indoor tennis court for France's royalty—the *Jeu de Paume* is the site where delegates met in 1789 to declare their independence, marking the beginning of the French Revolution (perhaps best commemorated in David's famous painting *The Tennis Court Oath,* which hangs in the *Louvre*). Previously home to the *Louvre*'s Impressionist collection (now in the *Musée d'Orsay;* see below), the extensively modernized museum houses exhibitions of contemporary works from 1960 on, including those of Takis, Broodthears, and Dubuffet. It also has video and conference areas, as well as a bookstore and cafeteria. Closed Mondays and weekday mornings. Admission charge. Pl. de la Concorde, 1er (phone: 47-03-12-50).

**RUE DE RIVOLI** Running along the north side of the *Louvre* and the *Jardin des Tuileries,* this elegant but car-clogged old street has perfume shops, souvenir stores, boutiques, bookstores, cafés, and such hotels as the *Meurice* and the *Inter-Continental* under its 19th-century arcades.

**LOUVRE** This colossus on the Seine, born in 1200 as a fortress and transformed over the centuries from Gothic mass to Renaissance palace, served as the royal residence in the 16th and 17th centuries. It was then supplanted by suburban *Versailles,* becoming a museum in 1793 after the French Revolution. It was Napoleon who later turned it into a glittering warehouse of artistic booty from the nations he conquered. Today its 200 galleries cover some 40 acres; to view all 297,000 items in the collections in no more than the most cursory fashion, it would be necessary to walk some 8 miles.

In addition to the *Mona Lisa, Venus de Milo,* and the *Winged Victory of Samothrace,* the *Louvre* has many delights that are easily overlooked—Vermeer's *Lace Maker* and Holbein's *Portrait of Erasmus,* for instance; not to mention van der Weyden's *Braque Triptych,* Ingres's *Turkish Bath,* Dürer's *Self-Portrait,* Cranach's naked and red-hatted *Venus,* and the exquisite 4,000-year-old Egyptian woodcarving known as the *Handmaiden of the Dead.* More of our favorites include Michelangelo's *The Dying Slave* and *The Bound Slave,* Goya's *Marquesa de la Solana,* Watteau's clown *Gilles* and his *Embarkation for Cythera,* Raphael's great portrait *Baldassare Castiglione,* Veronese's *Marriage at Cana,* Titian's masterpiece *Man with a Glove,* both *The Penitent Magdalen* and *The Card Sharps* by Georges de la Tour, Rembrandt's *Bathsheba,* and Frans Hals's *Bohemian Girl.* Try to save time for any one of David's glories: *Madame Récamier, The Oath of the Horatii, The Lictors Bringing Back to Brutus the Body of His Son,* or *The Coronation of Napoleon and Josephine.* And don't miss *Liberty Leading the People* and *The Bark of Dante,* both by Delacroix, and Courbet's *The Artist's Studio, Burial at Ornans,* and *Stags Fighting.*

Nor is the outside of this huge edifice to be overlooked. Note especially the *Cour Carrée* (the courtyard of the old *Louvre*), the southwest corner of which is the oldest part of the palace (dating from the mid-1550s) and a beautiful example of the Renaissance style that François I has so recently introduced from Italy. Renovation of the *Cour Carrée* and other sections of the museum are in progress and will continue through 1997, but most of the external walls have already been cleaned. Note, too, the *Colonnade*, which forms the eastern front of the *Cour Carrée*, facing the Place du Louvre; classical in style, it dates from the late 1660s, not too long before the Sun King left for *Versailles*. Newer wings of the *Louvre* embrace the palace gardens, in the midst of which stands the *Arc de Triomphe du Carrousel*, erected by Napoleon. From here the vista across the *Tuileries* and the Place de la Concorde and on up the Champs-Elysées to the *Arc de Triomphe* is one of the most beautiful in Paris. I. M. Pei's three glass pyramids, dating from 1989, sit center stage in the *Louvre*'s grand interior courtyard, and the largest of the trio now is the museum's main entrance. The controversial structure now houses the *Louvre*'s underground shops and galleries connecting the north and south wings (the addition increased the museum's exhibition space by nearly 80%). Last year the new *Richelieu Wing* opened, a stunning example of museum architecture just off the main *Louvre* entrance beneath the pyramid, as did the upscale *Carrousel du Louvre* shopping complex under the *Arc de Triomphe du Carrousel* (see *Shopping*).

Good guided tours in English, covering the highlights of the *Louvre*, are frequently available, but be sure to check in advance. Closed Tuesdays. Admission charge. Pl. du Louvre, 1er (phone: 40-20-51-51 for recorded information in French and English; 40-20-50-50 for more detailed information).

**PLACE VENDÔME** Just north of the *Tuileries* is one of the loveliest squares in Paris, the octagonal Place Vendôme, designed by Mansart in the 17th century. Now primarily a pedestrian zone, its arcades contain world-famous jewelers, perfumers, and banks, the *Ritz* hotel, and the *Ministère de Justice* (Ministry of Justice). The 144-foot column in the center is covered with bronze from the 1,200 cannon that Napoleon captured at Austerlitz in 1805. Just off Place Vendôme is the famous Rue du Faubourg-St-Honoré, one of the oldest streets in Paris, which now holds elegant shops selling the world's most expensive made-to-order items. To the north is the Rue de la Paix, noted for its jewelers.

**LA MADELEINE** Starting in 1764, the *Eglise Ste-Marie-Madeleine* (Church of St. Mary Magdalene) was built and razed twice before the present structure was commissioned by Napoleon in 1806 to honor his armies. The design of the recently cleaned and restored church is based on that of a Greek temple, with 65-foot-high Corinthian columns supporting the sculptured frieze. The bronze doors are adorned with illustrations of the Ten Commandments, and inside there are many distinctive murals and sculptures. From its portals, the view extends down Rue Royale to Place de la Concorde and over to the dome of *Les Invalides*. Nearby are some of Paris's most tantalizing food shops. Open daily. Free concerts are held two Sundays per month at 4 PM. Pl. de la Madeleine, 8e (phone: 42-65-52-17).

**OPÉRA/PALAIS GARNIER** When it was completed in 1875, this imposing rococo edifice was touted as the largest theater in the world (though with a capacity of only 2,156, it holds fewer people than the *Vienna Opera House* or *La Scala* in Milan). Designed by Charles Garnier, it covers nearly three acres and took 13 years to complete. The façade is decorated with sculpture, including a copy of Carpeaux's *The Dance* (the original is now in the *Musée d'Orsay*). The ornate interior has an impressive grand staircase, a beautiful foyer, lavish marble from every quarry in France, and Chagall's controversially decorated dome. These days the opera house is home to the *Ballet de l'Opéra de Paris*, while most operatic performances are now held at the *Opéra de la Bastille* (below). Visitors may explore the building's magnificent interior and enjoy its special exhibitions. Closed the month of August and on days when there are special performances. Admission charge. Pl. de l'Opéra, 9e (phone: 47-42-53-71).

**BASILIQUE DU SACRÉ-COEUR (BASILICA OF THE SACRED HEART) AND MONT-MARTRE** Built on the Butte Montmartre—the highest of Paris's seven hills—the white-domed *Basilique du Sacré-Coeur* provides an extraordinary view from its steps, especially at dawn or sunset. The church's Byzantine interior is rich and ornate, though light and well proportioned. Note the huge mosaics, one depicting Christ and the Sacred Heart over the high altar; another, the Archangel Michael and Joan of Arc; and a third, of Louis XVI and his family. One of the largest and heaviest bells (19 tons) in Christendom is housed in the tall bell tower to the north. The church, including the cupola, is open daily. 35 Rue Chevalier-de-la-Barre, 18e (phone: 42-51-17-02).

The area around *Sacré-Coeur* was the artists' quarter of late-19th- and early-20th-century Paris, and the streets still look the same as they do in the paintings of Utrillo. The site of the last of Paris's vineyards, Montmartre contains old houses, narrow alleys, steep stairways, and carefree cafés enough to provide a full day's entertainment. And at night the district still comes alive as it did in the days of Toulouse-Lautrec, who immortalized Montmartre's notoriously frivolous Belle Epoque nightlife, particularly the dancers and personalities at the *Moulin Rouge*, in his paintings. The Place du Tertre, where Braque, Dufy, Modigliani, Picasso, Rousseau, and Utrillo once lived, is still charming, but go early in the day; later it fills up with tourists and mostly undertalented artists. Spare yourself most of the climb to *Sacré-Coeur* by taking the modern, glass funicular, for which the fare is one *Métro* ticket, or the Montmartre bus (marked with an icon of *Sacré-Coeur* on the front instead of the usual number) from Place St-Pierre. Butte Montmartre, 18e.

**LES HALLES** The Central Market ("the Belly of Paris") that once stood on this 80-acre site northeast of the *Louvre* was razed in 1969. Gone are the picturesque early-morning fruit-and-vegetable vendors, butchers in blood-spattered aprons, and truckers bringing the freshest produce from all over France. They have been usurped by trendy shops and galleries of youthful entrepreneurs and artisans, small restaurants with lots of charm, the world's largest subway station, acres of trellised gardens and playgrounds, and *Le Forum des Halles,* a vast, mainly underground complex of boutiques, as well as concert space and movie theaters. Touch-sensitive locator devices, which help visitors find products and services, are placed strategically throughout the complex. The area, though, has been known to attract some rough types, so stay alert here. Rue Pierre-Lescot and Rue Rambuteau, 1er.

**LE CENTRE NATIONAL D'ART ET DE CULTURE GEORGES-POMPIDOU (LE CENTRE GEORGES-POMPIDOU)** Better known as the *"Beaubourg,"* after the street it faces and the *quartier* it replaced, this stark six-level creation of steel and glass, with its exterior escalators and blue, white, and red pipes, created a stir the moment its construction began. Outside a computerized digital clock ticks off the seconds remaining until the 21st century. The wildly popular cultural center brings together contemporary art in all its forms—painting, sculpture, industrial design, music, literature, cinema, and theater—under one roof. In addition to housing the *Musée National d'Art Moderne* (National Museum of Modern Art) and the *Centre de Création Industrielle* (Industrial Design Center), it also boasts a public information library and the *Institut de Recherches et de Coordination Acoustique/Musique* (Institute for Acoustic and Musical Research). The scene in the front courtyard, which serves as an impromptu stage for jugglers, mimes, acrobats, and magicians, often rivals the exhibits inside, which this year include special exhibitions of the work of Constantin Brancusi and Louise Bourgeois. On the fifth floor there's a cafeteria-style restaurant, and you can step outside for one of the most exciting views in Paris.

A massive renovation project, expected to cost more than $100 million, begins this year with work on the exterior of the center and on adjoining areas and buildings. Work on the interior is not slated to begin until 1997. The center as a whole will remain open throughout the project; sections under renovation will close in turn. Closed Tuesdays, weekday mornings, and May 1. Admission charge for the *Musée National d'Art Moderne* and for special exhibitions only; no admission charge on Sundays. Entrances on Rue de Beaubourg and Rue St-Martin, 4e (phone: 44-78-12-33).

**LE MARAIS** A marshland until the 16th century, this district east of the *Louvre* in the 4th *arrondissement* became a fashionable neighborhood during the 17th century. As the aristocracy moved on it fell into disrepair, but over the last 30 years the Marais has been enjoying a complete face-lift. Preservationists have lovingly restored more than 100 of the magnificent old *hôtels* (in this sense the word means private mansions or townhouses) to their former grandeur. The *hôtels* are exquisitely beautiful, with murals on the walls and ceilings. Many host theater and music performances in their courtyards during the summer *Festival du Marais.* Among the *hôtels* to note are the *Hôtel Salé,* which now houses the *Musée Picasso* (see below); the *Hôtel de Soubise,* now the *Archives Nationales* (National Archives; 60 Rue des Francs-Bourgeois), with its 14th-century *Porte de Clisson* (58 Rue des Archives); as well as the *Hôtels d'Aumont* (7 Rue de Jouy); *Guénégaud,* designed by Mansart (60 Rue des Archives); *de Rohan* (87 Rue Vieille-du-Temple); *de Sens* (1 Rue du Figuier); and *de Sully* (62 Rue St-Antoine). The *Caisse Nationale des Monuments Historiques et des Sites* (National Commission for Historic Monuments and Sites), housed in the *Hôtel de Sully,* offers tours on weekends plus a pass good for a year of free visits to sites of interest in Paris and throughout France (phone: 44-61-21-50 for general information; 44-61-21-69/70 for information on tours). 4e.

**PLACE DES VOSGES** In the Marais district, the oldest square in Paris—and also one of the most beautiful—was completed in 1612 by order of Henri IV, with its houses elegantly "built to a like symmetry." Though many of the houses have been rebuilt inside, their original façades remain. Corneille and Racine lived here, and at No. 6 is the *Maison de Victor-Hugo,* once the writer's home and now a museum. It's closed Mondays and holidays. Admission charge (phone: 42-72-10-16). 4e.

**MUSÉE CARNAVALET** This once was the home of Mme. de Sévigné, a noted 17th-century writer, and is now a museum with beautifully arranged exhibits covering the history of the city of Paris from the days of Henri IV to the present. The museum's name is derived from that of an earlier owner of the building, the widow of François de Kernevenoy (corrupted to Carnavalet), tutor to Henri III, who bought the *hôtel* in 1572. It was built in 1550 by the architect Pierre Lescot and over the years had many embellishments added by other architects. The museum's expansion through the *lycée* (school) next door and into the neighboring *Hôtel Le Peletier de Saint-Fargeau* doubled the exhibition space, making it the largest museum in the world devoted to the history of a single capital city. The expansion created space for a major permanent exhibit on the French Revolution, and a new wing is set to open to house recent archaeological finds, including Neolithic canoes discovered during excavations at the Bercy development. Also watch for special exhibitions and occasional concerts. The gift shop offers a wealth of interesting items, from T-shirts to objets d'art; there's also an excellent bookstore. Closed Mondays. No admission charge on Sundays. 23 Rue de Sévigné, 3e (phone: 42-72-21-13).

**MUSÉE PICASSO** A portion of the collection with which Picasso could never bring himself to part is displayed here in the beautiful 17th-century Ḥôtel Salé (the building is as interesting as the artwork it houses). More than 200 paintings, 3,000 drawings and engravings, and other objets d'art related to the great artist are arranged here in chronological order. These works provide a panoramic overview of the career of perhaps the century's greatest artist. Especially interesting is Picasso's own collection of works by other artists, including Cézanne, Braque, and Rousseau. There are also films on Picasso's life and work. Be sure to see the lovely fountain by Simounet in the formal garden. Closed Tuesdays. Admission charge. 5 Rue de Thorigny, 3e (phone: 42-71-25-21).

**OPÉRA DE LA BASTILLE** In sharp contrast to Garnier's *Opéra* is the curved glass façade of 20th-century architect Carlos Ott's opera house. Set against the historic landscape of the Bastille quarter, this austere, futuristic structure houses over 30 acres of multipurpose theaters, shops, and urban promenades. It looks a lot like its namesake, the prison-fortress the storming of which ignited the French Revolution. Pl. de la Bastille, 11e (phone: 44-73-13-00).

**AMERICAN CENTER AND BERCY** A Parisian venue for performing artists from the US since 1931, the *American Center* reopened last year (after a seven-year hiatus) in a futuristic new building designed by Frank Gehry. The center (51 Rue de Bercy, 12e; phone: 44-73-77-77; fax: 44-73-77-55) comprises a theater, a cinema, a restaurant, a bookstore, classrooms, and performance and gallery spaces. Through an eclectic program of avant-garde dance, music, film, and art, it aims to encourage cross-cultural relations between the US and the rest of the world. It's closed Tuesdays. Admission charge for performances and special exhibits. 7e.

The *American Center* is located in eastern Paris's Bercy development, formerly a wine depot, now also the site of France's *Ministère des Finances* and the *Palais Omnisports de Paris-Bercy,* a large sports complex. The much-talked-about new *Bibliothèque Nationale* (National Library) is slated to open here next year.

**BOIS DE VINCENNES** Designed as a counterpart to the *Bois de Boulogne* (see below), this park and zoological garden was laid out during Napoleon III's time on the former hunting grounds of the 14th-century *Château de Vincennes,* which encompassed 2,300 acres on the city's east side. Visit the château and its lovely chapel, the large garden, and the zoo, with animals in their natural habitats. Located on the eastern edge of the *Bois de Vincennes* is the *Musée National des Arts Africains et Océaniens* (Museum of African and Polynesian Art; see *Museums*). 20e.

**CIMETIÈRE PÈRE-LACHAISE (PÈRE-LACHAISE CEMETERY)** With over 100,000 tombs, sepulchers, and monuments, this is the most famous of France's cemeteries. Set in a wooded park, it's the final resting place of such illustrious personalities as Oscar Wilde, Edith Piaf, Marcel Proust, and Sarah Bernhardt. Purchase a map at the entrance before following the bizarre parade of adoring fans to the grave of rock star Jim Morrison of the *Doors* (section 27). It's hard to miss the legions of resident cats. Open daily. No admission charge. Bd. de Ménilmontant at Rue de la Roquette, 20e (phone: 43-70-70-33).

**LA VILLETTE** The *Cité des Sciences et de l'Industrie* (City of Sciences and Industry), a celebration of technology, stands in the *Parc de la Villette* on the northeastern edge of the capital and houses a planetarium, the spherical *Géode* cinema (see *Film*), lots of hands-on displays, and a half-dozen exhibitions at any given time. Also here is the *Cinaxe,* a movie theater that simulates a rocket launch—a must for children, as is a nearby futuristic playground. The *Cité de la Musique* (see *Museums*) and several restaurants and snack bars are also on the park grounds. Closed Mondays. Admission charge. 30 Av. Cotentin-Cariou, 19e (phone: 40-05-70-00).

**BOIS DE BOULOGNE** Originally part of the Forest of Rouvre, on the western edge of Paris, this 2,140-acre park was planned along English lines by Napoleon. It's a great place to ride a horse or a bike, row a boat, trap shoot, go bowling, picnic on the grass, see horse races at *Auteuil* and *Longchamp,* visit a children's amusement park *(Jardin d'Acclimatation)* or a zoo, see a play, walk to a waterfall, or just smell the roses. A particularly lovely spot is the *Bagatelle* château and park; a former residence of Marie-Antoinette, it boasts a magnificent rose garden (on the Rte. de Sèvres in Neuilly, 16e; phone: 40-67-97-00). Avoid the *Bois* after dark, when it becomes a playground for prostitutes and transvestites who actively solicit passersby. Recent attempts by the French government to stop the nighttime activity by banning cars from the park have begun to alleviate the situation. The park is open daily; the château is closed November through mid-March. Admission charge to the château.

**PALAIS DE CHAILLOT** Built for the *Paris Exposition of 1937* (on the site of the old *Palais du Trocadéro* left over from the *Exposition of 1878*), this structure houses a theater, a *Cinémathèque* (phone: 47-04-24-24), and four museums—the *Musée du Cinéma* (Film Museum; phone: 45-53-74-39), the *Musée de l'Homme* (Museum of Man; phone: 44-05-72-72), with anthropological exhibits; the *Musée de la Marine* (Maritime Museum; phone: 45-53-31-70); and *Musée des Monuments Français* (Museum of French Monuments; phone: 44-05-39-10), featuring reproductions of monuments. The terraces offer excellent views across gardens, fountains, and the Seine to the *Eiffel Tower* on the Rive Gauche. Closed Tuesdays and major holidays. Admission charge. Pl. du Trocadéro, 16e.

LA RIVE GAUCHE (THE LEFT BANK)

**TOUR EIFFEL (EIFFEL TOWER)** It is impossible to imagine the Paris skyline without this mighty symbol, yet what has been called Gustave Eiffel's folly was never meant to be permanent. Originally built for the *Universal Exposition of 1889,* it was due to be torn down in 1909 but was saved because of the development of the wireless—the first transatlantic wireless telephones were operated from the 984-foot tower in 1916 (the addition of television antennae in 1957 brought the tower's height up to 1,051 feet). It was the tallest building in the world until New York's Empire State Building (1,284 feet) was completed in 1930. Extensive renovations have taken place in more recent years (including modernized elevators); and a post office, three restaurants, and a few boutiques have opened on the first-floor landing. We recommend the one-Michelin-star *Jules Verne* restaurant, though it is pricey and requires reservations a month or two in advance. It's open daily (phone: 45-55-61-44; fax: 47-05-29-41). On a really clear day it's possible to see for 50 miles. Open daily. Admission charge. *Champ-de-Mars,* 7e (phone: 45-50-34-56).

**LES INVALIDES** Founded by Louis XIV in the 1670s as an asylum for wounded and aged soldiers, this vast structure was initially intended to house 4,000; it more often was a refuge for twice that number. The classically balanced buildings were designed by Libéral Bruant and have more than 10 miles of corridors. The royal *Eglise du Dôme* (Church of the Dome), part of the complex, was constructed from 1675 to 1706 and is topped by an elaborate golden dome designed by Mansart. Besides being a masterpiece of the 17th century, the church contains the impressive red-and-green granite *Tombeau de Napoléon Ier* (Tomb of Emperor Napoleon I; admission charge). The monument is surrounded by 12 huge white marble statues, interspersed with 54 flags, each symbolizing one of Napoleon's victories. The church also has an impressive courtyard and noteworthy frescoes. In addition, at *Les Invalides* is the *Musée de l'Armée,* one of the world's richest museums, displaying arms and armor along with mementos of French military history. For yet another splendid Parisian view approach the building from the Pont Alexandre III (Alexander III Bridge). Open daily. Admission charge. Av. de Tourville, Pl. Vauban, 7e (phone: 45-55-37-70).

**MUSÉE RODIN** This is one of France's most complete and satisfying museum experiences. By ambling through one of the great 18th-century Parisian aristocratic homes and its grounds it's possible to follow the evolution of the career of Auguste Rodin, that genius of modern sculpture. Among the broad terraces and in the serene and elegant gardens are scattered fabled statues such as *The Thinker* and the *Bourgeois de Calais;* the superb statues of Honoré de Balzac and Victor Hugo; the stunning *Gate of Hell,* on which the master labored a lifetime; *Les Bavardes,* a sculpture by Rodin's mistress Camille Claudel; and more. Rodin's celebrated Ugolin group is placed dramatically in the middle of a pond. The museum boutique sells reproductions of the major works. Closed Mondays. Admission charge. 77 Rue de Varenne, 7e (phone: 47-05-01-34).

**MONTPARNASSE** In the early 20th century this neighborhood south of the *Jardin du Luxembourg* (Luxembourg Gardens) hosted a colony of avant-garde painters, writers, and Russian political exiles. Here Hemingway, Picasso, and Scott and Zelda Fitzgerald sipped and supped in such bars and cafés as *La Closerie des Lilas* (see *Nightclubs and Nightlife*); *Le Dôme* (108 Bd. du Montparnasse, 14e; phone: 43-35-25-81); *La Rotonde* (105 Bd. du Montparnasse; phone: 43-26-48-26 or 43-26-68-84); and *La Coupole* and *Le Sélect* (see *Eating Out* for both). The cafés, small restaurants, and winding streets still exist in the shadow of the *Tour Montparnasse* complex (see below). 14e.

**TOUR MONTPARNASSE (MONTPARNASSE TOWER)** Each day the fastest elevator in Europe whisks Parisians and tourists alike up 59 stories (for a fee) to catch a view *down* at the *Eiffel Tower.* The shopping center here boasts all the famous names, and the surrounding office buildings are the headquarters of some of France's largest companies. 33 Av. du Maine, 15e, and Bd. de Vaugirard, 14e (phone: 45-38-52-56).

**MUSÉE D'ORSAY** This imposing former railway station has been transformed into one of the shining examples of modern museum design. Its eclectic collection includes not only the Impressionist paintings formerly displayed in the *Jeu de Paume* (see above), but also less sacred 19th-century achievements in sculpture, photography, and the applied arts, which together provide an excellent overview of the Victorian aesthetic. Masterpieces by Degas, Toulouse-Lautrec, Monet, and others hang in specially designed spaces, and no detail of light, humidity, or acoustics has been left to chance, making this voyage around the art world a very comfortable one. Don't miss the museum's pièce de résistance—the van Goghs on the top floor, glowing under the skylight. Closed Mondays. Admission charge is reduced on Sundays. 1 Rue de Bellechasse, 7e (phone: 40-49-48-14).

**EGLISE ST-GERMAIN-DES-PRÉS (CHURCH OF ST-GERMAIN-IN-THE-FIELDS) AND THE QUARTIER ST-GERMAIN-DES-PRÉS** Probably the oldest church in Paris, it once belonged to an abbey of the same name. The original basilica, completed in AD 558, was destroyed and rebuilt many times. The Romanesque steeple and its massive tower date from 1014. Inside the choir and sanctuary are as they were in the 12th century, and the marble shafts used in the slender columns are 14 centuries old. Pl. St-Germain-des-Prés, 6e (phone: 43-25-41-71).

Surrounding the church is the Quartier St-Germain-des-Prés, long a center for Paris's "fashionable" intellectuals and artists, with art galleries, boutiques, and renowned cafés for people watching (though not necessarily for dining), such as the *Flore* (172 Bd. St-Germain, 6e; phone: 45-48-55-26), Sartre's favorite, and *Les Deux Magots* (6 Pl. St-Germain-des-Prés, 6e; phone: 45-48-55-25), once a Hemingway haunt.

**QUARTIER LATIN (LATIN QUARTER)** Extending from the *Jardin du Luxembourg* and the *Panthéon* to the Seine, this famous neighborhood still maintains its unique atmosphere. A focal point for *Sorbonne* students since the Middle Ages, it's a mad jumble of narrow streets, old churches, and academic buildings. Boulevard St-Michel and Boulevard St-Germain are its main arteries, both lined with cafés, bookstores, and boutiques of every imaginable kind. There are also some charming old side streets, such as the Rue de la Huchette, off Place St-Michel, and Rue St-André-des-Arts, which starts on the opposite side of Place St-Michel. And don't miss the famous *bouquinistes* (bookstalls) along the Seine, around the Place St-Michel on the Quai des Grands-Augustins and the Quai St-Michel.

**PALAIS ET JARDIN DU LUXEMBOURG (LUXEMBOURG PALACE AND GARDENS)** Built for Marie de Médicis in 1615 in what once were the southern suburbs of Paris, this Renaissance palace became a prison during the French Revolution and now houses the national *Sénat* (Senate). The palace is closed to the public except for a group tour organized by the *Caisse Nationale des Monuments Historiques et* *des Sites* (see *Le Marais,* above) on the first Sunday of each month. The classic formal gardens, with lovely statues and the famous Médicis fountain, are popular with students and with neighborhood children, who play around the artificial lake or in the special children's park paved with rubber. 15 Rue de Vaugirard, 6e (phone: 42-34-20-60).

**PANTHÉON** Originally built by Louis XV in 1764 as a church dedicated to Paris's patron saint, Geneviève, in 1791 it was declared a "non-religious Temple of Fame dedicated to all the gods," where the *grands hommes* of French liberty (the first *grand femme* only arrived in 1885) would be interred. The tombs of Victor Hugo, the Résistance leader Jean Moulin, Rousseau, Voltaire, and Emile Zola, are among those here. The impressive interior also features murals depicting the life of Ste. Geneviève. Closed some holidays. Admission charge. Pl. du Panthéon, 5e (phone: 43-54-34-51).

**MUSÉE NATIONAL DU MOYEN-AGE/THERMES DE CLUNY (CLUNY NATIONAL MUSEUM OF THE MIDDLE AGES/ROMAN BATHS OF CLUNY)** One of the last remaining examples of medieval domestic architecture in Paris, the 15th-century residence of the abbots of Cluny, which was built on the site of 3rd century Gallo-Roman baths and later became the home of Mary Tudor, is now a museum of medieval arts and crafts. The most famous work displayed here is the celebrated *Lady and the Unicorn* tapestry. Closed Tuesdays. Admission charge. 6 Pl. Paul-Painlevé, 5e (phone: 43-25-62-00).

**MOSQUÉE DE PARIS (PARIS MOSQUE)** Dominated by a 130-foot-high minaret in gleaming white marble, this is one of the most beautiful structures of its kind in the world. Take off your shoes before entering the pebble-lined gardens full of flowers and dwarf trees. The *Salle de Prières* (Hall of Prayer), with its lush Oriental carpets, is open to the public, but it's closed Fridays (the weekly prayer day for Muslims) and during lunch hours. Admission charge. Next door is a restaurant and a patio for sipping Turkish coffee and tasting Oriental sweets. Pl. du Puits-de-l'Ermite, 5e (phone: 45-35-97-33).

**EGLISE ST-SÉVERIN (CHURCH OF ST. SÉVERIN)** This church still retains its beautiful Flamboyant Gothic ambulatory, considered a masterpiece of its kind, and lovely old stained glass windows dating from the 15th and 16th centuries. The small garden and the restored charnel house also are of interest. 3 Rue des Prêtres, 5e (phone: 43-25-96-63).

**EGLISE ST-JULIEN-LE-PAUVRE (CHURCH OF ST. JULIAN THE POOR)** One of the smallest and oldest churches (12th to 13th century) in Paris offers a superb view of Notre-Dame from the charming Place René-Viviani. 1 Rue St-Julien-le-Pauvre, 5e (no phone).

ILE DE LA CITÉ

The birthplace of Paris, settled by Gallic fishermen about 250 BC, this island in the Seine is so rich in historical monuments that an entire day could be spent here and on the neighboring Ile St-Louis (see below). A walk all around the islands, along the lovely, tree-shaded quays on both banks of the Seine, opens up one breathtaking view (of the *Cathédrale de Notre-Dame,* the *Louvre,* the Pont Neuf) after another.

**CATHÉDRALE DE NOTRE-DAME DE PARIS (CATHEDRAL OF OUR LADY OF PARIS)** It is said that druids once worshiped on this consecrated ground. Later the Romans built their temple here, and many Christian churches followed. In 1163 the foundations were laid for the present cathedral, one of the world's finest examples of Gothic architecture. By 1270, when the funeral of Louis IX (St. Louis) was held here, the cathedral was essentially complete, but construction continued until 1345, working from the plans of a single anonymous architect. Henri IV and Napoleon both were crowned here. At press time a 10-year restoration project was beginning, the first major work on the cathedral since the mid-19th century. Unfortunately for visitors, scaffolding is expected to cover the exterior throughout this year while the façade undergoes a high-tech cleaning process. Take a guided tour (offered in English at noon Tuesdays and Wednesdays and in French at noon other weekdays, 2:30 PM Saturdays, and 2 PM Sundays) or quietly explore on your own, but be sure to climb the 225-foot towers (closed during lunch hours) for a marvelous view of the city, and try to see the splendid 13th-century stained glass rose windows at sunset. Open daily. Pl. du Parvis de Notre-Dame, 4e (phone: 43-54-22-63).

**PALAIS DE JUSTICE AND LA SAINTE-CHAPELLE (PALACE OF JUSTICE AND HOLY CHAPEL** This monumental complex was first the seat of the Roman military government, then the headquarters of the early kings of the Capetian dynasty, and finally the law courts. In the 13th century Louis IX built a new palace, adding *Sainte-Chapelle* to house the "Sacred Crown of Thorns" and other holy relics. Its 15 soaring stained glass windows (plus a later rose window), with more than 1,100 brilliantly colored and exquisitely detailed miniature scenes of biblical life, are among the unquestioned masterpieces of medieval French art, and the graceful, gleaming 247-foot spire is one of the city's most beautiful and understated landmarks—particularly stunning on a sunny day. Closed holidays. Admission charge. 4 Bd. du Palais, 1er (phone: 43-54-30-09).

**CONCIERGERIE** This remnant of the former royal palace sits like a fairytale castle on the Ile de la Cité. It served as a prison during the revolution, and visitors can still see the cells where Marie-Antoinette, the Duke of Orléans, Mme. du Barry, and others of lesser fame awaited the guillotine. Documents and engravings dating from the time of Ravaillac, the 17th-century royal assassin, also illustrate the past of this sinister palace. Don't miss the Girondins' chapel, where the moderate Girondin deputies shared their last meal. Closed holidays. Admission charge. 4 Bd. du Palais, 1er (phone: 43-54-30-06).

## ILE ST-LOUIS

Walk across the footbridge behind *Notre-Dame* and you're in a charming, tranquil village. This "enchanted isle" has managed to keep its provincial charm despite its central location. Follow the main street, Rue St-Louis-en-l'Ile, down the middle of the island, past courtyards, balconies, old doors, curious stairways, the ornate *Eglise St-Louis* (St. Louis Church), built between 1664 and 1726, and discreet plaques bearing the names of illustrious former residents (including Mme. Curie, Voltaire, Baudelaire, Gautier, and Daumier). Pause along the way for some famous (and fabulous) *Berthillon* ice cream, either at their shop (see *Shopping*) or at one of the other small cafés that serve it. Then take the quay back along the banks of the Seine.

# Sources and Resources

TOURIST INFORMATION

In Paris the *Office de Tourisme de Paris* (127 Champs-Elysées, 8e; phone: 49-52-53-54 for general information; 49-52-53-56 for a recorded message in English on current events and exhibitions) is the place to go for information, brochures, maps, or hotel reservations. It's closed on *New Year's Day*, May 1, and *Christmas* only. If you call the office, be prepared for a four- to five-minute wait before someone answers. Other tourist offices, all closed Sundays, are found at the *Eiffel Tower* (phone: 45-51-22-15; closed October through April) and train stations: *Gare du Nord* (15 Rue de Dunkerque, 10e; phone: 45-26-94-82); *Gare de Lyon* (Pl. Louis-Armand, 12e; phone: 43-43-33-24); *Gare de l'Est* (Pl. du 11-Novembre 1918, 10e; phone: 46-07-17-73); *Gare Montparnasse* (17 Bd. de Vaugirard, 15e; phone: 43-22-19-19); and *Gare d'Austerlitz* (53 Quai d'Austerlitz, 13e; phone: 45-84-91-70). The *US Embassy* is at 2 Av. Gabriel (phone: 42-96-12-02 or 42-61-80-75).

In the US, the *French Government Tourist Office* answers phone inquiries only via its information line, 900-990-0040 (cost is 50¢ per minute). There are tourist office branches at 9454 Wilshire Blvd., Suite 715, Beverly Hills, CA 90212 (phone: 310-271-6665; fax: 310-276-2835); 676 N. Michigan Ave., Suite 3360, Chicago, IL 60611 (phone: 312-751-7800; fax: 312-337-6339); 628 Fifth Ave., New York, NY 10020 (phone: 212-757-1125 or 212-315-0888; fax: 212-247-6468); and 610 Fifth Ave., Suite 222, New York, NY 10020 (for mail requests only). The *French Embassy* is at 4101 Reservoir Rd. NW, Washington, DC 20007-2185 (phone: 202-944-6000).

**ENTRY REQUIREMENTS** A US citizen needs a current passport for a stay of up to 90 days.

**TIME** The time in France is six hours later than in US East Coast cities. France observes daylight saving time.

**LANGUAGE** French is the official language, though in many cases you can get by in English.

**ELECTRIC CURRENT** 220 volts, 50 cycles, AC.

**MONEY** The French franc (F) equals 100 centimes. One-centime coins are no longer minted, so all prices are rounded to the nearest fivecentime denomination. At press time about 5.30 francs bought $1 US.

**TIPPING** Hotel and restaurant bills include a 12% to 15% service charge. The doorman who helps with luggage should receive 5F per piece; the room service waiter 10F; the chambermaid should get 10F per day. Taxi drivers are rarely tipped by the French but may expect it from an American; 15% will suffice.

**BANKING/BUSINESS HOURS** Banks are open weekdays from 9 AM to 5 PM. Business hours generally run from 9 AM to 6 PM, with a generous break of up to two and a half hours for lunch beginning at noon or 1 PM.

**NATIONAL HOLIDAYS** *New Year's Day* (January 1), *Easter Sunday* (April 16), *Easter Monday* (April 17), *Labor Day* (May 1), *VE Day* (May 8), *Ascension Thursday* (May 25), *Whitmonday* (June 5), *Bastille Day* (July 14), the *Feast of the Assumption* (August 15), *All Saints' Day* (November 1), *Armistice Day* (November 11), and *Christmas Day* (December 25).

**LOCAL COVERAGE** *Paris Selection,* in both French and English, is the official tourist office magazine. It lists events, sights, tours, some hotels, restaurants, shopping, nightclubs, and other information. Far more complete are the weekly guides *L'Officiel des Spectacles, 7 à Paris,* and *Pariscope.* All are in simple French (*Pariscope* even has a section in English) and are available at newsstands. English-language magazines are *Boulevard,* sold at newsstands; the monthly *WHERE,* distributed in hotels; and, available free at English-language bookstores and other locations, the monthly *Paris Free Voice,* and the biweeklies *Paris City* and *France-USA Contacts.* Among the city's English-language bookstores are *W. H. Smith and Sons, Brentano's,* and *Shakespeare and Company* (see *Shopping* for all three).

**TELEPHONE** All phone numbers in Paris begin with the prefix 4 (incorporated into the numbers given here); in the area surrounding Paris, they are preceded by either 3 or 6. When calling a number in the Paris region (including the Ile-de-France) from Paris, dial only the 8-digit number. When calling a number from outside the Paris region, dial 1, then the 8-digit number. The country code for France is 33. Dial 18 for emergency assistance.

## GETTING AROUND

**AIRPORTS** *Aéroport Charles-de-Gaulle* (Roissy, 14 miles/23 km northeast of Paris; phone: 48-62-12-12 or 48-62-22-80) has two terminals: *Aérogare 1,* for foreign airlines, and *Aérogare 2,* predominantly for *Air France* flights. The two terminals are connected by a free shuttle bus. *Air France* airport buses (phone: 42-99-20-18; 49-38-57-57 for a multilingual recorded message), open to passengers of all airlines, leave for the city, stopping at the *Palais des Congrès* (*Métro:* Porte Maillot) and the *Arc de Triomphe* (*Métro:* Charles de Gaulle-Etoile), every 12 minutes from 5:40 AM to 11 PM and take about 40 minutes; there's also an hourly bus that goes to the *Gare Montparnasse* on the Rive Gauche and takes about 45 minutes. The *RATP* (see *Bus,* below) operates the *Roissybus* (city bus No. 352), departing from the *Opéra/Palais Garnier* (Pl. de l'Opéra, 9e) for the airport every 15 minutes from 5:45 AM to 11:30 PM daily; the trip takes about 45 minutes, and at press time the one-way fare was 30F (about $5.15). For more information call 48-04-18-24 or the main *RATP* information number. *Roissy-Rail,* part of the *RER* B suburban train line, runs between the airport and the *Gare du Nord* every 15 minutes and takes about 35 minutes. (A shuttle bus connects the airport to Roissy station, and from there to the *Gare du Nord* is by train.) For more details, call the general *SNCF* information number (see *Train,* below).

*Aéroport d'Orly* (9 miles/14 km south of Paris; phone: 49-75-52-52 or 49-75-15-15) has two terminals: *Orly Ouest,* mainly for domestic flights and flights to Geneva, and *Orly Sud,* for international flights. The two terminals are connected by a free shuttle. *Air France* buses (phone: 43-23-97-10; 49-38-57-57 for a multilingual recorded message) leave *Orly* for a terminus on the Esplanade des Invalides (*Métro: Invalides)* every 12 minutes from 5:50 AM to 11 PM and take about 40 minutes. Another *RATP* service (see *Bus,* below) is *Orlybus* (city bus No. 215), which links the airport to *Place Denfert-Rochereau* in southern Paris, leaving every 13 minutes daily from 5:45 AM to 11:30 PM; the trip takes about 30 minutes, and the one-way fare at press time was 27F (about $4.65). *Orlyval* is a service which connects by monorail the two *Orly* terminals with the Antony station on the *RER* C line, which links the suburbs with major stops in the city. The monorail shuttle departs every five to seven minutes from *Orly Sud* from 6:30 AM to 9:15 PM daily except Sunday, when hours are 7 AM to 10:55 PM. The trip takes 30 to 45 minutes, depending on the stop; at press time the combined fare for the shuttle and the *RER* trip into Paris was 45F (about $7.80). A more direct service is *Orly-Rail,* part of the *RER* C suburban train line, which makes various stops in the city such as *Luxembourg, St-Michel,* and *Invalides,* with a shuttle bus from *Orly* station to the airport. The service runs every 15 or 30 minutes depending on the time of day and takes 35 to 50 minutes, according to the stop. For more details on *Orlyval* or *Orly-Rail* call the general *SNCF* information number (see *Train,* below).

*Air France* buses linking *Charles de Gaulle* and *Orly* airports run every 20 minutes and take from 50 to 75 minutes.

**BOAT** The *Batobus,* operated by *Bateaux Parisiens* (Pont d'Iéna, Port de la Bourdonnais, 7e, phone: 44-11-33-44; and Quai Montebello, 5e, phone: 43-26-92-55), carries passengers along the Seine daily from mid-April through September 26; stops (watch for the signs on the quays) are near the *Eiffel Tower,* the *Musée d'Orsay,* the *Louvre, Notre-Dame,* and the *Hôtel de Ville* (just east of the *Louvre*). The fare is 12F (about $2.10) for each leg of the trip, or 60F (about $10.35) for an all-day, unlimited travel pass; tickets may be purchased at the stops along the quays.

**BUS** They're slow, but good for sightseeing; a few do not run on Sundays and holidays. *Métro* tickets are valid on all city buses, but you will need a new ticket if you change buses. Unlike the *Métro,* buses charge by distance; two tickets are sometimes needed for a ride across town (into a different zone). The standard fare at press time was about 7F (around $1.20), but it's best to buy a *carnet* (booklet) of 10 tickets, only 41F (around $7.10); one of the special tourist passes for short stays in Paris; or a *carte orange,* a pass permitting either a week or a month of unlimited travel (see *Métro,* below, for more on tickets and passes). Bus lines are numbered, and both stops and buses have signs indicating routes. The Paris *Régional Autorité du Transit Provincial* (*RATP;* Regional Rapid Transit Authority; phone: 43-46-14-14 for general information), which operates the *Métro* and bus system, has designated certain bus lines as being of particular interest to tourists; look for a panel on the front of the bus reading (in English), "This bus is good for sightseeing." On Sundays and holidays, a special *RATP* sightseeing bus, the *Balabus,* runs from the *Grande Arche de la Défense,* west of Paris, all the way east to the *Gare de Lyon.* The total trip time is 75 minutes; you can board the bus at any stop marked "Balabus Bb." The *RATP* has tourist offices at Place de la Madeleine, next to the flower market (8e; phone: 40-06-71-45) and on the Rive Gauche at 53 *bis* Quai des Grands-Augustins near Place St-Michel (6e; phone: 40-46-44-50 or 40-46-43-60); both organize bus tours in Paris and the surrounding region.

**CAR RENTAL** Book when making your plane reservation, or contact *Avis* (phone: 46-10-60-60, main reservations number in France; 5 Rue Bixio, 7e, phone: 44-18-10-50; *Charles de Gaulle* airport, phone: 48-62-34-34; and *Orly* airport, phone: 49-75-44-91), *Budget* (phone: 45-72-1115), *Europcar* (phone: 46-51-44-03), or *Hertz* (phone: 47-88-51-51). Many car rental agencies also have offices in train stations.

**MÉTRO** Operating from 5:30 AM to about 1 AM, the *Métro* system is generally safe (although pickpockets abound in certain areas), clean, quiet, and easy to use, and since the *RATP* has been sponsoring cultural events and art exhibits in some 200 of Paris's 368 *Métro* stations, at times it is even entertaining. Different lines are identified by the names of their terminals at either end. Every station has clear directional maps, some with push-button devices that light up the proper route after a destination button is pushed. Handy streetside bus and *Métro* directions are now available in some *Métro* stations from *SITU (Système d'Information des Trajets Urbains),* a computer that prints out the fastest routing onto a wallet-size piece of paper, complete with the estimated length of the trip, free of charge. High-traffic spots such as the *Châtelet Métro* station, the *Gare Montparnasse,* and the Boulevard St-Germain now sport *SITU* machines.

Keep your ticket (you may be asked to show it to one of the controllers who regularly patrol the *Métro*) and don't cheat; there are spot checks. Tickets cost about 7F (around $1.20); a *carnet* (10-ticket book) is available at a reduced rate, about 41F (around $7.10).

The same tickets can be used on buses, but on the *Métro* you will need only one ticket per ride. The *RATP* offers several economical tourist passes: The *Formule I* card is a one-day pass providing unlimited travel on the *Métro,* bus, and suburban trains; the *Paris-Visite* card entitles the bearer to three or five consecutive days of unlimited travel, plus discounts at several Paris attractions. A two-zone *Formule I* card (covering metropolitan Paris) costs 27F (about $4.70); three-day *Paris-Visite* cards cost 90F (about $15.50), and five-day cards cost 145F (about $25). The cards may be purchased upon presentation of your passport at 44 *Métro* stations, the four regional express stations, the six *SNCF* stations (see *Train,* below), or at the *RATP*'s tourist offices (see *Bus,* above); the cards also may be purchased in the US from *Marketing Challenges International* (10 E. 21st St., Suite 600, New York, NY 10010; phone: 212-529-9069; fax: 212-529-4838). The *carte orange,* a commuter pass, is available weekly (beginning on Mondays) or monthly (beginning the first of the month), and like the tourist passes provides unlimited travel. Though actually more economical than the tourist passes, the *carte orange* does require a small (passport-size) photo to attach to the card. For a two-zone pass (covering metropolitan Paris), the weekly *carte orange* cost 63F (about $10.90) at press time and the monthly pass sold for 219F (about $37.75). They are available at all *Métro* stations.

**TAXI** Taxis can be found at stands at main intersections, outside train stations and official buildings, and in the streets. A taxi is available if the entire "TAXI" sign is illuminated (with a white light); the small light *beside* the roof light signifies availability after dark; and no light means the driver is off duty. Be aware that Parisian cab drivers are notoriously selective about where they will go and how many passengers they will allow in their cabs. A foursome will inevitably have trouble since, by law, no one may ride in the front seat, but, also by law, a cab at a taxi stand must take you wherever you want to go. You also can call *Taxi Bleu* (phone: 49-36-10-10) or *Radio Taxi* (phone: 47-39-33-33); dispatchers usually speak at least some English. The meter starts running from the time the cab is dispatched, and a tip of about 15% is customary. Fares increase at night and on Sundays and holidays.

**TOURS** *Cityrama* (4 Pl. des Pyramides, 1er; phone: 42-60-30-14) and *Paris Vision* (214 Rue de Rivoli, 1er; phone: 42-60-31-25) offer well-planned, informative tours on bubble-top, double-decker buses equipped with earphones for commentary in English. Reserve through any travel agent or your hotel's concierge. Both *Cityrama* and *Paris Vision,* among other operators, also offer organized "Paris by Night" group tours, which include at least one *"spectacle"*—a performance featuring women in minimal, yet elaborate, costumes, lavish sets and effects, and sophisticated striptease.

Another great way to see Paris is from the Seine, by boat. Prices are reasonable for a day or evening cruise on a modern, glass-enclosed river rambler, which provides a constantly changing picture of the city. Contact *Bateaux-Mouches* (Pont d'Alma, 7e; phone:

42-25-96-10); *Bateaux Parisiens* (see *Boat,* above); or *Vedettes Pont-Neuf* (Pl. Vert-Galant, 1er; phone: 46-33-98-38). *Paris Canal* (19-21 Quai de la Loire, Bassin de la Villette, 19e; phone: 42-40-96-97) and *Canauxrama* (13 Quai de la Loire, Bassin de la Villette, 19e; phone: 42-39-15-00) offer three-hour barge trips starting on the Seine and navigating through some of the city's old canals and locks (*Paris Canal* offers a subterranean route under the *Bastille*). *Yachts de Paris* (Port de Javel-Hunt, 15e; phone: 44-37-10-20) offers romantic, first class dinner cruises which feature menus devised by two-Michelin-star chef Gérard Besson.

**TRAIN** Paris has six main *SNCF* (*Société Nationale des Chemins de Fer,* the French national railroad) train stations, each one serving a different area of the country. Trains heading north depart from *Gare du Nord* (15 Rue de Dunkerque, 10e; phone: 49-95-10-00); east, *Gare de l'Est* (Pl. du 11-Novembre 1918, 10e; phone: 40-18-20-00); southeast, *Gare de Lyon* (Pl. Louis-Armand, 12e; phone: 40-19-60-00); southwest, *Gare d'Austerlitz* (53 Quai d'Austerlitz, 13e; phone: 45-84-14-18); west, *Gare Montparnasse* (17 Bd. de Vaugirard, 15e; phone: 40-48-10-00); west and northwest, *Gare St-Lazare* (20 Rue St-Lazare, 8e; phone: 42-85-88-00). For general information call 45-82-50-50; for reservations, 45-65-60-60 (there's usually someone who can speak English). For additional information in English contact the tourist office within each station (see *Tourist Information*).

The *TGV (Train à Grand Vitesse),* the world's fastest train, has cut two hours off the usual four-hour ride between Paris and Lyons; it similarly shortens traveling time from Paris to Marseilles, the Côte d'Azur, the Atlantic Coast, the English Channel at Calais, and Switzerland. Most *TGVs* leave from the *Gare de Lyon,* except for the Atlantic Coast run, which departs from the *Gare Montparnasse,* and the Lille-Calais run, which leaves from the *Gare du Nord* and connects at Calais to the "Chunnel," the trans-Channel tunnel connecting France and Great Britain. Reserved seats are necessary on all *TGVs;* tickets can be purchased from machines in all main train stations.

## LOCAL SERVICES

**BABY-SITTING** Many hotels arrange babysitters. Agencies recommended by the *Paris Tourist Office* are *Baby-sitters, Inc.* (45-30-03-22); *Baby-sitting Services* (phone: 46-37-51-24); and *SOS Maman* (phone: 46-47-89-98), which specializes in last-minute sitters. Whether the sitter is hired directly or through an agency, ask for and check references.

**DENTIST (ENGLISH-SPEAKING)** Dr. Edward Cohen (20 Rue de la Paix; phone: 42-61-65-64) and Dr. Gérard Gautier (47 Av. Hoche; phone: 47-66-17-10). The *American Hospital* (see *Medical Emergency,* below) also provides dental services.

**DRY CLEANER/TAILOR** Dry cleaners are available throughout the city. Note that many have two different *pressings* (price schedules), one for "economic" service, another for faster, more expensive service.

The less expensive prices may be posted outside, but unless you specify, your clothes will be given the expensive treatment. *John Baillie, Real Scotch Tailor* (1 Rue Auber at Pl. de l'Opéra, 2e; phone: 47-42-49-17) is a reputable firm that offers French-style tailoring, despite its name.

**LIMOUSINE SERVICE** *Compagnie des Limousines* (37 Rue Acacias, 17e; phone: 43-80-79-41) and *Executive Car/Carey Limousine* (25 Rue d'Astorg, 8e; phone: 42-65-54-20; fax: 42-65-25-93).

**MEDICAL EMERGENCY** The *American Hospital* (63 Bd. Victor Hugo, Neuilly-sur-Seine 92200; phone: 46-41-25-25) provides advanced equipment and 24-hour emergency service. All of the staff speaks English and the hospital maintains an extensive network of English-speaking specialists. *SOS Médecins* (phone: 47-07-77-77) provides 24-hour house calls by doctors.

**MESSENGER SERVICE** Most hotels will arrange for pickups and deliveries.

**NATIONAL/INTERNATIONAL COURIER** *DHL Worldwide Express* (phone: 800-225-5345 in the US; 05-20-25-25, toll-free, in France) and *Federal Express* (phone: 800-238-5355 in the US; 05-33-33-55, toll-free, in France) .

**OFFICE EQUIPMENT RENTAL** *International Computer Location* (43 Rue Beaubourg, 3e; phone: 42-72-07-00) offers rentals of Macintosh computers.

**PHOTOCOPIES** In addition to the numerous small outlets specializing in photocopies, facilities are available in many stationery stores and post offices.

**POST OFFICE** The main post office in Paris (52 Rue du Louvre, 1er; phone: 40-28-20-00; fax: 40-28-20-81) is open weekdays from 8 AM to 7 PM and Saturdays from 8 AM to noon. Branch offices have similar hours. Stamps also are sold at hotels, *tabacs* (tobacco shops), and some newsstands, as well as from public vending machines.

**SECRETARY/STENOGRAPHER (ENGLISH-SPEAKING)** *Régis Business Center* (72 Rue du Faubourg-St-Honoré; phone: 40-07-80-07).

**TELECONFERENCE FACILITIES** *Hôtel Méridien* (81 Bd. Gouvion-St-Cyr, 17e; phone: 40-68-34-34), among other hotels.

**TELEX AND FAX SERVICES** *Poste Publique de Télex* (7 Rue Feydeau, 2e; phone: 42-33-20-12), a special *PTT* office where you can send a fax or telex, is open daily (closed mornings on holidays); faxes also may be sent from any of the city's other post offices. Prices are astronomical (at press time, around $50 for two pages to the US).

**TRANSLATOR** For a list of accredited translators contact the *Consulate* of the *American Embassy* (2 Rue St-Florentin, 1er; phone: 42-96-14-88 or 42-61-80-75).

**OTHER** Tuxedo rental: *Au Cor de Chasse* (40 Rue de Buci, 6e; phone: 43-26-51-89).

# SPECIAL EVENTS

In Paris during summer and fall the word "festival" translates into a musical orgy.

---

**FAVORITE FÊTE**

**Festival Estival and Festival d'Automne** The former, in July and August, brings a musical kaleidoscope of Gregorian chants, Bartók string quartets, Rameau opera, and more to the city's most picturesque and acoustically delightful churches. The *Festival d'Automne,* which takes up where the *Estival* leaves off, concentrates on the contemporary, generally focusing on one or two main themes or composers and including a certain number of new works. Its moving spirit is Pierre Boulez, France's top musical talent. The *Festival d'Automne* also features theater and dance performances. For information, contact the *Festival Estival de Paris* (20 Rue Geoffroy-l'Asnier, Paris 75004; phone: 48-04-98-01) and the *Festival d'Automne* (156 Rue de Rivoli, Paris 75001; phone: 42-96-12-27).

---

Fashion shows come to Paris in January, when press and buyers pass judgment on the spring and summer haute couture collections; later, in February and March, more buyers arrive for the ready-to-wear shows (fall and winter clothes), which also are open to the trade only. March brings the year's first *Foire Nationale à la Brocante et aux Jambons* (National Flea Market and Regional Food Products Fair), an event that is repeated in September; it's held on the Ile de Chatou, an island in the Seine west of Paris, accessible by the *RER* suburban train.

The running of the *Prix du Président de la République,* the year's first big horse race, takes place at *Auteuil,* in the *Bois de Boulogne,* in April. Late April through early May brings the *Foire de Paris,* a big international trade fair, to the *Parc des Expositions* (Porte de Versailles, 15e). In late April or May, the *Paris Marathon* is run; late May through early June is the time for the illustrious *Championnats Internationaux de France,* better known as the *French Open* tennis championship (in France it's informally called the *Roland Garros,* after the stadium in which it's held; 16e). Horse races crowd the calendar in June—there's the *Prix de Diane/Hermès* at *Chantilly,* the *Grand Prix de Paris* at *Longchamp,* the *Grande Steeplechase de Paris* at *Auteuil,* and the *Grand Prix de St-Cloud* (see *Horse Racing,* below, for details on all four). In the middle of June, the *Festival du Marais* begins a month's worth of music and dance performances in the courtyards of the Marais district's old townhouses. *Bastille Day* (July 14), which commemorates the fall of the *Bastille* and the beginning of the French Revolution in 1789, is celebrated with music, fireworks, parades (including one that goes down the Champs-Elysées), and dancing till dawn in many neighborhoods.

Cyclists arrive in Paris for the finish of the three-week *Tour de France* in late July. Also in July, press and buyers arrive to view the fall and winter haute couture collections, but the ready-to-wear shows (spring and summer clothes) wait until September and October, because August for Parisians is vacation time.

In even-numbered years the *Biennale des Antiquaires,* a major antiques event, comes to the *Grand Palais* from late September through early October. Every year on the first Sunday of October, the last big horse race of the season, the *Prix de l'Arc de Triomphe,* is run at *Longchamp* (see *Horse Racing*). The first Saturday in October also brings the *Fête des Vendanges à Montmartre,* a celebration of the harvest of the city's last remaining vineyard, in Montmartre. The *Salon Mondial de l'Automobile* (World Motor Show) takes place at the *Parc des Expositions* in even-numbered years, usually in October. On November 11, ceremonies at the *Arc de Triomphe* and a parade mark *Armistice Day;* the *Open de Paris* tennis tournament is also played this month. The *Salon du Cheval et du Poney* (Horse and Pony Show) comes to the *Parc des Expositions* in early December; then comes *Noël* (Christmas), which is celebrated most movingly with a *La Veille de Noël* (Christmas Eve) midnight mass at *Notre-Dame.* At midnight a week later, the *Nouvel An* (New Year) bows in to spontaneous street revelry in the Quartier Latin and along the Champs-Elysées.

## MUSEUMS

Besides those described in *Special Places*, the following museums and sites may be of interest (unless otherwise indicated, an admission fee is charged).

**BIBLIOTHÈQUE-MUSÉE DE L'OPÉRA (OPERA LIBRARY AND MUSEUM)** These trace the history of opera in Paris from its 17th-century origins. Closed Sundays, holidays, and two weeks around *Easter. Opéra/Palais Garnier,* Pl. de l'Opéra, 9e (phone: 47-42-07-02).

**CATACOMBES (CATACOMBS)** Dating from the Gallo-Roman era, these also contain the remains of Danton, Robespierre, and many others. Bring a flashlight. Closed weekday mornings, during lunch hours on weekends, Mondays, and holidays. 1 Pl. Denfert-Rochereau, 14e (phone: 43-22-47-63).

**CITÉ DE LA MUSIQUE** Comprising concert halls, the *Conservatoire National Supérieur de la Musique,* and other music-related facilities, this complex also contains a music museum with a collection of 700 rare instruments. Closed Mondays. In the *Parc de la Villette,* 211 Av. Jean-Jaurès, 19e (phone: 40-05-80-00).

**CRYPTE ARCHÉOLOGIQUE DE NOTRE-DAME (ARCHAEOLOGICAL CRYPT OF NOTRE-DAME)** Exhibits in this ancient crypt on which the cathedral was built include floor plans that show the evolution of the cathedral and earlier religious structures built on this spot. Open daily. Under the square in front of *Notre-Dame,* at Parvis de Notre-Dame, 4e (phone: 43-29-83-51).

**EGOUTS (SEWERS)** This underground city of tunnels has become an incredibly popular attraction, with lines that sometimes take an hour. Open daily. Pl. de la Résistance, in front of 93 Quai d'Orsay, 7e (phone: 47-05-10-29).

**MANUFACTURE DES GOBELINS** The famous tapestry factory has been in operation since the 15th century. Guided tours of the workshops take place Tuesdays, Wednesdays, and Thursdays (except holidays) from 2 to 3 PM. 42 Av. des Gobelins, 13e (phone: 43-37-12-60).

**MÉMORIAL DE LA DÉPORTATION (DEPORTATION MEMORIAL)** In a tranquil garden in the shadow of Notre-Dame at the tip of Ile de la Cité, this monument is dedicated to the 200,000 French citizens of all religions and races who died in Nazi concentration camps during World War II. Pl. de l'Ile-de-France, 4e.

**MÉMORIAL DU MARTYR JUIF INCONNU (MEMORIAL TO THE UNKNOWN JEWISH MARTYR)** A moving tribute to Jews killed during the Holocaust, this renovated memorial includes a museum displaying World War II documents and photographs. Closed Saturdays and Jewish holidays; the museum also is closed Sundays and other holidays. 17 Rue Geoffroy-l'Asnier, 4e (phone: 42-77-44-72).

**MUSÉE DES ANTIQUITÉS NATIONALES (MUSEUM OF NATIONAL ANTIQUITIES)** Archaeological specimens from prehistoric through Merovingian times, including an impressive Gallo-Roman collection, are exhibited. Closed during lunch hours and Tuesdays. Pl. du Château, St-Germain-en-Laye (phone: 34-51-53-65).

**MUSÉE DES ARTS AFRICAINS ET OCÉANIENS (MUSEUM OF AFRICAN AND POLYNESIAN ART)** One of the world's finest collections of African and Polynesian art. Closed during lunch hours and Tuesdays. 293 Av. Daumesnil, 12e (phone: 43-43-14-54).

**MUSÉE DES ARTS DE LA MODE ET DU TEXTILE (MUSEUM OF FASHION AND TEXTILE ARTS)** Adjacent to the *Musée National des Arts Décoratifs* (see below), this museum chronicles the history of the fashion and textile industries with opulent exhibits. Closed Mondays and Tuesdays. 109 Rue de Rivoli, 1er (phone: 42-60-32-14).

**MUSÉE DES ARTS ET TRADITIONS POPULAIRES (MUSEUM OF POPULAR ARTS AND TRADITIONS)** Traditional arts and crafts from rural France are featured. Closed Tuesdays. 6 Av. du Mahatma-Gandhi, *Bois de Boulogne,* 16e (phone: 44-17-60-00).

**MUSÉE BALZAC** The house where the writer lived, with a garden leading to one of the prettiest little alleys in Paris. Closed Mondays and holidays. 47 Rue Raynouard, 16e (phone: 42-24-56-38).

**MUSÉE CERNUSCHI** A collection of Chinese art. Closed Mondays and holidays. 7 Av. Vélasquez, 8e (phone: 45-63-50-75).

**MUSÉE DE LA CHASSE ET DE LA NATURE (MUSEUM OF HUNTING AND NATURE)** Art, weapons, and tapestries relating to the hunt are displayed in the beautiful 17th-century *Hôtel Guénégaud.* Of particular interest is the courtyard, now decorated with sculpture, where horses once were kept. Closed during lunch hours, Tuesdays, and holidays. 60 Rue des Archives, 3e (phone: 42-72-86-43).

**MUSÉE COGNACQ-JAY** In a stunningly beautiful mansion in the Marais district, this museum displays art, snuffboxes, and watches from the 17th and 18th centuries. Closed Mondays. 8 Rue Elzévir, 3e (phone: 40-27-07-21).

**MUSÉE DES COLLECTIONS HISTORIQUES DE LA PRÉFECTURE DE POLICE (MUSEUM OF THE HISTORICAL COLLECTIONS OF THE POLICE PREFEC-TURE)** On the second floor of this modern police station are historic arrest orders (for Charlotte Corday, among others), collections of contemporary engravings, and guillotine blades. Closed Sundays. 1 *bis* Rue des Carmes, 5e (phone: 43-29-21-57).

**MUSÉE DAPPER** This museum mounts splendid temporary exhibitions of African art in a charming former private house near the *Arc de Triomphe.* Open daily. 50 Av. Victor-Hugo, 16e (phone: 45-00-01-50).

**MUSÉE EUGÈNE-DELACROIX** A permanent collection of Delacroix's work as well as temporary exhibits of works by his contemporaries are displayed in the former studio and garden of the great painter. The museum was scheduled to reopen early this year after being closed for renovations. Closed Tuesdays. 6 Rue de Furstemberg, 6e (phone: 43-54-04-87).

**MUSÉE GRÉVIN** Waxworks of French historical figures, from Charlemagne to present day political leaders and celebrities. 10 Bd. Montmartre, 9e (phone: 47-70-85-05). A branch devoted to the Belle Epoque is in the *Forum des Halles* shopping complex. Pl. Carrée, 1er (phone: 40-26-28-50). Both branches are closed mornings.

**MUSÉE GUIMET** The *Louvre*'s Far Eastern collection. The museum's boutique, with reproductions inspired by the collection, is also well worth a visit. Closed Tuesdays. 6 Pl. d'Iéna, 16e (phone: 47-23-61-65).

**MUSÉE GUSTAVE-MOREAU** A collection of works by the early symbolist. Closed Tuesdays and during lunch hours Thursdays through Sundays. 14 Rue de la Rochefoucauld, 9e (phone: 48-74-38-50).

**MUSÉE DE L'INSTITUT DU MONDE ARABE (MUSEUM OF THE INSTITUTE OF THE ARAB WORLD)** Arab and Islamic arts from the 9th through the 19th century. Closed Mondays. 23 Quai St-Bernard, 5e (phone: 40-51-38-38).

**MUSÉE JACQUEMART-ANDRÉ** Eighteenth-century French decorative art and European Renaissance treasures, as well as frequent special exhibitions. Closed Mondays and Tuesdays. 158 Bd. Haussmann, 8e (phone: 42-89-04-91).

**MUSÉE MARMOTTAN** Superb Monets, including the nine masterpieces that were stolen in a daring 1985 robbery. All were recovered in a villa in Corsica and were cleaned, some for the first time, before being rehung. Closed Mondays. 2 Rue Louis-Boilly, 16e (phone: 42-24-07-02).

**MUSÉE DE LA MODE ET DU COSTUME (MUSEUM OF FASHION AND COSTUME)**
A panorama of French contributions to fashion. Closed Mondays
and Tuesday mornings. In the elegant *Palais Galliera,* 10 Av. Pierre-
Ier-de-Serbie, 16e (phone: 47-20-85-23).

**MUSÉE DE LA MONNAIE (MUSEUM OF CURRENCY)** More than 2,000 coins
and 450 medallions, plus historic coinage machines. Closed mornings, Mondays, and holidays. 11 Quai de Conti, 6e (phone: 40-46-
55-35).

**MUSÉE DE MONTMARTRE** Formerly artist Maurice Utrillo's house, it's now
home to a rich collection of paintings, drawings, and documents
depicting life in this quarter. Closed Mondays. 12 Rue Cortot, 18e
(phone: 46-06-61-11).

**MUSÉE NATIONAL DES ARTS DÉCORATIFS (NATIONAL MUSEUM OF DECO-
RATIVE ARTS)** Furniture and applied arts from the Middle Ages to
the present, Oriental carpets, Dubuffet paintings and drawings, and
three centuries of French posters. The *Galerie Art Nouveau–Art
Deco* features the celebrated 1920s designer Jeanne Lanvin's bedroom and bath. Closed mornings, Mondays, and Tuesdays. 107 Rue
de Rivoli, 1er (phone: 42-60-32-14).

**MUSÉE NISSIM DE CAMONDO** A former manor house filled with beautiful furnishings and art objects from the 18th century. Closed during lunch hours and Mondays, Tuesdays, and holidays. 63 Rue de
Monceau, 8e (phone: 45-63-26-32).

**MUSÉE DE SÈVRES** Just outside Paris, next door to the Sèvres factory, it
boasts one of the world's finest collections of porcelain. Closed
Tuesdays. 4 Grand-Rue, Sèvres (phone: 45-34-99-05).

**MUSÉE DU VIN (WINE MUSEUM)** Housed in a 14th-century abbey whose
interior was destroyed during the Revolution, the museum chronicles the history of wine and describes the wine-making process
through displays, artifacts, and a series of wax figure tableaux.
Closed mornings. Admission charge includes a glass of wine. 5-7
Pl. Charles-Dickens, 16e (phone: 45-25-63-26).

**PAVILLON DES ARTS** Located in the mushroom-shaped buildings overlooking the *Forum des Halles* complex, this space mounts a variety of art exhibits, from paintings to sculpture, ancient to modern.
Closed mornings, Mondays, and holidays. 101 Rue Rambuteau, 1er
(phone: 42-33-82-50).

**VIDÉOTHÈQUE DE PARIS** A treasure trove of information about the City
of Light, this extensive computerized video archive contains thousands of films, documentaries, and videos dating from the turn of
the century to the present. Closed mornings and Mondays. 2 Grand
Galerie, 1er (phone: 44-76-62-00).

GALLERIES
Although fine galleries can be found all over the city, Paris's best
are clustered on the Rive Droite around the *Centre Georges-Pom-*

*pidou* and the Place de la Concorde, and on the Rive Gauche on or near the Rue de Seine. Here are some of our favorites:

**ADRIEN MAEGHT** Works by a prestigious list of artists that includes Miró, Matisse, Calder, and Chagall are displayed in this Rive Gauche gallery. 42 and 46 Rue du Bac, 7e (phone: 45-48-45-15).

**AGATHE GAILLARD** The best in photography, including works by Cartier-Bresson and the like. 3 Rue du Pont-Louis-Philippe, 4e (phone: 42-77-38-24).

**ARTCURIAL** Sculptures and prints by early moderns, such as Braque and Delaunay, are featured. The bookshop has an extensive, multilingual collection of art books. 9 Av. Matignon, 8e (phone: 42-99-16-16).

**BEAUBOURG** Well-known names in the Paris art scene, including Niki de Saint-Phalle, César, Tinguely, and Klossowski are found here. 23 Rue du Renard, 4e (phone: 42-71-20-50).

**CAROLINE CORRE** Exhibitions by contemporary artists, specializing in unique, handmade artists' books. 53 Rue Berthe, 18e (phone: 42-55-37-76).

**CLAUDE BERNARD** Francis Bacon, David Hockney, and Raymond Mason are among the artists exhibited here. 5 Rue des Beaux-Arts, 6e (phone: 43-26-97-07).

**DANIEL MALINGUE** Works by the Impressionists, as well as such notable Parisian artists from the 1930s to the 1950s as Foujita and Fautrier. 26 Av. Matignon, 8e (phone: 42-66-60-33).

**DANIEL TEMPLON** Major contemporary American and Italian artists. 30 Rue Beaubourg, 3e (phone: 42-72-14-10).

**DARTHEA SPEYER** Contemporary painting is featured in this gallery run by a former American embassy attaché. 6 Rue Jacques-Callot, 6e (phone: 43-54-78-41).

**GALERIE DE FRANCE** A prestigious gallery located in a majestic space features the works of historical avant-garde artists such as Brancusi and Gabo, as well as such contemporary artists as Matta, Aillaud, and Arroyo. 52 Rue de la Verrerie, 4e (phone: 42-74-38-00).

**HERVÉ ODERMATT CAZEAU** Early moderns—among them Picasso, Léger, and Pissarro—and antiques. 85 *bis* Rue du Faubourg-St-Honoré, 8e (phone: 42-66-92-58).

**JEAN FOURNIER** This dealer defended abstract expressionism in 1955 and remains faithful to the cause in his main gallery, where he also exhibits the works of promising young artists. 44 Rue Quincampoix, 4e (phone: 42-77-32-31).

**LELONG** The great moderns on view here include Tapiès, Bacon, Alechinsky, Donald Judd, and Voss. 13-14 Rue de Téhéran, 8e (phone: 45-63-13-19).

**MARWAN HOSS** In an elegant space near the *Tuileries* are displayed works by Hartung, Henri Hayden, Julio Gonzalez, and Zao Wou-Ki. 12 Rue d'Alger, 1er (phone: 42-96-37-96).

**NIKKI DIANA MARQUARDT** A spacious gallery of contemporary work opened by an enterprising dealer from the Bronx, New York. 9 Pl. des Vosges, 4e (phone: 42-78-21-00).

**THORIGNY** Marcel Duchamp, Man Ray, and other early avant-garde greats are exhibited here along with promising new artists. 13 Rue de Thorigny, 3e (phone: 48-87-60-65).

**YVON LAMBERT** A dealer with an eye for the avant-avant-garde, he also exhibits the works of major artists from the 1970s and 1980s, including Jammes, Lewitt, Serra, and Schnabel. 108 Rue Vieille-du-Temple, 3e (phone: 42-71-09-33).

**ZABRISKIE** Early and contemporary photography by Atget, Brassaï, Arbus, and others. 37 Rue Quincampoix, 4e (phone: 42-72-35-47).

## SHOPPING

From street trends to classic haute couture, Paris sets the styles the world copies. Prices are generally high, but more than a few people are willing to pay for the quality of the merchandise, not to mention the cachet of a Paris label.

The big department stores are excellent places to get an idea of what's available. They include *Galeries Lafayette* (40 Bd. Haussmann, 9e; phone: 42-82-34-56; and other locations); *Printemps* (64 Bd. Haussmann, 9e; phone: 42-82-50-00); *La Samaritaine* (19 Rue de la Monnaie, 1er; phone: 40-41-20-20); *Le Bazar de l'Hôtel de Ville* (*BHV;* 52 Rue de Rivoli, 4e; phone: 42-74-90-00); and *Au Bon Marché,* located in two buildings on Rue de Sèvres (main store, 22 Rue de Sèvres, 7e, phone: 44-39-80-00; the supermarket annex, *La Grande Epicerie,* at 38 Rue de Sèvres, phone: 44-39-81-00).

Three major shopping centers—*Porte Maillot* (Pl. de la Porte Maillot, 16e and 17e, phone: 45-74-29-09); *Maine Montparnasse* (at the intersection of Bd. du Montparnasse and Rue de Rennes, 6e); and the *Forum des Halles* (Rue Pierre-Lescot and Rue Rambuteau, 1er; phone: 44-76-96-56)—also are worth a visit, as is the lovely *Galerie Vivienne* (main entrance at 4 Rue des Petits-Champs, 2e; phone: 42-60-08-23), one of Paris's glass-roofed *galeries,* the 19th-century precursors of the modern-day shopping mall. Two new luxury shopping venues have opened recently: the *Carrousel du Louvre,* an underground complex beneath the museum, ranks among the world's most elegant shopping malls, with 50 fine stores and a central atrium containing an inverted version of the I. M. Pei pyramids (main entrance at 99 Rue de Rivoli, beneath the *Arc de Triomphe du Carrousel,* 1er; phone: 46-92-47-47); the complex is closed Tuesdays, when the museum is also closed. And *Passy Plaza,* located in the posh Passy district, is one of Paris's largest shopping centers (53 Rue de Passy, 16e; phone: 40-50-09-07).

*Haute joaillerie*—the jewelry with the most splendid designs and the highest prices—is sold on Place Vendôme. Haute couture can be found in the streets around the Champs-Elysées: Avenue George-V, Avenue Montaigne, Rue François-I, and Rue du Faubourg-St-Honoré. Boutiques are especially numerous on Avenue Victor-Hugo (16e), Rue de Passy (16e), Boulevard des Capucines (2e and 9e), in the St-Germain-des-Prés area (6e), in the neighborhood of the *Opéra* (9e), around the Place des Victoires (1er and 2e), on or near the Rue des Rosiers in the Marais district (4e), and in the shopping centers *Forum des Halles, Passy Plaza,* and *Carrousel du Louvre.* Rue de Rivoli is a souvenir shoppers' destination, the best place to find scarves decorated with Eiffel Towers and handkerchiefs imprinted with maps of the *Métro* system; it also abounds in shops selling perfume and other gifts. The Rue de Paradis (10e) is lined with crystal and china shops that offer amazing prices: Try *Boutique Paradis,* No. 1 *bis; L'Art et La Table,* No. 3; *Porcelain Savary,* No. 9; *Arts Céramiques,* No. 15; and *Cristallerie Paradis,* No. 17.

The best (and most expensive) antiques dealers are along the Rue du Faubourg-St-Honoré on the Rive Droite. On the Rive Gauche, there's *Le Carré Rive Gauche,* an association of more than 100 antiques shops in the area bordered by Quai Voltaire, Rue de l'Université, Rue des Sts-Pères, and Rue du Bac (all 7e). *Villages d'antiquaires,* which are something like shopping centers for antiques, have their prototype in the giant *Louvre des Antiquaires* (2 Pl. du Palais-Royal, 1er; phone: 42-97-27-00), 250 different shops housed in an old department store; it's closed Mondays and, in the summer, also on Sundays. Other *villages d'antiquaires* are *La Cour aux Antiquaires* (54 Rue du Faubourg-St-Honoré, 8e; phone: 42-66-38-60; closed Sundays and Monday mornings), *Village Suisse* (78 Av. Suffren, 15e; phone: 43-06-69-90; closed Tuesdays and Wednesdays), *Village St-Honoré* (91 Rue St-Honoré, 1er; phone: 42-36-57-45; closed Sundays), and *Village St-Paul* (entrance on Rue St-Paul just off the Quai des Célestins, 4e; phone: 48-87-91-02).

Antiques and curio collectors should also explore Paris's several flea markets, which include the *Puces de la Porte de Montreuil* (Av. de la Porte de Montreuil, 11e), which is held weekends and Mondays year-round and is especially good for secondhand clothing; the *Puces de la Porte de Vanves* (at Av. Georges-Lafenestre and Marc-Sangnier, 14e; *Métro:* Porte de Vanves), held weekends year-round, for furniture and fine bric-a-brac (try to arrive early on Saturday morning); and the largest and best known, *Marché aux Puces de St-Ouen* (more commonly called the *Puces de Clignancourt;* between Porte de St-Ouen and Porte de Clignancourt, 18e), which is held weekends and Mondays year-round and offers an admirable array of antiques. The *Marché Biron* for fine bric-a-brac is one of the best of the smaller markets that make up the *Puces de Clignancourt.* Bargaining is a must at all the flea markets.

Paris boasts about 70 open-air and covered food markets, plus about 10 market streets and the central market—*Les Halles de Rungis,* 13e, successor to *Les Halles,* and now the world's largest wholesale market. Most numerous are the open-air roving markets that set up early in the morning two or three days a week on sidewalks or islands of major boulevards, only to tear down again at 1:30 PM. Most markets and market streets are closed Mondays. Among the best is the *Marché Batignolles* (17e, near Pl. Clichy), noteworthy for its reasonable prices and plethora of stands. More food shops line the streets surrounding the market. A typically tantalizing Rive Gauche market is the morning market that begins at the eastern end of Rue de Buci and winds around the corner onto Rue de Seine (6e). Paris's most popular market street is Rue Mouffetard (5e), which is criticized by locals for its high prices, dubious quality, and circus atmosphere. But the steep, winding street—about halfway between the *Jardin du Luxembourg* and the *Jardin des Plantes*—still has an old-fashioned flavor. The hustle and bustle of *Les Halles,* the vast central market that once occupied the same neighborhood, survives at the busy market on Rue Montorgueil (1er and 2e); some of Paris's chefs still do their marketing here. The open-air roving market under the elevated *Métro* in the center of Boulevard de Grenelle (15e), extending to La Motte–Picquet *Métro* stop, though not necessarily the best for bargains, offers excellent high-quality items. Paris's most enjoyable market is probably the one set up on Wednesday and Saturday mornings on the Avenue du Président-Wilson (16e), between Place d'Iéna and Place de l'Alma, both of which have *Métro* stops. Other good roving markets appear in the Place Monge (5e) on Wednesdays, Fridays, and Sundays; on the Boulevard Raspail (6e) on Tuesdays, Fridays, and Sundays (when all goods are guaranteed to be organic); and on the Boulevard Edgar-Quinet (14e) on Wednesdays and Saturdays.

Below is a sampling of the wealth of shops in Paris, many of which have more than one location in the city. Most shops are open from 9 AM to 6 or 7 PM, with a one hour lunch break starting at 12:30 or 1 PM. Some shops are open on Sundays from 9 AM to 5 PM. Smaller shops usually are closed Sundays and sometimes a half day on Mondays; they often open slightly later (around 10 AM) and have a longer midday break. Department stores and other large emporia are open from about 9:30 AM to 6:30 or 7 PM (usually with no midday break), Mondays through Saturdays, and may stay open as late as 9 or 10 PM one or more days of the week.

## TIPS FOR SAVVY SHOPPERS

In Paris, *soldes* (sales) take place during the first weeks in January and in late June and July. Any shop labeled *dégriffé* (the word means "without the label") offers year-round discounts on brand-name clothing, often last season's styles. Discount shops also are known as "stock" shops. The French Value Added Tax (VAT) can be refunded on most purchases made by foreigners, provided a minimum is spent in one store.

**Absinthe** Chic is the word here—everything from one-of-a-kind silk hats to the latest clothes from up-and-coming designers. Near the Place des Victoires, at 74 Rue Jean-Jacques Rousseau, 1er (phone: 42-33-54-44).

**Accessoire** Very feminine footwear, often seen on the pages of *Elle* magazine. 6 Rue du Cherche-Midi, 6e (phone: 45-48-36-08) and other locations.

**Agatha** One of the best sources for chic costume jewelry. In the *Carrousel du Louvre* complex, entrance at 99 Rue de Rivoli, 1er (phone: 42-96-03-09) and other locations.

**Agnès B** Supremely wearable, trendy, casual clothes. Five stores on the block-long Rue du Jour, 1er: menswear at No. 3 (phone: 42-33-04-13); clothes for young children and infants at No. 4 (phone: 40-39-96-88); articles for the home at No. 5 (phone: 49-53-52-80); womenswear at No. 6 (phone: 45-08-56-56); and *Lolita,* for girls, at No. 10 (phone: 40-26-36-87). Also at 17 Av. Pierre-Ier-de-Serbie, 16e (phone: 47-20-22-44); 81 Rue d'Assas, 6e (phone: 46-33-70-20); and a new location with women's and children's clothing at 6 Rue Vieux-Colombier, 6e (phone: 44-39-02-60).

**Après-Midi de Chien** Women's and children's wear in what the French call "Anglo-Saxon"–style—tweedy jackets, jodhpurs, and print skirts. 10 Rue du Jour, 1er (phone: 40-26-92-78) and other locations.

**Arnys** Elegant, conservative men's clothing. 14 Rue de Sèvres, 6e (phone: 45-48-76-99).

**Azzedine Alaïa** Clothing by the Tunisian designer who redefined "body-conscious." 7 Rue de Moussy, 4e (phone: 42-72-19-19).

**Baccarat** High-quality porcelain and crystal. 30 *bis* Rue de Paradis, 10e (phone: 47-70-64-30), and 11 Pl. de la Madeleine, 8e (phone: 42-65-36-26).

**La Bagagerie** Perhaps the best bag and belt boutique in the world. 12 Rue Tronchet, 8e (phone: 42-65-03-40), and other locations.

**Au Bain Marie** Beautiful kitchenware and table accessories, with an emphasis on Art Deco designs. 8 Rue Boissy-d'Anglas, 8e (phone: 42-66-59-74).

**Balenciaga** Ready-to-wear and haute couture from the classic design house. 10 Av. George-V, 8e (phone: 47-20-21-11).

**Barthélémy** In a city of great cheese stores, this is at the top of almost everyone's *fromagerie* list. 51 Rue de Grenelle, 7e (phone: 45-48-56-75).

**Berthillon** Heavenly ice cream—Parisians often line up outside. Flavors, which change with the season, include wild strawberry, calvados crunch, and candied chestnut. Closed Mondays, Tuesdays, school holidays, and the month of August. 31 Rue St-Louis-en-l'Ile, 4e (phone: 43-54-31-61). Several cafés on the Ile St-Louis also serve scoops of Berthillon.

**Biba** Designer-label women's clothes, such as Gaultier and Junko Shimada. 18 Rue de Sèvres, 6e (phone: 45-48-89-18).

**Boucheron** One of several fine jewelers clustered around the elegant Place Vendôme. 26 Pl. Vendôme, 1er (phone: 42-61-58-16).

**Boutique Le Flore** You'll find silver-plated eggcups and other bistro accoutrements in this annex of the celebrated *Café Le Flore*. 26 Rue St-Benoît, 6e (phone: 45-44-33-40).

**Brentano's** A variety of British and American fiction and nonfiction, including travel, technical, and business books. 37 Pl. de l'Opéra, 2e (phone: 42-61-52-50).

**Cacharel** Fashionable ready-to-wear in great prints for children and adults. 34 Rue Tronchet, 8e (phone: 47-42-12-61); 5 Pl. des Victoires, 1er (phone: 42-33-29-88); and other locations.

**Carel** Beautiful shoes. 12 Rond-Point des Champs-Elysées, 8e (phone: 45-62-30-62), and other locations.

**Carita** Paris's most extensive—and friendliest—beauty/hair salon. 11 Rue du Faubourg-St-Honoré, 8e (phone: 42-68-13-40).

**Cartier** The legendary jeweler. 11-13 Rue de la Paix, 2e (phone: 42-61-58-56), and other locations.

**Castelbajac** Trendy designer clothes for men and women. 31 Pl. du Marché St-Honoré, 1er (phone: 42-60-78-40), and other locations.

**Caves Taillevent** One of Paris's best and most fairly priced wine shops, run by the owners of the three-star restaurant of the same name. 199 Rue du Faubourg-St-Honoré, 8e (phone: 45-61-14-09).

**Céline** A popular high-fashion women's boutique for clothing and accessories. 24 Rue François-Ier, 8e (phone: 47-20-22-83); 3 Av. Victor-Hugo, 16e (phone: 45-01-70-48); and other locations.

**Cerruti** For women's clothing, 15 Pl. de la Madeleine, 8e (phone: 47-42-10-78); for men's, 27 Rue Royale, 8e (phone: 42-65-68-72).

**Chanel** Classic women's fashions, inspired by the late, legendary Coco Chanel, now under the direction of Karl Lagerfeld. There are three individual buildings (one for shoes, another for clothing and cosmetics, and a third for watches) at 42 Av. Montaigne, 8e (phone: 47-23-74-12). Other locations include 29-31 Rue Cambon, 1er (phone: 42-86-28-00), headquarters for haute couture as well as ready-to-wear and accessories, and 5 Pl. Vendôme, 1er (phone: 42-86-28-00), which sells only Chanel watches.

**Chantal Thomass** Ultra-feminine fashions and sexy lingerie. Near the Palais-Royal, at 1 Rue Vivienne, 1er (phone: 40-15-02-36), and other locations.

**Charles Jourdan** Sleek, high-fashion footwear. 86 Av. des Champs-Elysées, 8e (phone: 45-62-29-28); 5 Pl. de la Madeleine, 1er (phone: 42-61-50-07); and other locations.

**Charley** Featuring an excellent selection of lingerie, plus personal attention and relatively low prices. 14 Rue du Faubourg-St-Honoré, 8e (phone: 47-42-17-70).

**Charvet** Paris's answer to Jermyn Street. An all-in-one men's shop, where shirts (they stock more than 4,000) and ties are the house specialties. 28 Pl. Vendôme, 1er (phone: 42-60-30-70).

**La Châtelaine** Where all of Paris shops for exquisite (and costly) toys and clothing for children. 170 Av. Victor-Hugo, 16e (phone: 47-27-44-07).

**Chaumet** Crownmakers for most of Europe's royalty. Expensive jewels, including antique watches covered with semi-precious stones. 12 Pl. Vendôme, 1er (phone: 42-60-32-82), and 46 Av. George-V, 8e (phone: 49-52-08-25).

**Chloé** Fashion for women. 54-56 Rue du Faubourg-St-Honoré, 8e (phone: 44-94-33-00).

**Christian Dior** One of the most famous couture houses in the world. Men's fashion, articles for the home, cosmetics, and *Baby Dior* (clothing for infants) are also here. 28-30 Av. Montaigne, 8e (phone: 40-73-54-44).

**Christian Lacroix** This designer offers the "hautest" of haute couture. 26 Av. Montaigne, 8e (phone: 47-23-44-40), and 73 Rue du Faubourg-St-Honoré, 8e (phone: 42-65-79-08).

**Christofle** The internationally famous silversmith. 9 Rue Royale, 8e (phone: 49-33-43-00).

**Claude Montana** Ready-to-wear and haute couture from this au courant designer. For both men's and women's clothes, 3 Rue des Petits-Champs, 1er (phone: 40-20-02-14); for women's clothes only, 31 Rue de Grenelle, 7e (phone: 42-22-69-56).

**Coesnon** Arguably one of Paris's finest charcuteries, in spite of its diminutive size, with the very best terrines, pâtés, *boudin blanc aux truffles,* and other temptations. 30 Rue Dauphine, 6e (phone: 43-54-35-80).

**Commes des Garçons** Asymmetrical-style clothing for both *des filles* and *des garçons.* 40-42 Rue Etienne-Marcel, 1er (phone: 42-33-05-21).

**Comptoirs de la Tour d'Argent** Glassware, napkins, silver items, and other objects bearing the celebrated restaurant's logo. 2 Rue de Cardinal-Lemoine, 5e (phone: 46-33-45-58).

**Corinne Cobson** The daughter of the founders of *Dorothée Bis* (see below) is making a name for herself with her youthful, cheerfully sexy women's clothing. 43 Rue de Sèvres, 6e (phone: 40-49-02-04).

**Courrèges** Another bastion of haute couture. 40 Rue François-Ier, 8e (phone: 47-20-70-44), and 46 Rue du Faubourg-St-Honoré, 8e (phone: 42-65-37-75).

**Cristalleries de Saint Louis** Handmade lead crystal at good prices. They will pack and ship purchases. 13 Rue Royale, 8e (phone: 40-17-01-74).

**Dalloyau** Fine purveyor of pastries and inventor of the incredibly delicious *gâteau opéra,* a confection of coffee and chocolate cream frosted with the darkest of chocolate and topped with edible gold leaf. 99-101 Rue du Faubourg-St-Honoré, 8e (phone: 43-59-18-10); 2 Pl. Edmond-Rostand, 6e (phone: 43-29-31-10); and other locations.

**Debauve et Gallais** The decor of this shop, housed in an 1800 building, is as fine as the delicious chocolates sold here. 30 Rue des Sts-Pères, 7e (phone: 45-48-54-67).

**Didier Lamarthe** Elegant handbags and accessories. 219 Rue du Faubourg-St-Honoré, 1er (phone: 42-96-09-90).

**Diners En Ville** Irresistible antique glassware, dishes, and tablecloths. 27 Rue de Varenne, 7e (phone: 42-22-78-33).

**Dominique Morlotti** A current favorite of Paris's best-dressed men. 25 Rue St-Sulpice, 6e (phone: 43-54-89-89).

**Dorothée Bis** Colorful women's knit sportswear. 33 Rue de Sèvres, 6e (phone: 42-22-02-90), and other locations.

**Les Drugstores Publicis** A uniquely French version of the American drugstore, with an amazing variety of goods—perfume, books, records, foreign newspapers, magazines, film, cigarettes, food, and more, all wildly overpriced. 149 Bd. St-Germain, 6e (phone: 42-22-92-50); 133 Av. des Champs-Elysées, 8e (phone: 47-23-54-34); and 1 Av. Matignon, 8e (phone: 43-59-38-70).

**E. Dehillerin** An enormous selection of professional cookware. 18-20 Rue Coquillière, 1er (phone: 42-36-53-13).

**Elle** A clothes and home furnishings boutique run by the magazine that sums up Parisian feminine style. 30 Rue St-Sulpice, 6e (phone: 43-26-46-10).

**Emanuel Ungaro** Haute couture for women. 2 Av. Montaigne, 8e (phone: 47-23-61-94).

**Emmanuelle Khanh** Feminine clothes in lovely fabrics, including embroidered linen. 2 Rue de Tournon, 6e (phone: 46-33-41-03).

**Erès** Avant-garde sportswear, including chic bathing suits, for men and women. 2 Rue Tronchet, 8e (phone: 47-42-24-55).

**Fauchon** No discussion of Parisian food is complete without a mention of this gastronomic institution, considered *the* place to buy a huge variety of fine food and wine, from *oeufs en gelée* to condiments and candy. The complex of shops and restaurants occupies Nos. 26, 28, and 30 Pl. de la Madeleine, 8e (central phone: 47-42-60-11).

**Floriane** Smart and well-made clothes for children and infants. 45 Rue de Sèvres, 6e (phone: 45-49-97-61), and other locations.

**Franck et Fils** A department store for women's designer clothes, ranging from Yves Saint Laurent to Thierry Mugler. 80 Rue de Passy, 16e (phone: 46-47-86-00).

**Fratelli Rossetti** All kinds of shoes, made from buttery-soft leather, for men and women. 54 Rue du Faubourg-St-Honoré, 8e (phone: 42-65-26-60).

**Galignani** This shop, with books in English and French, has been run by the same family since the early 19th century. 224 Rue de Rivoli, 1er (phone: 42-60-76-07).

**Georges Rech** One of the most popular makers of classy, very Parisian styles, and at more affordable prices than other similar labels. 273 Rue du Faubourg-St-Honoré, 1er (phone: 42-61-41-14); 54 Rue Bonaparte, 6e (phone: 43-26-84-11); and other locations.

**Gianni Versace** This mega-store adorned with Empire antiques sells the designer's men's, women's, and children's lines. Across from the *Palais de l'Elysée* at 62 Rue du Faubourg-St-Honoré, 8e (phone: 47-42-88-02). A smaller Rive Gauche outlet featuring only women's clothing is located at 66 Rue des Sts-Pères, 6e (phone: 45-49-22-66).

**Giorgio Armani** The legendary Italian designer has two shops on the elegant Place Vendôme, 1er: No. 6 (phone: 42-61-55-09), for his top-of-the-line clothes, and *Emporio Armani,* No. 25 (phone: 42-61-02-34), for his less expensive line.

**Givenchy** Beautifully tailored clothing by the master couturier. 3 and 8 Av. George-V, 8e (phone: 47-20-81-31).

**Guerlain** For fine perfume and cosmetics. 2 Pl. Vendôme, 1er (phone: 42-60-68-61); 68 Champs-Elysées, 8e (phone: 45-62-52-57); 29 Rue de Sèvres, 6e (phone: 42-22-46-60); and 93 Rue de Passy, 16e (phone: 42-91-60-02).

**Guy Laroche** Classic, conservative couture. 30 Rue du Faubourg-St-Honoré, 8e (phone: 42-65-62-74), and 29 Av. Montaigne, 8e (phone: 40-69-69-50).

**Hanae Mori** The grande dame of Japanese designers in Paris. 9 Rue du Faubourg-St-Honoré, 8e (phone: 47-23-52-03), and 5 Pl. de l'Alma, 8e (phone: 40-70-05-73).

**Hédiard** A pricey but choice food shop, notable for its assortment of coffees and teas. There's a chic tearoom upstairs. 21 Pl. de la Madeleine, 8e (phone: 42-66-44-36).

**Hermès** For very high quality classic clothes, scarves, handbags, shoes, saddles, and other accessories. 24 Rue du Faubourg-St-Honoré, 8e (phone: 40-17-47-17).

**Hôtel des Ventes Drouot-Richelieu** Paris's huge auction house often offers good buys. 9 Rue Drouot, 9e (phone: 48-00-20-20).

**Hugo Boss** Fine men's clothes and accessories at reasonable prices. 2 Pl. des Victoires, 1er (phone: 40-28-91-64).

**IGN (French National Geographic Institute)** All manner of maps are sold here. 136 *bis* Rue Grenelle, 7e, and 107 Rue La Boëtie, 8e (phone for both: 42-56-06-68).

**Inès de la Fressange** The former Chanel model has opened this chic shop, which sells everything from classic white silk shirts to furniture gilded with her signature oak leaf. 14 Av. de Montaigne, 8e (phone: 47-23-08-94).

**Issey Miyake** An "in" shop, selling women's clothing made by the Japanese artist-designer. Miyake's latest collections are at 3 Pl. des Vosges, 4e (phone: 48-87-01-86); a lower-priced line is featured at *Plantation,* 17 Bd. Raspail, 7e (phone: 45-48-12-32).

**Jean-Paul Gaultier** Designer clothes for men and women. 6 Rue Vivienne, 2e (phone: 42-86-05-05).

**Jil Sander** The first boutique in Paris from the leading German womenswear designer. 52 Av. Montaigne, 8e (phone: 44-95-06-70).

**John Lobb** What are said to be the finest men's shoes in the world (and probably the most expensive) are sold here. 51 Rue François-Ier, 8e (phone: 45-62-06-34).

**Junko Shimada** Formfitting clothes from the chic Japanese designer. 54 Rue Etienne-Marcel, 2e (phone: 42-36-36-97).

**Karl Lagerfeld** Women's clothing in a more adventurous spirit than those he designs for Chanel. 19 Rue du Faubourg-St-Honoré, 8e (phone: 42-66-64-64).

**Kenzo** Avant-garde fashions by the Japanese designer. A *Kenzo* children's shop is located in the passageway next to the store. 3 Pl. des Victoires, 1er (phone: 40-39-72-03). *Kenzo Studio,* with a lower-priced sportswear line, is at 60 Rue de Rennes, 6e (phone: 45-44-27-88).

**Kitchen Bazaar** Specializes in everything imaginable for the smart kitchen. 11 Av. du Maine, 15e (phone: 42-22-91-17). A second store, *Kitchen Bazaar Autrement,* features kitchen utensils from all over the world. 6 Av. du Maine, 15e (phone: 45-48-89-00).

**Lalique** The famous crystal. 11 Rue Royale, 8e (phone: 42-66-52-40), and in the *Carrousel du Louvre,* entrance at 99 Rue de Rivoli, 1er (phone: 42-86-01-51).

**Lanvin** Another fabulous designer, with several spacious, colorful boutiques under one roof. For women's and men's clothes, 15 and 22 Rue du Faubourg-St-Honoré, 8e (phone: 44-71-33-33); for men's clothes only, 2 Rue Cambon, 1er (phone: 42-60-38-83).

**Legrand Fille et Fils** Fine wines and spirits and articles for the *cave* and table, such as *rattes* (wrought-iron candle holders used in real wine cellars), plus excellent maps of French wine regions. 1 Rue Banque, 2e (phone: 42-60-07-12).

**Lenôtre** Specializes in pastries and other desserts—from exquisite éclairs and fruit mousses to charlottes and chocolates. 44 Rue d'Auteuil, 16e (phone: 45-24-52-52), and several other locations.

**Lescêne-Dura** Everything for the wine lover or maker, except the wine itself. 63 Rue de la Verrerie, 4e (phone: 42-72-08-74).

**Limoges-Unic** Two stores on Rue de Paradis (10e), the first selling more expensive items, the second offering many varieties of Limoges china as well as a good selection of typically French Porcelaine de Paris. No. 12 (phone: 47-70-54-49), and No. 58 (phone: 47-70-61-49).

**Lolita Lempicka** Iconoclastic, formfitting womenswear. 3 *bis* Rue de Rosiers, 4e (phone: 42-74-42-94), and other locations.

**Louis Vuitton** High-quality luggage and handbags. The agreeable, efficient, and well-mannered staff at the modern Avenue Montaigne branch are a pleasure after the chilly reception at the original Avenue Marceau shop. 54 Av. Montaigne, 8e (phone: 45-62-47-00), and 78 *bis* Av. Marceau, 8e (phone: 47-20-47-00).

**Lumicrystal** In the building where artist Jean-Baptiste-Camille Corot lived and died, this fine china and crystal store carries Baccarat, Daum, Limoges, and Puiforcat. 22 Rue de Paradis, 10e (phone: 47-70-27-97).

**La Maison du Chocolat** Robert Linxe, perhaps the most talented chocolate maker in Paris, produces delicate, meltingly delicious confections. 225 Rue du Faubourg-St-Honoré, 8e (phone: 42-27-39-44).

**La Maison de l'Escargot** This shop prepares (and sells) more than 10 tons of snails annually, following a well-guarded secret recipe. 68 Rue Fondary, 15e (phone: 45-77-93-82).

**Maison de la Truffe** The world's largest retailer of truffles. There are fresh black truffles from November through March, and the fresh white variety are offered from mid-October through December; the rest of the year they're preserved. 19 Pl. de la Madeleine, 8e (phone: 42-65-53-22).

**Maria Luisa** Haute couture and daring new looks from Paris's top designers are the stock in trade here. 2 Rue Cambon, 1er (phone: 47-03-96-15).

**Marie Mercié** Fashionable hats, including turbans and velvet berets. 56 Rue Tiquetonne, 2e (phone: 40-26-60-68), and 23 Rue St-Sulpice, 6e (phone: 43-26-45-83).

**Marithé & François Girbaud** Not just jeans at this shop for men and women. 38 Rue Etienne-Marcel, 2e (phone: 42-33-54-69).

**Maud Frizon** Sophisticated, imaginative shoes and handbags. 83 Rue des Sts-Pères, 6e (phone: 42-22-06-93).

**Max Mara** Carries six distinct collections of Italian ready-to-wear, from classic chic to trendy, at surprisingly affordable prices. 37 Rue du Four, 6e (phone: 43-29-91-10); 265 Rue du Faubourg-St-Honoré, 1er (phone: 40-20-04-58); and other locations.

**Michel Swiss** The best place to buy perfume in the city, offering a voluminous selection, cheerful service, and excellent discounts. American visitors who spend more than 2,700F (about $466 at press time) get a refund of 25%; the VAT refund brings the total discount to almost 44%. 16 Rue de la Paix, 2e (phone: 42-61-71-71).

**Miss Maud** High-style shoes for young folks' feet. 90 Rue du Faubourg-St-Honoré, 8e (phone: 42-65-27-96), and other locations.

**Missoni** Innovative Italian knitwear. 43 Rue du Bac, 7e (phone: 45-48-38-02).

**Moholy-Nagy** The grandson of Bauhaus artist László Moholy-Nagy creates superb shirts, most in cotton, for men and women. 2 *Galerie Vivienne,* 2e (phone: 40-15-05-33).

**M.O.R.A.** One of Paris's "professional" cookware shops, though it sells to amateurs as well. Just about any piece of equipment you can imagine, and an interesting selection of cookbooks in French. 13 Rue Montmartre, 1er (phone: 45-08-19-24).

**Morabito** Magnificent handbags and luggage at steep prices. 1 Pl. Vendôme, 1er (phone: 42-60-30-76).

**Motsch et Fils** Fine hatmaker for men and women since 1887—the film star Jean Gabin was a customer. 42 Av. George-V, 8e (phone: 47-23-79-22).

**Muriel Grateau** An eclectic shop, with silk blouses and fine table linen. Jardin du Palais-Royal, under the arcade, 1er (phone: 40-20-90-30).

**Les Must de Cartier** Actually two boutiques, on either side of the *Ritz* hotel, offering such Cartier items as lighters and watches at prices that, though not low, are almost bearable when you deduct the 25% VAT. 7-23 Pl. Vendôme, 1er (phone: 42-61-55-55).

**Au Nain Bleu** The city's greatest toy store. 408 Rue du Faubourg-St-Honoré, 8e (phone: 42-60-39-01).

**Nina Ricci** Women's fashions, as well as the famous perfume. 39 Av. Montaigne, 8e (phone: 49-52-56-00).

**L'Olivier** Olives and olive products, with a variety of olive oils, plus other fine cooking oils, from hazelnut to walnut. 23 Rue de Rivoli, 4e (phone: 48-04-56-59).

**Paco Rabanne** Men's and women's clothes by a French designer famous for dresses mixing fabric and metals. 7 Rue du Cherche-Midi, 6e (phone: 42-22-87-80).

**Papier Plus** One of Paris's finest *papeteries* (stationery stores). 9 Rue du Pont Louis-Philippe, 4e (phone: 42-77-70-49).

**Per Spook** One of the city's best younger designers. 40 Av. Montaigne, 8e (phone: 42-99-60-00), and other locations.

**Au Petit Matelot** Classic sportswear, outdoor togs, and nautical accessories for men, women, and children. Especially terrific are their Tyrolean-style olive or navy loden coats. 27 Av. de la Grande-Armée, 16e (phone: 45-00-15-51).

**Pierre Balmain** Women's fashions from the classic couturier. 44 Rue François-Ier, 8e (phone: 47-20-98-79), and other locations.

**Pierre Cardin** The famous designer's own boutique. 27 Av. de Marigny, 8e (phone: 42-66-92-25), and other locations.

**Poilâne** Considered by many French to sell the best bread in the country; the large and crusty, round country-style loaves dubbed *pain Poilâne* are delicious with soup, pâté, cheese, or cassoulet. 8 Rue du Cherche-Midi, 6e (phone: 45-48-42-59).

**Popy Moreni** Unusually designed unisex clothes inspired by commedia dell'arte costumes. On one of the loveliest squares in the city. 13 Pl. des Vosges, 4e (phone: 42-77-09-96).

**Porthault** Expensive but exquisite bed and table linen. 18 Av. Montaigne, 8e (phone: 47-20-75-25).

**Puiforcat** Art Deco tableware in a beautiful setting. 22 Rue François-Ier, 8e (phone: 47-20-74-27).

**Robert Clergerie** Among Paris's finest footwear, these slightly chunky, thick-soled shoes and boots will actually stand up to the perils of cobblestone streets. 5 Rue du Cherche-Midi, 6e (phone: 45-48-75-47), and other locations.

**Romeo Gigli** Men's and women's arty ready-to-wear and haute couture. 46 Rue de Sévigné, 3e (phone: 48-04-57-05).

**Shakespeare and Company** This legendary English-language bookstore, opposite Notre-Dame, is something of a tourist attraction in itself. 37 Rue de la Bûcherie, 5e (phone: 43-26-96-50).

**Sidonie Larizzi** Heavenly handmade women's shoes. 8 Rue Marignan, 8e (phone: 43-59-38-87).

**Sonia Rykiel** Stunning sportswear and knits. 175 Bd. St-Germain, 6e (phone: 49-54-60-60), and other locations.

**Souleiado** Vibrant, traditional Provençal fabrics made into scarves, shawls, totes, tableware, even bathing suits. 78 Rue de Seine, 6e (phone: 43-54-62-25), and 83 Av. Paul-Doumer, 16e (phone: 42-24-99-34).

**Stéphane Kélian** High-fashion, high-quality, and high-priced (but not completely unreasonable) men's and women's shoes. 66 Av. des Champs-Elysées, 8e (phone: 42-25-56-96), and other locations.

**Tartine et Chocolat** Clothing for children, from infancy to 12 years old, and dresses for moms-to-be. 90 Rue de Rennes, 6e (phone: 42-22-67-34).

**Ted Lapidus** A compromise between haute couture and fine ready-to-wear. 23 Rue du Faubourg-St-Honoré, 8e (phone: 44-60-89-91); 35 Rue François-Ier, 8e (phone: 47-20-56-14); and other locations.

**Thierry Mugler** Dramatic ready-to-wear for women. 10 Pl. des Victoires, 2e (phone: 42-60-06-37), and other locations.

**Trussardi** Italian ready-to-wear from a designer whose leather goods and canvas carryalls are much appreciated by the French and Japanese. 21 Rue du Faubourg-St-Honoré, 8e (phone: 42-65-11-40).

**La Tuile à Loup** Crafts from the provinces, including Burgundy pottery and Normandy lace. 35 Rue Daubenton, 5e (phone: 47-07-28-90).

**Valentino** Ready-to-wear and haute couture fashions for men and women from the Italian designer. 17-19 Av. Montaigne, 8e (phone: 47-23-64-61).

**Van Cleef & Arpels** One of the world's great jewelers. 22 Pl. Vendôme, 1er (phone: 42-61-58-58).

**Vicky Tiel** Strapless evening gowns decorated with beads and bows, as well as contemporary sweaters and baseball jackets. 21 Rue Bonaparte, 6e (phone: 44-07-15-99).

**Victoire** Ready-to-wear from up-and-coming designers such as André Walker, with attractive accessories and jewelry. 10 and 12 Pl. des Victoires, 2e (phone: 42-60-96-21 or 42-61-09-02), and other locations.

**Virgin Megastore** The British have taken over the Parisian market in CDs, audiocassettes, and videocassettes. Though the selection is staggering, the store is usually so crowded that browsing is impossible. 56-60 Champs-Elysées, 8e, and in the *Carrousel du Louvre,* entrance at 99 Rue de Rivoli, 1er (phone: 49-53-50-00 for both stores).

**Walter Steiger** Some of the capital's most expensive footwear for men and women. The flagship shop displays satin slippers like precious jewels—with prices to match. 83 Rue du Faubourg-St-Honoré, 8e (phone: 42-66-65-08).

**W. H. Smith and Sons** The largest English-language bookstore in Paris (with more space now that the upstairs tearoom has been converted into additional shelf space). It sells the Sunday *New York Times,* in addition to many British and American magazines. 248 Rue de Rivoli, 1er (phone: 42-60-37-97).

**Yohji Yamamoto** This Japanese designer offers highly unusual outerwear. For women, 25 Rue du Louvre, 1er (phone: 42-21-42-93); for men, 47 Rue Etienne-Marcel, 1er (phone: 45-08-82-45).

**Yves Saint Laurent** The world-renowned designer's flagship boutique is here, on the Rue du Faubourg-St-Honoré. 38 Rue du Faubourg-St-Honoré, 8e (phone: 42-65-74-59); 6 Pl. St-Sulpice, 6e (phone: 43-29-43-00); and other locations.

## BEST DISCOUNT SHOPS

If you (like us) are among those shoppers who believe that the eighth deadly sin is buying retail, you'll treasure the following inexpensive outlets, including some of Paris's best *dépôt-vente* shops, where merchandise is sold on consignment, at a discount. Several discount designer fashion outlets line the Rue d'Alésia (14e), from *Sonia Rykiel* at No. 64, to *Chevignon* at No. 122.

**Anna Lowe** Yves Saint Laurent, Valentino, and others, at a discount. 35 Av. Matignon, 8e (phone: 43-59-96-61).

**Anne Parée** Great buys on French perfume, Dior scarves, men's ties, Limoges china, and Vuarnet sunglasses. A 40% discount (including VAT) is given on purchases totaling 1,500F (at press time, about $260) or more. Mail order, too. 10 Rue Duphot, 1er (phone: 42-60-03-26).

**Bab's** High fashion at reasonable prices. 29 Av. Marceau, 16e (phone: 47-20-84-74), and 89 *bis* Av. des Ternes, 17e (phone: 45-74-02-74).

**Bidermann** Menswear from Kenzo, Courrèges, and more in a warehouse of a store in the Marais. 114 Rue de Turenne, 3e (phone: 44-61-17-00).

**Boëtie 104** Good buys on men's and women's shoes. 104 Rue La Boëtie, 8e (phone: 43-59-72-38).

**Cacharel Stock** Surprisingly current Cacharel fashions at about a 40% discount. 114 Rue d'Alésia, 14e (phone: 45-42-53-04).

**Catherine Baril** Women's ready-to-wear by designers such as Chanel and Jean-Louis Scherrer. 14 Rue de la Tour, 16e (phone: 45-20-95-21). The men's store down the street carries labels such as Armani and Hermès. 25 Rue de la Tour, 16e (phone: 45-27-11-46).

**Chercheminippes** One of the best Parisian *dépôt-vente* shops for high-quality children's clothes. The women's *dépôt-vente* collections just down the street are also worth a visit. Children's clothes, 160 Rue du Cherche-Midi, 6e (phone: 42-22-33-89), plus two stores for women, at No. 109 (phone: 42-22-45-23) and No. 111 (phone: 42-22-53-76).

**Dépôt des Grandes Marques** A third-floor shop near the stock market, featuring up to 50% markdowns on Louis Féraud, Cerruti, Renoma, and similar labels. 15 Rue de la Banque, 2e (phone: 42-96-99-04).

**Dorothée Bis Stock** The well-known sportswear at about 40% off. 74 Rue d'Alésia, 14e (phone: 45-42-17-11).

**Eiffel Shopping** Another bastion of fine French perfumes at discounted prices, it also stocks Lalique crystal, watches, and upscale costume jewelry. 9 Av. de Suffren, 7e (phone: 45-66-55-30).

**Eve Cazes Bijoux d'Occasion** A gem expert has opened a *dépôt-vente* for pre-owned fine jewelry, including pieces by Chaumet and Van Cleef & Arpels. Prices are about 40% lower than new. 20 Rue de Miromesnil, 8e (phone: 42-65-95-44).

**Jean-Louis Scherrer** Haute couture labels by Scherrer and others at about half their original prices. 29 Av. Ledru-Rollin, 12e (phone: 46-28-39-27).

**Kashiyama** Check out the upper level of this store for the previous season's clothes from Paris's hottest young designers, sold at a discount here. 80 Rue Jean-Jacques-Rousseau, 1er (phone: 40-26-46-46).

**Mendès** Less-than-wholesale prices on haute couture, especially Saint Laurent and Lanvin. 65 Rue Montmartre, 2e (phone: 42-36-83-32).

**Miss Griff** The very best of haute couture in small sizes (up to size 10) at small prices. Alterations, too. 19 Rue de Penthièvre, 8e (phone: 42-65-10-00).

**Mouton à Cinq Pattes** Ready-to-wear clothing for men, women, and children at 50% off original prices. 8 and 18 Rue St-Placide, 6e (phone: 45-48-86-26), and other locations.

**Nina Ricci Stock** Discounted fashions by this designer. 17-19 Rue François-Ier, 8e (phone: 47-23-78-88).

**Réciproque** Billed as the largest *dépôt-vente* in Paris, this outlet features names like Chanel, Alaïa, Lanvin, and Scherrer, as well as fine objets d'art. Several hundred square yards of display area are arranged by designer and by size. Five locations on the Rue de la Pompe, 16e: No. 89 for artworks; No. 93 for women's evening-wear; No. 95 for women's sportswear; No. 103 for men's clothing and accessories (phone: 47-04-30-28 for these four); and No. 123 for women's coats and accessories (phone: 47-27-30-28).

**Soldes Trois** Lanvin fashions at about half their normal retail cost. 3 Rue de Vienne, 8e (phone: 42-94-99-67).

**Sonia Rykiel** Rykiel's clothes at half price. 64 Rue d'Alésia, 14e (phone: 43-95-06-13).

---

### SECOND BESTS

If haute couture prices paralyze your pocketbook, several shops in the city offer pre-owned, high-style clothes with down-to-earth price tags. *L'Astucerie* (105 Rue de Javel, 15e; phone: 45-57-94-74) offers designerwear and accessories, from Hermès scarves and Kelly bags to Vuitton luggage; *La Marette* (25 Galerie Vivienne, 2e; phone: 42-60-08-19) carries designer items including a selection of stylish children's outfits and accessories; *Didier Ludot,* under the arcades of the *Jardin du Palais-Royal* (19-24 Galerie Montpensier, 1er; phone: 42-96-06-56), offers an array of museum-quality designer fashions, most from the 1940s, 1950s, and 1960s; and *Troc'Eve* (25 Rue Violet, 15e; phone: 45-79-38-36) also has an impressive stock of pre-owned designer clothes in perfect condition.

## SPORTS AND FITNESS

**BICYCLING** Rentals are available in the *Bois de Boulogne* and the *Bois de Vincennes,* or contact *Paris-Vélo* (2 Rue du Fer-à-Moulin, 5e; phone: 47-07-67-45). For a membership fee, you can take advantage of group outings in Paris and the surrounding region, maps of cycling routes in the area, and other information especially for cyclists from the *Fédération Française de Cyclotourisme* (*FFCT;* 8 Rue Jean-Marie-Jégo, 13e; phone: 44-16-88-88); contact them for a detailed brochure in English. In addition to renting bicycles, both *Bicyclub* (8 Pl. de la Porte-de-Champerret, 17e; phone: 47-66-55-92) and *Paris by Cycle* (78 Rue de l'Ouest, 14e; phone: 40-47-08-04 for rentals and for excursions outside Paris; 48-87-60-01 for Paris tours) offer organized bicycle tours. *Bicyclub* can arrange group and individual tours in Paris and the surrounding region, while *Paris by Cycle* arranges guided group tours of the city and of Versailles, as well as bike trips alternating with horseback rides. *Mountain Bike Trip* (6 Pl. Etienne-Pernet, 15e; phone: 48-42-57-87 or 49-29-93-91) also arranges group rides in and around Paris. The world-famous *Tour de France* bicycle race takes place in July, ending in Paris.

**FITNESS CENTERS** The *Gymnase Club* (208 Rue de Vaugirard, 15e; phone: 47-83-99-45; and many other locations); *Club Quartier Latin* (19 Rue de Pontoise, 5e; phone: 43-54-82-45); *Club Jean de Beauvais* (5 Rue de Jean-de-Beauvais, 5e; phone: 46-33-16-80); *Espace Beaujon* (208 Rue du Faubourg-St-Honoré, 8e; phone: 42-89-12-32); and *Espace Vit'Halles* (48 Rue Rambuteau; phone: 42-77-21-71) are open daily to non-members for a fee.

**GOLF** Although there are no 18-hole courses within the city, several major layouts are close by. *Golf Club de Chantilly* (phone: 44-57-04-43), 25 miles (41 km) north of Paris in Chantilly, is an elegant club only five minutes from the historic château. In July and August non-members may play for a fee every day except Thursdays; the rest of the year non-members may play weekdays except Thursdays. *Golf National* (2 Av. du Golf; phone: 30-43-36-00), a huge public golf complex comprising three courses, in St-Quentin-en-Yvelines, 19 miles (30 km) from Paris, is owned and operated by the *Fédération Française de Golf* (see below). *Golf des Yvelines* (phone: 34-86-48-89), 28 miles (45 km) from Paris in La Queue-lès-Yvelines, is a par 72 forest course set in a park. Its clubhouse is in a château. *Urban Cély Golf Club* (Le Château, Rte. de St-Germain, Cély-en-Bière; phone: 64-38-03-07; fax: 64-38-08-78) is a perfectly manicured and landscaped course (18 holes, 6,500 yards, par 72) with a beautiful clubhouse that resembles a medieval castle. Electric carts are available. It's close to Fontainebleau, Barbizon, and Milly-la-Forêt.

The *Fédération Française de Golf* (69 Av. Victor-Hugo, 16e; phone: 45-02-13-55) and the *French Ministry of Tourism* have set up a system whereby travelers and others who are not members of a local golf club can play. Greens fees vary according to the day and season, but are usually higher on weekends. Call ahead to reserve. In addition, there is a nine-hole municipal course at the *St-Cloud* racecourse (1 Rue du Camp Canadien, St-Cloud; phone: 47-71-39-22), west of the city.

**HORSE RACING** If Paris has a sporting passion, it's horses. The French invented the pari-mutuel betting system (based on equally distributed winnings) and in and around the city there are eight tracks, a half-dozen racing sheets, and several hundred places to bet during a season that runs year-round.

Opened in 1870 for steeplechase only, *Auteuil* (*Bois de Boulogne;* phone: 45-27-12-25) features over 40 permanent obstacles spread across 30 acres. More than 60,000 Parisians turn out for the fashionable *Grande Steeplechase de Paris* on the third Sunday in June (this is where Hemingway took Ezra Pound to the races). The temple of thoroughbred racing since 1855, *Longchamp* (*Bois de Boulogne;* phone: 44-30-75-00) is its most prestigious racetrack and the one for which hopeful entries train at nearby Maisons-Laffitte, Enghien, Chantilly, Evry, and St-Cloud. The track's two highlight events are the *Grand Prix de Paris* in late June, which carries a purse of one million francs, and the *Prix de l'Arc de Triomphe* in early October, which at five millions francs is one of Europe's most lucrative races. *St-Cloud* (phone: 46-02-62-29), located west of Paris in the chic suburb of St-Cloud, offers flat racing from spring to fall, with the prestigious *Grand Prix de St-Cloud* held the first Sunday in July. A taxi ride into the woods, the *Champs de Courses de Vincennes* (*Bois de Vincennes;* phone: 49-77-17-17) is the scene of night racing, particularly trotting. Popular with diehard bettors, the track has a rough reputation. The major highlight of the Vincennes season is the *Prix d'Amérique* for trotters, in the dead cold of January.

From late April through early September, a number of other historic tracks around Paris open for selected racing dates. In late spring, races are scheduled in Fontainebleau; and the French equivalent of *Ascot,* the *Prix de Diane/Hermès,* is held at *Chantilly* (phone: 44-62-91-00), about 25 miles (40 km) north of Paris, as part of the *Grande Semaine.*

**JOGGING** There are a number of places where you can jog happily; one of the most pleasant is the 2,500-acre *Bois de Boulogne.* Five more centrally located parks are the *Jardin du Luxembourg* and the *Jardin des Tuileries* (see *Special Places* for both); the *Parc du Champ-de-Mars* (behind the Eiffel Tower, 7e); *Parc Monceau* (Bd. de Courcelles, 8e); and the *Jardin des Plantes* (Pl. Valhubert, 5e).

**SOCCER** There are matches from early August through mid-June at *Parc des Princes* (24 Rue du Commandant-Guilbaud, 16e; phone: 42-88-02-76).

**SQUASH** *Stadium Squash Club* (44 Av. d'Ivry, 13e; phone: 45-85-39-06) has 14 air conditioned courts.

**SWIMMING** Among pools in Paris open to visitors (all of the following charge admission) are the indoor *Piscine des Halles* (10 Pl. de la Rotonde, 1er; phone: 42-36-98-44), open daily; the indoor *Piscine Pontoise* (19 Rue de Pontoise, 5e; phone: 43-54-82-45), open daily; the outdoor *Butte-aux-Cailles* (5 Pl. Paul-Verlaine, 13e; phone: 45-89-60-05), open daily; the outdoor *Stade Nautique Robert-Keller* (14 Rue de l'Ingénieur-Robert-Keller, 15e; phone: 45-77-12-12), closed Mondays; the indoor *Jean-Taris* (16 Rue Thouin, 5e; phone: 43-25-54-03), open daily; the indoor *Tour Montparnasse* (beneath the tower at 66 Bd. du Montparnasse, 15e; phone: 45-38-65-19), open daily; *Piscine Georges-Vallerey* (148 Av. Gambetta, 20e; phone: 40-31-15-20), which is covered, but can be converted to open-air in good weather, open daily; *Aquaboulevard* (5 Rue Louis-Armand, 15e; phone: 40-60-10-00), a combination health club/water park, with facilities such as a wave pool, manmade beach, and water slides, open daily.

**TENNIS** On the outskirts of Paris are several top-flight tennis clubs. Lessons are available in English on the on the seven outdoor and four indoor courts at *Tennis Club Vitis* (159 Rue de la République, La Défense-Puteaux; phone: 47-73-04-01). Weekly instruction sessions are available in English on the 20 courts at *Tennis Club de Longchamp,* down the road from *Stade Roland-Garros* in the *Bois de Boulogne* (19 Bd. Anatole-France; phone: 46-03-84-49). *Tennis Forest Hill* (111 Av. Victor-Hugo, Aubervilliers, Seine-St-Denis; phone: 47-29-91-91) offers instruction, in French only, on eight indoor courts. It's closed in August. *Tennis de Villepinte* (Rue du Manège, Villepinte, Seine-St-Denis; phone: 43-83-23-31) has two outdoor and five indoor courts. Weekend and extended courses in English are available. *UCPA* (Rue de Tournezy, Bois-le-Roi, Seine-et-Marne; phone: 64-87-83-00), with 14 outdoor courts (two covered), offers a seven-hour weekend instruction program (though it's not always available in English).

In addition to those right outside the capital, six courts are available in the *Jardin du Luxembourg* for a nominal fee, but be certain to arrive early, as this is a popular spot. For general information on courts in Paris, call the *Ligue Régionale de Paris* (74 Rue de Rome, 17e; phone: 45-22-22-08), or the *Fédération Française de Tennis* (*Stade Roland-Garros,* 2 Av. Gordon-Bennett, 16e; phone: 47-43-48-00).

## THEATER AND OPERA

The most complete listings of theaters, operas, concerts, and movies are found in two weekly publications, *L'Officiel des Spectacles* and *Pariscope,* both available at newsstands. The season generally extends from September through May. Less expensive than in New York, tickets can be obtained at each box office; at any of the large *FNAC* stores (136 Rue de Rennes, 6e, phone: 49-54-30-00; in the *Forum des Halles,* 1er, phone: 40-41-40-00; also other locations); at the two *Virgin Megastores* (52-60 Champs-Elysées, 8e, and the *Carrousel du Louvre* shopping center, 99 Rue de Rivoli, 1er; phone:

49-53-50-00 for both); through brokers (*American Express* and *Thomas Cook* are good ones); or through your hotel's concierge. Tickets also can be purchased at high-tech *Billetel* machines at the *Galeries Lafayette* (see *Shopping*), near the *Centre Georges-Pompidou* (6 Bd. de Sébastopol; phone: 48-04-95-27), and other locations. Insert a credit card into a slot in the *Billetel* and choose from over 100 upcoming theater events and concerts. The device will spew out a display of dates, seats, and prices, from which you can order your tickets, which then will be printed on the spot and charged to your account. Half-price, day-of-performance theater tickets are available at *Kiosque* (15 Place de la Madeleine, 8e); it's closed mornings and Mondays. The curtain usually goes up at 8:30 PM.

What follows is a selection of our favorite Parisian theaters and opera houses.

---

### CENTER STAGE

**La Comédie-Française** The undisputed dowager queen of French theater, as much a national monument as the *Eiffel Tower,* it presents lavish productions of great classics by Corneille, Racine, Molière, Rostand, and the happy few 20th-century playwrights like Anouilh, Giraudoux, and Sartre who have been received into the inner circle of French culture. The *CF* is polishing up its fin de siècle image (the theater itself was entirely renovated last year), but even at its stodgiest, it's well worth seeing. 2 Rue de Richelieu, 1er (phone: 40-15-00-15). The company also presents contemporary plays in the renovated 350-seat *Théâtre du Vieux-Colombier* (21 Rue du Vieux-Colombier, 6e; phone: 42-22-77-48).

**L'Odéon–Théâtre de L'Europe** The chameleon-like *Odéon* has, for years, been the joker in the French theatrical pack. After the turbulent period when it hosted the fabled company under the direction of the late Jean-Louis Barrault and Madeleine Renaud and ranked among the most popular houses in the city, it became an annex of the *Comédie-Française.* Now it can be seen in yet another incarnation, as the *Théâtre de l'Europe.* Headed by one of Europe's foremost directors, Giorgio Strehler of Milan's *Piccolo Teatro,* it has become a kind of theatrical Common Market, with original-language productions from all over Europe. Pl. de l'Odéon, 6e (phone: 44-41-36-36).

**Opéra in Paris** In a futuristic opera house on the Place de la Bastille, the *Opéra de la Bastille* began regular performances in 1990 under the baton of Myung-Whun Chung, while the *Opéra/Palais Garnier,* at the melodramatic end of Place de l'Opéra, now hosts the best in ballet, as well as a classic opera repertoire (see *Special Places* for details on both opera houses). The other mainstays of Paris opera are the *Théâtre National de l'Opéra Comique,* at the *Salle Favart* (Pl. Boieldieu, 9e; phone: 42-96-12-20), and the *Théâtre du Châtelet/Théâtre Musicale de Paris* (1 Pl. du Châtelet, 1er; phone: 40-28-28-98), in the old *Châtelet* theater. The latter, once the stronghold of the frothy operetta, now does everything from early Offenbach to late Verdi, importing productions from other European opera companies as well. The touch is light and stylish, the accent utterly French. The *Opéra Comique* isn't especially comic. It's smaller and its performers are generally less well known than those at the *Palais Garnier,* but it has a wider repertoire.

Known for its continually evolving and inventive style, the *Théâtre des Amandiers* (7 Av. Pablo-Picasso; phone: 46-14-70-00) is in Nanterre, a working class suburb of Paris. Recent presentations have included such time-honored classics as the Oedipus trilogy by Sophocles, but a trip to the box office can turn up any number of theatrical surprises. The theater is about 20 minutes by the *RER* city-rail from downtown Paris. New formats, odd curtain times, and a constant redefining of theater and its audience are the trademarks of the *Théâtre National de Chaillot* (Pl. du Trocadéro et du 11-Novembre, 6e; phone: 47-27-81-15), whose repertory ranges from *Hamlet* to *Faust* for children—performed by marionettes—to new texts by Algerian workers, plus contemporary musical happenings. And *Théâtre du Soleil* (La Cartoucherie de Vincennes, Rte. du Champ de Manoeuvres, Bois de Vincennes, 12e; phone: 43-74-24-08 or 43-74-87-63), housed in an old cartridge factory, always has had a colorful, sweeping style with a popular mood and political overtones. That was true in the dazzling production *1789,* which made the troupe's international reputation during that other year of French upheaval, 1968, and in the more recent Shakespeare series as well. *Bouffes du Nord* (37 *bis* Bd. de la Chapelle, 10e; phone: 46-07-34-50) is a magical place, where the simple stagings and excellent acoustics lend power to the Peter Brook company's productions, from Shakespeare to the *Mahabharata.* The *Théâtre Marie-Stuart* (4 Rue Marie-Stuart, 2e; phone: 45-08-17-80) produces contemporary drama, including some American works (though they're performed in French).

Paris's many café-theaters offer amusing songs, sketches, satires, and takeoffs on topical issues and events. Among them are *Café de la Gare* (41 Rue Vieille-du-Temple, 4e; phone: 42-78-52-51) and *Café d'Edgar* (58 Bd. Edgar-Quinet, 14e; phone: 42-79-97-97). In addition, several vessels moored along the quays offer theatrical performances, ranging from classical French plays to magic shows. The *Péniche Opéra* boat (200 Quai de Jemmapes; phone: 43-49-08-15) is berthed on the Canal St-Martin on the Rive Droite; it's closed during the summer. Nearby is the *Metamorphosis* (35 Quai de la Tournelle, 5e; phone: 42-61-33-70), which offers magic shows. At the Quai Malaquais, on the Rive Gauche, are *L'Ouragan* (phone: 40-46-01-24) and the *Mare au Diable* (phone: 40-46-90-67).

## MUSIC

July and August bring the *Festival Estival*, which is followed by the *Festival d'Automne* (see *Special Events* for both). The *Orchestre de Paris* is based at the *Salle Pleyel*, Paris's *Carnegie Hall* (252 Rue du Faubourg-St-Honoré, 8e; phone: 45-63-07-96). The *Nouvelle Orchestre Philharmonic* performs at a variety of venues, including the *Grand Auditorium* at *Maison de Radio France* (116 Av. du Président-Kennedy, 16e; phone: 42-30-22-22). Classical concerts and recitals also take place at the *Salle Gaveau* (45 Rue La Boëtie, 8e; phone: 49-53-05-07); the *Théâtre des Champs-Elysées* (15 Av. Montaigne, 8e; phone: 49-52-50-50), and the *Palais des Congrès* (2 Pl. Porte Maillot, 17e; phone: 40-68-22-22). Special concerts frequently are held in Paris's many places of worship, with moving music at high mass on Sundays.

The *Palais des Congrès* and the *Olympia* (28 Bd. des Capucines, 9e; phone: 47-42-25-49) are the places to see well-known international pop and rock artists. Innovative contemporary music is the province of the *Institut de Recherche et de Coopération Acoustique Musique* (*IRCAM;* 31 Rue du Cloître-St-Merri, 4e; phone: 44-78-48-43), whose musicians can be heard in various auditoriums of the *Centre Georges-Pompidou* (see *Special Places*). The *Musée Carnavalet* (see *Special Places*) rents out its concert hall to various music groups.

## NIGHTCLUBS AND NIGHTLIFE

Typically lavish *Folies-Bergère*–style stage shows are a featured part of the "Paris by Night" group tours offered by a number of tour operators (see *Tours*). In addition, most music halls offer a package (usually far from discount) that includes dinner, dancing, and a half bottle of champagne. To save money, try going to one of these places on your own, skipping dinner and the champagne (both usually are way below par), and sitting at the bar to see the show. The most famous extravaganzas occur nightly at *Crazy Horse* (12 Av. George-V, 8e; phone: 47-23-32-32); *Lido* (116 *bis* Champs-Elysées, 8e; phone: 40-76-56-10); *Moulin Rouge* (Pl. Blanche, 18e; phone: 46-06-00-19); and *Paradis Latin* (28 Rue du Cardinal-Lemoine, 5e; phone: 43-29-07-07). An amusing evening also can be spent at such smaller cabarets as *Au Lapin Agile* (22 Rue des Saules, 18e; phone: 46-06-85-87) and *Michou* (80 Rue des Martyrs, 18e; phone: 46-06-16-04). Reserve a few days in advance for any of the above.

There's one big difference between discotheques and so-called private clubs. The latter, fashionable "in" spots such as *Le Palace* (8 Rue Faubourg-Montmartre, 9e; phone: 42-46-10-87); *Régine* (49 Rue de Ponthieu, 8e; phone: 43-59-21-13); *Chez Castel* (15 Rue Princesse, 6e; phone: 43-26-90-22); *Olivia Valère* (40 Rue de Colisée, 8e; phone: 42-25-11-68); *L'Arc* (12 Rue de Presbourg; phone: 45-00-45-00); and *Les Bains* (7 Rue du Bourg-l'Abbé, 3e; phone: 48-87-01-80) superscreen potential guests. To gain entrance, go with a member or regular, dress to fit in with the crowd, and show up early and on a weeknight, when your chances of getting past the gatekeeper are at least 50-50. (One expensive way to get into *Régine,*

*Chez Castel,* or *Les Bains* is to have your hotel make dinner reservations there for you.) Just as much fun and usually more hospitable are *Le Balajo* (9 Rue de Lappe, 11e; phone: 47-00-07-87), where the "in" crowd dances to music from rumba to rock; *Keur Samba* (73 Rue de la Boëtie, 8e; phone: 43-50-03-10), for an African mood; *Le Café Vogue* (50 Rue de la Chaussée-d'Antin, 9e; phone: 42-80-69-40), a restaurant and disco that is, as its name suggests, a favorite haunt of fashion models and other beautiful people; *Chapelle des Lombards* (19 Rue de Lappe, 11e; phone: 43-57-24-24), for a Brazilian beat; *Le Cirque* (49 Rue de Ponthieu, 8e; phone: 42-25-12-13), a mainly gay nightclub; *Niel's* (27 Av. des Ternes, 17e; phone: 47-66-45-00), chic and popular with the film crowd; and *L'Ecume des Nuits,* in the *Méridien* hotel (see *Checking In*).

A natural choice for an American in Paris is the celebrated *Harry's New York Bar* (5 Rue Daunou, 2e; phone: 42-61-71-14), which has been serving classic cocktails to transatlantic transplants like Ernest Hemingway, Gertrude Stein, and George Gershwin since 1911; a *Harry's* tradition decrees that on the night of a US presidential election, only card-carrying Americans are allowed in the place, where they can watch election returns on the bar's TV set. Other pleasant, popular spots for a nightcap include *Bar de la Closerie des Lilas* (171 Bd. du Montparnasse, 6e; phone: 43-26-70-50); *Fouquet's* (99 Champs-Elysées, 8e; phone: 47-23-70-60); *Ascot Bar* (66 Rue Pierre-Charron, 8e; phone: 43-59-28-15); *Bar Anglais* in the *Plaza-Athénée* hotel (see *Checking In*); and *Pub Winston Churchill* (5 Rue de Presbourg, 16e; phone: 40-67-17-37).

Jazz buffs can choose from among the *Caveau de la Huchette* (5 Rue de la Huchette, 5e; phone: 43-26-65-05); *Le Bilboquet* (13 Rue St-Benoît, 6e; phone: 45-48-81-84); *New Morning* (7-9 Rue des Petites-Ecuries, 10e; phone: 45-23-51-41); *La Villa* (in *La Villa* hotel, 29 Rue Jacob, 6e; phone: 43-26-60-00); *Le Petit Journal* (71 Bd. St-Michel, 6e; phone: 43-26-28-59); *Arbuci* (25 Rue de Buci, 6e; phone: 45-23-51-41); *Le Petit Opportune* (15 Rue des Lavandières-Sainte-Opportune; phone: 42-36-01-36); *Le Baiser Salé* (58 Rue des Lombards, 1er; phone: 42-33-37-71); and *Au Duc des Lombards* (42 Rue des Lombards, 1er; phone: 42-33-22-88). The latter, along with *New Morning,* is the best of the bunch.

*Enghien-les-Bains,* 8 miles (13 km) away in Enghien-les-Bains (3 Av. de Ceinture; phone: 34-12-90-00), is the only casino in the Paris vicinity. Open from 3 PM to about 4 AM, it's easily reached by train from the *Gare du Nord.*

# Best in Town

## CHECKING IN
Paris offers a broad choice of accommodations, from luxurious palaces with every service to more humble budget hotels. Below is our selection from all categories; for a double room expect to spend $450 or more (sometimes much more) per night in the "palace" hotels, which we've listed as very expensive; from $250 to $450

in the expensive ones; $150 to $250 in the moderate places; and less than $150 in the inexpensive hotels.

Hotel rooms usually are at a premium in Paris. In order to reserve your first choice we advise making reservations at least a month in advance, even farther ahead for the smaller, less expensive places. Watch for the dates of special events, when hotels are even more crowded than usual.

Street addresses of the hotels below are followed by the number of their *arrondissement* (neighborhood). Unless otherwise noted all hotels listed feature air conditioning, TV sets, telephones, and private baths in the rooms. Some less expensive hotels may have private baths in only some of their rooms; it's a good idea to confirm whether your room has a private bath when making a reservation. All hotels listed are open year-round and accept major credit cards unless otherwise indicated.

For an unforgettable experience we begin with our favorite Paris hostelries, followed by our cost and quality choices, listed by price category.

## GRAND HOTELS

**Bristol** Headquarters to dignitaries visiting the *Palais de l'Elysée* (Elysée Palace, the French White House), just a few steps down the street, this elegant establishment boasts 154 rooms and 41 suites, all beautifully decorated, and a one-Michelin-star restaurant with two dining rooms—one for summer and another for winter. The first is a light, airy glassed-in room overlooking the garden; the second is a richly wood-paneled room, a reassuring reminder of Old Europe craftsmanship. The open and exquisite elevator recalls an earlier age, the marvelously designed marble bathrooms are veritable oases of comfort, and the service is nothing short of superb. An elegant and comfortable lobby and bar add to the charm; there's also a new fitness center and business center, as well as a heated pool on the sixth-floor terrace, an amenity seldom found in Paris hotels. 112 Rue du Faubourg-St-Honoré, 8e (phone: 42-66-91-45; 800-223-6800; 212-838-3110 in New York City; fax: 42-66-68-68).

**Crillon** Today's heavy traffic gives the Place de la Concorde a frenetic atmosphere far at odds with its 18th-century spirit. But here, within the Sienese marble foyers and the 163 elegant rooms and suites (plus three master suites) of this Relais & Châteaux member, guests are largely insulated from the world outside. Diplomats from nearby Embassy Row, observed by ever-present journalists, buy and sell countries in the bar (considered one of the city's most sophisticated meeting places), or dine in the two restaurants, *L'Obélisque* and the two-

Michelin-star *Les Ambassadeurs* (see *Eating Out*). Rooms facing the street, though rather noisy, have a view *sans pareil;* those on the courtyards are just as nice and more tranquil. 10 Pl. de la Concorde, 8e (phone: 42-65-24-24; 800-888-4747; fax: 44-71-15-02).

**George V** The lobby is a League of Nations of private enterprise; it also seems to be where the *Cannes Film Festival* crowd spends the other 11 months of the year, so numerous are the movie folk who stay in the hotel's 298 rooms and 53 suites and dine in its two restaurants, including the one-Michelin-star *Les Princes.* The *Eiffel Tower* is just across the river, the Champs-Elysées just down the block, and the *Arc de Triomphe* around the corner; most of the rest of Paris can be seen from the windows of rooms on the higher floors. Even those who can't afford one of them—or the tranquil chambers facing the gracious courtyard—should be sure to stop for an utterly lyrical croissant at breakfast or a mean martini in the lively and chic bar. 31 Av. George-V, 8e (phone: 47-23-54-00; fax: 47-20-40-00).

**Lancaster** If location is everything, this charming 19th-century townhouse has it all: It's steps from the Champs-Elysées and two blocks from the Faubourg-St-Honoré. Admired by literati, dignitaries, socialites, Americans in the know, and even the haughtiest of Parisians, this Savoy Group establishment exudes an air of gentility, calm, and, above all, coziness. Aside from its handsome 18th-century antiques and objets d'art, every one of its only 50 rooms and nine suites (with no more than 10 rooms on each floor) has individual charm. Try to book accommodations on the sixth (top) floor, where there's sure to be a view of the *Eiffel Tower, Sacré-Coeur,* or the hotel's delightful garden from a balcony or a terrace. There's an old-fashioned bar with garden murals, a delightful spot for taking mid-morning coffee, afternoon tea, or a post-prandial liqueur, and a relaxed and refined restaurant, with alfresco dining when the weather permits. If the pleasure of truly personal service and gracious surroundings with nary a glimmer of glitz are your preference, this is the right place. 7 Rue de Berri, 8e (phone: 40-76-40-76; 800-223-6800; fax: 42-76-40-10).

**Lutétia** The only real palace hotel on the Rive Gauche, this aristocrat of elegantly ornamented stone with 286 rooms and 21 suites has reigned at the corner of Rue de Sèvres and Boulevard Raspail since 1910. From gray-striped balloon awnings and bowers of sculpted stone flowers framing its graceful arched windows to the regal red lobby appointed with crystal chandeliers, Art Deco skylights, and intricately carved wrought iron, this is a quintessentially Parisian place. It also offers some of the most fantastic views in Paris from its upper floors. The best perspective is from No. 71, a seventh-floor corner room whose balcony commands a view of nearly all of Paris's most famous monuments. There's also a restaurant, the one-Michelin-star *Le Paris,* and a brasserie. Business facilities include 24-hour room service, meeting rooms for up to 450, an English-speaking concierge, foreign currency exchange, secretarial services in English, audiovisual equipment, photocopiers, translation services, and express checkout. 45 Bd. Raspail, 6e (phone: 49-54-46-46; fax: 49-54-46-00).

**Plaza-Athénée** This European hotel is ever elegant and charming—from the 215 rooms and 41 suites done in Louis XV and XVI style to the *Relais Plaza* grill, where *tout Paris* seems to be eternally lunching, and the idyllic one-Michelin-star *Régence* restaurant, which is like a set for some Parisian *Mikado,* with its chirping birds, pools, and bridge. There's also the *Bar Anglais,* a classic Parisian spot for cocktails. A little more sedate and a little more French than the *George V* (above), this property is a haute bastion that takes its dignity very seriously (a discreet note in each bathroom offers an unobtrusive route in and out of the hotel for those in jogging togs). 25 Av. Montaigne, 8e (phone: 47-23-78-33; fax: 47-20-20-70).

**Ritz** The Rive Droite establishment that César Ritz made synonymous with all the finer things in life is such a Paris legend that, seeing it for the first time, it's almost hard to believe it still exists, much less reigns as majestically as ever over the Place Vendôme. Marcel Proust wrote most of *Remembrance of Things Past* here, and Georges-Auguste Escoffier put France at the top of the culinary Olympus from its kitchen, still highly rated today as the two-Michelin-star *L'Espadon* restaurant. The *Ritz Club* is a nightclub and discotheque open to guests and club members only, and there's a deluxe spa. But even if you can't afford to stay in one of the 142 rooms or 45 suites, have a glass of champagne in the elegant bar. 15 Pl. Vendôme, 1er (phone: 42-60-38-30; fax: 42-60-23-71).

**VERY EXPENSIVE**

**Grand** Part of the Inter-Continental chain, this property has long been a favorite of Americans abroad, with its "meeting place of the world," the *Café de la Paix.* It has 545 rooms and luxurious suites, plus cheerful bars, two restaurants, and a prime location next to the *Opéra/Palais Garnier.* There is also a fitness center. Business facilities include 24-hour room service, meeting rooms for up to 1,200, an English-speaking concierge, foreign currency exchange, secretarial services in English, audiovisual equipment, photocopiers, cable television news, and express checkout. 2 Rue Scribe, 9e (phone: 40-07-32-32; 800-327-0200; fax: 42-66-12-51).

**Inter-Continental** The 452 rooms and suites have been meticulously restored to re-create turn-of-the-century elegance with modern conveniences. The cozy, top-floor Louis XVI "garret" rooms look out over the *Tuileries*. There's an American-style coffee shop, a grill, and a popular bar. Business facilities include 24-hour room service, meeting rooms for up to 1,000, an English-speaking concierge, foreign currency exchange, secretarial services in English, audiovisual equipment, photocopiers, translation services, and express checkout. 3 Rue de Castiglione, 1er (phone: 44-77-11-11; fax: 44-77-14-60).

**Pont Royal** Right in the midst of Paris's most exclusive antiques and shopping district, this former 18th-century *hôtel particulier* (private home) has been a well-kept secret. Each of the 78 spacious rooms and suites is tastefully appointed with fine French antiques and sumptuous fabrics. The formal dining room, *Les Antiquaires,* serves first-rate fare. Business facilities include an English-speaking concierge, foreign currency exchange, secretarial services in English, and computers. Closed for renovations at press time, the hotel was scheduled to reopen early this year. 7 Rue Montalembert, 7e (phone: 45-44-38-27; fax: 45-44-92-07).

**Prince de Galles** An excellent location (a next-door neighbor of the pricier *George V*) and impeccable style make this Sheraton member a good choice. All 173 rooms and suites are individually decorated, there's a restaurant and oak-paneled bar, and parking is available. Business facilities include 24-hour room service, meeting rooms for up to 150, an English-speaking concierge, foreign currency exchange, secretarial services in English, audiovisual equipment, photocopiers, computers, translation services, and express checkout. 33 Av. George-V, 8e (phone: 47-23-55-11; fax: 47-20-96-92).

**Raphaël** Less well-known among the top Paris hotels is this spacious, stately place, with a Turner in the lobby downstairs and paneling painted with sphinxes in the generous guestrooms. Its 87 rooms, including 38 suites, attract film folk and the like, and for those who savor strolling down the Champs-Elysées, it's only a short walk away. Most, but not all, of the rooms are air conditioned. There's a restaurant. Business facilities include 24-hour room service, meeting rooms for up to 150, an English-speaking concierge, foreign currency exchange, secretarial services in English, audiovisual equipment, photocopiers, computers, translation services, and express checkout. 17 Av. Kléber, 16e (phone: 44-28-00-28; fax: 45-01-21-50).

**Relais Carré d'Or** For longer stays, this hostelry provides all the amenities of a luxury hotel, plus a variety of accommodations—from studios to multi-room apartments—all with modern kitchens, marble bathrooms, and lovely, understated furnishings. Most have balconies overlooking the hotel's garden or Avenue George-V. There's also a restaurant. Business facilities include 24-hour room service, meeting rooms for up to 30, an English-speaking concierge, foreign currency exchange, secretarial services in English, audiovisual equipment, photocopiers, computers, cable television news, translation services, and express checkout. 46 Av. George-V, 8e (phone: 40-70-05-05; fax: 47-23-30-90).

**Royal Monceau** This elegant, impeccably decorated 180-room, 39-suite hotel has three restaurants (including *Le Jardin du Royal Monceau;* see *Eating Out*), two bars, a fitness center, a pool, a Jacuzzi, and a beauty salon. The rooms are spacious, and the Sunday brunch is a delight. Business facilities include 24-hour room service, meeting rooms for up to 250, an English-speaking concierge, foreign currency exchange, secretarial services in English, audiovisual equipment, photocopiers, computers, translation services, and express checkout. Not far from the *Arc de Triomphe,* at 37 Av. Hoche, 8e (phone: 45-61-98-00; fax: 45-63-28-93).

**La Trémoille** Built in 1886, this former *hôtel particulier* is a true gem. Each of the 110 spacious rooms is beautifully appointed. The atmosphere is one of understated elegance, and the location, just off Avenue Montaigne, a bonus. There's a restaurant. Business facilities include a meeting room for up to 10, an English-speaking concierge, secretarial services in English, and audiovisual equipment. 14 Rue de la Trémoille, 8e (phone: 47-23-34-20; fax: 40-70-01-08).

### EXPENSIVE

**Abbaye St-Germain** On a quiet street, this small, delightful place once was a convent. The lobby has exposed stone arches, and the 46 elegant rooms (we especially admire No. 4, whose doors open onto the charming courtyard) are furnished with antiques, tastefully selected fabrics, and marble baths; none is air conditioned. Unfortunately, there continue to be some complaints about the service. There's no restaurant. Business facilities include an English-speaking concierge, foreign currency exchange, and photocopiers. 10 Rue Cassette, 6e (phone: 45-44-38-11; fax: 45-48-07-86).

**Balzac** Very private, this luxurious, charming hotel has 70 rooms and suites, plus the Paris branch of Milan's *Bice* restaurant. The nocturnally inclined can dance until dawn in the discotheque. Business facilities include 24-hour room service, an English-speaking concierge, foreign currency exchange, and photocopiers. Ideally located off the Champs-Elysées, at 6 Rue Balzac, 8e (phone: 45-61-97-22; fax: 45-25-24-82).

**Colbert** Decorated in pastel tones, each of the 34 rooms and two suites in this Rive Gauche hostelry has a balcony and a mini-bar, but no air conditioning. There's no restaurant, but breakfast is included. There is a meeting room for up to 20. 7 Rue de l'Hôtel-Colbert, 5e (phone: 43-25-85-65; 800-755-9313; fax: 43-25-80-19).

**Duc de St-Simon** In two big townhouses in a beautiful, quiet backwater off the Boulevard St-Germain, this elegant 29-room, five-suite establishment veritably screams Proust. None of the rooms is air conditioned, and there's no restaurant. Business facilities include foreign currency exchange and photocopiers. No credit cards accepted. A five-minute walk from the *Musée d'Orsay,* at 14 Rue de St-Simon, 7e (phone: 45-48-35-66; fax: 45-48-68-25).

**L'Hôtel** Small, but chic, this Rive Gauche hostelry is favored by experienced international travelers with an eye for the offbeat, and, though it's growing a bit shabby around the edges, it still has great charm. It's also where Oscar Wilde died (room No. 16 is a re-creation of the room in which he lived briefly in 1900) and where the Argentine writer Jorge Luis Borges lived. The 24 rooms and three suites are tiny, but beautifully appointed with antiques, fresh flowers, and marble baths; they also have mini-bars and safes. The attractive restaurant serves first-rate fare. Business facilities include meeting rooms for up to 50, an English-speaking concierge, foreign currency exchange, secretarial services in English, photocopiers, translation services, and express checkout. 13 Rue des Beaux-Arts, 6e (phone: 43-25-27-22; fax: 43-25-64-81).

**Jeu de Paume** The architect-owner of this former *jeu de paume* (tennis court) has artfully married old and new in this addition to the Ile St-Louis's collection of exclusive hotels. High-tech lighting, modern artwork, and a sleek glass elevator are set against ancient ceiling beams and limestone brick hearths. Each of the comfortable 30 rooms and two suites overlooks the lovely garden; none is air conditioned. There is also a music salon, but no restaurant. Business facilities include 24-hour room service, meeting rooms for up to 30, foreign currency exchange, secretarial services in English, and photocopiers. 54 Rue St-Louis-en-l'Ile, 4e (phone: 43-26-14-18; fax: 40-46-02-76).

**Méridien** *Air France*'s modern, well-run hotel is American style, but with all the expected French flair. The 1,025 rooms are on the small side, but they're tastefully decorated, quiet, and boast good views. There are four attractive restaurants (one, *Le Clos Longchamp,* has a Michelin star, while another serves Japanese fare), a shopping arcade, three lively bars, and a chic nightclub, *L'Ecume des Nuits.* Business facilities include 24-hour room service, meeting rooms for up to 2,000, an English-speaking concierge, foreign currency exchange, secretarial services in English, audiovisual equipment, photocopiers, translation services, and express checkout. 81 Bd. Gouvion-St-Cyr, 17e (phone: 40-68-34-34; fax: 40-68-31-31).

**Méridien Montparnasse** With 952 rooms, this ultramodern giant has a futuristic lobby, efficient service, a coffee shop, two bars, the one-Michelin-star *Montparnasse 25* restaurant, and in summer, a garden restaurant. There is also an excellent, ample Sunday brunch. Business facilities include 24-hour room service, meeting rooms for up to 2,000, an English-speaking concierge, foreign currency exchange, secretarial services in English, audiovisual equipment, photocopiers, computers, translation services, and express check-out. In the heart of Montparnasse, at 19 Rue du Commandant-René-Mouchotte, 14e (phone: 44-36-44-36; fax: 44-36-49-00).

**Meurice** Refined Louis XV and XVI elegance and a wide range of services are offered for a franc or two less than the other "palaces." The hotel, a member of the CIGA chain, has 179 rooms and 35 especially nice suites, a popular bar, the one-Michelin-star restaurant *Le Meurice* overlooking the Rue de Rivoli, and the chandeliered *Pompadour* tearoom. Business facilities include 24-hour room service, meeting rooms for up to 150, an English-speaking concierge, foreign currency exchange, secretarial services in English, audio-visual equipment, photocopiers, computers, cable television news, and translation services. Ideally located at 228 Rue de Rivoli, 1er (phone: 44-58-10-10; fax: 44-58-10-15).

**Montaigne** This unpretentious establishment is a true find. Each of its 29 rooms is comfortable, clean, and chicly decorated. There's a bar and a breakfast room, but no restaurant. 6 Av. Montaigne, 8e (phone: 47-20-30-50; fax: 47-20-94-12).

**Montalembert** Privacy is the hallmark of this exquisite little place, whose 56 rooms and suites are available in two styles—traditional, with restored period armoires and sleigh beds, or contemporary, with straight geometric lines and fireplaces. (If you're over six feet tall ask for one of the modern rooms—the beds are longer.) Bathrooms are small, but high-tech. The hotel's *Le Montalembert* restaurant serves delicious fare; there's also a cozy bar. Business facilities include 24-hour room service, meeting rooms for up to 30, an English-speaking concierge, foreign currency exchange, secretarial services in English, audiovisual equipment, photocopiers, and express checkout. On the Rive Gauche, at 3 Rue Montalembert, 7e (phone: 45-48-68-11; 800-628-8929; fax: 42-22-58-19).

**Le Parc Victor Hugo** A sumptuous 122-room hotel, decorated in the style of an English country house, it features a large interior garden. Its excellent restaurant, *Le Relais du Parc,* was set up by super-chef Joël Robuchon, whose own three-Michelin-star, self-named establishment is next door. 55 Av. Raymond-Poincaré, 16e (phone: 44-05-66-66; fax: 44-05-66-00).

**Paris Hilton International** Of the 455 modern rooms here, those facing the river have the best views. *Le Western* serves American staples like T-bone steaks, apple pie à la mode, and brownies (mostly to French diners), and the coffee shop is a magnet for homesick Americans. Business facilities include 24-hour room service, meeting rooms for up to 1,000, an English-speaking concierge, foreign currency exchange, secretarial services in English, audiovisual equipment, photocopiers, translation services, and express checkout. A few steps from the *Eiffel Tower,* at 18 Av. de Suffren, 15e (phone: 42-73-92-00; 800-932-3322; fax: 47-83-62-66).

**Pavillon de la Reine** Under the same ownership as the *Relais Christine* (see below), the Marais's only luxury hotel is similarly appointed.

It's blessed with a supreme location on the elegant Place des Vosges, and the 55 rooms (most are on the small side) look out on a garden or courtyard. There's no restaurant. Business facilities include 24-hour room service, foreign currency exchange, and photocopiers. 28 Pl. des Vosges, 3e (phone: 42-77-96-40; fax: 42-77-63-06).

**Régina** This hotel's 116 rooms and 14 suites are spacious and furnished with antiques. The restaurant has a lovely garden, and there's also a bar and a small fitness center. Business facilities include an English-speaking concierge, two meeting rooms, photocopiers, and translation services. Centrally located, overlooking the *Louvre* and the *Tuileries*, at 2 Pl. des Pyramides, 1er (phone: 42-60-31-10; fax: 50-15-95-16).

**Relais Christine** Formerly a 16th-century cloister, this lovely place boasts 34 rooms and 17 suites with modern fixtures and lots of old-fashioned charm. Ask for a room with a courtyard or garden view; the suites and the ground-floor room with a private *terrasse* are particularly luxurious. There's no restaurant. Business facilities include meeting rooms for up to 20, foreign currency exchange, and photocopiers. 3 Rue Christine, 6e (phone: 43-26-71-80; fax: 43-26-89-38).

**Relais Médicis** With the same owners as the *Relais Saint-Germain* (see below), this elegant 16-room establishment in an 18th-century building boasts marble bathrooms and beamed ceilings. There's no restaurant. 23 Rue Racine, 6e (phone: 43-26-00-60; fax: 40-46-83-39).

**Relais Saint-Germain** In a 17th-century building, this hostelry with 19 guestrooms and one suite is ideally situated on the Rive Gauche, just steps from the Boulevard St-Germain and the area's best shops, eateries, and galleries. It is attractively decorated, and charming down to its massive ceiling beams and huge flower bouquets. A rare find. There's a breakfast parlor, but no restaurant. 9 Carrefour de l'Odéon, 6e (phone: 43-29-12-05; fax: 46-33-45-30).

**Résidence Maxim's** No expense has been spared to create sybaritic splendor in Pierre Cardin's luxurious venture, a distinguished favorite of the rich and famous. Its clever decor combines modern statuary with Belle Epoque appointments. There are 37 suites and four rooms, as well as a classic lobby, a secluded bar (*Le Maximin,* open late), and *L'Atmosphère,* a world class restaurant. Business facilities include 24-hour room service, meeting rooms for up to 70, an English-speaking concierge, foreign currency exchange, secretarial services in English, audiovisual equipment, photocopiers, cable television news, translation services, and express checkout. Near the Champs-Elysées and the *Palais de l'Elysée,* at 42 Av. Gabriel, 8e (phone: 45-61-96-33; fax: 42-89-06-07).

**Résidence du Roy** This establishment offers 36 self-contained studios, suites, and duplexes, complete with kitchen facilities. There's no restaurant. Business facilities include meeting rooms for up to 20, an English-speaking concierge, audiovisual equipment, photocopiers, and express checkout. Within easy reach of the Champs-Elysées, at 8 Rue François-Ier, 8e (phone: 42-89-59-59; fax: 40-74-07-92).

**St. James Paris** Like something out of an Evelyn Waugh novel, this secluded 19th-century château is located in a residential neighborhood within a stroll of the *Bois de Boulogne.* The 17 rooms and 31 suites (including four penthouse suites opening onto a winter garden), the walled courtyard with a regal fountain, the library bar, the health club, the elegant restaurant overlooking a rose garden, and the more relaxed grill—all give one a sense of being a guest at an English country estate. Though the place is billed as a private club, hotel guests are welcome to stay after paying a temporary membership fee of about $10. (Non-members not staying at the hotel, however, may not dine or sip cocktails here.) Business facilities include 24-hour room service, meeting rooms for up to 35, an English-speaking concierge, foreign currency exchange, secretarial services in English, audiovisual equipment, photocopiers, computers, translation services, and express checkout. 5 Pl. Chancelier-Adenauer, 16e (phone: 47-04-29-29; 212-956-0200 in the US; fax: 45-53-00-61; 212-956-2555 in the US).

**San Régis** Guests are made to feel at home at this elegant place with a comfortable ambience. There are 34 rooms and 10 suites, all beautifully appointed, as well as a restaurant and bar. Business facilities include an English-speaking concierge, foreign currency exchange, photocopiers, computers, and cable television news. 12 Rue Jean-Goujon, 8e (phone: 44-95-16-16; fax: 45-61-05-48).

**Sofitel CNIT La Défense** The city's sights and pleasures are easily reached from this modern luxury hotel in suburban La Défense. The 147 rooms and six suites are outfitted with mini-bars and other up-to-date amenities. There's also a shopping arcade, a bar, and the one-Michelin-star restaurant, *Les Communautés.* Business facilities include meeting rooms, English-speaking staff, photocopiers, and express checkout. Steps away from the *Centre National des Industries et des Techniques* (*CNIT;* National Center for Industry and Technology) and the *Grande Arche,* at 2 Pl. de la Défense, La Défense (phone: 46-92-10-10; 800-763-4835; fax: 46-92-10-50).

**Le Stendhal** Named for the famous novelist who died here, this luxurious hostelry's 21 rooms feature antiques, Jacuzzis, and mini-bars. The suites are particularly charming—especially Nos. 52 and 53. There's a cozy bar, but no restaurant. Near the Place Vendôme, at 22 Rue Danielle-Casanova, 2e (phone: 44-58-52-52; fax: 44-58-52-00).

**Tuileries** With a good location in a "real" neighborhood in the heart of the city, this 26-room, four-suite hotel has a well-tended look and attractive, carved wood bedsteads. All rooms have mini-bars and safes. There's no restaurant. This is also one of the few Parisian members of the Relais de Silence, an association of hotels that meet requirements for being especially quiet. 10 Rue St-Hyacinthe, 1er (phone: 42-61-04-17 or 42-61-06-94; fax: 49-27-91-56).

**Le Vernet** Guests staying in the 60 modern rooms and three suites here have complimentary access to the fitness center at the elegant *Royal*

*Monceau* (see above), its sister establishment. There's an excellent restaurant, the one-Michelin-star *Les Elysées.* Business facilities include 24-hour room service, meeting rooms for up to 15, an English-speaking concierge, foreign currency exchange, audiovisual equipment, photocopiers, computers, translation services, and express checkout. A few steps from the *Arc de Triomphe,* at 25 Rue Vernet, 8e (phone: 44-31-98-00; fax: 44-31-85-69).

**de Vigny** A small, elegant 25-room, 12-suite Relais & Châteaux member, it features lots of mahogany and chintz. Suite 504 has its own stairway leading to a glass-roofed *salon* with a spectacular view. There's a bar, but no restaurant; this is one of the few hotels in the neighborhood where nonsmoking rooms and parking are available. 9 Rue Balzac, 8e (phone: 40-75-04-39; fax: 40-75-05-81).

**Westminster** This establishment, which in recent years has regained some of its lost luster, has a traditional decor complete with wood paneling, marble fireplaces, and parquet floors. Some of the 101 rooms (including 16 suites) overlook the street; others look down into an inner courtyard. There's also a one-Michelin-star restaurant, *Le Céladon,* and a bar. Business facilities include 24-hour room service, meeting rooms for up to 70, an English-speaking concierge, foreign currency exchange, secretarial services in English, audiovisual equipment, photocopiers, and translation services. Between the *Opéra/Palais Garnier* and the *Ritz,* at 13 Rue de la Paix, 2e (phone: 42-61-57-46; fax: 42-60-30-66).

### MODERATE

**Angleterre** Its 29 classic, unpretentious rooms and one suite (none air conditioned) are in what was the British Embassy in the 18th century; the building is now a national monument. There's no restaurant. Business facilities include an English-speaking concierge, foreign currency exchange, and photocopiers. 44 Rue Jacob, 6e (phone: 42-60-34-72; fax: 42-60-16-93).

**Bretonnerie** This restored, 17th-century townhouse with 28 rooms and one suite (none air conditioned) takes itself seriously, with dark wood furnishings and several beamed attic rooms that overlook the narrow streets of the fashionable Marais area. There's no restaurant. 22 Rue Ste-Croix-de-la-Bretonnerie, 4e (phone: 48-87-77-63; fax: 42-77-26-78).

**Brighton** This 69-room, one-suite hotel facing the *Tuileries* is decorated in pure 19th-century style; many of the spacious rooms overlook the gardens. Some smaller and less expensive rooms in the charming attic have great views, and the suite, with its gilt mosaic bathroom, is a bargain. There's no restaurant. Business facilities include an English-speaking staff and photocopiers. 218 Rue de Rivoli, 1er (phone: 42-60-30-03; fax: 42-60-41-78).

**Britannique** A Quaker mission house during World War I, this hotel now offers 40 rooms, all equipped with mini-bars, hair dryers, and satellite TV, but not air conditioning. There's no restaurant. Within minutes of the *Louvre* and *Notre-Dame,* at 20 Av. Victoria, 1er (phone: 42-33-74-59; 800-755-9313; fax: 42-33-82-65).

**Danube St-Germain** The 40 rooms and six elegant suites, all with four-poster bamboo beds, are comfortable, and some of them overlook an attractive courtyard typical of the Rive Gauche. None of the rooms is air conditioned, and 10 lower-priced rooms have baths, but shared toilets and no TV sets. There's no restaurant. Business facilities include foreign currency exchange and photocopiers. American Express only accepted. 58 Rue Jacob, 6e (phone: 42-60-34-70; fax: 42-60-81-18).

**Deux Continents** The cozy red sitting room of this quiet 40-room establishment on the Rive Gauche looks invitingly onto the street. Eleven of the rooms are air conditioned. There's no restaurant. 25 Rue Jacob, 6e (phone: 43-26-72-46).

**Deux Iles** On the historic Ile St-Louis, this beautifully restored 17th-century house has a garden with a Portuguese fountain, but no restaurant. Though small, the 17 rooms are nicely decorated with French provincial fabrics and Louis XIV ceramic tiles in the bathrooms; none is air conditioned. Business facilities include foreign currency exchange. No credit cards accepted. 59 Rue St-Louis-en-l'Ile, 4e (phone: 43-26-13-35; fax: 43-29-60-25).

**Ferrandi** This no-frills hostelry with a winding wood staircase and a quiet lounge is popular with international business travelers. The 41 rooms and one suite (none air conditioned) have antique furnishings. There's no restaurant. 92 Rue du Cherche-Midi, 6e (phone: 42-22-97-40; fax: 45-44-89-97).

**Fleurie** This lovely, family-run hotel in a former 18th-century townhouse has 29 well-equipped rooms with mini-bars and safes. The service is friendly, and there's a bar, but no restaurant. 32-34 Rue Grégoire-de-Tours, 6e (phone: 43-29-59-81; fax: 43-29-68-44).

**Grand Hôtel de l'Univers** Modern and tucked away on a quiet street, this hotel has 34 rooms, all with mini-bars and safes. There's no restaurant. Near St-Germain-des-Prés and the Quartier Latin, at 6 Rue Grégoire-de-Tours, 6e (phone: 43-29-37-00; fax: 40-51-06-45).

**Grandes Ecoles** The sort of place that people recommend only to the right friends (even the proprietress wants to keep it a secret). Insulated from the street by a delightful courtyard and garden, it is a simple, 19th-century private house that's long on atmosphere even though the 48 rooms offer plain comforts (they lack air conditioning and TV sets, and some do not have private baths). There aren't many like it in Paris, but beware: Booking is difficult, and the owner has been known to give away reserved rooms. There's no restaurant. 75 Rue Cardinal-Lemoine, 5e (phone: 43-26-79-23; fax: 43-25-28-15).

**Le Jardin des Plantes** In addition to a magnificent setting across from Paris's botanical gardens, near the *Sorbonne,* this hotel offers 33 airy rooms with mini-bars and hair dryers, some with safes; some also have alcoves large enough for extra beds for children. None of the rooms is air conditioned. Art exhibits and classical music concerts are held on Sundays in the vaulted cellar. There's also a sauna in the basement, but no restaurant. 5 Rue Linné, 5e (phone: 47-07-06-20; fax: 47-07-62-74).

**Lenox St-Germain** Small and tastefully done, this hotel has 32 rooms (none air conditioned) and a cozy bar, but no restaurant. It's popular with the fashion crowd. Between the busy St-Germain area and the boutiques nearby, at 9 Rue de l'Université, 7e (phone: 42-96-10-95; fax: 42-61-52-83).

**Littré** This 93-room, four-suite Rive Gauche hotel has old-fashioned elegance, spacious rooms (with large beds, a rarity in Paris, but no air conditioning) and huge bathrooms. There's no restaurant, but room-service meals are available, and there's an English-style bar. Business services also are offered. No credit cards accepted. 9 Rue Littré, 6e (phone: 45-44-38-68; fax: 45-44-88-13).

**Lord Byron** On a quiet street off the Champs-Elysées, it has a pleasant courtyard and 30 comfortable, homey rooms (none air conditioned). The staff is friendly and speaks good English. There's no restaurant. 5 Rue de Chateaubriand, 8e (phone: 43-59-89-98; fax: 42-89-46-04).

**Lutèce** Here are 23 smallish but luxurious rooms (one split-level; none air conditioned) on the charming Ile St-Louis. The decor is positively ravishing, with exquisite toile fabric and wallpaper and raw wood beams. There's no restaurant. No credit cards accepted. 65 Rue St-Louis-en-l'Ile, 4e (phone: 43-26-23-52; fax: 43-29-60-25).

**Madison** This place offers 55 large, bright rooms, with such amenities as mini-bars and safes; some have balconies. There's no restaurant. 143 Bd. St-Germain, 6e (phone: 40-51-60-00; fax: 40-51-60-01).

**Des Marroniers** An excellent location in the heart of the Rive Gauche makes this 37-room hotel a real bargain. The rooms are not air conditioned. There's a garden courtyard and pretty breakfast room, but no restaurant. No credit cards accepted. 21 Rue Jacob, 6e (phone: 43-25-30-60; fax: 40-46-83-56).

**Novanox** This 27-room hotel is ultramodern, with high-tech furniture, but it offers old-fashioned extras such as brioches for breakfast, served on an outdoor terrace. All the rooms have mini-bars and safes, but no air conditioning. There's a bar, but no restaurant. Service is exceptionally friendly. 155 Bd. du Montparnasse, 6e (phone: 46-33-63-60; fax: 43-26-61-72).

**Odéon** Small (29 rooms), modernized, and charming, it's in the heart of the St-Germain area on the Rive Gauche. There's no restaurant. 13 Rue de St-Sulpice, 6e (phone: 43-25-70-11; fax: 43-29-97-34).

**Parc St-Séverin** An interesting little hotel on the Rive Gauche, it has 27 rooms (none air conditioned), including a top-floor penthouse with a wraparound balcony. The decor is modern but understated, and the overall ambience is appealing, even though the neighborhood is not the quietest in Paris. There's no restaurant. 22 Rue de la Parcheminerie, 5e (phone: 43-54-32-17; fax: 43-54-70-71).

**Pavillon Bastille** There's a 17th-century fountain in the courtyard of this small, 19th-century *hôtel particulier*. The 24 smallish rooms and one suite are all cheerfully decorated in contemporary style and equipped with mini-bars. There's a bar and a breakfast room, but no restaurant. Conveniently located near the Place de la Bastille, at 65 Rue de Lyon, 12e (phone: 43-43-65-65; fax: 43-43-96-52).

**Perreyve** This quiet, 30-room hotel with understated, traditional decor is ideally located near the *Jardin du Luxembourg*. There's no restaurant. 63 Rue Madame, 6e (phone: 45-48-35-01; fax: 42-84-03-30).

**Pierre et Vacances** In a sleepy corner of Montmartre, this residential hotel charges nightly, weekly, and monthly rates. The apartments have kitchens, and some overlook a peaceful garden; none is air conditioned. There's no restaurant. Near the leafy square of the *Théâtre de l'Atelier*, at 10 Pl. Charles-Dullin, 18e (phone: 42-57-14-55; fax: 42-54-48-87).

**Récamier** An amazing bargain for those who manage to reserve a room, this is a simple, clean, and very peaceful 30-room hotel right on the elegant Place St-Sulpice. The rooms are not air conditioned and have no TV sets; eight share baths (though all have private toilet facilities). There's no restaurant. 3 *bis* Pl. St-Sulpice, 6e (phone: 43-26-04-89).

**Regent's Garden** This small hotel has 39 spacious rooms, some with large marble fireplaces, and three suites; none of the accommodations is air conditioned, but all have amenities such as mini-bars and hair dryers. A country atmosphere pervades, and the young hoteliers who run the place make guests feel completely at home. There's also a garden and parking, but no restaurant. On a quiet street near the *Arc de Triomphe,* at 6 Rue Pierre-Demours, 17e (phone: 45-74-07-30; fax: 40-55-01-42).

**Royal St-Honoré** Newly renovated, the 68-room, seven-suite hotel is one of the city's best values for this prime location. Some rooms have terraces overlooking the *Jardin des Tuileries.* There's no restaurant. Business services include an English-speaking concierge, meeting rooms for up to 27, photocopiers, computer modems, and translation services. 221 Rue Saint-Honoré, 1er (phone: 42-60-32-79; fax: 42-60-47-44).

**St-Germain-des-Prés** In the heart of one of Paris's loveliest districts, this comfortable 30-room hotel is a good bargain. Request a room on the courtyard, as the street can be noisy. There's no restaurant. 36 Rue Bonaparte, 6e (phone: 43-26-00-19; fax: 40-46-83-63).

**Le St-Grégoire** A small 18th-century mansion on the Rive Gauche, this hostelry has an intimate, cozy atmosphere, a warm fire in the hearth, a restaurant, and 19 tastefully furnished rooms and one suite. Two of the rooms have terraces overlooking a garden, and only two of the rooms are air conditioned. There's no restaurant. 43 Rue de l'Abbé-Grégoire, 6e (phone: 45-48-23-23; fax: 45-48-33-95).

**St-Louis Marais** This tiny hotel is a short walk from the Place des Vosges, the quays along the Seine, and the Bastille nightclubs. Dating from the 18th century, when it was part of the Celestine Convent, it has 15 small rooms with safes and hair dryers (no TV sets or air conditioning). There's no restaurant, and historical landmark status has barred the installation of an elevator. No credit cards accepted. On a quiet residential street on the edge of the chic Marais, at 1 Rue Charles-V, 4e (phone: 48-87-87-04; fax: 48-87-33-26).

**Sofitel Porte de Sèvres** Located in southwest Paris, this modern luxury hotel features 635 comfortably furnished rooms with all the conveniences (such as mini-bars). There's also a glass-enclosed fitness center and pool with marvelous views, the one-Michelin-star *Relais de Sèvres* restaurant, a brasserie, a jazz bar, and even a movie theater. Business facilities include an English-speaking concierge, a business center with meeting rooms for up to 2,000, photocopiers, computers, translation services, and express checkout. Right by the *Parc des Expositions,* at the Porte de Versailles, 8 Rue Louis-Armand, 15e (phone: 40-60-33-11; 800-763-4835; fax: 45-57-04-22).

**Solférino** A cozy place with Oriental rugs scattered about. The 34 tiny rooms have floral wallpaper; none has air conditioning or a TV set. There's a plant-filled breakfast and sitting room, but no restaurant. 91 Rue de Lille, 7e (phone: 47-05-85-54; fax: 45-55-51-16).

**Suède** A delightful hotel in a quiet area, just around the corner from the prime minister's residence. All 40 rooms and one suite are beautifully appointed (none has air conditioning or a TV set); those overlooking the garden are smaller but much prettier. There's no restaurant, but breakfast is served in a simple salon or, in good weather, in the beautiful courtyard. 31 Rue Vaneau, 7e (phone: 47-05-18-65; fax: 47-05-69-27).

**Villa des Artistes** Quiet luxury is the drawing card of this popular Quartier Latin hotel with 59 rooms and its own patio-garden. There's no restaurant. 9 Rue de la Grande-Chaumière, 6e (phone: 43-26-60-86; fax: 43-54-73-70).

### INEXPENSIVE

**Bersoly's Saint-Germain** This quiet hotel near the *Musée d'Orsay* attracts artists and antiques dealers. Each of the 16 rooms (none with air conditioning) is named for a famous painter. There's no restaurant. 28 Rue de Lille, 7e (phone: 42-60-73-79; fax: 49-27-05-55).

**Caron de Beaumarchais** Named after the 18th-century playwright who once lived on this street, this elegant new hotel in the Marais district has 19 rooms, all with fax lines, cable TV, safes, and mini-bars, and some with small balconies. There's a breakfast room that opens onto a small garden, but no restaurant. 12 Rue Vieille-du-Temple, 4e (phone: 42-72-34-12; fax: 42-72-34-63).

**Delavigne** With a good location (down the street from the *Odéon* theater) and an enlightened manager who says he isn't interested in simply handing out keys, but enjoys introducing foreigners to Paris, this 34-room hotel is a good value. None of the rooms is air conditioned. There's no restaurant. 1 Rue Casimir-Delavigne, 6e (phone: 43-29-31-50; fax: 43-29-78-56).

**Deux Avenues** A quiet 32-room hotel offering friendly service, near a lively street market. There's no restaurant. 38 Rue Poncelet, 17e (phone: 42-27-44-35; fax: 47-63-95-48).

**Esmeralda** Some of this hotel's 19 rooms look directly at *Notre-Dame* over the gardens of *Eglise St-Julien-le-Pauvre,* one of Paris's oldest churches. The oak beams and furniture enhance the medieval atmosphere. Don't look for air conditioning or TV sets here, though the rooms do have safes and hair dryers, and all but three have private baths. Small and friendly, it's especially popular with the theatrical crowd. There's no restaurant. No credit cards accepted. 4 Rue St-Julien-le-Pauvre, 5e (phone: 43-54-19-20; fax: 40-51-00-68).

**Familia** With friendly management and 30 rooms (none air conditioned), this simple hotel is a great bargain. The rooms feature such amenities as mini-bars and hair dryers. There's no restaurant. Near the *Sorbonne,* at 11 Rue des Ecoles, 5e (phone: 43-54-55-27; fax: 43-29-61-77).

**Jeanne d'Arc** This little place doesn't get top marks for decor, and its facilities are simple, but somehow word of its appeal has spread from Minnesota to Melbourne. It's well placed, near the Place des Vosges, and the management is friendly. There's no restaurant. On a quiet street in the Marais, at 3 Rue de Jarente, 4e (phone: 48-87-62-11; fax: 48-87-37-31).

**Marais** Ideal for families traveling with children, this simple, 39-room hotel with friendly management has several connecting rooms available. None of the rooms is air conditioned. There's no restaurant. Near the *Bastille,* at 2 *bis* Rue Commines, 3e (phone: 48-87-78-27; fax: 48-87-09-01).

**Oriental** This simple but comfortable 32-room hotel is near *Notre-Dame.* There's no restaurant. 2 Rue d'Arras, 5e (phone: 43-54-38-12; fax: 40-51-86-78).

**Prima-Lepic** The cheerful young owners have decorated the 38 rooms in this Montmartre hotel with pretty floral wallpapers and one-of-a-kind furnishings—a wicker chair, a mirrored armoire, a 1930s lamp (no air conditioning, though). No. 56, on the top floor, looks out over Paris, and travelers with children should make special note of room No. 2, which connects to an adjoining room. The public spaces are charming, too. There's no restaurant. 29 Rue Lepic, 18e (phone: 46-06-44-64; fax: 46-06-66-11).

**Le Vieux Marais** This agreeable Marais hostelry has 30 pretty, if not very large, rooms; none is air conditioned. The breakfast room (there's no restaurant) has an impressive wall-size engraving of the Place des Vosges; the real thing is not far away. Near the *Centre Georges-Pompidou,* at 8 Rue du Plâtre, 4e (phone: 42-78-47-22; fax: 42-78-34-32).

**Welcome** Overlooking the Boulevard St-Germain, it's simple but comfortable. There are 30 rooms; those on the street are relatively noisy, in spite of double windows, and none is air conditioned. The sixth floor garret rooms are very romantic, with great views. There's no restaurant. No credit cards accepted. 66 Rue de Seine, 6e (phone: 46-34-24-80; fax: 40-46-81-59).

---

## EATING OUT

Paris considers itself the culinary capital of the world, and you will never forget food for long here. Whether you grab a fresh croissant and café au lait for breakfast or splurge on an epicurean fantasy for dinner, this is the city in which to indulge all your gastronomic dreams. Remember, too, that there is no such thing as "French" food; rather, Paris is a gastronomic mosaic, where one can try cuisines from Provence, Alsace, Normandy, Brittany, and other regions.

For a dinner for two, including service, but not wine, a very expensive restaurant will charge $250 or more; an expensive one, $150 to $200; a moderate one, $100 to $150; an inexpensive one, $50 to $100; and a very inexpensive one, $50 or less. A service charge of 15% usually is included in the bill, but it's customary to leave a small additional tip for good service. Street addresses of the restaurants below are followed by their *arrondissement* number. Unless otherwise noted all restaurants listed below are open for lunch and dinner.

Although the city of Paris has passed a law requiring that all restaurants provide nonsmoking areas, nonsmokers can't claim victory yet. The general dearth of space in Paris restaurants, combined with the large numbers of French people who smoke (around 80% of the population, according to one recent survey), means that nonsmokers are still rarely seated very far from a smoker. And, what's more, compliance with the law is erratic: Ask restaurateurs in Paris about what is known there as the law *"à l'Américaine,"* and most will just laugh!

### REMEMBER, CALL AHEAD

To save frustration and embarrassment, always *reconfirm* dinner reservations before noon on the appointed day. Also remember that some of the better restaurants do not accept credit cards, and many close over the weekend, as well as for part or all of July or August. It's best to check ahead on these matters to avoid disappointment at the restaurant of your choice. It's also worth remembering that many

restaurants offer special lunch menus at considerably lower prices.

For an unforgettable culinary experience we begin with our favorites, followed by our cost and quality choices, listed by price category.

## HAUTE GASTRONOMIE

**L'Ambroisie** Promoted to three-star status by Michelin in 1988, this elegant establishment is the showcase for chef Bernard Pacaud's equally elegant cuisine. The menu is limited to only a few sublime entrées, such as a fresh truffle in puff pastry, rack of Pauillac lamb in a truffle crust, and *crème de homard aux Saint-Jacques* (lobster with sea scallops in a cream sauce). Closed Sundays, Mondays, two weeks in February, and the first three weeks in August. Reservations necessary. Major credit cards accepted. 9 Pl. des Vosges, 4e (phone: 42-78-51-45).

**Amphyclès** A protégé and former sous chef of super-chef Joël Robuchon (see below), Philippe Groult prepares fine contemporary cuisine, which bears both bourgeois and southern French influences. There are splendid creamy soups, lamb stew with rosemary, lobster salad with sweet red peppers, and a rock lobster risotto. If the brightly lit modern decor of his small two-Michelin-star establishment is forgettably neutral, the food is unquestionably memorable. Closed Saturday lunch, Sundays, and most of July. Reservations necessary. Major credit cards accepted. Near the Place des Ternes, at 78 Av. des Ternes, 17e (phone: 40-68-01-01; fax: 40-68-91-88).

**L'Arpège** The minimalist decor of this two-Michelin-star establishment belies the succulent, generous cuisine prepared by chef Alain Passard. Peppery tuna filet, veal sweetbreads with rosemary, and lemon soufflé flavored with cloves are just a few of the possibilities. The prix fixe lunch menu is a relative bargain. Closed Saturdays and Sunday lunch. Reservations necessary. Major credit cards accepted. 84 Rue de Varenne, 7e (phone: 45-51-47-33; fax: 44-18-98-39).

**Guy Savoy** In spite of the fact that he now operates several bistros throughout Paris (see *La Butte Chaillot,* below), Savoy, unlike many globe-trotting celebrity chefs, still mans the kitchen at his handsome, two-Michelin-star restaurant. The menu is small and constantly changing, with such recent successes as a peppery, jellied duck foie gras served with celery-root purée, and *volaille con-*

*fite et laquée au vinaigre* (chicken stewed in and glazed with vinegar). Inventive desserts (which may be ordered in half portions) include a grapefruit terrine with tea-flavored sauce. There had been some complaints about high prices, some disappointing dishes, and chilly service, but the restaurant seems to be back on track now. Closed weekends and most of August. Reservations necessary. Major credit cards accepted. 18 Rue Troyon, 17e (phone: 43-80-40-61; fax: 46-22-43-09).

**Joël Robuchon** A legend in his own time, Joël Robuchon is already ranked in France among the greatest chefs of any era, alongside Taillevent, Carême, and Escoffier. Robuchon's revolutionary cuisine, which he calls *moderne,* is neither traditional French nor nouvelle cuisine, but a happy medium. Like nouvelle cuisine, Robuchon's creations are lighter than traditional recipes, employing less butter and cream. They're based on intense reductions of vegetable, fish, and meat essences, as well as highly flavored, typically French ingredients such as truffles (a Robuchon favorite—the finest available pop up frequently in his signature dishes). But Robuchon also favors earthy, bistro-style ingredients that would never find their way onto the usual nouvelle cuisine menu. Mere words can't do justice to menu offerings such as *gratin de macaroni aux truffes et foie gras* (macaroni with truffles and foie gras) and *langouste rôtie au cumin et au romarin* (roast rock lobster with cumin and rosemary), both served topped with aged Parmesan and chopped fresh truffles. Robuchon's three-Michelin-star restaurant now goes by his name (it was formerly *Jamin*) and has a new locale, in a turn-of-the-century townhouse with the warm feel of a Victorian British country estate. Robuchon has said he'll retire in 1996 (at the ripe old age of 50), depriving the world of his genius, so now is the time to experience it. Closed weekends and the month of July. Reservations necessary far in advance. Major credit cards accepted. 55 Av. Raymond-Poincaré, 16e (phone: 47-27-12-27).

**Lasserre** The waiters are in tails, the ceiling glides open to reveal the stars, the decanted burgundy is poured over the flame of a candle to detect sediment, and the impeccable service makes diners feel that somehow they deserve all this. The two-Michelin-star cuisine—heavy on foie gras, caviar, truffles, and rich sauces—is traditional French at its most heavenly, and the wine cellar is a virtual museum of French oenology. Not surprisingly, making dinner reservations here is akin to booking seats for a sold-out Broadway musical, so think way ahead. Closed Sundays, Monday lunch, and the month of August. Reservations necessary. Major credit cards accepted. 17 Av. Franklin-Roosevelt, 8e (phone: 43-59-53-43; fax: 45-63-72-23).

**Lucas-Carton** The lush, plush Belle Epoque dining room, under the chef/owner Alain Senderens, is the perfect place to sample a few bites of truffle salad, lobster with vanilla, or anything else on the ever-changing menu. Diners also have the opportunity to order each course with a perfectly matched glass of wine. Senderens's quirky and innovative cooking combines many tenets of nouvelle cuisine with Asian influences, and Michelin lost no time in awarding it three stars. The utensils and serving pieces are almost as alluring as the food. The prix fixe lunch menu is a good value. Closed weekends, most of August, and December 24 through January 3. Reservations necessary. Major credit cards accepted. 9 Pl. de la Madeleine, 8e (phone: 42-65-22-90; fax: 42-65-06-23).

**Michel Rostang** Rostang seems to be at the top of his form these days, with an inventive repertoire that takes its inspiration from the cuisine of Savoie, Lyons, and Provence. The restaurant has two dining rooms, one of which has a large glass wall overlooking the kitchen. Specialties include *oeufs de caille en coque d'oursin* (quail's eggs in a sea urchin shell), *feuilleté de canard et foie gras au chou rouge* (duck and foie gras in puff pastry with a red cabbage sauce), and Scottish salmon with sesame seeds and artichokes. Desserts include warm chocolate tart, and pears roasted in sauternes. Closed Saturday lunch, Sundays, and the first two weeks of August. Reservations necessary. Major credit cards accepted. 20 Rue Rennequin, 17e (phone: 47-63-40-77; fax: 47-63-82-75).

**Taillevent** Named after a famed medieval chef, this three-Michelin-star dining room occupies a distinguished 19th-century mansion complete with fine paintings, porcelain dinnerware, and aristocratic decor, making it look as if the French Revolution was really just a bad dream. Longtime chef Claude Deligne has retired, but the traditions he established and many of his recipes are being kept alive by Philippe Legendre, who also has added new items to the menu. The rabbit in pastry with spinach and *sarriette* (summer savory), the sea-urchin mousse, and the many stunning desserts are sure to please, while the wine list is one of the city's best and most reasonably priced. One of the hardest-to-get restaurant reservations in France—but do try. Closed weekends, part of February, and most of August. Reservations necessary. Major credit cards accepted. 15 Rue Lamennais, 8e (phone: 45-61-12-90; fax: 42-25-95-18).

**La Tour d'Argent** For many, this place is touristy, overrated, and overpriced, but Paris's senior three-Michelin-star restaurant continues to amaze and entertain with its cuisine and the most romantic view of any restaurant in the city. The gold-toned room brings to mind Cole Porter's "elegant, swellegant party"; in fact, Porter occasionally dined here, as have a host of other luminaries, from Franklin Roosevelt to Paul McCartney, Greta Garbo to the Aga Khan. The specialty here is a Charente duck pressed at tableside just as it was a century ago; also not to be missed are the classic quenelles in mornay sauce with fresh black truffles. The spectacular wine list is one of France's best. As this restaurant has a reservations book thicker than the Manhattan telephone directory, it's often impossible to get dinner reservations at certain times of the year. Best tip: Book a windowside table for lunch on a weekday, when there's a prix fixe menu; the view of *Notre-Dame* and the Seine is just as splendid by daylight. Closed Mondays. Reservations necessary. Major credit cards accepted. 15 Quai de la Tournelle, 5e (phone: 43-54-23-31; fax: 44-07-12-04).

**Vivarois** Claude Peyrot is unquestionably one of France's finest chefs. His small, elegant establishment features *la cuisine du marché,* meaning that offerings vary according to what is available at the market. A splendid grilled turbot with capers is usually on the menu. Michelin has awarded it two stars. Closed weekends and the month of August. Reservations necessary. Major credit cards accepted. 192 Av. Victor-Hugo, 16e (phone: 45-04-04-31; fax: 4503-09-84).

---

### VERY EXPENSIVE

**Les Ambassadeurs** A two-Michelin-star establishment that offers a soul-satisfying meal gracefully presented in an elegant dining room with 20-foot-high ceilings, massive crystal chandeliers, and stunning views of the Place de la Concorde. Delicious dishes such as *gratin dauphinois de homard avec crème au caviar* (potato gratin with lobster in caviar sauce) and veal sweetbreads in a light wine sauce are perfectly complemented by one of the exceptional wines from the *cave.* Open daily. Reservations necessary. Major credit cards accepted. In the *Crillon Hotel,* 10 Pl. de la Concorde, 8e (phone: 44-71-16-16; fax: 44-71-15-02).

**L'Ami Louis** The archetypal Parisian bistro, small and charmingly unassuming, but with huge portions of generally marvelous, if extremely expensive food (though these days the place seems to be coasting on its reputation and its appealing ambience). Specialties include foie gras, roast chicken, spring lamb, ham, and burgundy wines. A favorite among Americans, this is the place to sample authentic French fries. Closed Mondays, Tuesdays, and most of July and August. Reservations necessary. Major credit cards accepted. 32 Rue de Vertbois, 3e (phone: 48-87-77-48).

**Le Grand Véfour** Established in 1760 in the stately courtyard of the *Palais-Royal,* this restaurant has rich carpets and mirrors framed by ornate frescoes, where the choice two-Michelin-star dishes are named for dignitaries who have discussed affairs of state here since the time of Robespierre. The delectable dishes, such as crayfish with olive oil and spices, or potato-truffle terrine, are every bit as enthralling as the restaurant's rich history. In honor of both, gentlemen still are required to wear jackets and ties. The prix fixe lunch menu is a good value. Closed Saturday lunch, Sundays, and the month of August. Reservations necessary. Major credit cards accepted. 17 Rue de Beaujolais, 1er (phone: 42-96-56-27; fax: 42-86-80-71).

**Laurent** This *grande luxe* restaurant has regained its former glory under chef Philippe Braun, who trained with super-chef Joël Robuchon. The finest ingredients are cooked to perfection—the freshest fish served with rare morel mushrooms, and game in season—and the wine list is one of Paris's best. Closed Saturday lunch, Sundays, and part of August. Reservations necessary. Major credit cards accepted. Near the Champs-Elysées, at 41 Av. Gabriel, 8e (phone: 42-25-00-39; fax: 45-62-45-21).

**Maxim's** Paris's most celebrated Belle Epoque restaurant was one century old in 1991; unfortunately, it has seen better days—it's now often half empty, with a façade that could use a face-lift. In fact, there are rumors that owner Pierre Cardin may be thinking of selling. But, with scenes like tableaux from Colette around its elegant salons, *Maxim's* always will be *Maxim's,* and with care could recapture its past glory. The service is impeccable, with excellent sommeliers to help with the extensive and intelligent wine list. The food is sometimes surprisingly good; try the *Challans canard aux cerises* (Challans duck with cherries). Fridays remain a strictly black-tie-only tradition, with an orchestra for dancing from 9:30 PM to 2 AM. Closed Sundays in July and August. Reservations necessary. Major credit cards accepted. 3 Rue Royale, 8e (phone: 42-65-27-94; fax: 40-17-02-91).

**Pré Catelan** This dreamy dinner palace is a wonderful special occasion spot—particularly in summer, when guests can dine on the flower-decked terrace. The food—which has earned two Michelin stars—lives up to the promise of the ambience. Offerings include pumpkin soup with crayfish, braised whole sole, and rack of lamb with coriander. Closed Sunday dinner, Mondays, and two weeks in February. Reservations necessary. Major credit cards accepted. Rte. de Suresnes, *Bois de Boulogne,* 16e (phone: 45-24-55-58; fax: 45-24-43-25).

### EXPENSIVE

**Apicius** Jean-Pierre Vigato's highly original recipes have earned this restaurant two Michelin stars. Favorites include *tourte de canard* (duck in pastry), potato purée with truffles, and *crème brûlée* made with cherries. Closed weekends and the month of August. Reservations necessary. Major credit cards accepted. 122 Av. de Villiers, 17e (phone: 43-80-19-66; fax: 44-40-09-57).

**L'Assiette** The chef, Lulu, is very much present in her slightly scruffy bistro, which attracts a fashionable clientele for delicious and generous servings of roast duck, potato salad with fresh truffles, and *coquilles St-Jacques* (sea scallops in cream sauce). The wine list is sublime. Closed Mondays, Tuesdays, and the month of August. Reservations necessary. Major credit cards accepted. 181 Rue du Château, 14e (phone: 43-22-64-86).

**Auberge des Deux Signes** This place was once the cellars of the priory of *St-Julien-le-Pauvre;* try to get an upstairs table overlooking the gardens. Auvergnat cooking (ham, charcuterie, cabbage, and potato dishes) is prepared with a light touch. Closed Saturday lunch, Sundays, and the month of August. Reservations necessary. Major credit cards accepted. 46 Rue Galande, 5e (phone: 43-25-46-56; fax: 46-33-20-49).

**Beauvilliers** With its intimate dining rooms and hydrangea-rimmed summer terraces, this one-Michelin-star restaurant is one of the most romantic spots in Paris. The rich, generous fare, prepared in the classic tradition of the restaurant's namesake, a famous 18th-century chef, complements the setting. Try the rabbit and parsley terrine, *turbot au jus de jarret* (turbot cooked in veal shank gravy), and the remarkable praline chocolate cake. Closed Sundays and Monday lunch. Reservations necessary. Major credit cards accepted. On the northern slope of the Butte Montmartre, at 52 Rue Lamarck, 18e (phone: 42-54-54-42; fax: 42-62-70-30).

**Bistro 121** Hearty food and excellent wines are offered in a modern setting that's always chic and crowded. Try one of the many first-rate fish dishes or an original creation such as *canard au fruit de la passion* (duck with passion fruit). Open daily until midnight. Reservations advised. Major credit cards accepted. 121 Rue de la Convention, 15e (phone: 45-57-52-90).

**Le Carré des Feuillants** Alain Dutournier of *Au Trou Gascon* (see below) has set up shop in the heart of the city, offering such creations as *perdreau sauvage* (wild partridge) with cumin, apricots, and fresh coriander. Michelin has awarded the establishment two stars. The prix fixe lunch menu is a good value. Closed Saturday lunch, Sundays, and the month of August. Reservations necessary. Major credit cards accepted. 14 Rue de Castiglione, 1er (phone: 42-86-82-82; fax: 42-86-07-71).

**Chez Benoît** A pretty, unpretentious bistro with wonderful, old-fashioned Lyonnaise cooking and exquisite wines. Just about at the top of the bistro list, it's rated one Michelin star. Closed weekends and the month of August. Reservations necessary. No credit cards accepted. 20 Rue St-Martin, 4e (phone: 42-72-25-76; fax: 42-72-45-68).

**Chez Pauline** In this quintessential bistro, which has earned one Michelin star, ask to be seated in the tiny, wood-paneled downstairs room, brightened by large mirrors and fresh flowers. Try the oysters in a watercress sauce or the assortment of seafood with a saffron sauce, and save room for dessert—the mille-feuille (layered puff pastry) of orange with raspberry sauce is sublime. Closed Saturday dinner, Sundays, the month of July, two weeks in August, and from December 24 through January 2. Reservations advised; make them well in advance. Major credit cards accepted. 5 Rue Villedo, 1er (phone: 42-96-20-70; fax: 49-27-99-99).

**Chiberta** Elegant and modern, this two-Michelin-star restaurant boasts the nouvelle cuisine of Philippe da Silva. Try the goat cheese ravioli, or the fish with ginger and mango in puff pastry. Closed weekends, the month of August, and December 24 through January 3. Reservations necessary. Major credit cards accepted. 3 Rue Arsène-Houssaye, 8e (phone: 45-63-77-90; fax: 45-62-85-08).

**La Coquille** This is a classic bistro, where the service is unpretentious and warm, and the food consistent, although the seafood (except the scallops) is usually overcooked. From October through mid-May, as its name suggests, the restaurant specializes in *coquilles St-Jacques,* a version that consists of scallops roasted with butter, shallots, and parsley. Closed Sundays, Mondays, late July through early August, and December 23 through January 3. Reservations advised. Major credit cards accepted. 6 Rue du Débarcadère, 17e (phone: 45-72-10-73).

**Le Divellec** This bright and airy, two-Michelin-star place serves exquisitely fresh seafood. Try the sea bass, the *rouget* (mullet), or the sautéed turbot. The latter is served with thick strips of pasta flavored with squid ink—an unusual and delicious concoction. Closed Sundays, Mondays, the month of August, and December 24 through January 3. Reservations necessary. Major credit cards accepted. 107 Rue de l'Université, 7e (phone: 45-51-91-96; fax: 45-51-31-75).

**Drouant** Founded in 1880, this perennial favorite has an ambitious chef who favors classic French recipes, particularly fish dishes and *agneau de Pauillac,* a traditional lamb specialty from the Médoc region. Last year, Michelin awarded it a coveted second star. Open daily. Reservations necessary. Major credit cards accepted. 18 Rue Gaillon, 2e (phone: 42-65-15-16; fax: 49-24-02-15).

**Duquesnoy** Jean-Paul Duquesnoy, one of Paris's most promising young chefs, is in his element in this enchanting, two-Michelin-star establishment. Warm, carved woods and tasteful decor set the stage for specialties that include squab with foie gras, and fresh sardines grilled with almond butter; for dessert, the *crème brûlée* with walnuts is a delight. Closed Saturday lunch, Sundays, and three weeks in August. Reservations necessary. Major credit cards accepted. 6 Av. Bosquet, 7e (phone: 47-05-96-78; fax: 44-18-90-57).

**Elysée-Lenôtre** Arguably one of Paris's most elegant dining rooms, this restaurant in a former private house on the Champs-Elysées serves fine traditional cuisine with a focus on seafood. Closed Saturday lunch and most of August. Reservations advised. Major credit cards accepted. 10 Av. des Champs-Elysées, 8e (phone: 42-65-85-10; fax: 42-65-76-23).

**Faucher** Chef-owner Gérard Faucher has drawn praise (and one Michelin star) for his light touch with fish dishes and desserts. Closed Saturday lunch, Sundays, and one week in August. Reservations necessary. Major credit cards accepted. 123 Av. Wagram, 17e (phone: 42-27-61-50; fax: 46-22-25-72).

**Faugeron** Awarded two stars by Michelin, this place combines a nouvelle cuisine approach with bistro influences and more generous portions. Specializing in such simple, but exquisitely prepared, dishes as soft-boiled eggs with truffle purée and slices of sea scallops with lentils, it offers excellent service, a first-rate wine list, and one of Paris's prettiest settings, in what was once a school. Closed weekends (except Saturday dinner October through April), and the month of August. Reservations necessary. Major credit cards accepted. 52 Rue de Longchamp, 16e (phone: 47-04-24-53; phone: 47-55-62-90).

**La Ferme St-Simon** Among our favorites for wholesome *cuisine d'autrefois* (old-fashioned cooking), this one-Michelin-star place offers nothing very chichi, just well-prepared, authentic dishes—the kinds you'd expect from a traditional Rive Gauche restaurant. Leave room for dessert; the owner once was a top assistant to France's famed pastry chef Gaston Lenôtre. It's also a perfect place for lunch. Closed Saturday lunch, Sundays, and three weeks in August. Reservations advised. Major credit cards accepted. 6 Rue de St-Simon, 7e (phone: 45-48-35-74; fax: 40-49-07-31).

**Gérard Besson** Michelin has given this small, formal eatery two stars. The service is impeccable and the classic menu includes specialties such as *ris de veau poêlé à la truffe* (veal sweetbreads sautéed with truffles). Closed Sundays, and from September through December for lunch. Reservations necessary. Major credit cards accepted. 5 Rue Coq-Héron, 1er (phone: 42-33-14-74; fax: 42-33-85-71).

**Goumard-Prunier** Chef Jean-Claude Goumard relies on a network of Breton and Mediterranean fishermen to provide the finest seafood obtainable; his inventive creations, such as scallop mille-feuilles, have earned him two Michelin stars. Closed Sundays and Mondays. Reservations necessary. Major credit cards accepted. 9 Rue Duphot, 1er (phone: 42-60-36-07; fax: 42-60-04-54).

**Jacques Cagna** This establishment has a quintessentially Rive Gauche look and a mix of nouvelle and classic dishes, which Michelin has awarded two stars. The talented eponymous chef always provides an interesting menu at these charming premises near the Seine. Closed weekends (except Saturday dinner twice a month), three weeks in August, and *Christmas* week. Reservations necessary. Major credit cards accepted. 14 Rue des Grands-Augustins, 6e (phone: 43-26-49-39; fax: 43-54-54-48).

**Le Jardin du Royal Monceau** With the arrival of chef Bernard Guilhaudin, this attractive garden restaurant in one of Paris's best hotels has begun to reap accolades. Many dished have an Asian accent, such as crayfish with mango and papaya. Open daily. Reservations advised. Major credit cards accepted. At the *Royal Monceau Hotel,* 35 Av. Hoche, 8e (phone: 45-62-96-02; fax: 45-63-04-03).

**Jean-Claude Ferrero** This inventive chef prepares eclectic cuisine, from authentic bouillabaisse to chicken with asparagus, and game in season. The restaurant is one of the city's prettiest and is favored by the diplomatic crowd. Closed weekends (except Saturday dinner October through March), two weeks in May, and most of August. Reservations advised. Major credit cards accepted. 38 Rue Vital, 16e (phone: 45-04-42-42).

**Ledoyen** This grand dowager of Paris restaurants has been given a breath of life by a new chef, Ghislaine Arabian, who favors hearty, classic dishes such as *coquilles St-Jacques* (sea scallops in cream sauce). Last year, her efforts were rewarded with a second Michelin star. There's also an excellent, more moderately priced lunch menu. The view from the upstairs dining room—of the Champs-Elysées but with the trees blocking the traffic—is superb. Closed weekends and most of August. Reservations necessary. Major credit cards accepted. Carré des Champs-Elysées, 8e (phone: 47-42-23-23; fax: 47-42-55-01).

**La Marée** Its exterior is unobtrusive, but there is great comfort within— also the freshest of fish, the best restaurant wine values in Paris, and fabulous desserts. Michelin has awarded it one star. Closed weekends, holidays, and the month of August. Reservations advised. Major credit cards accepted. 1 Rue Daru, 8e (phone: 43-80-20-00; fax: 48-88-04-04).

**Miravile** Gilles Epié's one-Michelin-star cuisine features such memorable dishes as *lapin aux olives* (rabbit with olives) and other Provençal-inspired recipes. Closed Saturday lunch and Sundays. Reservations necessary. Major credit cards accepted. 72 Quai de l'Hôtel-de-Ville, 4e (phone: 42-74-72-22; fax: 42-74-67-55).

**Morot-Gaudry** This one-Michelin-star restaurant is perched on the top floor of a 1920s building with a great view of the *Eiffel Tower,* especially from the flowered terrace. Among the inventive dishes is *pigeon en papillote* (squab steamed in its own juices); many dishes have a Mediterranean accent. Closed weekends. Reservations necessary. Major credit cards accepted. 8 Rue de la Cavalerie, 15e (phone: 45-67-06-85; fax: 45-67-55-72).

**Au Petit Marguery** This true, family-run bistro on the Rive Gauche serves excellent old-fashioned cuisine and *petit crus* wines. Closed Sundays, Mondays, the month of August, and December 23 through *New Year's Day.* Reservations advised. Major credit cards accepted. 9 Bd. du Port Royal, 13e (phone: 43-31-58-59).

**Le Petit Montmorency** In his location near the Champs-Elysées, Daniel Bouché presents one of the most consistent menus in Paris, offering such specialties as a fresh truffle roasted in pastry (in winter) and a *soufflé aux noisettes* (hazelnut soufflé). Closed weekends and the month of August. Reservations necessary. Major credit cards accepted. 26 Rue Jean-Mermoz, 8e (phone: 42-25-11-19).

**Pile ou Face** The name means "heads or tails," but you won't be taking any chances at this one-Michelin-star bistro; super-fresh ingredients come from the owners' own farm. Try the *lapin en marmelade de romarin* (rabbit in a rich, rosemary-flavored sauce). Closed weekends, the month of August, and *Christmas* through *New Year's Day*. Reservations advised. Major credit cards accepted. 52 *bis* Rue Notre-Dame-des-Victoires, 2e (phone: 42-33-64-33; fax: 42-36-61-09).

**Le Port Alma** This elegant establishment, with a view of the *Eiffel Tower* offers some of the finest seafood in town, such as baby clams in a thyme-flavored cream sauce. Closed Sundays and the month of August. Reservations necessary. Major credit cards accepted. 10 Av. de New-York, 16e (phone: 47-23-75-11).

**La Timonerie** At this one-Michelin-star restaurant, specialties include *filet de maquereau* (mackerel filet) with an herb salad, and a superb chocolate tart. Especially recommended is the very affordable prix fixe lunch. Closed Sundays, Mondays, and one week in August. Reserve at least three days in advance. MasterCard and Visa accepted. 35 Quai de la Tournelle, 5e (phone: 43-25-44-42).

**Le Toit de Passy** Not only is the food here good (Michelin has awarded chef Yannick Jacquot one star), but the rooftop view in one of Paris's more exclusive districts is spectacular. Try specialties such as *pigeonneau en croûte de sel* (squab in a salt crust) while dining outdoors. Closed Saturday lunch, Sundays, and *Christmas* week. Reservations necessary. Major credit cards accepted. 94 Av. Paul-Doumer, 16e (phone: 45-24-55-37; fax: 45-20-94-57).

**Le Train Bleu** The pricey traditional cuisine is adequate, but it's really the setting that makes this place worthwhile—in a train station whose Baroque decor is so gorgeous that the spot has been declared a national monument. Open daily. Reservations advised. Major credit cards accepted. *Gare de Lyon,* 20 Bd. Diderot, 12e (phone: 43-43-38-39; fax: 43-43-97-96).

**Au Trou Gascon** Alain Dutournier created this restaurant's inspired and unusual cooking, featuring southwestern French specialties and augmented by a vast choice of regional wines and armagnacs. He now has set up operations in a more elegant neighborhood at *Le Carré des Feuillants* (see above), while his wife holds down the fort at this one-Michelin-star restaurant. Closed weekends, the month of August, and *Christmas* week. Reservations advised. Major credit cards accepted. 40 Rue Taine, 12e (phone: 43-44-34-26; fax: 43-07-80-55).

**Vancouver** One of Paris's newest seafood restaurants, this modern establishment has already won a Michelin star for dishes with a Pacific flair, such as sweet and sour shrimp with fresh edible seaweed, and crayfish wrapped in coriander leaves. Closed weekends and most

---

of August. Reservations advised. Major credit cards accepted. 4
Rue Arsène-Houssaye, 8e (phone: 42-56-77-77; fax: 44-71-15-02).

MODERATE

**Ambassade d'Auvergne** The young chef here creates delicious, classic
Auvergnat dishes with an innovative touch. Try the lentil salad and
the sliced ham or the *aligot* (a purée of potatoes and young cantal
cheese); for dessert, opt for a slice of one of the wonderful cakes.
Closed August 1 through 16. Reservations advised. Major credit
cards accepted. 22 Rue du Grenier-St-Lazare, 3e (phone: 42-72-
31-22; fax: 42-78-85-47).

**Atelier Maître Albert** Unlike most other eateries on the Rive Gauche, this
one is pleasantly roomy, with a prix fixe menu of classic French
cuisine and a cozy log fire in winter. The spectacle of *Notre-Dame*
looming up before diners as they walk out the door and onto the
quay adds the finishing stroke to a charming meal. Closed Sunday
dinner. Reservations advised. Major credit cards accepted. 1 Rue
Maître-Albert, 5e (phone: 46-33-13-78).

**L'Auberge Nicolas Flanel** Believed to be the oldest restaurant in Paris (an
inn opened in the half-timbered building in 1407), its menu includes
such good, simple fare as grilled tuna and leg of lamb. Closed Saturday lunch, Sundays, and the first two weeks in August. Reservations advised. MasterCard and Visa accepted. 51 Rue de Montmorency, 3e (phone: 42-71-77-78).

**L'Avenue** This chic brasserie, as fashionable as the district, offers grilled
meat, raw oysters, and old-fashioned desserts in a dining room with
a view of the *Eiffel Tower.* Closed most of August. Reservations
advised. Major credit cards accepted. 41 Av. Montaigne, 8e (phone:
40-70-14-91).

**Balzar** Perhaps because of its location next to the *Sorbonne,* this mirrored brasserie always has attracted well-heeled intellectuals. The
steaks and *pommes frites* are definitely worth a visit. Open until
midnight; closed the month of August, and *Christmas* through *New
Year's Day.* Reservations necessary (and often difficult to get). Major
credit cards accepted. 49 Rue des Ecoles, 5e (phone: 43-54-13-67).

**Baracane** This reasonably priced bistro has excellent cuisine from southwestern France. Try the *lentilles au magret d'oie sechée* (lentils
with dried goose breast) or the cassoulet. Closed Saturday lunch,
Sundays, and most of August. Reservations necessary. MasterCard
and Visa accepted. 38 Rue des Tournelles, 4e (phone: 42-71-43-
44).

**Bistro de la Grille** The decor of this old-fashioned spot is right out of a
Cartier-Bresson photo, and the excellent food, from the raw oysters to the *andouillette* (grilled tripe sausage), is as classic as the
setting. The *première étage* (upstairs) is preferable to the noisy
downstairs. Closed most of August. Reservations advised. Master-
Card and Visa accepted. In the chic St-Germain-des-Prés district,
at 14 Rue Mabillon, 6e (phone: 43-54-16-87).

**Le Bistrot d'à Côté Flaubert** Michel Rostang, impresario of the topflight restaurant that bears his name (see above), here offers *cuisine de terroir* (back-to-basics regional fare) in a turn-of-the-century bistro. Closed Saturday lunch, Sundays, and the first two weeks of August. Reservations advised. Major credit cards accepted. 10 Rue Gustave-Flaubert, 17e (phone: 42-67-05-81; fax: 47-63-82-75).

**Le Bistrot du Sommelier** The wine list is sublime in this bistro operated by 1992's *Meilleur Sommelier du Monde* (World's Best Sommelier), and there's hearty bourgeois cuisine to match. The special wine-lover's menu at dinner features six dishes served with six different wines. Closed weekends, the month of August, and *Christmas* through *New Year's Day.* Reservations advised. Major credit cards accepted. 97 Bd. Haussmann, 8e (phone: 42-65-24-85; fax: 42-94-03-26).

**Le Boeuf sur le Toit** A haunt of Jean Cocteau, Antoine de St-Exupéry, and other Paris artists and writers in the 1940s, this eatery is managed by the Flo group, well known for good value in atmospheric surroundings, although here these far outrank the classic brasserie fare. The piano bar is open until 2 AM. Open daily. Reservations advised. Major credit cards accepted. Off the Champs-Elysées, at 34 Rue du Colisée, 8e (phone: 43-59-83-80; fax: 45-63-45-40).

**Bofinger** This magnificent Belle Epoque place is one of Paris's oldest brasseries, and its beauty makes up for the occasionally mediocre food. Ask to be seated on the ground floor, and order onion soup and *choucroute* (sauerkraut)—you won't be disappointed. Open daily. Reservations advised. Major credit cards accepted. 15 Rue de la Bastille, 4e (phone: 42-72-87-82; fax: 42-72-97-68).

**Brasserie Lipp** This famous brasserie (a beer hall distinguished by its brass dispensers), where the Paris intelligentsia have flocked for over a century, is fashionable for a late supper of *choucroute* and Alsatian beer and for people watching inside and out, although guests not known to the staff sometimes receive less than welcoming treatment. Closed July and August. Reservations advised. Major credit cards accepted. 151 Bd. St-Germain, 6e (phone: 45-48-53-91).

**Brissemoret** Popular with Parisians, this pleasant eatery features basic, high-quality food: excellent foie gras, raw salmon marinated in fresh herbs, and great sauces—try the breast of duck in wine sauce. Closed weekends and most of August. Reservations necessary. Major credit cards accepted. 5 Rue St-Marc, 2e (phone: 42-36-91-72).

**La Butte Chaillot** A starkly modern bistro in a posh district, one of several restaurants operated by celebrated chef Guy Savoy (also see his self-named restaurant, above), features such old-fashioned dishes as roast chicken with mashed potatoes, and an unusual lentil soup with crayfish. Closed *Christmas* and *New Year's Day.* Reservations advised. Major credit cards accepted. 112 Av. Kléber, 16e (phone: 47-27-88-88; fax: 47-04-85-70).

**La Cagouille** This Rive Gauche bistro prepares fish to one-Michelin-star perfection; try the steamed clams or the *bar* (sea bass) with vegetables. Closed three weeks in August and *Christmas* through *New Year's Day*. Reservations advised. Major credit cards accepted. 12 Pl. Constantin-Brancusi, 14e (phone: 43-22-09-01; fax: 45-38-57-29).

**Le Caméléon** In a true bistro atmosphere—with marble tables, moleskin banquettes, and the spirit of 1920s Montparnasse, as well as moderate prices—try the superb casserole-roasted veal and *morue provençale* (salt cod in tomato sauce with garlic mayonnaise). Closed Sundays, Mondays, and the month of August. Reservations advised. No credit cards accepted. 6 Rue de Chevreuse, 6e (phone: 43-20-63-43).

**Campagne et Provence** The bistro alternative to the fine *Miravile* (see above), this tiny Quartier Latin spot has a lovely *tapenade de lapin* (rabbit with olive purée) and a garlicky mixed green salad. Closed Saturday lunch, Sundays, Mondays, and most of August. Reservations necessary. MasterCard and Visa accepted. 25 Quai de la Tournelle, 5e (phone: 43-54-05-17; fax: 42-74-67-55).

**Canard'avril** This friendly place features such southwestern French specialties as roast duck, cassoulet, foie gras, and potatoes sautéed with garlic; there's also a good selection of fish dishes. Closed weekends. Reservations advised. MasterCard and Visa accepted. 5 Rue Paul-Lelong, 2e (phone: 42-36-26-08).

**Le Caroubier** A family-run couscous restaurant, it has some of the best hand-rolled couscous grains in town, accompanied by good vegetables, grilled meat, and a delicious *pastilla,* a flaky pastry with a spicy meat filling. Pour the vegetable broth on the delicate couscous, add a little hot pepper sauce, and you'll feel as if you've been transported to Morocco. Closed Sunday dinner, Mondays, and the month of August. Reservations advised. MasterCard and Visa accepted. 122 Av. du Maine, 14e (phone: 43-20-41-49).

**Chez Marius** A real find—the rotund chef really loves his work, and the three-dish prix fixe dinner is a great deal. Specialties are bouillabaisse and grilled fish. The atmosphere is Old Europe cozy though there have been complaints of late about the service. Closed Saturday lunch, Sundays, most of August, and a week at *Christmas*. Reservations advised. Major credit cards accepted. 5 Rue Bourgogne, 7e (phone: 47-05-96-19).

**La Coupole** A big, brassy brasserie, once the haunt of Hemingway, Josephine Baker, and Picasso, it's now owned by the Flo group. The atmosphere is still great, and the food improving. Open until 2 AM; closed the month of August and *Christmas Eve.* Reservations advised. Major credit cards accepted. 102 Bd. du Montparnasse, 14e (phone: 43-20-14-20; fax: 43-35-46-14).

**Fontaine de Mars** A simple, family-style restaurant with dishes from southwestern France, such as salad with *magret de canard* (slices of smoked duck breast) and chicken with morel mushrooms. In summer, there's outdoor dining on the patio. Closed Sundays and the month of August. Reservations advised. Major credit cards accepted. Near the *Eiffel Tower*, at 129 Rue St-Dominique, 7e (phone: 47-05-46-44; fax: 45-50-31-92).

**Fouquet's Bastille** Sister restaurant to the Champs-Elysées institution (see *Cafés*, below), this postmodern brasserie next to the *Opéra de la Bastille* serves traditional fare, such as shellfish platters and simple *plats du jour*, with a modern touch. Closed Saturday lunch, Sundays, and the month of August. Reservations advised. Major credit cards accepted. 130 Rue de Lyon, 12e (phone: 43-42-18-18).

**Au Gamin de Paris** Combining the coziness of a classic bistro with the chic of a historic Marais building, it serves well-prepared, imaginative food. Specialties include grilled salmon and *magret de canard;* for dessert, try the *crème brûlée* or *tarte tatin* (caramelized apple tart). Open daily. Reservations unnecessary. Major credit cards accepted. 51 Rue Vieille-du-Temple, 4e (phone: 42-78-97-24).

**Le Grizzli** The wonderful food here is southwestern French in accent, featuring duck and plenty of garlic. Closed Sundays and Monday lunch. Reservations advised. Major credit cards accepted. 7 Rue St-Martin, 4e (phone: 48-87-77-56).

**Jo Goldenberg** The best-known eating house in the Marais's quaint Jewish quarter, with good, albeit overpriced, chopped liver and cheesecake and a range of Eastern European Jewish specialties. Try the mushroom and barley soup. It's also a fine place to sip mint tea at the counter in the middle of a busy day. Open daily. Reservations unnecessary. Major credit cards accepted. 7 Rue des Rosiers, 4e (phone: 48-87-20-16).

**Le Maraîcher** This tiny Marais eatery has excellent bourgeois cooking (try the cassoulet). Closed Sundays, Monday lunch, the month of August, and *Christmas* week. Reservations advised. Major credit cards accepted. 5 Rue Beautrellis, 4e (phone: 42-71-42-49).

**Marie et Fils** Marie and her son have found a successful formula: great bistro food, an authentic Rive Gauche atmosphere, and reasonable prices. Reservations advised. MasterCard and Visa accepted. Closed Sundays and Monday lunch. 34 Rue Mazarine, 6e (phone: 43-26-69-49).

**Moissonier** Over the past 30 years little has changed (except the prices) on the menu of this Lyonnaise restaurant, across the street from what was once Paris's wine depot. The seafood, tripe dishes, and beaujolais may not be anything new, but this is bourgeois cuisine par excellence. Closed Sunday dinner and Mondays. Reservations advised. MasterCard and Visa accepted. 28 Rue Fossés-St-Bernard, 5e (phone: 43-29-87-65).

**Le Muniche** St-Germain's best brasserie is a bustling place with a rather extensive menu. Open daily until 1:30 AM. Reservations advised.

Major credit cards accepted. 22 Rue Guillaume-Apollinaire, 6e (phone: 47-34-01-06).

**Ostréade** Seafood is king at this bustling, loft-like Montparnasse brasserie. Try the salad of potatoes and baby clams or the whole roast fish, and don't miss the tiny Breton oysters known as *boudeuses.* Open daily. Reservations necessary. Major credit cards accepted. 11 Bd. de Vaugirard, 15e (phone: 43-21-87-41).

**Le Poquelin** The excellent bourgeois cooking includes *magret de canard en croûte d'épices* (duck breast in a spicy crust). Closed Saturday lunch, Sundays, and three weeks in August. Reservations advised. Major credit cards accepted. 17 Rue Molière, 1er (phone: 42-96-22-19; fax: 42-96-05-72).

**Robert et Louise** With warm paneled decor and high standards in the kitchen, this family-run bistro is a great place to try *boeuf bourguignon* or open-fire–grilled *côte de boeuf.* Also good are the *fromage blanc* and the *vin en pichet.* Closed Sundays, holidays, and the month of August. Reservations advised for Friday and Saturday dinner. No credit cards accepted. 64 Rue Vieille-du-Temple, 3e (phone: 42-78-55-89).

**La Rôtisserie du Beaujolais** A de rigueur spot for Paris's "in" set is Claude Terrail's casual canteen on the quay in the shadow of his three-star gastronomic temple, *La Tour d'Argent.* Most of the restaurant's meat, produce, and cheese comes from Lyons; try the offerings with a superb Georges Duboeuf beaujolais. Closed Mondays. No reservations. Major credit cards accepted. 19 Quai de la Tournelle, 5e (phone: 43-54-17-47).

**La Rôtisserie d'en Face** Comfortably low-key decor, tiled floors, and an open, uncluttered atmosphere provide the backdrop for the bistro fare of noted chef Jacques Cagna (also see his self-named restaurant, above), such as grilled chicken, roast leg of lamb, and thick steaks. Closed Saturday lunch and Sundays. Reservations advised. MasterCard and Visa accepted. 2 Rue Christine, 6e (phone: 43-26-40-98; fax: 43-54-54-48).

**La Tour de Monthléry** This bistro offers great bourgeois cooking. Closed weekends and the month of August. Reservations necessary. MasterCard and Visa accepted. In *Les Halles,* at 5 Rue des Prouvaires, 1er (phone: 42-36-21-82).

**Le Valencay** A small, popular bistro with classic bourgeois fare and wines by the glass or the bottle. Closed Sundays and the month of August. No reservations. Major credit cards accepted. 11 Bd. du Palais, 4e (phone: 43-54-64-67).

**Yvan** Creative bistro fare, such as squab with polenta, and sardines with tomatoes, along with a wonderful cheese selection, keep this restaurant almost always full. The place also boasts a stylish atmosphere and very reasonable prices. Closed Saturday lunch and Sundays. Reservations necessary. Major credit cards accepted. 1 *bis* Rue Jean-Mermoz, 8e (phone: 43-59-18-40; fax: 45-63-78-69).

**Les Zygomates** This friendly bistro occupies a converted fin de siècle charcuterie with lots of mirrors and marble counters. The menu includes fish, as well as classic bistro meat dishes and gooey chocolate desserts. Closed Saturday lunch, Sundays, most of August, and December 26 through January 4. Reservations necessary. MasterCard and Visa accepted. In an out-of-the-way location, at 7 Rue Capri, 12e (phone: 40-19-93-04).

### INEXPENSIVE

**L'Ami Jean** This place offers good Basque cooking. Closed Saturday dinner and Sundays. No reservations. No credit cards accepted. 27 Rue Malar, 7e (phone: 47-05-86-89).

**Astier** An honest-to-goodness neighborhood spot that always is packed, it offers the staples of bourgeois cooking, lovingly prepared and remarkably inexpensive. Closed weekends, late April through mid-May, and late August through early September. Reservations advised. Major credit cards accepted. 44 Rue Jean-Pierre-Timbaud, 11e (phone: 43-57-16-35).

**Auberge de Jarente** This Basque restaurant is the place to sample classic *pipérade* (omelette with ham and tomato) and cassoulet. Closed Sundays, Mondays, and the month of August. Reservations advised. Major credit cards accepted. In the heart of the Marais district, at 7 Rue de Jarente, 4e (phone: 42-77-49-35).

**Brasserie Fernand** A nondescript hole-in-the-wall place that produces surprisingly tasty dishes. The pot-au-feu, steaks with shallots, and fish pâté all are first-rate, but the real lure is the huge tub of chocolate mousse served for dessert—a chocoholic's fantasy come true. Open daily for dinner only. Reservations advised. MasterCard and Visa accepted. 13 Rue Guisarde, 6e (phone: 43-54-61-47).

**Cartet** This tiny, friendly place serves Lyonnaise specialties with a focus on charcuterie and meat, such as *côtes de veau aux morilles* (veal chops with morel mushrooms). Closed weekends and the month of August. Reservations advised. Major credit cards accepted. 62 Rue de Malte, 11e (phone: 48-05-17-65).

**Casa Olympe** Dominique Nahmias, the former *doyenne* of *Olympe,* has her own restaurant again, a chic and intimate place in a charming neighborhood. Her copious servings of fine bistro classics with a Mediterranean touch, such as *lapin au pistou* (rabbit with garlic-basil sauce), at reasonable prices (the menu is prix fixe only) have made reservations difficult to get, but keep trying. Closed weekends and most of August. Reservations necessary. Major credit cards accepted. 48 Rue Saint-Georges, 9e (phone: 42-85-26-01; fax: 45-26-49-33).

**Le Grand Colbert** This restaurant near the lovely *Galerie Vivienne* has murals on the walls, copper light fixtures, and big banquettes—in short, authentic turn-of-the-century decor—and good brasserie specialties like herring with potatoes in vinaigrette and duck *confit* with garlic-laden potatoes. Closed mid-July through mid-August. Reservations advised. Major credit cards accepted. 2 Rue Vivienne, 2e (phone: 42-86-87-8; fax: 42-86-82-65).

**La Lozère** Here you'll find authentic country cooking from the Lozère region in the south of France, with an emphasis on charcuterie and cassoulet. Closed Sundays, Mondays, and the month of August. Reservations advised. No credit cards accepted. 4 Rue Hautefeuille, 6e (phone: 43-54-26-64).

**Le Passage** This bistro serves 70 excellent wines by the glass (try the chinon), and has a varied menu of bistro classics like *foie de veau sauté* (sautéed calf's liver) and friendly service. Closed Saturday lunch, Sundays, and most of August. Reservations advised. MasterCard and Visa accepted. 18 Passage de la Bonne-Graine, 11e (phone: 47-00-73-30).

**Polidor** Regulars here, who have included such starving artists as Paul Verlaine, James Joyce, Ernest Hemingway, and, more recently, Jean-Paul Belmondo, still keep their napkins in numbered pigeonholes. The *Collège de Pataphysique,* founded by Raymond Queneau and Eugène Ionesco, continues to meet here regularly for the good family-style food. But a drawback to this customer loyalty is that foreigners are banished to the back room. Closed the month of August. Reservations unnecessary. No credit cards accepted. 41 Rue Monsieur-le-Prince, 6e (phone: 43-26-95-34).

**La Route du Beaujolais** This is a barn-like workers' bistro serving Lyonnaise specialties and beaujolais wines. Don't miss the charcuterie and the fresh bread here, and try the *tarte tatin* for dessert. Closed Saturday lunch and Sundays. Reservations unnecessary. MasterCard and Visa accepted. On the Rive Gauche, at 17 Rue de Lourmel, 15e (phone: 45-79-31-63).

**Thoumieux** This family-run bistro has been reliable for decades. Come here for tripe, cassoulet, and *boudin aux châtaignes* (blood sausage with chestnuts). Open daily. Reservations advised. MasterCard and Visa accepted. 79 Rue St-Dominique, 7e (phone: 47-05-49-75; fax: 47-05-36-96).

**Aux Tonneaux des Halles** Wine by the glass, an old-fashioned setting, and typical bistro dishes like *navarin d'agneau* (lamb stew) make this a popular spot among Parisians. Closed Sundays and Mondays. Reservations advised. MasterCard and Visa accepted. 28 Rue Montorgueil, 1er (phone: 42-33-36-19).

**Le Trumilou** The formidable proprietress sets the tone of this robust establishment on the Seine, which serves huge, steaming portions of game in season, *truite aux amandes* (trout with almonds), and chicken, all beneath a frieze of some excruciatingly bad rustic oil paintings. Try the *charlotte aux marrons* (chestnut parfait) for dessert. The amazingly cheerful service is another plus. Closed Mondays. Reservations unnecessary. Major credit cards accepted. 84 Quai de l'Hôtel-de-Ville, 4e (phone: 42-77-63-98).

**Bistro de la Gare** Michel Oliver's restaurants offer a choice of three appetizers and three main courses with *pommes frites,* excellent for a quick lunch. Open daily. No reservations. Major credit cards accepted. Ten locations, including 1 Rue du Four, 6e (phone: 43-25-87-76); 59 Bd. du Montparnasse, 6e (phone: 45-48-38-01); and 30 Rue St-Denis, 1er (phone: 40-26-82-80).

**Chartier** This huge, turn-of-the-century place serves lots of down-to-earth food for the price. The famous pot-au-feu is still served on Mondays. Open daily. No reservations. No credit cards accepted. 7 Rue du Faubourg-Montmartre, 9e (phone: 47-70-86-29).

**Drouot** A favorite of locals, the younger member of the Chartier family (see above) proffers simple fare at bargain prices. To avoid a long wait for a table, arrive before 9 PM. Open daily. No reservations. No credit cards accepted. 103 Rue de Richelieu, 2e (phone: 42-96-68-23).

**Le Petit Gavroche** A hole-in-the-wall bistro-cum-restaurant with a lively clientele and a classic menu. Closed Sundays. Reservations unnecessary. No credit cards accepted. 15 Rue Ste-Croix-de-la-Bretonnerie, 4e (phone: 48-87-74-26).

**Le Petit St-Benoît** Here is French cooking at its simplest, in a plain little place with tiled floors and curlicued hat stands. Closed weekends. Reservations unnecessary. No credit cards accepted. 4 Rue St-Benoît, 6e (phone: 42-60-27-92).

**Au Pied de Fouet** This former coach house has had its habitués, including celebrities as diverse as Graham Greene, Le Corbusier, and Georges Pompidou. Service is fast and friendly, and the daily specials are reliably good. Save room for the marvelous desserts, such as *charlotte au chocolat.* Arrive early; it closes at 9 PM. Closed Saturday dinner, Sundays, two weeks at both *Easter* and *Christmas,* and the month of August. No reservations. No credit cards accepted. 45 Rue de Babylone, 7e (phone: 47-05-12-27).

---

## CAFÉS

Paris without cafés would be like Madrid without *tapas* bars, Dublin without pubs, or New York without delis. The corner café is the glue that holds the French neighborhood together; it's a place for coffee and gossip, or just a spot to sit and watch the world go by. Reservations are never needed; just claim a table, and it's yours for as long as the spirit moves you. And, possibly best of all, it's almost always easy on the wallet. Of the more than 5,000 cafés in Paris, the following are our favorites:

**Café Costes** Philippe Starck's postmodern design, inspired by Fritz Lang's *Metropolis,* helped make this café the trendiest of trendsetters for *branché* (with-it) Parisians; now its fame is such that it has rated a mention in *Time* magazine. Open daily. Major credit cards accepted. In the Beaubourg district, near the *Centre Georges-Pompidou,* at 4 Rue Berger, 1er (phone: 45-08-54-38/9).

**Café de la Paix** Designed by Charles Garnier to complement his baroque *Opéra,* this grande dame is best for afternoon tea; keep your eye out for the elusive pastry cart (the service in general can be elusive at times). Open daily until 1:30 AM. Major credit cards accepted. Two entrances, at 12 Bd. des Capucines and 2 Rue Scribe, 9e (phone: 40-07-32-32).

**Fouquet's** Arguably Paris's best-located café—it's part of the eponymous regal restaurant, now an official historic monument—this institution on the Champs-Elysées is far from perfect: The drinks are too expensive; the sidewalk is often too crowded; and the downstairs dining is forgettable one night and downright mediocre the next. But if there is still magic in the world, it can be found here at dusk, when the lights come up on the *Arc de Triomphe.* Open daily 9 PM to midnight. Major credit cards accepted. 99 Av. des Champs-Elysées, 8e (phone: 47-23-70-60).

**Ma Bourgogne** Beneath the vaulted arcades of the Place des Vosges, this is a great spot for an afternoon stop, not so much for the food as for the view of Paris's most beautiful square. Try their specialty of sausages from Auvergne with a glass of burgundy or bordeaux. Closed Mondays. MasterCard and Visa accepted. 19 Pl. des Vosges, 4e (phone: 42-78-44-64).

**La Palette** A Rive Gauche hangout on a tiny square, with outdoor tables during the summer, it stays lively with a young crowd until 2 AM. Closed Sundays, holidays, and the month of August. No credit cards accepted. 43 Rue de Seine, 6e (phone: 43-26-68-15).

**Le Piano Zinc** Tiny and authentic, this hole-in-the-wall place with a classic, zinc-topped, horseshoe-shaped bar has a regular and eclectic clientele of artists and workers. Central to Marais shopping, museums, designer boutiques, and the *Hôtel de Ville,* it's well worth a detour. Closed the month of August. No credit cards accepted. 49 Rue des Blancs-Manteaux, 3e (phone: 42-74-32-42).

**La Rhumerie** This longtime hangout of Rive Gauche literati has a pleasant, elevated terrace, salads and Caribbean-style cuisine for light lunches, and 15 varieties of mostly rum-based punch. Open daily until 2 AM. MasterCard and Visa accepted. 166 Bd. Saint-Germain, 6e (phone: 43-54-28-94).

**Le Sélect** Opened in 1925 at the height of the Jazz Age, this was the first Montparnasse café to stay open all night. Edna St. Vincent Millay, Erik Satie, and Leonard Foujita adored the place; in 1927 Isadora Duncan got into a fistfight here with an American newspaperman. (History records the dancer won by a decision.) The café hasn't changed much since, and it has some of the liveliest early-morning and late-night scenes imaginable. Open daily until 2 AM. MasterCard and Visa accepted. 99 Bd. du Montparnasse, 6e (phone: 42-22-65-27 or 45-48-38-24).

**Le Voltaire** An often-overlooked gem, this tiny café along the Seine has a rich literary history: It's where Baudelaire wrote *Les Fleurs du Mal* (he lived at 19 Quai Voltaire), Wagner wrote *Die Meistersinger* (his home was at No. 22), and the eponymous Voltaire died. Closed Sundays, Mondays, and the month of August. No credit cards accepted. Opposite the *Louvre* and near the *Musée d'Orsay,* at 27 Quai Voltaire, 7e (phone: 42-61-17-49).

---

WINE BARS

Though wine bars are now a Parisian institution, they actually originated among oenophilic Londoners. They vary widely in decor and the types of wines they purvey, but all offer wines by the glass only and a convivial atmosphere; if food is served, it's simple and specially chosen to accompany the wine. While some wine bars offer very expensive wines and edibles, all have some inexpensive wines on their lists. Unless otherwise noted, reservations are unnecessary; however, at lunch hour, if you don't have a reservation and want only a glass of wine, some very busy places may ask you to stand at the bar. The following are some of our favorites among Paris's true wine bars:

**Bistrot des Augustins** Just across the street from the booksellers on the quays, this old-fashioned café with an excellent *plat du jour* at lunch has fine beaujolais and other wines by the glass. Closed the month of August. No credit cards accepted. 39 Quai des Grands-Augustins, 6e (phone: 43-54-41-65).

**Le Bouchon du Marais** One of the capital's newer wine bars, it specializes in Loire Valley wines (the owner has a vineyard in Chinon) and simple light snacks. Closed Sundays, the month of August, and daily from 3 to 7 PM. No credit cards accepted. 15 Rue François-Miron, 4e (phone: 48-87-44-13).

**Caves Saint-Gilles** This Spanish wine bar serves generous *tapas* (try the *pipérade,* a Basque omelette), rioja and sangria by the glass, and an ample *plat du jour.* Closed the month of August. Reservations accepted for a full meal at lunch only. No credit cards accepted. Appropriately located near the *Musée Picasso,* at 4 Rue St-Gilles, 3e (phone: 48-87-22-62).

**La Cloche des Halles** The dim lighting and dark wood paneling at this cozy establishment add to the pleasure of sampling the wine here. Those with hunger pangs can order the generous cheese platter or try a plate of charcuterie. Closed Saturday evenings, Sundays, and the month of August. 28 Rue Coquillière, 1er (phone: 42-36-93-89).

**L'Ecluse** This unassuming wine bar overlooking the Seine has fathered several other, more sophisticated places, on the Rue François-Ier, at the *Madeleine,* at the *Opéra* (both the *Palais Garnier* and the *Bastille*), in *Le Forum des Halles,* and in Neuilly. Its red velvet benches and wooden tables—not to mention its bordeaux and its fresh, homemade foie gras and spectacular chocolate cake—remain unchanged. Open daily. Major credit cards accepted. 15 Quai des Grands-Augustins, 6e (phone: 46-33-58-74), and several other locations.

**L'Enoteca** This wine bar in the Marais features a vast assortment of Italian wines by the glass or bottle, along with Italian fare at lunch. Closed part of August. Major credit cards accepted. 25 Rue Charles-V, 4e (phone: 42-78-91-44).

**Espace Hérault** Attached to the Hérault *département*'s tourist office, it features wines and simple dishes from Languedoc. Closed Saturday mornings, Sundays, the month of August, and daily between 2 and 7:30 PM. Major credit cards accepted. 8 Rue de la Harpe, 5e (phone: 43-33-00-56).

**Au Franc Pinot** A restaurant has operated on this spot for 350 years, making this Paris's oldest wine bar. In a lovely setting on the Ile St-Louis, it offers regional wines, many from the Loire, and delicious snacks. Closed Sundays, Mondays, the month of August, and daily from 3 to 7 PM. Major credit cards accepted. 1 Quai Bourbon, 4e (phone: 43-29-46-98).

**Jacques Melac** An old-fashioned wine bar run by a young, extravagantly mustachioed man from the Auvergne, who bottles and sells his own rustic wines and even stages a harvest celebration in honor of the restaurant's vineyard. Closed weekends and the month of August. MasterCard and Visa accepted. 42 Rue Léon-Frot, 11e (phone: 43-70-59-27).

**Juveniles** This friendly spot has excellent wine and top-quality snacks, as well as several fine sherries. The British owners have a loyal Anglo-American following. Closed Sundays. MasterCard and Visa accepted. 47 Rue de Richelieu, 1er (phone: 47-97-46-49).

**Millésimes** An ideal location next to the renovated St-Germain-des-Prés covered market, plus a wide choice of wines and good *tartines* (open-face sandwiches) and charcuterie platters, have made this one of the most popular wine bars on the Rive Gauche. Open 7 AM to 1 AM; closed Sundays. MasterCard and Visa accepted. 7 Rue Lobineau, 6e (phone: 46-34-21-15).

**Le Pain et Le Vin** Operated by four top Parisian chefs, including Alain Dutournier of *Le Carré des Feuillants* and *Au Trou Gascon* (see *Eating Out* for both), this place features 40 wines by the glass and daily hot lunch specials. Closed Sundays, the month of August, and daily between 3 and 7 PM. Major credit cards accepted. 1 Rue d'Armaillé, 17e (phone: 47-63-88-29).

**Relais Chablisien** As the name implies, this wine bar, with its wood-beamed ceilings and warm atmosphere, specializes in chablis. Sandwiches and excellent *plats du jour* also are available. Closed weekends and two weeks in August. Reservations advised for meals. Major credit cards accepted. 4 Rue Bertin-Poirée, 1er (phone: 45-08-53-73).

**Le Repaire de Bacchus** A tiny wine bar specializing in unusual regional wines, displayed in crowded rows. You can buy wine by the bottle to take home or on a picnic, or sip it at the counter with cheese and charcuterie. Closed Sundays and Mondays. MasterCard and Visa accepted. 13 Rue du Cherche-Midi, 6e (phone: 45-44-01-07).

**Le Rouge-Gorge** Near the antiques shops of the St-Paul *quartier,* this place has changing, thematic menus that feature the wines and foods of a particular region for two-week periods. Some patrons have complained of indifferent service, however. Closed Sundays and the month of August. No credit cards accepted. 8 Rue St-Paul, 4e (phone: 48-04-75-89).

**Le Rubis** A tiny corner bar, it has an old-fashioned atmosphere and a selection of about 30 wines. With your glass of wine try the pork *rillettes,* savory meat pies made on the premises. Closed Saturdays after 4 PM, Sundays, and two weeks in August. No credit cards accepted. 10 Rue du Marché-St-Honoré, 1er (phone: 42-61-03-34).

**Le Sancerre** A hospitable spot featuring nothing but Sancerre wines—red, white, and rosé. Simple lunches of omelettes, charcuterie, apple tarts, and *petits goûters* (snacks) such as goat cheese marinated in olive oil are the perfect accompaniment for the excellent wine. Open 7 AM to 8:30 PM; closed Saturday afternoons and evenings, Sundays, and the month of August. Major credit cards accepted. 22 Av. Rapp, 7e (phone: 45-51-75-91).

**Au Sauvignon** The couple who run this tiny corner bar seem to be in perpetual motion, pouring the sauvignon blanc (or the white quincy and beaujolais nouveau in November and January) and carving up chunky *tartines* with bread from the famous *Poilâne* bakery not far away. Closed Sundays, two weeks in January, *Easter,* and the month of August. No credit cards accepted. 80 Rue des Sts-Pères, 7e (phone: 45-48-49-02).

**La Tartine** An old, authentic bistro where Trotsky was once known to sip a glass or two of wine. There's a colorful local clientele and a good selection of mostly inexpensive wines by the glass. Closed Tuesdays, Wednesday mornings, and most of August. No credit cards accepted. 24 Rue de Rivoli, 4e (phone: 42-72-76-85).

**Taverne Henri IV** A selection of nearly 20 wines is offered by the glass, along with generous servings of simple food such as open-face sandwiches of ham, cheese, sausage, or the more exotic terrine of wild boar. Closed Saturday evenings, Sundays, and most of August. No credit cards accepted. On the Pont Neuf, at 13 Pl. du Pont-Neuf, 1er (phone: 43-54-27-90).

**Willi's** An enterprising Englishman set up this smart little wine bar, a pleasant walk through the *Palais Royal* gardens from the *Louvre.* The wine selection—a list of 150—is one of the best in Paris, with an emphasis on Côtes du Rhône. The chef creates some appetizing salads as well as *plats du jour.* Closed Sundays. Major credit cards accepted. 13 Rue des Petits-Champs, 1er (phone: 42-61-05-09).

## TEAROOMS

In Paris taking tea provides a revitalizing mid-afternoon break from frantic sightseeing and window shopping. The *salon de thé* originally was the refuge of patrician Parisian ladies, who lingered over ambrosial pastries and fragrant, steaming cups of *cerise* (cherry) tea between social calls. Today, tearooms still lure Parisians and visitors alike to partake of their caloric treats. *L'Arbre à Canelle* (57 Passage des Panoramas, 2e; phone: 45-08-55-87) offers scrumptious chocolate pear and apple tart in a stylish setting. Those with discriminating tea tastes frequent *A La Cour de Rohan* (59-61 Rue St-André-des-Arts, 6e; phone: 43-25-79-67), which offers over 20 varieties described in almost religious detail. You'll find a *plus raffiné* Belle Epoque atmosphere at *Ladurée* (16 Rue Royale, 8e; phone: 42-60-21-79), where it would be a shame to ignore the masterfully decorated petits fours, marrons glacés, and macaroons. Nowhere in Paris is tea taken more seriously than at *Mariage Frères* (30-32 Rue du Bourg-Tibourg, 4e; phone: 42-72-28-11; and 13 Rue des Grands-Augustins, 6e; phone: 40-51-82-50); with a supply of 450 different kinds of tea, it's perhaps wisest to close your eyes and choose a blend at whim. Neoclassical art and classical music contribute to the tranquil ambience at *A Priori Thé* (35-37 *Galerie Vivienne,* 2e; phone: 42-97-48-75), set in one of Paris's lovely *passages* (glass-roofed shopping arcades). In another *passage* is the new *Thé S. F.* (Passage du Grand Cerf, 2e; phone: 40-28-08-76), which features 45 teas, a scrumptious chocolate terrine, scones, and cheesecake; quiches and a cheese platter are also available. The *Tea Caddy* (14 Rue Julien-le-Pauvre, 5e; phone: 43-54-15-56), one of the oldest tea shops in Paris, is very British—from its name to its fine teas and scones. *Tea and Tattered Pages* (24 Rue Mayet, 6e; phone: 40-65-94-35), a combination tearoom and used-English-books store, is a great place to pick up some reading material for a rainy day. And the *Crillon* hotel (see *Checking In*) is one of the city's most elegant spots in which to take very expensive afternoon tea, complete with an assortment of sublime pastries.

## AND FOR CHOCOHOLICS

The best hot chocolate in Paris, if not the universe, is served at *Angelina* (226 Rue de Rivoli, 1er, phone: 42-60-82-00; 86 Av. de Longchamp, 16e, phone: 47-04-89-42; 40 Bd. Haussmann, 9e, phone: 42-82-34-56; and in the *Palais des Congrès, Porte Maillot,* 17e, phone: 40-68-22-50). To accompany your cup of sweet ambrosia order *chocolat l'Africain,* a dessert made with delicious dark chocolate.

# Prague

## At-a-Glance

### SEEING THE CITY

To experience the drama of Prague visit the *Zlatá Praha* (Golden Prague) restaurant on the eighth floor of the *Inter-Continental* hotel (see *Eating Out*). From here there's a spectacular view of *Prague Castle,* particularly beautiful at sunset, when it is a black silhouette and the last rays of sun splash red and gold into the Vltava River. A trip up Petřín Hill in the funicular offers a fine view in the opposite direction.

### SPECIAL PLACES

Historical Prague was originally five independent towns, and each of these five districts—Nové Město (New Town), Staré Město (Old Town), Malá Strana (Lesser Quarter), Hradčany, and Vyšehrad—retains its individual character.

A few Czech words that may help with your navigations: *Náměstí* is the word for square or place; *ulice* and *ulička* mean street; and *třída* means avenue.

#### NOVÉ MĚSTO (NEW TOWN)

Prague's New Town dates from 1348, when it was established by King Charles IV. Wenceslas Square, with its profusion of shops, hotels, and restaurants, is the center of the modern city of Prague and a logical starting point for seeing the city.

**VÁCLAVSKÉ NÁMĚSTÍ (WENCESLAS SQUARE)** St. Václav ("Good King Wenceslas"), seated on his horse, guards this square, which is really a boulevard. Dominated by the *National Museum,* Wenceslas Square—2,475 by 198 feet—is the central thoroughfare of the city, lined with Art Nouveau hotels, restaurants, cafés, and rather pricey shops.

**NÁRODNÍ MUZEUM (NATIONAL MUSEUM)** The imposing neo-Renaissance façade and the interior decorations of this building reflect the spirit of late-19th-century Czech nationalism in which it was built. Its façade still bears the machine-gun markings made by Russian troops, who mistook it for *Parliament* during the 1968 invasion. Inside are paintings on Czech historical themes, fossils, stamps, and archaeological items. Closed Tuesdays. Admission charge the first Monday of the month. 68 Václavské náměstí (phone: 269451, ext. 376).

**KARLOVO NÁMĚSTÍ (CHARLES SQUARE)** Now a park surrounded by old buildings, the New Town's oldest square—and Prague's largest—was the central market around which the town was proudly planned by Charles IV in 1348. On the north side is the oldest building in the New Town, the *Novoměstská radnice* (New Town Hall), site of

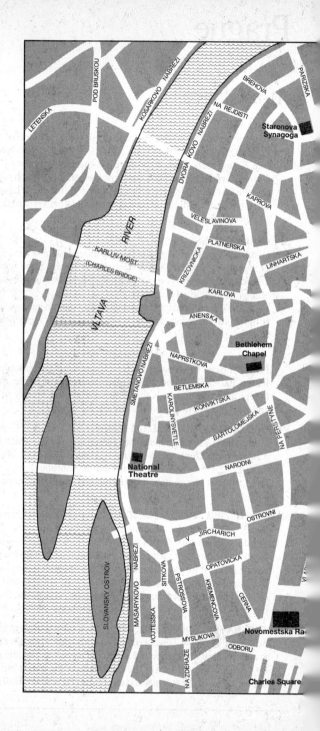

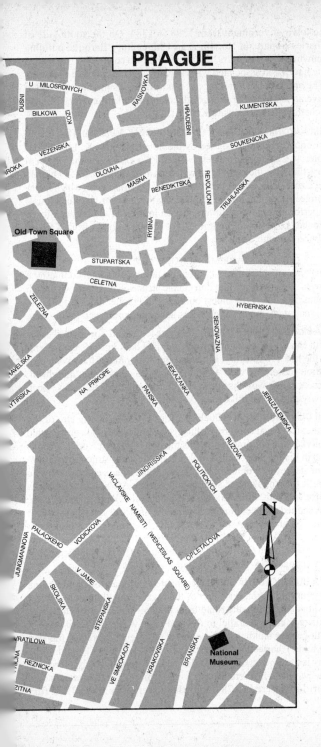

# PRAGUE

U MILOSRDNYCH

DUSNI

BILKOVA

KOZI

RASNOVKA

HRADEBNI

KLIMENTSKA

VEZENSKA

IROKA

SOUKENICKA

DLOUHA

MASNA

BENEDIKTSKA

REVOLUCNI

TRUHLARSKA

RYBNA

Old Town Square

STUPARTSKA

CELETNA

ZELEZNA

HYBERNSKA

SENOVAZNA

HAVELSKA

YTIRSKA

NA PRIKOPE

PANSKA

NEKAZANKA

JERUZALEMSKA

RUZOVA

JINDRISSKA

POLITICKYCH

JUNGMANNOVA

PALACKEHO

VODICKOVA

VACLAVSKE NAMESTI (WENCESLAS SQUARE)

OPLETALOVA

N

V JAME

SKOLSKA

STEPANSKA

VRATILOVA

REZNICKA

VE SMECKACH

KRAKOVSKA

BRANSKA

National Museum

ZITNA

the town government from 1398 to 1784. On the south side of Charles Square, at No. 40, is an 18th-century Baroque building known as *Faust's House*. Ever since the 14th century houses on this site have been associated with alchemy and other occult practices. (The origin of the Faust legend is uncertain; it sometimes is said to have arisen from the strange adventures of a 16th-century English alchemist named Edward Kelley.)

**MUZEUM ANTONÍNA DVOŘÁKA (ANTON DVOŘÁK MUSEUM)** This lovely Baroque building, designed by the noted architect K. I. Dienzenhofer, was a summer residence called *Villa America* in the 18th century. Fittingly, the building now houses mementos of Anton Dvořák, the Czech composer of the great *New World Symphony* (which incorporates American folk tunes). During the summer Dvořák's music is performed in the sculpture garden in back of the house. Closed Mondays. Admission charge. 20 Ke Karlovu, not far from Karlovo náměstí (phone: 298214).

STARÉ MĚSTO (OLD TOWN)

Walk here just before dusk, when the narrow, winding, cobblestone streets seem to merge into dim Gothic arcades. The Old Town, which contains most of the oldest buildings in Prague, dates from 1120. A great many medieval exteriors have been preserved in this area.

**PRAŠNÁ BRÁNA (POWDER TOWER)** This gate to the Old Town, used in the 17th century to store gunpowder, was first built in 1475, then rebuilt in the late 19th century. It marked the beginning of the royal coronation route. The view from the top (186 steps up) is delightful. Recent repair work has been completed, and the statues have been newly gilded. Na příkopě.

**OBECNÍ DŮM (MUNICIPAL HOUSE)** Built in 1905–11 on the site of the Bohemian royal court by architects Antonína Balsánek and Osvald Polívka, this building represents the best of the Art Nouveau tradition in Prague. Start with a walk around the white structure to appreciate its freshly painted ironwork and stained-glass entryway. Inside you'll find the work of such notable Czech Art Nouveau artists as Alfons Mucha, Josef Saloun, and Jan Preisler. Walk upstairs to see the stained glass ceiling in *Smetanova Síň* (Smetana Hall), where concerts are held. Ask to see the lavish, lavender mayoral room painted by Alfons Mucha. If there's time, listen to the jazz quartet that plays in the *Café Nouveau* (see *Eating Out*). 5 Náměstí republiky (phone: 248-11057).

**CELETNÁ ULICE (CELETNÁ STREET)** Renovated Baroque townhouses line this curving street, once part of the royal coronation route. Today, visitors can follow the route from the *Powder Tower* to Old Town Square, running parallel to Zelezná ulice where the *Carolinum*, a 14th-century building that was part of the original university founded by King Charles IV (9 Zelezná ulice), is located. Also along the way is the *Stavovské Divadlo* (Estates Theater; 6 Ovocný), formerly the *Tyl Theater*, where Mozart's masterpiece *Don Giovanni* had its world premiere in 1787 and where scenes from the 1984 film

*Amadeus* were shot. Recent renovations have restored the original magnificence to this musical landmark.

**STAROMĚSTSKÉ NÁMĚSTÍ (OLD TOWN SQUARE)** The center of Prague's Old Town, this important square was given a face-lift in time for the 1988 celebration of the 40th anniversary of the Communist takeover. The monument to Jan Hus (John Huss) was erected in 1915, 500 years after the religious reformer was burned at the stake. Every hour on the hour crowds gather to watch the *Old Town Hall*'s astronomical clock (built in 1490), with its mechanical figures of the 12 apostles, and allegorical memento mori figures performing their solemn march. The *Town Hall* itself was founded in 1338 and rebuilt many times (parts of it were destroyed by fire during the final days of World War II). The many interesting features within include a dungeon and a well in the cellar, and a 15th-century council chamber adorned with 60 imaginative coats of arms belonging to the guilds of Prague and still used by the city government. Guided tours—some in English—are given hourly. On the east side of the square is the *Kostel Panny Marie před Týnem* (Church of Our Lady at Týn), dating from 1365, with its twin Gothic spires. Once the property of the Hussites and later of the Jesuits, this beautiful church combines a Gothic exterior with a Baroque interior. Tycho de Brahe, the Danish astronomer, was buried here in 1601. A pretty little café, *U Týna,* is under the arches at 15 Staroměstské náměstí (phone: 231-0525). Nearby is the *Dům u Kammeného Zvonu* (House of the Stone Bell; phone: 231-7677), a Gothic structure that serves as a municipal art exhibition hall, where concerts also are performed. Closed Mondays.

This is "Kafka territory." A bust of the writer commemorates the site of his birth in 1883, at 5 U Radnice. He grew up in the Italian-style plaster house next to the *Old Town Hall,* and his father ran a dry-goods shop on the ground floor of the Rococo *Goltz-Kinský Palace* on Old Town Square. The palace is also where young Kafka attended school.

On the north side of the square is the *Kostel Sv. Mikuláše* (Church of St. Nicholas); built in 1732–35 by architect Kilián Ignác Dienzenhofer, it houses statuary by Antonína Braun. This is also the site of frequent organ and choir concerts. Check listings posted on the door for dates and times.

**JOSEFOV (THE JEWISH QUARTER)** Walk north from the *Old Town Hall* on Pařížská třída and turn left on Cervená to see the *Staronová Synagóga* (Old-New Synagogue), the oldest functioning synagogue in Europe (1270). One of Prague's most beautiful examples of the early Gothic style, it is truly inspiring, with its fluted pillars and sculptural decorations.

Jewish traders founded the Prague ghetto as early as the 9th century, and it became a center of Jewish culture by the 17th century. Parts of the ghetto were demolished in 1896 when Pařížská třída was being reconstructed in Art Noveau style. Only six synagogues and the cemetery remain, all belonging to the *Statní Zidovský*

*Muzeum* (State Jewish Museum; 17 Listopadu; phone: 248-10099). All the properties are closed Saturdays.

In the restored *Pinkasová Synagóga* (Pinkas Synagogue; 3 Siroká), the names of 77,297 Jewish men, women, and children murdered by the Nazis were painted on the interior walls. These names were "accidentally" plastered over during renovations that took place when the Communist regime severed relations with Israel in 1967. At present artisans have restored two-thirds of the names. Ironically, during the war the Nazis attempted to turn the entire Jewish quarter into a museum of the very culture they were seeking to destroy. The *Vysoká Synagóga* (High Synagogue; Cervená ulice) houses a textile collection including some very fine hand-embroidered Torah mantles. The *Maislová Synagóga* (Maisel Synagogue; 9 Maislová) displays silver and pewter artifacts such as seder plates and Torah pointers.

Also here is the *Starý Zidovský Hřbitov* (Old Jewish Cemetery), with its 12,000 15th- to 18th-century tombstones. The oldest preserved tomb dates from 1438; burials continued here until 1787, when a new cemetery was built in Prague. In the *Ceremonial Hall* connected to the cemetery is an intensely moving collection of drawings and paintings by children in the *Theresienstadt* concentration camp.

Nearby, in the *Jewish Town Hall,* is the only kosher restaurant in town, the *Koscher Restaurace Shalom* (18 Maislová; phone: 248-10929).

**KLÁŠTER SV. ANEŽKY (CONVENT OF ST. AGNES)** In a partly reconstructed Gothic convent, collections of 19th-century Czech paintings, porcelain, glass, silver, and pewter are on display. Look for the paintings of Antonína Mánes (1784–1843) for an artist's view of Prague and its environs before the modern age. Closed Mondays. 17 Milosrdných ulice (phone: 248-10835).

**BETLÉMSKÁ KAPLE (BETHLEHEM CHAPEL)** Here, on the southern edge of the Old Town, the church reformer Jan Hus (John Huss) preached his revolutionary ideas from 1402 until his martyrdom in 1415. To the Czechs, Hus is a symbol of freedom from oppression and is revered as a national hero. The present chapel is a painstaking 1950–54 reconstruction of the original Gothic building, and the wooden threshold of the pulpit, once trod by Hus himself, is now protected under glass. Open daily. Betlémské náměstí.

**KARLŮV MOST (CHARLES BRIDGE)** One of the oldest and most beautiful bridges in Europe was built of stone between the Old Town and the Lesser Quarter in 1357 by Charles IV. Lined on both sides by 30 fine statues of the Baroque period (1683–1714), its Lesser Quarter end has two towers; the higher one may be climbed for a spectacular view. The bridge is a favorite strolling place day and night, and it offers views of the castle, the Vltava River, and the lovely island of Kampa, with its chestnut trees. Vendors now sell souvenirs here, and there are usually musicians playing for contributions.

## MALÁ STRANA (LESSER QUARTER)

Sometimes called Little Town, this is Prague's Baroque soul, founded in 1257 as the second (after the Old Town) of the royal towns. During the 17th and 18th centuries foreign noblemen and the Catholic church engaged some outstanding architects and artists to embellish what is the city's most picturesque quarter. Full of old palaces—including the magnificent *Wallenstein Palace,* where concerts are held during the summer—the Malá Strana is a maze of crooked cobblestone lanes lined with old churches, museums, inns, wine cellars, and charming little parks. It is best just to wander around and discover the nooks and crannies for yourself.

**MALOSTRANSKÉ NÁMĚSTÍ (LESSER QUARTER SQUARE)** Surrounded by 16th-century houses with arcades, the square—like the entire Malá Strana—is dominated by the Jesuit *Kostel Sv. Mikuláše* (Church of St. Nicholas). Designed by famous 18th-century architects, the Dienzenhofers and Anselmago Lurago, this is the finest Baroque building in Prague.

**VALDŠTEJNSKÝ PALÁC (WALLENSTEIN PALACE)** Northwest of the *Church of St. Nicholas* is this magnificent Baroque palace begun in 1623 by Italian architects for Albrecht Wallenstein, the great Hapsburg general. Unfortunately, the frescoes inside can't be seen because the building also houses the *Ministry of Culture,* but the public concerts in the garden with its *sala terrena* (patio) are an experience that should not be missed. The garden, consisting of a lake, a cave, and hundreds of roses, rhododendron, magnolias, and Japanese cherry blossom trees, was landscaped in 1623. The statues here are actually replicas of originals created by Dutch master Adrian de Vries in 1626. Be sure to visit the *Valdštejnská Jiždarna* (Wallenstein Riding Academy; 3 Valdštejnská; phone: 536814), which often holds special art exhibitions. Open daily from May through September. Valdštejnské náměstí.

**KOSTEL PANNY MARIE VÍTĚZNÉ (CHURCH OF OUR LADY OF VICTORY)** A favorite pilgrimage site that dates from the 17th century and houses the *Bambino di Praga* (The Infant Jesus of Prague, called the *Jezulátko* in Czech) by an anonymous artist. The renowned statue was brought to Prague from Spain at the beginning of the 16th century. 13 Karmelitská.

**NERUDOVÁ ULICE (NERUDA STREET)** Leading from the Malá Strana to *Prague Castle* and lined on both sides by Baroque façades is one of the most beautiful streets in town. Many townhouses on this street, named after 19th-century writer Jan Neruda, have preserved the old signs used before numbers were introduced: a red eagle, three violins, a golden goblet, and so on.

## HRADČANY (CASTLE DISTRICT)

Near *Prague Castle,* which probably was begun in the 9th century, is the district of Hradčany, officially founded in 1320.

**PRAŽSKÝ HRAD (PRAGUE CASTLE)** This castle, actually a complex of buildings, has been a Slav stronghold, a residence of the Kings of

Bohemia, and the present seat of the president of the republic; it is the history of the Czech nation in stone. With three dizzyingly walled courtyards, the castle is best grasped with the help of a *Cedok* walking tour (see *Seeing the City*, above). Perhaps most interesting is the interior of the vaulted Gothic *Vladislav Hall*, where jousting tournaments once took place. Closed Mondays (phone: 333-73368 for general information on all buildings within the complex).

**KATEDRÁLA SV. VÍTA (ST. VITUS'S CATHEDRAL)** Dominating the castle is this Gothic mausoleum of the Czech kings. The original building was designed in 1344 by Mathias Arras and Petr Parléř and finally completed in 1929. It is the repository for the Czech crown jewels, which are rarely on public display. However, they were shown during the last week of January 1993 to commemorate the birth of the new Czech Republic. Admission charge for crypt where Charles IV, his four wives, and King Rudolf are buried, as well as for the main tower.

**ZLATÁ ULIČKA (GOLDEN LANE)** Just north of the castle, this charming cobblestone lane lined with little houses and shops is famous as the legendary street of alchemists who tried to turn lead into gold. Franz Kafka worked at No. 24 in 1917; it is now a souvenir shop.

**NÁRODNÍ GALÉRIE (NATIONAL GALLERY)** From European Old Masters to Picasso, a very rich collection of paintings adorns this museum in the Baroque *Sternberk Palace* on Castle Square. Closed Mondays. Admission charge. 15 Hradčanské náměstí (phone: 352-4413).

**KLÁŠTER SV. JIŘÍ (ST. GEORGE'S MONASTERY)** An extensive collection of Czech Gothic art, superbly installed in the first convent founded in Bohemia. Closed Mondays. Admission charge. 33 Sv. Jiřské náměstí (no phone).

**LORETA (LORETTO CHURCH)** Built in 1626, this structure was so named because it was modeled after a pilgrimage church in Loretto, Italy. It also is famous for the 1694 carillon in its clock tower and for the "Loretto Treasury," a collection of extremely valuable 16th- to 18th-century jewelry and religious applied arts. Closed Mondays. Admission charge. Loretánské náměstí (phone: 536228).

**PETŘÍN GARDENS** The site of the newly restored 180-foot *Petřín Tower* (modeled after the *Eiffel Tower*), these captivating gardens offer the perfect respite for the weary traveler. Also located here is a mirrored *bludiště* (labyrinth), in addition to a diorama that depicts the 1648 battle between Bohemia and Sweden. Open daily. Admission charge. To reach the gardens, take the funicular on Ujezd.

**BELVEDERE (QUEEN ANNA'S SUMMER HOUSE)** Originally designed in 1537 for Anna, wife of King Ferdinand I, this is the most important Renaissance building north of the Alps. The garden contains a "singing fountain" (water drips into a bell-like metal bowl, producing a musical sound) designed by Tomáš Jaroš in 1564. The palace is now the site of numerous art exhibitions. Closed Mondays. Admission charge. Chotkovy sady (phone: 241-97411).

**STRAHOVSKÝ KLÁŠTER (STRAHOV MONASTERY)** West of the castle, high above the green slopes of Petřín Hill, is a gigantic monastery, built between 1140 and 1784, which once rivaled the castle itself in magnificence and whose garden provides a lovely view of Prague. Today, *Strahov* houses the *Památník Národního Písemnictví* (Museum of Czech Literature); two Baroque library halls as well as a painting gallery also may be seen. Closed Mondays. Admission charge. 1 Strahovské nádvoří (phone: 245-11137).

## VYŠEHRAD

High on the cliffs above the Vltava River on the side opposite Hradčany, this fortress and the town around it probably were founded in the 9th century. However, no one knows how old Vyšehrad really is; it may be much older.

**VYŠEHRAD FORTRESS** Walk around the grounds, which include a park, the 11th-century *Rotunda of St. Martin,* and the *Church of St. Peter and St. Paul.*

**VYŠEHRAD CEMETERY** This is the burial place of the country's greats; Anton Dvořák, Karel Capek, Jan Kubelík, Jan Neruda, and Bedřich Smetana are just a few of the prominent names. Open daily. Next to the *Church of St. Peter and St. Paul* (phone: 296-6512).

## ENVIRONS

**KUTNÁ HORA** Set in a lovely area just 42 miles (67 km) southeast of Prague, it is a former silver-mining town that boomed in the 13th century, when its rich deposits were used to help create the splendor of the Bohemian court. During the 14th century it was the second-largest town in the country. Here coins were minted by craftsmen imported from Florence. Here also is the *Vlašský Dvůr,* a 13th-century palace where the craftsmen worked, a fine coin museum, a church whose vault is lined entirely with human skulls, and the unusual Gothic roof of *St. Barbara's Church.* A one-day bus excursion—"Treasures of Bohemian Gothic"—includes a tour of Kutná Hora with a stop at *Cesky Sternberk,* a 13th-century hilltop castle. For further information, contact *Cedok* (see *Tourist Information*).

**KARLŠTEJN, KŘIVOKLÁT, AND KONOPIŠTĚ CASTLES** About 17½ miles (28 km) southwest of Prague is the most visited castle in the Czech Republic, 14th-century *Karlštejn Castle.* Built by Charles IV, it is the depository of the great wealth he attained as Holy Roman emperor. The castle underwent massive reconstruction in the 19th century, and today is the site of the *Chapel of the Holy Rood* with its magnificent display of crown jewels. Also of interest is the *Audience Hall,* where the king greeted his supplicants, and *Luxembourg Hall,* which features a tapestry that traces the royal family tree. Within the palace complex is the *Church of the Virgin* where *Relic Scenes* (ca. 1357), one of the earliest known portraits in European art, is on display. *St. Catherine's Chapel,* with an oratory encrusted in semi-precious stones, and the *Chapel of the Holy Cross* are also on the grounds.

About 2 miles (3 km) from *Karlštejn* is *Křivoklát Castle.* Set in a forest preserve near the Berounka River, it was used as a hunting lodge by Czech kings from the 13th to the 16th century. Later it was turned into a prison for political offenders. The permanent collection on display here includes sculpture and paintings from the late Gothic period, as well as arms, carriages, and sleighs dating from the 17th to the 19th century.

*Konopiště Castle,* located 26½ miles (42 km) from the city near the small town of Benešov, is a Renaissance château surrounded by landscaped gardens and a park. It offers a fine collection of 15th- and 16th-century armor, porcelain, and other precious objects.

All three castles are closed Mondays. There is an admission charge to all three, and English-language tours are available. Tickets can be purchased in advance from the concert and tourist activities booking agency *BTI* (16 Na příkopě; phone: 242-15031; fax: 248-10368). Most major travel agencies, including *Cedok* (see *Tourist Information*) offer half-day bus excursions from Prague. The castles also are accessible by public transportation—trains leave the *Praha Hlavní Nádraží* station (see *Getting Around*) in Prague hourly for Karlštejn, where you can transfer to trains for the other two sites. Be sure to check train return schedules before your departure.

**LIDICE** Also quite popular is the village of Lidice, only 13 miles (21 km) from Prague. The town was totally destroyed by the Nazis in 1942 in reprisal for the killing of a Nazi police governor. All local men were shot on sight, all women sent to concentration camps, and all young blond children shipped to Germany for adoption. Today the village (a national monument) has been preserved exactly as it was—so the ruins can serve as a reminder of Nazi atrocities and a memorial to its victims. *Cedok* (see *Tourist Information*) offers motorcoach trips which include *Terezín,* set up by the Nazis as a "model" transfer point to concentration camps with its own orchestra and children's school. The area also is accessible by public transportation.

# Sources and Resources

## TOURIST INFORMATION

For general information, brochures, maps, and tour bookings contact *Cedok* (18 Na příkopě; phone: 241-9711; fax: 242-25491); or the *Prague Information Service* (20 Na příkopě; phone: 544444). The latter can arrange for private guides as well as concert and theater tickets at its office at 4 Panská (phone: 242-12212 or 242-12757). *Rekrea* (26-28 Pařížská; phone: 248-11749 or 248-10385) is much smaller than *Cedok,* yet it offers many services—and a much warmer welcome. *IFB Bohemia* (25 Václavské náměstí; phone: 242-27253; fax: 242-278442), another tourist agency, also is helpful, as is *Pragotour* (23 U Obecního domu; phone: 248-10973; fax: 248-11651). The *American Hospitality Center* (8 Melantrichová;

phone: 267770; fax: 269384) offers tourist information and will assist travelers in finding accommodations and in reserving theater and concert tickets. The *US Embassy and Consulate* is at 15 Tržiště, Prague (phone: 531200; fax: 510001).

In the US, contact *Cedok* (10 E. 40th St., New York, NY 10016; phone: 212-689-9720; 800-800-8891; fax: 212-481-0597). The *Czech Embassy and Consulate* is at 3900 Spring of Freedom St. NW, Washington, DC 20008 (phone: 202-363-6315; fax: 202-966-8540).

**ENTRY REQUIREMENTS** A US citizen needs only a current passport for a visit of up to 30 days.

**TIME** The time in the Czech Republic is six hours later than in US East Coast cities. The Czech Republic follows daylight saving time.

**LANGUAGE** Czech is the official language of the Czech Republic. Those engaged in tourism speak English, and Russian is usually understood. German is also becoming an increasingly popular second language.

**ELECTRIC CURRENT** 220 volts, 50 cycles, AC.

**MONEY** The Czech currency is called the koruna (kč). At press time $1 US bought about 28 korun.

**TIPPING** Restaurant bills don't include service charges, and at least 10% should be added; taxi drivers also expect 10% tips; 5 to 10 korun should be given to porters and doormen.

**BANKING/BUSINESS HOURS** Banks generally are open weekdays from 8 AM to 4 PM; some are open until 6 PM twice a week and until noon once a week. Throughout the city are numerous *Chequepoints* where travelers may exchange currency. Very often these places charge a much higher commission rate than do banks. On the flip side are the ubiquitous black marketeers who are in the business of exchanging money—and ripping off unsuspecting tourists. No matter how tempting their deals may sound, steer clear. Most other businesses are open weekdays from 8 AM to 4 PM.

**NATIONAL HOLIDAYS** *New Year's Day* (January 1), *Easter Sunday* (April 16), *Easter Monday* (April 17), *Anniversary of WW II Liberation* (May 8), *National Holiday* (July 5–6), *Proclamation of Czechoslovak Republic* (October 28), *Christmas Day* (December 25), and *Boxing Day* (December 26).

**LOCAL COVERAGE** You can find the English-language newspapers *Prognosis* and *The Prague Post* in larger hotels and at newsstands. Both are produced by American expatriates and have complete entertainment listings. *Prognosis* is biweekly, *The Prague Post* is weekly. *PRO*, a weekly Czech entertainment magazine, has culture and entertainment listings in an English-language section.

**TELEPHONE** The city code for Prague is 2. Most public phones now operate with phone cards, which can be purchased at the *Main Post Office* (14 Jindřišská ulice; phone: 242-28584) and at newspaper kiosks. When calling from one area to another within the Czech Republic dial 0 + city code + local number. The country code for the Czech Republic is 42. In an emergency, dial 155 for an ambulance and 158 for the police.

## GETTING AROUND

**AIRPORT** *Praha-Ruzyně Airport,* about 40 minutes from downtown by taxi, handles both domestic and international flights (for information call 334-1111). Buses connecting the airport and downtown leave from the *Vltava Travel Bureau* (25 Revoluční třída in Prague; contact the *Czechoslovak Airline—CSA*—counter at the airport. There is also an inexpensive shuttle bus serving the airport and major hotels; more information can be obtained from the *Cedok* counter at the airport.

**BUS/TRAM** Public transportation is relatively inexpensive and good. Tickets are sold at newsstands and tobacco shops—not on the bus or tram. You punch your ticket yourself once aboard. For destinations outside of Prague buses depart from *Autobusové Nádraží Florenc* (Florenc Bus Station). For information call 242-11057.

**CAR RENTAL** *Avis* is located at 9 Elišky Krásno-Horské (phone: 232-2459; fax: 231-7865); there also is an office at *Praha-Ruzyně Airport. Budget* has offices at the airport (phone/fax: 316-5214) and at the *Inter-Continental* hotel (see *Checking In*). There are *Hertz* branches at the airport (phone: 312-0717) and at the *Atrium* and *Diplomat* hotels (see *Checking In* for both). *Avanti Car* is at 178 Evropská (phone: 316-5204). Limos (both Lincoln and Cadillac) are available from *Exclusive Luxury Limo Service* (4 Na marně; phone: 342791; fax: 311-5031).

**CARRIAGE RIDES** A ride in a *fiakr* (horse-drawn carriage) is a romantic way to see the city. You can find them drawn up at Old Town Square.

**METRO** Built in cooperation with the Russians and still expanding, the subway system, which runs daily, is fast, safe, and clean. The same 6-koruna (about 20¢) ticket used for the metro, buses, and trams can be purchased in metro stations, tobacco shops, and at hotel desks. One-, two-, three-, four-, and five-day metro passes also are available.

**TAXI** Reasonably priced taxis are available at major hotels or through *Profi Taxi* (phone: 610-45555).

**TRAIN** The main train station, *Praha Hlavní Nádraží* (2 Wilsonová třída; phone: 242-17654) is also called the *Woodrow Wilson Station* in honor of the US president's efforts for peace at the end of World War I and his subsequent involvement in negotiating the 1919 Treaty of Versailles, which officially recognized Czechoslovakia as an independent nation.

**TOURS** For an unsurpassed perspective on the city, consider the "Prague by Balloon" tour offered by *Buddy Bombard's Great Balloon Adventures* (6727 Curran St., McLean, VA 22101; phone: 703-448-9407; 800-862-8537). The six-day tour features daily treetop-level sightseeing excursions that lift off from Old Town Square. Terrestrial and aquatic trips (via motorcoach and boat) are also included in the package.

Any exploration should begin with "Historical Prague," a two-hour tour of the city by motorcoach, with a multilingual guide, offered by *Cedok* (18 Na příkopě; phone: 241-9711; fax: 242-25491). A three-hour bus and walking tour of "Historical Prague" leaves from the *Cedok* branch office (6 Bílkova; phone: 231-6619) opposite the *Inter-Continental* hotel.

Seeing the city by steamship is yet another option. *Pražská Paroplavební Společnost* (Prague Passenger Ships; phone: 298309; fax: 249-13862) runs the historic steamship *Vyšehrad,* which leaves regularly from Rašínovo nábřeží, close to the Palackého Bridge, and travels to the Barrandov Cliffs, the *Prague Zoo,* and the Slapy Dam. Lunch, coffee, and dinner cruises are available.

## LOCAL SERVICES

Most hotels will try to arrange for any special services a traveler might require.

**DENTIST (ENGLISH-SPEAKING)** The number to call for emergency dental care is 261374, although English is not always spoken; it's best to ask the service desk at any major hotel to make the call for you. English is spoken at *AAA Dentist* (1969 Zvoncovitá; phone: 644-3443).

**EMERGENCY** The number to call for an ambulance is 155, although English is not always spoken; it's best to ask the service desk at any major hotel to make the call for you. The 24-hour medical emergency number for foreigners is 249148; doctors on call at the *Fakulta Polyklinik* (32 Karlovo náměstí) speak English and/or German. The *Diplomatic Health Center* (2 Roenteenova; phone: 529-22146, weekdays; 529-22191, evenings and weekends) also treats foreign travelers. A 24-hour first-aid service is located at 5 Palackého (phone: 242-22520/1). The police emergency number is 158. For less urgent police matters call the station at 6 Bartolomějská (phone: 241-31111). English may not be spoken; ask your hotel service desk for assistance. Emergency road service is provided by *Yellow Angels* (phone: 154).

**LOST AND FOUND** A drop-off and pick-up depot is located at 5 Bolzanov (phone: 236-8887).

**PHARMACY** The pharmacy at 7 Na příkopě (phone: 242-10229) is open around the clock. Other pharmacies alternate in staying open 24 hours a day; ask at your hotel desk for a schedule.

**POST OFFICE** The *Hlavní Pošta* (Main Post Office) is open 24 hours and is located just off Wenceslas Square (14 Jindřišská ulice; phone: 242-28584).

## SPECIAL EVENTS

*Pražské Jaro* (Prague Spring), held every year from mid-May to early June since 1946, presents operas and concerts featuring internationally known soloists, orchestras, and chamber ensembles (also see *Music*). The *International Jazz Festival Prague,* one of the major

European jazz festivals, takes place in even-numbered years. Previous festivals have featured Chick Corea, Stephane Grappelli, and Czech bands led by Gustav Brom and Milan Svoboda. For information, contact the *Pražské Jaro Agency,* the Czech arts and entertainment agency (18 Hellichová; phone: 533474; fax: 536040). Prague also hosts several smaller jazz events during the year—the *Prague Jazz Celebration Festival* in the spring and the *Jazz on the Island Festival* in June. For further information contact *Cedok* (see *Tourist Information*) or *BTI* (16 Na příkopě; phone: 242-15031; fax: 248-10368).

## MUSEUMS

In addition to the museums mentioned in *Special Places,* we recommend the following (all charge admission):

**BERTRAMKA/PAMÁTNÍK W. A. MOZARTA (VILLA BERTRAMKA/W. A. MOZART MUSEUM)** A 17th-century mansion in the Smíchov district, where Mozart stayed, is now a museum devoted to the composer and the city of Prague. Closed Tuesdays. 169 Mozartova (phone: 543893).

**LOBKOVICKÝ PALÁC (LOBKOVIC PALACE)** Housed in an 18th-century building, this museum is devoted to the country's Baroque period. Piano and orchestra concerts are held on Wednesdays, Thursdays, and Fridays during the summer. Closed Mondays. Jiřská ulice, behind *Prague Castle* (phone: 537306).

**MUZEUM HLAVNÍHO MĚSTA PRAHY (MUSEUM OF THE CITY OF PRAGUE)** This museum documents the history of the city from its beginnings in the 9th century until the present. The highlight is a scale model of Prague in the years 1826 through 1837, which shows the Jewish ghetto before its eventual destruction. Closed Mondays. 52 Na poříčí (phone: 242-23180).

**UMĚLECKOPRŮMYSOLOVÉ MUZEUM (MUSEUM OF THE DECORATIVE ARTS)** Beautiful inlaid cabinets, tapestries, porcelain, and pewterware traditionally found in the country's castles and stately mansions are displayed here. The objects date from the Renaissance to the mid-19th century. The museum also houses (though it's not on display) the largest glass collection in the world. Closed Mondays. 2 17 Listopadu (phone: 248-11241).

## SHOPPING

Bohemian glass and crystal are world famous and are available here at much lower prices than outside the country. Try *Moser* (12 Na příkopě; phone: 242-11293); *Bohemia* in the Old Town Square (2 Pařížská; phone: 248-11023); *Krystal* (30 Václavské náměstí; phone: 242-28355); and *Crystalex* (6 Malé náměstí; phone: 242-28459). For chandeliers visit *Lustry* (19 Jindřišská; phone: 268386).

Many Europeans and Americans living in Europe buy entire sets of glassware and china in Prague's department stores, which have improved dramatically in recent years. Department stores also carry clothing, hats, and other local items at incredible prices, although imported items are less of a bargain. Head first to Prague's largest department store, *Kotva* (8 Náměstí republiky; phone: 248-01111); others are *Kmart* (26 Národní; phone: 242-27971); *Bíla labuť* (23 Na příkopě; phone: 248-11364); and *Krone* (21 Václavské náměstí; phone: 242-30477). All of the above (except *Bíla labuť*) are now under *Kmart* ownership.

For costume jewelry stop in at *Royal Bijou* (12 Na příkopě; phone: 242-10552); for the real thing try *Klenoty* (9 Václavské náměstí; phone: 242-13207). *Garnet* (28 Václavské náměstí; no phone) specializes in the stone of the same name, native to Bohemia.

The best place to see what local artisans are up to is the Charles Bridge, where you'll find marionettes, wooden toys, and handmade jewelry that's all the rage; crafts can also be bought in the Wenceslas Square area at *Lidová jizba* (14 Václavské náměstí; no phone). Another wonderful selection of wooden toys and ceramics can be found at *Dřevěné Hračky* (26 Karlova; phone: 242-10886).

The *Central European Gallery* (19 Husová; phone: 236-0700; fax: 269086) carries a fine selection of posters and works by local graphic artists. *Galérie Maislová* (17 Maislová; phone: 231-8196; fax: 231-8754) features fine antiques; *Antikvariat* (7 Dlážděná; no phone) sells used books, graphic arts, sheet music, and paper money. Sheet music can be found at 30 Jungmannovo náměstí, and musical instruments at 17 Jungmannovo náměstí. The *Globe Bookstore and Café* is run by Americans (14 Strossmayerovo náměstí; phone: 357-9161).

## SPORTS AND FITNESS

**FITNESS CENTERS** *Plavecký Stadión* (74 Podolská; phone: 612-14343), a 20-minute drive south of Prague in Podolí, has an Olympic-size pool, steamroom, and sauna. In addition, several larger hotels, including the *Atrium, Diplomat, Forum Praha, Inter-Continental,* and *Panorama,* have fitness centers for guests (see *Checking In* for all).

**JOGGING** A good place is *Stromovka Park,* a 15-minute walk or five-minute ride northeast of downtown.

**SOCCER** Games are played at *Sparta Stadium* (98 Mílady Horakové; phone: 322110); you can purchase tickets there.

**SQUASH AND TENNIS** There are indoor-outdoor courts at *Sparta Stadium* (see above), *Centrálni Tenisový Dvorec* (Central Tennis Courts; Stvanice; phone: 231-1270), and at the *Tennis Club Průhonice* (400 Průhonice; phone: 643-6501). Courts are available to guests at the *Atrium, Forum Praha,* and *Inter-Continental* hotels (see *Checking In* for all three).

## THEATER

Although theater is usually performed in Czech, don't miss this special experience which transcends all languages:

---

### CENTER STAGE

**Laterna Magika** This unique theater experience is an amalgam of cinema, opera, theater, dance, and circus. One of

---

the most intriguing spectacles on the Continent, its name, "Magic Lantern," conveys the swirling, kaleidoscopic style of the performances. It's not necessary to understand Czech to enjoy the hypnotic beauty of these shows; children in particular find them fascinating. This theater is also of interest because of the role it played in the 1989 "velvet revolution." In the first days of the demonstrations that overthrew the Communist regime, the *Laterna Magika* troupe offered the theater to playwright (later president) Václav Havel and the other dissidents masterminding the revolution. Every night reporters from around the world would squeeze into the theater to hear Havel's latest words on the progress of negotiations with the Communists. 4 Národní (phone: 249-14129; fax: 242-27567).

---

Also popular with foreigners are the pantomime productions at the *Divadlo Na Zábradlí* (Theater on the Balustrade; 5 Anenské náměstí; phone: 242-21933). Other theaters include the *Národní Divadlo* (National Theater; 2 Národní; phone: 249-12673) for the classics (in Czech); the *Nová Scéna,* the *National Theater*'s architecturally controversial offshoot next door; and the recently renovated *Stavovské Divadlo* (Estates Theater; 6 Ovocný; phone: 242-14339), which offers some simultaneous translations and where Mozart's *Don Giovanni* premiered in 1787.

For a taste of Old Bohemia and Moravia, reserve a place at the *Folklore Show of the Czech Song and Dance Ensemble* (25 Pohořelec; phone: 245-11027). The troupe has successfully combined traditional folk dance with modern dance, black theater, and pantomime for an all-around enjoyable experience. Music is adapted from that of Czech greats Anton Dvořák, Leoš Janáček, and Bedřich Smetana.

## MUSIC

Prague is a city that Mozart loved, and where Dvořák and Smetana worked and composed their music. It is still a very musical city.

---

### HIGH NOTES

**Pražské Jaro (Prague Spring)** This doyen of European music festivals has been an annual event since 1946. Internationally known conductors, soloists, orchestras, chamber ensembles, and opera companies from Eastern Europe are always on the program, as are some fine Russian artists (who invariably go on to give sold-out performances at *Carnegie Hall* in New York). The festival takes place from mid-May to early June. 18 Hellichová (phone: 533474; fax: 536040).

---

Concerts can be heard at the *Stavovské Divadlo* (see *Theater,* above); *Smetanova Síň* (Smetana Hall) in *Obecní Dům* (Municipal House; 5 Náměstí republiky; phone: 245-10950); the *Palác Kul-*

*tury* (Palace of Culture; 65 Květná ulice; phone: 611-72354); and *Dvořáková Síň* (Dvořák Hall) of the *Rudolfinum* (12 Alšovo nábřeží; phone: 248-93352), the home of the renowned *Czech Philharmonic Orchestra.* Operas are performed at the *Národní Divadlo* (see *Theater,* above), and the *Státní Opera Praha* (Prague State Opera; 4 Wilsonová třída; phone: 242-27693), formerly the *Smetanovo Divadlo.*

## NIGHTCLUBS AND NIGHTLIFE

In the past several years Prague has seen an explosion of new clubs and discos. Begin the night at around 9 PM for a grab bag of jazz, blues, and rock, at the *Malostranská Beseda* (Malostranské náměstí; phone: 231-3123 or 231-4535). Have a beer, watch TV, or dance the night away at *Borat* (18 Ujezd; phone: 538362). The *Bunkr Café* (2 Lodecká; phone: 231-0735) is a favorite among the young American crowd, and the *Rock Club Bunkr* next door features local and international live bands. For dancing, drinks, and a view of the Vltava River, there is the slick *Lávka Klub* (1 Novotného Lávka; phone: 245-11026). The *Rock Café* (20 Národní; phone: 249-14416) is a popular, high-volume club with live music and a disco. Run by Americans, another fairly recent addition to the club scene is *Radost* (120 Bělohradská; phone: 258938), with disco nightly. The attached *FX Café* serves vegetarian fare and great cappuccino.

For jazz buffs the *Reduta Jazz Club* (20 Národní; phone: 249-12246), a cozy cellar with plush furniture and a smoky, dark atmosphere, has everything from Dixieland to swing to contemporary jazz-fusion nightly except Sundays. It was here that US President Clinton jammed on the sax during his first official visit to the city. The *Jazz Art Club* (40 Vinohradská) offers not only jazz, but a music store and an offbeat bar. The *Viola Café* (7 Národní; phone: 242-20844), a favorite among former dissidents, features live music on Saturdays. *Aghartha* (5 Krakouská; phone: 224558) is a funky club with a shop and a café.

For extravagant floor shows don't miss *Lucerna* (61 Malá Stěpánská; phone: 235-0888) and *Revue Alhambra* at the *Ambassador/Zlatá Husa* hotel (see *Checking In*). *Club Penguin* (5 Zborovská; phone: 545660) has been known to spin waltz music if the crowd is right. Those with a penchant for gambling should try the casinos at the *Ambassador/Zlatá Husa, Forum Praha,* and *Jalta* hotels (see *Checking In*).

# Best in Town

## CHECKING IN

Hotel reservations may be made directly, through *Cedok* (see *Tourist Information*), or through your travel agent. One intriguing Prague option is called a "botel" (boat plus hotel), several of which are anchored in the Vltava River. Each has about 80 rooms, which are charming though somewhat cramped. All have mini-bars. They are the *Admirál* (Hořejší nábřeží; phone: 245-11697; fax: 549616); the

*Albatros* (L. Svobody nábřeží; phone: 248-112141; fax: 248-11214); and the *Racek* (Dvorecká louka; phone: 612-14383; fax: 612-14390).

The *Prague Travelers Service* (phone: 800-626-4160 in the US) arranges apartment rentals for $60 to $120 per night (for a two-room unit). Also available for considerably less money are private apartments. Contact the *Ave Travel Agency* (8 Wilsonová třída; phone: 242-23262; fax: 242-23463). Another option is *American-International Homestays* (1515 W. Penn St., Iowa City, IA 52240; phone: 319-626-2125), which arranges stays with families in Prague and several other Eastern European cities.

For all accommodations advance bookings are essential; the influx of tourists has created a greater-than-ever shortage of space in Prague. *Cedok* accepts bookings for non-deluxe hotels only on a half-board basis (meal vouchers can be used outside the hotel). Expect to pay from $200 to $300 per night for a double room at a very expensive hotel; $100 to $200 at an expensive property; $50 to $100 at a moderate place; and $20 to $50 at the inexpensive botels. Be aware that the Czech government had imposed a 23% tax on hotel rooms, so check in advance to see whether or not it has been included in the price you are quoted. In all of the following hotels, guestrooms have private baths unless otherwise specified. All telephone numbers are in the 2 city code unless otherwise indicated.

### VERY EXPENSIVE

**Ambassador/Zlatá Husa** The *Ambassador* has joined forces with its somewhat shabbier cousin and is now a larger hotel that offers 172 rooms and 17 suites. A few of the floors have been completely renovated; others exude a somewhat faded Old World charm, with Louis XIV–style furniture and chandeliers. Amenities include four restaurants, a café, two wine cellars, two bars, a disco, a casino, and the popular floor show *Revue Alhambra*. 5 Václavské náměstí (phone: 242-12185; fax: 242-23563).

**Diplomat** Now managed by Vienna International, this favorite among businesspeople, only a 10-minute drive from the city center, has 387 rooms (5 for the disabled) and 12 suites. (Nonsmokers should ask for a room on the sixth floor.) There are two restaurants, a club/restaurant, and a nightclub. The fitness center is equipped with a sauna, solarium, whirlpool bath, and gym. Business facilties include meeting rooms for up to 250, secretarial services in English, audio-visual equipment, photocopiers, and cable television news. 15 Evropská (phone: 243-94111; fax: 341731).

**Esplanade** One of the more evocative, pre-World War II hostelries in town, this 64-room and six-suite establishment has a very friendly family atmosphere, a well-trained staff, two excellent restaurants, and a nightclub. There's a meeting room for up to 20. Business facilties include secretarial services in English. Near the *National Museum* and the main train station, at 19 Washingtonová (phone: 242-11715; fax: 242-29306).

**Inter-Continental** A nine-story, 398-room, newly renovated modern property, conveniently located on the river at the edge of the Old Town. The rooms on the upper floors afford superb views of *Prague Castle* and the Old Town, as do the two restaurants, including *Zlatá Praha* (Golden Prague; see *Eating Out*). There are also two bars, a nightclub, a café, a wine cellar, 24-hour room service, and a parking garage. For the health-conscious there are a fitness center, a squash court, a sauna, and a solarium. Business facilities include meeting rooms for up to 100, audiovisual equipment, photocopiers, cable television news, and translation services. 5 Náměstí Curieových (phone: 248-81111; 800-327-0200; fax: 248-10071).

**Jalta** A favorite of Americans, it has 79 rooms, each with satellite TV and a mini-bar. The staff is friendly and helpful, and the *Jalta Club* has disco music for dancing. There's also a restaurant and casino. The hotel's second floor has been redesigned as a center with three meeting rooms for up to 150, secretarial services in English, audiovisual equipment, photocopiers, computers, and cable television news. 45 Václavské náměstí (phone: 242-29133; fax: 242-13866).

**Palace Praha** Offering the finest accommodations in the nation's capital, this is the city's most beautiful—and most expensive—hotel. Built at the beginning of the century in ornate Art Nouveau style, this luxurious property near the Old Town has been renovated to its original grandeur. From the sartorially splendid doorman to the elegantly decorated 115 rooms and 10 suites, this establishment does its best to pamper and impress its chic international clientele. There's a restaurant that serves excellent French fare and an upscale cafeteria with that rare find, a salad bar (see *Eating Out* for the latter). A piano bar, a sauna, and a solarium round out the amenities. Business facilties include a meeting room for up to 100, secretarial services in English, audiovisual equipment, and photocopiers. 12 Panská (phone: 240-93111; fax: 242-21240).

### EXPENSIVE

**Atrium** This huge, 788-room property just outside the city center offers the most up-to-date facilities and the most services in town. Highlights include a large, airy atrium; five restaurants; a café; two nightclubs; the *Casino de France;* and a fitness center with a pool, a solarium, a sauna, and tennis courts. The large conference center makes this the choice for businesspeople. Business facilities include meeting rooms, secretarial services in English, audiovisual equipment, photocopiers, and cable television news. 1 Pobřežní (phone: 248-12018; fax: 248-11896).

**Forum Praha** Opposite the *Palace of Culture* conference center/concert hall, and a short taxi ride from the city center, this large, modern tower has 492 doubles and 39 suites, all with satellite TV. Other amenities include two restaurants, a beer hall, a bar, a café, a nightclub, a casino, a fitness center and swimming pool, a squash court, a bowling alley, gift shops, and a parking garage. Business facilties include meeting rooms for up to 750, secretarial services in

English, audiovisual equipment, photocopiers, and translation services. 1 Kongresová ulice (phone: 619-19111; 800-327-0200; fax: 612-11673).

**Panorama** Just four metro stops from the center of town, this large (400-room) hotel offers a pool, three saunas, a gym, a good Czech restaurant, a meeting room for up to 15, a bar, a café, and a disco. 7 Milevská (phone: 611-61111; fax: 426263).

**Paříž Praha** This lovely Art Nouveau–style, 100-room hotel has a lounge bar, and a café. The rooms are not up to the level of the public areas, but a new executive floor for the business traveler includes 10 deluxe rooms, two suites with mini-bars, fax, audiovisual equipment, photocopiers, computers, and secretarial and translation services. The hotel also has a contract with the neighboring *Municipal House* office building, which allows for the use of 12 meeting rooms. 1 U Obecního domu (phone: 242-22151; fax: 242-25475).

**Prague Penta** Geared toward the business traveler, this hotel is one of the best and most modern in town. The 306 rooms (including 12 suites and a duplex) offer satellite TV and mini-bars. Guests enjoy the *Pavilion* restaurant, a bar, and a *bierstube*. Other amenities include a fitness center with gym, sauna, solarium, and massage. Business facilties include 11 conference rooms for up to 250, secretarial services in English, audiovisual equipment, photocopiers, computers, cable television news, and translation services. V. Celnice (phone: 248-10396; 800-225-3456; fax: 231-3133).

**Ungelt** This tiny hostelry is set in a 600-year-old building that was originally a customs hall. It's located in the Old Town Square area of centuries-old Romanesque and Gothic buildings. The 10 apartment-style suites are in great demand, due to this establishment's Old World ambience; reserve months ahead. There are a restaurant and a bar on the premises. 1 Stupartská (phone: 248-11330; fax: 231-8505).

**U Raků** What looks like a simple mountain cabin is actually an exclusive, Old Europe–style retreat hidden from the bustle of Prague behind *Loretto Church*. The five rooms and one suite, each furnished in a different style, have expansive garden views. Because of high demand, reservations must be made three to four months in advance. 10 Cernínská (phone: 351453; fax: 353074).

**U Tří Pštrosů (At the Three Ostriches)** Located at the Malá Strana end of the Charles Bridge, this pretty, 16th-century house is the oldest and most charming hostelry in Prague and one of the most exclusive places in all of Eastern Europe. The 18 rooms and suites must be booked several months in advance, particularly for summer visits. The restaurant also is one of the city's most delightful; it serves Czech specialties at lunch and dinner and features fine service. 12 Dražického náměstí (phone: 242-21240).

**Villa Voyta** Located 15 minutes by taxi from the city center, this Art Nouveau–style villa offers 13 elegant rooms and two luxury suites. A good restaurant serves Czech and continental dishes, and there are a bar, a wine cellar, and a café. Business facilities include secretarial services in English, audiovisual equipment, a photocopier, and a computer. 124 K Novému dvoru (phone: 472-5511 or 472838; fax: 472-9426)

**Evropa** A wonderfully ornate Art Nouveau–style establishment on Wenceslas Square, it offers good value in once exquisite, now faded, surroundings. The 88 rooms are homey, and the four suites are sparsely and eclectically furnished, making their spaciousness seem almost surreal. The lackadaisical service and offbeat ambience may not appeal to everyone, but the place has a certain quirky charm. There is a cocktail bar and gallery on the second floor, and the restaurant is a replica of a dining room on the *Titanic* (see *Eating Out*). 25 Václavské náměstí; phone: 242-28117; fax: 242-24544).

**International** This monolithic building, once a base for Soviet army brass and now a hotel, has 240 comfortable, if nondescript, rooms (including 69 suites). Ask for a room in one of the wings, which are considerably larger. There are two restaurants serving Czech and continental fare, a wine cellar, a bar, and a café. The hotel is 15 minutes by metro from the center of Prague, at 15 Koulová (phone: 243-93111; fax: 311-8300).

**St. Monica** Located about 20 minutes from the city center, this charming stucco villa sits on a hill overlooking the Vltava River. It has 24 guestrooms, most with sunny balconies, and a cozy breakfast room. The attentive staff goes out of its way to make travelers welcome. 31A Vlnita (phone: 464465; fax: 464120).

---

## EATING OUT

Prague has thousands of eating places—outdoor cafés, wine cellars, pubs, and international restaurants. In most cases reservations are necessary, particularly during the *Easter* holidays and in summertime, but be aware that they aren't always honored when you arrive. Czech cuisine is hearty and good, although it is weak on fresh produce, which is slowly making inroads. Specialties include *knedlíky* (dumplings, both plain and filled with fruit or meat); *knedlozelo-vepřo* (dumplings, sauerkraut, and pork); *svíčková* (beef marinated in cream sauce); *uzené maso* (smoked pork with potato dumplings and spinach); and roast goose or duck. A pub favorite is *smažený sýr,* which quite literally means breaded and fried cheese; its cousin, *smažený hermelín,* is a variation using a local version of camembert.

Wines from southern Moravia are the best; sample *tři grácie* red, rosé, or white. In Prague, as elsewhere in the country, you have the choice of eating in either *pivnice* (beer halls), where the only drink is beer and dishes are quite basic, or in a *vinárna* (wine restaurant), where you can order wine and the fare is a bit more distinctive. There also are the more traditional restaurants, where you have many choices of food and drink.

Restaurant prices in Prague generally are quite reasonable; we have rated a dinner for two at $30 and up as expensive (excluding wine, drinks, and tip); $20 to $30 as moderate; and $10 to $20 as inexpensive. Remember, too, that you always can eat for almost nothing at a street stall, or "hall in the wall," a type of fast-food place featuring grilled sausages. Approach the *parek v rohlíku* with caution, as you would New York City street hot dogs. The *bramborák,* a greasy but delicious fried potato pancake is worth a try. Many less expensive restaurants do *not* accept credit cards. Unless otherwise specified all places below are open for lunch and dinner. All telephone numbers are in the 2 city code.

### EXPENSIVE

**Club Kampa** This eatery, located in the Malá Strana (Lesser Quarter) not far from *Wallenstein Palace,* is set in an 18th-century building with high vaulted ceilings. The menu (recited by elegantly attired waiters) features traditional Czech fare, done to perfection. Try the wild duck with cumin-flavored sauerkraut. Open daily. Reservations advised. Major credit cards accepted. 14 Na kampě (phone: 539985).

**David** Located near the *US Embassy,* this well-run dining spot is very popular with diplomats. A menu in every imaginable language features carefully prepared continental and Czech dishes. Try the poultry kebabs and the smoked swordfish appetizer. Open daily. Reservations necessary. Major credit cards accepted. 21 Tržiště (phone: 539325).

**Evropa Restaurant and Café** This hotel dining room was once the best in Prague. The prix fixe dinner of either Czech or French fare is still dependably good, and the decor, a replica of a dining room on the *Titanic,* is stupendous. Food is prepared at your table, and cognac is available in fishbowl-size snifters. The decor in the café is equally marvelous, although the pastries are only so-so. Open daily. Reservations necessary in the dining room; unnecessary in the café. Major credit cards accepted. In the *Evropa Hotel,* 25 Václavské náměstí (phone: 242-28119). Note: The café is inexpensive.

**Florianův Dvůr** Fresco-adorned walls and stained glass contribute to the atmosphere, while the exquisitely prepared French fare delights the palate. The health-conscious menu features lamb, rabbit, fresh fish, and nouvelle cuisine. The fresh salads are a treat, and the wine cellar, stocked with fine French and Moravian wines, comes highly recommended. Reservations advised. Major credit cards accepted. 16 Ujezd (phone: 530502).

**Opera Grill** Convenient to the *National Theater,* it serves excellent traditional Czech food and boasts a fine wine cellar. After dinner a specialty is brandy served in a giant crystal snifter. Open daily for dinner only. Reservations necessary. Major credit cards accepted.

35 Karolíny Světlé (another entrance at 24 Divadelní; phone: 265508).

**Parnas** Also near the *National Theater,* this former 1920s jazz club offers live piano music, romantic views of the Vltava River and *Prague Castle,* and excellent food and service. Specialties include Norwegian salmon and Czech roast duck as well as pasta dishes. The *crème caramel* is not to be missed for dessert. Open daily. Reservations necessary. Major credit cards accepted. 2 Smetanovo nábřeží (phone: 242-27614).

**Principe** This excellent dining spot, popular with businesspeople, is authentically Italian; even the menu is written in that language. Specialties include lasagna, veal scaloppine, steaks with green peppercorns and cream, and other favorites. The ambience is cheerful and contemporary, and the service is good. There's a garden for summer dining. Open daily. Reservations necessary. American Express accepted. 23 Anglická (phone: 259614).

**Reykjavík** Not far from the Charles Bridge, this nautical-style place offers some of the best seafood in Prague. Owned by a Scandinavian expatriate, its specialty is excellently prepared salmon. Other dishes include creatively prepared vegetarian platters. One of the city's liveliest spots, the bar is crowded with folks waiting for tables. Open daily. No reservations. Major credit cards accepted. 20-180 Karlova (phone: 265776).

**Svatá Klára (St. Clare)** Three hundred years ago Count Václav Vojtěch spent his evenings in the wine cellar of his Baroque château. Today foreign diplomats and others in the know frequent this *vinárna.* It's cozier now than it was in the count's day, with its fireplace, fine service, accomplished cuisine, and selection of Moravian wines. Specialties range from fondue *bourguignon* to *palačinky* (crêpes) *flambé,* a classic Czech dessert. Open weekdays for dinner only. Reservations necessary. No credit cards accepted. 9 U Trojského zámku (phone: 664-10405).

**U Labutí (At the Swans)** It's hard to believe that this dining spot right on Castle Square once was home to the steeds of the local princes. The royal stables have been transformed into a charming eatery with old-fashioned nooks, vaulted ceilings, and window casings dating from the 14th century. The service is excellent, and the Czech specialties are superb. Game dishes are featured, and venison prepared with a variety of sauces is a specialty. The Bohemian plate, which includes several different types of meat, is also quite good. Open daily for dinner only. Reservations necessary. Major credit cards accepted. 11 Hradčanské náměstí (phone: 539476).

**U Malířů (At the Painters)** A combination of 16th-century decor and 20th-century culinary expertise makes this restaurant, a Franco-Czech venture opened five years ago, one of the finest dining experiences in Prague. The superbly prepared, French-style dishes are pleasingly authentic, thanks to weekly deliveries of lobsters, asparagus, truffles, and other luxuries from Parisian markets. There's also a choice selection of French wines. This is one of the most expensive places in town, but the memorable meals are worth every koruna. Closed Sundays. Reservations necessary. Major credit cards accepted. 11 Maltézské náměstí. (phone: 245-10269).

**U Mecenáše (At the Art Patron's)** A small, medieval-style wine restaurant, it has vaulted ceilings, comfortable booths, and a cozy, romantic atmosphere. Political types such as German Chancellor Helmut Kohl have dined in the elegant Queen Anne–style back room. The fare is quite good, particularly the beef and pork dishes; there's also game, duck, and goose. Open daily for dinner only. Reservations necessary. Major credit cards accepted. 10 Malostranské náměstí, next to *St. Nicholas Church* (phone: 533881).

**U Modré Kachničky (At the Blue Duck)** Featuring an eclectic Art Nouveau decor, this Malá Strana restaurant is one of Prague's most romantic. Service is gracious and the food—venison, boar, rabbit, and pheasant—divine. Open daily. Reservations advised. Major credit cards accepted. 6 Nebovidská (phone: 203822).

**U Pavouka (At the Spider)** Vaulted ceilings and wood-paneled rooms add to the charm here. When the elegant dining room is full, as it usually is, ask to be seated in the beautifully appointed cocktail area. Classic Czech and continental dishes are served; try the "Goulash Spider" (beef in cheese sauce, flambéed with brandy). A snack bar and a garden restaurant offer a separate menu of traditional Czech dishes. Open daily. Reservations necessary. Major credit cards accepted. In the courtyard of 17 Celetná (phone: 248-11436).

**U Zlaté Hrušky (At the Golden Pear)** Set in an 18th-century house near *Prague Castle,* this small, charming eatery is popular with tourists. Game dishes are the specialty here, but the beefsteak in wine sauce is delicious. Open daily. Reservations necessary. Major credit cards accepted. 3 Nový Svět (phone: 531133).

**U Zlatého Rožně (At the Golden Skewer)** A favorite of people associated with the foreign embassies nearby, it has an eclectic menu of cuisines—from Icelandic fish to Chinese and Czech specialties—all superbly prepared. Try the chicken with pineapple and almonds or the broiled salmon. Open daily. Reservations necessary. American Express accepted. 22 Ceské armády (phone: 243-11161).

**Vinárna v Zátiší** Located between Old Town Square and the Charles Bridge, this restaurant run by an Englishman specializes in roast beef, salmon, and other international dishes. Popular with businesspeople are the fixed-price lunches and dinners. Open daily. Reservations necessary. No credit cards accepted. 1 Liliová on Betlémské náměstí (phone: 242-28977).

**Zlatá Praha (Golden Prague)** Good Czech and international fare and a spectacular view of *Prague Castle* are the attractions at this elegant dining room atop the *Inter-Continental* hotel. Open daily. Reservations necessary. Major credit cards accepted. 5 Náměstí Curieových (phone: 248-81111).

**Myslivna (Hunting Lodge)** True to its name, this eatery specializes in well-prepared game—venison, boar, hare, pheasant, and duck—from the Bohemian woods. The quail is a must. Open daily. Reservations necessary. Major credit cards accepted. 21 Jagellonská, Vinohrady (phone: 627-0209).

**Nebozízek (The Little Auger)** The funicular from Ujezd in the Malá Strana takes diners to this pleasant restaurant in a park facing *Prague Castle.* It offers good Czech specialties, Chinese dishes, and seafood. Open daily. Reservations necessary. Major credit cards accepted. 411 Petřínské sady (phone: 537905).

**Palace Hotel Cafeteria** This upscale spot has a good salad bar, making it a lifesaver for vegetarians and a refreshing change for everyone else. Open daily. Reservations unnecessary. Major credit cards accepted. 12 Panská (phone: 240-93111).

**Penguin's** A bit out of central Prague, this modern, elegant dining place serves continental and Czech fare and some of the freshest vegetables in town. The turtle soup is authentic, and the steaks are first-rate. A popular spot for local artists and sports figures. Open daily. Reservations advised. Major credit cards accepted. 5 Zborovská (phone: 545660).

**Sumická Vinárna** In addition to the Moravian wine that you can order by the carafe, this well-run wine cellar serves traditional pork, beef, and veal dishes. The background Gypsy music adds to the enjoyment. Open daily. Reservations advised. Major credit cards accepted. 12 Mikulandská (phone: 291568).

**U Cerveného Kola (At the Red Wheel)** It may take some effort to find this small spot, located in an open courtyard, and even more to get in, since it is always crowded—but it is well worth the trouble. Steaks are a specialty, and the chicken is superb. Open daily. Reservations unnecessary. Major credit cards accepted. 2 Anežská (phone: 248-11118).

**U Cížků (At the Bluebird's)** Popular with the business crowd and with tour groups, this classic Bohemian restaurant serves good and hearty portions of Czech staples. Try the pork with three kinds of dumplings. Open daily. Reservations necessary. Major credit cards accepted. 34 Karlovo náměstí (phone: 298891).

**U Dlouhé** The brightly lit, wood-paneled *pivnice* (beer hall) upstairs and cozy, vaulted *vinárna* (wine bar) downstairs offer the visitor the best of both worlds. The management pays special attention to details, from the charming, 1920s-style menu to the friendly attitude of the waiters. Czech specialties are a highlight of the menu, including thick potato soup and the *posvícenská mísa,* a combination of duck and corned beef with bread and bacon dumplings. Rabbit prepared several ways tops the game menu, and a garden plate is available for vegetable fans. Open daily. Reservations advised. Major credit cards accepted. 35 Dlouhá (phone: 321-6125).

**U Kalicha (The Chalice)** A popular pilsner beer hall and restaurant, which is disappointingly modern in character (but full of literary allusions). This is where Good Soldier Svejk, a character in a series of novels by Jaroslav Hašek, arranged to meet his World War I buddies "at 6 o'clock after the war." Terrific Czech dishes are served. Open daily. Reservations advised. Major credit cards accepted. 12 Na bojišti (phone: 290701).

**U Modré Růže (At the Blue Rose)** A small restaurant with a cozy, romantic atmosphere featuring game and fish. Specialties include the rabbit stuffed with spinach and the Norwegian salmon. Open daily. Reservations advised. Major credit cards accepted. 16 Rytířská (phone: 263886).

**U Sedmi Andělů (At the Seven Angels)** This Old Town eatery is furnished in a spare and elegant style—with a Baroque accent. Try the *síp amorův,* a specialty platter of grilled meat. Folk music nightly. Closed Sundays. No reservations. Major credit cards accepted. 20 Jilská (phone: 260104).

**U Zelené Záby (At the Green Frog)** The quiet atmosphere is perfect for talking and drinking at this wine cellar housed in a building more than eight centuries old. The house specialty is grilled meat with sauerkraut. Open daily. Reservations necessary. No credit cards accepted. 8 U Radnice (phone: 242-28133).

**Vinárna u Maltézských Rytířu (Wine Tavern at the Knights of Malta)** Located in a former hospice of the Knights of Malta religious order (it was also a dance hall after World War I), this cozy, Renaissance-style wine cellar with only three tables and eight bar stools serves delicately prepared Czech and international dishes. You also can dine in one of the two simple saloons that seat about 30. Open daily. Reservations advised. Major credit cards accepted. 10 Prokopská (phone: 536357).

### INEXPENSIVE

**Café Nouveau** As you sip your frothy cappuccino, take in the Jugenstil murals, ironwork, and stylized light fixtures of this café in the famed *Obecní Dům* (Municipal House). The service is a mite slow, but no one cares if you sit and read a newspaper for hours. In the evening relax to the soothing sounds of the jazz quartet or classical combo, or sit upstairs in the bar to take in the view. Croissant sandwiches, pasta dishes, and a wide variety of fresh salads comprise the menu. Open daily. No reservations or credit cards accepted. 5 Náměstí republiky (phone: 248-11057).

**Kmotra (The Godfather)** Pizza served in a relaxed atmosphere plus steaks and helpings from the salad bar. Try the house pizza specialty, *kmotra.* There is a café upstairs. Open daily. No reservations or credit cards accepted. 12 V Jirchářích (phone: 249-15809).

**Mikulka's Pizzeria** This small eatery with great pizza is a favorite with Americans. Also try the pasta, ice cream, and cappuccino. Open daily. Reservations unnecessary. No credit cards accepted. 16 Benediktská (phone: 231-5727).

**Saté Grill** Conveniently located near *Prague Castle,* this small, simple grill serves Indonesian specialties, including *satay,* noodles, and salad. It's a popular place for lunch. Open daily. Reservations unnecessary. No credit cards accepted. 3 Pohořelec (phone: 532113).

**U Cerného Slunce (At the Black Sun)** In an alley right off Old Town Square, this 17th-century wine cellar offers atmospheric decor and good, simple dishes made from pork, chicken, and beef. Open daily. Reservations necessary. No credit cards accepted. 9 Kamzíková (phone: 242-24746).

**U Cerveného Raka (At the Red Lobster)** A small, pretty place for lunch or dinner, its international menu includes steaks, seafood, lobster and shrimp cocktails, and a variety of desserts. Open daily. No reservations or credit cards accepted. 30 Karlova (phone: 265538).

**U Fleků (Fleck's Inn)** One of Prague's most famous old pubs (no one knows quite how old it is, but it was in existence in 1499), it specializes in strong, dark beer (probably the best brew you'll ever quaff) and good goulash. A huge place, filled with music and guests who love to sing along, it's a favorite among Germans and other tourists. Open daily. Reservations advised. Major credit cards accepted. 11 Křemencová (phone: 249-15119).

**U Pavlice** A cheery, traditional tavern serving hearty fare and robust brews. Open daily. Reservations unnecessary. No credit cards accepted. 1 Fügnerovo náměstí (phone: 290373).

**U Radnice (At the Town Hall)** Under the arcades just southeast of Old Town Square, this typical beer cellar caters to businesspeople at lunch and dinner. Though not a full-fledged restaurant, it serves one of the best duck dinners in town. Open daily. Reservations unnecessary. No credit cards accepted. 2 Malé náměstí (phone: 242-28136).

**U Sv. Tomáše** Prague's oldest beer hall—a large vaulted room with wooden tables, lots of students, and huge steins of beer. The best dish is a plate of pork, sauerkraut, and dumplings. Open daily. Reservations unnecessary. No credit cards accepted. 12 Letenská (phone: 531632).

**U Zeleného Caje (At the Green Tea House)** This charming tea house near *Prague Castle* serves 60 different blends of tea and coffee as well as baked goods. For nonsmokers only. Open daily. No reservations or credit cards accepted. 19 Nerudová (phone: 532683).

**Vltava** Located on a bank of the river, this place offers excellent fish and a great view of *Prague Castle* and the Vltava from its patio. The Czech menu boasts a fairly wide variety of beef, pork, and chicken dishes. Open daily. Reservations unnecessary. No credit cards accepted. 2 Rašínovo nábřeží (phone: 294964).

# Rome

## At-a-Glance

### SEEING THE CITY

The magnificent overview of Rome and the surrounding hill towns from Piazzale Garibaldi at the top of Monte Gianicolo (Janiculum Hill) is best at sunset. There's another splendid panorama from the dome of the *Basilica di San Pietro.* For a view of Rome dominated by the basilica, go to the Colle del Pincio (Pincio Hill), next to the *Villa Borghese,* above Piazza del Popolo. To see the city and the basilica from an unusual angle, look through the keyhole in the gate to the priory of the *Cavalieri di Malta* (Knights of Malta), at Piazza dei Cavalieri di Malta on Monte Aventino (Aventine Hill).

### SPECIAL PLACES

Rome cannot be seen in a day, a week, or even a year. If your time is limited to a few days, an organized tour is your best bet (see *Getting Around*). After your organized excursion grab a pair of comfortable walking shoes and a map and explore on your own. The ancient center of the city is very close to Piazza Venezia, the heart of the modern city, making Rome delightfully walkable.

The "must sees" below are organized under the headings "Ancient Rome," "Papal Rome," and "Modern Rome," with a separate section on "Piazze, Palazzi, and Other Sights." Elements of all categories often are found in one location, however. A bit of trivia: The initials "SPQR," seen on buildings throughout the city, stand for *Senatus Populus que Romanus* (Senate and People of Rome). They've been used since ancient times to indicate public structures.

Most museums, monuments, and archaeological sites run by the state or city are closed on Sunday afternoons, and many close Mondays as well. Also, many attractions close for a two- to four-hour break in the afternoons. Because of ongoing strikes and personnel shortages, opening and closing hours change often. The numerous restorations under way mean that some museums are closed and others have only limited displays. Check with your hotel, the *Ente Provinciale per il Turismo* (*EPT;* Provincial Tourist Office), or the daily newspapers before starting out. The *EPT* (see *Tourist Information*) publishes an annual pamphlet in four languages with information on Rome's museums and monuments, including addresses, phone numbers, and schedules. Where possible, we have listed operating schedules that seem relatively reliable.

*Warning:* Pickpockets work all around the city, but are especially busy on such bus lines as the No. 56 to Via Veneto and Nos. 62, 64, and 492 to the *Vatican,* and at the most popular tourist spots, even though plainclothes police scour these areas. Beware of gangs of children who may surround you and make straight for your wallet or purse. They haunt the Tiber bridges, the *Colosseo,* and the quay-side walk to the *Porta Portese.* On Via del Corso, carry your shoulder bag on the arm *away* from passing vehicular traffic to avoid bag snatchers on motor scooters. Do not hang purses on *caffè* or restaurant chairs. Avoid carrying your passport and any significant amount of money, and be sure to store valuables in a hotel safe-deposit box.

## ANCIENT ROME

**COLOSSEO (COLOSSEUM)** The grandest and most celebrated of all Rome's monuments, this amphitheater is a logical starting point for a tour of ancient Rome. The enormous arena, one-third of a mile in circumference and 137 feet high, was built between AD 72 and 81. At the time, 50,000 spectators regularly would pack the stadium for an afternoon of gory fun. Hundreds of professional gladiators did battle to the death and numerous unarmed condemned criminals wrestled hungry lions here; on state occasions the *Colosseo* was flooded and naval battles staged. Gladiatorial contests were held here until 404; animal combats were stopped toward the middle of the 6th century. The *Colosseo* was abused by later generations. It was a fort in the Middle Ages, and Renaissance construction workers regularly chopped away at the structure when they needed marble for the *Basilica di San Pietro* and assorted palazzi, destroying a large chunk of the outer wall. Buttresses were erected by Pius VIII (1800–23) to keep the structure from caving in on itself. Later, the luxuriant vegetation (420 exotic species that prompted two books on the *Colosseo*'s flora and countless rhapsodies by Dickens, Byron, and other famous writers) was entirely weeded out. The floor was then excavated to reveal the locker rooms underneath—with separate but equal facilities for lions and men.

The lions have long since been replaced by stray cats, but the allure of the structure is as strong as ever. Visitors instinctively appreciate the genius of the engineers who found a way to erect such a gigantic structure on marshy ground, and who designed it so that immense and often rowdy crowds could enter and exit with ease through its 80 doors. Now in the midst of being restored, it remains the very symbol of Rome's grandeur. It's easy to understand why Romans said that should the *Colosseo* fall, Rome—and the world—would follow. Closed Wednesday and Sunday afternoons. Admission charge to the upper level. Piazzale del Colosseo.

**MONTE PALATINO (PALATINE HILL)** Adjacent to the *Colosseo* and the *Foro Romano* (Roman Forum), the Palatine Hill is where Rome began. The Emperors of Rome subsequently built their palaces here, turning the hill into an imperial preserve (its Latin name is the source of the word "palace"). Other great men—including Cicero, Crassus, and Mark Antony—also lived here. In ruins by the Middle Ages, the ancient structures were incorporated into the sumptuous *Villa Farnese* in the 16th century, and the *Orti Farnesiani* (Farnese Gardens) were laid out, the first botanical gardens in the world.

The Palatine Hill is a lovely spot for a walk or a picnic, offering fine views of ancient and modern Rome. Fields of flowers are

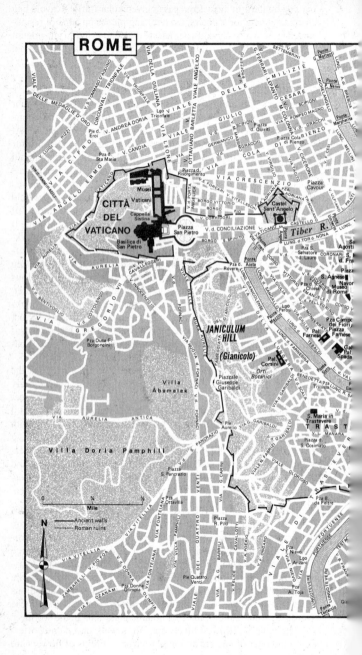

# ROME

CITTÀ DEL VATICANO

Musei Vaticani

Cappella Sistina

Piazza San Pietro

Basilica di San Pietro

Castel Sant'Angelo

Tiber R.

JANICULUM HILL (Gianicolo)

Villa Abamelek

Villa Doria Pamphili

Orti Botanici

Pal. Corsini

Piazzale Giuseppe Garibaldi

Pal. Farnese

Pal. Spada

Gal. Pal. Spada

S. Maria in Trastevere

TRAST

Piazza d. S. Cosimato

Piazza S. Pancrazio

Piazza Ottavilla

Piazza R. Pilo

Ple Quattro Venti

0 ¼ ½
Mile

N
— Ancient walls
···· Roman ruins

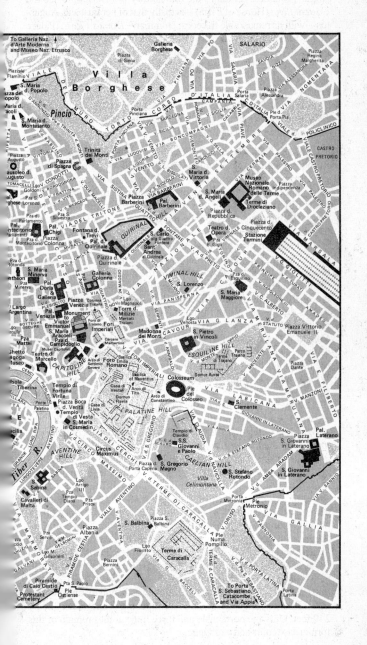

scattered with ruins of the luxurious villas that once covered most of the hill. They stand next to the foundations of the mud huts where Rome's founders settled in the 8th century BC. Be sure to see the *Casa di Livia* (House of Livia)—actually that of her husband, Augustus—with its remarkable frescoes; Domitian's *Domus Flavia* (Palace of the Flavians), designed by his favorite architect, Rabirius; the impressive stadium; the view from the terrace of the *Palazzo di Settimio Severo* (Palace of Septimius Severus); and the remains of the *Orti Farnesiani* at the top, with another superb panorama of the nearby *Foro Romano* and *Fori Imperiali* (Imperial Forums). Closed Tuesday and Sunday afternoons. Admission charge includes the *Foro Romano*. Enter at Via di San Gregorio or by way of the *Foro Romano* on Via dei Fori Imperiali.

**FORO ROMANO (ROMAN FORUM)** Following in the footsteps of early Romans, climb down from the Palatine Hill to the low area that grew from a meeting ground of hilltop tribes into the commercial, civil, and religious center of ancient Rome. Actually made up of many different forums, it was once an agglomeration of open-air markets, shopping malls, public meeting spots, and large ceremonial structures, including three triumphal arches, two public halls, half a dozen temples, and numerous monuments and statues. Along its Via Sacra, Julius Caesar returned from the wars in triumphal processions, and at its *Rostra* (Platform), Mark Antony harangued the crowd after Caesar was killed. Still embedded in the floor of the *Basilica Emilia* (Aemilian Basilica) are the coins that melted in fires during the sack of Rome in the 5th century. During the Middle Ages the forum was covered with dirt and garbage and called *Campo Vaccino* (Cow Field); when excavations began in the 19th century, a good deal of it was 20 feet underground. Today much of the forum lies beneath the roaring traffic of Via dei Fori Imperiali. What is left is a white, open jungle of fallen columns and headless statues.

Highlights today include the triumphal *Arco di Settimio Severo* (Arch of Septimius Severus), built by that emperor in AD 203; the *Arco di Tito* (Arch of Titus), adorned with scenes depicting his victories; the *Tempio di Antonino e Faustina* (Temple of Antoninus and Faustina), with its 10 magnificent marble columns—and a 16th-century Baroque façade; the eight columns of the *Tempio di Saturno* (Temple of Saturn), which was built in 497 BC and was the site of the *Saturnalia,* the precursor of our *Mardi Gras;* three splendid Corinthian columns of the *Tempio di Castore e Polluce* (Temple of Castor and Pollux), erected in 484 BC; and the *Tempio di Vesta* (Temple of Vesta) and the nearby *Casa delle Vestali* (House of the Vestal Virgins), where highly esteemed women guarded the sacred flame of Vesta and their virginity. The *Basilica di Massenzio* (Basilica of Maxentius)—otherwise known as the *Basilica di Constantino* (Basilica of Constantine) because it was begun by one emperor and finished by the other)—still has imposing proportions: 328 by 249 feet. Only the north aisle and three huge arches remain of this former law court and exchange.

As this is one of the city's most bewildering archaeological sites, a guide is extremely useful, especially for short-term visitors. A detailed plan and portable taped tour (in English) are available at the entrance. Keep in mind that this neighborhood becomes extremely hot at midday in summer. Closed Tuesday and Sunday afternoons. Admission charge includes *Monte Palatino*. Entrance on Via dei Fori Imperiali, opposite Via Cavour.

**FORI IMPERIALI (IMPERIAL FORUMS)** Next to the *Foro Romano* and now divided in two by Via dei Fori Imperiali is the civic center begun by Caesar to meet the demands of the expanding city when the *Foro Romano* became too congested. It was completed by Augustus, with further additions by later emperors, and abandoned in the Middle Ages. Sections of the *Fori Imperiali* were excavated by Mussolini, who then partially paved them over when he constructed Via dei Fori Imperiali in 1932.

Two of the major sights of this area are a forum and a market built by Emperor Trajan. Although the *Foro di Traiano* (Trajan's Forum) is not open to visitors, it can be seen either from the side-walk that surrounds it or from the market. It's noteworthy for the formidable 138-foot-high *Colonna Traiana* (Trajan's Column), composed of 19 blocks of marble. The column is decorated with a spiral frieze depicting the Roman army under Trajan during the campaign against the Dacians. Some 2,500 figures appear to be climbing toward the top where, since 1588, a statue of St. Peter has stood instead of the original one of Trajan. The market (entered at 94 Via IV Novembre) is a three-story construction that once housed about 150 shops and commercial exchanges. Now it is mostly empty, with terraces and huge vaulted rooms where the city's supplies of wheat and olive oil were once stored. However, it is still worth a look. Closed Mondays. Admission charge for *Mercati Traiani* (Trajan's Market). Entrance to the forums is on Via XXIV Maggio.

**CARCERE MAMERTINO (MAMERTINE PRISON)** Just off Via dei Fori Imperiali between the *Foro Romano* and the *Campidoglio* (City Hall) is the prison where the Gallic rebel leader Vercingetorix died and where, according to legend, St. Peter was imprisoned by Nero and used a miraculous spring to baptize his fellow inmates. From 509 to 27 BC it was a state prison where many were tortured and slaughtered. Much later the prison became a chapel called *San Pietro in Carcere*. The gloomy dungeons below, made of enormous stone blocks, are among the oldest structures in Rome. Open daily, with a short closing (12:30 to 2 PM). Admission charge. Via San Pietro in Carcere off Via dei Fori Imperiali.

**CIRCO MASSIMO (CIRCUS MAXIMUS)** A few ruins dot the open grassy valley that once was the site of the great 4th-century BC arena. Originally one-third of a mile long and big enough to accommodate 250,000 spectators, the horseshoe-shaped racetrack was the model for later Roman circuses. The obelisks that once decorated a long central dais here are now in Rome's Piazza del Laterano and Piazza del Popolo. The medieval tower is one of the few remains of the great fortresses built by the Frangipane family. Behind the Palatine Hill.

**PANTHEON** This best-preserved ancient Roman building, sometimes called *La Rotonda,* was founded in 27 BC by Agrippa, who probably dedicated it to the seven planetary divinities, and was rebuilt by Hadrian in AD 125. It became a Christian church in 606 and contains the tombs of Raphael and the first two Kings of Italy. The building is remarkable for its circular plan combined with a Greek-style rectangular porch of 16 Corinthian columns, for the masterful engineering of its immense dome (which is wider than that of the *Basilica di San Pietro*), and for its balanced proportions (the diameter of the interior and the height of the dome are the same). Closed Mondays. No admission charge. Piazza della Rotonda.

**TERME DI CARACALLA (BATHS OF CARACALLA)** This grandiose tribute to the human body was built on 27 acres by Emperor Caracalla in the 3rd century AD. Each of the sunken, mosaic-covered floors visible today was the bottom of a single, huge pool. Each of the pools was heated to a different temperature by an elaborate underground central-heating system, and the whole complex was open to the public. For a nominal fee, the citizens of Rome could pass from tub to tub, soaking in the steaming water of the circular *caldarium,* rubbing elbows with friends in the *tepidarium,* and talking brisk business in the *frigidarium.* Changing rooms, dry steamrooms, gymnasiums, a snack bar, and a library flanked the pool rooms. Located in the southern part of the city, near the beginning of Via Appia Antica, what's left are sunbaked walls and some wall paintings, but the vast scale makes a picturesque ruin. Closed Sunday and Monday afternoons. Admission charge. Enter on Viale delle Terme di Caracalla, just short of Piazzale Numa Pompilio.

**MURA DI ROMA ANTICA (ANCIENT ROMAN WALLS)** Set in the 3rd-century *Mura Aureliane* (Aurelian Walls), which snake around the city for 12 miles, the magnificent gates at the *Porta San Sebastiano* mark the beginning of Via Appia Antica (see below). They were rebuilt in the 5th century and restored again in the 6th century. Every Sunday morning guided walks (in Italian only) are conducted along the walls from the ancient Roman wall to *Porta Latina,* affording good views of the *Terme di Caracalla,* Via Appia Antica, and the Alban Hills in the distance. The *Museo delle Mura* (Museum of the Walls), housed within two medieval towers of the gate, contains local archaeological finds. Closed Mondays as well as Sunday, Wednesday, and Friday afternoons; the museum closes for an afternoon break (1:50 to 4 PM) on Tuesdays, Thursdays, and Saturdays. Admission charge. 18 *Porta San Sebastiano* (phone: 704-75284).

**VIA APPIA ANTICA (APPIAN WAY)** Portions of this famous 2,300-year-old road are still paved with the well-laid stones of the Romans. By 190 BC the Via Appia Antica extended all the way from Rome to Italy's southeastern coast. Although its most famous sights are the *Catacombe di San Callisto* (see below), many other interesting ruins are scattered along the first 10 miles (16 km) of the route. Via Appia

Antica was used as a graveyard by patrician families because Roman law forbade burial within the city walls. Among the sights worth seeing is the *Chiesa di Santa Maria in Palmis,* better known as the *Domine Quo Vadis Chapel,* about a half mile beyond *Mura di Roma Antica.* It was built in the mid-9th century on the site where (according to legend) St. Peter, fleeing from Nero, had a vision of Christ. St. Peter said, "*Domine quo vadis?*" ("Lord, whither goest thou?"). Christ replied that he was going back to Rome to be crucified again because Peter had abandoned the Christians in a moment of danger. Peter then returned to Rome to face his own martyrdom. The marble-lined *Tomba di Cecilia Metella* (Tomb of Cecilia Metella), where the daughter of a Roman general is buried, is a very picturesque ruin not quite 2 miles (3 km) from *Mura di Roma Antica.* The tomb is closed Sunday and Monday afternoons. No admission charge. From here a bus will take you back to the center of Rome.

**CATACOMBE DI SAN CALLISTO (CATACOMBS OF ST. CALIXTUS)** Of all the catacombs in Rome, these are the most famous. Catacombs are burial places in the form of galleries, or tunnels—miles of them, arranged in as many as five tiers—carved underground. Marble or terra cotta slabs mark the openings where the bodies were laid to rest. Early pagans, Jews, and Christians prayed and were buried in the catacombs from the 1st through the 4th centuries. After Christianity became the official religion of Rome, the catacombs became places of pilgrimage because they contained the remains of so many early martyrs, including St. Cecilia, St. Eusebius, and many popes (though these remains were later moved to churches for safekeeping). Take a guided bus tour or a public bus. At the catacombs guides (who are often priests) conduct regular tours in English. Closed Wednesdays and for an afternoon break (noon to 2:30 PM). Admission charge. 110 Via Appia Antica.

**BASILICA DI SAN CLEMENTE (BASILICA OF ST. CLEMENT)** This basilica is one of Rome's most complex buildings, a physical testimony to the city's long history. Beneath this 12th-century structure near the *Colosseo* are a frescoed church and vestiges of several other buildings, including a 1st-century Mithraic temple dedicated to Apollo (the Roman sun god) and a house where early Christians worshiped. The church was built in the 4th century after Emperor Constantine put an end to the persecution of Christians. Open daily, with a midday closing (noon to 3:30 PM). Admission charge to the below-ground areas. On the corner of Via San Giovanni Laterano and Piazza San Clemente (phone: 704-51018).

**ANTIQUITIES MUSEUMS** West of the city center, not far from the train station, are three neighboring museums which among them display a great number of Rome's splendid antiquities. The first museum is set in the *Terme di Diocleziano* (Baths of Diocletian; 79 Via Enrico de Nicola; phone: 488-0530), which were the largest baths in the empire, built in AD 305 to hold 3,000 people. The site now houses the *Chiesa di Santa Maria degli Angeli* (Church of St. Mary of the Angels), adapted by Michelangelo from the hall of the baths' *tep-*

*idarium.* Although part of the museum is presently closed, visitors can view much of its impressive collection, including the *Trono Ludovisi* (Ludovisi Throne), a finely carved marble throne belonging to an aristocratic family prominent during the Renaissance; tour the *Chiostro Grande* (Great Cloister), which also was designed by Michelangelo; and stroll through the 16th-century gardens. The museum is closed Mondays and afternoons. Admission charge.

Next door to the *Terme di Diocleziano,* on Piazza della Repubblica, is *Il Planetario* (The Planetarium), a brick Roman rotunda (built around AD 300) that houses about a dozen ancient marble and bronze statues of gods and goddesses as well as a splendid bronze figure of a gladiator. Formerly linked with the *Terme di Diocleziano,* the building served as a planetarium (hence the name) and then a movie theater until the 1980s. It's open daily. No admission charge (no phone).

The third antiquities museum is the new *Museo Nazionale Romano* (National Museum of Rome), which is scheduled to open early this year. Set in the huge, bright pink *Palazzo Massimo,* across from *Il Planetario,* it contains a large number of historic artifacts and treasures, including a collection of Roman coins and several restored marble statues dating to the days of the Roman Empire. At press time its operating schedule was not yet determined; contact the tourist office (see *Tourist Information*) for an update. There's an admission charge. The museum is on Piazza dei Cinquecento, to the right of the *Stazione Termini* (Central Railway Station).

**CASTEL SANT'ANGELO** Dramatically facing the 2nd-century Ponte Sant' Angelo (St. Angelo Bridge)—lined with statues of angels (including two reproductions of originals by Bernini)—this imposing monument was built by Hadrian in AD 139 as a burial place for himself and his family (thus, it is also known as the *Tomba di Adriano*— Hadrian's Tomb). It has undergone many alterations, including the addition of the square wall with bastions at each corner named after the four evangelists. Later converted into a fortress and prison, the building has seen a lot of history: Popes took refuge here from antipapal forces (a secret passage connects it to the *Vatican*), some of the victims of the Borgias met their ends here, Benvenuto Cellini was imprisoned here for some time, and the last act of Puccini's opera *Tosca* takes place here. It is now a national museum containing relics, artworks, ancient weapons, a prison cell, and a restored 300-year-old papal bathroom with a tub. Closed Mondays and afternoons. Admission charge. Lungotevere Castello.

**TEATRO DI MARCELLO (THEATER OF MARCELLUS)** Begun by Julius Caesar, completed by Augustus, and named after the latter's nephew, this was the first stone theater in Rome and is said to have been the model for the *Colosseo.* It seated from 10,000 to 14,000 spectators and was in use for over 300 years. During the Middle Ages it became a fortress, and during the 16th century the Savelli family transformed it into a palace, which later passed to the powerful Orsini family. The sumptuous apartments at the top still are inhabited by the Orsinis, whose emblem, a bear *(orso),* adorns the gateway on

Via di Monte Savello, where the theater's stage once stood. Every summer a concert series is performed here in the evenings; contact the tourist office (see *Tourist Information*) for more details. The theater is closed to the public except during performances. Via del Teatro di Marcello.

**LARGO ARGENTINA** Just west of Piazza Venezia are the remains of four Roman temples, still unidentified, which are among the oldest ruins in Rome. Julius Caesar was assassinated nearby, in the *Teatro di Pompeo* (Pompey's Theater); the Senate was meeting here temporarily because of fire damage to the *Foro Romano*. The area is slated for much-needed restoration. Visits must be arranged in advance with the *Soprintendenza Comunale ai Monumenti Antichi* (Superintendent of Antiquities, Monuments, and Excavations; 29 Via del Portico d'Ottavia; phone: 671-02070). No admission charge. Corso Vittorio Emanuele II.

**PIRAMIDE DI CAIO CESTIO (PYRAMID OF GAIUS CESTIUS)** Rome's only pyramid is located in the southern part of the city, near the Protestant cemetery. Covered with white marble and 121 feet high, it contains a burial chamber decorated with frescoes and inscriptions. Piazzale Ostiense. The interior can be visited only with special permission from the *Soprintendenza Comunale ai Monumenti Antichi* (see above). No admission charge. Piazzale Ostiense.

PAPAL ROME

**CITTÀ DEL VATICANO (VATICAN CITY)** Vatican City, the world's second-smallest country (the smallest is also in Rome, the Sovereign Military Order of Malta, on Via Condotti), occupies less than 1 square mile within the city and is headquarters of the Roman Catholic church. An independent state under the sovereignty of the pope since the Lateran Treaties were concluded in 1929, the *Vatican* has its own newspaper *(Osservatore Romano)*, its own currency, railway, and radio station, as well as its own post office and stamps. (Since Italian post offices function so badly, do all your mailing from here. *Vatican* stamps may be used in Rome but not elsewhere in Italy, while Italian stamps may *not* be used in *Vatican* mailboxes. Souvenir packets of stamps can be purchased at the *Servizio Filatelico*—Philatelic Service—in the office building to the left of the *Basilica di San Pietro,* entered under the *Arco delle Campane*—Arch of the Bells.) The *Vatican*'s extraterritorial rights cover other major basilicas (such as *Basilica di Santa Maria Maggiore* and the *Chiesa di San Giovanni in Laterano*—see below for both), the pope's summer home at *Castel Gandolfo,* and a few other buildings. Vatican City is governed politically by the pope and protected by an army of Swiss Guards (formed in 1506 by Pope Julius II), whose uniforms were designed by Raphael. The *Vatican*'s central telephone number is 6982; most of its operators speak English.

General audiences are held by the pope every Wednesday at 10 or 11 AM, usually in the *Sala Nervi* (Nervi Auditorium), within the *Vatican* walls. Special audiences can be arranged for groups of 25 to 50 persons. Given John Paul II's propensity for travel, however, it is a good idea to check on his whereabouts before trekking off to see him. To arrange for free tickets to papal audiences, write to Bishop Dino Monduzzi (*Prefettura della Casa Pontificia,* Città del Vaticano 00120, Italy). Be sure to include your address in Rome. Reservations will be confirmed by mail before the audience, but tickets will be delivered by messenger the day before. Last-minute bookings (space permitting) can be made in person on Mondays and Tuesdays from 9 AM to noon at the *Prefettura* office, located at the bronze doors of the right wing of the colonnade of Piazza San Pietro. Tickets also are available through the *North American College* (30 Via dell'Umiltà; no phone) and the *Chiesa di Santa Susanna* (Church of St. Susan; 14 Via XX Settembre; phone: 482-7510).

Guided tours in English of Vatican City's underground excavations, the gardens, and the *Cappella Sistina* (Sistine Chapel) are offered daily year-round. Sign up at the *Ufficio Scavi* (Excavations Office; near the *Arco delle Campane;* phone: 698-85318) for a 90-minute tour of the pre-Constantine necropolis in the *Vatican,* where it is believed that St. Peter is buried. You can also see a wall of the original, smaller medieval church (closed Sundays; admission charge). Book a tour of the gardens at the *Ufficio Informazioni* (Vatican Tourist Information Office; see *Tourist Information*). Tours are offered daily (except Wednesdays and Sundays) at around 10 AM. There's an admission charge. Ask at the information office about guided tours of the *Cappella Sistina* (or make prior arrangements for a group visit through a travel agency). The tourist office also can arrange visits to the famous *Laboratorio del Mosaico* (Vatican Mosaic Workshop), where students have been making miniature and full-size mosaic pictures for centuries.

**PIAZZA SAN PIETRO (ST. PETER'S SQUARE)** This 17th-century architectural masterpiece was created by Gian Lorenzo Bernini, the foremost practitioner of the Baroque style in Rome. The vast, open, elliptical area is framed by two colonnades, each four deep in Doric columns, leading to the façade of the *Basilica di San Pietro* (see below). Atop the colonnades are statues of saints. An 83½-foot obelisk, shipped from Heliopolis, Egypt, to Rome by Caligula, marks the center of the square and is flanked by two fountains that are still fed by the nearly 400-year-old *Acqua Paola* aqueduct. Find the circular paving stone between the obelisk and one of the fountains and turn toward a colonnade: From this vantage point it will appear to be only a single row of columns.

**BASILICA DI SAN PIETRO (ST. PETER'S BASILICA)** The first church here was built by Constantine on the site where it is believed St. Peter was martyred and subsequently buried. Some 11 centuries later the church was totally reconstructed. Michelangelo deserves a great deal of the credit for the existing church, but not all of it: Bramante began the plans in the early 16th century, with the dome of the *Pantheon* in mind; Michelangelo finished the plans in mid-century, thinking of Brunelleschi's dome on the *Duomo* in Florence. Giacomo della Porta took over the project at Michelangelo's death, actually raising the dome by the end of the century. In the early 17th century Carlo Maderno made some modifications to the structure and completed the façade, and by the middle of the century Bernini was working on his colonnades.

The door farthest to the right of the portico is the Holy Door, opened and closed by the pope at the beginning and end of each *Jubilee Year,* usually only four times a century. (It was last opened in 1983.) The door farthest to the left is by the modern Italian sculptor Giacomo Manzù and dates from the 1960s. Among the treasures and masterpieces inside the basilica are the famous *Pietà* by Michelangelo (now encased in bulletproof glass since its mutilation and restoration in 1972); the *Baldacchino* by Bernini, a colossal, seven-story Baroque amalgam of architecture and decorative sculpture weighing 46 tons; and Arnolfo di Cambio's 13th-century statue of St. Peter, whose toes have been kissed smooth by the faithful. Also inside is the *Museo Storico* (Historical Museum; phone: 698-83410), which houses part of the *Vatican*'s treasures. The interior of the basilica is gigantic and so overloaded with decoration that it takes some time to get a sense of the whole. *Note:* Visitors must obey a strict dress code. Although casual clothing is permitted, shorts, miniskirts, and revealing tops are prohibited.

The vast dome can be seen from nearly everywhere in the city, just as the entire city is visible from the summit of the dome. Visitors may go up into the dome by elevator, then take a staircase to the top for a panoramic view of Rome or a bird's-eye view of the pope's backyard. The basilica, the dome, and the *Museo Storico* are open daily. Separate admission charges to the latter two. Piazza San Pietro.

**MUSEI VATICANI (VATICAN MUSEUMS)** The *Vatican*'s museum complex houses one of the most impressive collections in the world, embracing works of art of every epoch. It also contains some masterpieces created on the spot, foremost of which is the extraordinary *Cappella Sistina* (Sistine Chapel), with Michelangelo's Old Testament frescoes on the ceiling (painted from 1508 to 1512) and his *Last Judgment* on the altar wall (1534–41). The splendid $13-million restoration of the ceiling, a 10-year project involving the removal of centuries of soot, has revealed unexpected vibrancy in Michelangelo's colors. Air conditioning and lighting systems also have been installed in the chapel, and footnotes have been added to art histories. The second phase of the project—restoration of the *Last Judgment*—was completed last year, and other frescoes are in the process of being restored.

While Michelangelo was painting the ceiling of the chapel for Pope Julius II, the 25-year-old Raphael was working on the *Stanza della Segnatura* (Hall of the Signature), one of the magnificent *Raphael Rooms* commissioned by the same pope, which would occupy the painter until his death at the age of 37. Half of the rooms in the *Museo Gregorio Etrusco* (Gregorian-Etruscan Museum), which houses the *Vatican*'s Etruscan collection—including the famous *Tomba Regolini-Galassi* (Regolini-Galassi Tomb) from

Cerveteri, two Etruscan carts, and an extensive funereal dowry of pots, jewelry, and votive offerings—are now open to the public. The remaining rooms are still closed for renovation, and at press time no date had been set for reopening. Also part of the *Vatican* museum complex are the *Museo Pio-Clementino* (Pius-Clementinus Museum), containing Greco-Roman antiquities, including such marvelous statues as *Laocoön and His Sons* and the *Apollo Belvedere;* the *Pinacoteca* (Picture Gallery); the *Biblioteca* (Library); and the *Gregoriano-Profano* (Gregorian Profane), *Pio-Cristiano* (Christian), and *Missionario-Etnologico* (Missionary-Ethnological) sectors. Closed Sundays (except the last Sunday of the month), all Catholic holidays, and afternoons from October through June (except during *Easter* week). No admission charge on the last Sunday of the month. Entrance on Viale Vaticano (phone: 698-83333).

## CHIESA DI SAN GIOVANNI IN LATERANO (CHURCH OF ST. JOHN LATERAN)

Founded by Pope Melchiades in the 4th century, this is the cathedral of Rome—the pope's parish church, in effect. Over the centuries it has suffered barbarian vandalism, an earthquake, and several fires. Most recently it was the target of a terrorist bombing in 1993, which caused structural damage inside the courtyard. The interior of the church was largely rebuilt in the 17th century by Borromini, who maintained the 16th-century wooden ceiling. The principal façade belongs to the 18th century. Older sections are the lovely cloisters, dating from the 13th century, and the baptistry, which dates back to the time of Constantine. The adjoining *Palazzo di San Giovanni Laterano* was built in the 15th century on the site of an earlier palace, destroyed by fire, that had been the home of the popes from Constantine's day to the Avignon Captivity. A small museum houses a collection of papal robes, uniforms, coats of arms, and the original 1929 *Lateran Treaty,* which created the sovereign state of Vatican City and recognized Roman Catholicism as Italy's state religion. The church has reopened, but at press time the museum remained closed due to the damage sustained in the bombing; call for current information (phone: 698-86433). In front of the palace and church is the *Scala Santa* (Holy Staircase), traditionally believed to have come from the palace of Pontius Pilate in Jerusalem and to have been ascended by Christ at the time of the Passion. The 28 marble steps, climbed by worshipers on their knees, lead to the *Cappella di San Lorenzo* (Chapel of St. Lawrence; also known as the *Sancta Sanctorum*), once the popes' private chapel; while it's closed to the public, it is visible through the grating. In the piazza is the oldest obelisk in Rome. Piazza di San Giovanni in Laterano.

## BASILICA DI SANTA MARIA MAGGIORE (BASILICA OF ST. MARY MAJOR)

This 5th-century church, rebuilt in the 13th century, has an 18th-century façade and the tallest campanile in Rome. It has particularly interesting 5th-century mosaics and a ceiling that was, according to tradition, gilded with the first gold to arrive from the New World. Piazza di Santa Maria Maggiore.

**PIAZZA DEL CAMPIDOGLIO** The Capitoline, the smallest of the original seven hills, was the political and religious center of ancient Rome. In the 16th century Michelangelo designed the harmonious square seen today, with its delicate, star-patterned pavement. At the center is a copy of the magnificent 2nd-century bronze equestrian statue of Marcus Aurelius (the original is in the museum in the *Palazzo dei Conservatori*). The piazza is flanked on three sides by palaces: the *Palazzo Nuovo* and *Palazzo dei Conservatori* (Palace of the Magistrates)—facing each other and together making up the *Musei Capitolini* (Capitoline Museums)—and between the two, the *Palazzo Senatorio* (Senate Building), which houses officials of the municipal government. The *Musei Capitolini* (phone: 671-02475) are famous for their especially valuable collection of ancient sculptures, including the *Capitoline Venus,* the *Dying Gaul,* a bronze statue (known as the *Spinario*) of a boy removing a thorn from his foot, and the *Capitoline Wolf,* an Etruscan bronze to which Romulus and Remus were added during the Renaissance. Closed Sundays and Mondays. Admission charge.

**PIAZZA DI SPAGNA (SPANISH STEPS)** One of the most picturesque settings of 18th-century Rome was named after a palace that housed the Spanish Embassy to the Holy See. The famous Piazza di Spagna actually was built by the French to connect their quarter above with the Spanish area below. One of Rome's finest French churches, *Trinità dei Monti* (Holy Trinity on the Hill), hovers at the top of the 138 steps, as does an ancient obelisk placed there by Pius VI in 1789. At the bottom of the steps—which in the spring are covered with hundreds of pots of azaleas—is the *Fontana della Barcaccia* (Barcaccia Fountain), the oldest architectural feature of the square, believed to have been designed by either Pietro Bernini or his son, Gian Lorenzo.

Over the years the steps have become a meeting place for young people, crafts sellers, caricature sketchers, and musicians. The house where John Keats spent the last three months of his life and died, in February 1821, is on Piazza di Spagna at No. 26. It is now the *Keats-Shelley Memorial House,* a museum dedicated to the English Romantic poets, containing a library of more than 9,000 volumes of their works. Open weekdays, with a short closing (12:30 to 2:30 PM). Admission charge. 26 Piazza di Spagna (phone: 678-4235).

**VIA CONDOTTI** The Roman version of New York City's Fifth Avenue, this street is lined with the city's most exclusive shops, including *Gucci, Bulgari,* and *Ferragamo* (see *Shopping*). Only a few blocks long, it begins at the foot of Piazza di Spagna, ends at Via del Corso, and is a favorite street for window shopping and the ritual evening *passeggiata,* or promenade, since it is—like much of the area— pedestrians-only. Via Condotti's name derives from the water conduits built under it by Gregory XIII in the 16th century.

One of Via Condotti's landmarks is the famous *Caffè Greco,* long a hangout for Romans and foreigners (see *Bars and Caffès*).

Another noteworthy spot, at No. 68, is the smallest sovereign state in the world, consisting of one historic palazzo. If you peek into its charming courtyard, you'll see cars with license plates bearing the letters "SMOM" (Sovereign Military Order of Malta), denoting an order founded during the Crusades.

**PIAZZA DEL POPOLO** This semicircular plaza at the foot of Pincio Hill was designed in neoclassical style by Valadier between 1816 and 1820. At its center is the second-oldest obelisk in Rome, dating from the 13th century BC. Two twin-domed churches, *Santa Maria di Montesanto* (St. Mary of Montesanto) and *Santa Maria dei Miracoli* (St. Mary of the Miracles), face a ceremonial gate where Via Flaminia enters Rome. Next to the gate is the remarkable early-Renaissance *Chiesa di Santa Maria del Popolo* (Church of St. Mary of the People), containing two paintings by Caravaggio, sculptures by Bernini, and frescoes by Pinturicchio, among others. The piazza's two open-air *caffès, Rosati* and *Canova,* are favorite meeting places (see *Bars and Caffès*).

**PIAZZA NAVONA** This historic square, built on the site of Emperor Domitian's stadium, is a fine example of Roman Baroque. In the center is Bernini's fine *Fontana dei Fiumi* (Fountain of the Rivers), the huge figures representing the Nile, Ganges, Danube, and Plata. On the west side of the square is the *Chiesa di Sant'Agnese in Agone* (Church of St. Agnes in Agony), the work of a Bernini assistant, Borromini, which contains statuary and frescoes from the same period. During the *Christmas* season the square is lined with booths selling sweets, toys, and nativity figures.

**PIAZZA FARNESE** This square is dominated by the *Palazzo Farnese,* the most beautiful 16th-century palace in Rome. Commissioned by Cardinal Alessandro Farnese (later Pope Paul III), it was begun in 1514 by Sangallo the Younger, continued by Michelangelo, and completed by Della Porta in 1589. Opera fans will know it as the location of Scarpia's apartment in the second act of Puccini's *Tosca.* Today it is occupied by the *French Embassy* and can be visited only with special permission. Send your request a few days in advance of the date you want to visit, along with a copy of the first page of your passport, to the *Ufficio Culturale* (Cultural Office; Ambasciata di Francia, Piazza Farnese, Rome; phone: 686011). However, anyone is welcome to sit outside the palazzo on the long stone bench in front. The two fountains on the square incorporate Egyptian granite bathtubs from the *Terme di Caracalla.*

**PIAZZA CAMPO DEI FIORI** Very near Piazza Farnese, one of Rome's most colorful squares is the scene of a general market every morning (except Sundays). In the center—surrounded by delicious cheeses, salamis, ripe fruit and vegetables, and *fiori* (flowers) of every kind— is a statue of the philosopher Giordano Bruno, who was burned at the stake here for heresy in 1600. Watch your wallet or purse—this is a favorite hangout for pickpockets.

**PIAZZA MATTEI** This delightful small square on the edge of the ancient Jewish ghetto contains the famous *Fontana delle Tartarughe* (Fountain of the Tortoises), sculpted in 1585 by Giacomo della Porta and Taddeo Landini. Four naked boys lean against the base and life-size bronze tortoises adorn the marble basin. The water moves in several directions, creating a magical effect.

**PIAZZA DEL QUIRINALE** The *Palazzo del Quirinale,* built by the popes in the late 16th and early 17th centuries as a summer residence, became the royal palace after the unification of Italy, and is now the official residence of the President of Italy. The *Fontana dei Dioscuri* (Fountain of the Dioscuri) has ancient Roman statues depicting Castor and Pollux (who were known as the Dioscuri) dominating wild horses; the granite basin is from the *Foro Romano* and was once used for watering livestock. The square affords a marvelous view of Rome and the *Basilica di San Pietro.* A band plays daily at 4 PM in winter and 4:30 PM in summer.

**FONTANA DI TREVI (TREVI FOUNTAIN)** Designed by Nicola Salvi and completed in 1762, the fountain took 30 years to build and was the last important monumental Baroque work in Rome. Set in a tiny square reached by narrow, cobblestone streets, it depicts a colossal Oceanus riding a chariot drawn by sea horses surrounded by a fantasy of gods and tritons. According to legend, you will return to Rome if you stand with your back to the fountain and throw a coin over your left shoulder into the water. Piazza di Trevi.

**PIAZZA BARBERINI** At the foot of Via Veneto, this square has two of Bernini's famous fountains: the *Fontana del Tritone* (Triton Fountain), which depicts a triton kneeling upon a scallop shell supported by four dolphins; and the *Fontana delle Api* (Fountain of the Bees), with three Barberini bees (the family's crest) spurting thin jets of water into a basin below.

**CHIESA DI SAN CARLO ALLE QUATTRO FONTANE (CHURCH OF ST. CHARLES AT THE FOUR FOUNTAINS)** A masterful achievement of fantastical Roman Baroque architecture, this tiny church and its adjacent convent, begun in 1634, were Borromini's first important commission. The dome of the church features unusual geometric coffers that make it appear to float above the curved walls. The crypt, with curves echoing the church above, and the small convent are true lessons in architectural economy. The church façade, completed in 1668, was Borromini's last work. Open daily, with a long closing (noon to 4 PM). At the corner of Via del Quirinale and Via delle Quattro Fontane.

**CHIESA DI SANT'IVO ALLA SAPIENZA (CHURCH OF ST. IVES OF KNOWLEDGE)** With its star-shaped church, elaborate white marble corkscrew campanile, and courtyard of noble proportions, this is considered Borromini's masterpiece. The dome has six windows, so the church is filled with light. Commissioned by Pope Urban VIII, the church— the original seat of the *Università La Sapienza di Roma* (Roman

University of Knowledge)—was completed in 1650 after eight years of work. Open Sunday mornings only. 40 Corso Rinascimento.

**VILLA BORGHESE** In the northern section of the city, this former estate of Cardinal Scipione Borghese is Rome's most magnificent park, with hills, lakes, villas, and vistas. It is a wonderful place for a picnic in the shade of an umbrella pine. Two museums are here: the *Galleria Borghese* (phone: 854-8577), housed in the cardinal's small palace and noted for its Caravaggios (including the dramatic *Madonna and Child with St. Anne*), its Bernini sculptures, and Antonio Canova's statue of the reclining Pauline Borghese; and the *Galleria Nazionale d'Arte Moderna* (National Gallery of Modern Art; phone: 322-4152), with a collection of works by modern Italian artists. At press time half of the *Galleria Borghese* was closed for restoration; part of its collection, including masterpieces by Caravaggio, Bernini, and Raphael, is displayed in the *San Michele a Ripa* building complex (22 Via di San Michele in Trastevere; no phone) along the Tiber River. Both galleries are closed Mondays. Admission charge to the *Galleria Borghese*. *San Michele a Ripa* is closed Mondays and for a long afternoon break (1 to 4 PM). Admission charge. Enter the *Villa Borghese* through the *Porta Pinciana*, at the top of Via Veneto, or walk up Pincio Hill from Piazza del Popolo. The main entrance is at Piazzale Flaminio, just outside the *Porta del Popolo*.

**CIMITERO PROTESTANTE (PROTESTANT CEMETERY)** In the southern part of the city, behind the *Piramide di Caio Cestio*, is the Protestant cemetery where many non-Catholics who lived and died in Rome are buried: Keats (look for his gravestone, with the inscription, "Here lies one whose name is writ in water"), Shelley, Trelawny, Goethe's illegitimate son, and the Italian Communist leader Antonio Gramsci. The cemetery is another favorite haunt of pickpockets, so keep tabs on your wallet or purse. 6 Via Caio Cestio.

**GHETTO E SINAGOGA (JEWISH GHETTO AND SYNAGOGUE)** On the banks of the Tiber River, near the Ponte Garibaldi (Garibaldi Bridge), is this vibrant, though somewhat shabby section of town, once a walled ghetto, today rich with tiny shops and restaurants offering Roman-Jewish specialties. The synagogue is located by the Tiber; next door is the *Museo di Arte Ebraica* (Museum of Hebraic Art), a permanent exhibit of ritual objects from the 16th to the 19th century plus documents of recent history. Closed Saturdays and Jewish holidays. Admission charge. On the Lungotevere dei Cenci (phone: 687-5051).

**ISOLA TIBERINA (TIBER ISLAND)** In the oldest part of the city, between Trastevere and the Jewish ghetto, this small, 900-foot-long island in the Tiber grew, according to legend, from a seed of grain tossed into the river after the Etruscan kings were forced out. Noteworthy is the *Chiesa di San Bartolomeo* (Church of St. Bartholomew), built on the site of the earliest-known temple to Asclepius, the Greek god of healing. This is where victims of the city's 3rd-century plague were sent, and today a hospital still operates here. There also is a tiny park on the marble-paved, downriver point of the island, a good spot to read or enjoy a picnic. The *Antico Caffè dell'Isola* (Via di Quattro Capi; no phone) offers snacks; next door is the popular trattoria *Sora Lella* (see *Eating Out*).

## MODERN ROME

**MONUMENTO A VITTORIO EMANUELE II (MONUMENT TO VICTOR EMMANUEL II)** Sometimes called the *Vittoriano,* this most conspicuous landmark of questionable taste was completed in 1911 to celebrate the unification of Italy. Built of white Brescian marble and overwhelming Capitoline Hill, it is often derided by Romans as the "wedding cake" or the "typewriter." It contains Italy's *Tomba del Milite Ignoto* (Tomb of the Unknown Soldier) from World War I. Turn your back to the monument and note the 15th-century *Palazzo Venezia* to your left. Formerly Mussolini's official residence (and home to Pope Paul II before that), it was from the small balcony of this building that the dictator made his speeches. Piazza Venezia.

**VIA VITTORIO VENETO** Popularly known as Via Veneto, this wide street extends from a handsome gate in the ancient Roman wall, the *Porta Pinciana,* down past the *US Embassy* to Piazza Barberini. Recently spruced up with flowers, trees, and other greenery, the area also boasts several fashionable shops and restaurants; however, the elegant atmosphere is becoming marred by more and more hamburger joints springing up alongside the smart *caffès.* Late at night the street can attract a mixed crowd—from down-and-out actors and decadent Roman nobility to seedy gigolos and male prostitutes. Well-to-do Americans stay in the fine hotels, and young people flock to the discos in the area, which, along with adjacent Via Bissolati with its many foreign airline offices, is well patrolled by police.

**PORTA PORTESE** Rome's flea market takes place on the edge of Trastevere on Sundays from dawn to about 1 or 2 PM. It's a colorful, crowded, and chaotic happening. Genuine antiques are few and far between—and they're usually scooped up before most people are out of bed. Still, you'll find some interesting junk, new and secondhand clothes, shoes, jeans, items brought by Eastern European immigrants, pop records, used tires and car parts, black-market cigarettes—everything from Sicilian puppets to old postcards and broken bidets. Keep a sharp eye on your wallet or purse here. Via Portuense.

## OUT OF TOWN

**ESPOSIZIONE UNIVERSALE DI ROMA (EUR)** Mussolini's ultramodern quarter southwest of the city center was designed for an international exhibition that was supposed to take place in 1942 but never did. It's now a fashionable garden suburb and the site of international congresses and trade shows as well as of some remarkable sports installations built for the *1960 Olympic Games,* including the *Palazzo dello Sport* (Sports Building). Also noteworthy here is the *Museo della Civiltà Romana* (Museum of Roman Civilization; 10 Piazza Giovanni Agnelli; phone: 592-6135). Although half the museum remained closed for renovations at press time, it's still worth seeing for its thorough reconstruction of ancient Rome during the time of Constantine. The museum is closed Mondays and Sunday, Wednesday, Friday, and Saturday afternoons; on Tuesdays and Thursdays it also closes for a short break (1:30 to 3 PM). Admission charge.

**OSTIA ANTICA (ANCIENT OSTIA)** This immense excavation site about 15 miles (24 km) southwest of Rome was the great trading port of the ancient city, much closer to the mouth of the Tiber than it is today. The ruins—picturesquely set among pines and cypresses—first were uncovered in 1914, and new treasures are being discovered constantly. They reveal a great deal about the building methods and management of the far-flung Roman Empire.

A visit takes at least half a day. Among the chief sites are Piazzale delle Corporazioni (Corporations' Square), once 70 commercial offices, with mottoes and emblems in black and white mosaics indicating that the merchants were shipwrights, caulkers, rope makers, furriers, and shipowners from all over the ancient world; the *Capitolium* (a temple); the *Foro* (Forum); baths; apartment blocks; several private houses, most notably the *Casa di Amore e Psiche* (House of Cupid and Psyche); and the restored theater. This one-time community boasted remarkable cultural and religious diversity, obvious today from the remains of its synagogue, several Christian chapels, and a number of temples to the Persian sun god, Mithras. The site is open daily. Admission charge. A local museum (phone: 565-0022) traces the development of Ostia Antica and displays some outstanding statues, busts, and frescoes. It is open daily. Admission charge included in the park entry fee. To reach Ostia Antica, take either the *metropolitana*'s *Linea B* towards *EUR,* transferring to the local train at *Stazione della Magliana* (Magliana Station); an *ACOTRAL* bus from Via Giolitti; or the *Tiber II* boat (see *Getting Around*).

**CASTELLI ROMANI (ROMAN CASTLES)** Rome's "castles" are actually 13 hill towns set in the lovely Alban Hills region southeast of the city, an area where popes and powerful families built fortresses, palaces, and other retreats. The mountains, the volcanic lakes of Nemi and Albano, chestnut groves, olive trees, and vines producing the famous Castelli wine make the area a favorite day trip for Romans. Particularly charming are Frascati, known for its villas and its wines; Grottaferrata, famous for its fortified monastery, which can be visited; beautiful Lago di Nemi (Lake Nemi), with its vivid blue waters and wooded surroundings, where the goddess Diana was worshiped; and Monte Cavo (Mt. Cavo), a mountain whose summit offers a panorama of the *Castelli* from a height of 3,124 feet. The *Castelli Romani* are best seen on an organized tour or by car—but beware of Sunday traffic.

### EXTRA SPECIAL

**Fountain fans should not miss Tivoli, a charming hilltop town on the Aniene, a tributary of the Tiber, about**

20 miles (32 km) east of Rome. It's famous for its villas, gardens, and, above all, cascading waters—all immortalized by Fragonard's 18th-century landscapes. Called Tibur by the ancient Romans, it was even then a resort for wealthy citizens, who bathed in its thermal waters, considered therapeutic to this day.

The *Villa d'Este,* built for a cardinal in the 16th century, is the prime attraction—or, rather, its terraced gardens are. They contain some 500 fountains, large and small, including the jets of water lining the famous Viale delle Cento Fontane (Avenue of the Hundred Fountains) and the two-story *Fontana dell'Organo* (Organ Fountain), so named because it once worked a hydraulic organ. The villa and gardens are open daily. Admission charge. Nearby, the *Villa Gregoriana,* built by Pope Gregory XVI in the 19th century, has sloping gardens and lovely cascades, which are best on Sundays, since most of the water is used for industrial purposes on other days. It's open daily. Admission charge.

Only 4 miles (6 km) southwest of Tivoli is *Villa Adriana* (Hadrian's Villa), the most sumptuous ancient Roman villa, almost a city in itself. It was built from AD 125 to 134 by the Emperor Hadrian, an amateur architect who enjoyed this stately pleasure dome for only four years before his death. Every detail of the villa's dozens of buildings, two swimming pools, two libraries, gymnasium, theater, thermal baths, courtyards, and tree-lined avenues was perfect. Each window was placed for the best possible view, jets of water spouted strategically in every corner, statues from all over the empire surrounded the pools, and romantic nooks were sculpted out of nature to appear as if they'd always been there. Still standing in a huge, rambling, and somewhat abandoned archaeological park are numerous buildings, including a marine theater—a delightful little island construction accessible by bridges. There's a scale model of the entire original layout at the entrance gate. The villa is closed Mondays. Admission charge.

You can see Tivoli with a guided tour or take an *ACOTRAL* bus from Via Gaeta or a train from the

*Stazione Termini* (Central Railway Station). The *Villa Adriana* also can be reached by bus from Via Gaeta, but note that while one bus, which leaves every hour, stops first at the *Villa Adriana* and then at Tivoli, the other, which leaves every half hour, goes directly to Tivoli—to reach the *Villa Adriana,* you must get off at a crossroads and walk about a half mile. If you rent a car (a wiser choice), take the Autostrada per l'Aquila to the Tivoli exit, then follow the signs; the town is about an hour's drive from the city.

# Sources and Resources

## TOURIST INFORMATION

The *Ente Provinciale per il Turismo* (*EPT;* Provincial Tourist Office) for Rome and Lazio has a main information office (5 Via Parigi; phone: 488-99253) that is open weekdays. There are branches at the *Stazione Termini* (phone: 487-1270), in the customs area at *Aeroporto Leonardo da Vinci* (Leonardo da Vinci Airport, at Fiumicino; phone: 650-10255), and at the Feronia "Punto Blu" and Frascati Est service areas of the A1 and A2 highways, respectively, for those arriving by car (no phone). All branches stock useful (and free) booklets, maps, and hotel listings. Ask for *Carnet,* the English-language monthly listing of events.

The *Ufficio Informazioni* (Vatican Tourist Information Office) is on the left side of Piazza San Pietro, facing the basilica (phone: 698-84866). It's closed on some Catholic holidays. The *US Embassy* is at 119 Via Veneto (phone: 46741).

In the US, the *Ente Nazionale Italiano di Turismo* (Italian Government Travel Office) has several branches (500 N. Michigan Ave., Suite 1046, Chicago, IL 60611; phone: 312-644-0990; 12400 Wilshire Blvd., Suite 550, Los Angeles, CA 90025; phone: 310-820-0098; fax: 310-820-6357; and 630 Fifth Ave., Suite 1565, New York, NY 10111; phone: 212-843-6880; fax: 212-586-9249). The *Italian Embassy* is at 1601 Fuller St. NW, Washington, DC 20009 (phone: 202-328-5500).

**ENTRY REQUIREMENTS** A US citizen needs a current passport for a stay of up to 90 days.

**TIME** The time in Italy is six hours later than in US East Coast cities. Italy observes daylight saving time.

**LANGUAGE** Italian is the official tongue.

**ELECTRIC CURRENT** 220 volts, 50 cycles, AC, but there are some 110-volt outlets. Sometimes both voltages are found in hotel guestrooms.

**MONEY** The Italian currency unit is the lira (abbreviated either L. or Lit.); the plural of lira is lire. At press time the lira traded at 1,626 to the American dollar.

**TIPPING** Keep a handful of lire notes ready. Despite the 15% to 18% service charges at hotels and the 15% usually added to restaurant bills, you'll be expected to give 1,000 to 1,500 L. or more to chambermaids for each night you stay, and at least 1,500 L. to bellhops for each bag they carry. Waiters and wine stewards get an extra 10% of the bill. When eating or drinking at a café counter the procedure is to pay at the cash register first, then take the small receipt over to the counter, where you leave it with 100 to 200 L. (depending on what you're having). Then place your order. Taxi drivers receive 15% of the meter, hairdressers 15% of the bill. Even service station attendants expect about 1,000 L. for cleaning windshields and giving directions. Theater ushers are tipped 1,000 L.

**BANKING/BUSINESS HOURS** Most banks are open weekdays from 8:30 AM to 1:30 PM and 3:30 to 4:15 PM (some are open from 2:30 to 3:30 PM). On days preceding holidays, banking hours are from 8:30 to 11:30 AM. Government offices generally operate from 8 AM to 2 PM. Most other businesses are open from 9 AM to 1 PM and again from 3:30 or 4 to 7:30 or 8 PM. (Places that remain open all day generally close at 6:30 PM.)

**NATIONAL HOLIDAYS** *New Year's Day* (January 1), *Epiphany* (January 6), *Good Friday* (April 14), *Easter Sunday* (April 16), *Easter Monday* (April 17), *Liberation Day* (April 25), *Labor Day* (May 1), *Ferragosto/Feast of the Assumption* (August 15), *All Saints' Day* (November 1), *Feast of the Immaculate Conception* (December 8), *Christmas Day* (December 25), and *St. Stephen's Day* (December 26).

**LOCAL COVERAGE** The *International Herald Tribune,* now also printed in Rome, is available at most newsstands in the city center; it often lists major events in Italy in its Saturday "Weekend" section. *A Guest in Rome* is published by the *Golden Key Association of Concierges. La Repubblica, Corriere della Sera,* and *Il Messaggero* are daily newspapers that list local events on weekends; *La Repubblica* has an interesting Thursday supplement called "TrovaRoma" that lists the week's events, shows, theater, new movies, and more. *Wanted in Rome,* a useful biweekly publication sold at downtown newsstands, details the latest happenings.

The Rome telephone directory's *TuttoCittà* supplement is an invaluable resource. It lists every street in the city and contains detailed maps of each zone as well as postal codes, bus routes, locations of taxi stands, and other useful information.

There are many useful English-language books about Rome, some of which are available in Italy. (However, you should purchase them in the US whenever possible, as the prices are far more reasonable.) They include *Italian Hours* by Henry James (Ecco Press; $10.50), first published in 1909; and Georgina Masson's *Companion Guide to Rome* (HarperCollins; $19), which provides handy information on the city presented in an amusing, readable style. An excellent source for readers who can understand Italian is the two-volume *A Piedi nella Roma Antica* (Edizoni Iter; 18,000 lire/about $12 per volume), describing several walking tours through various sections of Rome. The best map of the city is *A-Z Roma Autostradario* (Guidaverde Editrice; 35,000 lire/about $22).

**TELEPHONE** The city code for Rome is 6. When calling from one area to another within Italy dial 0 + city code + local number. The country code for Italy is 39. In an emergency, dial 112 for an ambulance; 113 for the police.

## GETTING AROUND

**AIRPORTS** *Aeroporto Leonardo da Vinci* (phone: 6595; also called *Fiumicino Airport*) in Fiumicino, about 16 miles (26 km) from downtown Rome, handles both international and domestic traffic. Check in at least 40 minutes before your flight or risk losing your reservation. The trip between the airport and downtown Rome takes between a half hour and 45 minutes by taxi, depending on traffic. *Ferrovie Italiane dello Stato (FS)*—also known as *Italian State Railways*—provides the quickest and least expensive service between the airport and the city. The *Servizio Navetta* (also called the *Collegamento Non-Stop*) express train runs between the airport and Rome's *Stazione Termini;* the trip takes about 30 minutes and costs 12,000 lire (about $7.40) each way. Trains leave the airport for Rome from 7:50 AM to 10:25 PM, and leave *Stazione Termini* for the airport from 7 AM to 8:50 PM. The local *Servizio Metropolitana* train runs between the airport and *Stazione Tiburtina* (Tiburtina Station) in Rome, making several stops en route. The fare is 7,000 lire ($4.30); the trip takes about 40 minutes. Trains leave the airport from 6:55 AM to 10:50 PM, and leave *Tiburtina* for the airport between 6 AM and 10 PM. *Aeroporto Ciampino* (Ciampino Airport; phone: 794921), located about 8 miles (13 km) from downtown, handles mostly charter traffic.

**BOAT** The *Tiber II* carries 300 passengers on half-day cruises along the river to Ostia Antica and back (water levels and weather permitting). From May to September the *Acquabus* also plies the river. For information and reservations for both, contact either *Tourvisa* (phone: 445-0284) or the *EPT* (see *Tourist Information*). To rent a boat, contact *Acquario* (41 Via V. Brunelli; phone: 501-0360); charters are available from *Axa-Riga Yachts* (191 Via Eschillo, Room 51; phone: 509-0222; fax: 509-17530).

**BUS** *ATAC (Azienda Tramvie e Autobus Comune di Roma),* the city bus company, is the (weak) backbone of Rome's public transportation system. Most central routes can be extremely crowded, pickpockets are rampant, and some lines discontinue service after 9 PM, midnight, or 1 AM. During August the number of buses in use is greatly reduced while drivers are on vacation. Tickets, which currently cost 1,280 lire (about 80¢), must be purchased before boarding and are available at some newsstands, tobacco shops, and bars. (Be aware that these outlets frequently exhaust their ticket supply, and the fine for riding without a ticket is steep.) You also can buy a single ticket (also costing 1,280 lire) that can be used on all three forms of local transportation—buses, subways, and trains. Remember to get on the bus via the back doors, stamp your ticket in the machine, and exit via the middle doors (the front doors are used only by *abbonati*, season-ticket holders). There are no transfer tickets, but all tickets are valid for 90 minutes.

Consider buying day passes, called "Big," at the *ATAC* information booth in Piazza dei Cinquecento or at principal bus stations, such as those at Piazza San Silvestro and Piazza Risorgimento; they cost 4,000 lire (about $2.60). A weekly pass called the *Carta Settimanale per Turisti* is also economical; costing 10,000 lire (about $6), it may be purchased only at the *ATAC*'s *Ufficio Informazioni* (Information Office; Largo Giovanni Montemartini) and at the information booth in Piazza dei Cinquecento. Tourists will appreciate the tiny, electric-powered No. 119 bus, which loops through downtown Rome between Piazza del Popolo and close to Piazza Navona, passing Piazza di Spagna. Route maps—*Roma in Metrobus*—are sold at the *ATAC* information booth and at the *Ufficio Informazioni,* as well as at some newsstands. For information, call 46951. Bus service to points out of town is run by *ACOTRAL.* For information, call 593-5551.

**CAR RENTAL** Major car rental firms such as *Avis* (phone: 470-1229 in Rome, 167-863063 toll-free in Italy), *Budget* (phone: 488-1905), *Europcar* (phone: 481-9103 or 482-5701), and *Hertz* (phone: 321-6886), as well as several reliable Italian companies such as *Auto Maggiore* (8/A Via Po; phone: 229351), have offices in the city, at the airport, and at railway stations. *Tropea* (60 Via San Basilio; phone: 488-1189) has rental and chauffeur-driven cars.

**HORSE-DRAWN CARRIAGES** Rome's *carrozzelle* accommodate up to five passengers and are available at major city squares (Piazze San Pietro, di Spagna, Venezia, and Navona), in front of the *Colosseo,* near the *Fontana di Trevi,* on Via Veneto, and in the *Villa Borghese.* They can be hired by the half hour, hour, half day, or full day. Arrange the price with the driver before boarding.

**SCOOTERS AND MOPEDS** Pollution and insufferable traffic jams have made scooters and mopeds popular alternatives to cars for some Romans. But a word to the two-wheeled: Some Italian automobile drivers consider these vehicles a nuisance and often are loath to give them their fair share of the roadway. Use extreme caution—and wear a solid helmet. To rent a moped, scooter, or motorbike, try *Scoot-a-long* (302 Via Cavour; phone: 678-0206); *Scooters for Rent* (66 Via della Purificazione, near Piazza Barberini; phone: 488-5485), which also rents bikes; or *St. Peter Scooters* (43 Via Porta Castello, near the *Basilica di San Pietro;* phone: 687-5714).

**SUBWAY** The *metropolitana,* Rome's subway, consists of two lines. *Linea A* runs roughly east to west, from the *Stazione Ottaviano* (Ottaviano Station) near the *Vatican,* across the Tiber, through the historic center (Piazza di Spagna, Piazza Barberini, the *Stazione Termini,* and San Giovanni), and over to the eastern edge of the city past Cinecittà, the filmmaking center, to the Alban Hills. *Linea B,* which is partly an underground and partly a surface railroad, runs north to south, connecting the *Tiburtina* train station (where numerous long-distance trains stop) with the *Stazione Termini* and the *Colosseo* and, with a stop at the *Ostiense* station at Piazza Piramide to connect with the train to *Aeroport Leonardo da Vinci,* down to the southern suburb of *EUR.* Tickets, which cost 1,280 lire (about 80¢), are sold at some newsstands, tobacco shops, bars, and at most stations. Only a few stations are staffed with ticket sellers, however; most have ticket-dispensing machines that accept only coins, so be prepared. Subway entrances are marked by a large red "M."

**TAXI** Cabs can be hailed in the street or found at numerous stands, which are listed in the yellow pages. The *Radio Taxi* telephone numbers are 3570, 3875, 4994, and 88177. Taxi rates are quite expensive (and increase regularly); drivers are required to show you, if asked, the current list of added charges. After 10 PM a night surcharge is added, there are surcharges for holidays and for suitcases, and an additional surcharge is added for trips to the airport at Fiumicino. Don't hire free-lance taxis; drivers usually are unlicensed and charge up to double the price of the regular taxi fare.

**TOURS** A quick and interesting tour on Bus No. 110 covers some 45 major sights in three hours. Although there is no guide, a short brochure in English gives the highlights. The bus leaves Piazza dei Cinquecento around 3 PM (2 PM in winter). It runs daily in season and on weekends only the rest of the year. For additional details, either call 46951 or check with the *ATAC* booth in the square. The Roman Catholic, pro-ecumenical Fathers of Atonement (30 Via Santa Maria dell'Anima; phone: 687-9552) lead walking tours of the city and the *Vatican* on Friday mornings. They also offer lectures on Thursday mornings. Both are given in English; there's no charge, but a donation is appreciated.

*Secret Walks in Rome* (6 Via dei Quattro Cantoni; phone: 397-28728) offers imaginative tours of the city. Excursions include bicycle tours of Rome and half-day walking tours focusing on wines and wine shops. Advance reservations required.

For those especially interested in art history and archaeology, a team of professionals in both fields is available to take individuals or groups on private English-language tours of Rome, or on one- and two-day trips outside the city. For information, contact Peter Zalewski (6 Via Cristoforo Colombo, Marcellina di Roma; phone: 774-425451; fax: 774-425122). An English-speaking German, Ruben Popper (12 Via dei Levii; phone: 761-0901), who has lived in Rome for more than 30 years, also leads city tours (mostly walking).

For a bird's-eye view of the city, take a helicopter tour, which leaves from the *Centro Sperimentale d'Aviazione* at *Aeroporto dell' Urbe* (Urbe Airport; 825 Via Salaria; phone: 8864-0035). A minimum of five passengers is required for the breathtaking—but pricey—20-minute ride; reserve a week in advance.

**TRAIN** Rome's main train station is the *Stazione Termini* (Piazza dei Cinquecento; phone: 4775, information). There are several suburban stations. The ones most often used by visitors are the *Stazione Ostiense* (Ostiense Station; Piazzale dei Partigiani; phone: 575-0732), one of the stations from which trains depart for *Aeroporto Leonardo da Vinci;* and the *Stazione Tiburtina* (Tiburtina Station; Circonvolazione Nomentana). Because of the increase in crime in many of Italy's train stations, the police have anticrime units patrolling all trains and stations, but remain alert anyway.

## LOCAL SERVICES

**CONVENTION CENTERS** *Centro Internazionale Roma (CIR)*, at the *Hotel Ergife* (619 Via Aurelia; phone: 6644; fax: 663-2689) has eight meeting rooms for up to 800; *Palazzo Brancaccio* (7 Via Monte Oppio; phone: 487-3177) is centrally located and available for conferences of up to 390 people; *Palazzo dei Congressi* (Piazzale Kennedy in *EUR;* phone: 591-2735; fax: 592-4044) has 30 meeting rooms for up to 4,000. Also centrally located is the *Palazzo Taverna* (36 Via di Monte Giordano; phone: 683-3785), which is available for receptions and business lunches for up to 1,200. The *Castello Orsini-Odescalchi* (Orsini-Odescalchi Castle), 25 miles (40 km) from Rome in Bracciano (phone: 902-4050 or 902-4003), is a 15th-century palace, richly furnished and decorated with frescoes, that can be rented for receptions of up to 500.

**DRY CLEANER** *Campo dei Fiori* (38 Piazza Campo dei Fiori; phone: 687-9096); *Mosea* (23 Via Belisario; phone: 482-7255); and *Tintoria Maddalena* (40 Piazza Maddalena; phone: 654-3348).

**LIMOUSINE SERVICE** *Biancocavallo* (200 Via Fiume Giallo; phone: 520-2957); *Capitol* (33 Via del Galoppatoio; phone: 320-0428); *Coop. UARA* (261 Via Panisperna; phone: 679-2320); *Italo Mazzei Roma* (123 Via Trionfale; phone: 397-28158); *Nazionale* (32/B Via Milano; phone: 481-8587; fax: 481-4530); and *Traiano* (19 Via Sant'Agata dei Goti; phone: 679-1518; fax: 678-7996).

**MEDICAL EMERGENCY** *Casa di Cura Privata Salvator Mundi* (67 Viale della Mura Gianicolensi; phone: 588961); *Rome American Hospital* (67 Via Longoni; phone: 22551).

**MESSENGER SERVICE** *Romana Recapiti* (phone: 559-0993) and *Speedy Boys* (phone: 372-5656).

**OFFICE EQUIPMENT RENTAL** *Executive Service* (68 Via Savoia; phone: 854-3241) and *International Services Agency* (35 Piazza di Spagna; phone: 684-0287 or 684-0288). For computer rentals: *ATEC* (127 Via Madonna del Riposa; phone: 663-6741; fax: 620537); *Cardinale* (74 Via T. Prisco; phone: 789978; fax: 781-1677); and *Tecmatica* (4 Via Sante Bargellini; phone: 439-5264; fax: 434628).

**OFFICE SPACE RENTAL** For fully equipped offices contact: *Amministrazione Principe Livio Odescalchi* (80 Piazza SS. Apostoli; phone: 679-2154); *Center Office* (132 Via del Tritone; phone: 488-1995;

fax: 474-7641); *International Business Centre* (121 Piazzale di Porta Pia; phone: 886-3051); and *Tiempo* (50 Via Barberini; phone: 482-5151).

**PHOTOCOPIES** *Centro Copia Palombi* (54 Piazza dei Santi Apostoli; phone: 678-1125), which also has a fax service; *Centro Copie Serpenti* (127 Via dei Serpenti; phone/fax: 482-0207); and *Fotoprint Artistica* (32 Via Boncompagni; phone: 482-0207).

**POST OFFICE** The most efficient post office for international mail is the *Vatican Post Office* (Vatican City; phone: 698-83406); Rome's main branch is the *Ufficio Postale Centrale, Roma Centro Corrispondenza* (19 Piazza San Silvestro; phone: 6771). *Note:* Italian stamps may *not* be used in Vatican mailboxes.

**SECRETARY/STENOGRAPHER (ENGLISH-SPEAKING)** *Agenzia Copisteria* (20 Lungotevere Prati; phone: 688-02575); *Executive Service* (78 Via Savoia; phone: 854-3241; fax: 884-0738); and *Rome at Your Service* (95 Via Torino; phone: 484429; and 75 Via V. E. Orlando; phone: 484583). *Copisteria al Tritone* (17 Via Crispi; phone: 679-7190) has word-processing facilities, a fax machine, and limited secretarial services in English.

**TAILOR** *Caraceni* (61/B Via Campania; phone: 488-2594; and 50 Via Sardegna; phone: 474-4023); *Cifonelli* (68 Via Sella; phone: 488-1827); and *Coccurello* (7 Via Manfredi; phone: 808-2360), for smaller budgets.

**TELEX/FACSIMILE TRANSMISSIONS** Telexes, faxes, and telegrams can be sent 24 hours a day from 18 Piazza San Silvestro (phone: 160), next to the main post office.

**TRANSLATOR** *Agenzia Barberini* (5 Piazza Barberini; phone: 474-1738 or 481-8873; fax: 488-5491); *Alfa International* (29 Via Lucrezio Caro; phone: 323-0077; fax: 322-2038); *Executive Service;* and *Rome at Your Service* (see *Secretary/Stenographer,* above, for the last two). For simultaneous translations, contact the *Centro Congressi* (23 Via Sallustiana; phone: 485990; fax: 482-0024) or *STOC* (44 Via G. de Ruggiero; phone: 540-5621; and 203 Via Laurentina; phone: 540-3741).

**OTHER** Tuxedo rental: *Misano* (87 Via Nazionale; phone: 488-2005).

## SPECIAL EVENTS

During *La Settimana Santa* (Holy Week), the city swarms with visitors. Religious ceremonies abound, particularly on *Venerdì Santo* (Good Friday), when the pope conducts the famous *Via Crucis* (Way of the Cross) procession to the ruins of the *Colosseo,* where Christian martyrs met their deaths. On *Easter Sunday* itself Romans go to mass, then indulge in a huge family feast (often featuring roast lamb and concluding with a dove-shaped cake). The celebration continues through the next day, which is known as *Pasquetta* (Little Easter); on this day almost everything in the city closes down, and it seems like the entire population is out picnicking in the sunshine.

The arrival of spring is celebrated in April with a colorful display of potted azaleas covering Piazza di Spagna, and in May a picturesque street nearby, Via Margutta, is the site of an exhibition of paintings by artists of varied talents. The *Fiera di Via Margutta* (Via Margutta Art Fair) is repeated in the fall. Also in May, the *Villa Borghese*'s lush Piazza di Siena becomes the site of the *Concorso Ippico Internazionale* (International Horse Show), and soon after that is the *Campionato Internazionale di Tennis* (Italian Open) tennis tournament (see *Tennis*). An antiques show also takes place in spring and fall along charming Via dei Coronari (near Piazza Navona), and there's the *Mostra Internazionale di Rose* (International Rose Show) in late spring at the delightful Roseto Comunale on Aventine Hill. In late May or June the vast *Fiera di Roma,* a national industrial exhibition, takes place at the fairgrounds along Via Cristoforo Colombo. For one boisterous week in late July, when the richest Romans have fled to the sea or the mountains, the teeming Trastevere quarter becomes a sprawling outdoor trattoria for *La Festa di Noantri* (The Feast of Ourselves). Rows of tables stretch for blocks, musicians stroll, and piazze become dance floors and open-air cinemas. The *noantri* of the celebration are the people of Trastevere, who consider themselves the only true Romans and choose to honor their neighborhood when the rest of town has fled the heat.

For *Natale* (Christmas), relatively modest decorations go up around the city, almost all churches display their sometimes movable, elaborate *presepi* (nativity scenes), and a colorful toy and candy fair is held in Piazza Navona. The season, including the fair, lasts through the *Festa dell'Epifania* (Feast of the Epiphany; January 6), when children receive gifts from a witch known as the Befana to add to those Babbo Natale (Father Christmas) or the Gesù Bambino (Baby Jesus) brought them at *Christmas.* The intervening *Capodanno* (New Year's Eve) is celebrated with a bang here as in much of the rest of Italy—firecrackers snap, crackle, and pop from early evening on.

There are also innumerable characteristic *feste* or *sagre* (festivals, usually celebrating some local food or beverage at the height of its season) in the many hill towns surrounding Rome, particularly in the Castelli Romani, about 15 miles (24 km) south of the city. The most notable of these are *L'Infiorata* (The Flowering) at Genzano di Roma in June and the *Sagra dell'Uva* (Rite of the Grapes) at Marino in October.

## MUSEUMS

In addition to those described in *Special Places,* Rome has many other interesting museums. Included in the following list are churches that should be seen because of their artistic value. Unless otherwise indicated, the churches are open daily and do not charge admission. You will, however, need a supply of 500-lire coins to operate the electric lights that illuminate the frescoes and other paintings in many churches. The museums and galleries listed below are closed Mondays and charge admission unless otherwise specified (though some waive their admission charges on Sundays). Always check the operating schedules before setting out; many places close for several hours in the afternoon.

**CHIESA DI SAN LUIGI DEI FRANCESI (CHURCH OF ST. LOUIS OF THE FRENCH)** The French national church, built in the 16th century, contains three Caravaggios, including the famous *Calling of St. Matthew.* Via della Dogana Vecchia.

**CHIESA DI SAN PIETRO IN VINCOLI (CHURCH OF ST. PETER IN CHAINS)** Erected in the 5th century to preserve St. Peter's chains, this church contains Michelangelo's magnificent statue of Moses. Piazza di San Pietro in Vincoli.

**CHIESA DI SANT'AGOSTINO (CHURCH OF ST. AUGUSTINE)** The *Madonna of the Pilgrims* by Caravaggio and the *Prophet Isaiah* by Raphael are found in this 15th-century church. Piazza di Sant'Agostino.

**CHIESA DI SANT'ANDREA AL QUIRINALE (CHURCH OF ST. ANDREW OF THE QUIRINAL)** A Baroque church by Bernini, to be compared with the *Chiesa di San Carlo alle Quattro Fontane* (see *Special Places*), Borromini's church on the same street. Via del Quirinale.

**CHIESA DI SANT'ANDREA DELLA VALLE (CHURCH OF ST. ANDREW OF THE VALLEY)** This fine 17th-century church was designed by Carlo Maderno and Carlo Rainaldi and has an elegant cupola (Rome's second-highest after the *Basilica di San Pietro*) that dominates the skyline. Giorgio Lanfranco's celebrated fresco, *The Glory of Paradise,* is inside. Both the exterior and interior recently were cleaned. Piazza Sant'Andrea.

**CHIESA DI SANTA MARIA D'ARACOELI (CHURCH OF ST. MARY OF THE ALTAR OF HEAVEN)** In this Romanesque-Gothic church are frescoes by Pinturicchio and a 14th-century staircase built in thanksgiving for the end of a plague. Piazza d'Aracoeli.

**CHIESA DI SANTA MARIA IN COSMEDIN (CHURCH OF ST. MARY IN COSMEDIN)** This Romanesque church is known for the *Bocca della Verità* (Mouth of Truth) in its portico—a Roman drain or treasury cover in the shape of a god's face whose mouth, according to legend, will bite off the hand of anyone telling a lie. Piazza della Bocca della Verità.

**CHIESA DI SANTA MARIA SOPRA MINERVA (CHURCH OF ST. MARY OVER MINERVA)** Built over a Roman temple to the goddess Minerva, this church has a Gothic interior (unusual for Rome), frescoes by Filippino Lippi (which have been freshly restored), and two versions of Michelangelo's statue of *St. John the Baptist.* Piazza della Minerva.

**CHIESA DI SANTA MARIA IN TRASTEVERE (CHURCH OF ST. MARY IN TRASTEVERE)** Another recently restored ancient church, this one was the first in Rome dedicated to the Virgin, with 12th- and 13th-century mosaics. Piazza Santa Maria in Trastevere.

**CHIESA DI SANTA MARIA DELLA VITTORIA (CHURCH OF ST. MARY OF THE VICTORY)** It is Baroque to the core, especially in Bernini's *Cappella Cornaro* (Cornaro Chapel). Via XX Settembre.

**CHIESA DI SANTA SABINA (CHURCH OF ST. SABINA)** A simple 5th-century basilica, it offers original cypress doors, a 13th-century cloister and bell tower, and stunning views of the city. Piazza Pietro d'Illiria.

**GALLERIA COLONNA** The Colonna family collection of mainly 17th-century Italian paintings, including some works by Veronese and Tintoretto, are displayed in the *Palazzo Colonna,* where the family still lives. Open Saturday mornings only; closed in August. *Palazzo Colonna,* 17 Via della Pilotta (phone: 679-4362).

**GALLERIA DORIA PAMPHILI** Displayed here is the Doria Pamphili family's private collection of Italian and foreign paintings from the 15th to the 17th century, including Caravaggio's *Mary Magdalene.* Closed Mondays, Wednesdays, and Thursdays. *Palazzo Doria Pamphili,* 1/A Piazza del Collegio Romano (phone: 679-4365).

**GALLERIA NAZIONALE D'ARTE ANTICA (NATIONAL GALLERY OF ANCIENT ART)** This museum exhibits paintings by Italian artists from the 13th through the 18th century plus some Dutch and Flemish works. *Palazzo Barberini,* 13 Via delle Quattro Fontane (phone: 481-4591).

**GALLERIA NAZIONALE D'ARTE MODERNA (NATIONAL GALLERY OF MODERN ART)** Particularly noteworthy are works by pre–World War I Italian painters and the futurists. 131 Viale Belle Arti (phone: 322-4151).

**GALLERIA PALAZZO CORSINI** Displayed in a regal palace are paintings, classical sculptures, and other artworks, all created in the 16th and 17th centuries. 10 Via della Lungara (phone: 654-2323).

**GALLERIA SPADA** Renaissance art and Roman marble work from the 2nd and 3rd centuries; also two huge, rare antique globes that were used on Dutch ships in the 16th century. The building itself is noteworthy for its exterior, designed by Borromini. *Palazzo Spada,* 3 Piazza Capo di Ferro (phone: 686-1158).

**MUSEO BARRACCO (BARRACCO MUSEUM)** This fine, extensively restored 19th-century mansion houses a rich collection of fascinating pre–Roman era sculptures. 168 Corso Vittorio Emanuele II (phone: 654-0848).

**MUSEO NAPOLEONICO (NAPOLEONIC MUSEUM)** Housed here is memorabilia of the emperor's family during their rule in Rome. Closed weekends and for an afternoon break (2 to 5 PM). 1 Via Zanardelli (phone: 654-0286).

**MUSEO NAZIONALE DI VILLA GIULIA (VILLA GIULIA NATIONAL MUSEUM)** The country's most important Etruscan collection is displayed in a 16th-century villa by Vignola. 9 Piazzale di Villa Giulia (phone: 320-1951).

**MUSEO DI PALAZZO VENEZIA (MUSEUM AT PALAZZO VENEZIA)** Tapestries, paintings, sculpture, ceramics, and other art objects, as well as important temporary exhibits. A hall of medieval art recently reopened after a 10-year renovation. 118 Via del Plebescito (phone: 679-8865).

## GALLERIES
Rome has many art galleries with interesting shows of Italian and foreign artists. They generally close Mondays and for an afternoon break (1 to 4 PM). The following offer an excellent selection of contemporary and modern art:

**GABBIANO** 51 Via della Frezza (phone: 322-7049).

**GALLERIA L'ARCADIA** 70/A Via Babuino (phone: 679-1023).

**GALLERIA GIULIA** 148 Via Giulia (phone: 688-02061).

**GALLERIA IL SEGNO** 4 Via di Capo Le Case (phone: 679-1387).

**L'ISOLA** 5 Via Gregoriana (phone: 678-4678).

## SHOPPING
In Rome you'll find the great couturiers, but even though their designs will cost less here than back home, don't expect any bargain-basement finds. The best buys are in high-quality, hand-finished leather goods, jewelry, fabrics, shoes, and sweaters. Almost all stores observe the Anglo-Saxon rite of *prezzi fissi* (fixed prices). A particularly good time to shop is in early January, when most stores in Rome lower their prices significantly (sometimes by as much as 50%) for several weeks.

The chicest shopping area is around the bottom of Piazza di Spagna, beginning with elegant Via Condotti, which runs east to west and is lined with Rome's most exclusive shops. Via del Babuino, which connects Piazza di Spagna to Piazza del Popolo, has traditionally been known for its antiques shops, but is also a high-fashion street, as is nearby Via Bocca di Leone, where there are a number of designers' boutiques. Running parallel to Via Condotti are several more streets—such as Via Borgognona, Via delle Carrozze, and Via Frattina—mostly pedestrian zones with more fashionable boutiques. These streets end at Via del Corso, the main street of Rome, which runs north to south and is lined with shops geared to the younger set. There are some fine shops along Via del Tritone, Via Sistina, and in the Via Veneto area, and small, chic boutiques around the *Pantheon,* Campo dei Fiori, and Via del Governo Vecchio. On the other side of the river toward the *Vatican* are two popular shopping streets that are slightly less expensive—Via Cola di Rienzo and Via Ottaviano. Also explore Via Nazionale, near the *Stazione Termini.*

Antiques hunters should stroll along Via del Babuino, Via dei Coronari, Via del Governo Vecchio, Via Margutta, and Via Giulia. Rome's finest food shops are on Via della Croce and Via Cola di Rienzo.

If shopping is entertainment, Rome's street markets are its best theater. Most of the country's most intriguing goods can be found here. High-quality shoes, new and secondhand clothes, a few genuine antiques, and lots of interesting junk are sold at the city's gigantic Sunday morning labyrinth at the *Porta Portese,* which operates from 5 AM (the bargain hour) until 1 PM. If you wish to join the fray, stuff a little cash in a tight inside pocket, leave camera and purse at home, and prepare to shuffle through the packed streets. The vast clothing market at the weekday shops and stands on Via Sannio, near San Giovanni, is the place for good buys on a wide assortment of casual clothes—army surplus, jeans, down jackets, mode-of-the-moment sweaters; beware of imitations.

One of the most rewarding Roman experiences is to pore over new and used books, modern reproductions of etchings of Rome's monuments, and the occasional authentic antique print in the stalls at Piazza di Fontanella Borghese, which are open weekday mornings. Fine prints also may be found at the following auction houses: *L'Antonina* (23 Piazza Mignanelli; phone: 679-4009); *Christie's* (114 Piazza Navona; phone: 687-2787); *Finarte* (54 Via Margutta; phone: 320-7630); *Semenzato* (93 Piazza di Spagna; phone: 676-6479); and *Sotheby's* (90 Piazza di Spagna; phone: 678-1798).

Store hours in Rome can be capricious, but shops usually are open from 8:30 AM to 1 PM and 3 or 3:30 to 6 or 7 PM; however, an increasing number are staying open through midday and closing at 5 PM. Many shops also are open on Saturdays (usually from 10 AM to 1 PM, and from 3 to 6 or 7 PM). Major department stores and shopping centers are open Mondays through Saturdays from 9:30 AM to 6:30 PM (or later), and usually skip the midday break. Many shops are closed on Sundays, and smaller establishments may be closed for a half or full day on Mondays as well. Department stores (and some shops), however, may be open on Sundays, and also may stay open late (until around 8 PM) at least one day a week.

Below are some of our favorite shops in Rome:

**Apolloni** Mostly 17th- and 18th-century paintings, sculpture, and furnishings. 133 Via del Babuino (phone: 679-2429).

**Armando Rioda** Hand-crafted copies of Italy's luxury leather goods at lower prices than the originals. 90 Via Belsiana (phone: 678-4435).

**Arturo Ferrante** Rare antiquities, also paintings and furnishings. 42-43 Via del Babuino (phone: 678-3613).

**Balloon** Italian-designed, low-cost women's shirts made of Chinese silk. 35 Piazza di Spagna (phone: 678-0110) and 495 Via Flaminia Vecchia (phone: 333-3352).

**Bassetti** High-fashion ready-to-wear for both men and women at discounted prices; the best clothes bargain in the Eternal City. 5 Via Monterone (phone: 689-2878).

**Battistoni** Men's elegant but conservative clothing. 61/A Via Condotti (phone: 678-6241).

**Beltrami** Sophisticated women's clothing. 19 Via Condotti (phone: 679-1330).

**Beppino Rampin** Custom-made shoes and boots for men and women. 31 Via Quintino Sella (phone: 474-0469).

**Bertè** Old and new toys. 107-111 Piazza Navona (phone: 678-5011).

**Borsalino** World-renowned hats. 157/B Via IV Novembre (phone: 679-4192).

**Bottega Veneta** Fine leather goods in the firm's trademark soft, basketweave design. 16/B Via San Sebastianello (phone: 678-2535).

**Bruno Magli** Top-quality shoes and boots, classic elegance. Three locations: 70 Via Veneto (phone: 488-4355); 1 Via del Gambero (phone: 679-3802); and 237 Via Cola di Rienzo (phone: 324-1759).

**Buccellati** For connoisseurs: A fine jeweler with a unique way of working with gold. 31 Via Condotti (phone: 679-0329).

**Bulgari** One of the world's most famous high-style jewelers. 10 Via Condotti (phone: 679-3876).

**Carlo Pasquali** Old prints, engravings, original lithographs, and drawings. Near the *Fontana di Trevi* at 25 Largo di Brazzà (no phone).

**Cerruti 1881** This trendy clothier is a favorite among Italian men. 20 Piazza San Lorenzo in Lucina (phone: 687-1505).

**Cesari** Exquisite upholstery and other decorator fabrics. 195 Via del Babuino (phone: 361-0495).

**Davide Cenci** Italian diplomats and their spouses buy their pin-striped suits, tweeds, and trench coats here. 1-7 Via Campo Marzio (phone: 699-0681).

**Fallani** Antiquities, ancient coins, and archeological items. 58/A Via del Babuino (phone: 320-7982).

**Fendi** Canvas and leather bags, genuine and faux furs, luggage, costume jewelry, and clothing. 36-40 Via Borgognona (phone: 679-7641/2/3).

**Ferragamo** Classic shoes. Women's: 73 Via Condotti (phone: 679-1565); men's: 66 Via Condotti (phone: 678-1130).

**Franco Maria Ricci** Sumptuously printed coffee-table books by a discriminating publisher, sold in an elegant setting. 4/D Via Borgognona (phone: 679-3466).

**Fratelli Merola** Handmade gloves of fine leather, produced in their own atelier. 143 Via del Corso (phone: 679-1961).

**Galleria dell'Antiquariato Europeo** Porcelain, bronzes, marbles. 76 Via Margutta (phone: 320-7729) and 112 Via dei Pastini (phone: 678-0195).

**Galleria delle Stampe Antiche** Old prints. 38 Via del Governo Vecchio (no phone).

**Galtrucco** All kinds of fabrics, especially pure silk. 23 Via del Tritone (phone: 678-9022).

**Gherardini** Fine leather fashions. 48/B Via Belsiana (phone: 679-5501).

**Gianfranco Ferré** High fashion for women. 42/B Via Borgognona (phone: 679-0050).

**Gianni Versace** The Milanese designer's Rome outlets. 41 Via Borgognona and 29 Via Bocca di Leone (phone: 678-0521).

**Giorgio Armani** Smart, fashionable clothing for men and women. 140 Via del Babuino (phone: 678-8454) and 77 Via Condotti (phone: 699-1460).

**Gucci** Men's and women's shoes, luggage, handbags, and other leather goods. Be prepared to wait. 8 Via Condotti (phone: 678-9340).

**Laura Biagiotti** Elegant womenswear. 43 Via Borgognona, corner of Via Belsiana (phone: 679-1205).

**Libreria Editrice Vaticana** A vast selection of books on art, archaeology, religion, and theology (some in English) at the *Vatican*'s own publisher's outlet. Next to the *Vatican* post office in Piazza San Pietro (phone: 6982).

**Lion Bookshop** The city's oldest English-language bookstore, chock-full of volumes on Rome's history, travel, and food. 181 Via del Babuino (phone: 322-5837).

**Mario Valentino** Fine shoes and leather goods. 84/A Via Frattina (phone: 679-1242).

**Marisa Pignataro** Outstanding knit dresses and tops in pure wool. 20 Via dei Greci (phone: 678-5443).

**Massoni** Fine handmade jewelry with a distinctive look. 48 Largo Goldoni (phone: 679-0182).

**Medison** One of the city's best custom shirtmakers for men. 6 Via Gregoriana (phone: 678-9618).

**Missoni** High-fashion knitwear for men and women in unique weaves of often costly blended yarns. 78 Piazza di Spagna (phone: 679-2555).

**Ai Monasteri** Products ranging from bath oils to honey to liqueurs from some 20 monasteries. 76 Piazza Cinque Lune (phone: 688-02783).

**Myricae** Hand-painted ceramics and such, made by Italian artisans from Sardinia to Deruta. 36 Via Frattina (phone: 679-5335).

**Nazareno Gabrielli** Excellent leather goods. 36-37 Via Condotti (phone: 679-0862).

**Perrone** Leather and fabric gloves. 92 Piazza di Spagna (phone: 678-3101).

**Petochi** Imaginative jewelry and grand old clocks. 23 Piazza di Spagna (phone: 679-3947).

**Pineider** Italy's famed stationer. 68-69 Via Due Macelli (phone: 678-9013).

**Polidori** Exclusive menswear and tailoring (21 Via Condotti and 4/C Via Borgognona). Finest pure silks and other fabrics (4/A Via Borgognona; phone: 678-4842).

**Prada** Fine-quality leather goods, including bags, shoes, and luggage, at relatively reasonable prices. 28-31 Via Nazionale (phone: 488-2413).

**Le Quattro Stagioni** Handmade ceramics by artisans from all over Italy. Shipping to the US can be arranged. 30/B Via dell'Umiltà (no phone).

**Richard Ginori** This shop has sold fine porcelain dinnerware and vases since 1735. 87-90 Via Condotti (phone: 678-1013) and 177 Via del Tritone (phone: 679-3836).

**Ritz** The classic look of Tuscany in women's clothing, including dressy loden coats. 188-189 Via del Babuino (phone: 361-2057).

**De Sanctis** Gift items, including Murano glass objects, Ginori porcelain, Florentine ceramics, and Alessi stainless household items. 80-84 Piazza Navona (phone: 688-06810).

**Al Sogno Giocattoli** Huge stuffed animals and a wide selection of amusing toys. 53 Piazza Navona (phone: 686-4198).

**Tanino Crisci** Chic women's shoes. 1 Via Borgognona (phone: 679-5461).

**Trimani** Founded in 1821, this is Rome's oldest and most famous wine shop. 20 Via Goito (phone: 446-9661).

**Valentino** Bold, high-fashion clothes for men. 12 Via Condotti (phone: 678-3656). Branches include a womenswear shop (15-18 Via Bocca di Leone; phone: 679-5862); *Oliver,* a shop for men, women, and children (61 Via del Babuino; phone: 679-8314); and an haute couture salon (24 Via Gregoriana; no phone).

## SPORTS AND FITNESS

**AUTO RACING** At the *Autodromo di Roma* (*Valle Lunga* racetrack, Campagnano di Roma, Via Cassia, Km 34; phone: 904-1027). Take a bus from Via Lepanto.

**BICYCLING** A pleasant excursion through Rome by bicycle is along the Villa Circuit, which travels 18 miles (29 km) from one major public park to another, all former private estates. You can get a perspective of the city that few tourists—and even fewer Romans—ever see. Start on the silent residential Aventine Hill, cross the Tiber, and climb up Monte Gianicolo to the vast *Villa Doria Pamphili.* Dozens of muskrats, descendants of a single pair brought here as part of an experiment, waddle and paddle around the lake in the park's center. Pass by the *Basilica di San Pietro,* cross the river again, and pedal through the gardens of the *Villa Borghese.* From the *Villa Borghese* due north to Via Salaria, it's a short ride to our final suggested stop—the wooded, aristocratic *Villa Ada. Nino Collati* (81 Via del Pellegrino; phone: 654-1084) rents bikes, including tandems. Bicycles are also available at *Bike Rome* (phone: 322-5240), located in the parking lot of the *Villa Borghese;* at Piazza San Silvestro and Piazza del Popolo; and on Via di Porta Castello near Piazza San Pietro. Be sure to take the same precautions when biking as when riding a scooter or moped (see *Getting Around*).

**FITNESS CENTERS** Rome has relatively few fitness centers and gyms, and those that exist tend to be cramped. An exception is the roomy, well-equipped, and (unusual for Rome) air conditioned *Roman Sport Center* (in the underground passage to the *metropolitana* stop at the top of Via Veneto in the *Villa Borghese,* 33 Via del Galoppatoio; phone: 320-1667). Although it is a private club, its American owner allows visitors to attend aerobics classes and to use the pool, squash court, sauna, Jacuzzi, and two gyms. Another private club, the *Navona Health Center* (39 Via dei Banchi Nuovi; phone: 689-6104), also opens its three-room gym in an ancient historical palazzo to non-members. Another fitness center accessible to the public is the *Barbara Bouchet Bodyshop* (162 Viale Parioli; phone: 808-5686).

**GOLF** Of the several courses in and around Rome, two are truly outstanding. The *Circolo del Golf Roma* (716A Via Appia Nuova; phone: 780-3407), 7 miles (11 km) southeast of Rome, is a rough, windy course loved by golf devotees (accuracy is a must). In the background are ruins of several ancient aqueducts. It's closed Mondays; book well ahead for weekends. At *Olgiata* (15 Largo Olgiata; phone: 378-9968), every hole has a character all its own. The *West* course is for international tournaments, the nine-hole *East* course for duffers. It's also closed Mondays; visitors may not play on weekends.

**HORSE RACING** Trotting races take place at the *Ippodromo Tor di Valle* (Via del Mare, Km 9.3; phone: 529-0269). Flat races are held at the *Ippodromo delle Capannelle* (1255 Via Appia, Km 12; phone: 718-3143) in the spring and fall.

**HORSEBACK RIDING** There are several riding schools and clubs inside the capital, and dozens more in the countryside surrounding the city. A regional branch of the *Associazione Nazionale per il Turismo Equestre* (*ANTE;* National Association for Equestrian Tourism; 5 Via A. Borelli; phone: 444-1179 or 494-0969) arranges special events for riders and can provide a complete list of local facilities. For lessons at various levels of proficiency, rentals by the hour (sometimes a subscription for several hours is required), or guided rides in the country, contact the *Centro Ippico Monte del Pavone* (Via Valle di Baccano; phone: 904-1378) or *Società Ippica Romana* (30 Via dei Monti della Farnesina; phone: 324-0591 or 324-0592). For weekend or week-long riding vacations, contact *Turismo Verde* (20 Via Fortuny; phone: 320-3464).

**JOGGING** There are two tracks in the *Villa Borghese;* enter at the top of Via Veneto or from Piazza del Popolo. The *Villa Doria Glori* (in the Parioli quarter) has a 1,180-meter track, which is illuminated at night;

the large *Villa Pamphili,* on the top of Monte Gianicolo (Janiculum Hill), has three tracks, as does the *Villa Ada* (off Via Salaria), which once was Mussolini's private park; and the *Villa Torlonia* (off Via Nomentana) has a pretty track flanked by palm and acacia trees. These villas are generally safe places to run, even at night.

**SOCCER** Two highly competitive teams, *Roma* and *Lazio,* play on Sundays from September through May at the *Stadio Olimpico* (Olympic Stadium at the *Foro Italico;* 1 Via dei Gladiatori; phone: 36851), site of the final game of the 1990 *World Cup.*

**SWIMMING** The pools at the *Cavalieri Hilton International* (see *Checking In*) and the *Aldrovandi Palace* (15 Via Ulisse Aldrovandi; phone: 322-3993) hotels are open to non-guests for a fee. Public pools include the *Piscina Olimpica* (*Foro Italico;* phone: 323-6076) and the *Piscina delle Rose* (20 Viale America, *EUR;* phone: 592-1862). Swimming in the sea near Rome is dangerous because of the high levels of pollution. Southeast of Ostia, at Castel Fusano and Castel Porziano, are stretches of free beach which are fine for a stroll, but are not suitable for swimming. Lago di Bracciano (Lake Bracciano), about 20 miles (32 km) north of Rome, is good for swimming, but there are no changing facilities. Note that the lake can get very crowded on weekends.

There are several water parks in the area, complete with swimming and wading pools, Jacuzzi-type basins, long, snaking water slides, and playpens for small children. Among them are: *Acqualand,* 30 miles (48 km) southeast of Rome near Anzio (41 Via dei Faggi, Lavinio; phone: 987-8247); *Acquasplash,* 20 miles (32 km) from the city (Via Palo Laziale, Ladispoli; phone: 991-2942); and *Acquapiper,* 15 miles (24 km) from Rome near Tivoli (Via Maremanna Inferiore; phone: 774-326538).

**TENNIS** Most courts belong to private clubs. Those at the *Cavalieri Hilton International* (see *Checking In*) and at the *Sheraton Roma* (Viale del Pattinaggio; phone: 5453) hotels are open to non-guests for a fee. Public courts are occasionally available at the *Foro Italico* (phone: 321-9021). Also open to the public are the *Società Ginnastica Roma* (5 Via del Muro Torto; phone: 488-5566), which has five courts; and, in the Via Appia Antica area, the four-court *Oasi di Pace* (2 Via degli Eugenii; phone: 718-4550), which also has a swimming pool.

The *Campionato Internazionale di Tennis* (Italian Open) takes place in Rome in May, and although tickets for the semifinals and finals are difficult to come by without advance purchase (at least four months ahead), daytime tickets for same-day events are relatively easy to obtain at the *Foro Italico* box office (phone: 36851). For information on purchasing advance tickets, contact the *Federazione Italiana Tennis* (70 Viale Tiziano; phone: 323-3807 or 324-0578).

**WINDSURFING** Sailboards and lessons are available at Castel Porziano (*primo cancello,* or first gate); in Fregene at the *Stabilimento La Baia* (phone: 665-61647) and the *Miraggio Sporting Club* (phone:

665-61802); and at the *Centro Surf Bracciano* at Lago di Bracciano (no phone).

## THEATER

Italy has been a land of patrons and performers since the days of the Medicis. Now, in areas where the aristocracy is too impoverished to treat, the government has rushed in, and virtually every fair-size city has its *teatro stabile* (repertory theater). As a result, ticket prices are far more reasonable than in the US, which is why you'll often see *esaurito* ("sold out") pasted across the poster outside the theater. During the theater season, approximately October through May, check *A Guest in Rome* or any daily newspaper for listings (see *Local Coverage*).

The *Teatri di Roma* (Theaters of Rome), the city's government-subsidized regional theaters, premiere most contemporary Italian plays, as well some foreign works. The *Teatri di Roma* perform at three principal locations, each a splendid historic theater building—the recently restored *Teatro Argentina* (Argentine Theater; Largo Argentina; phone: 688-04601), the lovely old *Teatro Valle* (Valley Theater; 23/A Via Teatro Valle; phone: 688-03794), and the *Teatro Quirino* (Quirinale Theater; 73 Piazza dell'Oratorio; phone: 679-4585). Another major theater is the *Teatro Eliseo* (Eliseo Theater; 183/E Via Nazionale; phone: 488-2114), which presents both classic and avant-garde works. A season of classical drama (in Italian and sometimes Greek) is held each July in the open-air *Teatro Romano di Ostia Antica* (Roman Theater of Ostia Antica; phone: 565-1913). The *Teatro Sistina* (Sistine Theater; 129 Via Sistina; phone: 482-6841) is Rome's best music hall. The charming, turn-of-the-century cabaret theater *Salone Margarita* (Margarita Lounge; 75 Via Due Macelli; phone: 679-8269) offers late-night shows and occasional Sunday afternoon concerts. Check the newspapers for the *Cinema Pasquino* (in Trastevere at Vicolo del Piede; phone: 580-3622) and the *Cinema Alcazar* (14 Via Merry del Val; phone: 588-0099), which often have English-language movies.

## MUSIC

Aside from Italian opera, Rome offers visitors a wealth of musical experiences. Check *A Guest in Rome* or the daily newspaper for information about performances (see *Local Coverage*).

Established in 1566 and named for the patron saint of music, the *Accademia Nazionale di Santa Cecilia* (National Academy of St. Cecilia; 4 Via della Conciliazione; phone: 679-0389) serves a host of functions. Besides managing Rome's symphony orchestra in residence and staging concerts in the *Vatican*'s stark *Pio Auditorium* on Sunday afternoons (with reprises on Monday and Tuesday evenings) from October through June, it orchestrates popular Bach-to-Berg chamber performances in the academy's own delightful hall on Friday evenings and presents evening concerts in summer in the hilltop Piazza del Campidoglio.

The regular season at the *Teatro dell'Opera* (Opera Theater; 1 Piazza Beniamino Gigli, corner of Via Firenze; phone: 481-7003) runs December through May. The best way to get tickets for good seats is through your hotel concierge or major travel agencies. Tickets also are sold at the box office several days before a performance, but they go fast—and be prepared to wait in line. The *Rome Ballet* also performs at the *Teatro dell'Opera.* Between October and May concerts and ballets are offered at the *Teatro Olimpico* (Olympic Theater; 17 Piazza Gentile da Fabriano; phone: 323-4890). The *Istituzione Universitaria dei Concerti* (University Institute of Music) holds concerts at the renovated *Aula Magna IUC* (50 Lungotevere Flaminio; phone: 361-0051/2) and at the university's *Aula Magna* (1 Piazzale Aldo Moro; phone: 361-0051). Other concerts occasionally are held at the *Auditorio del Gonfalone* (Banner Auditorium; 32 Via del Gonfalone; phone: 687-5952) and elsewhere around Rome by the *Coro Polifonico Romano* (Roman Polyphonic Chorus). Still other musical groups use the *Teatro Ghione* (Ghione Theater; 37 Via delle Fornaci; phone: 637-2294). There are concerts in many churches throughout the year, especially around *Christmas,* and during the summer there are occasional musical performances in the parks and piazze.

## NIGHTCLUBS AND NIGHTLIFE

Nightspots slip into and out of fashion so easily that visitors would do well to check Thursday's "TrovaRoma" supplement to the daily *La Repubblica* for an up-to-date survey of what's going on. Since the 1950s the few nightclubs here have clustered around Via Veneto and Piazza di Spagna, but they are pricey, with high minimums. For the younger set on the lookout for disco, jazz, and general hanging-out spots, a walk through Trastevere or the Testaccio area around Rome's old general markets and slaughterhouse (the newer bohemian area now that Trastevere has become gentrified) will turn up a host of intriguing places.

Among the nightclubs, the small, swanky, expensive restaurant and piano bar *Tartarughino* (near Piazza Navona at 1 Via della Scrofa; phone: 686-4131) is popular with the political set; there's no dancing. A slightly younger crowd gathers at fashionable *Gilda* (near Piazza di Spagna at 97 Via Mario de' Fiore; phone: 678-4838), known for its live music and pricey restaurant. Also popular are the *Open Gate* (4 Via San Nicola da Tolentino; phone: 488-4604 or 482-4464) and, off Via Veneto, *Jackie O* (11 Via Boncompagni; phone: 488-5754), which has an expensive restaurant, a piano bar, and a disco.

The disco *Piper* (9 Via Tagliamento; phone: 841-4459) has been packing people in, literally, for generations. The show here changes every night. *Le Stelle* (22 Via Cesare Beccaria; phone: 361-1240) plays pop, rap, soul, and funk until dawn. The *Bulli e Pupi* disco (on Aventine Hill at 11/A Via San Saba; phone: 578-2022) is not for executives, but for their offspring. The posh *Hostaria dell'Orso* (25 Via dei Soldati; phone: 683-07074) has something for everyone—the dimly lit, comfortable *Blu Bar* on the main floor offers laid-back piano or guitar music, and *La Cabala* upstairs is a disco for titled young Romans. It's in one of Rome's loveliest centuries-old buildings, not far from Piazza Navona (closed Sundays). There also is a restaurant (see *Eating Out*). *Veleno* (27 Via Sardegna, off Via Veneto; phone: 493583), which often has "theme" evenings, packs in the motor-scooter crowd. For live music and dancing in downtown historical Rome, there is the very special *Casanova* (36 Piazza Rondanini; phone: 654-7314). The live music at *Club 84* (84 Via Emilia; phone: 482-7538) lures dancers of all ages. *L'Alibi* disco (44 Via di Monte Testaccio; no phone) attracts a gay clientele. *Alien* (17 Via Velletri; phone: 841-2212), is another popular disco, located near the *Porta Pia. Yes Brazil* (in Trastevere at 103 Via San Francesco a Ripa; phone: 581-6267) offers live music from 7 to 9 PM and Latin disco after until 1 AM. *Caffè Latino* (96 Via di Monte Testaccio; phone: 574-4020) also has live music (including blues). Things get hot at *Regine* (50 Via del Moro; no phone), where there is live Caribbean music and South American food. *Zelig* (74 Via Monterone; phone: 687-9209) is a disco for the younger crowd.

*Karaoke,* that Japanese import where audience members perform onstage to recorded background music, has hit the Eternal City; good *karaoke* bars include *I Soliti Ignoti* (Via delle Tre Cannelle; phone: 678-9424) and the *Karaoke Club* (2 Via Ludovisi; phone: 489-04044).

Especially good jazz can be heard (despite the noise of diners in its restaurant) at *St. Louis Music City* (13/A Via del Cardello; phone: 474-50706) and the *Sax Club* (51 Vicolo dei Modelli; phone: 699-42260), near the *Fontana di Trevi.* Also try well-regarded *Caffè Caruso* (36 Via Monte Testaccio; phone: 574-5019), which plays both disco and jazz.

If you're just an amiable barfly who might like to strike up a pleasant conversation in English, the place to go is the bar at the *D'Inghilterra* hotel (see *Checking In*); there is no music except for the tinkling of ice cubes, but the bartender is one of the nicest in town. Other American haunts include the *Little Bar* (54/A Via Gregoriana; phone: 699-22243) and a pub called *Jeff Flynn's* (12 Via Zamardelli; phone: 686-1990). The *Fox Pub* (9 Via di Monterone; no phone) is jumping nightly around happy hour (from 9:30 to 10:30 PM), when drinks are very inexpensive. Many hotels have pleasant piano bars, including the *Excelsior, Holiday Inn Crowne Plaza Minerva, Majestic,* and *Plaza* (see *Checking In* for all).

*Caffè Picasso* (Piazza della Pigna; no phone) is a relaxing, upscale hangout for young intellectuals and hip artists; it also features a rotating art exhibit. *La Vetrina* (20 Via della Vetrina; no phone) is another bohemian enclave, complete with live music, art exhibits, and occasional poetry readings.

# Best in Town

## CHECKING IN

Of the more than 500 hotels in Rome, the following are recommended either for some special charm, location, or bargain price in their category. Those without restaurants are noted, although all serve breakfast if desired. All have private baths, air conditioning, TV sets, and telephones in the rooms unless otherwise stated. In high season prices can be staggering; expect to pay more than $500 for a double room per night in the hotels listed as very expensive; from $300 to $500 for hotels in the expensive price range; from $150 to $300 in the moderate category; and less than $150 in the inexpensive category. Off-season rates are about 10% lower. All telephone numbers listed below are in the 6 city code unless otherwise indicated.

### VERY EXPENSIVE

**Cavalieri Hilton International** It's far from the historic center of Rome at the top of a lovely hill (Monte Mario) overlooking much of the city, but shuttle buses to Via Veneto and the Piazza di Spagna run hourly during shopping hours. The swimming pool is especially desirable in summer, and the rooftop restaurant, *La Pergola,* wins high praise from food critics. A 387-room resort, it further offers tennis, a sauna, and other diversions. Business facilities include meeting rooms for up to 2,100, an English-speaking concierge, foreign currency exchange, secretarial services in English, audiovisual equipment, photocopiers, translation services, and express checkout. 101 Via Cadlolo (phone: 31511; 800-HILTONS; fax: 315-12241).

**Excelsior** Big (383 rooms), bustling, but efficient, this member of the CIGA chain dominates Via Veneto, next to the *US Embassy.* It's a favorite with Americans, and the bar is a popular meeting place; there's also a restaurant. Business facilities include 24-hour room service, meeting rooms for up to 400, an English-speaking concierge, foreign currency exchange, secretarial services in English, audiovisual equipment, photocopiers, computers, translation services, and express checkout. 125 Via Veneto (phone: 4708; 800-221-2340; fax: 482-6205).

**Le Grand** The pride of the CIGA chain, this old-fashioned, luxurious property is truly grand. It has 171 large and well-appointed rooms, and the food served in *Le Restaurant* (see *Eating Out*) is considered among the best in Rome. There also are two cozy bars, and afternoon tea is served to the strains of soothing harp music. Business facilities include 24-hour room service, meeting rooms for up to 400, an English-speaking concierge, foreign currency exchange, secretarial services in English, audiovisual equipment, photocopiers, computers, translation services, and express checkout. 3 Via Vittorio Emanuele Orlando (phone: 4709; 800-221-2340; fax: 474-7307).

**Hassler Villa Medici** At the top of the Piazza di Spagna and within easy striking distance of the best shopping in Rome, this hotel is favored by a loyal clientele of Hollywood stars and European royalty. The guestrooms could stand some refurbishing, and the public rooms have seen better days, yet the bar remains a popular and traditional meeting place for local personalities. Each of the 85 rooms is individually decorated, and half overlook the city; a small number of penthouse suites with private terraces afford breathtaking views. The service is friendly and efficient. The rooftop restaurant has splendid views and serves a Sunday brunch popular with Romans and other lovers of Rome. Business facilities include meeting rooms for up to 180, an English-speaking concierge, foreign currency exchange, secretarial services in English, audiovisual equipment, photocopiers, translation services, and express checkout. 6 Piazza Trinità dei Monti (phone: 678-2651; fax: 678-9991).

## EXPENSIVE

**Ambasciatori Palace** Across the street from the *US Embassy,* it has 145 generally spacious rooms, old-fashioned amenities, a restaurant, and a convenient location. Business facilities include 24-hour room service, meeting rooms for up to 200, an English-speaking concierge, foreign currency exchange, secretarial services in English, audiovisual equipment, photocopiers, cable television news, translation services, and express checkout. 70 Via Veneto (phone: 47493; fax: 474-3601).

**Atlante Star** Near the *Vatican,* this modern 61-room hotel boasts a magnificent rooftop terrace. The *Roof-Garden Les Etoiles* restaurant offers a sweeping view of Rome with the *Basilica di San Pietro* in the foreground. Parking is available as well. Business facilities include 24-hour room service, meeting rooms for up to 83, an English-speaking concierge, foreign currency exchange, secretarial services in English, audiovisual equipment, photocopiers, computers, translation services, and express checkout. 34 Via Vitelleschi (phone: 687-9558; fax: 687-2300).

**Boston** The roof garden is just one of the selling points of this 120-room hostelry, well located between Via Veneto and Piazza di Spagna and across from a parking garage. Although there is no restaurant, the breakfast buffet is a delightful plus. Business facilities include meeting rooms for up to 25 and an English-speaking concierge. 47 Via Lombardia (phone: 473951; 800-223-9862; fax: 482-1019).

**Forum** Few hotels anywhere in the world can boast rooms with such views. The roof garden and adjacent rooftop restaurant, which abut the wall of a medieval church tower, overlook the *Foro Romano* and *Fori Imperiali.* The 81 rooms are comfortably sized; the service is pleasant; and all around are lively restaurants in the Subura quarter. It's also within walking distance of Piazza Venezia and near a *metropolitana* (subway) stop. 25 Via Tor de' Conti (phone: 679-2446; fax: 678-6479).

**Holiday Inn Crowne Plaza Minerva** Any resemblance to US members of this chain begins and ends with its moniker. Located in the historical section of the city, adjacent to the *Pantheon,* it offers 118 rooms,

13 junior suites, and three presidential suites, all with color satellite TV and electronic safes. The suites are elegantly decorated with Napoleonic-period furnishings—even the meeting rooms have fine frescoes and statues. There's a restaurant, a comfortable piano bar, and a rooftop terrace that offers alfresco dining in summer with a unique view of the *Pantheon* and the ancient city. Business facilities include meeting rooms for up to 250, an English-speaking concierge, foreign currency exchange, secretarial services in English, audiovisual equipment, photocopiers, translation services, and express checkout. 69 Piazza della Minerva (phone: 684-1888; 800-HOLIDAY; fax: 679-4165).

**D'Inghilterra** Popular with knowledgeable travelers—Anatole France, Mark Twain, and Ernest Hemingway have stayed here. Some of the 102 rooms in this venerable place are small —inevitable in older, downtown hotels—so be sure to ask for one of the larger ones. Some top-floor suites have flowered terraces. There is a small and *simpatico* restaurant, and the bar is always crowded. Business facilities include meeting rooms for up to 50, an English-speaking concierge, audiovisual equipment, photocopiers, computers, and express checkout. Near Piazza di Spagna, in the middle of the central shopping area. 14 Via Bocca di Leone (phone: 672161; fax: 684-0828).

**Lord Byron** Once a private villa, this small (47 rooms) elite inn in the fashionable Parioli residential district still maintains its club-like atmosphere. There isn't a swimming pool or spa—nothing but discreet personal attention, subdued opulence, and what general opinion holds is the finest restaurant in the capital, *Relais le Jardin* (see *Delightful Dining*). Business facilities include 24-hour room service, meeting rooms for up to 100, an English-speaking concierge, foreign currency exchange, secretarial services in English, audiovisual equipment, photocopiers, translation services, and express checkout. 5 Via Giuseppe de Notaris (phone: 322-0404; fax: 322-0405).

**Majestic** The lobbies and some of the halls are richly adorned with frescoes, sumptuous carpeting, and draperies; the 105 rooms and baths are well appointed and spacious. On the premises is the turn-of-the-century *La Veranda* dining room. The service is professional, and the downtown location across from the *US Embassy* and close to airline offices is particularly convenient in this traffic-bound city. 50 Via Veneto (phone: 486841; fax: 488-0984).

**Plaza** This property in a 19th-century historic building has aged gracefully. Its lobby, with a stained glass ceiling, period wallpaper, and plush furniture, is one of Rome's prettiest, and the old-fashioned bar at one end is a great place for a nightcap. Former guests include Empress Carlota of Mexico and Sir Edmund Hillary. All but 11 of the 207 spacious guestrooms have private baths. Although some of the rooms could use refurbishing, this hotel is a good choice because of its location near Via Condotti and its ambience. There is no restaurant, but a complimentary breakfast is offered. Business facilities include 24-hour room service, an English-speaking concierge, foreign currency exchange, secretarial services in English, audiovisual equipment, photocopiers, translation service, and express checkout. 126 Via del Corso (phone: 396-672101; fax: 684-1575).

**Raphael** Behind Piazza Navona, it's a favorite of Italian politicians (it's near the *Senate* and the *Chamber of Deputies*). Several of the 83 rooms are small, and some could use a bit of refurbishing, but loyal patrons love the antiques in the lobby, the cozy bar, the restaurant, and the location. The roof terrace has one of Rome's finest views. Business facilities include two English-speaking concierges, foreign currency exchange, secretarial services in English, photocopiers, translation services, and express checkout. 2 Largo Febo (phone: 650881; fax: 687-8993).

**Rex** This 50-room hotel close to the *Teatro dell'Opera* is named for the fabled pre–World War II Italian luxury liner (the ship in Fellini's *Amarcord*), which gives an idea of the Art Deco aura to which it aspires. There's a bar but no restaurant; breakfast is included in the room rate. Business facilities include meeting rooms for up to 110 and photocopiers. 149 Via Torino (phone: 488-1568 or 482-4828; fax: 488-2743).

**Sole al Pantheon** One of Rome's most venerable hostelries—and one of the more sought after and priciest in town—this 28-room hotel is also among the most convenient because of its entrance on Piazza della Rotonda, facing the *Pantheon.* Be sure to ask for a room with a view—a few on the top floor have whirlpool baths, balconies, and panoramas of the spectacular skyline. Don't be put off by the kitschy downstairs lobby. There is no restaurant. Business facilities include an English-speaking concierge, foreign currency exchange, photocopiers, translation services, and express checkout. 63 Piazza della Rotonda (phone: 678-0441; fax: 684-0689).

### MODERATE

**Columbus** In a restored 15th-century palace right in front of the *Basilica di San Pietro,* this 107-room hotel (under the same ownership as the *Rex* hotel—see above) offers antique furniture, paintings, a handsome restaurant, a garden, and a lot of atmosphere for the price. 33 Via della Conciliazione (phone: 686-5435; fax: 686-4874).

**Fontana** A restored 13th-century monastery next to the *Fontana di Trevi,* it offers 30 cell-like rooms (no TV sets)—though 10 have great views of the fabulous fountain—and a lovely rooftop bar and restaurant. It's a bargain in every way. Business facilities include meeting rooms for up to 35, an English-speaking concierge, and secretarial services in English. 96 Piazza di Trevi (phone: 678-6113).

**Gregoriana** In the heart of Rome's high-fashion district, on the street of the same name, this tiny gem (19 rooms) attracts a stylish crowd. Its Art Deco–like decor features room letters (rather than numbers) created by the late illustrator Erté. There's no restaurant, though a continental breakfast is included. No credit cards accepted. 18 Via Gregoriana (phone: 679-4269; fax: 678-4258).

**Locarno** Near Piazza del Popolo and Piazza di Spagna, this Belle Epoque hotel often attracts artists, writers, and intellectuals. The 36 rooms have Victorian furniture, and many are large enough to accommodate sofas and desks. A pleasant plus: Bikes are available to guests free of charge. Although the hotel does not have a restaurant, drinks and breakfast are served on the terrace during warm weather. Business facilities include meeting rooms for up to 15, an English-speaking concierge, secretarial services in English, photocopiers, and express checkout. 22 Via della Penna (phone: 361-0841; fax: 321-5249).

**Manfredi** Located on a charming street chockablock with artists' studios and galleries, this is the perfect romantic hideaway for those who don't fancy big hotels. The 15 elegant rooms—decorated in dusty rose and cream—are soundproofed from the noise of the busy street below. There's a small breakfast room but no restaurant. 61 Via Margutta (phone: 310-7676; fax: 320-7736).

**La Residenza** On a quiet street just behind Via Veneto, this old-fashioned place feels much more like a private villa than a hotel. The 27 rooms are comfortable and artistically decorated (all but two have private baths). Full American breakfast is included, but there's no restaurant. Book well in advance. Business facilities include meeting rooms for up to 25, an English-speaking concierge, foreign currency exchange, secretarial services in English, photocopiers, and translation services. No credit cards accepted. 22 Via Emilia (phone: 488-0789; fax: 485721).

**Sant'Anselmo** In a small palazzo-style building on Aventine Hill, this bargain hotel has 46 rooms (all but three with private baths) and a family atmosphere, but no restaurant or air conditioning. Nearby are two other similar properties under the same management—the *San Pio* with 65 guestrooms (no air conditioning) and the *Aventino* with 23 rooms (no air conditioning, no TV sets). Reservations are necessary well in advance. Business facilities include meeting rooms for up to 50, an English-speaking concierge, foreign currency exchange, secretarial services in English, and photocopiers. 2 Piazza di Sant'Anselmo (phone: 578-3214; fax: 578-3604).

**Teatro di Pompeo** The hotel's foundation was originally laid in 55 BC and is said to have supported the *Teatro di Pompeo* (Pompey's Theater), where Julius Caesar met his untimely end. It's on a quiet street and offers 12 charming rooms, with hand-painted tiles and beamed ceilings. There's no restaurant. Business facilities include meeting rooms for up to 20, an English-speaking concierge, foreign currency exchange, audiovisual equipment, and photocopiers. 8 Largo del Pallaro (phone: 687-2566; fax: 654-5531).

**Trevi** In a renovated palazzo only a few steps from the fabled fountain, this four-story hotel has 20 guestrooms but no restaurant. 20 Vicolo del Babuccio (phone: 678-9543; fax: 684-1407).

**Casa Stefazio** Here is a great bargain: a bed-and-breakfast place set in a sprawling, tree-shaded house and run by Orazio and Stefania Azzola, a hospitable Italian couple. The five bedrooms are attractive and comfortable, and there is a surprising number of amenities: several lovely gardens, a tennis court, a pool, a sauna, and a billiards table on the premises, and horseback riding nearby. The food, prepared by Cordon Bleu chef Orazio, is sumptuous (dinner is available upon request). The property is a 45-minute bus ride from the city center, but the privacy, greenery, and quiet are powerful compensations. Open April through December. 553 Via della Marcigliana (phone/fax: 871-20042).

**Fortis Guest House** This small, friendly hotel offers 22 guestrooms, 17 with private baths or showers. The accommodations are basic (no air conditioning or TV sets), but the property is well managed, the ambience is homey, and the location (in the Prati quarter across the Tiber River) is pleasant and convenient. There is no restaurant. 7 Via Fornovo (phone: 321-2256; fax: 321-2222).

**Margutta** This 21-room hotel near Piazza del Popolo has an English-speaking concierge but no restaurant. The rooms are basically furnished (no TV sets, phones, or air conditioning), but all have private baths. The two rooms on the roof (Nos. 50 and 51) feature fireplaces and are surrounded by terraces. 34 Via Laurina (phone: 679-8440).

---

## EATING OUT

Although influenced by Greece and Asia Minor, the ancient Romans were the originators of the first fully developed cuisine of the Western world.

Roman gastronomy was developed in humble kitchens, based on such staples as lentils and chick-peas. Unfortunately, the old-fashioned, inexpensive trattorie are becoming rare, replaced by growing numbers of mediocre Chinese restaurants and fast-food emporiums, so don't be surprised if your favorite casual dining spot is now all tarted up and pricey. Be aware, too, that fad menus continue to show up everywhere. In addition, some chefs are cutting corners—for example, using truffle-flavored pastes in dishes described on the menu as *con tartufi* (with truffles). The trendy dessert continues to be *tiramisù,* a Tyrolean calorie bombe of mascarpone cheese, liqueur, and coffee; easy to prepare, it is elbowing out better and more interesting desserts. Worst of all, an increasing number of desserts are factory-made frozen confections, rather than freshly prepared dishes.

The bright side is the new generation of well-trained cooks who are reviving forgotten regional dishes and devising new, less fatty, and more refined versions of old standbys; they call their fare *cucina creativa* (creative cuisine).

Traditional Roman cooking is robust and hearty. Cholesterol and calorie counters guiltily succumb to steaming dishes of *spaghetti all'amatriciana* (with tomato, special bacon, and tangy pecorino—sheep's-milk cheese), deep-fried *filetti di baccalà* (salt cod filets), or *coda alla vaccinara* (oxtail stewed in tomato, onion, and celery). Restaurants usually offer abundant fresh fish, particularly on Tuesdays and Fridays, but prices are steep. (All restaurants are required to identify frozen fish as well as other frozen ingredients—look for the word *congelato.*) Don't hesitate to try the *antipasto marinara* (a mixture of seafoods in a light sauce of olive oil, lemon, parsley, and garlic), the *spaghetti alle vongole* (with clam sauce—the shells included), and as a main course, trout from the nearby lakes or (at a higher price) rockfish from the Mediterranean.

Veal is typically Roman, served as saltimbocca (literally "hop into the mouth," flavored with ham, sage, and marsala wine) or roasted with the fresh rosemary that grows in every garden. *Abbacchio al forno* is milk-fed baby lamb roasted with garlic and rosemary, and *abbacchio brodettato,* ever harder to find, is lamb stew topped by a tangy sauce of egg yolks and lemon juice. *Abbacchio scottadito* ("finger burning") are tiny grilled lamb chops. On festive occasions *maialetto* (suckling pig) may appear on the menu; it is stuffed with herbs, roasted, and thickly sliced. Its street-stand version, *la porchetta,* is eaten between thick slabs of country bread. Another traditional meat dish is *bollito misto* (boiled beef, tongue, chicken, and pig's trotter). Watch too for such Roman specialties as *trippa* (tripe flavored with mint, parmigiano cheese, and tomato sauce), *coniglio* (rabbit), *capretto* (kid), *coratella* (lamb's heart), *animelle* (sweetbreads), and in season, *cinghiale* (wild boar). Dried boar sausages are popular in antipasti, along with salamis; the local Roman salami is prepared with tasty fennel seeds.

Among the traditional pasta dishes is the incredibly simple *spaghetti alla carbonara* (with egg, salt pork, and pecorino cheese). *Penne all'arrabbiata* are short pasta in a tomato-and- garlic sauce with hot peppers. The familiar *fettuccine all'Alfredo* depends upon the quality of the egg pasta in a rich sauce of cream, butter, and parmigiano.

Fresh seasonal vegetables are served in many ways: as a separate first course; as the base for a savory antipasto; accompanying the main dish; or even munched raw—for instance, *finocchio al pinzimonio* (fennel dipped into purest olive oil, seasoned with salt and pepper)—after a particularly heavy meal to "clean the palate." Several local greens are unknown to visitors, such as *agretti, bieta, cicoria,* and *broccolo romano*—the last two often boiled briefly, then sautéed with olive oil, garlic, and hot red peppers. Salad ingredients include red radicchio, wild aromatic herbs, and the juicy tomatoes so cherished during the sultry summer months, when they are served with ultra-aromatic basil—the sun's special gift to Mediterranean terraces and gardens (don't spoil their wonderful taste by adding vinegar). Tomatoes also are stuffed with rice and roasted. Yellow, red, and green sweet peppers, eggplant, mushrooms, green and broad beans, and zucchini are favorite vegetables for antipasto, while asparagus and artichokes are especially prized in season. The latter are stuffed with mint and garlic and stewed in olive oil *alla romana,* or opened out like a flower and deep fried *alla giudia* (Jewish-style).

After such a meal, Romans normally have fresh fruit for dessert, although there is no shortage of sweet desserts, such as *montebianco* (a rich chestnut-purée confection), zuppa inglese (a trifle-like dessert consisting of liqueur-soaked strips of cake served with pudding), and of course, gelato (ice cream). For a final *digestivo,* bottles brought to the table may include sambuca (it has an aniseed base), grappa (made from the third and fourth grape pressings and normally over 60 proof), and an herbal liqueur to aid digestion known as *amaro* (which means bitter, but is more often quite sweet).

Most dining is à la carte, although a *menù turistico* is offered at some unpretentious trattorie for reasonable prices, and a few tony establishments have a *menù degustazione* (sampler menu) that is sometimes (but not always) less expensive. An even better value are the quick-service, often cafeteria-style, *rosticcerie* and *tavole calde* (literally "hot tables"). There are also several small wine-tasting establishments that offer inexpensive light snacks at lunch with a glass of fine wine; some also serve pasta or a mixed vegetable platter (see *Bars and Caffès,* below).

Dinner for two (with wine) will cost more than $200 in restaurants listed below as very expensive; $120 to $200 in restaurants described as expensive; $75 to $120 in moderate places; and less than $75 in inexpensive spots. Restaurants serve lunch and dinner unless otherwise noted. Always ask prices when ordering wine. Good Italian wines can cost $30 or more per bottle. All telephone numbers are in the 6 city code unless otherwise indicated.

For an unforgettable dining experience, we begin with our favorites (we admit that they're pricey), followed by our cost and quality choices, listed by price category.

---

### DELIGHTFUL DINING

**Checchino dal 1887** Serious diners flock to this bustling place (which has earned a Michelin star) for traditional Roman specialties and samples from the city's best wine cellar. The current generation of Mariani brothers, Francesco and Elio (whose family has run the restaurant since 1887), are consummately professional. The *spaghetti alla carbonara* and *all'amatriciana* alone are worth a visit. Other notable specialties include oxtail stew with celery and the unlikely sounding *rigatoni con pajatta* (pasta in a tomato sauce with lamb's intestines). The ubiquitous pecorino cheese is served with raw acacia honey for dessert. Closed Sunday dinner, Mondays, August, and a week at *Christmas.* Reservations necessary. Major credit cards accepted. 30 Via Monte Testaccio (phone: 574-6318 or 574-3816).

**Relais le Jardin** The sumptuous dining room of the *Lord Byron* hotel has been hailed as Rome's foremost restaurant by a wide consensus of Italian food critics and restaurant guides. Chef Antonio Sciullo's creations transform the unlikely into the surprising and sometimes sublime. The menu follows the seasons—you might find zucchini blossoms stuffed with bean purée, ravioli with a delicate pigeon ragout, or watercress flan with scallops. The dessert soufflé has a crunchy hazelnut topping. Service is appropriately sophisticated, as are the wines. Closed Sundays and August. Reservations necessary. Major credit cards accepted. *Lord Byron Hotel,* 5 Via Giuseppe de Notaris (phone: 322-0404).

### VERY EXPENSIVE

**Alberto Ciarla** Acclaimed chef Alberto is renowned for what he does with fresh fish, although his herbed pasta sauces also are a delight, and the pâté of wild game in season is divine. Be sure to leave room for one of his picture-perfect desserts. (The restaurant recently began offering a slightly less expensive prix fixe menu.) The ever-large, noisy crowd brightens up the somber all-black decor, and in good weather there are a few outdoor tables on a Trastevere street. Open for dinner only; closed Sundays. Reservations advised. Major credit cards accepted. 40 Piazza San Cosimato (phone: 581-8668).

**Antica Enoteca Capranica** A 16th-century palace that has served as housing for seminary students and as a wine shop is now one of Rome's smartest dining spots. The food, prepared under the watchful eye of famed chef Angelo Paracucchi, is light and elegantly presented. The menu changes seasonally, but specialties might include ravioli stuffed with ricotta and zucchini, boiled meat, and seafood. The knowledgeable sommelier can help you select just the right wine to go with your meal. Closed Sundays. Reservations advised. Major credit cards accepted. 99 Piazza Capranica (phone: 684-0992).

**Le Restaurant** This outstanding dining room at the *Grand* hotel serves continental and regional specialties that change with the seasons. The decor, flowers, and waiters in tails all reflect the *Grand* approach to luxury. Open daily. Reservations necessary. Major credit cards accepted. 3 Via Vittorio Emanuele Orlando (phone: 4709).

**La Rosetta** Famous for its excellent fish dishes, this swanky, one-Michelin-star bistro is small, jam-packed, and chic. The chef grills, fries, boils, or bakes to perfection any—or a mixture of all—of the seafood flown in from his native Sicily. Try the *pappardelle al pescatore* (wide noodles in a piquant tomato sauce with mussels, clams, and parsley) or Sicilian-style *pasta con le sarde* (with sardine chunks and wild fennel). Closed weekends and August. Reservations necessary. Major credit cards accepted. 9 Via della Rosetta (phone: 656-1002 or 683-08841).

**El Toulà** The well-heeled, well-traveled, and aristocratic literally rub elbows here (the place is small) for Cortina- and Venice-inspired fare. The menu changes continually, but chef Daniele Repetti can be counted on to prepare excellent seafood year-round (such as poppy seed–daubed salmon in oyster sauce) and game (including venison) in winter. Try the *menù degustazione*. There's an impressive list of 500 wines, and the desserts are exceptional. Prices are lower at midday. Closed Saturday lunch, Sundays, and August. Reservations necessary. Major credit cards accepted. 29/B Via della Lupa (phone: 687-3750 or 687-3498).

### EXPENSIVE

**Alvaro al Circo Massimo** Let Alvaro suggest what's best—be it fresh fish, game such as *fagiano* (pheasant) or *faraona* (guinea hen), or mushrooms (try grilled *porcini*). The ambience is rustic; there are outdoor tables during the summer. Closed Mondays. Reservations advised. Major credit cards accepted. 53 Via dei Cerchi (phone: 678-6112).

**Andrea** The best dining place in the Via Veneto area. In season there's fettuccine with artichoke sauce; always on the menu is ricotta-stuffed fresh ravioli. Also try the *insalata catalan,* a Spanish-style seafood salad. Pleasant service, a good house wine, and rich desserts are other pluses. Closed Sundays, Monday lunch, and three weeks in August. Reservations necessary. Major credit cards accepted. 26 Via Sardegna (phone: 474-0557).

**Dal Bolognese** The menu is nearly as long as the list of celebrities who frequent this eatery, run by two brothers from Bologna. Try the homemade *tortelloni* (pasta twists stuffed with ricotta cheese) and the popular *bollito misto.* There are tables outdoors in good weather. Closed Sunday dinner, Mondays, and two weeks in August. Reservations necessary. Major credit cards accepted. 1 Piazza del Popolo (phone: 361-1426).

**Camponeschi** In summer dinner is served on an outdoor terrace overlooking the *Palazzo Farnese* and a tranquil square with ancient Roman fountains. Some say the view is better than the pricey fare, which tends to be refined, well-prepared versions of traditional Italian dishes. Others swear by such rarified offerings as corn polenta with Alba truffles or partridge *en croûte.* Open for dinner only; closed Sundays. Reservations advised. Major credit cards accepted. 50 Piazza Farnese (phone: 687-4927).

**Il Capitello** This elegant addition to the ancient Campo dei Fiori area is an understated 50-table dining room crowned by a frescoed ceiling; piano music in the background adds to the ambience. The menu is decidedly Calabrian: Try the spicy pasta dishes and the fresh seafood. Closed Sundays. Reservations necessary. Major credit cards accepted. 4 Campo dei Fiori (phone: 683-00073).

**Al Fogher** This special restaurant not far from Via Veneto offers a taste of Venice in the heart of Rome. Every ingredient is carefully selected to ensure peak freshness and taste, and the dishes are meticulously prepared. Good choices include *taglioni* flavored with cinnamon, ham, and lemon; *fegato alla veneta* (liver with onions and white wine); and *osso buco* (veal shanks). Be sure to save room for the wonderful homemade desserts, including apple strudel, *panna cotta* topped with seasonal fruit, and *crème brûlée*. There's also a fine wine list, and the atmosphere is quiet and elegant, almost somber. Closed Saturday lunch, Sundays, and August. Reservations advised. American Express accepted. 13/b Via Tevere (phone: 841-7032).

**Hostaria dell'Orso** Although this restaurant housed in an elegant 14th-century building is widely known as a tourist place, the traditional Italian fare is quite good. Upstairs is a disco (see *Nightclubs and Nightlife*), and downstairs is a piano bar. Closed Sundays. Reservations necessary. Major credit cards accepted. 25 Via dei Soldati (phone: 683-07074).

**La Lampada** Specialties here are truffles and wild mushrooms, but don't expect the former to be fresh beyond the autumn/winter season. The risotto is made with white truffles, the carpaccio with a grating of both black and white truffles (from Norcia and Alba, respectively). Closed Sundays. Reservations necessary. Major credit cards accepted. 25 Via Quintino Sella (phone: 481-5673).

**Quinzi e Gabrieli** Seafood, prepared as simply as possible, is a very serious subject here. In season the oyster bar is popular; the small dining room seats only 22. Open for dinner only; closed Sundays and August. Reservations necessary. Major credit cards accepted. Near the *Pantheon,* at 6 Via delle Coppelle (phone: 687-9389).

**Romolo** In this famed tavern in the heart of Trastevere, near a particularly picturesque ancient city gate, the painter Raphael supposedly courted (and painted) the baker's daughter—the resulting portrait is called *La Fornarina.* The fare and the good wine list cling to the traditional, with such hearty dishes as *spaghetti alla boscaiolo* (with mushrooms and tomato) and *mozzarella alla Fornarina* (melted cheese wrapped in prosciutto and accompanied by a fried artichoke). Closed Mondays and August. Reservations necessary, especially in summer. Major credit cards accepted. 8 Via di Porta Settimiana (phone: 581-8284).

**Taverna Flavia** It's been fashionable with the movie crowd, journalists, and politicians for over 30 years. Owner Mimmo likes autographed pictures—one entire room is devoted to Elizabeth Taylor—and the *Sardi's* style survives, despite the demise of "Hollywood on the Tiber" long ago. Good pasta dishes and fine grilled fish are served until quite late. Closed Saturday lunch, Sundays, and August. Reservations necessary. Major credit cards accepted. 9-11 Via Flavia (phone: 474-5214).

**Taverna Giulia** This reliable old favorite is set in a 600-year-old building. Genoese specialties include pesto over *trofie* noodles, wild mushroom soup, *stoccafisso* (dried cod), and smoked fish. Closed

Sundays and August. Reservations advised. Major credit cards accepted. 26 Vicolo dell'Oro (phone: 686-9768).

**Vecchia Roma** Located steps away from some of the finest monuments of ancient Rome, this is where tradition reigns. The menu offers a broad selection of justifiably beloved favorites like prosciutto with melon, veal in a tuna sauce, grilled baby lamb chops, and fresh country salad greens; there's also an impressive wine list. The setting is classic trattoria: whitewashed walls, rustic furniture, and an agreeably old-fashioned air. It is especially pleasant in warm weather, when tables are set up outdoors under giant market umbrellas, but it's comfortable inside as well (thanks to air conditioning—a rarity in Rome restaurants). Closed Wednesdays and two weeks in August. Reservations advised. Major credit cards accepted. 18 Piazza Campitelli (phone: 686-4604).

### MODERATE

**Il Barroccio** *Pane rustico* (crusty country-style bread) is made here daily, and Tuscan-style beans are slow-baked in a wood-burning oven. This is the place to try *crostini* (fried bread offered with an assortment of toppings) in all its permutations, *bruschette* (slices of toast covered with tomatoes and herbs), and pizza. Across the street at No. 123 is its twin, *Er Faciolaro,* owned by the same people. One or the other always is open during conventional hours. Reservations necessary on weekends. Major credit cards accepted. 13 Via dei Pastini (phone: 679-3797).

**La Campana** This 400-year-old, truly Roman restaurant has become a beloved institution. The waiters can help you decipher the handwritten menu, which tempts most with *carciofi alla romana* (fresh artichokes in garlic and oil), *tonnarelli alla chitarra* (homemade pasta in an egg-and-cheese sauce), lamb, truffle-topped poultry dishes, and homemade desserts. Closed Mondays and August. Reservations advised. Major credit cards accepted. 18 Vicolo della Campana (phone: 686-7820).

**La Cannaccia** Sicilian owner Salvatore Ruggieri has gone overboard decorating his trattoria; fortunately, the fare is more straightforward. The fresh swordfish is a favorite. Closed Sundays and part of August. No reservations or credit cards accepted. 63 Via della Guglia (no phone).

**La Carbonara** On the square where Rome's most colorful morning food market has been held for centuries, this is where *spaghetti alla carbonara* is said to have been invented. The windows of the ancient palazzo look out over the scene; inside are high-ceilinged, woodbeamed rooms—try for a table near the window. The menu is as authentically Roman as the decor. Closed Tuesdays. Reservations advised for dinner in summer. Major credit cards accepted. 23 Campo dei Fiori (phone: 686-4783). Moderate.

**Il Cardinale** In a restored bicycle shop off stately Via Giulia, decorated in a somewhat precious turn-of-the-century style, this popular spot specializes in regional dishes: pasta with green tomato or artichoke sauce, grilled eels, a sweetbread casserole with mushrooms, and *aliciotti con l'indivia* (an anchovy and endive dish). Closed Sundays and August. Reservations advised. Visa accepted. 6 Via delle Carceri (phone: 686-9336).

**Cesarina** Year in and year out diners return for the *bollito misto*, well prepared from the rich cart of meat and sausage, with green sauce. In summer the fresh fish may appeal more, as will the air conditioning. Year-round the pasta Bolognese-style is a traditional favorite. Closed Sundays. Reservations necessary. Major credit cards accepted. 109 Via Piemonte (phone: 488-0828).

**Le Colline Emiliane** Eateries like this are becoming a rarity: Service is prompt, the decor is simple, and homemade pasta is the specialty— the *maccheroncini al funghetto* (large macaroni with mushrooms) is delicious. Closed Fridays and August. Reservations advised in winter. No credit cards accepted. Near Via Veneto at 22 Via degli Avignonesi (phone: 481-7538).

**Costanza** This spacious trattoria, a longtime Roman favorite is now among the smartest eateries in the capital. The stuffed homemade pasta—varieties change with the seasons—is delectable; look for ravioli plump with puréed artichoke, or try the wild *porcini* mushrooms on pasta. The antipasto offerings are of the highest quality. The rustic decor—terra cotta floors and white walls—includes a bit of the *Teatro di Pompeo*, still visible on the back wall. Don't bother with the handful of outdoor tables in summer unless you arrive very early in the evening or don't mind a long wait. Closed Sundays and August. Reservations advised. Major credit cards accepted. 65 Piazza Paradiso (phone: 686-1717 or 688-01002).

**Er Cuccurucù** A garden overlooking the Tiber provides one of Rome's most pleasant summer settings for dining alfresco, while inside all is cozy and rustic. The antipasti are good, as is the meat grilled over an open wood fire. Ask for the *bruschetta con pomodori* (toasted country bread smothered in fresh tomatoes and oregano), homemade pasta with wild mushroom sauce, and a *spiedino misto* (a grilled kebab with big chunks of veal, pork, and sausage interspersed with onions and peppers). Closed Mondays in winter, Sundays in summer, and July 15 to September 15. Reservations advised. Major credit cards accepted. 10 Via Capoprati (phone: 325-2571).

**Il Dito e la Luna** Sicilian fare and *cucina creativa* are featured at this lovely restaurant with white walls, terra cotta floors, and antique furnishings. Specialties include *lasagnette con scampi, pomodori, e zucchini* (flat pasta with shrimp, tomatoes, and zucchini), *anitra in pasta sfoglia* (duck in puff pastry with an orange sauce), and a good selection of homemade desserts. Open for dinner only; closed Sundays and August 11 to 31. Reservations advised. No credit cards accepted. 51 Via dei Sabelli (phone: 494-0276).

**Il Drappo** Drapes softly decorate the two small rooms of this *ristorantino* run by a Sardinian brother-sister team that offers delicate versions of the island's fare, fragrant with wild fennel, myrtle, and herbs. The innovative menu always begins with mixed antipasti, including *carta di musica* (hors d'oeuvres on crisp wafers). Try the classic Sardinian dessert *seadas* (cheese-stuffed, fried cake in a special dark honey). Open for dinner only; closed Sundays and two weeks in August. Reservations necessary. Major credit cards accepted. 9 Vicolo del Malpasso (phone: 687-7365).

**La Fiorentina** This favorite Roman pizzeria, with its wood-burning oven and grill, is in residential Prati on the *Vatican* side of the river. It serves pizza even at lunchtime, a rarity in Italy. There are tables on the street in good weather. Closed Wednesdays and Thursday lunch. Reservations advised. Major credit cards accepted. 22 Via Andrea Doria (phone: 312310).

**La Gensola** Located in Trastevere, this *simpatico* Sicilian trattoria offers delicious antipasti based on eggplant, and the pasta with broccoli is superb. Closed Saturday lunch, Sundays, and a week at *Christmas*. No reservations or credit cards accepted. 63 Via della Guglia (no phone).

**Giggetto al Portico d'Ottavia** In Rome's Jewish ghetto, this is the place to sample the delicious and well-prepared fried artichokes that most Roman menus identify as *alla giudia,* as well as zucchini flowers stuffed with mozzarella and *crostini.* This place is a continual favorite, even if the waiters do tend to be cheerless. The experience is absolutely authentic. Closed Mondays. Reservations advised. Major credit cards accepted. 21/A Via del Portico d'Ottavia (phone: 686-1105).

**Il Gladiatore** This old-fashioned, cozy trattoria overlooking the *Colosseo* is known for its fresh fish. Closed Wednesdays. No reservations. Major credit cards accepted. 5 Piazza Colosseo (phone: 700-0531).

**Da Mario** A favorite, with such Tuscan specialties as Francovich soup, Florentine steaks, and delicious game in season, all prepared with care and dedication by Mario himself. Try the famed *ribollita* (twice-boiled vegetable soup, which depends upon a deep purple cabbage for its special taste). Service is brusquely Tuscan; the decor is dark and old-fashioned; and the location is near Piazza di Spagna. Closed Sundays and August. Reservations advised. Major credit cards accepted. 55 Via della Vite (phone: 678-3818).

**Nino** A reliable place, frequented by artists, actors, and aristocrats, near Piazza di Spagna. The authentic Tuscan fare is simply but ably prepared, and the service is serious. Specialties: *zuppa di fagioli alla Francovich* (thick Tuscan white-bean soup with garlic), *bistecca alla fiorentina* (thick, succulent T-bone steak), and *castagnaccio* (semisweet chestnut cake). There's an excellent wine list. Closed Sundays. Reservations advised. Major credit cards accepted. 11 Via Borgognona (phone: 679-5676).

**Osteria Picchioni** Serving the most expensive—some say the best—pizza in town, this family-style, old-fashioned trattoria uses only top-quality ingredients; unfortunately, the decor runs to plastic flowers. Watch out for the prices—a plate of spaghetti with truffles can run around $100! Closed Wednesdays and August. Reservations necessary. No credit cards accepted. 16 Via del Boschetto (phone: 488-5261).

**Otello alla Concordia** A delightful trattoria in the middle of the Piazza di Spagna shopping area, it has certain tables reserved for habitués and a colorful courtyard for fine-weather dining. The menu is Roman and changes daily, depending a great deal on the season. Closed Sundays and for two weeks beginning at *Christmas.* No reservations. Major credit cards accepted. 81 Via della Croce (phone: 679-1178).

**Paris** The Cappellanti family adds a creative zing to traditional Roman-Jewish and Roman dishes such as deep-fried artichokes (in season) and *pasta e ceci* (with chick-peas). The delicious desserts are homemade—a rarity in Rome nowadays. Closed Sunday dinner, Mondays, and August. Reservations necessary. Major credit cards accepted. 7/A Piazza San Calisto (phone: 581-5378).

**Pierluigi** The fish is fresh, the piazza is charming, the prices are reasonable, and in summer the dining is alfresco. As a result, this popular trattoria in the heart of old Rome is usually full. Closed Mondays and Tuesday lunch. Reservations necessary. Major credit cards accepted. 144 Piazza de' Ricci (phone: 686-1301/2).

**Piperno** A summer dinner outdoors on this quiet Renaissance *piazzetta,* next to the *Palazzo Cenci*—which still reeks "of ancient evil and nameless crimes"—is sheer magic. Indoors it is modern and less magical, and the classic Roman-Jewish cooking can be a bit heavy. The great specialty is *fritto vegetariano* (zucchini flowers, mozzarella cheese, salt cod, rice and potato balls, and artichokes *alla giudia*). Closed Sunday dinner, Mondays, *Easter,* August, and *Christmas.* Reservations necessary. Major credit cards accepted. 9 Monte de' Cenci (phone: 688-02772).

**Polese** This place offers good value. You can choose to eat outside under the trees of the spacious square or inside the intimate rooms of a Borgia palace. Begin with *bresaola con rughetta* (cured beef with arugula, seasoned with olive oil, lemon, and freshly grated black pepper), and continue with the *pasta al pesto.* Closed Tuesdays. No reservations. Major credit cards accepted. 40 Piazza Sforza Cesarini (phone: 686-1709).

**Al Pompiere** Visiting firemen and other travelers adore this bright, old-fashioned restaurant (whose name means "The Fireman"), situated in a 16th-century palazzo near the Campo dei Fiori. The menu includes deep-fried artichokes, mozzarella-stuffed zucchini blossoms, and osso buco (veal shanks). Closed Sundays and July 24 to September 1. Reservations advised for dinner. No credit cards accepted. 38 Via Santa Maria Calderari (phone: 686-8377).

**Quadrifoglio** The spicy and flavorful Neapolitan fare—like *vermicelli con colatura di alici* (with anchovy paste) and *tortino di alici e* *patate* (anchovy and potato tarts)—served in this award-winning restaurant is in sharp contrast to its spartan decor. Don't pass up the rich pastries. Closed Saturday dinner, Sundays, and August. Reservations advised. Major credit cards accepted. 7 Via Marche (phone: 484575).

**Settimio all'Arancio** Simple but good food, served right in the heart of downtown Rome, near the old Jewish ghetto. It's always crowded. Particularly noteworthy is the *fusilli con melanzane* (pasta with eggplant). Closed Sundays and August. Reservations advised. Major credit cards accepted. 50 Via dell'Arancio (phone: 687-6119).

**Sora Lella** On Isola Tiberina (Tiber Island), this trendy, always-crowded trattoria serves authentic, hearty Roman dishes such as *pasta e ceci* (with chick-peas), *penne all'arrabbiata,* tiny sautéed lamb chops, and beans with pork rind. Ring the bell to gain entry. Closed Sundays and July. No reservations or credit cards accepted. 16 Via di Quattro Capi (phone: 686-1601).

**La Tana de Noantri** There is delightful dining at this Trastevere trattoria, both in the garden in summer and in the rustic indoor room the rest of the year. The pasta and meat dishes respect Roman tradition (as does the pizza), and the fish is always fresh. Closed Tuesdays. Reservations advised. Major credit cards accepted. 1-3 Via della Paglia (phone: 580-6404).

**La Tavernetta** It looks like a take-out pasta shop, but there are actually four narrow dining rooms set one above the other. At this tiny, tidy spot between Piazza di Spagna and Piazza Barberini, the homemade pasta is nearly perfect and seafood is the specialty. Closed Mondays and August. Reservations advised. Major credit cards accepted. 3-4 Via del Nazareno (phone: 679-3124).

**Toto alle Carrozze** A trattoria with a banquet spread of strictly Roman antipasti, good pasta, and Roman fish and meat dishes. This is a *giovedì gnocchi, sabato trippa* (Thursday gnocchi, Saturday tripe) kind of traditional place. Closed Sundays. No reservations. Major credit cards accepted. Just off Via del Corso at 10 Via delle Carrozze (phone: 678-5558).

**Tullio** Up a narrow hill, just a few yards from Via Veneto, this Tuscan trattoria serves superb *ribollita* (Tuscan vegetable soup) and baked beans *al fiasco* (in the bottle). It's a custom to place a straw-covered bottle of chianti on the table—diners pay only for what they drink. Try the grilled steak Florentine-style. Closed Sundays and August. Reservations advised. Major credit cards accepted. 26 Via di San Nicola da Tolentino (phone: 474-5560).

**Le Volte** Under the frescoed ceiling of the 16th-century *Palazzo Rondanini,* diners can enjoy linguine in lobster sauce, pizza baked in a wood-burning oven, and wild boar with polenta (in autumn and winter). Closed Tuesdays and two weeks in August. Reservations advised. Major credit cards accepted. 47 Piazza Rondanini (phone: 687-7408).

**Buca di Ripetta** This delightfully old-fashioned trattoria is always packed with locals, who flock here for the delicious food, including a variety of pasta dishes, vegetable soup, and osso buco (veal shanks). The atmosphere is lively and friendly. Closed Sunday dinner, Mondays, and August. Reservations advised. No credit cards accepted. 36 Via di Ripetta (phone: 321-9391).

**Fiaschetteria Beltramme** The fashion crowd—plus painters, potters, plumbers, and frame makers—crams into this tiny place to enjoy the home-cooked broth, spaghetti, boiled beef, and oxtail Roman-style. The strictly traditional menu may take some deciphering, but the staff will be happy to translate. No fancy decor, not even a telephone—just good food and a pleasant house wine from Frascati. Closed Sundays and August. No reservations or credit cards accepted. Between Piazza del Popolo and Via Condotti at 39 Via della Croce (no phone).

**Grotte Teatro di Pompeo** Julius Caesar met his untimely end nearby—some say right here, amid the massive and still visible stone vaults of the *Teatro di Pompeo.* The *zuppa di verdura* (vegetable soup) is untheatrical but wholesome, and the *fettuccine verdi alla gorgonzola* (green noodles in a rich cheese sauce) is a wonderful pasta choice. Try the typically Roman osso buco *con funghi* (with wild mushrooms) or the saltimbocca. Closed Mondays and August. Reservations unnecessary. Visa accepted. 73 Via del Biscione (phone: 688-03686).

**Lucifero Pub** A fondue-and-beer tavern tucked into a side street off the Campo dei Fiori, it offers an inexpensive alternative to pizza. Open daily. No reservations or credit cards accepted. 28 Via dei Cappellari (phone: 654-5536).

**Pizzeria Panattoni** Popular with university students, this always-crowded eatery in Trastevere is nicknamed "The Morgue" because of its long, white marbles tables. But there's nothing morbid about the delicious pizza, garlic bread, *supplì al telefono* (rice balls stuffed with cheese), and baked beans served here. Closed Wednesdays. No reservations or credit cards accepted. 53 Viale Trastevere (phone: 580-0919).

**La Sagrestia** The best pizza in town—or at least a top contender—with pies fresh from the wood-burning oven. There's also good pasta and draft beer at this ever-crowded and cheery place, with a kitschy decor. Closed Wednesdays and a week in mid-August. Reservations advised for large groups. Major credit cards accepted. Near the *Pantheon* at 89 Via del Seminario (phone: 679-7581).

**Trearchi da Gioachino** Among the declining numbers of true Roman trattorie, this one stands out. The chef, who comes from the Abruzzo region, prepares such tasty specialties as homemade ravioli, *pappardelle* noodles with hare sauce and lamb, and other pasta made in various delectable ways. Closed Sundays and August. Reservations advised. Major credit cards accepted. 233 Via dei Coronari (phone: 686-5890).

———————————

## BARS AND CAFFÈS

Perhaps no other institution reflects the relaxed Italian lifestyle as much as the ubiquitous *caffè* (or bar, as it is called in Rome). From small emporiums with three tin tables (where locals perpetually argue world politics and the Sunday soccer results) to sprawling drawing rooms to tearooms to wine bars, life slows to sit and sip. Romans order Campari, cappuccino, or a light lunch and put the world on hold. Inside they meet friends and suitors, read the paper, or write the great Italian novel. Some regulars even get their mail at their local *caffè*. Outside, in summer, the *caffè* is for appraising the passing spectacle. Remember that prices are usually far higher outdoors than in, so when you're charged $6 or $7 for an espresso, don't grumble—just think of it as rent for the sidewalk table. You can stay the whole afternoon if you like. Also increasingly popular are small wine bars, which offer samples of regional and continental wines as well as light fare, making for an ideal lunch. Most of these places do not take credit cards or reservations; those listed below are open daily unless otherwise indicated.

Filled with busts and statues of such famous habitués as Stendhal, Schopenhauer, Casanova, and Mark Twain, *Caffè Greco* (86 Via Condotti; phone: 678-2554) today is a haven for such luminaries as couturier Valentino and members of the Bulgari clan, whose shop is nearby. Even the waiters, who dress in tails, look as if they're being preserved for posterity. Another of our favorites is *Babington's* (23 Piazza di Spagna; phone: 678-6027), an English tearoom in the heart of the former artists' quarter, where art and antiques dealers of the nearby streets gather by the welcoming wood fire for light lunches or rich, homemade tea cakes, scones, and skillfully brewed tea (closed Tuesdays). Rome's runaway favorite for cappuccino is *Eustachio il Caffè* (82 Piazza Sant'Eustachio; phone: 656-1309), which has been in the same location since 1938 (closed Mondays). For one of the city's best *cornetti* (a sweetish croissant, not on any list of low-cholesterol food), walk across the piazza to the *Bernasconi Caffè*. *Tre Scalini* (28 Piazza Navona; phone: 688-01996) is a perennial favorite with both Romans and foreigners, particularly in summer, when the cone-seekers are often three deep at the ice cream counter inside. The setting is incomparable, the cast of characters colorful, and the renowned specialty (*tartufo,* a grated bitter chocolate–covered chocolate ice-cream ball swathed in whipped cream) is sinfully delicious.

For a pre-lunch or -dinner *aperitivo,* try fashionable *Baretto* (Via Condotti), *Rosati* (5/A Piazza del Popolo; phone: 322-5859; closed Tuesdays), or *Canova* (Piazza del Popolo; no phone); all also offer light lunches and late-night snacks. Currently *alla moda* is the little *Bar della Pace* (Piazza della Pace, behind Piazza Navona; no phone), popular with the young crowd and open until 3 AM. *Ciampini*

———————————

(Piazza Trinità dei Monti; phone: 678-5678) boasts a fine hilltop view of the entire city, as well as excellent food.

Wine shops–cum–wine bars serve light lunches of well-prepared vegetables, pasta, cheese, and good wine (November through March, try a glass of the wonderful *vini novelli*) for around $15 to $20 per person. They are scattered all over old Rome but are tiny and dark. Simply look for their sign: *Enoteca.* The shops usually have only a few tables and close before 8 PM. Try the *Bottega del Vino da Bleve* (9/A Via Santa Maria del Pianto; phone: 683-00475) in downtown Rome; tiny *Cul de Sac 1* (73 Piazza Pasquino; phone: 688-01094), which re-creates the atmosphere of an old *osteria; Il Piccolo* (74 Via del Governo Vecchio; no phone) near Piazza Navona; or *Spiriti* (5 Via di Sant'Eustachio; phone: 689-2499).

On summer evenings the after-dinner crowd often moves toward one of the many *gelaterie* in Rome, some of which are much more than ice-cream parlors, since they serve exotic long drinks and *semifreddi* (semisoft ice cream). Perhaps the best-known *gelateria* in town is the very crowded *Giolitti* (40 Via Uffici del Vicario; phone: 699-1243), not far from Piazza Colonna—try any of the fresh fruit flavors (closed Mondays). Others include the sleek, high-tech *Gelateria della Palma* (at the corner of Via della Maddalena and Via delle Coppelle; no phone), *Fiocco di Neve* (51 Via del Pantheon; no phone), and *Caffè di Rienzo* (5 Piazza della Rotonda; phone: 687-7404)—all near the *Pantheon;* the lively *Gelofestival* (29 Viale Trastevere, in Trastevere; phone: 581-3363); and the more sedate *Biancaneve* (1 Piazza Pasquale Paoli, where Corso Vittorio Emanuele II meets the Lungotevere dei Fiorentini; phone: 688-06227). Favorites in the fashionable Parioli residential district are *Gelateria Duse* (1/E Via Eleonora Duse; no phone) and the *Casina delle Muse* (Piazzale delle Muse; no phone) for a fabulous *granita di caffè con panna* (iced coffee with whipped cream). In the Jewish ghetto try *Dolce Roma* (20/B Via Portico d'Ottavia; phone: 587-972) for chocolate-chip cookies and Austrian pastries. The *Gran Caffè Europeo* (33 Piazza San Lorenzo in Lucina; no phone) is another place for indulging in high-calorie pastries.

# St. Petersburg

## At-a-Glance

SEEING THE CITY

The best panorama of the city, and the best place to start a tour, is from the colonnade surrounding the gilded dome of *St. Isaac's Cathedral,* which is visible from at least 15 miles (24 km) away on a clear day. The mesmerizing 360° view from the colonnade is just reward for the bracing journey it takes to get there—you must first climb the spiral staircase inside a tower, then negotiate the metal catwalk that covers the final 40 feet to the colonnade. Small signs in Russian help visitors get their bearings. To the *sever* (north), far below the cathedral's dramatic statuary, is Senatskaya Ploshchad (Senate, formerly Decembrists', Square), a park that leads to the *Bronze Horseman,* St. Petersburg's most famous monument; the mighty Neva River and Vasilyevskiy Island are beyond. Moving clockwise around the colonnade, a number of St. Petersburg landmarks come into view: the *Admiralty,* the birthplace of the Baltic fleet; Dvortsovaya Ploshchad (Palace Square), graced with the famed *Winter Palace* and the *Hermitage* museum; the *Peter and Paul Fortress;* and the cruiser *Aurora* docked on the Neva beyond. To the south is Isaakievskaya Ploshchad (St. Isaac's Square) and *Mariya Palace,* the home of St. Petersburg's City Council. As you look toward the west, notice the intricate network of canals and the huge cranes towering over the Gulf of Finland, a reminder that this was and still is a busy port city. The colonnade is closed Wednesdays; admission charge and a steep fee for the use of cameras and videorecorders.

There are other interesting vantage points as well. Beside the Neva, opposite the *Peter and Paul Fortress,* you get a sense of where and how the city began. At the *Admiralty Building,* where the city's three major avenues converge, you can grasp St. Petersburg's layout and planning. In Palace Square, the site of czarist splendor and bloody revolution, you can get in touch with the city's political history; and on Nevsky Prospekt at Yekaterinskiy Canal, you can feel the contemporary pulse of the city.

### BE PREPARED!

At press time, prompted by the increase in reported cases of diphtheria in Russia, travelers are advised to update their immunizations before entering this region. For further information, call the US State Department's *Citizen's Emergency Center* at 202-647-5225. Visitors should also be aware of increased

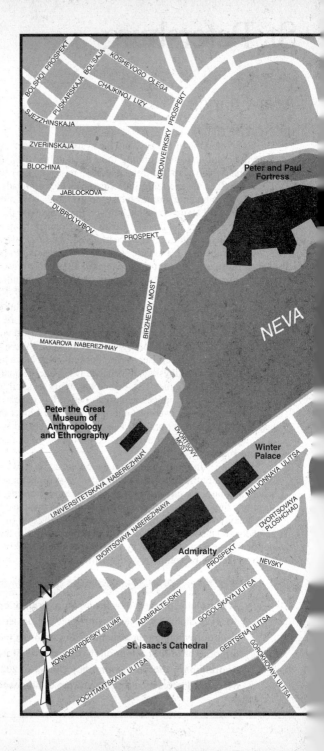

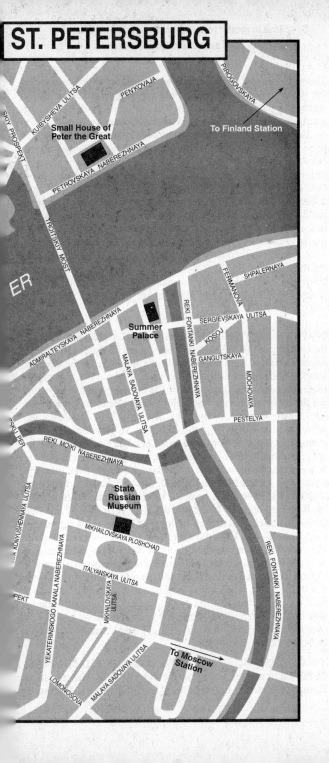

## SPECIAL PLACES

The major sites of St. Petersburg are spread out over a number of
the 101 islands that interconnect to form the city, but all are easily
reached by public transportation. You can sightsee on your own or
arrange tours through your hotel's service bureau.

Today, it has become almost commonplace for streets and squares
to be renamed, and hotels and restaurants to have changed hands.
Now that many streets and squares have reverted to their prerevolutionary names, getting around St. Petersburg may cause some
confusion for the visitor. However, locals—most especially taxi
drivers—will steer you in the right direction. Fortunately, many
buildings retain small white plaques with elegant lettering (albeit
in the Cyrillic alphabet) indicating prerevolutionary street names
that have either been revived or are expected to be.

A few Russian words to assist you in your navigating: *Ulitsa* is
the Russian word for street; *prospekt* means avenue; *bulvar* means
boulevard; *naberezhnaya* is embankment; *proyezd* means passage;
*shosse* means highway; and *ploshchad* is the word for square.

### DOWNTOWN

**PETROPAVLOVSKAYA KREPOST (PETER AND PAUL FORTRESS)** Before Peter
the Great chose this site to build a new capital for Russia, he ordered
a fortress built to bar the Swedish fleet's approach. As the threat of
attack decreased, the fortress, established in May 1703, came to be
used as a prison for opponents of the czarist regime. The list of
political prisoners over the centuries includes Peter the Great's own
son, Alexei; Fyodor Dostoyevsky, before his exile to Siberia; the
writer Maxim Gorky; and the anarchist Mikhail Bakunin. The
*Petropavlovskaya Sobor* (Cathedral of Sts. Peter and Paul), with its
tall, extremely slender golden spire, stands in the center of the
fortress. It is the burial place of the Romanov czars from Peter the
Great to Alexander III, with the exception of Peter II. (Grand Duke
Vladimir Kirillovich Romanov, the most recently deceased head of
the Romanov dynastic house in exile, died in April 1992 and was
buried in a special Romanov vault in the fortress, although not in
the cathedral.) In 1924 the *Peter and Paul Fortress* became a
museum. The main branch of the *State Museum of the History of
St. Petersburg and Petrograd* is also on the premises. There is a
cannon salute fired here at noon daily, a tradition carried on from
the 18th century, when it was used to notify citizens of the exact
time. Closed Wednesdays and the last Tuesday of the month. Admission charge. 3 *Petropavlovskaya Krepost* on Zayachy Island, just
over the Troitskiy Most (Trinity Bridge) near Kamennoostrovskiy
Prospekt (phone: 238-4540).

**LETNIY SAD; DVORETS-MUZEY PETRA I (SUMMER GARDEN; PALACE-MUSEUM
OF PETER I)** Across the Neva from the fortress, on the Naberezhnaya
Kutuzova (Kutuzov Embankment), is a 30-acre park, laid out in

1704, and an unpretentious summer palace built in the Dutch style for Peter the Great. The park, filled with classical sculptures, is a favorite open space for St. Petersburgers, particularly during the summer's long *White Nights.* The palace is open May through the first week of November; closed Tuesdays. Admission charge (phone: 312-9436 or 312-9666). The park is open year-round, although the outdoor sculptures are covered during the winter. The park's entrance is at 2 Pestelya Ulitsa.

**GOSUDARSTVENNIY ERMITAZH; ZIMNIY DVORETS (STATE HERMITAGE; WINTER PALACE)** Built during the 18th-century reigns of Elizabeth and Catherine the Great, the *Winter Palace* was designed by Italian architect Bartolomeo Rastrelli. The grandiose Baroque palace and four adjacent buildings now house one of the finest art collections in the world. The splendor of the room decorations—parquet floors, molded and painted ceilings, elaborate furniture, and decorative objects of malachite, lapis lazuli, and jasper—dazzle the eye as much as do works such as Gainsborough's *Duchess of Beaufort;* Renoir's *Girl with a Fan;* Ingres's *Portrait of Count Guriev;* Brueghel's *Fair;* Rembrandt's *Old Man in Red;* Titian's *Danaë;* Holbein's *Portrait of a Young Man;* and a wonderful, little-known Michelangelo sculpture, the *Crouching Boy.* Don't overlook the private dining room, where members of the provisional government were arrested on the evening of November 7, 1917. A great deal of space is allotted to Russian history and culture, and exhibits run the gamut from exquisite antique silver and a map of Russia set with semi-precious stones to turn-of-the-century paintings with such fetching titles as *The Dairymaid Spurned* and *The Volunteer Shall Return No More.* Unfortunately, the dazzling *Gold Treasure Room*— which holds the exquisite jewels of Catherine the Great and a spectacular collection of Scythian gold—was closed at press time, so check before you go. There are no museum tours conducted in English, but you can book an English-speaking guide through your hotel. The museum is closed Mondays. Admission charge. 34 Dvortsovaya Naberezhnaya (phone: 219-8625 or 311-3420).

**DVORTSOVAYA PLOSHCHAD (PALACE SQUARE)** The heart of St. Petersburg is this square with its red granite *Alexander Column* in the center. It was erected in 1832 as a monument to the victory over Napoleon in 1812. This square, the site of Bloody Sunday in 1905, is closely associated with the revolutionary movement. The climax of the October Revolution in 1917 was the storming of the *Winter Palace* from here. Each year there are parades and demonstrations to mark the event, although, not surprisingly, these gatherings have diminished in intensity in recent years. Several enterprising local souls will rent horses to tourists for a gallop around the square and a dramatic photo.

**MEDNIY VSADNIK (BRONZE HORSEMAN/PETER THE GREAT MONUMENT)** The famous bronze statue of Peter the Great, designed by French sculptor E. M. Falconet, stands in the center of grassy *Senatskaya Ploshchad* (Senate, formerly Decembrists', Square) to the west of the *Admiralty Building*. The statue, commissioned by Catherine the Great, depicts Peter astride a horse whose hoofs are trampling a writhing snake (said to be a symbolic representation of Sweden). The monument inspired Pushkin to write *The Bronze Horseman,* and the statue in turn takes its nickname from the poem.

**ISAAKIEVSKIY SOBOR (ST. ISAAC'S CATHEDRAL)** St. Petersburg's largest church—and one of the world's largest domed structures—stands to the south of Dekabristov Ploshchad, across Gertsena Ulitsa from the *Astoria* hotel. The cathedral is filled with mosaics and decorated with various kinds of minerals and semi-precious stones. Malachite and lapis lazuli columns form a part of the massive gilded iconostasis before the altar. A museum under the Soviet regime, it's now used as a church on Russian Orthodox holidays and other special occasions. Closed Wednesdays. The colonnade around the dome offers the best views of the city. Closed Wednesdays; admission charge and a steep fee for the use of cameras and video recorders. Isaakievskaya Ploshchad (phone: 315-9732).

**ALEKSANDRO-NEVSKAYA LAVRA (ALEXANDER NEVSKY MONASTERY)** The monastery's *Troitskiy Sobor* (Trinity Cathedral) was built in 1722 to house the remains of St. Alexander Nevsky, which were brought here from Vladimir. In 1922 the silver sarcophagus containing the saint's ashes was moved to the *Hermitage*. The monastery also has ten other churches, four cemeteries (known here as necropolises), and a seminary. The *Muzey Gorodskikh Skulptur* (Museum of Urban Sculpture), which has models and site photographs of most of the city's monuments, is under renovation, and at press time there was no date set for its reopening. The 18th-century necropolis includes the graves of Peter I's sister and Mikhail Lomonosov, the scientist and poet who founded *Moscow University.* The 19th-century necropolis includes the graves of Dostoyevsky, Tchaikovsky, Mussorgsky, Rimsky-Korsakov, and Borodin. You must buy a ticket to enter these cemeteries, but you may visit the interesting modern necropolis opposite the cathedral without charge. Note its unusual grave markers, such as the propeller of the plane in which a pilot met his death and a miniature rig for three oil field workers. The monastery is closed Thursdays. Admission charge for both the monastery and the museum. Since the grounds are never closed, they are a nice place to walk during the *White Nights,* the June arts festival. There are daily services in the cathedral. Near the *Aleksandra Nevskovo* metro stop. 1 Aleksandra Nevskovo Ploshchad (phone: 277-1716).

**VOLKOVSKOYE ORTHODOX CEMETERY** This necropolis, also known as the *Literatorskiye Mostki* (Literary Stage), holds the graves of several famous Russian writers (Alexander Kuprin, Ivan Turgenev, and Alexander Blok), scientists (Dmitri Mendeleyev and Ivan Pavlov), and other prominent native sons. Closed Thursdays. No admission charge. 30 Rastanniy Proyezd (phone: 166-2383).

**GOSUDARSTVENNIY RUSSKIY MUZEY (RUSSIAN STATE MUSEUM)** After the *Tretyakov Gallery* in Moscow, this is the largest collection of Russian art in the world. There are some 300,000 examples of painting, sculpture, decorative art, and folk art, all housed in the former *Mikhailovskiy Palace.* You need not have a doctorate in Russian art to appreciate this collection, since many works are interpretations of classical themes. Closed Tuesdays. Admission charge. 4-2 Inzhenernaya Ulitsa (phone: 314-3448 or 314-4153).

**KHRAM SPASA NA KROVI (CHURCH OF THE BLOOD OF THE SAVIOR)** This church was built in the Old Russian style, similar to *St. Basil's* in Moscow, at the end of the 19th century on the spot where Alexander II was assassinated. The exterior is covered with mosaics. The church has been closed for the past two years for renovations. The best views of it are from the pleasant *Mikhailovskiy Garden* just to the east beyond the elegant wrought-iron fence, or from one of the footbridges spanning the Yekaterinskiy Canal to the south. Just north of the *Russian State Museum* at 2A Yekaterinskovo Kanala Naberezhnaya (phone: 314-4053).

**KAZANSKIY SOBOR (KAZAN CATHEDRAL)** Freed from its Soviet role as a dubious museum devoted to the history of religion and atheism (not necessarily in that order), this majestic cathedral is once again holding religious services. Originally modeled on *St. Peter's* in Rome and named for the famous icon *Our Lady of Kazan* that was once on the premises (its current whereabouts are unknown), *Kazan Cathedral*'s most noticeable features are its embracing Corinthian arcades. The dramatic architecture and enormous dome are best appreciated inside, where there are a number of trophies and banners from the Napoleonic Wars. The great Russian Field Marshal Kutuzov prayed here before going off to war and is buried on that spot. Closed Wednesdays; no admission charge, but a donation for restoration is appreciated. Services are held on Saturdays and Sundays. 2 Kazanskaya Ploshchad, off Nevsky Prospekt (phone: 314-5856).

**BRIDGES OF ST. PETERSBURG** From the large, impressive Troitskiy Most (Trinity Bridge) over the Neva to the multitude of smaller spans connecting the islands, St. Petersburg's bridges are not only useful but beautiful and historic. The stone turrets and chains of the Lomonosov Bridge over the Fontanka are examples of the earliest bridges. This heavy style soon gave way to light, airy ironwork decorated with lions, gilded griffins, sphinxes, and other delightful creatures. There are hundreds of these bridges, large and small, and they give a unified aspect to the city. The most famous, perhaps, is the Anichkov, which spans the Fontanka River at Nevsky Prospekt and has four sculptures by Peter Klodt. To allow ships to pass, the bridges are raised at various times during the night.

**SMOLNIY MONASTYR (SMOLNY MONASTERY AND INSTITUTE)** The cathedral and convent of the monastery were built in the 18th century by Czarina Elizabeth, and the institute was founded during the reign of Catherine II (the Great) as a school for young ladies of the nobility. The room at the institute where Lenin later lived has been turned into a museum featuring paintings by several St. Petersburg artists. Tours of the interiors are available by special arrangement, but the park may be visited at any time. Classical musicians and the church choir perform at the *Cathedral and Exhibition Complex* here on Saturday and Sunday nights. The complex is closed Thursdays. Admission charge. 3 Rastrelli Ploshchad (phone: 311-3690). The museum is closed Sundays. Admission charge to the exhibitions. Along the Neva between Smolnaya Ulitsa and Smolniy Prospekt, about seven blocks east of the *Sernysevskaya* metro stop (phone: 278-1461).

## PISKAREVSKOYE KLADBISHSCHE (PISKAREVSKOYE MEMORIAL CEMETERY)
An eternal flame and small museum are located at the entrance to these memorial grounds commemorating the 900-day siege of St. Petersburg (then called Leningrad) during World War II. Some 500,000 of those who died before the ring of the blockade was broken in 1943 were buried in mass graves here. The museum contains photographs and documents chronicling the heroism of the city's residents. North of the *Smolny Monastery and Institute,* across the Neva in the northeast sector of the city. Open daily. 74 Nepokorennykh Prospekt (phone: 247-5716).

## KREYSER *AVRORA* (CRUISER *AURORA*)
The Communists claim a blank shot fired from this cruiser signaled the start of the October Revolution, but local journalists say the original *Aurora* was sunk and this is just a replica. The cruiser is permanently moored in the Neva, opposite the *St. Petersburg* hotel. Closed Mondays and Fridays. Admission charge. 4 Petrovskaya Naberezhnaya (phone: 230-8440 or 230-5202).

ENVIRONS

## TSARSKOYE SELO (THE CZAR'S VILLAGE)
This town is the site of the *Yekaterinskiy Palace,* named for Peter the Great's wife, Catherine I. Built during the reigns of Elizabeth and Catherine II and set in a 1,482-acre park, the palace has a stunning aqua façade, decorated with gold-and-white ornaments. Part of the building now is a museum, with exhibitions of furniture and china and displays explaining the palace's history. The *Pushkinskiy Litsey Muzey* (Pushkin Lyceum Museum for Noblemen's Children; 2 Komsomolskaya Ulitsa; phone: 276-6411), located near the railroad station, about a half mile from the palace, is filled with manuscripts, rare books, and the personal belongings of poet Alexander Pushkin, who studied at the school for the nobility attached to the palace. The village was renamed Pushkin from 1937 (the 100th anniversary of his death) until recently. Both museums are closed Tuesdays and the last Monday of every month. Admission charge. Trains and taxis are available at the *Vitebskiy Station* in St. Petersburg; trains leave every 20 minutes. The trip takes about 30 minutes (get off at the *Detskoe Selo Station* in Pushkin/Tsarskoye Selo). From *Detskoe Selo* buses and taxis are available to take you to the museums. First-time visitors will probably find it more enjoyable to arrange for an English-speaking guide and taxi driver through their hotel concierge. The palace is at 7 Komsomolskaya Ulitsa, 14 miles (22 km) south of St. Petersburg along Zabalkanskiy Prospekt (phone: 314-5594).

**PAVLOVSK** One of the most beautifully restored palaces in Russia is less than 2 miles (3 km) from the *Pushkin Lyceum Museum.* The 1,500-acre compound, originally the village's hunting grounds, is now one of the largest landscaped parks in Europe. The land and palace were a gift from Catherine II to her son Paul in 1777. After crossing a quaint wooden bridge, visitors enter the park through cast-iron gates. The palace interior is light and elegant. The grounds are wonderful for casual strolls; you can also sunbathe or rent boats along the nearby Slavyanka River. The palace is closed Sundays and the first Monday of every month. Admission charge. (Check with your hotel before going, since many offer combined tours of Tsarskoye Selo and *Pavlovsk.*) The palace is at 20 Revolyutsii Ulitsa (phone: 470-2155). The palace grounds are 15 miles (24 km) south of St. Petersburg along Zabalkanskiy Prospekt.

**PETRODVORETS** On the southern shore of the Gulf of Finland, Peter the Great built *Petrodvorets,* the *Grand Palace,* which he hoped would rival *Versailles.* Originally designed by the French architect Alexandre Jean-Baptiste Leblond, today the building reflects the Russian Baroque style of architect Bartolomeo Rastrelli, who altered the original building under the direction of Peter's daughter, Elizabeth. It was Peter himself, however, who drafted the 300-acre layout and the spectacular system of fountains that cascade through the park and gardens. The 129 fountains in this elaborate system begin on the Ropshinskiy Heights 13 miles (21 km) away; unfortunately, most of the fountains are currently under renovation and it is not clear when the entire system will be fully operative again. The most impressive is the *Samson Fountain,* directly in front of the *Grand Palace,* depicting Samson ripping open the jaws of a lion as a spray of water rises from the mouth. Three other palaces stand on the grounds. *Montplaisir,* completed in 1723, is said to have been Peter the Great's favorite palace; it was later a residence of Catherine the Great. The *Hermitage Pavilion* and *Marly Palace* date from the same era. All the builings were badly damaged during World War II but have been carefully restored by art historians and craftsmen following photographs and original plans. *Petrodvorets* is about 20 miles (32 km) southwest of the city. It can be reached by car (leave the city via Stasek Prospekt), taxi, or, in summer, by hydrofoil down the Neva into the gulf (board at the dock across from the *Hermitage* museum). The palace is closed Mondays and the last Tuesday of every month. Admission charge. 2 Kominterna Ulitsa (phone: 427-5390 or 427-9527).

# Sources and Resources

## TOURIST INFORMATION

The *St. Petersburg Tourist Company* (11 Isaakievskaya Ploshchad; phone: 315-5129 for information; 272-7887 for guides; fax: 312-0996) operates out of the old *Intourist* headquarters opposite *St. Isaac's Cathedral.* Its services include reserving hotel rooms; booking tickets for concerts, exhibitions, and special events; arranging tours of museums, palaces, and other special attractions; and providing English-speaking guides. However, the major hotels and the burgeoning number of private companies associated with them often offer better deals and with less red tape. The *US Consulate* is at 15 Furshtadtskaya Ulitsa (phone: 812-275-1701).

In the US contact *Intourist USA* (610 Fifth Ave., Suite 603, New York, NY 10020; phone: 212-757-3884; 800-982-8416; fax: 212-459-0031). The *Russian Embassy* is at 1825 S. Phelps Pl. NW, Washington, DC, 20008 (phone: 202-939-8907).

**ENTRY REQUIREMENTS** A US citizen needs a valid passport and a visa to enter Russia. At present there are three kinds of visas: tourist, ordinary (for business or family visits), and transit. A visa application can be filed through a travel agent or directly with a consular office in the US; allow a minimum of 14 days before your departure. An itinerary that describes the time and duration of all stops within the country, travel arrangements, and hotel reservations must be submitted along with a fee (there is an additional fee for processing within a week or for a 24-hour turnaround); processing fees vary between consular offices.

**LANGUAGE** Russian, the official language, uses the Cyrillic alphabet. Tourism industry personnel and workers in the hotel and restaurant industries speak English.

**ELECTRIC CURRENT** 220 volts, 50 cycles, AC.

**MONEY** One ruble is made up of 100 kopecks. At press time $1 US was worth about 3,385 rubles. Although the ruble is convertible, the exchange rate is very unstable, so check rates before departing. Many prices are quoted in US dollars or German marks.

Economic turmoil, including frequent and steep price increases for many goods and services, makes it impossible to provide accurate information on prices, including the cost of basic services such as public transportation and the telephone. New currency regulations came into force on January 1, 1994 that require all businesses to accept cash payments in rubles only. Payment by credit card can be made in dollars. The measure was aimed at putting an end to economic segregation between shops and restaurants that accepted foreign (hard) currency and those that accepted rubles. However, businesses can request payment in rubles at their own fixed rate, which may be considerably higher than the bank's. Travelers are advised to pay by credit card to avoid an unfavorable exchange rate.

**TIME** The time in most of western Russia, including St. Petersburg, is eight hours later than in US East Coast cities. In western-central Russia the time is 16 hours later than in the US East Coast. Russia follows daylight saving time.

**TIPPING** Tipping is not officially sanctioned, though tips are not refused.

**BANKING/BUSINESS HOURS** There are banking branches for currency exchange at major hotels, open weekdays from 9 AM to 5 PM. Most other businesses are open weekdays from 9 AM to 5 or 6 PM.

**NATIONAL HOLIDAYS** *New Year's Day* (January 1), Russian Orthodox *Christmas* (January 8), *Soviet Army Day* (February 23), *International Women's Day* (March 8), *Day of Spring and Labor* (May 1), *Victory Day* (May 9), *Independence Day* (June 12), and *Anniversary of the 1917 Bolshevik Revolution* (November 7).

**LOCAL COVERAGE** English-language publications such as the *St. Petersburg Press,* the *International Herald Tribune, Time, Newsweek,* and other European and North American dailies and weeklies often can be purchased at kiosks and hotels, although not necessarily on the day of publication. For local coverage of the economy and Western business ventures, Russia's premier publication is the English-language edition of *Commersant,* available at hotels and kiosks throughout the city. In addition, several US newspapers, including *The New York Times,* now publish editions in Russian.

Although good transportation and city maps are available in hotels and at newsstands and book kiosks for very reasonable prices, it is helpful to take along a *Falkplan* map of St. Petersburg (Falk-Verlag; $6.95), available in the US. This pocket map is designed to be used in sections and includes a street name index and gazetteer for monuments, museums, hotels, and theaters.

**TELEPHONE** The city code for St. Petersburg is 812. When calling from one area to another within Russia dial 8 + city code + local number. The country code for Russia is 7.

Only some—mostly Western—hotels have telephone systems allowing you to dial direct. To make a long-distance call from your room, dial "8" and wait for a second dial tone. Then dial "1" and then "0" for an international line (followed by the country code, city or area code, and local number). In most hotels built during the Soviet era, you will have to place such calls through your hotel operator, service bureau, or business center. But beware: The costs of international calls range from high to excessive, so check carefully beforehand. In an emergency, dial 03 for an ambulance and 02 for the police.

## GETTING AROUND

St. Petersburg has a small but exceedingly good subway system, the metro, which is supplemented by a network of bus, trolley, and tram routes that enable visitors to move about the city with relative ease. Good, inexpensive transportation maps are generally available in hotels and at street kiosks, although English-language versions may be hard to find.

**AIRPORT** St. Petersburg's *Pulkovo-2 International Airport* is about 45 minutes from downtown by taxi; the fare can cost from several dollars up to $25 depending on whom you ask, so bargain before entering a cab (see *Taxi,* below).

**BOATS** In summer hydrofoils and excursion boats ply the Neva, the canals, and the smaller rivers. There are two docks opposite the *Winter Palace* museum on the Neva River, one for cruises to the *Smolny Convent and Institute* (about an hour), the other for hydrofoils to *Petrodvorets,* Peter the Great's summer palace (about 25 minutes). Boat trips on the Neva are also available from a dock in front of the *St. Petersburg* hotel (5-2 Pirogovskaya Naberezhnaya). The boat trip along the Fontanka and Moika rivers and Kyukov Canal (about two hours) leaves from the dock near the Anchikov Bridge, where Nevsky Prospekt crosses the Fontanka. Cruises are inexpensive. In the summer tickets should be purchased in advance at kiosks near the docks.

**BUS/TROLLEY/TRAM** The costs of tickets for St. Petersburg's public transportation system are rising all the time, but they still remain a bargain for tourists because of the falling value of the ruble. Tickets must be bought in advance either from vending machines located near the bus stops or from nearby kiosks. Bus stops are marked by the letter "A," trams and trolleys by the letter "T." Route numbers are posted on signs and match the number on the front of the bus. Maps showing the various bus, tram, and trolley routes are available at hotels and street kiosks. However, for those without at least a passing knowledge of Russian, the public transit system can be confusing.

**CAR RENTAL** There are now many places to rent cars and chauffeured cars, including at major hotels. Rates can be exorbitant, so shop around. Fords are available through *Svit Automobile Rental* (*Pribaltiskaya Hotel;* phone: 356-9329 or 356-1074; fax: 356-0094 or 356-3845) and Nissans through *Innis Automobile Rental* (*Astoria Hotel;* phone: 210-5858, fax: 210-5859). At press time *Hertz* was the only major Western agency in St. Petersburg, located at the *Grand Hotel Europe* (see *Checking In*) and at its affiliated *Interavto* office (9-11 Ispolkomskaya Ulitsa; phone: 277-4032; fax: 274-2662 or 277-4677). The main rental agency is *Intourist Transport* (5 Sedova Ulitsa; phone: 567-8246). It's highly recommended that visitors, particularly first-timers, rent a car with a driver. St. Petersburg's roads are absolutely horrible—many have crater-sized potholes, particularly those near the trolley tracks. In addition, Russian drivers pay little, if any, attention to traffic laws or rules of common driving courtesy. Street patterns, especially near the canals and the Neva River, are hard to fathom.

**METRO** The subway system runs daily and is inexpensive. Since St. Petersburg is built on marshy land, the stations for the 25-mile (40-km) metro are exceptionally deep. In fact, some escalator rides up from the platforms can take a full two minutes. Stand to the right on down escalators; the left side is for "runners." Coming up you can stand on either side.

**TAXI** Once the easiest way to get around town, cabs have become expensive and unsafe for foreigners. Requesting limousine service is preferable, since many limousines are owned either by the hotels or private companies. In addition, make sure you agree on the fare *before* you get into a cab—bargaining is essential.

---

### BE ALERT!

**There has been an increasing number of reports of tourists being robbed by bands of young people, commonly known as Russian "mafia," who lurk outside major hotels and restaurants posing as taxi drivers. The best advice is never get into a cab with other passengers, and walk away if anything looks or sounds suspicious.**

---

**TRAIN** The five railway stations are *Moscow Station* (2 Vosstaniya Ploshchad; phone: 168-04374 or 277-0800); *Finland Station* (6 Lenina Ploshchad; phone: 168-7685); *Warsaw Station* (118 Obvodnovo Kanala Naberezhnaya; phone: 168-2611 or 259-1972); *Baltic Station* (120 Obvodnovo Kanala Naberezhnaya; phone: 168-2259); and *Vitebskiy Station* (52 Zagorodniy Prospekt; phone: 168-5390). Station names indicate the primary destination of trains leaving from there. For example, trains leaving from *Moscow Station* travel to Moscow. Tickets can be purchased daily at the above stations or at the *Rail Kassa* (24 Griboyedova Kanala Naberezhnaya). For general information about arrival and departure times, call 168-0111. For ticket information and advance reservations, call 162-3344 (for trains within the former Soviet Union) or 274-2092 (international).

For those who want to explore St. Petersburg and beyond, *Cox & Kings* provides a 14-day tour from the city on their *Bolshoi Express* with steam locomotive which includes stops at Volgograd, Sukhara, Samarkand, and Moscow. Accommodations and meals are provided. For more information contact *Cox & Kings* (511 Lexington Ave., New York, NY 10017; phone: 212-935-3854).

## LOCAL SERVICES

**BUSINESS SERVICES** Most major hotels now have their own business centers, with services including fax and photocopying machines, typing, translation, and direct-dial international telephones. The newest is the *American Business Center* at the *Nevsky Palace* hotel. Some hotels also offer conference and audiovisual facilities. See individual hotel listings in *Checking In.* You don't have to be a guest at most hotels to use their business services.

**DENTIST** *Dental Polyclinic No. 3* (phone: 213-7551, days; 213-5550, nights) has 24-hour emergency service with an English-speaking staff. *Polyclinic No. 2* (see *Medical Emergency,* below) has a dental facility that is open weekdays, with an "on call" dentist available nights and weekends (phone: 110-0654). All facilities have Western-trained personnel and equipment. Patients must pay in hard currency only.

---

**MEDICAL EMERGENCY** All major hotels have a doctor on call, and translators are provided for those doctors who do not speak English. *Polyclinic No. 2* (22 Moskovskiy Prospekt; phone: 292-6272, fax: 292-5939) has its own ambulance service, and its medical staff will make house/hotel calls. The 24-hour emergency number is 110-1102. The clinic is closed Sundays. The *American Medical Center* (77 Reki Fontanki; phone: 310-3611) dispenses immediate outpatient care.

For extreme medical problems *Lenfinmed* (77 Reki Fontanki Naberezhnaya; phone: 310-9611), a joint Russian-Finnish venture, will airlift patients to Helsinki for treatment. Also contact the *US Consulate* (15 Furshtadtskaya Ulitsa; phone: 275-1701) for further information.

**PHARMACY** Most hotels now have a good selection of over-the-counter drugs and health-care products available in their shops. For prescription drugs try *Polyclinic No. 2*'s *Damian Pharmacy* (phone: 110-1744 or 110-1272; fax: 292-5939); closed weekends and public holidays. *Lenfinmed* (see above) operates its own pharmacy.

## SPECIAL EVENTS

*St. Petersburg Spring,* March 31 to April 7, is a week of festivities celebrating the end of winter. The major annual arts festival in St. Petersburg is called the *White Nights,* and is held the third week in June to coincide with the longest days of the year. This far north the sun does not set until 10 or 11 at night and rises again at 2 or 3 in the morning. Information on what will be offered during the festival is spotty at best; traditionally there have been performances by the *Kirov Academic Theater of Opera and Ballet* (see *Theater*), by the *Maly Theater Opera and Ballet,* and by various top Russian singers and musicians. Evening cruises to watch the sun set for its brief rest are becoming increasingly popular.

## MUSEUMS

St. Petersburg is a major art center; many of the best-known museums are listed in *Special Places.* In addition, you may enjoy visiting—either individually or on a guided tour—some of the following. Note: The hours for many of these museums can change with little or no notice; be sure to check before you go. Most museums charge either a nominal entrance fee or ask for a donation for upkeep and/or repair.

**BOTANICHESKIY MUZEY (BOTANICAL MUSEUM)** Founded in 1824, the garden has more than 3,000 varieties of tropical and subtropical plants. There is a separate orangery with varieties of trees. Both are closed Fridays. 2 Professora Popova Ulitsa (phone: 234-1764, 234-8470 or 234-0673).

**ETNOGRAFICHESKIY MUZEY (ETHNOGRAPHIC MUSEUM)** Located near the *Russian State Museum,* this museum houses a beautiful collection of clothing, household goods, and folk articles associated with the daily life and customs of the peoples of the republics that once made up the Soviet Union. Closed Mondays and the last Friday of every month. 4-1 Inzhenernaya Ulitsa (phone: 219-1174 or 210-3652).

**KITAYSKIY DVORETS (CHINESE PALACE)** Commissioned by Catherine the Great (who lived here for only two months), this exotically adorned building, located in the suburb of Oraninbaum (known as Lomonosov in Soviet times), is considered just as important—and impressive—as the *Summer Palace*. Peter the Great also lived here before ascending to the throne. Off the usual tourist track, this palace was spared during the Nazi occupation of World War II, so its splendid original details are still intact. Open in summer only (exact dates vary from year to year depending on the weather; it's best to check before you go); closed Tuesdays and the last Monday of each month (phone: 422-3753 or 422-4796).

**KREPOST ORESHEK (ORESHEK FORTRESS)** A former czarist prison where Lenin's older brother was executed, this out-of-the-way museum has exhibits on the fortress's history and on modern life in Schlies-selburg, its suburban island home. Take the train from *Finland Station* to *Petrokrepost Station* and then a hydrofoil to the island. Open from mid-May through mid-September (dates vary depending on the weather, so call ahead). Closed Tuesdays and the last Monday of each month. Schliesselburg (phone: 238-4686 or 238-4720).

**LITERATURNIY-MEMORIALNIY MUZEY ANNI AKHMATOVOI (ANNA AKHMA-TOVA LITERARY AND MEMORIAL MUSEUM)** In a wing of the illustrious *Sheremetyev Palace*, the apartment where the famous Russian poetess lived for many years is now a museum. English audiotapes are for sale at the entrance. Closed Mondays and the last Wednesday of each month. 34 Reki Fontanki Naberezhnaya (phone: 272-5895 or 272-1811).

**MEMORIALNIY LITERATURNIY MUZEY-KVARTIRA DOSTOYEVSKOVO (DOS-TOYEVSKY LITERARY MEMORIAL APARTMENT-MUSEUM)** Home of the celebrated writer during the last years of his life. Closed Mondays and the last Wednesday of each month. 5-2 Kuznechniy Pereulok (phone: 311-4031).

**MEMORIALNIY MUZEY-KVARTIRA A. BLOKA (ALEXANDER BLOK MEMORIAL APARTMENT-MUSEUM)** The furniture and rooms have been re-created as they were when the distinguished Russian poet lived—and died—here. Closed Wednesdays. 57 Deskaloristov (phone: 113-8616 or 113-8633).

**MEMORIALNIY MUZEY-KVARTIRA A. S. PUSHKINA (A. S. PUSHKIN MEMOR-IAL APARTMENT-MUSEUM)** The house where Pushkin lived during the last months of his life (he died from wounds received in a duel). English-speaking guides must be arranged for in advance. English-language books and audiotapes are available at the entrance for an additional charge. Special shoe coverings (located in bins on the way upstairs to the museum) must be worn in the apartment. Closed Tuesdays and the last Friday of each month. 12 Reki Moiki Naberezhnaya (phone: 314-0006).

**MENSHIKOVSKIY MUZEY-DVORETS (MENSHIKOV PALACE)** This branch of the *Hermitage* offers insights into the Russian domestic scene—palatial style—along with art from the time of Peter the Great. Closed Mondays. 15 Universitetskaya Naberezhnaya (phone: 213-1112).

**MUZEY ANTROPOLOGII I ETNOGRAFII IMENI PETRA VELIKOVO (PETER THE GREAT MUSEUM OF ETHNOGRAPHY AND ANTHROPOLOGY)** An exhibition of rarities, curiosities, and oddities of nature, started by Peter the Great and occupying the building that formerly was the *Kunstkamera* (Chamber of Curiosities). Closed Fridays, Saturdays, and the last Thursday of every month. 3 Universitetskaya Naberezhnaya (phone: 218-1412).

**MUZEY ARKTIKI I ANTARKTIKI (MUSEUM OF THE ARCTIC AND THE ANTARCTIC)** The only museum of its kind in the world, it offers an introduction to the history of the exploration of the North and South Poles. Closed Mondays and Tuesdays. 24A Marata Ulitsa (phone: 311-2549).

**MUZEY ARTILLERII, INZHENERNIKH VOISK I VOISK SVYAZI (MUSEUM OF ARTILLERY, ENGINEERS, AND SIGNALS)** A military museum of old arms, including a good collection of 16th-century weapons that belonged to the czars. Housed in the city's former arsenal, built in 1860. Closed Mondays, Tuesdays, and the last Thursday of every month. 7 Park Lenina (phone: 232-0209).

**MUZEY DOMIK PETRA I (PETER THE GREAT'S COTTAGE)** The modest dwelling used by Peter the Great while the *Peter and Paul Fortress* was being constructed nearby in the early 18th century. A must-see for history buffs, the small cottage has been refurbished with period antiques and replicas of maps and implements Peter used when he was designing the city. Closed Tuesdays and the last Monday of every month. 6 Petrovskaya Naberezhnaya (phone: 232-4576 or 238-9070).

**PUSHKINSKIY DOM/MUZEY RUSSKOI LITERATURI (PUSHKIN HOUSE/MUSEUM OF RUSSIAN LITERATURE)** The most comprehensive collection in Russia of manuscripts by Russian poets from the 12th to the 20th centuries. Closed Mondays. On Basil's Island at 4 Makarova Naberezhnaya (phone: 218-0502).

**TEATRALNIY MUZEY (THEATRICAL MUSEUM)** A variety of exhibits and descriptions of Russian theater and theatrical life. Closed Tuesdays and the last Friday of each month. 6 Ostrovskaya Ploshchad (phone: 311-2195).

**TSENTRALNIY VOENNO-MORSKOI MUZEY (CENTRAL NAVAL MUSEUM)** A collection of ship models begun by Peter the Great in 1709 and more, housed in the former stock exchange building. Closed Mondays, Tuesdays, and the last Thursday of each month. 4 Pushkinskaya Ploshchad (phone: 218-2501).

# SHOPPING

St. Petersburg does not offer the variety of goods that Moscow does, and the prices are a bit higher, but it is a good source for souvenirs. Department stores and souvenir shops as well as an outdoor crafts market near the *State Circus* (be careful of pickpockets in this area) all offer a wide selection of Russian mementos: festively painted wooden dolls that stack inside each other, amber jewelry from the nearby Baltics, wooden toys, balalaikas, painted wooden eggs, shawls, vodka, caviar, and crystal and china from St. Petersburg's famed porcelain factory. This is also an excellent place to look for furs—coats, hats, muffs, and pelts—as Russia's main fur auctions are held in this city three times a year.

Located in all of the major hotels are stores selling souvenirs as well as toiletries, soft drinks, film, alcohol, snacks, and the most essential item for tourists—bottled water. The best of these outlets are in the *Astoria* and *Pribaltiskaya* hotels (see *Checking In*).

A recent phenomena on the Russian shopping scene is the non-newsstand kiosk. These tiny outlets, which resemble oversized phone booths, have been popping up on every street corner. Though the emphasis is on Western goods, some surprisingly good deals can be found on spirits, caviar, hats, lacquered objects, and other souvenirs.

Be sure to make time to go to the *Kuznechiy Rynok* (3 Kuznech-naya Ulitsa), St. Petersburg's best farmers' market, where merchants from all parts of the former Soviet Union come to sell their wares under a big tent. Georgians stand over what looks like an alchemist's selection of obscure spices; gold-toothed *babushkas* proffer their prized pickles, pickled garlic (a Russian phenomenon), homemade goat cheese, and honey; and Uzbeks are on hand with bright bouquets of fresh flowers. Prices at the farmers' market are tradition-ally much higher than in the stores, but the array is impressive. Open daily from 7 AM to 6 PM.

Most of the city's department stores and shops are open Mondays through Saturdays from 10 AM to 9 PM. The newly renovated *Gostiny Dvor* (35 Nevsky Prospekt; phone: 312-4165 or 312-4174), a large, old-fashioned establishment that dates from the 18th century, is St. Petersburg's version of Moscow's *GUM* department store. Other major department stores include *Dom Leningradskikh Torgovel (DLT)*, which specializes in everything related to children, including clothes and toys (21-23 Bolshaya Konyushennaya Ulitsa; phone: 312-2627); *Moskovskiy* (205-220 Zabalkanskiy Prospekt; phone: 293-4455); and the *Tsentr Firmennikh Torgovel* (Trade Firm Center; 1 Oktyabrskiy Prospekt; phone: 352-1134). The following are some of St. Petersburg's finer small shops.

**Andrei Ananov** Exquisite animal figurines, priceless egg medallions, and picture frames are the subjects favored by Andrei Ananov, a goldsmith who has excelled in the art form developed by Peter Carl Fabergé. Even if you can't splurge on a perfect gold-and-silver egg pendant, take time to browse around the upscale shop if only to appreciate the workmanship. 1-7 Mikhailovskaya Ulitsa (phone: 312-0072).

**Ariadna** A cooperative that sells contemporary works by local artists. Closed Wednesdays. 32 Reki Moiki Naberezhnaya (phone: 312-7831).

**Dom Knigi (House of Books)** The largest bookstore in St. Petersburg, with posters, reproductions, and postcards on the second floor. The building itself is of interest because it was the Russian headquarters of the Singer Sewing Machine Company early in this century. It has some wonderful Art Nouveau details as well as distinctive metalwork sculpture on its roof. 13 Nevsky Prospekt (phone: 311-5473).

**Galereya** Drawings, Russian boxes, wooden dolls, ceramic sculptures, painted samovars, and folk art by talented young Russians. Closed Sundays and Mondays. 10 Pushkinskaya Ulitsa, Apartment 10 (on the third floor; phone: 164-4857).

**Griffon** Paintings, drawings, and photographs by professional artists, as well as souvenirs. 38 Bolshaya Morskaya Ulitsa (phone: 314-4815).

**Izdeliya Khudozhestuennikh Promislov (Arts and Handicrafts)** Traditional Russian handicrafts including ceramics, wooden dolls, and lacquered boxes. 51 Nevsky Prospekt (phone: 113-1495).

**Komissionniy Antikvarniy Magazin (Antiquarian Secondhand Bookshop)** Old and rare books in a variety of languages. There's also an excellent collection of antique ruble notes and maps. 18 Nevsky Prospekt (phone: 312-6676).

**Leningrad** A good selection of artwork, books, and some souvenirs. 52 Nevsky Prospekt (phone: 311-1651).

**Mikha Rossi (Furs of Russia)** This is the place to shop for a sable hat, a mink coat, or that special rabbit, *shapka*. Prices are high, but the selection is extensive. 57 Nevsky Prospekt (phone: 117-0163).

**Nasledie (Heritage)** The art shop of the St. Petersburg branch of the *Russian Cultural Foundation* offers superior quality souvenirs including painted eggs and nesting dolls as well as paintings, drawings, and jewelry. Closed Sundays and Mondays. 116 Nevsky Prospekt (phone: 279-5067).

**Nevsky 20 Gallery** Attached to the *Blok Library,* this place features a good variety of works by amateur St. Petersburg artists. One side is primarily a gallery; paintings may be purchased on the other side (signs in English explain which is which). Open daily. 20 Nevsky Prospekt (phone: 311-0106).

**Norka (Mink)** A cooperative offering a wide choice of opulent fur coats, hats, and muffs, along with other small fur souvenirs—all made in the traditional Russian style. 34 Bolshaya Morskaya Ulitsa (phone: 273-4404).

**Palitra (Palette)** A cooperative selling works of fine and applied art. Closed Mondays. 166 Nevsky Prospekt (phone: 274-0911).

**Passage** A very old, beautiful department store, catering mainly to women. Open weekdays only. 48 Nevsky Prospekt (phone: 311-7084).

**Petersburg** An exquisite antiques shop, with everything from furniture, icons, and paintings to silverware, porcelain, and toys. Drop in for a browse, even if you can't afford the hefty price tags or don't have the patience for the paperwork you would have to complete in order to get a purchase through customs. Open daily. 54 Nevsky Prospekt (phone: 311-4020).

**Plakat (Poster)** St. Petersburg's best selection of posters, plus a reasonable selection of paintings, greeting cards, and other graphics. Open daily. 38 Lermontovskiy Prospekt (next to the *Sovietskaya* hotel).

**Polyarnaya Zvezda (Polar Star)** A fine selection of semi-precious stones, such as malachite, tigereye, and carnelian. Open weekdays only. 158 Nevsky Prospekt (phone: 277-0980).

**Rapsodiya** Musical paraphernalia, including recordings and books in Russian, German, English, and French. Open weekdays only. 13 Bolshaya Konyushennaya Ulitsa (phone: 314-4801).

**Souvenirs** More traditional Russian and Central Asian handicrafts. 92 Nevsky Prospekt (phone: 272-7793).

**Vakhont** Located on the site where the famed Fabergé made his baubles and jewel-encrusted eggs for Russian royalty, this store features a wide selection of amber necklaces and gold and silver jewelry. 24 Gertsena Ulitsa (phone: 314-6447).

**Vostochniye Sladosti (Far East Sweets)** Specializing in Middle Eastern sweets, including that all-time favorite, halvah. Open daily. 104 Nevsky Prospekt (phone: 273-7436).

**Yeliseyev's** This grand old food emporium, unimaginatively labeled *Gastronom No. 1* during the Soviet years, has regained its former name and been restored to its original splendor. At the turn of the century this was St. Petersburg's showcase for imported European and Asian delicacies, but don't visit the early Art Nouveau building expecting to find the brimming cornucopia it was when the millionaire Yeliseyev brothers were in charge. In fact, today the opulent stained glass, ornate tile-hung interior, and bronze façade seem downright overblown when compared with its limited selection of goods. Open daily. 52 Nevsky Prospekt (no phone).

## SPORTS

Hundreds of sporting events are held each year in St. Petersburg's major sports arenas: the *Sankt Petersburgskiy Sportivno-Kontsertniy Kompleks* (St. Petersburg Sports and Concert Complex; 8 Yuria Gagarina Prospekt; phone: 298-4847 or 298-2164), which seats 25,000; *Kirovskiy Stadion* (Kirov Stadium; 1 Morskoi Prospekt; phone: 235-4877 or 235-5494); the *Dvorets Sporta Yubileiny* (Jubilee Palace of Sports; 18 Dobrolyubov Prospekt; phone: 238-4122 or 238-4067); and *Zimniy Stadion* (Winter Stadium; 2 Manezhnaya

Ploshchad; phone: 210-4688 or 315-5110). Soccer and ice hockey are the two main professional sports in town. Your hotel service bureau can provide schedules and tickets for events.

For those who prefer participating over spectating, the *Kirovskiy Stadion* (see above) offers (for a fee) horseback riding, track and field facilities, tennis courts and equipment, and bowling. In winter you can rent cross-country skis and ski the surrounding grounds. Tennis courts and equipment also can be rented at *The Tennis Club* (23 Konstantinovskiy Proyezd; phone: 235-0407) and the *BAST Sports Centre* (16 Raevskovo Proyezd; phone: 552-5512 or 552-3936).

The *World Class Fitness Centre* at the *Astoria* hotel (phone: 210-5869; closed Sundays) has a gym, a sauna, a pool, a solarium, and massage facilities. The same company operates the *World Class Health Club* at the *Grand Hotel Europe* (phone: 119-6200; open daily), which offers a sauna, a pool, a gym, a solarium, massage, a hairdresser, and a sports shop. The *BAST Sports Centre* (see above) also has an exercise room, sauna, and massage facilities, as well as an English-speaking staff.

For true fitness freaks the world's only nighttime marathon is run during the *White Nights,* in the third week of June. The date and route vary from year to year, so it's best to check in advance.

## THEATER

It's easiest to arrange tickets through your hotel service bureau, which will also have schedules of performances at all the theaters in town. Performances begin early, usually at 7 PM for the theater and 7:30 PM for the circus and puppet shows. During intermission be sure to try the theater buffet, which includes open-faced salami and sturgeon sandwiches, cakes, cookies, soft drinks, and other snacks.

Many of the best resident theater, ballet, and opera companies tour Western countries, other parts of Russia, or parts of the former Soviet Union during the summer months. However, their stand-ins are just as talented. Here are some of our favorites.

---

### CENTER STAGE

**Mariinski Teatr i Operi (Marinsky Opera and Ballet Theater)**
The most famous troupe in St. Petersburg is the theater and ballet company simply known as the *Kirov* during Soviet times (formally known as the *Akademicheskiy Teatr Operi i Baleta imeni S. M. Kirova*—Kirov Academic Theater of Opera and Ballet). Such legends as Nijinski, Pavlova, Nureyev, and Baryshnikov have danced with this troupe, which is noted for its adherence to strict classical ballet traditions. In fact, many critics regard the *Kirov* as the foremost European ballet company—in the East or West— even better than Moscow's *Bolshoi.* Under the direction of Marius Petipa, the company gave the premiere perfor-

mances of Tchaikovsky's *Sleeping Beauty* and *Swan Lake* in 1890 and 1895, respectively. The company declined after the Russian Revolution, then experienced a rebirth under storied ballet teacher Agrippina Vaganova. Renamed the *Kirov* in 1935, today its performances are held in the beautiful *Marinsky Theater.* Tickets can be difficult to get, so book as far in advance as possible. (Some people have had luck just showing up at the theater or at the booking desk in their hotel early on the day of the performance and asking for a *single* ticket.) 1 Teatralnaya Ploshchad (phone: 314-9083 for general inquiries; 114-5424 for administration; 114-4344 for the box office).

---

The *Pushkin* (2 Ostrovskaya Ploshchad; phone: 312-1545) is the top theater in St. Petersburg. Recend productions have often been satirical and have touched on topics strictly forbidden only a short time ago. Other major theaters include the *Sankt Petersburgskiy Konservatoriya imeni Rimskovo-Korskikov* (St. Petersburg Rimsky-Korsakov Conservatory—but tell your driver the *"Konservatoria"*; 3 Teatralnaya Ploshchad; phone: 312-2519 or 312-2507); *Akademicheskiy Maly Teatr Operi u Baleta* (Small Academic Theater of Opera and Ballet—but tell your driver the *"Maly Teatr"*; 1 Mikhailovskaya Ploshchad, better known as Arts Square; phone: 312-2040 or 314-3758); *Bolshoi Teatr Kukol* (Grand Puppet Theater; 10 Nekrasova Ulitsa; phone: 272-8215); *Tsirk* (Circus; 3 Reki Fontanki Naberezhnaya; phone: 210-4411 or 210-4390); and the *Bolshoi Konsertniy Zal* (Grand Concert Hall; 6 Ligovskiy Prospekt; phone: 277-7400 or 277-6960).

## MUSIC

Tickets and performance schedules for concerts can be obtained through your hotel service bureau. Concerts usually begin at 7:30 PM. The major halls are the *Sankt Petersburgskaya Filarmoniya* (St. Petersburg Philharmonic; 2 Mikhailovskaya Ulitsa; phone: 312-2001); the *Maly Zal imeni Glinki* (Glinka Small Hall) of the *Sankt Petersburgskiy Filarmoniya* (30 Nevsky Prospekt; phone: 312-4585); the *Sankt Petersburgskiy Kontsertniy Zal* (St. Petersburg Concert Hall; 1 Lenina Ploshchad; phone: 542-0944); the *Dzhaz Tsentr* (Jazz Center; 27 Zagorodniy Prospekt; phone: 164-8565); the *Gosudarstvenniy i Vistavochnii Kompleks Smolniy Sabor* (Smolny Cathedral and Exhibition Complex; 3-1 Rastrelli Ploshchad; phone: 271-9182 for the box office; 311-3560 for administration); and the *Sankt Petersburgskiy Sportivno-Kontsertniy Kompleks* (St. Petersburg Sports and Concerts Complex; 8 Yuria Gagarina Prospekt; phone: 298-4847 or 298-4659).

## NIGHTCLUBS AND NIGHTLIFE

St. Petersburg is known for its lively nightlife, and locals often mock Moscow for its failure to live up to the second city's reputation as a "happening place." Over the years several famous Russian rock bands have emerged from smoky underground bars in the city, and

---

you might catch a rising star in one of these hot new venues: the *Art Club Café* (3 Canal Griboyedova; phone: 314-5273), the *Indie Club* (223 Obukhovskoye Oborony Prospekt; no phone), the *Tam-tam Club* (49 Maly Prospekt; no phone), and *Rock Around the Clock* (27 Sadovo Ulitsa; phone: 310-0439). Check the listings in the English-language newspaper *St. Petersburg Press,* available in the lobby of all major hotels. The *Dzhazkafe* (Jazz Café; 27 Zagorodniy Prospekt; phone: 113-5345) features local artists performing some cool numbers. The *Grand Hotel Europe* (see *Checking In*) has a nightclub on the fifth floor with two dance levels; also try the lobby bar with its wood-paneled walls and library atmosphere. Casinos in St. Peterburg are not recommended for foreigners, as they are usually seedy and fraught with unsavory characters.

# Best in Town

CHECKING IN
Major hotels accept direct private bookings or those made through Western travel agencies. The *Grand Hotel Europe* and the *Astoria* have both been remodeled recently and are the city's best—and most expensive. Package deals, arranged in advance through a travel agent, offer the best value. Most hotels have banks, shops, postcard and stamp kiosks, service bureaus, beauty parlors and barber shops, newsstands, restaurants, and business centers.

Youth hostels do exist; it is best to arrange for these in advance. An inexpensive hostel for travelers of all ages also has opened in a former dormitory on Sovyetskaya Ulitsa (phone: 277-0569). For information, contact *Russian Youth Hostels and Tourism* (409 N. Pacific Coast Highway, Building 106, Suite 390, Redondo Beach, CA 90277; phone: 310-379-4316; fax: 310-379-8420). For bed and breakfast accommodations, contact *Room with the Russians,* which has an office in London (Station Chambers, High St. N., London E6 11E, England; phone: 81-472-2694; fax: 81-964-0272). The organization provides a driver who will greet you at the airport and take you to your destination; all of the participating families have at least one English-speaking member, and some provide evening meals. The agency can arrange for apartment rentals as well. *American-International Homestays* (1515 W. Penn St., Iowa City, IA 52240; phone: 319-626-2125) organizes stays with Russian families in St. Petersburg and several other Eastern European cities. *IBV Bed & Breakfast Systems* (13113 Ideal Dr., Silver Spring, MD 20906; phone: 301-942-3770; fax: 301-933-0024) also can arrange a home visit with a local family.

Accommodations in St. Petersburg hotels usually are available in three classes: first class double rooms, deluxe two-room suites, and deluxe three-room suites. The dramatically fluctuating Russian economy makes it difficult to provide accurate rates for hotels; we suggest that you check costs—and the latest exchange rate—immediately prior to your departure. Be aware that the Russian government has imposed a 23% tax on rooms; check in advance to see if it is included in your room rate. In all of the following hotels, guestrooms have private baths unless otherwise specified. All telephone numbers are in the 812 city code unless otherwise indicated.

### DELUXE

**Astoria** Built in 1912 in the heart of downtown St. Petersburg, and extensively refurbished in 1991, this is still one of the city's best. The 436 rooms in the hotel, which incorporates the former *Angleterre* next door, are decorated with antique furniture; many of them afford good views of *St. Isaac's Cathedral* and the *Mariya Palace* on St. Isaac's Square. Potted plants dot the elegant public rooms, and everything and everyone, including the doormen, are impeccable and impressive. Hitler planned to hold his victory banquet here after his armies captured the city; the arrangements, however, were premature (the invitation once hung in the lobby). There are three restaurants (the *Winter Garden* is the most elegant; see *Eating Out*), three bars, two cafés, 24-hour room service, an art salon, a fitness center with pool and sauna, a hair salon, and three shops. Business facilities include meetings rooms for up to 180, an English-speaking concierge, foreign currency exchange, secretarial services in English, audiovisual equipment, photocopiers, cable television news, and translation services. 39 Gertsena Ulitsa (phone: 210-5032; fax: 315-9668).

**Grand Hotel Europe** Simply the best. With a fleet of Volvo limousines that greets guests at the airport, a glass-enclosed atrium shining with marble, a bar with a harpist and 33 types of vodka, this hotel is rivaled only by Moscow's *Metropol* as the country's finest. Formerly the *Evropeyskaya,* it was designed by Swedish architect Fyodor Lidvall at the turn of the century. The Swedish-Russian joint venture that restored the building has made it one of Europe's premier hotels. There are 301 guestrooms, some decorated with antiques, others in an Art Nouveau style. Even if you're not a guest, be sure to stop for coffee or a drink at the hotel's first-floor bar, an elegant respite from the sometimes overwhelming crush of shoppers on Nevsky Prospekt around the corner. In addition to European grandeur, the hotel has its own water-cleaning system (tap water in St. Petersburg is unfit to drink), three restaurants (including the *Europe;* see *Eating Out*), a nightclub, two cafés, a health club, a sauna, a wood-paneled billiard room, 24-hour room service, and a row of boutiques and shops. Business facilities include an English-speaking concierge, secretarial services in English, audiovisual equipment, computers, cable television news, and translation services. Located off Nevsky Prospekt at 1-7 Mikhailovskaya Ulitsa (phone: 119-6200 for information/switchboard; 1-800-THE-OMNI; fax: 119-0002 for reservations).

**Hotelship Peterhof** This four-star floating hotel affords a comfortable and efficient setting. All 91 cabins come equipped with satellite TV sets. There is a good restaurant featuring seafood specialties. Business facilities include meetings rooms for up to 150, secretarial services in English, audiovisual equipment, and photocopiers. On the

Makarov Pier near the Tuckhkov Bridge (phone: 850-1459; fax: 850-1406).

**Nevsky Palace** Opened in 1993, this beautiful Art Nouveau hotel is the result of the renovation of two 19th-century buildings that once housed the old *Hermes* hotel, which later was renamed the *Baltiskaya* and became the home of the famous acting Smoilovs. A museum commemorating the Smoilovs' work with the *Alexandrinsky Drama Theater* has been opened in the second floor rooms where they once lived. The Austrian-owned property is now run by the Marco Polo hotel chain, which also runs the *Palace* and *Presnaya* in Moscow. There are 287 rooms, including 30 suites, all decorated in lively blue and pink pastels. Guests can request one of the 49 nonsmoking rooms on the seventh floor. All accommodations feature direct-dial telephones, satellite TV, and the benefits of the in-house water-purification system. There is a sauna, a whirlpool, and an outdoor sun terrace offering a splendid view of the *Virgin of Vladimir Cathedral.* The hotel also boasts the *Admiralty,* one of the best restaurants in the city, and the rooftop *Landskrona* (see *Eating Out* for both). Business facilities include meeting rooms for up to 180, secretarial services in English, audiovisual equipment, photocopiers, and translation services. 57 Nevsky Prospekt (phone: 275-2001; 222-715-55300 in Vienna; fax: 113-1470).

### FIRST CLASS

**Commodore** Located near the St. Petersburg harbor, this renovated wing of the former *Leningrad* hotel features 800 rooms, two restaurants, and three bars. Business facilities include secretarial services in English, photocopiers, and translation services. 1 Morskoy Slavy Ploshchad (phone: 119-6666; fax: 119-6667).

**Helen** This Finnish-Russian joint venture on the banks of the beautiful Fontanka River is ideal for the budget-conscious traveler in search of Western-quality accommodations. A favorite of many British, German, and Scandinavian travelers, the hotel projects a clean and modern atmosphere and has a personable staff—it's a welcome relief from the sprawling, dingy, and chaotic atmosphere of most Russian-managed hotels. The 275 rooms are quiet, cozy, and tastefully decorated with cheerful prints, Finnish furniture and fixtures, radios and color TV sets; the bathrooms can be a bit spartan. A breakfast buffet is included in the price. There's a modest cafeteria, a typically loud Russian restaurant, and a swinging bar on the fifth floor (open until 5 AM), with a good view of the river. Several buses and minibuses offer tourist excursions and sightseeing tours. 43-1 Lermontovskiy Prospekt (phone: 259-2026; fax: 113-0860; in Helsinki phone: 694-8022; fax: 694-8471).

**Pribaltiskaya** This huge (1,200 rooms—including a number of three-room suites), Swedish-built hotel is located on Vasilyevskiy Island, overlooking the Gulf of Finland. Of special note are two duplex corner suites, complete with spiral staircases, pianos, chandeliers, kitchens, and dining areas. There are several restaurants with floor ·

shows and dancing, a bar, a nightclub with live jazz, a casino, a sauna with a massage room, a beauty salon, a duty-free shop, car rental facilities, a plane/train ticket desk, and dry-cleaning services. In addition, this establishment is distinguished from every other hotel in town by its bowling alley. Business facilities include meeting rooms for up to 120, foreign currency excahnge, secretarial services in English, photocopiers, translation services, and express checkout. About 8 miles (13 km) from the city center at 14 Korablestroitelaya Ulitsa (phone: 356-0001; fax: 356-0372).

---

## EATING OUT

The food situation throughout Russia is getting better, and the advent of new, privatized restaurants has added a competitive edge to the city's dining scene. The fare, service, and atmosphere in St. Petersburg establishments have improved over what was offered just two years ago.

Russia has many notable dishes—although many are heavy on oil and sour cream—from the familiar beef Stroganoff, chicken Kiev, and borscht to *pelmyeni* (Siberian dumplings stuffed with spicy meat) and *ovoschvey* (vegetable stew). Most Russian meals start with an array of appetizers known as *zakuski,* such as caviar, canned crab, sliced meat, smoked fish, marinated mushrooms, mushrooms baked in a sour cream sauce known here as *julienne,* sliced tomatoes and cucumbers, and salad *stolichnaya* (a potato salad with meat). Be sure to save room for the main course; you could easily fill up on appetizers alone.

Travelers should *not* drink water from public fountains, tap water, or the water served at restaurant tables; a parasite, called *giardia lambia,* is prevalent in the St. Petersburg water system. It can cause violent intestinal illness requiring hospitalization if not properly treated. There is an incubation period of about two weeks; therefore, this illness should not be confused with the usual travelers' maladies. You can avoid this parasite by taking minimal precautions; cooked food, tea, coffee, bottled water, and soft drinks are quite safe. If you order the local mineral water, be warned that it is often very salty. Russian restaurants rarely serve wine, but they often have local champagne, which is really quite good, especially if you insist on the dry variety (ask for brut or *suhoy*).

Meals at major restaurants in St. Petersburg can be booked in advance through your hotel service bureau, or you can reserve on your own—that is, if you speak Russian. You can request a prix fixe menu, or you can order à la carte. Most of the hotels have dining rooms with live bands, dancing, and, occasionally, a floor show. Reservations at hotel restaurants also should be made in advance with the hotel service bureau. There are many cafés in St. Petersburg, providing a good opportunity to mix with local residents. As in other Russian cities, privately owned establishments have become popular here.

The dramatically fluctuating Russian economy makes it difficult to provide accurate prices for restaurants; we suggest that you check costs—and the current exchange rate—immediately prior to going. With the new monetary regulations now in effect, all transactions are in rubles only; however, an increasing number of restaurants now accept major credit cards as well. Unless otherwise specified, all restaurants are open for lunch and dinner. All telephone numbers are in the 812 city code unless otherwise indicated.

**Admiralty** The dining room of the *Nevsky Palace* hotel offers Russian fare, with such specialties as beluga sturgeon, beef Stroganoff, and roast breast of duck. Save room for the tempting cheesecake. Open daily. Reservations advised. Major credit cards accepted. 57 Nevsky Prospekt (phone: 275-2001).

**Austeria** Located in the *Peter and Paul Fortress,* this place recalls the era of Peter the Great. The fare, too, has an Old Russian flavor. Try the *file austeria* (fried beef stuffed with onions and nuts and served with fried potatoes, onions, and carrots) or the *rulet starorusskiy* (roast veal roll with hard-boiled eggs, onions, and carrots). Live music is played most nights. Open daily. Reservations advised. No credit cards accepted. Ioannovskiy Ravelin, *Peter and Paul Fortress* (phone: 238-4262).

**Chayka** The first foreign-owned restaurant to have opened in the city, this Russian-German joint venture specializes in German fare (beefsteaks and sausages) and German beer. The interior has a nautical decor (*chayka* is Russian for sea gull). Open daily until the wee hours. No reservations. MasterCard accepted. 14 Canal Griboyedova. (phone: 312-4631).

**Chopsticks** A delightful Chinese eatery featuring deliciously prepared Szechuan and Cantonese specialties. Try the lemon chicken, chicken with cashew nuts, eggplant in garlic sauce, and fresh fried broccoli, served with hot jasmine tea. The fried banana with caramel sauce makes a sweet ending to any meal. Open daily. Reservations necessary. Major credit cards accepted. Located next to the *Grand Hotel Europe,* on the corner of Nevsky Prospekt (phone: 119-6000).

**Demyanova Ukha** A small spot with rustic decor and a menu consisting primarily of fish and seafood. Open daily. Reservations necessary. No credit cards accepted. 53 Gorkova Ulitsa (phone: 232-8090).

**Europe** This dining hall in the *Grand Hotel Europe* has a well-prepared menu including tempting seafood, beef, chicken, veal, and duck entrées. Sunday brunch is special: five long tables filled with pâté, meats, crêpes, pasta, and desserts including fruit and cheese. Open daily. Reservations advised. Major credit cards accepted. 1-7 Mikhailovskaya Ulitsa (phone: 119-6200).

**Fortezia** A Russian-Belgian venture, this cozy spot seats only 45 in three small dining rooms (the smallest has only two tables, set under portraits of Peter the Great and his wife, Catherine). Traditional Russian food is the bill of fare. Closed Mondays. Reservations advised. No credit cards accepted. 7 Kuibysheva Ulitsa (phone: 233-9468).

**Gino Genelli** Originally opened as an ice cream parlor (though considering that ice cream is a Russian specialty, the selection here is not wide), this glitzy, little (it has only eight tables), subterranean place now serves a variety of hamburgers. An Italian-Russian joint venture, it's not a bad place to go to pretend you never left the USA. Open daily. Reservations unnecessary. No credit cards accepted. 14 Kanala Griboyedova (no phone).

**Hermitage** For good traditional Russian fare and old-fashioned decor, visit this café in Tsarskoye Selo, a mile (1.6 km) from the *Yekaterinskiy Palace* and its park. Try the *zharkoye russkoye* (roast meat). Open daily. Reservations advised. Major credit cards accepted. 27 Kominterna Ulitsa (phone: 476-6255).

**Imperial** Traditional Russian dishes are served in this ornately decorated dining room (the walls are covered with paintings and photographs of Russian nobility and other prerevolutionary bigwigs). Try the *suvorov* (a beef and mushroom stew baked in a clay pot). The service, from tuxedo-clad waiters, is fast and efficient. Open daily. Reservations advised. No credit cards accepted. 53 Kamennoostrovskiy Prospekt, on the main road to Vyborg on the north side of the Neva (phone: 234-1594 or 234-1742).

**Ismailov** Come here for some of the best traditional Russian food in town—and the best floor show (Gypsy love songs, cossack dancing, and Russian folk songs). The prix fixe menu starts with a groaning table of cold *zakuski*, hot *blini*, caviar, and creamed mushroom crêpes. There are usually three entrées from which to choose, followed by dessert and coffee. Open daily. Reservations necessary. No credit cards accepted. Corner of Sovietskaya Ulitsa and Krasnoarmeyskaya Ulitsa (phone: 292-6838).

**John Bull Pub** Located in what used to be an ice cream parlor, this English-style pub offers draft beer (John Bull bitter) on tap and snacks. Traditional Russian meals are served in the adjacent dining room, but be warned that the service can be very slow. The pub and restaurant are open daily. Reservations advised. Major credit cards accepted. 79 Nevsky Prospekt (phone: 164-9877).

**Landskrona** This recently opened Swedish restaurant is poised to become one of St. Petersburg's best. The menu features such innovative fare as smoked breast of pheasant and poached lobster and crabmeat. Sitting high atop the *Nevsky Palace* hotel, it affords spectacular views of the city. At press time the owners were considering outdoor dining during the summer months. Open daily. Reservations advised. Major credit cards accepted. 57 Nevsky Prospekt (phone: 275-2001).

**Literaturniy Kafé** In this city rich in culture and vibrating with social change, there's no better place to get a feel for the current arts scene than this, the favorite gathering spot of St. Petersburg's cultural elite, both present and past (Pushkin left the café to fight his fatal duel). The white-walled first-floor room is elegant and serene, with meals accompanied by a classical quartet; St. Petersburg's best poets, writers, and artists congregate upstairs. The food is good, although the selection can be rather limited, and the service is notoriously slow. Pass on the soups, which tend to be watery and rather greasy; stick with the cold appetizers and the steak with mushrooms. Also try *salat slavyanskiy* (a salad of sliced beef and potatoes mixed with a variety of fresh vegetables, hard-boiled eggs, and mayonnaise). Open daily. Reservations necessary. No credit cards accepted. There is a small cover charge. 18 Nevsky Prospekt (phone: 312-6057).

**Metropol** One of St. Petersburg's oldest dining establishments, it was founded in the 19th century and still tries to maintain that era's charm—although it's becoming increasingly more difficult to justify that effort as prices rise and upkeep does not keep pace. (It is resting on laurels earned when there was little competition, and now food and service can be erratic.) The place is as large as an airplane hangar (10 halls); Russian fare is served in Baroque surroundings, and live music adds to the ambience. The prix fixe menu generally consists of a huge selection of cold appetizers (including crab and caviar), soup, a choice of hot entrées such as chicken Kiev, and dessert, all washed down with champagne or vodka. Specialties include *kotlety po-kievskiy* (chicken served with mashed potatoes) and *file pikantnoye* (beef stew served with boiled cabbage and carrots). The desserts are wonderful. Open daily. Reservations advised. No credit cards accepted. 22 Sadovaya Ulitsa (phone: 310-2281).

**Na Fontanke** Located in the center of St. Petersburg, this is one of the best dining spots in town. The menu offers such specialties as *langet na-Fontanke* (fried beef served with boiled potatoes and peas) and *salat Sankt-Petersburgskiy* (salad prepared from an old Russian recipe). The prix fixe menu is determined by what's fresh in the market that day, but generally includes a full table of cold appetizers (the marinated mushrooms are the best in town), a choice of hot entrée (the steaks topped with tomatoes and cheese are good), and dessert. You can request a vegetarian meal in advance, but more than likely you'll wind up with fried fish. There's a piano player and violinist. Open daily. Since there are only 10 tables, reservations are necessary. No credit cards accepted. 77 Reki Fontanki Naberezhnaya (phone: 310-2547).

**Nevsky** For traditional Russian food and hospitality in modern surroundings, visit this first-class dining establishment in the city center. Specialties include *eskalop* (veal served with fried potatoes and olives). There's a variety show, along with live music performed by different orchestras in three separate dining rooms. Open daily. Reservations necessary. Major credit cards accepted. 71 Nevsky Prospekt (phone: 311-3093).

**Petrovskiy** An old ship that has been moored permanently and transformed into a restaurant and bar. The dark blue decor recalls the 18th century, as does the food. A house specialty is *myaso po-preobrazhenskiy* (fried, beef-filled pastry, served with peas, onions, and tomato sauce). Open daily. Reservations advised. Major credit cards accepted. Opposite house No. 3 on Mytninskaya Naberezhnaya (phone: 238-4793).

**Pizza Express** A Russian-Finnish venture, this eatery serves 13 kinds of pizza, from Americano (ham, pineapple, and blue cheese) to Milano (tuna, clams, onions, and capers), made from Finnish products and served in Russian surroundings (or—astonishingly—delivered to your hotel door). The menu also includes a full range of other entrées, including pork dishes and beef Stroganoff. Cocktails are served. Paintings by local artists are for sale, too. Open daily. Reservations advised. Major credit cards accepted. 23 Podolskaya Ulitsa (phone: 292-2666).

**Sadko** Still one of the best restaurants in St. Petersburg, with traditional German fare and a flashy, predominantly Russian clientele. Try the *spätzle* (thick noodles), *räucheraal* (smoked eel), or sauerbraten (pot roast marinated with herbs). Desserts are just as good. Open daily. Major credit cards accepted. Next to the *Grand Hotel Europe* at Nevsky Prospekt and Mikhailovskaya Ulitsa (phone: 210-3198).

**Saint Petersburg** This first-class dining spot is located on the Yekaterinskiy Canal on one of the city's prettiest streets, between Nevsky Prospekt and the *Church of the Blood of the Savior.* A German-Russian joint venture (the flags of both countries billow over the entrance), it is outfitted in brass and wood with the clubbish feel of a New York steakhouse, although the prix fixe menu consists of page after page of traditional Russian fare. Specialties include Peter's soup (cabbage) and chicken Nicholas I (cutlets stuffed with mushrooms, cheese, and nuts). The wine list features a wide assortment of French and Italian vintages. A folk orchestra performs throughout the evening. Open daily. Reservations necessary (book a day or two in advance). Major credit cards accepted. 5 Yekaterinskovo Kanala Naberezhnaya (phone: 314-4947).

**Schvabskiy Domik** Also known as the *Schwäbisch Hut,* this stylish eatery serves genuine Schwäbisch food and light German wines from Baden and Württemberg. There are two separate dining rooms with different menus and entrances. Open daily. Reservations necessary. Major credit cards accepted. 28-19 Krasnogvardeyskiy Prospekt (phone: 528-2211).

**Senat** This former Russian-Dutch eatery has been revamped into a French bistro-style restaurant offering seafood classics such as filet of sole with mussels in white wine sauce. Open daily. Reservations necessary. Major credit cards accepted. 1-3 Galernaya Ulitsa (phone: 314-9253).

**Tbilisi Café** A little out of the way on the north side of the Neva River (and north of the *Peter and Paul Fortress*), this festive Georgian eatery is a favorite with foreigners and tour groups. Georgian art and tapestries adorn the stone walls, and there are many ceramics and miniatures on display. The staff seems genuinely delighted to serve foreigners, but the food occasionally can be bland and uninspired. (Purists in search of authentic fare will not find it here—too many Russian dishes appear among the Georgian specialties.) Open daily. Reservations advised for dinner. No credit cards accepted. 10 Sytninskaya Ulitsa (phone: 232-9391).

**Tête-à-Tête** This former barbershop has become a luxurious dining room that is intimate, lamplit, and graced with plenty of antiques and chandeliers with real candles—all of which make diners feel as though they've stepped back into Old St. Petersburg. The menu features continental fare, including sturgeon, a house specialty. A tailcoated jazz pianist works wonders on the grand piano in the corner. Open daily. Reservations necessary. No credit cards accepted. 65 Bolshoi Prospekt, Petrogradskaya Storona, on the north side of the Neva (phone: 232-7548).

**Troika** Excellent food and first-rate entertainment served up in a red and gold Baroque setting. There are several courses offered here, from caviar to crab, right through to the ice cream and vodka and champagne. The nightly variety show is one of the best in town—traditional Russian folk songs, dancing, and music; after intermission, however, the whole thing turns into a tacky sex show. Open daily. Reservations advised. No credit cards accepted. 27 Zagorodniy Prospekt (phone: 113-5376).

**Vostok** This is still the only dining establishment in St. Petersburg serving Indian fare. A joint Russian-Indian venture, it offers good and spicy dishes prepared over an open fire. There is a variety show and casino. Open daily. Reservations advised. No credit cards accepted. *Primorskiy Park,* near the lake (phone: 235-5984 or 235-2804).

**Winter Garden** The Doric columns, marble floors, fountain, and lush foliage are quite enough to ensure a delightful experience at this dining room in the *Astoria* hotel. Add an orchestra and well-prepared traditional Russian fare, and you've got the makings of a truly memorable meal. Reservations advised. Major credit cards accepted. At the *Astoria Hotel,* 39 Gertsena Ultisa (phone: 210-5838).

# Stockholm

## At-a-Glance

### SEEING THE CITY

The best aerial view of Stockholm is from planes circling the city before landing; if you can't have that, ascend to the observation gallery atop the 419-foot *Kaknästornet*, a TV tower on the eastern edge of town (Järget Norrandjurgården; phone: 789-2435). A bird's-eye view is the only way to comprehend fully the city's idyllic setting. A vista of wooded islands and winding waterways enhanced by twisting copper spires and turreted roofs stretches almost as far as the eye can see. The tower is open daily; admission charge.

### SPECIAL PLACES

Most of central Stockholm can be explored on foot, while sightseeing barges provide a fascinating "under the bridges" perspective on the city (see *Getting Around,* below).

#### DOWNTOWN

**VASA MUSEET (VASA MUSEUM)** When the man-of-war *Vasa* was launched in 1628 during the peak era of Swedish power, it was intended as the flagship of the *Royal Swedish Navy.* But the warship foundered on the way out of the harbor on its maiden voyage. This tragic—and embarrassing—mishap was but a dim memory when the wreck was rediscovered in 1956. A five-year salvage operation raised the remarkably well-preserved warship and some 24,000 historic items aboard it from the harbor bottom. The cleaned and refurbished *Vasa* and its fittings are housed in the museum. A short film detailing the salvage operation precedes regular guided tours in English. Open daily. Admission charge. Djurgården (phone: 442-8000).

**SKANSEN** This folklore center and summer meeting place for people of all ages is within walking distance of the *Vasa Museet.* Opened in 1891, *Skansen* was the prototype for outdoor museums throughout the world. More than 150 buildings of historic interest, brought here from various regions of Sweden, shed light on the daily lives of Swedes through the ages. In summer, craftspeople demonstrate glass blowing, weaving, and other traditional skills. *Skansen's* hilltop setting also houses a zoo; concerts, open-air dancing, and shows enliven the summer scene. A traditional *Christmas* market is held on three Sundays during the holiday season. Open daily. Admission charge. Djurgården (phone: 442-8000).

**GAMLA STAN (OLD TOWN)** The influential political figure Birger Jarl founded the city of Stockholm on the central island of Gamla Stan in 1252. This old quarter, a warren of small buildings jumbled together in crooked rows, is unmistakably medieval in character.

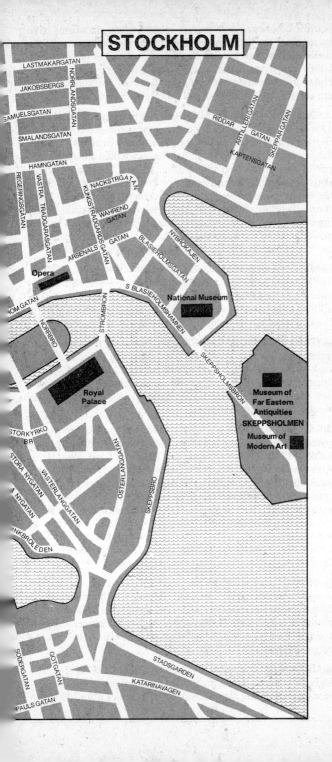

Narrow lanes open onto market squares where merchants have traded since the 13th century. Even today this remains one of the liveliest districts of the city. Careful renovation has preserved the buildings that now house about 300 small shops, restaurants, nightclubs, artists' studios, and boutiques. South of Stockholm's modern center; accessible by several short bridges.

**STOCKHOLMS SLOTT (ROYAL PALACE)** Built during the late 17th and early 18th centuries, this palace is no longer the home of the royal family, which now resides at *Drottningholm Slott* (see below). Parts of the *Stockholms Slott* and the *Royal Treasury* within are open to the public when there are no official functions here. The palace features Baroque and rococo furnishings and collections of tapestry and china; the crown jewels can be seen in the treasury. There are also small shops where "royal" souvenirs can be purchased. A colorful changing of the guard ceremony takes place in summer at 1 PM Sundays, noon the rest of the week. Closed Mondays. Admission charge. At the foot of Norrbro Bridge, in Gamla Stan (phone: 789-8500).

**NATURHISTORISKA RIKSMUSEET (SWEDISH MUSEUM OF NATURAL HISTORY)** The highlight here is a planetarium called *Cosmonova,* where computer-controlled video projectors let visitors experience a fantastic million-mile journey into space. Open daily. Admission charge. Frescati (phone: 666-4040; 666-5130, planetarium reservations).

**STOR-KYRKAN (STOCKHOLM CATHEDRAL)** A short walk from the *Stockholms Slott,* through the Gamla Stan, takes you to the cathedral, built in the 13th century and rebuilt between 1736 and 1742. Its ornate interior includes a masterful wood sculpture, *Saint George and the Dragon* by Bernt Nötke, dating from 1479. Behind the *Stockholms Slott* on Trångsund.

**STADSHUSET (CITY HALL)** The red brick façade of this seat of Stockholm government is a masterpiece of understatement. The building, dedicated in 1923, contains a spectacular *Gyllene Hallen* (Golden Hall), whose walls are covered with mosaics depicting Swedish history, made up of nearly 18 million gilded tiles. Guided tours (in English) are offered daily, official functions permitting, at 10 AM and noon, with additional tours offered June through August at 11 AM and 2 PM. The 320-foot *Stadshusettornet* (City Hall Tower) offers an impressive panorama of the city; open daily from May through September. Admission charge includes both. 1 Hantverkargatan (phone: 785-9059).

**POSTMUSEUM (POSTAL MUSEUM)** An outstanding collection of postage stamps is housed in this lovely old building. The highlights of the collection are two rare 1847 Mauritius stamps and a quarter-sheet of four-skilling banco. There's also an authentic 19th-century mail coach. Closed Mondays. Admission charge. In Gamla Stan, 6 Lilla Nygatan (phone: 781-1755).

**OSTASIATISKA MUSEET (MUSEUM OF FAR EASTERN ANTIQUITIES)** Surprisingly, Sweden has a long tradition of sinological studies. The Chinese exhibition here includes Stone Age ceramics from 2000 BC; a rich collection of jade pieces; carvings in wood, ivory, and horn; lacquer; and everyday paraphernalia such as mirrors and dress hooks. The museum also has collections of fine arts and handicrafts from Japan, Korea, and India. Closed Mondays. Admission charge. Skeppsholmen (phone: 666-4250).

**OSTERMALMS SALUHALL** This large covered market is where Stockholm's gourmets buy fresh meat, fish, and delicatessen goods. Steeped in atmosphere, the market offers visitors a taste of typical Swedish market trading. There are salad bars and health food counters here too. Ask at *Lisa Elmquist's* for her recipe for *gravlax* (dill-cured salmon). A few blocks east of the city center on Ostermalmstorg.

**KUNGSTRÄDGÅRDEN (ROYAL GARDEN)** This broad tree-lined avenue-cum-park with its dancing fountains in summer and ice skating in winter is an ideal place to engage in the pleasures of people watching. In the summer there often is a show at the bandstand. *Kungsträdgårdsgatan.*

**SANDHAMN AND THE ARCHIPELAGO** By the *Stadshuset* and opposite the *Grand* hotel one can see smart white steamships bobbing at their moorings. These genuine turn-of-the-century steam vessels are lovingly preserved and still contribute to the heavy summer traffic out to the archipelago. You will not have touched the heart of the city until you have made the steamer trip out to an island paradise such as the yachting center of Sandhamn or the charming town of Vaxholm with its 16th-century fortress (now a museum). Several steamer operators offer frequent trips of varying lengths to the islands, and there's daily ferry service to Sandhamn throughout the summer. For details, contact *Strommakanal AB* (22 Skeppsbron; phone: 233375 for schedules; 241100 for steamer rental). Local tourist offices also can provide information and schedules.

**KULTURHUSET (HOUSE OF CULTURE)** This modern center features exhibitions of art, handicrafts, and design. Tourists may find its reading library of foreign newspapers particularly useful. There is a cafeteria on the top floor. Closed Mondays. 3 Sergelstorg (phone: 700-0100).

**MODERNA MUSEET (MUSEUM OF MODERN ART)** Special exhibitions of contemporary works complement the permanent collection of 20th-century art. Closed Mondays. Admission charge. Jarlaplan (phone: 666-4250).

## SUBURBS

**MILLESGÅRDEN** Many of the finest works of sculptor Carl Milles (1875–1955), best known for his statues at New York City's Rockefeller Center, are displayed in the garden of his former home on fashionable Lidingö Island overlooking central Stockholm. The waterside residence also contains the sculptor's own collection, including some of the classical Greek and Roman statues that influenced his work. Closed Mondays. Admission charge. Take the subway to Ropsten, where buses leave frequently for *Millesgården.* 2 Carl Milles väg, on Lidingö (phone: 765-0553).

**DROTTNINGHOLMS SLOTT (DROTTNINGHOLM PALACE)** This 17th-century palace was built for dowager Queen Hedvig Eleonora on the island of Lovön just 5 miles west of Stockholm. The French-style palace and its beautiful gardens resemble Versailles but deserve recognition in their own right. The *Kina Slott* (Chinese Pavilion), a small rococo summer house in the park, also is open to visitors, as is the *Drottningholms Slottsteater* (Drottningholm Court Theater; see below). The palace and grounds are reached by road or by the steamer that departs from Klara Mälarstrand, an embankment near the *Stadshuset.* Visitors also can take the subway to Brommaplan and then change to Mälaröbuses, which stop here. Palace open daily May through September; *Kina Slott* open daily April through mid-October. Admission charge. Lovön (phone: 759-0310).

**DROTTNINGHOLMS SLOTTSTEATER (DROTTNINGHOLM COURT THEATER)** On the palace grounds, this superb rococo building deserves separate mention as one of the most perfectly preserved 18th-century theaters anywhere. During summer months the theater's original stage sets and machinery are used for performances of period operas and ballets. But the 450-seat auditorium and theater museum are worth a visit at any time. Guided tours are available. Open daily May through September. Admission charge. Lovön (phone: 759-0406).

**WALDEMARSUDDE** This beautiful retreat in an exquisite setting was the home of the late Prince Eugen of Norway and Sweden, an accomplished artist. His fine collection of paintings and sculpture, both his own work and that of other Scandinavian artists, is exhibited here. Closed Mondays. Admission charge. Djurgården (phone: 662-1833).

# Sources and Resources

## TOURIST INFORMATION

For general tourist information, stop by *Sverigehuset* (Sweden House; *Kungsträdgården;* phone: 789-2490; fax: 789-2491), where the *Sverige Turistbyrå* (Swedish Tourist Board) and the *Stockholm Information Service* provide maps and literature. The *Stockholmskortet* (Stockholm Card)—valid for one adult and two children, and good for a free sightseeing tour in summer, unlimited use of public transportation, and admission to most museums—can be bought for one-, two- or three-day periods (175, 350, and 525 kronor, respectively; that's roughly $22.50, $45, and $67.50). It's available at *Sweden House* and at other tourist information centers: *Hotellcentralen* at the *Stockholms Centralstation* (Stockholm Central Railway Station, on Klarabergsviadukten a short walk southwest from Sergels Torg); phone: 240880); at the *Kaknästornet* (Kaknäs TV tower; Djurgården; phone: 667-8030); and in the summer at *Stadshuset* (City Hall). Special tourist discount tickets for subways, buses, and streetcars (including the Stockholm Card) can be purchased at major bus and subway stations, as well as at *Pressbyrån* newsstands. The

*US Embassy and Consulate* is at 101 Strandvägen (phone: 783-5300).

In the US, contact the *Swedish Travel & Tourism Council* (655 Third Ave., New York, NY 10017; phone: 212-949-2333; fax: 212-697-0835). The *Swedish Embassy* is at 600 New Hampshire Ave. NW, Suite 1200, Washington, DC 20037 (phone: 202-944-5600).

**ENTRY REQUIREMENTS** A US citizen needs a current passport for a stay of up to 90 days. The 90-day period begins on the date of entry into any one of the Nordic countries, which besides Sweden include Denmark, Finland, Iceland, and Norway.

**TIME** The time in Sweden is six hours later than in US East Coast cities. Sweden observes daylight saving time.

**LANGUAGE** Swedish is the official tongue, but many people have a firm command of English.

**ELECTRIC CURRENT** 220 volts, 50 cycles, AC.

**MONEY** The Swedish krona (SEK) equals 100 öre. There were about 7.50 kronor to one American dollar at press time.

**TIPPING** A 13% service charge is automatically tacked on to restaurant tabs; hotels add 15%.

**BANKING/BUSINESS HOURS** Most banks are open weekdays from 9:30 AM to 3 PM, with some centrally located banks open to 5 PM. Smaller branches of the central banks also are open from 4:30 to 6 PM one evening per week. Most other businesses are open weekdays from 7:30 or 9 AM until 4 or 5:30 PM. Stores are open weekdays from 9:30 AM to 6 PM, and Saturdays to 1 or 2 PM.

**NATIONAL HOLIDAYS** *New Year's Day* (January 1), *Twelfth Day* (January 6), *Good Friday* (April 14), *Easter Sunday* (April 16), *Easter Monday* (April 17), *Ascension Thursday* (May 25), *Whitmonday* (June 5), *All Saints' Day* (November 1), *Labor Day* (November 4), *Christmas Day* (December 25), and *Boxing Day* (December 26).

**LOCAL COVERAGE** There are no English-language newspapers published in Sweden, though the *International Herald Tribune* and British papers are available at *Gallerian* (a shopping arcade, accessible from Hamngatan and Regeringsgatan) and at newsstands. National dailies sometimes produce English-language sections for tourists in summer. Most hotels supply copies of *Stockholm This Week,* a free English-language review of current activities in the city.

**TELEPHONE** The city code for Stockholm and surrounding areas is 8. When calling from one area to another within Sweden dial 0 + city code + local number. The country code for Sweden is 46. Dial 90000 for emergency assistance.

## GETTING AROUND

**AIRPORTS** *Arlanda Internationell Flygplats* (Arlanda International Airport), which serves both domestic and international flights, is a 30-

to 45-minute drive from downtown. Several taxi companies offer a flat rate into Stockholm, including *SAS Limousine* (797-3700), which offers travelers arriving from abroad on a scheduled flight a 12% reduction upon presentation of their airline tickets. The *City Terminal,* next to the *Centralstation,* has regular airport bus service, with an intermediate stop at a restaurant called *Jarva Krog* (the one-way fare is 50 kronor, or $6.25). There are two other airport bus routes serving Stockholm's northwestern (*Kista/Barkaby*) and western (*Bromma*) suburbs during peak hours. A free bus service is operated between domestic and international terminals at the airport, and there is a direct bus route between the airport and the trade fair site at Alvsjö.

*Bromma Flygplats* (Bromma Airport), which serves a few local airlines as well as charter and international flights, is a 15-minute trip from downtown. There is no bus service to the airport.

**BOAT** A number of companies offer "under the bridges" sightseeing tours, with commentary in English and other languages, in boats similar to the *bateaux mouches* of Paris. One such is *Stockholm Sightseeing* (22 Skeppsbron; phone: 240470).

**CAR RENTAL** All major international firms are represented.

**FERRY SERVICE** Small ferryboats operate regularly between Räntmästartrappan by the Gamla Stan and Allmänna Gränd on Djurgården, and in summer between Nybroplan downtown and Allmänna Gränd. They're inexpensive and great fun.

**SUBWAY, BUS, AND TRAIN** The Stockholm subway, with entrances marked by *Tunnelbana* signs, is a clean (except for graffiti), efficient, extensive, and super-quick means of intracity transportation. The newer stations have been designed by leading artists. Subways run until 2 AM. *Djurgårdslinjen,* a special line that uses museum-piece street cars, takes passengers from the city center out to the island of Djurgården, site of several museums and an amusement park.

All parts of the city are linked by bus routes, but during morning and evening rush hours progress can be slow despite special bus-only traffic lanes.

*Centralstation,* the main station for commuter and international trains, buses, and *Tunnelbana,* is at Vasagatan (toll-free local phone: 020-757575, for domestic train information; 020-227940, for information on international trains). The basic ticket (good for one hour from purchase time) costs 12 krona ($1.50). Special tourist discount tickets offer lower fares on subways, buses, and streetcars (see *Tourist Information,* above); also available is the 10-ride "clipp card," which costs 85 krona (about $10.60).

**TAXI** Taxis are expensive but plentiful, except during rush hours and inclement weather. The break-up of Stockholm's taxi monopoly in 1990 has resulted in lower fares. Since each taxi company sets its own fees, it is advisable to check the fare before entering the vehicle. Most taxis now display a small notice on the window showing current rates. Several companies have introduced fixed rates or eliminated pick-up charges, so it pays to shop around. Some, but not all, companies include a tip in the metered fare. Nighttime rates tend to be 25% higher that those charged during the day.

Licensed taxis now have yellow-number license plates and an authorization certificate displayed in the window. Taxis can be hailed in the street—an illuminated roof sign indicates they are available—but the easiest way is to call one of the major companies: *Taxi Stockholm* (phone: 150000; 150200, in the suburbs; and 150400, for advance bookings or a tourist taxi with a bilingual driver); *Taxi Kurir* (phone: 300000); *Taxi Ett* (phone: 670-0000); or *Top Cab* (phone: 333333). *Taxi Kurir, Taxi Ett,* and *Top Cab* all offer a 10% to 15% discount to women riding alone. Note that calling for a taxi usually involves a pick-up fee.

## LOCAL SERVICES

**DENTIST (ENGLISH-SPEAKING)** Marianne Dalheim (1 Kungsholmstorg; phone: 651-5252), practice closed early July to mid-August. For emergencies the public dental clinic (22 Fleminggatan; phone: 654-0590) is open daily from 8 AM to 7 PM; no appointments accepted.

**DRY CLEANER** *Johansson & Källström* (89-91 Drottninggatan; phone: 322790).

**LIMOUSINE SERVICE** *Limousine Service AB* (63 Norrtullgatan; phone: 233345).

**MEDICAL EMERGENCY** *City Akuten* (3 Holländargatan; phone: 117177).

**MESSENGER SERVICE** *Adena Picko's* (phone: 730-0000); for delivery by taxi call: 612-6000.

**NATIONAL/INTERNATIONAL COURIER** *DHL Worldwide Express* (in the *Wennergren Center* at 170 Sveavägen; phone: 690-0200). Express mail service to foreign destinations is available at post offices.

**OFFICE EQUIPMENT RENTAL** *Ljus & AV-teknik* (40 Riddargatan; phone: 663-5255) rents audiovisual equipment; *Teco Kontorsservice AB* (25 Rålambsvägen; phone: 618-5400) rents electronic typewriters (one-month minimum).

**PHARMACY** *CW Scheele* (64 Klarabergsgatan; phone: 218934) has 24-hour service.

**PHOTOCOPIES** *ABA Kopiering* (67 Regeringsgatan; phone: 205042).

**POST OFFICE** The main post office (28-34 Vasagatan; phone: 781-2040) is open weekdays from 8 AM to 6:30 PM and Saturdays from 10 AM to 2 PM. A nearby post office in the *Stockholms Centralstation* (phone: 102609) is open weekdays from 7 AM to 10 PM.

**SECRETARY/STENOGRAPHER (ENGLISH-SPEAKING)** *Kontorsvikarien* (45 Sveavägen; phone: 247680); *Proffice* (*World Trade Center,* 70 Klarabergsviadukten; phone: 787-1800).

**TELECONFERENCE FACILITIES** *Swedish Telecommunications Administration* (phone: 020-781110 toll-free within Sweden) can provide teleconference facilities at its head office in Farsta, a southern suburb of Stockholm.

**TELEX** The main telecenter is in the main hall of the *Central Railway Station* (phone: 106439). To send a telex by phone dial 0021 and ask for Phonotelex.

**TRANSLATOR** Contact the *Språktjänst* (Swedish Trade Council; 19 Storgatan; phone: 783-8700).

SPECIAL EVENTS

*Valborgsmässoafton* (Walpurgis Night, April 30) heralds the arrival of spring and is celebrated with bonfires in public places. *Första Maj* (Labor Day, May 1) is an occasion for parades and political speeches. *Midsommardagen* (Midsummer Day) is a charming festival (originally an ancient pagan rite) occurring around the June 21 summer solstice. It's celebrated with folk dances, raising the maypole, general merrymaking, and heavy drinking (though Stockholm tends to empty out during this time since many residents go to celebrate in the archipelago or the countryside). The month of July sees *Sommar Stockholm* (Summer Stockholm), a festival of athletic contests, music, and drama. The annual 10-day *Stockholms Vatten Festival* (Stockholm Water Festival), held in August, features aquatic events and fireworks displays. The Nobel Prize festivities take place annually in December, but it is difficult to gain admittance to anything but the public lectures of the prize winners. On *Luciadagen* (Feast of St. Lucia, December 13), Swedish children traditionally wake their parents in the early morning hours to serve them saffron buns and coffee. Some of Stockholm's major hotels celebrate the day by sending "Lucia maidens" with wreaths of candles on their heads to serve the traditional breakfast to guests in their rooms. There also are special evening festivities at *Skansen* (see *Special Places*).

MUSEUMS

Stockholm has more than 50 museums, art galleries, and historic buildings. Most museums, including those listed below, are closed Mondays and charge admission. Those of note not listed in *Special Places* include the following.

**HALLWYLSKA MUSEET** Collections of weapons, paintings, and Chinese porcelain. 4 Hamngatan (phone: 666-4499).

**HISTORISKA MUSEET AND KUNGLIGA MYNTKABINETTET (MUSEUM OF NATIONAL ANTIQUITIES AND THE ROYAL COIN CABINET)** Thirty rooms cover 10,000 years of history. The second floor houses the coin collection. The new Gold Room features nearly 700 pounds of exquisite gold and silver artifacts from the Viking and medieval eras. 13-17 Narvavägen (phone: 783-9400).

**MEDELTIDSMUSEUM (STOCKHOLM MEDIEVAL MUSEUM)** This museum explores the development of Stockholm from 1250 to 1550. At Strömparterren Norrbro (phone: 700-0593).

**NATIONALMUSEUM (NATIONAL MUSEUM OF FINE ARTS)** Opened in 1794, it contains works by Brueghel, El Greco, Rembrandt, Rubens, and Swedish artists. Södra Blasieholmshamnen (phone: 666-4250).

**NORDISKA MUSEET (NORDIC MUSEUM)** Over a million objects illustrate life in Sweden since the 16th century. Djurgården (phone: 666-4600).

**RIDDARHOLMSKYRKAN (RIDDARHOLM CHURCH)** Founded in the 13th century, this pantheon contains the tombs of Swedish kings and other famous Swedes. Riddarholmen, across the bridge from the Gamla Stan (phone: 789-8500).

**RIDDARHUSET (HOUSE OF NOBILITY)** Exhibitions pertaining to Swedish nobility in a historic, 17th-century building. Riddarhustorget (phone: 100857).

**STRINDBERG MUSEET** Sweden's most famous playwright, August Strindberg (1849–1912), lived here in the years leading up to his death. 85 Drottninggatan (phone: 411-3789 or 411-5354).

**VIN & SPIRITHISTORISKA MUSEET (WINE AND SPIRITS HISTORICAL MUSEUM)** The history of alcoholic beverages in Sweden: distillation, distribution, and customs. 100 Dalagatan (phone: 744-7070).

## SHOPPING

Shopping is a major pastime of affluent Swedes, which is evidenced by the capital city's many richly stocked department stores, trendy boutiques, and exclusive shops. Stockholm's main shopping district is the area around Sergelstorg (Sergel Square), Hamngatan, Kungsgatan, Stureplan, and the market square, Hötorget, and adjoining streets. *Nordiska Kompaniet* (18-20 Hamngatan; phone: 762-8000), called *NK* by locals, is one of Europe's greatest and grandest department stores. Department stores usually have a shopping service with English-speaking clerks. Two large indoor shopping arcades downtown, *Sturegallerian,* at Stureplan, and *Gallerian,* accessible from Hamngatan and Regeringsgatan, save tourists from getting red noses from window shopping outdoors in the depth of winter. Best buys are Swedish glass, textiles, ceramics, stainless steel housewares, furs, and Swedish crafts. Try the Gamla Stan for antiques. The usual store hours are weekdays from 9:30 AM to 6 PM, and Saturdays from 9:30 AM to 2 PM. Some shops stay open an hour later during winter months.

The following Stockholm stores are our favorites:

***Amoress*** Exclusive furs and leather jackets. 5 Norrlandsgatan (phone: 212200).

***Carl Malmsten*** The largest exponent of Swedish modern furniture. 5B Strandvägen (phone: 233380).

***Georg Jensen Silver AB*** Specializes in silverware, glassware, and porcelain. 13 Birger Jarlsgatan (phone: 611-3822).

**Klockargården** An interesting range of Swedish folk handicrafts, including hand-painted cabinets, wall hangings from Dalarna (Dalecarlia), and handmade brushes. 55 Kungsgatan (phone: 214726).

**Kodak Image Center** They carry a range of photographic supplies and equipment and offer a one-hour photo developing service. Two locations: 16 Hamngatan (phone: 214042) and 21 Sergelgatan (phone: 219167).

**Svensk Hemslöjd** More handicrafts, run by the *Swedish Handicraft Society.* 44 Sveavägen (phone: 232115).

**Svenskt Glas Butik & Galleri** Stunning displays of Swedish crystal and glass artwork. 8 Birger Jarlsgatan (phone: 679-7909).

**Svenskt Tenn** Outstanding pewter designs, as well as fabrics for the home. 5A Strandvägen (phone: 670-1600).

## SPORTS AND FITNESS

**BASKETBALL** Swedish basketball has had quite a lift from imported American players in recent years. The top local teams are the Stockholm *Capitals,* Solna *Vikings,* and *Alvik.* Games are played at various stadiums; check with the tourist information offices for schedules and ticket information.

**FITNESS CENTER** *World Class Hälsostudion* (68 Luntmakargatan; phone: 673-5410) offers weights and exercise equipment, sunbeds, and massage.

**GOLF** There are some fine 18-hole courses in the Stockholm region: *Drottningholm* (on the island of Lovön, 5 miles west of the city center; phone: 759-0085), *Lidingö* (on the island of Lidingö, east of Stockholm; phone: 765-7911), and *Djursholm* (in the wealthy Djursholm district of the city; phone: 755-1477) are among the best. During July, the Swedish vacation month, foreign visitors may play these courses if they show a membership card from their home club and evidence of their official handicap.

**ICE HOCKEY** Swedish teams are very competitive internationally and players are known for their good skating ability. Stockholm's top teams, *AIK* and *Djurgården,* play at the *Globe Arena* (Johanneshov; phone: 600-3400) from November through March.

**JOGGING** *Djurgården* (Animal Park), an island virtually free of buildings save museums, is a 10-minute walk from the center of town.

**SOCCER** The sport is known here as *fotboll* (football). The season is split into spring and autumn. *AIK* plays at *Råsunda Fotbollstadion* (Råsunda Soccer Stadium), Solna; *Djurgården* at the *Olympic* Stadium; and *Hammarby* at *Söder Stadion.* For schedule information call *Sverigehuset* (see *Tourist Information* above).

**TENNIS** Future Stefan Edbergs and lesser mortals can keep up their game at the *Kunglig Tennishallen* (Royal Tennis Hall; 75 Lidingövägen; phone: 667-0350), which also has squash courts.

**TROTTING** A popular spectator sport, with gambling permitted. *Solvalla Stadion* (Solvalla Stadium) at the border of the western suburbs of Bromma and Sundyberg (phone: 635-9000) has regular meetings during most of the year.

## THEATER

Few non-Swedish-speaking visitors would wish to sit through Strindberg in the original or hear *A Chorus Line* in Swedish, but those who do will find the current program at the *Dramaten* (Royal Dramatic Theater; at Nybroplan; phone: 667-0680, reservations; 660-6811, information) and other theaters in *Stockholm This Week.* The regular theater and opera season runs from the end of August to mid-June.

## MUSIC

The *Operan* (Royal Opera House; just off Gustav Adolfs Torg; phone: 248240 for reservations; 203515 for other information) offers performances during the season (see *Theater*), with both local talent and prominent international singers. In summer there are performances at *Drottningholms Slottsteater* (Drottningholm Court Theater; see *Special Places*). During the season there are also frequent concerts at the *Konserthuset* (Concert Hall; Hötorget; phone: 102110); *Berwaldhallen* (Berwald Hall; 69 Strandvägen; phone: 784-1800); and *Kulturhuset* (House of Culture; 3 Sergelstorg; phone: 700-0100). In summer there are outdoor concerts in several city parks and at *Skansen.* Recitals take place at the cathedral, other churches in Gamla Stan, and elsewhere in the city center, including *Engelbrekts Kyrka, Adolf Fredriks Kyrka, Gustav Vasas Kyrka,* and *Jakobs Kyrka.* Last-minute tickets are sold at the kiosk on Norrmalmstorg.

## NIGHTCLUBS AND NIGHTLIFE

Top discos are *Sturecompagniet* (4 Sturegatan; phone: 611-7800); *Café Opera* (Operahuset; phone: 676-5807); and *Landbyska Verket* (24 Birger Jarlsgatan; phone: 678-0009). You might rub shoulders with Swedish pop stars and international tennis aces at these trendy spots. Otherwise the plethora of discos is a fast-changing scene. The palatial (and painstakingly restored) rooms of *Berns* (phone: 614-0550, restaurant; 614-0720, floor show), the classic nightspot in downtown *Berzelli Park,* have helped make the spacious bar a popular watering hole again. *Börsen* (6 Jakobsgatan; phone: 787-8500) is another exclusive nighclub with a floor show. Be aware that alcohol, heavily controlled and taxed by a state monopoly, is extremely expensive in Sweden (some Swedes travel abroad just to go on drinking holidays).

# Best in Town

## CHECKING IN

Stockholm hotels have a high rate of occupancy all year round, so it's wise to book well in advance. If you do arrive without a hotel reservation *Hotellcentralen* on the lower floor at the *Centralstation*, on Klarabergsviadukten a short walk southwest of Sergels Torg (phone: 240880), is the official accommodations agency. Those visiting from mid-June through August and on weekends should ask about the special rates offered by most hotels. From June 15 through August 16, reduced rates in first class hotels and a complimentary Stockholm Card (see *Tourist Information*) are offered. A double room will cost $200 to $400 per night at one of the hotels listed below as expensive, and $125 to $200 at places described as moderate. Although we don't list an inexpensive category, the city has numerous pensions and youth hostels; contact the local tourist offices for information. Unless otherwise noted, hotels listed all offer private baths, TV sets, and telephones. All telephone numbers are in the 8 city code unless otherwise indicated.

### EXPENSIVE

**Clas på Hörnet** A rarity in the city, this 18th-century country inn has 10 uniquely decorated rooms, each furnished in period style. There is an excellent restaurant and a good smaller dining room, also called *Clas på Hörnet* (see *Eating Out*). 20 Surbrunnsgatan (phone: 165130; fax: 612-5315).

**Diplomat** The hotel is located in a splendid Art Nouveau building from the early 20th century, located at the edge of the diplomatic quarter and offering a superb view of the harbor. The 133 sophisticated rooms are individually decorated, and a genuine turn-of-the-century atmosphere pervades the hotel. There is a cocktail bar and the elegant *Tea House* restaurant. Business facilities include meeting rooms for up to 30, an English-speaking concierge, foreign currency exchange, secretarial services in English, photocopiers, cable television news, translation services, and express checkout. 7C Strandvägen (phone: 663-5800; fax: 783-6634).

**Grand** This establishment remains steeped in European tradition and old-fashioned luxury. Opposite the *Stockholms Slott* (Royal Palace), it is the most exclusive hotel in town. The beautiful Venetian-style *Bolinderska Palatset* (Bolinder Palace), built in 1877, is part of the hotel and contains a number of elegant suites. The *Grand* hotel has played host to Nobel Prize winners and their families every year since 1901. There are 321 rooms, two restaurants, a winter garden, and a bar. Business facilities include 24-hour room service, meeting rooms for up to 700, an English-speaking concierge, foreign currency exchange, secretarial services in English, photocopiers, and audiovisual equipment. 8 Södra Blasieholmhamnen (phone: 221020; 800-223-6800; fax: 611-8686).

**Mälardrottningen** Formerly the luxurious private yacht of the late heiress Barbara Hutton, it's now an unusual 59-room hotel with an exclusive restaurant and cocktail bar on its bridge. Business services include meeting rooms for up to 18, foreign currency exchange, audiovisual equipment, and photocopiers. Moored at Riddarholmen (phone: 243600; fax: 243676).

**Radisson SAS Royal Viking** The special features of this modern 319-room property include three duplex suites with whirlpool baths and saunas, a glass-roofed winter garden, shops and restaurants, an exotic "Bermuda pool" sauna and bar, and the *Sky Bar* on the top floor, which has a lovely view. Business facilities include a banquet room for up to 350, a meeting room for up to 130, an English-speaking concierge, foreign currency exchange, secretarial services in English, photocopiers, cable television news, and audiovisual equipment. It offers a very convenient location right next to the airport bus terminal and near the *Centralstation.* 1 Vasagatan (phone: 141000; 800-333-3333; fax: 108180).

**Radisson SAS Strand** On the waterfront, this delightful old-fashioned place has 138 rooms with high ceilings and a decor that combines old Swedish furniture with modern textiles and lighting. The atrium *Piazza* lounge and restaurant are designed to resemble the courtyard of an Italian palazzo. Business facilities include 24-hour room service, meeting rooms for up to 90, an English-speaking concierge, foreign currency exchange, secretarial services in English, audiovisual equipment, photocopiers, cable television news, and express checkout. 9 Nybrokajen (phone: 678-7800; 800-333-3333; fax: 611-2436).

**Reisen** An interesting old building in the Gamla Stan, it offers modern facilities and a view of the harbor from some rooms. The hotel has 114 rooms, a grill room, a piano bar, a sauna, and a small pool in its medieval cellar. Business facilities include meeting rooms for up to 50, foreign currency exchange, photocopiers, and audiovisual equipment. 12-14 Skeppsbron (phone: 223260; fax: 201559).

**Sergel Plaza** This elegant 406-room hotel, which features 18th-century artwork and antiques in some of its public places, has much to recommend it. It is located in the heart of the city's business and shopping district and offers a wide range of facilities: a fine restaurant with 18th-century decor, a piano bar with nightly entertainment, and a spa (with a sauna, massages, a solarium, and whirlpool baths). Business facilities include 24-hour room service, meeting rooms for up to 200, an English-speaking concierge, foreign currency exchange, secretarial services in English, audiovisual equipment, photocopiers, cable television news, translation services, and express checkout. 9 Brunkebergstorg (phone: 226600; fax: 215070).

### MODERATE

**Adlon** Centrally located, small, and unpretentious, it has 69 rooms. Only breakfast is served in the dining room. Business facilities include an English-speaking concierge, foreign currency exchange, photocopiers, and cable television news; the hotel can arrange for meeting rooms and secretarial services in English at the nearby *Norra Latin Conference Center.* 42 Vasagatan (phone: 245400; fax: 208610).

**Prize** Centrally located in the *World Trade Center,* with nice—though small—accommodations, it keeps rates modest by dispensing with unnecessary frills and offering 158 pleasant, basic rooms (only seven are double occupancy, but all rooms have a foldaway bed). There's a breakfast room, but no restaurant. Business and conference facilities can be arranged through the *World Trade Center.* 1 Kungsbron (phone: 149450; fax: 149848).

## EATING OUT

The *smörgåsbord,* a seemingly endless array of delicacies, ranging from smoked salmon and dozens of varieties of herring to lingonberry jam and honey, put Swedish food on the map (the most extravagant versions, called *julbord,* are served at *Christmastime*). You also might want to try other more exotic Swedish specialties, such as elk or moose steaks accompanied by red currant or rowan-berry jelly. *Surströmming,* fermented (and strong-smelling) Baltic herring, has as many detractors as fans. If you'd like to sample some in the traditional way, eat them on a slice of *norrland* bread with Swedish *mandel* potatoes—and a necessary glass of *snaps* to wash it all down. Yellow pea-and-pork soup and Kalles cod roe on open-face sandwiches are other popular treats. Recent years have seen the growth of fast-food pizzerias, kebab and hamburger restaurants, and self-service cafeterias in Stockholm. But this new food culture has done little to harm the more established (and expensive) restaurants. A three-course dinner for two, with wine and service, will cost $175 or more at an expensive restaurant, $80 to $175 at a moderate place, and $65 or less at an inexpensive one. One way to cut costs: Look for the words *Dagens rätt* (today's special) on the menu. Additional tipping beyond the service charge is not expected. Most restaurants accept major credit cards and all are open for lunch and dinner unless otherwise noted. All telephone numbers are in the 8 city code.

For an unforgettable culinary experience we begin with our favorite Stockholm dining spot, followed by our cost and quality choices of restaurants, listed by price category.

---

### DELIGHTFUL DINING

**Operakällaren** Sunday—the traditional day to eat *smörgås-bord*—is the best time to visit this large, beautifully designed dining palace facing the sea from inside the *Operan* (Royal Opera House). This is the special *smörgåsbord,* piled with seafood from all the waters of the North, that is the pride of Scandinavia. *Operabaren* and *Café Opera,* in the same building, are favorite meeting places of Stockholm intellectuals. Open daily. Reservations necessary. At the *Operan,* just off Gustav Adolfs Torg (phone: 676-5800 or 411-1125).

---

**Aurora** An intimate hideaway that serves traditional Swedish fare. Open daily. Reservations advised. 11 Munkbron (phone: 219359).

**La Brochette** Delightfully and authentically French, this place offers a varied menu of well-prepared food served in an inviting but constantly crowded dining room. A good selection of wines is available. Open daily. Reservations advised. 27 Storgatan (phone: 662-2000).

**Clas på Hörnet** Delicious Swedish and international fare is served in the formal dining room of this 18th-century hostelry. There also is a separate informal eatery, *Skänkrummet,* which offers a limited menu of traditional Swedish dishes at reasonable prices. Both open daily. Reservations necessary in the formal dining room; no reservations at *Skänkrummet.* 20 Surbrunnsgatan (phone: 165130).

**Erik's** Located in the Gamla Stan, this dining spot is highly praised by food columnists. It is an expensive haunt for those who love good food—Swedish specialties such as herring and other fish dishes predominate—and have the means to enjoy it. Closed Sundays. Reservations advised. 17 Osterlånggatan (phone: 238500).

**Den Gyldene Freden** True to its name, "The Golden Peace," this elegant 273-year-old establishment is a study in serenity. It features rooms named for famous Swedes who have dined here in the past. Food is strictly traditional—fish and game dishes—and unforgettable. Closed Sundays. Reservations advised. 51 Osterlånggatan (phone: 109046).

**Martini** Centrally located, this fashionable dining room serves continental cuisine. Open daily. Reservations advised. 4 Norrmalmstorg (phone: 679-8220).

**Nils Emil's** The elegant decor and small size of this congenial spot conspire with the superb Swedish food to make dining here an intimate experience. Closed Sundays and from late June to mid-August. Reservations necessary. 122 Folkkungagatan (phone: 640-7209).

**Riche** A ritzy up-market place, it features traditional Swedish dishes and nouvelle French cuisine. Closed Sundays. Reservations advised. 4 Birger Jarlsgatan (phone: 679-6840).

**Ulriksdals Inn** In the park of *Ulriksdals Slott* (Ulriksdals Palace), it features a fine lunchtime *smörgåsbord* as well as French and international fare. Closed Sunday dinner. Reservations necessary. *Slottspark,* Solna (phone: 850815).

**Wärdshuset Godthem** A 100-year-old inn in the *Djurgården* features a good, varied menu, a pleasant view, and a welcoming staff. A meal here is an experience in 19th-century hospitality. Open daily. Reservations advised. 9 Rosendalsvägen (phone: 661-0722).

**La Famiglia** Well-prepared pasta dishes are served in a friendly atmosphere. Several celebrity guests, including Frank Sinatra and Tina

Turner, have autographed the chairs in which they sat. Open daily for dinner. Reservations necessary. 45 Alströmergatan (phone: 650-6310).

**De Fyras Krog** The four intimate dining rooms here are each furnished in a different historic style. The food is wholesome traditional Swedish fare. Open for dinner only; closed Sundays. Reservations advised. 22 Tavastgatan (phone: 658-6405).

**Hanna's Krog** One of those unpretentious neighborhood restaurants that proves an overnight success. Locals rave about the traditional Swedish food served here. Closed for lunch on weekends. Reservations advised. 80 Skånegatan, 3 miles (5 km) outside the city (phone: 643-8225).

### INEXPENSIVE

**Coco and Carmen** In a former bakery, this small hospitable restaurant has authentic 1920s furnishings. Serving reasonably priced light dishes such as cheese pie, toast *skagen,* soups, salads, and herring, it caters to a very genteel clientele but leans more toward friendliness than stuffiness. Closed weekends. Reservations advised. 7 Banergatan (phone: 660-9954).

---

### OLD TOWN RESTAURANTS

There are several cellar restaurants in the narrow lanes of the Gamla Stan, tucked into in centuries-old vaults where each nook and cranny seems to have a story of its own. The food is excellent, and the menus normally include delicacies from the traditional Swedish kitchen, such as raw spiced salmon or snow grouse. Our two favorites are *Diana* (2 Brunnsgränd; phone: 107310), an unconventional spot that attracts a mixed clientele, and *Fem Små Hus* (10 Nygränd; phone: 100482), "Five Small Houses" interconnected to form a honeycomb of vaults, arches, and alcoves. Both are open daily.

# Vienna

## At-a-Glance

### SEEING THE CITY

The *Donauturm* (Danube Tower; phone: 235368-32) is an 846-foot-high column whose express purpose is to provide panoramic views. Located in the *Donaupark* (Danube Park), across the river from the city's center, it has an observation platform and two revolving restaurants at its summit. All three overlook the green expanse of the park and the adjacent United Nations City, and, across the river, the spires and domes of the Innere Stadt and the *Wienerwald* beyond. On a clear day, the horizon sweeps from the Alps to the plains of Hungary. The tower is open daily; admission charge. The last elevator to the summit leaves an hour before closing.

For a view of a Vienna that still resembles a Canaletto cityscape stand on the terrace of the *Oberes Belvedere* (Upper Belvedere Palace). The entrance to this an enchanting public garden is at 27 Prinz-Eugen-Strasse, near the *Südbahnhof* (South Railway Station). Good views also can be had from the *Stephansdom* towers (see below).

### SPECIAL PLACES

The Innere Stadt (Old Town), encircled by the Danube Canal and the Ring boulevards, spans about a square mile and is best explored on foot. Its main street is the Kärntnerstrasse, and its heart is the Stephansplatz, the cathedral square.

A brief language note: The German character "β," which is interchangeable with "ss," usually appears on signs, such as those with the word *Straβe* (street) or *Schloβ* (castle or fortress); these words can also be written *Strasse* and *Schloss*.

### DOWNTOWN

**STEPHANSDOM (ST. STEPHEN'S CATHEDRAL)** The most important Gothic structure in Austria, the cathedral has a soaring, ornate spire that's a trademark of Vienna. Its roof is a dramatically sloped wedge whose intricately patterned inlay gleams in the sun. The *Stephansdom* was the site of the famous double marriage in 1515 between the Hapsburgs and the Bohemian and Hungarian dynasties, a union that laid the foundations of the Austrian Empire. Climb a spiral stone staircase to the south tower, go down to the catacombs on a guided tour, or take an elevator up the north tower for a look at the cathedral's giant bell, the Pummerin, and another good view of Vienna. Guided tours of the cathedral are offered Mondays through Saturdays at 10:30 AM and 3 PM and Sundays and holidays at 3 PM. Tours also are offered at 7 PM from June through September. There is a fee for

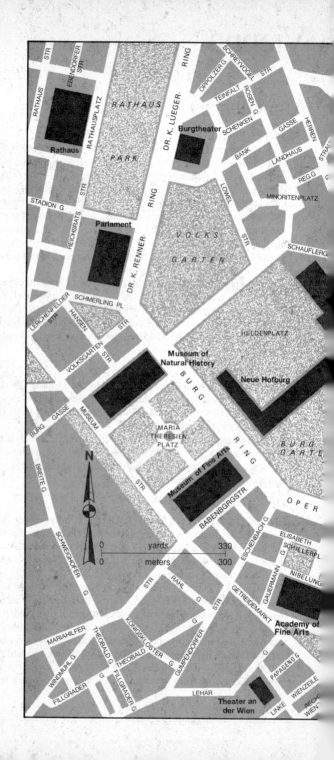

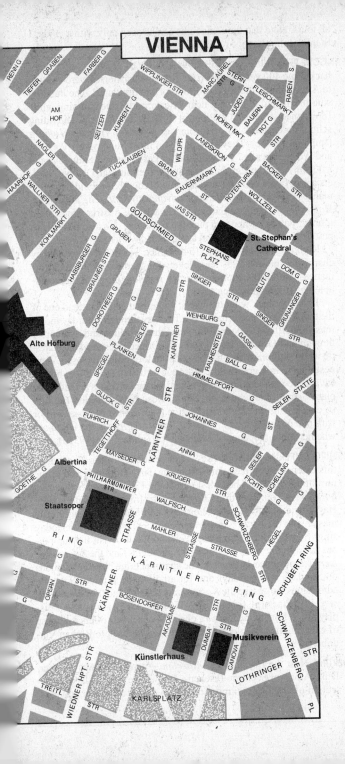

# VIENNA

- RENN G
- TIEFER GRABEN
- FARBER G
- WIPPLINGER STR
- MARC AUREL STR
- STERN G
- FLEISCHMARKT
- RABEN S
- AM HOF
- JUDEN G
- BAUERN STR
- ROT G
- NAGLER G
- HOHER MKT
- LANDSKRON G
- WILDPR
- BRAND
- BACKER STR
- HAARHOF
- WALLNER STR
- TUCHLAUBEN
- BAUERNMARKT
- ROTENTURM
- WOLLZEILE
- KOHLMARKT
- GOLDSCHMIED G
- JAS STR
- ST
- St. Stephan's Cathedral
- HABSBURGER G
- GRABEN
- STEPHANS PLATZ
- DOM G
- BRAUNER STR
- SINGER STR
- BLUT G
- GRUNANGER
- Alte Hofburg
- DOROTHEER G
- SEILER
- SINGER STR
- GASSE
- PLANKEN
- KÄRNTNER STR
- WEIHBURG
- RAUHENSTEIN
- BALL G
- SEILER STATTE
- SPIEGEL
- GLUCK G
- STR
- HIMMELPFORT
- FUHRICH
- JOHANNES
- SEILER
- ST
- G
- TEGETTHOF G
- KÄRNTNER STRASSE
- ANNA
- FICHTE
- SCHELLING
- Albertina
- MAYSEDER G
- KRUGER
- PHILHARMONIKER STR
- Staatsoper
- WALFISCH
- SCHWARZENBERG
- HEGEL
- SCHUBERT RING
- GOETHE
- MAHLER
- STRASSE
- STRASSE
- RING
- KÄRNTNER RING
- OPERN G
- STR
- KÄRNTNER
- BÖSENDORFER
- AKADEMIE
- DUMBA STR
- SCHWARZENBERG
- Musikverein
- Künstlerhaus
- CANOVA
- STR
- WIEDNER HPT. STR
- TREITL
- KARLSPLATZ
- LOTHRINGER
- PL

all tours. Note that the catacombs can be seen only with a guide. 1 Stephanspl. (phone: 515-52563).

**SPANISCHE REITSCHULE (SPANISH RIDING SCHOOL)** This institution dates back some 400 years to when the first Spanish horses were brought to Austria under the aegis of Emperor Maximilian II. The imperial stud originated at Lipizza near Trieste; today the stunning white Lipizzaners are raised at Piber in southeastern Austria. The riding school holds about 50 performances a year in Vienna's *Hofburg* (Imperial Palace). They take place on most Sundays at 10:45 AM and Wednesdays at 7 PM, with shorter performances Saturdays at 9 AM from April through June and September through October. Tickets are in fierce demand, and the rule of thumb for Sunday performances is to write *six months in advance* to *Spanische Reitschule, Hofburg,* Josefsplatz (Gate 2), Vienna 1010, Austria. Don't send money; you pay when you pick the tickets up. It's also possible to buy tickets from a local travel agent such as *American Express* (21-23 Kärntner Strasse; phone: 5154056; fax: 5154070), although they charge a minimum 22% fee. Tickets for Wednesday night performances and for the shorter Saturday morning programs are available only through agencies.

If you're stuck without tickets, you might want to attend one of the training sessions, usually held Tuesday through Saturday mornings from 10 AM to noon from April through June and September through mid-October. Traditionally uniformed riders lead the majestic white stallions through their paces to the strains of classic Viennese music in a great white Baroque hall. There is a fee, but no advance reservations are taken—stand in line for tickets at the Josefsplatz Gate 2. The school was due to close for renovation last fall, so check with the city tourist office (see *Tourist Information*) or with one of the *Austrian National Tourist Offices* in the US to see whether it has reopened. 1 Michaelerpl. (phone: 533-90310).

**HOFBURG (IMPERIAL PALACE)** The winter residence of the Hapsburgs, this extensive complex dates from the early Gothic period to the turn of the century. The oldest part is the 13th-century *Schweizerhof* (Swiss Court), with its *Burgkapelle* (Imperial Chapel). Here Haydn and Schubert were choirboys and Mozart a young music master, and the *Wiener Sängerknaben* (Vienna Boys' Choir) today sings Sunday morning masses. You should also visit the sumptuous *Kaiserappartements* (Imperial Apartments) and the *Schatzkammer* (Treasury; see *Museums*). The apartments are closed afternoons on Sundays and holidays and for a half-hour at noon. Separate admission charges for the *Kaiserappartements* and the *Schatzkammer.* 1 Michaelerpl. (phone: 587-5554, ext. 515). An open-air display just in front of the *Hofburg* on the Michaelplatz offers a glimpse of excavations of settlement remnants dating back to Roman Vindobona.

**ALBERTINA** Near the *Hofburg,* the *Albertina*—named after its founder, Duke Albert of Sachsen-Teschen—houses the world's largest collection of graphic arts: more than a million etchings, engravings, color prints, sketches, and woodcuts. The highlight is a complete collection of Albrecht Dürer's etchings. Closed Friday, Saturday, and Sunday afternoons and most holidays; closed all day Sundays in July and August. No admission charge on Sundays from September through March. 1 Augustinerstr. (phone: 534830).

**KUNSTHISTORISCHES MUSEUM (MUSEUM OF FINE ARTS)** The heart of the great Hapsburg collection survived two world wars intact and appears here today in most of its imperial glory. One of the most dramatic exhibits in Europe is the roomful of paintings by Pieter Brueghel the Elder, which represents more than half the known body of work of this strange genius. The grotesque *Peasant Wedding,* the icily beautiful *Hunters in the Snow,* the lunatic *Battle between Carnival and Lent*—they're all here. Here, too, are some of Rubens's finest works, including the great Ildefonso altar painting; the portrait of a nude, fur-swathed Hélène Fourment, his second wife; and a splendid self-portrait that is one of his last paintings. You'll also find a stunning assortment of Albrecht Dürers and fine works by Velázquez, Titian, Rembrandt, Holbein, Van Dyck, Giorgione, Cranach, and Raphael. On the premises are a café and a gift shop. Closed Mondays and major holidays. Certain collections are open Tuesday and Friday evenings until 9 PM. Admission charge. 5 Maria-Theresienpl. (phone: 521770).

## BEYOND THE CENTER

**SCHLOSS SCHÖNBRUNN (SCHÖNBRUNN PALACE)** West of the center of town, this vast palace was the summer residence of the Hapsburgs. The palace has 1,441 rooms, and the grounds are vast. Among the many sights are the royal apartments and gala rooms, the rococo palace theater (once the stage for Max Reinhardt's world-famed acting school), the dazzling collection of imperial carriages, the beautifully groomed Baroque park and gardens, and the *Gloriette*— a colonnaded structure with a panoramic hilltop view. Centered around the graceful pavilion where the Empress Maria Theresa used to take her morning coffee is Europe's oldest zoo, once the imperial menagerie, with several thousand exotic animals. The palace is open daily and on summer evenings; the park and zoo are open year-round; the *Gloriette* is open from May through October. Separate admission charges to the zoo and palace. Schönbrunner-Schloss-Str. (phone: 81113, ext. 238). Zoo entrance at Hietzinger Tor (phone: 877-1236).

**PRATER AND RIESENRAD** The *Prater* was once the private game preserve of the Hapsburg princes, but the Emperor Joseph II opened this immense green space to the public in 1766. Ideal for strolling or bicycling, its Hauptallée is a 3-mile-long boulevard flanked by lovely chestnut trees and leading to the *Lusthaus,* once the imperial hunting lodge, now a good restaurant with terrace dining in the summer (254 Freudenau; phone: 218-9565). In summer, veer left at the *Lusthaus* onto Aspernallee or Schwarzenstockallee and wend your way to *Gustav Lindmayer's Fischrestaurant* (50 Dammhaufen;

phone: 218-9580), where you can sit on the banks of the Danube and enjoy a bowl of *Fischbeuschl* soup and a pilsner. It's closed Mondays and from December through February.

At the entrance to the *Prater* amusement park stands the *Riesenrad,* the great iron Ferris wheel, a landmark since the end of the 19th century and almost as much a symbol of Vienna as the *Stephansdom* spire. The panorama of Vienna is stunning as you swing to the top of the wheel's orbit—and *Third Man* devotees will remember a menacing Orson Welles standing precariously by an open car door. The park is closed in February and November (phone: 262130).

**GRINZING** It's a charming little suburb not quite half an hour north of downtown Vienna, but the name stands for a whole aspect of Viennese life. Grinzing is where the Viennese go for food, wine, and merriment—and perhaps to remind themselves of the hearty country pleasures at the root of so much of Austrian life. The food is the traditional *Brathendl* or *Backhendl* (tender young grilled or fried chicken); the wine is *Heurigen,* which means "from this year." You can buy both food and wine at refreshment stands. In warm weather people sit outside under an arbor; in winter there may be a crackling fire. Many Viennese arrive with elaborate box lunches. Take the No. 38 tram instead of driving, to avoid the heavy traffic. (Also see *Nightclubs and Nightlife,* below.)

## EXTRA SPECIAL

The *Wienerwald,* the Vienna Woods of Johann Strauss waltzes, is a vast, unspoiled forest to the west and south of the city. The nearer edges are popular for Sunday outings, the deeper recesses for serious hiking or bike riding (bikes can be rented). There are numerous well-marked trails. To reach them take trolley No. 38 to Grinzing and continue by bus No. 38A to Kahlenberg, the starting point for many hiking trails. Or take the No. 43 tram from downtown to Neuwaldegg; from there it's a 90-minute hike—one-third of it uphill—to the *Sophienalpe* hotel (13 Sophienalpe; phone: 462432), where you can stay the night or just dine on wild boar and *Millirahmstrudel,* a cottage cheese pastry served hot with vanilla sauce.

A day's excursion to the south end of the woods can take you to the 12th-century *Heiligenkreuz* (Holy Cross) Cistercian monastery, a harmonious mix of Romanesque and Gothic. En route you'll go through the lovely wooded Helenental valley and along the Seegrotte, Europe's largest underground lake, then to the vineyards outside the towns of Perchtoldsdorf

and Gumpoldskirchen, and past one of the Prince
of Liechtenstein's Austrian castles. Rent a car and
drive the route yourself, or contact *Wiener Rund-
fahrten* (Vienna Sightseeing Tours; 411 Stelzham-
mergasse; phone: 712-46830; fax: 712-468377) or
*Cityrama*, the primary agent for *Gray Line* tours (1
Börsegasse; phone: 534130; fax: 534-1322).

# Sources and Resources

## TOURIST INFORMATION

The *Wiener Tourismusverband* (Vienna City Tourist Office; behind
the *Staatsoper* at 38 Kärntnerstrasse; phone: 211140) is open daily.
The *US Embassy* is at 16 Boltzmanngasse (phone: 31339).

In the US, the *Austrian National Tourist Office* accepts mail and
telephone inquiries (PO Box 491938, Los Angeles, CA 90049;
phone: 310-477-3332; 800-252-0468; fax: 310-477-5141; and PO
Box 1142, Times Square Station, New York, NY 10108; phone:
212-944-6890; fax: 212-730-4568). The *Austrian Embassy* is at
3524 International Ct. NW, Washington, DC 20008 (phone: 202-
895-6700).

**ENTRY REQUIREMENTS** A US citizen needs a current passport for a stay of
up to 90 days.

**TIME** The time in Austria is six hours later than in US East Coast cities.
Austria observes daylight saving time.

**LANGUAGE** German is the written language and is taught in schools, but
numerous regional dialects exist. English, taught as the second language, is understood in major tourist areas.

**ELECTRIC CURRENT** 220 volts, 50 cycles, AC.

**MONEY** The Austrian schilling (AS internationally, S or OS in Austria)
equals 100 groschen. At press time there were about 11 schillings
to $1 US.

**TIPPING** Service charges of 10% to 15% appear on restaurant and hotel
bills, but also leave a small amount of change for the waiter or the
chambermaid. Porters and bellhops should receive 10 AS per bag,
doormen about 5, and taxi drivers 10% of the fare.

**BANKING/BUSINESS HOURS** Most banks are open weekdays from 8 AM
to 3 PM (to 5 or 5:30 PM on Thursdays); branch offices close from
12:30 to 1:30 PM but otherwise keep the same hours as main offices.
The Meinl Bank AG in Vienna (8A Stephanspl.) stays open weekdays until 5 PM. Money can be changed daily from 7 AM to 10 PM
at the capital's *Westbahnhof* and *Südbahnhof* railway stations and
at the airport around the times of international flights. A number of
automatic money changers are available 24 hours a day for currency exchange into Austrian schillings; one is on Vienna's Kärnt-

nerstrasse (across from the *Opera House*). Currencies accepted are British, French, German, Italian, and US.

Most businesses are open Mondays through Thursdays from 8 AM to 4 PM, and Fridays until noon.

**NATIONAL HOLIDAYS** *New Year's Day* (January 1), *Epiphany* (January 6), *Easter Sunday* (April 16), *Easter Monday* (April 17), *Labor Day* (May 1), *Ascension Thursday* (May 25), *Whitmonday* (June 5), *Feast of Corpus Christi* (June 15), *Feast of the Assumption* (August 15), *Flag Day* (October 26), *All Saints' Day* (November 1), *Feast of the Immaculate Conception* (December 8), *Christmas Day* (December 25), and *St. Stephen's Day* (December 26).

**LOCAL COVERAGE** *Falter,* a weekly calendar of events, and *Wiener,* a monthly magazine, list everything going on, albeit in German; they're available at the *Shakespeare & Co.* bookstore (2 Sterngasse; phone: 5355053) or at any newsstand. The tourist office issues a free multilingual monthly program called *Hallo Wien* listing helpful information and events of note. A calendar of events is posted in every hotel and in other places throughout the city. Be sure to pick up a list of museum hours, as they tend to change. Freytag and Berndt publishes a good map of Vienna, which includes a brief guide to the city in English. The *Falk Plan* is a gorgeous, intricate, fold-out map that comes in two sizes. It is available at many of the city's bookstores.

*Blue Danube Radio* is an English-language mix of news, pop music, and lists of events broadcast between 6 AM and 1 AM; tune to 103.8 FM.

**TELEPHONE** The city code for Vienna is 1 when calling from outside Austria, and 222 when calling from within the country. When calling from one area to another within Austria, dial 0 + city code + local number. The country code for Austria is 43. In an emergency, dial 133 for the police.

## GETTING AROUND

**AIRPORT** Vienna's *Flughafen Schwechat* (Schwechat Airport) handles international and domestic flights. It is approximately 20 minutes from downtown by taxi or bus. Airport buses (phone: 580-033369) run to and from the *City Air Terminal* next to the *Wien Hilton International* every 20 minutes during the day; at night they run according to flight schedules (one-way fare is 60 schillings, or about $5). There is also hourly bus service during the day from *Flughafen Schwechat* to the *Südbahnhof* and *Westbahnhof* rail terminals (phone: 71101 for information). An hourly train runs from the airport to *Wien-Mitte,* a subway and rail station across from the *City Air Terminal,* and *Wien-Nord,* a subway and rail station at the northernmost tip of the *Prater;* the trip takes half an hour (phone: 1717 for information). *Mazur Shuttle,* a minibus to and from the airport, will drop you off or pick you up at your hotel. Make arrangements through the airline, your hotel, the desk at the airport (phone: 604-9191 or 604-2233), or the city office (phone: 604-2233).

**BOAT** From April through October, the *Donau Dampfschiffahrtsge-sellschaft* (*DDSG;* Danube Steamship Company; 265 Handelskai; phone: 21750, ext. 454) provides sightseeing boat trips along the canal. Boats depart frequently for one- to two-and-a-half-hour excursions from Schwedenbrücke (Swedes' Bridge), on the Danube at the *Schwedenplatz* subway stop.

**CAR RENTAL** Represented are *Hertz* (17 Kärntner Ring; phone: 512-8677); *Avis* (in the Opernpassage, an underground passage leading to and from the *Staatsoper* house; phone: 587-6241); and *Europcar Inter-Rent* (14 Kärntner Ring; phone: 505-42000).

**FIACRE** A horse-drawn carriage, as Viennese as the Hapsburgs, is a favorite mode of transportation to weddings and carnival balls or just for trundling about the Innere Stadt. The public transport map marks Fiacre stands; three reliable coachmen are Martin Stelzel (32 Gumpendorferstr.; phone: 5877037); Rudi Glück (16-7 Gestetten-gasse; phone: 722-9804); and Johann Paukner (13-8 Mohsgasse; phone: 787918).

**SUBWAY, BUS, TRAIN, AND TRAM** The public transport office in the Opern-passage sells a beautiful multilingual transport map that marks all the routes of the *U-Bahn* (subway), *Stadtbahn* (city railway), *Schnell-bahn* (rapid transit), *Strassenbaum* (tram), and *Bus* (bus), and explains the mysteries of tickets, passes, stamping machines, and the like. Buy tickets at any of the city's tobacco kiosks, which are marked Tabak/Trafik, or from a machine at reduced prices. Single rides cost AS 20 (about $1.85), but it's possible to buy passes—good for unlimited rides on all public transport for a day—at tobacconists' counters in the airport and at rail stations (AS 50, roughly $4.60) or three days (AS 130/$12).

**TAXI** Call radio taxis at 31300, 60160, 81400, or 91091. Taxis are metered; there is a 10-schilling ($1) surcharge for summoning cabs by phone, as well as for trips after 11 PM and on Sundays and holidays. There's also a special surcharge for taxi rides to and from the airport, which is outside the city limits, although many taxi agencies also offer special rates to the airport.

**WATER TAXIS** River taxis ply the Danube; each boat holds up to eight passengers. People who have motorboat licenses can hire one without a skipper. The water taxis are moored on the canal near the Salz-torbrücke (phone: 639669).

## LOCAL SERVICES

**DENTIST (ENGLISH-SPEAKING)** Peter Bischof (16 Schwarzspanierstr.; phone: 422215).

**DRY CLEANER/TAILOR** Generally this can be arranged through your hotel; otherwise, try the nearest *Phoebus Kleiderreinigung* (branches are listed by district in the city phone book).

**LIMOUSINE SERVICE** *Austrian Chauffeur Limousines,* at the *Vienna Hilton* hotel (Am Stadtpark; phone: 71100-1929).

**MEDICAL EMERGENCY** Dial 141 for medical emergency (evenings and weekends only); dial 53116 for the *Medical Center* (24 hours daily).

**MESSENGER SERVICE** *Funktrans Botendienst* (3 Hornbostelgasse; phone: 59909); or call a taxi (phone: 31300, 60160, or 40100) and ask for *Botendienst* (messenger service).

**NATIONAL/INTERNATIONAL COURIER** *DHL Worldwide Express* (59-61 Ungargasse; phone: 711810).

**OFFICE EQUIPMENT RENTAL** Contact *Dorfmeister* (17 Kärntnerstr.; phone: 512-36070) or the business centers at the *Vienna Hilton* and *Vienna Plaza* hotels (see *Checking In*).

**PHARMACY** *Cottage Apotheke* (1 Hasenauerstr.; phone: 342215) and *Internationale Apotheke* (17 Kärntnerring; phone: 512-2825) both have English-speaking staff members. *Apotheke zum rothen Krebs* (4 Lichtensteg; phone: 533-6791 and 533-8540) offers homeopathic as well as pharmaceutical medicines. All pharmacies take turns for the night shift.

**PHOTOCOPIES** *Melzer* (48 Kirchengasse; phone: 523-8244).

**POST OFFICE** Daily, 24-hour service is provided at the main post office (2 Barbaragasse; phone: 512-76810) and at branches in the *Westbahnhof* (phone: 891150) and *Südbahnhof* (phone: 501810) railroad stations.

**SECRETARY/STENOGRAPHER (ENGLISH-SPEAKING)** Contact *All Languages* (2a Fichtegasse; phone: 513-9128).

**TELECONFERENCE FACILITIES** Available at the *Austria Center* (6 Am Hubertusdamm; phone: 23690).

**TELEX** *Central Telegraphic Post Office* (1 Börsepl.; phone: 533-3455); your hotel also may have facilities.

**TRANSLATOR** *All Languages* (see *Secretary/Stenographer,* above).

**OTHER** Word processing services: the business centers of the *Vienna Hilton* and *Vienna Plaza* hotels (see *Checking In*).

## SPECIAL EVENTS

They may have venerable histories, but Vienna's major festivals are anything but staid.

---

### FAVORITE FÊTES

**Wiener Festwochen (Vienna Festival Weeks)** This orgy of music and theater lasts for five weeks, generally running from early May to mid-June. Mehta, Levine, and Abbado come to town, along with theater groups from all over Europe. There are new productions at the *Staatsoper,* premieres of new plays, art exhibitions, symposia, and plain old songfests—and every one of the city's 23 *Bezirke* (districts) sponsors special programs. For information and tick-

---

ets contact *Büro der Wiener Festwochen* (11 Lehárgasse, Vienna 1060; phone: 586-167626; fax: 586-167649).

**Silvester (New Year's Eve)** If you've spent all your life hating *New Year's Eve,* here's a spectacular way to get over the grudge—spend it in Vienna. It requires substantial planning—and money—to procure hard-to-get tickets to performances, but the reward is a *New Year's* you won't soon forget. It's best to write for tickets many months in advance, but concierges at the city's better hotels often manage to conjure up tickets to "sold out" events.

A perfect *New Year's* celebration begins with the exuberant performance of *Die Fledermaus* at the *Staatsoper* or *Volksoper* (see *Music*). From there move on to the *Kaiserball* (Imperial Ball) at the *Hofburg* for a glimpse of the old *Ballsäle* (Imperial Ballroom)—but don't stay long, as the party has become too commercial. (For tickets contact *Kongresszentrum Hofburg,* Vienna 1014; phone: 587-366623; fax: 535-6426.) Then it's on to the *Palais Schwarzenberg* hotel, where 150 guests are entertained royally in the old palace ballroom. At midnight the fireworks display rivals a *Fourth of July* extravaganza, and there's something special about dancing in the *New Year* to the strains of "The Blue Danube Waltz" rather than "Auld Lang Syne." At about 2 AM a Tirolean oompah band marches through the palace, trumpeting away, and all the guests march behind. (For tickets contact the *Palais Schwarzenberg,* 9 Schwarzenbergpl., Vienna 1030; phone: 784515; fax: 784714.)

The festivities begin again early on *New Year's Day.* At 11 AM in the *Musikverein* the *Wiener Philharmoniker* rouses celebrants with the *Neujahrskonzert* (New Year's Concert), a program of waltzes and polkas by both Strausses. Tickets for the performance, which run from $25 to $400, are nearly impossible to procure, but you may get lucky if you order a year in advance. (For more information contact *Musikverein,* 12 Bösendorferstr., Vienna 1010; phone: 505-8190; fax: 505-9409.) The day's climax is the evening performance of Beethoven's Ninth by the *Wiener Symphoniker* (Vienna Symphony). Hearing hundreds of voices sing the "Ode to Joy" movement in the *Konzerthaus* (see *Music*)—where the composer first conducted it—is a genuine thrill. (For more information contact *Wiener Konzerthausgesellschaft,* 20 Lothringerstr., Vienna 1030; phone: 712-4686; fax: 713-1709.)

Another special Viennese celebration is *Fasching,* which loosely describes the carnival period from *New Year's Eve* until *Ash Wednesday,* the beginning of *Lent.* For some two months the city hosts a series of *Fasching* balls, ranging from the *New Year's Eve Kaiser-*

*ball* (see above) to the *Ball der Wiener Instalateure* (Vienna Plumbers Guild Ball) at a large hotel. The season's highlight is the *Opera Ball,* which is held in the *Staatsoper* house in February or March with celebrities and diplomats on hand. Other old favorites include the *Wiener Philharmoniker Ball* (Vienna Philharmonic Ball), held in the *Musikverein* concert hall; the *Wiener Artze Ball* (Vienna Physicians Ball); the *Jägerball vom Grünen Kreuz* (Huntsmen's Ball of the Green Cross); and the *Maskenball des Wiener Männergesangvereins* (Fool's Night of the Vienna Men's Choir). All are open to the general public, as is November's *Champagnerball* (Champagne Ball), which marks the opening of the European ball season. A complete schedule and ticket information are available from the *Vienna Tourist Board* (see *Tourist Information*).

## MUSEUMS

Besides those mentioned in *Special Places,* Vienna has numerous other interesting museums. Note that the *Technisches Museum für Industrie und Gewerbe* (Museum of Technology) will be closed for renovations until 1996. Unless otherwise indicated all the museums listed are closed Mondays and charge admission.

**AKADEMIE DER BILDENDEN KÜNSTE, GEMÄLDEGALERIE (PICTURE GALLERY OF THE ACADEMY OF FINE ARTS)** Twentieth-century art, mainly Austrian painters. 3 Schillerpl. (phone: 588-16225).

**EPHESOS-MUSEUM (EPHESUS MUSEUM OF ARCHAEOLOGY)** Ancient artifacts discovered in Ephesus, Turkey. Closed Tuesdays. Heldenpl. (phone: 52177).

**FIGARO-HAUS (FIGARO HOUSE/MOZART MEMORIAL)** The composer's home from 1784 to 1787. 5 Domgasse (phone: 513-6294).

**HISTORISCHES MUSEUM DER STADT WIEN (VIENNA HISTORICAL MUSEUM)** Three floors of exhibitions on the city's history and culture. 1 Karlspl. (phone: 505-8747).

**JOHANN STRAUSS MUSEUM** Strauss lived here in the 1860s; his piano, organ, and other belongings are on view. 54 Praterstr. (phone: 240121).

**JÜDISCHES MUSEUM DER STADT WIEN (VIENNA CITY JEWISH MUSEUM)** Permanent and temporary exhibitions highlight Jewish history and culture in Austria and Europe, housed in a newly renovated 16th-century former section of the venerable *Dorotheum* auction house. A bookstore and café are on the premises. Closed Saturdays. 11 Dorotheergasse (phone: 5350431).

**KUNSTHAUS WIEN** Permanent and traveling exhibitions of works by artist Friedensreich Hundertwasser, displayed in a most unique building, with wavy multicolored walls punctuated by pillars and towers. A café and gift shop are on the premises. 13 Untere Weisbergerstr. (phone: 7120491).

**KÜNSTLERHAUS (HOUSE OF ARTISTS)** Traveling art exhibitions from all over. 5 Karlspl. (phone: 5879-6630).

**NATURHISTORISCHES MUSEUM (MUSEUM OF NATURAL HISTORY)** Collections of rocks, crystals, minerals, and fossils. Closed Tuesdays. Maria-Theresien-Pl. (phone: 521770).

**NEUE BERG SAMMLUNG ALTER MUSIKINSTRUMENTE (NEW HOFBURG COLLECTIONS OF WEAPONS AND ANCIENT MUSICAL INSTRUMENTS)** A good display of medieval musical instruments. Closed Tuesdays. Heldenpl. (phone: 52177).

**OSTERREICHISCHE GALERIE DES 19 UND 20 JAHRHUNDERTS (AUSTRIAN GALLERY OF 19TH- AND 20TH-CENTURY ART)** Works by *Jugendstil* (Art Nouveau) painters and Austrian Expressionists such as Oskar Kokoschka, Gustav Klimt, Egon Schiele, and others. 27 Oberes Belvedere, Prinz-Eugen-Str. (phone: 784-1580).

**OSTERREICHISCHES BAROCKMUSEUM AND OSTERREICHISCHES MUSEUM MITTELALTERLICHER KUNST (AUSTRIAN MUSEUM OF BAROQUE AND MEDIEVAL ART)** Newly remodeled galleries displaying Austrian Baroque and medieval art. Unteres Belvedere, 6A Rennweg (phone: 784-1580).

**SCHATZKAMMER (TREASURY)** Among the gems on display is the custom-made imperial crown of Emperor Rudolf II. Closed Tuesdays. In the *Hofburg;* entrance by the Swiss Court (phone: 512-10656).

**SCHUBERT MUSEUM** The birthplace of the composer (1797–1828). 54 Nussdorfer Str. (phone: 345-9924).

**SECESSION** The works of *Jugendstil* (Art Nouveau) artists, who seceded from the traditionalists in 1897, including movement cofounder Gustav Klimt's *Beethoven Frieze,* are on exhibit in the artists' former meeting place and gallery, built in 1898. 12 Friedrichstr. (phone: 587-5307).

**SIGMUND-FREUD-HAUS** Freud's collection of books and photos, in the house in which he lived from 1891 to 1938. 19 Berggasse (phone: 3191596).

**UHRENMUSEUM DER STADT WIEN (VIENNA CITY CLOCK MUSEUM)** More than 900 timepieces. 2 Schulhof (phone: 533-2265).

**WAGENBURG (IMPERIAL COACH COLLECTION)** More than 150 old carriages, some from the *Imperial Court* in the time of Maria Theresa (1740–80). *Schloss Schönbrunn* (phone: 8773244).

## SHOPPING

The center for shopping in Vienna is the area around Kärntnerstrasse, Graben, and Kohlmarkt; most department stores are on Mariahilferstrasse. Among the best buys are knitwear, glassware, crystal, porcelain, petit point, musical instruments and scores, fur hats, riding gear, and, of course, lederhosen (leather shorts, often with suspenders), loden coats, and *Sachertorte.*

Vienna also is a haven for antiques aficonados. On the Dorotheergasse, a lovely old street off the Graben, antiques shops have proliferated in the shadow of the great *Dorotheum* (17 Dorotheergasse;

phone: 515600; fax: 515-600443), Europe's oldest auction house. Stop in at the strongholds of the Hofstätter, Vienna's leading antiques dynasty; *Reinhold* (12 Bräunerstr.; phone: 533-5069) is their sculpture and furniture branch. Also arrange to attend at least one auction at the *Dorotheum.* If you're unused to auctions, you can pay a *Sensal,* a licensed bidder—they are absolutely honest—to bid for you for a small fee. On Saturday, try the less rarefied end of the spectrum: The *Flohmarkt* (flea market) at *Naschmarkt* in the 6th district is reached easily from the *Kettenbrückengasse* station. While you're in the neighborhood, visit the *Naschmarkt* itself, an outdoor fruit and vegetable market held daily except Sundays between Linke and Rechte Wienzeile.

For those longing for the mall there's always *Ringstrassen Galerien,* a flashy glass-and-chrome shopping center filled with designer boutiques, restaurants, and cafés, all wrapped around a central atrium occupied by a *Marché Mövenpick,* a food court of sorts. It's on Kärntner Ring between the *Bristol* and *ANA Grand* hotels, with entrances on Kärntnerstrasse, Academiestrasse, and Mahlerstrasse.

A Value Added Tax (VAT) of 10% to 32% is included in the price of many items. Department stores and finer shops provide a tax refund packet that includes a refund form and a list of border points (including Vienna's *Schwechat Airport*) where refund offices are located.

All stores in Vienna are open weekdays from 9 AM to 6 PM and Saturday mornings till noon; most are closed Sundays.

**A. E. Köchert** Fine jewelry. 15 Neuer Markt (phone: 512-58280).

**Anton Heldwein** One of the city's best-known jewelry stores. 13 Graben (phone: 512-5781).

**Doblinger Musikhaus** A treasure trove of things musical, especially hard-to-find sheet music and scores. 10 Dortheergasse (phone: 5150300).

**Eduard Kettner** Hunting clothes, accessories, and gear. 12 Seilergasse (phone: 513-2239).

**F. and J. Votruba** A century-old dynasty that deals in musical items, including instruments, scores, records, and anything else you can think of. 4 Lerchenfelder Gürtel (phone: 5237473).

**Haben** Famous for its fine jewelery. 2 Kärntnerstr. (phone: 512-6730).

**Lanz** Known for dirndls and lederhosen. 10 Kärntnerstr. (phone: 512-2456).

**Lobmeyr** Fine crystal is the specialty here. 26 Kärntnerstr. (phone: 512-0508).

**Loden Plankl** A very reputable, if expensive, place for dirndls, lederhosen, and other regional wear. 6 Michaelerpl. (phone: 533-8032).

**Osterreichische Werkstätten** Austrian handicrafts. 6 Kärntnerstr. (phone: 512-2418).

**Resi Hammerer** The place for haute-couture loden and sports apparel for women. 29-31 Kärntnerstr. (phone: 512-6952).

**Der Reiter** A superb selection of riding equipment. 43 Heinestr. (phone: 214-2410).

**Rosenthal-Studio** China and silver—and a beautiful wall mosaic outside. 16 Kärntnerstr. (phone: 512-3994).

**Sacher Confiserie** The official *Sachertorte* outlet since 1832. Kärntnerstr., around the corner from the main entrance of the *Sacher* hotel (phone: 514560).

**Schloss Augarten** Maker of the world-famous porcelain. 1 Obere Augartenstr. (phone: 211-2444). Also at 3 Stock-im-Eisen-Platz (phone: 512-1494) and 99 Mariahilfer Strasse (phone: 596-1311).

**Smejkal** One of the best of many places in Vienna that specialize in petit point embroidery. In the underground Opernpassage (phone: 587-2102) and at 7 Zedlitzgasse (phone: 512-6813).

**Tostmann Trachten** Dirndls (off the rack or made to order) and other national costumes. 3A Schottengasse (phone: 533-53310).

## SPORTS AND FITNESS

**GOLF** You can tee off at the *Wiener Golfclub* (Vienna Golf Club; 65A Freudenau; phone: 218-9564).

**HORSEBACK RIDING** A good riding center is the *Wiener Reitinstitut* (17 Barmherzigengasse; phone: 713-5111).

**HORSE RACING** There's racing year-round at two beautiful tracks in the *Prater:* the *Freudenau* (phone: 218-9517), where there's flat and steeplechase racing, and the *Krieau* (phone: 587-7257), where there's harness racing.

**JOGGING** *Stadtpark,* which separates the *Inter-Continental* from the *Hilton* hotel, *Volksgarten,* and *Burggarten* are all good, central venues for running. Farther out, but still within the city limits, are the *Prater* and the *Lainzer Tiergarten.* The latter—a 5,300-acre nature preserve—is closed during the winter.

**TENNIS** The *Floridsdorfer Tennis Club* (5 Lorettopl.; phone: 381283) has 15 sand courts, including two indoors. There's also *Vereinigte Tennisanlagen* (Prater Hauptallée; phone: 218-1811), pleasantly situated in the *Prater,* with its own restaurant.

**WALKING** The Austrian national sport. There is a several-hundred-kilometer circuit of walking and hiking trails in the *Wienerwald,* excellently marked and serviced by numerous inexpensive inns.

## THEATER

Two famous old theaters are worth a visit, even if you have only a rudimentary knowledge of German: the beautiful *Theater in der Josefstadt* (26 Josefstädterstr.; phone: 402-5127) and the musical house *Theater an der Wien* (Vienna Theater; 6 Linke Wienzeile;

phone: 58830, ext. 265), where such classics as Beethoven's *Fidelio* and Lehár's *The Merry Widow* had their premieres. The *Burgtheater* (National Theater; 2 Dr. Karl Lueger Ring; phone: 51444-2959; fax: 51444-2969), one of Europe's great theaters and most accomplished companies, features classical repertory in an imposing, colonnaded Baroque palace. The same company performs a somewhat flashier modern repertory at the *Akademietheater* (Academy Theater; 1 Lisztstr.; phone: 51444-2959; fax: 51444-2969). Tickets for the *Burgtheater* and *Akademietheater* are available from two months to 10 days in advance from the *Osterreichischer Bundestheaterverband/Bestellbüro* (Austrian Federal Theater Association; 3 Hanuschgasse, Vienna 1010; phone: 513-1513; fax: 514-442969). Telephone sales start six days before the performance.

Vienna also has an established English-language company, the *English Theater* (12 Josefsgasse; phone: 402-1260), which is housed in a lovely neo-Baroque building.

## MUSIC

The ultimate Viennese musical experience is a concert by the *Wiener Philharmoniker* (Vienna Philharmonic Orchestra), whose headquarters are at the *Weiner Musikverein* (12 Bösendorferstr.; phone: 5058681; fax: 5059409). During July and August, when the box office is closed, tickets can be ordered by fax. The other major concert hall, with three separate auditoriums, is the *Konzerthaus* (20 Lothringerstr.; phone: 7121211; fax: 7131709).

Another quintessential Viennese musical group is the *Wiener Sängerknaben* (Vienna Boys' Choir). The choir performs at the *Konzerthaus* Friday afternoons at 3:30 in May, June, September, and October; it also sings mass in the *Burgkapelle* (City Chapel) of the *Hofburg* most Sunday and religious holiday mornings at 9:15, though not in July or August. Tickets should be ordered at least eight weeks in advance from *Verwaltung der Hofmusikkapelle* (Hofburg, Vienna 1010; phone: 533-9927); tickets are picked up and paid for at the *Burgkapelle* on the Friday before the performance between 11 AM and noon (or on Sunday no later than 9 AM). The remaining tickets are sold at the *Burgkapelle* every Friday afternoon, starting at 5 PM (get there at least an hour early) for the following Sunday morning. Standing room is free.

The *Staatsoper* (State Opera, 2 Opern Ring; phone: 514-442959) is one of the most important opera houses in the world. During the course of the long season (September through June) most of the great names in contemporary opera make an appearance. The *Volksoper* (People's Opera, 78 Währingerstr.; phone: 51444-2956) specializes in light opera, Viennese operetta, and musicals. Written requests for tickets to the *Staatsoper* and *Volksoper* should be sent three weeks in advance to the *Osterreichischer Bundestheaterverband/Bestellbüro* (see *Theater,* above). Telephone sales start six days before the performance; local ticket sales usually start a week before the performance.

Devoted music lovers might enjoy a tour of the homes of the great composers—Beethoven, Schubert, Mozart, Haydn, Strauss—

who lived and worked in Vienna. Tours are offered by *Cityrama* (1 Börsegasse; phone: 534130; fax: 534-1322) and several other major travel agencies.

## NIGHTCLUBS AND NIGHTLIFE

The most traditional Viennese night on the town is at one of the *Heurigen* in Grinzing: These rustic taverns on the outskirts of town specialize in new wine, old wooden tables, and aging musicians playing *Schrammelmusik* (Viennese folk music). They can be recognized by a tuft of greenery hanging over the door. Cobenzlgasse is the main street of *Heurigen*-dom: Try the *Altes Presshaus* (No. 19; phone: 3223930), the *Grinzinger Hauermandl* (No. 20; phone: 322-0444), or the *Grinzinger Weinbottich* (No. 28; phone: 324237). If dancing cheek to cheek is more your style try the *Johann Strauss* (phone: 5339367; fax: 533-3163), an old riverboat moored near the Marienbrücke (Mary Bridge) on the Danube Canal; a string orchestra provides music for dancing on board from 8:30 to 11 PM. The *Eden-Bar* (2 Liliengasse; phone: 512-7450), an "in" spot with music and a lively, classy crowd, is open until 4 AM. Another sophisticated spot is the *Tanz Café* in the *Volksgarten* (phone: 630518). The reigning disco is the *Queen Anne* (12 Johannesgasse; phone: 512-0203). Vienna is one of the few major European cities with legal gambling; its *Casino Wien* is in the *Palais Esterházy* (41 Kärntnerstr.; phone: 512-48360). The so-called Bermuda Drieck (Bermuda Triangle) north of *Stephansdom* (between Seitenstettengasse, Ruprechtsplatz, and Judengasse) is home to many cafés, wine bars, and trendy restaurants.

# Best in Town

## CHECKING IN

The nicest place to stay in Vienna is in the Innere Stadt—or just on the edge of it. Don't be put off by first impressions; many of the hotels appear more old than quaint, but they do have a particular Viennese charm. A double room costs from about $245 to $450 in hotels listed as expensive; $125 to $245 in those listed as moderate; and less than $125 at those rated inexpensive. Unless otherwise noted hotel rooms have private baths, TV sets, and telephones, and breakfast is included in the rate. All telephone numbers are in the 1 city code when calling from outside of Austria and in the 222 city code when calling from within the country unless otherwise indicated.

For an unforgettable experience in Vienna we begin with our favorites, followed by our cost and quality choice of hotels, listed by price category.

---

### GRAND AND BABY GRAND HOTELS

**Bristol** It's across the square from the *Staatsoper*, with 133 rooms and 13 suites (ask for one with a view of the opera house). Among the luxurious touches are lots of polished wood, bathrooms with twin sinks, and bathtubs large enough to do the backstroke. Other amenities include instant 24-hour room service, one of the great hotel bars of Europe, and two restaurants, one of which is the well-known *Korso* (see *Eating Out*). Business facilities include meeting rooms for up to 200, an English-speaking concierge, foreign currency exchange, secretarial services, audiovisual equipment, photocopiers, computers, cable television news, and translation services. 1 Kärntner Ring (phone: 515160; 800-223-6800 or 212-838-3110 in the US; fax: 515-16550).

**Imperial** This regal building, built in 1867 as a private palace for the Duke of Württemberg and at one time a favorite of such discriminating egoists as Hitler and Wagner, manages to be at once majestic and modern. Now owned by the CIGA group, it offers 145 superb rooms and the impeccable, heel-clicking service that has always been a tradition here. There's complimentary limousine airport pick-up service, and business facilities include 24-hour room service, meeting rooms for up to 635, an English-speaking concierge, foreign currency exchange, secretarial services, audiovisual equipment, and cable television news. 16 Kärntner Ring (phone: 501100; 800-223-6800 or 212-838-3110 in the US; fax: 501-10410).

**Im Palais Schwarzenberg** Small, exclusive, and perfectly sedate, this 38-room establishment sits in the middle of a manicured park, in a palace still owned by one of Austria's oldest families. Ask for a room overlooking the lovely garden. It's the only hotel in Vienna that's a member of the distinguished Relais & Châteaux hotel group, and its dining room is one of the city's most elegant (see *Eating Out*). There's also a cozy bar with a wood-burning fireplace, and five clay tennis courts. Business facilities include 24-hour room service, meeting rooms for up to 200, an English-speaking concierge, foreign currency exchange, audiovisual equipment, and cable television news. Near the city center, at 9 Schwarzenbergpl. (phone: 784515; 800-323-7500 or 708-290-6172 in the US; fax: 784714).

**Sacher** The quintessential European hotel, this rococo monument to good living stands behind the *Staatsoper* and is a kind of "mission control" for Vienna's rich musical life. The 118 rooms are all elegant, and the service uniformly superb. The concierge is fabled for producing tickets (albeit sometimes at staggering prices) to Vienna's most noteworthy musical events. The hotel's *Anna Sacher* restaurant is a center of Viennese social life (see *Eating*

*Out*), and its elegant coffeehouse, *Café Hotel Sacher,* made the *Sachertorte* a legend. Business facilities include 24-hour room service, meeting rooms for up to 120, an English-speaking concierge, foreign currency exchange, audiovisual equipment, and cable television news. 4 Philharmonikerstr. (phone: 51456; 800-323-7500 or 708-290-6172 in the US; fax: 514-57810).

---

## EXPENSIVE

**ANA Grand Wien** Located on the Kärntner Ring steps away from the *Staatsoper,* Vienna's newest luxury hotel is a marriage of tradition and technology, owned and operated by *All Nippon Airways.* The century-old *Grand Hotel* building was completely reconstructed to create this new property, which has 205 rooms and suites equipped with international direct dialing, satellite TV, electronic safes, refrigerators, trouser presses, and coffee and tea service. *Le Ciel* restaurant serves French and Viennese cuisine in a traditional setting, with terrace dining in the summer. A Japanese restaurant and three bars, one of them a sidewalk café in summer, are also on the premises. In addition there's 24-hour room service and the *Grand Café* coffee shop is open around the clock. A skyway links the hotel to a new upscale shopping mall. The executive floor has such special amenities as butlers and suites with balconies. Other business facilities include meeting rooms for up to 600, an English-speaking concierge, and a business center with complete secretarial and office services. 9 Kärntner Ring (phone: 515800; 800-262-4683; fax: 5151313).

**SAS Palais** This 155-room, 15-suite Belle Epoque palace on the Ring has been lovingly restored by *Scandinavian Airlines.* The result is a luxury hotel with a fine restaurant (*Le Siècle;* see *Eating Out*) and a fitness center complete with an indoor pool. Business facilities include meeting rooms for up to 800 and cable television news. 32 Weihburggasse (phone: 515170; fax: 512-2216).

**Vienna Hilton International** Right across from the *Stadtpark,* this 603-room high-rise has a lobby that's become a crossroads of sorts, its turn-of-the-century *Klimt Bar* attracting a loyal following for coffee and cocktails. The hotel's new *Arcadia* restaurant (see *Eating Out*) as well as its Asian eatery *Mangostin* are popular, too. Also on the premises are fitness facilities, a hair salon, a coffee shop, and a shopping arcade. Business facilities include two executive floors, 24-hour room service, meeting rooms for up to 1,000, an English-speaking concierge, foreign currency exchange, secretarial services, audiovisual equipment, a photocopier, laptop computers, cable television news, and express checkout. Am Stadtpark (phone: 717000; 800-445-8667; fax: 713-0691).

**Vienna Inter-Continental** At one end of the elegant *Stadtpark,* this imposing 495-room member of the worldwide chain has become a landmark where the Viennese love to eat, dance, and gossip. Among its many features are the *Vier Jahreszeiten* restaurant (see *Eating Out*), which serves imaginative Austrian and international cuisine, a beauty salon, and a fitness room. Business facilities include 24-hour room service, meeting rooms for up to 1,200, an English-speaking concierge, foreign currency exchange, audiovisual equipment, and cable television news. 28 Johannesgasse (phone: 711220; 800-327-0200; fax: 713-4489).

**Vienna Marriott** Glassy and modern, this American-style hotel on the Ring, opposite the *Stadtpark,* is an attractive oasis of openness in a city of fairly forbidding hotel lobbies. There are 310 rooms, a restaurant, a waterfall to sip drinks by, and a pool, a whirlpool, and a sauna. Business facilities include 24-hour room service, meeting rooms for up to 600, foreign currency exchange, audiovisual equipment, and cable television news. 12A Park Ring (phone: 515180; 800-228-9290; fax: 515186722).

**Vienna Plaza** Opened in 1988, this is a very European *Hilton,* with 223 large yet cozy rooms that offer such extras as bathrobes, hair dryers, fresh fruit, and the *International Herald Tribune* delivered every morning. The cheery *Le Jardin* restaurant serves continental, American, or Viennese breakfasts, lunches, and Sunday brunches, and the award-winning *La Scala* is a good dinner choice (see *Eating Out*). There's also a fitness room, a gift shop, and free parking on the premises. Business facilities include 24-hour room service, meeting rooms for up to 250, an English-speaking concierge, foreign currency exchange, secretarial services, audiovisual equipment, photocopiers, computers, cable television news, and translation services. 11 Schottenring (phone: 313900; 800-445-8667; fax: 313-90160).

### MODERATE

**Astoria** In the pedestrian shopping haven behind the *Staatsoper,* this 108-room hotel has a lobby with a lively international atmosphere, and a popular restaurant (see *Eating Out*) upstairs. Business facilities include meeting rooms for up to 40, foreign currency exchange, audiovisual equipment, and cable television news. 32 Kärntnerstr. (phone: 515770; 800-448-8355; fax: 515-7782).

**Biedermeier im Sünnhof** This charming 203-room hotel complex, complete with restaurants and shops, is set in several beautifully restored houses. Business facilities include meeting rooms for up to 100 and audiovisual equipment. 28 Landstrasser Hauptstr. (phone: 716710; 800-448-8355; fax: 71671503).

**Kaiserin Elisabeth** In a building that dates from the 14th century, this 63-room hotel is conveniently located just off the Kärntnerstrasse. There's a bar but no restaurant (though several of Vienna's better dining spots are on the same street). 3 Weihburggasse (phone: 515260; 800-448-8355; fax: 515267).

**König von Ungarn** In one form or another this fine old house has been in the hotel business since 1764. It has 25 rooms and boasts a glass-roofed atrium with a three-story century-old tree around which coffee and cocktails are served, and a restaurant. Business facilities include meeting rooms for up to 20 and an English-speaking concierge. 10 Schulerstr. (phone: 515840; fax: 515848).

**Römischer Kaiser** This handsome Baroque building was erected in 1684 as the private palace of the imperial chancellor, then served as a military academy; it has been a hotel since the turn of the century and is today part of the Best Western chain. There are 24 rooms and a charming little café on the front doorstep. Business facilities include an English-speaking concierge and cable television news. 16 Annagasse (phone: 512-77510; 800-528-1234; fax: 512-775113).

**Am Stephansplatz** Though this 62-room hotel's architecture is modern and without character, its location in the heart of Vienna and its charming first-floor café are appealing. Just five paces across the pedestrian mall from the main portal of the *Stephansdom,* it's perched above a subway station that has a medieval chapel within. 9 Stephanspl. (phone: 534050; fax: 534-05711).

**Pension Wiener** When Sam and Helen Thau retired, they sold their posh *Hôtel de France* on the Ring and opened this small 11-room hostelry atop a quiet downtown office building. If you like your Viennese *Gemütlichkeit* with a little Jewish mothering and all the modern conveniences, this is the place. There is no restaurant. No credit cards accepted. 16 Seilergasse (phone: 512-48160; fax: 513-9858).

**Wandl** In the heart of Vienna, behind the Baroque *Peterskirche* (which has a famous crèche every *Christmas*), this pleasant, modest 138-room hotel has been family-owned for generations. It has no restaurant. No credit cards accepted. 9 Peterspl. (phone: 534550; fax: 534-5577).

#### INEXPENSIVE

**Schweizerhof** Just behind a marvelous clock on which statues of Vienna's greats—from Marcus Aurelius to Josef Haydn—march at midday, this 55-room hotel is a slice of old Vienna. There's no restaurant. 22 Bauernmarkt (phone: 533-1931; fax: 533-0214).

---

## EATING OUT

Viennese cooking ranks among the best in Europe, but be forewarned: There's nothing light about it. At some point make sure to buy a sausage from a street stand (the best *Würstelstand* is outside the main Creditanstalt-Bankverein, at 6 Schottengasse) and to visit at least one *Heurigen* (a rustic tavern), one coffeehouse, and one *Beisel* (a cozy, inexpensive neighborhood restaurant, open all hours).

The highlights of Viennese cuisine include Wiener schnitzel (a lightly breaded veal cutlet), *Rindsgulasch* (beef goulash), and *Tafelspitz* (boiled beef with vegetables and horseradish sauce). Desserts in Vienna are positively sinful, especially baked ones such as strudel, *Sachertorte,* and *Linzertorte* (a tart of raspberry jam and almonds), and there are always mounds of *Schlag* (whipped cream). Coffee comes in many varieties, of which the most popular are *Mokka* (black), *Brauner* (with milk), *Melange* or *Milchkaffee* (with foamy hot milk), and *Einspänner* (with whipped cream in a glass).

A meal for two will cost from $100 to $200 or more in restaurants described as expensive; $60 to $100 in those rated moderate; and below $60 in those listed as inexpensive. Although a 10% tip is included in most menu prices, leave up to an additional 10% for particularly good service. Be aware that many restaurants in Vienna do not accept credit cards, so it's advisable to check before making a reservation. Unless otherwise indicated restaurants are open for lunch and dinner and all telephone numbers are in the 1 city code when calling from outside of Austria and the 222 city code when calling from within the country.

For an unforgettable culinary experience we begin with our favorites, followed by our cost and quality choice of restaurants, listed by price category.

---

### DELIGHTFUL DINING

**Anna Sacher** The venerable hotel restaurant has changed little since it was founded by Franz Sacher, inventor of the *Sachertorte*. It's superbly elegant and it reeks of tradition—the zither music doesn't hurt, either. Dinner here before or after the opera is the quintessence of Vienna. Ordering *Tafelspitz* and wearing a tie will put the waiter on your side from the start. Since you can buy a *Sachertorte* to take out around the corner, for dessert have some *Palatschinken*—thin crêpes filled with jam or chocolate and sprinkled with powdered sugar. Open daily. Reservations necessary well in advance. Major credit cards accepted. 4 Philharmonikerstr. (phone: 514560; fax: 514-57810).

**Zu den Drei Husaren (The Three Hussars)** Decorated in the typical old-style Viennese abundance of plush velour and drapery, this place is famous for the huge procession of hors d'oeuvres wheeled by your table. After a recent slump it is back up to standard, with new, lighter dishes. Sample its definitive schnitzel, but be sure to leave room for the special dessert, *Husaren Pfannkuchen* (crêpes). There's piano music in the evenings. Closed from mid-July to mid-August. Reservations necessary. Major credit cards accepted. At the rear of the *Sacher Hotel,* 4 Weihburggasse (phone: 512-10920; fax: 512-109218).

---

### EXPENSIVE

**Altwienerhof** Specializing in traditional and nouvelle Austrian cooking, this place has one of the best wine cellars in town. Closed Sundays. Reservations necessary. Visa accepted. 6 Herklotzgasse (phone: 892-60000).

**Arcadia** This restaurant in the *Vienna Hilton* is great for breakfast and lunch buffets, Viennese coffee in the afternoon, and dinner, when it features an extensive selection of lamb specialties. It also offers an after-theater menu and a large selection of Austrian wines. Dine on the terrace or in the non-smoking section (still a relative rarity in Europe). Open daily. Reservations advised. Major credit cards accepted. Am Stadtpark (phone: 717000).

**Astoria** In the heart of the city's cultural scene, this first class restaurant in the hotel of the same name is a local favorite. Specialties include Viennese dishes and local game in season. Closed weekends. Reservations advised. 32 Kärntnerstr. (phone: 515770).

**Kervanseray** Many say this is the best fish restaurant in Vienna. Fresh seafood, including lobster, is flown in daily. Turkish dishes also are a specialty. Enjoy a drink at the attached *Hummerbar.* Closed Sundays. Reservations necessary. Major credit cards accepted. 9 Mahlerstrasse (phone: 512-8843; fax: 5138130).

**Korso** Some of the best food in Vienna is served at this lovely Belle Epoque dining spot in the *Bristol* hotel. Try the soufflés. Closed Saturday lunch and three weeks in August. Reservations necessary. 2 Mahlerstr. (phone: 515-16546).

**Im Palais Schwarzenberg** This elegant dining room overlooks the formal gardens of the palace-hotel of the same name. The menu is French-flavored—a welcome respite from an excess of schnitzels and *Schlag*—and the service is perfect. Open daily. Reservations necessary. 9 Schwarzenbergpl. (phone: 798-4515).

**La Scala** Awarded a Michelin star in 1991 only two years after opening, this establishment is well on its way to becoming one of Vienna's best dining spots. Tirolean-born chef Werner Matt, the man who introduced nouvelle cuisine to Austria, continues to create innovative dishes as well as homemade pasta and traditional *Tafelspitz.* Open daily. Reservations necessary. Major credit cards accepted. In the *Vienna Plaza Hotel,* 11 Schotten Ring (phone: 313900).

**Le Siècle** The *SAS Palais* hotel's impressive dining room serves Scandinavian specialties and other international fare. Open daily. Reservations necessary, except in July and August. 32 Weihburggasse (phone: 515170).

**Steirereck** This rustically furnished dining spot is one of the best in town (it's a member of the prestigious Relais & Château group). The menu features refined dishes from the province of Styria. The lamb is very good, as are the venison, hare, and other game in season. Closed weekends. Reservations advised. American Express and Visa accepted. 2 Rasumofskygasse (phone: 713-3168).

**Vier Jahreszeiten** The elegant "Four Seasons" dining room in the *Vienna Inter-Continental* hotel offers light versions of traditional Viennese and international fare. Closed Saturday lunch and Sunday dinner.

Reservations necessary, except in July and August. 28 Johannesgasse (phone: 71122-143).

**Do & Co** The deli cases here are full of delicious seafood, salads, and spreads to eat in or take away. Open daily. Reservations unnecessary. Major credit cards accepted. 3 Akademiestr. (phone: 512-6474).

**Figlmüller** A Viennese incarnation of a prewar Broadway eatery, serving up platters overflowing with thin, tender pork schnitzels in a bustling but friendly atmosphere. A good place to sample traditional Viennese food and *Gemütlichkeit.* Closed Saturday dinner, Sundays, and August. Reservations advised. 5 Wollzeile (phone: 512-6177). In warm weather, try *Figlmüller's* garden restaurant in Grinzing. Closed Sundays and January through March. Reservations advised. 55 Grinzingerstr. (phone: 324257).

**Griechenbeisl** Vienna's oldest pub, with traditional Austrian food, is touristy but oozes charm. Viennese *schrammel* music is featured in the evenings. Open daily. Reservations advised. 11 Fleischmarkt (phone: 533-1941).

**Zimmermann** This *Heuriger* is absolutely delightful. Its several cozy rooms surround a flower-filled courtyard, and both food and atmosphere are topnotch. Closed Sundays. Reservations advised. No credit cards accepted. 5 Armbrustergasse (phone: 372211).

**Zum Weissen Rauchfangkehrer** A homey place with good food and rustic furnishings—wooden benches, hanging iron lamps, and painted glass—on a street of elegant restaurants. For dessert take a deep breath and ask the waiter for *Brandteigschokoladecremekrapfen.* Your reward for saying that mouthful will be one of the best chocolate cream puffs ever. Open daily. Reservations unnecessary. 4 Weihburggasse (phone: 512-3471).

**Zu den Drei Hacken** Favored by aficionados of Wiener schnitzel and dark wood paneling. The *Gebackenen* camembert (baked camembert cheese) is simply wonderful. Closed Saturday dinner and Sundays. Reservations advised. 28 Singerstr. (phone: 512-5895).

**Trzesniewski** No visit to Vienna is complete without a meal at this ever-thronged sandwich bar, offering endless varieties of miniature open sandwiches from great bins of assorted Viennese goodies. Dark bread, draft beer, and *Apfelsaft* (apple cider) are highlights. Open weekdays until 7:30 PM; closed Saturday afternoons and Sundays. No reservations. No credit cards accepted. 1 Dorotheergasse (phone: 512-3291).

---

### VIENNA'S BEST CAFÉS

If you had only an hour to see Vienna, the best way to get a feel for the city would be to sit in one of its cafés. The Viennese café is a cross between a living room, office, club, and street corner, a place where habitués lounge by the hour. *Jause*—the Viennese version of five o'clock tea—is generally the liveliest time of day. The emphasis is always on coffee, but other beverages, snacks, and pastries are available too, especially at the *Konditoreien* (pastry shops), where luscious sweets are temptingly arranged in refrigerated glass cases. Some of the city's most famous cafés are *Hawelka* (6 Dorotheergasse; phone: 512-8230), one of the few that stay open late, serving *Büchteln* (warm jelly-filled sweet rolls) between 10 PM and midnight; *Landtmann* (4 Dr.-Karl-Lueger-Ring; phone: 630621); *Café Central* (14 Herrengasse; phone: 5333763); *Café Bräunerhof* (2 Stallburggasse; phone: 512-3893); and the *Hotel Imperial* café (16 Kärntner Ring; phone: 501-10389), which regularly features music to inhale pastries by. Among the best *Konditoreien* are *Demel* (14 Kohlmarkt; phone: 535-1717) and the *Hotel Sacher*'s café (phone: 51457-846), home of the *Sachertorte*.

# Warsaw

## At-a-Glance

### SEEING THE CITY

For a general sense of Warsaw's postwar reconstruction and continuing modernization take the elevator to the 30th-floor terrace of the *Pałac Kulturi i Nauki* (Palace of Culture and Science) on Plac Defilad (Defilad Square). From here, on a clear day (rare in this heavily polluted metropolis), you can see beyond the outskirts of the city, which are marked by heavy industry, modern buildings, and new housing estates. There is a small charge for the elevator ride. The best view of the Old Town and the castle is from the east side of the river.

### SPECIAL PLACES

The Old Town is west of the Wisła (Vistula) River and just north of the Śląsko-Dąbrowski Most (Slasko-Dabrowski Bridge). Most sights and activities of interest to tourists are found between this area and *Łazienki Park*, south of Plac na Rozdrożu.

As you make your way through the city it's helpful to remember that *ulica* is the Polish word for street, *aleja* is the word for avenue, and *plac* means square. Though streets renamed by the Communists have been changed, taxi drivers and locals are aware of both names and are happy to help bewildered visitors.

#### STARE MIASTO (OLD TOWN)

**ZAMEK KRÓLEWSKI (ROYAL CASTLE)** Warsaw's most important historical monument, its *Royal Castle*, built between the 14th and 18th centuries, was blown up by the Nazis in their campaign to wipe Poland off the map. Painstakingly rebuilt, its imposing silhouette forms an impressive background to the *Kolumna Zygmunta* (King Sigismund III Column) in the middle of Plac Zamkowy (Castle Square). The *Royal Castle* has rejoined the ranks of the most beautiful palaces in Europe. In addition, it boasts 17th-century paintings of Warsaw by Canaletto. Closed Mondays. Admission charge. Adjacent to Plac Zamkowy (phone: 635-3995).

**KOLUMNA ZYGMUNTA (KING SIGISMUND III COLUMN)** This, the oldest monument in Warsaw (1644), stands in the center of Plac Zamkowy at the edge of the Old Town. At the top is the bronze statue of the 16th-century Polish king who built his castle here. The column was nearly destroyed by the Nazis, but the statue survived and the monument was reerected shortly after the war.

**POD BLACHĄ** A tin-roofed Baroque palace noted for its attic, crowned with a richly ornamented cartouche bearing coats of arms. Near Plac Zamkowy.

**RYNEK STAREGO MIASTA (OLD TOWN MARKET SQUARE)** The most beautiful square in Warsaw, it is enclosed by 17th- and 18th-century Baroque burgher houses that were re-created using bits of ornamentation recovered after the Nazi destruction. No. 28, housing the *Historical Museum of the City of Warsaw* (phone: 635-1625), is considered among the best preserved. Closed Mondays. The square is filled with flowers and alive with little shops and cafés. Each side is named for a Warsaw burgher of the late 18th century who fought for civil rights.

**KATEDRA SW. JANA (ST. JOHN'S CATHEDRAL)** The site of a parish church since the early 14th century, the cathedral was virtually destroyed by the Nazis, then rebuilt in the Gothic style. It is beloved by the city's deeply religious Roman Catholics. The crypts contain the remains of illustrious Poles, including romantic novelist Henryk Sienkiewicz (1846–1916), who won the Nobel Prize for *Quo Vadis?*. In 1992, 51 years after his death, the remains of pianist Ignacy Jan Paderewski were interred here, fulfilling his wish to be buried in a free Poland. Ulica Swiętojańska.

**BARBAKAN (BARBICAN)** This brick wall with turrets was built to encircle and defend the Old Town in the mid-16th century and later reconstructed. Today it marks the dividing line between the old and the newer sections of the city. There are fine views of the Vistula River from the top.

**TRAKT KRÓLEWSKI (ROYAL ROUTE)** About 6 miles (10 km) long, this thoroughfare begins at Plac Zamkowy (Castle Square) and heads south to *Lazienki Park* and on to *Wilanów Palace*. The street, whose name changes from Ulica Krakówskie Przedmieście to Ulica Nowy Swiat to Aleje Ujazdowskie along the way, is lined with palaces of Poland's nobility, Baroque houses, museums, government and university buildings, embassies, churches, restaurants, and shops. Located near the statue to the romantic 19th-century poet Adam Mickiewicz is the *Radziwiłł Palace* (46-48 Ulica Krakówskie Przedmieście), now the *Council of Ministers,* where the Soviet bloc's Warsaw Pact was signed, and years later where the "round-table" agreement transferred power from the Communists to the Solidarity-led opposition.

## ELSEWHERE IN THE CITY

**NOWE MIASTO (NEW TOWN)** New in relative terms only, it was built adjacent to the expanding Old Town in the early 15th century. At 16 Ulica Freta is the house where chemist Marie Curie was born in 1867. The long Rynek Nowego Miasta (New Town Market Square) boasts a beautiful well in its center.

**WORLD WAR II MONUMENTS** So extensive was the heroic resistance to the Nazis that even the churches and cemeteries of Warsaw were scenes of fierce fighting. Bullet holes still can be seen on some façades. The city's *Monument to the Heroes of Warsaw* stands in Plac Teatralny (Theater Square) in front of the *Teatr Wielki* (see *Music*). It is sort of a new version of the mermaid Syrena, a fight-

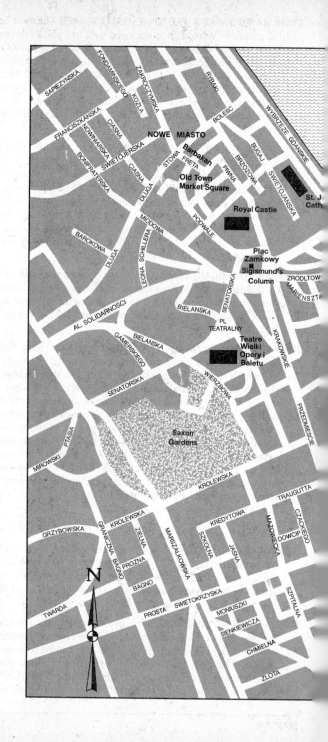

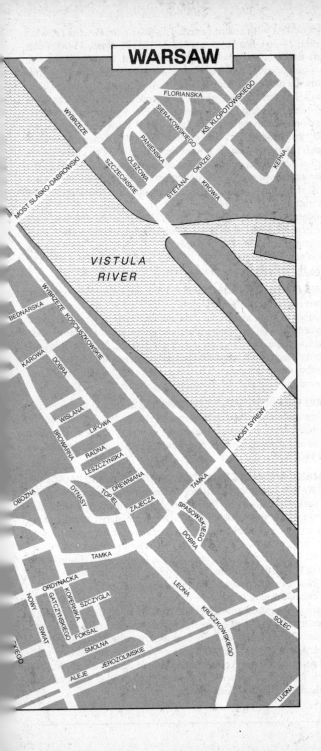

ing goddess with sword raised. The *Więzienia Pawiak* (Pawiak Prison; 24-26 Ulica Dzielna; phone: 311317), where 35,000 Poles were executed and another 65,000 detained, is today a museum commemorating the victims. The *Muzeum Walki i Męczenistwa* (Museum of Struggle and Martyrdom; Aleje Szucha; phone: 244929) also celebrates the struggle for independence. At the intersection of Ulica Długa and Ulica Miodowa on Plac Krasińskich is a strik-ing monument to the heroes of the 63-day Warsaw Uprising in 1944. Still intact near the middle of the intersection is the manhole through which the fighters escaped from the Old Town. The ghetto where the Jewish population was walled up in 1940 is remembered by the *Pomnik Boharterów Getta* (Monument to the Heroes of the Ghetto) on a grassy square at Ulica Zamenhofa and Ulica Anielewicza. The *Zydowki Institut Historyczny* (Jewish Historical Institute; 79 Aleje Solidarnośći; phone: 279227) has an exhibit on the ghetto as well as extensive archives on Jews in Poland; closed weekends. A mar-ble monument marks Umschlagplatz (Ulica Stawki at Ulica Dubois), the square where hundreds of thousands of Jews were loaded onto railway cars en route to death camps.

**CMENTARZ ZYDOWSKI (JEWISH CEMETERY)** Somehow this large cemetery survived the Nazi destruction of the city. Though overgrown, it is possible to walk among the headstones, many of which go back two centuries. Of the hundreds of thousands of Jews who once called Warsaw home, there are now only about 300 left. A visit to this final resting place, which had no succeeding generation to tend it, is heartbreaking, but a must. There is often an English-speaking care-taker at the entrance. 49-51 Okopowa (phone: 382622).

**CMENTARZ WOJSKOWY (ARMY CEMETERY)** The memorial to the Polish officers massacred by the Soviets at Katyn in 1940 is here, as are the birch crosses marking the graves of young couriers who died in the resistance to the Nazi occupation. 43-45 Powązkoska (phone: 332140).

**PARK LAZIENKI AND PAŁAC NA WODZIE (LAZIENKI PARK AND PALACE ON THE WATER)** The splendid *Palace on the Water* in Warsaw's loveli-est park was built in the 18th century for Stanisław August Ponia-towski, last of the Polish kings. The Nazis plundered its collections and devastated the building, but the interiors have been copied care-fully and restored. There are some 18 other buildings and monu-ments in the spacious park, including the *Biały Domek* (Little White House), once the residence in exile of the future King Louis XVIII of France. In warm weather the monument to Chopin at the south-ern end of the park is the scene of Sunday afternoon concerts of his music. At the southern end of the gardens is the *Conservatory*, a place to enjoy a cup of coffee, a slice of chocolate cake, and piano music. The park is open daily to dusk; the palace is closed Mon-days. Admission charge to the palace. The *Belvedere Palace*, offi-cial residence of the President of the State Council, is in *Belvedere Park*, adjacent to *Lazienki Park*. Southeast of Plac na Rozdrożu, along Aleje Ujazdowskie (phone: 218212).

**OGRÓD SASKI (SAXON GARDENS)** In the center of the city, next to Plac Piłsudskiego and the *Grób Nieznanego Żołnierza* (Monument to the Unknown Soldier), this is the oldest garden in Warsaw. Planted at the end of the 18th century in the English style, it has many rare trees and an artificial lake. Open daily. No admission charge.

**WILANÓW PALACE AND PARK** This Polish version of *Versailles* was built in the late 17th century as a summer residence for King Jan Sobieski III and his French-born wife, Marysieńka; it is now a branch of the *Muzeum Narodowe* (National Museum). The Baroque palace was restored after World War II and contains period furniture, china, old clocks, portraits, and other mementos of the Sobieski family. The French-style gardens are lovely, with Baroque terraces leading to a small lake. The *Muzeum Plakatów* (Poster Museum; phone: 422606), with an interesting collection of Polish graphic art, is in a building on the grounds. The palace is closed Tuesdays; the museum is closed Mondays. Admission charge to both. Ulica Wiertnicza, just south of the city, less than 6 miles (10 km) from the Old Town. Reached by express bus B or bus No. 180 from Ulica Marszałkowska (phone: 420795).

ENVIRONS

**OJCIEC POPIŁUSZKO JRÓB (FATHER POPIELUSZKO TOMB)** Next to the *Kościół Sw. Stanisława Kostki* (Church of St. Stanislawa Kostka) in the Zoliborz section, due north of central Warsaw, is the tomb of Father Popieluszko, a national hero and martyr, who fought for workers' rights and national independence alongside the Solidarity trade union. He was killed by the state police in 1984, and a simple granite cross has become a pilgrimage site for many Poles and visiting dignitaries. Ulica Hozjusza, off Ulica Krasińskiego, Zoliborz.

**POD CHOPIN (CHOPIN'S HOME)** Thirty-three miles (53 km) west of Warsaw in Zelazowa Wola is the Chopin family manor, where the composer was born in 1810. The house, set on lovely grounds, has been turned into a museum, and concerts of the composer's work are held on the lawn on Sundays during the summer. Usually performed by a four- or five-piece chamber ensemble, the concerts are presented in a delightful Renaissance setting, and the music is sublime. Diehard fans may want to travel 6 miles (10 km) north of Zelazowa Wola to the village of Brochów to see the mid-16th-century Renaissance church where Chopin was baptized. Leave Warsaw by Route E30 (2) in the direction of Pozan (phone: 828-22300). For more information, contact *Orbis* (see *Tourist Information,* below).

# Sources and Resources

## TOURIST INFORMATION

Maps and information have become widely available, especially at gift shops in hotels and the Old Town. The *Informacja Turystyczna* (*IT Center;* 1-13 Plac Zamkowy; phone: 635-1887) is across from the *Royal Castle. Orbis,* the Polish national tourist agency, also can be helpful (142 Ulica Marszałkowska; phone: 278031; and 16 Ulica Brack; phone: 277603). The *US Embassy* is at Aleje Ujazdowskie 29-31 (phone: 628-3041; fax: 625-7290).

In the US, contact the *Polish National Tourist Office* (275 Madison Ave., New York, NY 10016; phone: 212-338-9412; fax: 212-338-9283; and 333 N. Michigan Ave., Suite 224, Chicago, IL 60601; phone: 312-236-9013; fax: 312-236-1125). The *Polish Embassy* is at 2224 Wyoming Ave. NW, Washington, DC 20008 (phone: 202-232-4517).

**ENTRY REQUIREMENTS** A valid passport is required for a US citizen; no visa is necessary for a stay of up to 90 days.

**TIME** The time in Poland is six hours later than in US East Coast cities. Poland follows daylight saving time.

**LANGUAGE** Polish is the official language, but German and some English also are spoken; Russian and Ukrainian are widely understood.

**ELECTRIC CURRENT** 220 volts, 50 cycles, AC.

**MONEY** The złoty (zł) is made up of 100 groszy. At press time $1 US bought about 2.44 złoty, but the exchange rate is very unstable, so check rates before departing. Many prices are quoted in US dollars or German marks.

When entering and leaving Poland you must declare how much currency (of any country) you have with you; no import or export of Polish currency is allowed. Unused złotys must be left at the border—there are exchange counters at most transportation centers.

**TIPPING** The usual tip is 10% of hotel, restaurant, hairdresser, and taxi bills. Service charges are not included in most bills.

**BANKING/BUSINESS HOURS** Banks generally are open weekdays from 8 AM to 4 PM. Most other businesses keep the same hours.

**NATIONAL HOLIDAYS** *New Year's Day* (January 1), *Easter Sunday* (April 16), *Easter Monday* (April 17), *May Day* (May 1), *Constitution Day* (May 3), *Corpus Christi* (June 15), *Feast of the Assumption* (August 15), *All Souls' Day* (November 1), *Independence Day* (November 11), and *Christmas Day* (December 25).

**LOCAL COVERAGE** The *Warsaw Voice* is an English-language newspaper. The *International Herald Tribune, USA Today, Time, Newsweek,* and other major English-language periodicals are available in hotels and larger bookshops. *What, Where, When Warszawa* and *Welcome to Warsaw* are monthly English-language magazines with useful listings distributed free at major hotels and travel agencies.

Several good English-language guidebooks to the country and city are published. The 120-page *Destination Poland* is free from the *Polish National Tourist Office* (see *Tourist Information,* above). The complex street layout makes a city map useful, and several new ones have updated street names. We also recommend carrying a Polish-English dictionary.

**TELEPHONE** The city codes for Warsaw are 22 (for six-digit numbers) and 2 (for seven-digit numbers). When calling from one area to another within Poland dial 0 + city code + local number. The country code for Poland is 48. In an emergency, dial 999 for an ambulance and 997 for the police.

## GETTING AROUND

The Old Town, the Vistula River embankment, and the whole Royal Route of Ulica Krakówskie Przedmieście, Ulica Nowy Swiat, and Aleje Ujazdowskie are best seen on foot. But Poland's capital is a very big city, so at some point you will probably want to use cabs or municipal transportation.

**AIRPORT** Warsaw's new international terminal and its domestic airport are collectively known as *Okęcie* (phone: 606-7381) and are about five minutes apart by shuttle bus. *Okęcie* is about a 20-minute cab ride from downtown. Some hotels have courtesy buses. Regular buses between the airport and major hotels are provided by *AirportCity* (phone: 268211).

**BUS/TRAM** Avoid them if possible during rush hours, but they are the least expensive way to get around. Route signs are at each stop. Buy your ticket before boarding at a nearby tobacco or newspaper kiosk, then cancel it in a special machine on the coach. It's a good idea to buy extra tickets since kiosks often are closed.

**CAR RENTAL** The major rental car companies now operate in Poland, although better rates can be obtained by making reservations in advance. Most are located at the airport and several hotels. The main *Orbis S.A./Hertz* location is near the *Forum* hotel (27 Ulica Nowogrodzka; phone: 621-1360); *Avis* is at *Okęcie Airport* (phone: 650-4872); *Budget* is at 65-79 Jerozolimskie Aleje (phone: 630-6946).

**TAXI** Cabs may be hailed on the street or more easily at taxi stands. To order a taxi by phone, call 919. Make sure the driver turns on the meter at the outset of the ride. Be aware, too, that, because of inflation, the price that appears on the meter is multiplied several hundred times; a sign on the taxi window will tell you which figure is used. Cabs also are fine for extended sightseeing surveys of the city; rates are reasonable if you agree on them before setting off. Choose *Radio Taxi* (phone: 919), *Plus Taxi* (phone: 9621), or *Express Taxi* (phone: 9626).

**TRAIN** The main train station is on Aleje Jerozolimskie, in the center of town (phone: 200361 for local schedules and fare information; 204512 for international schedules and fare information). A *PolRailPass* is available in Poland at *Orbis* travel agencies (see above). Although there is an increased police presence, be aware of professional bands of pickpockets who lie in wait for Western travelers as they board trains.

## LOCAL SERVICES

Most hotels will try to arrange any special services a traveler might require, such as a translator.

**DENTIST (ENGLISH-SPEAKING)** Ask the service desk at any major hotel to recommend a dentist in an emergency.

**MEDICAL EMERGENCY** The number to call is 999. English generally is not spoken, so it's best to ask the service desk at any major hotel to make the call for you. There is also an *American Medical Center* for outpatient care at the *St. Vincent International Medical Center* (18 Ulica Wołoska; phone: 483711 or 483704).

**PHARMACY** Some pharmacies stay open 24 hours a day; ask at your hotel desk.

**POST OFFICE** The main post office (31-33 Ulica Swiętokrzyska) is in the center town and is open 24 hours daily.

## SPECIAL EVENTS

An *International Book Fair* is held here each May, and there is an *International Poster Biennale* in June during even-numbered years. The *"Warsaw Autumn" International Festival of Modern Music* is an important September event, and the *Jazz Jamboree* held in late October is the oldest such festival in Central and Eastern Europe. The *International Chopin Competition* for pianists (held every five years) will next take place in October 1995, and the *Henryk Wieniawski International Competition* for violinists is held annually in September.

## MUSEUMS

In addition to those described in *Special Places,* Warsaw has a number of other interesting museums. Most charge a nominal admission.

**CENTRUM SZTUKI WSPÓŁCZESNEJ (CONTEMPORARY ART MUSEUM)** Exhibits of modern art and installations with a partially renovated castle as the dramatic backdrop. Closed Mondays. 6 Aleje Ujazdowskie (phone: 628-1271).

**JOHN PAUL II COLLECTION** Formerly the *Museum of Revolutionary Politics,* it now houses Old Master paintings contributed by the Porczyński family. Closed Mondays. 1 Plac Bankowy (phone: 202725).

**MUZEUM ARCHEOLOGICNZE (ARCHAEOLOGICAL MUSEUM)** Tools and other relics of prehistoric Baltic peoples, as well as changing exhibitions. Closed Saturdays. 52 Ulica Długa (phone: 313221).

**MUZEUM ETNOGRAFICZNE (ETHNOGRAPHIC MUSEUM)** Exhibits on peasant life, folk art, and costumes. Closed Mondays. 1 Ulica Kredytowa (phone: 277641).

**MUZEUM HISTORYCZNE WARSZAWY (WARSAW HISTORICAL MUSEUM)** Pictures and exhibits trace the history of Warsaw through the centuries. A 20-minute presentation compiled from captured Nazi film (narrated in English) documents the devastation of the city; shown daily at noon. Closed Mondays. 28 Rynek Starego Miasta (phone: 635-1625).

**MUZEUM MARII SKŁODOWSKIEJ-CURIE (MARIE SKŁODOWSKA-CURIE MUSEUM)** The Polish chemist's home before she moved to Paris. Closed Saturdays. 16 Ulica Freta (phone: 318092).

**MUZEUM NARODOWE (NATIONAL MUSEUM)** Poland's greatest art collection. Above all, don't miss the huge painting of the *Battle of Grunwald* by Jan Matejko, which shows the defeat of the Knights of the Teutonic Order in the 15th century. During World War II the Polish government ordered that the painting, like all other national treasures, be hidden, and though the Nazis offered a whopping reward for its return, there wasn't a single taker. Closed Sundays and Mondays. 3 Aleje Jerozolimskie (phone: 211031).

**TOWARZYSTWO IM. FRYDERYKA CHOPINA (CHOPIN'S DRAWING ROOM)** Composer Frederic Chopin lived briefly in a second-floor room of the former *Pałac Raczyński* (Raczynski Palace), now the *Akademia Sztuk Pieknych* (Academy of Fine Arts). Concerts are occasionally held in the room, which is decorated with Empire-style furnishings. Nearby, on Ulica Krakówskie Przedmieście, is *Kościół Sw. Krzyza* (Holy Cross Church), where Chopin's heart is buried in one of the columns. Closed Mondays. 1 Ulica Okólnik (phone: 275471).

## SHOPPING

Shops in Warsaw generally are open from 11 AM to 7 PM, but department stores open earlier and close later. Avoid the crowds by shopping before 3 PM. Leather, linen, and folk art, which ranges from wonderful woodcarvings to handsome handwoven rugs, are good buys here, as is amber and sterling silver jewelry. A good place to look for old and new jewelry is along the side streets of the Old Town. Check the small shops as well as the new larger ones. Warsaw's main shopping thoroughfare is Ulica Nowy Swiat (New World Street), not terribly elegant by Western standards. On Sunday mornings there is an interesting antiques flea market in the Wola District on Ulica Obozowa near Ulica Ciołka. (There are restrictions on the quantity and types of items you can take out of Poland, particularly on things made before 1945; check with authorities before your trip.)

The country's national currency is the złoty. Dollars and other Western money can be converted most easily at the many private exchanges marked *"kantor."* Hotels and banks also generally have exchanges. The following are some shops of particular interest.

**Arex** A good collection of Polish folk crafts and paintings. 5A Ulica Copina (phone: 296624).

**Art** Stylized folk art and works of modern art. 1-7 Ulica Krakówskie Przedmieście (no phone).

**Arteon** Located behind the *Marriott* hotel, this shop sells beautiful silver and amber jewelry. 65-79 Aleje Jerozolimskie (phone: 650-5053).

**Bazar Rózyckiego** Sought-after items such as fur coats are for sale here; prices are negotiable. Ulica Targowa (no phone).

**Canaletto** Another good shop for amber and silver jewelry. 89 Ulica Krakówskie Przedmieście (no phone).

**Cepelia** Shops that sell souvenirs and folk art. Several locations: 2 and 5 Plac Konstytucji, 10 Rynek Starego Miasta, and 3 Ulica Bracka (phone: 215838 for all).

**Desa** Specialists in Polish antiques. Locations at 34-50 Ulica Marszałkowska (phone: 628-7705) and 48 and 51 Ulica Nowy Swiat (phone: 274760).

**Edward Magdziarz** One of finest collections of stained-glass lamps in Warsaw. 64 Ulica Nowy Swiat (no phone).

**Mix** This is where Poles go to buy good-quality jewelry. Many are one-of-a-kind pieces. 47A Ulica Krucza (phone: 296668).

**Silver Line** Amber and silver jewelry in traditional and modern settings. 59 Ulica Nowy Swiat (phone: 266355).

**Stadion Dziesięciolecia (10th Anniversary Stadium)** One of the largest weekend bazaars in Eastern Europe, favored by traders from the former Soviet Union. The stadium is on the east side of the Vistula River on Wybrzeże Szczecińskie (no phone).

**Zapiecek** In the Old Town, this modern art gallery features the work of local artists. 1 Ulica Zapiecek (phone: 319918).

## SPORTS AND FITNESS

**HORSE RACING** The *Służewiec* racecourse, on the southern extremity of the city, is one of the largest in Europe. Races are held on Wednesdays, Saturdays, and Sundays in summer.

**SOCCER** Played at the *Skra* and *Warszawa* soccer stadiums. *Legia,* the best and most popular Warsaw team, also plays at various stadiums around the country.

**SWIMMING** In summer there is swimming at the *Legia* pool (Ulica Łazienkowska) and the indoor pool at the *Pałac Kultury i Nauki* (Palace of Culture and Science; 6 Plac Defilad). The *Marriott* hotel (see *Checking In*) also has a pool (there's a fee for non-guests). There are no public beaches, and swimming is not permitted—or advised—in the badly polluted river.

## THEATER

Advance booking for theater or cinema tickets can be made at the box office or through the *Informacja Turystyczna* (1-13 Plac Zamkowy; phone: 635-1887), the *ZASP* ticket office (25 Aleje Jerozolimskie; phone: 266164 or 285995), or the ticket office in *Kino Wisła* (Plac Wilsona; phone: 392365). The city's foremost drama theaters include the *Polski* (2 Ulica Karasia; phone: 267992), *Dramatyczny* (in the *Palace of Culture and Science;* Plac Defilad; phone: 263872), *Ateneum* (2 Ulica Jaracza; phone: 625-7330), and *Zydowski* (12-16 Plac Grzybowski; phone: 206081 or 207025). There are several children's theaters in Warsaw, including the *Lalka* puppet theater (in the *Palace of Culture and Science;* Plac Defilad; phone: 204950).

## MUSIC

Opera and ballet are performed at Warsaw's *Teatr Wielki Opery i Baletu* (Grand Theater of Opera and Ballet; Plac Teatralny; phone: 263001). The prestigious *International Chopin Competition* for pianists is held every five years at the *Filharmonia Narodowa* (5 Ulica Jasna; phone: 265712 or 267281). Operettas are staged at the *Operetka* (49 Nowogrodzka Ulica; phone: 628-0360).

## NIGHTCLUBS AND NIGHTLIFE

You'll need a fairly sophisticated knowledge of Polish to appreciate the humor at Warsaw's popular satirical cafés, but you might try one for the atmosphere.

For jazz and some international food, try *Akwarium* (49 Ulica Emilii Plater; phone: 205072), a modern nightspot near the *Palace of Culture and Science.* One of the city's best private clubs is *SARP* (13 Foksal; no phone), which is run by the association of Polish architects and artists; you must be taken there by a member. Young crowds frequent *Riviera Remont* (12 Ulica Waryńskiego; phone: 257497).

Though Las Vegas has nothing to fear, gambling is popular at the casinos at the *Orbis-Grand, Marriott,* and *Victoria Inter-Continental* hotels (see *Checking In* for all three), where there are slot machines, blackjack, and roulette tables. There is an admission charge.

# Best in Town

## CHECKING IN

Recent openings have improved the Warsaw hotel situation, but with less than a dozen recommendable properties, booking well in advance is strongly advised, especially during the summer. Expect to pay more than $200 per night for a double room in a very expensive hotel; from $120 to $200 in the expensive range; $70 to $120 in the moderate category; and less than $70 at an inexpensive place. Prices include breakfast. In all of the following hotels, guestrooms have private baths unless otherwise specified and major credit cards are accepted.

Another option is the bed and breakfast type of accommodation, but in Warsaw such places don't offer the breakfast. What they do provide, however, is the rare chance for a glimpse into the lives of typical Poles. Bookings and information are available through the *Syrena* travel agency (17 Ulica Krucza; phone: 628-7540).

All telephone numbers are in the 22 or 2 city code unless otherwise indicated.

### VERY EXPENSIVE

**Bristol** This 1901 Art Nouveau establishment reopened in late 1992 after being left unattended under Communist management. Now a Forte property, it is continuing to gain status as the country's grande dame (it boasts such famous former guests as Marlene Dietrich, Douglas Fairbanks, Charles de Gaulle, and John F. Kennedy). Lovingly restored, all 163 rooms and 43 suites feature marble baths, air conditioning, direct-dial telephones, and satellite TV. There's a health club with a pool, gym, sauna, and solarium, as well as beauty treatment facilities. There are three restaurants: The *Malinowa* features traditional Polish specialties, the *Marconi* has an Italian menu, and the *Café Bristol* serves morning coffee and afternoon tea. Business facilities include meeting rooms for up to 50, an English-speaking concierge, foreign currency exchange, secretarial services in English, audiovisual equipment, photocopiers, cable television news, and translation services. 42-44 Ulica Kraków skie Przedmieście (phone: 625-2525; 800-225-5843; fax: 625-2577).

### EXPENSIVE

**Forum** The Inter-Continental chain's second link in Warsaw is larger than the *Victoria* (see below) but not as nice. Its 751 rooms are of modest size and sparsely decorated. Guests enjoy three restaurants, a bar, and 24-hour room service. It has a casino and a central location, near the *Palace of Culture and Science.* Business facilities include meeting rooms for up to 200, audiovisual equipment, photocopiers, cable television news, and translation services. 24-26 Ulica Nowogrodzka (phone: 210271; 800-327-0200; fax: 258157).

**Jan II Sobieski** A splash of color on the Warsaw cityscape, this addition is cheerful and well appointed. Conveniently located a few blocks from the city center, its 419 rooms and suites are attractive in a streamlined way, with satellite TV, direct-dial telephones, and other amenities. The large restaurant features Polish and international fare. Business facilities include meeting rooms for up to 200 and computers. Plac Artura Zawiszy (phone: 658-4444; fax: 659-8828).

**Marriott** It may not have the patina of age, but the creature comforts and convenience offered by this hotel provide a welcome Western respite in this Eastern European capital. The five-star hotel occupies the top 20 stories of a 40-story skyscraper smack in the middle of town. Its 525 spacious rooms—complete with color TV sets (CNN, too)—are decorated in soft pastels; bathrooms come complete with thick terry-cloth towels and hair dryers. Best of all is the English-speaking staff, which is unfailingly polite and helpful (it's said that none of the employees ever worked in a hotel or restaurant before—*Marriott*'s way of avoiding the surly service that was common in Communist Poland). There are several restaurants from which to choose. The *Lila Weneda* coffee shop—where plenty of East-West wheeling and dealing takes place—serves a truly first-rate buffet breakfast, which is included in the room rate. Afternoon tea (try the pastries) or snacks can be enjoyed on the mezzanine lounge overlooking a large, light-filled atrium and the lobby. And for those who crave a game of chance, there's a casino. Business facilities include meeting rooms for up to 300, audiovisual equipment, photocopiers, and translation services. 65-79 Aleje Jerozolimskie (phone: 630-6306; 800-228-9290; fax: 300050).

**Mercure** This ultramodern French venture is in a less congested area of Warsaw, between the city center and the Old Town. There are 242 well-appointed rooms, which feature satellite TV and direct-dial telephones, and two restaurants. Business facilities include meeting rooms for up to 220, secretarial services in English, audiovisual equipment, photocopiers, and translation services. 22 Aleje Jana Pawła II (phone: 200201; 800-221-4542; fax: 208779).

**Novotel** A joint venture with the French hotel chain, this hotel offers 153 simple but comfortable rooms with satellite TV, along with shops and restaurants. On the down side, the location near the airport is neither attractive nor convenient to the city center. Business facilities include meeting rooms for up to 50, audiovisual equipment, and cable television news. 1 Ulica Sierpnia (phone: 464051; 800-221-4542; fax: 463686).

**Orbis-Europejski** For a sense of Old World Warsaw, this is the place to stay. The 239 rooms—including singles and doubles, with or without private bath—and suites are functionally modern, although the four-story building is over a hundred years old. A café looks out on the *Saxon Gardens* and the *Gróbieznanego Zołnierza* (Monument to the Unknown Soldier). Business facilities include meeting rooms for up to 150 and cable television news. 13 Ulica Krakówskie Przedmieście (phone: 265051; fax: 26111).

**Orbis-Holiday Inn** One of the first joint ventures of the US and the Polish capital, it has 338 rooms—spartan by most Western standards but adequate. There are three restaurants and a sauna. Business facilities include meeting rooms for up to 100, audiovisual equipment, photocopiers, cable television news, and translation services. 2 Ulica Złota (phone: 200341; 800-HOLIDAY; fax: 300569).

**Victoria Inter-Continental** One of Warsaw's top hotels, it is close to the *Teatr Wielki* and *Saxon Gardens*. Its 365 rooms are comfortable (although the furniture is a little frayed at the edges) and feature satellite TV; the *Canaletto* restaurant specializes in Polish dishes. There is a swimming pool and a casino. Business facilities include meeting rooms for up to 50, audiovisual equipment, photocopiers, cable television news, and translation services. 11 Ulica Królewska (phone: 279271; 800-327-0200; fax: 279856).

### MODERATE

**Maria** A small private hotel, a bit out of the way but accessible by taxi or public transportation. The 22 rooms and suites are modern and complete with satellite TV. There's good Polish fare at the restaurant. 71 Aleje Jana Pawła II (phone: 384062; fax: 383840).

**Orbis-Grand** The more than 366 rooms with satellite TV are rather plain, but the midtown location is a plus. The hotel has a rooftop café with glass-enclosed terrace and a pool. On the eighth floor is a disco, so the seventh floor is to be avoided. 28 Ulica Krucza (phone: 294051; fax: 219724).

**Orbis-Solec** Located near the Vistula River embankment, this hotel features 147 motel-modern rooms with satellite TV. A restaurant serves delicious Polish fare. 1 Ulica Zagórna (phone: 259241; fax: 216442).

## EATING OUT

Food shortages are no longer a fact of life in Poland, so while not yet a culinary wonder, Warsaw is brimming with restaurants. Some of the new ones are excellent, but those that probably interest residents the most are the more than half-dozen *McDonald's* and *Burger King* outlets scattered throughout the city.

Warsaw restaurants serve dinner relatively early, and by 10:30 PM most kitchens are dark. Dinner for two (including wine, drinks, and tip) will cost $50 to $60 at restaurants described as very expensive; $25 to $50 at restaurants in the expensive category; $15 to $25 at places listed as moderate; and under $10 at inexpensive spots. All places are open for lunch and dinner unless otherwise noted, and all telephone numbers are in the 22 or 2 city code.

### VERY EXPENSIVE

**Belvedere** Elegant continental dining in a lovely setting in *Lazienki Park*. Open daily. Reservations necessary. Major credit cards accepted. Nowa Oranzeria (phone: 414806).

**Fukier** Traditional Polish and continental fare as well as some vegetarian dishes are featured in this Old Town dining room. The favorite dish here is *bigos* (traditional Polish hunters' stew of pork, beef, and sauerkraut). Live music most nights. Open daily. Reservations necessary. Major credit cards accepted. 27 Rynek Starego Miasta (Old Town Market Sq.; phone: 311013).

**Zajazd Napoleonski** In a neighborhood not exactly meant for strolling, this is a small, 25-room hotel and restaurant. The uniformed, white-gloved staff serves superb French fare with great style. Closed Sundays for lunch. Reservations advised. Major credit cards accepted. Ulica Płowiecka (phone: 153454 or 153068).

### EXPENSIVE

**Bazyliszek** Easily Warsaw's premier restaurant, best known for its wild game and Old Town location. It's on the second floor over a snack bar and has an Old Warsaw ambience, with a decor that features hussars' armor and wooden beams. A horse and carriage usually is waiting outside to take you for a romantic ride through the city after dinner. Open daily. Reservations necessary. No credit cards accepted. 5 Rynek Starego Miasta (Old Town Market Sq.; phone: 311841).

**Gessler** Lovely, especially in the summer when the restaurant opens into the *Saxon Gardens.* The menu is traditionally Polish. Try the smoked trout soup, herring, and other fresh fish dishes. The homemade ice cream is also worth a taste—or two. Open daily. Reservations necessary for dinner. Major credit cards accepted. 37 Ulica Senatorska (phone: 270663).

**Montmarte** Fine French bistro food in a pleasant setting across from the *Polish Stock Exchange,* housed in the old Communist Party head-quarters. The steaks are first-rate, as are the soups and salads with cheese and bread. Open daily. Reservations advised. Major credit cards accepted. 7 Ulica Nowy Swiat (phone: 628-6315).

**Świętoszek** An Old Town cellar restaurant where Polish fare is well represented. Don't miss the *blini* with caviar. Open daily. Reservations necessary. No credit cards accepted. 6-8 Jezuicka (phone: 315634).

### MODERATE

**Da Elio** One of Warsaw's many new Italian eateries specializing in home-made pasta (the gnocchi are great), with a salad bar. Open daily. Reservations advised. Major credit cards accepted. 20A Ulica Zurawia (phone: 290602).

**Nowe Miasto** Warsaw's first vegetarian restaurant boasts a pleasant wicker dining room and patio on the New Town Market Square. Ingredients used in all dishes, including salads, soups, and crêpes, are made from organically grown produce. Open daily. Reservations advised. Major credit cards accepted. 13 Rynek Nowego Miasta (phone: 314379).

**Rycerska** Good Polish fare is served in a rustic atmosphere with medieval armor and original paintings. Open daily. Reservations advised. Major credit cards accepted. 9-11 Ulica Szeroki Dunaj (phone: 313668).

**Wilanów** Traditional Polish cooking served in a modern setting, some distance from the town center near the *Wilanów Palace.* Open daily. Reservations advised. Major credit cards accepted. 27 Ulica Wiert-nicza (phone: 421852).

### INEXPENSIVE

**Bambola** Poland's first homegrown restaurant chain serves first-rate pizza. Open daily. No reservations or credit cards accepted. Locations at 111 Aleje Jerozolimskie and 42B Ulica Nowy Swiat serve pasta and salad as well. Pizza only at 16 Ulica Puławska and 36 Ulica Przemysłowa.

**Staropolska** Near the university, this restaurant is a mainstay among academic types. Although the menu is limited, it has one of the best cold buffets in Warsaw, with veal in aspic and steak tartare. Also sample the broth with hard-boiled egg and sausage, called *zurek staropolski.* Old *Beatles* tapes or European disco music plays continuously. Open daily. Reservations advised. No credit cards accepted. 8 Ulica Krakówskie Przedmieście (phone: 269070).

### VERY SPECIAL

One corner of the Old World still thrives in this other-wise drab culinary capital. It's called *E. Wedel* (8 Szpi-talna, on the corner of Wojciecha Górskiego; no phone). The name is stenciled on the front window, and there is a sign that says *"Pijalnia Czekolady,"* which roughly translates as "Chocolate Pump Room." The place consists of two small rooms right out of a *mittel* European stage set: one is mint green, the other is pink. The *only* thing served here is very good, thick hot chocolate (in porcelain cups), for less than 50¢ per cup. No smoking is allowed. Right next door (on Szpitalna) is a faded but still elegant (by local standards) candy shop, also owned by *E. Wedel.*

Also not to be missed is the tiny bakery *Blikle 1869* (35 Ulica Nowy Swiat; phone: 226-4568), a Warsaw tradition since 1869. The *mazurki* and *babkas* are Polish classics, and the *paczki* (light, spongy jelly doughnuts) are irresistible. For something cooler try *Dr. Oetker* (35 Aleje Jana Pawła II; no phone), where ice cream sundaes are the order of the day.

# Zurich

## At-a-Glance

### SEEING THE CITY

The most enchanting view of the city and lake is from Quai Bridge, where river and lake join. From here you can see both sides of the Altstadt (Old City), with its church towers, bridges, and medieval façades. Turn and you'll see the lake, dotted with sailboats, and, on a day when there's a föhn (a warm Alpine wind), a picture-book view of the Alps. For another view of the city try the *Sonnenbergterasse,* the terrace of the *Sonnenberg* hotel on Zurichberg on the eastern edge of town, or have a drink or a meal at the hotel's restaurant (Am Dolder; phone: 262-0062).

### SPECIAL PLACES

Zurich is a strollers' city, and visitors no longer need to avoid the *Platzpromenade,* a park north of the *Hauptbahnhof* (Main Railway Station) which once was the city's center of drug activity. The area around the *Hauptbahnhof* is relatively safer than it was at that time, but as is the case in most major cities it always pays to be aware of your personal safety and surroundings.

On both sides of the Limmat River, the Altstadt's cobblestone streets and narrow lanes are dotted with small antiques shops, high fashion boutiques, and art galleries. Many of the buildings have their date of construction hewn into their stone doorways. A good starting point is Münsterhof, a former pig market where excavations have uncovered layers of housing and burial sites dating back to the 12th century.

### DOWNTOWN/ALTSTADT

**BAHNHOFSTRASSE** One of the most beautiful—and expensive—shopping streets in the world, it runs from the lake to the main railway station. It's a shopper's and stroller's paradise, with rows of banks, shops, and cafés. There is a colorful flower and vegetable market at the lake end on Tuesday and Friday mornings, and a flea market is held on the Bürkliplatz Saturdays from 7 AM to 4 PM from May through September.

**MUSEUM DER ZEITMESSUNG BEYER (BEYER'S MUSEUM OF TIME MEASUREMENT)** Inside the oldest watch shop in Switzerland is the Beyer family's private collection, which includes rare and interesting items from 1400 BC to the present. Closed weekends. No admission charge. 31 Bahnhofstr. (phone: 221-1080).

**FRAUMÜNSTER (LADIES CHURCH)** This 12th-century church at Münsterhof is noted for its chapel, with marvelous stained glass windows created by Marc Chagall. Try to see them in the morning light; dur-

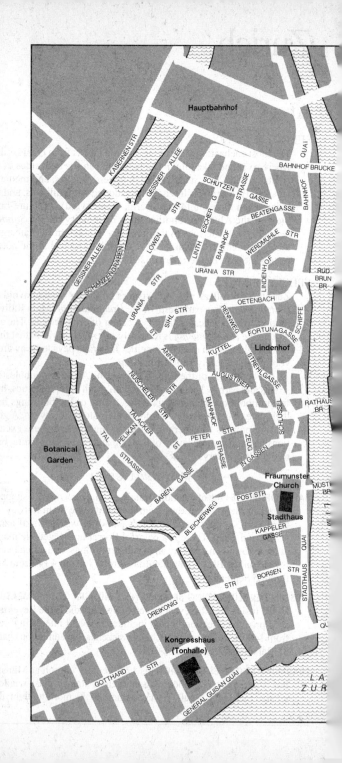

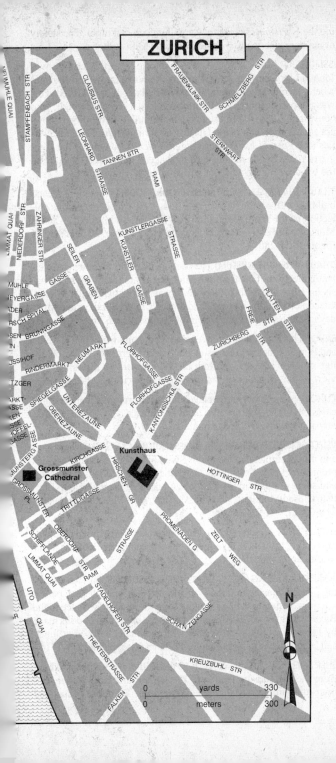

ing the *Christmas* season they are illuminated at night. The stately organ here also is justly famous. On the Münsterhof.

**GROSSMÜNSTER (CATHEDRAL)** According to legend, this church was founded by Charlemagne, whose horse bowed down on the spot where the city's patron saints, martyrs Felix and Regula, died. This was the parish church of Reformation leader Ulrich Zwingli, who converted Zurich to Protestantism in the mid-16th century. Its towers are a Zurich landmark. During the spring *Sechseläuten* festivities (see *Special Events*) the *Weggliwerfen* (throwing of the *Weggli,* or rolls) by the members of the bakers' guild takes place from the windows of the adjacent guild building. 4 Zwinglipl.

**ZUNFTHAUS "ZUR MEISEN" ("ZUR MEISEN" GUILDHOUSE)** A splendid rococo building with a wrought-iron gate houses the excellent ceramic collection of the *Historisches Museum* (Historical Museum). Closed Mondays and daily at lunch. No admission charge. 20 Münsterhof (phone: 221-2807).

**KUNSTHAUS (FINE ARTS MUSEUM)** The permanent exhibits feature an excellent collection of art from the Middle Ages to today, with emphasis on 19th- and 20th-century European works by Monet, Munch, Giacometti, Rodin, Chagall, and others. Closed Sundays and Mondays. Admission charge. 1 Heimpl. (phone: 251-6765).

**LINDENHOF** This romantic tree-covered lookout point was a fort in Celtic and Roman times; a Freemason lodge stands here now. A few climbing, crooked alleys away from the *Fraumünster,* it offers a lovely view of the Altstadt and is a favorite spot for lovers after dark.

**NÄGELIHOF** A delightful little enclave, this reconstructed square features cafés, shops, movie theaters, and an unusual view of the *Grossmünster* towers. Off 42 Limmatquai.

**SCHWEIZERISCHES LANDESMUSEUM (SWISS NATIONAL MUSEUM)** The largest and most complete collection of Swiss historical artifacts includes prehistoric finds, a reconstructed Celtic tomb, Carolingian frescoes, and some old paintings of Zurich. A brochure is available in English. Closed Mondays. No admission charge. 2 Museumstr. (phone: 218-6565).

**ST. PETERHOFSTATT** Another small, charming square surrounded by buildings dating from the 13th through the 15th centuries. Between Münsterhof and Lindenhof.

**WOHNMUSEUM BÄRENGASSE (BÄRENGASSE HOUSE MUSEUM)** Two charming private houses from the 17th and 18th centuries display period interiors, with interesting furniture from the late Renaissance to the Biedermeier period. The basement houses a collection of dolls made by the famous Swiss artist Sacha Morgenthaler. Closed at lunch and Mondays. Admission charge. 22 Bärengasse (phone: 211-1716).

**ZÜRICHER SPIELZEUGMUSEUM (ZURICH TOY MUSEUM)** A permanent exhibit from the antiques collection of the same Franz Carl Weber who owns the famous toy shop (see *Shopping*). There are occasional special exhibitions. Closed mornings and Sundays. No admission charge. 15 Fortunagasse (phone: 211-9305).

OUTSIDE THE CITY CENTER

**SAMMLUNG E. G. BÜHRLE (E. G. BÜHRLE COLLECTION)** Housed in his private villa, the important art collection of the late industrialist Emil Bührle includes French Impressionist paintings, medieval sculptures, and other works, mainly from the 19th century. Open Tuesday and Friday afternoons and Wednesday evenings. Admission charge. 172 Zollikerstr. (phone: 422-0086).

**BOTANISCHER GARTEN DER UNIVERSITÄT ZÜRICH (ZURICH UNIVERSITY BOTANICAL GARDEN)** Rare plants from all over the world thrive here. There's also a good cafeteria with a large terrace. Open daily; hours vary by season. No admission charge. Near the Bührle villa at 107 Zollikerstr. (phone: 385-4411).

**MUSEUM RIETBERG** One of the most important collections of non-European art in Europe—the items are mainly Indian, Southeast Asian, Chinese, Japanese, and African—is set in the enchanting *Wesendonck Villa* outside the city center. Richard Wagner was often a guest here, and his love affair with the hostess inspired *Tristan and Isolde*. The villa is surrounded by a magnificent private park. There's a guidebook in English. Closed Mondays. No admission charge Wednesday evenings and Sundays. 15 Gablerstr. (phone: 202-4528).

**ZOO DOLDER (DOLDER ZOO)** Some 250 species of animals, including a black rhino, snow leopards, and an Asian elephant family. Open daily. Admission charge. 221 Zürichbergstr. (phone: 252-7100).

ENVIRONS

**SCHAFFHAUSEN AND STEIN AM RHEIN** Schaffhausen, 35 miles (56 km) north of Zurich, is a wonderfully preserved medieval town, with a photogenic fortress and the Rheinfall, Europe's largest waterfall. The best view is from the district of Neuhausen, perhaps from the terrace restaurant of the *Bellevue* hotel (phone: 532-2121). Stein am Rhein, 13 miles (21 km) farther east, is a delight, with its intricately painted housefronts and the *Klostermuseum St. Georgen* (St. George Cloister Museum; phone: 54-412142), housed in a former monastery. It's closed public holidays and November through February. If possible, return to Zurich through the gentle wine country around Stammheim, with villages of half-timbered houses, vineyards, and orchards.

---

**EXTRA SPECIAL**

What better way to spend a sunny day than cruising in a boat on the Zürichsee (Lake Zurich). Of the many boat trips possible the best is probably the one that takes in the small town of Rapperswil. Boats depart from Bürkliplatz, at the lake end of Bahnhofstrasse.

> In summer there are special lunch cruises. For information call *Zürichsee Schiffahrtsgesellschaft* (phone: 482-1033) or the *Zurich Tourist Office* (see below).

# Sources and Resources

TOURIST INFORMATION
For general information, brochures, and maps, contact the *Verkehrsverein Zürich* (Zurich Tourist Office) in the *Hauptbahnhof* (Main Railway Station; phone: 211-1131; fax: 211-3981; open daily). The *US Consulate* is at 141 Zollikerstr. (phone: 422-2566). In the US, the *Swiss National Tourist Office* has three branches (150 N. Michigan Ave., Suite 2930, Chicago, IL 60601; phone: 312-630-5840; fax: 312-630-5848; 222 N. Sepulveda Blvd., Suite 1570, El Segundo, CA 90245; phone: 310-335-5980; fax: 310-335-5982; and 608 Fifth Ave., New York, NY 10020; phone: 212-757-5944; fax: 212-757-6116). The *Swiss Embassy* is at 2900 Cathedral Ave. NW, Washington, DC 20008 (phone: 202-745-7900).

ENTRY REQUIREMENTS A US citizen needs a current passport for a stay of up to 90 days.

TIME The time in Switzerland is six hours later than in US East Coast cities. Switzerland observes daylight saving time.

LANGUAGE German, French, Italian, and Romansh, a Romance language derived from Latin, are all spoken in Switzerland. The more than two dozen Swiss dialects, called collectively Schweizerdeutsch, vary from region to region. English is widely understood.

ELECTRIC CURRENT 220 volts, 50 cycles, AC.

MONEY The Swiss franc (SFr) equals 100 centimes or rappen. The exchange rate at press time was 1.28 Swiss francs to the dollar.

TIPPING A 15% service charge is included in hotel, restaurant, and bar bills, as well as taxi fares, so that only porters and bellhops require tips (about 1 SFr per bag).

BANKING/BUSINESS HOURS Most banks are open weekdays from 8:30 AM to 4:30 PM. Most other businesses are open weekdays from 9 AM to 5 PM, but many offices close between noon and 2 PM.

NATIONAL HOLIDAYS *New Year's Day* and the day after (January 1 and 2), *Good Friday* (April 14), *Easter Sunday* (April 16), *Easter Monday* (April 17), *Ascension Thursday* (May 25), *Whitmonday* (June 5), *Independence Day* (August 1), *Jeûne Fédéral* (Fasting Day, the first Thursday in September; September 7 this year), and *Christmas* (celebrated December 25 and 26).

LOCAL COVERAGE The *Zürich News,* which comes out every other Friday, has a detailed listing of events in English and German. It is available at all hotels and at the tourist office. The *Shopping Guide Zürich* is a monthly publication in German, English, and French available at hotels and selected shops. There is no local English-language newspaper, but the *International Herald Tribune* is available at most large kiosks and in the train station.

**TELEPHONE** The city code for Zurich and surrounding areas is 1. When calling from one area to another within Switzerland dial 0 + city code + local number. The country code for Switzerland is 41. In an emergency dial 144 for an ambulance; 117 for the police.

## GETTING AROUND

**AIRPORT** The *Lufthafen Kloten* (Kloten Airport), about 10 minutes from the center of town by train and 20 minutes by car, handles domestic and international flights. Terminal A handles flights within Europe; Terminal B handles all others. Trains to the airport leave every 20 minutes from the *Hauptbahnhof,* Zurich's main train station; the stop is called *Kloten.* A Swiss Transport Pass, available for four, eight, or 15 days, provides unlimited train, boat, bus, and tram rides; a *Swiss Card* provides 50% discounts. Both are available at the tourist office (see *Tourist Information*) and the *Hauptbahnhof* (see *Train,* below). For airport information call 812-7111.

**BICYCLES** Available for rent at most railroad stations, bicycles—which can be taken onto passenger trains for a small fee and returned at any station—provide an inexpensive and delightful means of transportation.

**BUS** The supermodern blue streetcar/trams (*VBZ*) are best. Fares range from 1.90 francs (about $1.50) for a short trip to 3.20 ($2.50) for a longer one. Automatic machines at every stop issue tickets for exact change; you cannot pay on board trams or buses, and you are fined if found without a ticket. If you intend to use public transportation a lot, it pays to get a one-day pass (6.40 francs, roughly $5) or a season ticket. An informative multilingual brochure giving rates, routes, and other details is available at information booths marked *VBZ* in the underground *Shopville* at the main railroad station, at Paradeplatz and Bellevueplatz, or at the *Zurich Tourist Office.*

**CAR RENTAL** Represented at the airport and in the city are *Avis* (17 Gartenhofstr.; phone: 241-7070); *Europcar* (53 Josefstr.; phone: 271-5656); *Hertz* (33 Lagerstr.; phone: 242-8484); and *Avag* (123 Sihlfeldstr.; phone: 242-2200), a local firm whose rates are sometimes lower.

**TAXI** Among the most expensive in the world (the tip is included in the fare), taxis can be flagged down; the light on top indicates availability. You also can call *Züritaxiphone* (phone: 271-1111) or *Taxi Central* (phone: 272-4444).

**TRAIN** The main train station is the *Hauptbahnhof* (at the northern end of Bahnhofstrasse, at 15 Bahnhofplatz; phone: 211-5010).

## LOCAL SERVICES

**DENTIST (ENGLISH-SPEAKING)** Dr. Terance McDermott (123 Klosbachstr.; phone: 252-4452); *General Dental Service* (phone: 363-3100).

**DRY CLEANER/TAILOR** *Terlinden* (29 Löwenstr. and other locations; phone: 211-0811).

**LIMOUSINE SERVICE** *Alpine Limousine* (41 Hagenbuchenweg, Wangen-Zurich; phone: 784-3006); *Rolls-Royce Limousine Service* (phone: 077-781737); *Welti Furrer Car Hire* (31A Pfingstweidstr.; phone: 444-1444).

**MEDICAL EMERGENCY** *University Hospital* (100 Rämistr.; phone: 255-1111). Dial 144 for an ambulance.

**MESSENGER SERVICE** *DHL Worldwide Express* (13-19 Schützenstr., Urdorf; phone: 734-5757); *Federal Express* (3 Feldeggstr., Glattbrugg; phone: 811-0404); *Kurier AG* (49 Klausstr.; phone: 383-6666).

**NATIONAL/INTERNATIONAL COURIER** *DHL Worldwide Express; Federal Express* (see *Messenger Service,* above, for both).

**OFFICE EQUIPMENT RENTAL** *E. Brender AG* (104 Bahnhofstr.; phone: 211-7447).

**PHARMACY** *Bellevue Apotheke* (14 Theaterstr.; Bellvueplatz; phone: 252-5600), open 24 hours.

**PHOTOCOPIES** *Copyquick* (10 Tessinerplatz and various other locations throughout the city; phone: 202-2818).

**POST OFFICE** The main post office (*Sihlpost*) is open Mondays through Saturdays from 6:30 AM to 11 PM, and Sundays from 9 AM to 11 PM (95-99 Kasernenstr.; phone: 245-4111).

**SECRETARY/STENOGRAPHER** *World-Wide Business Centers* (32 Rennweg; phone: 214-6111).

**TELEX** *World-Wide Business Centers* (see *Secretary/Stenographer,* above).

**TRANSLATOR** *Bureau Rochat* (231 Seestr., Küsnacht; phone: 910-7877); *World-Wide Business Centers* (see *Secretary/Stenographer,* above).

**OTHER** Office space rental, fully equipped: *World-Wide Business Centers* (see *Secretary/Stenographer,* above). Camera and photographic rental: *Foto Ganz* (40 Bahnhofstr.; phone: 211-7673). Men's and women's formal wear rental: *Atelier Claire Schärer* (197 Seefeldstr.; phone: 383-1206).

## SPECIAL EVENTS

*Fasnacht* (Mardi Gras), the Zurich version of pre-Lenten *Carnival,* is celebrated with masked processions and costume balls in late February or early March. The city's most colorful event, the *Sechseläuten* (Six Bells), generally on the third Monday in April, celebrates the end of winter with a bang—a giant snowman called the *Böög,* stuffed with firecrackers, burns and explodes on Bellevueplatz as the 6 o'clock bells ring and costumed guild members gallop on horses around the bonfire. This ceremony is preceded by a picturesque procession of medieval guilds in traditional costumes and carriages. Membership in these fraternities is inherited by the males in certain old Zurich families.

The *Juni (June) Festival* features top musical and theatrical events for the entire month, but is held only every three years and will not occur again until 1997. *1 August,* a national holiday, marks the anniversary of the founding of the *Confederatio Helvetica* (Helvetic, or Swiss Confederation) in 1291; it's celebrated with fireworks and bonfires.

## MUSEUMS

Besides those described in *Special Places,* there are several noteworthy museums in Zurich.

**HAUS FÜR KONSTRUKTIVE UND KONKRETE KUNST (FOUNDATION FOR CONSTRUCTIVIST AND CONCRETE ART)** High-quality international exhibits of 20th-century works. Closed Mondays. Admission charge. 317 Seefeldstr. (phone: 381-3808).

**HELMHAUS** Changing exhibitions of contemporary Swiss art. Closed Mondays. Admission charge. 31 Limmatquai (phone: 251-6177).

**JOHANN JACOBS (SUCHARD) MUSEUM** Rotating exhibitions and displays present the cultural history of coffee. Closed Mondays through Thursdays. No admission charge. 17 Seefeldquai/Feldeggstr. (phone: 383-5651).

**MEDIZINHISTORISCHES MUSEUM DER UNIVERSITÄT ZÜRICH (ZURICH UNIVERSITY MEDICAL HISTORY MUSEUM)** An interesting collection, housed at the university. Closed Mondays. No admission charge. 69 Rämistr. (phone: 257-2298).

**MUSEUM BELLERIVE** Excellent changing exhibits in a charming villa on Lake Zurich showcase the largest collection of decorative arts in Switzerland. Closed Mondays. Admission charge. 3 Höschgasse (phone: 383-4376).

**MUSEUM FÜR GESTALTUNG (MUSEUM OF FORM AND FUNCTION)** Varying exhibitions on environmental design, architecture, graphics, photography, and other aspects of visual communications. Closed Mondays. Admission charge. 60 Ausstellungstr. (phone: 271-6700).

**VÖLKERKUNDEMUSEUM DER UNIVERSITÄT ZÜRICH (ZURICH UNIVERSITY ETHNOLOGICAL MUSEUM)** An interesting collection of non-European cultural artifacts. Closed Mondays. No admission charge, except for the occasional concerts held of traditional music from non-European cultures. In the botanical garden at the university, 40 Pelikanstr. (phone: 221-3191).

## SHOPPING

The major hunting ground for shoppers is the ultra-elegant Bahnhofstrasse and its side streets (Storchengasse, In Gassen, and Rennweg). The Altstadt is full of fashion boutiques, art galleries, and antiques shops, and there is more casual shopping along Limmatquai. In rainy weather, you might want to try *Shopville* under the *Hauptbahnhof* (Main Railway Station). Look for antiques along the Kirchgasse, Stüssihofstatt, Schipfe, Rindermarkt, and Oberdorfstrasse, or at the two flea markets—the *Flohmarkt* on the Bürkliplatz is open from 7 AM to 4 PM Saturdays from May through October, and the *Rosenhof* market in the Niederdorf is open from 10 AM to 9 PM Thursdays and from 10 AM to 4 PM Saturdays from April through December.

Switzerland's best buys are watches, which can be purchased in Zurich even though most are made in Geneva. The *Peter Ineichen* salerooms house an eclectic collection of antique clocks and watches. Other good values are chocolate, embroidery and linen, optical instruments, and the wonderful (and ubiquitous) Swiss Army knives. *Jelmoli* and *Globus,* both on Bahnhofstrasse, are the two best-known department stores (the former offers more solid quality and greater variety, the latter features more trendy merchandise at lower prices). General shopping hours are weekdays from 9 AM to 6:30 PM (to 9 PM on Thursdays), and Saturdays from 9 AM to 4 PM. Other stores to explore:

**Agathe** Supremely wearable, elegant women's clothing. 3 Neumarkt (phone: 251-6373).

**Babar Palace** King Babar, the beloved elephant of children's books, reigns supreme in this tiny shop. His royal visage appears on every item of first-rate children's togs. 2 Storchengasse (phone: 221-3522) and 81 Zürichbergstr. (phone: 252-1730).

**Bally** Famous for shoes. Several locations throughout the city, including 66 Bahnhofstr. (phone: 211-3515).

**Buch & Antiquariat Falk & Falk** Old books, prints, and manuscripts sold in a medieval house. 28 Kirchgasse (phone: 252-6773).

**Bucherer** This three-level shop features a large selection of watches and jewelry. 50 Bahnhofstr. (phone: 211-2635).

**Café Schober** Cakes, cookies made in 16th-century molds, chocolates, and homemade marmalades. 4 Napfgasse (phone: 251-8060).

**Cashmere House** All kinds of luxury fashion items. 50 Augustinergasse (phone: 211-3075).

**Chronometric Beyer** The oldest watch shop in Switzerland also boasts the country's largest selection. 31 Bahnhofstr. (phone: 221-1080).

**Cigarren Weber** Owned for three generations by the Weber family, this welcoming shop is stocked with some of the world's finest (and costliest) tobacco. 70 Bahnhofstr. (phone: 211-2375).

**F. C. Weber** Toys—including trains and cars—and, yes, cuckoo clocks. 62 Bahnhofstr. (phone: 211-2961).

**Grieder** A scaled down, boutique-style department store with high quality fashions for women and men. 30 Bahnhofstr. (phone: 211-3360).

**Gübelin** Fine watches and jewelry. 36 Bahnhofstr. (phone: 221-3888).

**Hannes B** Upscale menswear. 2 Wühre (phone: 211-8655).

**Kalin & Co.** Specialists in knives and scissors. 4 Poststr. (phone: 211-2367).

**Keinath** Fine old silver and other antiques. Near the *Storchen* hotel, 19 Wühre (phone: 211-9750).

**Leinen Langenthal** Bed, table, and kitchen linen from a long-established Swiss factory, plus gift items. 29 Strehlgasse (phone: 221-3104).

**Medieval Art & View** Books on the music, art, and food of the Middle Ages. 29 Spiegelg. (phone: 252-4720).

**Meister** Crystal, silver, and jewels. 28 Bahnhofstr. at Paradepl. (phone: 221-2730).

**Merkur** A virtual supermarket of Swiss chocolate, as well as coffees and coffee-drinking accoutrements. At many locations, including 106 Bahnhofstr. (phone: 211-5372).

**Musik Hug** Musical instruments, including alphorns (long wooden horns typical of German Switzerland) and wooden spoons called *Löffeli*. 28-30 Limmatquai (phone: 251-6850).

**Orell Füssli** This bookstore has become the largest in Switzerland since it bought out *Daeniker's,* the city's oldest English-language bookstore, in 1991. 4 Füsslistr. (phone: 221-1060).

**Parfumerie Schindler** A true shrine for perfume lovers, with a large selection and attentive service. 26 Bahnhofstr. (phone: 221-1855).

**Pastorini** Creative and educational toys. 3 Weinpl. (phone: 211-7426).

**The Pen House** Offers a variety of fine fountain pens and other writing tools. 81 Löwenstr. (phone: 212-2595).

**Pic + Asso** A bewilderingly large selection of games, toys, and gadgets. 26 Rennweg. (phone: 211-0064).

**Schade Uhren** Antique watches and clocks. 5 Waaggasse (phone: 221-1042).

**Schweizer Heimatwerk** Top-quality Swiss handicrafts. At various locations, including the airport and 2 Bahnhofstr. (phone: 221-0837).

**Sibler** A dazzling shop filled with unusual but very functional cookware. 16 Münsterhof (phone: 211-5550).

**Spitzenhaus** Traditional handmade lace and embroidered organdy. 14 Börsenstr. (phone: 211-5576).

**Sprüngli** More than a century old, this place is famous for chocolates and pastry. There's also a café (see *Eating Out*). 21 Bahnhofstr. at Paradepl. (phone: 211-0795); at the airport (no phone); and at the *Hauptbahnhof,* 49 Löwenstr. (phone: 211-9612).

**Stäheli** Centrally located, this shop is another good source for English-language books. 70 Bahnhofstr. (phone: 201-3302).

**Sträuli** Alpine sweaters and warm scarves. 30 Rennweg (phone: 211-0096).

**Sturzenegger Broderie** Fine Swiss embroidery, knitwear, and linen—from tablecloths to lingerie. 48 Bahnhofstr. (phone: 211-2820).

**Teehaus Wühre** An enchanting small tea shop with a wide selection of its own blends. 15 Wühre (phone: 211-6114).

**Teuscher** Great chocolates. 9 Storchengasse (phone: 211-5153). The company also has its own tea and coffee shop called *Schober* at 4 Napfgasse (phone: 251-8060).

**Travel Book Shop** Books about all aspects of travel—many in English—sold by world traveler Gisela Treichler and her informed staff. 20 Rindermarkt (phone: 252-3883).

**Wohnshop Bazar** Decorations, gadgets, gifts, bags, cards, and more. 32 Schifflände (phone: 261-8100).

## SPORTS AND FITNESS

**FITNESS CENTERS** The *Atmos Fitness Club* in the *Zürich* hotel (42 Neumühlequai; phone: 363-4040), the *John Valentine Fitness Club* (3 Blaufahnens; phone: 262-4200), and the *TSI Luxor Squash and Fitness Club* (35 Glärnischstr.; phone: 202-3838) are open to visitors for a fee.

**GOLF** There are no public courses, but several clubs accept visitors: *Dolder Golf Club* (66 Kurhausstr.; phone: 261-5045); *Golf & Country Club Zurich* (Zumikon; phone: 918-0051); *Golf & Country Club Schönenberg* (Schönenberg; phone: 788-1624); and *Golf & Country Club Breitenloo* (9 Untere Zäune; phone: 836-4080).

**HIKING** There are dozens of marked trails on the outskirts of town.

**JOGGING** Run along the Zürichsee (Lake Zurich) on either side of Bellevue Bridge, or in the Dolder district of the city, in the woods of the Zürichberg (Mt. Zurich). There are seven *Vita Parcours* (woodland jogging routes with exercise stops in scenic spots). Try the one called *Allmend Flutern,* closest to the city (for details contact the tourist office).

**SAILING AND ROWING** Boats can be rented along the Seequai, the upper Limmatquai, and the Stadthausquai.

**SKATING** The outdoor ice rink at Dolder (36 Adlisbergstr.) is open from October through March.

**SKIING** From December through March nearby skiing is good; there are accessible runs within an hour of Zurich at Flumserberg and Hoch-Ybrig Mountains. Equipment rental is available at all major ski shops, department stores, and ski resorts. The more famous Alpine ski resorts are further away; Davos and Gstaad, both two-hour drives, are among the closest of these.

**SOCCER** Several national and international matches are played at *Hardturm* (321 Hardturmstr.) and *Letzigrund* (47 Herdenstr.) stadiums. For information, call the tourist office.

**SWIMMING** Two good beaches, Mythenquai and Tiefenbrunnen, are right on the lake; Tiefenbrunnen is popular with topless bathers. There's an attractive pool at Dolder on Zürichberg (Mt. Zurich). In winter several indoor public pools are open in town, including *City* (71 Sihlstr.; phone: 211-3844) and *Oerlikon* (100 Wallisellenstr.; phone: 312-4690).

**TENNIS AND SQUASH** Courts may be rented hourly at 10 municipal tennis facilities and several private tennis clubs, as well as at the more than 15 squash centers around town. For information, call the tourist office.

## THEATER

There are two main stages: *Schauspielhaus* (34 Rämistr.; phone: 265-5858) produces plays in classical German, and *Theater am Neumarkt* (5 Neumarkt; phone: 221-2283) features avant-garde works. There also are twice-yearly productions of the *British Comedy Club* and of guest companies. See listings in local publications. Theater tickets are also available (from September through June only) through *Billetzentrale* at Werdmühleplatz (phone: 221-2283).

## MUSIC

Top-quality operas, ballets, and operettas are presented at the *Opernhaus* (1 Falkenstr.; phone: 262-0909). Classical concerts are given regularly by the *Tonhalle Orchester* and visiting orchestras at the *Tonhalle* (7 Claridenstr.; phone: 206-3440). There are also frequent concerts and recitals in the *Konservatorium* (Conservatory; 6 Florhofgasse; phone: 221-2283) and in several churches, mainly *Fraumünster, Grossmünster* (see *Special Places* for both) and *Peterskirche* (St. Peter's) in St. Peterhofstatt. Jazz is also fairly popular (see *Nightclubs and Nightlife*); rock, pop, and folk concerts are somewhat more rare. For live country music visit the *Hotel Hirschen* (see *Nightclubs and Nightlife*). The central ticket office for most cultural events is *Billetzentrale* (see *Theater*).

## NIGHTCLUBS AND NIGHTLIFE

Zurich is far from the most swinging town in Europe; the latest that most public establishments can stay open is 2 AM. There are some finds, though. The newest night spot is *Kaufleuten* (see *Eating Out*), a complex of restaurants and music clubs. *Diagonal* discotheque (Gen. Guisan-Quai; phone: 201-2410) remains one of the best, and if you are the guest of the *Baur au Lac* hotel, you can get a temporary membership. The *Joker-Club* (5 Gotthardstr.; phone: 202-2262) has great live music and dancing; it often offers shows as well. *Roxy* (11 Beatengasse; phone: 211-5457) and *Le Paragraphe* (43 Dufourstr.; phone: 251-9422) are favorites of the young crowd. The *Birdwatcher's Club* (16 Schützengasse; phone: 211-5058) is a swank semiprivate club that opens at 5 PM and becomes a lively disco by 9. *Blackout Airport* (phone: 814-1087), though out of town near the airport, is still a nocturnal hot spot, and the *Petit Prince* (21 Bleicherweg; phone: 201-1739) has disco dancing with international shows. *Polygon* (17 Marktgasse; phone: 252-1110) offers spirited variety shows, with dancing into the wee hours.

Jazz and Dixieland fans should drop in for a set at the *Casa Bar* (30 Münstergasse; phone: 261-2002) or *Moods* (5 Sihlamtsstr.;

phone: 201-8130). Everyone should experience a little Swiss folk music; plan on spending at least one night at a small bar in the Altstadt such as *Wolf Bierhalle* (132 Limmatquai; no phone), where spirited bands of costumed men yodel and joke with the audience. Be prepared to down steins of beer and share a table with locals. Another Altstadt Swiss music bar that attracts locals is *Elpli* (15 Ankengasse; phone: 251-1026), where yodelers let loose as patrons down *Alpermilch* ("Alpine milk"), a particularly potent milk-based house drink. A restaurant called *Börse* (5 Leicherweg; phone: 211333) has different weekly bands that specialize in a type of Swiss folk music called *Ländlehr* as well as American country-and-western music (live country music is also offered at the *Hotel Hirschen* bar (13 Niederdorferstr.; phone: 251-4252).

# Best in Town

## CHECKING IN

For a double room expect to pay $280 or more per night at hotels listed as very expensive, $210 to $280 at hotels in the expensive category; $120 to $200 at places described as moderate; and $75 to $100 at inexpensive places (slightly less if you choose a room without a private bath. Most hotel rooms have private baths, phones, and TV sets. Continental breakfast or buffet is included at most places, and several smaller hotels offer reduced rates in winter. Reservations are necessary during the week. All telephone numbers are in the 1 city code unless otherwise indicated.

### VERY EXPENSIVE

**Baur au Lac** The most prestigious establishment in the city center, owned by the same family for generations, offers understated Old World luxury, beautiful gardens facing the lake, and a celebrity-dotted guest list; its 160 rooms always are full. It features adjacent parking and a fashionable restaurant, the *Grill Room* (though this is currently closed and not expected to open till sometime in 1996). Business facilities include 24-hour room service, meeting rooms, an English-speaking concierge, foreign currency exchange, secretarial services in English, audiovisual equipment, photocopiers, computers, cable television news, and translation services. 1 Talstr. (phone: 221-1650; 800-223-6800; fax: 211-8139).

**Dolder Grand** On a forested mountainside minutes by hotel car from downtown Zurich, this romantic old 200-room Gothic fantasy is a member of the Leading Hotels of the World group. Golf, tennis, woodland pathways, panoramic views over city and lake, world class cuisine, an ice rink, and an open-air pool with artificial waves are among the draws. Business facilities include 24-hour room service, meeting rooms for up to 895, an English-speaking concierge, audiovisual equipment, photocopiers, computers, cable television news, translation services, and express checkout. 65 Kurhausstr. (phone: 251-6231; 800-223-6800; fax: 251-8829).

**Ascot** Across from the *Enge* train station, which connects to the *Hauptbahnhof* (Main Railway Station) and *Kloten Airport,* this renovated hotel is just a short walk from the city's business and banking center. All 70 rooms and four suites have attractive balconies and mini-bars. There is bus service to and from the airport each morning, as well as a parking garage, the *Lawrence* restaurant and bar, summer dining in the garden, and room service from 7 AM to 11 PM. Business facilities include meeting rooms for up to 45, an English-speaking concierge, foreign currency exchange, secretarial services in English, audiovisual equipment, fax and copy machines, and computers. 9 Tessinerpl. (phone: 201-1800; fax: 202-7210).

**Carlton Elite** This long established 80-room hotel is central to banks and shopping. It has a pub and an excellent Italian restaurant. A few of the top-floor rooms have private roof gardens; split-level suites are available, too. Business facilities include meeting rooms for up to 300, an English-speaking concierge, and audiovisual equipment. 41 Bahnhofstr. (phone: 211-6560; fax: 211-3019).

**Central Plaza** Centrally located, this 100-room hostelry is bright and cheery. Several popular restaurants and bars contribute to a lively ambience. Business facilities include an English-speaking concierge, foreign currency exchange, secretarial services in English, translation services, audiovisual equipment, photocopiers, and cable television news. 1 Central (phone: 251-5555; fax: 251-8535).

**Dolder Waldhaus** Under the same ownership as the *Dolder Grand* (above), this lovely establishment overlooks a lake, mountains, and the city. Each of its 100 spacious, well-appointed rooms is equipped with a mini-bar; some have kitchenettes. Tennis courts, a nine-hole golf course, an ice skating rink, and an indoor/outdoor pool are nearby, and there are two restaurants and a cocktail bar, as well as terrace dining during the summer. Business facilities include meeting rooms for up to 48, foreign currency exchange, audiovisual equipment, photocopiers, and computers. In a wooded residential area on the outskirts of town, at 20 Kurhausstr. (phone: 251-9360; fax: 251-0029).

**Schweizerhof** Popular with frequent business travelers, this lovely establishment has 115 soundproof, well-appointed rooms, each equipped with such extras as a mini-bar, trouser press, and hair dryer, and adorned with a fresh pink rose every day. The fine French restaurant also serves traditional Swiss dishes, and there's a cocktail bar, coffee shop, and caviar boutique. Business facilities include meeting rooms for up to 50, an English-speaking concierge, foreign currency exchange, audiovisual equipment, computers, secretarial services in English, translation services, cable television news, and express checkout. In the heart of the city, at 7 Bahnhofpl. (phone: 211-8640; fax: 211-3505).

**Splügenschloss** A few steps from the lake, this charming member of the Relais & Châteaux hotel group in a turn-of-the-century building has 55 cozy rooms and suites, all luxuriously furnished (some with balconies). There's a pleasant restaurant with a French-accented menu, a bar, and a meeting room for up to 30. 2 Splügenstr. (phone: 201-0800; fax: 201-4286).

**St. Gotthard** In addition to its terrific location on the upper end of Bahnhofstrasse near the *Hauptbahnhof* (Main Railway Station), this first class hotel, which opened in 1889, features 135 modern rooms and the *Hummer Bar,* a very good seafood restaurant. 87 Bahnhofstr. (phone: 211-5500; fax: 211-2419).

**Swissôtel** Within walking distance of the *ZÜSPA Exhibition Center* and connected to downtown by several tram lines, this place, operated by *Swissair,* offers 333 rooms and 11 suites, a pool, a fitness center, and a solarium, plus several restaurants and bars, one with a splendid panoramic view. Business facilities include 24-hour room service, meeting rooms for up to 700, an English-speaking concierge, foreign currency exchange, secretarial services in English, audiovisual equipment, photocopiers, computers, cable television news, translation services, and underground parking. Am Marktpl., Zurich-Oerlikon (phone: 311-4341; fax: 312-4468).

**Tiefenau** Privacy prevails in this quiet 150-year-old townhouse near the *Kunsthaus* (Fine Arts Museum). Some of the 27 bed/sitting rooms are very large; most are furnished with antiques. There is a garden and a good, candlelit restaurant, *Au Gourmet* (see *Eating Out*). 8-10 Steinwiesstr. (phone: 251-2409; fax: 251-2476).

**Zum Storchen** Built in the 14th century, this is Zurich's oldest hotel and its most romantically situated: in the heart of the Altstadt on the Limmat River. The 80 rooms, except for the corner ones, tend to be small and spartan, but those with a river view are much in demand (and require reservations far in advance). *La Rôtisserie* is a pleasant restaurant. Business facilities include meeting rooms for up to 45, an English-speaking concierge, audiovisual equipment, and cable television news. 2 Am Weinpl. (phone: 211-5510; fax: 211-6451).

**Zurich Airport Hilton** Although it's only five minutes from the airport, this large establishment is surrounded by beautiful, tranquil woodlands. All 288 rooms are soundproof and air conditioned. There are two restaurants, a running track, and a sauna, solarium, and massage center. Business facilities include meeting rooms for up to 320, an English-speaking concierge, foreign currency exchange, secretarial services in English, audiovisual equipment, photocopiers, computers, cable television news, translation services, and express check-out. There's underground parking. 10 Hohenbühlstr. (phone: 810-3131; 800-HILTONS; fax: 810-9366).

### MODERATE

**Ammann** A small, friendly (and attractively priced) modern hotel in the heart of the historic Altstadt. There are 24 rooms, a large suite, and a restaurant. 4-6 Kirchgasse (phone: 252-7240; fax: 262-4370).

**Helmhaus** Centrally located in a historic building, this superbly run establishment is an excellent value. There are 24 modern, cheerful rooms, but no restaurant. 30 Schiffländepl. (phone: 251-8810; fax: 251-0430).

**Opéra** Next to the opera house, this place has a large, pleasant lobby/sitting room and 67 modern rooms (the best are on the top floor). There's no restaurant. 5 Dufourstr. (phone: 251-9090; fax: 251-9001).

**Pullman Continental** Close to the *Hauptbahnhof* (Main Railway Station), it has 180 comfortable rooms, all equipped with telephones, radio, color TV sets, air conditioning, and hair dryers. There are two bars and two restaurants, including *Diff,* a favorite with locals who come to dine and dance. Business facilities include meeting rooms for up to 120, foreign currency exchange, cable television news, an English-speaking concierge, photocopiers, computers, secretarial services in English, translation services, and audiovisual equipment. There's a parking garage. 60 Stampfenbachstr. (phone: 363-3363; 800-221-4542; fax: 363-3318).

**Renaissance** This is a topnotch business hotel with reasonable rates. There are 204 rooms, three restaurants, a wine bar with live entertainment, and a health center with an indoor pool, whirlpool, steambath, sauna, and solarium. Jogging, tennis, and squash facilities are nearby. Business facilities include 24-hour room service, an English-speaking concierge, computers, photocopiers, audiovisual equipment, secretarial services in English, translation services, meeting rooms for up to 430, and a foreign currency exchange. There's garage parking. In Zurich's business quarter, five minutes from the airport and next to the *ZÜSPA Exhibition Center.* 1 Talackerstr. (phone: 810-8500; 800-228-9898; fax: 810-8755).

**Wellenberg** In the center of the Altstadt, this modern establishment has 46 bright, cleverly decorated and comfortable rooms and wonderful views of the Hirschenplatz. There's an outdoor terrace, and the small dining room offers a bountiful buffet breakfast and snacks (but no complete meals) to guests only. 10 Niederdorfstr. (phone: 262-4300; fax: 251-3130).

#### INEXPENSIVE

**Limmathof** Perfectly located and rather modest, it's near the *Hauptbahnhof* (Main Railway Station) and offers 55 no-frills (but pleasant) modern rooms and a restaurant. No credit cards accepted. 142 Limmatquai (phone: 261-4220; fax: 262-0217).

**Schifflände** A small (20 rooms) and simple but comfortable hotel in the Bellevue neighborhood by the Limmatquai. There is a restaurant on the premises. 18 Schifflände (phone: 262-4050; fax: 262-4367).

---

## EATING OUT

The culinary traditions of Germany, Italy, and France all meet in Switzerland, but some specialties are singularly Swiss. The people of Zurich like *geschnetzeltes Kalbsfleisch* (minced veal or calf's liver with cream), *Leberspiessli* (roasted calf liver with bacon), and *Kalbsbratwurst* (a delicious veal sausage). Fondue, the national dish, is made with a combination of several cheeses and white wine. Also try the crisp hash-brown potato "pancake" called *Rösti.* Desserts feature fresh cream and delicious Swiss chocolate; try *Zuger Kirschtorte,* a cake soaked in kirsch, a cherry brandy. And visit at least one of the many tearooms for which Zurich is famous; they serve tea or coffee with a choice of pastries.

Most restaurants serve wine by the glass at reasonable prices, but plain water rarely is seen on the table; order mineral water (still or carbonated) if you wish.

For a dinner for two without drinks expect to pay $120 or more at an expensive restaurant; $75 to $110 at a moderate place; and less than $65 at an inexpensive one. A service charge is included in all bills, but it is customary to leave a small additional tip (around 10% to 20% at better restaurants). Unless otherwise noted restaurants are open for lunch and dinner, major credit cards are accepted, and all telephone numbers are in the 1 city code.

### EXPENSIVE

**Casa Ferlin** For three decades a loyal clientele has come here to enjoy Angelo Ferlin's mouth-watering green and white ravioli and veal piccata. Closed weekends and mid-July to mid-August. Reservations necessary. 38 Stampfenbachstr. (phone: 362-3509).

**Flühgasse** The food served in this enchanting 16th-century inn is among the best in Zurich. The emphasis is on light Swiss dishes. Closed weekends. Reservations necessary. 214 Zollikerstr. (phone: 381-1215).

**Haus zum Rüden** Located in one of the most spectacular of Zurich's medieval houses (originally the town mint, dating back to the 13th century), this dining spot has a Gothic interior and a fabulous view of the Limmat. Delicious seafood is served on festive tables with fresh flowers and fine linen. For the famished and well-heeled, there is also a seven-course gourmet menu. Closed Sundays in summer. Reservations advised. 42 Limmatquai (phone: 261-9566).

**Kaufleuten** In a 19th-century landmark building, this large and very popular place attracts a stylish crowd of all ages. It includes a discotheque, bar, and restaurant; the menu is Mediterranean, but there are also two sushi chefs at work during lunch and early dinner. Closed Friday and Saturday lunch. Reservations advised, especially on weekends. 18 Pelikanstr. (phone: 221-1506).

**Königstuhl** Zurich's cognoscenti haunt this restaurant, where chef Marc Zimmermann prepares sophisticated fare such as baked potatoes filled with smoked salmon and caviar, rabbit terrine, and lobster ravioli. There is a moderately priced bistro on the main floor (the main restaurant is on the second floor), plus a chic bar that serves champagne by the glass. Open daily. Reservations necessary. 3 Stüssihofstr. (phone: 261-7618).

**Kronenhalle** The best-known place in Zurich, where "everybody" goes, from local artists to visiting celebrities; the walls are covered with original Picassos, Mirós, and other works from the owner's collection. The bill of fare features international food with Swiss specialties. Try the chocolate mousse. Open daily. Reservations necessary. 4 Rämistr. (phone: 251-6669).

**Petermann's Kunststuben** Creative young chef-owner Horst Petermann, who is rated among the top *toques* in the country, prepares memorable Swiss gastronomic creations at this cozy, flower-filled place, the recipient of two Michelin stars. Don't miss the apricot flan. Closed Sundays and Mondays. Reservations necessary. Located in the suburb of Küsnacht, 160 Seestr. (phone: 910-0715).

### MODERATE

**Barrique** A wine bar, it attracts a lively crowd that comes to try wines by the glass and reasonably priced daily specials. Closed Sundays. No reservations. In the Altstadt, 17 Marktgasse (phone: 252-5895).

**Belvoirpark** This dining establishment serves as a training ground for some of Europe's premier young chefs. An extensive international menu and topnotch service usually impresses even the most jaded of restaurant critics. Closed Sundays and Mondays. Reservations necessary. No credit cards accepted. 125 Seestr. (phone: 202-1054).

**Blaue Ente** In an old grain mill, the "Blue Duck" is Zurich's liveliest and trendiest restaurant, offering imaginative French and Italian fare. Open daily. Reservations necessary. 223 Seefeldstr. (phone: 422-7706).

**Brasserie Lipp** All the Alsace specialties found at the original branch in Paris, including *choucroute* and cassoulet, are served; there are also daily specials. After dining, go upstairs to the *Jules Verne* bar for a panoramic view of the city. Closed Sundays from August through mid-September. Reservations advised. 9 Uraniastr. (phone: 211-1155).

**California** This offbeat place has menus in English, California wines, and American food (steaks, burgers, and the like). A small garden enhances its informal, friendly atmosphere. Closed at lunch on weekends. Reservations advised. 125 Asylstr. (phone: 381-5680).

**Le Dézaley** Fondue fans should make a stop at this lively dining room, which serves the delicious dish in convivial surroundings. Your waiter also can recommend one of the regional specialties from the Lake Geneva area, called Waadtländ by Swiss Germans. Order some dry Vaudoise wine to go with your meal. Closed Sundays. Reservations necessary. 7 Römergasse, next to *Grossmünster* church (phone: 251-6129).

**Goethestübli** Located on the second floor of an 18th-century inn where Goethe once lived, this is a cozy place to try traditional fare. Venison with *knöpfli* (egg noodles), and *fogasch* (a sweet fish resembling perch and pike) in beer batter are served in season. Closed weekends. Reservations advised. 7 Glockengasse (phone: 221-2120).

**Au Gourmet** The place to go for intimate dining by candlelight. International fare is served at this dining spot in the charming *Tiefenau* hotel. In the summer, there's dining in the garden. Open daily. Reservations advised. 8-10 Steinwiesstr. (phone: 251-2409).

**Kropf** This Art Nouveau beer hall, an institution housed in a 15th-century burgher's house complete with a fancy Baroque ceiling, serves plenty of hearty Swiss/German/Austrian food. Here you'll find one of the best schnitzels with *Rösti* in town, served by motherly waitresses. There's dining on the pleasant terrace in summer. Closed Sundays. Reservations advised. American Express accepted. 16 In Gassen, near Paradelpl. (phone: 221-1805).

**Oepfelchammer** Werner and Rosa Maria Hausmann's charming restaurant, in a 14th-century house with an enchanting atmosphere, has excellent "Old Zurich" specialties and good wines. Try the veal cutlet in a light cream sauce, and save room for the savory baked apples in puff pastry. For the adventurous, a lively student fraternity room here welcomes anybody to partake of a glass of wine at two long wooden tables—provided you first show your prowess at chinning the ancient wood beams, which also earns you the right to carve your initials in them. Closed Sundays in winter. Reservations necessary. Visa accepted. 12 Rindermarkt (phone: 251-2336).

**Pinte Vaudoise** Swiss cheese specialties such as fondue and raclette (potatoes and cheese) are offered in a cozy, paneled tavern in the *Villette* hotel. Closed Sundays. Reservations advised. No credit cards accepted. 4 Kruggasse (phone: 252-6009).

**Wolfbach** This small, excellent restaurant specializes in freshwater fish. Closed Sundays and Mondays. Reservations advised. 35 Wolfbachstr., near the *Kunsthaus* (phone: 252-5180).

**Zum Grobe Ernst** An unpretentious spot, cozy yet sophisticated, it features a menu that is equally unassuming. Hearty selections such as fresh seafood salad or the house specialty, *Knusperiges mit Knoblauch und Rosemaria* (garlic-and-rosemary roasted game hen with gratin potatoes), are served. Good wine is sold by the glass. Open daily. Reservations advised. 16 Stüssihofstatt, in the Altstadt (phone: 251-2055).

**Zunfthaus zur Schmiden** More than half a century old, this former blacksmith's guildhouse has an exquisite sculpted wooden ceiling and ceramic chimneys. The kitchen produces traditional Swiss dishes; an excellent veal schnitzel with *Rösti* is the house specialty. Open daily. Reservations advised. No credit cards accepted. 20 Marktgasse (phone: 251-5287).

### INEXPENSIVE

**Belcanto** In the city's *Opernhaus* (Opera House), this place is open from morning to midnight, with a menu ranging from light snacks to full meals. There's an outdoor terrace and an interesting ambience, especially before performances. Open daily. Reservations advised for dinner before the opera. Theater Pl. (phone: 251-6951).

**Bodega Española** There's a lively, popular *tapas* bar downstairs and a more sedate restaurant upstairs. Squeeze in at a wooden table and sip Rioja wine while people watching. The paella is a good choice. Open daily. Reservations advised for upstairs only. No credit cards accepted. 15 Münstergasse (phone: 251-2310).

**Café Opus** Opened in 1993 on the site of the historic *Kindli* restaurant and beer hall, this spot features traditional Viennese coffee house chairs, marble tables, a wall of books, and 25 different periodicals. Besides the soups, desserts, and assorted international fare, patrons come for the musical, theatrical, and literary events. Open daily. Reservations advised for performance times. Major credit cards accepted. 1 Pfalzgasse (phone: 211-4182).

**Cantina Tina** Budget-conscious diners come to this popular bar and Italian restaurant for fresh soups, salads, pasta, and Italian desserts. Open daily. Reservations unnecessary. 10 Niederdorfstr. (phone: 251-6170).

**Chueche Café** It's a perfect spot for an espresso or a toasted cheese sandwich. In a charming location in the Altstadt by the river, the café and the adjacent bar (*Le Philosophe*) and French bistro (*Mère Catherine*) all have the same owner. Open daily. No reservations. No credit cards accepted. 1 Nägelihof (phone: 262-1600).

**Gleich** A vegetarian's delight serving imaginative, high-quality dishes, this place is famous for homemade fruit tarts and special juices. No alcohol is served. Closed Saturday dinner and Sundays. Reservations advised for lunch. No credit cards accepted. 9 Seefeldstr. (phone: 251-3203).

**Hiltl Vegi** The oldest vegetarian restaurant in town serves delicious salads and Indian curries. There's a daily "Indian buffet," and 55 varieties of fresh brewed tea are poured in the upstairs tearoom. Open daily. Reservations advised for lunch. No credit cards accepted. 28 Sihlstr. (phone: 221-3870).

**James Joyce Pub** This classic pub was renamed after one of Zurich's most prominent writers-in-residence. Moved from the venerable *Jury's* hotel in Dublin, the bar is a perfect setting for a pint of Guinness or a glass of Cardinale, a light Swiss beer. Try the Bloom's lunch—black bread with gorgonzola cheese and a glass of beaujolais. Closed Sundays. Reservations unnecessary. 8 Pelikanstr. (phone: 221-1828).

**Risotteria** This no-frills café on the lower level of an old guildhouse features at least a dozen types of risotto, including risotto with gorgonzola cheese and risotto with smoked salmon and basil. Open daily. Reservations advised. No credit cards accepted. 54 Limmatquai (phone: 261-6565).

**Schober** A gilded, picture-postcard delight and now a designated historic landmark, this is the oldest café in town. Cold snacks and marvelous sweets are available to eat here or to take with you. A favorite for Sunday brunch. Closed evenings. Reservations unnecessary. No credit cards accepted. 4 Napfgasse, on a quaint square near *Grossmünster* (phone: 251-8060).

**Sprüngli** For a tasty breakfast, light lunch, or afternoon hot chocolate, this is the city's most famous and elegant café/candy shop. The chocolate truffles and pralines are delicious, and there's wonderful pastry to eat in or carry out. Closed for dinner and Sundays. Reservations unnecessary. Credit cards accepted in the retail shop only. 21 Bahnhofstr. at Paradepl. (phone: 211-0795) and 49 Löwenstr. (phone: 211-9612).

# Climate Chart

*Average Temperatures (in °F)*

| City | January | April | July | October |
|------|---------|-------|------|---------|
| Amsterdam | 34–40 | 43–52 | 59–70 | 49–56 |
| Athens | 43–55 | 52–68 | 73–91 | 59–75 |
| Barcelona | 43–55 | 52–64 | 70–82 | 59–70 |
| Berlin | 27–36 | 40–56 | 58–76 | 43–56 |
| Bratislava | 27–36 | 43–61 | 61–79 | 45–59 |
| Brussels | 31–40 | 41–58 | 54–74 | 45–59 |
| Bucharest | 19–34 | 41–64 | 60–86 | 43–65 |
| Budapest | 25–34 | 44–63 | 61–82 | 45–61 |
| Copenhagen | 28–36 | 37–52 | 57–72 | 45–54 |
| Dublin | 34–47 | 40–56 | 52–68 | 48–53 |
| Edinburgh | 34–43 | 40–52 | 52–65 | 45–54 |
| Frankfurt | 29–38 | 43–61 | 59–77 | 45–58 |
| Geneva | 29–40 | 41–59 | 59–77 | 45–58 |
| Helsinki | 16–27 | 30–43 | 55–72 | 37–46 |
| Lisbon | 46–57 | 54–68 | 63–81 | 57–72 |
| London | 36–45 | 40–56 | 56–72 | 45–58 |
| Madrid | 36–48 | 45–64 | 63–88 | 50–66 |
| Milan | 32–41 | 50–64 | 68–84 | 52–63 |
| Moscow | 3–16 | 34–50 | 55–74 | 37–49 |
| Munich | 23–34 | 38–58 | 56–74 | 40–56 |
| Oslo | 19–28 | 34–50 | 55–72 | 37–48 |
| Paris | 34–43 | 43–60 | 58–76 | 46–60 |
| Prague | 23–36 | 38–58 | 55–75 | 41–55 |
| Rome | 41–52 | 50–66 | 68–86 | 55–72 |
| St. Petersburg | 8–20 | 32–47 | 55–70 | 39–49 |
| Stockholm | 23–30 | 34–46 | 57–72 | 41–48 |
| Vienna | 25–34 | 43–59 | 59–77 | 45–57 |
| Warsaw | 21–32 | 37–54 | 58–75 | 41–55 |
| Zurich | 27–36 | 40–59 | 58–77 | 43–58 |

# Weights and Measures

|  | Metric Unit | Abbreviation | US Equivalent |
|---|---|---|---|
| Length | 1 millimeter | mm | .04 inch |
|  | 1 meter | m | 39.37 inches |
|  | 1 kilometer | km | .62 mile |
| Capacity | 1 liter | l | 1.057 quarts |
| Weight | 1 gram | g | .035 ounce |
|  | 1 kilogram | kg | 2.2 pounds |
|  | 1 metric ton | MT | 1.1 tons |
| Temperature | 0° Celsius | C | 32° Fahrenheit |

## CONVERSION TABLES

### METRIC TO US MEASUREMENTS

|  | Multiply: | by: | to convert to: |
|---|---|---|---|
| Length | millimeters | .04 | inches |
|  | meters | 3.3 | feet |
|  | meters | 1.1 | yards |
|  | kilometers | .6 | miles |
| Capacity (liquid) | liters | 2.11 | pints |
|  | liters | 1.06 | quarts |
|  | liters | .26 | gallons |
| Weight | grams | .04 | ounces |
|  | kilograms | 2.2 | pounds |

### US TO METRIC MEASUREMENTS

|  | Multiply: | by: | to convert to: |
|---|---|---|---|
| Length | inches | 25.0 | millimeters |
|  | feet | .3 | meters |
|  | yards | .9 | meters |
|  | miles | 1.6 | kilometers |
| Capacity | pints | .47 | liters |
|  | quarts | .95 | liters |
|  | gallons | 3.8 | liters |
| Weight | ounces | 28.0 | grams |
|  | pounds | .45 | kilograms |

### SPECIAL MEASUREMENTS

|  | British | US |
|---|---|---|
| Weight | stone | 14 pounds |
| Capacity | Imperial gallon | 1.2 US gallons |

### TEMPERATURE

| Celsius to Fahrenheit | $(°C \times 9/5) + 32 = °F$ |
|---|---|
| Fahrenheit to Celsius | $(°F - 32) \times 5/9 = °C$ |

# Index